The
Hutchinson
Pocket Encyclopedia

D0234401

Editorial Director
Michael Upshall

Project Editor
Frances Lass

Editors
Ingrid von Essen
Edith Harkness
Tony Germing
Sarah MacLeod

Design
Behram Kepardia
Terry Caven

The
Hutchinson
Pocket Encyclopedia

Helicon Publishing Limited
42 Hythe Bridge Street
Oxford OX1 2EP

set in Century Old Style

Computer typesetting and page make-up by
Æsthetex Ltd, Edinburgh

Printed and bound by Cox & Wyman Ltd

ISBN   0 09 174416 0

British Library Cataloguing in Publication Data
A catalogue for this book is available from the British
Library.

This edition published 1992 by TSP by arrangement
with Helicon Publishing Ltd

How to use this book

Arrangement of entries

Entries are ordered alphabetically, as if there were no spaces between words. Thus, entries for words beginning 'gold' follow the order:

> gold
> Golden Fleece
> goldfinch

However, we have avoided a purely mechanical alphabetization in cases where a different order corresponds more with human logic. For example, sovereigns with the same name are grouped according to country before number, so that King George II of England is placed before George III of England, and not next to King George II of Greece. Words beginning 'Mc' and 'Mac' are treated as if they begin 'Mac'; and 'St' and 'Saint' are both treated as if they were spelt 'Saint'.

Foreign names

Names of foreign sovereigns and places are usually shown in their English form, except where the foreign name is more familiar; thus, there are entries for Charles V of Spain, but Juan Carlos (not John Charles), and for Florence, not Firenze. Cross-references have been provided in cases where confusion is possible.

Cross-references

are shown by a ⇨ symbol immediately preceding the reference. Cross-referencing is selective; a cross-reference is shown when another entry contains material directly relevant to the subject matter of an entry, and where the reader may not otherwise think of looking. Common alternative spellings, where there is no agreed consistent form, are also shown; thus there ia a cross-reference to Muhammad at Mohammed.

Units

Si (metric) units are used throughout for scientific entries. Measurements of distances, temperatures, sizes, and so on, usually include an approximate imperial equivalent. Entries are also included for a wide variety of measurements no longer in common use.

Science and technology

Entries are generally placed under the same name by which they are better known, with the technical term given a cross-reference. To make it easier for the non-specialist to understand, technical terms are frequently explained when used within the text of an entry, even though they may have their own entry elsewhere.

Chinese names

Pinyin, the preferred system for transcribing Chinese names of people and places, is generally used: thus, there is an entry at Mao Zedong, not Mao Tse-tung; an exception is made for a few names which are more familiar in their former (Wade-Giles) form, such as Sun Yat-sen and Chiang Kai-Shek. Where confusion is likely, Wade-Giles forms are given as cross-references.

Aachen (French *Aix-la-Chapelle*) German cathedral city and spa in the *Land* of North Rhine–Westphalia, 72 km/45 mi SW of Cologne; population (1988) 239,000.

Aalborg (Danish *Ålborg*) port in Denmark 32 km/20 mi inland from the Kattegat, on the S shore of the Limfjord; population (1990) 155,000. One of Denmark's oldest towns, it has a castle and the fine Budolfi church. It is the capital of Nordjylland county in Jylland (Jutland).

aardvark nocturnal mammal *Orycteropus afer*, order Tubulidentata, found in central and southern Africa. A timid, defenceless animal about the size of a pig, it has a long head, piglike snout, and large asinine ears. It feeds on termites, which it licks up with its long sticky tongue.

Aarhus (Danish *Århus*) second-largest city of Denmark, on the E coast overlooking the Kattegat; population (1990) 261,400. It is the capital of Aarhus county in Jylland (Jutland) and a shipping and commercial centre.

abacus method of calculating with a handful of stones on 'a flat surface' (Latin *abacus*), familiar to the Greeks and Romans, and used by earlier peoples, possibly even in ancient Babylon; it still survives in the more sophisticated bead-frame form of the Russian *schoty* and the Japanese *soroban*.

Abadan Iranian oil port on the E side of the Shatt-al-Arab; population (1986) 294,000. Abadan is the chief refinery and shipping centre for Iran's oil industry, nationalized 1951.

abalone edible marine snail of the worldwide genus *Haliotis*, family Haliotidae. Abalones have flattened, oval, spiralled shells, which have holes around the outer edge and a bluish mother-of-pearl lining. This lining is used in ornamental work.

Abbasid dynasty family of rulers of the Islamic empire, whose ⟡caliphs reigned in Baghdad 750–1258. They were descended from Abbas, the prophet Muhammad's uncle, and some of them, such as Harun al-Rashid and Mamun (reigned 813–33), were outstanding patrons of cultural development. Later their power dwindled, and in 1258 Baghdad was burned by the Tatars.

abdomen in invertebrates, the part of the body below the ⟡thorax, containing the digestive organs; in insects and other arthropods, it is the hind part of the body. In mammals, the abdomen is separated from the thorax by the diaphragm, a sheet of muscular tissue; in arthropods, commonly by a narrow constriction. In insects and spiders, the abdomen is characterized by the absence of limbs.

Abdullah ibn Hussein 1882–1951. King of Jordan from 1946. He worked with the British guerrilla leader T E ⟡Lawrence in the Arab revolt of World War I. Abdullah became king of Trans-Jordan 1946; on the incorporation of Arab Palestine (after the 1948–49 Arab-Israeli War) he renamed the country the Hashemite Kingdom of Jordan. He was assassinated.

Abelard Peter 1079–1142. French scholastic philosopher who worked on logic and theology. His romantic liaison with his pupil ⟡Héloîse caused a medieval scandal. Details of his controversial life are contained in the autobiographical *Historia Calamitatum Mearum/The History of My Misfortunes*.

Aberdeen city and seaport on the E coast of Scotland, administrative headquarters of Grampian region; population (1991) 201,100. It has shore-based maintenance and service depots for the North Sea oil rigs. Industries include agricultural machinery, paper, and textiles; fishing; shipbuilding; granite-quarrying; and engineering. It is Scotland's third largest city.

Aberdeen George Hamilton Gordon, 4th Earl of Aberdeen 1784–1860. British Tory politician, prime minister 1852–55 when he resigned because of the criticism aroused by the miseries and mismanagement of the Crimean War.

aberration, optical any of a number of defects that impair the image in an optical instrument. Aberration occurs because of minute variations in lenses and mirrors, and because different parts of the light ⟡spectrum are reflected or refracted by varying amounts. In *chromatic aberration* the image is surrounded by coloured fringes, because light of different colours is brought to different focal points by a lens. In *spherical aberration* the image is blurred because different parts of a spherical lens or mirror have different focal lengths. In *astigmatism* the image appears elliptical or cross-shaped because of an irregularity in the curvature of the lens. In *coma* the images appear progressively elongated towards the edge of the field of view.

Abidja'n port and former capital (to 1983) of the Republic of Ivory Coast, W Africa; population (1982) 1,850,000. Products include coffee, palm oil, cocoa, and timber (mahogany). It was replaced as capital by Yamoussoukro.

Abkhazia autonomous republic in Georgia, situated on the Black Sea; area 8,600 sq km/3,320 sq mi; population (1989) 526,000; capital Sukhumi. Abkhazia, a Georgian kingdom from the 4th century, was inhabited traditionally by Abkhazis, an ethnic group converted from Christianity to Islam in the 17th century. By the 1980s some 17% of the population were Muslims and two-thirds were of Georgian origin. In March–April and July 1989, Abkhazis demanded secession from Georgia and reinstatement as a full Union republic; violent interethnic clashes erupted in which at least 20 people died. Georgian nationalists, however, wanted the republic to be incorporated as part of Georgia. The dispute triggered nationalist demonstrations throughout Georgia.

abolitionism in UK and US history, a movement culminating in the late 18th and early 19th centuries that aimed first to end the slave trade, and then to abolish the institution of ◊slavery and emancipate slaves. In the UK, the leading abolitionist was William ◊Wilberforce, who secured passage of a bill abolishing the slave trade 1807.

abominable snowman or *yeti* legendary creature, said to resemble a human, with long arms and a thickset body covered with reddish-grey hair. Reports of its existence in the Himalayas have been made since 1832, and they gained substance from a published photograph of a huge footprint in the snow 1951. No further 'evidence' has been found.

abortion ending of a pregnancy before the fetus is developed sufficiently to survive outside the uterus. Loss of a fetus at a later gestational age is termed premature stillbirth. Abortion may be accidental (miscarriage) or deliberate (termination of pregnancy).

In the UK a deliberate abortion must be carried out under the terms of the 1967 Abortion Act, which states that two doctors must agree that termination of the pregnancy is necessary, and the operation must be performed on approved premises. In April 1990, after 15 unsuccessful attempts to alter the 1967 act, Parliament approved a measure to lower the time limit on abortions to 24 weeks.

Abraham *c.* 2300 BC. In the Old Testament, founder of the Jewish nation. In his early life he was called Abram. God promised him heirs and land for his people in Canaan (Israel), renamed him Abraham ('father of many nations'), and tested his faith by a command (later retracted) to sacrifice his son Isaac.

Abraham, Plains of plateau near Québec, Canada, where the British commander ◊Wolfe defeated the French under ◊Montcalm, 13 Sept 1759, during the French and Indian War (1754–63). The outcome of the Battle of the Plains of Abraham established British supremacy in Canada.

abrasive substance used for cutting and polishing or for removing small amounts of the surface of hard materials. There are two types: natural and artificial abrasives, and their hardness is measured using the ◊Mohs' scale.

Abruzzi mountainous region of S central Italy, comprising the provinces of L'Aquila, Chieti, Pescara, and Teramo; area 10,800 sq km/4,169 sq mi; population (1990) 1,272,000; capital L'Aquila.

abscissa in ◊coordinate geometry, the x-coordinate of a point – that is, the horizontal distance of that point from the vertical or y-axis. For example, a point with the coordinates (3,4) has an abscissa of 3.

absolute value or *modulus* in mathematics, the value, or magnitude, of a number irrespective of its sign. It is written $|n|$, and defined as the positive squareroot of n^2. For example, 5 and –5 have the same absolute value: $|5| = |-5| = 5$. It is also often written mod n.

absolute zero lowest temperature theoretically possible, zero degrees kelvin, equivalent to –273.16°C/–459.67°F, at which molecules are motionless. Although the third law of ◊thermodynamics indicates the impossibility of reaching absolute zero exactly, a temperature within 3×10^{-8} kelvin of it was produced 1984 by Finnish scientists.

absolutism or *absolute monarchy* system of government in which the ruler or rulers have unlimited power. The principle of an absolute monarch, given a right to rule by God (see ◊divine right of kings), was extensively used in Europe during the 17th and 18th centuries.

absorption in science, the taking up of one substance by another, such as a liquid by a solid (ink by blotting paper) or a gas by a liquid (ammonia by water). In biology, absorption describes the passing of nutrients or medication into and through tissues such as intestinal walls and blood vessels. In physics, absorption is the phenomenon by which a substance retains radiation of particular wavelengths; for example, a piece of blue glass absorbs all visible light except the wavelengths in the blue part of the spectrum; it also refers to the partial loss of energy resulting from light and other electromagnetic waves passing through a medium.

abstract art nonrepresentational art. Ornamental art without figurative representation occurs in most cultures. The modern abstract movement in sculpture and painting emerged in Europe and North America between 1910 and 1920.

Abstract Expressionism US movement in abstract art that emphasized the act of painting, the expression inherent in paint itself, and the interaction of artist, paint, and canvas. Abstract Expressionism emerged in New York in the early 1940s. Arshile Gorky, Franz Kline, Jackson Pollock, and Mark Rothko are associated with the movement.

1988	Best Picture: *Rain Man*; Best Director: Barry Levinson *Rain Man*; Best Actor: Dustin Hoffman *Rain Man*; Best Actress: Jodie Foster *The Accused*
1989	Best Picture: *My Left Foot*; Best Director: Oliver Stone *Born on the 4th of July*; Best Actor: Daniel Day-Lewis *My Left Foot*; Best Actress: Jessica Tandy *Driving Miss Daisy*
1990	Best Picture: *Dances with Wolves*; Best Director: Kevin Costner *Dances with Wolves*; Best Actor: Jeremy Irons *Reversal of Fortune*; Best Actress: Kathy Bates *Misery*
1991	Best Picture: *The Silence of the Lambs*; Best Director: Jonathan Demme *The Silence of the Lambs*; Best Actor: Anthony Hopkins *The Silence of the Lambs*; Best Actress: Jodie Foster *The Silence of the Lambs*

Abu Dhabi sheikdom in SW Asia, on the Arabian Gulf, capital of the ◊United Arab Emirates. Formerly under British protection, it has been ruled since 1971 by Sheik Sultan Zayed bin al-Nahayan.

Abuja city in Nigeria that began construction 1976 as a replacement for Lagos. Shaped like a crescent, it was designed by the Japanese architect Kenzo Tange.

Abu Simbel former site of two ancient temples cut into the rock on the banks of the Nile in S Egypt during the reign of Ramses II, commemorating him and his wife Nefertari. The temples were moved, in sections, 1966–67 before the site was flooded by the Aswan High Dam.

abyssal zone dark ocean area 2,000–6,000 m/ 6,500–19,500 ft deep; temperature 4°C/39°F. Three-quarters of the area of the deep ocean floor lies in the abyssal zone, which is too far from the surface for photosynthesis to take place.

Abyssinia former name of ◊Ethiopia.

acacia any of a large group of shrubs and trees of the genus *Acacia* of the legume family Leguminosae. Acacias include the thorn trees of the African savanna and the gum arabic tree *A. senegal* of N Africa, and several North American species of the SW USA and Mexico. Acacias are found in warm regions of the world, particularly Australia.

Academy Award annual award in many categories, given since 1927 by the American Academy of Motion Picture Arts and Sciences. Arguably the film community's most prestigious accolade, the award is a gold-plated statuette, which has been nicknamed 'Oscar' since 1931.

acanthus any herbaceous plant of the genus *Acanthus* with handsome lobed leaves. Twenty species are found in the Mediterranean region and Old World tropics.

Acapulco or *Acapulco de Juárez* port and holiday resort in S Mexico, on the Pacific coast; population (1990) 592,200. Founded 1550, it has a fine natural harbour and is popular for its deep-sea fishing and skin diving facilities.

ACAS acronym for ◊*Advisory, Conciliation, and Arbitration Service.*

acceleration rate of change of the velocity of a moving body. It is usually measured in metres per second per second ($m\ s^{-2}$). Because velocity is a ◊vector quantity (possessing both magnitude and direction) a body travelling at constant speed may be said to be accelerating if its direction of motion changes. According to Newton's second law of motion, a body will only accelerate if it is acted upon by an unbalanced, or resultant, ◊force.

Acceleration due to gravity is the acceleration of a body falling freely under the influence of the Earth's gravitational field; it varies slightly at different latitudes and altitudes. The value adopted internationally for gravitational acceleration is $9.806\ m\ s^{-2}$.

accelerator in physics, a device to bring charged particles (such as ◊protons) up to high speeds and energies, at which they can be of use in industry, medicine, and pure physics: when high-energy particles collide with other particles, the fragments formed reveal the nature of the fundamental forces of nature. For particles to achieve the energies required, successive applications of a high voltage are given to electrodes placed in the path of the particles. During acceleration, the particles are confined within a circular or linear track using a magnetic field.

accordion musical instrument of the reed organ type comprising left and right wind chests connected by flexible bellows. The right hand plays melody on a piano-style keyboard while the left hand has a system of push buttons for selecting single notes or chord harmonies.

Accra capital and port of Ghana; population of greater Accra region (1984) 1,420,000. The port trades in cacao, gold, and timber. Industries include engineering, brewing, and food processing.

accumulator in electricity, a storage battery – that is, a group of rechargeable secondary cells. A familiar example is the lead-acid car battery which consists of connected cells with lead and lead oxide electrodes immersed in strong sulphuric acid. Chemical changes induced in the electrodes during charging are reversed when the battery discharges, releasing the stored electricity.

acetone common name for ⮑propanone.

acetylene common name for ⮑ethyne.

Achaea in ancient Greece, and also today, an area of the N Peloponnese. The *Achaeans* were the predominant society during the Mycenaean period and are said by Homer to have taken part in the siege of Troy.

Achebe Chinua 1930– . Nigerian novelist whose themes include the social and political impact of European colonialism on African people, and the problems of newly independent African nations. His novels include the widely acclaimed *Things Fall Apart* 1958 and *Anthills of the Savannah* 1987.

Achilles Greek hero of Homer's *Iliad*. He was the son of Peleus, king of the Myrmidons in Thessaly, and the sea nymph Thetis, who rendered him invulnerable, except for the heel by which she held him, by dipping him in the river Styx. He was killed by Paris who shot a poisoned arrow into Achilles' heel.

acid compound that, in solution in an ionizing solvent (usually water), gives rise to hydrogen ions (H+ or protons). In modern chemistry, acids are defined as substances that are proton donors and accept electrons to form ionic bonds. Acids react with ⮑bases to form salts, and they act as solvents. Strong acids are corrosive; dilute acids have a sour or sharp taste, although in some organic acids this may be partially masked by other flavour characteristics.

acid rain acidic rainfall, thought to be caused principally by the release into the atmosphere of sulphur dioxide (SO_2) and oxides of nitrogen. Sulphur dioxide is formed from the burning of fossil fuels, such as coal, that contain high quantities of sulphur; nitrogen oxides are contributed from various industrial activities and from car exhaust fumes.

aclinic line the magnetic equator, an imaginary line near the equator, where the compass needle balances horizontally, the attraction of the north and south magnetic poles being equal.

acne skin eruption, mainly occurring among adolescents and young adults, caused by inflammation of the sebaceous glands.

Aconcagua extinct volcano in the Argentine Andes, the highest peak in the Americas; 6,960 m/22,834 ft. It was first climbed by Vines and Zeebruggen 1897.

acoustics in general, the experimental and theoretical science of sound and its transmission; in particular, that branch of the science that has to do with the phenomena of sound in a particular space such as a room or theatre.

Acre or *'Akko* seaport in Israel; population (1983) 37,000. Taken by the Crusaders 1104, it was captured by Saladin 1187 and retaken by Richard I (the Lionheart) 1191. Napoleon failed in a siege 1799. British field marshal Allenby captured the port 1918.

acropolis citadel of an ancient Greek town. The Acropolis of Athens contains the ruins of the Parthenon and surrounding complexes, built there during the days of the Athenian empire.

acrylic fibre synthetic fibre often used as a substitute for wool. It was first developed 1947 but not produced in great volumes until the 1950s.

actinide chemical element with atomic numbers 89–105. All actinides are radioactive, and synthetic above uranium (atomic number 92). They are grouped because of their chemical similarities, and also by analogy with the rare-earth elements (lanthanides).

actinium rare radioactive element, atomic number 89, relative atomic mass of most stable isotope 227; the first of the actinide series and a weak emitter of high-energy alpha-rays. It is made by bombarding radium with neutrons.

action and reaction in physical mechanics, equal and opposite effects produced by a force acting on an object. For example, the pressure of expanding gases from the burning of fuel in a rocket engine (a force) produces an equal and opposite reaction, which causes the rocket to move.

action painting or *gesture painting* in US art, a dynamic school of Abstract Expressionism. It emphasized the importance of the physical act of painting, sometimes expressed with both inventiveness and aggression. Jackson ⮑Pollock was the leading exponent.

Actium, Battle of naval battle in which Octavian defeated the combined fleets of ⮑Mark Antony and ⮑Cleopatra 31 BC to become the undisputed ruler of the Roman world (as the emperor ⮑Augustus). The site is at Akri, a promontory in WYGreece.

activation energy in chemistry, the energy required in order to start a chemical reaction. Some elements and compounds will react together merely by bringing them into contact (spontaneous reaction). For others it is necessary to supply energy in order to start the reaction, even if there is ultimately a net output of energy. This initial energy is the activation energy.

act of Congress in the USA, a bill or resolution passed by both houses of Congress, the Senate and the House of Representatives, which becomes law with the signature of the president. If vetoed by the president, it may still become law if it returns to Congress again and is passed by a majority of two-thirds in each house.

act of Parliament in Britain, a change in the law originating in Parliament and called a statute. Before an act receives the royal assent and becomes law it is a *bill*. An act of Parliament may be either public (of general effect), local, or private. The body of English statute law comprises all the acts passed by Parliament: the existing list opens with the Statute of Merton, passed in 1235. An act (unless it is stated to be for a definite period and then to come to an end) remains on the statute book until it is repealed.

acupuncture system of inserting long, thin metal needles into the body at predetermined points to relieve pain, as an anaesthetic in surgery, and to assist healing. The needles are rotated manually or electrically. The method was developed in ancient China and is increasingly popular in the West.

Adam family of Scottish architects and designers. *William Adam* (1689–1748) was the leading Scottish architect of his day, and his son *Robert Adam* (1728–1792) is considered one of the greatest British architects of the late 18th century. He designed interiors for many great country houses and earned a considerable reputation as a furniture designer. With his brother *James Adam* (1732–1794), also an architect, he speculatively developed the Adelphi near Charing Cross, London, largely rebuilt 1936.

Adam in the Old Testament, founder of the human race. Formed by God from dust and given the breath of life, Adam was placed in the Garden of Eden, where ◊Eve was created from his rib and given to him as a companion. Because she tempted him, he tasted the forbidden fruit of the Tree of Knowledge of Good and Evil, for which trespass they were expelled from the Garden.

Adams Gerry (Gerard) 1948– . Northern Ireland politician, president of Provisional Sinn Féin (the political wing of the IRA) from 1978. He was elected member of Parliament for Belfast West 1983 but declined to take up his Westminster seat, stating that he did not believe in the British government.

Adams John 1735–1826. 2nd president of the USA 1797–1801, and vice president 1789–97. He was born in Quincy, Massachusetts. He was a member of the Continental Congress 1774–78 and signed the Declaration of Independence. In 1779 he went to France and negotiated the treaties that ended the American Revolution.

Adams John Quincy 1767–1848. 6th president of the USA 1825–29. Eldest son of President John Adams, he was born in Quincy, Massachusetts, and became US minister in The Hague, Berlin, St Petersburg, and London. He negotiated the Treaty of Ghent to end the ◊War of 1812 (fought between Britain and the USA) on generous terms for the USA. In 1817 he became ◊Monroe's secretary of state, formulated the ◊Monroe Doctrine 1823, and was elected president by the House of Representatives, despite receiving fewer votes than his main rival, Andrew ◊Jackson.

Adamson Robert R 1821–1848. Scottish photographer who, with David Octavius Hill, produced 2,500 ◊calotypes (mostly portraits) in five years from 1843.

adaptation in biology, any change in the structure or function of an organism that allows it to survive and reproduce more effectively in its environment. In ◊evolution, adaptation is thought to occur as a result of random variation in the genetic make-up of organisms (produced by ◊mutation and ◊recombination) coupled with ◊natural selection.

adaptive radiation in evolution, the formation of several species, with adaptations to different ways of life, from a single ancestral type. Adaptive radiation is likely to occur whenever members of a species migrate to a new habitat with unoccupied ecological niches. It is thought that the lack of competition in such niches allows sections of the migrant population to develop new adaptations, and eventually to become new species.

adder European venomous snake, the common ◊viper *Vipera berus*. Growing to about 60 cm/24 in in length, it has a thick body, triangular head, a characteristic V-shaped mark on its head and, often, zigzag markings along the back. It feeds on small mammals and lizards. The puff adder *Bitis arietans* is a large, yellowish, thick-bodied viper up to 1.6 m/5 ft long, living in Africa and Arabia.

addiction state of dependence on drugs, alcohol, or other substances. Symptoms include uncontrolled craving, tolerance, and symptoms of withdrawal when access is denied. Habitual use produces changes in chemical processes in the brain; when the substance is withheld, severe neurological manifestations, even death, may follow.

Addis Ababa or *Adis Abeba* capital of Ethiopia; population (1984) 1,413,000. It was founded 1887 by Menelik, chief of Shoa, who ascended the throne of Ethiopia 1889. The city is the headquarters of the ◊Organization of African Unity.

additive in food, any natural or artificial chemical added to prolong the shelf life of processed foods (salt or nitrates), alter the colour or flavour of food, or improve its food value (vitamins or minerals). Many chemical additives are used and they are subject to regulation, since individuals may be affected by constant exposure even to traces of certain additives and may suffer side effects ranging from headaches and hyperactivity to cancer. Within the European Community, approved additives are given an official ◊E number.

Adelaide capital and industrial city of South Australia; population (1990) 1,049,100. Industries include oil refining, shipbuilding, and the manufacture of electrical goods and cars.

Aden (Arabic *'Adan*) main port and commercial centre of Yemen, on a rocky peninsula at the SW corner of Arabia, commanding the entrance to the Red Sea; population (1984) 318,000. The city's economy is based on oil refining, fishing, and shipping. A British territory from 1839, Aden became part of independent South Yemen 1967; it was the capital of South Yemen until 1990.

Adenauer Konrad 1876–1967. German Christian Democrat politician, chancellor of West Germany 1949–63. With the French president de Gaulle he achieved the postwar reconciliation of France and Germany and supported all measures designed to strengthen the Western bloc in Europe.

adenoids masses of lymphoid tissue, similar to ◊tonsils, located in the upper part of the throat, behind the nose. They are part of a child's natural defences against the entry of germs but usually shrink and disappear by the age of ten.

adhesive substance that sticks two surfaces together. Natural adhesives (glues) include gelatin in its crude industrial form (made from bones, hide fragments, and fish offal) and vegetable gums. Synthetic adhesives include thermoplastic and thermosetting resins, which are often stronger than the substances they join; mixtures of epoxy resin and hardener that set by chemical reaction; and elastomeric (stretching) adhesives for flexible joints. Superglues are fast-setting adhesives used in very small quantities.

adjective grammatical ◊part of speech for words that describe nouns (for example, *new* and *beautiful*, as in 'a new hat' and 'a beautiful day'). Adjectives generally have three degrees (grades or levels for the description of relationships): the positive degree (*new*, *beautiful*), the comparative degree (*newer*, *more beautiful*), and the superlative degree (*newest*, *most beautiful*).

admiral any of several species of butterfly in the same family (Nymphalidae) as the ◊tortoiseshells. The red admiral *Vanessa atalanta*, wingspan 6 cm/2.5 in, is found worldwide in the northern hemisphere. It migrates south each year from northern areas to subtropical zones.

adobe in architecture, building with earth bricks. The formation of earth bricks ('adobe') and the construction of walls by enclosing earth within moulds (*pisé de terre*) are the two principal methods of earth building. The techniques are commonly found in Spain, Latin America, and the SW USA.

Adonis in Greek mythology, a beautiful youth beloved by the goddess ◊Aphrodite. He was killed while boar-hunting but was allowed to return from the lower world for six months every year to rejoin her. The anemone sprang from his blood.

adrenaline or *epinephrine* hormone secreted by the medulla of the adrenal glands. Adrenaline and noradrenaline (secreted alongside adrenaline) constrict the blood vessels of the belly and skin so that more blood is available for the heart, lungs, and voluntary muscles, an emergency preparation for the stress reaction 'fight or flight'.

Adrian IV (Nicholas Breakspear) *c.* 1100–1159.

Pope 1154–59, the only British pope. He secured the execution of Arnold of Brescia; crowned Frederick I Barbarossa as German emperor; and refused Henry II's request that Ireland should be granted to the English crown in absolute ownership.

Adriatic Sea large arm of the Mediterranean Sea, lying NW to SE between the Italian and the Balkan peninsulas. The W shore is Italian; the E is Croatian, Yugoslav, and Albanian. The sea is about 805 km/500 mi long, and its area is 135,250 sq km/52,220 sq mi.

adsorption taking-up of a gas or liquid at the surface of another substance, usually a solid (for example, activated charcoal adsorbs gases). It involves molecular attraction at the surface, and should be distinguished from ◊absorption (in which a uniform solution results from a gas or liquid being incorporated into the bulk structure of a liquid or solid).

adverb grammatical ◊part of speech for words that modify or describe verbs ('She ran *quickly*'), adjectives ('a *beautifully* clear day'), and adverbs ('They did it *really* well'). Most adverbs are formed from adjectives or past participles by adding *-ly* (*quick: quickly*) or *-ally* (*automatic: automatically*).

Advisory, Conciliation, and Arbitration Service (ACAS) in the UK, the independent body set up under the Employment Protection Act 1975 to improve industrial relations.

advocate (Latin *advocatus*, one summoned to one's aid, especially in a lawcourt) professional pleader in a court of justice. A more common term for a professional advocate is ◊barrister or counsel.

Aegean Islands islands of the Aegean Sea, but more specifically a region of Greece comprising the Dodecanese islands, the Cyclades islands, Lesvos, Samos, and Chios; population (1991) 460,800; area 9,122 sq km/3,523 sq mi.

Aegean Sea branch of the Mediterranean between Greece and Turkey; the Dardanelles connect it with the Sea of Marmara. The numerous islands in the Aegean Sea include Crete, the Cyclades, the Sporades, and the Dodecanese.

Aeneas in Classical legend, a Trojan prince who became the ancestral hero of the Romans. According to Homer, he was the son of Anchises and the goddess Aphrodite. During the Trojan War he owed his life to the frequent intervention of the gods. The legend on which Virgil's epic poem the *Aeneid* is based describes his escape from Troy and his eventual settlement in Latium, on the Italian peninsula.

aerial or *antenna* in radio and television broadcasting, a conducting device that radiates or receives electromagnetic waves. The design of an aerial depends principally on the wavelength of the signal. Long waves (hundreds of metres in wavelength) may employ long wire aerials; short waves (several centimetres in wavelength) may employ rods and dipoles; microwaves may also use dipoles – often with reflectors arranged like a toast rack – or highly directional parabolic dish aerials.

aerobic in biology, a description of those living organisms that require oxygen (usually dissolved in water) for the efficient release of energy contained in food molecules, such as glucose. They include almost all living organisms (plants as well as animals) with the exception of certain bacteria.

aerodynamics branch of fluid physics that studies the forces exerted by air or other gases in motion – for example, the airflow around bodies (such as land vehicles, bullets, rockets, and aircraft) moving at speed through the atmosphere.

aeronautics science of travel through the Earth's atmosphere, including aerodynamics, aircraft structures, jet and rocket propulsion, and aerial navigation.

aeroplane (North American **airplane**) powered heavier-than-air craft supported in flight by fixed wings. Aeroplanes are propelled by the thrust of a jet engine or airscrew (propeller). They must be designed aerodynamically, since streamlining

ensures maximum flight efficiency. For the history of aircraft and aviation, see ⟩flight.

aerosol particles of liquid or solid suspended in a gas. Fog is a common natural example. Aerosol cans, which contain pressurized gas mixed with a propellant, are used to spray liquid in the form of tiny drops of such products as scents and cleaners. Most aerosols used chlorofluorocarbons (CFCs) as propellants until these were found to cause destruction of the ⟩ozone layer in the stratosphere.

Aeschylus *c.* 525–c. 456 BC. Greek dramatist, widely regarded as the founder of Greek tragedy (with ⟩Euripides and ⟩Sophocles). By the introduction of a second actor he made true dialogue and dramatic action possible. Aeschylus wrote some 90 plays between 499 and 458 BC, of which seven survive. These are *The Suppliant Women* performed about 490 BC, *The Persians* 472 BC, *Seven against Thebes* 467 BC, *Prometheus Bound c.* 460 BC, and the ⟩*Oresteia* trilogy 458 BC.

Aesop traditional writer of Greek fables. According to the historian Herodotus, he lived in the reign of Amasis of Egypt (mid-6th century BC) and was a

aeroplane

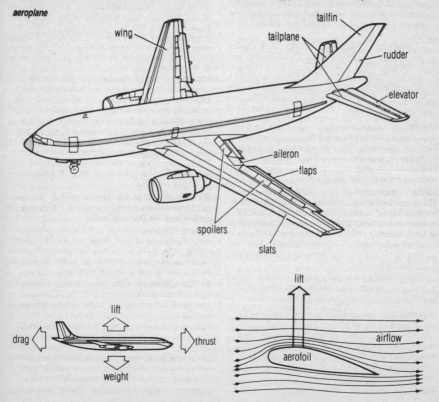

slave of Iadmon, a Thracian. The fables, for which no evidence of his authorship exists, are anecdotal stories using animal characters to illustrate moral or satirical points.

Aesthetic movement English artistic movement of the late 19th century, dedicated to the doctrine of 'art for art's sake' – that is, art as self-sufficient, not needing to justify its existence by serving any particular use. Artists associated with the movement include Aubrey Beardsley and James Whistler. The writer Oscar Wilde was, in his twenties, an exemplary aesthete.

aesthetics branch of philosophy that deals with the nature of beauty, especially in art. It emerged as a distinct branch of enquiry in the mid-18th century.

affidavit legal document, used in court applications and proceedings, in which a person swears that certain facts are true. In England, an affidavit is usually sworn before a solicitor or commissioner for oaths.

Afghan hound breed of fast hunting dog resembling the ◊saluki, though more thickly coated, first introduced to the West by British army officers serving on India's North-West Frontier along the Afghanistan border in the late 19th century. The Afghan hound is about 70 cm/28 in tall and has a long, silky coat.

Afghanistan Republic of; country in S central Asia, bordered N by Tajikistan, Turkmenistan, and Uzbekistan, W by Iran, and S and E by Pakistan; *area* 652,090 sq km/251,707 sq mi; *capital* Kābul; *physical* mountainous in centre and NE, plains in N and SW; *head of state* Burhanuddin Rabbani president from June 1992; *head of government* Usted Sabour Farred (prime minister) from 1992; *political system* military emergency republic; *exports* dried and fresh fruit, rare minerals, natural gas, karakul lamb skins, Afghan coats; *population* (1989) 15,590,000 (more than 5 million have become refugees since 1979); *language* Pushtu; *recent history* full independence recovered 1919 after Third Afghan War with Britain. Constitutional monarchy established 1963, overthrown 1973. Treaty of friendship signed with USSR 1978. Reforms introduced, opposed by conservative Muslims. Guerrilla resistance by the mujaheddin led to Soviet invasion 1979. Partial withdrawal 1986 was completed 1989; civil war between government and mujaheddin continued.

Afghan Wars three wars waged between Britain and Afghanistan to counter the threat to British India from expanding Russian influence in Afghanistan: *First Afghan War* 1838–42, when the British garrison in Kābul was wiped out; *Second Afghan War* 1878–80, when General ◊Roberts captured Kābul and relieved Kandahar; *Third Afghan War* 1919, when peace followed the dispatch by the UK of the first aeroplane ever seen in Kābul.

AFL–CIO abbreviation for ◊*American Federation of Labor and Congress of Industrial Organizations*.

Africa second largest of the continents, three times the area of Europe; *area* 30,097,000 sq km/11,620,451 sq mi; *largest cities* (population over 1 million) Cairo, Algiers, Lagos, Kinshasa, Abidjan, Cape Town, Nairobi, Casablanca, El Gîza, Addis Ababa, Luanda, Dar es Salaam, Ibadan, Douala, Mogadishu; *physical* dominated by a uniform central plateau comprising a southern tableland with a mean altitude of 1,070 m/3,000 ft that falls northwards to a lower elevated plain with a mean altitude of 400 m/1,300 ft. Although there are no great alpine regions or extensive coastal plains, Africa has a mean altitude of 610 m/2,000 ft, two times greater than Europe. The highest points are Mount Kilimanjaro 5,900 m/19,364 ft, and Mount Kenya 5,200 m/17,058 ft; the lowest point is Lac Assal in Djibouti –144 m/–471 ft. Compared with other continents, Africa has few broad estuaries or inlets and therefore has proportionately the shortest coastline (24,000 km/15,000 mi). The geographical extremities of the continental mainland are Cape Hafun in the E, Cape Almadies in the W, Ras Ben Sekka in the N, and Cape Agulhas in the S. The Sahel is a narrow belt of savanna and scrub forest which covers 700 million hectares of W and central Africa; 75% of the continent lies within the tropics; *features* Great Rift Valley, containing most of the great lakes of E Africa (except Lake Victoria); Atlas Mountains in NW; Drakensberg mountain range in SE; Sahara Desert (world's largest desert) in N; Namib, Kalahari, and Great Karoo deserts in S; Nile, Zaîre, Niger, Zambezi, Limpopo, Volta, and Orange rivers; *products* has 30% of the world's minerals including diamonds (51%) and gold (47%); produces 11% of the world's crude petroleum, 58% of the world's cocoa (Ivory Coast, Ghana, Cameroon, Nigeria) 23% of the world's coffee (Uganda, Ivory Coast, Zaire, Ethiopia, Cameroon, Kenya), 20% of the world's groundnuts (Senegal, Nigeria, Sudan, Zaire), and 21% of the world's hardwood timber (Nigeria, Zaire, Tanzania, Kenya); *population* (1988) 610 million.

African art art of sub-Saharan Africa, from prehistory onwards, ranging from the art of ancient civilizations to the new styles of post-imperialist African nations. Examples of historic African art are bronze figures from Benin and Ife (in Nigeria) dating from about 1500 and, also on the W coast, in the same period, bronze or brass figures for weighing gold, made by the Asante.

African National Congress (ANC) multiracial nationalist organization formed in South Africa 1912 to extend the franchise to the whole population and end all racial discrimination there. Its president is Nelson ◊Mandela. Although originally nonviolent, the ANC was banned by the government from 1960 to Jan 1990, and in exile in Mozambique developed a military wing, **Umkhonto we Sizwe**, which engaged in sabotage and guerrilla training. The armed struggle was suspended Aug 1990.

African violet herbaceous plant *Saintpaulia*

ionantha from tropical central and E Africa, with velvety green leaves and scentless purple flowers. Different colours and double varieties have been bred.

Afrikaans language an official language (with English) of the Republic of South Africa and Namibia. Spoken mainly by the Afrikaners – descendants of Dutch and other 17th-century colonists – it is a variety of the Dutch language, modified by circumstance and the influence of German, French, and other immigrant as well as local languages.

Agadir resort and seaport in S Morocco, near the mouth of the river Sus; population (1984) 110,500. It was rebuilt after being destroyed by an earthquake 1960.

Agamemnon in Greek mythology, a Greek hero, son of Atreus, king of Mycenae. He married Clytemnestra, and their children included Electra, Iphigenia, and ▷Orestes. He led the capture of Troy, received Priam's daughter Cassandra as a prize, and was murdered by Clytemnestra and her lover, Aegisthus, on his return home. His children Orestes and Electra later killed the guilty couple.

agaric fungus of typical mushroom shape. Agarics include the field mushroom *Agaricus campestris* and the cultivated edible mushroom *A. brunnesiens*. Closely related is the often poisonous *Amanita* genus, including the fly agaric *Amanita muscaria*.

agate banded or cloudy type of ▷chalcedony, a silica, SiO_2, that forms in rock cavities. Agates are used as ornamental stones and for art objects.

agnosticism belief that the existence of God cannot be proven; that in the nature of things the individual cannot know anything of what lies behind or beyond the world of natural phenomena. The term was coined 1869 by T H ▷Huxley.

agoraphobia ▷phobia involving fear of open spaces and crowded places. The anxiety produced can be so severe that some sufferers are confined to their homes for many years.

agouti small rodent of the genus *Dasyprocta*, family Dasyproctidae. It is found in the forests of Central and South America. The agouti is herbivorous, swift-running, and about the size of a rabbit.

Agra city of Uttar Pradesh, India, on the river Jumna, 160 km/100 mi SE of Delhi; population (1981) 747,318. A commercial and university centre, it was the capital of the Mogul empire 1527–1628, from which period the Taj Mahal dates.

Agricola Gnaeus Julius AD 37–93. Roman general and politician. Born in Provence, he became Consul of the Roman Republic AD 77, and then governor of Britain AD 78–85. He extended Roman rule to the Firth of Forth in Scotland and won the battle of Mons Graupius.

agricultural revolution sweeping changes that took place in British agriculture over the period

1750–1850 in response to the increased demand for food from a rapidly expanding population. Recent research has shown these changes to be only part of a much larger, ongoing process of development.

agriculture practice of farming, including the cultivation of the soil (for raising crops) and the raising of domesticated animals. Crops are for human nourishment, animal fodder, or commodities such as cotton and sisal. Animals are raised for wool, milk, leather, dung (as fuel), or meat. The units for managing agricultural production vary from small holdings and individually owned farms to corporate-run farms and collective farms run by entire communities.

Agriculture developed in the Middle East and Egypt at least 10,000 years ago. Farming communities soon became the base for society in China, India, Europe, Mexico, and Peru, then spread throughout the world. Reorganization along more scientific and productive lines took place in Europe in the 18th century in response to dramatic population growth.

Mechanization made considerable progress in the USA and Europe during the 19th century. After World War II, there was an explosive growth in the use of agricultural chemicals: herbicides, insecticides, fungicides, and fertilizers. However, there was also a reaction against some forms of intensive agriculture because of the pollution and habitat destruction caused. One result of this was a growth of alternative methods, including organic agriculture.

agronomy study of crops and soils, a branch of agricultural science. Agronomy includes such topics as selective breeding (of plants and animals), irrigation, pest control, and soil analysis and modification.

AH with reference to the Muslim calendar, abbreviation for *anno hegirae* (Latin 'year of the flight' – of ▷Muhammad, from Mecca to Medina).

Ahmedabad or *Ahmadabad* capital of Gujarat, India; population (1981) 2,515,195. It is a cotton-manufacturing centre, and has many sacred buildings of the Hindu, Muslim, and Jain faiths.

Aidan, St *c.* 600–651. Irish monk who converted Northumbria to Christianity and founded Lindisfarne monastery on Holy Island off the NE coast of England. His feast day is 31 Aug.

aid, development money given or lent on concessional terms to developing countries or spent on maintaining agencies for this purpose. In the late 1980s official aid from governments of richer nations amounted to $45–60 billion annually whereas voluntary organizations in the West received about $2.4 billion a year for the Third World. The World Bank is the largest dispenser of aid. It transferred $467 billion to developing countries in 1990. All industrialized United Nations (UN) member countries devote a proportion of their gross national product to aid. In 1990, the UK's aid budget was 0.31% of GNP, the USA's was 0.15%.

aid, foreign another name for development aid; see entry above.

AIDS (acronym for *a*cquired *i*mmune *d*eficiency *s*yndrome) the gravest of the sexually transmitted diseases, or STDs. It is caused by the human immunodeficiency virus (HIV), now known to be a ◊retrovirus, an organism first identified 1983. HIV is transmitted in body fluids, mainly blood and sexual secretions.

The estimated incubation period is 9.8 years. Some AIDS victims die within a few months of the outbreak of symptoms, some survive for several years; roughly 50% are dead within three years. There is no cure for the disease, although the new drug ◊zidovudine (AZT) is claimed to delay the onset of AIDS and diminish its effects. The search continues for an effective vaccine.

The HIV virus originated in Africa, where the total number of cases up to Oct 1988 was 19,141. In the UK, 2,256 people had died of AIDS by Dec 1990, and between 30,000 and 50,000 people were thought to be carriers of the disease. Altogether 1,276 new cases of AIDS were reported in the UK in 1990, a 51% increase over the 1988 figure. In the USA, there were 100,777 deaths from AIDS by Dec 1990, and 161,075 persons with the disease. One million Americans are thought to be infected with the virus. By the year 2000 the World Health Organization expects that 15–20 million adults and 10 million children will have been infected with HIV.

air see ◊atmosphere.

aircraft any aeronautical vehicle, which may be lighter than air (supported by buoyancy) or heavier than air (supported by the dynamic action of air on its surfaces). ◊Balloons and ◊airships are lighter-than-air craft. Heavier-than-air craft include the ◊aeroplane, glider, autogyro, and helicopter.

aircraft carrier ocean-going naval vessel with a broad, flat-topped deck for launching and landing military aircraft.

The first purpose-designed aircraft carrier was the British HMS *Hermes*, completed 1913. Carriers such as HMS *Ark Royal*, completed 1938, played a major role in World War II. Aircraft carriers have always remained popular with major powers, such as the USA and the former USSR (until its demise 1991). Examples include the USSR's *Komsomolsk* 1979 (40,000 tonnes, 15 fixed-wing aircraft, 20 helicopters), the USA's *Eisenhower* 1979 (81,600 tonnes, 95 aircraft), and the British *Invincible* 1980 (19,500 tonnes).

air-cushion vehicle (ACV) craft that is supported by a layer, or cushion, of high-pressure air. The ◊hovercraft is one form of ACV.

Airedale terrier breed of large ◊terrier dog, about 60 cm/2 ft tall, with a rough red-brown coat. It originated about 1850 in England, as a cross of the otter hound and Irish and Welsh terriers.

airlock airtight chamber that allows people to pass between areas of different pressure; also an air bubble in a pipe that impedes fluid flow. An airlock may connect an environment at ordinary pressure and an environment that has high air pressure (such as a submerged caisson used for tunnelling or building dams or bridge foundations).

An airlock may also permit someone wearing breathing apparatus to pass into an airless environment (into water from a submerged submarine or into the vacuum of space from a spacecraft).

air sac in birds, a thin-walled extension of the lungs. There are nine of these and they extend into the abdomen and bones, effectively increasing lung capacity. In mammals, it is another name for the alveoli in the lungs, and in some insects, for widenings of the trachea.

airship or *dirigible* any aircraft that is lighter than air and power-driven, consisting of an elliptical balloon that forms the streamlined envelope or hull and has below it the propulsion system (propellers), steering mechanism, and space for crew, passengers and/or cargo. The balloon section is filled with lighter-than-air gas, either the nonflammable helium or, before helium was industrially available in large enough quantities, the easily ignited and flammable hydrogen.

Ajaccio capital and second-largest port of Corsica; population (1982) 55,279. Founded by the Genoese 1492, it was the birthplace of Napoleon; it has been French since 1768.

Ajax Greek hero in Homer's *Iliad*. Son of Telamon, king of Salamis, he was second only to Achilles among the Greek heroes in the Trojan War. When ◊Agamemnon awarded the armour of the dead Achilles to ◊Odysseus, Ajax is said to have gone mad with jealousy, and then committed suicide in shame.

Ajman smallest of the seven states that make up the ◊United Arab Emirates; area 250 sq km/96 sq mi; population (1985) 64,318.

Akbar Jalal ud-Din Muhammad 1542–1605. Mogul emperor of N India from 1556, when he succeeded his father. He gradually established his rule throughout N India. He is considered the greatest of the Mogul emperors.

Akhenaton another name for ◊Ikhnaton, pharaoh of Egypt.

Akihito 1933– . Emperor of Japan from 1989, succeeding his father Hirohito (Showa). His reign is called the Heisei ('achievement of universal peace') era.

Akkad northern Semitic people who conquered the Sumerians in 2350 BC and ruled Mesopotamia. The ancient city of Akkad in central Mesopotamia, founded by Sargon I, was an imperial centre in the 3rd millennium BC; the site is unidentified, but it was on the Euphrates River.

Akron city in Ohio, USA, on the Cuyahoga River,

56 km/35 mi SE of Cleveland; population (1990) 660,000. Known as the 'Rubber Capital of the World,' it is home to the headquarters of several major tyre and rubber companies, although production there ended by 1982.

Aksum ancient Greek-influenced Semitic kingdom that flourished 1st–6th centuries AD and covered a large part of modern Ethiopia as well as the Sudan. The ruins of its capital, also called Aksum, lie NW of Aduwa, but the site has been developed as a modern city.

Alabama state in S USA; nickname Heart of Dixie/ Cotton State; *area* 134,700 sq km/51,994 sq mi; *capital* Montgomery; *physical* Cumberland Plateau in the N; the Black Belt, or Canebrake, which is excellent cotton-growing country, in the centre; and S of this, the coastal plain of Piny Woods; Alabama and Tennessee rivers; Appalachian mountains; *products* cotton still important though no longer prime crop; soya beans, peanuts, wood products, coal, iron, chemicals, textiles, paper; *population* (1990) 4,040,600; *history* first settled by the French in the early 18th century, it was ceded to Britain 1763, passed to the USA 1783, and became a state 1819. It was one of the Confederate States in the American Civil War.

alabaster naturally occurring fine-grained white or light-coloured translucent form of gypsum, often streaked or mottled. It is a soft material, used for carvings, and ranks second on the ¢Mohs' scale of hardness.

Alamein, El, Battles of in World War II, two decisive battles in the western desert, N Egypt. In the *First Battle of El Alamein* 1–27 July 1942 the British 8th Army under Auchinleck held the German and Italian forces under Rommel. In the *Second Battle of El Alamein* 23 Oct–4 Nov 1942 ¢Montgomery defeated Rommel.

Alamo, the mission fortress in San Antonio, Texas, USA. It was besieged 23 Feb–6 March 1836 by ¢Santa Anna and 4,000 Mexicans; they killed the garrison of about 180, including Davy ¢Crockett and Jim ¢Bowie.

Alaric c. 370–410. King of the Visigoths. In 396 he invaded Greece and retired with much booty to Illyria. In 400 and 408 he invaded Italy, and in 410 captured and sacked Rome, but died the same year on his way to invade Sicily.

Alaska largest state of the USA, on the NW extremity of North America, separated from the lower 48 states by British Columbia; nickname Last Frontier; *total area* 1,530,700 sq km/ 591,004 sq mi; *land area* 1,478,457 sq km/ 570,833 sq mi; *capital* Juneau; *physical* much of Alaska is mountainous; Rocky Mountains include Mount McKinley (Denali), 6,194 m/20,322 ft, the highest peak in North America, and Mount Katmai, a volcano that erupted 1912 and formed the Valley of Ten Thousand Smokes. Caribou thrive in the

Arctic tundra, and elsewhere there are extensive forests; Yukon River; Little Diomede Island, only 4 km/2.5 mi from Russian Big Diomede/Ratmanov Island; *products* oil, natural gas, coal, copper, iron, gold, tin, fur, salmon fisheries and canneries, lumber; *population* (1990) 550,000; including 9% American Indians, Aleuts, and Inuits; *history* various groups of Indians crossed the Bering land bridge 60,000–15,000 years ago; the Eskimo began to settle the Arctic coast from Siberia about 2000 BC; the Aleuts settled the Aleutian archipelago about 1000 BC. The first European to visit Alaska was Vitus Bering 1741. Alaska was a Russian colony from 1744 until purchased by the USA 1867 for $7,200,000; gold was discovered five years later. It became a state 1959. Valuable mineral resources have been exploited from 1968, especially in the Prudhoe Bay area to the SE of Point Barrow. An oil pipeline (1977) runs from Prudhoe Bay to the port of Valdez. Oilspill from a tanker in Prince William Sound caused great environmental damage 1989.

Alba Celtic name for Scotland.

Albania Republic of; country in SE Europe, bordered W and SW by the Adriatic and Mediterranean seas, N and E by Yugoslavia, and SE by Greece; *area* 28,748 sq km/11,097 sq mi; *capital* Tiranë; *physical* mainly mountainous, with rivers flowing E–W, and a narrow coastal plain; *head of state* Ramiz Alia from 1982; *head of government* Vilson Ahmeti from 1991; *political system* emergent democracy; *exports* crude oil, bitumen, chrome, iron ore, nickel, coal, copper wire, tobacco, fruit, vegetables; *population* (1990 est) 3,270,000; *languages* Albanian, Greek; *recent history* communist republic proclaimed under Enver Hoxha 1946. Albania admitted into Comecon 1949; broke off relations with USSR 1961 and China 1978. Diplomatic relations with the West restored 1985. Albania attended the conference of Balkan states 1988. First free multiparty elections held 1991. Former communist officials arrested on corruption charges 1992.

albatross large seabird, genus *Diomedea*, with long narrow wings adapted for gliding and a wingspan of up to 3 m/10 ft, mainly found in the southern hemisphere. It belongs to the order Procellariiformes, the same group as petrels and shearwaters.

Albee Edward 1928– . US playwright. His internationally performed plays are associated with the Theatre of the Absurd and include *The Zoo Story* 1960, *The American Dream* 1961, and *Who's Afraid of Virginia Woolf?* 1962.

Albert Prince Consort 1819–1861. Husband of British Queen ¢Victoria from 1840; a patron of the arts, science, and industry. Albert was the second son of the Duke of Saxe Coburg-Gotha and first cousin to Queen Victoria, whose chief adviser he became. He planned the Great Exhibition of 1851; the profit was used to buy the sites in London of all the South

Kensington museums and colleges and the Royal Albert Hall, built 1871. He died of typhoid.

Alberta province of W Canada; *area* 661,200 sq km/255,223 sq mi; *capital* Edmonton; *physical* Rocky Mountains; dry, treeless prairie in centre and S; mixed forest towards the N. The valley of the Peace River is the most northerly farming land in Canada (except for Inuit pastures), and there are good grazing lands in the foothills of the Rockies; *products* coal; wheat, barley, oats, sugar beet in the south; more than a million head of cattle; oil and natural gas; *population* (1991) 2,501,400; *history* in the 17th century much of the area was part of a grant to the ◊Hudson's Bay Company for the fur trade. Alberta became a province 1905.

Albertville resort town at the entrance to the Val d'Arly in the *département* of Savoie, SE France; population (1981) 17,500; scene of the 1992 Winter Olympics.

albinism rare hereditary condition in which the body has no tyrosinase, one of the enzymes that form the pigment melanin, normally found in the skin, hair, and eyes. As a result, the hair is white and the skin and eyes are pink. The skin and eyes are abnormally sensitive to light, and vision is often impaired.

Albion ancient name for Britain used by the Greeks and Romans. It was mentioned by Pytheas of Massilia (4th century BC), and is probably of Celtic origin, but the Romans, having in mind the white cliffs of Dover, assumed it to be derived from *albus* (white).

albumin or *albumen* any of a group of sulphur-containing ◊proteins. The best known is in the form of egg white; others occur in milk, and as a major component of serum.

alchemy supposed technique of transmuting base metals, such as lead and mercury, into silver and gold by the philosopher's stone, a hypothetical substance, to which was also attributed the power to give eternal life.

Alcibiades 450–404 BC. Athenian general. Handsome and dissolute, he became the archetype of capricious treachery for his military intrigues against his native state with Sparta and Persia; the Persians eventually had him assassinated. He was brought up by ◊Pericles and was a friend of ◊Socrates, whose reputation as a teacher suffered from the association.

alcohol any member of a group of organic chemical compounds characterized by the presence of one or more aliphatic OH (hydroxyl) groups in the molecule, and which form ◊esters with acids. The main uses of alcohols are as solvents for gums, resins, lacquers, and varnishes; in the making of dyes; for essential oils in perfumery; and for medical substances in pharmacy. Alcohol (ethanol) is produced naturally in the ◊fermentation process and is consumed as part of alcoholic beverages.

alcoholic liquor intoxicating drink. ◊Ethanol (ethyl alcohol), a colourless liquid C_2H_5OH, is the basis of all common intoxicants. *Wines, ciders, and sherry* contain alcohol produced by direct fermentation with yeasts of the sugar in the fruit forming the basis of the drink. *Malt liquors* are beers and stouts, in which the starch of a grain is converted to sugar by malting, and the sugar then fermented into alcohol by yeasts. Fermented drinks contain less than 20% alcohol. *Spirits* are distilled from malted liquors or wines, and can contain up to 55% alcohol.

Alcott Louisa May 1832–1888. US author. Her children's classic *Little Women* 1869 drew on her own home circumstances, the heroine Jo being a partial self-portrait. *Good Wives* 1869 was among its sequels.

Alcuin 735–804. English scholar. Born in York, he went to Rome 780, and in 782 took up residence at Charlemagne's court in Aachen. From 796 he was abbot of Tours. He disseminated Anglo-Saxon scholarship, organized education and learning in the Frankish empire, and gave a strong impulse to the Carolingian Renaissance.

aldehyde any of a group of organic chemical compounds prepared by oxidation of primary alcohols, so that the OH (hydroxyl) group loses its hydrogen to give an oxygen joined by a double bond to a carbon atom (the aldehyde group, with the formula CHO). The name is made up from *al*cohol *dehyd*rogenation – that is, alcohol from which hydrogen has been removed. Aldehydes are usually liquids and include methanal (formaldehyde), ethanal (acetaldehyde), and benzaldehyde.

alder any tree or shrub of the genus *Alnus*, in the birch family Betulaceae, found mainly in cooler parts of the northern hemisphere and characterized by toothed leaves and catkins.

alderman Anglo-Saxon term for the noble governor of a shire; after the Norman Conquest the office was replaced with that of sheriff. From the 19th century aldermen were the senior members of the borough or county councils in England and Wales, elected by the other councillors, until the abolition of the office 1974; the title is still used in the City of London.

Aleppo (Syrian *Halab*) ancient city in NW Syria; population (1981) 977,000. There has been a settlement on the site for at least 4,000 years.

Aletsch most extensive glacier in Europe, 23.6 km/14.7 mi long, beginning on the southern slopes of the Jungfrau in the Bernese Alps, Switzerland.

Aleutian Islands volcanic island chain in the N Pacific, stretching 1,200 mi/1,900 km SW of Alaska, of which it forms part; population 6,000 Aleuts plus a large US defence establishment. There are 14 large and more than 100 small islands running along the Aleutian Trench. The islands are mountainous, barren, and treeless.

A level or *Advanced level* in the UK, examinations

taken by some students in no more than four subjects at one time, usually at the age of 18 after two years' study.

Alexander III (Orlando Barninelli) Pope 1159–81. His authority was opposed by Frederick I Barbarossa, but Alexander eventually compelled him to render homage 1178. He supported Henry II of England in his invasion of Ireland, but imposed penance on him after the murder of Thomas à ◊Becket.

Alexander VI (Rodrigo Borgia) 1431–1503. Pope 1492–1503. Of Spanish origin, he bribed his way to the papacy, where he furthered the advancement of his illegitimate children, who included Cesare and Lucrezia ◊Borgia.

Alexander I 1777–1825. Tsar from 1801. Defeated by Napoleon at Austerlitz 1805, he made peace at Tilsit 1807, but economic crisis led to a break with Napoleon's continental system and the opening of Russian ports to British trade; this led to Napoleon's ill-fated invasion of Russia 1812.

Alexander II 1818–1881. Tsar from 1855. He embarked on reforms of the army, the government, and education, and is remembered as 'the Liberator' for his emancipation of the serfs 1861, but he lacked the personnel to implement his reforms. However, the revolutionary element remained unsatisfied, and Alexander became increasingly autocratic and was assassinated by an anarchistic terrorist group, the ◊Nihilists.

Alexander III 1845–1894. Tsar from 1881, when he succeeded his father, Alexander II. He pursued a reactionary policy, promoting Russification and persecuting the Jews. He married Dagmar (1847–1928), daughter of Christian IX of Denmark and sister of Queen Alexandra of Britain, 1866.

Alexander I *c.* 1078–1124. King of Scotland from 1107, known as **the Fierce**. He ruled to the N of the rivers Forth and Clyde while his brother and successor David ruled to the S. He assisted Henry I of England in his campaign against Wales 1114 but defended the independence of the church in Scotland.

Alexander II 1198–1249. King of Scotland from 1214, when he succeeded his father William the Lion. Alexander supported the English barons in their struggle with King John after ◊Magna Carta. By the treaty of Newcastle 1244 he pledged allegiance to Henry III of England.

Alexander III 1241–1285. King of Scotland from 1249, son of Alexander II. In 1263, by military defeat of Norwegian forces, he extended his authority over the Western Isles, which had been dependent on Norway. He strengthened the power of the central Scottish government.

Alexander I Karageorgevich 1888–1934. Regent of Serbia 1912–21 and king of Yugoslavia 1921–34, as dictator from 1929. Second son of ◊Peter I, King of Serbia, he was declared regent for his father 1912 and on his father's death became king of the state of South Slavs – Yugoslavia – that had come into being 1918.

Alexander Nevski, St 1220–1263. Russian military leader, son of the grand duke of Novgorod. In 1240 he defeated the Swedes on the banks of the Neva (hence Nevski), and 1242 defeated the Teutonic Knights on the frozen Lake Peipus.

Alexander the Great 356–323 BC. King of Macedonia and conqueror of the large Persian empire. As commander of the vast Macedonian army he conquered Greece 336. He defeated the Persian king Darius in Asia Minor 333, then moved on to Egypt, where he founded Alexandria. He defeated the Persians again in Assyria 331, then advanced further east to reach the Indus.

Alexandra 1872–1918. Last tsarina of Russia 1894–1917. She was the former Princess Alix of Hessen and granddaughter of Britain's Queen Victoria. She married ◊Nicholas II and, from 1907, fell under the spell of ◊Rasputin, a 'holy man' brought to the palace to try to cure her son of haemophilia. She was shot with the rest of her family by the Bolsheviks in the Russian Revolution.

Alexandria or *El Iskandariya* city, chief port, and second largest city of Egypt, situated between the Mediterranean and Lake Maryut; population (1986) 5,000,000. It is linked by canal with the Nile and is an industrial city (oil refining, gas processing, and cotton and grain trading). Founded 331 BC by Alexander the Great, Alexandria was the capital of Egypt for over 1,000 years. The Library of Alexandria, founded 330 BC, was the world's first state-funded scientific institution and comprised a museum, teaching facilities, and a library containing 700,000 scrolls.

Alexandria, school of group of writers and scholars of Alexandria who made the city the chief centre of culture in the Western world from about 331 BC to AD 642. They include the poets Callimachus, Apollonius Rhodius, and Theocritus; Euclid, pioneer of geometry; Eratosthenes, the geographer; Hipparchus, who developed a system of trigonometry; the astronomer Ptolemy, who gave his name to the Ptolemaic system of astronomy that endured for over 1,000 years; and the Jewish philosopher Philo. The Gnostics and Neo-Platonists also flourished in Alexandria.

Alexius I (Comnenus) 1048–1118. Byzantine emperor 1081–1118. The Latin (W European) Crusaders helped him repel Norman and Turkish invasions, and he devoted great skill to buttressing the threatened empire.

Alexius III (Angelos) died *c.* 1210. Byzantine emperor 1195–1203. He gained power by deposing and blinding his brother Isaac II, but Isaac's Venetian allies enabled him and his son Alexius IV to regain power as co-emperors.

Alexius IV (Angelos) 1182–1204. Byzantine

emperor from 1203, when, with the aid of the army of the Fourth Crusade, he deposed his uncle Alexius III. He soon lost the support of the Crusaders, and was overthrown and murdered by another Alexius, Alexius Mourtzouphlus (son-in-law of Alexius III) 1204.

alfalfa or *lucerne* perennial tall herbaceous plant *Medicago sativa* of the pea family Leguminosae. It is native to Eurasia and bears spikes of small purple flowers in late summer. It is now a major fodder crop, generally processed into hay, meal, or silage.

Alfonsín Foulkes Raúl Ricardo 1927– . Argentine politician, president 1983–89, leader of the moderate Radical Union Party (UCR). As president from the country's return to civilian government, he set up an investigation of the army's human-rights violations. Economic problems caused him to seek help from the International Monetary Fund and introduce austerity measures.

Alfred the Great c. 848–c. 900. King of Wessex from 871. He defended England against Danish invasion, in 878 being forced to retire to the stronghold of ♢Athelney, from where he finally emerged to win the victory of Edington, Wiltshire. By the Peace of Wedmore 878 the Danish leader Guthrum (died 890) agreed to withdraw from Wessex and from Mercia W of Watling Street. A new landing in Kent encouraged a revolt of the East Anglian Danes, which was suppressed 884–86, and a final foreign invasion was defeated 892–96. Alfred founded the first English navy, and put into operation a legal code.

algae (singular *alga*) diverse group of plants (including those commonly called seaweeds) that shows great variety of form, ranging from single-celled forms to multicellular seaweeds of considerable size and complexity. Algae were formerly included within the division Thallophyta, together with fungi and bacteria. Their classification changed with increased awareness of the important differences existing between the algae and Thallophyta, and also between the groups of algae themselves; many botanists now place each algal group in a separate class or division of its own.

Algarve ancient kingdom in S Portugal, the modern district of Faro, a popular holiday resort; population (1981) 323,500. The Algarve became part of the Portuguese kingdom 1189, after five centuries of Muslim rule.

algebra system of arithmetic applying to any set of non-numerical symbols (usually letters), and the axioms and rules by which they are combined or operated upon; sometimes known as *generalized arithmetic*.

Algeria Democratic and Popular Republic of; country in N Africa, bordered E by Tunisia and Libya, SE by Niger, SW by Mali, NW by Morocco, and N by the Mediterranean Sea; *area* 2,381,741 sq km/ 919,352 sq mi; *capital* al-Jazair (Algiers); *physical* coastal plains backed by mountains in N; Sahara Desert in S; *head of state* Ali Kafi from 1992; *head of government* Sid Ahmed Ghozali from 1992; *political system* transitional; *exports* oil, natural gas, iron, wine, olive oil; *population* (1990 est) 25,715,000 (Arab 83%, Berber 17%); *languages* Arabic (official); Berber, French; *recent history* independence from France achieved 1962 after eight years of civil war. Ahmed Ben Bella, leader of the National Liberation Front (FLN) elected president of the republic but deposed 1965 by a military coup. Limited political pluralism introduced 1989. 1991 elections won by Fundamentalist Islamic Salvation Front (FIS); military took control 1992.

Algiers (Arabic *al-Jazair*; French *Alger*) capital of Algeria, situated on the narrow coastal plain between the Atlas Mountains and the Mediterranean; population (1984) 2,442,300. Founded by the Arabs AD 935, Algiers was taken by the Turks 1518 and by the French 1830.

Algiers, Battle of bitter conflict in Algiers 1954–62 between the Algerian nationalist population and the French colonial army and French settlers. The conflict ended with Algerian independence 1962.

ALGOL (acronym for *algo*rithmic *l*anguage) in computing, an early high-level programming language, developed in the 1950s and 1960s for scientific applications. A general-purpose language, ALGOL is best suited to mathematical work and has an algebraic style. Although no longer in common use, it has greatly influenced more recent languages, such as ADA and PASCAL.

algorithm procedure or series of steps that can be used to solve a problem. In computer science, it describes the logical sequence of operations to be performed by a program. A flow chart is a visual representation of an algorithm.

Ali c. 598–660. 4th caliph of Islam. He was born in Mecca, the son of Abu Talib, uncle to the prophet Muhammad, who gave him his daughter Fatima in marriage. On Muhammad's death 632, Ali had a claim to succeed him, but this was not conceded until 656. After a stormy reign, he was assassinated. Around Ali's name the controversy has raged between the Sunni and the Shi'ites (see ♢Islam), the former denying his right to the caliphate and the latter supporting it.

Ali Muhammad. Adopted name of Cassius Marcellus Clay, Jr 1942– . US boxer. Olympic light-heavyweight champion 1960, he went on to become world professional heavyweight champion 1964, and was the only man to regain the title twice.

Alia Ramiz 1925– . Albanian communist politician, head of state from 1982 and party leader from 1985. He gradually relaxed the isolationist policies of his predecessor Hoxha and following public unrest introduced political and economic reforms, including free elections 1991, when he was elected executive president.

alibi in law, a provable assertion that the accused was at some other place when a crime was committed. In Britain it can usually only be used as a defence in a ◊crown court trial if the prosecution is supplied with details before the trial.

Aligarh city in Uttar Pradesh, N central India; population (1981) 320,861. Industries include agricultural manufacturing and processing, engineering, and textiles. The city is also named Koil; Aligarh is the name of a nearby fort.

alimentary canal in animals, the tube through which food passes; it extends from the mouth to the anus. It is a complex organ, adapted for digestion. In human adults, it is about 9 m/30 ft long, consisting of the mouth cavity, pharynx, oesophagus, stomach, and the small and large intestines.

alimony in the USA, money allowance given by court order to a former spouse after separation or ◊divorce. The right has been extended to relationships outside marriage and is colloquially termed palimony. Alimony is separate and distinct from court orders for child support. In the UK the legal term is ◊maintenance.

aliphatic compound any organic chemical compound in which the carbon atoms are joined in straight chains, as in hexane (C_6H_{14}), or in branched chains, as in 2–methylpentane ($CH_3CH(CH_3)CH_2CH_2CH_3$).

alkali in chemistry, a compound classed as a ◊base that is soluble in water. Alkalis neutralize acids and are soapy to the touch. The hydroxides of metals are alkalis; those of sodium (sodium hydroxide, NaOH) and of potassium (potassium hydroxide, KOH) being chemically powerful; both were derived from the ashes of plants.

alkali metal any of a group of six metallic elements with similar chemical bonding properties: lithium, sodium, potassium, rubidium, caesium, and francium. They form a linked group in the ◊periodic table of the elements. They are univalent (have a valency of one) and of very low density (lithium, sodium, and potassium float on water); in general they are reactive, soft, low-melting-point metals.

alkaline-earth metal any of a group of six metallic elements with similar bonding properties: beryllium, magnesium, calcium, strontium, barium, and radium. They form a linked group in the ◊periodic table of the elements. They are strongly basic, bivalent (have a valency of two), and occur in nature only in compounds. They and their compounds are used to make alloys, oxidizers, and drying agents.

alkaloid any of a number of physiologically active and frequently poisonous substances contained in some plants. They are usually organic bases and contain nitrogen. They form salts with acids and, when soluble, give alkaline solutions.

alkane member of a group of ◊hydrocarbons having the general formula C_nH_{2n+2}, commonly known as **paraffins**. Lighter alkanes, such as methane, ethane, propane, and butane, are colourless gases; heavier ones are liquids or solids. In nature they are found in natural gas and petroleum. As alkanes contain only single covalent bonds, they are said to be saturated.

alkene member of the group of ◊hydrocarbons having the general formula C_nH_{2n}, formerly known as **olefins**. Lighter alkenes, such as ethene and propene, are gases, obtained from the cracking of oil fractions. Alkenes are unsaturated compounds, characterized by one or more double bonds between adjacent carbon atoms. They react by addition.

alkyne member of the group of ◊hydrocarbons with the general formula C_nH_{2n-2}, formerly known as the **acetylenes**. They are unsaturated compounds, characterized by one or more triple bonds between adjacent carbon atoms. Lighter alkynes, such as ethyne, are gases; heavier ones are liquids or solids.

Allah Islamic name for God.

Allahabad ('city of god') historic city in Uttar Pradesh state, NE India, 580 km/360 mi SE of Delhi, on the Yamuna River where it meets the Ganges and the mythical Seraswati River; population (1981) 642,000. A Hindu religious festival is held here every 12 years with the participants washing away sin and sickness by bathing in the rivers.

allegory in literature, the description or illustration of one thing in terms of another; a work of poetry or prose in the form of an extended metaphor or parable that makes use of symbolic fictional characters.

allele one of two or more alternative forms of a ◊gene at a given position (locus) on a chromosome, caused by a difference in the ◊DNA. Blue and brown eyes in humans are determined by different alleles of the gene for eye colour.

Allen Woody. Adopted name of Allen Stewart Konigsberg 1935– . US film writer, director, and actor, known for his cynical, witty, often self-deprecating parody and offbeat humour. His films include *Sleeper* 1973, *Annie Hall* 1977 (for which he won three Academy Awards), *Manhattan* 1979, and *Hannah and Her Sisters* 1986, all of which he directed, wrote, and appeared in. From the late 1970s, Woody Allen has mixed his output of comedies with straight dramas, such as *Interiors* 1978 and *Another Woman* 1988, but *Crimes and Misdemeanors* 1990 broke with tradition by combining humour and straight drama.

Allende (Gossens) Salvador 1908–1973. Chilean left-wing politician. Elected president 1970 as the candidate of the Popular Front alliance, Allende never succeeded in keeping the electoral alliance together in government. His failure to solve the country's economic problems or to deal with political subversion allowed the army, backed by the

CIA, to stage the 1973 coup which brought about the death of Allende and many of his supporters.

allergy special sensitivity of the body that makes it react, with an exaggerated response of the natural immune defence mechanism, especially with ▷histamines, to the introduction of an otherwise harmless foreign substance (*allergen*).

The person subject to hay fever in summer is allergic to one or more kinds of pollen. Many asthmatics are allergic to certain kinds of dust or to microorganisms in animal fur or feathers. Others come out in nettle rash or are violently sick if they eat shellfish or eggs. Drugs such as antihistamines and corticosteroids are used.

Allies, the in World War I, the 23 countries allied against the Central Powers (Germany, Austria-Hungary, Turkey, and Bulgaria), including France, Italy, Russia, the UK, Australia and other Commonwealth nations, and, in the latter part of the war, the USA; and in World War II, the 49 countries allied against the ▷Axis powers (Germany, Italy, and Japan), including France, the UK, Australia and other Commonwealth nations, the USA, and the USSR.

alligator reptile of the genus *Alligator*, related to the crocodile. There are two species: *A. mississipiensis*, the Mississippi alligator of the southern states of the USA, and *A. sinensis* from the swamps of the lower Chang Jiang River in China. The former grows to about 4 m/12 ft, but the latter only to 1.5 m/5 ft. Alligators lay their eggs in sand; they feed on fish and mammals but seldom attack people.

alloy metal blended with some other metallic or nonmetallic substance to give it special qualities, such as resistance to corrosion, greater hardness, or tensile strength. Useful alloys include bronze, brass, pewter, solder, steel, and stainless steel.

allspice spice prepared from the dried berries of the evergreen pimento tree or West Indian pepper tree *Pimenta dioica* of the myrtle family, cultivated chiefly in Jamaica.

alluvial deposit layer of broken rocky matter, or sediment, formed from material that has been carried in suspension by a river or stream and dropped as the velocity of the current changes. River plains and deltas are made entirely of alluvial deposits.

Alma-Ata formerly (to 1921) *Vernyi*, capital of the republic of Kazakhstan; population (1991) 1,151,300. Industries include engineering, printing, tobacco processing, textile manufacturing, and leather products.

Almohad Berber dynasty 1130–1269 founded by the Berber prophet Muhammad ibn Tumart (c. 1080–1130). The Almohads ruled much of Morocco and Spain, which they took by defeating the ▷Almoravids; they later took the area that today forms Algeria and Tunis. Their policy of religious 'purity' involved the forced conversion and massacre of the Jewish population of Spain. The Almohads were themselves defeated by the Christian kings of Spain 1212, and in Morocco 1269.

almond tree *Prunus amygdalus*, family Rosaceae, related to the peach and apricot. Dessert almonds are the kernels of the fruit of the sweet variety *P. amygdalus dulcis*, which is also the source of a low-cholesterol culinary oil. Oil of bitter almonds, from the variety *P. amygdalus amara*, is used in flavouring. Almond oil is also used for cosmetics, perfumes, and fine lubricants.

Almoravid Berber dynasty 1056–1147 founded by the prophet Abdullah ibn Tashfin, ruling much of Morocco and Spain in the 11th–12th centuries. The Almoravids came from the Sahara and in the 11th century began laying the foundations of an empire covering the whole of Morocco and parts of Algeria; their capital was the newly founded Marrakesh. In 1086 they defeated Alfonso VI of Castile to gain much of Spain. They were later overthrown by the ▷Almohads.

aloe plant of the genus *Aloe* of African plants, family Liliaceae, distinguished by their long, fleshy, spiny-edged leaves. The drug usually referred to as 'bitter aloes' is a powerful cathartic prepared from the juice of the leaves of several of the species.

alpaca domesticated South American hoofed mammal *Lama pacos* of the camel family, found in Chile, Peru, and Bolivia, and herded at high elevations in the Andes. It is bred mainly for its long, fine, silky wool, and stands about 1 m/3 ft tall at the shoulder with neck and head another 60 cm/2 ft.

alphabet set of conventional symbols used for writing, based on a correlation between individual symbols and spoken sounds, so called from *alpha* (α) and *beta* (β), the names of the first two letters of the classical Greek alphabet. The earliest known alphabet is from Palestine, about 1700 BC. Alphabetic writing now takes many forms, for example the Hebrew *aleph-beth* and the Arabic script, both written from right to left; the Devanagari script of the Hindus, in which the symbols 'hang' from a line common to all the symbols; and the Greek alphabet, with the first clearly delineated vowel symbols.

Alpha Centauri or *Rigil Kent* the brightest star in the constellation Centaurus and the third brightest star in the sky. It is actually a triple star (see ▷binary star); the two brighter stars orbit each other every 80 years, and the third, Proxima Centauri, is the closest star to the Sun.

alpha particle positively charged, high-energy particle emitted from the nucleus of a radioactive ▷atom. It is one of the products of the spontaneous disintegration of radioactive elements (see ▷radioactivity) such as radium and thorium, and is identical with the nucleus of a helium atom – that is, it consists of two protons and two neutrons. The process of emission, *alpha decay*, transforms one element into another, decreasing the atomic (or

alpaca

proton) number by two and the atomic mass (or nucleon number) by four.

Alps mountain chain, the barrier between N Italy and France, Germany, and Austria. Famous peaks include *Mont Blanc*, the highest at 4,809 m/ 15,777 ft; *Matterhorn* in the Pennine Alps, 4,479 m/ 14,694 ft; *Eiger* in the Bernese Alps/Oberland, 3,970 m/13,030 ft; and *Jungfrau*, 4,166 m/13,673 ft.

Alsace region of France; area 8,300 sq km/ 3,204 sq mi; population (1986) 1,600,000. It consists of the *départements* of Bas-Rhin and Haut-Rhin, and its capital is Strasbourg.

Alsace-Lorraine area of NE France, lying W of the river Rhine. It forms the French regions of ◊Alsace and ◊Lorraine. The former iron and steel industries are being replaced by electronics, chemicals, and precision engineering.

Alsatian breed of dog known officially from 1977 as the *German shepherd*. It is about 63 cm/26 in tall and has a wolflike appearance, a thick coat with many varieties of colouring, and a distinctive gait.

Altamira caves decorated with Palaeolithic wall paintings, the first such to be discovered, in 1879. The paintings are realistic depictions of bison, deer, and horses in polychrome (several colours). The caves are near the village of Santillana del Mar in Santander province, N Spain.

alternation of generations typical life cycle of terrestrial plants and some seaweeds, in which there are two distinct forms occurring alternately: *diploid* (having two sets of chromosomes) and *haploid* (one set of chromosomes). The diploid generation produces haploid spores by ◊meiosis, and is called the sporophyte, while the haploid generation produces gametes (sex cells), and is called

the gametophyte. The gametes fuse to form a diploid ◊zygote which develops into a new sporophyte; thus the sporophyte and gametophyte alternate.

alternative energy see ◊energy, alternative

alternative medicine see ◊medicine, alternative.

alternator electricity generator that produces an alternating current.

Althing parliament of Iceland, established about 930, and the oldest in the world. It was dissolved 1800, revived 1843 as an advisory body, and became a legislative body again 1874. It has an upper and a lower house comprising one-third and two-thirds of its members respectively.

altimeter instrument used in aircraft that measures altitude, or height above sea level. The common type is a form of aneroid ◊barometer, which works by sensing the differences in air pressure at different altitudes. This must continually be recalibrated because of the change in air pressure with changing weather conditions. The ◊radar altimeter measures the height of the aircraft above the ground, measuring the time it takes for radio pulses emitted by the aircraft to be reflected. Radar altimeters are essential features of automatic and blind-landing systems.

Altiplano densely populated upland plateau of the Andes of South America, stretching from S Peru to NW Argentina. The height of the Altiplano is 3,000–4,000 m/10,000–13,000 ft.

alto voice or instrument between tenor and soprano. The sound of the traditional male alto voice is trumpet-like and penetrating; the female contralto is rich and mellow in tone. The alto range is centred on the octave above middle C on the piano.

aluminium lightweight, silver-white, ductile and malleable, metallic element, symbol Al, atomic number 13, relative atomic mass 26.9815. It is the third most abundant element (and the most abundant metal) in the Earth's crust, of which it makes up about 8.1% by mass. It is an excellent conductor of electricity and oxidizes easily. Because of its rapid oxidation a great deal of energy is needed in order to separate aluminium from its ores, and the pure metal was not readily obtainable until the middle of the 19th century. Commercially, it is prepared by the electrolysis of ◊bauxite.

Alzheimer's disease common manifestation of ◊dementia, thought to afflict one in 20 people over 65. Attacking the brain's 'grey matter', it is a disease of mental processes rather than physical function, characterized by memory loss and progressive intellectual impairment.

Amal radical Lebanese ◊Shi'ite military force, established by Musa Sadr in the 1970s. The movement split into extremist and moderate groups 1982, but both sides agreed on the aim of increasing Shi'ite political representation in Lebanon.

American Indians: major tribes

Area	Tribe
North America	
Arctic	Inuit, Aleut
Sub-Arctic	Algonquin, Cree, Ottawa
NE Woodlands	Huron, Iroquois, Mohican, Shawnee (Tecumseh)
SE Woodlands	Cherokee, Choctaw, Creek, Hopewell, Natchez, Seminole
Great Plains	Blackfoot, Cheyenne, Comanche, Pawnee, Sioux
NW Coast	Chinook, Tlingit, Tsimshian
Desert West	Apache, Navajo, Pueblo, Hopi, Mojave, Shoshone
Central America	
	Maya, Toltec, Aztec, Mexican

amalgam any alloy of mercury with other metals. Most metals will form amalgams, except iron and platinum. Amalgam is used in dentistry for filling teeth, and usually contains copper, silver, and zinc as the main alloying ingredients. This amalgam is pliable when first mixed and then sets hard.

Amazon South American river, the world's second longest, 6,570 km/4,080 mi, and the largest in volume of water. Its main headstreams, the Marañón and the Ucayali, rise in central Peru and unite to flow E across Brazil for about 4,000 km/2,500 mi. It has 48,280 km/30,000 mi of navigable waterways, draining 7,000,000 sq km/2,750,000 sq mi, nearly half the South American land mass. It reaches the Atlantic on the equator, its estuary 80 km/50 mi wide, discharging a volume of water so immense that 64 km/40 mi out to sea, fresh water remains at the surface. The Amazon basin covers 7.5 million sq km/3 million sq mi, of which 5 million sq km/2 million sq mi is tropical forest containing 30% of all known plant and animal species. It is the wettest region on Earth; average rainfall 2.54 m/8.3 ft a year. Independent estimates and Landsat surveys indicated a deforestation of 12% by 1985 (up from 0.6% in 1975).

Amazon in Greek mythology, a member of a group of legendary female warriors living near the Black Sea, who cut off their right breasts to use the bow more easily. Their queen, Penthesilea, was killed by Achilles at the siege of Troy. The term Amazon has come to mean a strong, fierce woman.

Amazonia those regions of Brazil, Colombia, Ecuador, Peru, and Bolivia lying within the basin of the Amazon River.

amber fossilized resin from coniferous trees of the Middle Tertiary period. It is often washed ashore on the Baltic coast with plant and animal specimens preserved in it; many extinct species have been found preserved in this way. It ranges in colour from red to yellow, and is used to make jewellery.

ambergris fatty substance, resembling wax, found in the stomach and intestines of the sperm ◊whale. It is found floating in warm seas, and is used in perfumery as a fixative.

Amenhotep III King of Egypt (c. 1400 BC) who built great monuments at Thebes, including the temples at Luxor. Two portrait statues at his tomb were known to the Greeks as the colossi of Memnon; one was cracked, and when the temperature changed at dawn it gave out an eerie sound, then thought supernatural. His son **Amenhotep IV** changed his name to ◊Ikhnaton.

America western hemisphere of the Earth, containing the continents of ◊North America and ◊South America, with ◊Central America in between. This great land mass extends from the Arctic to the Antarctic, from beyond 75° N to past 55° S. The area is about 42,000,000 sq km/16,000,000 sq mi, and the estimated population is over 500 million.

American Civil War 1861–65; see ◊Civil War, American.

American Federation of Labor and Congress of Industrial Organizations (AFL–CIO) federation of North American trade unions, currently representing about 20% of the workforce in North America.

American football see ◊football, American

American Independence, War of alternative name of the ◊American Revolution.

American Indian one of the aboriginal peoples of the Americas. Columbus named them Indians 1492 because he believed he had found a new route to India. The Asian ancestors of the Indians are thought to have entered North America on the land bridge, Beringia, exposed by the lowered sea level between Siberia and Alaska during the last ice age, 60,000–35,000 BC.

American Revolution revolt 1775–83 of the British North American colonies that resulted in the establishment of the United States of America. It was caused by colonial resentment at the attitude that commercial interests of any colony should be subordinate to those of the mother country; and by the unwillingness of the colonists to pay for a standing army. It was also fuelled by the colonists' antimonarchist sentiment and a desire to participate in the policies affecting them.

American Samoa see ◊Samoa, American.

americium radioactive metallic element of the ◊actinide series, symbol Am, atomic number 95, relative atomic mass 243.13; it was first synthesized 1944. It occurs in nature in minute quantities in ◊pitchblende and other uranium ores, where it is produced from the decay of neutron-bombarded plutonium, and is the element with the highest atomic number that occurs in nature. It is synthesized in quantity only in nuclear reactors by the bombardment of plutonium with neutrons.

amethyst variety of ◊quartz, SiO_2, coloured violet by the presence of small quantities of manganese; used as a semiprecious stone. Amethysts are found chiefly in the Ural Mountains, India, the USA, Uruguay, and Brazil.

Amin (Dada) Idi 1926– . Ugandan politician, president 1971–79. He led the coup that deposed Milton Obote 1971, expelled the Asian community 1972, and exercised a reign of terror over his people. He fled when insurgent Ugandan and Tanzanian troops invaded the country 1979.

amine any of a class of organic chemical compounds in which one or more of the hydrogen atoms of ammonia (NH_3) have been replaced by other groups of atoms.

amino acid water-soluble organic ◊molecule, mainly composed of carbon, oxygen, hydrogen, and nitrogen, containing both a basic amine group (NH_2) and an acidic carboxyl (COOH) group. When two or more amino acids are joined together, they are known as ◊peptides; ◊proteins are made up of interacting polypeptides (peptide chains consisting of more than three amino acids) and are folded or twisted in characteristic shapes.

Amis Kingsley 1922– . English novelist and poet. His works include *Lucky Jim* 1954, a comic portrayal of life in a provincial university, and *Take a Girl Like You* 1960. He won the UK's Booker Prize 1986 for *The Old Devils*. He is the father of Martin Amis.

Amis Martin 1949– . English novelist. His works are characterized by their savage wit and include *The Rachel Papers* 1974, *Money* 1984, *London Fields* 1989, and *Time's Arrow* 1991.

Amman capital and chief industrial centre of Jordan; population (1986) 1,160,000. It is a major communications centre, linking historic trade routes across the Middle East.

Ammon in Egyptian mythology, the king of the gods, the equivalent of ◊Zeus or ◊Jupiter. The name is also spelled Amen/Amun, as in the name of the pharaoh Tutankh*amen*. In art, he is represented as a ram, as a man with a ram's head, or as a man crowned with feathers.

ammonia NH_3, a colourless pungent-smelling gas, lighter than air and very soluble in water. It is made on an industrial scale by the ◊Haber process, and used mainly to produce nitrogenous fertilizers, some explosives, and nitric acid.

ammonite extinct marine ◊cephalopod mollusc of the order Ammonoidea, related to the modern nautilus. The shell was curled in a plane spiral and made up of numerous gas-filled chambers, the outermost containing the body of the animal. Many species flourished between 200 million and 65 million years ago, ranging in size from that of a small coin to 2 m/6 ft across.

amnesia loss or impairment of memory. As a clinical condition it may be caused by disease or injury to the brain, or by shock; in some cases it may be a symptom of an emotional disorder.

amnesty release of political prisoners under a general pardon, or a person or group of people from criminal liability for a particular action; for example, the occasional amnesties in the UK for those who surrender firearms that they hold illegally.

Amnesty International human-rights organization established in the UK 1961 to campaign for the release of political prisoners worldwide; it is politically unaligned. It has 700,000 members, and section offices in 43 countries. The organization was awarded the Nobel Peace Prize 1977.

amniocentesis sampling the amniotic fluid surrounding a fetus in the womb for diagnostic purposes. It is used to detect Down's syndrome and other genetic abnormalities.

amoeba (plural *amoebae*) one of the simplest living animals, consisting of a single cell and belonging to the ◊protozoa group. The body consists of colourless protoplasm. Its activities are controlled by the nucleus, and it feeds by flowing round and engulfing organic debris. It reproduces by ◊binary fission. Some species of amoeba are harmful parasites.

ampere SI unit (abbreviation amp, symbol A) of electrical current. Electrical current is measured in a similar way to water current, in terms of an amount per unit time; one ampere represents a flow of about 6.28×10^{18} ◊electrons per second, or a rate of flow of charge of one coulomb per second.

amphetamine or *speed* powerful synthetic ◊stimulant. Benzedrine was the earliest amphetamine marketed, used as a pep pill in World War II to help soldiers overcome fatigue, and until the 1970s amphetamines were prescribed by doctors as an appetite suppressant for weight loss; as an antidepressant, to induce euphoria; and as a stimulant, to increase alertness. Indications for its use today are very restricted because of severe side effects, including addiction and distorted behaviour.

amphibian member of the vertebrate class Amphibia, which generally spend their larval (tadpole) stage in fresh water, transferring to land at maturity (after ◊metamorphosis) and generally returning to water to breed. Like fish and reptiles, they continue to grow throughout life, and cannot maintain a temperature greatly differing from that of their environment. The class includes salamanders, frogs, and toads.

amphitheatre large oval or circular building used by the Romans for gladiatorial contests, fights of wild animals, and other similar events; it is a structure with an open space surrounded by rising rows of seats; the arena of an amphitheatre is completely surrounded by the seats of the spectators, hence the name (Greek *amphi* 'around'). The ◊Colosseum in Rome, completed AD 80, held 50,000 spectators.

Amritsar industrial city in the Punjab, India; population (1981) 595,000. It is the holy city of ◊Sikhism. In 1919 it was the scene of the Amritsar Massacre 1919 when British troops opened fire on a crowd assembled to protest against the arrest of two Indian National Congress leaders; 379 Indians were killed. In 1984 armed demonstrators were evicted from the Golden Temple by the Indian army under General Dayal, 325 being killed. Subsequently, Indian prime minister Indira Gandhi was assassinated in reprisal.

Amsterdam capital of the Netherlands; population (1991) 1,02,400. Canals cut through the city link it with the North Sea and the Rhine, and as a Dutch port it is second only to Rotterdam. There is shipbuilding, printing, food processing, banking, and insurance.

Amundsen Roald 1872–1928. Norwegian explorer who in 1903–06 became the first person to navigate the ◊Northwest Passage. Beaten to the North Pole by US explorer Robert Peary 1910, he reached the South Pole ahead of Captain Scott 1911.

Amur river in E Asia. Formed by the Argun and Shilka rivers, the Amur enters the Sea of Okhotsk. At its mouth at Nikolaevsk it is 16 km/10 mi wide. For much of its course of over 4,400 km/2,730 mi it forms, together with its tributary, the Ussuri, the boundary between Russia and China.

Anabaptist member of any of various 16th-century radical Protestant sects. They believed in adult rather than child baptism, and sought to establish utopian communities. Anabaptist groups spread rapidly in N Europe, particularly in Germany, and were widely persecuted.

anabolic steroid any hormone of the ◊steroid group that stimulates tissue growth. Its use in medicine is limited to the treatment of some anaemias and breast cancers; it may help to break up blood clots. Side effects include aggressive behaviour, masculinization in women, and, in children, reduced height.

It is used in sports, such as weightlifting and athletics, to increase muscle bulk for greater strength and stamina, but it is widely condemned because of the side effects. In 1988 the Canadian sprinter Ben Johnson was stripped of an Olympic gold medal for taking anabolic steroids.

anaconda South American snake *Eunectes murinus*, a member of the python and boa family, the Boidae. One of the largest snakes, growing to 9 m/30 ft or more, it is found in and near water, where it lies in wait for the birds and animals on which it feeds. The anaconda is not venomous, but kills its prey by coiling round it and squeezing until the creature suffocates.

anaemia condition caused by a shortage of haemoglobin, the oxygen-carrying component of red blood cells. The main symptoms are fatigue, pallor, breathlessness, palpitations, and poor resistance to infection. Treatment depends on the cause.

anaerobic (of living organisms) not requiring oxygen for the release of energy from food molecules such as glucose. Anaerobic organisms include many bacteria, yeasts, and internal parasites. In

plants, yeasts, and bacteria, anaerobic respiration results in the production of alcohol and carbon dioxide, a process that is exploited by both the brewing and the baking industries (see ◊fermentation).

anaesthetic drug that produces loss of sensation or consciousness; the resulting state is *anaesthesia*, in which the patient is insensitive to stimuli. Anaesthesia may also happen as a result of nerve disorder.

analgesic agent for relieving ◊pain. Opiates alter the perception or appreciation of pain and are effective in controlling 'deep' visceral (internal) pain. Non-opiates, such as ◊aspirin, ◊paracetamol, and NSAIDs (nonsteroidal anti-inflammatory drugs), relieve musculoskeletal pain and reduce inflammation in soft tissues.

analogue computer computing device that performs calculations through the interaction of continuously varying physical quantities, such as voltages (as distinct from the more common ◊digital computer, which works with discrete quantities). An analogue computer is said to operate in real time (corresponding to time in the real world), and can therefore be used to monitor and control other events as they happen.

analytical chemistry branch of chemistry that deals with the determination of the chemical composition of substances. *Qualitative analysis* determines the identities of the substances in a given sample; *quantitative analysis* determines how much of a particular substance is present.

anarchism political belief that society should have no government, laws, police, or other authority, but should be a free association of all its members. It does not mean 'without order'; most theories of anarchism imply an order of a very strict and symmetrical kind, but they maintain that such order can be achieved by cooperation. Anarchism must not be confused with nihilism (a purely negative and destructive activity directed against society); anarchism is essentially a pacifist movement.

anatomy study of the structure of the body and its component parts, especially the human body, as distinguished from physiology, which is the study of bodily functions.

ANC abbreviation for ◊*African National Congress*, South African nationalist organization.

Anchorage port and largest city of Alaska, USA, at the head of Cook Inlet; population (1990) 226,340. Established 1918, Anchorage is an important centre of administration, communication, and commerce. Oil and gas extraction and fish canning are also important to the local economy.

anchovy small fish *Engraulis encrasicholus* of the ◊herring family. It is fished extensively, being abundant in the Mediterranean, and is also found on the Atlantic coast of Europe and in the Black Sea. It grows to 20 cm/8 in.

ancien régime the old order; the feudal, absolute

monarchy in France before the French Revolution 1789.

ancient art art of prehistoric cultures and the ancient civilizations around the Mediterranean that predate the classical world of Greece and Rome: for example, Sumerian and Aegean art. Artefacts range from simple relics of the Palaeolithic period, such as pebbles carved with symbolic figures, to the sophisticated art forms of ancient Egypt and Assyria: for example, mural paintings, sculpture, and jewellery.

Andalusia (Spanish *Andalucía*) fertile autonomous region of S Spain, including the provinces of Almería, Cádiz, Córdoba, Granada, Huelva, Jaén, Málaga, and Seville; area 87,300 sq km/ 33,698 sq mi; population (1986) 6,876,000. Málaga, Cádiz, and Algeciras are the chief ports and industrial centres. The *Costa del Sol* on the S coast has many tourist resorts.

Andaman and Nicobar Islands two groups of islands in the Bay of Bengal, between India and Myanmar, forming a Union Territory of the Republic of India; capital Port Blair; area 8,300 sq km/ 3,204 sq mi; population (1991) 278,000. The economy is based on fishing, timber, rubber, fruit, and rice.

Andersen Hans Christian 1805–1875. Danish writer of fairy tales, such as 'The Ugly Duckling', 'The Snow Queen', 'The Little Mermaid', and 'The Emperor's New Clothes'. A gothic inventiveness, strong sense of wonder, and a redemptive evocation of material and spiritual poverty have given these stories perennial and universal appeal.

Andes great mountain system or *cordillera* that forms the western fringe of South America, extending through some 67° of latitude and the republics of Colombia, Venezuela, Ecuador, Peru, Bolivia, Chile, and Argentina. The mountains exceed 3,600 m/12,000 ft for half their length of 6,500 km/ 4,000 mi.

Andhra Pradesh state in E central India; *area* 276,700 sq km/106,845 sq mi; *capital* Hyderabad; *products* rice, sugar cane, tobacco, groundnuts, cotton; *population* (1991) 66,304,900; *languages* Telugu, Urdu, Tamil; *history* formed 1953 from the Telegu-speaking areas of Madras, and enlarged 1956 from the former Hyderabad state.

Andorra Principality of; country in the E Pyrenees, bordered N by France and S by Spain; *area* 468 sq km/181 sq mi; *capital* Andorra-la-Vella; *physical* mountainous, with narrow valleys; *head of state* Joan Martí i Alanis (bishop of Urgel, Spain) and François Mitterrand (president of France); *head of government* Oscar Riba Reig from 1989; *political system* feudal coprincipality; *exports* main industries tourism and tobacco; *population* (1990) 51,000 (Andorran 30%, Spanish 61%; French 6%); *languages* Catalan (official); Spanish, French; *recent history* Democratic Party of Andorra formed 1976 was first Andorran political organization (the country was ruled jointly by France

and the bishops of Urgel since the 13th century). The first prime minister was appointed 1981. With appointment of Executive Council, executive and legislative powers were separated 1982.

Andrea del Sarto (Andrea d'Agnola) 1486–1531. Italian Renaissance painter active in Florence, one of the finest portraitists and religious painters of his time. His style is serene and noble, characteristic of High Renaissance art.

Andreotti Giulio 1919– . Italian politician. In 1989 he became prime minister for the sixth time, having headed previous governments 1972–73 and four successive governments 1976–79. In addition, he has been defence minister eight times, and foreign minister five times.

Andrew (full name Andrew Albert Christian Edward) 1960– . Prince of the UK, Duke of York, second son of Queen Elizabeth II. He married Sarah Ferguson 1986; their first daughter, Princess Beatrice, was born in 1988, and their second daughter, Princess Eugenie, was born in 1990. Prince Andrew is a naval helicopter pilot.

Andrew, St New Testament apostle, brother of Simon Peter. According to tradition, he went with John to Ephesus, preached in Scythia, and was martyred at Patras on an X-shaped cross (*St Andrew's cross*). He is the patron saint of Scotland. Feast day 30 Nov.

Androcles traditionally, a Roman slave who fled from a cruel master into the African desert, where he encountered and withdrew a thorn from the paw of a crippled lion. Recaptured and sentenced to combat a lion in the arena, he found his adversary was his old friend. The emperor Tiberius was said to have freed them both.

androgen general name for any male sex hormone, of which ◊testosterone is the most important. They are all ◊steroids and are principally involved in the production of male secondary sexual characters (such as facial hair in humans).

Andropov Yuri 1914–1984. Soviet communist politician, president of the USSR 1983–84. As chief of the KGB 1967–82, he established a reputation for efficiently suppressing dissent. As president, he introduced economic reforms, but died Feb 1984.

anemone any plant of the genus *Anemone* of the buttercup family Ranunculaceae. The function of petals is performed by its sepals. The garden anemone *A. coronaria* is white, blue, red, or purple. The Eurasian white wood anemone *A. nemorosa*, or windflower, grows in shady woods, flowering in spring.

aneroid barometer kind of ◊barometer.

Aneto, Pico highest peak of the Pyrenees Mountains, rising to 3,400 m/11,052 ft in the Spanish province of Huesca.

aneurysm weakening in the wall of an artery, causing it to balloon outwards, with the risk of rupture and serious, often fatal, blood loss. If detected in time and accessible, some aneurysms can be excised.

angel in Jewish, Christian, and Muslim belief, a supernatural being intermediate between God and humans. The Christian hierarchy has nine orders: *Seraphim*, *Cherubim*, *Thrones* (who contemplate God and reflect his glory), *Dominations*, *Virtues*, *Powers* (who regulate the stars and the universe), *Principalities*, *Archangels*, and *Angels* (who minister to humanity). In traditional Catholic belief every human being has a guardian angel. The existence of angels was reasserted by Pope John Paul II 1986.

Angel Falls highest waterfalls in the world, on the river Caroní in the tropical rainforest of Bolivár Region, Venezuela; total height 978 m/3,210 ft. They were named after the aviator and prospector James Angel who flew over the falls and crash-landed nearby 1935.

angelfish any of a number of unrelated fishes. The freshwater *angelfish*, genus *Pterophyllum*, of South America, is a tall, side-to-side flattened fish with a striped body, up to 26 cm/10 in long, but usually smaller in captivity. The *angelfish* or *monkfish* of the genus *Squatina* is a bottom-living shark up to 1.8 m/6 ft long with a body flattened from top to bottom. The *marine angelfishes*, *Pomacanthus* and others, are long narrow-bodied fish with spiny fins, often brilliantly coloured, up to 60 cm/2 ft long, living around coral reefs in the tropics.

angelica any plant of the genus *Angelica* of the carrot family Umbelliferae. Mostly Eurasian in distribution, they are tall, perennial herbs with divided leaves and clusters of white or greenish flowers. The roots and fruits have long been used in cooking and for medicinal purposes.

Angelico Fra (Guido di Pietro) *c.* 1400–1455. Italian painter of religious scenes, active in Florence. He was a monk and painted a series of frescoes at the monastery of San Marco, Florence, begun after 1436.

Angevin relating to the reigns of the English kings Henry II, and Richard I (also known, with the later English kings up to Richard III, as the *Plantagenets*). Angevin derives from Anjou, the region in France controlled by English kings at this time. The *Angevin Empire* comprised the territories (including England) that belonged to the Anjou dynasty.

angina or *angina pectoris* severe pain in the chest due to impaired blood supply to the heart muscle because a coronary artery is narrowed. Faintness and difficulty in breathing accompany the pain. Treatment is by drugs such as nitroglycerin and amyl nitrite; rest is important.

angiosperm flowering plant in which the seeds are enclosed within an ovary, which ripens to a fruit. Angiosperms are divided into ▷monocotyledons (single seed leaf in the embryo) and ▷dicotyledons

(two seed leaves in the embryo). They include the majority of flowers, herbs, grasses, and trees except conifers.

angle pair of rays (half-lines) that share a common endpoint but do not lie on the same line. Angles are measured in ▷degrees (°) or ▷radians, and are classified generally by their degree measures. *Acute angles* are less than 90°; *right angles* are exactly 90°; *obtuse angles* are greater than 90° but less than 180°; *reflex angles* are greater than 180° but less than 360°. Angles can be measured by using a protractor. No angle is classified as having a measure of 180°, as by definition such an 'angle' is actually a straight line.

Angle member of the Germanic tribe that invaded Britain in the 5th century; see ▷Anglo-Saxon.

Anglican Communion family of Christian churches including the Church of England, the US Episcopal Church, and those holding the same essential doctrines, that is the Lambeth Quadrilateral 1888 Holy Scripture as the basis of all doctrine, the Nicene and Apostles' Creeds, Holy Baptism and Holy Communion, and the historic episcopate.

angling fishing with rod and line. It is the biggest participant sport in the UK. Competition angling exists and world championships take place for most branches of the sport. The oldest is the World Freshwater Championship, inaugurated 1957.

Anglo-Irish Agreement or *Hillsborough Agreement* concord reached 1985 between the UK premier Margaret Thatcher and Irish premier Garret FitzGerald. One sign of the improved relations between the two countries was increased cooperation between police and security forces across the border with Northern Ireland. The pact also gave the Irish Republic a greater voice in the conduct of Northern Ireland's affairs. However, the agreement was rejected by Northern Ireland Unionists as a step towards renunciation of British sovereignty. In March 1988 talks led to further strengthening of the agreement.

Anglo-Saxon one of the several Germanic invaders (Angles, Saxons, and Jutes) who conquered much of Britain between the 5th and 7th centuries. After the conquest a number of kingdoms were set up, commonly referred to as the *Heptarchy*; these were united in the early 9th century under the overlordship of Wessex. The Norman invasion 1066 brought Anglo-Saxon rule to an end.

Anglo-Saxon art painting and sculpture of England from the 7th century to 1066. Sculpted crosses and ivories, manuscript painting, and gold and enamel jewellery survive. The relics of the Sutton Hoo ship burial, 7th century, and the *Lindisfarne Gospels*, about 690 (both British Museum, London), have typical Celtic ornamental patterns, but in manuscripts of southern England a different style emerged in the 9th century, with delicate, lively pen-and-ink figures and heavily decorative foliage borders.

Anglo-Saxon language group of dialects spoken by the Anglo-Saxon peoples who, in the 5th to 7th centuries, invaded and settled in Britain. Anglo-Saxon is traditionally known as Old English. See ◊English language.

Angola People's Republic of; country in SW Africa, bordered W by the Atlantic Ocean, N and NE by Zaire, E by Zambia, and S by Namibia; *area* 1,246,700 sq km/481,226 sq mi; *capital* and chief port Luanda; *physical* narrow coastal plain rises to vast interior plateau with rainforest in NW; desert in S; *head of state and government* José Eduardo dos Santos from 1979; *political system* socialist republic; *exports* oil, coffee, diamonds, palm oil, sisal, iron ore, fish; *population* (1989 est) 9,733,000 (largest ethnic group Ovimbunduu); *languages* Portuguese (official); Bantu dialects; *recent history* independence from Portugal achieved 1975; a struggle for power followed between People's Movement for the Liberation of Angola (MPLA), supported by the USSR and Cuba, and National Front for the Liberation of Angola (FNLA) and National Union for the Total Independence of Angola (UNITA) supported by the West and South Africa. MPLA gained control 1976. Guerrilla raids continued until 1988 when a peace treaty providing for the withdrawal of all foreign troops was signed with South Africa and Cuba. Ceasefire broke down 1989; peace agreement signed and civil war officially ended 1991.

Angry Young Men group of British writers who emerged about 1950 after the creative hiatus that followed World War II. They included Kingsley Amis, John Wain, John Osborne, and Colin Wilson.

angstrom unit (symbol A) of length equal to 10^{-10} metre or one-hundred-millionth of a centimetre, used for atomic measurements and the wavelengths of electromagnetic radiation. It is named after the Swedish scientist A J Ångström.

Ångström Anders Jonas 1814–1874. Swedish physicist who worked in spectroscopy and solar physics. He discovered 1862 that the Sun's spectrum contains hydrogen. His map of the solar spectrum was published 1868; he also studied the aurora borealis ('northern lights'). Ångström's method of measuring wavelengths of light (based on the angstrom unit) has been extensively used.

Anguilla island in the E Caribbean; *area* 160 sq km/62 sq mi; *capital* The Valley; *physical* white coral-sand beaches; 80% of its coral reef has been lost through tourism (pollution and souvenir sales); *government* from 1982, governor, executive council, and legislative house of assembly (chief minister Emile Gumbs from 1984); *exports* lobster, salt; *population* (1988) 7,000; *languages* English, creole; *history* a British colony from 1650, Anguilla was long associated with St Christopher–Nevis but revolted against alleged domination by the larger

island and in 1969 declared itself a republic. A small British force restored order, and Anguilla retained a special position at its own request, since 1980 a separate dependency of the UK.

Anhui or **Anhwei** province of E China, watered by the Chang Jiang (Yangtze River); *area* 139,900 sq km/54,000 sq mi; *capital* Hefei; *products* cereals in N; cotton, rice, tea in S; *population* (1990) 56,181,000.

anhydride chemical compound obtained by the removal of water from another compound; usually a dehydrated acid. For example, sulphur(VI) oxide (sulphur trioxide, SO_3) is the anhydride of sulphuric acid (H_2SO_4).

aniline $C_6H_5NH_2$ or **phenylamine** one of the simplest aromatic chemicals (a substance related to benzene, with its carbon atoms joined in a ring). When pure, it is a colourless oily liquid; it has a characteristic odour, and turns brown on contact with air. It occurs in coal tar, and is used in the rubber industry and to make drugs and dyes. It is highly poisonous.

animal or **metazoan** member of the kingdom Animalia, one of the major categories of living things, the science of which is zoology. Animals are all ◊heterotrophs (they obtain their energy from organic substances produced by other organisms); they have eukaryotic cells (the genetic material is contained within a distinct nucleus) bounded by a thin cell membrane rather than the thick cell wall of plants. Most animals are capable of moving around for at least part of their life cycle.

animism in psychology and physiology, the view of human personality that attributes human life and behaviour to a force distinct from matter. In religious theory, the conception of a spiritual reality behind the material one: for example, beliefs in the soul as a shadowy duplicate of the body capable of independent activity, both in life and death. In anthropology, the concept of spirits residing in all natural phenomena and objects.

anion ion carrying a negative charge. An electrolyte, such as the salt zinc chloride ($ZnCl_2$), is dissociated in aqueous solution or in the molten state into doubly-charged Zn^{2+} zinc ◊cations and singly charged Cl- anions. During electrolysis, the zinc cations flow to the cathode (to become discharged and liberate zinc metal) and the chloride anions flow to the anode (to liberate chlorine gas).

anise plant *Pimpinella anisum*, of the carrot family Umbelliferae, whose fragrant seeds are used to flavour foods.

Ankara (formerly *Angora*) capital of Turkey; population (1990) 2,559,500. Industries include cement, textiles, and leather products. It replaced Istanbul (then in Allied occupation) as capital 1923.

Annapurna mountain 8,075 m/26,502 ft in the Himalayas, Nepal. The N face was first climbed by a French expedition (Maurice Herzog) 1950 and the S by a British team 1970.

Anne 1665–1714. Queen of Great Britain and Ireland 1702–14. She was the second daughter of James, Duke of York, who became James II, and Anne Hyde. She succeeded William III 1702. Events of her reign include the War of the Spanish Succession, Marlborough's victories at Blenheim, Ramillies, Oudenarde, and Malplaquet, and the union of the English and Scottish parliaments 1707. She was succeeded by George I.

Anne (full name Anne Elizabeth Alice Louise) 1950– . Princess of the UK, second child of Queen Elizabeth II, declared Princess Royal 1987. She is an excellent horsewoman, winning a gold medal at the 1976 Olympics, and is actively involved in global charity work, especially for children. In 1973 she married Capt Mark Phillips (1949–), of the Queen's Dragoon Guards; they separated 1989 and were divorced 1992. Their son Peter (1977–) was the first direct descendant of the Queen not to bear a title. They also have a daughter, Zara (1981–).

annealing process of heating a material (usually glass or metal) for a given time at a given temperature, followed by slow cooling, to increase ductility and strength. It is a common form of ⟡heat treatment.

annelid any segmented worm of the phylum Annelida. Annelids include earthworms, leeches, and marine worms such as lugworms.

Anne of Austria 1601–1666. Queen of France from 1615 and regent 1643–61. Daughter of Philip III of Spain, she married Louis XIII of France (whose chief minister, Cardinal Richelieu, worked against her). On her husband's death she became regent for their son, Louis XIV, until his majority.

Anne of Cleves 1515–1557. Fourth wife of ⟡Henry VIII of England 1540. She was the daughter of the Duke of Cleves, and was recommended to Henry as a wife by Thomas ⟡Cromwell, who wanted an alliance with German Protestantism against the Holy Roman Empire. Henry did not like her looks, had the marriage declared void after six months, pensioned her, and had Cromwell beheaded.

anno Domini in the Christian chronological system, refers to dates since the birth of Jesus, denoted by the letters AD. There is no year 0, so AD 1 follows immediately after the year 1 BC (before Christ). The system became the standard reckoning in the Western world after being adopted by the English historian Bede in the 8th century. The abbreviations CE (Common Era) and BCE (before Common Era) are often used instead by scholars and writers as objective, rather than religious, terms.

annual percentage rate (APR) the charge (including ⟡interest) for granting consumer credit, expressed as an equivalent once-a-year percentage figure of the amount of the credit granted. It is usually approximately double the flat rate of interest, or simple interest. In the UK, lenders are legally required to state the APR when advertising loans.

annual plant plant that completes its life cycle within one year, during which time it germinates, grows to maturity, bears flowers, produces seed, and then dies. Examples include the common poppy *Papaver rhoeas* and groundsel *Senecio vulgaris*. Among garden plants, some that are described as 'annuals' are actually ⟡perennials, although usually cultivated as annuals because they cannot survive winter frosts.

Annunciation in the New Testament, the announcement to Mary by the archangel Gabriel that she was to be the mother of Christ; the feast of the Annunciation is 25 March (also known as Lady Day).

anode in chemistry, the positive electrode of an electrolytic ⟡cell, towards which negative particles (anions), usually in solution, are attracted. See ⟡electrolysis.

anodizing process that increases the resistance to corrosion of a metal, such as aluminium, by building up a protective oxide layer on the surface. The natural corrosion resistance of aluminium is provided by a thin film of aluminium oxide; anodizing increases the thickness of this film and thus the corrosion protection.

anorexia lack of desire to eat, especially the pathological condition of *anorexia nervosa*, usually found in adolescent girls and young women, who may be obsessed with the desire to lose weight. Compulsive eating, or ⟡bulimia, often accompanies anorexia.

Anouilh Jean 1910–1987. French dramatist. His plays, influenced by the Neo-Classical tradition, include *Antigone* 1942, *L'Invitation au château/Ring Round the Moon* 1947, *Colombe* 1950, and *Becket* 1959, about St Thomas à Becket and Henry II.

Anschluss (German 'union') the annexation of Austria with Germany, accomplished by the German chancellor Adolf Hitler 12 March 1938.

Anselm, St *c.* 1033–1109. Medieval priest and philosopher. Born in Piedmont, he was educated at the abbey of Bec in Normandy, which as abbot (from 1078) he made a centre of scholarship in Europe. He was appointed archbishop of Canterbury by William II of England 1093, but was later forced into exile; he was recalled by Henry I and came to an agreement which gave the king the right of temporal investiture and the clergy that of spiritual investiture. Anselm holds an important place in the development of Scholasticism. He was canonized 1494.

ant insect belonging to the family Formicidae, and to the same order (Hymenoptera) as bees and wasps. Ants are characterized by a conspicuous 'waist' and elbowed antennae. About 10,000 different species are known; all are social in habit, and all construct nests of various kinds. Ants are found in all parts of the world, except the polar regions.

antacid any substance that neutralizes stomach

anteater

acid, such as sodium bicarbonate or magnesium hydroxide ('milk of magnesia'). Antacids are weak ◊bases, swallowed as solids or emulsions. They may be taken between meals to relieve symptoms of hyperacidity, such as pain, bloating, nausea, and 'heartburn'.

Antalya Mediterranean port on the W coast of Turkey and capital of a province of the same name; population (1990) 378,200. The port trades in agricultural and forest produce.

Antananarivo (formerly *Tananarive*) capital of Madagascar, on the interior plateau, with a rail link to Tamatave; population (1986) 703,000. Industries include tobacco, food processing, leather goods, and clothing.

Antarctica continent surrounding the South Pole, arbitrarily defined as the region lying S of the Antarctic Circle. Occupying 10% of the world's surface, Antarctica contains 90% of the world's ice and 70% of its fresh water; *area* 13,900,000 sq km/ 5,400,000 sq mi (the size of Europe and the USA combined); *physical* formed of two blocs of rock with an area of about 8 million sq km/ 3 million sq mi, Antarctica is covered by a cap of ice that flows slowly towards its 22,400 km/ 14,000 mi coastline, reaching the sea in high ice cliffs. The most southerly shores are near the 78th parallel in the Ross and Weddell seas. E Antarctica is a massive bloc of ancient rocks that surface in the Transantarctic Mountains of Victoria Land. Separated by a deep channel, W Antarctica is characterized by the mountainous regions of Graham Land, the Antarctic Peninsula, Palmer Land, and Ellsworth Land; the highest peak is Vinson Massif (5,139 m/16,866 ft). Little more than 1% of the land is ice-free. With an estimated volume of 24 million cu m/5.9 million cu mi, the ice-cap has a mean thickness of 1,880 m/6,170 ft and in places reaches depths of 5,000 m/16,000 ft or more. Each annual layer of snow preserves a record of global conditions, and where no melting at the surface of the bedrock has occurred the ice can be a million years old; *features* Mount Erebus on Ross Island is the world's southernmost active volcano; the Ross Ice Shelf is formed by several glaciers coalescing in the Ross Sea; *products* cod, Antarctic icefish, and krill are fished in Antarctic waters. Whaling, which began in the early 20th century, ceased during the 1960s as a result of overfishing. Petroleum, coal, and minerals, such as palladium and platinum exist, but their exploitation is prevented by a 50-year ban on commercial mining agreed by 39 nations

1991; *population* no permanent residents; settlement limited to scientific research stations with maximum population of 2,000 to 3,000 during the summer months. Sectors of Antarctica are claimed by Argentina, Australia, Chile, France, the UK, Norway, and New Zealand.

Antarctic Peninsula mountainous peninsula of W Antarctica extending 1,930 km/1,200 mi N towards South America; originally named Palmer Land after a US navigator, Capt Nathaniel Palmer, who was the first to explore the region 1820. It was claimed by Britain 1832, Argentina 1940, and Chile 1942. Its name was changed to the Antarctic Peninsula 1964.

Antarctic Treaty international agreement aiming to promote scientific research and keep Antarctica free from conflict. It dates from 1961 and in 1991 a 50-year ban on mining activity was secured.

anteater mammal of the family Myrmecophagidae, order Edentata, native to Mexico, Central America, and tropical South America. An anteater lives almost entirely on ants and termites. It has toothless jaws, an extensile tongue, and claws for breaking into the nests of its prey.

antelope any of numerous kinds of even-toed, hoofed mammals belonging to the cow family, Bovidae. Most antelopes are lightly built and good runners. They are grazers or browsers, and chew the cud. They range in size from the dik-diks, only 30 cm/1 ft high, to the eland, which can be 1.8 m/ 6 ft at the shoulder.

antenna in zoology, an appendage ('feeler') on the head. Insects, centipedes, and millipedes each have one pair of antennae but there are two pairs in crustaceans, such as shrimps. In insects, the antennae are usually involved with the senses of smell and touch.

antenna in radio and television, another name for ◊aerial.

anther in a flower, the terminal part of a stamen in which the ◊pollen grains are produced. It is usually borne on a slender stalk or filament, and has two lobes, each containing two chambers, or pollen sacs, within which the pollen is formed.

Anthony, St *c.* 251–356. Also known as Anthony of Thebes. He was the founder of Christian monasticism. At the age of 20, he renounced all his possessions and began a hermetic life of study and prayer.

anthracite hard, dense, shiny variety of ◊coal, containing over 90% carbon and a low percentage of ash and impurities, which causes it to burn without flame, smoke, or smell.

anthrax cattle and sheep disease occasionally transmitted to humans, usually via infected hides and fleeces. It may develop as black skin pustules or severe pneumonia.

anthropology study of humankind, which developed following 19th-century evolutionary theory to investigate the human species, past and present, physically, socially, and culturally.

antibiotic drug that kills or inhibits the growth of bacteria and fungi. It is derived from living organisms such as fungi or bacteria, which distinguishes it from synthetic antimicrobials.

antibody protein molecule produced in the blood by ♢lymphocytes in response to the presence of invading substances, or ♢antigens, including the proteins carried on the surface of microorganisms. Antibody production is only one aspect of ♢immunity in vertebrates.

Antichrist in Christian theology, the opponent of Christ. The appearance of the Antichrist was believed to signal the Second Coming, at which Christ would conquer his opponent. The concept may stem from the idea of conflict between Light and Darkness, which is present in Persian, Babylonian, and Jewish literature and which influenced early Christian thought.

anticline in geology, a fold in the rocks of the Earth's crust in which the layers or beds bulge upwards to form an arch (seldom preserved intact).

anticoagulant substance that suppresses the formation of blood clots. Common anticoaguiants are heparin, produced by the liver and lungs, and derivatives of coumarin. Anticoagulants are used medically in treating heart attacks, for example. They are also produced by blood-feeding animals, such as mosquitoes, leeches, and vampire bats, to keep the victim's blood flowing.

anticyclone area of high atmospheric pressure caused by descending air, which becomes warm and dry. Winds radiate from a calm centre, taking a clockwise direction in the northern hemisphere and an anticlockwise direction in the southern hemisphere. Anticyclones are characterized by clear weather and the absence of rain and violent winds. In summer they bring hot, sunny days and in winter they bring fine, frosty spells, although fog and low cloud are not uncommon in the UK. *Blocking anticyclones*, which prevent the normal air circulation of an area, can cause summer droughts and severe winters.

antidepressant any drug used to relieve symptoms in depressive illness. The two main groups are the tricyclic antidepressants (TCADs) and the monoamine oxidase inhibitors (MAOIs), which act by altering chemicals available to the central nervous system. Both may produce serious side effects and are restricted.

antifreeze substance added to a water-cooling system (for example, that of a car) to prevent it freezing in cold weather. The most common types of antifreeze contain the chemical ethylene ♢glycol, an organic alcohol with a freezing point of about –15°C/5°F. The addition of this chemical depresses the freezing point of water significantly. A solution containing 33.5% by volume of ethylene glycol will

not freeze until about –20°C/–4°F. A 50% solution will not freeze until –35°C/–31°F.

antigen any substance that causes the production of ♢antibodies. Common antigens include the proteins carried on the surface of bacteria, viruses, and pollen grains. The proteins of incompatible blood groups or tissues also act as antigens, which has to be taken into account in medical procedures such as blood transfusions and organ transplants.

Antigone in Greek legend, a daughter of Jocasta, by her son ♢Oedipus. She defied her uncle King Creon of Thebes in giving burial rites to her brother Polynices and later killed herself in the cave where she was imprisoned by her uncle.

Antigua and Barbuda State of; country comprising three islands (Antigua, Barbuda, and uninhabited Redonda) in the E Caribbean; *area* Antigua 280 sq km/108 sq mi, Barbuda 161 sq km/62 sq mi, and Redonda 1 sq km/0.4 sq mi; *capital* and chief port St John's; *physical* low-lying tropical islands with volcanic outcrop on W Antigua; *head of state* Elizabeth II from 1981 represented by governor general; *head of government* Vere C Bird from 1981; *political system* liberal democracy; *exports* sea-island cotton, rum, lobsters; *population* (1989) 83,500; *language* English; *recent history* became an associated state within the Commonwealth 1967 and fully independent 1981. Antigua Labour Party (ALP) in power since 1984.

antihistamine any substance that counteracts the effects of histamine. Antihistamines may be naturally produced (such as vitamin C and epinephrin) or synthesized (pseudepinephrin).

anti-inflammatory any substance that reduces swelling in soft tissues. Antihistamines relieve allergic reactions; aspirin and NSAIDs are effective in joint and musculoskeletal conditions; rubefacients (counterirritant liniments) ease painful joints, tendons, and muscles.

Antilles the whole group of West Indian islands, divided N–S into the *Greater Antilles* (Cuba, Jamaica, Haiti–Dominican Republic, Puerto Rico) and *Lesser Antilles*, subdivided into the Leeward Islands (Virgin Islands, St Kitts–Nevis, Antigua and Barbuda, Anguilla, Montserrat, and Guadeloupe) and the Windward Islands (Dominica, Martinique, St Lucia, St Vincent and the Grenadines, Barbados, and Grenada).

antimatter in physics, a form of matter in which most of the attributes (such as electrical charge, magnetic moment, and spin) of ♢elementary particles are reversed. Such particles (antiparticles) can be created in particle accelerators, such as those at ♢CERN in Geneva, Switzerland, and at Fermilab in the USA.

antimony silver-white, brittle, semimetallic element (a metalloid), symbol Sb (from Latin *stibium*), atomic number 51, relative atomic mass 121.75. It occurs chiefly as the ore stibnite, and is used to make alloys harder; it is also used in photo-sensitive substances in colour photography, optical electronics, fireproofing, pigment, and medicine.

Antioch ancient capital of the Greek kingdom of Syria, founded 300 BC by Seleucus Nicator in memory of his father Antiochus, and famed for its splendour and luxury. Under the Roman and Byzantine empires it was an early centre of Christianity. It was captured by the Arabs 637. After a five-month siege 1098 Antioch was taken by the crusaders, who held it until 1268. The site is now occupied by the Turkish town of ▷Antakya.

Antiochus III the Great *c*. 241–187 BC. King of Syria from 223 BC, nephew of Antiochus II. He secured a loose suzerainty over Armenia and Parthia 209, overcame Bactria, received the homage of the Indian king of the Kabul valley, and returned by way of the Persian Gulf 204. He took possession of Palestine, entering Jerusalem 198. He crossed into NW Greece, but was decisively defeated by the Romans at Thermopylae 191 and at Magnesia 190. He had to abandon his domains in Anatolia, and was killed by the people of Elymais.

Antiochus IV *c*. 215–164 BC. King of Syria from 175 BC, known as Antiochus Epiphanes, the Illustrious; second son of Antiochus III. He occupied Jerusalem about 170, seizing much of the Temple treasure, and instituted worship of the Greek type in the Temple in an attempt to eradicate Judaism. This produced the revolt of the Hebrews under the Maccabees; Antiochus died before he could suppress it.

Antiochus VII Sidetes *c*. 159–129 BC. King of Syria from 138 BC. The last strong ruler of the Seleucid dynasty, he took Jerusalem 134, reducing the Maccabees to subjection, and fought successfully against the Parthians.

antioxidant any substance that prevents deterioration by oxidation in fats, oils, paints, plastics, and rubbers. When used as ▷food additives, antioxidants prevent fats and oils from becoming rancid when exposed to air, and thus extend their shelf life.

antiparticle in nuclear physics, a particle corresponding in mass and properties to a given ▷elementary particle but with the opposite electrical charge, magnetic properties, or coupling to other fundamental forces. For example, an electron carries a negative charge whereas its antiparticle, the positron, carries a positive one. When a particle and its antiparticle collide, they destroy each other, in the process called 'annihilation', their total energy being converted to lighter particles and/or photons. A substance consisting entirely of antiparticles is known as ▷antimatter.

antipodes places at opposite points on the globe. In the UK, Australia and New Zealand are called the Antipodes.

antipope rival claimant to the elected pope for

the leadership of the Roman Catholic Church, for instance in the Great Schism 1378–1417 when there were rival popes in Rome and Avignon.

antipyretic any drug, such as aspirin, used to reduce fever.

anti-Semitism literally, prejudice against Semitic people (see ▷Semite), but in practice it has meant prejudice or discrimination against, and persecution of, the Jews as an ethnic group. Historically this was practised for almost 2,000 years by European Christians. Anti-Semitism was a tenet of Hitler's Germany, and in the Holocaust 1933–45 about 6 million Jews died in concentration camps and in local extermination ▷pogroms, such as the siege of the Warsaw ghetto. After World War II, the creation of Israel 1948 provoked Palestinian anti-Zionism, backed by the Arab world. In Europe, as well as in Islamic nations, anti-Semitism exists and is promulgated by neofascist groups.

antiseptic any substance that kills or inhibits the growth of microorganisms. The use of antiseptics was pioneered by Joseph ▷Lister. He used carbolic acid (▷phenol), which is a weak antiseptic; substances such as TCP are derived from this.

antiviral any drug that acts against viruses, usually preventing them from multiplying. Most viral infections are not susceptible to antibiotics. Antivirals have been difficult drugs to develop, and do not necessarily cure viral diseases.

antler 'horn' of a deer, often branched, and made of bone rather than horn. Antlers, unlike true horns, are shed and regrown each year. Reindeer of both sexes grow them, but in all other types of deer, only the males have antlers.

ant lion larva of one of the insects of the family Myrmeleontidae, order Neuroptera, which traps ants by waiting at the bottom of a pit dug in loose, sandy soil. Ant lions are mainly tropical, but also occur in parts of Europe and in the USA.

Antofagasta port of N Chile, capital of the region of Antofagasta; population (1990) 218,800. The area of the region is 125,300 sq km/48,366 sq mi; its population (1982) 341,000.

Antonello da Messina *c*. 1430–1479. Italian painter, born in Messina, Sicily, a pioneer of the technique of oil painting, which he is said to have introduced to Italy from N Europe. Flemish influence is reflected in his technique, his use of light, and sometimes in his imagery. Surviving works include bust-length portraits and sombre religious paintings.

Antonine Wall Roman line of fortification built AD 142–200. It was the Roman Empire's NW frontier, between the Clyde and Forth rivers, Scotland.

Antoninus Pius 86–161. Roman emperor who had been adopted 138 as Hadrian's heir, and succeeded him later that year. He enjoyed a prosperous reign, during which he built the Antonine Wall. His daughter married ♢Marcus Aurelius Antoninus.

Antonioni Michelangelo 1912– . Italian film director, famous for his subtle presentations of neuroses and personal relationships among the leisured classes. His work includes *L'Avventura* 1960, *Blow Up* 1966, and *The Passenger* 1975.

Antrim county of Northern Ireland; *area* 2,830 sq km/1,092 sq mi; *towns* Belfast (county), Larne (port); *physical* Antrim borders Lough Neagh, and is separated from Scotland by the 32-km/20-mi-wide North Channel; Giant's Causeway of natural hexagonal basalt columns, which, in legend, was built to enable the giants to cross between Ireland and Scotland; *products* potatoes, oats, linen, synthetic textiles; *population* (1981) 642,000.

Antwerp (Flemish *Antwerpen*, French *Anvers*) port in Belgium on the river Scheldt, capital of the province of Antwerp; population (1991) 467,500. One of the world's busiest ports, it has shipbuilding, oil-refining, petrochemical, textile, and diamond-cutting industries. The province of Antwerp has an area of 2,900 sq km/1,119 sq mi; population (1987) 1,588,000.

Anubis in Egyptian mythology, the jackal-headed god of the dead, son of Osiris. Anubis presided over the funeral cult, including embalming, and led the dead to judgement.

ANZAC (acronym for *A*ustralian and *N*ew *Z*ealand *A*rmy *C*orps) general term for all troops of both countries serving in World War I and to some extent those in World War II. The date of their World War I landing in Gallipoli, Turkey, 25 April 1915, is marked by a public holiday, *Anzac Day*, in both Australia and New Zealand.

Anzio seaport and resort on the W coast of Italy, 53 km/33 mi SE of Rome; population (1984) 25,000. It is the site of the Roman town of Antium and the birthplace of Emperor Nero. In World War II, it was the scene of the beachhead invasion of Italy 22 Jan–23 May 1944 by Allied troops.

aorta the chief ♢artery, the dorsal blood vessel carrying oxygenated blood from the left ventricle of the heart in birds and mammals. It branches to form smaller arteries, which in turn supply all body organs except the lungs. Loss of elasticity in the aorta provides evidence of ♢atherosclerosis, which may lead to heart disease.

Aouita Said 1960– . Moroccan runner. Outstanding at middle and long distances, he won the 1984 Olympic and 1987 World Championship 5,000-metres title, and has set many world records. In 1985 he held world records at both 1,500 and 5,000 metres, the first person for 30 years to hold both. He has since broken the 2 miles, 3,000 metres, and 2,000 metres world records.

Aoun Michel 1935– . Lebanese soldier and Maronite Christian politician, president 1988–90. As commander of the Lebanese army, he was made president without Muslim support, his appointment precipitating a civil war between Christians and Muslims. His unwillingness to accept a 1989 Arab League–sponsored peace agreement increased his isolation until the following year when he surrendered to military pressure.

Aouzu Strip disputed territory 100 km/60 mi wide on the Chad–Libya frontier, occupied by Libya 1973. Lying to the N of the Tibesti massif, the area is rich in uranium and other minerals.

apartheid racial-segregation policy of the government of South Africa, which was legislated 1948, when the Afrikaner National Party gained power. Nonwhites (Bantu, coloured or mixed, or Indian) do not share full rights of citizenship with the 4.5 million whites (for example, the 23 million black people cannot vote in parliamentary elections), and many public facilities and institutions were until 1990 (and in some cases remain) restricted to the use of one race only; the establishment of ♢Black National States is another manifestation of apartheid. In 1991 President de Klerk repealed the key elements of apartheid legislation.

apatosaurus large plant-eating dinosaur, formerly called *brontosaurus*, which flourished about 145 million years ago. Up to 21 m/69 ft long and 30 tonnes in weight, it stood on four elephantlike legs and had a long tail, long neck, and small head.

ape ♢primate of the family Pongidae, closely related to humans, including gibbon, orang-utan, chimpanzee, and gorilla.

Apennines chain of mountains stretching the length of the Italian peninsula. A continuation of the Maritime Alps, from Genoa it swings across the peninsula to Ancona on the E coast, and then back to the W coast and into the 'toe' of Italy. The system is continued over the Strait of Messina along the N Sicilian coast, then across the Mediterranean Sea in a series of islands to the Atlas Mountains of N Africa. The highest peak is Gran Sasso d'Italia at 2,914 m/9,560 ft.

aperture in photography, an opening in the camera that allows light to pass through the lens to strike the film. Controlled by shutter speed and the iris diaphragm, it can be set mechanically or electronically at various diameters.

aphid any of the family of small insects, Aphididae, in the order Homoptera, that live by sucking sap from plants. There are many species, often adapted to particular plants.

Aphrodite in Greek mythology, the goddess of love (Roman Venus, Phoenician Astarte, Babylonian Ishtar); said to be either a daughter of Zeus (in Homer) or sprung from the foam of the sea (in Hesiod). She was the unfaithful wife of Hephaestus, the god of fire, and the mother of Eros.

Apia capital and port of Western ♢Samoa, on the N coast of Upolu island, in the W Pacific; population

(1981) 33,000. It was the final home of the writer Robert Louis Stevenson.

Apocrypha appendix to the Old Testament of the Bible, not included in the final Hebrew canon but recognized by Roman Catholics. There are also disputed New Testament texts known as Apocrypha.

Apollinaire Guillaume. Pen name of Guillaume Apollinaire de Kostrowitsky 1880–1918. French poet of aristocratic Polish descent. He was a leader of the avant-garde in Parisian literary and artistic circles. His novel *Le Poète assassiné/The Poet Assassinated* 1916, followed by the experimental poems *Alcools/Alcohols* 1913 and *Calligrammes/Word Pictures* 1918, show him as a representative of the Cubist and Futurist movements.

Apollo in Greek and Roman mythology, the god of sun, music, poetry, prophecy, agriculture, and pastoral life, and leader of the Muses. He was the twin child (with Artemis) of Zeus and Leto. Ancient statues show Apollo as the embodiment of the Greek ideal of male beauty.

a posteriori (Latin 'from the latter') in logic, an argument that deduces causes from their effects; inductive reasoning; the converse of ▷a priori.

apostle in the New Testament, any of the chosen 12 ▷disciples sent out by Jesus after his resurrection to preach the Gospel. In the earliest days of Christianity the term was extended to include some who had never known Jesus in the flesh, notably St Paul.

Appalachians mountain system of E North America, stretching about 2,400 km/1,500 mi from Alabama to Québec, composed of very ancient eroded rocks. The chain includes the Allegheny, Catskill, and Blue Ridge mountains, the last-named having the highest peak, Mount Mitchell, 2,045 m/6,712 ft. The eastern edge has a fall line to the coastal plain where Philadelphia, Baltimore, and Washington stand.

appeal in law, an application for a rehearing of all or part of an issue that has already been dealt with by a lower court or tribunal. The outcome can be a new decision on all or part of the points raised, or the previous decision may be upheld. In criminal cases, an appeal may be against conviction and either the prosecution or the defence may appeal against sentence.

appendicitis inflammation of the appendix, a small, blind extension of the bowel in the lower right abdomen. In an acute attack, the pus-filled appendix may burst, causing a potentially lethal spread of infection. Treatment is by removal (appendectomy).

apple fruit of *Malus pumila*, a tree of the family Rosaceae. There are several hundred varieties of cultivated apples, grown all over the world. All are derived from the wild crab apple.

Appleton layer band containing ionized gases

in the Earth's upper atmosphere, above the ▷E layer (formerly the Kennelly–Heaviside layer). It is named after the English physicist Edward Appleton.

application in computing, a program or job designed for the benefit of the end user, such as a payroll system or a ▷word processor. The term is used to distinguish such programs from those that control the computer or assist the programmer, such as a compiler.

Appomattox village in Virginia, USA, scene of the surrender 9 April 1865 of the Confederate army under Robert E Lee to the Union army under Ulysses S Grant, which ended the American Civil War.

apricot fruit of *Prunus armeniaca*, a tree of the rose family Rosaceae, closely related to the almond, peach, plum, and cherry. It has yellow-fleshed fruit. Although native to the Far East, it has long been cultivated in Armenia, from where it was introduced into Europe and the USA.

a priori (Latin 'from what comes before') in logic, an argument that is known to be true, or false, without reference to experience; the converse of ▷a posteriori.

Apulia English form of ▷Puglia, region of Italy.

Aqaba, Gulf of gulf extending for 160 km/100 mi between the Negev and the Red Sea; its coastline is uninhabited except at its head, where the frontiers of Israel, Egypt, Jordan, and Saudi Arabia converge. The two ports of Eilat (Israeli 'Elath') and Aqaba, Jordan's only port, are situated here.

aquaculture or *fish farming* raising fish (including molluscs and crustaceans) under controlled conditions in tanks and ponds, sometimes in off-shore pens. It has been practised for centuries in the Far East, where Japan alone produces some 100,000 tonnes of fish a year. In the 1980s one-tenth of the world's consumption of fish was farmed.

aqualung or *scuba* underwater breathing apparatus worn by divers, developed in the early 1940s by French diver Jacques Cousteau. Compressed-air cylinders strapped to the diver's back are regulated by a valve system and by a mouth tube to provide air to the diver at the same pressure as that of the surrounding water (which increases with the depth).

aquamarine blue variety of the mineral beryl. A semiprecious gemstone, it is used in jewellery.

Aquarius zodiacal constellation a little south of the celestial equator near Pegasus. Aquarius is represented as a man pouring water from a jar. The Sun passes through Aquarius from late Feb to early March. In astrology, the dates for Aquarius are between about 20 Jan and 18 Feb (see ▷precession).

aquatint printmaking technique, usually combined with ▷etching to produce areas of subtle tone as well as more precisely etched lines. Aquatint became common in the late 18th century.

aqueduct any artificial channel or conduit for water, often an elevated structure of stone, wood, or iron built for conducting water across a valley. The Greeks built a tunnel 1,280 m/4,200 ft long near Athens, 2,500 years ago. Many Roman aqueducts are still standing, for example the one at Nîmes in S France, built about AD 18 (which is 48 m/160 ft high). The longest aqueduct in Britain is the Pont Cysylltau in Clwyd, Wales, opened 1805. It is 307 m/1,007 ft long, with 19 arches up to 36 m/121 ft high.

aquifer any rock formation containing water that can be extracted by a well. The rock of an aquifer must be porous and permeable (full of interconnected holes) so that it can absorb water.

Aquinas St Thomas c. 1226–1274. Neapolitan philosopher and theologian, the greatest figure of the school of ⍉Scholasticism. He was a Dominican monk, known as the 'Angelic Doctor'. In 1879 his works were recognized as the basis of Catholic theology. His *Summa contra Gentiles/Against the Errors of the Infidels* 1259–64 argues that reason and faith are compatible. He assimilated the philosophy of Aristotle into Christian doctrine.

Aquino (Maria) Corazon (born Cojuangco) 1933– . President of the Philippines 1986–92, and instrumental in the nonviolent overthrow of President Ferdinand Marcos 1986. She sought to rule in a conciliatory manner, but encountered opposition from left (communist guerrillas) and right (army coup attempts), and her land reforms have been seen as inadequate.

Aquitaine region of SW France; capital Bordeaux; area 41,300 sq km/15,942 sq mi; population (1986) 2,718,000. It comprises the *départements* of Dordogne, Gironde, Landes, Lot-et-Garonne, and Pyrénées-Atlantiques. Red wines (Margaux, St Julien) are produced in the Médoc district, bordering the Gironde. Aquitaine was an English possession 1152–1452.

Arab any of a Semitic (see ⍉Semite) people native to the Arabian peninsula, but now settled throughout North Africa and the nations of the Middle East. The term Arab was first recorded 853 BC but was not widely used until the end of the 6th century AD. The 7th century saw the rise of Islam and by the 8th century non-Arab converts were being assimilated by the Arabs. Arabic became the principal language of the Arab Empire. In 1258 the empire was broken up by the Mongols and it was not until the decline of the Ottoman Empire at the end of World War I that the Arab nations emerged again as separate, if not independent, states.

Arab Emirates see ⍉United Arab Emirates.

Arabian Sea NW branch of the ⍉Indian Ocean.

Arabic language major Semitic language of the Hamito-Semitic family of W Asia and North Africa, originating among the Arabs of the Arabian peninsula. It is spoken today by about 120 million people in the Middle East and N Africa. Arabic script is written from right to left.

Arabic numerals symbols 0, 1, 2, 3, 4, 5, 6, 7, 8, 9, early forms of which were in use among the Arabs before being adopted by the peoples of Europe during the Middle Ages in place of ⍉Roman numerals.

Arab-Israeli Wars series of wars between Israel and various Arab states in the Middle East since the founding of the state of Israel 1948; *First Arab-Israeli War* 14 Oct 1948–13 Jan/24 March 1949. As soon as the independent state of Israel had been proclaimed by the Jews, it was invaded by combined Arab forces. The Israelis defeated them and went on to annex territory until they controlled 75% of what had been Palestine under British mandate; *Second Arab-Israeli War* 29 Oct–4 Nov 1956. After Egypt had taken control of the Suez Canal and blockaded the Straits of Tiran, Israel, with British and French support, invaded and captured Sinai and the Gaza Strip, from which it withdrew under heavy US pressure after the entry of a United Nations force; *Third Arab-Israeli War* 5–10 June 1967, the *Six-Day War*. It resulted in the Israeli capture of the Golan Heights from Syria; the eastern half of Jerusalem and the West Bank from Jordan; and, in the south, the Gaza Strip and Sinai peninsula as far as the Suez Canal; *Fourth Arab-Israeli War* 22–24 Oct 1973, the 'October War' or *Yom Kippur War*, so called because the Israeli forces were taken by surprise on the Day of ⍉Atonement. It started with the recrossing of the Suez Canal by Egyptian forces who made initial gains, though there was some later loss of ground by the Syrians in the north; *Fifth Arab-Israeli War* From 1978 the presence of Palestinian guerrillas in Lebanon led to Arab raids on Israel and Israeli retaliatory incursions, but on 6 June 1982 Israel launched a full-scale invasion. By 14 June Beirut was encircled, and ⍉Palestine Liberation Organization (PLO) and Syrian forces were evacuated (mainly to Syria) 21–31 Aug, but in Feb 1985 there was a unilateral Israeli withdrawal from the country without any gain or losses incurred. Israel maintains a 'security zone' in S Lebanon and supports the South Lebanese Army militia as a buffer against Palestinian guerrilla incursions.

Arabistan former name of the Iranian province of Khuzestan, revived in the 1980s by the 2 million Sunni Arab inhabitants who demand autonomy. Unrest and sabotage 1979–80 led to a pledge of a degree of autonomy by Ayatollah Khomeini.

Arab League organization of Arab states established in Cairo 1945 to promote Arab unity, primarily in opposition to Israel. The original members were Egypt, Syria, Iraq, Lebanon, Transjordan (Jordan 1949), Saudi Arabia, and Yemen. In 1979 Egypt was suspended and the league's headquarters transferred to Tunis in protest against the

Egypt-Israeli peace, but Egypt was readmitted as a full member May 1989, and in March 1990 its headquarters returned to Cairo.

arachnid or *arachnoid* type of arthropod, including spiders, scorpions, and mites. They differ from insects in possessing only two main body regions, the cephalothorax and the abdomen.

Arafat Yassir 1929– . Palestinian nationalist politician, cofounder of al-ᗯFatah 1956 and president of the ᗯPalestine Liberation Organization (PLO) from 1969. In the 1970s his activities in pursuit of an independent homeland for Palestinians made him a prominent figure in world politics, but in the 1980s the growth of factions within the PLO effectively reduced his power. His support for Saddam Hussein after Iraq's invasion of Kuwait 1990 weakened his international standing.

Aragón autonomous region of NE Spain including the provinces of Huesca, Teruel, and Zaragoza; area 47,700 sq km/18,412 sq mi; population (1986) 1,215,000. Its capital is Zaragoza, and products include almonds, figs, grapes, and olives. Aragón was an independent kingdom 1035–1479.

Aral Sea inland sea divided between Kazakhstan and Uzbekistan, the world's fourth largest lake; former area 62,000 sq km/24,000 sq mi, but decreasing. Water from its tributaries, the Amu Darya and Syr Darya, has been diverted for irrigation and city use, and the sea is disappearing, with long-term consequences for the climate.

Aramaic language Semitic language of the Hamito-Semitic family of W Asia, the everyday language of Palestine 2,000 years ago, during the Roman occupation and the time of Jesus.

Ararat double-peaked mountain on the Turkish-Iranian border; the higher, Great Ararat, 5,137 m/16,854 ft, was the reputed resting place of Noah's Ark after the Flood.

Arbil Kurdish town in a province of the same name in N Iraq; population (1985) 334,000. Occupied since Assyrian times, it was the site of a battle 331 BC at which Alexander the Great defeated the Persians under Darius III. In 1974 Arbil became the capital of a Kurdish autonomous region set up by the Iraqi government.

arbitrageur in finance, a person who buys securities (such as currency or commodities) in one country or market for immediate resale in another market, to take advantage of different prices.

arbitration submission of a dispute to a third, unbiased party for settlement. It may be personal litigation, a trade-union issue, or an international dispute.

arc in geometry, a section of a curved line or circle. The arcs of a circle are classified thus: a *semicircle*, which is exactly half of the circle; *minor arcs*, which are less than the semicircle; and *major arcs*, which are greater than the semicircle.

arch curved structure of masonry that supports the weight of material over an open space, as in a bridge or doorway. The first arches consisted of several wedge-shaped stones supported by their mutual pressure. The term is also applied to any curved structure that is an arch in form only.

archaeology study of history (primarily but not exclusively the prehistoric and ancient periods), based on the examination of physical remains. Principal activities include preliminary field (or site) surveys, excavation (where necessary), and the classification, dating, and interpretation of finds. Since 1958 radiocarbon dating has been used to establish the age of archaeological strata and associated materials.

archaeopteryx extinct primitive bird, known from fossilized remains, about 160 million years old, found in limestone deposits in Bavaria, Germany. It is popularly known as 'the first bird', although some earlier bird ancestors are now known. It was about the size of a crow and had feathers and wings, but in many respects its skeleton is reptilian (teeth and a long, bony tail) and very like some small meat-eating dinosaurs of the time.

archery use of the bow and arrow, originally in hunting and warfare, now as a competitive sport. The world governing body is the Fédération Internationale de Tir à l'Arc (FITA) founded 1931.

Archimedes c. 287–212 BC. Greek mathematician who made major discoveries in geometry, hydrostatics, and mechanics. He formulated a law of fluid displacement (Archimedes' principle), and is credited with the invention of the Archimedes' screw, a cylindrical device for raising water.

Archimedes' principle in physics, law stating that an object wholly or partly submerged in a fluid displaces a volume of fluid that weighs the same as the apparent loss in weight of the object (which, in turn, equals the upwards force, or upthrust, experienced by that object).

Archimedes' screw one of the earliest kinds of pump, thought to have been invented by Archimedes. It consists of a spiral screw revolving inside a close-fitting cylinder. It was once commonly used to lift water from canals. The screw is still used to lift water in the Nile delta in Egypt.

archipelago group of islands, or an area of sea containing a group of islands. The islands of an archipelago are usually volcanic in origin, and they sometimes represent the tops of peaks in areas around continental margins flooded by the sea.

architecture art of designing structures. The term covers the design of the visual appearance of structures; their internal arrangements of space; selection of external and internal building materials; design or selection of natural and artificial lighting systems, as well as mechanical, electrical, and plumbing systems; and design or selection of decorations and furnishings. Architectural style may emerge from evolution of techniques and styles particular to a culture in a given time period with or without identifiable individuals as architects, or may be attributed to specific individuals or groups of architects working together on a project.

arc lamp or *arc light* electric light that uses the illumination of an electric arc maintained between two electrodes. The British scientist Humphry Davy developed an arc lamp 1808, and its main use in recent years has been in cinema projectors. The lamp consists of two carbon electrodes, between which a very high voltage is maintained. Electric current arcs (jumps) between the two, creating a brilliant light.

arc minute, arc second units for measuring small angles, used in geometry, surveying, map-making, and astronomy. An arc minute is one-sixtieth of a degree, and an arc second one-sixtieth of an arc minute. Small distances in the sky, as between two close stars or the apparent width of a planet's disc, are expressed in minutes and seconds of arc.

Arctic, the that part of the northern hemisphere surrounding the North Pole; arbitrarily defined as the region lying N of the Arctic Circle (66° 32″N) or N of the tree line. There is no Arctic continent; the greater part of the region comprises the Arctic Ocean, which is the world's smallest ocean. Arctic climate, fauna, and flora extend over the islands and N edges of continental land masses that surround the Arctic Ocean (Svalbard, Iceland, Greenland, Siberia, Scandinavia, Alaska, and Canada); *area* 36,000,000 sq km/14,000,000 sq mi; *physical* pack-ice floating on the Arctic Ocean occupies almost the entire region between the North Pole and the coasts of North America and Eurasia, covering an area that ranges in diameter from 3,000 km/1,900 mi to 4,000 km/2,500 mi. The pack-ice reaches a maximum extent in Feb when its outer limit (influenced by the cold Labrador Current and the warm Gulf Stream) varies from 50°N along the coast of Labrador to 75°N in the Barents Sea N of Scandinavia. In spring the pack-ice begins to break up into ice floes which are carried by the south-flowing Greenland Current to the Atlantic Ocean. Arctic ice is at its minimum area in Aug. The greatest concentration of icebergs in Arctic regions is found in Baffin Bay. They are derived from the glaciers of W Greenland, then carried along Baffin Bay and down into the N Atlantic where they melt off Labrador and Newfoundland. The Bering Straits are icebound for more than six months each year, but the Barents Sea between Scandinavia and Svalbard is free of ice and is navigable throughout the year. Arctic coastlines, which have emerged from the sea since the last Ice Age, are characterized by deposits of gravel and disintegrated rock. The area covered by the Arctic icecap shrank 2% 1978–87. (Countries with Arctic coastlines established the International Arctic Sciences Committee 1987 to study ozone depletion and climatic change);

natural resources the Arctic is rich in coal, oil and natural gas, and mineral resources including gold, silver, copper, uranium, lead, zinc, nickel, and bauxite. Because of climatic conditions, the Arctic is not suited to navigation and the exploitation of these resources. Murmansk naval base on the Kola Peninsula is the largest in the world; *population* there are about 1 million aboriginal people including the Aleuts of Alaska, North American Indians, the Lapps of Scandinavia and Russia, the Yakuts, Samoyeds, Komi, Chukchi, Tungus, and Dolgany of Russia, and the Inuit of Siberian Russia, the Canadian Arctic and Greenland.

Arctic Circle imaginary line that encircles the North Pole at latitude 66° 32″ N. Within this line there is at least one day in the summer during which the Sun never sets, and at least one day in the winter during which the Sun never rises.

Arctic Ocean ocean surrounding the North Pole; area 14,000,000 sq km/5,400,000 sq mi. Because of the Siberian and North American rivers flowing into it, it has comparatively low salinity and freezes readily.

Arcturus or *Alpha Boötis* brightest star in the constellation Boötes and the fourth brightest star in the sky. Arcturus is a red giant about 28 times larger than the Sun and 70 times more luminous, 34 light years away from Earth.

Ardennes wooded plateau in NE France, SE Belgium, and N Luxembourg, cut through by the river Meuse; also a *département* of ▷Champagne-Ardenne. There was heavy fighting here in World Wars I and II.

Ares in Greek mythology, the god of war (Roman ▷Mars). The son of Zeus and Hera, he was worshipped chiefly in Thrace.

Argentina Republic of; country in South America, bordered W and S by Chile, NW by Bolivia, and E by Paraguay, Brazil, Uruguay, and the Atlantic Ocean; *area* 2,780,092 sq km/1,073,116 sq mi; *capital* Buenos Aires (to move to Viedma); *physical* mountains in W, forest in N, pampas (treeless plains) in E central area, Patagonian plateau in S; rivers Colorado, Paraná, Uruguay, Rio de la Plata estuary; *territories* part of Tierra del Fuego; disputed claims to S Atlantic islands and part of Antarctica; *head of state and government* Carlos Menem from 1989; *political system* emergent democratic federal republic; *exports* livestock products, cereals, wool, tannin, peanuts, linseed oil, minerals (coal, copper, molybdenum, gold, silver, lead, zinc, barium, uranium); the country has huge resources of oil, natural gas, hydroelectric power; *population* (1990 est) 32,686,000 (mainly of Spanish or Italian origin, only about 30,000 American Indians surviving); *languages* Spanish (official); English, Italian, German, French; *recent history* independence from Spain achieved 1816. Juan Perón elected president 1946, overthrown 1955. He returned to power 1973 but died the following year. A coup 1976 resulted in rule by a military junta. Defeat in the Falklands War with the UK led to General Galtieri's removal from power 1983. Full diplomatic relations with the UK restored 1990.

argon colourless, odourless, nonmetallic, gaseous element, symbol Ar, atomic number 18, relative atomic mass 39.948. It is grouped with the ▷inert gases, since it was long believed not to react with other substances, but observations now indicate that it can be made to combine with boron fluoride to form compounds. It constitutes almost 1% of the Earth's atmosphere, and was discovered 1894 by British chemists John Rayleigh (1842–1919) and William Ramsay after all oxygen and nitrogen had been removed chemically from a sample of air. It is used in electric discharge tubes and argon lasers.

Argonauts in Greek legend, the band of heroes who accompanied ▷Jason when he set sail in the *Argo* to find the ▷Golden Fleece.

Argus in Greek mythology, a giant with 100 eyes. When he was killed by Hermes, Hera transplanted his eyes into the tail of her favourite bird, the peacock.

aria solo vocal piece in an opera or oratorio, often in three sections, the third repeating the first after a contrasting central section.

Ariadne in Greek mythology, the daughter of Minos, King of Crete. When Theseus came from Athens as one of the sacrificial victims offered to the Minotaur, she fell in love with him and gave him a ball of thread, which enabled him to find his way out of the labyrinth.

Arias Sanchez Oscar 1940– . Costa Rican politician, president 1986–90, secretary general of the left-wing National Liberation Party (PLN) from 1979. He advocated a neutralist policy and in 1987 was the leading promoter of the Central American Peace Plan (see ▷Nicaragua). He lost the presidency to Rafael Angel Calderón 1990. He was awarded the Nobel Peace Prize 1987.

Aries zodiacal constellation in the northern hemisphere between Pisces and Taurus, near Auriga, represented as the legendary ram whose golden fleece was sought by Jason and the Argonauts. Its most distinctive feature is a curve of three stars of decreasing brightness. The brightest of these is Hamal or Alpha Arietis, 65 light years from Earth.

Ariosto Ludovico 1474–1533. Italian poet who wrote Latin poems and comedies on Classical lines, including the poem ▷*Orlando Furioso* 1516, published 1532, an epic treatment of the *Roland* story, the perfect poetic expression of the Italian Renaissance.

Aristarchus of Samos *c.* 280–264 BC. Greek astronomer. The first to argue that the Earth moves around the Sun, he was ridiculed for his beliefs. He was also the first astronomer known to estimate the sizes of the Sun and Moon and their distances from the Earth.

Aristides *c.* 530–468 BC. Athenian politician. He was one of the ten Athenian generals at the battle of Marathon 490 BC and was elected chief archon, or magistrate. Later he came into conflict with the democratic leader Themistocles, and was exiled about 483 BC. He returned to fight against the Persians at Salamis 480 BC and in the following year commanded the Athenians at Plataea.

Aristophanes *c.* 448–380 BC. Greek comedic dramatist. Of his 11 extant plays (of a total of over 40), the early comedies are remarkable for the violent satire with which he ridiculed the democratic war leaders. He also satirized contemporary issues such as the new learning of Socrates in *The Clouds* 423 BC and the power of women in *Lysistrata* 411 BC.

Aristotle 384–322 BC. Greek philosopher who advocated reason and moderation. He maintained that sense experience is our only source of knowledge, and that by reasoning we can discover the essences of things, that is, their distinguishing qualities. In his works on ethics and politics, he suggested that human happiness consists in living in conformity with nature. He derived his political theory from the recognition that mutual aid is natural to humankind, and refused to set up any one constitution as universally ideal.

arithmetic branch of mathematics involving the study of numbers. The fundamental operations of arithmetic are addition, subtraction, multiplication, division, and, dependent on these four, raising to ▷powers and extraction of roots. Percentages, fractions, and ratios are developed from these operations. Fractions arise in the process of measurement.

arithmetic progression or *arithmetic sequence* sequence of numbers or terms that have a common difference between any one term and the next in the sequence. For example, 2, 7, 12, 17, 22, 27, . . . is an arithmetic sequence with a common difference of 5.

Arizona state in SW USA; nickname Grand Canyon State; *area* 294,100 sq km/113,500 sq mi; *capital* Phoenix; *towns* Tucson, Scottsdale, Tempe, Mesa, Glendale, Flagstaff; *physical* Colorado Plateau in N and E, desert basins and mountains in S and W, Colorado River, Grand Canyon; *products* cotton under irrigation, livestock, copper, molybdenum, silver, electronics, aircraft; *population* (1990) 3,665,000; including 4.5% American Indians (Navajo, Hopi, Apache), who by treaty own 25% of the state; *famous people* Cochise, Wyatt Earp, Geronimo, Barry Goldwater, Zane Grey, Percival Lowell, Frank Lloyd Wright; *history* part of New Spain 1715; part of Mexico 1824; passed to the USA after Mexican War 1848; territory 1863; statehood achieved 1912.

Arkansas state in S central USA; nickname Wonder State/Land of Opportunity; *area* 137,800 sq km/53,191 sq mi; *capital* Little Rock; *towns* Fort Smith, Pine Bluff, Fayetteville; *physical*

Ozark Mountains and plateau in W, lowlands in E; Arkansas River; many lakes; Hot Springs National Park; ***products*** cotton, soya beans, rice, oil, natural gas, bauxite, timber, processed foods; ***population*** (1990) 2,350,700; ***famous people*** Johnny Cash, J William Fulbright, Douglas MacArthur, Winthrop Rockefeller; ***history*** explored by de Soto 1541; European settlers 1648, who traded with local Indians; part of Louisiana Purchase 1803; statehood achieved 1836.

Arkwright Richard 1732–1792. English inventor and manufacturing pioneer who developed a machine for spinning cotton (he called it a 'spinning frame') 1768. He set up a water-powered spinning factory 1771 and installed steam power in another factory 1790. This was part of the first phase of the ⇨Industrial Revolution.

Armada fleet sent by Philip II of Spain against England 1588. See ⇨Spanish Armada.

armadillo mammal of the family Dasypodidae, with an armour of bony plates on its back. Some 20 species live between Texas and Patagonia and range in size from the fairy armadillo at 13 cm/5 in to the giant armadillo, 1.5 m/4.5 ft long. Armadillos feed on insects, snakes, fruit, and carrion. Some can roll into an armoured ball if attacked; others rely on burrowing for protection.

Armagh county of Northern Ireland; ***area*** 1,250 sq km/483 sq mi; ***towns*** Armagh (county), Lurgan, Portadown, Keady; ***physical*** smallest county of Northern Ireland; flat in N, with many bogs; low hills in S; chief rivers Bann and Blackwater, flowing into Lough Neagh, and the Callan tributary of the Blackwater; ***products*** chiefly agricultural: apples, potatoes, flax; ***population*** (1981) 119,000.

armature in a motor or generator, the wire-wound coil that carries the current and rotates in a magnetic field. (In alternating-current machines, the armature is sometimes stationary.) The pole piece of a permanent magnet or electromagnet and the moving, iron part of a ⇨solenoid, especially if the latter acts as a switch, may also be referred to as armatures.

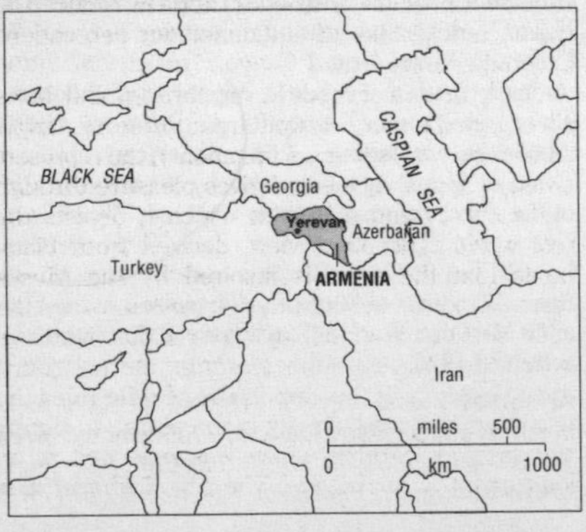

Armenia Republic of; country in SE Europe, bordered N by Georgia, E by Azerbaijan, S by Iran, and W by Turkey; ***area*** 29,800 sq km/11,506 sq mi; ***capital*** Yerevan; ***physical*** mainly mountainous (including Mount Ararat), wooded; ***head of state*** Levon Ter-Petrossian from 1990; ***head of government*** Vazguen Manukyan from 1990; ***political system*** emergent democracy; ***products*** copper, molybdenum, cereals, cotton, silk; ***population*** (1991) 3,580,000 (Armenian 90%, Azerbaijani 5%, Russian 2%, Kurd 2%); ***language*** Armenian; ***recent history*** became independent republic 1918; occupied by Red Army 1920; made a constituent republic of USSR 1936. Popular demonstrations in Yerevan 1988 called for transfer of Nagorno-Karabakh from Azerbaijan to Armenian control; civil war broke out with neighbouring Azerbaijan 1989–91 over Nagorno-Karabakh; Red Army intervened. In 1991 Armenia boycotted Soviet Union constitutional referendum; overwhelming vote for independence. Nagorno-Karabkh ceasefire signed but broken; Nagorno-Karabakh declared its independence 1991. Armenia joined new Commonwealth of Independent States (CIS) Dec 1991; recognized as independent state by USA Jan 1992; admitted into Conference on Security and Cooperation in Europe (CSCE).

Armenian member of the largest ethnic group inhabiting Armenia. There are Armenian minorities in Azerbaijan, as well as in Turkey and Iran. Christianity was introduced to the ancient Armenian kingdom in the 3rd century. There are 4–5 million speakers of Armenian, which belongs to the Indo-European family of languages.

armistice cessation of hostilities while awaiting a peace settlement. 'The Armistice' refers specifically to the end of World War I between Germany and the Allies 11 Nov 1918. On 22 June 1940 French representatives signed an armistice with Germany in the same railway carriage at Compiègne as in 1918. No armistice was signed with either Germany or Japan 1945; both nations surrendered and there was no provision for the suspension of fighting. The Korean armistice, signed at Panmunjom 27 July 1953, terminated the Korean War 1950–53.

armour body protection worn in battle. Body armour is depicted in Greek and Roman art. Chain mail was developed in the Middle Ages but the craft of the armourer in Europe reached its height in design in the 15th century, when knights were completely encased in plate armour that still allowed freedom of movement. Medieval Japanese armour was articulated, made of iron, gilded metal, leather, and silk. Contemporary bulletproof vests and riot gear are forms of armour. The term is used in a modern context to refer to a mechanized armoured vehicle, such as a tank.

arms trade sale of weapons from a manufacturing country to another nation. Nearly 50% of the world's arms exports end up in the Middle East, and most of the rest in Third World countries. Iraq, for instance, was armed in the years leading up to the 1991 Gulf War mainly by the USSR but also by France, Brazil, and South Africa.

Armstrong Louis ('Satchmo') 1901–1971. US jazz cornet and trumpet player and singer. His Chicago recordings in the 1920s with the Hot Five and Hot Seven brought him recognition for his warm and pure trumpet tone, his skill at improvisation, and his quirky, gravelly voice. From the 1930s he also appeared in films.

Armstrong Neil Alden 1930– . US astronaut. In 1969, he became the first person to set foot on the Moon, and said, 'That's one small step for a man, one giant leap for mankind.' The Moon landing was part of the ⏃Apollo project.

army organized military force for fighting on the ground. A national army is used to further a political policy by force either within the state or on the territory of another state. Most countries have a national army, maintained by taxation, and raised either by conscription (compulsory military service) or voluntarily (paid professionals). Private armies may be employed by individuals and groups.

Arnhem city in the Netherlands, on the river Rhine SE of Utrecht, capital of Gelderland province; population (1991) 131,700. It produces salt, chemicals, and pharmaceuticals. It was the scene of an airborne operation by the Allies in World War II, 17–26 Sept 1944, to secure a bridgehead over the Rhine, thereby opening the way for a thrust towards the Ruhr. The operation was only partially successful, with 7,600 casualties.

Arnold Matthew 1822–1888. English poet and critic. His poems, characterized by their elegiac mood and pastoral themes, include *The Forsaken Merman* 1849, *Thyrsis* 1867 (commemorating his friend Arthur Hugh Clough), *Dover Beach* 1867, and *The Scholar Gypsy* 1853. Arnold's critical works include *Essays in Criticism* 1865 and 1888, and *Culture and Anarchy* 1869, which attacks 19th-century philistinism. His father **Thomas Arnold** (1795–1842) was the headmaster of Rugby School 1828–42. His regime has been graphically described in Thomas Hughes's *Tom Brown's Schooldays* 1857. He emphasized training of character, and his influence on public school education was profound.

aromatic compound organic chemical compound in which some of the bonding electrons are delocalized (shared among several atoms within the molecule and not localized in the vicinity of the atoms involved in bonding). The commonest aromatic compounds have ring structures, the atoms comprising the ring being either all carbon or containing one or more different atoms (usually nitrogen, sulphur, or oxygen). Typical examples are benzene (C_6H_6) and pyridine (C_6H_5N).

Arp Hans or Jean 1887–1966. French abstract

painter and sculptor. He was one of the founders of the ⏃Dada movement about 1917, and later was associated with the Surrealists.

arrest apprehension and detention of a person suspected of a crime. In Britain an arrest may be made on a magistrate's warrant, but a police constable is empowered to arrest without warrant in all cases where he or she has reasonable ground for thinking a serious offence has been committed.

Arrhenius Svante August 1859–1927. Swedish scientist, the founder of physical chemistry. Born near Uppsala, he became a professor at Stockholm in 1895, and made a special study of electrolysis. He wrote *Worlds in the Making* and *Destinies of the Stars*, and in 1903 received the Nobel Prize for Chemistry. In 1905 he is reputed to have predicted global warming as a result of carbon dioxide emission from burning fossil fuels.

arrowroot starchy substance derived from the roots and tubers of various tropical plants with thick, clumpy roots. The true arrowroot *Maranta arundinacea* was used by the Indians of South America as an antidote against the effects of poisoned arrows.

arsenic brittle, greyish-white, semimetallic element (a metalloid), symbol As, atomic number 33, relative atomic mass 74.92. It occurs in many ores and occasionally in its elemental state, and is widely distributed, being present in minute quantities in the soil, the sea, and the human body. In larger quantities, it is poisonous. The chief source of arsenic compounds is as a by-product from metallurgical processes. It is used in making semiconductors, alloys, and solders.

arson malicious and wilful setting fire to property. In Britain arson is covered by the Criminal Damage Act 1971.

art in the broadest sense, all the processes and products of human skill, imagination, and invention; the opposite of nature. In contemporary usage, definitions of art usually reflect aesthetic criteria, and the term may encompass literature, music, drama, painting, and sculpture. Popularly, the term is most commonly used to refer to the visual arts. In Western culture, aesthetic criteria introduced by the ancient Greeks still influence our perceptions and judgements of art.

Two currents of thought run through our ideas about art. In one, derived from Aristotle, art is concerned with *mimesis* ('imitation'), the representation of appearances, and gives pleasure through the accuracy and skill with which it depicts the real world. The other view, derived from Plato, holds that the artist is inspired by the Muses (or by God, or by the inner impulses, or by the collective unconscious) to express that which is beyond appearances – inner feelings, eternal truths, or the essence of the age. In the Middle Ages the term 'art' was used, chiefly in the plural, to signify a branch of learning which was regarded as an instrument of knowledge. The seven **liberal arts** consisted of the *trivium*, that is grammar, logic, and rhetoric, and the *quadrivium*, that is arithmetic, music, geometry, and astronomy. In the visual arts of Western civilizations, painting and sculpture have been the dominant forms for many centuries. This has not always been the case in other cultures. Islamic art, for example, is one of ornament, for under the Muslim religion artists were forbidden to usurp the divine right of creation by portraying living creatures. In some cultures masks, tattoos, pottery, and metalwork have been the main forms of visual art. Recent technology has made new art forms possible, such as photography and cinema, and today electronic media have led to entirely new ways of creating and presenting visual images. See also ⊳ancient art, ⊳medieval art, and individual movements, such as ⊳Romanticism, ⊳Cubism, and ⊳Impressionism.

Art Deco style in art and architecture that emerged in Europe in the 1920s and continued through the 1930s, using rather heavy, geometric simplification of form. It was a self-consciously modern style, with sharp lines, and dominated the decorative arts.

Artemis in Greek mythology, the goddess (Roman Diana) of chastity, the Moon, and the hunt. She is the twin sister of ⊳Apollo. Her cult centre was at Ephesus.

arteriosclerosis nontechnical term for ⊳atherosclerosis.

artery vessel that carries blood from the heart to the rest of the body. It is built to withstand considerable pressure, having thick walls that are impregnated with muscle and elastic fibres. During contraction of the heart muscles, arteries expand in diameter to allow for the sudden increase in pressure that occurs; the resulting ⊳pulse or pressure wave can be felt at the wrist. Not all arteries carry oxygenated (oxygen-rich) blood; the pulmonary arteries convey deoxygenated (oxygen-poor) blood from the heart to the lungs.

artesian well well in which water rises from its ⊳aquifer under natural pressure. Such a well may be drilled into an aquifer that is confined by impermeable beds both above and below. If the water table (the top of the region of water saturation) in that aquifer is above the level of the well head, hydrostatic pressure will force the water to the surface. The artesian well is named after Artois, a French province, where the phenomenon was first observed.

arthritis inflammation of the joints, with pain, swelling, and restricted motion. Many conditions may cause arthritis, including gout and trauma to the joint. *Osteoarthritis*, a degenerative condition, tends to affect larger, load-bearing joints, such as the knee and hip. It appears in later life, especially in those whose joints may have been subject to earlier stress or damage. Joint replacement surgery is nearly always successful.

arthropod member of the phylum Arthropoda; an invertebrate animal with jointed legs and a segmented body with a horny or chitinous casing (exoskeleton), which is shed periodically and replaced as the animal grows. Included are arachnids such as spiders and mites, as well as crustaceans, millipedes, centipedes, and insects.

Arthur 6th century AD. Legendary British king and hero in stories of ⊳Camelot and the quest for the ⊳Holy Grail. Arthur is said to have been born in Tintagel, Cornwall, and buried in Glastonbury, Somerset.

Arthur Chester Alan 1830–1886. 21st president of

artesian well

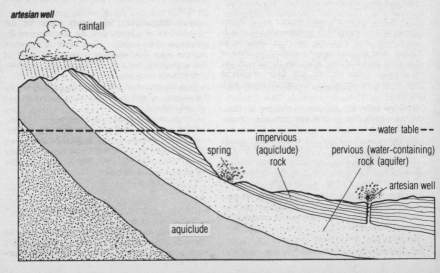

the USA 1881–85, a Republican. In 1880 he was chosen as James ♢Garfield's vice president, and was his successor when Garfield was assassinated the following year.

artichoke either of two plants of the composite or sunflower family Compositae. The common or globe artichoke *Cynara scolymus* is native to the Mediterranean, and is a form of thistle. It is tall, with purplish blue flowers; the bracts of the unopened flower are eaten. The Jerusalem artichoke *Helianthus tuberosus* is a sunflower, native to North America. It has edible tubers.

article grammatical ♢part of speech. There are two articles in English: the *definite article the*, which serves to specify or identify a noun (as in 'This is *the* book I need'), and the *indefinite article a* or (before vowels) *an*, which indicates a single unidentified noun ('They gave me *a* piece of paper and *an* envelope').

artificial insemination (AI) introduction by instrument of semen from a sperm bank or donor into the female reproductive tract to bring about fertilization. Originally used by animal breeders to improve stock with sperm from high-quality males, in the 20th century it has been developed for use in humans, to help the infertile. In ♢in vitro fertilization, the egg is fertilized in a test tube and then implanted in the womb. In zygote intrafallopian transfer (ZIFT) the mixed egg and sperm are reintroduced into the fallopian tube.

artificial intelligence (AI) branch of science concerned with creating computer programs that can perform actions comparable with those of an intelligent human. Current AI research covers such areas as planning (for robot behaviour), language understanding, pattern recognition, and knowledge representation.

artificial respiration maintenance of breathing when the natural process is suspended. If breathing is permanently suspended, as in paralysis, an ♢*iron lung* is used; in cases of electric shock or apparent drowning, for example, the first choice is the expired-air method, the *kiss of life* by mouth-to-mouth breathing until natural breathing is resumed.

artificial selection in biology, selective breeding of individuals that exhibit the particular characteristics that a plant or animal breeder wishes to develop. In plants, desirable features might include resistance to disease, high yield (in crop plants), or attractive appearance. In animal breeding, selection has led to the development of particular breeds of cattle for improved meat or milk production.

artillery collective term for military ♢firearms too heavy to be carried. Artillery can be mounted on ships or aeroplanes and includes cannons and missile launchers.

Art Nouveau art style of about 1890–1910 in Europe, named after a shop in Paris that opened 1895,

which makes marked use of sinuous lines, stylized flowers and foliage, and flame shapes. In England, it appears in the illustrations of Aubrey Beardsley; in Spain, in the architecture of Antonio Gaudi; in France, in the architecture of Hector Guimard and the art glass of René Lalique; in Belgium, in the houses and shops of Victor Horta; in the USA, in the lamps and metalwork of Louis Comfort Tiffany, and in Scotland, the interior and exterior designs of Charles Rennie Mackintosh.

Arts and Crafts movement English social movement, largely antimachine in spirit, based in design and architecture and founded by William Morris in the latter half of the 19th century. It was supported by the architect A W Pugin and by John ♢Ruskin and stressed the importance of handcrafting. The Art Nouveau style succeeded it.

Aruba island in the Caribbean, the westernmost of the Lesser Antilles; an overseas part of the Netherlands; *area* 193 sq km/75 sq mi; *population* (1989) 62,400; *history* Aruba obtained separate status from the other Netherlands Antilles 1986 and has full internal autonomy.

arum any plant of the genus *Arum*, family Araceae, especially the Old World genus *Arum*. The arum called the trumpet lily *Zantedeschia aethiopica*, an ornamental plant, is a native of South Africa.

Arunachal Pradesh state of India, in the Himalayas on the borders of Tibet and Myanmar; *area* 83,600 sq km/32,270 sq mi; *capital* Itanagar; *products* rubber, coffee, spices, fruit, timber; *population* (1991) 858,400; *languages* 50 different dialects; *history* formerly nominally part of Assam, known as the renamed Arunachal Pradesh ('Hills of the Rising Sun'). It became a state 1986.

Arvand River Iranian name for the ♢Shatt al-Arab waterway.

Aryan languages 19th-century name for the ♢Indo-European languages; the languages of the Aryan peoples of India. The name Aryan is no longer used by language scholars because of its association with the Nazi concept of white supremacy.

asbestos any of several related minerals of fibrous structure that offer great heat resistance because of their nonflammability and poor conductivity. Commercial asbestos is generally made from chrysolite, a serpentine mineral, tremolite (a white amphibole), and riebeckite (a blue amphibole, also known as crocidolite when in its fibrous form). Asbestos usage is now strictly controlled because exposure to its dust can cause cancer.

Ascension British island of volcanic origin in the S Atlantic, a dependency of ♢St Helena since 1922; population (1982) 1,625. The chief settlement is Georgetown.

ASCII (acronym for American standard code for information interchange) in computing, a coding system in which numbers (between 0 and 127) are assigned to letters, digits, and punctuation symbols. For example, 45 represents a hyphen and 65 a capital A. The first 32 codes are used for control functions, such as carriage return and backspace. Strictly speaking, ASCII is a seven-bit code, but an eighth bit (binary digit) is often used to provide ⬦parity or to allow for extra characters. The system is widely used for the storage of text and for the transmission of data between computers. Although computers work in binary code, ASCII numbers are usually quoted as decimal or ⬦hexadecimal numbers.

ascorbic acid $C_6H_8O_6$ or **vitamin C** a relatively simple organic acid found in fresh fruits and vegetables. It is soluble in water and destroyed by prolonged boiling, so soaking or overcooking of vegetables reduces their vitamin C content. Lack of ascorbic acid results in scurvy.

ASEAN acronym for ⬦Association of South East Asian Nations.

asepsis practice of ensuring that bacteria are excluded from open sites during surgery, wound dressing, blood sampling, and other medical procedures.

asexual reproduction in biology, reproduction that does not involve the manufacture and fusion of sex cells, nor the necessity for two parents. The process carries a clear advantage in that there is no need to search for a mate nor to develop complex pollinating mechanisms; every asexual organism can reproduce on its own. Asexual reproduction can therefore lead to a rapid population build-up.

ash any tree of the worldwide genus *Fraxinus*, belonging to the olive family Oleaceae, with winged fruits. *F. excelsior* is the European species; its timber is of importance. The ⬦mountain ash or rowan belongs to the family Rosaceae.

Ashcroft Peggy 1907–1991. English actress. Her Shakespearean roles included Desdemona in *Othello* (with Paul Robeson) and Juliet in *Romeo and Juliet* 1935 (with Laurence Olivier and John Gielgud), and she appeared in the British TV play *Caught on a Train* 1980 (BAFTA award), the series *The Jewel in the Crown* 1984, and the film *A Passage to India* 1985.

Ashdown Paddy (Jeremy John Durham) 1941– . English politician, leader of the Social and Liberal Democratic Party from 1988. He served in the Royal Marines as a commando, and was a member of the Diplomatic Service 1971–76. He became a Liberal member of Parliament 1983. His constituency is Yeovil, Somerset.

Ashkenazi (plural *Ashkenazim*) a Jew of German or E European descent, as opposed to a Sephardi, of Spanish, Portuguese, or N African descent.

Ashkenazy Vladimir 1937– . Russian-born pianist and conductor. His keyboard technique differs slightly from standard Western technique. In 1962 he was joint winner of the Tchaikovsky Competition with John Ogdon.

Ashkhabad capital of Turkmenistan; population (1989) 402,000. Ashkhabad was founded as a Russian military fort 1881. Industries include glass, carpets ('Bukhara' carpets are made here), cotton; the spectacular natural setting has been used by the film-making industry.

Ashton Frederick 1904–1988. British choreographer, director of the Royal Ballet, London 1963–70. He studied with Marie Rambert before joining the Vic-Wells (now Royal) Ballet 1935 as chief choreographer. His major works include *Façade* 1931 and *Les Rendezvous* 1933 for Rambert; *Cinderella* 1948, *Ondine* 1958, *La Fille mal gardée* 1960, *Marguerite and Armand* 1963, and *A Month in the Country* 1976.

Ash Wednesday first day of Lent, the period in the Christian calendar leading up to Easter; in the Roman Catholic Church the foreheads of the congregation are marked with a cross in ash, as a sign of penitence.

Asia largest of the continents, occupying one-third of the total land surface of the world; *area* 44,000,000 sq km/17,000,000 sq mi; *largest cities* (population over 5 million) Tokyo, Shanghai, Osaka, Beijing, Seoul, Calcutta, Bombay, Jakarta, Bangkok, Tehran, Hong Kong, Delhi, Tianjin, Karachi; *physical* lying in the eastern hemisphere, Asia extends from the Arctic Circle to just over 10° S of the equator. The Asian mainland, which forms the greater part of the Eurasian continent, lies entirely in the northern hemisphere and stretches from Cape Chelyubinsk at its N extremity to Cape Piai at the S tip of the Malay Peninsula. From Dezhneva Cape in the E, the mainland extends W over more than 165° longitude to Cape Baba in Turkey. Containing the world's highest mountains and largest inland seas, Asia can be divided into five physical units: 1) at the heart of the continent, a central triangle of plateaus at varying altitudes (Tibetan Plateau, Tarim Basin, Gobi Desert), surrounded by huge mountain chains which spread in all directions (Himalayas, Karakoram, Hindu Kush, Pamirs, Kunlun, Tien Shan, Altai); 2) the W plateaus and ranges (Elburz, Zagros, Taurus, Great Caucasus mountains) of Afghanistan, Iran, N Iraq, Armenia, and Turkey; 3) the lowlands of Turkestan and Siberia which stretch N of the central mountains to the Arctic Ocean and include large areas in which the subsoil is permanently frozen; 4) the fertile and densely populated E lowlands and river plains of Korea, China, and Indochina, and the islands of the East Indies and Japan; 5) the southern plateaus of Arabia, and the Deccan, with the fertile alluvial plains of the Euphrates, Tigris, Indus, Ganges, Brahmaputra, and Irrawaddy rivers; *features* Mount Everest at 8,872 m/29,118 ft is the world's highest mountain; Dead Sea –394 m/–1,293 ft is the world's lowest point below sea level; *products* 62% of the population are employed in agriculture; Asia produces 46% of the world's cereal crops (91% of the world's rice); other crops include mangoes (India), groundnuts (India, China), 84% of the world's copra (Philippines, Indonesia), 93% of the world's rubber (Indonesia, Malaysia, Thailand), tobacco (China), flax (China, Russia), 95% of the world's jute (India, Bangladesh, China), cotton (China, India, Pakistan), silk (China, India), fish (Japan, China, Korea, Thailand); China produces 55% of the world's tungsten; 45% of the world's tin is produced by Malaysia, China, and Indonesia; Saudi Arabia is the world's largest producer of oil; *population* (1988) 2,996,000; the world's largest, though not the fastest growing population, amounting to more than half the total number of people in the world; between 1950 and 1990 the death rate and infant mortality were reduced by more than 60%; annual growth rate 1.7%; projected to increase to 3,550,000 by 2000.

Asia Minor historical name for *Anatolia*, the Asian part of Turkey.

AS level General Certificate of Education *A*dvanced *S*upplementary examinations introduced in the UK 1988 as the equivalent to 'half an ◊A level' as a means of broadening the sixth form (age 16–18) curriculum, and including more students in the examination system.

Asmara or *Asmera* capital of Eritrea, Ethiopia; 64 km/40 mi SW of Massawa on the Red Sea; population (1984) 275,385. Products include beer, clothes, and textiles. In 1974 unrest here precipitated the end of the Ethiopian Empire.

Asoka lived *c.* 273–238 BC. Indian emperor, and Buddhist convert from Hinduism. He issued edicts, carved on pillars and rock faces throughout his dominions, promoting wise government and the cultivation of moral virtues according to Buddhist teachings. Many still survive, and are among the oldest deciphered texts in India.

asp any of several venomous snakes, including *Vipera aspis* of S Europe, allied to the adder, and the Egyptian cobra *Naja haje*, reputed to have been used by the Egyptian queen Cleopatra for her suicide.

asparagus any plant of the genus *Asparagus*, family Liliaceae, with small scalelike leaves and many needlelike branches. Native to Eurasia, *A. officinalis* is cultivated, and the young shoots are eaten as a vegetable.

aspen any of several species of ◊poplar tree, genus *Populus*. The European quaking aspen *P. tremula* has flattened leafstalks that cause the leaves to flutter with every breeze. The soft wood is used for matches and paper pulp.

asphalt mineral mixture containing semisolid brown or black ◊bitumen, used in the construction industry. Asphalt is mixed with rock chips to form paving material, and the purer varieties are used for insulating material and for waterproofing masonry. It can be produced artificially by the distillation of ◊petroleum.

aspidistra Asiatic plant of the genus *Aspidistra* of

the lily family Liliaceae. The Chinese *A. elatior* has broad, lanceolate leaves and, like all members of the genus, grows well in warm indoor conditions.

aspirin acetylsalicylic acid, a popular pain-relieving drug (◊analgesic) developed in the early 20th century for headaches and arthritis. It inhibits ◊prostaglandins, and is derived from the white willow tree *Salix alba*.

In the long term, even moderate use may cause stomach bleeding, kidney damage, and hearing defects, and aspirin is no longer considered suitable for children under 12, because of a suspected link with a rare disease, Reye's syndrome. However, recent medical research suggests that an aspirin a day may be of value in preventing heart attack and thrombosis.

Asquith Herbert Henry, 1st Earl of Oxford and Asquith 1852–1928. British Liberal politician, prime minister 1908–16. As chancellor of the Exchequer he introduced old-age pensions 1908. He limited the right of the House of Lords to veto legislation by the Parliament Act 1911. His endeavours to pass the Home Rule for Ireland Bill led to the ◊Curragh 'Mutiny' and incipient civil war. Unity was re-established by the outbreak of World War I 1914, and a coalition government was formed May 1915. However, his attitude of 'wait and see' was not adapted to all-out war, and in Dec 1916 he was replaced by Lloyd George.

ass any of several horselike, odd-toed, hoofed mammals of the genus *Equus*, family Equidae. Species include the African wild ass *E. asinus*, and the Asian wild ass *E. hemionus*. They differ from horses in their smaller size, larger ears, tufted tail, and characteristic bray. Donkeys and burros are domesticated asses.

Assad Hafez al 1930– . Syrian Ba'athist politician, president from 1971. He became prime minister after a bloodless military coup 1970, and the following year was the first president to be elected by popular vote. Having suppressed dissent, he was re-elected 1978 and 1985. He is a Shia (Alawite) Muslim.

Assam state of NE India; *area* 78,400 sq km/ 30,262 sq mi; *capital* Dispur; *towns* Guwahati; *products* half India's tea is grown and half its oil produced here; rice, jute, sugar, cotton, coal; *population* (1991) 24,294,600, including 12 million Assamese (Hindus), 5 million Bengalis (chiefly Muslim immigrants from Bangladesh), Nepalis, and 2 million indigenous people (Christian and traditional religions); *language* Assamese; *history* after Burmese invasion 1826, Britain took control; and made Assam a separate province 1874; included in the Dominion of India, except for most of the Muslim district of Silhet, which went to Pakistan 1947. Ethnic unrest started in the 1960s when Assamese was declared the official language. After protests, the Gara, Khasi, and Jainitia tribal hill districts became the state of Meghalaya 1971; the

Mizo hill district became the Union Territory of Mizoram 1972. There were massacres of Muslim Bengalis by Hindus 1983. In 1987 members of the Bodo ethnic group began fighting for a separate homeland. Direct rule was imposed by the Indian government Nov 1990 following separatist violence from the Marxist-militant United Liberation Front of Assam (ULFA), which had extorted payments from tea-exporting companies. In March 1991 it was reported that the ULFA, operating from the jungles of Myanmar, had been involved in 97 killings, mainly of Congress I politicians, since 27 Nov 1990.

assassination murder, usually of a political, royal, or public person. The term derives from a sect of Muslim fanatics in the 11th and 12th centuries known as *hashshashin* ('takers of hashish'). They were reputed either to smoke cannabis before they went out to murder, or to receive hashish as payment.

assault intentional act or threat of physical violence against a person. In English law it is both a crime and a ◊tort (a civil wrong). The kinds of criminal assault are common (ordinary); aggravated (more serious, such as causing actual bodily harm); or indecent (of a sexual nature).

assay in chemistry, the determination of the quantity of a given substance present in a sample. Usually it refers to determining the purity of precious metals.

assembly code computer-programming language closely related to a computer's internal codes. It consists chiefly of a set of short mnemonics, which are translated, by a program called an assembler, into ◊machine code for the computer's ◊central processing unit (CPU) to follow directly. In assembly language, for example, 'JMP' means 'jump' and 'LDA' means 'load accumulator'. Assembly code is used by programmers who need to write very fast or efficient programs.

asset in business accounting, a term that covers the land or property of a company or individual, payments due from bills, investments, and anything else owned that can be turned into cash. On a company's balance sheet, total assets must be equal to or greater than liabilities (money and services owed).

asset stripping sale or exploitation by other means of the assets of a business, often one that has been taken over for that very purpose. The parts of the business may be potentially more valuable separately than together.

Association of South East Asian Nations (ASEAN) regional alliance formed in Bangkok 1967; it took over the nonmilitary role of the Southeast Asia Treaty Organization 1975. Its members are Indonesia, Malaysia, the Philippines, Singapore, Thailand, and (from 1984) Brunei; its headquarters are in Jakarta, Indonesia.

Assyria empire in the Middle East *c.* 2500–612 BC,
in N Mesopotamia (now Iraq); early capital Ashur, later Nineveh. It was initially subject to Sumer and intermittently to Babylon. The Assyrians adopted in the main the Sumerian religion and structure of society. At its greatest extent the empire included Egypt and stretched from the E Mediterranean coast to the head of the Persian Gulf.

Astaire Fred. Adopted name of Frederick Austerlitz 1899–1987. US dancer, actor, singer, and choreographer who starred in numerous films, including *Top Hat* 1935, *Easter Parade* 1948, and *Funny Face* 1957, many containing inventive sequences he designed and choreographed himself. He made ten classic films with the most popular of his dancing partners, Ginger Rogers. He later played straight dramatic roles in such films as *On the Beach* 1959.

astatine nonmetallic, radioactive element, symbol At, atomic number 85, relative atomic mass 210. It is a member of the ◊halogen group, and is very rare in nature. Astatine is highly unstable, with many isotopes.

aster any plant of the large genus *Aster*, family Compositae, belonging to the same subfamily as the daisy. All asters have starlike flowers with yellow centres and outer rays (not petals) varying from blue and purple to white and the genus comprises a great variety of size. Many are cultivated as garden flowers, including the Michaelmas daisy *A. novabelgii*. The sea aster *A. tripolium* grows wild on sea cliffs in the south of England.

asteroid or *minor planet* any of many thousands of small bodies, composed of rock and iron, that orbit the Sun. Most lie in a belt between the orbits of Mars and Jupiter, and are thought to be fragments left over from the formation of the ◊Solar System. About 100,000 may exist, but their total mass is only a few hundredths the mass of the Moon.

asthma difficulty in breathing due to spasm of the bronchi (air passages) in the lungs. Attacks may be provoked by allergy, infection, stress, or emotional upset. It may also be increasing as a result of air pollution and occupational hazards. Treatment is with ◊bronchodilators to relax the bronchial muscles and thereby ease the breathing, and in severe cases by inhaled ◊steroids that reduce inflammation of the bronchi.

astigmatism aberration occurring in lenses, including that in the eye. It results when the curvature of the lens differs in two perpendicular planes, so that rays in one plane may be in focus while rays in the other are not. With astigmatic eyesight, the vertical and horizontal cannot be in focus at the same time; correction is by the use of a cylindrical lens that reduces the overall focal length of one plane so that both planes are seen in sharp focus.

Astor prominent US and British family. *John Jacob Astor* (1763–1848) was a US millionaire. His great-grandson *Waldorf Astor*, 2nd Viscount

Astor (1879–1952), was Conservative member of Parliament for Plymouth 1910–19, when he succeeded to the peerage. He was chief proprietor of the British *Observer* newspaper. His US-born wife Nancy Witcher Langhorne (1879–1964), **Lady Astor**, was the first woman member of Parliament to take a seat in the House of Commons 1919, when she succeeded her husband for the constituency of Plymouth. Government policy was said to be decided at Cliveden, their country home.

astronomical unit unit (symbol AU) equal to the mean distance of the Earth from the Sun: 149,597,870 km/92,955,800 mi. It is used to describe planetary distances. Light travels this distance in approximately 8.3 minutes.

astronomy science of the celestial bodies: the Sun, the Moon, and the planets; the stars and galaxies; and all other objects in the universe. It is concerned with their positions, motions, distances, and physical conditions; and with their origins and evolution. Astronomy thus divides into fields such as astrophysics, celestial mechanics, and cosmology. See also ◊radio astronomy and ◊X-ray astronomy.

astrophysics study of the physical nature of stars, galaxies, and the universe. It began with the development of spectroscopy in the 19th century, which allowed astronomers to analyse the composition of stars from their light. Astrophysicists view the universe as a vast natural laboratory in which they can study matter under conditions of temperature, pressure, and density that are unattainable on Earth.

Asturias autonomous region of N Spain; area 10,600 sq km/4,092 sq mi; population (1986) 1,114,000. Half of Spain's coal comes from the mines of Asturias. Agricultural produce includes maize, fruit, and livestock. Oviedo and Gijón are the main industrial towns.

Asunción capital and port of Paraguay, on the Paraguay River; population (1984) 729,000. It produces textiles, footwear, and food products. Founded 1537, it was the first Spanish settlement in the La Plata region.

Aswan winter resort town in Upper Egypt; population (1985) 183,000. It is near the High Dam, built 1960–70, which keeps the level of the Nile constant throughout the year without flooding. It produces steel and textiles.

asylum, political in international law, refuge granted in another country to a person who, for political reasons, cannot return to his or her own country without putting themselves in danger. A person seeking asylum is a type of ◊refugee. In the UK, a House of Lords ruling 1988 held that an applicant for asylum must be able to justify objectively his or her fears of persecution if returned to the country of origin.

asymptote in ◊coordinate geometry, a straight line toward which a curve approaches more and more closely but never reaches. The x and y axes are asymptotes to the rectangular ◊hyperbola, graph of xy = constant.

Atacama desert in N Chile; area about 80,000 sq km/31,000 sq mi. There are mountains inland, and the coastal area is rainless and barren. The Atacama has silver and copper mines, and extensive nitrate deposits.

Atatürk Kemal ('Father of the Turks'). Name assumed 1934 by Mustafa Kemal Pasha 1881–1938. Turkish politician and general, first president of Turkey from 1923. After World War I he established a provisional rebel government and in 1921–22 the Turkish armies under his leadership expelled the Greeks who were occupying Turkey. He was the founder of the modern republic, which he ruled as virtual dictator, with a policy of consistent and radical westernization.

atheism nonbelief in, or the positive denial of, the existence of a God or gods. A related concept is ◊agnosticism. The first openly atheistic book published in Britain was *Answer to Dr Priestley's Letters to a Philosophical Unbeliever* 1782 by Matthew Turner, a Liverpool doctor.

Athelstan *c.* 895–939. King of the Mercians and West Saxons. Son of Edward the Elder and grandson of Alfred the Great, he was crowned king 925 at Kingston upon Thames. He subdued parts of Cornwall and Wales, and defeated the Welsh, Scots, and Danes at Brunanburh 937.

Athena in Greek mythology, the goddess (Roman Minerva) of war, wisdom, and the arts and crafts, who was supposed to have sprung fully grown from the head of Zeus. Her chief cult centre was Athens, where the Parthenon was dedicated to her.

Athens (Greek *Athinai*) capital city of Greece and of ancient Attica; population (1981) 885,000, metropolitan area (1991) 3,096,800. Situated 8 km/5 mi NE of its port of Piraeus on the Gulf of Aegina, it is built around the rocky hills of the Acropolis 169 m/555 ft and the Areopagus 112 m/368 ft, and is overlooked from the northeast by the hill of Lycabettus, 277 m/909 ft high. It lies in the south of the central plain of Attica, watered by the mountain streams of Cephissus and Ilissus. It has less green space than any other European capital (4%) and severe air and noise pollution; *features* The Acropolis dominates the city. Remains of ancient Greece include the Parthenon, the Erechtheum, and the temple of Athena Nike. Near the site of the ancient Agora (marketplace) stands the Theseum, and south of the Acropolis is the theatre of Dionysus. To the southeast stand the gate of Hadrian and the columns of the temple of Olympian Zeus. Nearby is the marble stadium built about 330 BC and restored 1896; *history* The site was first inhabited about 3000 BC, and Athens became the capital of a united Attica before 700 BC. Captured and sacked by the Persians 480 BC, subsequently under Pericles it was the first city of Greece in power and culture. After the death of Alexander the Great the city fell into comparative decline, but it flourished as an intellectual centre until AD 529. In 1458 it was captured by the Turks who held it until 1833; it was chosen as the capital of Greece 1834.

atherosclerosis thickening and hardening of the walls of the arteries, associated with atheroma, a deposit of yellowish fatty matter on lining of the artery wall. The blood flow decreases and blood pressure rises. The condition causes coronary heart disease, stroke, and several other diseases of middle/old age.

athletics competitive track and field events consisting of running, throwing, and jumping disciplines. *Running events* range from sprint races (100 metres) and hurdles to the marathon (26 miles 385 yards). *Jumping events* are the high jump, long jump, triple jump, and pole vault (men only). *Throwing events* are javelin, discus, shot put, and hammer throw (men only).

Atlanta capital and largest city of Georgia, USA; population (1990) 394,000, metropolitan area 2,010,000. It was founded 1837 and was partly destroyed by General ⟡Sherman 1864. There are Ford and Lockheed assembly plants, and it is the headquarters of Coca-Cola. In 1990 it was chosen as the host city for the 1996 summer Olympic Games.

Atlantic Ocean ocean lying between Europe and Africa to the E and the Americas to the W, probably named after the legendary island Atlantis; area of basin 81,500,000 sq km/31,500,000 sq mi; including the Arctic Ocean and Antarctic seas, 106,200,000 sq km/41,000,000 sq mi. The average depth is 3 km/2 mi; greatest depth the Milwaukee Depth in the Puerto Rico Trench 8,648 m/28,374 ft. The Mid-Atlantic Ridge, of which the Azores, Ascension, St Helena, and Tristan da Cunha form part, divides it from N to S. Lava welling up from this central area annually increases the distance between South America and Africa. The N Atlantic is the saltiest of the main oceans, and has the largest tidal range. In the 1960s–80s average wave heights increased by 25%, the largest from 12 m/39 ft to 18 m/59 ft.

Atlas in Greek mythology, one of the ⟡Titans who revolted against the gods; as a punishment, Atlas was compelled to support the heavens on his head and shoulders. Growing weary, he asked ⟡Perseus to turn him into stone, and he was transformed into Mount Atlas.

Atlas Mountains mountain system of NW Africa, stretching 2,400 km/1,500 mi from the Atlantic coast of Morocco to the Gulf of Gabes, Tunisia, and lying between the Mediterranean on the N and the Sahara on the S. The highest peak is Mount Toubkal 4,167 m/13,670 ft.

atmosphere mixture of gases that surrounds the Earth, prevented from escaping by the pull of the Earth's gravity. Atmospheric pressure decreases with height in the atmosphere. In its lowest layer, the atmosphere consists of nitrogen (78%) and oxygen (21%), both in molecular form (two atoms bounded together). The other 1% is largely argon, with very small quantities of other gases, including water vapour and carbon dioxide. The atmosphere plays a major part in the various cycles of nature (the ⟡water cycle, ⟡carbon cycle, and ⟡nitrogen cycle). It is the principal industrial source of nitrogen, oxygen, and argon, which are obtained by fractional distillation of liquid air.

atmosphere or *standard atmosphere* in physics, a unit (symbol atm) of pressure equal to 760 torr, 1013.25 millibars, or 1.01325×10^5 newtons per square metre. The actual pressure exerted by the atmosphere fluctuates around this value, which is assumed to be standard at sea level and 0°C/32°F, and is used when dealing with very high pressures.

atom smallest unit of matter that can take part in a chemical reaction, and which cannot be broken down chemically into anything simpler. An atom is made up of protons and neutrons in a central nucleus surrounded by electrons (see ⟡atomic structure). The atoms of the various elements differ in atomic number, relative atomic mass, and chemical behaviour. There are 109 different types of atom, corresponding with the 109 known elements as listed in the ⟡periodic table of the elements.

Atoms are much too small to be seen even by the microscope (the largest, caesium, has a diameter of 0.0000005 mm/0.00000002 in), and they are in constant motion. Belief in the existence of atoms dates back to the ancient Greek natural philosophers. The first scientist to gather evidence for the existence of atoms was John Dalton, in the 19th century, who believed that every atom was a complete unbreakable entity. Ernest Rutherford showed by experiment that an atom in fact consists of a nucleus surrounded by negatively charged particles called electrons.

atom bomb bomb deriving its explosive force from nuclear fission (see ⟡nuclear energy) as a result of a neutron chain reaction, developed in the 1940s in the USA into a usable weapon. The development of the hydrogen bomb in the 1950s rendered the early atom bomb obsolete. See ⟡nuclear warfare.

atomic clock timekeeping device regulated by various periodic processes occurring in atoms and molecules, such as atomic vibration or the frequency of absorbed or emitted radiation.

atomic mass unit or *dalton unit* (symbol amu or u) unit of mass that is used to measure the relative mass of atoms and molecules. It is equal to one-twelfth of the mass of a carbon-12 atom, which is equivalent to the mass of a proton or 1.66×10^{-27} kg. The ⟡relative atomic mass of an atom has no units; thus oxygen-16 has an atomic mass of 16 daltons, but a relative atomic mass of 16.

atomic number or *proton number* the number (symbol Z) of protons in the nucleus of an atom.

It is equal to the positive charge on the nucleus. In a neutral atom, it is also equal to the number of electrons surrounding the nucleus. The 109 elements are arranged in the ◊periodic table of the elements according to their atomic number.

atomic structure internal structure of an ◊atom. The core of the atom is the **nucleus**, a dense body only one ten-thousandth the diameter of the atom itself. The simplest nucleus, that of hydrogen, comprises a single stable positively charged particle, the **proton**. Nuclei of other elements contain more protons and additional particles of about the same mass as the proton but with no electrical charge, called **neutrons**. Each element has its own characteristic nucleus with a unique number of protons, the atomic number. The number of neutrons may vary. Where atoms of a single element have different numbers of neutrons, they are called ◊isotopes. Although some isotopes tend to be unstable and exhibit ◊radioactivity, they all have identical chemical properties.

The nucleus is surrounded by a number of moving **electrons**, each of which has a negative charge equal to the positive charge on a proton, but which weighs only $1/1,839$ times as much. In a neutral atom, the nucleus is surrounded by the same number of electrons as it contains protons. The chemical properties of an element are determined by the ease with which its atoms can gain or lose electrons. This is dependent on both the number of electrons associated with the nucleus and the force exerted on them by its positive charge.

Atonement, Day of Jewish holy day (**Yom Kippur**) held on the tenth day of Tishri (Sept–Oct), the first month of the Jewish year. It is a day of fasting, penitence, and cleansing from sin, ending the Ten Days of Penitence that follow **Rosh Hashanah**, the Jewish New Year.

ATP abbreviation for **adenosine triphosphate**, a nucleotide molecule found in all cells. It can yield large amounts of energy, and is used to drive the thousands of biological processes needed to sustain life, growth, movement, and reproduction. Green plants use light energy to manufacture ATP as part of the process of ◊photosynthesis. In animals, ATP is formed by the breakdown of glucose molecules, usually obtained from the carbohydrate component of a diet, in a series of reactions termed ◊respiration. It is the driving force behind muscle contraction and the synthesis of complex molecules needed by individual cells.

Attica (Greek **Attiki**) region of Greece comprising Athens and the district around it; area 3,381 sq km/ 1,305 sq mi. It is renowned for its language, art, and philosophical thought in Classical times.

Attila c. 406–453. King of the Huns in an area from the Alps to the Caspian Sea from 434, known to later Christian history as the 'Scourge of God'. He twice attacked the Eastern Roman Empire to increase the quantity of tribute paid to him, 441–443 and

447–449, and then attacked the Western Roman Empire 450–52.

Attlee Clement (Richard), 1st Earl 1883–1967. British Labour politician. In the coalition government during World War II he was Lord Privy Seal 1940–42, dominions secretary 1942–43, and Lord President of the Council 1943–45, as well as deputy prime minister from 1942. As prime minister 1945–51 he introduced a programme of nationalization and a new system of social services.

Attorney General principal law officer. In the UK, principal law officer of the crown and head of the English Bar; the post is one of great political importance. In the USA, it is the chief law officer of the government and head of the Department of Justice.

aubergine or **eggplant** plant *Solanum melongena*, a member of the nightshade family Solanaceae. The aubergine is native to tropical Asia. Its purple-skinned, sometimes white, fruits are eaten as a vegetable.

Auckland largest city in New Zealand, situated in N North Island; population (1989) 850,900. It fills the isthmus that separates its two harbours (Waitemata and Manukau), and its suburbs spread north across the Harbour Bridge. It is the country's chief port and industrial centre, having iron and steel plants, engineering, car assembly, textiles, food processing, sugar refining, and brewing.

Auden W(ystan) H(ugh) 1907–1973. English-born US poet. He wrote some of his most original poetry, such as *Look, Stranger!* 1936, in the 1930s when he led the influential left-wing literary group that included Louis MacNeice, Stephen Spender, and Cecil Day Lewis. He moved to the USA 1939, became a US citizen 1946, and adopted a more conservative and Christian viewpoint, for example in *The Age of Anxiety* 1947.

audit official inspection of a company's accounts by a qualified accountant as required by law each year to ensure that the company balance sheet reflects the true state of its affairs.

Augustine of Hippo, St 354–430. One of the early Christian leaders and writers known as the Fathers of the Church. He was converted to Christianity by Ambrose in Milan and became bishop of Hippo (modern Annaba, Algeria) 396. Among Augustine's many writings are his *Confessions*, a spiritual autobiography, and *De Civitate Dei/The City of God*, vindicating the Christian church and divine providence in 22 books.

Augustine, St first archbishop of Canterbury, England. He was sent from Rome to convert England to Christianity by Pope Gregory I. He landed at Ebbsfleet in Kent 597, and soon after baptized Ethelbert, King of Kent, along with many of his subjects. He was consecrated bishop of the English at Arles in the same year, and appointed archbishop 601, establishing his see at Canterbury. Feast day 26 May.

Augustus 63 BC–AD 14. Title of Octavian (Gaius Julius Caesar Octavianus), first of the Roman emperors. He joined forces with Mark Antony and Lepidus in the Second Triumvirate. Following Mark Antony's liaison with the Egyptian queen Cleopatra, Augustus defeated her troops at Actium 31 BC. As emperor (from 27 BC) he reformed the government of the empire, the army, and Rome's public services, and was a patron of the arts. The period of his rule is known as the Augustan Age.

auk any member of the family Alcidae, consisting of marine diving birds including razorbills, puffins, murres, and guillemots. Confined to the northern hemisphere, they feed on fish and use their wings to 'fly' underwater in pursuit.

Aung San 1916–1947. Burmese politician. He was a founder and leader of the Anti-Fascist People's Freedom League, which led Burma's fight for independence from Great Britain. During World War II he collaborated first with Japan and then with the UK. In 1947 he became head of Burma's provisional government but was assassinated the same year by political opponents; Burma (now Myanmar) became independent 1948.

Aurangzeb or **Aurungzebe** 1618–1707. Mogul emperor of N India from 1658. Third son of Shah Jahan, he made himself master of the court by a palace revolution. His reign was the most brilliant period of the Mogul dynasty, but his despotic tendencies and Muslim fanaticism aroused much opposition.

Aurelian (Lucius Domitius Aurelianus) *c.* 214–275 AD. Roman emperor from 270. A successful soldier, he was chosen emperor by his troops on the death of Claudius II. He defeated the Goths and Vandals, defeated and captured Zenobia of Palmyra, and was planning a campaign against Parthia when he was murdered. The *Aurelian Wall*, a fortification surrounding Rome, was built by Aurelian 271. It was made of concrete, and substantial ruins exist. The *Aurelian Way* ran from Rome through Pisa and Genoa to Antipolis (Antibes) in Gaul.

Aurelius Antoninus Marcus. Roman emperor; see ⋄Marcus Aurelius Antoninus.

aurochs (plural *aurochs*) extinct species of long-horned wild cattle *Bos primigenius* that formerly roamed Europe, SW Asia, and N Africa. It survived in Poland until 1627. It is depicted in many cave paintings, and is considered the ancestor of domestic cattle.

aurora coloured light in the night sky near the Earth's magnetic poles, called *aurora borealis*, 'northern lights', in the northern hemisphere and *aurora australis* in the southern hemisphere. An aurora is usually in the form of a luminous arch with its apex towards the magnetic pole followed by arcs, bands, rays, curtains, and coronas, usually green but often showing shades of blue and red, and sometimes yellow or white. Auroras are caused at heights of over 100 km/60 mi by a fast stream of charged particles from solar flares and low-density 'holes' in the Sun's corona. These are guided by the Earth's magnetic field towards the north and south magnetic poles, where they enter the upper atmosphere and bombard the gases in the atmosphere, causing them to emit visible light.

Auschwitz (Polish *Oswiecim*) town near Kraków in Poland, the site of a notorious ⋄concentration camp used by the Nazis in World War II to exterminate Jews and other political and social minorities, as part of the 'final solution'.

Austen Jane 1775–1817. English novelist who described her raw material as 'three or four families in a Country Village'. *Sense and Sensibility* was published 1811, *Pride and Prejudice* 1813, *Mansfield Park* 1814, *Emma* 1816, *Northanger Abbey* and *Persuasion* 1818, all anonymously. She observed speech and manners with wit and precision, revealing her characters' absurdities in relation to high standards of integrity and appropriateness.

Austerlitz, Battle of battle 2 Dec 1805 in which the French forces of Emperor Napoleon defeated those of Alexander I of Russia and Francis II of Austria at a small town in Czechoslovakia (formerly in Austria), 19 km/12 mi E of Brno.

Australasia loosely applied geographical term, usually meaning Australia, New Zealand, and neighbouring islands.

Australia Commonwealth of; country occupying the smallest continent in the world, situated S of Indonesia, between the Pacific and Indian oceans; *area* 7,682,300 sq km/2,966,136 sq mi; *capital* Canberra; *physical* the world's smallest, flattest, and driest continent (40% lies in the tropics, one-third is desert, and one-third is marginal grazing); Great Sandy Desert; Gibson Desert; Great Victoria Desert; Simpson Desert; the Great Barrier Reef (largest coral reef in the world, stretching 2,000 km/1,250 mi off E coast of Queensland); Great Dividing Range and Australian Alps in the E; Darling, Lachlan, Murrumbridgee, and Murray rivers; Lake Eyre basin and Nullarbor Plain in S; *territories* Norfolk Island, Christmas Island, Cocos (Keeling) Islands, Ashmore and Cartier Islands,

Coral Sea Islands, Heard Island and McDonald Islands, Australian Antarctic Territory; *head of state* Elizabeth II from 1952 represented by governor general; *head of government* Paul Keating from 1991; *political system* federal constitutional monarchy; Australia is an independent sovereign nation within the Commonwealth; *exports* world's largest exporter of sheep, wool, diamonds, alumina, coal, lead and refined zinc ores, and mineral sands; other exports include cereals, beef, veal, mutton, lamb, sugar, nickel (world's second largest producer), iron ore; principal trade partners are Japan, the USA, and EC member states; *population* (1990 est) 16,650,000; *languages* English, Aboriginal; *recent history* Commonwealth of Australia created 1901; autonomy from the UK in internal and external affairs achieved 1942. Australia joined New Zealand and the USA as a signatory to the Anzus Pacific security treaty 1951. In 1967 Aborigines were given full citizenship rights. The Northern Territory attained self-government 1978. The last vestiges of British legal authority in Australia were eliminated 1986. Free-trade agreement with New Zealand signed 1988.

Australia: history

30,000–10,000 BC	Aboriginal immigration from S India, Sri Lanka, and SE Asia.
AD 1606	First European sightings of Australia include Dutch ship *Duyfken* off Cape York.
1770	Captain Cook claimed New South Wales for Britain.
1788	Sydney founded.
19th century	The great age of exploration: coastal surveys (Bass, Flinders), interior (Sturt, Eyre, Leichhardt, Burke and Wills, McDouall Stuart, Forrest). Also the era of the bushrangers, overlanders and squatters, and individuals such as William Buckley and Ned Kelly.
1804	Castle Hill Rising by Irish convicts in New South Wales.
1813	Barrier of the Blue mountains crossed.
1825	Tasmania seceded from New South Wales.
1829	Western Australia formed.
1836	South Australia formed.
1840–68	Convict transportation ended.
1851–61	Gold rushes (Ballarat, Bendigo).
1851	Victoria seceded from New South Wales.
1855	Victoria achieved government.
1856	New South Wales, South Australia, Tasmania achieved government.
1859	Queensland formed from New South Wales and achieved government.
1860	(National) Country Party founded.
1890	Western Australia achieved government.
1891	Depression gave rise to the Australian Labor Party.
1899–1900	South African War – forces offered by the individual colonies.
1901	Creation of the Commonwealth of Australia.
1911	Site for capital at Canberra acquired.
1914–18	World War I – Anzac troops in Europe including Gallipoli.
1939–45	World War II – Anzac troops in Greece, Crete, and N Africa (El Alamein) and the Pacific (Battle of the Coral Sea).
1941	Curtin's appeal to USA for help in World War II marks the end of the special relationship with Britain.
1944	Liberal Party founded by Menzies.
1948–75	Two million new immigrants, the majority from continental Europe.
1950–53	Korean War – Australian troops formed part of the United Nations forces.
1964–72	Vietnam War – Commonwealth troops in alliance with US forces.
1966–74	Mineral boom typified by the Poseidon nickel mine.
1967	Australia became a member of ASEAN.
1973	Britain entered the Common Market, and in the 1970s Japan became Australia's chief trading partner.
1974	Whitlam abolished 'white Australia' policy.
1975	Constitutional crisis; Prime Minister Whitlam dismissed by the governor general.
1975	United Nations trust territory of Papua New Guinea became independent.
1978	Northern Territory achieved self-government.
1979	Opening of uranium mines in Northern Territory.
1983	Hawke convened first national economic summit to seek consensus on economic policy to deal with growing unemployment.
1986	Australia Act passed by UK government, eliminating last vestiges of British legal authority in Australia.
1988	Labor foreign minister Bill Hayden appointed governor general designate. Free trade agreement signed with New Zealand.
1989	Andrew Peacock returned as Liberal Party leader. National Party leader, Ian Sinclair, replaced by Charles Blunt.
1990	Hawke won a record fourth election victory.

Australian Aborigine any of the 500 groups of indigenous inhabitants of the continent of Australia, who migrated to this region from S Asia about 40,000 years ago. They were hunters and gatherers, living throughout the continent in small kin-based groups before European settlement. Several hundred different languages developed, the most important being Aranda (Arunta), in central Australia, and Murngin, in Arnhem Land. In recent years there has been a movement for the recognition of Aborigine rights and campaigning against racial discrimination in housing, education, wages, and medical facilities.

Australian Antarctic Territory islands and territories S of 60° S, between 160° E and 45° E longitude, excluding Adélie Land; area 6,044,000 sq km/ 2,332,984 sq mi of land and 75,800 sq km/ 29,259 sq mi of ice shelf.

Australian Capital Territory territory ceded to Australia by New South Wales 1911 to provide the site of ⟨⟩Canberra, with its port at Jervis Bay, ceded 1915; area 2,400 sq km/926 sq mi; population (1987) 261,000.

Austral Islands alternative name for ⟨⟩Tubuai Islands, part of ⟨⟩French Polynesia.

Austria Republic of; country in central Europe, bordered E by Hungary, SE by Slovenia, SW by Italy, W by Switzerland, NW by Germany, and NE by Czechoslovakia; *area* 83,500 sq km/ 32,374 sq mi; *capital* Vienna; *physical* mountainous, with Alps in W and S and Danube river basin in E; *head of state* Thomas Klestil from 1992; *head of government* Franz Vranitzky from 1986; *political system* democratic federal republic; *exports* lumber, textiles, clothing, iron and steel, paper, machinery and transport equipment, foodstuffs; *population* (1990 est) 7,595,000; *language* German; *recent history* part of the Habsburg empire until 1918. Incorporated into Hitler's Third Reich 1938. Under Allied occupation the constitution was reinstated 1945, and independence was formally recognized 1955. Austria applied for membership of the European Community 1989; application endorsed 1991.

Austrian Succession, War of the war 1740–48 between Austria (supported by England and Holland) and Prussia (supported by France and Spain).
1740 The Holy Roman emperor Charles VI died and the succession of his daughter Maria Theresa was disputed by a number of European powers. Frederick the Great of Prussia seized *Silesia* from Austria.
1743 At *Dettingen* an army of British, Austrians, and Hanoverians under the command of George II was victorious over the French.
1745 An Austro-English army was defeated at *Fontenoy* but British naval superiority was confirmed, and there were gains in the Americas and India.

1748 The war was ended by the Treaty of Aix-la-Chapelle.

Austro-Hungarian Empire Dual Monarchy established by the Habsburg Franz Joseph 1867 between his empire of Austria and his kingdom of Hungary (including territory that became Czechoslovakia as well as parts of Poland, the Ukraine, Romania, Yugoslavia, and Italy). It collapsed autumn 1918 with the end of World War I. Only two king-emperors ruled: Franz Joseph 1867–1916 and Charles 1916–18.

authoritarianism rule of a country by a dominant elite who repress opponents and the press to maintain their own wealth and power. They are frequently indifferent to activities not affecting their security, and rival power centres, such as trade unions and political parties, are often allowed to exist, although under tight control. An extreme form is ⟨⟩totalitarianism.

autism, infantile rare syndrome, generally present from birth, characterized by a withdrawn state and a failure to develop normally in language or social behaviour, although the autistic child may, rarely, show signs of high intelligence in other areas, such as music. Many have impaired intellect, however. The cause is unknown, but is thought to involve a number of interacting factors, possibly including an inherent abnormality of the child's brain.

autochrome in photography, a single-plate additive colour process devised by the ⟨⟩Lumière brothers 1903. It was the first commercially available process, in use 1907–35.

autocracy form of government in which one person holds absolute power. The autocrat has uncontrolled and undisputed authority. Russian government under the tsars was an autocracy extending from the mid-16th century to the early 20th century.

autogiro or *autogyro* heavier-than-air craft that supports itself in the air with a rotary wing, or rotor. The Spanish aviator Juan de la Cierva designed the first successful autogiro 1923. The autogiro's rotor provides only lift and not propulsion; it has been superseded by the helicopter, in which the rotor provides both. The autogiro is propelled by an orthodox propeller.

autoimmunity in medicine, condition where the body's immune responses are mobilized not against 'foreign' matter, such as invading germs, but against the body itself. Diseases considered to be of autoimmune origin include myasthenia gravis, rheumatoid ⟨⟩arthritis, and ⟨⟩lupus erythematosus.

automatic pilot control device that keeps an aeroplane flying automatically on a given course at a given height and speed. Devised by US business executive Lawrence Sperry 1912, the automatic pilot contains a set of gyroscopes that provide references for the plane's course. Sensors detect when the plane deviates from this course and send signals to the control surfaces – the ailerons, elevators, and rudder – to take the appropriate action. Autopilot is also used in missiles.

automation widespread use of self-regulating machines in industry. Automation involves the addition of control devices, using electronic sensing and computing techniques, which often follow the pattern of human nervous and brain functions, to already mechanized physical processes of production and distribution; for example, steel processing, mining, chemical production, and road, rail, and air control.

automaton mechanical figure imitating human or animal performance. Automatons are usually designed for aesthetic appeal as opposed to purely functional robots. The earliest recorded automaton is an Egyptian wooden pigeon of 400 BC.

autonomic nervous system in mammals, the part of the nervous system that controls the involuntary activities of the smooth muscles (of the digestive tract, blood vessels), the heart, and the glands. The *sympathetic* system responds to stress, when it speeds the heart rate, increases blood pressure and generally prepares the body for action. The *parasympathetic* system is more important when the body is at rest, since it slows the heart rate, decreases blood pressure, and stimulates the digestive system.

autonomy in politics, term used to describe political self-government of a state or, more commonly, a subdivision of a state. Autonomy may be based upon cultural or ethnic differences and often leads eventually to independence.

autopsy or *post-mortem* examination of the internal organs and tissues of a dead body, performed to try to establish the cause of death.

autotroph any living organism that synthesizes organic substances from inorganic molecules by using light or chemical energy. Autotrophs are the primary producers in all food chains since the materials they synthesize and store are the energy sources of all other organisms. All green plants and many planktonic organisms are autotrophs, using sunlight to convert carbon dioxide and water into sugars by ◊photosynthesis.

autumn crocus any member of the genus *Colchicum*, family Liliaceae. One species, the mauve meadow saffron *C. autumnale*, yields colchicine, which is used in treating gout and in plant breeding (it causes plants to double the numbers of their chromosomes, forming polyploids).

Auvergne ancient province of central France and a modern region comprising the *départements* of Allier, Cantal, Haute-Loire, and Puy-de-Dôme; *area* 26,000 sq km/10,036 sq mi; *capital* Clermont-Ferrand; *physical* mountainous, composed chiefly of volcanic rocks in several masses; *products* cattle, wheat, wine, and cheese; *population* (1986) 1,334,000; *history* named after the ancient Gallic

Avenni tribe whose leader, Vercingetorix, led a revolt against the Romans 52 BC. In the 14th century the Auvergne was divided into a duchy, dauphiny, and countship. The duchy and dauphiny were united by the dukes of Bourbon before being confiscated by Francis I 1527. The countship united with France 1615.

auxin plant hormone that promotes stem and root growth in plants. Auxins influence many aspects of plant growth and development, including cell enlargement, inhibition of development of axillary buds, tropisms, and the initiation of roots. *Synthetic auxins* are used in rooting powders for cuttings, and in some weedkillers, where high auxin concentrations cause such rapid growth that the plants die. They are also used to prevent premature fruitdrop in orchards. The most common naturally occurring auxin is known as indoleacetic acid, or IAA. It is produced in the shoot apex and transported to other parts of the plant.

avatar in Hindu mythology, the descent of a deity to Earth in a visible form, for example the ten avatars of ◊Vishnu.

Avebury Europe's largest stone circle (diameter 412 m/1,352 ft), in Wiltshire, England. It was probably constructed in the Neolithic period 3,500 years ago, and is linked with nearby Silbury Hill. The village of Avebury was built within the circle, and many of the stones were used for building material.

Averroës (Arabic *Ibn Rushd*) 1126–1198. Arabian philosopher who argued for the eternity of matter and against the immortality of the individual soul. His philosophical writings, including commentaries on Aristotle and on Plato's *Republic*, became known to the West through Latin translations. He influenced Christian and Jewish writers into the Renaissance, and reconciled Islamic and Greek thought in that philosophic truth comes through reason. St Thomas Aquinas opposed this position.

Avicenna (Arabic *Ibn Sina*) 979–1037. Arabian philosopher and physician. He was the most renowned philosopher of medieval Islam. His *Canon Medicinae* was a standard work for many centuries. His philosophical writings were influenced by al-Farabi, Aristotle, and the neo-Platonists, and in turn influenced the scholastics of the 13th century.

Avignon city in Provence, France, capital of Vaucluse *département*, on the river Rhône NW of Marseilles; population (1982) 174,000. An important Gallic and Roman city, it has a 12th-century bridge (only half still standing), a 13th-century cathedral, 14th-century walls, and two palaces built during the residence here of the popes, Le Palais Vieux (1334–42) and Le Palais Nouveau (1342–52). Avignon was papal property 1348–1791.

avocado tree *Persea americana* of the laurel family, native to Central America. Its dark-green, thick-skinned, pear-shaped fruit has buttery-textured flesh and is used in salads.

avocet wading bird, genus *Recurvirostra*, family Recurvirostridae, with a characteristic long, narrow, upturned bill used in sifting water as it feeds in the shallows. It is about 45 cm/18 in long, and has long legs, partly webbed feet, and black and white plumage. There are four species.

Avogadro's hypothesis in chemistry, the law stating that equal volumes of all gases, when at the same temperature and pressure, have the same numbers of molecules. This law was first propounded by Italian physicist Amadeo Avogadro (1776–1856).

Avon county in SW England; *area* 1,340 sq km/ 517 sq mi; *towns* Bristol (administrative headquarters), Bath, Weston-super-Mare; *physical* lowlying basin bordered by Cotswold Hills in NE and Mendip Hills in S; river Avon flows W into Severn estuary; *products* aircraft and other engineering, tobacco, chemicals, printing, dairy products; *population* (1987) 919,800; *history* formed 1974 from the city and county of Bristol, part of S Gloucestershire, and part of N Somerset.

Avon any of several rivers in England and Scotland. The Hampshire Avon rises E of Devizes, Wiltshire, and flows S through the Salisbury Plain, entering the English Channel at Christchurch. It is 77 km/ 48 mi long. The Bristol Avon rises in the SE Cotswolds and flows W for 120 km/75 mi, entering the Severn river estuary at Avonmouth, Bristol. The Warwickshire Avon rises near Naseby in central England and flows SW for 154 km/96 mi. It is a tributary of the river Severn.

Awe longest (37 km/23 mi) of the Scottish freshwater lochs, in Strathclyde, SE of Oban. It is drained by the river Awe into Loch Etive.

axiom in mathematics, a statement that is assumed to be true and upon which theorems are proved by using logical deduction. The Greek mathematician Euclid used a series of axioms that he considered could not be demonstrated in terms of simpler concepts to prove his geometrical theorems.

axis in geometry, one of the lines by which a point on a graph is located, as in a *coordinate axis*; or a line alongside which an object may be symmetrical, as in an *axis of symmetry*; or a line about which an object or plane figure may revolve, as in an *axis of rotation*.

Axis alliance of Nazi Germany and Fascist Italy before and during World War II. The *Rome–Berlin Axis* was formed 1936, when Italy was being threatened with sanctions because of its invasion of Ethiopia (Abyssinia). It became a full military and political alliance May 1939. A ten-year alliance between Germany, Italy, and Japan (*Rome–Berlin–Tokyo Axis*) was signed Sept 1940 and was subsequently joined by Hungary, Bulgaria, Romania, and the puppet states of Slovakia and Croatia. The Axis collapsed with the fall of Mussolini and the surrender of Italy 1943 and Germany and Japan 1945.

axolotl aquatic larval form ('tadpole') of any of several North American species of salamander, belonging to the family Ambystomatidae. Axolotls are remarkable because they can breed without changing to the adult form and will only metamorphose into adult salamanders in response to the drying-up of their ponds. The adults then migrate to another pond.

Ayacucho capital of a province of the same name in the Andean Mountains of central Peru; population (1988) 94,200. The last great battle against Spanish troops in the war of independence was fought near here Dec 1824.

ayatollah honorific title awarded to Shi'ite Muslims in Iran by popular consent, as, for example, to Ayatollah Ruhollah ♢Khomeini.

aye-aye nocturnal tree-climbing prosimian *Daubentonia madagascariensis* of Madagascar, related to the lemurs. The aye-aye has large forward-looking eyes, powerful rodentlike teeth, and large ears. Its fingers are long and slender, particularly the middle finger which is used to dig insects out of tree trunks. It is just over 1 m/3 ft long, including a tail 50 cm/20 in long.

Ayer A(lfred) J(ules) 1910–1989. English philosopher. He wrote *Language, Truth and Logic* 1936, an exposition of the theory of 'logical positivism', presenting a criterion by which meaningful statements (essentially truths of logic, as well as statements derived from experience) could be distinguished from meaningless metaphysical utterances (for example, claims that there is a God or that the world external to our own minds is illusory). Later works included *Probability and Evidence* 1972 and *Philosophy in the Twentieth Century* 1982.

Ayers Rock (Aboriginal *Uluru*) vast ovate mass of pinkish rock in Northern Territory, Australia; 335 m/1,110 ft high and 9 km/6 mi around. It is named after Henry Ayers, a premier of South Australia. For the Aborigines, whose paintings decorate its caves, it has magical significance.

azalea any of various deciduous flowering shrubs, genus *Rhododendron*, of the heath family Ericaceae.

There are several species native to Asia and North America, and from these many cultivated varieties have been derived. Azaleas are closely related to the evergreen ▷rhododendrons of the same genus.

Azerbaijan Republic of; country in SE Europe, on the Caspian Sea, bordered N by the Russian Federation and Georgia, W by Armenia, and S by Iran; *area* 86,600 sq km/33,436 sq mi; *capital* Baku; *physical* ranges from semidesert to Caucasus Mountains in N; *head of state* Yakub Mamedov (interim) from 1992; *head of government* Hassan Hasanov from 1990; *political system* socialist pluralist; *products* oil, iron, copper, fruit, vines, cotton, silk, carpets; *population* (1990) 7,145,600 (Azerbaijani 78%, Russian 8%, Armenian 8%); *language* Turkic; *recent history* became independent republic 1918; occupied by Red Army 1920; made a constituent republic of USSR 1936. Dispute with neighbouring Armenia over Nagorno-Karabakh and Nakhichevan resulted in violent clashes 1988–89. Soviet troops despatched to Baku to restore order; state of emergency declared 1990. In 1991 Azerbaijani leadership gave initial support to attempted anti-Gorbachev coup in Moscow; Azerbaijan declared itself independent; Nagorno-Karabakh ceasefire signed but broken; Nagorno-Karabakh declared its independence. Azerbaijan joined Commonwealth of Independent States (CIS) Dec 1991. Admitted into Conference on Security and Cooperation in Europe (CSCE) 1992. Signed cooperation agreement with Turkey; joined Economic Cooperation Organization (ECO).

Azerbaijani or *Azeri* native of the Azerbaijan region of Iran (population 5,500,000) or of the Republic of Azerbaijan (formerly a Soviet republic) (population 6,000,000). Azerbaijani is a Turkic language belonging to the Altaic family. Of the total population of Azerbaijanis, 70% are Shi'ite Muslims and 30% Sunni Muslims.

Azerbaijan, Iranian two provinces of NW Iran, *Eastern Azerbaijan* (capital Tabriz), population (1986) 4,114,000, and *Western Azerbaijan* (capital Orúmiyeh), population 1,972,000. Azerbaijanis in Iran, as in the Republic of Azerbaijan, are mainly Shi'ite Muslim ethnic Turks, descendants of followers of the Khans from the Mongol Empire.

Azores group of nine islands in the N Atlantic, belonging to Portugal; area 2,247 sq km/867 sq mi; population (1987) 254,000. They are outlying peaks of the mid-Atlantic Ridge and are volcanic in origin. The capital is Ponta Delgada on the main island, San Miguel.

Azov (Russian *Azovskoye More*) inland sea of Europe forming a gulf in the NE of the Black Sea, between Ukraine and Russia; area 37,555 sq km/ 14,500 sq mi. Principal ports include Rostov-on-Don, Kerch, and Taganrog. Azov is a good source of freshwater fish.

Aztec member of an ancient Mexican civilization that migrated south into the valley of Mexico in the 12th century, and in 1325 began reclaiming lake marshland to build their capital, Tenochtitlán, on the site of present-day Mexico City. Under Montezuma I (reigned from 1440), the Aztecs created a tribute empire in central Mexico. After the conquistador Cortès landed 1519, Montezuma II (reigned from 1502) was killed and Tenochtitlán subsequently destroyed. Nahuatl is the Aztec language; it belongs to the Uto-Aztecan family of languages.

Baabda capital of the province of Jebel Lubnan in central Lebanon, to the SE of Beirut, and site of the country's presidential palace.

Baader-Meinhof gang popular name for the West German guerrilla group the *Rote Armee Fraktion/ Red Army Faction*, active from 1968 against what it perceived as US imperialism. The three main founding members were Andreas Baader, Gudrun Ensslin, and Ulrike Meinhof.

Baal divine title given to their chief male gods by the Phoenicians, or Canaanites. Their worship as fertility gods, often orgiastic and of a phallic character, was strongly denounced by the Hebrew prophets.

Ba'ath Party ruling political party in Iraq and Syria. Despite public support of pan-Arab unity and its foundations 1943 as a party of Arab nationalism, its ideology has been so vague that it has fostered widely differing (and often opposing) parties in Syria and Iraq.

Babangida Ibrahim 1941– . Nigerian politician and soldier, president from 1985. He became head of the Nigerian army in 1983 and in 1985 led a coup against President Buhari, assuming the presidency himself.

Babbage Charles 1792–1871. English mathematician who devised the precursor of the computer. He designed an analytical engine, a general-purpose mechanical computing device for performing different calculations according to a program input on punched cards (an idea borrowed from the Jacquard loom). This device was never built, but it embodied many of the principles on which present digital computers are based.

babbler bird of the thrush family Muscicapidae with a loud babbling cry. Babblers, subfamily Timaliinae, are found in the Old World, and there are some 250 species in the group.

Babel Hebrew name for the city of ⇨Babylon,

chiefly associated with the *Tower of Babel* which, in the Genesis story in the Old Testament, was erected in the plain of Shinar by the descendants of Noah. It was a ziggurat, or staged temple, seven storeys high (100 m/300 ft) with a shrine of Marduk on the summit. It was built by Nabopolassar, father of Nebuchadnezzar, and was destroyed when Sennacherib sacked the city 689 BC.

baboon large monkey, genus *Papio*, with a long doglike muzzle and large canine teeth, spending much of its time on the ground in open country. Males, with head and body up to 1.1 m/3.5 ft long, are larger than females and dominant males rule the 'troops' in which baboons live. They inhabit Africa and SW Arabia.

Babylon capital of ancient Babylonia, on the bank of the lower Euphrates River. The site is now in Iraq, 88 km/55 mi S of Baghdad and 8 km/5 mi N of Hilla, which is built chiefly of bricks from the ruins of Babylon. The *Hanging Gardens of Babylon*, one of the ⇨Seven Wonders of the World, were probably erected on a vaulted stone base, the only stone construction in the mud-brick city. They formed a series of terraces, irrigated by a hydraulic system.

Bacall Lauren. Stage name of Betty Joan Perske 1924– . Striking US actress who became an overnight star when cast by Howard Hawks opposite Humphrey Bogart in *To Have and Have Not* 1944. She and Bogart married in 1945, and starred together in *The Big Sleep* 1946 and several other films. She also appeared in *The Cobweb* 1955, *Harper* 1966, and *The Shootist* 1976.

Baccalauréat French examination providing the school-leaving certificate and qualification for university entrance, also available on an international basis as an alternative to English ⇨A levels.

Bacchus in Greek and Roman mythology, the god of fertility (see ⇨Dionysus) and of wine; his rites (the *Bacchanalia*) were orgiastic.

Bach Johann Sebastian 1685–1750. German composer. He was a master of ⇨counterpoint, and his music epitomizes the Baroque polyphonic style. His orchestral music includes the six *Brandenburg Concertos*, other concertos for keyboard instrument and violin, and four orchestral suites. Bach's keyboard music, for clavier and organ, his fugues, and his choral music are of equal importance. He also wrote chamber music and songs.

bacillus member of a group of rodlike ⇨bacteria that occur everywhere in the soil and air. Some are responsible for diseases such as anthrax or for causing food spoilage.

background radiation radiation that is always present in the environment. By far the greater proportion (87%) of it is emitted from natural sources. Alpha and beta particles and gamma radiation are emitted by the traces of radioactive minerals that occur naturally in the ground, the underlying rocks, the bricks and stones of buildings, and even in the human body, and by radioactive gases such as radon and thoron, which are found in soil and may seep upwards into buildings. Radiation from space (cosmic radiation) also contributes to the background level.

Bacon Francis 1561–1626. English politician, philosopher, and essayist. He became Lord Chancellor 1618, and the same year confessed to bribe-taking, was fined £40,000 (which was later remitted by the king), and spent four days in the Tower of London. His works include *Essays* 1597, characterized by pith and brevity; *The Advancement of Learning* 1605, a seminal work discussing scientific method; the *Novum Organum* 1620, in which he redefined the task of natural science, seeing it as a means of empirical discovery and a method of increasing human power over nature; and *The New Atlantis* 1626, describing a utopian state in which scientific knowledge is systematically sought and exploited.

Bacon Francis 1909–1992. British painter, born in Dublin. He moved to London in 1925 and taught himself to paint. He practised abstract art, then developed a distorted Expressionist style with tortured figures presented in loosely defined space. From 1945 he focused on studies of figures, as in his series of screaming popes based on the portrait of Innocent X by Velázquez.

Bacon Roger 1214–1292. English philosopher, scientist, and a teacher at Oxford University. In 1266, at the invitation of his friend Pope Clement IV, he began his *Opus Majus/Great Work*, a compendium of all branches of knowledge. In 1268 he sent this with his *Opus Minus/Lesser Work* and other writings to the pope. In 1277 Bacon was condemned and imprisoned by the church for 'certain novelties' (heresy) and not released until 1292. He was interested in alchemy, the biological and physical sciences and magic. Many discoveries have been credited to him, including the magnifying lens. He foresaw the extensive use of gunpowder and mechanical cars, boats, and planes.

bacteria (singular *bacterium*) microscopic unicellular organisms with prokaryotic cells (see ◇prokaryote). Bacteria usually reproduce by ◇binary fission, and since this may occur approximately every 20 minutes, a single bacterium is potentially capable of producing 16 million copies of itself in a day.

bacteriophage virus that attacks ◇bacteria. Such viruses are now of use in genetic engineering.

Baden former state of SW Germany, which had Karlsruhe as its capital. Baden was captured from the Romans in 282 by the Alemanni; later it became a margravate and in 1806, a grand duchy. A state of the German empire 1871–1918, then a republic, and under Hitler a *Gau* (province), it was divided between the *Länder* of Württemberg-Baden and Baden in 1945 and in 1952 made part of ◇Baden-Württemberg.

Baden-Powell Robert Stephenson Smyth, 1st Baron Baden-Powell 1857–1941. British general, founder of the Scout Association. He fought in defence of Mafeking (now Mafikeng) during the Second South African War. After 1907 he devoted his time to developing the Scout movement, which rapidly spread throughout the world. He was created a peer in 1929.

Baden-Württemberg administrative region (German *Land*) of Germany; *area* 35,800 sq km/13,819 sq mi; *capital* Stuttgart; *towns* Mannheim, Karlsruhe, Freiburg, Heidelberg, Heilbronn, Pforzheim, Ulm; *physical* Black Forest; Rhine boundary S and W; source of the Danube; see also ◇Swabia; *products* wine, jewellery, watches, clocks, musical instruments, textiles, chemicals, iron, steel, electrical equipment, surgical instruments; *population* (1988) 9,390,000; *history* formed 1952 (following a plebiscite) by the merger of the *Länder* Baden, Württemberg-Baden, and Württemberg-Hohenzollern.

badger large mammal of the weasel family with molar teeth of a crushing type adapted to a partly vegetable diet, and short strong legs with long claws suitable for digging. The Eurasian *common badger Meles meles* is about 1 m/3 ft long, with long, coarse, greyish hair on the back, and a white face with a broad black stripe along each side. Mainly a woodland animal, it is harmless and nocturnal, and spends the day in a system of burrows called a 'sett'. It feeds on roots, a variety of fruits and nuts, insects, worms, mice, and young rabbits.

badminton racket game similar to lawn ◇tennis but played on a smaller court and with a shuttlecock (a half-sphere of cork or plastic with a feather or nylon skirt) instead of a ball. The object of the game is to prevent the opponent from being able to return the shuttlecock. World championships were first staged 1977 in singles, doubles, and mixed doubles and are now held every two years.

Baffin William 1584–1622. English explorer and navigator. In 1616, he and Robert Bylot explored Baffin Bay, NE Canada, and reached latitude 77° 45′ N, which for 236 years remained the 'furthest north'. Later he made surveys of the Red Sea and Persian Gulf.

badger

Baghdad historic city and capital of Iraq, on the river Tigris; population (1985) 4,649,000. Industries include oil refining, distilling, tanning, tobacco processing, and the manufacture of textiles and cement. Founded 762, it became Iraq's capital 1921.

bagpipe ancient wind instrument used outdoors and incorporating a number of reed pipes powered from a single inflated bag. Known in Roman times, it is found in various forms throughout Europe including Ireland and Greece. The most famous, that of the Highlands, is the Scottish national instrument.

Baha'i religion founded in the 19th century from a Muslim splinter group, Babism, by the Persian ◊Baha'ullah. His message in essence was that all great religious leaders are manifestations of the unknowable God and all scriptures are sacred. There is no priesthood: all Baha'is are expected to teach, and to work towards world unification. There are about 4.5 million Baha'is worldwide.

Bahamas Commonwealth of the; country comprising a group of islands in the Caribbean, off the SE coast of Florida; *area* 13,864 sq km/ 5,352 sq mi; *capital* Nassau on New Providence; *physical* 700 tropical coral islands (only 30 are inhabited) and about 1,000 cays; *head of state* Elizabeth II from 1973 represented by governor general; *head of government* Lynden Oscar Pindling from 1967; *political system* constitutional monarchy; *exports* cement, pharmaceuticals, petroleum products, crayfish, salt, aragonite, rum, pulpwood; over half the islands' employment comes from tourism; *population* (1990 est) 251,000; *languages* English and some creole; *recent history* independence was achieved from Britain 1964. The first national assembly elections were held 1967 and full independence was reached 1973.

Bahrain State of; country comprising a group of islands in the Arabian Gulf, between Saudi Arabia and Iran; *area* 688 sq km/266 sq mi; *capital* Manama on the largest island (also called Bahrain); *physical* 35 islands, composed largely of sand-covered limestone; generally poor and infertile soil; flat and hot; a causeway links Bahrain to mainland Saudi Arabia; *head of state and government* Sheik Isa bin Sulman al-Khalifa from 1961; *political system* absolute emirate; *exports* oil, natural gas, aluminium, fish; *population* (1990 est) 512,000 (two-thirds are nationals); *languages* Arabic (official); Farsi, English, Urdu; *recent history* a British protectorate 1861–1968, Bahrain became an independent state 1971. A national assembly was elected and dissolved; the emir assumed virtually absolute power 1975. Bahrain joined the United Nations coalition that ousted Iran from occupation of Kuwait in the Gulf War 1991.

Baikal Russian *Baykal Ozero* largest freshwater lake in Asia (area 31,500 sq km/12,150 sq mi) and deepest in the world (up to 1,740 m/5,710 ft), in S Siberia, Russia. Fed by more than 300 rivers, it is drained only by the Lower Angara. It has sturgeon fisheries and rich fauna.

bail the setting at liberty of a person in legal custody on an undertaking (usually backed by some security, given either by that person or by someone else) to attend at a court at a stated time and place. If the person does not attend, the bail may be forfeited.

Bailey David 1938– . British fashion photographer, chiefly associated with *Vogue* magazine from the 1960s. He has published several books of his work, exhibited widely, and also made films.

bailiff officer of the court whose job, usually in the county courts, is to serve notices and enforce the court's orders involving seizure of the goods of a debtor.

Baird John Logie 1888–1946. Scottish electrical engineer who pioneered television. In 1925 he gave the first public demonstration of television and in 1926 pioneered fibre optics, radar (in advance of Robert ◊Watson-Watt), and 'noctovision', a system for seeing at night by using infrared rays.

Bakelite first synthetic ◊plastic, created by Leo Baekeland in 1909. Bakelite is hard, tough, and heatproof, and is used as an electrical insulator. It is made by the reaction of phenol with formaldehyde, producing a powdery resin that sets solid when heated. Objects are made by subjecting the resin to compression moulding (simultaneous heat and pressure in a mould).

Baker James (Addison), III 1930– . US Republican politician. Under President Reagan, he was White House chief of staff 1981–85 and Treasury secretary 1985–88. After managing Bush's successful presidential campaign 1988, Baker was appointed secretary of state 1989 and played a prominent role in the 1990–91 Gulf crisis, and the subsequent search for a lasting Middle East peace settlement.

Baku capital city of the Republic of Azerbaijan, industrial port (oil refining) on the Caspian Sea; population (1987) 1,741,000. It is a major oil centre and is linked by pipelines with Batumi on the Black Sea. In Jan 1990 there were violent clashes between the Azeri majority and the Armenian minority, and Soviet troops were sent to the region. Over 13,000 Armenians subsequently fled from the city.

Bakunin Mikhail 1814–1876. Russian anarchist, active in Europe. In 1848 he was expelled from France as a revolutionary agitator. In Switzerland in the 1860s he became recognized as the leader of the anarchist movement. In 1869 he joined the First International (a coordinating socialist body) but, after stormy conflicts with Karl Marx, was expelled 1872.

Balaclava, Battle of in the Crimean War, an engagement on 25 Oct 1854 near a town in Ukraine, 10 km/6 mi SE of Sevastopol. It was the scene of the ill-timed *Charge of the Light Brigade* of British cavalry against the Russian entrenched artillery. Of the 673 soldiers who took part, there were 272 casualties. *Balaclava helmets* were knitted hoods worn here by soldiers in the bitter weather.

balance apparatus for weighing or measuring mass. The various types include the **beam balance** consisting of a centrally pivoted lever with pans hanging from each end, and the **spring balance**, in which the object to be weighed stretches (or compresses) a vertical coil spring fitted with a pointer that indicates the weight on a scale. Kitchen and bathroom scales are balances.

balance of payments in economics, a tabular account of a country's debit and credit transactions with other countries. Items are divided into the **current account**, which includes both visible trade (imports and exports) and invisible trade (such as transport, tourism, interest, and dividends), and the **capital account**, which includes investment in and out of the country, international grants, and loans. Deficits or surpluses on these accounts are brought into balance by buying and selling reserves of foreign currencies.

balance of power in politics, the theory that the best way of ensuring international order is to have power so distributed among states that no single state is able to achieve a dominant position. The term, which may also refer more simply to the actual distribution of power, is one of the most enduring concepts in international relations. Since the development of nuclear weapons, it has been asserted that the balance of power has been replaced by a **balance of terror**.

Balanchine George 1904–1983. Russian-born US choreographer. After leaving the USSR in 1924, he worked with ▷Diaghilev in France. Moving to the USA in 1933, he became a major influence on dance, starting the New York City Ballet in 1948.

Balboa Vasco Núñez de 1475–1519. Spanish ▷conquistador. He founded a settlement at Darien (now Panama) 1511 and crossed the Isthmus in search of gold, reaching the Pacific Ocean (which he called the South Sea) on 25 Sept 1513, after a 25-day expedition. He was made admiral of the Pacific and governor of Panama but was removed by Spanish court intrigue, imprisoned and executed.

baldness loss of hair from the upper scalp, common in older men. Its onset and extent are influenced by genetic make-up and the level of male sex ▷hormones. There is no cure, and expedients such as hair implants may have no lasting effect. Hair loss in both sexes may also occur as a result of ill health or radiation treatment. **Alopecia**, a condition in which the hair falls out, is different from the 'male-pattern baldness' described above.

Baldwin James 1924–1987. US writer, born in New York City, who portrayed the condition of black Americans in contemporary society. His works include the novels *Go Tell It on the Mountain* 1953, *Another Country* 1962, and *Just Above My Head* 1979; the play *The Amen Corner* 1955; and the autobiographical essays *Notes of a Native Son* 1955 and *The Fire Next Time* 1963. He was active in the civil-rights movement.

Baldwin Stanley, 1st Earl Baldwin of Bewdley 1867–1947. British Conservative politician, prime minister 1923–24, 1924–29, and 1935–37; he weathered the general strike 1926, secured complete adult suffrage 1928, and handled the ▷abdication crisis of Edward VIII 1936, but failed to prepare Britain for World War II.

Balearic Islands (Spanish **Baleares**) group of Mediterranean islands forming an autonomous region of Spain; including ▷Majorca, ▷Minorca, ▷Ibiza, Cabrera, and Formentera. **area** 5,000 sq km/1,930 sq mi; **capital** Palma de Mallorca; **products** figs, olives, oranges, wine, brandy, coal, iron, slate; tourism is crucial; **population** (1986) 755,000; **history** a Roman colony from 123 BC, the Balearic Islands were an independent Moorish kingdom 1009–1232; they were conquered by Aragón 1343.

Balfour Arthur James, 1st Earl of Balfour 1848–1930. British Conservative politician, prime minister 1902–05 and foreign secretary 1916–19, when he issued the Balfour Declaration 1917 and was involved in peace negotiations after World War I, signing the Treaty of Versailles.

Balfour Declaration letter, dated 2 Nov 1917, from the British foreign secretary A J Balfour to Lord Rothschild (chair, British Zionist Federation) stating: 'HM government view with favour the establishment in Palestine of a national home for the Jewish people.' It led to the foundation of Israel 1948.

Bali island of Indonesia, E of Java, one of the Sunda Islands; **area** 5,800 sq km/2,240 sq mi; **capital** Denpasar; **physical** volcanic mountains; **features** Balinese dancing, music, drama; one million tourists a year (1990); **products** gold and silver work, woodcarving, weaving, copra, salt, coffee; **population** (1989) 2,787,000; **history** Bali's Hindu culture goes back to the 7th century; the Dutch gained control of the island by 1908.

Baliol John de c. 1250–1314. King of Scotland 1292–96. As an heir to the Scottish throne on the death of Margaret, the Maid of Norway, he received support for his cause from the English king, Edward I, against 12 other claimants. Having paid homage to Edward, Baliol was proclaimed king but soon rebelled and gave up the kingdom when English forces attacked Scotland.

Balkans peninsula of SE Europe, stretching into the Mediterranean Sea between the Adriatic and Aegean seas, comprising Albania, Bosnia-Herzegovina, Bulgaria, Croatia, Greece, Romania, Slovenia, Turkey-in-Europe, and Yugoslavia. It is joined to the rest of Europe by an isthmus 1,200 km/750 mi wide between Rijeka on the west and the mouth of the Danube on the Black Sea to the east.

Balkan Wars two wars 1912–13 and 1913 (preceding World War I) which resulted in the expulsion by the Balkan states of Ottoman Turkey from Europe, except for a small area around Istanbul.

Ball John died 1381. English priest, one of the leaders of the ▷Peasants' Revolt 1381, known as 'the mad priest of Kent'. A follower of John Wycliffe and a believer in social equality, he was imprisoned for disagreeing with the archbishop of Canterbury. During the revolt he was released from prison, and when in Blackheath, London, preached from the text 'When Adam delved and Eve span, who was then the gentleman?' When the revolt collapsed he escaped but was captured near Coventry and executed.

ballad popular poem that tells a story. Of simple metrical form and dealing with some strongly emotional event, the ballad is halfway between the lyric and the epic. Most English ballads date from the 15th century. Poets of the Romantic movement both in England and in Germany were greatly influenced by the ballad revival, as seen in, for example, the *Lyrical Ballads* 1798 of Wordsworth and Coleridge.

Ballesteros Seve(riano) 1957– . Spanish golfer who came to prominence 1976 and has won several leading tournaments in the USA, including the Masters Tournament. He has also won the British Open three times: in 1979, 1984, and 1988.

ballet theatrical representation in dance form in which music also plays a major part in telling a story or conveying a mood. Some such form of entertainment existed in ancient Greece, but Western ballet as we know it today first appeared in Italy. From there it was brought by Catherine de' Medici to France in the form of a spectacle combining singing, dancing, and declamation. In the 20th century Russian ballet has had a vital influence on the Classical tradition in the West, and ballet developed further in the USA through the work of George Balanchine and American Ballet Theater, and in the UK through the influence of Marie Rambert. ▷Modern dance is a separate development.

ballistics study of the motion and impact of projectiles such as bullets, bombs, and missiles. For projectiles from a gun, relevant exterior factors include temperature, barometric pressure, and wind strength; and for nuclear missiles these extend to such factors as the speed at which the Earth turns.

balloon lighter-than-air craft that consists of a gasbag filled with gas lighter than the surrounding air and an attached basket, or gondola, for carrying passengers and/or instruments. In 1783, the first successful human ascent was in Paris, in a hot-air balloon designed by the ▷Montgolfier brothers. In 1785, a hydrogen-filled balloon designed by J A C Charles travelled across the English Channel.

ballot the process of voting in an election. In political elections in democracies ballots are usually secret: voters indicate their choice of candidate on a voting slip which is placed in a sealed ballot box. *Ballot rigging* is a term used to describe elections that are fraudulent because of interference with the voting process or the counting of ▷votes.

ball valve valve that works by the action of external pressure raising a ball and thereby opening a hole. An example is the valve used in lavatory cisterns, where the ball floats on the water surface, rising as the cistern fills, and at the correct level a flat rubber washer at the other end of the valve is pushed against the water-inlet pipe, cutting off the flow.

balsam any of various garden plants of the genus *Impatiens* of the balsam family. They are usually annuals with spurred red or white flowers and pods that burst and scatter their seeds when ripe. In medicine and perfumery, balsam refers to various oily or gummy aromatic plant resins, such as balsam of Peru from the Central American tree *Myroxylon pereirae*.

Baltic Sea large shallow arm of the North Sea, extending NE from the narrow Skagerrak and Kattegat, between Sweden and Denmark, to the Gulf of Bothnia between Sweden and Finland. Its coastline is 8,000 km/5,000 mi long, and its area, including the gulfs of Riga, Finland, and Bothnia, is 422,300 sq km/163,000 sq mi. Its shoreline is shared by Denmark, Germany, Poland, the Baltic States, Russia, Finland, and Sweden.

Baltic States collective name for the states of ▷Estonia, ▷Latvia, and ▷Lithuania, former constituent republics of the USSR (from 1940). They regained independence Sept 1991.

Baltimore industrial port and largest city in Maryland, USA, on the W shore of Chesapeake Bay, NE of Washington DC; population (1990) 736,000. Industries include shipbuilding, oil refining, food processing, and the manufacture of steel, chemicals, and aerospace equipment. The city dates from 1729.

Baltistan region in the Karakoram range of NE Kashmir, held by Pakistan since 1949. It is the home of Balti Muslims of Tibetan origin. The chief town is Skardu, but Ghyari is of greater significance to Muslims as the site of a mosque built by Sayyid Ali Hamadani, a Persian who brought the Shia Muslim religion to Baltistan in the 14th century.

Baluchistan mountainous desert area, comprising a province of Pakistan, part of the Iranian province of Sistán and Balúchestan, and a small area of Afghanistan. The Pakistani province has an area of 347,200 sq km/134,019 sq mi and a population (1985) of 4,908,000; its capital is Quetta. Sistán and Balúchestan has an area of 181,600 sq km/70,098 sq mi and a population (1986) of 1,197,000; its capital is Zahedan. The port of Gwadar in Pakistan is strategically important, on the Indian Ocean and the Strait of Hormuz.

Balzac Honoré de 1799–1850. French novelist. His first success was *Les Chouans/The Chouans* and *La Physiologie du mariage/The Physiology of Marriage* 1829, inspired by Walter Scott. This was the beginning of the long series of novels *La Comédie humaine/The Human Comedy*. He also wrote the Rabelaisian *Contes drolatiques/Ribald Tales* 1833.

Bamako capital and port of Mali on the river Niger; population (1976) 400,000. It produces pharmaceuticals, chemicals, textiles, tobacco, and metal products.

bamboo any of numerous plants of the subgroup Bambuseae within the grass family Gramineae, mainly found in tropical and subtropical countries. Some species grow as tall as 36 m/120 ft. The stems are hollow and jointed and can be used in furniture, house, and boat construction. The young shoots are edible; paper is made from the stem.

banana any of several treelike tropical plants of the genus *Musa*, family Musaceae, which grow up to 8 m/25 ft high. The edible banana is the fruit of a sterile hybrid form.

Banda Hastings Kamuzu 1902– . Malawi politican, president from 1966. He led his country's independence movement and was prime minister of Nyasaland (the former name of Malawi) from 1963. He became Malawi's first president 1966 and 1971 was named president for life; his rule has been authoritarian.

Bandaranaike Sirimavo (born Ratwatte) 1916– . Sri Lankan politician, who succeeded her husband Solomon Bandaranaike to become the world's first female prime minister 1960–65 and 1970–77, but was expelled from parliament 1980 for abuse of her powers while in office. She was largely responsible for the new constitution 1972.

Bandar Seri Begawan formerly *Brunei Town* capital of Brunei; population (1983) 57,600.

bandicoot small marsupial mammal inhabiting Australia and New Guinea. There are about 11 species, family Peramelidae, rat- or rabbit-sized and living in burrows. They have long snouts, eat insects, and are nocturnal. A related group, the rabbit bandicoots or bilbys, is reduced to a single species that is now endangered and protected by law.

Bandung commercial city and capital of Jawa Barat province on the island of Java, Indonesia; population (1980) 1,463,000. Bandung is the third largest city in Indonesia and was the administrative centre when the country was the Netherlands East Indies.

Bangalore capital of Karnataka state, S India; population (1981) 2,600,000. Industries include electronics, aircraft and machine-tools construction, and coffee.

Bangkok capital and port of Thailand, on the river Chao Phraya; population (1990) 6,019,000. Products include paper, ceramics, cement, textiles, and aircraft. It is the headquarters of the Southeast Asia Treaty Organization (SEATO).

Bangladesh People's Republic of (formerly *East Pakistan*); country in S Asia, surrounded on three sides by India and bordered to the south by the Bay of Bengal; *area* 144,000 sq km/55,585 sq mi; *capital* Dhaka (formerly Dacca); *physical* flat delta of rivers Ganges and Brahmaputra; some 75% of the land is less than 3 m/10 ft above sea level; hilly in extreme SE and NE; *head of state* Abdur Rahman Biswas from 1991; *head of government* Begum Khaleda Zia from 1991; *political system* emergent democracy; *exports* jute, tea, garments, fish products; *population* (1991 est) 107,992,100; *language* Bangla (Bengali); *recent history* formed into eastern province of Pakistan on partition of British India 1947. Bangladesh emerged from civil war as an independent nation 1971; under martial law 1975–76 and 1982–86. Islam became state religion 1988. Mass protests against government of President Ershad led to his resignation 1990; Abdur Rahman Biswas elected president Sept 1991.

Bangui capital and port of the Central African Republic, on the river Ubangi; population (1988) 597,000. Industries include beer, cigarettes, office machinery, and timber and metal products.

Banjul capital and chief port of Gambia, on an island at the mouth of the river Gambia; population (1983) 44,536. Established 1816 as a settlement for freed slaves, it was known as Bathurst until 1973.

bank financial institution that uses funds deposited with it to lend money to companies or individuals, and also provides financial services to its customers. In terms of assets, seven of the world's top ten banks were Japanese in 1988. A *central bank* (in the UK, the Bank of England) issues currency for the government, in order to provide cash for circulation and exchange.

Bank of England UK central bank founded by act of Parliament 1694. It was entrusted with the note issue 1844 and nationalized 1946. It is banker to the clearing banks and the UK government. As the government's bank, it manages and arranges the financing of the ⟩public-sector borrowing requirement and the national debt, implements monetary policy and exchange-rate policy through intervention in foreign-exchange markets, and supervises the UK banking system.

bankruptcy process by which the property of a person (in legal terms, an individual or corporation) unable to pay debts is taken away under a court order and divided fairly among the person's creditors, after preferential payments such as taxes and wages. Proceedings may be instituted either by the debtor (voluntary bankruptcy) or by any creditor for a substantial sum (involuntary bankruptcy). Until 'discharged', a bankrupt is severely restricted in financial activities.

Bannister Roger Gilbert 1929– . English athlete, the first person to run a mile in under four minutes. He achieved this feat at Oxford, England, on 6 May 1954 in a time of 3 min 59.4 sec.

Banting Frederick Grant 1891–1941. Canadian physician who discovered a technique for isolating the hormone insulin 1921 when, experimentally, he and his colleague Charles Best tied off the ducts of the ▷pancreas to determine the function of the cells known as the islets of Langerhans. This allowed for the treatment of diabetes. Banting and John J R Macleod (1876–1935), his mentor, shared the 1923 Nobel Prize for Medicine, and Banting divided his prize with Best.

Bantu languages group of related languages spoken widely over the greater part of Africa south of the Sahara, including Swahili, Xhosa, and Zulu. Meaning 'people' in Zulu, the word Bantu itself illustrates a characteristic use of prefixes: *mu-ntu* 'man', *ba-ntu* 'people'.

Bantustan or *homeland* name until 1978 for a ▷Black National State in the Republic of South Africa.

banyan tropical Asian fig tree *Ficus benghalensis*, family Moraceae. It produces aerial roots that grow down from its spreading branches, forming supporting pillars that have the appearance of separate trunks.

baobab tree of the genus *Adansonia*, family Bombacaceae. It has rootlike branches, hence its nickname 'upside-down tree', and a disproportionately thick girth, up to 9 m/30 ft in diameter. The pulp of its fruit is edible and is known as monkey bread.

baptism immersion in or sprinkling with water as a religious rite of initiation. It was practised long before the beginning of Christianity. In the Christian baptism ceremony, sponsors or godparents make vows on behalf of the child, which are renewed by the child at confirmation. It is one of the seven sacraments. The *amrit* ceremony in Sikhism is sometimes referred to as baptism.

Baptist member of any of several Protestant and evangelical Christian sects that practise baptism by immersion only upon profession of faith. Baptists seek their authority in the Bible. They originated among English Dissenters who took refuge in the Netherlands in the early 17th century, and spread by emigration and, later, missionary activity. Of the world total of approximately 31 million, some 26.5 million are in the USA and 265,000 in the UK.

bar unit of pressure equal to 10^5 pascals or 10^6 dynes/cm^2, approximately 750 mmHg or 0.987 atm. Its diminutive, the *millibar* (one-thousandth of a bar), is commonly used by meteorologists.

Bar, the in law, the profession of ▷barristers collectively. To be *called to the Bar* is to become a barrister. Prospective barristers in the UK must not only complete a course of study in law but also be admitted to one of the four Inns of Court before they can be 'called'. The General Council of the Bar and of the Inns of Court (known as the Bar Council) is the professional governing body of the Bar.

barb general name for fish of the genus *Barbus* and some related genera of the family Cyprinidae. As well as the ▷barbel, barbs include many small tropical Old World species, some of which are familiar aquarium species. They are active egg-laying species, usually of 'typical' fish shape and with barbels at the corner of the mouth.

Barbados island country in the Caribbean, one of the Lesser Antilles; *area* 430 sq km/166 sq mi; *capital* Bridgetown; *physical* most easterly island of the West Indies; surrounded by coral reefs; subject to hurricanes June–Nov; *head of state* Elizabeth II from 1966 represented by governor general; *head of government* Erskine Lloyd Sandiford from 1987; *political system* constitutional monarchy; *exports* sugar, rum, electronic components, clothing, cement; *population* (1990 est) 260,000; *languages* English and Bajan (Barbadian English dialect); *recent history* British colony 1627; developed as a sugar plantation economy. Independence from Britain was achieved 1961; full independence within the Commonwealth was reached 1966.

Barbary ape tailless, yellowish-brown macaque monkey *Macaca sylvanus*, found in the mountains and wilds of Algeria and Morocco. It was introduced to Gibraltar, where legend has it that the British will leave if the ape colony dies out.

Barbie Klaus 1913–1991. German Nazi, a member of the ▷SS from 1936. During World War II he was involved in the deportation of Jews from the occupied Netherlands 1940–42 and in tracking down Jews and Resistance workers in France 1942–45. He was arrested 1983 and convicted of crimes against humanity in France 1987.

barbiturate hypnosedative drug, commonly known as a 'sleeping pill', consisting of any salt or ester of barbituric acid $C_4H_4O_3N_2$. They work by depressing brain activity. Most barbiturates, being highly addictive, are no longer prescribed and are listed as controlled substances.

Barbizon school French school of landscape painters of the mid-19th century, based at Barbizon in the forest of Fontainebleau. Members included Jean-François Millet, Diaz de la Peña (1807–1876), and Théodore Rousseau (1812–1867). They aimed to paint fresh, realistic scenes, sketching and painting their subjects in the open air.

Barbour John *c.* 1316–1395. Scottish poet whose chronicle poem *The Brus* is among the earliest Scottish poetry.

Barbuda one of the islands that form the state of ▷Antigua and Barbuda.

Barcelona capital, industrial city (textiles, engineering, chemicals), and port of Catalonia, NE Spain; population (1991) 1,653,200. As the chief centre of anarchism and Catalonian nationalism, it was prominent in the overthrow of the monarchy 1931 and was the last city of the republic to surrender to Franco 1939. In 1992 the city hosted the Summer Olympics.

Bardeen John 1908–1991. US physicist who won a Nobel prize 1956, with Walter Brattain and William Shockley, for the development of the transistor

1948. In 1972 he became the first double winner of a Nobel prize in the same subject (with Leon Cooper and John Schrieffer) for his work on superconductivity.

Bardot Brigitte 1934– . French film actress whose sensual appeal did much to popularize French cinema internationally. Her films include *Et Dieu créa la femme/And God Created Woman* 1950, *Viva Maria* 1965, and *Shalako* 1968.

Barebones Parliament English assembly called by Oliver ◊Cromwell to replace the 'Rump Parliament' July 1653. It consisted of 140 members nominated by the army and derived its name from one of its members, Praise-God Barbon. Although they attempted to pass sensible legislation (civil marriage; registration of births, deaths, and marriages; custody of lunatics), its members' attempts to abolish tithes, patronage, and the court of chancery, and to codify the law, led to the resignation of the moderates and its dissolution Dec 1653.

Bari capital of Puglia region, S Italy, and industrial port on the Adriatic; population (1988) 359,000. It is the site of Italy's first nuclear power station; the part of the town known as Tecnopolis is the Italian equivalent of ◊Silicon Valley.

Barisal river port and capital city of Barisal region, S Bangladesh; population (1981) 142,000. It trades in jute, rice, fish, and oilseed.

baritone male voice pitched between bass and tenor centred in the octave below middle C and rising to the F or G above. The range is well-suited to ◊lieder.

barium soft, silver-white, metallic element, symbol Ba, atomic number 56, relative atomic mass 137.33. It is one of the alkaline-earth metals, found in nature as barium carbonate and barium sulphate. As the sulphate it is used in medicine: taken as a suspension (a 'barium meal'), its progress is followed by using X-rays to reveal abnormalities of the alimentary canal. Barium is also used in alloys, pigments, and safety matches and, with strontium, forms the emissive surface in cathode-ray tubes. It was first discovered in barytes or heavy spar.

bark protective outer layer on the stems and roots of woody plants, composed mainly of dead cells. To allow for expansion of the stem, the bark is continually added to from within, and the outer surface often becomes fissured or is shed as scales. The bark from the cork oak *Quercus suber* is economically important and harvested commercially. The spice ◊cinnamon and the drugs cascara (used as a laxative and stimulant) and ◊quinine all come from bark.

barley cereal belonging to the grass family (Gramineae). Cultivated barley *Hordeum vulgare* comprises three main varieties – six-rowed, four-rowed, and two-rowed. Barley was one of the earliest cereals to be cultivated, about 5000 BC in Egypt, and no other cereal can thrive in so wide a range of climatic conditions; polar barley is sown and reaped well within the Arctic Circle in Europe. Barley is no longer much used in bread-making, but it is used in soups and stews and as a starch. Its high-protein form finds a wide use for animal feeding, and its low-protein form is used in brewing and distilling alcoholic beverages.

bar mitzvah in Judaism, initiation of a boy, which takes place at the age of 13, into the adult Jewish community; less common is the *bat* or *bas mitzvah* for girls aged 12. The child reads a passage from the Torah in the synagogue on the Sabbath, and is subsequently regarded as a full member of the congregation.

barnacle marine crustacean of the subclass Cirripedia. The larval form is free-swimming, but when mature, it fixes itself by the head to rock or floating wood. The animal then remains attached, enclosed in a shell through which the cirri (modified legs) protrude to sweep food into the mouth. Barnacles include the stalked *goose barnacle Lepas anatifera* found on ships' bottoms, and the *acorn barnacles*, such as *Balanus balanoides*, common on rocks.

barometer instrument that measures atmospheric pressure as an indication of weather. Most often used are the *mercury barometer*, in which the weight of the column of mercury is balanced by the pressure of the atmosphere on the lower end, and the *aneroid barometer*, in which a change of atmospheric pressure causes a metal box that contains the vacuum to be squeezed or to expand slightly.

Barons' Wars civil wars in England:
1215–17 between King ◊John and his barons, over his failure to honour ◊Magna Carta
1264–67 between ◊Henry III (and the future ◊Edward I) and his barons (led by Simon de ◊Montfort)
1264 14 May *Battle of Lewes* at which Henry III was defeated and captured
1265 4 Aug Simon de Montfort was defeated by Edward I at Evesham and killed.

Baroque style of art and architecture characterized by extravagance in ornament, asymmetry of design, and great expressiveness. It dominated European *art* for most of the 17th century, with artists such as the painter Rubens and the sculptor Bernini. In *architecture*, it often involved large-scale designs, such as Bernini's piazza in Rome and the palace of Versailles in France. In *music*, the Baroque period lasted from about 1600 to 1750, and its composers included Monteverdi, Vivaldi, J S Bach, and Handel.

barracuda large predatory fish *Sphyraena barracuda* found in the warmer seas of the world. It can grow over 2 m/6 ft long, and has a superficial resemblance to a pike. Young fish shoal but the older ones are solitary. The barracuda has very sharp shearing teeth, and may attack people.

Barras Paul François Jean Nicolas, Count

barometer

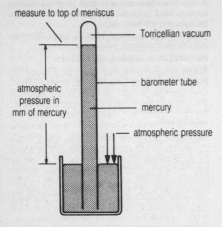

measure to top of meniscus

Torricellian vacuum

atmospheric pressure in mm of mercury

barometer tube

mercury

atmospheric pressure

1755–1829. French revolutionary. He was elected to the National Convention 1792 and helped to overthrow Robespierre 1794. In 1795 he became a member of the ruling Directory (see ¢>French Revolution). In 1796 he brought about the marriage of his former mistress, Joséphine de Beauharnais, with Napoleon and assumed dictatorial powers. After Napoleon's coup d'état 19 Nov 1799, Barras fell into disgrace.

barrel unit of liquid capacity, the value of which depends on the liquid being measured. It is used for petroleum, a barrel of which contains 159 litres/ 35 imperial gallons; a barrel of alcohol contains 189 litres/41.5 imperial gallons.

Barrett Browning Elizabeth 1806–1861. English poet. In 1844 she published *Poems* (including 'The Cry of the Children'), which led to her friendship with and secret marriage to Robert Browning 1846. The *Sonnets from the Portuguese* 1847 were written during their courtship. Later works include *Casa Guidi Windows* 1851 and the poetic novel *Aurora Leigh* 1857.

Barrie J(ames) M(atthew) 1860–1937. Scottish playwright and novelist, author of *The Admirable Crichton* 1902 and the children's fantasy *Peter Pan* 1904.

barrister in the UK, a lawyer qualified by study at the ¢>Inns of Court to plead for a client in court. In Scotland such lawyers are called ¢>advocates. Barristers also undertake the writing of opinions on the prospects of a case before trial. They act for clients through the intermediary of ¢>solicitors.

Barrois de Chamorro Violeta. President of Nicaragua from 1990; see ¢>Chamorro.

barrow burial mound, usually composed of earth but sometimes of stones, examples of which are

found in many parts of the world. The two main types are *long*, dating from the New Stone Age, or Neolithic, and *round*, dating from the later Mesolithic peoples of the early Bronze Age.

Barry Charles 1795–1860. English architect of the Neo-Gothic Houses of Parliament at Westminster, London, 1840–60, in collaboration with Augustus ¢>Pugin.

Barthes Roland 1915–1980. French critic and theorist of ¢>semiology, the science of signs and symbols. One of the French 'new critics' and an exponent of ¢>structuralism, he attacked traditional literary criticism in his early works, including *Le Degré zéro de l'ecriture/Writing Degree Zero* 1953 and *Sur Racine/On Racine* 1963.

Bartók Béla 1881–1945. Hungarian composer who developed a personal musical language, combining folk elements with mathematical concepts of tone and rhythmic proportion. His large output includes six string quartets, concertos, an opera, and graded teaching pieces for piano.

Bartolommeo Fra, also called *Baccio della Porta* c. 1472–c. 1517. Italian religious painter of the High Renaissance, active in Florence. His painting of *The Last Judgement* 1499 (Museo di San Marco, Florence) influenced Raphael.

Baryshnikov Mikhail 1948– . Latvian-born dancer, now based in the USA. He joined the Kirov Ballet 1967 and became one of their most brilliant soloists. After defecting in Canada 1974, he danced with various companies, and later joined the American Ballet Theater (ABT) as principal dancer, partnering Gelsey Kirkland. He left to join the New York City Ballet 1978–80, but rejoined ABT as director 1980–90. From 1990 he has danced for various companies.

basal metabolic rate (BMR) amount of energy needed by an animal just to stay alive. It is measured when the animal is awake but resting, and includes the energy required to keep the heart beating, sustain breathing, repair tissues, and keep the brain and nerves functioning. Measuring the animal's consumption of oxygen gives an accurate value for BMR, because oxygen is needed to release energy from food.

basalt commonest volcanic ¢>igneous rock, and the principal rock type on the ocean floor; it is basic, that is, it contains relatively little silica: under 50%. It is usually dark grey, but can also be green, brown, or black.

base in mathematics, the number of different single-digit symbols used in a particular number system. In our usual (decimal) counting system of numbers (with symbols 0, 1, 2, 3, 4, 5, 6, 7, 8, 9) the base is 10. In the ¢>binary number system, which has only the symbols 1 and 0, the base is two. A base is also a number that, when raised to a particular power (that is, when multiplied by itself a particular number of times as in $10^2 = 10 \times 10 = 100$), has a

⯈logarithm equal to the power. For example, the logarithm of 100 to the base ten is 2.

In geometry, the term is used to denote the line or area on which a polygon or solid stands.

base in chemistry, a substance that accepts protons, such as the hydroxide ion (OH⁻) and ammonia (NH_3). Bases react with acids to give a salt. Those that dissolve in water are called ⯈alkalis.

baseball national summer game of the USA, derived in the 19th century from the English game of rounders. Baseball is a bat-and-ball game played between two teams, each of nine players, on a pitch ('field') marked out in the form of a diamond, with a base at each corner. The ball is struck with a cylindrical bat, and the players try to score ('make a run') by circuiting the bases. A 'home run' is a circuit on one hit.

Basel or *Basle* (French *Bâle*) financial, commercial, and industrial (dyes, vitamins, agrochemicals, dietary products, genetic products) city in Switzerland; population (1990) 171,000. Basel was a strong military station under the Romans. In 1501 it joined the Swiss confederation and later developed as a centre for the Reformation.

base pair in biochemistry, the linkage of two base (purine or pyrimidine) molecules in ⯈DNA. They are found in nucleotides, and form the basis of the genetic code.

base rate in economics, the rate of interest to which most bank lending is linked, the actual rate depending on the status of the borrower. A prestigious company might command a rate only 1% above base rate, whereas an individual would be charged several points above.

Bashkir autonomous republic of Russia, with the Ural Mountains on the east; *area* 143,600 sq km/ 55,430 sq mi; *capital* Ufa; *products* minerals, oil, natural gas; *population* (1982) 3,876,000; *language* Russian, Bashkir (c. 25%); *history* annexed by Russia 1557; became the first Soviet autonomous republic 1919. Since 1989 Bashkirs have been demanding greater independence.

Bashō pen name of Matsuo Munefusa 1644–1694. Japanese poet who was a master of the *haiku*, a 17-syllable poetic form with lines of 5, 7, and 5 syllables, which he infused with subtle allusiveness. His *Oku-no-hosomichi/The Narrow Road to the Deep North* 1694, an account of a visit to northern and western Honshu, consists of haiku interspersed with prose passages.

BASIC (acronym for *b*eginner's *a*ll-purpose *s*ymbolic *i*nstruction *c*ode) high-level computer-programming language, developed 1964, originally designed to take advantage of multiuser systems (which can be used by many people at the same time). The language is relatively easy to learn and is popular among microcomputer users.

Basie Count (William) 1904–1984. US jazz band leader, pianist, and organist who developed the big-band sound and a simplified, swinging style of music. He led impressive groups of musicians in a career spanning more than 50 years. Basie's compositions include 'One O'Clock Jump' and 'Jumpin at the Woodside'.

basil or *sweet basil* plant *Ocimum basilicum* of the mint family Labiatae. A native of the tropics, it is cultivated in Europe as a culinary herb.

basilica Roman public building; a large roofed hall flanked by columns, generally with an aisle on each side, used for judicial or other public business. The earliest known basilica, at Pompeii, dates from the 2nd century BC. This architectural form was adopted by the early Christians for their churches.

basketball ball game between two teams of five players on an indoor enclosed court. The object is, via a series of passing moves, to throw the large inflated ball through a circular hoop and net positioned at each end of the court, 3.05 m/10 ft above the ground. The first world championship for men was held in 1950, and in 1953 for women. They are now held every four years.

Basle alternative form of ⯈Basel, city in Switzerland.

Basque member of a people who occupy the ⯈Basque Country of central N Spain and the extreme SW of France. The Basques are a pre-Indo-European people who largely maintained their independence until the 19th century. During the Spanish Civil War 1936–39, they were on the republican side defeated by Franco. Their language (*Euskara*) is unrelated to any other language. The Basque separatist movement ETA (*Euskadi ta Askatasuna* 'Basque Nation and Liberty') and the French organization *Iparretarrak* ('ETA fighters from the north side') have engaged in guerrilla activity from 1968 in an attempt to secure a united Basque state.

Basque Country (Basque *Euskal Herria*) homeland of the Basque people in the W Pyrenees, divided by the Franco-Spanish border. The Spanish Basque Country (Spanish *País Vasco*) is an autonomous region (created 1979) of central N Spain, comprising the provinces of Vizcaya, Alava, and Guipúzcoa (Basque *Bizkaia, Araba,* and *Gipuzkoa*); area 7,300 sq km/2,818 sq mi; population (1988) 2,176,790. The French Basque Country (French *Pays Basque*) comprises the arrondissements of Labourd, Basse-Navarre, and Soule (Basque *Lapurdi, Nafarroa Beherea,* and *Zuberoa*). To Basque nationalists, Euskal Herria also includes the autonomous Spanish province of Navarre.

Basque Provinces see ⯈Basque Country.

Basra (Arabic *al-Basrah*) principal port in Iraq, in the Shatt-al-Arab delta, 97 km/60 mi from the Persian Gulf, founded in the 7th century; population (1977) 1.5 million (1991) 850,000. Exports include wool, oil, cereal, and dates. Aerial bombing during the Gulf War destroyed bridges, factories, power stations, water-treatment plants, sewage-treatment plants, and the port. A Shi'ite rebellion March 1991 was crushed by the Iraqi army, causing further death and destruction.

bass the lowest male voice, ranging from middle C to the C two octaves below.

bass long-bodied scaly sea fish *Morone labrax* found in the N Atlantic and Mediterranean. They grow to 1 m/3 ft, and are often seen in shoals.

Basse-Normandie or *Lower Normandy* coastal region of NW France lying between Haute-Normandie and Brittany (Bretagne). It includes the *départements* of Calvados, Manche, and Orne; area 17,600 sq km/6,794 sq mi; population (1986) 1,373,000. Its capital is Caen. Apart from stock farming, dairy farming, and textiles, the area produces Calvados (apple brandy).

basset type of dog with a long low body, wrinkled forehead, and long pendulous ears, originally bred in France for hunting hares.

Basseterre capital and port of St Kitts-Nevis, in the Leeward Islands; population (1980) 14,000. Industries include data processing, rum, clothes, and electrical components.

bassoon double-reed ⟨⟩woodwind instrument, the bass of the oboe family. It doubles back on itself in a tube about 2.5 m/7.5 ft long. Its tone is rich and deep.

Bass Strait channel between Australia and Tasmania, named after British explorer George Bass; oil was discovered there in the 1960s.

Bastille castle of St Antoine, built about 1370 as part of the fortifications of Paris. It was made a state prison by Cardinal ⟨⟩Richelieu and was stormed by the mob that set the French Revolution in motion 14 July 1789. Only seven prisoners were found in the castle when it was stormed; the governor and most of the garrison were killed, and the Bastille was razed.

Basutoland former name for ⟨⟩Lesotho, a kingdom in southern Africa.

bat flying mammal in which the forelimbs are developed as wings capable of rapid and sustained flight. There are two main groups of bats: *megabats*, or *flying foxes*, which eat fruit, and *microbats*, which mainly eat insects. Although by no means blind, many microbats rely largely on echolocation for navigation and finding prey, sending out pulses of high-pitched sound and listening for the echo. Bats are nocturnal, and those native to temperate countries hibernate in winter. There are about 1,000 species of bats forming the order Chiroptera, making this the second-largest mammalian order; bats make up nearly one-quarter of the world's mammals. Although bats are widely distributed, bat populations have declined alarmingly and many species are now endangered. Since 1981 bats have been protected by law in Britain.

Bataan peninsula in Luzon, the Philippines, which was defended against the Japanese in World War II by US and Filipino troops under General MacArthur 1 Jan–9 April 1942. MacArthur was evacuated, but some 67,000 Allied prisoners died on the *Bataan Death March* to camps in the interior.

Bates H(enry) W(alter) 1825–1892. English naturalist and explorer who spent 11 years collecting animals and plants in South America and identified 8,000 new species of insects. He made a special study of ⟨⟩camouflage in animals, and his observation of insect imitation of species that are unpleasant to predators is known as *Batesian mimicry*.

Bathurst former name (until 1973) of ⟨⟩Banjul, capital of the Gambia.

Batista Fulgencio 1901–1973. Cuban dictator 1933–44 and 1952–59, whose authoritarian methods enabled him to jail his opponents and amass a large personal fortune. He was overthrown by rebel forces led by Fidel ⟨⟩Castro 1959.

battery any energy-storage device allowing release of electricity on demand. It is made up of one or more electrical ⟨⟩cells. Primary-cell batteries are disposable; secondary-cell batteries are rechargeable. The common dry cell relies on chemical changes occurring between the electrodes – a central carbon rod and an outer zinc casing – and the ammonium chloride electrolyte to produce electricity.

baud in engineering, a unit of electrical signalling speed equal to one pulse per second, measuring the rate at which signals are sent between electronic devices such as telegraphs and computers; 300 bauds is about 300 words a minute.

Baudelaire Charles Pierre 1821–1867. French poet whose work combined rhythmical and musical perfection with a morbid romanticism and eroticism, finding beauty in decadence and evil. His first book of verse was *Les Fleurs du mal/Flowers of Evil* 1857.

Baudouin 1930– . King of the Belgians from 1951. In 1950 his father, ⟨⟩Leopold III, abdicated and Baudouin was known until his succession July 1951 as *Le Prince Royal*. In 1960 he married Fabiola de Mora y Aragón (1928–), member of a Spanish noble family.

Bauhaus German school of Modern architecture and design founded 1919 by the architect Walter ⟨⟩Gropius at Weimar in Germany in an attempt to fuse all arts, design, architecture, and crafts into a unified whole. Moved to Dessau under political pressure 1925, it was closed by the Nazis 1933 because of 'decadence'. Associated with the Bauhaus were the artists Klee and Kandinsky and the architect Mies van der Rohe.

bauxite principal ore of ⟨⟩aluminium, formed by the ⟨⟩chemical weathering of rocks in tropical climates. To produce aluminium the ore is processed into a white powder (alumina), which is then smelted by passing a large electric current through it. The chief producers of bauxite are Australia, Guinea, Jamaica, Russia, Kazakhstan, Surinam, and Brazil.

Bavaria (German *Bayern*) administrative region (German *Land*) of Germany; *area* 70,600 sq km/27,252 sq mi; *capital* Munich; *towns* Nuremberg, Augsburg, Würzburg, Regensburg; *features* largest of the German *Länder*; forms the Danube basin; festivals at Bayreuth and Oberammergau; *products* beer, electronics, electrical engineering, optics, cars, aerospace, chemicals, plastics, oil refining, textiles, glass, toys; *population* (1988) 11,000,000; *famous people* Lucas Cranach, Adolf Hitler, Franz Josef Strauss, Richard Strauss; *religion* 70% Roman Catholic, 26% Protestant; *history* the last king, Ludwig III, abdicated 1918, and Bavaria declared itself a republic.

bay various species of ◊laurel, genus *Laurus*. The aromatic evergreen leaves are used for flavouring in cookery. There is also a golden-leaved variety.

Bayern German name for ◊Bavaria, region of Germany.

Bay of Pigs inlet on the S coast of Cuba about 145 km/90 mi SW of Havana. It was the site of an unsuccessful invasion attempt by 1,500 US-sponsored Cuban exiles 17–20 April 1961; 1,173 were taken prisoner.

bayonet short sword attached to the muzzle of a firearm. The bayonet was placed inside the barrel of the muzzle-loading muskets of the late 17th century. The *sock* or ring bayonet, invented 1700, allowed a weapon to be fired without interruption, leading to the demise of the pike.

BBC abbreviation for ◊*British Broadcasting Corporation*.

BCG (abbreviation for *bacillus of Calmette and Guérin*) bacillus used as a vaccine to confer active immunity to ◊tuberculosis (TB).

beagle short-haired hound with pendant ears, sickle tail, and a bell-like voice for hunting hares on foot ('beagling').

Beaker people people thought to be of Iberian origin who spread out over Europe from the 3rd millennium BC. They were skilled in metalworking, and are identified by their use of distinctive earthenware beakers with stamped designs, of which the bell-beaker type was widely distributed throughout Europe. They favoured inhumation (burial of the intact body), in a trench or under a round ◊barrow, or secondary burials in some form of chamber tomb. A beaker accompanied each burial, to hold a drink for the deceased on their final journey.

bean any seed of numerous leguminous plants. Beans are rich in nitrogenous or protein matter and are grown both for human consumption and as food for cattle and horses. Varieties of bean are grown throughout Europe, the USA, South America, China, Japan, SE Asia, and Australia.

bear large mammal with a heavily built body, short powerful limbs, and a very short tail. Bears breed once a year, producing one to four cubs. In northern regions they hibernate, and the young are born in the winter den. They are found mainly in North America and N Asia. The skin of the polar bear is black to conserve 80–90% of the solar energy trapped and channelled down the hollow hairs of its fur.

bear in business, a speculator who sells stocks or shares on the stock exchange expecting a fall in the price in order to by them back at a profit; the opposite of a ◊bull. In a bear market, prices fall and bears prosper.

Beardsley Aubrey (Vincent) 1872–1898. British illustrator. His meticulously executed black-and-white work displays the sinuous line and decorative mannerisms of Art Nouveau and was often charged with being grotesque and decadent. He became known through the *Yellow Book* magazine and his drawings for Oscar Wilde's *Salome* 1894.

bearing device used in a machine to allow free movement between two parts, typically the rotation of a shaft in a housing. *Ball bearings* consist of two rings, one fixed to a housing, one to the rotating shaft. Between them is a set, or race, of steel balls. They are widely used to support shafts, as in the spindle in the hub of a bicycle wheel.

bearing the direction of a fixed point, or the path of a moving object, from a point of observation on the Earth's surface, expressed as an angle from the north. Bearings are taken by ◊compass and are measured in degrees (°), given as three-digit numbers increasing clockwise. For instance, north is 00°, northeast is 045°, south is 180°, and southwest is 225°.

beat regular variation in the loudness of the sound when two notes of nearly equal pitch or ◊frequency are heard together. Beats result from the ◊interference between the sound waves of the notes. The frequency of the beats equals the difference in frequency of the notes.

Beat Generation or *Beat movement* beatniks of the 1950s and 1960s, usually in their teens and early twenties, who rejected conventional lifestyles and opted for life on the road, drug experimentation, and antimaterialist values; and the associated literary movement whose members included William S Burroughs, Lawrence Ferlinghetti, Allen ◊Ginsberg, and Jack ◊Kerouac (who is credited with coining the term).

Beatles, the English pop group 1960–70. The members, all born in Liverpool, were John Lennon (1940–80, rhythm guitar, vocals), Paul McCartney (1942– , bass, vocals), George Harrison (1943– , lead guitar, vocals), and Ringo Starr (formerly Richard Starkey, 1940– , drums). Using songs written largely by Lennon and McCartney, the Beatles dominated rock music and pop culture in the 1960s.

Beaufort scale

Number and description	Features	Air speed mi per hr	m per sec
0 calm	smoke rises vertically; water smooth	less than 1	less than 0.3
1 light air	smoke shows wind direction; water ruffled	1–3	0.3–1.5
2 slight breeze	leaves rustle; wind felt on face	4–7	1.6–3.3
3 gentle breeze	loose paper blows around	8–12	3.4–5.4
4 moderate	branches sway	13–18	5.5–7.9
5 fresh breeze	small trees sway, leaves blown off	19–24	8.0–10.7
6 strong breeze	whistling in telephone wires; sea spray	25–31	10.8–13.8
7 moderate gale	large trees sway	32–38	13.9–17.1
8 fresh gale	twigs break from trees	39–46	17.2–20.7
9 strong gale	branches break from trees	47–54	20.8–24.4
10 whole gale	trees uprooted, weak buildings collapse	55–63	24.5–28.4
11 storm	widespread damage	64–72	28.5–32.6
12 hurricane	widespread structural damage	above 73	above 32.7

Beaton Cecil 1904–1980. English portrait and fashion photographer, designer, illustrator, diarist, and conversationalist. He produced portrait studies and also designed scenery and costumes for ballets, and sets for plays and films.

Beatrix 1936– . Queen of the Netherlands. The eldest daughter of Queen Juliana, she succeeded to the throne on her mother's abdication 1980. In 1966 she married West German diplomat Claus von Amsberg (1926–), who was created Prince of the Netherlands. Her heir is Prince Willem Alexander (1967–).

Beaufort scale system of recording wind velocity, devised by Francis Beaufort 1806. It is a numerical scale ranging from 0 to 17, calm being indicated by 0 and a hurricane by 12; 13–17 indicate degrees of hurricane force.

Beauvoir Simone de 1908–1986. French socialist, feminist, and writer who taught philosophy at the Sorbonne university in Paris 1931–43. Her book *Le Deuxième sexe/The Second Sex* 1949 became a seminal work for many feminists.

beaver aquatic rodent *Castor fiber* with webbed hind feet, a broad flat scaly tail, and thick waterproof fur. It has very large incisor teeth and fells trees to feed on the bark and to use the logs to construct the 'lodge', in which the young are reared, food is stored, and where much of the winter is spent.

Beaverbrook (William) Max(well) Aitken, 1st Baron Beaverbrook 1879–1964. British financier, newspaper proprietor, and politician, born in Canada. He bought a majority interest in the *Daily Express* 1919, founded the *Sunday Express* 1921, and bought the London *Evening Standard* 1929. He served in Lloyd George's World War I cabinet and Churchill's World War II cabinet. Between the wars he used his newspapers, in particular the *Daily Express*, to campaign for empire and free trade and against Prime Minister Baldwin.

bebop or *bop* hot jazz style, rhythmically complex, virtuosic, and highly improvisational, developed in New York 1945–55 by Charlie Parker, Dizzy Gillespie, Thelonius Monk, and other black musicians disaffected with dance bands and racism, and determined to create music that would be too difficult for white people to play.

Bechuanaland former name until 1966 of ⍛Botswana.

Becker Boris 1967– . German tennis player. In 1985 he became the youngest winner of a singles title at Wimbledon at the age of 17. He has won the title three times and helped West Germany to win the Davis Cup 1988 and 1989. He also won the US Open 1989.

Becket St Thomas à 1118–1170. English priest and politician. He was chancellor to ⍛Henry II 1155–62, when he was appointed archbishop of Canterbury. From 1164 he opposed Henry's attempt to regulate the relations between church and state, and in consequence Becket was assassinated. He was canonized 1172, and his shrine became the busiest centre of pilgrimage in England until the Reformation.

Beckett Samuel 1906–1989. Irish novelist and dramatist who wrote in French and English. His *En attendant Godot/Waiting for Godot* 1952 is possibly the most universally known example of Theatre of the Absurd, in which life is taken to be meaningless. This genre is taken to further extremes in *Fin de Partie/Endgame* 1957 and *Happy Days* 1961. Nobel Prize for Literature 1969.

becquerel SI unit (symbol Bq) of ⍛radioactivity, equal to one radioactive disintegration (change in the nucleus of an atom when a particle or ray is given off) per second.

Becquerel Antoine Henri 1852–1908. French physicist who discovered penetrating radiation coming from uranium salts, the first indication of ⟷radioactivity, and shared a Nobel prize with Marie and Pierre ⟷Curie 1903.

bed in geology, a single ⟷sedimentary rock unit with a distinct set of physical characteristics or contained fossils, readily distinguishable from those of beds above and below. Well-defined partings called *bedding planes* separate successive beds or strata.

bedbug flattened wingless red-brown insect *Cimex lectularius* with piercing mouthparts. It hides by day in crevices or bedclothes, and emerges at night to suck human blood.

Bede c. 673–735. English theologian and historian, known as *the Venerable Bede*, active in Durham and Northumbria. He wrote many scientific, theological, and historical works. His *Historia Ecclesiastica Gentis Anglorum/Ecclesiastical History of the English People* 731 is a seminal source for early English history.

Bedfordshire county in S central England; *area* 1,240 sq km/479 sq mi; *towns* Bedford (administrative headquarters), Luton, Dunstable; *features* Whipsnade Zoo 1931, near Dunstable, a zoological park (200 hectares/500 acres) belonging to the London Zoological Society; Woburn Abbey, seat of the duke of Bedford; *products* cereals, vegetables, agricultural machinery, electrical goods; *population* (1991) 514,200; *famous people* John Bunyan, John Howard, Joseph Paxton.

Bedouin Arab of any of the nomadic peoples occupying the desert regions of Arabia and N Africa, now becoming increasingly settled. Their traditional trade was the rearing of horses and camels.

bee four-winged insect of the superfamily Apoidea in the order Hymenoptera, usually with a sting. There are over 12,000 species, of which fewer than 1 in 20 are social in habit. The *hive* or *honey bee Apis mellifera* establishes perennial colonies of about 80,000, the majority being infertile females (workers), with a few larger fertile males (drones), and a single very large fertile female (the queen).

beech any tree of the genera *Fagus* and *Nothofagus*, family Fagaceae. The common beech *F. sylvaticus*, found in European forests, has a smooth grey trunk and edible nuts, or 'mast', which are used as animal feed or processed for oil. The timber is used in furniture.

Beecham Thomas 1879–1961. British conductor and impresario. He established the Royal Philharmonic Orchestra 1946 and fostered the works of such composers as Delius, Sibelius, and Richard Strauss.

Beelzebub in the New Testament, the leader of the devils, sometimes identified with Satan and sometimes with his chief assistant (see ⟷devil). In the Old Testament Beelzebub was a fertility god worshipped by the Philistines and other Semitic groups (Baal).

beer alcoholic drink made from water and malt (fermented barley or other grain), flavoured with hops. Beer contains between 1% and 6% alcohol. One of the oldest alcoholic drinks, it was brewed in ancient China, Egypt, and Babylon. The medieval distinction between beer (containing hops) and *ale* (without hops) has now fallen into disuse and beer has come to be used strictly as a generic term including ale, stout, and lager. *Stout* is top-fermented, but is sweet and strongly flavoured with roasted grain; *lager* is a light beer, bottom fermented and matured over a longer period (German *Lager*, 'store').

Beersheba industrial town in Israel; population (1987) 115,000. It is the chief centre of the Negev desert and has been a settlement from the Stone Age.

beet plant of the genus *Beta* of the goosefoot family Chenapodiaceae. The common beet *B. vulgaris* is used in one variety to produce sugar, and another, the mangelwurzel, is grown as cattle fodder. The beetroot, or red beet, *B. rubra* is a salad plant.

Beethoven Ludwig van 1770–1827. German composer and pianist whose mastery of musical expression in every genre made him the dominant influence on 19th-century music. Beethoven's repertoire includes concert overtures; the opera *Fidelio*; five piano concertos and two for violin (one unfinished); 32 piano sonatas, including the *Moonlight* and *Appassionata*; 17 string quartets; the Mass in D *Missa solemnis*; and nine symphonies, as well as many youthful works. He usually played his own piano pieces and conducted his orchestral works until he was hampered by deafness 1801; nevertheless he continued to compose.

beetle common name of insects in the order Coleoptera (Greek 'sheath-winged') with leathery forewings folding down in a protective sheath over the membranous hindwings, which are those used for flight. They pass through a complete metamorphosis. They include some of the largest and smallest of all insects: the largest is the *Hercules beetle Dynastes hercules* of the South American rainforests, 15 cm/6 in long; the smallest is only 0.05 cm/0.02 in long. Comprising more than 50% of the animal kingdom, beetles number some 370,000 named species, with many not yet described.

Begin Menachem 1913–1992. Israeli politician. He was leader of the extremist Irgun Zvai Leumi organization in Palestine from 1942, and prime minister of Israel 1977–83, as head of the right-wing Likud party. In 1978 Begin shared a Nobel Peace Prize with President Sadat of Egypt for work on the ⟷Camp David Agreements for a Middle East peace settlement.

begonia any plant of the genus *Begonia* of the tropical and subtropical family Begoniaceae. Begonias have fleshy and succulent leaves, and some have large, brilliant flowers. There are numerous species native to the tropics, in particular South America and India.

Behan Brendan 1923–1964. Irish dramatist. His early experience of prison and knowledge of the workings of the ⏵IRA (recounted in his autobiography *Borstal Boy* 1958) provided him with two recurrent themes in his plays. *The Quare Fellow* 1954 was followed by the tragicomedy *The Hostage* 1958, first written in Gaelic.

behaviour therapy in psychology, the application of behavioural principles, derived from learning theories, to the treatment of clinical conditions such as ⏵phobias, ⏵obsessions, sexual and interpersonal problems. For example, in treating a phobia the person is taken into the feared situation in gradual steps. Over time, the fear typically reduces, and the problem becomes less acute.

Behn Aphra 1640–1689. English novelist and playwright, the first woman in England to earn her living as a writer. Her writings were criticized for their explicitness; they frequently present events from a woman's point of view. Her novel *Oronooko* 1688 is an attack on slavery.

Behrens Peter 1868–1940. German architect. He pioneered the adaptation of architecture to industry, and designed the AEG turbine factory in Berlin 1909, a landmark in industrial design. He taught ⏵Le Corbusier and Walter ⏵Gropius.

Beiderbecke Bix (Leon Bismarck) 1903–1931. US jazz cornetist, composer, and pianist. A soloist with King Oliver, Louis Armstrong, and Paul Whiteman's orchestra, Beiderbecke was the first acknowledged white jazz innovator. He was inspired by the classical composers Debussy, Ravel, and Stravinsky.

Beijing or *Peking* capital of China; part of its NE border is formed by the Great Wall of China; population (1989) 6,800,000. The municipality of Beijing has an area of 17,800 sq km/6,871 sq mi and a population (1990) of 10,819,000. Industries include textiles, petrochemicals, steel, and engineering.

Beirut or *Beyrouth* capital and port of ⏵Lebanon, devastated by civil war in the 1970s and 1980s, when it was occupied by armies of neighbouring countries; population (1988 est) 1,500,000. The city is divided into a Christian eastern and a Muslim western sector by the Green Line.

Bekka, the or *El Beqa'a* governorate of E Lebanon separated from Syria by the Anti-Lebanon mountains. The Bekka Valley has been of strategic importance in the Syrian struggle for control of N Lebanon. In the early 1980s the valley was penetrated by Shia Muslims who established an extremist Hezbollah stronghold with the support of Iranian Revolutionary Guards. Zahlé and the ancient city of Baalbek are the chief towns.

Belarus, Republic of (or *Byelorussia* or *Belorussia*) country in E central Europe bordered NW by Lithuania and Latvia, NE and E by the Russian Federation, S by Ukraine, and E by Poland; *area* 208,000 sq km/80,290 sq mi; *capital* Mensk

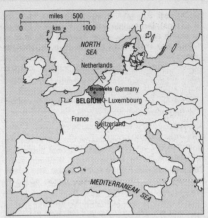

(Minsk); *physical* more than 25% forested, rivers W Dvina, Dnieper and tributaries; Pripet Marshes in E; *head of state* Stanislav Shushkevich from 1991; *head of government* Vyacheslav Kebich from 1990; *political system* emergent democracy; *products* peat, agricultural machinery, fertilizers, glass, textiles, leather, salt, electrical goods, meat dairy products; *population* (1990) 10,200,000; *languages* Belorussian, Russian; *recent history* briefly independent from Russia 1918–19. Occupied by Nazi Germany 1941–44. Became founding member of United Nations 1945. Republican sovereignty declared 1990; independence from USSR declared 1991. ⏵Commonwealth of Independent States (CIS) formed in Mensk Dec 1991. USA recognized independence Jan 1992.

Belau, Republic of (formerly *Palau*) self-governing island group in Micronesia; area 500 sq km/193 sq mi; population (1988) 14,000. There are 26 larger islands (eight inhabited) and about 300 islets. It has been part of the US Trust Territory of the Pacific Islands since 1947, becoming internally self-governing 1980.

Belfast industrial port (shipbuilding, engineering, electronics, textiles, tobacco) and capital of Northern Ireland since 1920; population (1985) 300,000. Since 1968 it has been heavily damaged by civil disturbances.

Belgian Congo former name (1908–60) of ⏵Zaire.

Belgium Kingdom of; country in N Europe, bordered NW by the North Sea, SW by France, E by Luxembourg and Germany, and NE by the Netherlands; *area* 30,510 sq km/11,784 sq mi; *capital* Brussels; *physical* flat coastal plain in NW, central rolling hills, hills and forest in SE; forested plateau of the Ardennes; rivers Scheldt and Meuse; *head of state* King Baudouin from 1951; *head of government* Jean-Luc Dehaene from 1992; *political system* liberal democracy; *exports* iron, steel, textiles, manufactured goods, petrochemicals, vehicles, diamonds; *population*

(1990 est) 9,895,000 (comprising Flemings and Walloons); *languages* in the N (Flanders) Flemish (a Dutch dialect, known as *Vlaams*) 55%; in the S (Wallonia) Walloon (a French dialect) 32%; bilingual 11%; German (E border) 0.6%; all are official; *recent history* became an independent kingdom 1830. Invaded by Germany 1914 and 1940 in world wars I and II. Since 1945 Belgium has been a major force for international cooperation in Europe, being a founding member of the Benelux Economic Union 1948; of the Council of Europe and NATO 1949, and of the European Community (EC) 1957. Steps towards regional autonomy were taken 1971, 1974, and 1980, when regional assemblies were created for Flanders and Wallonia and a three-member executive for Brussels.

Belgrade (Serbo-Croatian *Beograd*) capital of Yugoslavia and Serbia, and Danube river port linked with the port of Bar on the Adriatic; population (1981) 1,470,000. Industries include light engineering, food processing, textiles, pharmaceuticals, and electrical goods.

Belize (formerly *British Honduras*) country in Central America, bordered N by Mexico, W and S by Guatemala, and E by the Caribbean Sea; *area* 22,963 sq km/8,864 sq mi; *capital* Belmopan; *physical* tropical swampy coastal plain, Maya Mountains in S, over 90% under forest; world's second longest barrier reef; *head of state* Elizabeth II from 1981 represented by governor general; *head of government* George Price from 1989; *political system* constitutional monarchy; *exports* sugar, citrus fruits, rice, fish products, bananas; *population* (1990 est) 180,400 (including Mayan minority in the interior); *languages* English (official); Spanish (widely spoken), creole dialects; *recent history* became a British colony (British Honduras) 1862. Self-government was achieved 1964. In 1970 the capital was moved from Belize City to the new town of Belmopan. In 1973 the name Belize was adopted. In 1975 British troops were sent to defend the long-disputed frontier with Guatemala; negotiations begun 1977 were inconclusive. Full independence was achieved 1981. Diplomatic relations with Guatemala established 1991.

Belize City chief port of Belize, and capital until 1970; population (1991) 46,000. After the city was destroyed by a hurricane 1961 it was decided to move the capital inland, to Belmopan.

Bell Alexander Graham 1847–1922. Scottish-born US scientist and inventor of the telephone. He patented his invention 1876, and later experimented with a type of phonograph and, in aeronautics, invented the tricycle undercarriage.

belladonna or *deadly nightshade* poisonous plant *Atropa belladonna*, found in Europe and Asia. The dried powdered leaves contain ◊alkaloids. Belladonna extract acts medicinally as an anticholinergic (blocking the passage of certain nerve impulses), and is highly toxic in large doses.

bellflower general name for many plants of the family Campanulaceae, notably those of the genus *Campanula*. The Canterbury bell *C. medium* is the garden variety, originally from S Europe. The ◊harebell is also a *Campanula*.

Bellini family of Italian Renaissance painters, founders of the Venetian school. *Jacopo* (*c.* 1400–1470) was father to Gentile and Giovanni. Little of his work has survived, but two of his sketchbooks (now in the British Museum and the Louvre) contain his ideas and designs; *Gentile* (*c.* 1429–1507) assisted in the decoration of the Doge's Palace 1474 and worked in the court of Muhammad II at Constantinople (a portrait of the sultan is in the National Gallery, London). His also painted processional groups (Accademia, Venice); *Giovanni* (*c.*1430–1516), Gentile's younger brother, studied under his father, and painted portraits and various religious subjects. Giovanni Bellini's early works show the influence of his brother-in-law, Mantegna. His style developed from the static manner of mid-15th century Venetian work towards a High Renaissance harmony and grandeur, as in the altarpiece 1505 in Sta Zaccaria, Venice. He introduced softness in tone, harmony in composition, and a use of luminous colour that influenced the next generation of painters (including his pupils Giorgione and Titian). He worked in oil rather than tempera, a technique adopted from Antonello da Messina.

Bellow Saul 1915– . Canadian-born US novelist. Novels such as *Herzog* 1964, *Humboldt's Gift* 1975, and *The Dean's December* 1982 show his method of inhabiting the consciousness of a central character, frequently a Jewish-American intellectual, to portray an individual's frustration with the ongoing events of an indifferent society. His finely styled works and skilled characterizations won him the Nobel Prize for Literature 1976.

Belmopan capital of Belize from 1970; population (1991) 4,000. It replaced Belize City as administrative centre of the country.

Belo Horizonte industrial city (steel, engineering, textiles) in SE Brazil, capital of the fast-developing state of Minas Gerais; population (1991) 2,103,300. Built in the 1890s, it was Brazil's first planned modern city.

Belorussia see ◊Belarus, Republic of.

Ben Ali Zine el Abidine 1936– . Tunisian politician, president from 1987. After training in France and the USA, he returned to Tunisia and became director-general of national security. He was made minister of the interior and then prime minister under the ageing president for life, Habib ◊Bourguiba, whom he deposed 1987 by a bloodless coup with the aid of ministerial colleagues. He ended the personality cult established by Bourguiba and moved toward a pluralist political system.

Benares alternative transliteration of ◊Varanasi, holy city in India.

Ben Bella Ahmed 1916– . Algerian politician. He was leader of the National Liberation Front (FLN) from 1952, the first prime minister of independent Algeria 1962–63, and its first president 1963–65. In 1965 Ben Bella was overthrown by Col Houari ⟁Boumédienne and detained until 1979. He founded a new party, Mouvement pour la Démocratie en Algérie, in 1985, and returned to Algeria 1990 after nine years in exile.

Benedict, St c. 480–c. 547. Founder of Christian monasticism in the West and of the Benedictine order. He founded the monastery of Monte Cassino, Italy. Here he wrote out his rule for monastic life, and was visited shortly before his death by the Ostrogothic king Totila, whom he converted to the Christian faith. His feast day is 11 July.

Benelux (acronym from **Be**lgium, the **Ne**therlands, and **Lux**embourg) customs union agreed by Belgium, the Netherlands, and Luxembourg 1948, fully effective 1960. It was the precursor of the European Community.

Beneš Eduard 1884–1948. Czechoslovak politician. He worked with Tomáš ⟁Masaryk towards Czechoslovak nationalism from 1918 and was foreign minister and representative at the League of Nations. He was president of the republic from 1935 until forced to resign by the Germans; he headed a government in exile in London during World War II. He returned home as president 1945 but resigned again after the Communist coup 1948.

Bengal former province of British India, divided 1947 into ⟁West Bengal, a state of India, and East Bengal, from 1972 ⟁Bangladesh. A famine in 1943, caused by a slump in demand for jute and a bad harvest, resulted in more than 3 million deaths.

Bengal, Bay of part of the Indian Ocean lying between the east coast of India and the west coast of Myanmar (Burma) and the Malay Peninsula. The Irrawaddy, Ganges, and Brahmaputra rivers flow into the bay. The principal islands are to be found in the Andaman and Nicobar groups.

Bengali person of Bengali culture from Bangladesh and India (W Bengal, Tripura). There are 80–150 million speakers of Bengali, an Indo-Iranian language belonging to the Indo-European family. It is the official language of Bangladesh and of the state of Bengal, and is also used by emigrant Bangladeshi and Bengali communities in such countries as the UK and the USA. Bengalis in Bangladesh are predominantly Muslim, whereas those in India are mainly Hindu.

Benghazi or **Banghazi** historic city and industrial port in N Libya on the Gulf of Sirte; population (1982) 650,000. It was controlled by Turkey between the 16th century and 1911, and by Italy 1911–42; a major naval supply base during World War II.

Ben-Gurion David. Adopted name of David Gruen 1886–1973. Israeli statesman and socialist politician, one of the founders of the state of Israel, the country's first prime minister 1948–53, and again 1955–63.

Benin People's Republic of; country in W Africa, bordered E by Nigeria, N by Niger and Burkina Faso, W by Togo, and S by the Gulf of Guinea; *area* 112,622 sq km/43,472 sq mi; *capital* Porto Novo (official), Cotonou (de facto); *physical* flat to undulating terrain; Niger River in NE; hot and humid in S, semi-arid in N; *head of state and government* Nicéphore Soglo from 1991; *political system* socialist pluralist republic; *exports* cocoa, peanuts, cotton, palm oil, petroleum, cement, sea products; *population* (1990 est) 4,840,000; *languages* French (official); Fon 47% and Yoruba 9% in S; six major tribal languages in N; *recent history* independence from France was achieved 1960. A period of acute political instability was followed by a military regime 1972; this was replaced by civilian rule from 1977. The country's name was changed from Dahomey to Benin 1975. The first multiparty elections were held 1991.

Benin former African kingdom 1200–1897, now part of Nigeria. It reached the height of its power in the 14th–17th centuries when it ruled the area between the Niger Delta and Lagos. Benin traded in spices, ivory, palm oil, and slaves until its decline and eventual incorporation into Nigeria. The oba (ruler) of Benin continues to rule his people as a divine monarch. The present oba is considered an enlightened leader and one who is helping his people to become part of modern Nigeria.

Bennett (Enoch) Arnold 1867–1931. English novelist. He became a London journalist 1893 and editor of *Woman* 1896. His many novels include *Anna of the Five Towns* 1904, *The Old Wives' Tale* 1908, and the trilogy *Clayhanger, Hilda Lessways*, and *These Twain* 1910–16.

Ben Nevis highest mountain in the British Isles (1,342 m/4,406 ft), in the Grampians, Scotland.

Bentham Jeremy 1748–1832. English philosopher, legal and social reformer, and founder of ⟁utilitarianism. The essence of his moral philosophy is found in the pronouncement of his *Principles of Morals and Legislation* (written 1780, published 1789): that the object of all legislation should be 'the greatest happiness for the greatest number'.

Benz Karl Friedrich 1844–1929. German automobile engineer who produced the world's first petrol-driven motor vehicle. He built his first model engine 1878 and the petrol-driven car 1885.

benzene C_6H_6 clear liquid hydrocarbon of characteristic odour, occurring in coal tar. It is used as a solvent and in the synthesis of many chemicals.

benzodiazepine any of a group of mood-altering drugs (tranquillizers), for example Librium and Valium. They are addictive and interfere with the process by which information is transmitted between brain cells, and various side effects arise from continued use. They were originally developed as a muscle relaxant, and then excessively prescribed in the West as anxiety-relaxing drugs.

Beowulf Anglo-Saxon poem (composed *c.* 700), the only complete surviving example of Germanic folk epic. It exists in a single manuscript copied about 1000 in the Cottonian collection of the British Museum. The hero Beowulf delivers the Danish king Hrothgar from the water demon Grendel and its monstrous mother, and, returning home, succeeds his cousin Heardred as king of the Geats. After 50 years of prosperity, he is killed in slaying a dragon.

Berber member of a non-Semitic Caucasoid people of North Africa who since prehistoric times inhabited Barbary, the Mediterranean coastlands from Egypt to the Atlantic. Their language, Berber (a member of the Afro-Asiatic language family), is spoken by about one-third of Algerians and nearly two-thirds of Moroccans, 10 million people. Berbers are mainly agricultural, but some are still nomadic.

Bérégovoy Pierre 1925– . French socialist politician, prime minister from 1992. A close ally of François ◊Mitterrand, he was named chief of staff 1981 after managing the successful presidential campaign. He was social affairs minister 1982–84 and finance minister 1984–86 and 1988–92.

Berg Alban 1885–1935. Austrian composer. He studied under Arnold ◊Schoenberg and was associated with him as one of the leaders of the serial, or 12-tone, school of composition. His output includes orchestral, chamber, and vocal music as well as two operas, *Wozzeck* 1925, a grim story of working-class life, and the unfinished *Lulu* 1929–35.

bergamot small, evergreen tree *Citrus bergamia* of the rue family Rutaceae. From the rind of its fruit a fragrant orange-scented essence used as a perfume is obtained. The sole source of supply is S Calabria, Italy, but the name comes from the town of Bergamo, in Lombardy.

Bergen industrial port (shipbuilding, engineering, fishing) in SW Norway; population (1991) 213,300. Founded 1070, Bergen was a member of the ◊Hanseatic League.

Bergman Ingmar 1918– . Swedish stage producer (from the 1930s) and film director (from the 1950s). His work deals with complex moral, psychological, and metaphysical problems and is tinged with pessimism. His films include *Wild Strawberries* 1957, *The Seventh Seal* 1957, *Persona* 1966, and *Fanny and Alexander* 1982.

Bergman Ingrid 1917–1982. Swedish actress whose films include *Intermezzo* 1939, *Casablanca*, *For Whom the Bell Tolls* both 1943, and *Gaslight* 1944, for which she won an Academy Award.

Beria Lavrenti 1899–1953. Soviet politician who in 1938 became minister of the interior and head of the Soviet police force that imprisoned, liquidated, and transported millions of Soviet citizens. On Stalin's death 1953, he attempted to seize power but was foiled and shot after a secret trial.

Bering Vitus 1681–1741. Danish explorer, the first

European to sight Alaska. He died on Bering Island in the Bering Sea, both named after him, as is the Bering Strait, which separates Asia (Russia) from North America (Alaska).

Bering Sea section of the N Pacific between Alaska and Siberia, from the Aleutian Islands north to the Bering Strait.

Bering Strait strait between Alaska and Siberia, linking the N Pacific and Arctic oceans.

Berkeley Busby. Stage name of William Berkeley Enos 1895–1976. US choreographer and film director who used ingenious and extravagant sets and teams of female dancers to create large-scale kaleidoscopic patterns through movement and costume when filmed from above, as in *Gold Diggers of 1933* and *Footlight Parade* 1933.

berkelium synthesized, radioactive, metallic element of the actinide series, symbol Bk, atomic number 97, relative atomic mass 247. It was first produced 1949 by Glenn Seaborg and his team at the University of California at Berkeley, USA, after which it is named.

Berkshire or *Royal Berkshire* county in S central England; *area* 1,260 sq km/486 sq mi; *towns* Reading (administrative headquarters), Eton, Slough, Maidenhead, Ascot, Bracknell, Newbury, Windsor; *features* rivers Thames and Kennet; Inkpen Beacon, 297 m/975 ft; Bagshot Heath; Ridgeway Path, walkers' path (partly prehistoric) running from Wiltshire across the Berkshire Downs into Hertfordshire; Windsor Forest and Windsor Castle; Eton College; Royal Military Academy at Sandhurst; atomic-weapons research establishment at Aldermaston; the former main UK base for US cruise missiles at Greenham Common, Newbury; *products* general agricultural and horticultural goods, electronics, plastics, pharmaceuticals; *population* (1991) 716,500; *famous people* Jethro Tull, William Laud, Stanley Spencer.

Berlin industrial city (machine tools, electrical goods, paper, printing) and capital of the Federal Republic of Germany; population (1990) 3,102,500. The Berlin Wall divided the city from 1961 to 1989, but in Oct 1990 Berlin became the capital of a unified Germany once more with East and West Berlin reunited as the 16th *Land* (state) of the Federal Republic.

Berlin Irving. Adopted name of Israel Baline 1888–1989. Russian-born US composer who wrote over 1,500 songs including such hits as 'Alexander's Ragtime Band' 1911, 'Always' 1925, 'God Bless America' 1939, and 'White Christmas' 1942, and the musicals *Top Hat* 1935, *Annie Get Your Gun* 1950, and *Call Me Madam* 1953. He also wrote film scores such as *Blue Skies* and *Easter Parade*.

Berlin blockade in June 1948, the closing of entry to Berlin from the west by Soviet forces. It was an attempt to prevent the other Allies (the USA, France, and the UK) unifying the western part of

Germany. The British and US forces responded by sending supplies to the city by air for over a year (the *Berlin airlift*). In May 1949 the blockade was lifted; the airlift continued until Sept. The blockade marked the formal division of the city into Eastern and Western sectors.

Berlin Wall dividing barrier between East and West Berlin 1961–89, erected by East Germany to prevent East Germans from leaving for West Germany. Escapers were shot on sight.

Berlioz (Louis) Hector 1803–1869. French romantic composer, the founder of modern orchestration. Much of his music was inspired by drama and literature and has a theatrical quality. He wrote symphonic works, such as *Symphonie fantastique* 1830–31 and *Roméo et Juliette* 1839; dramatic cantatas including *La Damnation de Faust* 1846 and *L'Enfance du Christ* 1854; sacred music; and three operas.

Bermuda British colony in the NW Atlantic; *area* 54 sq km/21 sq mi; *capital* and chief port Hamilton; *features* consists of about 150 small islands, of which 20 are inhabited, linked by bridges and causeways; Britain's oldest colony; *products* Easter lilies, pharmaceuticals; tourism and banking are important; *currency* Bermuda dollar; *population* (1988) 58,100 *language* English; *religion* Christian; *government* under the constitution of 1968, Bermuda is a fully self-governing British colony, with a governor, senate, and elected House of Assembly (premier from 1982 John Swan, United Bermuda Party); *history* the islands were named after Juan de Bermudez, who visited them in 1515, and were settled by British colonists in 1609. Indian and African slaves were transported from 1616, and soon outnumbered the white settlers. Racial violence 1977 led to intervention, at the request of the government, by British troops.

Bern (French *Berne*) capital of Switzerland and of Bern canton, in W Switzerland on the Aare River; population (1990) 134,600; canton 945,600. It joined the Swiss confederation 1353 and became the capital 1848. Industries include textiles, chocolate, pharmaceuticals, light metal, and electrical goods.

Bernadotte Jean-Baptiste Jules 1764–1844. Marshal in Napoleon's army who in 1818 became ▷Charles XIV of Sweden. Hence, Bernadotte is the family name of the present royal house of Sweden.

Bernard Claude 1813–1878. French physiologist and founder of experimental medicine. Bernard first demonstrated that digestion is not restricted to the stomach, but takes place throughout the small intestine. He discovered the digestive input of the pancreas, several functions of the liver, and the vasomotor nerves which dilate and contract the blood vessels and thus regulate body temperature. This led him to the concept of the *milieu intérieur* ('internal environment') whose stability is essential to good health.

Bernese Oberland or *Bernese Alps* mountainous area in the S of Berne canton. It includes

the Jungfrau, Eiger, and Finsteraarhorn peaks. Interlaken is the chief town.

Bernhardt Sarah. Stage name of Rosine Bernard 1845–1923. French actress who dominated the stage of her day, frequently performing at the Comédie-Française in Paris. She excelled in tragic roles, including Cordelia in Shakespeare's *King Lear*, the title role in Racine's *Phèdre*, and the male roles of Hamlet and of Napoleon's son in Edmond Rostand's *L'Aiglon*.

Bernini Giovanni Lorenzo 1598–1680. Italian sculptor, architect, and painter, a leading figure in the development of the Baroque style. His work in Rome includes the colonnaded piazza in front of St Peter's Basilica (1656), fountains (as in the Piazza Navona), and papal monuments. His sculpture includes *The Ecstasy of St Theresa* 1645–52 (Sta Maria della Vittoria, Rome) and numerous portrait busts.

Bernoulli's principle law stating that the speed of a fluid varies inversely with pressure, an increase in speed producing a decrease in pressure (such as a drop in hydraulic pressure as the fluid speeds up flowing through a constriction in a pipe) and vice versa. The principle also explains the pressure differences on each surface of an aerofoil, which gives lift to the wing of an aircraft. The principle was named after Swiss mathematician and physicist Daniel Bernoulli.

Bernstein Leonard 1918–1990. US composer, conductor, and pianist, one of the most energetic and versatile of US musicians in the 20th century. His works, which established a vogue for realistic, contemporary themes, include symphonies such as *The Age of Anxiety* 1949, ballets such as *Fancy Free* 1944, and scores for musicals, including *Wonderful Town* 1953, *West Side Story* 1957, and *Mass* 1971 in memory of President J F Kennedy.

Berri Nabih 1939– . Lebanese politician and soldier, leader of Amal ('Hope'), the Syrian-backed Shi'ite nationalist movement. He became minister of justice in the government of President ▷Gemayel 1984. In 1988 Amal was disbanded after defeat by the Iranian-backed Hezbollah ('Children of God') during the Lebanese civil wars, and Berri joined the cabinet of Selim Hoss 1989. In Dec 1990 Berri was made minister of state in the newly formed Karami cabinet.

Berry Chuck (Charles Edward) 1926– . US rock-and-roll singer, prolific songwriter, and guitarist. His characteristic guitar riffs became staples of rock music, and his humorous storytelling lyrics were also emulated. He had a string of hits in the 1950s and 1960s beginning with 'Maybellene' 1955.

Bertolucci Bernardo 1940– . Italian film director whose work combines political and historical perspectives with an elegant and lyrical visual appeal. His films include *The Spider's Stratagem* 1970, *Last Tango in Paris* 1972, *1900* 1976, *The Last*

Emperor 1987, for which he received an Academy Award, and *The Sheltering Sky* 1990.

Berzelius Jöns Jakob 1779–1848. Swedish chemist who accurately determined more than 2,000 relative atomic and molecular masses. He devised (1813–14) the system of chemical symbols and formulae now in use and proposed oxygen as a reference standard for atomic masses. His discoveries include the elements cerium (1804), selenium (1817), and thorium (1828).

Bessarabia region in SE Europe, divided between Moldova and Ukraine. Bessarabia was annexed by Russia 1812, but broke away at the Russian Revolution to join Romania. The cession was confirmed by the Allies, but not by Russia, in a Paris treaty of 1920; the USSR reoccupied it 1940 and divided it between the Moldavian and Ukrainian republics (now independent Moldova and Ukraine). Romania recognized the position in the 1947 peace treaty.

Bessemer process the first cheap method of making ⬦steel, invented by Henry Bessemer in England 1856. It has since been superseded by more efficient steelmaking processes, such as the basic-oxygen process. In the Bessemer process compressed air is blown into the bottom of a converter, a furnace shaped like a cement mixer, containing molten pig iron. The excess carbon in the iron burns out, other impurities form a slag, and the furnace is emptied by tilting.

beta-blocker any of a class of drugs that block impulses that stimulate certain nerve endings (beta receptors) serving the heart muscles. This reduces the heart rate and the force of contraction, which in turn reduces the amount of oxygen (and therefore the blood supply) required by the heart. Beta-blockers are banned from use in competitive sports. They may be useful in the treatment of angina, arrhythmia, and raised blood pressure, and following myocardial infarctions. They must be withdrawn from use gradually.

beta decay the disintegration of the nucleus of an atom to produce a beta particle, or high-speed electron, and an electron-antineutrino. During beta decay, a proton in the nucleus changes into a neutron, thereby increasing the atomic number by one while the mass number stays the same. The mass lost in the change is converted into kinetic (movement) energy of the beta particle. Beta decay is caused by the weak nuclear force, one of the fundamental ⬦forces of nature operating inside the nucleus.

Betelgeuse or *Alpha Orionis* red supergiant star in the constellation of Orion and the tenth brightest star in the sky, although its brightness varies. It is over 300 times the diameter of the Sun, about the same size as the orbit of Mars, is over 10,000 times as luminous as the Sun, and lies 650 light years from Earth.

betel nut fruit of the areca palm *Areca catechu*, used together with lime and betel pepper as a masticatory stimulant by peoples of the East and Papua New Guinea. Chewing it results in blackened teeth and a mouth stained deep red.

Bethlehem (Hebrew *Beit-Lahm*) town on the W bank of the river Jordan, S of Jerusalem. Occupied by Israel in 1967; population (1980) 14,000. In the Bible it is mentioned as the birthplace of King David and Jesus.

Betjeman John 1906–1984. English poet and essayist, originator of a peculiarly English light verse, nostalgic, and delighting in Victorian and Edwardian architecture. His *Collected Poems* appeared in 1968 and a verse autobiography, *Summoned by Bells*, in 1960. He became poet laureate 1972.

Beuys Joseph 1921–1986. German sculptor and performance artist, one of the leaders of avant-garde art in Europe during the 1970s and 1980s. His sculpture makes use of unusual materials such as felt and fat. He was strongly influenced by his wartime experiences.

Bevan Aneurin (Nye) 1897–1960. British Labour politician, member of Parliament for Ebbw Vale 1929–60. As minister of health 1945–51, he inaugurated the National Health Service (NHS); he was minister of labour Jan–April 1951, when he resigned on the introduction of NHS charges and led a Bevanite faction against the government. He was a good speaker.

Bevin Ernest 1881–1951. British Labour politician. Chief creator of the Transport and General Workers' Union, he was its general secretary from 1921 to 1940, when he entered the war cabinet as minister of labour and national service. He organized the 'Bevin boys', chosen by ballot to work in the coal mines as war service, and was foreign secretary in the Labour government 1945–51.

Bhopal industrial city (textiles, chemicals, electrical goods, jewellery); capital of Madhya Pradesh, central India; population (1981) 672,000. Nearby Bhimbetka Caves, discovered 1973, have the world's largest collection of prehistoric paintings, which are about 10,000 years old. In 1984 some 2,600 people died from an escape of the poisonous gas methyl isocyanate from a factory owned by the US company Union Carbide; another 300,000 suffer long-term health problems.

Bhumibol Adulyadej 1927– . King of Thailand from 1946. Born in the USA and educated in Bangkok and Switzerland, he succeeded to the throne on the assassination of his brother. In 1973 he was active, with popular support, in overthrowing the military government of Marshal Thanom Kittikachorn and thus ended a sequence of army-dominated regimes in power from 1932.

Bhutan Kingdom of; country in SE Asia, bordered N by China and S by India; *area* 46,500 sq km/ 17,954 sq mi; *capital* Thimbu (Thimphu); *physical* occupies southern slopes of the Himalayas; cut by valleys formed by tributaries of the Brahmaputra; thick forests in south; **head of state and government** Jigme Singye Wangchuk from 1972; **political system** absolute monarchy; **exports** timber, talc, fruit and vegetables, cement, distilled spirits, calcium carbide; **population** (1990 est) 1,566,000 (Ngalops and Sharchops 75%, Nepalese 25%); **languages** Dzongkha (official, a Tibetan dialect); Sharchop, Bumthap, Nepali, English; **recent history** first hereditary monarchy installed 1907. National assembly installed 1953; the first cabinet was established 1968. Prodemocracy demonstrations took place 1990.

Bhutto Benazir 1953– . Pakistani politician, leader of the Pakistan People's Party (PPP) from 1984 (in exile until 1986), and prime minister of Pakistan 1988–90, when the opposition manoeuvred her from office and charged her with corruption. In May 1991 new charges were brought against her. She was the first female leader of a Muslim state.

Bhutto Zulfikar Ali 1928–1979. Pakistani politician, president 1971–73; prime minister from 1973 until the 1977 military coup led by General ⊳Zia ul-Haq. In 1978 Bhutto was sentenced to death for conspiring to murder a political opponent and was hanged the following year.

Biafra, Republic of African state proclaimed in 1967 when fears that Nigerian central government was increasingly in the hands of the rival Hausa tribe led the predominantly Ibo Eastern Region of Nigeria to secede under Lt Col Odumegwu Ojukwu. On the proclamation of Biafra, civil war ensued with the rest of the federation. In a bitterly fought campaign federal forces confined the Biafrans to a shrinking area of the interior by 1968, and by 1970 Biafra ceased to exist.

Bible the sacred book of the Jewish and Christian religions. The Hebrew Bible, recognized by both Jews and Christians, is called the ⊳**Old Testament** by Christians. The ⊳**New Testament** comprises books recognized by the Christian church from the 4th century as canonical. The Roman Catholic Bible also includes the ⊳**Apocrypha**.

bicycle pedal-driven two-wheeled vehicle used in ⊳cycling. It consists of a metal frame mounted on two large wire-spoked wheels, with handlebars in front and a seat between the front and back wheels. The bicycle is an energy-efficient, nonpolluting form of transport, and it is estimated that 800 million bicycles are in use throughout the world — twice the number of cars in existence. China, India, Denmark, and the Netherlands are countries with a high use of bicycles. More than 10% of road spending in the Netherlands is on cycleways and bicycle parking.

big-band jazz ⊳swing music created in the late 1930s and 1940s by bands of 13 or more players, such as those of Duke ⊳Ellington and Benny

⊳Goodman. Big-band jazz relied on fixed arrangements, where there is more than one instrument to some of the parts, rather than improvisation. Big bands were mainly dance bands, flourishing at a time when all dance music was live, and they ceased to be economically viable in the 1950s.

Big Bang in astronomy, the hypothetical 'explosive' event that marked the origin of the universe as we know it. At the time of the Big Bang, the entire universe was squeezed into a hot, superdense state. The Big Bang explosion threw this compacted material outwards, producing the expanding universe (see ⊳red shift). The cause of the Big Bang is unknown; observations of the current rate of expansion of the universe suggest that it took place about 15 billion years ago. The Big Bang theory began modern ⊳cosmology.

Big Bang in economics, popular term for the changes instituted in late 1986 to the organization and practices of the City of London as Britain's financial centre, including the liberalization of the London ⊳Stock Exchange. This involved merging the functions of jobber (dealer in stocks and shares) and broker (who mediates between the jobber and the public), introducing negotiated commission rates, and allowing foreign banks and financial companies to own British brokers/jobbers, or themselves to join the London Stock Exchange.

Bihar or **Behar** state of NE India; **area** 173,900 sq km/67,125 sq mi; **capital** Patna; **features** river Ganges in the N, Rajmahal Hills in the south; **products** copper, iron, coal, rice, jute, sugar cane, grain, oilseed; **population** (1991) 86,338,900; **language** Hindi, Bihari; **famous people** Chandragupta, Asoka; **history** the ancient kingdom of Magadha roughly corresponded to central and S Bihar. Many Bihari people were massacred as a result of their protest at the establishment of Bangladesh 1971.

Bihari member of a N Indian people, also living in Bangladesh, Nepal, and Pakistan, and numbering over 40 million. The Bihari are mainly Muslim. The Bihari language is related to Hindi and has several widely varying dialects. It belongs to the Indic branch of the Indo-European family. Many Bihari were massacred during the formation of Bangladesh, which they opposed.

Bikini atoll in the ⊳Marshall Islands, W Pacific, where the USA carried out 23 atomic- and hydrogen-bomb tests (some underwater) 1946–63.

Biko Steve (Stephen) 1946–1977. South African civil-rights leader. An active opponent of ⊳apartheid, he was arrested in Sept 1977; he died in detention six days later. Since his death in the custody of South African police, he has been a symbol of the anti-apartheid movement.

Bilbao industrial port (iron and steel, chemicals, cement, food) in N Spain, capital of Biscay province; population (1991) 372,200.

bilberry several species of shrubs of the genus *Vaccinium* of the heath family Ericaceae, closely related to North American blueberries.

bile brownish fluid produced by the liver. In most vertebrates, it is stored in the gall bladder and emptied into the small intestine as food passes through. Bile consists of bile salts, bile pigments, cholesterol, and lecithin. *Bile salts* assist in the breakdown and absorption of fats; *bile pigments* are the breakdown products of old red blood cells that are passed into the gut to be eliminated with the faeces.

billiards indoor game played, normally by two players, with tapered poles (cues) and composition balls (one red, two white) on a rectangular table covered with a green, feltlike cloth (baize). The table has six pockets, one at each corner and in each of the long sides at the middle. Scoring strokes are made by potting the red ball, potting the opponent's ball, or potting another ball off one of these two. The cannon (when the cue ball hits the two other balls on the table) is another scoring stroke.

bill of exchange form of commercial credit instrument, or IOU, used in international trade. In Britain, a bill of exchange is defined by the Bills of Exchange Act 1882 as an unconditional order in writing addressed by one person to another, signed by the person giving it, requiring the person to whom it is addressed to pay on demand or at a fixed or determinable future time a certain sum in money to or to the order of a specified person, or to the bearer.

bill of lading document giving proof of particular goods having been loaded on a ship. The person to whom the goods are being sent normally needs to show the bill of lading in order to obtain the release of the goods. For air freight, there is an *air waybill.*

Bill of Rights in the USA, the first ten amendments to the US ▷Constitution:
1 guarantees freedom of worship, of speech, of the press, of assembly, and to petition the government;
2 grants the right to keep and bear arms (which has hindered recent attempts to prevent illicit use of arms);
3 prohibits billeting of soldiers in private homes in peacetime;
4 forbids unreasonable search and seizure;
5 guarantees none be 'deprived of life, liberty or property without due process of law' or compelled in any criminal case to be a witness against him- or herself;
6 grants the right to speedy trial, to call witnesses, and to have defence counsel;
7 grants the right to trial by jury of one's peers;
8 prevents the infliction of excessive bail or fines, or 'cruel and unusual punishment';
9, 10 provide a safeguard to the states and people for all rights not specifically delegated to the central government.

Bill of Rights in Britain, an act of Parliament 1689 that established Parliament as the primary governing body of the country. The Bill of Rights embodied the Declarations of Rights which contained the conditions on which William and Mary were offered the throne. It made provisions limiting royal prerogative with respect to legislation, executive power, money levies, courts, and the army and stipulated Parliament's consent to many government functions.

binary fission in biology, a form of ▷asexual reproduction, whereby a single-celled organism, such as the amoeba, divides into two smaller 'daughter' cells. It can also occur in a few simple multicellular organisms, such as sea anemones, producing two smaller sea anemones of equal size.

binary number system or *binary number code* system of numbers to ▷base two, using combinations of the digits 1 and 0. Binary numbers play a key role in digital computers, in which they form the basis of the internal coding of information, the values of ▷bits (short for 'binary digits') being represented as on/off (1 and 0) states of switches and high/low voltages in circuits.

binary star pair of stars moving in orbit around their common centre of mass. Observations show that most stars are binary, or even multiple — for example, the nearest star system to the Sun, ▷Alpha Centauri.

binding energy in phyics, the amount of energy needed to break the nucleus of an atom into the neutrons and protons of which it is made.

binoculars optical instrument for viewing an object in magnification with both eyes; for example, field glasses and opera glasses. Binoculars consist of two telescopes containing lenses and prisms, which produce a stereoscopic effect as well as magnifying the image. Use of prisms has the effect of 'folding' the light path, allowing for a compact design.

binomial in mathematics, an expression consisting of two terms, such as $a + b$ or $a - b$.

binomial system of nomenclature in biology, the system in which all organisms are identified by a two-part Latinized name. Devised by the biologist ▷Linnaeus, it is also known as the Linnaean system. The first name is capitalized and identifies the ▷genus; the second identifies the ▷species within that genus.

biochemistry science concerned with the chemistry of living organisms: the structure and reactions of proteins (such as enzymes), nucleic acids, carbohydrates, and lipids.

biodegradable capable of being broken down by living organisms, principally bacteria and fungi. In biodegradable substances, such as food and sewage, the natural processes of decay lead to compaction and liquefaction, and to the release of nutrients that are then recycled by the ecosystem. Nonbiodegradable substances, such as glass, heavy metals, and most types of plastic, present serious problems of disposal.

bioengineering the application of engineering to biology and medicine. Common applications include the design and use of artificial limbs, joints, and organs, including hip joints and heart valves.

Bioko island in the Bight of Bonny, W Africa, part of Equatorial Guinea; area 2,017 sq km/786 sq mi; products include coffee, cacao, and copra; population (1983) 57,190. Formerly a Spanish possession, as *Fernando Po*, it was known 1973–79 as *Macías Nguema Bijogo*.

biological control control of pests such as insects and fungi through biological means, rather than the use of chemicals. This can include breeding resistant crop strains; inducing sterility in the pest; infecting the pest species with disease organisms; or introducing the pest's natural predator. Biological control tends to be naturally self-regulating, but as ecosystems are so complex, it is difficult to predict all the consequences of introducing a biological controlling agent.

biological warfare the use of living organisms, or of infectious material derived from them, to bring about death or disease in humans, animals, or plants. At least ten countries have this capability.

biology science of life. Strictly speaking, biology includes all the life sciences — for example, anatomy and physiology, cytology, zoology and botany, ecology, genetics, biochemistry and biophysics, animal behaviour, embryology, and plant breeding. During the 1990s an important focus of biological research will be the international Human Genome Project, which will attempt to map the entire genetic code contained in the 23 pairs of human chromosomes.

biomass the total mass of living organisms present in a given area. It may be specified for a particular species (such as earthworm biomass) or for a general category (such as herbivore biomass). Estimates also exist for the entire global plant biomass. Measurements of biomass can be used to study interactions between organisms, the stability of those interactions, and variations in population numbers.

bionics design and development of electronic or mechanical artificial systems that imitate those of living things. The bionic arm, for example, is an artificial limb (⟡prosthesis) that uses electronics to amplify minute electrical signals generated in body muscles to work electric motors, which operate the joints of the fingers and wrist.

biopsy removal of a living tissue sample from the body for diagnostic examination.

biotechnology industrial use of living organisms to manufacture food, drugs, or other products. The brewing and baking industries have long relied on the yeast microorganism for ⟡fermentation purposes, while the dairy industry employs a range of bacteria and fungi to convert milk into cheeses and yoghurts. ⟡Enzymes, whether extracted from cells or produced artificially, are central to most biotechnological applications.

birch any tree of the genus *Betula*, including about 40 species found in cool temperate parts of the northern hemisphere. Birches grow rapidly, and their hard, beautiful wood is used for veneers and cabinet work. The white or silver birch *Betula pendula* is of great use to industry because its timber is quick-growing and durable. The bark is used for tanning and dyeing leather, and an oil is obtained from it.

bird backboned animal of the class Aves, the biggest group of land vertebrates, characterized by warm blood, feathers, wings, breathing through lungs, and egg-laying by the female. There are nearly 8,500 species of birds, ranging from the largest living bird, the N African ostrich, which can reach a height of 2.74 m/9 ft and a weight of 156 kg/345 lb, to the smallest bird, the bee hummingbird of Cuba and the Isle of Pines, which measures 57 mm/2.24 in in length and weighs a mere 1.6 g/0.056 oz.

bird of paradise one of 40 species of crowlike birds, family Paradiseidae, native to New Guinea and neighbouring islands. Females are drably coloured, but the males have bright and elaborate plumage used in courtship display. Hunted almost to extinction for their plumage, they are now subject to conservation.

Birendra Bir Bikram Shah Dev 1945– . King of Nepal from 1972, when he succeeded his father Mahendra; he was formally crowned 1975. King Birendra has overseen Nepal's return to multiparty politics and introduced a new constitution 1990.

Birmingham industrial city in the West Midlands, second largest city of the UK; population (1991 est) 934,900, metropolitan area 2,632,000. Industries include motor vehicles, machine tools, aerospace control systems, plastics, chemicals, and food.

Birmingham commercial and industrial city (iron, steel, chemicals, building materials, computers, cotton textiles) and largest city in Alabama, USA; population (1990) 266,000.

birth control another name for ⟡family planning; see also ⟡contraceptive.

birth rate the number of live births per 1,000 of the population of an area over the period of a year. Birth rate is a factor in ⟡demographic transition. It is sometimes called *crude birth rate* because it takes in the whole population, including men and women who are too old to bear children. In the 20th century, the UK's birth rate has fallen from 28 per 1,000 to below 10 per 1,000 owing to increased use of contraception, better living standards, and falling infant mortality. The birth rate remains high in poor countries.

Biscay, Bay of bay of the Atlantic Ocean between N Spain and W France, known for rough seas and exceptionally high tides.

Bismarck Otto Eduard Leopold, Prince von 1815–1898. German politician, prime minister of Prussia 1862–90 and chancellor of the German Empire 1871–90. He pursued an aggressively expansionist policy, waging wars against Denmark 1863–64, Austria 1866, and France 1870–71, which brought about the unification of Germany.

Bismarck Archipelago group of over 200 islands in SW Pacific Ocean, part of ⏀Papua New Guinea; area 49,660 sq km/19,200 sq mi. The largest island is New Britain.

bismuth hard, brittle, pinkish-white, metallic element, symbol Bi, atomic number 83, relative atomic mass 208.98. It has the highest atomic number of all the stable elements (the elements from atomic number 84 up are radioactive). Bismuth occurs in ores and occasionally as a free metal (⏀native metal). It is a poor conductor of heat and electricity, and is used in alloys of low melting point and in medical compounds to soothe gastric ulcers.

bison large, hoofed mammal of the bovine family. There are two species, both brown. The *European bison* or *wisent Bison bonasus*, of which only a few protected herds survive, is about 2 m/7 ft high and weighs up to 1,100 kg/2,500 lb. The *North American bison* (often known as 'buffalo') *Bison bison* is slightly smaller, with a heavier mane and more sloping hindquarters. Formerly roaming the prairies in vast numbers, it was almost exterminated in the 19th century, but survives in protected areas.

Bissau capital and chief port of Guinea-Bissau, on an island at the mouth of the Geba river; population (1988) 125,000. Originally a fortified slave-trading centre, Bissau became a free port 1869.

bit in computing, the smallest unit of information; a binary digit or place in a binary number. A ⏀byte contains eight bits (four bits is sometimes called a nybble).

bittern any of several small herons, in particular the common bittern *Botaurus stellaris* of Europe and Asia. It is shy, stoutly built, has a streaked camouflage pattern and a loud, booming call. An inhabitant of marshy country, it is now quite rare in Britain.

bitumen impure mixture of hydrocarbons, including such deposits as petroleum, asphalt, and natural gas, although sometimes the term is restricted to a soft kind of pitch resembling asphalt.

bivalve marine or freshwater mollusc whose body is enclosed between two shells hinged together by a ligament on the dorsal side of the body.

Bizet Georges (Alexandre César Léopold) 1838–1875. French composer of operas, among them *Les Pêcheurs de perles/The Pearl Fishers* 1863, *La jolie Fille de Perth/The Fair Maid of Perth* 1866, and *Carmen* 1875. He also wrote the concert overture *Patrie* and incidental music to Alphonse Daudet's *L'Arlésienne*.

black English term first used 1625 to describe West Africans, now used to refer to Africans south of the Sahara and to people of African descent living outside Africa. In some countries such as the UK (but not in North America) the term is sometimes also used for people originally from the Indian subcontinent, for Australian Aborigines, and peoples of Melanesia.

Black Joseph 1728–1799. Scottish physicist and chemist who in 1754 discovered carbon dioxide (which he called 'fixed air'). By his investigations in 1761 of latent heat and specific heat, he laid the foundation for the work of his pupil James Watt.

Black and Tans nickname of a special auxiliary force of the Royal Irish Constabulary employed by the British 1920–21 to combat the Sinn Féiners (Irish nationalists) in Ireland; the name derives from the colours of the uniforms, khaki with black hats and belts.

blackberry prickly shrub *Rubus fruticosus* of the rose family, closely allied to raspberries and dewberries, that is native to northern parts of Europe. It produces pink or white blossoms and edible, black, compound fruits.

blackbird bird *Turdus merula* of the thrush family. The male is black with a yellow bill and eyelids, the female dark brown with a dark beak. About 25 cm/10 in long, it lays three to five blue-green eggs with brown spots. Its song is rich and flutelike.

black body in physics, a hypothetical object that completely absorbs all thermal (heat) radiation striking it. It is also a perfect emitter of thermal radiation.

black box popular name for the unit containing an aeroplane's flight and voice recorders. These monitor the plane's behaviour and the crew's conversation, thus providing valuable clues to the cause of a disaster. The box is nearly indestructible and usually painted orange for easy recovery. The name also refers to any compact electronic device that can be quickly connected or disconnected as a unit.

Blackburn industrial town (engineering) in Lancashire, England, 32 km/20 mi NW of Manchester; population (1981) 88,000.

Black Country central area of England, around and to the N of Birmingham. Heavily industrialized, it gained its name in the 19th century from its belching chimneys, but antipollution laws have changed its aspect.

blackcurrant variety of ⏀currant.

Black Death great epidemic of bubonic ⏀plague that ravaged Europe in the 14th century, killing between one-third and half of the population. The cause of the plague was the bacterium *Pasteurella pestis*, transmitted by fleas borne by migrating Asian black rats. The name Black Death was first used in England in the early 19th century.

blackfly plant-sucking insect, a type of ▷aphid.

Black Forest (German *Schwarzwald*) mountainous region of coniferous forest in Baden-Württemberg, W Germany. Bounded W and S by the Rhine, which separates it from the Vosges, it has an area of 4,660 sq km/1,800 sq mi and rises to 1,493 m/4,905 ft in the Feldberg. Parts of the forest have recently been affected by ▷acid rain.

black hole object in space whose gravity is so great that nothing can escape from it, not even light. Thought to form when massive stars shrink at the ends of their lives, a black hole sucks in more matter, including other stars, from the space around it. Matter that falls into a black hole is squeezed to infinite density at the centre of the hole. Black holes can be detected because gas falling towards them becomes so hot that it emits X-rays.

Black Muslim member of a religious group founded 1929 in the USA and led, from 1934, by Elijah Muhammad (then Elijah Poole) (1897–1975) after he had a vision of ▷Allah. Its growth from 1946 as a black separatist organization was due to Malcolm X (1926–1965), the son of a Baptist minister who, in 1964, broke away and founded his own Organization for Afro-American Unity, preaching 'active self-defence'. Under the leadership of Louis Farrakhan, the movement underwent a recent revival.

Black National State area in the Republic of South Africa set aside for development towards self-government by black Africans in accordance with ▷apartheid. Before 1980 these areas were known as *black homelands* or *bantustans*. They make up less than 14% of the country and tend to be in arid areas (though some have mineral wealth), and may be in scattered blocks. Those that achieved nominal independence are Transkei 1976, Bophuthatswana 1977, Venda 1979, and Ciskei 1981. They are not recognized outside South Africa owing to their racial basis.

Blackpool seaside resort in Lancashire, England, 45 km/28 mi N of Liverpool; population (1981) 148,000. The largest holiday resort in N England, the amusement facilities include 11 km/7 mi of promenades, known for their 'illuminations' of coloured lights, funfairs, and a tower 152 m/500 ft high. Political party conferences are often held here.

Black Power movement towards black separatism in the USA during the 1960s, embodied in the *Black Panther Party* founded 1966 by Huey Newton and Bobby Seale. Its declared aim was the establishment of a separate black state in the USA established by a black plebiscite under the aegis of the United Nations. Following a National Black Political Convention 1972, a National Black Assembly was established to exercise pressure on the Democratic and Republican parties.

Black Prince nickname of ▷Edward, Prince of Wales, eldest son of Edward III of England.

Black Sea (Russian *Chernoye More*) inland sea in SE Europe, linked with the seas of Azov and Marmara, and via the Dardanelles with the Mediterranean. Uranium deposits beneath it are among the world's largest.

Blackshirts term widely used to describe fascist paramilitary organizations. Originating with Mussolini's fascist Squadristi in the 1920s, it was also applied to the Nazi SS (*Schutzstaffel*) and to the followers of Oswald Mosley's British Union of Fascists.

blackthorn densely branched spiny European bush *Prunus spinosa*, family Rosaceae. It produces white blossom on black and leafless branches in early spring. Its sour, plumlike, blue-black fruit, the sloc, is used to flavour gin.

black widow North American spider *Latrodectus mactans*. The male is small and harmless, but the female is 1.3 cm/0.5 in long with a red patch below the abdomen and a powerful venomous bite. The bite causes pain and fever in human victims, but they usually recover.

bladder hollow elastic-walled organ in the ▷urinary systems of some fishes, most amphibians, some reptiles, and all mammals. Urine enters the bladder through two ureters, one leading from each kidney, and leaves it through the urethra.

bladderwort any of a large genus *Utricularia* of carnivorous aquatic plants of the family Lentibulariaceae. They have leaves with bladders that entrap small aquatic animals.

Blake William 1757–1827. English poet, artist, engraver, and visionary. His lyrics, as in *Songs of Innocence* 1789 and *Songs of Experience* 1794 express spiritual wisdom in radiant imagery and symbolism. Prophetic books like *The Marriage of Heaven and Hell* 1790, *America* 1793, and *Milton* 1804 yield their meaning to careful study. He created a new composite art form in engraving and hand-colouring his own works.

blank verse in literature, the unrhymed iambic pentameter or ten-syllable line of five stresses. First used by the Italian Gian Giorgio Trissino in his tragedy *Sofonisba* 1514–15, it was introduced to England about 1540 by the Earl of Surrey, and developed by Christopher Marlowe. More recent exponents of blank verse in English include Thomas Hardy, T S Eliot, and Robert Frost.

blasphemy written or spoken insult directed against religious belief or sacred things with deliberate intent to outrage believers. Blasphemy against Christianity is still an offence in English common law, despite several recommendations (for example by the Law Commission 1985) that the law of blasphemy should be abolished or widened to apply to all religious faiths.

blastula early stage in the development of a fertilized egg, when the egg changes from a solid mass of cells (the morula) to a hollow ball of cells (the blastula), containing a fluid-filled cavity (the blastocoel).

Blaue Reiter, der (German 'the Blue Rider') group of German Expressionist painters based in Munich, some of whom had left *die* ⟡*Brücke*. They were interested in the value of colours, in folk art, and in the necessity of painting 'the inner, spiritual side of nature', but styles were highly varied. Wassily Kandinsky and Franz Marc published a book of their views 1912, and there were two exhibitions 1911, 1912.

bleaching decolorization of coloured materials. The two main types of bleaching agent are the *oxidizing bleaches*, which bring about the ⟡oxidation of pigments, and include the ultraviolet rays in sunshine, hydrogen peroxide, and chlorine in household bleaches; and the *reducing bleaches*, which bring about ⟡reduction, and include sulphur dioxide.

Blenheim, Battle of battle on 13 Aug 1704 in which English troops under ⟡Marlborough defeated the French and Bavarian armies near the Bavarian village of Blenheim (now in west Germany) on the left bank of the Danube.

Blériot Louis 1872–1936. French aviator who, in a 24–horsepower monoplane of his own construction, made the first flight across the English Channel on 25 July 1909.

Bligh William 1754–1817. English sailor who accompanied Captain James ⟡Cook on his second voyage around the world 1772–74, and in 1787 commanded HMS *Bounty* on an expedition to the Pacific. On the return voyage the crew mutinied 1789, and Bligh was cast adrift in a boat with 18 men. He was appointed governor of New South Wales 1805, where his discipline again provoked a mutiny 1808 (the Rum Rebellion). He returned to Britain, and was made an admiral 1811.

blight any of a number of plant diseases caused mainly by parasitic species of ⟡fungus, which produce a whitish appearance on leaf and stem surfaces – for instance *potato blight Phytophthora infestans*. General damage caused by aphids or pollution is sometimes known as blight.

blimp airship: any self-propelled, lighter-than-air craft that can be steered. A blimp with a soft frame is also called a *dirigible*; a *zeppelin* is rigid-framed.

blindness complete absence or impairment of sight. It may be caused by heredity, accident, disease, or deterioration with age. Aids under development include electronic devices that convert print to recognizable mechanical speech, and sonic torches.

blind spot area where the optic nerve and blood vessels pass through the retina of the ⟡eye. No visual image can be formed as there are no light-sensitive cells in this part of the retina.

Blitzkrieg (German 'lightning war') swift military campaign, as used by Germany at the beginning of World War II 1939–41. The abbreviated *Blitz* was applied to the attempted saturation bombing of London by the German air force between Sept 1940 and May 1941.

Blixen Karen, born Karen Dinesen 1885–1962. Danish writer. Her autobiography *Out of Africa* 1937 is based on her experience of running a coffee plantation in Kenya. She wrote fiction, mainly in English, under the pen name Isak Dinesen.

Bloch Felix 1905–1983. Swiss-US physicist who invented the analytical technique of nuclear magnetic resonance (NMR) ⟡spectroscopy 1946. For this work he shared the Nobel Prize for Physics 1952 with US physicist Edward Purcell (1912–   ).

blockade cutting-off of a place by hostile forces by land, sea, or air so as to prevent any movement to or fro, in order to compel a surrender without attack or to achieve some other political aim (for example, the ⟡Berlin blockade 1948).

Bloemfontein capital of the Orange Free State and judicial capital of the Republic of South Africa; population (1985) 204,000. Founded 1846, the city produces canned fruit, glassware, furniture, and plastics.

blood liquid circulating in the arteries, veins, and capillaries of vertebrate animals; the term also refers to the corresponding fluid in those invertebrates that possess a closed ⟡circulatory system. Blood carries nutrients and oxygen to individual cells and removes waste products, such as carbon dioxide. It is also important in the immune response and, in many animals, in the distribution of heat throughout the body.

blood clotting complex series of events that prevents excessive bleeding after injury. The result is the formation of a meshwork of protein fibres (fibrin) and trapped blood cells over the cut blood vessels.

blood group any of the blood groups into which blood is classified according to antigenic activity. Red blood cells of one individual may carry molecules on their surface that act as ⟡antigens in another individual whose red blood cells lack these molecules. The two main antigens are designated A and B. These give rise to four blood groups: having A only (A), having B only (B), having both (AB), and having neither (O). Each of these groups may or may not contain the ⟡rhesus factor. Correct typing of blood groups is vital in transfusion, since incompatible types of donor and recipient blood will result in blood clotting, with possible death of the recipient.

bloodhound ancient breed of dog. Black and tan in colour, it has long, pendulous ears and distinctive wrinkled head and face. It grows to a height of about 65 cm/26 in at the shoulder. The breed originated as a hunting dog in Belgium in the Middle Ages, and its excellent powers of scent have been employed

blood

red cells

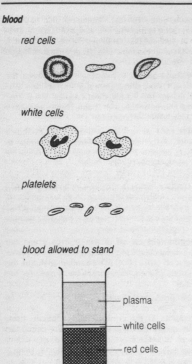

white cells

platelets

blood allowed to stand

- plasma
- white cells
- red cells

in tracking and criminal detection from very early times.

blood pressure pressure, or tension, of the blood against the inner walls of blood vessels, especially the arteries, due to the muscular pumping activity of the heart. Abnormally high blood pressure (see ◊hypertension) may be associated with various conditions or arise with no obvious cause; abnormally low blood pressure (hypotension) occurs in ◊shock and after excessive fluid or blood loss from any cause.

blood vessel specialist tube that carries blood around the body of multicellular animals. Blood vessels are highly evolved in vertebrates where the three main types, the arteries, veins, and capillaries, are all adapted for their particular role within the body.

Bloomsbury Group group of writers and artists based in Bloomsbury, London. The group included the artists Duncan ◊Grant and Vanessa Bell, and the writers Lytton ◊Strachey and Leonard (1880–1969) and Virginia ◊Woolf.

blowfly any fly of the genus *Calliphora*, also known as bluebottle, or of the related genus *Lucilia*, when it is greenbottle. It lays its eggs in dead flesh, on which the maggots feed.

Blücher Gebhard Leberecht von 1742–1819. Prussian general and field marshal, popularly known as 'Marshal Forward'. He took an active part in the patriotic movement, and in the War of German Liberation defeated the French as commander in chief at Leipzig 1813, crossed the Rhine to Paris 1814, and was made prince of Wahlstadt (Silesia).

bluebell name given in Scotland to the harebell *Campanula rotundifolia*, and in England to the wild hyacinth *Endymion nonscriptus*, belonging to the family Liliaceae.

blueberry any of various North American acid-soil shrubs of the genus *Vaccinium* of the heath family. The genus also includes huckleberries, bilberries, deerberries, and cranberries, many of which resemble each other and are difficult to distinguish from blueberries. All have small, elliptical short-stalked leaves, slender green or reddish twigs, and whitish bell-like blossoms. Only true blueberries, however, have tiny granular speckles on their twigs. Blueberries have black or blue edible fruits, often covered with a white powder.

bluebird three species of a North American bird, genus *Sialia*, belonging to the thrush subfamily, Turdinae. The eastern bluebird *Sialia sialis* is regarded as the herald of spring. About 18 cm/7 in long, it has a reddish breast, the upper plumage being sky-blue, and a distinctive song.

blue chip in business and finance, a stock that is considered strong and reliable in terms of the dividend yield and capital value. Blue-chip companies are favoured by stock-market investors more interested in security than in risk-taking.

bluegrass dense, spreading grass of the genus *Poa*, which is bluetinted and grows in clumps. Various species are known from the northern hemisphere. Kentucky bluegrass *P. pratensis*, introduced to the USA from Europe, provides pasture for horses.

blue-green algae or *cyanobacteria* single-celled, primitive organisms that resemble bacteria in their internal cell organization, sometimes joined together in colonies or filaments. Blue-green algae are among the oldest known living organisms and, with bacteria, belong to the kingdom Monera; remains have been found in rocks up to 3.5 billion years old. They are widely distributed in aquatic habitats, on the damp surfaces of rocks and trees, and in the soil.

blue gum either of two Australian trees: Tasmanian blue gum *Eucalyptus globulus* of the myrtle family, with bluish bark, a chief source of eucalyptus oil, or Sydney blue gum *E. saligna*, a tall, straight tree. The former is cultivated extensively in California and has also been planted in South America, India, parts of Africa, and S Europe.

Blue Mountains part of the ◊Great Dividing Range, New South Wales, Australia, ranging 600–1,100 m/2,000–3,600 ft and blocking Sydney from the interior until the crossing 1813 by surveyor William Lawson, Gregory Blaxland, and William Wentworth.

Blue Nile (Arabic *Bahr el Azraq*) river rising in the mountains of Ethiopia. Flowing W then N for 2,000 km/1,250 mi, it eventually meets the White Nile at Khartoum. The river is dammed at Roseires where a hydroelectric scheme produces 70% of Sudan's electricity.

Blue Ridge Mountains range extending from West Virginia to Georgia, USA, and including Mount Mitchell 2,045 m/6,712 ft; part of the ⟡Appalachians.

blues African-American music that originated in the rural American South in the late 19th century, characterized by a 12–bar construction and frequently melancholy lyrics. Blues guitar and vocal styles have played a vital part in the development of jazz and pop music in general.

blue shift in astronomy, a manifestation of the ⟡Doppler effect in which an object appears bluer when it is moving towards the observer or the observer is moving towards it (blue light is of a higher frequency than other colours in the spectrum). The blue shift is the opposite of the ⟡red shift.

Blunt Anthony 1907–1983. British art historian and double agent. As a Cambridge lecturer, he recruited for the Soviet secret service and, as a member of the British Secret Service 1940–45, passed information to the USSR. In 1951 he assisted the defection to the USSR of the British agents Guy ⟡Burgess and Donald Maclean (1913–1983). He was the author of many respected works on French and Italian art. Unmasked 1964, he was given immunity after his confession.

boa any of various nonvenomous snakes of the family Boidae, found mainly in tropical and subtropical parts of the New World. Boas feed mainly on small mammals and birds. They catch these in their teeth or kill them by constriction (crushing the creature within their coils until it suffocates). The boa constrictor *Constrictor constrictor* can grow up to 5.5 m/18.5 ft long, but rarely reaches more than 4 m/12Yft. Other boas include the anaconda and the emerald tree boa *Boa canina*, about 2 m/6 ft long and bright green.

Boadicea alternative spelling of British queen ⟡Boudicca.

boar wild member of the pig family, such as the Eurasian wild boar *Sus scrofa*, from which domestic pig breeds derive. The wild boar is sturdily built, being 1.5 m/4.5 ft long and 1 m/3 ft high, and possesses formidable tusks. Of gregarious nature and mainly woodland-dwelling, it feeds on roots, nuts, insects, and some carrion.

boat people illegal emigrants arriving by sea, especially those Vietnamese who left their country after the takeover of South Vietnam 1975 by North Vietnam. Some 160,000 Vietnamese fled to Hong Kong, many being attacked at sea by Thai pirates, and in 1989 50,000 remained there in cramped, squalid refugee camps. The UK government began forced repatriation 1990.

Boat Race annual UK rowing race between the crews of Oxford and Cambridge universities. It is held during the Easter vacation over a 6.8 km/4.25 mi course on the river Thames between Putney and Mortlake, SW London.

bobcat cat *Felis rufa* living in a variety of habitats from S Canada through to S Mexico. It is similar to the lynx, but only 75 cm/2.5 ft long, with reddish fur and less well-developed ear tufts.

bobsleighing or ***bobsledding*** sport of racing steel-bodied, steerable toboggans, crewed by two or four people, down mountain ice chutes at speeds of up to 130 kph/80 mph. It was introduced as an Olympic event 1924 and world championships have been held every year since 1931. Included among the major bobsleighing events are the Olympic Championships (the four-crew event was introduced at the 1924 Winter Olympics and the two-crew 1932) and the World Championships, the four-crew championship introduced in 1924 and the two-crew in 1931. In Olympic years winners automatically become world champions.

Boccaccio Giovanni 1313–1375. Italian poet, chiefly known for the collection of tales called the *Decameron* 1348–53.

Bodhidharma 6th century AD. Indian Buddhist and teacher. He entered China from S India about 520, and was the founder of the Ch'an school (⟡Zen is the Japanese derivation). Ch'an focuses on contemplation leading to intuitive meditation, a direct pointing to and stilling of the human mind.

bodhisattva in Mahāyāna Buddhism, someone who seeks enlightenment in order to help other living beings. A bodhisattva is free to enter ⟡nirvana but voluntarily chooses to be reborn until all other beings have attained that state.

Boeotia ancient district of central Greece, of which ⟡Thebes was the chief city. The *Boeotian League* (formed by 10 city states in the 6th century BC) superseded ⟡Sparta in the leadership of Greece in the 4th century BC.

Boer Dutch settler or descendant of Dutch and Huguenot settlers in South Africa.

Boer War the second of the ⟡South African Wars 1889–1902, waged between the Dutch settlers in South Africa and the British.

Boethius Anicius Manilus Severinus AD 480–524. Roman philosopher. While imprisoned on suspicion of treason by the emperor Theodoric the Great, he wrote treatises on music and mathematics and *De Consolatione Philosophiae/The Consolation of Philosophy*, a dialogue in prose. It was translated into European languages during the Middle Ages;

English translations by Alfred the Great, Geoffrey Chaucer, and Queen Elizabeth I.

bog type of wetland where decomposition is slowed down and dead plant matter accumulates as ⟡peat. Bogs develop under conditions of low temperature, high acidity, low nutrient supply, stagnant water, and oxygen deficiency. The typical bog plant is sphagnum moss; rushes, cranberry, and cotton grass also grow under these conditions; insectivorous plants such as sundews and bladderworts are common in bogs (insect prey make up for the lack of nutrients).

Bogarde Dirk. Stage name of Derek van den Bogaerde 1921– . English actor who appeared in comedies and adventure films such as *Doctor in the House* 1954 and *Campbell's Kingdom* 1957, before acquiring international recognition for complex roles in Joseph Losey's *The Servant* 1963 and *Accident* 1967, and Luchino Visconti's *Death in Venice* 1971.

Bogart Humphrey 1899–1957. US film actor who achieved fame as the gangster in *The Petrified Forest* 1936. He became an international cult figure as the tough, romantic 'loner' in such films as *The Maltese Falcon* 1941 and *Casablanca* 1943, a status resurrected in the 1960s and still celebrated today. He won an Academy Award for his role in *The African Queen* 1952.

Bogotá capital of Colombia, South America; 2,640 m/8,660 ft above sea level on the edge of the plateau of the E Cordillera; population (1985) 4,185,000. It was founded 1538.

Bohemia area of W Czechoslovakia, a kingdom of central Europe from the 9th century. It was under Habsburg rule 1526–1918, when it was included in Czechoslovakia. The name Bohemia derives from the Celtic Boii, its earliest known inhabitants.

boil small abscess originating around a hair follicle or in a sweat gland, most likely to form if resistance is low or diet inadequate.

boiler any vessel that converts water into steam. Boilers are used in conventional power stations to generate steam to feed steam ⟡turbines, which drive the electricity generators. They are also used in steamships, which are propelled by steam turbines, and in steam locomotives. Every boiler has a furnace in which fuel (coal, oil, or gas) is burned to produce hot gases, and a system of tubes in which heat is transferred from the gases to the water.

boiling point for any given liquid, the temperature at which the application of heat raises the temperature of the liquid no further, but converts it into vapour.

Bokassa Jean-Bédel 1921– . President of the Central African Republic 1966–79 and later self-proclaimed emperor 1977–79. Commander in chief from 1963, in Dec 1965 he led the military coup that gave him the presidency. On 4 Dec 1976 he proclaimed the Central African Empire and one

year later crowned himself as emperor for life. His regime was characterized by arbitrary state violence and cruelty. Overthrown in 1979, Bokassa was in exile until 1986. Upon his return he was sentenced to death, but this was commuted to life imprisonment 1988.

boletus genus of fleshy fungi belonging to the class Basidiomycetes, with thick stems and caps of various colours. The European *Boletus edulis* is edible, but some species are poisonous.

Boleyn Anne 1507–1536. Queen of England, the woman for whom Henry VIII broke with the pope and founded the Church of England (see ⟡Reformation). Second wife of Henry, she was married to him 1533 and gave birth to the future Queen Elizabeth I in the same year. Accused of adultery and incest with her half-brother (a charge invented by Thomas ⟡Cromwell), she was beheaded.

Bolger Jim (James) Brendan 1935– . New Zealand politician and prime minister from 1990. A successful sheep and cattle farmer, Bolger was elected to Parliament 1972. He held a variety of cabinet posts under Robert Muldoon's leadership 1977–84, and was an effective, if uncharismatic, leader of the opposition from March 1986, taking the National Party to electoral victory Oct 1990.

Bolingbroke title of Henry of Bolingbroke, ⟡Henry IV of England.

Bolingbroke Henry John, Viscount Bolingbroke 1678–1751. British Tory politician and political philosopher. He was foreign secretary 1710–14 and a Jacobite conspirator. He went into exile 1714, returning 1723, when he worked to overthrow Robert Walpole. His books, such as *Idea of a Patriot King* 1738 and *The Dissertation upon Parties* 1735, laid the foundations for 19th-century Toryism.

Bolívar Símon 1783–1830. South American nationalist, leader of revolutionary armies, known as *the Liberator*. He fought the Spanish colonial forces in several uprisings and eventually liberated his native Venezuela 1821, Colombia and Ecuador 1822, Peru 1824, and Bolivia (a new state named after him, formerly Upper Peru) 1825.

Bolivia Republic of; country in South America, bordered N and E by Brazil, SE by Paraguay, S by Argentina, and W by Chile and Peru; *area* 1,098,581 sq km/424,052 sq mi; *capital* La Paz (seat of government), Sucre (legal capital and seat of judiciary); *physical* high plateau of the Andes in the west between mountain ridges (the Altiplano), forest and lowlands in the east; lakes Titicaca and Poopó; *head of state and government* Jaime Paz Zamora from 1989; *political system* emergent democratic republic; *exports* tin, antimony (world's second largest producer), other nonferrous metals, oil, gas (piped to Argentina), agricultural products, coffee, sugar, cotton; *population* (1990 est) 6,730,000 (Quechua 25%, Aymara 17%, mestizo (mixed race) 30%, European 14%); *languages* Spanish, Aymara, Quechua (all official); *recent history* liberated from Spanish rule by Simón Bolívar 1825; name changed from Upper Peru to Bolivia. The country has suffered from repeated army coups to overthrow elected presidents, including the uprising by Che Guevara 1967. A worsening economy has made necessary economic aid from the USA and Europe.

Bolkiah Hassanal 1946– . Sultan of Brunei from 1967, following the abdication of his father, Omar Ali Saifuddin (1916–1986). As absolute ruler, Bolkiah also assumed the posts of prime minister and defence minister on independence 1984.

Böll Heinrich 1917–1985. German novelist. A radical Catholic and anti-Nazi, he attacked Germany's political past and the materialism of its contemporary society. His many publications include poems, short stories, and novels which satirized West German society, for example *Billard um Halbzehn/Billiards at Half-Past Nine* 1959 and *Gruppenbild mit Dame/Group Portrait with Lady* 1971. Nobel Prize for Literature 1972.

boll weevil small American beetle *Anthonomus grandis* of the weevil group. The female lays her eggs in the unripe pods or 'bolls' of the cotton plant, and on these the larvae feed, causing great destruction.

Bologna industrial city and capital of Emilia-Romagna, Italy, 80 km/50 mi north of Florence; population (1988) 427,000. It was the site of an Etruscan town, later of a Roman colony, and became a republic in the 12th century. It came under papal rule 1506 and was united with Italy 1860.

Bolshevik member of the majority of the Russian Social Democratic Party who split from the ⬦Mensheviks 1903. The Bolsheviks, under ⬦Lenin, advocated the destruction of capitalist political and economic institutions, and the setting-up of a socialist state with power in the hands of the workers. The Bolsheviks set the ⬦Russian Revolution 1917 in motion. They changed their name to the Russian Communist Party 1918.

Boltzmann constant in physics, the constant (symbol k) that relates the kinetic energy (energy of motion) of a gas atom or molecule to temperature. Its value is 1.380662×10^{-23} joules per Kelvin. It is equal to the gas constant R, divided by ⬦Avogadro's number.

bomb container filled with explosive or chemical material and generally used in warfare. There are also incendiary bombs and nuclear bombs and missiles (see ⬦nuclear warfare). Any object designed to cause damage by explosion can be called a bomb (car bombs, letter bombs). Initially dropped from aeroplanes (from World War I), bombs were in World War II also launched by rocket. The 1960s saw the development of missiles that could be launched from aircraft, land sites, or submarines. In the 1970s laser guidance systems were developed to hit small targets with accuracy.

Bombay industrial port (textiles, engineering, pharmaceuticals, diamonds), commercial centre, and capital of Maharashtra, W India; population (1981) 8,227,000. It is the centre of the Hindi film industry.

Bombay duck or *bummalo* small fish *Harpodon nehereus* found in the Indian Ocean. It has a thin body, up to 40 cm/16 in long, and sharp, pointed teeth. It feeds on shellfish and other small fish. It is valuable as a food fish, and is eaten, salted and dried, with dishes such as curry.

Bonaparte Corsican family of Italian origin that gave rise to the Napoleonic dynasty: see ⬦Napoleon I, ⬦Napoleon II, and ⬦Napoleon III. Others were the brothers and sister of Napoleon I: *Joseph* (1768–1844) whom Napoleon made king of Naples 1806 and Spain 1808; *Lucien* (1775–1840) whose handling of the Council of Five Hundred on 10 Nov 1799 ensured Napoleon's future; *Louis* (1778–1846) the father of Napoleon III, who was made king of Holland 1806–10; *Caroline* (1782–1839) who married Joachim Murat 1800; *Jerome* (1784–1860) made king of Westphalia 1807.

Bonar Law British Conservative politician; see ⬦Law, Andrew Bonar.

bond in chemistry, the result of the forces of attraction that hold together atoms of an element or elements to form a molecule. The principal types of bonding are ionic, covalent, metallic, and intermolecular (such as hydrogen bonding).

bond in commerce, a security issued by a government, local authority, company, bank, or other institution on fixed interest. Usually a long-term security, a bond may be irredeemable (with no date of redemption), secured (giving the investor a claim on the company's property or on a part of its assets), or unsecured (not protected by a lien).

Bond Alan 1938– . English-born Australian entrepreneur. He was chair of the Bond Corporation 1969–90 during the years when its aggressive takeover strategy gave the company interests in brewing, the media, mining, and retailing. The collapse of the Bond empire 1990 left thousands of investors impoverished and shook both Australian and international business confidence. Declared bankrupt April 1992 with debts of at least $10 million, Bond was imprisoned on criminal charges relating to the collapse of an Australian merchant bank.

Bond Edward 1935– . English dramatist. His early work aroused controversy because of the savagery of some of his imagery, for example, the stoning of a baby by bored youths in *Saved* 1965. Other works include *Early Morning* 1968, the last play to be banned in the UK by the Lord Chamberlain; *Lear* 1972, a reworking of Shakespeare's play; *Bingo* 1973, an account of Shakespeare's last days; and *The War Plays* 1985.

bone hard connective tissue comprising the ⇨skeleton of most vertebrate animals. It consists of a network of collagen fibres impregnated with inorganic salts, especially calcium phosphate. Enclosed within this solid matrix are bone cells, blood vessels, and nerves.

bone marrow substance found inside the cavity of bones. In early life it produces red blood cells but later on lipids (fat) accumulate and its colour changes from red to yellow.

bonito any of various species of medium-sized tuna, predatory fish of the genus *Sarda*, in the mackerel family. The ocean bonito *Katsuwonus pelamis* grows to 1 m/3 ft and is common in tropical seas. The Atlantic bonito *Sarda sarda* is found in the Mediterranean and tropical Atlantic and grows to the same length but has a narrower body.

Bonn industrial city (chemicals, textiles, plastics, aluminium) and seat of government of the Federal Republic of Germany, 18 km/15 mi SSE of Cologne, on the left bank of the Rhine; population (1988) 292,000.

Bonnard Pierre 1867–1947. French Post-Impressionist painter. With other members of *les Nabis*, he explored the decorative arts (posters, stained glass, furniture). He painted domestic interiors and nudes.

Bonnie Prince Charlie Scottish name for ⇨Charles Edward Stuart, pretender to the throne.

booby tropical seabird of the genus *Sula*, in the same family, Sulidae, as the northern ⇨gannet. There are six species, including the circumtropical brown booby *Sula leucogaster*. They inhabit coastal waters, and dive to catch fish. The name was given by sailors who saw the bird's tameness as stupidity.

boogie-woogie jazz played on the piano, using a repeated motif for the left hand. It was common in the USA from around 1900 to the 1950s. Boogie-woogie players included Pinetop Smith (1904–1929), Meade 'Lux' Lewis (1905–1964), and Jimmy Yancey (1898–1951). Rock-and-roll pianists like Jerry Lee Lewis adapted the style.

book portable written record. Substances used to make early books included leaves, bark, linen, silk, clay, leather, and papyrus. In about AD 100–150, the codex or paged book, as opposed to the roll or scroll, began to be adopted. Vellum (parchment of calfskin, lambskin, or kidskin) was generally used for book pages by the beginning of the 4th century, and its use lasted until the 15th. It was superseded by paper, which came to Europe from China (where it was made as early as AD 105, a mixture of bark and hemp fibres). Books only became widely available after the invention of the ⇨printing press in the 15th century. Printed text is also reproduced and stored in ⇨microform.

book-keeping process of recording commercial transactions in a systematic and established procedure. These records provide the basis for the

borage

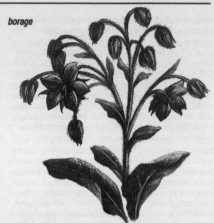

preparation of accounts. The earliest known work on double-entry book-keeping, a system in which each item of a business transaction is entered twice – as debit and as credit – was by Luca Pacioli, published in Venice 1494. The method had, however, been practised by Italian merchants for several hundred years before that date.

booklouse any of numerous species of tiny wingless insects of the order Psocoptera, especially *Atropus pulsatoria*, which live in books and papers, feeding on starches and moulds.

Boole George 1815–1864. English mathematician whose work *The Mathematical Analysis of Logic* 1847 established the basis of modern mathematical logic, and whose **Boolean algebra** can be used in designing computers.

boomerang hand-thrown, flat wooden hunting missile shaped in a curved angle, formerly used throughout the world but developed by the Australian Aborigines to a great degree of diversity and elaboration. It is used to kill game and as a weapon or, in the case of the returning boomerang, for recreation.

Boone Daniel 1734–1820. US pioneer who explored the Wilderness Road (East Virginia–Kentucky) 1775 and paved the way for the first westward migration of settlers.

boot or **bootstrap** in computing, the process of starting up a computer. Most computers have a small, built-in boot program that starts automatically when the computer is switched on — its only task is to load a slightly larger program, usually from a disc, which in turn loads the main ⇨operating system. In microcomputers the operating system is often held in the permanent ⇨ROM memory and the boot program simply triggers its operation.

Booth William 1829–1912. British founder of the Salvation Army 1878, and its first 'general'. His wife Catherine (1829–1890, born Mumford) and their eldest son, *William Bramwell Booth* (1856–1929), also played active roles in the organization.

bootlegging illegal manufacture, distribution, or sale of a product. The term originated in the USA, when the sale of alcohol to American Indians was illegal and bottles were hidden for sale in the legs of the jackboots of unscrupulous traders. The term was later used for all illegal liquor sales during the period of ◊Prohibition in the USA 1920–33, and is often applied to unauthorized commercial tape recordings and the copying of computer software.

Bophuthatswana Republic of; self-governing black 'homeland' within South Africa; *area* 40,330 sq km/15,571 sq mi; *capital* Mmbatho or Sun City, a casino resort frequented by many white South Africans; *features* divided into six 'blocks'; *exports* platinum, chromium, vanadium, asbestos, manganese; *currency* South African rand; *population* (1985) 1,627,000; *language* Setswana, English; *religion* Christian; *government* executive president elected by the Assembly: Chief Lucas Mangope; *recent history* first 'independent' Black National State from 1977, but not recognized by any country other than South Africa.

borage salad plant *Borago officinalis* native to S Europe and used in salads and medicinally. It has small blue flowers and hairy leaves. It is cultivated in Britain and occasionally naturalized.

Bordeaux port on the Garonne, capital of Aquitaine, SW France, a centre for the wine trade, oil refining, and aeronautics and space industries; population (1982) 640,000. Bordeaux was under the English crown for three centuries until 1453. In 1870, 1914, and 1940 the French government was moved here because of German invasion.

Border Allan 1955– . Australian cricketer, captain of the Australian team from 1985. He has played for Australia (New South Wales and Queensland) since 1978, and in England for Gloucestershire and Essex. He holds the world record (1992) for appearances in test matches (125) and one-day internationals (223).

Borders region of Scotland. *area* 4,700 sq km/ 1,815 sq mi; *towns* Newtown St Boswells (administrative headquarters), Hawick, Jedburgh; *features* river Tweed; Lammermuir, Moorfoot, and Pentland hills; home of the novelist Walter Scott at Abbotsford; Dryburgh Abbey, burial place of Field Marshal Haig and Scott; ruins of 12th-century Melrose Abbey; *products* knitted goods, tweed, electronics, timber; *population* (1991) 102,600; *famous people* Duns Scotus, James Murray, Mungo Park.

bore surge of tidal water up an estuary or a river, caused by the funnelling of the rising tide by a narrowing river mouth. A very high tide, possibly fanned by wind, may build up when it is held back by a river current in the river mouth. The result is a broken wave, a metre or a few feet high, that rushes upstream.

Borg Björn 1956– . Swedish tennis player who won the men's singles title at Wimbledon five times 1976–80, a record since the abolition of the challenge system 1922. He also won six French Open singles titles 1974–75 and 1978–81 inclusive.

Borges Jorge Luis 1899–1986. Argentine poet and short-story writer, an exponent of ◊magic realism. In 1961 he became director of the National Library, Buenos Aires, and was professor of English literature at the university there. He is known for his fantastic and paradoxical work *Ficciones/ Fictions* 1944.

Borgia Cesare 1476–1507. Italian general, illegitimate son of Pope ◊Alexander VI. Made a cardinal at 17 by his father, he resigned to become captain-general of the papacy, campaigning successfully against the city republics of Italy. Ruthless and treacherous in war, he was an able ruler (the model for Machiavelli's *The Prince*), but his power crumbled on the death of his father. He was a patron of artists, including Leonardo da Vinci.

Borgia Lucrezia 1480–1519. Duchess of Ferrara from 1501. She was the illegitimate daughter of Pope ◊Alexander VI and sister of Cesare Borgia. She was married at 12 and again at 13 to further her father's ambitions, both marriages being annulled by him. At 18 she was married again, but her husband was murdered 1500 on the order of her brother, with whom (as well as with her father) she was said to have committed incest. Her final marriage was to the duke of Este, the son and heir of the duke of Ferrara. She made the court a centre of culture and was a patron of authors and artists such as Ariosto and Titian.

Boris III 1894–1943. Tsar of Bulgaria from 1918, when he succeeded his father, Ferdinand I. From 1934 he was virtual dictator until his sudden and mysterious death following a visit to Hitler. His son Simeon II was tsar until deposed 1946.

Boris Godunov 1552–1605. See ◊Godunov Boris, tsar of Russia from 1598.

Bormann Martin 1900–1945. German Nazi leader. He took part in the abortive Munich putsch (uprising) 1923 and rose to high positions in the Nazi (National Socialist) Party, becoming party chancellor May 1941.

Born Max 1882–1970. German physicist who received a Nobel prize 1954 for fundamental work on the ◊quantum theory. He left Germany for the UK during the Nazi era.

Borneo third largest island in the world, one of the Sunda Islands in the W Pacific; area 754,000 sq km/ 290,000 sq mi. It comprises the Malaysian territories of ◊*Sabah* and ◊*Sarawak*; ◊*Brunei*; and, occupying by far the largest part, the Indonesian territory of ◊*Kalimantan*. It is mountainous and densely forested. In coastal areas the people of Borneo are mainly of Malaysian origin, with a few Chinese, and the interior is inhabited by the indigenous Dyaks. It was formerly under both Dutch

and British colonial influence until Sarawak was formed 1841.

boron nonmetallic element, symbol B, atomic number 5, relative atomic mass 10.811. In nature it is found only in compounds, as with sodium and oxygen in borax. It exists in two allotropic forms: brown amorphous powder and very hard, brilliant crystals. Its compounds are used in the preparation of boric acid, water softeners, soaps, enamels, glass, and pottery glazes. In alloys it is used to harden steel. Because it absorbs slow neutrons, it is used to make boron carbide control rods for nuclear reactors. It is a necessary trace element in the human diet. The element was named by Humphry Davy, who isolated it 1808, from *bor*ax + -on, as in carb*on*.

borough unit of local government in the UK from the 8th century until 1974, when it continued as an honorary status granted by royal charter to a district council, entitling its leader to the title of mayor.

Borromini Francesco 1599–1667. Italian Baroque architect, one of the two most important (with ◊Bernini, his main rival) in 17th-century Rome. Whereas Bernini designed in a florid, expansive style, his pupil Borromini developed a highly idiosyncratic and austere use of the Classical language of architecture. His genius may be seen in the cathedrals of San Carlo 1641 and San Ivo 1660, and the oratorio of St Filippo Neri 1650.

borstal in the UK, formerly a place of detention for offenders aged 15–21. The name was taken from Borstal prison near Rochester, Kent, where the system was first introduced 1908. From 1983 borstal institutions were officially known as youth custody centres, and were in 1988 replaced by *young offender institutions*.

borzoi large breed of dog originating in Russia, 75 cm/2.5 ft or more at the shoulder. It is of the greyhound type, white with darker markings, with a thick, silky coat.

Bosch Hieronymus (Jerome) 1460–1516. Early Netherlandish painter. His fantastic visions of weird and hellish creatures, as shown in *The Garden of Earthly Delights* about 1505–10 (Prado, Madrid), show astonishing imagination and a complex imagery. His religious subjects focused not on the holy figures but on the mass of ordinary witnesses, placing the religious event in a contemporary Netherlandish context and creating cruel caricatures of human sinfulness.

Bosnia-Herzegovina Republic of; country in central Europe bordered N and W by Croatia, E by the Yugoslavian republic of Serbia, and E and S by the Yugoslavian republic of Montenegro; *area* 51,000 sq km/19,725 sq mi; *capital* Sarajevo; *physical* barren, mountainous country, part of the Dinaric Alps, limestone gorge; *population* (1986) 4,360,000; *political system* emergent democracy; *head of state* Alija Izetbegović from 1990; *products* citrus fruits and vegetables; iron, steel, and leather goods; *language* Serbian variant of Serbo-Croat; *recent history* became a constituent republic of Yugoslavia 1945; ruling communists routed by nationalists in elections 1990; Serbia-Croatia conflict spread into Bosnia-Herzegovina with the predominantly Serb Yugoslav army taking border areas from 1991 onwards. The republic declared its sovereignty but this was rejected by the Serbs, who wished to remain in the rump Yugoslav federation 1991. Violent ethnic clashes ensued centring on the capital. The EC and the USA officially recognized Bosnia's independence in April 1992, but violence continued to escalate.

boson in physics, an elementary particle whose spin can only take values that are whole numbers or zero. Bosons may be classified as ◊gauge bosons (carriers of the four fundamental forces) or ◊mesons. All elementary particles are either bosons or ◊fermions.

Bosporus (Turkish *Karadeniz Boğazı*) strait 27 km/17 mi long, joining the Black Sea with the Sea of Marmara and forming part of the water division between Europe and Asia; its name may be derived from the Greek legend of Io. Istanbul stands on its W side. The *Bosporus Bridge* 1973, 1,621 m/5,320 ft, links Istanbul and Turkey-in-Asia. In 1988 a second bridge across the straits was opened, linking Asia and Europe.

Boston industrial and commercial centre, capital of Massachusetts, USA; population (1990) 574,300; metropolitan area 4,171,600. It is a publishing centre and industrial port on Massachusetts Bay, but the economy is dominated by financial and health services and government. Boston and Northeastern universities are here; Harvard University and the Massachusetts Institute of Technology are in neighbouring Cambridge, across the Charles River.

Boston Tea Party protest 1773 against the British

tea tax imposed on colonists in Massachusetts, America, before the ▷American Revolution.

Boswell James 1740–1795. Scottish biographer and diarist. He was a member of Samuel ▷Johnson's London Literary Club and the two men travelled to Scotland together 1773, as recorded in Boswell's *Journal of the Tour to the Hebrides* 1785. His classic English biography *Life of Samuel Johnson* was published 1791.

Bosworth, Battle of last battle of the Wars of the ▷Roses, fought on 22 Aug 1485. Richard III, the Yorkist king, was defeated and slain by Henry of Richmond, who became Henry VII. The battlefield is near the village of Market Bosworth, 19 km/12 mi W of Leicester, England.

botany the study of plants. It is subdivided into a number of specialized studies, such as the identification and classification of plants (taxonomy), their external formation (plant morphology), their internal arrangement (plant anatomy), their microscopic examination (plant histology), their functioning and life history (plant physiology), and their distribution over the Earth's surface in relation to their surroundings (plant ecology). Palaeobotany concerns the study of fossil plants, while economic botany deals with the utility of plants. Horticulture, agriculture, and forestry are branches of botany.

Botany Bay inlet on the E coast of Australia, 8 km/5 mi S of Sydney, New South Wales. Chosen 1787 as the site for a penal colony, it proved unsuitable. Sydney now stands on the site of the former settlement. The name Botany Bay continued to be popularly used for any convict settlement in Australia.

Botha Louis 1862–1919. South African soldier and politician, a commander in the Second South African War (Boer War). In 1907 Botha became premier of the Transvaal and in 1910 of the first Union South African government. On the outbreak of World War I 1914 he rallied South Africa to the Commonwealth, suppressed a Boer revolt, and conquered German South West Africa.

Botha P(ieter) W(illem) 1916– . South African politician, prime minister from 1978. Botha initiated a modification of ▷apartheid, which later slowed in the face of Afrikaner (Boer) opposition. In 1984 he became the first executive state president. In 1989 he unwillingly resigned both party leadership and presidency after suffering a stroke, and was succeeded by F W de Klerk.

Botham Ian (Terrence) 1955– . English cricketer whose test record places him among the world's greatest all-rounders. He has played county cricket for Somerset, Worcestershire, and Durham as well as playing in Australia. He played for England 1977–89 and returned to the England side 1991.

Bothwell James Hepburn, 4th Earl of Bothwell *c*. 1536–1578. Scottish nobleman, third husband of ▷Mary Queen of Scots, 1567–70, alleged to have arranged the explosion that killed Darnley, her previous husband, 1567.

bo tree or *peepul* Indian ▷fig tree *Ficus religiosa*, said to be the tree under which the Buddha became enlightened.

Botswana Republic of; country in central southern Africa, bordered S and E by South Africa, W and N by Namibia, and NE by Zimbabwe; *area* 582,000 sq km/225,000 sq mi; *capital* Gaborone; *physical* Kalahari Desert in SW, plains in E, fertile lands and Okavango Swamp, remarkable for its wildlife, in N; *head of state and government* Quett Ketamile Joni Masire from 1980; *political system* democratic republic; *exports* diamonds (world's third largest producer), copper, nickel, meat products, textiles; *population* (1990 est) 1,218,000 (Bamangwato 80%, Bangwaketse 20%); *languages* English (official); Setswana (national); *recent history* became a British protectorate 1885. Independence achieved 1966 and new constitution came into effect; name changed from Bechuanaland to Botswana. Since independence Botswana has earned a reputation for stability.

Botticelli Sandro 1445–1510. Florentine painter of religious and mythological subjects. He was patronized by the ruling ▷Medici family, for whom he painted *Primavera* 1478 and *The Birth of Venus* about 1482–84 (both in the Uffizi, Florence). From the 1490s he was influenced by the religious fanatic ▷Savonarola and developed a harshly expressive and emotional style.

botulism rare, often fatal type of ▷food poisoning. Symptoms include muscular paralysis and disturbed breathing and vision. It is caused by a toxin produced by the bacterium *Clostridium botulinum*, sometimes found in improperly canned food.

Boudicca Queen of the Iceni (native Britons), often referred to by the Latin form *Boadicea*. Her husband, King Prasutagus, had been a tributary of the Romans, but on his death AD 60 the territory of the Iceni was violently annexed. Boudicca was scourged and her daughters raped. Boudicca raised the whole of SE England in revolt, and before the main Roman armies could return from campaigning in Wales she burned London, St Albans, and Colchester. Later the Romans under governor Suetonius Paulinus defeated the British between London and Chester; they were virtually annihilated and Boudicca poisoned herself.

bougainvillea any plant of the genus of South American tropical vines *Bougainvillea*, of the four o'clock family Nyctaginaceae, now cultivated in warm countries throughout the world for the red and purple bracts that cover the flowers. They are named after the French navigator Louis Bougainville.

Boulez Pierre 1925– . French composer and conductor. He studied with ▷Messiaen and promoted contemporary music with a series of innovative *Domaine Musical* concerts and recordings in the 1950s, as conductor of the BBC Symphony and New York Philharmonic orchestras during the 1970s, and as founder and director of IRCAM, a music research studio in Paris opened 1977.

Boumédienne Houari. Adopted name of Mohammed Boukharouba 1925–1978. Algerian politician who brought the nationalist leader Ben Bella to power by a revolt 1962, and superseded him as president in 1965 by a further coup.

Boundary Peak highest mountain in Nevada, USA, rising to 4,006 m/13,143 ft on the Nevada–California frontier.

Bounty, Mutiny on the naval mutiny in the Pacific 1789 against British captain William ⟡Bligh.

Bourbon dynasty French royal house (succeeding that of Valois) beginning with Henry IV, and ending with Louis XVI, with a brief revival under Louis XVIII, Charles X, and Louis Philippe. The Bourbons also ruled Spain almost uninterruptedly from Philip V to Alfonso XIII and were restored in 1975 (⟡Juan Carlos); at one point they also ruled Naples and several Italian duchies. The Grand Duke of Luxembourg is also a Bourbon by male descent.

Bourdon gauge instrument for measuring pressure, invented by Eugène Bourdon 1849. The gauge contains a C-shaped tube, closed at one end. When the pressure inside the tube increases, the tube uncurls slightly causing a small movement at its closed end. A system of levers and gears magnifies this movement and turns a pointer, which indicates the pressure on a circular scale. Bourdon gauges are often fitted to cylinders of compressed gas used in industry and hospitals.

bourgeoisie (French) the middle classes. The French word originally meant 'the freemen of a borough'. It came to mean the whole class above the workers and peasants, and below the nobility. Bourgeoisie (and *bourgeois*) has also acquired a contemptuous sense, implying commonplace, philistine respectability. By socialists it is applied to the whole propertied class, as distinct from the proletariat.

Bourgogne region of France that includes the *départements* of Côte-d'Or, Nièvre, Sâone-et-Loire, and Yonne; area 31,600 sq km/12,198 sq mi; population (1986) 1,607,000. Its capital is Dijon. It is renowned for its wines, such as Chablis and Nuits-Saint-Georges, and for its cattle (the Charolais herd-book is maintained at Nevers). A former independent kingdom and duchy (English name ⟡Burgundy), it was incorporated into France 1477.

Bournonville August 1805–1879. Danish dancer and choreographer. He worked with the Royal Danish Ballet for most of his life, giving Danish ballet a worldwide importance. His ballets, many

of which have been revived in the last 50 years, include *La Sylphide* 1836 (music by Lövenskjöld) and *Napoli* 1842.

bovine spongiform encephalopathy (BSE) disease of cattle, allied to scrapie, that renders the brain spongy and may drive an animal mad. It has been identified only in the UK, where more than 26,000 cases had been confirmed between the first diagnosis Nov 1986 and April 1991. The organism causing it is unknown; it is not a conventional virus because it is more resistant to chemicals and heat, cannot be seen even under an electron microscope, cannot be grown in tissue culture, and does not appear to provoke an immune response in the body. BSE is very similar to, and may be related to, Creutzfeld-Jakob disease and kuru, which affect humans.

bower bird New Guinean and N Australian bird of the family Ptilonorhynchidae, related to the ⟡birds of paradise. The males are dull-coloured, and build elaborate bowers of sticks and grass, decorated with shells, feathers, or flowers, and even painted with the juice of berries, to attract the females. There are 17 species.

bowfin North American fish *Amia calva* with a swim bladder highly developed as an air sac, enabling it to breathe air. It is the only surviving member of a primitive group of bony fishes.

Bowie David. Stage name of David Jones 1947– . British pop singer, songwriter, and actor. He became a glam-rock star with the release of the album *The Rise and Fall of Ziggy Stardust and the Spiders from Mars* 1972, and collaborated in the mid-1970s with the electronic virtuoso Brian Eno (1948–) and Iggy Pop. He has also acted in plays and films, including Nicolas Roeg's *The Man Who Fell to Earth* 1976.

bowls outdoor and indoor game popular in Commonwealth countries. It has been played in Britain since the 13th century at least and was popularized by Francis Drake, who is reputed to have played bowls on Plymouth Hoe as the Spanish Armada approached 1588. There are two popular forms: *lawn bowls*, played on a flat surface, and *crown green bowls*, played on a rink with undulations and a crown at the centre of the green. The World Championship was first held in 1966 for men and in 1969 for women.

box any of several small evergreen trees and shrubs, genus *Buxus*, of the family Buxaceae, with small, leathery leaves. Some species are used as hedge plants and for shaping into garden ornaments.

boxer breed of dog, about 60 cm/2 ft tall, with a smooth coat and a set-back nose. The tail is usually docked. Boxers are usually brown but may be brindled or white.

Boxer member of the *I ho ch'üan* ('Righteous Harmonious Fists'), a society of Chinese nationalists dedicated to fighting European influence. The *Boxer Rebellion* or *Uprising* 1900 was instigated by the Dowager Empress Tzu Hsi (1834–1908). European and US legations in Beijing were besieged and thousands of Chinese Christian converts and missionaries murdered. An international punitive force was dispatched, Beijing was captured 14 Aug 1900, and China agreed to pay a large indemnity.

boxing fighting with gloved fists, almost entirely a male sport. The sport dates from the 18th century, when fights were fought with bare knuckles and untimed rounds. Each round ended with a knockdown. Fighting with gloves became the accepted form in the latter part of the 19th century after the formulation of the Queensberry Rules 1867.

Boycott Geoffrey 1940– . English cricketer born in Yorkshire. He was England's most prolific run-maker with 8,114 runs in test cricket until overtaken by David Gower in 1992. He was banned as a test player in 1982 for taking part in matches against South Africa.

Boyle Robert 1627–1691. Irish physicist and chemist who published the seminal *The Sceptical Chymist* 1661. He formulated *Boyle's law* 1662. He was the first chemist to collect a sample of gas, and was one of the founders of the Royal Society.

Boyle's law law stating that the volume of a given mass of gas at a constant temperature is inversely proportional to its pressure. For example, if the pressure of a gas doubles, its volume will be reduced by half, and vice versa.

Boyne, Battle of the battle fought 1 July 1690 in E Ireland, in which James II was defeated by William III and fled to France. It was the decisive battle of the War of English Succession, confirming a Protestant monarch. It took its name from the river Boyne which rises in County Kildare and flows 110 km/69 mi NE to the Irish Sea.

Brabant (Flemish *Braband*) former duchy of W Europe, comprising the Dutch province of ◇North Brabant and the Belgian provinces of Brabant and Antwerp. They were divided when Belgium became independent 1830. The present-day Belgian province of Brabant has an area of 3,400 sq km/1,312 sq mi and a population (1987) of 2,245,900.

bracken large fern, especially *Pteridium aquilinum*, abundant in the northern hemisphere. A perennial rootstock throws up coarse fronds.

bract leaflike structure in whose axil a flower or inflorescence develops. Bracts are generally green and smaller than the true leaves. However, in some plants they may be brightly coloured and conspicuous, taking over the role of attracting pollinating insects to the flowers, whose own petals are small; examples include poinsettia *Euphorbia pulcherrima* and bougainvillea.

Bradbury Malcolm 1932– . British novelist and critic whose writings include comic and satiric portrayals of academic life. He became professor of American studies at the University of East Anglia 1970, and his major work is *The History Man* 1975, set in a provincial English university. Other works include *Rates of Exchange* 1983.

Bradford industrial city (engineering, machine tools, electronics, printing) in West Yorkshire, England, 14 km/9 mi W of Leeds; population (1981) 281,000. It has the National Museum of Photography, Film, and Television 1983 (with Britain's largest cinema screen 14 x 20 m). From the 13th century, Bradford developed as a great wool- and, later, cloth-manufacturing centre, but the industry declined from the 1970s.

Bradman Donald George 1908– . Australian test cricketer with the highest average in test history. From 52 test matches he averaged 99.94 runs per innings. He only needed four runs from his final test innings to average 100 but was dismissed second ball.

Bragança capital of a province of the same name in NE Portugal, 176 km/110 mi NE of Oporto. Population (1981) 13,900. It was the original family seat of the House of Braganza which ruled Portugal 1640–1910.

Braganza the royal house of Portugal whose members reigned 1640–1910; another branch were emperors of Brazil 1822–89.

Brahma in Hinduism, the creator of the cosmos, who forms with Vishnu and Siva the Trimurti, or three aspects of the absolute spirit.

Brahman in Hinduism, the supreme being, an abstract, impersonal world-soul into whom the atman, or individual soul, will eventually be absorbed when its cycle of rebirth is ended.

Brahmaputra river in Asia 2,900 km/1,800 mi long, a tributary of the Ganges.

Brahms Johannes 1833–1897. German composer, pianist, and conductor. Considered one of the greatest composers of symphonic music and of songs, his works include four symphonies; ◇lieder (songs); concertos for piano and for violin; chamber music; sonatas; and the choral *A German Requiem* 1868. He performed and conducted his own works.

Braille system of writing for the blind. Letters are represented by a combination of raised dots on paper or other materials, which are then read by touch. It was invented 1829 by Louis *Braille* (1809–1852).

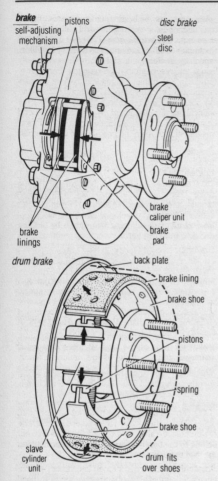

brake
self-adjusting
mechanism
pistons
disc brake
steel
disc
brake
caliper unit
brake
pad
brake
linings
drum brake
back plate
brake lining
brake shoe
pistons
spring
brake shoe
slave
cylinder
unit
drum fits
over shoes

brain in higher animals, a mass of interconnected ⟡nerve cells, forming the anterior part of the ⟡central nervous system, whose activities it coordinates and controls. In ⟡vertebrates, the brain is contained by the skull. An enlarged portion of the upper spinal cord, the *medulla oblongata*, contains centres for the control of respiration, heartbeat rate and strength, and blood pressure. Overlying this is the *cerebellum*, which is concerned with coordinating complex muscular processes such as maintaining posture and moving limbs. The cerebral hemispheres (*cerebrum*) are paired outgrowths of the front end of the forebrain, in higher vertebrates, greatly developed and involved in the integration of all sensory input and motor output, and in intelligent behaviour.

brake device used to slow down or stop the movement of a moving body or vehicle. The mechanically applied caliper brake used on bicycles uses a scissor action to press hard rubber blocks against the wheel rim. The main braking system of a car works hydraulically: when the driver depresses the brake pedal, liquid pressure forces pistons to apply brakes on each wheel.

Bramah Joseph 1748–1814. British inventor of a flushing water closet 1778, an 'unpickable' lock 1784, and the hydraulic press 1795. The press made use of ⟡Pascal's principle (that pressure in fluid contained in a vessel is evenly distributed) and employed water as the hydraulic fluid; it enabled the 19th-century bridge-builders to lift massive girders.

Bramante Donato *c.* 1444–1514. Italian Renaissance architect and artist. Inspired by Classical designs, he was employed by Pope Julius II in rebuilding the Vatican and St Peter's in Rome.

bramble any prickly bush of a genus *Rubus* belonging to the rose family Rosaceae. Examples are ⟡blackberry, raspberry, and dewberry.

Brancusi Constantin 1876–1957. Romanian sculptor, active in Paris from 1904, a pioneer of abstract forms and conceptual art. He developed increasingly simplified natural or organic forms, such as the sculpted head that gradually came to resemble an egg (*Sleeping Muse* 1910, Musée National d'Art Moderne, Paris).

Brandenburg administrative *Land* (state) of Germany; *area* 25,000 sq km/10,000 sq mi; *capital* Potsdam; *towns* Cottbus, Brandenburg, Frankfurt-on-Oder; *products* iron and steel, paper, pulp, metal products, semiconductors; *population* (1990) 2,700,000; *history* the Hohenzollern rulers who took control of Brandenburg in 1415 later acquired the powerful duchy of Prussia and became emperors of Germany. At the end of World War II, Brandenburg lost over 12,950 sq km/5,000 sq mi of territory when Poland advanced its frontier to the line of the Oder and Neisse rivers. The remainder, which became a region of East Germany, was divided 1952 into the districts of Frankfurt-on-Oder, Potsdam, and Cottbus. When Germany was reunited 1990, Brandenburg reappeared as a state of the Federal Republic.

Brando Marlon 1924– . US actor whose casual style, mumbling speech, and use of ⟡Method acting earned him a place as a distinctive actor. He won best-actor Academy Awards for *On the Waterfront* 1954 and *The Godfather* 1972.

Brandt Willy. Adopted name of Karl Herbert Frahm 1913– . German socialist politician, federal chancellor (premier) of West Germany 1969–74. He played a key role in the remoulding of the Social Democratic Party (SPD) as a moderate socialist force (leader 1964–87). As mayor of West Berlin 1957–66, Brandt became internationally known during the Berlin Wall crisis 1961. Nobel Peace Prize 1971.

brandy alcoholic drink distilled from fermented grape juice (wine). The best-known examples are produced in France, notably Armagnac and Cognac. Brandy can also be prepared from other fruits, for example, apples (Calvados) and cherries (Kirschwasser). Brandies contain up to 55% alcohol.

Branson Richard 1950– . British entrepreneur whose Virgin company developed quickly, diversifying from retailing records to the airline business.

Braque Georges 1882–1963. French painter who, with Picasso, founded the Cubist movement around 1907–10. They worked together at L'Estaque in the south of France and in Paris. Braque began to experiment in collages and invented a technique of gluing paper, wood, and other materials to canvas. His later work became more decorative.

Brasília capital of Brazil from 1960, 1,000 m/ 3,000 ft above sea level; population (1991) 1,841,000. It was designed by Lucio Costa (1902–1963), with Oscar Niemeyer as chief architect, as a completely new city to bring life to the interior.

brass metal ◊alloy of copper and zinc, with not more than 5% or 6% of other metals. The zinc content ranges from 20% to 45%, and the colour of brass varies accordingly from coppery to whitish yellow. Brasses are characterized by the ease with which they may be shaped and machined; they are strong and ductile, resist many forms of corrosion, and are used for electrical fittings, ammunition cases, screws, household fittings, and ornaments.

brass instrument in music, any instrument made of brass or other metal that is directly blown through a 'cup' or 'funnel' mouthpiece. Brass instruments include trumpet, trombone, tuba, French horn, cornet, and flugelhorn.

Bratislava (German *Pressburg*) industrial port (engineering, chemicals, oil refining) in Czechoslovakia, on the river Danube; population (1991) 441,500. It was the capital of Hungary 1526–1784 and is now capital of the Slovak Socialist Republic and second largest city in Czechoslovakia.

Brazil Federative Republic of; country in South America, bordered SW by Uruguay, Argentina, Paraguay, and Bolivia; W by Peru and Colombia; N by Venezuela, Guyana, Surinam, and French Guiana; and E by the Atlantic Ocean; *area* 8,511,965 sq km/3,285,618 sq mi; *capital* Brasília; *physical* densely forested Amazon basin covers northern half of the country with a network of rivers; south is fertile; enormous energy resources both hydroelectric and nuclear (uranium ore); *head of state and government* Fernando Afonso Collor de Mello from 1989; *political system* emergent democratic federal republic; *exports* coffee, sugar, soya beans, cotton, textiles, timber, motor vehicles, iron, chrome, manganese, tungsten and other ores, as well as quartz crystals, industrial diamonds, gemstones; world's sixth largest arms exporter; *population* (1990 est) 153,770,000 (including 200,000 Indians, survivors of 5 million, especially in Rondonia and Mato Grosso, mostly living on reservations); *languages* Portuguese (official); 120 Indian languages; *recent history* independence achieved from Portugal 1822; monarchy abolished and republic established 1889. Free political parties abolished by President General Castelo Branco 1964; legalized again 1979. Power was transferred from the president to the congress 1988.

Brazil nut seed, rich in oil and highly nutritious, of the gigantic South American tree *Bertholletia excelsa*. The seeds are enclosed in a hard outer casing, each fruit containing 10–20 seeds arranged like the segments of an orange. The timber of the tree is also valuable.

brazing method of joining two metals by melting an ◊alloy into the joint. It is similar to soldering but takes place at a much higher temperature. Copper and silver alloys are widely used for brazing, at temperatures up to about 900°C/1,650°F.

Brazzaville capital of the Congo, industrial port (foundries, railway repairs, shipbuilding, shoes, soap, furniture, bricks) on the river Zaîre, opposite Kinshasa; population (1984) 595,000. There is a cathedral 1892 and the Pasteur Institute 1908. It stands on Pool Malebo (Stanley Pool).

breadfruit fruit of the tropical trees *Artocarpus communis* and *A. altilis* of the mulberry family Moraceae. It is highly nutritious and when baked is said to taste like bread. It is native to many South Pacific islands.

bream deep-bodied, flattened fish *Abramis brama* of the carp family, growing to about 50 cm/1.6 ft, typically found in lowland rivers across Europe. The sea breams are also deep-bodied flattened fish, but belong to the family Sparidae, and are unrelated to the true breams.

Breathalyzer trademark for an instrument indicating the amount of alcohol in a person's system, used by police to check suspect drivers. The suspect breathes into a plastic bag connected to a tube containing a chemical (such as diluted solution of potassium dichromate in 50% sulphuric acid) that changes colour in the presence of alcohol. Breath testing was introduced in the UK in 1967.

breathing in terrestrial animals, the muscular movements whereby air is taken into the lungs and then expelled, a form of gas exchange. Breathing is sometimes referred to as external respiration, for true respiration is a cellular (internal) process.

Brecht Bertolt 1898–1956. German dramatist and poet who aimed to destroy the 'suspension of disbelief' usual in the theatre and to express Marxist ideas. He adapted John Gay's *Beggar's Opera* as *Die Dreigroschenoper/The Threepenny Opera* 1928, set to music by Kurt Weill. Later plays include *Mutter Courage/Mother Courage* 1941, set during the Thirty Years' War, and *Der kaukasische Kreidekreis/The Caucasian Chalk Circle* 1949.

Bremen industrial port (iron, steel, oil refining, chemicals, aircraft, shipbuilding, cars) in Germany, on the Weser 69 km/43 mi from the open sea; population (1988) 522,000.

Brenner Pass lowest of the Alpine passes, 1,370 m/4,495 ft; it leads from Trentino–Alto Adige, Italy, to the Austrian Tirol, and is 19 km/12 mi long.

Brest naval base and industrial port (electronics, engineering, chemicals) on *Rade de Brest* (Brest Roads), a great bay at the western extremity of Bretagne, France; population (1983) 201,000. Occupied as a U-boat base by the Germans 1940–44, the town was destroyed by Allied bombing and rebuilt.

Bretagne region of NW France, see ▷Brittany.

Breton André 1896–1966. French author, among the leaders of the ▷Dada art movement. *Les Champs magnétiques/Magnetic Fields* 1921, an experiment in automatic writing, was one of the products of the movement. He was also a founder of ▷Surrealism, publishing *Le Manifeste de surréalisme/Surrealist Manifesto* 1924. Other works include *Najda* 1928, the story of his love affair with a medium.

Breton language member of the Celtic branch of the Indo-European language family; the language of Brittany in France, related to Welsh and Cornish, and descended from the speech of Celts who left Britain as a consequence of the Anglo Saxon invasions of the 5th and 6th centuries. Officially neglected for centuries, Breton is now a recognized language of France.

Bretton Woods Conference the United Nations Monetary and Financial Conference 1944, which led to the creation 1945 of the International Monetary Fund and the International Bank for Reconstruction and Development.

Breuer Marcel 1902–1981. Hungarian-born architect and designer who studied and taught at the ▷Bauhaus school in Germany. His tubular steel chair 1925 was the first of its kind. He moved to England, then to the USA, where he was in partnership with Walter Gropius 1937–40. His buildings show an affinity with natural materials; the best known is the Bijenkorf, Rotterdam, the Netherlands (with Elzas) 1953.

brewing making of beer, ale, or other alcoholic beverage from ▷malt and ▷barley by steeping (mashing), boiling, and fermenting.

Brezhnev Leonid Ilyich 1906–1982. Soviet leader. A protégé of Stalin and Khrushchev, he came to power (after he and ▷Kosygin forced Khrushchev to resign) as general secretary of the Soviet Communist Party (CPSU) 1964–82 and was president 1977–82. Domestically he was conservative; abroad the USSR was established as a military and political superpower during the Brezhnev era, extending its influence in Africa and Asia.

Brian known as *Brian Boru* ('Brian of the Tribute') 926–1014. High king of Ireland from 976, who took Munster, Leinster, and Connacht to become ruler of all Ireland. He defeated the Norse at Clontarf, thus ending Norse control of Dublin, although he was himself killed. He was the last high king with jurisdiction over most of Scotland. His exploits were celebrated in several chronicles.

brick common building material, rectangular in shape, made of clay that has been fired in a kiln. Bricks are made by kneading a mixture of crushed clay and other materials into a stiff mud and extruding it into a ribbon. The ribbon is cut into individual bricks, which are fired at a temperature of up to about 1,000°C/1,800°F. Bricks may alternatively be pressed into shape in moulds.

bridge structure that provides a continuous path or road over water, valleys, ravines, or above other roads. The basic designs and composites of these are based on the way they bear the weight of the structure and its load. *Beam*, or *girder*, bridges are supported at each end by the ground with the weight thrusting downwards. *Cantilever* bridges are a complex form of girder. *Arch* bridges thrust outwards but downwards at their ends; they are in compression. *Suspension* bridges use cables under tension to pull inwards against anchorages on either side of the span, so that the roadway hangs from the main cables by the network of vertical cables. Some bridges are too low to allow traffic to pass beneath easily, so they are designed with movable parts, like swing and draw bridges.

bridge card game derived from whist. First played among members of the Indian Civil Service about 1900, bridge was brought to England in 1903. It is played in two forms: auction bridge and contract bridge.

Bridgetown port and capital of Barbados, founded 1628; population (1987) 8,000. Sugar is exported through the nearby deep-water port.

Bridgewater Francis Egerton, 3rd Duke of 1736–1803. Pioneer of British inland navigation. With James ▷Brindley as his engineer, he constructed 1762–72 the *Bridgewater canal* from Worsley to Manchester and on to the Mersey, a distance of 67.5 km/42 mi.

brill flatfish *Scophthalmus laevis*, living in shallow water over sandy bottoms in the NE Atlantic and Mediterranean. It is a freckled sandy brown, and grows to 60 cm/2 ft.

Brindley James 1716–1772. British canal builder, the first to employ tunnels and aqueducts extensively, in order to reduce the number of locks on a direct-route canal. His 580 km/360 mi of canals included the Bridgewater (Manchester–Liverpool) and Grand Union (Manchester–Potteries) canals.

Brinell hardness test test of the hardness of a substance according to the area of indentation made by a 10 mm/0.4 in hardened steel or sintered tungsten carbide ball under standard loading conditions in a test machine. The resulting Brinell number is equal to the load (kg) divided by the surface area (mm²) and is named after its inventor Johann Brinell.

Brisbane industrial port (brewing, engineering, tanning, tobacco, shoes; oil pipeline from Moonie), capital of Queensland, E Australia, near the mouth of Brisbane River, dredged to carry ocean-going ships; population (1990) 1,301,700.

bristletail primitive wingless insect of the order Thysanura. Up to 2 cm/0.8 in long, bristletails have a body tapering from front to back, two long antennae, and three 'tails' at the rear end. They include the *silverfish Lepisma saccharina* and the *firebrat Thermobia domestica*. Two-tailed bristletails constitute another insect order, the Diplura. They live under stones and fallen branches, feeding on decaying material.

Bristol industrial port (aircraft engines, engineering, microelectronics, tobacco, chemicals, paper, printing), administrative headquarters of Avon, SW England; population (1991 est) 370,300. The old docks have been redeveloped for housing, industry, yachting facilities, and the National Lifeboat Museum.

Britain or *Great Britain* island off the NW coast of Europe, one of the British Isles. It consists of ⟡England, ⟡Scotland, and ⟡Wales, and is part of the ⟡United Kingdom. The name is derived from the Roman name Britannia, which in turn is derived from ancient Celtic name of the inhabitants, *Bryttas*.

Britain, ancient period in the history of the British Isles (excluding Ireland) from prehistory to the Roman occupation. After the last glacial retreat of the Ice Age about 15,000 BC, Britain was inhabited by hunters who became neolithic farming villagers. They built stone circles and buried their chiefs in ⟡barrow mounds. Around 400 BC Britain was conquered by the ⟡Celts and 54 BC by the Romans under Julius Caesar; ⟡Boudicca led an uprising against their occupation. The Romans withdrew in the 5th century AD.

Britain, Battle of World War II air battle between German and British air forces over Britain lasting 10 July–31 Oct 1940. Losses Aug–Sept were, for the RAF: 832 fighters totally destroyed; for the Luftwaffe: 668 fighters and some 700 bombers and other aircraft.

British Antarctic Territory colony created in 1962 and comprising all British territories S of latitude 60° S: the South Orkney Islands, the South Shetland Islands, the Antarctic Peninsula and all adjacent lands, and Coats Land, extending to the South Pole; total land area 660,000 sq km/170,874 sq mi. Population (exclusively scientific personnel): about 300.

British Broadcasting Corporation (BBC) the UK state-owned broadcasting network. It operates television and national and local radio stations, and is financed solely by the sale of television viewing licences; it is not allowed to carry advertisements. Overseas radio broadcasts (World Service) have a government subsidy.

British Columbia province of Canada on the Pacific. *area* 947,800 sq km/365,851 sq mi; *capital* Victoria; *towns* Vancouver, Prince George, Kamloops, Kelowna; *physical* Rocky Mountains and Coast Range; deeply indented coast; rivers include the Fraser and Columbia; over 80 lakes; more than half the land is forested; *products* fruit and vegetables; timber and wood products; fish; coal, copper, iron, lead; oil and natural gas; hydroelectricity; *population* (1991) 3,185,900; *history* Captain Cook explored the coast in 1778; a British colony was founded on Vancouver Island in 1849, and the gold rush of 1858 extended settlement to the mainland; it became a province in 1871. In 1885 the Canadian Pacific Railroad linking British Columbia to the E coast was completed.

British Commonwealth of Nations former official name of the ⟡Commonwealth.

British Council semiofficial organization set up 1935 (royal charter 1940) to promote a wider knowledge of the UK, excluding politics and commerce, and to develop cultural relations with other countries.

British Empire various territories all over the world conquered or colonized by Britain from about 1600, most now independent or ruled by other powers; the British Empire was at its largest at the end of World War I, with over 25% of the world's population and area. The ⟡Commonwealth is composed of former and remaining territories of the British Empire.

British Honduras former name (1862–1973) of ⟡Belize.

British Indian Ocean Territory British colony in the Indian Ocean directly administered by the Foreign and Commonwealth Office. It consists of the Chagos Archipelago some 1,900 km/1,200 mi NE of Mauritius; *area* 60 sq km/23 sq mi; *features* lagoons; US naval and air base on Diego Garcia; *products* copra, salt fish, tortoiseshell; *population* (1982) 3,000; *history* purchased in 1965 for $3 million by Britain from Mauritius to provide a joint US/UK base. The islands of Aldabra, Farquhar, and Desroches, some 485 km/300 mi N of Madagascar, originally formed part of the British Indian Ocean Territory but were returned to the administration of the Seychelles in 1976.

British Isles group of islands off the NW coast of Europe, consisting of Great Britain (England, Wales, and Scotland), Ireland, the Channel Islands, the Orkney and Shetland islands, the Isle of Man, and many other islands that are included in various counties, such as the Isle of Wight, Scilly Isles, Lundy Island, and the Inner and Outer Hebrides. The islands are divided from Europe by the North Sea, Strait of Dover, and the English Channel, and face the Atlantic to the west.

British Somaliland British protectorate comprising over 176,000 sq km/67,980 sq mi of territory on the Somali coast of E Africa from 1884 until the independence of Somalia in 1960. British authorities were harassed by Somali nationalists under the leadership of Muhammad bin Abdullah Hassan.

British Virgin Islands part of the ⟡Virgin Islands group in the West Indies.

Brittany (French *Bretagne*, Breton *Breiz*) region of NW France in the Breton peninsula between the Bay of Biscay and the English Channel; area 27,200 sq km/10,499 sq mi; population (1987) 2,767,000. Its capital is Rennes and includes the *départements* of Côtes-du-Nord, Finistère, Ille-et-Vilaine, and Morbihan. It is a farming region. *history* Brittany was the Gallo-Roman province of Armorica after being conquered by Julius Caesar 56 BC. It was devastated by Norsemen after the Roman withdrawal. It was established under the name of Brittany in the 5th century AD by Celts fleeing the Anglo-Saxon invasion of Britain. It became a strong, expansionist state that maintained its cultural and political independence, despite pressure from the Carolingians, Normans, and Capetians. By 1547 it had been formally annexed by France, and the ⟡Breton language was banned in education. A separatist movement developed after World War II, and there has been guerrilla activity.

Britten (Edward) Benjamin 1913–1976. English composer. He often wrote for the individual voice; for example, the role in the opera *Peter Grimes* 1945, based on verses by George Crabbe, was created for Peter ⟡Pears. Among his many works are the *Young Person's Guide to the Orchestra* 1946; the chamber opera *The Rape of Lucretia* 1946; *Billy Budd* 1951; *A Midsummer Night's Dream* 1960; and *Death in Venice* 1973.

brittle-star any member of the echinoderm class Ophiuroidea. A brittle-star resembles a starfish, and has a small, central, rounded body and long, flexible, spiny arms used for walking. The small brittle-star *Amphipholis squamata* is greyish, about 4.5 cm/2 in across, and found on sea bottoms worldwide. It broods its young, and its arms can be luminous.

broadbill primitive perching bird of the family Eurylaimidae, found in Africa and S Asia. Broadbills are forest birds and are often found near water. They are gregarious and noisy, have brilliant coloration and wide bills, and feed largely on insects.

broadcasting the transmission of sound and vision programmes by ⟡radio and ⟡television. Broadcasting may be organized under private

enterprise, as in the USA, or may operate under a compromise system, as in Britain, where there is a television and radio service controlled by the state-regulated ⟡British Broadcasting Corporation (BBC) and also the commercial ⟡Independent Television Commission (known as the Independent Broadcasting Authority before 1991).

Broads, Norfolk area of navigable lakes and rivers in England, see ⟡Norfolk Broads.

broccoli variety of ⟡cabbage.

Brodsky Joseph 1940– . Russian poet who emigrated to the USA in 1972. His work, often dealing with themes of exile, is admired for its wit and economy of language, particularly in its use of understatement. Many of his poems, written in Russian, have been translated into English (*A Part of Speech* 1980). More recently he has also written in English. He was awarded the Nobel Prize for Literature in 1987 and became US poet laureate 1991.

Broglie Louis de, 7th Duc de Broglie 1892–1987. French theoretical physicist. He established that all subatomic particles can be described either by particle equations or by wave equations, thus laying the foundations of wave mechanics. He was awarded the 1929 Nobel Prize for Physics.

bromeliad any tropical or subtropical plant of the pineapple family Bromeliaceae, usually with stiff leathery leaves and bright flower spikes. Bromeliads are native to tropical America, where there are some 1,400 species. Some are terrestrial, growing in habitats ranging from scrub desert to tropical forest floor. Others are epiphytes and grow on trees.

bromine dark, reddish-brown, nonmetallic element, a volatile liquid at room temperature, symbol Br, atomic number 35, relative atomic mass 79.904. It is a member of the ⟡halogen group, has an unpleasant odour, and is very irritating to mucous membranes. Its salts are known as bromides.

bronchitis inflammation of the bronchi (air passages) of the lungs, usually caused initially by a viral infection, such as a cold or flu. It is aggravated by environmental pollutants, especially smoking, and results in a persistent cough, irritated mucus-secreting glands, and sputum.

Brontë three English novelists, daughters of a Yorkshire parson. *Charlotte* (1816–1855), notably with *Jane Eyre* 1847 and *Villette* 1853, reshaped autobiographical material into vivid narrative. *Emily* (1818–1848) in *Wuthering Heights* 1847 expressed the intensity and nature mysticism which also pervades her poetry (*Poems* 1846). The more modest talent of *Anne* (1820–1849) produced *Agnes Grey* 1847 and *The Tenant of Wildfell Hall* 1848.

brontosaurus former name of a type of large, plant-eating dinosaur, now better known as ⟡apatosaurus.

bronze alloy of copper and tin, yellow or brown in

colour. It is harder than pure copper, more suitable for casting, and also resists corrosion. Bronze may contain as much as 25% tin, together with small amounts of other metals, mainly lead.

Bronze Age stage of prehistory and early history when bronze became the first metal worked extensively and used for tools and weapons. It developed out of the Stone Age, preceded the Iron Age and may be dated 5000–1200 BC in the Middle East and about 2000–500 BC in Europe. Recent discoveries in Thailand suggest that the Far East, rather than the Middle East, was the cradle of the Bronze Age.

Bronzino Agnolo 1503–1572. Italian painter active in Florence, court painter to Cosimo I, Duke of Tuscany. He painted in a Mannerist style and is best known for portraits and the allegory *Venus, Cupid, Folly and Time* (c. 1545) (National Gallery, London).

Brook Peter 1925– . English director who created experimental productions with the Royal Shakespeare Company in the 1960s. His later productions transcend Western theatre conventions and include *The Conference of the Birds* 1973, based on a Persian story, and *The Mahabarata* 1985/88, a cycle of three plays based on the Hindu epic. His films include *Lord of the Flies* 1962 and *Meetings with Remarkable Men* 1979.

Brooke Rupert (Chawner) 1887–1915. English poet, symbol of the World War I 'lost generation'. His five war sonnets, the best known of which is 'The Patriot', were published posthumously. Other notable works include 'Grantchester' and 'The Great Lover'.

broom any shrub of the family Leguminisae, especially species of the *Cytisus* and *Spartium*, often cultivated for their bright yellow flowers. In Britain the yellow-flowered Scots broom *Cytisus scoparius* predominates.

Brown Capability (Lancelot) 1715–1783. English landscape gardener. He acquired his nickname because of his continual enthusiasm for the 'capabilities' of natural landscapes. He advised on gardens of stately homes, including Blenheim, Oxfordshire; Stowe, Buckinghamshire; and Petworth, W Sussex, sometimes also contributing to the architectural designs.

Brown Ford Madox 1821–1893. British painter associated with the ⚪Pre-Raphaelite Brotherhood. His pictures include *The Last of England* 1855 (Birmingham Art Gallery) and *Work* 1852–65 (City Art Gallery, Manchester), packed with realistic detail and symbolic incident.

Brown John 1800–1859. US slavery abolitionist. With 18 men, on the night of 16 Oct 1859, he seized the government arsenal at Harper's Ferry in W Virginia, apparently intending to distribute weapons to runaway slaves who would then defend the mountain stronghold, which Brown hoped would become a republic of former slaves. On 18 Oct

the arsenal was stormed by US Marines under Col Robert E ⚪Lee. Brown was tried and hanged on 2 Dec, becoming a martyr and the hero of the popular song 'John Brown's Body' c. 1860.

brown dwarf hypothetical object less massive than a star, but heavier than a planet. Brown dwarfs would not have enough mass to ignite nuclear reactions at their centres, but would shine by heat released during their contraction from a gas cloud. Because of the difficulty of detection, no brown dwarfs have been spotted with certainty, but some astronomers believe that vast numbers of them may exist throughout the Galaxy.

Browne Thomas 1605–1682. English author and physician. Born in London, he travelled widely in Europe before settling in Norwich in 1637. His works display a richness of style as in *Religio Medici/The Religion of a Doctor* 1643, a justification of his profession; *Vulgar Errors* 1646, an examination of popular legend and superstition; *Urn Burial* and *The Garden of Cyrus* 1658; and *Christian Morals*, published posthumously in 1717.

Browning Robert 1812–1889. English poet, married to Elizabeth Barret Browning. His work is characterized by the use of dramatic monologue and an interest in obscure literary and historical figures. It includes the play *Pippa Passes* 1841 and the poems 'The Pied Piper of Hamelin' 1842, 'My Last Duchess' 1842, 'Home Thoughts from Abroad' 1845, and 'Rabbi Ben Ezra' 1864.

Browns Ferry site of a nuclear power station on the Alabama River, central Alabama, USA. A nuclear accident in 1975 resulted in the closure of the plant for 18 months. This incident marked the beginning of widespread disenchantment with nuclear power in the USA.

Brownshirts the SA (*Sturmabteilung*), or Storm Troops, the private army of the German Nazi party, who derived their name from the colour of their uniform.

Bruce one of the chief Scottish noble houses. ⚪Robert I (Robert the Bruce) and his son, David II, were both kings of Scotland descended from Robert de Bruis (died 1094), a Norman knight who arrived in England with William the Conqueror 1066.

Bruce Robert. King of Scotland; see ⚪Robert I.

Bruce Robert de, 5th Lord of Annandale 1210–1295. Scottish noble, one of the unsuccessful claimants to the throne at the death of Alexander II 1290. His grandson was ⚪Robert I (the Bruce).

brucellosis disease of cattle, goats, and pigs, also known when transmitted to humans as **undulant fever** since it remains in the body and recurs. It was named after Australian doctor David Bruce (1855–1931), and is caused by bacteria (genus *Brucella*) present in the milk of infected cattle.

Brücke, die German Expressionist art movement 1905–13, formed in Dresden. Ernst Ludwig

Kirchner was one of its founders, and Emil Nolde was a member 1906–07. Influenced by African art, they strove for spiritual significance, using raw colours to express different emotions. In 1911 the ▷*Blaue Reiter* took over as the leading group in German art.

Bruckner (Joseph) **Anton** 1824–1896. Austrian Romantic composer. He was cathedral organist at Linz 1856–68, and from 1868 he was professor at the Vienna Conservatoire. His works include many choral pieces and 11 symphonies, the last unfinished. His compositions were influenced by Richard ▷Wagner and Beethoven.

Brueghel family of Flemish painters. *Pieter Brueghel the Elder* (c. 1525–1569) was one of the greatest artists of his time. He painted satirical and humorous pictures of peasant life, many of which include symbolic details illustrating folly and inhumanity, and a series of Months (five survive), including *Hunters in the Snow* (Kunsthistorisches Museum, Vienna).

Bruges (Flemish *Brugge*) historic city in NW Belgium; capital of W Flanders province, 16 km/10 mi from the North Sea, with which it is connected by canal; population (1991) 117,100. Bruges was the capital of medieval ▷Flanders and was the chief European wool manufacturing town as well as its chief market.

Brundtland Gro Harlem 1939– . Norwegian Labour politician. Environment minister 1974–76, she briefly took over as prime minister 1981, and was elected prime minister in 1986 and again in 1990. She chaired the World Commission on Environment and Development which produced the *Brundtland Report* 1987.

Brunei the Islamic Sultanate of; country on the N coast of Borneo, surrounded to the landward side by Sarawak and bordered N by the South China Sea; *area* 5,765 sq km/2,225 sq mi; *capital* Bandar Seri Begawan; *physical* flat coastal plain with hilly lowland in W and mountains in E; 75% of the area is forested; Limbang valley splits Brunei in two, and its cession to Sarawak 1890 is disputed by Brunei; *head of state and government* HM Muda Hassanal Bolkiah Mu'izzaddin Waddaulah, Sultan of Brunei, from 1968; *political system* absolute monarchy; *exports* liquefied natural gas (world's largest producer) and oil, both expected to be exhausted by the year 2000; *population* (1990 est) 372,000 (65% Malay, 20% Chinese – few Chinese granted citizenship); *languages* Malay (official); Chinese (Hokkien), English; *history* Brunei became a British protectorate 1888; independence was achieved 1984.

Brunei Town former name (until 1970) of ▷Bandar Seri Begawan, Brunei.

Brunel Isambard Kingdom 1806–1859. British engineer and inventor. In 1833 he became engineer to the Great Western Railway, which adopted the 2.1 m/7 ft gauge on his advice. He built the Clifton Suspension Bridge over the river Avon at Bristol and the Saltash Bridge over the river Tamar near Plymouth. His shipbuilding designs include the *Great Western* 1838, the first steamship to cross the Atlantic regularly; the *Great Britain* 1843, the first large iron ship to have a screw propeller; and the *Great Eastern* 1857, which laid the first transatlantic telegraph cable.

Brunel Marc Isambard 1769–1849. British engineer and inventor, father of Isambard Kingdom Brunel. He constructed the Rotherhithe tunnel under the river Thames in London from Wapping to Rotherhithe 1825–43.

Brunelleschi Filippo 1377–1446. Italian Renaissance architect. One of the earliest and greatest Renaissance architects, he pioneered the scientific use of perspective. He was responsible for the construction of the dome of Florence Cathedral (completed 1438), a feat deemed impossible by many of his contemporaries.

Bruno Giordano 1548–1600. Italian philosopher. He entered the Dominican order of monks 1563, but his sceptical attitude to Catholic doctrines forced him to flee Italy 1577. After visiting Geneva and Paris, he lived in England 1583–85, where he wrote some of his finest works. He was arrested by the ▷Inquisition 1593 in Venice and burned at the stake for his adoption of Copernican astronomy and his heretical religious views.

Brunswick (German *Braunschweig*) industrial city (chemical engineering, precision engineering, food processing) in Lower Saxony, Germany; population (1988) 248,000. It was one of the chief cities of N Germany in the Middle Ages and a member of the ▷Hanseatic League. It was capital of the duchy of Brunswick from 1671.

Brussels (Flemish *Brussel*; French *Bruxelles*) capital of Belgium, industrial city (lace, textiles, machinery, chemicals); population (1987) 974,000 (80% French-speaking, the suburbs Flemish-speaking). It is the headquarters of the European Economic Community and since 1967 of the international secretariat of ▷NATO. First settled in the 6th century, and a city from 1312, Brussels became the capital of the Spanish Netherlands 1530 and of Belgium 1830.

Brussels sprout one of the small edible buds along the stem of a variety (*Brassica oleracea* var. *gemmifera*) of ▷cabbage.

Brussels, Treaty of pact of economic, political, cultural, and military alliance established 17 March 1948, for 50 years, by the UK, France, and the Benelux countries, joined by West Germany and Italy 1955. It was the forerunner of the North Atlantic Treaty Organization and the European Community.

Brutus Marcus Junius *c.* 78–42 BC. Roman soldier, a supporter of ▷Pompey (against Julius Caesar) in the civil war 49–48, when Caesar seized sole power. Pardoned by Caesar and raised to high office by him, Brutus nevertheless plotted Caesar's assassination to restore the purity of the republic. Brutus committed suicide when he was defeated (with ▷Cassius) by ▷Mark Antony, Caesar's lieutenant, at Philippi 42 BC.

bryony either of two hedgerow climbing plants found in Britain: *white bryony Bryonia dioca* belonging to the gourd family Cucurbitaceae, and *black bryony Tamus communis* of the yam family Dioscoreaceae.

bryophyte member of the Bryophyta, a division of the plant kingdom containing three classes: the Hepaticae (▷liverwort), Musci (▷moss), and Anthocerotae (hornwort). Bryophytes are generally small, low-growing, terrestrial plants with no vascular (water-conducting) system as in higher plants. Their life cycle shows a marked ▷alternation of generations. Bryophytes chiefly occur in damp habitats and require water for the dispersal of the male gametes (antherozoids).

bubble chamber in physics, a device for observing the nature and movement of atomic particles, and their interaction with radiations. It is a vessel filled with a superheated liquid through which ionizing particles move and collide. The paths of these particles are shown by strings of bubbles, which can be photographed and studied. By using a pressurized liquid medium instead of a gas, it overcomes drawbacks inherent in the earlier ▷cloud chamber. It was invented by Donald Glaser 1952.

bubble memory in computing, a memory device based on the creation of small 'bubbles' on a magnetic surface. Bubble memories typically store up to 4 megabits (4 million ▷bits) of information. They are not sensitive to shock and vibration, unlike other memory devices such as disc drives, yet, like magnetic discs, they are nonvolatile and do not lose their information when the computer is switched off.

Bucaramanga industrial (coffee, tobacco, cacao, cotton) and commercial city in N central Colombia; population (1985) 493,929. It was founded by the Spanish 1622.

buccaneer member of any of various groups of seafarers who plundered Spanish ships and colonies on the Spanish American coast in the 17th century. Unlike true pirates, they were acting on (sometimes spurious) commission.

Bucharest (Romanian *Bucureşti*) capital and largest city of Romania; population (1985) 1,976,000, the conurbation of Bucharest district having an area of 1,520 sq km/587 sq mi and a population of 2,273,000. It was originally a citadel built by Vlad the Impaler (see ▷Dracula) to stop the advance of the Ottoman invasion in the 14th century. Bucharest became the capital of the princes of Wallachia 1698 and of Romania 1861. Savage

fighting took place in the city during Romania's 1989 revolution.

Buchenwald site of a Nazi ▷concentration camp 1937–45 at a village NE of Weimar, E Germany.

Buckingham George Villiers, 1st Duke of Buckingham 1592–1628. English courtier, adviser to James I and later Charles I. After Charles's accession, Buckingham attempted to form a Protestant coalition in Europe, which led to war with France, but he failed to relieve the Protestants (▷Huguenots) besieged in La Rochelle 1627. This added to his unpopularity with Parliament, and he was assassinated.

Buckingham George Villiers, 2nd Duke of Buckingham 1628–1687. English politician, a member of the ▷Cabal under Charles II. A dissolute son of the first duke, he was brought up with the royal children. His play *The Rehearsal* satirized the style of the poet Dryden, who portrayed him as Zimri in *Absalom and Achitophel*.

Buckinghamshire county in SE central England; *area* 1,880 sq km/726 sq mi; *towns* Aylesbury (administrative headquarters), Buckingham, High Wycombe, Beaconsfield, Olney, Milton Keynes; *features* Chequers (country seat of the prime minister); Burnham Beeches and the church of the poet Gray's 'Elegy' at Stoke Poges; Cliveden, a country house designed by Charles Barry (now a hotel, it was used by the newspaper-owning Astors for house parties); Bletchley Park, home of World War II code-breaking activities, now used as a training post for GCHQ (Britain's electronic surveillance centre); Open University at Walton Hall; homes of the poets William Cowper at Olney and John Milton at Chalfont St Giles, and of the Tory prime minister Disraeli at Hughenden; Stowe gardens; *products* furniture, chiefly beech; agricultural goods; *population* (1991) 619,500; *famous people* William Herschel, George Gilbert Scott, Edmund Waller, John Hampden, Ben Nicholson.

buckminsterfullerene form of carbon made up of molecules (buckyballs) consisting of 60 carbon atoms arranged in 12 pentagons and 20 hexagons to form a perfect sphere. It was named after the US architect and engineer Buckminster ▷Fuller because of its structural similarity to the geodesic dome that he designed. See ▷fullerene.

buckwheat any of several plants of the genus *Fagopyrum*, family Polygonaceae. The name usually refers to *F. esculentum*, which grows to about 1 m/3 ft and can grow on poor soil in a short summer. The highly nutritious black, triangular seeds (groats) are consumed by both animals and humans. They can be eaten either cooked whole or or as a cracked meal (kasha) or ground into flour, often made into pancakes.

buckyball popular name for a molecule of ▷buckminsterfullerene.

bud undeveloped shoot usually enclosed by protective scales; inside is a very short stem and numerous undeveloped leaves, or flower parts, or both. Terminal buds are found at the tips of shoots, while axillary buds develop in the axils of the leaves, often remaining dormant unless the terminal bud is removed or damaged. Adventitious buds may be produced anywhere on the plant, their formation sometimes stimulated by an injury, such as that caused by pruning.

Budapest capital of Hungary, industrial city (chemicals, textiles) on the river Danube; population (1989) 2,115,000. Buda, on the right bank of the Danube, became the Hungarian capital 1867 and was joined with Pest, on the left bank, 1872.

Buddha 'enlightened one', title of Prince *Gautama Siddhārtha c.* 563–483 BC. Religious leader, founder of Buddhism, born at Lumbini in Nepal. At the age of 29 he left his wife and son and a life of luxury, to escape from the material burdens of existence. After six years of austerity he realized that asceticism, like overindulgence, was futile, and chose the middle way of meditation. He became enlightened under a bo, or bodhi, tree near Buddh Gaya in Bihar, India. He began teaching at Varanasi, and founded the Sangha, or order of monks. He spent the rest of his life travelling around N India, and died at Kusinagara in Uttar Pradesh.

Buddhism one of the great world religions, which originated in India about 500 BC. It derives from the teaching of the Buddha, who is regarded as one of a series of such enlightened beings; there are no gods. The chief doctrine is that of *karma*, good or evil deeds meeting an appropriate reward or punishment either in this life or (through reincarnation) a long succession of lives. The main divisions in Buddhism are *Theravāda* (or Hīnayāna) in SE Asia and *Mahāyāna* in N Asia; *Lamaism* in Tibet and *Zen* in Japan are among the many Mahāyāna sects. Its symbol is the lotus. There are over 247.5 million Buddhists worldwide.

buddleia any shrub or tree of the tropical genus *Buddleia*, family Buddleiaceae. The purple or white flower heads of the butterfly bush *B. davidii* attract large numbers of butterflies.

budgerigar small Australian parakeet *Melopsittacus undulatus* that feeds mainly on grass seeds. Normally it is bright green, but yellow, white, blue, and mauve varieties have been bred for the pet market.

Buenos Aires capital and industrial city of Argentina, on the S bank of the Río de la Plata; population (1991) 2,961,000, metropolitan area 7,950,400. It was founded 1536, and became the capital 1853.

buffalo either of two species of wild cattle. The Asiatic water buffalo *Bubalis bubalis* is found domesticated throughout S Asia and wild in parts of India and Nepal. It likes moist conditions. Usually grey or black, up to 1.8 m/6 ft high, both sexes carry large horns. The African buffalo *Syncerus*

caffer is found in Africa, south of the Sahara, where there is grass, water, and cover in which to retreat. There are a number of subspecies, the biggest up to 1.6 m/5 ft high, and black, with massive horns set close together over the head. The name is also commonly applied to the American ◊bison.

bug in entomology, an insect belonging to the order Hemiptera. All these have two pairs of wings with forewings partly thickened. They also have piercing mouthparts adapted for sucking the juices of plants or animals, the 'beak' being tucked under the body when not in use.

bug in computing, an error in a program. It can be an error in the logical structure of a program or a syntax error, such as a spelling mistake. Some bugs cause a program to fail immediately; others remain dormant, causing problems only when a particular combination of events occurs. The process of finding and removing errors from a program is called *debugging.*

bugle in music, a valveless brass instrument with a shorter tube and less flared bell than the trumpet. The bugle has long been used as a military instrument for giving a range of signals based on the tones of a harmonic series.

Bukharin Nikolai Ivanovich 1888–1938. Soviet politician and theorist. A moderate, he was the chief Bolshevik thinker after Lenin. Executed on Stalin's orders for treason 1938, he was posthumously rehabilitated 1988.

Bulawayo industrial city and railway junction in Zimbabwe; population (1982) 415,000. It lies at an altitude of 1,355 m/4,450 ft on the river Matsheumlope, a tributary of the Zambezi, and was founded on the site of the kraal (enclosed village), burned down 1893, of the Matabele chief, Lobenguela. It produces agricultural and electrical equipment. The former capital of Matabeleland, Bulawayo developed with the exploitation of gold mines in the neighbourhood.

bulb underground bud with fleshy leaves containing a reserve food supply and with roots growing from its base. Bulbs function in vegetative reproduction and are characteristic of many monocotyledonous plants such as the daffodil, snowdrop, and onion. Bulbs are grown on a commercial scale in temperate countries, such as England and the Netherlands.

Bulganin Nikolai 1895–1975. Soviet politician and military leader. His career began in 1918 when he joined the Cheka, the Soviet secret police. He helped to organize Moscow's defence in World War II, became a marshal of the USSR 1947, and was minister of defence 1947–49 and 1953–55. On the fall of Georgi Malenkov he became prime minister (chair of Council of Ministers) 1955–58 until ousted by Nikita Khrushchev.

Bulgaria People's Republic of; country in SE Europe, bordered N by Romania, W by Yugoslavia,

S by Greece, SW by Turkey, and E by the Black Sea; *area* 110,912 sq km/42,812 sq mi; *capital* Sofia; *physical* lowland plains in N and SE separated by mountains that cover three-quarters of the country; Balkan and Rhodope mountains; Danube River in N; *head of state* Zhelyo Zhelev from 1990; *head of government* Filip Dimitrov from 1991; *political system* emergent democracy; *exports* textiles, leather, chemicals, nonferrous metals, timber, machinery, tobacco, cigarettes (world's largest exporter); *population* (1990 est) 8,978,000 (including 900,000–1,500,000 ethnic Turks, concentrated in S and NE); *languages* Bulgarian, Turkish; *recent history* became a kingdom independent of Turkish rule 1908. Soviet invasion of German-occupied Bulgaria 1944; monarchy abolished and communist-dominated people's republic proclaimed 1946. A Soviet-style constitution was adopted 1947. Multicandidate elections were introduced 1987; opposition parties allowed to form 1989. New constitution adopted 1991; first noncommmunist government formed under Filip Dimitrov. Relations with West greatly improved during 1992.

bulimia condition of continuous, uncontrolled hunger. Considered a counteraction to stress or depression, this eating disorder is found chiefly in young women. When compensated for by forced vomiting or overdoses of laxatives, the condition is called *bulimia nervosa*. It is sometimes associated with ◊anorexia.

bull in finance, a speculator who buys stocks or shares on the stock exchange expecting a rise in the price in order to sell them later at a profit; the opposite of a ◊bear. In a bull market, prices rise and bulls profit.

Bull John. Imaginary figure personifying England; see ◊John Bull.

bulldog British dog of ancient but uncertain origin. The head is broad and square, with deeply wrinkled cheeks, small folded ears, and the nose laid back between the eyes. The bulldog grows to about 45 cm/18 in at the shoulder.

bullfighting the national 'sport' of Spain (where there are more than 400 bullrings), which is also popular in Mexico, Portugal, and much of Latin America. It involves the ritualized taunting of a bull in a circular ring, until its eventual death at the hands of the matador. Originally popular in Greece and Rome, it was introduced into Spain by the Moors in the 11th century.

bullfinch Eurasian finch *Pyrrhula pyrrhula*, with a thick head and neck, and short heavy bill. It is small and blue-grey or black, the males being reddish and the females brown on the breast. Bullfinches are 15 cm/6 in long, and usually seen in pairs. They feed on tree buds as well as seeds and berries, and are usually seen in woodland. They also live in the Aleutians and on the Alaska mainland.

bull terrier heavily built, smooth-coated breed of dog, usually white, originating as a cross between a terrier and a bulldog. It grows to about 40 cm/16 in tall, and was formerly used in bull-baiting. Pit bull terriers are used in illegal dog fights.

bulrush either of two plants: the great reed mace or cat's tail *Typha latifolia* with chocolate-brown tight-packed flower spikes reaching up to 15 cm/6 in long; and a type of sedge *Scirpus lacustris* with tufts of reddish-brown flowers at the top of a rounded, rushlike stem.

bumblebee any large ◊bee, 2–5 cm/1–2 in long, usually dark-coloured but banded with yellow, orange, or white, belonging to the genus *Bombus*.

Bunker Hill, Battle of the first significant engagement in the ◊American Revolution, 17 June 1775, near a small hill in Charlestown (now part of Boston), Massachusetts, USA; the battle actually took place on Breed's Hill. Although the colonists were defeated they were able to retreat to Boston and suffered fewer casualties than the British.

bunsen burner gas burner used in laboratories, consisting of a vertical metal tube through which a fine jet of fuel gas is directed. Air is drawn in through airholes near the base of the tube and the mixture is ignited and burns at the tube's upper opening.

bunting any of a number of sturdy, finchlike, passerine birds with short, thick bills, of the family Emberizidae, especially the genera *Passerim* and *Emberiza*. Most of these brightly coloured birds are native to the New World. Some live in the Old World, such as the ◊ortolan and the ◊*yellowhammer*.

Buñuel Luis 1900–1983. Spanish ◊Surrealist film director. He collaborated with Salvador Dali on *Un Chien andalou* 1928 and *L'Age d'or/The Golden Age* 1930, and established his solo career with *Los olvidados/The Young and the Damned* 1950. His works are often anticlerical, with black humour and erotic imagery.

Bunyan John 1628–1688. English author. A Baptist, he was imprisoned in Bedford 1660–72 for unlicensed preaching. During a second jail sentence 1675 he started to write *The Pilgrim's Progress*, the first part of which was published 1678. Other works include *Grace Abounding* 1666, *The Life and Death of Mr Badman* 1680, and *The Holy War* 1682.

bur or *burr* in botany, a type of 'false fruit' or ◊pseudocarp, surrounded by numerous hooks; for instance, that of burdock *Arctium*, where the hooks are formed from bracts surrounding the flowerhead. Burs catch in the feathers or fur of passing animals, and thus may be dispersed over considerable distances.

burdock any of the bushy herbs belonging to the genus *Arctium* of the family Compositae, characterized by hairy leaves and ripe fruit enclosed in ◊burs with strong hooks. It is a common roadside weed in Britain.

bureaucracy organization whose structure and operations are governed to a high degree by written rules and a hierarchy of offices; in its broadest sense, all forms of administration, and in its narrowest, rule by officials.

Burgenland federal state of SE Austria, extending from the Danube south along the western border of the Hungarian plain; area 4,000 sq km/1,544 sq mi; population (1989) 267,200. It is a largely agricultural region adjoining the Neusiedler See, and produces timber, fruit, sugar, wine, lignite, antimony, and limestone. Its capital is Eisenstadt.

Burgess Anthony. Pen name of Anthony John Burgess Wilson 1917– . British novelist, critic, and composer. His prolific work includes *A Clockwork Orange* 1962, set in a future London terrorized by teenage gangs, and the panoramic *Earthly Powers* 1980. His vision has been described as bleak and pessimistic, but his work is also comic and satiric, as in his novels featuring the poet Enderby.

Burgess Shale Site site of unique fossil-bearing rock formations created 530 million years ago by a mud slide, in Yoho National Park, British Columbia, Canada. The shales in this corner of the Rocky Mountains contain more than 120 species of marine invertebrate fossils. The site was discovered 1909.

burgh (burh or borough) term originating in Germanic lands in the 9th–10th centuries referring to a fortified settlement, usually surrounding a monastery or castle. Later, it was used to mean new towns, or towns that enjoyed particular privileges relating to government and taxation and whose citizens were called *burghers*.

burgh former unit of Scottish local government, abolished 1975; the terms *burgh* and *royal burgh* once gave mercantile privilege but are now only an honorary distinction.

Burgh Hubert de, died 1243. English justiciar and regent of England. He was a supporter of King John against the barons, and ended French intervention in England by his defeat of the French fleet in the Strait of Dover 1217. He reorganized royal administration and the Common Law.

Burghley William Cecil, Baron Burghley 1520–1598. English politician, chief adviser to Elizabeth I as secretary of state from 1558 and Lord High Treasurer from 1572. He was largely responsible for the religious settlement of 1559, and took a leading role in the events preceding the execution of Mary Queen of Scots 1587.

burglary offence committed when a trespasser enters a building intending to steal, do damage to property, grievously harm any person, or rape a woman. Entry needs only be effective so, for example, a person who puts their hand through a broken shop window to steal something may be guilty of burglary.

Burgundy ancient kingdom and duchy in the valleys of the rivers Saône and Rhône, France. The Burgundi were a Teutonic tribe that overran the country about 400. From the 9th century to the death of Duke Charles the Bold 1477, Burgundy was the nucleus of a powerful principality. On Charles's death the duchy was incorporated into France. The capital of Burgundy was Dijon. Today the region to which it corresponds is ⟨⟩Bourgogne.

Burke Edmund 1729–1797. British Whig politician and political theorist, born in Dublin, Ireland. In Parliament from 1765, he opposed the government's attempts to coerce the American colonists, for example in *Thoughts on the Present Discontents* 1770, and supported the emancipation of Ireland, but denounced the French Revolution, for example in *Reflections on the Revolution in France* 1790.

Burkina Faso the People's Democratic Republic of (formerly *Upper Volta*); country in W Africa, bordered E by Niger, NW and W by Mali, S by Ivory Coast, Ghana, Togo, and Benin; *area* 274,122 sq km/105,811 sq mi; *capital* Ouagadougou; *physical* landlocked plateau with hills in W and SW; headwaters of the river Volta; semi-arid in N, forest and farmland in S; *head of state and government* Blaise Compaoré from 1987; *political system* transitional; *exports* cotton, groundnuts, livestock, hides, skins, sesame, cereals; *population* (1990 est) 8,941,000; *languages* French (official); about 50 native Sudanic languages spoken by 90% of population; *recent history* independence achieved from France 1960. A series of coups has rocked the country between military and civilian rule. Burkina Faso was given its present name, 'land of upright men', 1984.

Burlington Richard Boyle, 3rd Earl of Burlington 1694–1753. British architectural patron and architect; one of the premier exponents of the Palladian style in Britain. His buildings, such as Chiswick House, London, 1725–29, are characterized by absolute adherence to the Classical rules. His major protégé was William ⟨⟩Kent.

Burman member of the largest ethnic group in Myanmar (formerly Burma). The Burmans, speakers of a Sino-Tibetan language, migrated from the hills of Tibet, settling in the areas around Mandalay by the 11th century AD.

burn in medicine, destruction of body tissue by extremes of temperature, corrosive chemicals, electricity, or radiation. *First-degree burns* may cause reddening; *second-degree burns* cause blistering and irritation but usually heal spontaneously; *third-degree burns* are disfiguring and may be life-threatening.

Burne-Jones Edward Coley 1833–1898. English painter. In 1856 he was apprenticed to the Pre-Raphaelite painter Dante Gabriel ⟨⟩Rossetti, who remained a dominant influence. His paintings, inspired by legend and myth, were characterized by elongated forms as in *King Cophetua and the Beggar Maid* 1880–84 (Tate Gallery, London). He later moved towards Symbolism. He also designed tapestries and stained glass in association with William ◇Morris.

Burnett Frances (Eliza) Hodgson 1849–1924. English writer who emigrated with her family to the USA 1865. Her novels for children include the rags-to-riches tale *Little Lord Fauntleroy* 1886 and the sentimental *The Secret Garden* 1909.

Burney Frances (Fanny) 1752–1840. English novelist and diarist, daughter of musician Dr Charles Burney (1726–1814). She achieved success with *Evelina*, published anonymously 1778, became a member of Dr ◇Johnson's circle, received a post at court from Queen Charlotte, and in 1793 married the French émigré General d'Arblay. She published three further novels, *Cecilia* 1782, *Camilla* 1796, and *The Wanderer* 1814; her diaries and letters appeared 1842.

Burns Robert 1759–1796. Scottish poet who used the Scots dialect at a time when it was not considered suitably 'elevated' for literature. Burns's first volume, *Poems, Chiefly in the Scottish Dialect*, appeared 1786. In addition to his poetry, Burns wrote or adapted many songs, including 'Auld Lang Syne'.

Burroughs Edgar Rice 1875–1950. US novelist. He wrote *Tarzan of the Apes* 1914, the story of an aristocratic child lost in the jungle and reared by apes, and followed it with over 20 more books about the Tarzan character. He also wrote about life on Mars.

Burroughs William S 1914– . US novelist. He 'dropped out' and, as part of the ◇Beat Generation, wrote *Junkie* 1953, describing his addiction to heroin; *The Naked Lunch* 1959; *The Soft Machine* 1961; and *Dead Fingers Talk* 1963. His later novels include *Queer* and *Mind Wars*, both 1985.

Burton Richard Francis 1821–1890. British explorer and translator (he knew 35 oriental languages). He travelled mainly in the Middle East and NE Africa, often disguised as a Muslim; made two attempts to find the source of the Nile, 1855 and 1857–58 (on the second, with John Speke, he reached Lake Tanganyika); and wrote many travel books. He translated oriental erotica and the *Arabian Nights* 1885–88.

Burton Richard. Stage name of Richard Jenkins 1925–1984. Welsh actor of stage and screen. He had a rich, dramatic voice, and appeared in several films (including *Cleopatra* 1962 and *Who's Afraid of Virginia Woolf?* 1966) with the US actress Elizabeth Taylor, to whom he was intermittently married. Among his later films are *Equus* 1977 and *Nineteen Eighty-Four* 1984.

Burundi Republic of; country in E central Africa, bordered N by Rwanda, W by Zaire, S by Lake Tanganyika, and SE and E by Tanzania; **area** 27,834 sq km/10,744 sq mi; **capital** Bujumbura; **physical** landlocked grassy highland straddling watershed of Nile and Congo; Lake Tanganyika,

Great Rift Valley; **head of state and government** Pierre Buyoya from 1987; **political system** one-party military republic; **exports** coffee, cotton, tea, nickel, hides, livestock, cigarettes, beer, soft drinks; **population** (1990 est) 5,647,000 (of whom 15% are the Nilotic Tutsi, still holding most of the land and political power, 1% are Pygmy Twa, and the remainder Bantu Hutu); **languages** Kirundi (a Bantu language) and French (official); Kiswahili; **recent history** separated from Ruanda-Urundi as Burundi 1962; given independence as a monarchy under King Mwambutsa IV. Declared a republic 1966. The constitution of 1981 provided for a national assembly. Conflict continues between rival ethnic groups, with some 24,000 Hutus killed by Tutsis 1988.

Bush George 1924– . 41st president of the USA from 1989, a Republican. He was director of the Central Intelligence Agency (CIA) 1976–81 and US vice president 1981–89. As president, he responded to the Soviet leader Gorbachev's diplomatic initiatives, and his dispatch of US troops to depose his former ally, General ◇Noriega of Panama, proved a popular move at home. Success in the 1991 Gulf War against Iraq also raised Bush's standing, but he attracted widespread criticism for inadequate US commitments to the global environment at the 1992 Earth Summit.

bushbuck antelope *Tragelaphus scriptus* found over most of Africa S of the Sahara. Up to 1 m/3 ft high, the males have keeled horns twisted into spirals, and are brown to blackish. The females are generally hornless, lighter, and redder. All have white markings, including stripes or vertical rows of dots down the sides. Rarely far from water, bushbuck live in woods and thick brush.

Bushman former name for the Kung, San, and other hunter-gatherer groups (for example, the Gikwe, Heikom, and Sekhoin) living in and around the Kalahari Desert in southern Africa. They number approximately 50,000 and speak San and other languages of the Khoisan family. They are characteristically small-statured and brown-skinned.

bushmaster large snake *Lachesis muta*. It is a type of pit viper, and is related to the rattlesnakes. Up to 4 m/12 ft long, it is found in wooded areas of South and Central America, and is the largest venomous snake in the New World. When alarmed, it produces a noise by vibrating its tail among dry leaves.

bushranger Australian armed robber of the 19th century. The first bushrangers were escaped convicts. The last gang was led by Ned Kelly and his brother Dan in 1878–80. They form the subject of many Australian ballads.

Bustamante (William) Alexander (born Clarke) 1884–1977. Jamaican socialist politician. As leader of the Labour Party, he was the first prime minister of independent Jamaica 1962–67.

bustard bird of the family Otididae, related to

cranes but with a rounder body, a thicker neck, and a relatively short beak. Bustards are found on the ground on open plains and fields. The bustard has been extinct in Britain for some time, and the great Indian bustard is endangered.

butane C_4H_{10} one of two gaseous alkanes (paraffin hydrocarbons) having the same formula but differing in structure. Normal butane is derived from natural gas; isobutane is a by-product of petroleum manufacture. Liquefied under pressure, it is used as a fuel for industrial and domestic purposes.

Buthelezi Chief Gatsha 1928– . Zulu leader and politician, chief minister of KwaZulu, a black 'homeland' in the Republic of South Africa from 1970. He is the founder (1975) and president of ◊Inkatha, a paramilitary organization secretly in receipt of South African government funds.

Butler Samuel 1835–1902. English author who made his name 1872 with a satiric attack on contemporary utopianism, *Erewhon*, but is now remembered for his autobiographical *The Way of All Flesh* written 1872–85 and published 1903.

buttercup plant of the genus *Ranunculus* of the buttercup family with divided leaves and yellow flowers. Species include the common buttercup *R. acris* and the creeping buttercup *R. repens*.

butterfly insect belonging, like moths, to the order Lepidoptera, in which the wings are covered with tiny scales, often brightly coloured. There are some 15,000 species of butterfly, many of which are under threat throughout the world because of the destruction of habitat.

butterwort insectivorous plant, genus *Pinguicula*, of the bladderwort family, with purplish flowers and a rosette of flat leaves covered with a sticky secretion that traps insects.

buzzard any of a number of species of medium-sized hawks with broad wings, often seen soaring. The *common buzzard Buteo buteo* of Europe and Asia is about 55 cm/1.8 ft long with a wingspan of over 1.2 m/4 ft. It preys on a variety of small animals up to the size of a rabbit.

Byatt A(ntonia) S(usan) 1936– . English novelist and critic. Her fifth novel, *Possession*, won the 1990 Booker Prize. *The Virgin in the Garden* 1978 is a confident, zestfully handled account of a varied group of characters putting on a school play during Coronation year, 1953. It has a sequel, *Still Life* 1985.

Byelorussian or *Belorussian* 'White Russian' native of Belarus. Byelorussian, a Balto-Slavic language belonging to the Indo-European family, is spoken by about 10 million people, including some in Poland. It is written in the Cyrillic script. Byelorussian literature dates to the 11th century AD.

Byrd Richard Evelyn 1888–1957. US aviator and explorer. The first to fly over the North Pole (1926), he also flew over the South Pole (1929), and led five overland expeditions in Antarctica.

Byrd William 1543–1623. English composer. His church choral music (set to Latin words, as he was a firm Catholic), notably masses for three, four, and five voices, is among the greatest Renaissance music. He also composed secular vocal and instrumental music.

Byrds, the US pioneering folk-rock group 1964–73. Emulated for their 12–string guitar sound, as on the hits 'Mr Tambourine Man' (a 1965 version of Bob Dylan's song) and 'Eight Miles High' 1966, they moved towards country rock in the late 1960s.

Byron George Gordon, 6th Baron Byron 1788–1824. English poet who became the symbol of Romanticism and political liberalism throughout Europe in the 19th century. His reputation was established with the first two cantos of *Childe Harold* 1812. Later works include *The Prisoner of Chillon* 1816, *Beppo* 1818, *Mazeppa* 1819, and, most notably, the satirical *Don Juan* 1819–24. He left England in 1816, spending most of his later life in Italy.

byte in computing, a basic unit of storage of information. A byte contains 8 ◊bits and can specify 256 values, such as the numbers from 0 to 255, or 256 colours at one byte per pixel (picture element). Three bytes (24 bits) can specify 16,777,216 values. Twenty-four-bit colour graphics with 16.8 million colours can provide a photo-realistic colour display.

Byzantine Empire the *Eastern Roman Empire* 395–1453, with its capital at Constantinople (formerly Byzantium, modern Istanbul). Syria, Egypt, and N Africa were in the 7th–8th centuries lost to the Muslims, who twice besieged Constantinople (673– 77,718). Under the Macedonian dynasty (867–1056) the empire reached the height of its prosperity, and defeated the Bulgars (1018). In 1071–73 most of Anatolia was conquered by the Seljuk Turks. The Greek Orthodox Church had broken with the papacy in 867, and the Fourth Crusade sacked Constantinople 1204 and created a new Latin (W European) Empire. The Byzantine Empire was restored 1261–1453, when the Turks captured Constantinople and founded the ◊Ottoman Empire.

Byzantine style style in the visual arts and architecture that originated in the 4th–5th centuries in Byzantium (the capital of the Eastern Roman Empire), and spread to Italy, throughout the Balkans, and to Russia, where it survived for many centuries. It is characterized by heavy stylization, strong linear emphasis, the use of rigid artistic stereotypes and rich colours such as gold. Byzantine artists excelled in mosaic work and manuscript painting. In architecture, the dome supported on pendentives was in widespread use.

Byzantium (modern Istanbul) ancient Greek city on the Bosporus, founded as a colony of the Greek city of Megara, near Corinth, about 660 BC. In AD 330 the capital of the Roman Empire was transferred there by Constantine the Great, who renamed it ◊Constantinople.

C high-level general-purpose computer-programming language popular on minicomputers and microcomputers. Developed in the early 1970s from an earlier language called BCPL, C was first used as the language of the operating system ⟡Unix, though it has since become widespread beyond Unix. It is useful for writing fast and efficient systems programs, such as operating systems (which control the operations of the computer).

Cabal, the group of politicians, the English king Charles II's counsellors 1667–73, whose initials made up the word by coincidence – Clifford (Thomas Clifford 1630–1673), Ashley (Anthony Ashley Cooper, 1st Earl of ⟡Shaftesbury), ⟡Buckingham (George Villiers, 2nd Duke of Buckingham), Arlington (Henry Bennett, 1st Earl of Arlington 1618–1685), and ⟡Lauderdale (John Maitland, Duke of Lauderdale).

cabbage plant *Brassica oleracea* of the cress family Cruciferae, allied to the turnip and wild mustard, or charlock. It is a table vegetable, cultivated as early as 2000 BC, and the numerous commercial varieties include kale, Brussels sprouts, common cabbage, savoy, cauliflower, sprouting broccoli, and kohlrabi.

cabinet in politics, the group of ministers holding a country's highest executive offices who decide government policy. In Britain the cabinet system originated under the Stuarts. Under William III it became customary for the king to select his ministers from the party with a parliamentary majority. The US cabinet, unlike the British, does not initiate legislation, and its members, appointed by the president, must not be members of Congress.

cable television distribution of broadcast signals through cable relay systems. Narrow-band systems were originally used to deliver services to areas with poor regular reception; systems with wider bands using coaxial and fibreoptic cable are increas-ingly used for distribution and development of home-based interactive services.

Caboto Giovanni or *John Cabot* 1450–1498. Italian navigator. Commissioned, with his three sons, by Henry VII of England to discover unknown lands, he arrived at Cape Breton Island on 24 June 1497, thus becoming the first European to reach the North American mainland (he thought he was in NE Asia). In 1498 he sailed again, touching Greenland, and probably died on the voyage.

cacao tropical American evergreen tree *Theobroma cacao* of the Sterculia family, now also cultivated in W Africa and Sri Lanka. Its seeds are cocoa beans, from which ⟡cocoa and chocolate are prepared.

cactus (plural *cacti*) plant of the family Cactaceae, although the term is commonly applied to many different succulent and prickly plants. True cacti have a woody axis (central core) overlaid with an enlarged fleshy stem, which assumes various forms and is usually covered with spines (actually reduced leaves). They all have special adaptations to growing in dry areas. Some species have been introduced to the Old World, for example, in the Mediterranean area.

CAD (acronym for computer-*aided* *design*) the use of computers in creating and editing design drawings. CAD also allows such things as automatic testing of designs and multiple or animated three-dimensional views of designs. CAD systems are widely used in architecture, electronics, and engineering, for example in the motor-vehicle industry, where cars designed with the assistance of computers are now commonplace. A related development is ⟡CAM (computer-assisted

UK Cabinet

Prime Minister
Lord President of the Council and Leader of the House of Lords
Lord Chancellor
Secretary of State for Foreign and Commonwealth Affairs
Chancellor of the Exchequer
Home Secretary
Secretary of State for Trade and Industry
Secretary of State for Defence
Secretary of State for Wales
Lord Privy Seal and Leader of the House of Commons
Secretary of State for Social Services
Secretary of State for Northern Ireland
Minister of Agriculture, Fisheries and Food
Secretary of State for the Environment
Secretary of State for Employment
Secretary of State for Education and Science
Chief Secretary to the Treasury
Secretary of State for Scotland
Secretary of State for Energy
Chancellor of the Duchy of Lancaster
Secretary of State for Transport

manufacture).

caddis fly insect of the order Trichoptera. Adults are generally dull brown, mothlike, with wings covered in tiny hairs. Mouthparts are poorly developed, and many caddis flies do not feed as adults. They are usually found near water.

cadenza in music, an unaccompanied bravura passage (requiring elaborate, virtuoso execution) in the style of an improvisation for the soloist during a concerto.

Cadiz Spanish city and naval base, capital and seaport of the province of Cadiz, standing on Cadiz Bay, an inlet of the Atlantic, 103 km/64 mi S of Seville; population (1991) 156,600. After the discovery of the Americas 1492, Cadiz became one of Europe's most vital trade ports. The English adventurer Francis ◊Drake burned a Spanish fleet here 1587 to prevent the sailing of the ◊Armada.

cadmium soft, silver-white, ductile, and malleable metallic element, symbol Cd, atomic number 48, relative atomic mass 112.40. Cadmium occurs in nature as a sulphide or carbonate in zinc ores. It is a toxic metal that, because of industrial dumping, has become an environmental pollutant. It is used in batteries, electroplating, and as a constituent of alloys used for bearings with low coefficients of friction; it is also a constituent of an alloy with a very low melting point.

caecilian tropical amphibian of wormlike appearance. There are about 170 species known, forming the amphibian order Apoda (also known as Caecilia or Gymnophiona). Caecilians have a grooved skin that gives a 'segmented' appearance, have no trace of limbs, and mostly live below ground. Some species bear live young, others lay eggs.

Caedmon 7th century. Earliest known English poet. According to the Northumbrian historian Bede, when Caedmon was a cowherd at the Christian monastery of Whitby, he was commanded to sing by a stranger in a dream, and on waking produced a hymn on the Creation. The poem is preserved in some manuscripts. Caedmon became a monk and may have composed other religious poems.

Caernarvon or *Caernarfon* administrative headquarters of Gwynedd, N Wales, situated on the SW shore of the Menai Strait; population (1981) 10,000. Formerly a Roman station, it is now a market town and port. The first Prince of Wales (later ◊Edward II) was born in Caernarvon Castle; Edward VIII was invested here 1911 as was Prince Charles in 1969.

Caesar Gaius Julius *c.* 100–44 BC. Roman statesman and general. He formed with Pompey and Crassus the First Triumvirate 60 BC. He conquered Gaul 58–50 and invaded Britain 55 and 54. He fought against Pompey 49–48, defeating him at Pharsalus. After a period in Egypt Caesar returned to Rome as dictator from 46. He was assassinated by conspirators on the Ides of March 44.

Caesarean section surgical operation to deliver a baby by cutting through the mother's abdominal and intrauterine walls. It may be recommended for almost any obstetric complication implying a threat to mother or baby. In the USA in 1990, about 25% of all births were by Caesarean section.

caffeine ◊alkaloid organic substance found in tea, coffee, and kola nuts; it stimulates the heart and central nervous system. When isolated, it is a bitter crystalline compound, $C_8H_{10}N_4O_2$. Too much caffeine (more than six average cups of tea or coffee a day) can be detrimental to health.

Cage John 1912– . US composer. A pupil of Arnold ◊Schoenberg, he maintained that all sounds should be available for musical purposes; for example, he used 24 radios, tuned to random stations, in *Imaginary Landscape No 4* 1951. He also worked to reduce the control of the composer over the music, introducing randomness (aleatory music) and inexactitude and allowing sounds to 'be themselves'. Cage's unconventional ideas have had a profound impact on 20th-century music.

Cagliari capital and port of Sardinia, Italy, on the Gulf of Cagliari; population (1988) 222,000. Founded by the Phoenicians, it was taken by the Romans in the second Punic War. Industries include cement, superphosphates, flour milling, and sugar refining; agriculture is important.

Cagney James 1899–1986. US actor who moved to films from Broadway. Usually associated with gangster roles (*The Public Enemy* 1931), he was an actor of great versatility, playing Bottom in *A Midsummer Night's Dream* 1935 and singing and dancing in *Yankee Doodle Dandy* 1942.

Cahora Bassa largest hydroelectric scheme in Africa, created as a result of the damming of the Zambezi River to form a reservoir 230 km/144 mi long in W Mozambique.

Cairo capital of Egypt, on the E bank of the Nile 13 km/8 mi above the apex of the delta and 160 km/100 mi from the Mediterranean; the largest city in Africa and in the Middle East; population (1985) 6,205,000; metropolitan area (1987) 13,300,000. Industries include textiles, iron and steel, food and tobacco processing, and consumer goods.

Cajun member of a French-speaking community of Louisiana, USA, descended from French-Canadians who, in the 18th century, were driven there from Nova Scotia (then known as Acadia, from which the name Cajun comes). *Cajun music* has a lively rhythm and features steel guitar, fiddle, and accordion.

calabash tropical South American evergreen tree *Crescentia cujete*, family Bignoniaceae, with gourds 50 cm/20 in across, which are used as water containers. The Old World tropical vine bottle gourd *Lagenaria siceraria* of the gourd family Cucurbitaceae is sometimes called calabash, and it produces equally large true gourds.

Calabria mountainous earthquake region occupying the 'toe' of Italy, comprising the provinces of Catanzaro, Cosenza, and Reggio; capital Catanzaro; area 15,100 sq km/5,829 sq mi; population (1990) 2,153,700. Reggio is the industrial centre.

calcite colourless, white, or light-coloured common rock-forming mineral, calcium carbonate, CaCO₃. It is the main constituent of ⟩limestone and marble, and forms many types of invertebrate shell.

calcium soft, silvery-white metallic element, symbol Ca, atomic number 20, relative atomic mass 40.08. It is one of the ⟩alkaline-earth metals. It is the fifth most abundant element (the third most abundant metal) in the Earth's crust. It is found mainly as its carbonate CaCO₃, which occurs in a fairly pure condition as chalk and limestone (see ⟩calcite). Calcium is an essential component of bones, teeth, shells, milk, and leaves, and it forms 1.5% of the human body by mass.

calculator pocket-sized electronic computing device for performing numerical calculations. It can add, subtract, multiply, and divide; many calculators also compute squares and roots, and have advanced trigonometric and statistical functions. Input is by a small keyboard and results are shown on a one-line computer screen, typically a ⟩liquid crystal display (LCD) or a light-emitting diode (LED). The first electronic calculator was manufactured by the Bell Punch Company in the USA 1963.

calculus branch of mathematics that permits the manipulation of continuously varying quantities, used in practical problems involving such matters as changing speeds, problems of flight, varying stresses in the framework of a bridge, and alternating current theory. *Integral calculus* deals with the method of summation or adding together the effects of continuously varying quantities. *Differential calculus* deals in a similar way with rates of change. Many of its applications arose from the study of the gradients of the tangents to curves.

Calcutta largest city of India, on the river Hooghly, the westernmost mouth of the river Ganges, some 130 km/80 mi N of the Bay of Bengal. It is the capital of West Bengal; population (1981) 9,166,000. It is chiefly a commercial and industrial centre (engineering, shipbuilding, jute, and other textiles). Calcutta was the seat of government of British India 1773–1912. There is severe air pollution.

Calderón de la Barca Pedro 1600–1681. Spanish dramatist and poet. After the death of Lope de Vega 1635, he was considered to be the leading Spanish dramatist. Most celebrated of the 118 plays is the philosophical *La vida es sueño/Life is a Dream* 1635.

calendar division of the year into months, weeks, and days and the method of ordering the years. From year one, an assumed date of the birth of Jesus, dates are calculated backwards (BC 'before Christ' or BCE 'before common era') and forwards

(AD, Latin *anno Domini* 'in the year of the Lord', or CE 'common era'). The *lunar month* (period between one new moon and the next) naturally averages 29.5 days, but the Western calendar uses for convenience a *calendar month* with a complete number of days, 30 or 31 (Feb has 28). For adjustments, since there are slightly fewer than six extra hours a year left over, they are added to Feb as a 29th day every fourth year (*leap year*), century years being excepted unless they are divisible by 400. For example, 1896 was a leap year; 1900 was not. 1996 is the next leap year.

Calgary city in Alberta, Canada, on the Bow River, in the foothills of the Rockies; at 1,048 m/3,440 ft it is one of the highest Canadian towns; population (1986) 671,000. It is the centre of a large agricultural region and is the oil and financial centre of Alberta and W Canada. Founded as Fort Calgary by the North West Mounted Police 1875, it was reached by the Canadian Pacific Railway 1885 and developed rapidly after the discovery of oil 1914. The 1988 Winter Olympic Games were held here.

Cali city in SW Colombia, in the Cauca Valley 975 m/3,200 ft above sea level; population (1985) 1,398,276. Cali was founded 1536. It has textile, sugar, and engineering industries.

California Pacific-coast state of the USA; nicknamed the Golden State (originally because of its gold mines, more recently because of its orange groves and sunshine); *area* 411,100 sq km/158,685 sq mi; *capital* Sacramento; *cities* Los Angleles, San Diego, San Francisco, San José, Fresno; *physical* Sierra Nevada, including Yosemite and Sequoia national parks, Lake Tahoe, Mount Whitney (4,418 m/14,500 ft, the highest mountain in the lower 48 states); the Coast Range; Death Valley (282 ft/86 m below sea level, the lowest point in the western hemisphere); Colorado and Mojave deserts; Monterey Peninsula; Salton Sea; the San Andreas fault; huge, offshore underwater volcanoes with tops 5 mi/8 km across; *products* leading agricultural state with fruit (peaches, citrus, grapes in the valley of the San Joaquin and Sacramento rivers), nuts, wheat, vegetables, cotton, and rice, all mostly grown by irrigation, beef cattle, timber, fish, oil, natural gas, aerospace technology, electronics (Silicon Valley), food processing, films and television programmes, great reserves of energy (geothermal) in the hot water that lies beneath much of the state; *population* (1990) 29,760,000, the most populous state of the USA (white 69.9%, Hispanic 25.8%, Asian and Pacific islander, including many Vietnamese, 9.6%, black 7.4%, American Indian 0.8%; *famous people* Luther Burbank, Walt Disney, William Randolph Hearst, Jack London, Marilyn Monroe, Richard Nixon, Ronald Reagan, John Steinbeck; *history* colonized by Spain 1769; ceded to the USA after the Mexican War 1848; became a state 1850. The discovery of gold in the Sierra Nevada Jan 1848 was followed by the gold rush 1849–56.

californium synthesized, radioactive, metallic element of the actinide series, symbol Cf, atomic number 98, relative atomic mass 251. It is produced in very small quantities and used in nuclear reactors as a neutron source. The longest-lived isotope, Cf-251, has a half-life of 800 years.

Caligula Gaius Caesar AD 12–41. Roman emperor, son of Germanicus and successor to Tiberius AD 37. Caligula was a cruel tyrant and was assassinated by an officer of his guard. Believed to have been mentally unstable, he is remembered for giving a consulship to his horse Incitatus.

caliph title of civic and religious heads of the world of Islam. The first caliph was Abu Bakr. Nominally elective, the office became hereditary, held by the Ummayyad dynasty 661–750 and then by the ◊Abbasid dynasty. After the death of the last Abbasid 1258, the title was claimed by a number of Muslim chieftains in Egypt, Turkey, and India. The most powerful of these were the Turkish sultans of the Ottoman Empire.

Callaghan (Leonard) James, Baron Callaghan 1912– . British Labour politician. As chancellor of the Exchequer 1964–67, he introduced corporation and capital-gains taxes, and resigned following devaluation. He was home secretary 1967–70 and prime minister 1976–79 in a period of increasing economic stress. In 1980 he resigned the party leadership under left-wing pressure, and in 1985 announced that he would not stand for Parliament in the next election.

Callas Maria. Adopted name of Maria Kalogeropoulos 1923–1977. US lyric soprano, born in New York of Greek parents. With a voice of fine range and a gift for dramatic expression, she excelled in operas including *Norma*, *La Sonnambula*, *Madame Butterfly*, *Aïda*, *Lucia di Lammermoor*, and *Medea*.

calligraphy art of handwriting, regarded in China and Japan as the greatest of the visual arts, and playing a large part in Islamic art because the depiction of the human and animal form is forbidden. Printing and the typewriter reduced the need for calligraphy in the West. In the UK there was a 20th-century revival inspired by Edward Johnston (1872–1944) and Irene Wellington (1904–1984).

calorie c.g.s. unit of heat, now replaced by the ◊joule (one calorie is approximately 4.2 joules). It is the heat required to raise the temperature of one gram of water by 1°C. In dietetics, the calorie or kilocalorie is equal to 1,000 calories.

calotype paper-based photograph using a wax paper negative, the first example of the ◊negative/positive process invented by the English photographer Fox Talbot around 1834.

Calvin John (also known as *Cauvin* or *Chauvin*) 1509–1564. French-born Swiss Protestant church reformer and theologian. He was a leader of the Reformation in Geneva and set up a strict religious community there. His theological system is known as Calvinism, and his church government as ◊Presbyterianism. Calvin wrote (in Latin) *Institutes of the Christian Religion* 1536 and commentaries on the New Testament and much of the Old Testament.

Calvinism Christian doctrine as interpreted by John Calvin and adopted in Scotland, parts of Switzerland, and the Netherlands; by the ◊Puritans in England and New England, USA; and by the subsequent Congregational and Presbyterian churches in the USA. Its central doctrine is predestination, under which certain souls (the elect) are predestined by God through the sacrifice of Jesus to salvation, and the rest to damnation. Although Calvinism is rarely accepted today in its strictest interpretation, the 20th century has seen a Neo-Calvinist revival through the work of Karl Barth.

calypso West Indian satirical ballad with a syncopated beat. Calypso is a traditional song form of Trinidad, a feature of its annual carnival, with roots in W African praise singing. It was first popularized in the USA by Harry Belafonte (1927–) in 1956.

calyx collective term for the ◊sepals of a flower, forming the outermost whorl of the perianth. It surrounds the other flower parts and protects them while in bud. In some flowers, for example, the campions *Silene*, the sepals are fused along their sides, forming a tubular calyx.

cam part of a machine that converts circular motion to linear motion or vice versa. The *edge cam* in a car engine is in the form of a rounded projection on a shaft, the camshaft. When the camshaft turns, the cams press against linkages (plungers or followers) that open the valves in the cylinders.

CAM (acronym for computer-aided manufacture) the use of computers to control production processes; in particular, the control of machine tools and ◊robots in factories. In some factories, the whole design and production system has been automated by linking ◊CAD (computer-aided design) to CAM.

Camargue marshy area of the ◊Rhône delta, S of Arles, France; about 780 sq km/300 sq mi. Bulls and horses are bred here, and the nature reserve, which is known for its bird life, forms the southern part.

cambium in botany, a layer of actively dividing cells (lateral meristem), found within stems and roots, that gives rise to secondary growth in perennial plants, causing an increase in girth. There are two main types of cambium: *vascular cambium*, which gives rise to secondary ◊xylem and ◊phloem tissues, and *cork cambium* (or phellogen), which gives rise to secondary cortex and cork tissues (see ◊bark).

Cambodia State of (formerly *Kmer Republic* 1970–76, *Democratic Kampuchea* 1976–79, *People's Republic of Kampuchea* 1979–89);

country in SE Asia, bordered N and NW by Thailand, N by Laos, E and SE by Vietnam, and SW by the South China Sea; *area* 181,035 sq km/ 69,880 sq mi; *capital* Phnom Penh; *physical* mostly flat forested plains with mountains in SW and N; Mekong River runs N–S; *head of state* Prince Sihanouk from 1991; *head of government* Hun Sen from 1985; *political system* transitional; *exports* rubber, rice, pepper, wood, cattle; *population* (1990 est) 6,993,000; *languages* Khmer (official); French; *recent history* independence was achieved from France 1953. Vietnamese invasion 1978; the country was known as the People's Republic of Kampuchea until Vietnamese forces were fully withdrawn. Peace agreement 1991 provided for UN Transitional Authority in Cambodia (UNTAC) to administer country in transition period. Communism abandoned 1991.

Cambrian period of geological time 590–505 million years ago; the first period of the Palaeozoic era. All invertebrate animal life appeared, and marine algae were widespread. The earliest fossils with hard shells, such as trilobites, date from this period.

Cambridge city in England, on the river Cam (a river sometimes called by its earlier name, Granta), 80 km/50 mi N of London; population (1989) 101,000. It is the administrative headquarters of Cambridgeshire. The city is centred on Cambridge University (founded 12th century), whose outstanding buildings, including Kings College Chapel, back onto the river.

Cambridgeshire county in E England; *area* 3,410 sq km/1,316 sq mi; *towns* Cambridge (administrative headquarters), Ely, Huntingdon, Peterborough; *features* rivers: Ouse, Cam, Nene; Isle of Ely; Cambridge University; at RAF Molesworth, near Huntingdon, Britain's second cruise missile base was deactivated Jan 1989; *products* mainly agricultural; *population* (1991) 640,700; *famous people* Oliver Cromwell, Octavia Hill, John Maynard Keynes.

camel large cud-chewing mammal of the eventoed hoofed order Artiodactyla. Unlike typical ruminants, it has a three-chambered stomach. It has two toes which have broad soft soles for walking on sand, and hooves resembling nails. There are two species, the single-humped *Arabian camel Camelus dromedarius* and the twin-humped *Bactrian camel Camelus bactrianus* from Asia. They carry a food reserve of fatty tissue in the hump, can go without drinking for long periods, can feed on salty vegetation, and withstand extremes of heat and cold, thus being well adapted to desert conditions.

camellia any oriental evergreen shrub with roselike flowers of the genus *Camellia*, tea family Theaceae. Numerous species, including *C. japonica* and *C. reticulata*, have been introduced into Europe, the USA, and Australia.

Camelot legendary seat of King ◊Arthur.

cameo small relief carving of semiprecious stone, shell, or glass. A pale-coloured surface layer is carved to reveal a darker ground. Fine cameos were produced in ancient Greece and Rome, during the Renaissance, and in the Victorian era. They were used for decorating goblets and vases, and as jewellery.

camera apparatus used in ◊photography, consisting of a light-proof box with a lens at one end and sensitized film at the other. The lens collects rays of light reflected from the subject and brings them together as a sharp image on the film; it has marked numbers known as ◊apertures, or F stops, that reduce or increase the amount of light. Apertures also control depth of field. A shutter controls the amount of time light has to affect the film. There are small-, medium-, and large-format cameras; the format refers to the size of recorded image and the dimensions of the print obtained.

camera obscura darkened box with a tiny hole for projecting the inverted image of the scene outside on to a screen inside. For its development as a device for producing photographs, see ◊photography.

Cameron Julia Margaret 1815–1879. British photographer. She made lively, revealing portraits of the Victorian intelligentsia using a large camera, fiveminute exposures, and wet plates. Her subjects included Charles Darwin and Alfred Tennyson.

Cameroon Republic of; country in W Africa, bordered NW by Nigeria, NE by Chad, E by the Central African Republic, S by Congo, Gabon, and Equatorial Guinea, and W by the Atlantic; *area* 475,440 sq km/183,638 sq mi; *capital* Yaoundé; *physical* desert in far N in Lake Chad basin, mountains in W, dry savanna plateau in the intermediate area, and dense tropical rainforest in S; *head of state and government* Paul Biya from 1982; *political system* transitional; *exports* cocoa, coffee, bananas, cotton, timber, rubber, groundnuts, gold, aluminium, crude oil; *population* (1990 est) 11,109,000; *languages* French and English in pidgin variations (official); 163 indigenous languages; *recent history* German rule was established by treaty 1884. The country was captured by Allied forces in World War I and divided between Britain and France. French Cameroon became an independent republic 1960; the S part of British Cameroon joined 1961 (the N part merged with Nigeria). New constitution made Cameroon a unitary state, the United Republic of Cameroon, 1972; name changed to Republic of Cameroon 1984.

Camorra Italian secret society formed about 1820 by criminals in the dungeons of Naples and continued once they were freed. It dominated politics from 1848, was suppressed 1911, but many members eventually surfaced in the US ◊Mafia. The Camorra still operates in the Naples area.

camouflage colours or structures that allow an

animal to blend with its surroundings to avoid detection by other animals. Camouflage can take the form of matching the background colour, of countershading (darker on top, lighter below, to counteract natural shadows), or of irregular patterns that break up the outline of the animal's body. More elaborate camouflage involves closely resembling a feature of the natural environment, as with the stick insect; this is closely akin to ◊mimicry.

Campaign for Nuclear Disarmament (CND) nonparty-political British organization advocating the abolition of nuclear weapons worldwide. CND seeks unilateral British initiatives to help start the multilateral process and end the arms race. It was founded 1958.

Campania agricultural region (wheat, citrus, wine, vegetables, tobacco) of S Italy, including the volcano ◊Vesuvius; capital Naples; industrial centres Benevento, Caserta, and Salerno; area 13,600 sq km/5,250 sq mi; population (1990) 5,853,900. There are ancient sites at Pompeii, Herculaneum, and Paestum.

Campbell Donald Malcolm 1921–1967. British car and speedboat enthusiast, son of Malcolm Campbell, who simultaneously held the land-speed and water-speed records. In 1964 he set the world water-speed record of 444.57 kph/276.3 mph on Lake Dumbleyung, Australia, with the turbojet hydroplane *Bluebird*, and achieved the land-speed record of 648.7 kph/403.1 mph at Lake Eyre salt flats, Australia. He was killed in an attempt to raise his water-speed record on Coniston Water, England.

Campbell Malcolm 1885–1948. British racing driver who, at one time, held both land- and water-speed records. His car and boat were both called *Bluebird*. His son Donald Campbell emulated his feats.

Campbell-Bannerman Henry 1836–1908. British Liberal politician, prime minister 1905–08. It was during his term of office that the South African colonies achieved self-government, and the Trades Disputes Act 1906 was passed. He began the conflict between Commons and Lords that led to the Parliament Act of 1911. He resigned 1908.

Camp David Agreements two framework agreements signed 1978 by Israeli prime minister Begin and Egyptian president Sadat at Camp David, Maryland, USA, under the guidance of US president Carter, covering an Egypt–Israel peace treaty and phased withdrawal of Israel from Sinai, which was completed 1982, and an overall Middle East settlement including the election by the West Bank and Gaza Strip Palestinians of a 'self-governing authority'. This issue has stalled repeatedly over questions of who should represent the Palestinians and what form the self-governing body should take.

camphor $C_{10}H_{16}O$ volatile, aromatic ◊ketone

substance obtained from the camphor tree *Cinnamomum camphora*. It is distilled from chips of the wood, and is used in insect repellents and medicinal inhalants and liniments, and in the manufacture of celluloid.

Campin Robert, also known as the **Master of Flémalle** c. 1378–1444. Netherlandish painter of the early Renaissance, active in Tournai from 1406, one of the first northern masters to use oil. Several altarpieces are attributed to him. Rogier van der Weyden was his pupil.

Camus Albert 1913–1960. Algerian-born French writer. A journalist in France, he was active in the Resistance during World War II. His novels, which owe much to ◊existentialism, include *L'Etranger/ The Outsider* 1942, *La Peste/The Plague* 1948, and *L'Homme révolté/The Rebel* 1952. He was awarded the Nobel Prize for Literature 1957.

Canaan ancient region between the Mediterranean and the Dead Sea, called in the Bible the 'Promised Land' of the Israelites. It was occupied as early as the 3rd millennium BC by the Canaanites, a Semitic-speaking people who were known to the Greeks of the 1st millennium BC as Phoenicians. The capital was Ebla (now Tell Mardikh, Syria).

Canada Dominion of; country occupying the northern part of the North American continent, bordered S by the USA, N by the Arctic Ocean, NW by Alaska, E by the Atlantic Ocean, and W by the Pacific Ocean; **area** 9,970,600 km/3,849,803 sq mi; *capital* Ottawa; *physical* world's second largest country; Rocky Mountains in W, with low-lying plains (Great Plains or Prairies) in interior and rolling hills in E; Canadian Shield in E; Great Lakes in S; Niagara Falls; St Lawrence Seaway; Mackenzie River. The climate varies from temperate in the S to arctic in the N; *head of state* Elizabeth II from 1952 represented by governor general; *head of*

government Brian Mulroney from 1984; *political system* federal constitutional monarchy; *exports* wheat, timber, pulp, newsprint, fish (salmon), furs, oil, natural gas, aluminium, asbestos, coal, copper, iron, zinc, nickel (world's largest producer), uranium (world's largest producer), motor vehicles and parts, industrial and agricultural machinery, fertilizers, chemicals; *population* (1990 est) 26,527,000, including 300,000 North American Indians, some 300,000 Métis (people of mixed race), and 19,000 Inuit (or Eskimo); *languages* English, French (both official); North American Indian languages and the Inuit Inuktitut; *recent history* the Dominion of Canada, a member of the British Commonwealth, was founded 1867 (having been ceded to Britain by France 1763); Newfoundland joined 1949. The Canada Act 1982 removed Britain's last legal control over Canadian affairs.

canal artificial waterway constructed for drainage, irrigation, or navigation. *Irrigation canals* carry water for irrigation from rivers, reservoirs, or wells, and are designed to maintain an even flow of water over the whole length. *Navigation and ship canals* are constructed at one level between ◊locks, and frequently link with rivers or sea inlets to form a waterway system. The Suez Canal 1869 and the Panama Canal 1914 eliminated long trips around continents and dramatically shortened shipping routes.

Canaletto Antonio (Giovanni Antonio Canale) 1697–1768. Italian painter celebrated for his paintings of views (*vedute*) of Venice (his native city), popular with foreign patrons. He also painted the river Thames and London 1746–56.

canary bird *Serinus canaria* of the finch family, found wild in the Canary Islands and Madeira. It is greenish with a yellow underside. Canaries have been bred as cage birds in Europe since the 15th century, and many domestic varieties are yellow or orange.

Canary Islands (Spanish *Canarias*) group of volcanic islands 100 km/60 mi off the NW coast of Africa, forming the Spanish provinces of Las Palmas and Santa Cruz de Tenerife; area 7,300 sq km/2,818 sq mi; population (1986) 1,615,000. The chief centres are Santa Cruz on Tenerife (which also has the highest peak in extracontinental Spain, Pico de Teide, 3,713 m/12,186 ft), and Las Palmas on Gran Canaria. The province of Santa Cruz comprises Tenerife, Palma, Gomera, and Hierro; the province of Las Palmas comprises Gran Canaria, Lanzarote, and Fuerteventura. There are also six uninhabited islets. The Northern Hemisphere Observatory (1981) is on the island of La Palma, the first in the world to be controlled remotely. Observation conditions are exceptionally good because there is no moisture, no artificial light pollution, and little natural airglow.

Canberra capital of Australia (since 1908), situated in the Australian Capital Territory, enclosed within New South Wales, on a tributary of the Murrumbidgee River; area (Australian Capital Territory including the port at Jervis Bay) 2,432 sq km/939 sq mi; population (1988) 297,300.

cancer group of diseases characterized by abnormal proliferation of cells. Cancer (malignant) cells are usually degenerate, capable only of reproducing themselves (tumour formation). Malignant cells tend to spread from their site of origin by travelling through the bloodstream or lymphatic system.

Cancer faintest of the zodiacal constellations (its brightest stars are fourth magnitude). It lies in the northern hemisphere, between Leo and Gemini, and is represented as a crab. Cancer's most distinctive feature is the star cluster Praesepe, popularly known as the Beehive. The Sun passes through the constellation during late July and early Aug. In astrology, the dates for Cancer are between about 22 June and 22 July (see ◊precession).

candela SI unit (symbol cd) of luminous intensity, which replaced the old units of candle and standard candle. It measures the brightness of a light itself rather than the amount of light falling on an object, which is called *illuminance* and measured in ◊lux.

Candida albicans yeastlike fungus present in the human digestive tract and in the vagina, which causes no harm in most healthy people. However, it can cause problems if it multiplies excessively, as in vaginal candidiasis or ◊thrush, the main symptom of which is intense itching. The most common form of thrush is oral, which often occurs in those taking steroids or prolonged courses of antibiotics.

cane reedlike stem of various plants such as the sugar cane, bamboo, and, in particular, the group of palms called rattans, consisting of the genus *Calamus* and its allies. Their slender stems are dried and used for making walking sticks, baskets, and furniture.

Canetti Elias 1905– . Bulgarian-born writer. He was exiled from Austria as a Jew 1938 and settled in England 1939. His books, written in German, include *Die Blendung/Auto da Fé* 1935. He was awarded the Nobel Prize for Literature 1981.

cannabis dried leaves and female flowers (marijuana) and resin (hashish) of certain varieties of ◊hemp *Cannabis sativa*, which are smoked or eaten and have an intoxicating effect. Cultivation of cannabis is illegal in the UK and USA except under licence.

canning food preservation in hermetically sealed containers by the application of heat. Originated by Nicolas Appert in France 1809 with glass containers, it was developed by Peter Durand in England 1810 with cans made of sheet steel thinly coated with tin to delay corrosion. Cans for beer and soft drinks are now generally made of aluminium.

Canning Charles John, 1st Earl 1812–1862. British

administrator, first viceroy of India from 1858. As governor general of India from 1856, he suppressed the Indian Mutiny with a fair but firm hand which earned him the nickname 'Clemency Canning'. He was the son of George Canning.

Canning George 1770–1827. British Tory politician, foreign secretary 1807–10 and 1822–27, and prime minister 1827. He was largely responsible, during the Napoleonic Wars, for the seizure of the Danish fleet and British intervention in the Spanish peninsula. During his second term as foreign secretary he supported the national movements in Greece and South America. When Wellington, Peel, and other Tories refused to serve under him as prime minister, he formed a coalition with the Whigs. He died in office.

canoeing sport of propelling a lightweight, shallow boat, pointed at both ends, by paddles or sails. Currently, canoes are made from fibreglass, but original boats were of wooden construction covered in bark or skin. Canoeing was popularized as a sport in the 19th century.

canon in music, an echo form for two or more parts repeating and following a leading melody at regular time intervals to achieve a harmonious effect. It is often found in classical music, for example ◊Vivaldi and J S ◊Bach.

canonization in the Catholic church, the admission of one of its members to the Calendar of ◊Saints. The evidence of the candidate's exceptional piety is contested before the Congregation for the Causes of Saints by the Promotor Fidei, popularly known as the *devil's advocate*. Papal ratification of a favourable verdict results in beatification, and full sainthood (conferred in St Peter's basilica, the Vatican) follows after further proof.

canon law rules and regulations of the Christian church, especially the Greek Orthodox, Roman Catholic, and Anglican churches. Its origin is sought in the declarations of Jesus and the apostles. In 1983 Pope John Paul II issued a new canon law code reducing offences carrying automatic excommunication, extending the grounds for annulment of marriage, removing the ban on marriage with non-Catholics, and banning trade union and political activity by priests.

Canopus or *Alpha Carinae* second brightest star in the sky (after Sirius), lying in the constellation Carina. It is a yellow-white supergiant about 120 light years from Earth, and thousands of times more luminous than the Sun.

Canova Antonio 1757–1822. Italian Neo-Classical sculptor, based in Rome from 1781. He received commissions from popes, kings, and emperors for his highly finished marble portrait busts and groups. He made several portraits of Napoleon. His reclining marble *Pauline Borghese* 1805–07 (Borghese Gallery, Rome) is a fine example of

cool, polished Classicism. He executed the tombs of popes Clement XIII, Pius VII, and Clement XIV. His marble sculptures include *Cupid and Psyche* (Louvre, Paris) and *The Three Graces*.

Cantabria autonomous region of N Spain; area 5,300 sq km/2,046 sq mi; population (1986) 525,000; capital Santander. There is mining, steel manufacturing, and fishing.

cantata in music, an extended work for voices, from the Italian, meaning 'sung', as opposed to ◊sonata ('sounded') for instruments. A cantata can be sacred or secular, sometimes uses solo voices, and usually has orchestral accompaniment. The first printed collection of sacred cantata texts dates from 1670.

Canterbury historic cathedral city in Kent, England, on the river Stour, 100 km/62 mi SE of London; population (1984) 39,000. The Roman Durovernum, Canterbury was the Saxon capital of Kent. In 597 King Ethelbert received Augustine's mission to England here, and the city has since been the metropolis of the Anglican Communion and seat of the archbiship of Canterbury.

cantilever beam or structure that is fixed at one end only, though it may be supported at some point along its length; for example, a diving board. The cantilever principle, widely used in construction engineering, eliminates the need for a second main support at the free end of the beam, allowing for more elegant structures and reducing the amount of materials required. Many large-span bridges have been built on the cantilever principle.

canton in France, an administrative district, a subdivision of the *arrondissement*; in Switzerland, one of the 23 subdivisions forming the Confederation.

Canton alternative spelling of Kwangchow or ◊Guangzhou in China.

Canute c. 995–1035. King of England from 1016, Denmark from 1018, and Norway from 1028. Having invaded England 1013 with his father, Sweyn, king of Denmark, he was acclaimed king on his father's death 1014 by his ◊Viking army. Canute defeated ◊Edmund II Ironside at Assandun, Essex, 1016, and became king of all England on Edmund's death. He succeeded his brother Harold as king of Denmark 1018, compelled King Malcolm to pay homage by invading Scotland about 1027, and conquered Norway 1028. He was succeeded by his illegitimate son Harold I.

capacitor or *condenser* device for storing electric charge, used in electronic circuits; it consists of two or more metal plates separated by an insulating layer called a dielectric.

Cape Canaveral promontory on the Atlantic coast of Florida, USA, 367 km/228 mi N of Miami, used as a rocket launch site by ◊NASA. It was known as Cape Kennedy 1963–73. The ◊Kennedy Space Center is nearby.

Cape Cod hook-shaped peninsula in SE Massachusetts, USA; 100 km/60 mi long and 1.6–32 km/1–20 mi wide; population (1980) 150,000. Its beaches and woods make it a popular tourist area. It is separated from the rest of the state by the Cape Cod Canal. The islands of Martha's Vineyard and Nantucket are just S of the cape. Basque and Norse fisherfolk are believed to have visited Cape Cod many years before the English Pilgrims landed at Provincetown 1620.

Cape Horn southernmost point of South America, in the Chilean part of the archipelago of ⟨⟩Tierra del Fuego; notorious for gales and heavy seas. It was named 1616 by Dutch explorer Willem Schouten (1580–1625) after his birthplace (Hoorn).

Čapek Karel 1890–1938. Czech writer whose works often deal with social injustice in an imaginative, satirical way. *R.U.R.* 1921 is a play in which robots (a term he coined) rebel against their controllers; the novel *Válka s Mloky/War with the Newts* 1936 is a science-fiction classic.

Capella or *Alpha Aurigae* brightest star in the constellation Auriga and the sixth brightest star in the sky. It consists of a pair of yellow giant stars 41 light years from Earth, orbiting each other every 104 days.

Cape of Good Hope South African headland forming a peninsula between Table Bay and False Bay, Cape Town. The first European to sail around it was Bartholomew Diaz 1488. Formerly named Cape of Storms, it was given its present name by King John II of Portugal.

Cape Province (Afrikaans *Kaapprovinsie*) largest province of the Republic of South Africa, named after the Cape of Good Hope; *area* 641,379 sq km/247,638 sq mi, excluding Walvis Bay; *capital* Cape Town; *towns* Port Elizabeth, East London, Kimberley, Grahamstown, Stellenbosch; *physical* Orange River; Drakensberg; Table Mountain (highest point Maclear's Beacon, 1,087 m/3,567 ft); Great Karoo Plateau; Walvis Bay; *products* fruit, vegetables, wine, meat, ostrich feathers, diamonds, copper, asbestos, manganese; *population* (1985) 5,041,000; officially including 44% coloured; 31% black; 25% white; 0.6% Asian; *history* Dutch traders established the first European settlement on the Cape 652, but it was taken by the British 1795, after the French Revolutionary armies had occupied the Netherlands, and was sold to Britain 1814. The Cape achieved self-government 1872. It was an original province of the Union 1910.

caper trailing shrub *Capparis spinosa*, native to the Mediterranean and belonging to the family Capparidaceae. Its flower buds are preserved in vinegar as a condiment.

Cape Town (Afrikaans *Kaapstad*) port and oldest town in South Africa, situated in the SW on Table Bay; population (1985) 776,617. Industries include horticulture and trade in wool, wine, fruit, grain,

and oil. It is the legislative capital of the Republic of South Africa and capital of Cape Province; it was founded 1652.

Cape Verde Republic of; group of islands in the Atlantic Ocean, off the W coast of Senegal (W Africa); *area* 4,033 sq km/1,557 sq mi; *capital* Praia; *physical* archipelago of ten volcanic islands, all but one inhabited; *head of state* Mascarenhas Monteiro from 1991; *head of government* Carlos Viega from 1991; *political system* socialist pluralist state; *exports* bananas, coffee, salt, fish; *population* (1990 est) 375,000 (including 100,000 Angolan refugees); *language* creole dialect of Portuguese; *recent history* independence was achieved from Portugal 1975. Union with Guinea-Bissau was provided for, but abandoned 1981. First multiparty elections held 1991; won by Movement for Democracy (MPD).

capillary narrowest blood vessel in vertebrates, 0.008–0.02 mm in diameter, barely wider than a red blood cell. Capillaries are distributed as *beds*, complex networks connecting arteries and veins. Capillary walls are extremely thin, consisting of a single layer of cells, and so nutrients, dissolved gases, and waste products can easily pass through them. This makes the capillaries the main area of exchange between the fluid (⟨⟩lymph) bathing body tissues and the blood.

capital in architecture, a stone placed on the top of a column, pier, or pilaster, and usually wider on the upper surface than the diameter of the supporting shaft. A capital consists of three parts: the top member, called the *abacus*, a block that acts as the supporting surface to the superstructure; the middle portion, known as the bell or *echinus*; and the lower part, called the necking or *astragal*.

capital in economics, accumulated or inherited wealth held in the form of assets (such as stocks and shares, property, and bank deposits). In stricter terms, capital is defined as the stock of goods used in the production of other goods, and may be *fixed capital* (such as buildings, plant, and machinery) that is durable, or *circulating capital* (raw materials and components) that is used up quickly.

capital gains tax income tax levied on the change of value of a person's assets after they are sold, including securities and real property.

capitalism economic system in which the principal means of production, distribution, and exchange are in private (individual or corporate) hands and competitively operated for profit. A *mixed economy* combines the private enterprise of capitalism and a degree of state monopoly, as in nationalized industries.

capital punishment punishment by death. Capital punishment, abolished in the UK 1965 for all crimes except treason, is retained in 92 countries and territories (1990), including the USA (37 states), China, and Islamic countries. Ireland abolished the death penalty for all offences 1990. Methods of execution include electrocution, lethal gas, hanging, shooting, lethal injection, garrotting, and decapitation.

Capone Al(phonse 'Scarface') 1898–1947. US gangster. During the ▷Prohibition period, he built a formidable criminal organization in Chicago. He was brutal in his pursuit of dominance, killing seven members of a rival gang in the St Valentine's Day massacre. He was imprisoned 1931–39 for income-tax evasion, the only charge that could be sustained against him.

Caporetto former name of Kobarid, Slovenia.

Capote Truman. Pen name of Truman Streckfus Persons 1924–1984. US novelist, journalist, and playwright. He wrote *Breakfast at Tiffany's* 1958; set a trend with the first 'nonfiction novel', *In Cold Blood* 1966, reconstructing a Kansas killing; and mingled recollection and fiction in *Music for Chameleons* 1980.

Cappadocia ancient region of Asia Minor, in E central Turkey. It was conquered by the Persians 584 BC but in the 3rd century BC became an independent kingdom. The region was annexed as a province of the Roman Empire AD 17. There are over 600 Byzantine cave churches cut into volcanic rock, dating mainly from the 10th and 11th centuries.

Capra Frank 1897–1991. Italian-born US film director. His films, satirical social comedies that often have idealistic heroes, include *It Happened One Night* 1934, *Mr Deeds Goes to Town* 1936, and *You Can't Take It With You* 1938, for each of which he received an Academy Award.

capriccio in music, a short instrumental piece, often humorous or whimsical in character. Well known or popular tunes often appear in a capriccio. The genre was popular in the 19th century.

Capricornus zodiacal constellation in the southern hemisphere next to Sagittarius. It is represented as a fish-tailed goat, and its brightest stars are third magnitude. The Sun passes through it late Jan to mid-Feb. In astrology, the dates for Capricornus (popularly known as Capricorn) are between about 22 Dec and 19 Jan (see ▷precession).

capsicum any pepper plant of the genus *Capsicum* of the nightshade family Solanaceae, native to Central and South America. The differing species produce green to red fruits that vary in size. The small ones are used whole to give the hot flavour of chilli, or ground to produce cayenne pepper; the large pointed or squarish pods, known as sweet peppers, are mild-flavoured and used as a vegetable.

capsule in botany, a dry, usually many-seeded fruit formed from an ovary composed of two or more fused ▷carpels, which splits open to release the seeds. The same term is used for the spore-containing structure of mosses and liverworts; this is borne at the top of a long stalk or seta.

capuchin monkey of the genus *Cebus* found in Central and South America, so called because the hairs on the head resemble the cowl of a Capuchin monk (a member of an independent branch of the Franciscan order). Capuchins live in small groups, feed on fruit and insects, and have a long tail that is semiprehensile and can give support when climbing through the trees.

capybara world's largest rodent *Hydrochoerus hydrochaeris*, up to 1.3 m/4 ft long and 50 kg/110 lb in weight. It is found in South America, and belongs to the guinea-pig family. The capybara inhabits marshes and dense vegetation around water. It has thin, yellowish hair, swims well, and can rest underwater with just eyes, ears, and nose above the surface.

car small, driver-guided, passenger-carrying motor vehicle; originally the automated version of the horse-drawn carriage, meant to convey people and their goods over streets and roads. From 1951 to 1991 the number of cars on British roads increased from 2 million to 20 million. Over 300 million motor vehicles are now produced each year worldwide. Most are four-wheeled and have water-cooled, piston-type internal-combustion engines fuelled by petrol or diesel. Variations have existed for decades that use ingenious and often nonpolluting power plants, but the motor industry long ago settled on this general formula for the consumer market. Experimental and sports models are streamlined, energy-efficient, and hand-built.

Caracas chief city and capital of Venezuela, situated on the Andean slopes, 13 km/8 mi S of its port La Guaira on the Caribbean coast; population of metropolitan area (1989) 3,373,100. Founded 1567, it is now a large industrial and commercial centre, notably for oil companies.

carambola small evergreen tree *Averrhoa carambola* of SE Asia. The fruits, called *star fruit*, are yellowish, about 12 cm/4 in long, with a five-pointed star-shaped cross-section. They may be eaten raw, cooked, or pickled, and are juicily acidic. The juice is also used to remove stains from hands and clothes.

carat unit for measuring the mass of precious stones; it is equal to 0.2 g/0.00705 oz, and is part of the troy system of weights. It is also the unit of purity in gold (US karat). Pure gold is 24-carat; 22-carat (the purest used in jewellery) is 22 parts gold and two parts alloy (to give greater strength).

Caravaggio Michelangelo Merisi da 1573–1610. Italian early Baroque painter, active in Rome 1592–1606, then in Naples, and finally in Malta. His life was as dramatic as his art (he had to leave Rome after killing a man). He created a forceful style, using contrasts of light and shade and focusing closely on the subject figures, sometimes using dramatic foreshortening. He painted from models, making portraits of real Roman people as saints and

caraway

Madonnas, which caused outrage. An example is *The Conversion of St Paul* (Sta Maria del Popolo, Rome).

caraway herb *Carum carvi* of the carrot family Umbelliferae. Native to northern temperate Eurasian regions, it is grown for its spicy, aromatic seeds, which are used in cookery, medicine, and perfumery.

carbohydrate chemical compound composed of carbon, hydrogen, and oxygen, with the basic formula $C_m(H_2O)_n$, and related compounds with the same basic structure but modified functional groups. As sugar and starch, carbohydrates form a major energy-providing part of the human diet.

carbon nonmetallic element, symbol C, atomic number 6, relative atomic mass 12.011. It is one of the most widely distributed elements, both inorganically and organically, and occurs in combination with other elements in all plants and animals. The atoms of carbon can link with one another in rings or chains, giving rise to innumerable complex compounds. It occurs in nature (1) in the pure state in the crystalline forms of graphite and diamond; (2) as calcium carbonate ($CaCO_3$) in carbonaceous rocks such as chalk and limestone; (3) as carbon dioxide (CO_2) in the atmosphere; and (4) as hydrocarbons in the fossil fuels petroleum, coal, and natural gas. Noncrystalline forms of pure carbon include charcoal and coal.

carbonate $CO_3{}^{2-}$ ion formed when carbon dioxide dissolves in water; any salt formed by this ion and another chemical element, usually a metal.

carbon cycle sequence by which ◊carbon circulates and is recycled through the natural world. The carbon element from carbon dioxide, released into the atmosphere by living things as a result of ◊respiration, is taken up by plants during ◊photosynthesis and converted into carbohydrates; the

oxygen component is released back into the atmosphere. The simplest link in the carbon cycle occurs when an animal eats a plant and carbon is transferred from, say, a leaf cell to the animal body. Today, the carbon cycle is in danger of being disrupted by the increased consumption and burning of fossil fuels, and the burning of large tracts of tropical forests, as a result of which levels of carbon dioxide are building up in the atmosphere and probably contributing to the ◊greenhouse effect.

carbon dating alternative name for ◊radiocarbon dating.

carbon dioxide CO_2 colourless, odourless gas, slightly soluble in water and denser than air. It is formed by the complete oxidation of carbon. It is present in the atmosphere and is produced naturally by respiration, decay of organic matter, and fermentation and artificially by chemical manufacturing and the burning of carbon fuels. Carbon dioxide is used to give sparkle to carbonated drinks, as a refrigerant (dry ice), and as a pressurizing medium, for example in fire extinguishers. See also ◊carbon cycle.

carbon fibre fine, black, silky filament of pure carbon produced by heat treatment from a special grade of Courtelle acrylic fibre, used for reinforcing plastics. The resulting composite is very stiff and, weight for weight, has four times the strength of high-tensile steel. It is used in the aerospace industry, cars, and electrical and sports equipment.

Carboniferous period of geological time 360–286 million years ago, the fifth period of the Palaeozoic era. In the USA it is divided into two periods: the Mississippian (lower) and the Pennsylvanian (upper). Typical of the lower-Carboniferous rocks are shallow-water ◊limestone, while upper-Carboniferous rocks have ◊delta deposits with ◊coal (hence the name). Amphibians were abundant, and reptiles evolved during this period.

carbon monoxide CO colourless, odourless gas formed when carbon is oxidized in a limited supply of air. It is a poisonous constituent of car exhaust fumes, forming a stable compound with haemoglobin in the blood, thus preventing the haemoglobin from transporting oxygen to the body tissues.

Carborundum trademark for a very hard, black abrasive, consisting of silicon carbide (SiC), an artificial compound of carbon and silicon. It is harder than ◊corundum but not as hard as ◊diamond.

carburation mixing of a gas, such as air, with a volatile hydrocarbon fuel, such as petrol, kerosene, or fuel oil, in order to form an explosive mixture. The process, which increases the amount of potential heat energy released during combustion, is used in internal-combustion engines. In most petrol engines the liquid fuel is atomized and mixed with air by means of a device called a **carburettor**.

carcinogen any agent that increases the chance of a cell becoming cancerous (see ◊cancer), including various chemical compounds, some viruses, X-rays, and other forms of ionizing radiation. The term is often used more narrowly to mean chemical carcinogens only.

carcinoma malignant ⟩tumour arising from the skin, the glandular tissues, or the mucous membranes that line the gut and lungs.

Cardiff (Welsh *Caerdydd*) capital of Wales (from 1955) and administrative headquarters of South and Mid Glamorgan, at the mouth of the Taff, Rhymney, and Ely rivers; population (1991) 272,600. Besides steelworks, there are car-component, flour-milling, paper, cigar, and other industries. The docks on the Bristol Channel were opened 1839 and greatly extended by the second marquess of Bute (1793–1848). They have now been redeveloped for industry. Llandaff, on the right bank of the river Taff, was included in Cardiff 1922.

cardinal in the Roman Catholic church, the highest rank next to the pope. Cardinals act as an advisory body to the pope and elect him. Their red hat is the badge of office. The number of cardinals has varied; there were 164 in 1991.

cardinal number in mathematics, one of the series of numbers 0, 1, 2, 3, 4, ... Cardinal numbers relate to quantity, whereas ordinal numbers (first, second, third, fourth, ...) relate to order.

Carey George Leonard 1935– . 103rd archbishop of Canterbury from 1991. A product of a liberal evangelical background, he was appointed bishop of Bath and Wells 1987.

Caribbean Sea W part of the Atlantic Ocean between the S coast of North America and the N coasts of South America. Central America is to the W and the West Indies are the islands within the sea, which is about 2,740 km/1,700 mi long and 650–1,500 km/400–900 mi wide. It is from here that the ⟩Gulf Stream turns towards Europe.

caribou the ⟩reindeer of North America.

caricature exaggerated portrayal of individuals or types, aiming to ridicule or otherwise expose the subject. Classical and medieval examples survive. Artists of the 18th, 19th, and 20th centuries have often used caricature as a way of satirizing society and politics. Notable exponents include the French artist Honoré Daumier and the German George Grosz.

British caricaturists include William Hogarth, Thomas Rowlandson, George Cruikshank, Edward Lear, Max Beerbohm, 'Giles' (Carl Ronald Giles), Ronald Searle, Ralph Steadman (1936–), and Peter Fluck and Roger Law (who created the three-dimensional puppets for their satirical television series *Spitting Image*).

caries decay and disintegration, usually of the substance of teeth (cavity) or bone. It is caused by acids produced when the bacteria that live in the mouth break down sugars in the food. Fluoride, a low sugar intake, and regular brushing are all protective. Caries forms mainly in the 45 minutes following an intake of sugary food, so the most dangerous diet for the teeth is one in which frequent sugary snacks and drinks are consumed.

Carinthia (German *Kärnten*) federal province of Alpine SE Austria, bordering Italy and Slovenia in the south; capital Klagenfurt; area 9,500 sq km/3,667 sq mi; population (1987) 542,000. It was an independent duchy from 976 and a possession of the Habsburg dynasty 1276–1918.

Carl XVI Gustaf 1946– . King of Sweden from 1973. He succeeded his grandfather Gustaf VI, his father having been killed in an air crash 1947. Under the new Swedish constitution, which became effective on his grandfather's death, the monarchy was stripped of all power at his accession.

Carlow county in the Republic of Ireland, in the province of Leinster; county town Carlow; area 900 sq km/347 sq mi; population (1991) 40,900. Mostly flat except for mountains in the south, the land is fertile, and well suited to dairy farming.

Carlsson Ingvar (Gösta) 1934– . Swedish socialist politician, leader of the Social Democratic Party, deputy prime minister 1982–86 and prime minister 1986–91.

Carlyle Thomas 1795–1881. Scottish essayist and social historian. His works include *Sartor Resartus* 1833–34, describing his loss of Christian belief, *French Revolution* 1837, *Chartism* 1839, and *Past and Present* 1843. His prose style was idiosyncratic, encompassing grand, thunderous rhetoric and deliberate obscurity. His suspicion of democracy together with a streak of anti-Semitism foreshadowed 20th-century fascist ideology.

Carnarvon alternative spelling of ⟩Caernarvon, a town in Gwynedd, NW Wales.

carnation any of numerous double-flowered cultivated varieties of a plant *Dianthus caryophyllus* of the pink family. The flowers smell like cloves; they are divided into flake, bizarre, and picotees, according to whether the petals exhibit one or more colours on their white ground, have the colour dispersed in strips, or have a coloured border to the petals.

Carnegie Andrew 1835–1919. US industrialist and philanthropist, born in Scotland, who developed the Pittsburgh iron and steel industries, making the USA the world's leading producer. He endowed public libraries, education, and various research trusts.

carnivore animal that eats other animals. Although the term is sometimes confined to those that eat the flesh of ⟩vertebrate prey, it is often used more broadly to include any animal that eats other animals, even microscopic ones. Carrion-eaters may or may not be included. The mammalian order

Carnivora includes cats, dogs, bears, badgers, and weasels.

Carnot Lazare Nicolas Marguerite 1753–1823. French general and politician. A member of the National Convention in the French Revolution, he organized the armies of the republic. He was war minister 1800–01 and minister of the interior 1815 under Napoleon. His work on fortification, *De la Défense de places fortes* 1810, became a military text-book. Minister of the interior during the Hundred Days, he was proscribed at the restoration of the monarchy and retired to Germany.

Caro Anthony 1924– . British sculptor who has made bold, large abstracts using ready-made angular metal shapes, often without bases. His works include *Fathom* (outside the Economist Building, London).

carob small Mediterranean tree *Ceratonia siliqua* of the legume family Leguminosae. Its 20-cm/8-in pods are used as animal fodder; they are also the source of a chocolate substitute. It is sometimes known as the *locust tree* and the pods as St John's bread.

Carolina two separate states of the USA; see ▷North Carolina and ▷South Carolina.

Caroline of Anspach 1683–1737. Queen of George II of Great Britain and Ireland. The daughter of the Margrave of Brandenburg-Anspach, she married George, Electoral Prince of Hanover, 1705, and followed him to England 1714 when his father became King George I. She was the patron of many leading writers and politicians such as Alexander Pope, John Gay, and the Earl of Chesterfield. She supported Sir Robert Walpole and kept him in power and acted as regent during her husband's four absences.

Caroline of Brunswick 1768–1821. Queen of George IV of Great Britain, who unsuccessfully attempted to divorce her on his accession to the throne 1820. First cousins, they were married 1795, but after the birth of Princess ▷Charlotte Augusta a separation was arranged. In July 1820 the government brought in a bill to dissolve the marriage, but Lord ▷Brougham's brilliant defence led to the bill's abandonment. On 19 July 1821 Caroline was prevented by royal order from entering Westminster Abbey for the coronation. She died 7 Aug, and her funeral was the occasion of popular riots.

Carolines scattered archipelago in Micronesia, Pacific Ocean, consisting of over 500 coral islets; area 1,200 sq km/463 sq mi. The chief islands are Ponape, Kusai, and Truk in the eastern group, and Yap and Belau in the western group.

Carolingian dynasty Frankish dynasty descending from ▷Pepin the Short (died 768) and named after his son Charlemagne; its last ruler was Louis V of France (reigned 966–87), who was followed by Hugh Capet (*c.* 938–996), first ruler of the Capetian dynasty.

carp fish *Cyprinus carpio* found all over the world. It commonly grows to 50 cm/1.8 ft and 3 kg/7 lb, but may be even larger. It lives in lakes, ponds, and slow rivers. The wild form is drab, but cultivated forms may be golden, or may have few large scales (mirror carp) or be scaleless (leather carp). *Koi* carp are highly prized and can grow up to 1 m/3 ft long with a distinctive pink, red, white, or black colouring.

Carpathian Mountains Central European mountain system, forming a ˙ semicircle through Czechoslovakia–Poland–Ukraine–Romania, 1,450 km/900 mi long. The central *Tatra Mountains* on the Czechoslovakia–Poland frontier include the highest peak, Gerlachovka, 2,663 m/8,737 ft.

carpel female reproductive unit in flowering plants (▷angiosperms). It usually comprises an ▷ovary containing one or more ovules, the stalk or style, and a stigma at its top which receives the pollen. A flower may have one or more carpels, and they may be separate or fused together. Collectively the carpels of a flower are known as the gynoecium.

carpetbagger in US history, derogatory name for any of the entrepreneurs and politicians from the North who moved to the Southern states during ▷Reconstruction 1861–65 after the Civil War.

Carreras José Maria 1946– . Spanish lyric tenor who made his operatic debut as Flavio in Bellini's *Norma* 1971 and specializes in French and Italian opera. In 1988 he made a successful comeback after suffering from leukaemia. Together with Placido ▷Domingo and Luciano ▷Pavarotti, he recorded a selection of operatic hits among which was 'Nessun Dorma', the anthem of the 1990 World Cup football series held in Rome.

Carrington Peter Alexander Rupert, 6th Baron Carrington 1919– . British Conservative politician. He was defence secretary 1970–74, and led the opposition in the House of Lords 1964–70 and 1974–79. While foreign secretary 1979–82, he negotiated independence for Zimbabwe, but resigned after failing to anticipate the Falklands crisis. He was secretary general of NATO 1984–88. He chaired EC-sponsored peace talks on Yugoslavia 1991.

Carroll Lewis. Pen name of Charles Lutwidge Dodgson 1832–1898. English author of children's classics *Alice's Adventures in Wonderland* 1865 and its sequel *Through the Looking-Glass* 1872. Among later works was the mock-heroic nonsense poem *The Hunting of the Snark* 1876. An Oxford don, he also published mathematical works.

carrot hardy European biennial *Daucus carota* of the family Umbelliferae. Cultivated since the 16th century for its edible root, it has a high sugar content and also contains carotene, which is converted by the human liver to vitamin A.

Carson City capital of Nevada, USA; population (1990) 40,400. Settled as a trading post 1851, it was named after the frontier guide Kit Carson 1858. It flourished as a boom town after the discovery of the nearby Comstock silver-ore lode 1859.

Cartagena or *Cartagena de los Indes* port, industrial centre, and capital of the department of Bolivar, NW Colombia; population (1985) 531,000. Plastics and chemicals are produced here.

cartel agreement among national or international firms to set mutually acceptable prices for their products. A cartel may restrict supply, or output, or raise prices to prevent entrants to the market and increase member profits. It therefore represents a form of oligopoly. OPEC, for example, is an oil cartel.

Carter Angela 1940–1992. English writer of the ◊magic realist school. Her novels include *The Magic Toyshop* 1967 (filmed by David Wheatley 1987) and *Nights at the Circus* 1984. She co-wrote the script for the film *The Company of Wolves* 1984, based on one of her stories. Her last novel before her death from lung cancer was *Wise Children* 1991.

Carter Jimmy (James Earl) 1924– . 39th president of the USA 1977–81, a Democrat. In 1976 he narrowly wrested the presidency from Gerald Ford. Features of his presidency were the return of the Panama Canal Zone to Panama, the Camp David Agreements for peace in the Middle East, and the Iranian seizure of US embassy hostages. He was defeated by Ronald Reagan 1980.

Cartesian coordinates in ◊coordinate geometry, the components of a system used to show the position of a point on a plane (two dimensions) or in space (three dimensions) with reference to a set of two or more axes.

Carthage ancient Phoenician port in N Africa; it lay 16 km/10 mi N of Tunis, Tunisia. A leading trading centre, it was in conflict with Greece from the 6th century BC, and then with Rome, and was destroyed by Roman forces 146 BC at the end of the ◊*Punic Wars*. About 45 BC, Roman colonists settled in Carthage, and it became the wealthy capital of the province of Africa. After its capture by the Vandals AD 439 it was little more than a pirate stronghold. From 533 it formed part of the Byzantine Empire until its final destruction by Arabs 698, during their conquest in the name of Islam.

Cartier Jacques 1491–1557. French navigator who was the first European to sail up the St Lawrence River 1534. He discovered the Magdalen Islands and Prince Edward Island and sailed up the St Lawrence River to the sites of Québec and Montréal, but failed in his aim to discover the Northwest Passage.

Cartier-Bresson Henri 1908– . French photographer, considered one of the greatest photographic artists. His documentary work was shot in black and white, using a small-format camera. His work is remarkable for its tightly structured composition and his ability to capture the decisive moment.

cartilage flexible bluish-white connective ◊tissue made up of the protein collagen. In cartilaginous fish it forms the skeleton; in other vertebrates it forms the greater part of the embryonic skeleton, and is replaced by ◊bone in the course of development, except in areas of wear such as bone endings, and the discs between the backbones. It also forms structural tissue in the larynx, nose, and external ear of mammals.

cartography art and practice of drawing ◊maps.

cartoon humorous or satirical drawing or ◊caricature; a strip cartoon or ◊comic strip; traditionally, the base design for a large fresco, mosaic, or tapestry, transferred to wall or canvas by tracing or picking out (pouncing). Surviving examples include Leonardo da Vinci's *Virgin and St Anne* (National Gallery, London).

Cartwright Edmund 1743–1823. British inventor. He patented the power loom 1785, built a weaving mill 1787, and patented a wool-combing machine 1789. He went bankrupt 1793 but was awarded £10,000 by the government 1809.

Caruso Enrico 1873–1921. Italian operatic tenor, acclaimed as one of the greatest singers in the history of opera. He made his debut in Naples 1894 and achieved international fame 1902. During his career he sang over 50 roles in French and Italian operas. He was one of the first opera singers to profit from gramophone recordings.

Carver George Washington 1864–1943. US agricultural chemist. Born a slave in Missouri, he was kidnapped and raised by his former owner, Moses Carver. He devoted his life to improving the economy of the US South and the condition of blacks. He advocated the diversification of crops, promoted peanut production, and was a pioneer in the field of plastics.

caryatid building support or pillar in the shape of a woman, the name deriving from the Karyatides, who were priestesses at the temple of Artemis at Karyai; the male equivalent is a *telamon* or *atlas*.

Casablanca (Arabic *Dar el-Beida*) port, commercial and industrial centre on the Atlantic coast of Morocco; population (1982) 2,139,000. It trades in fish, phosphates, and manganese. The Great Hassan II Mosque, completed 1989, is the world's largest; it is built on a platform (40,000 sq m/430,000 sq ft) jutting out over the Atlantic, with walls 60 m/200 ft high, topped by a hydraulic sliding roof, and a minaret 175 m/574 ft high.

Casals Pablo 1876–1973. Catalan cellist, composer, and conductor. As a cellist, he was celebrated for his interpretations of J S Bach's unaccompanied suites. He left Spain 1939 to live in Prades, in the French Pyrenees, where he founded an annual music festival. In 1956 he moved to Puerto Rico, where he launched the Casals Festival 1957, and toured extensively in the USA.

Casanova de Seingalt Giovanni Jacopo 1725–

1798. Italian adventurer, spy, violinist, librarian, and, according to his *Memoirs*, one of the world's great lovers. From 1774 he was a spy in the Venetian police service. In 1782 a libel got him into trouble, and after more wanderings he was appointed 1785 librarian to Count Waldstein at his castle of Dúx in Bohemia. Here Casanova wrote his *Memoirs* (published 1826–38, although the complete text did not appear until 1960–61).

casein main protein of milk, from which it can be separated by the action of acid, the enzyme rennin, or bacteria (souring); it is also the main component of cheese. Casein is used commercially in cosmetics, glues, and as a sizing for coating paper.

Cash Johnny 1932– . US country singer, songwriter, and guitarist. His early hits, recorded for Sun Records in Memphis, Tennessee, include the million-selling 'I Walk the Line' 1956. Many of his songs have become classics.

cash crop crop grown solely for sale rather than for the farmer's own use, for example, coffee, cotton, or sugar beet. Many Third World countries grow cash crops to meet their debt repayments rather than grow food for their own people. The price for these crops depends on financial interests, such as those of the multinational companies and the International Monetary Fund. In Britain, the most widespread cash crop is the potato.

cashew tropical American tree *Anacardium occidentale*, family Anacardiaceae. Extensively cultivated in India and Africa, it produces poisonous kidney-shaped nuts that become edible after being roasted.

cash flow input of cash required to cover all expenses of a business, whether revenue or capital. Alternatively, the actual or prospective balance between the various outgoing and incoming movements which are designated in total, positive or negative according to which is greater.

Caspian Sea world's largest inland sea, divided between Iran, Azerbaijan, Russia, Kazakhstan, and Turkmenistan; area about 400,000 sq km/155,000 sq mi, with a maximum depth of 1,000 m/3,250 ft. The chief ports are Astrakhan and Baku. It is now approximately 28 m/90 ft below sea level owing to drainage in the north and the damming of the Volga and Ural rivers for hydroelectric power.

Cassandra in Greek mythology, the daughter of Priam, king of Troy. Her prophecies (for example, of the fall of Troy) were never believed, because she had rejected the love of Apollo. She was murdered with Agamemnon by his wife Clytemnestra.

cassava or **manioc** plant *Manihot utilissima*, belonging to the spurge family Euphorbiaceae. Native to South America, it is now widely grown throughout the tropics for its starch-containing roots, from which tapioca and bread are made.

Cassiopeia prominent constellation of the northern hemisphere, named after the mother of Andromeda. It has a distinctive W-shape, and contains one of the most powerful radio sources in the sky, Cassiopeia A, the remains of a supernova (star explosion).

Cassius Gaius died 42 BC. Roman soldier, one of the conspirators who killed Julius ◊Caesar 44 BC. He fought at Carrhae 53, and with the republicans against Caesar at Pharsalus 48, was pardoned and appointed praetor, but became a leader in the conspiracy of 44, and after Caesar's death joined Brutus. He committed suicide after his defeat at Philippi 42.

Casson Hugh 1910– . British architect, professor at the Royal College of Art 1953–75, and president of the Royal Academy 1976–84. His books include *Victorian Architecture* 1948. He was director of architecture for the Festival of Britain 1948–51.

cassowary large flightless bird, genus *Casuarius*, found in New Guinea and N Australia, usually in forests. Related to the emu, the cassowary has a bare head with a horny casque, or helmet, on top, and brightly coloured skin on the neck. Its loose plumage is black and its wings tiny, but it can run and leap well and defends itself by kicking. Cassowaries stand up to 1.5 m/5 ft tall.

Castagno Andrea del *c.* 1421–1457. Italian Renaissance painter, active in Florence. In his frescoes in Sta Apollonia, Florence, he adapted the pictorial space to the architectural framework and followed ◊Masaccio's lead in perspective.

caste stratification of Hindu society into four main groups: **Brahmans** (priests), **Kshatriyas** (nobles and warriors), **Vaisyas** (traders and farmers), and **Sudras** (servants); plus a fifth group, **Harijan** (untouchables). No upward or downward mobility exists, as in classed societies. The system dates from ancient times, and there are more than 3,000 subdivisions.

Castile kingdom founded in the 10th century, occupying the central plateau of Spain. Its union with ◊Aragon 1479, based on the marriage of ◊Ferdinand and Isabella, effected the foundation of the Spanish state, which at the time was occupied and ruled by the ◊Moors. Castile comprised the two great basins separated by the Sierra de Gredos and the Sierra de Guadarrama, known traditionally as Old and New Castile. The area now forms the regions of ◊Castilla–León and ◊Castilla–La Mancha.

Castilian language member of the Romance branch of the Indo-European language family, originating in NW Spain, in the provinces of Old and New Castile. It is the basis of present-day standard Spanish (see ◊Spanish language) and is often seen as the same language, the terms *castellano* and *español* being used interchangeably in both Spain and the Spanish-speaking countries of the Americas.

Castilla–La Mancha autonomous region of central Spain; area 79,200 sq km/30,571 sq mi; population (1986) 1,665,000. It includes the provinces of Albacete, Ciudad Real, Cuenca, Guadalajara, and Toledo. Irrigated land produces grain and chickpeas, and merino sheep graze here.

Castilla–León autonomous region of central Spain; area 94,100 sq km/36,323 sq mi; population (1986) 2,600,000. It includes the provinces of Avila, Burgos, León, Palencia, Salamanca, Segovia, Soria, Valladolid, and -Zamora. Irrigated land produces wheat and rye. Cattle, sheep, and fighting bulls are bred in the uplands.

cast iron cheap but invaluable constructional material, most commonly used for car engine blocks. Cast iron is partly refined pig (crude) ◊iron, which is very fluid when molten and highly suitable for shaping by casting; it contains too many impurities (for example, carbon) to be readily shaped in any other way. Solid cast iron is heavy and can absorb great shock but is very brittle.

castle private fortress of a king or noble. The earliest castles in Britain were built following the Norman Conquest, and the art of castle building reached a peak in the 13th century. By the 15th century, the need for castles for domestic defence had largely disappeared, and the advent of gunpowder made them largely useless against attack. See also ◊château.

Castlereagh Robert Stewart, Viscount Castlereagh 1769–1822. British Tory politician. As chief secretary for Ireland 1797–1801, he suppressed the rebellion of 1798 and helped the younger Pitt secure the union of England, Scotland, and Ireland 1801. As foreign secretary 1812–22, he coordinated European opposition to Napoleon and represented Britain at the Congress of Vienna 1814–15.

Castor and Pollux/Polydeuces in Greek mythology, twin sons of Leda (by ◊Zeus), brothers of ◊Helen and ◊Clytemnestra. Protectors of mariners, they were transformed at death into the constellation Gemini.

castor-oil plant tall, tropical and subtropical shrub *Ricinus communis* of the spurge family Euphorbiaceae. The seeds, in North America called castor beans, yield the purgative castor oil and also ricin, one of the most powerful poisons known, which can be targeted to destroy cancer cells, while leaving normal cells untouched.

castration removal of the testicles. Male domestic animals, mainly stallions and bulls, may be castrated to prevent undesirable sires from reproducing, to moderate their aggressive and savage disposition and, for bulls, to improve their value as beef cattle (steers). Cockerels are castrated (capons) to improve their flavour and increase their size. The effects of castration can also be achieved by administration of hormones.

Castries port and capital of St Lucia, on the NW coast of the island in the Caribbean; population (1988) 53,000. It produces textiles, chemicals, tobacco, and wood and rubber products.

Castro (Ruz) Fidel 1927– . Cuban communist politician, prime minister 1959–76 and president from 1976. He led two unsuccessful coups against the right-wing Batista regime and led the revolution that overthrew the dictator 1959. From 1979 he was also president of the nonaligned movement, although promoting the line of the USSR, which subsidized his government. He has raised the standard of living for most Cubans but dealt harshly with dissenters.

cat small, domesticated, carnivorous mammal *Felis catus*, often kept as a pet or for catching small pests such as rodents. Found in many colour variants, it may have short, long, or no hair, but the general shape and size is constant. All cats walk on the pads of their toes, and have retractile claws. They have strong limbs, large eyes, and acute hearing. The canine teeth are long and well-developed, as are the shearing teeth in the side of the mouth.

catacomb underground cemetery, such as the catacombs of the early Christians. Examples include those beneath the basilica of St Sebastian in Rome, where bodies were buried in niches in the walls of the tunnels.

Catalan language member of the Romance branch of the Indo-European language family, an Iberian language closely related to Provençal in France. It is spoken in Catalonia in NE Spain, the Balearic Islands, Andorra, and a corner of SW France.

Catalonia (Spanish *Cataluña*, Catalan *Catalunya*) autonomous region of NE Spain; area 31,900 sq km/12,313 sq mi; population (1986) 5,977,000. It includes Barcelona (the capital), Gerona, Lérida, and Tarragona. Industries include wool and cotton textiles; hydroelectric power is produced.

catalyst substance that alters the speed of, or makes possible, a chemical or biochemical reaction but remains unchanged at the end of the reaction. ◊Enzymes are natural biochemical catalysts. In practice most catalysts are used to speed up reactions.

catalytic converter device for reducing toxic emissions from the ◊internal-combustion engine. It converts harmful exhaust products to relatively harmless ones by passing exhaust gases over a mixture of catalysts. *Oxidation catalysts* convert hydrocarbons into carbon dioxide and water; *three-way catalysts* convert oxides of nitrogen back into nitrogen.

catamaran twin-hulled sailing vessel, based on the aboriginal craft of South America and the Indies, made of logs lashed together, with an outrigger. A similar vessel with three hulls is known as a trimaran. Car ferries with a wave-piercing catamaran design are also in use in parts of Europe and North America. They have a pointed main hull and two outriggers and travel at a speed of 35 knots (84.5 kph/52.5 mph).

Catania industrial port and second largest city in Sicily; population (1988) 372,000. Founded 729 BC, it stands on lava from Mount Etna; it was rebuilt with local volcanic material after an earthquake 1693. It exports local sulphur; other industries include mechanical and chemical products, food processing, and fishing.

cataract eye disease in which the crystalline lens or its capsule becomes opaque, causing blindness. Fluid accumulates between the fibres of the lens and gives place to deposits of ◊albumin. These coalesce into rounded bodies, the lens fibres break down, and areas of the lens or the lens capsule become filled with opaque products of degeneration. In most cases the treatment is replacement of the lens with an artificial implant.

caterpillar larval stage of a ◊butterfly or ◊moth. Wormlike in form, the body is segmented, may be hairy, and often has scent glands. The head has strong biting mandibles, silk glands, and a spinneret.

catfish fish belonging to the order Siluriformes, in which barbels (feelers) on the head are well-developed, so giving a resemblance to the whiskers of a cat. Catfishes are found worldwide, mainly but not exclusively in fresh water, and are plentiful in South America.

cathedral Christian church containing the throne of a bishop or archbishop, which is usually situated on the south side of the choir. A cathedral is governed by a dean and chapter. Some British cathedrals, such as Lincoln and York, are referred to as 'minsters', the term originating in the name given to the bishop and cathedral clergy who were often referred to as a *monasterium*. There are cathedrals in most of the chief cities of Europe; UK cathedrals include Canterbury cathedral (spanning the Norman to Perpendicular periods), Exeter cathedral (13th-century Gothic), and Coventry cathedral (rebuilt after World War II, consecrated 1962).

Catherine II the Great 1729–1796. Empress of Russia from 1762, and daughter of the German prince of Anhalt-Zerbst. In 1745, she married the Russian grand duke Peter. Catherine was able to dominate him; six months after he became Tsar Peter III 1762, he was murdered in a coup and Catherine ruled alone. During her reign Russia extended its boundaries to include territory from wars with the Turks 1768–74, 1787–92, and from the partitions of Poland 1772, 1793, and 1795.

Catherine de' Medici 1519–1589. French queen consort of Henry II, whom she married 1533; daughter of Lorenzo de' Medici, Duke of Urbino; and mother of Francis II, Charles IX, and Henry III. At first outshone by Henry's mistress Diane de Poitiers (1490–1566), she became regent 1560–63

for Charles IX and remained in power until his death 1574.

Catherine of Aragon 1485–1536. First queen of Henry VIII of England, 1509–33, and mother of Mary I. Catherine had married Henry's elder brother Prince Arthur 1501 and on his death 1502 was betrothed to Henry, marrying him on his accession. She failed to produce a male heir and Henry divorced her without papal approval, thus beginning the English ◊Reformation.

Catherine of Braganza 1638–1705. Queen of Charles II of England 1662–85. Her childlessness and practice of her Catholic faith were unpopular, but Charles resisted pressure for divorce. She returned to Lisbon 1692 after his death.

cathode in chemistry, the negative electrode of an electrolytic ◊cell, towards which positive particles (cations), usually in solution, are attracted. See ◊electrolysis.

cathode-ray tube vacuum tube in which a beam of electrons is produced and focused onto a fluorescent screen. It is an essential component of television receivers, computer visual display units, and oscilloscopes.

Catholic Emancipation in British history, acts of Parliament passed 1780–1829 to relieve Roman Catholics of civil and political restrictions imposed from the time of Henry VIII and the Reformation.

CAT scan or *CT scan* (acronym for computerized axial tomography) in medicine, a sophisticated method of X-ray imaging. Quick and noninvasive, CAT scanning is an aid to diagnosis, helping to pinpoint problem areas without the need for exploratory surgery.

cattle any large, ruminant, even-toed, hoofed mammal of the genus *Bos*, family Bovidae, including wild species such as the yak, gaur, gayal, banteng, and kouprey, as well as domestic breeds. Asiatic water buffaloes *Bubalus*, African buffaloes *Syncerus*, and American bison *Bison* are not considered true cattle. Cattle were first domesticated in the Middle East during the Neolithic period, about 8000 BC. They were brought north into Europe by migrating Neolithic farmers. Cattle are bred for meat (beef cattle) or milk (dairy cattle).

Catullus Gaius Valerius *c.* 84–54 BC. Roman lyric poet, born in Verona of a well-to-do family. He moved in the literary and political society of Rome and wrote lyrics describing his unhappy love affair with Clodia, probably the wife of the consul Metellus, calling her Lesbia. His longer poems include two wedding songs. Many of his poems are short verses to his friends.

Caucasus series of mountain ranges between the Caspian and Black seas, in the republics of Russia, Georgia, Armenia, and Azerbaijan; 1,200 km/750 mi long. The highest peak is Elbruz, 5,633 m/18,480 ft.

cauliflower variety of ◊cabbage *Brassica oleracea*,

distinguished by its large, flattened head of fleshy, aborted flowers. It is similar to broccoli but less hardy.

cauterization in medicine, the use of special instruments to burn or fuse small areas of body tissue to destroy dead cells, prevent the spread of infection, or seal tiny blood vessels to minimize blood loss during surgery.

Cauvery or *Kaveri* river of S India, rising in the W Ghats and flowing 765 km/475 mi SE to meet the Bay of Bengal in a wide delta. It has been a major source of hydroelectric power since 1902 when India's first hydropower plant was built on the river.

Cavaco Silva Anibal 1939– . Portuguese politician, finance minister 1980–81, and prime minister and Social Democratic Party (PSD) leader from 1985. Under his leadership Portugal joined the European Community 1985 and the Western European Union 1988.

cavalier horseman of noble birth, but mainly used to describe a male supporter of Charles I in the English Civil War (Cavalier), typically with courtly dress and long hair (as distinct from a Roundhead); also a supporter of Charles II after the Restoration.

Cavalier poets poets of Charles I's court, including Thomas Carew, Robert Herrick, Richard Lovelace, and John Suckling. They wrote witty, light-hearted love lyrics.

Cavan agricultural county of the Republic of Ireland, in the province of Ulster; area 1,890 sq km/ 730 sq mi; capital Cavan; population (1991) 52,800. The river Erne divides it into a narrow, mostly low-lying peninsula, 30 km/20 mi long, and an eastern section of wild and bare hill country. The soil is generally poor, and the climate moist and cold.

cave roofed-over cavity in the Earth's crust usually produced by the action of underground water or by waves on a seacoast. Caves of the former type commonly occur in areas underlain by limestone, such as Kentucky and many Balkan regions, where the rocks are soluble in water. A *pothole* is a vertical hole in rock caused by water descending a crack and is thus open to the sky.

Celebrated caves include the Mammoth Cave in Kentucky, USA, 6.4 km/4 mi long and 38 m/125 ft high; the Caverns of Adelsberg (Postumia) near Trieste, Italy, which extend for many miles; Carlsbad Cave, New Mexico, the largest in the USA; the Cheddar Caves, England; Fingal's Cave, Scotland, which has a range of basalt columns; and Peak Cavern, England.

Cavell Edith Louisa 1865–1915. British matron of a Red Cross hospital in Brussels, Belgium, in World War I, who helped Allied soldiers escape to the Dutch frontier. She was court-martialled by the Germans and condemned to death.

Cavendish Henry 1731–1810. English physicist. He discovered hydrogen (which he called 'inflam-

mable air') 1766, and determined the compositions of water and of nitric acid. The Cavendish experiment (measurement of the gravitational attraction between lead and gold spheres) enabled him to discover the mass and density of the Earth.

caviar salted roe (eggs) of sturgeon, salmon, and other fishes. Caviar is prepared by beating and straining the egg sacs until the eggs are free from fats and then adding salt. Russia and Iran are the main exporters of the most prized variety of caviar, derived from Caspian Sea sturgeon. Iceland produces various high-quality, lower-priced caviars.

Cavour Camillo Benso di, Count 1810–1861. Italian nationalist politician. He was the editor of *Il* ◊*Risorgimento* from 1847. As prime minister of Piedmont 1852–59 and 1860–61, he enlisted the support of Britain and France for the concept of a united Italy achieved 1861; after expelling the Austrians 1859, he assisted Garibaldi in liberating S Italy 1860.

cavy short-tailed South American rodent, family Caviidae, of which the guinea-pig *Cavia porcellus* is an example. Wild cavies are greyish or brownish with rather coarse hair. They live in small groups in burrows, and have been kept for food since ancient times.

Cawnpore former spelling of ◊Kanpur, Indian city.

Caxton William *c.* 1422–1491. The first English printer. He learned the art of printing in Cologne, Germany, 1471 and set up a press in Belgium where he produced the first book printed in English, his own version of a French romance, *Recuyell of the Historyes of Troye* 1474. Returning to England 1476, he established himself in London, where he produced the first book printed in England, *Dictes or Sayengis of the Philosophres* 1477.

Cayenne capital and chief port of French Guiana, on Cayenne island at the mouth of the river Cayenne; population (1982) 38,135. It was founded 1634 and used as a penal settlement 1854–1946. Cayenne pepper is grown locally.

cayenne pepper condiment derived from the dried fruits of various species of ◊capsicum (especially *Capsicum frutescens*), a tropical American genus of plants of the family Solanaceae. It is wholly distinct in its origin from black or white pepper, which is derived from an East Indian plant (*Piper nigrum*).

cayman or *caiman*, large reptile, resembling the ◊crocodile.

Cayman Islands British island group in the West Indies; *area* 260 sq km/100 sq mi; *physical* three low-lying islands: Grand Cayman, Cayman Brac, and Little Cayman; *government* governor, executive council, and legislative assembly; *exports* seawhip coral, a source of ◊prostaglandins; shrimps; honey; jewellery; *population* (1988) 22,000; *language* English; *history* settled by military deserters in the 17th century, the islands became a pirate lair in the 18th century. Administered with Jamaica until 1962, when the Caymans became a separate colony, they are now a tourist resort, international financial centre, and tax haven.

CBI see ⊅Confederation of British Industry.

CD-ROM (abbreviation for *compact-disc read-only memory*) computer storage device developed from the technology of the audio ⊅compact disc. It consists of a plastic-coated metal disc, on which binary digital information is etched in the form of microscopic pits. This can then be read optically by passing a light beam over the disc. CD-ROMs typically hold about 550 ⊅megabytes of data, and are used in distributing large amounts of text and graphics, such as encyclopedias, catalogues, and technical manuals.

Ceauşescu Nicolae 1918–1989. Romanian politician, leader of the Romanian Communist Party (RCP), in power 1965–89. He pursued a policy line independent of and critical of the USSR. He appointed family members, including his wife *Elena Ceauşescu*, to senior state and party posts, and governed in an increasingly repressive manner, zealously implementing schemes that impoverished the nation. The Ceauşescus were overthrown in a bloody revolutionary coup Dec 1989 and executed.

Cebu chief city and port of the island of Cebu in the Philippines; population (1990) 610,400; area of the island 5,086 sq km/1,964 sq mi; population (1980) 1,234,000. The oldest city of the Philippines, Cebu was founded as San Miguel 1565 and became the capital of the Spanish Philippines.

Cecil Robert, 1st Earl of Salisbury 1563–1612. Secretary of state to Elizabeth I of England, succeeding his father, Lord Burghley; he was afterwards chief minister to James I (James VI of Scotland) whose accession to the English throne he secured 1603. He discovered the ⊅Gunpowder Plot, the conspiracy to blow up the king and Parliament. James I created him Earl of Salisbury 1605.

cedar any of an Old World genus *Cedrus* of coniferous trees of the pine family Pinaceae. The *cedar of Lebanon Cedrus libani* grows to great heights and age in the mountains of Syria and Asia Minor. Of the historic forests on Mount Lebanon itself, only a few stands of trees remain.

Ceefax one of Britain's two ⊅teletext systems (the other is Oracle), or 'magazines of the air', developed by the BBC and first broadcast in 1973.

celandine either of two plants belonging to different families, and resembling each other only in their bright yellow flowers. The *greater celandine Chelidonium majus* belongs to the poppy family, and is common in hedgerows. The *lesser celandine Ranunculus ficaria* is a member of the buttercup family, and is a familiar wayside and meadow plant in Europe.

Celebes English name for ⊅Sulawesi, island of Indonesia.

celery Old World plant *Apium graveolens* of the carrot family Umbelliferae. It grows wild in ditches and salt marshes and has a coarse texture and acrid taste. Cultivated varieties of celery are grown under cover to make them less bitter.

celestial sphere imaginary sphere surrounding the Earth, on which the celestial bodies seem to lie. The positions of bodies such as stars, planets, and galaxies are specified by their coordinates on the celestial sphere. The equivalents of latitude and longitude on the celestial sphere are called declination and right ascension (which is measured in hours from 0 to 24). The *celestial poles* lie directly above the Earth's poles, and the *celestial equator* lies over the Earth's equator. The celestial sphere appears to rotate once around the Earth each day, actually a result of the rotation of the Earth on its axis.

cell in biology, a discrete, membrane-bound portion of living matter, the smallest unit capable of an independent existence. All living organisms consist of one or more cells, with the exception of ⊅viruses. Bacteria, protozoa, and many other microorganisms consist of single cells, whereas a human is made up of billions of cells. Essential features of a cell are the membrane, which encloses it and restricts the flow of substances in and out; the jellylike material within, often known as ⊅protoplasm; the ⊅ribosomes, which carry out protein synthesis; and the ⊅DNA, which forms the hereditary material.

cell, electrical or *voltaic cell* or *galvanic cell* device in which chemical energy is converted into electrical energy; the popular name is ⊅'battery', but this actually refers to a collection of cells in one unit. The reactive chemicals of a *primary cell* cannot be replenished, whereas *secondary cells* – such as storage batteries – are rechargeable: their chemical reactions can be reversed and the original condition restored by applying an electric current. It is dangerous to attempt to recharge a primary cell.

Cellini Benvenuto 1500–1571. Italian sculptor and goldsmith working in the Mannerist style; author of an arrogant autobiography (begun 1558). Among his works is a graceful bronze *Perseus* 1545–54 (Loggia dei Lanzi, Florence) and a gold salt cellar made for Francis I of France 1540–43 (Kunsthistorisches Museum, Vienna), topped by nude reclining figures.

cello abbreviation for *violoncello*, a member of the violin family and fourth member of a string quartet. The cello has been much in demand as a solo instrument because of its exeptional range and brilliance of tone, and its repertoire extends from Bach to Beethoven, Dvořák, and Elgar.

cellular phone or *cellphone* mobile radio telephone, one of a network connected to the telephone system by a computer-controlled communication system. Service areas are divided into small 'cells', about 5 km/3 mi across, each with a separate low-power transmitter.

celluloid transparent or translucent, highly flammable, plastic material (a thermoplastic) made from cellulose nitrate and camphor. It was once used for toilet articles, novelties, and photographic film, but has now been replaced by the nonflammable substance ▷cellulose acetate.

cellulose complex ▷carbohydrate composed of long chains of glucose units. It is the principal constituent of the cell wall of higher plants, and a vital ingredient in the diet of ▷herbivores. Molecules of cellulose are organized into long, unbranched microfibrils that give support to the cell wall. No mammal produces the enzyme (cellulase) necessary for digesting cellulose; mammals such as rabbits and cows are only able to digest grass because the bacteria present in their gut manufacture the appropriate enzyme.

Celsius scale of temperature, previously called Centigrade, in which the range from freezing to boiling of water is divided into 100 degrees, freezing point being 0 degrees and boiling point 100 degrees.

Celt member of an Indo-European people that originated in Alpine Europe and spread to the Iberian peninsula and beyond. They were ironworkers and farmers. In the 1st century BC they were defeated by the Roman Empire and by Germanic tribes and confined largely to Britain, Ireland, and N France.

Celtic art style of art that originated about 500 BC, probably on the Rhine, and spread as the Celts moved westwards to Gaul and the British Isles and southwards to Italy and Turkey. Celtic manuscript illumination and sculpture from Ireland and Anglo-Saxon Britain of the 6th–8th centuries has intricate spiral and geometric ornament, as in *The Book of Kells* (Trinity College, Dublin) and the *Lindisfarne Gospels* (British Museum, London). Metalwork using curving incised lines and inlays of coloured enamel and coral survived at La Tène, a site at Lake Neuchâtel, Switzerland.

Celtic languages branch of the Indo-European family, divided into two groups: the *Brythonic* or *P-Celtic* (Welsh, Cornish, Breton, and Gaulish) and the *Goidelic* or *Q-Celtic* (Irish, Scottish, and Manx Gaelic). Celtic languages once stretched from the Black Sea to Britain, but have been in decline for centuries, limited to the so-called 'Celtic fringe' of W Europe.

cement any bonding agent used to unite particles in a single mass or to cause one surface to adhere to another. *Portland cement* is a powder obtained from burning together a mixture of lime (or chalk) and clay, and when mixed with water and sand or gravel, turns into mortar or concrete. In geology, a chemically precipitated material such as carbonate that occupies the interstices of clastic rocks is called cement.

Cenozoic or *Caenozoic* era of geological time that began 65 million years ago and is still in process. It is divided into the Tertiary and Quaternary periods. The Cenozoic marks the emergence of mammals as a dominant group, including humans, and the formation of the mountain chains of the Himalayas and the Alps.

censor in ancient Rome, either of two senior magistrates, high officials elected every five years to hold office for 18 months. Their responsibilities included public morality, a census of the citizens, and a revision of the senatorial list.

censorship the suppression by authority of material considered immoral, heretical, subversive, libellous, damaging to state security, or otherwise offensive. It is generally more stringent under totalitarian or strongly religious regimes and in wartime.

The British government uses the ▷D-notice and the ▷Official Secrets Act to protect itself. Laws relating to obscenity, libel, and blasphemy act as a form of censorship. The media exercise a degree of self-censorship. During the Gulf War 1991, access to the theatre of war was controlled by the US military: only certain reporters were allowed in and their movements were restricted.

census official count of the population of a country, originally for military call-up and taxation, later for assessment of social trends as other information regarding age, sex, and occupation of each individual was included. The first US census was taken in 1790 and the first in Britain in 1801. The most recent UK census was taken on 21 April 1991.

centaur in Greek mythology, a creature half-human and half-horse. Centaurs were supposed to live in Thessaly, and be wild and lawless; the mentor of Heracles, Chiron, was an exception.

centigrade common name for the ▷Celsius temperature scale.

centipede jointed-legged animal of the group Chilopoda, members of which have a distinct head and a single pair of long antennae. Their bodies are composed of segments (which may number nearly 200), each of similar form and bearing a single pair of legs. Most are small, but the tropical *Scolopendra gigantea* may reach 30 cm/1 ft in length. *Millipedes*, class Diplopoda, have fewer segments (up to 100), but have two pairs of legs on each.

Central African Republic country in Central Africa, bordered NE and E by Sudan, S by Zaire and Congo, W by Cameroon, and NW by Chad; *area* 622,436 sq km/240,260 sq mi; *capital* Bangui; *physical* most of the country is on a plateau, with rivers flowing N and S; dry in N, rainforest in SW; *head of state and government* André Kolingba from 1981; *political system* one-party military republic; *exports* diamonds, uranium, coffee, cotton, timber, tobacco; *population* (1990 est) 2,879,000 (more than 80 ethnic groups); *languages*

central nervous system

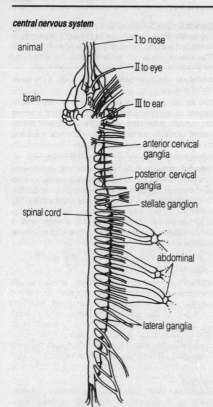

- I to nose
- animal
- II to eye
- brain
- III to ear
- anterior cervical ganglia
- posterior cervical ganglia
- stellate ganglion
- spinal cord
- abdominal
- lateral ganglia

Sangho (national), French (official); *recent history* independence was achieved from France 1960. A military coup 1965 led to Col Bokassa declaring himself president for life and emperor. He was deposed by former president David Dacko 1979, in turn deposed by General André Kolingba 1981. A new constitution was approved by referendum 1986; widespread demonstrations called for political reform 1990 and 1991.

Central America the part of the Americas that links Mexico with the Isthmus of Panama, comprising Belize, Costa Rica, El Salvador, Guatemala, Honduras, Nicaragua, and Panama. It is also an isthmus, crossed by mountains that form part of the Cordilleras, rising to a maximum height of 4,220 m/ 13,845 ft. There are numerous active volcanoes. Central America is about 523,000 sq km/ 200,000 sq mi in area and has a population (1980) estimated at 22,700,000, mostly Indians or mestizos (of mixed white-Indian ancestry). Tropical agricultural products and other basic commodities and raw materials are exported.

Central Asian Republics group of five republics:

⟡Kazakhstan, ⟡Kyrgyzstan, ⟡Tajikistan, ⟡Turkmenistan, and ⟡Uzbekistan. Formerly part of the Soviet Union, their independence was recognized 1991. All five republics belong to the Commonwealth of Independent States (CIS). They comprise a large part of the geographical region of ⟡Turkestan and are the home of large numbers of Muslims.

Central Command military strike force consisting of units from the US army, navy, and air force which operates in the Middle East and North Africa. Its headquarters are in Fort McDill, Florida. It was established 1979, following the Iranian hostage crisis and the Soviet invasion of Afghanistan, and was known as the Rapid Deployment Force until 1983. It commanded coalition forces in the Gulf War 1991.

Central Intelligence Agency (CIA) US intelligence organization established 1947. It has actively intervened overseas, generally to undermine left wing regimes or to protect US financial interests; for example, in the Congo (now Zaire) and Nicaragua. From 1980 all covert activity by the CIA has by law to be reported to Congress, preferably beforehand and must be authorized by the president. Robert Gates became CIA director 1991.

Central Lowlands one of the three geographical divisions of Scotland, occupying the fertile and densely populated plain that lies between two geological fault lines, which run nearly parallel NE–SW across Scotland from Stonehaven to Dumbarton and from Dunbar to Girvan.

central nervous system the part of the nervous system with a concentration of ⟡nerve cells which coordinates various body functions. In ⟡vertebrates, the central nervous system consists of brain and a dorsal nerve cord (the spinal cord within the spinal column. In worms, insects, and crustaceans, it consists of a paired ventral nerve cord with concentrations of nerve cells, known as *ganglia* in each segment, and a small brain in the head.

central processing unit (CPU) main component of a computer, the part that executes individual program instructions and controls the operation of other parts. It is sometimes called the central processor or, when contained on a single integrated circuit, a microprocessor.

Central Scotland region of Scotland, formed 1975 from the counties of Stirling, S Perthshire, and West Lothian; *area* 2,600 sq km/1,004 sq mi; *towns* Stirling (administrative headquarters), Falkirk, Alloa, Grangemouth; *features* Stirling Castle; field of Bannockburn; Loch Lomond; the Trossachs; *products* agriculture; industries including brewing and distilling, engineering, electronics; *population* (1991) 268,000; *famous people* William Alexander (founder of Nova Scotia), Rob Roy Macgregor.

Centre region of N central France; *area* 39,200 sq km/15,131 sq mi; population (1986

2,324,000. It includes the *départements* of Cher, Eure-et-Loire, Indre, Indre-et-Loire, Loire-et-Cher, and Loiret. Its capital is Orléans.

centre of mass or *centre of gravity* point in or near an object from which its total weight appears to originate and can be assumed to act. A symmetrical homogeneous object such as a sphere or cube has its centre of mass at its physical centre; a hollow shape (such as a cup) may have its centre of mass in space inside the hollow.

centrifugal force useful concept in physics, based on an apparent (but not real) force. It may be regarded as a force that acts radially outwards from a spinning or orbiting object, thus balancing the centripetal force (which is real). For an object of mass m moving with a velocity v in a circle of radius r, the centrifugal force F equals mv^2/r (outwards).

centripetal force force that acts radially inwards on an object moving in a curved path. For example, with a weight whirled in a circle at the end of a length of string, the centripetal force is the tension in the string. For an object of mass m moving with a velocity v in a circle of radius r, the centripetal force F equals mv^2/r (inwards). The reaction to this force is the centrifugal force.

cephalopod any predatory marine mollusc of the class Cephalopod, with the mouth and head surrounded by tentacles. Cephalopods are the most intelligent, the fastest-moving, and the largest of all animals without backbones, and there are remarkable luminescent forms which swim or drift at great depths. They have the most highly developed nervous and sensory systems of all invertebrates, the eye in some closely paralleling that found in vertebrates. Examples include octopus, squid, and cuttlefish. Shells are rudimentary or absent in most cephalopods.

ceramic nonmetallic mineral (clay) used to form articles that are then fired at high temperatures. Ceramics are divided into heavy clay products (bricks, roof tiles, drainpipes, sanitary ware), refractories or high-temperature materials (linings for furnaces used to manufacture steel, fuel elements in nuclear reactors), and pottery, which uses china clay, ball clay, china stone, and flint. Superceramics, such as silicon carbide, are lighter, stronger, and more heat-resistant than steel for use in motor and aircraft engines and have to be cast to shape since they are too hard to machine.

Cerberus in Greek mythology, the three-headed dog guarding the entrance to ◊Hades, the underworld.

cereal grass grown for its edible, nutrient-rich, starchy seeds. The term refers primarily to wheat, oats, rye, and barley, but may also refer to corn, millet, and rice. Cereals contain about 75% complex carbohydrates and 10% protein, plus fats and fibre (roughage). They store well. If all the world's cereal crop were consumed as wholegrain products directly by humans, everyone could obtain adequate protein and carbohydrate; however, a large proportion of cereal production in affluent nations is used as animal feed to boost the production of meat, dairy products, and eggs.

cerebral haemorrhage or *apoplectic fit* in medicine, a ◊stroke in which a blood vessel bursts in the brain, caused by factors such as high blood pressure combined with hardening of the arteries, or chronic poisoning with lead or alcohol. It may cause death or damage parts of the brain, leading to paralysis or mental impairment. The effects are usually long-term and the condition may recur.

cerebrum part of the vertebrate ◊brain, formed from the two paired cerebral hemispheres. In birds and mammals it is the largest part of the brain. It is covered with an infolded layer of grey matter, the cerebral cortex, which integrates brain functions. The cerebrum coordinates the senses, and is responsible for learning and other higher mental faculties.

Ceres in Roman mythology, the goddess of agriculture; see ◊Demeter.

cerium malleable and ductile, grey, metallic element, symbol Ce, atomic number 58, relative atomic mass 140.12. It is the most abundant member of the lanthanide series, and is used in alloys, electronic components, nuclear fuels, and lighter flints. It was discovered 1804 by the Swedish chemists Jöns Berzelius and Wilhelm Hisinger (1766–1852), and, independently, by Martin Klaproth. The element was named after the then recently discovered asteroid Ceres.

CERN nuclear research organization founded 1954 as a cooperative enterprise among European governments. It has laboratories at Meyrin, near Geneva, Switzerland. It was originally known as the *Conseil Européen pour la Recherche Nucléaire* but subsequently renamed *Organisation Européen pour la Recherche Nucléaire*, although still familiarly known as CERN. It houses the world's largest particle ◊accelerator, the ◊Large Electron-Positron Collider (LEP), with which notable advances have been made in ◊particle physics.

Cervantes Saavedra, Miguel de 1547–1616. Spanish novelist, playwright, and poet whose masterpiece *Don Quixote* (in full *El ingenioso hidalgo Don Quixote de la Mancha*) was published 1605. In 1613, his *Novelas ejemplares/Exemplary Novels* appeared, followed by *Viaje del Parnaso/The Voyage to Parnassus* 1614. A spurious second part of *Don Quixote* prompted Cervantes to bring out his own second part 1615, often considered superior to the first in construction and characterization.

cervical smear removal of a small sample of tissue from the cervix (neck of the womb) to screen for changes implying a likelihood of cancer. The procedure is also known as the *Pap test* after its originator, George Papanicolau.

cervix abbreviation for the Latin *cervix uteri*, the neck of the womb. The cervix is a cylindrical organ which connects the womb with the vagina. Made of fibrous tissue and some smooth muscle, it is less than 2.5 cm/1 in in diameter but can be stretched to enable childbirth.

Ceylon former name (until 1972) of ⟡Sri Lanka.

Cézanne Paul 1839–1906. French Post-Impressionist painter, a leading figure in the development of modern art. He broke away from the Impressionists' spontaneous vision to develop a style that captured not only light and life, but the structure of natural forms in landscapes, still lifes, portraits, and his series of bathers. His paintings of Mont Sainte-Victoire in Provence from the 1880s into the 1900s show an increasing fragmentation and a movement towards abstraction, with layers of colour and square brushstrokes.

CFC abbreviation for ⟡*chlorofluorocarbon*.

c.g.s. system or *CGS system* system of units based on the centimetre, gram, and second, as units of length, mass, and time respectively. It has been replaced for scientific work by the ⟡SI units to avoid inconsistencies in definition of the thermal calorie and electrical quantities.

Chaco province of Argentina; area 99,633 sq km/ 38,458 sq mi; population (1991) 838,300. Its capital is Resistencia, in the SE. The chief crop is cotton, and there is forestry.

Chad Republic of; country in central N Africa, bordered N by Libya, E by Sudan, S by the Central African Republic, and W by Cameroon, Nigeria, and Niger; *area* 1,284,000 sq km/495,624 sq mi; *capital* Ndjamena (formerly Port Lamy); *physical* mountains in NW, savanna and part of Sahara Desert in N; rivers in S flow NW to Lake Chad in marshy E; *head of state and government* Idriss Deby from 1990; *political system* transitional; *exports* cotton, meat, livestock, hides, skins; *population* (1990 est) 5,064,000; *languages* French, Arabic (both official); over 100 African dialects; *recent history* independence was achieved from France 1960; violent opposition from the Chadian National Liberation Front, backed by Libya, eventually drove the government into exile 1981. Fighting continued between Libyan-backed and French-backed forces until 1987. Full diplomatic relations were restored with Libya 1988. A new constitution was adopted 1990.

Chad, Lake lake on the NE boundary of Nigeria. It once varied in extent between rainy and dry seasons from 50,000 sq km/20,000 sq mi to 20,000 sq km/ 7,000 sq mi, but a series of droughts 1979–89 reduced its area by 80%. The S Chad irrigation project used the lake waters to irrigate the surrounding desert; the 4,000 km/2,500 mi of canals dug for the project are now permanently dry because of the shrinking size of the lake. The Lake Chad basin is being jointly developed for oil and natron by Cameroon, Chad, Niger, and Nigeria.

Chadwick James 1891–1974. British physicist. In 1932 he discovered the particle in the nucleus of an atom that became known as the neutron because it has no electric charge. In 1940 he was one of the British scientists reporting on the atom bomb. He received the Nobel Prize for Physics 1935.

chaffinch bird *Fringilla coelebs* of the finch family, common throughout much of Europe and W Asia. About 15 cm/6 in long, the male is olive-brown above, with a bright chestnut breast, a bluish-grey cap, and two white bands on the upper part of the wing; the female is duller.

Chagall Marc 1887–1985. Russian-born French painter and designer; much of his highly coloured, fantastic imagery was inspired by the village life of his boyhood and Jewish and Russian folk tradition. He also designed stained glass (for a chapel in Vence, S France 1950s and a synagogue in Jerusalem 1961), mosaics (for Israel's Knesset in the 1960s), the ceiling of the Paris Opera House 1964, and tapestries, and stage sets. He was an original figure, a precursor of Surrealism, as in *The Dream* (Metropolitan Museum of Art, New York).

Chain reaction in nuclear physics, a fission reaction that is maintained because neutrons released by the splitting of some atomic nuclei themselves go on to split others, releasing even more neutrons. Such a reaction can be controlled (as in a nuclear reactor) by using moderators to absorb excess neutrons. Uncontrolled, a chain reaction produces a nuclear explosion (as in an atom bomb).

Chaka alternative spelling of ⟡Shaka, Zulu chief.

Chalatenango department on the N frontier of El Salvador; area 2,507 sq km/968 sq mi; population (1981) 235,700; capital Chalatenango. It is largely controlled by socialist Farabundo Marti Liberation Front (FMLN) guerrilla insurgents.

chalcedony form of quartz, SiO_2, in which the crystals are so fine-grained that they are impossible to distinguish with a microscope (cryptocrystalline). Agate, onyx, tiger's eye, and carnelian are ⟡gem varieties of chalcedony.

Chamberlain (Arthur) Neville 1869–1940. British Conservative politician, son of Joseph Chamberlain. He was prime minister 1937–40. Trying to close the old Anglo-Irish feud, he agreed to return to Eire those ports that had been occupied by the navy. He also attempted to appease the demands of the European dictators, particularly Mussolini. In 1938 he went to Munich and negotiated with Hitler the settlement of the Czechoslovak question. He was ecstatically received on his return, and claimed that the Munich Agreement brought 'peace in our time'. Within a year, however, Britain was at war with Germany. He resigned 1940 following the defeat of the British forces in Norway.

Chamberlain Joseph 1836–1914. British politician,

reformist mayor of, and member of Parliament for, Birmingham; in 1886, he resigned from the cabinet over Gladstone's policy of home rule for Ireland, and led the revolt of the Liberal-Unionists. Chamberlain was one of the most colourful figures of British politics, and his monocle and orchid made him a favourite subject for political cartoonists.

chamber music music suitable for performance in a small room or chamber, rather than in the concert hall, and usually written for instrumental combinations, played with one instrument to a part, as in the string quartet.

chameleon any of some 80 or so species of lizard of the family Chameleontidae. Some species have highly developed colour-changing abilities, which are caused by changes in the intensity of light, of temperature, and of emotion altering the dispersal of pigment granules in the layers of cells beneath the outer skin.

chamois goatlike mammal *Rupicapra rupicapra* found in mountain ranges of S Europe and Asia Minor. It is brown, with dark patches running through the eyes, and can be up to 80 cm/2.6 ft high. Chamois are very sure-footed, and live in herds of up to 30 members. *Chamois leather*, used for cleaning glass, is now often made from the skin of sheep and goats rather than chamois as they are comparatively rare.

Chamorro Violeta Barrios de *c.* 1939–   . President of Nicaragua from 1990. With strong US support, she was elected to be the candidate for the National Opposition Union (UNO) 1989, winning the presidency from David Ortega Saavedra Feb 1990 and thus ending the period of Sandinista rule.

champagne sparkling white wine invented by Dom Pérignon, a Benedictine monk, 1668. It is made from a blend of grapes (*pinot noir* and *pinot chardonnay*) grown in the Marne River region around Reims and Epernay, in Champagne, NE France. After a first fermentation, sugar and yeast are added to the still wine, which, when bottled, undergoes a second fermentation to produce the sparkle. Sugar syrup may be added to make the wine sweet (*sec*) or dry (*brut*).

Champagne-Ardenne region of NE France; area 25,600 sq km/9,882 sq mi; population (1986) 1,353,000. Its capital is Reims, and it comprises the *départements* of Ardennes, Aube, Marne, and Haute-Marne. It has sheep and dairy farming and vineyards.

champignon any of a number of edible fungi of the family Agaricaceae. The *fairy ring champignon Marasmius oreades* is so called because its fruiting bodies (mushrooms) occur in rings around the outer edge of the underground mycelium (threadlike tubes) of the fungus.

Champlain Samuel de 1567–1635. French pioneer, soldier, and explorer in Canada. Having served in the army of Henry IV and on an expedition to the West Indies, he began his exploration of Canada 1603. In a third expedition 1608 he founded and named Québec, and was appointed lieutenant governor of French Canada 1612.

Champlain, Lake lake in NE USA (extending some 10 km/6 mi into Canada) on the New York–Vermont border; length 201 km/125 mi; area 692 sq km/430 sq mi. It is linked by canal to the St Lawrence and Hudson rivers.

Chancellor, Lord UK state official, originally the royal secretary, today a member of the cabinet, whose office ends with a change of government. The Lord Chancellor acts as Speaker of the House of Lords, may preside over the Court of Appeal, and is head of the judiciary.

chancellor of the Exchequer in the UK, senior cabinet minister responsible for the national economy. The office, established under Henry III, originally entailed keeping the Exchequer seal.

Chandigarh city of N India, in the foothills of the Himalayas; population (1981) 421,000. It is also a Union Territory; area 114 sq km/44 sq mi; population (1991) 640,725.

Chandler Raymond 1888–1959. US crime writer who created the hard-boiled private eye Philip Marlowe in books that include *The Big Sleep* 1939, *Farewell, My Lovely* 1940, and *The Long Goodbye* 1954. He also wrote numerous screenplays, notably *Double Indemnity* 1944 and *Strangers on a Train* 1951.

Changchun industrial city and capital of Jilin province, China; population (1989) 2,070,000. Machinery and motor vehicles are manufactured. It is also the centre of an agricultural district.

Chang Jiang or *Yangtze Kiang* longest river of China, flowing about 6,300 km/3,900 mi from Tibet to the Yellow Sea. It is a main commercial waterway.

Channel, English stretch of water between England and France, leading in the west to the Atlantic Ocean, and in the east via the Strait of Dover to the North Sea; also known as *La Manche* (French 'the sleeve') from its shape.

Channel Islands group of islands in the English Channel, off the NW coast of France; they are a possession of the British crown. They comprise the islands of Jersey, Guernsey, Alderney, Great and Little Sark, with the lesser Herm, Brechou, Jethou, and Lihou.

Channel Tunnel tunnel built beneath the English Channel, linking Britain with mainland Europe. It comprises twin rail tunnels, 50 km/31 mi long and 7.3 m/24 ft in diameter, located 40 m/130 ft beneath the seabed. Specially designed shuttle trains carrying cars and lorries will run between terminals at Folkestone, Kent, and Sangatte, W of Calais, France. It was begun 1986 and is scheduled to be operational 1993. The French and English sections were linked Dec 1990.

Channel tunnel

the Channel Tunnel route

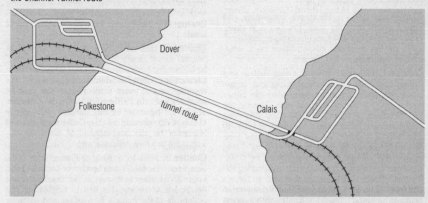

chanson de geste epic poetry of the High Middle Ages in Europe. It probably developed from oral poetry recited in royal or princely courts, and takes as its subject the exploits of heroes, such as those associated with Charlemagne and the crusades. The best known example is the *Chanson de Roland*.

Chaplin Charlie (Charles Spencer) 1889–1977. English film actor and director. He made his reputation as a tramp with a smudge moustache, bowler hat, and twirling cane in silent comedies from the mid-1910s, including *The Rink* 1916, *The Kid* 1920, and *The Gold Rush* 1925. His work often contrasts buffoonery with pathos, and his later films combine dialogue with mime and music, as in *The Great Dictator* 1940 and *Limelight* 1952. He was one of cinema's most popular and greatest stars.

char or **charr** fish *Salvelinus alpinus* related to the trout and salmon which is distinguished by its small scales and large, round, pinkish spots on its back and sides. It lives in the Arctic coastal waters, and also in Europe and North America in some upland lakes. It is one of Britain's rarest fish, and is at risk from growing acidification.

charcoal black, porous form of ⟡carbon, produced by heating wood or other organic materials in the absence of air. It is used as a fuel in the smelting of metals such as copper and zinc, and by artists for making black line drawings. *Activated charcoal* has been powdered and dried so that it presents a much increased surface area for adsorption; it is used for filtering and purifying liquids and gases, for example, in drinking-water filters and gas masks.

Chardin Jean-Baptiste-Siméon 1699–1779. French painter of naturalistic still lifes and quiet domestic scenes that recall the Dutch tradition. His work is a complete contrast to that of his contemporaries, the Rococo painters. He developed his own technique

using successive layers of paint to achieve depth of tone and is generally considered one of the finest exponents of the genre.

charge see ⟡electric charge.

Charge of the Light Brigade disastrous attack by the British Light Brigade of cavalry against the Russian entrenched artillery on 25 Oct 1854 during the Crimean War at the Battle of ⟡Balaclava.

Charlemagne Charles I **the Great** 742–814. King of the Franks from 768 and Holy Roman emperor from 800. By inheritance (his father was ⟡Pepin the Short) and extensive campaigns of conquest, he united most of W Europe by 804, when after 30 years of war the Saxons came under his control. He reformed the legal, judicial, and military systems; established schools; and promoted Christianity, commerce, agriculture, arts, and literature. In his capital, Aachen, scholars gathered from all over Europe.

Charles (full name Charles Philip Arthur George) 1948– . Prince of the UK, heir to the British throne, and Prince of Wales since 1958 (invested 1969). He is the first-born child of Queen Elizabeth II and the Duke of Edinburgh. He studied at Trinity College, Cambridge, 1967–70, before serving in the Royal Air Force and Royal Navy. He is the first royal heir since 1659 to have an English wife, Lady Diana Spencer, daughter of the 8th Earl Spencer. They have two sons and heirs, William (1982–) and Henry (1984–).

Charles (Mary) Eugenia 1919– . Dominican politician, prime minister from 1980; cofounder and first leader of the centrist Dominica Freedom Party (DFP). Two years after Dominica's independence the DFP won the 1980 general election and she became the Caribbean's first female prime minister.

Charles Jacques Alexandre César 1746–1823. French physicist who studied gases and made the first ascent in a hydrogen-filled balloon 1783. His work on the expansion of gases led to the formulation of ▷Charles's law.

Charles Ray 1930– . US singer, songwriter, and pianist whose first hits were 'I've Got A Woman' 1955, 'What'd I Say' 1959, and 'Georgia on My Mind' 1960. He has recorded gospel, blues, rock, soul, country, and rhythm and blues.

Charles I 1600–1649. King of Great Britain and Ireland from 1625, son of James I of England (James VI of Scotland). When he succeeded his father friction with Parliament began at once. He accepted the ▷Petition of Right 1628 but then dissolved Parliament and ruled without a parliament 1629–40 (the Eleven Years' Tyranny). During this time he raised money by expedients, such as ▷ship money, that alienated the nation, while the ▷Star Chamber suppressed opposition by persecuting the Puritans. When Charles attempted 1637 to force a prayer book on the English model on Presbyterian Scotland he found himself confronted with a nation in arms. The ▷Short Parliament, summoned 1640, refused funds, and the ▷Long Parliament later that year rebelled. Charles declared war on Parliament 1642 by raising his standard at Nottingham (see English ▷Civil War) but surrendered 1646 and was beheaded 1649. Charles's advisers were ▷Strafford and ▷Laud. He was the father of Charles II.

Charles II 1630–1685. King of Great Britain and Ireland from 1660, when Parliament accepted the restoration of the monarchy after the collapse of ▷Cromwell's Commonwealth; son of Charles I. His chief minister Clarendon, who arranged his marriage 1662 with Catherine of Braganza, was replaced 1667 with the ▷Cabal of advisers. His plans to restore Catholicism in Britain led to war with the Netherlands 1672–74, in support of Louis XIV of France, and a break with Parliament, which he dissolved 1681. He ruled without a parliament 1681–85, financed by Louis XIV. He was succeeded by James II.

Charles II *the Bald*; king of France. See ▷Charles II, Holy Roman emperor.

Charles V *the Wise* 1337–1380. King of France from 1364. He was regent during the captivity of his father, John II, in England 1356–60, and became king on John's death. He reconquered nearly all France from England 1369–80.

Charles VI *the Mad* or *the Well-Beloved* 1368–1422. King of France from 1380, succeeding his father Charles V; he was under the regency of his uncles until 1388. He became mentally unstable 1392, and civil war broke out between the dukes of Orléans and Burgundy. Henry V of England invaded France 1415, conquering Normandy, and in 1420 forced Charles to sign the Treaty of Troyes, recognizing Henry as his successor.

Charles VII 1403–1461. King of France from 1429. Son of Charles VI, he was excluded from the suc-cession by the Treaty of Troyes, but recognized by the south of France. In 1429 Joan of Arc raised the siege of Orléans and had him crowned at Reims. He organized France's first standing army and by 1453 had expelled the English from all of France except Calais.

Charles IX 1550–1574. King of France from 1560. Second son of Henry II and Catherine de' Medici, he succeeded his brother Francis II at the age of ten but remained under the domination of his mother's regency for ten years while France was torn by religious wars. In 1570 he fell under the influence of the ▷Huguenot leader Gaspard de Coligny (1517–1572); alarmed by this, Catherine instigated his order for the Massacre of St Bartholomew, which led to a new religious war.

Charles X 1757–1836. King of France from 1824. Grandson of Louis XV and brother of Louis XVI and Louis XVIII, he was known as the comte d'Artois before his accession. He fled to England at the beginning of the French Revolution, and when he came to the throne on the death of Louis XVIII, he attempted to reverse the achievements of the Revolution. A revolt ensued 1830, and he again fled to England.

Charles II *the Bald* 823–877. Holy Roman emperor from 875 and (as Charles II) king of France from 843. Younger son of Louis I (the Pious), he warred against his eldest brother, Emperor Lothair I. The Treaty of Verdun 843 made him king of the West Frankish Kingdom (now France and the Spanish Marches).

Charles V 1500–1558. Holy Roman emperor 1519–56. Son of Philip of Burgundy and Joanna of Castile, he inherited vast possessions, which led to rivalry from Francis I of France, whose alliance with the Ottoman Empire brought Vienna under siege 1529 and 1532. Charles was also in conflict with the Protestants in Germany until the Treaty of Passau 1552, which allowed the Lutherans religious liberty.

Charles VI 1685–1740. Holy Roman emperor from 1711, father of ▷Maria Theresa, whose succession to his Austrian dominions he tried to ensure, and himself claimant to the Spanish throne 1700, thus causing the War of the ▷Spanish Succession.

Charles (Karl Franz Josef) 1887–1922. Emperor of Austria and king of Hungary from 1916, the last of the Habsburg emperors. He succeeded his great-uncle Franz Josef 1916 but was forced to withdraw to Switzerland 1918, although he refused to abdi-cate. In 1921 he attempted unsuccessfully to regain the crown of Hungary and was deported to Madeira, where he died.

Charles II (Spanish *Carlos*) 1661–1700. King of Spain from 1665. The second son of Philip IV, he was the last of the Spanish Habsburg kings. Mentally handicapped from birth, he bequeathed his dominions to Philip of Anjou, grandson of Louis XIV, which led to the War of the ▷Spanish

Succession.

Charles X 1622–1660. King of Sweden from 1654, when he succeeded his cousin Christina. He waged war with Poland and Denmark and in 1657 invaded Denmark by leading his army over the frozen sea.

Charles XII 1682–1718. King of Sweden from 1697, when he succeeded his father, Charles XI. From 1700 he was involved in wars with Denmark, Poland, and Russia. He won a succession of victories until, in 1709 while invading Russia, he was defeated at Poltava in the Ukraine, and forced to take refuge in Turkey until 1714. He was killed while besieging Fredrikshall, Norway.

Charles XIV (Jean Baptiste Jules Bernadotte) 1763–1844. King of Sweden and Norway from 1818. A former marshal in the French army, in 1810 he was elected crown prince of Sweden under the name of Charles John (Carl Johan). Loyal to his adopted country, he brought Sweden into the alliance against Napoleon 1813, as a reward for which Sweden received Norway. He was the founder of the present dynasty.

Charles Edward Stuart the *Young Pretender* or *Bonnie Prince Charlie* 1720–1788. British prince, grandson of James II, son of James, the Old Pretender. In the Jacobite rebellion 1745 Charles won the support of the Scottish Highlanders; his army invaded England to claim the throne but was beaten back by the duke of ⟡Cumberland and routed at ⟡Culloden 1746. For five months he wandered through the Highlands with a price of £30,000 on his head before going into exile in France.

Charles Martel *c.* 688–741. Frankish ruler (Mayor of the Palace) of the E Frankish kingdom from 717 and the whole kingdom from 731. His victory against the Moors at Moussais-la-Bataille near Tours 732 earned him his nickname of Martel, 'the Hammer', because he halted the Islamic advance by the ⟡Moors into Europe.

Charles's law law stating that the volume of a given mass of gas at constant pressure is directly proportional to its absolute temperature (temperature in kelvin). It was discovered by Jacques Charles 1787, and independently by Joseph Gay-Lussac 1802.

Charleston capital and chief city of West Virginia, USA, on the Kanawha River; population (1990) 57,300. It is the centre of a region that produces coal, natural gas, salt, clay, timber, and oil, and it is an important chemical-producing centre. Charleston developed from a fort built 1788.

charlock or *wild mustard* annual plant *Sinapis arvensis* of the family Cruciferae. It is a common weed in Britain, reaching a height of 60 cm/2 ft, with yellow flowers.

Charlotte Amalie capital, tourist resort, and free port of the US Virgin Islands; population (1980) 11,756. It became a Danish colony 1672 and was named after the Danish queen. The main industries are tourism, handicrafts, and rum.

Charlottetown capital of Prince Edward Island, Canada; population (1986) 16,000. The city trades in textiles, fish, timber, vegetables, and dairy produce. It was founded by French settlers in the 1720s.

Charlton Bobby (Robert) 1937– . English footballer, younger brother of Jack Charlton, who scored a record 49 goals in 106 appearances. He spent most of his playing career with Manchester United and played in the England team that won the World Cup 1966. He was European Footballer of the Year 1966.

Charon in Greek mythology, the boatman who ferried the dead over the rivers Acheron and Styx to Hades, the underworld. A coin placed on the tongues of the dead paid for their passage.

Chartism radical British democratic movement, mainly of the working classes, which flourished around 1838–50. It derived its name from the People's Charter, a six-point programme comprising universal male suffrage, equal electoral districts, secret ballot, annual parliaments, and abolition of the property qualification for, and payment of, members of Parliament. Greater prosperity, lack of organization, and rivalry in the leadership led to its demise.

Charybdis in Greek mythology, a whirlpool formed by a monster of the same name on one side of the narrow straits of Messina, Sicily, opposite the monster Scylla.

château country house or important residence in France. The term originally applied to a French medieval castle, and the château was first used as a domestic building in the late 15th century; by the reign of Louis XIII (1610–43) fortifications such as moats and keeps were no longer used for defensive purposes, but merely as decorative features. The Loire valley contains some fine examples of châteaux.

Chateaubriand François René, vicomte de 1768–1848. French author. In exile from the French Revolution 1794–99, he wrote *Atala* 1801 (after his encounters with North American Indians) and the autobiographical *René*, which formed part of *Le Génie du christianisme/The Genius of Christianity* 1802. He later wrote *Mémoires d'outre tombe/Memoirs from Beyond the Tomb* 1849–50.

Chatterton Thomas 1752–1770. English poet whose medieval-style poems and brief life were to inspire English Romanticism. Born in Bristol, he studied ancient documents he found in the Church of St Mary Redcliffe and composed poems he ascribed to a 15th-century monk, 'Thomas Rowley', which were accepted as genuine. He committed suicide in London, after becoming destitute.

Chaucer Geoffrey *c.* 1340–1400. English poet. *The Canterbury Tales*, a collection of stories told by a group of pilgrims on their way to Canterbury, reveals his knowledge of human nature and his stylistic variety, from urbane and ironic to simple and bawdy. Early allegorical poems, including *The Book of the Duchess*, were influenced by French poems like the *Roman de la Rose*. His *Troilus and Criseyde* is a substantial narrative poem about the tragic betrayal of an idealized courtly love.

cheese food made from the **curds** (solids) of soured milk from cows, sheep, or goats, separated from the **whey** (liquid), then salted, put into moulds, and pressed into firm blocks. Cheese is ripened with bacteria or surface fungi, and kept for a time to mature before eating. There are six main types of cheese: **soft cheese**, which may be ripe or unripe; **semi-hard cheese** and **hard cheese**, both ripened by bacteria; **very hard cheese** made with skimmed milk; **processed cheese** made with dried skim milk powder and additives; and **whey cheese** made by heat coagulation of the proteins from whey.

cheetah large wild cat *Acinonyx jubatus* native to Africa, Arabia, and SW Asia, but now rare in some areas. Yellowish with black spots, it has a slim lithe build. It is up to 1 m/3 ft tall at the shoulder, and up to 1.5 m/5 ft long. It can reach 110 kph/70 mph, but tires after about 400 m/1,300 ft. Cheetahs live in open country where they hunt small antelopes, hares, and birds.

Chekhov Anton (Pavlovich) 1860–1904. Russian dramatist and writer of short stories. His plays concentrate on the creation of atmosphere and delineation of internal development, rather than external action. His first play, *Ivanov* 1887, was a failure, as was *The Seagull* 1896 until revived by Stanislavsky 1898 at the Moscow Art Theatre, for which Chekhov went on to write his finest plays: *Uncle Vanya* 1899, *The Three Sisters* 1901, and *The Cherry Orchard* 1904.

chelate chemical compound whose molecules consist of one or more metal atoms or charged ions joined to chains of organic residues by coordinate (or dative covalent) chemical ◊bonds.

Chelyabinsk industrial town and capital of Chelyabinsk region, W Siberia, Russia; population (1987) 1,119,000. It has iron and engineering works and makes chemicals, motor vehicles, and aircraft.

chemical warfare use in war of gaseous, liquid, or solid substances intended to have a toxic effect on humans, animals, or plants. Together with ◊biological warfare, it was banned by the Geneva Protocol 1925 and the United Nations in 1989 also voted for a ban. The total US stockpile 1989 was estimated at 30,000 tonnes and the Soviet stockpile at 50,000 tonnes. In June 1990, the USA and USSR agreed bilaterally to reduce their stockpile to 5,000 tonnes each by 2002. The USA began replacing its stocks with new nerve-gas ◊binary weapons.

chemistry science concerned with the composition of matter (gas, liquid, or solid) and of the changes that take place in it under certain conditions. *Organic chemistry* is the branch of chemistry that deals with carbon compounds. *Inorganic chemistry* deals with the description, properties, reactions, and preparation of the elements and their compounds, with the exception of carbon compounds. *Physical chemistry* is concerned with the quantitative explanation of chemical phenomena and reactions, and the measurement of data required for such explanations. This branch studies in particular the movement of molecules, and the effects of temperature and pressure, often with regard to gases and liquids.

chemotherapy any medical treatment with chemicals. It usually refers to treatment of cancer with cytotoxic and other drugs. The term was coined by the German bacteriologist Paul Ehrlich for the use of synthetic chemicals against infectious diseases.

Chengdu or *Chengtu* ancient city, capital of Sichuan province, China; population (1989) 2,780,000. It is a busy rail junction and has railway workshops, and textile, electronics, and engineering industries. It has well-preserved temples.

Chernobyl town in central Ukraine; site of a nuclear power station. In April 1986 a leak, caused by overheating, occurred in a non-pressurized boiling-water nuclear reactor. The resulting clouds of radioactive isotopes were traced as far away as Sweden; over 250 people were killed, and thousands of square miles contaminated.

cherry spherical smooth fruit of several species of trees of the rose family Rosaceae. Cultured cherries are varieties of the gean or wild cherry *Prunus avium* and the sour or morello cherry *P. cerasus*. Cherries are cultivated in temperate regions with warm summers. They grow best in deep fertile soil.

chervil any of several plants of the carrot family Umbelliferae. The garden chervil *Anthriscus cerefolium* has leaves with a sweetish odour, resembling parsley. It is used as a garnish and in soups. Chervil originated on the borders of Europe and Asia and was introduced to W Europe by the Romans.

Chesapeake Bay largest of the inlets on the Atlantic coast of the USA, bordered by Maryland and Virginia. It is about 320 km/200 mi in length and 6–64 km/4–40 mi in width.

Cheshire county in NW England; *area* 2,320 sq km/896 sq mi; *towns* Chester (administrative headquarters), Warrington, Crewe, Widnes, Macclesfield, Congleton; *physical* chiefly a fertile plain; rivers: Mersey, Dee, Weaver; *products* textiles, chemicals, dairy products; *population* (1991) 937,300; *famous people* Charles Dodgson (Lewis Carroll); the novelist Mrs Gaskell lived at Knutsford (the locale of *Cranford*).

chess board game originating as early as the 2nd

century AD. Two players use 16 pieces each, on a board of 64 squares of alternating colour, to try to force the opponent into a position where the main piece (the king) is threatened and cannot move to another position without remaining threatened.

Chesterton G(ilbert) K(eith) 1874–1936. English novelist, essayist, and satirical poet, author of a series of novels featuring as detective a naive priest, Father Brown. Other novels include *The Napoleon of Notting Hill* 1904 and *The Man Who Knew Too Much* 1922.

chestnut tree of the genus *Castanea*, belonging to the beech family Fagaceae. The Spanish or sweet chestnut *C. sativa* produces edible nuts inside husks; its timber is also valuable. ⬦Horse chestnuts are quite distinct, belonging to the genus *Aesculus*, family Hippocastanaceae. The chestnut is native to the Balkans and Italy; it was introduced to Britain in Roman times, but is not common elsewhere in northern Europe.

Chetnik member of a Serbian nationalist group that operated underground during the German occupation of Yugoslavia during World War II. Led by Col Draza Mihailović, the Chetniks initially received aid from the Allies, but this was later transferred to the communist partisans led by Tito. The term has also popularly been applied to Serb militia forces in the 1991–92 Yugoslav civil war.

Chiang Ching alternative transliteration of ⬦Jiang Qing, Chinese actress, third wife of Mao Zedong.

Chiang Kai-shek (Pinyin *Jiang Jie Shi*) 1887–1975. Chinese nationalist Guomindang (Kuomintang) general and politician, president of China 1928–31 and 1943–49, and of Taiwan from 1949, where he set up a US-supported right-wing government on his expulsion from the mainland by the Communist forces. He was a commander in the civil war that lasted from the end of imperial rule 1911 to the Second ⬦Sino-Japanese War and beyond, having split with the Communist leader Mao Zedong 1927.

Chicago financial and industrial city in Illinois, on Lake Michigan. It is the third largest US city; population (1990) 2,783,700, metropolitan area 8,065,000. Industries include iron, steel, chemicals, electrical goods, machinery, meatpacking and food processing, publishing, fabricated metals, machinery. The once famous stockyards are now closed. Chicago has the world's first skyscraper, built 1887–88, and some of the world's tallest modern skyscrapers, including the Sears Tower, 443 m/1,454 ft.

chickenpox or *varicella* common acute disease, caused by a virus of the ⬦herpes group and transmitted by airborne droplets. Chickenpox chiefly attacks children under the age of ten. The incubation period is two to three weeks. One attack normally gives immunity for life.

chickpea annual plant *Cicer arietinum*, family Leguminosae, which is grown for food in India and the Middle East. Its short, hairy pods contain edible pealike seeds.

Chiclayo capital of Lambayeque department, NW Peru; population (1988) 395,000. Founded 1720, it became a city 1835. Sugar cane, cotton, and rice are grown in irrigated areas around Chiclayo.

chicory plant *Cichorium intybus*, family Compositae. Native to Europe and W Asia, it has large, usually blue, flowers. Its long taproot is used dried and roasted as a coffee substitute. As a garden vegetable, grown under cover, its blanched leaves are used in salads. It is related to ⬦endive.

chiffchaff bird *Phylloscopus collybita* of the warbler family, found in woodlands and thickets in Europe and N Asia during the summer, migrating south for winter. About 11 cm/4.3 in long, olive above, greyish below, with an eyestripe and usually dark legs, it looks similar to a willow warbler but has a distinctive song.

chihuahua smallest breed of dog, 15 cm/10 in high, developed in the USA from Mexican origins. It may weigh only 1 kg/2.2 lb. The domed head and wide-set ears are characteristic, and the skull is large compared to the body. It can be almost any colour, and occurs in both smooth (or even hairless) and long-coated varieties.

Chihuahua capital of Chihuahua state, Mexico, 1,285 km/800 mi NW of Mexico City; population (1984) 375,000. Founded 1707, it is the centre of a mining district and has textile mills.

Chile Republic of; South American country, bordered N by Peru and Bolivia, E by Argentina, and S and W by the Pacific Ocean; *area* 756,950 sq km/292,257 sq mi; *capital* Santiago; *physical* Andes mountains along E border, Atacama Desert in N, arable land and forest in S; territories Easter Island, Juan Fernández Islands, part of Tierra del Fuego, part of Antarctica; *head of state and government* Patricio Aylwin from 1990; *political system* emergent democratic republic; *exports* copper (world's leading producer), iron, molybdenum (world's second largest producer), nitrate, pulp and paper, steel products, fishmeal, fruit; *population* (1990 est) 13,000,000 (the majority mestizo, of mixed American Indian and Spanish descent); *language* Spanish; *recent history* independence from Spain was achieved 1818. An extensive programme of nationalization and social reform launched by Dr Salvador Allende 1970 was halted by General Pinochet's military takeover 1973. In 1989 he agreed to constitutional changes to allow pluralist politics; Patricio Aylwin became head of state and government 1990.

chilli (North American *chili*) pod, or powder made from the pod, of a variety of ⬦capsicum, *Capsicum frutescens*, a hot, red pepper. It is widely used in cooking.

Chimbote largest fishing port in Peru; population (1981) 216,000. Originally a fishing village with a

natural harbour, Chimbote became a town 1895. It was largely destroyed by an earthquake 1970 and has been rebuilt. Industries include fish meal and fish oil, minerals, cast iron, and machine parts.

chimera or **chimaera** in Greek mythology, a fire-breathing animal with a lion's head, a goat's body, and tail in the form of a snake; hence any apparent hybrid of two or more creatures. The chimera was killed by the hero Bellerophon on the winged horse Pegasus.

chimpanzee highly intelligent African ape *Pan troglodytes* that lives mainly in rainforests but sometimes in wooded savanna. Chimpanzees are covered in thin but long black body hair, except for the face, hands, and feet, which may have pink or black skin. They normally walk on all fours, supporting the front of the body on the knuckles of the fingers, but can stand or walk upright for a short distance. They can grow to 1.4 m/4.5 ft tall, and weigh up to 50 kg/110 lb. They are strong and climb well, but spend time on the ground, living in loose social groups. The bulk of the diet is fruit, with some leaves, insects, and occasional meat. Chimpanzees can use 'tools', fashioning twigs to extract termites from their nests.

China People's Republic of; country in SE Asia, bordered N by Mongolia; NW by Kazakhstan; NE by the Russian Federation; SW by India and Nepal; S by Bhutan, Myanmar (formerly Burma), Laos, and Vietnam; SE by the South China Sea; and E by the East China Sea, North Korea, and the Russian Federation; *area* 9,596,960 sq km/ 3,599,975 sq mi; *capital* Beijing (Peking); *physical* two-thirds of China is mountains or desert (N and W), including the Gobi Desert in the N; the low-lying E is irrigated by rivers Huang He (Yellow River), Chang Jiang (Yangtze-Kiang), Xi Jiang (Si Kiang); *head of state* Yang Shangkun from 1988; *head of government* Li Peng from 1987;

political system communist republic; *exports* tea, livestock and animal products, silk, cotton, oil, minerals (world's largest producer of tungsten and antimony), chemicals, light industrial goods; *population* (1990 est) 1,130,065,000 (the majority are Han or ethnic Chinese; other ethnic groups include Tibetan, Uigur, and Zhuang); *languages* Chinese, including Mandarin (official), Cantonese, and other dialects; *recent history* the People's Republic of China was proclaimed by Mao Zedong 1949; a Soviet style constitution was adopted. The Great Leap Forward 1958–60 aimed to achieve 'true communism'. China entered the United Nations 1971; opened diplomatic relations with the USA 1979. Economic reforms, normalization of foreign relations, and prodemocracy demonstrations have characterized recent years.

china clay or **kaolin** white clay formed by the chemical weathering of feldspar, a mineral found in ⊳granite. China clay is used in making porcelain and as a filler in paper making and paints. It is mined in the USA, France, Czechoslovakia, and the UK, near St Austell, Cornwall.

China Sea area of the Pacific Ocean bordered by China, Vietnam, Borneo, the Philippines, and Japan. Various groups of small islands and shoals, including the Paracels, 500 km/300 mi E of Vietnam, have been disputed by China and other powers because they lie in oil-rich areas.

chinchilla South American rodent *Chinchilla laniger* found in high, rather barren areas of the Andes in Bolivia and Chile. About the size of a small rabbit, it has long ears and a long bushy tail, and shelters in rock crevices. These gregarious animals have thick, soft, silver-grey fur, and were hunted almost to extinction for it. They are now farmed and protected in the wild.

Chinese native to or an inhabitant of China and Taiwan, or a person of Chinese descent. The Chinese comprise more than 25% of the world's population.

Chinese language language or group of languages of the Sino-Tibetan family, spoken in China, Taiwan, Hong Kong, Singapore, and Chinese communities throughout the world. Varieties of spoken Chinese differ greatly, but all share a written form using thousands of ideographic symbols – characters – which have changed little in 2,000 years. Nowadays, *putonghua* ('common speech'), based on the educated Beijing dialect known as Mandarin Chinese, is promoted throughout China as the national spoken and written language.

Chinese Revolution series of great political upheavals in China 1911–49 that eventually led to Communist party rule and the establishment of the People's Republic of China. In 1912, a Nationalist revolt overthrew the imperial Manchu (or Ching) dynasty. Led by Sun Yat-sen 1923–25, and by Chiang Kai-shek 1925–49, the Nationalists, or Guomindang, were increasingly challenged by the growing Communist movement. The 10,000 km/6,000 mi **Long March** to the NW by the Communists 1934–35 to escape from attacks by the Nationalist forces resulted in Mao Zedong's emergence as Communist leader. During World War II 1939–45, the various Chinese political groups pooled military resources against the Japanese invaders. After World War II, the conflict reignited into open civil war 1946–49, until the Nationalists were defeated at Nanking and forced to flee to Taiwan. Communist rule was established in the People's Republic of China under the leadership of Mao.

chip or **silicon chip** another name for an ▷**integrated circuit**, a complete electronic circuit on a slice of silicon (or other semiconductor) crystal only a few millimetres square.

chipmunk any of several species of small ground squirrel with characteristic stripes along its side. Chipmunks live in North America and E Asia, in a variety of habitats, usually wooded, and take shelter in burrows. They have pouches in their cheeks for carrying food. They climb well but spend most of their time on or near the ground.

Chippendale Thomas *c.* 1718–1779. English furniture designer. He set up his workshop in St Martin's Lane, London 1753. His book *The Gentleman and Cabinet Maker's Director* 1754, was a significant contribution to furniture design. He favoured Louis XVI, Chinese, Gothic, and Neo-Classical styles, and worked mainly in mahogany.

Chirac Jacques 1932– . French conservative politician, prime minister to President Giscard d'Estaing 1974–76 and to President Mitterrand in a 'cohabitation' experiment 1986–88. The latter term was marked by economic decline, nationality reforms, and student unrest; he was replaced by Michel Rocard 1988. Chirac established the neo-Gaullist Rassemblement pour la République (RPR) 1976, and became mayor of Paris 1977.

Chirico Giorgio de' 1888–1978. Italian painter born in Greece, whose style presaged Surrealism in its use of enigmatic imagery and dreamlike settings, for example, *The Enigma of an Autumn Afternoon* 1910 and *Nostalgia of the Infinite* 1911.

chiropractic technique of manipulation of the spine and other parts of the body, based on the principle that disorders are attributable to aberrations in the functioning of the nervous system, which manipulation can correct.

Chissano Joaquim 1939– . Mozambique nationalist politician, president from 1986. When Mozambique achieved internal self-government 1974 he was appointed prime minister. After independence he served as foreign minister 1975–86, then succeeded Samora Machel as president.

Chittagong city and port in Bangladesh, 16 km/10 mi from the mouth of the Karnaphuli River, on the Bay of Bengal; population (1981) 1,388,476. Industries include steel, engineering, chemicals, and textiles.

chivalry code of gallantry and honour that medieval knights were pledged to observe. The word originally meant the knightly class of the feudal Middle Ages. Chivalry originated in feudal France and Spain, spreading rapidly to the rest of Europe and reaching its height in the 12th and 13th

Chinese dynasties

Dynasty	Dates	Major Events
Hsia	1994–1523 BC	Agriculture, bronze, first writing
Shang or Yin	1523–1027	First major dynasty; first Chinese calendar
Chou	1027–255	Developed society using money, iron, written laws; age of Confucius.
Qin	255–206	Unification after period of Warring States, building of Great Wall begun, roads built.
Han	AD 206–220	First centralized and effectively administered empire; introduction of Buddhism.
San Kuo (Three Kingdoms)	220–265	Division into three parts, prolonged fighting and eventual victory of Wei over Chu and Wu; Confucianism superseded by Buddhism and Taoism.
Tsin	265–420	Beginning of Hun invasions in the N
Sui	581–618	Reunification; barbarian invasions stopped; Great Wall refortified
T'ang	618–906	Centralized government; empire greatly extended; period of excellence in sculpture, painting and poetry.
Wu Tai (Five Dynasties)	907–960	Economic depression and loss of territory in N China, central Asia and Korea; first use of paper money
Sung	960–1279	Period of calm and creativity; printing developed (movable type); central government restored; N and W frontiers neglected and Mongol incursions begun.
Yüan	1260–1368	Beginning of Mongol rule in China, under Kublai Khan; Marco Polo visited China; dynasty brought to an end by widespread revolts, centred in Mongolia.
Ming	1368–1644	Mongols driven out by native Chinese, Mongolia captured by 2nd Ming emperor; period of architectural development; Beijing flourished as new capital.
Manchu	1644–1912	China once again under non-Chinese rule, the Qing conquered by nomads from Manchuria; trade with the West, culture flourished, but conservatism eventually led to the dynasty's overthrow by nationalistic revolutionaries under Sun Yatsen.

centuries. It was strengthened by the Crusades; the earliest orders of chivalry were the Knights Hospitallers and the Knights Templars, founded to serve pilgrims to the Holy Land. The principal virtues of the chivalric code were piety, honour, valour, courtesy, chastity, and loyalty.

chive or *chives* bulbous European perennial plant *Allium schoenoprasum* of the lily family Liliaceae. It has long, tubular leaves and dense, round flower heads in blue or lilac, and is used as a garnish for salads.

chlorine greenish-yellow, gaseous, nonmetallic element with a pungent odour, symbol Cl, atomic number 17, relative atomic mass 35.453. It is a member of the ◊halogen group and is widely distributed, in combination with the ◊alkali metals, as chlorates or chlorides.

chlorofluorocarbon (CFC) synthetic chemical that is odourless, nontoxic, nonflammable, and chemically inert. CFCs have been used as propellants in ◊aerosol cans, as refrigerants in refrigerators and air conditioners, and in the manufacture of foam boxes for take-away food cartons. They are partly responsible for the destruction of the ◊ozone layer. In June 1990 representatives of 93 nations, including the UK and the USA, agreed to phase out production of CFCs and various other ozone-depleting chemicals by the end of the 20th century.

chlorophyll green pigment present in most plants; it is responsible for the absorption of light energy during ◊photosynthesis. The pigment absorbs the red and blue-violet parts of sunlight but reflects the green, thus giving plants their characteristic colour.

chocolate powder, syrup, confectionery, or beverage derived from cacao seeds. See ◊cocoa and chocolate.

choir body of singers, normally divided into two or more parts, and commonly four (soprano, alto, tenor, bass). The words *choir* and *chorus* are frequently interchangeable, although all church groups use the former, while larger groups, which may have several hundred members, invariably use the latter.

cholera any of several intestinal diseases, especially *Asiatic cholera*, an infection caused by a bacterium *Vibrio cholerae* transmitted in contaminated water and characterized by violent diarrhoea and vomiting. It is prevalent in many tropical areas.

cholesterol white, crystalline ◊sterol found throughout the body, especially in fats, blood, nerve tissue, and bile; it is also provided in the diet by foods such as eggs, meat, and butter. A high level of cholesterol in the blood is thought to contribute to atherosclerosis (hardening of the arteries).

Chomsky Noam 1928– . US professor of linguistics. He proposed a theory of transformational generative grammar, which attracted widespread interest because of the claims it made about the relationship between language and the mind and the universality of an underlying language structure. He has been a leading critic of the imperialist tendencies of the US government.

Chongjin capital of North Hamgyong province on the NE coast of North Korea; population (1984) 754,000. It developed rapidly from a small fishing village under Japanese occupation 1910–45. There are metal industries, shipbuilding, and machine production.

Chongqing or *Chungking*, also known as *Pahsien* city in Sichuan province, China, that stands at the confluence of the ◊Chang Jiang and Jialing Jiang rivers; population (1984) 2,733,700. Industries include iron, steel, chemicals, synthetic rubber, and textiles. When both Beijing and Nanjing were occupied by the Japanese, it was the capital of China 1938–46.

Chopin Frédéric (François) 1810–1849. Polish composer and pianist. He made his debut as a pianist at the age of eight. As a performer, he revolutionized the technique of pianoforte-playing, turning the hands outwards and favouring a light, responsive touch. His compositions for piano, which include two concertos and other works with orchestra, are characterized by great volatility of mood, and rhythmic fluidity.

chorale traditional hymn tune of the German Protestant church, usually harmonized in four parts for singing by a congregation. It is slow and formal.

chord in music, a group of three or more notes sounded together. The resulting combination of tones may be either harmonious or dissonant.

chordate animal belonging to the phylum Chordata, which includes vertebrates, sea squirts, amphioxi, and others. All these animals, at some stage of their lives, have a supporting rod of tissue (notochord or backbone) running down their bodies.

choreography art of creating and arranging ballet and dance for performance; originally, in the 18th century, the art of dance notation. The system of recording dance movements in abstract symbols devised by the Hungarian Rudolf von Laban (1829–1958), known as Labanotation, was very influential.

Chou En-lai alternative transcription of ◊Zhou Enlai.

chough bird *Pyrrhocorax pyrrhocorax* of the crow family, about 38 cm/15 in long, black-feathered, and with red bill and legs. It lives on sea cliffs and mountains from Europe to E Asia, but is now rare.

chow chow breed of dog originating in China in ancient times. About 45 cm/1.5 ft tall, it has a broad neck and head, round catlike feet, a soft woolly undercoat with a coarse outer coat, and a mane. Its coat should be of one colour, and it has an unusual blue-black tongue.

Chrétien de Troyes lived second half of the 12th century. French poet, born in Champagne. His epics, which introduced the concept of the ⟡Holy Grail, include *Lancelot, ou le chevalier de la charrette*; *Perceval, ou le conte du Graal*, written for Philip, Count of Flanders; *Erec*; *Yvain, ou le chevalier au Lion*; and other Arthurian romances.

Christ the ⟡Messiah as prophesied in the Hebrew Bible, or Old Testament.

Christian IV 1577–1648. King of Denmark and Norway from 1588. He sided with the Protestants in the Thirty Years' War (1618–48), and founded Christiania (now Oslo, capital of Norway). He was succeeded by Frederick II 1648.

Christianity world religion derived from the teaching of Jesus in the first third of the 1st century, with a present-day membership of about 1 billion. It is divided into groups or denominations that differ in some areas of belief and practice. Its main divisions are the ⟡Roman Catholic, ⟡Eastern Orthodox, and ⟡Protestant churches; *beliefs* Christians believe in one God with three aspects: God the Father, God the Son (Jesus), and God the Holy Spirit, who is the power of God working in the world. God created everything that exists and showed his love for the world by coming to Earth as Jesus, and suffering and dying in order to be reconciled with humanity. Christians believe that three days after his death by crucifixion Jesus was raised to life by God's power, appearing many times in bodily form to his followers, and that he is now alive in the world through the Holy Spirit.

Christian Science or *the Church of Christ, Scientist* sect established in the USA by Mary Baker Eddy 1879. Christian Scientists believe that since God is good and is a spirit, matter and evil are not ultimately real. Consequently they refuse all medical treatment. The church has its own daily newspaper, the *Christian Science Monitor*.

Christie Agatha (born Miller) 1890–1976. English detective novelist who created the characters Hercule ⟡Poirot and Miss Jane ⟡Marple. She wrote more than 70 novels, including *The Murder of Roger Ackroyd* 1926 and *Ten Little Indians* 1939. Her play *The Mousetrap*, which opened in London 25 Nov 1952, is the longest continuous running show in the world.

Christmas 25 Dec, a Christian religious holiday, observed throughout the Western world and traditionally marked by feasting and gift-giving. In the Christian church, it is the day on which the birth of Jesus is celebrated, although the actual birth date is unknown. Many of its customs have a non-Christian origin and were adapted from celebrations of the winter ⟡solstice.

Christmas rose see ⟡hellebore.

Christopher, St patron saint of travellers. Traditionally he was a martyr in Syria in the 3rd century, and legend describes his carrying the Christ child over the stream; despite his great strength he found the burden increasingly heavy and was told that the child was Christ bearing the sins of all the world. His feast day, 25 July, was dropped from the Roman Catholic liturgical calendar 1969.

chromatic scale musical scale proceeding by semitones. All 12 notes in the octave are used rather than the 7 notes of the diatonic scale.

chromatography technique used for separating the components of a mixture. This is brought about by means of two immiscible substances, one of which (the *mobile phase*) transports the sample mixture through the other (the stationary phase). The mobile phase may be a gas or a liquid; the stationary phase may be a liquid or a solid, and may be in a column, on paper, or in a thin layer on a glass or plastic support. The components of the mixture are absorbed or impeded by the stationary phase to different extents and therefore become separated.

chromium hard, brittle, grey-white, metallic element, symbol Cr, atomic number 24, relative atomic mass 51.996. It takes a high polish, has a high melting point, and is very resistant to corrosion. It is used in chromium electroplating, in the manufacture of stainless steel and other alloys, and as a catalyst. Its compounds are used for tanning leather and for ⟡alums. In human nutrition it is a vital trace element. In nature, it occurs chiefly as chrome iron ore or chromite (Fe,Cr_2O_4). Kazakhstan, Zimbabwe, and Brazil are sources.

chromosome structure in a cell nucleus that carries the ⟡genes. Each chromosome consists of one very long strand of DNA, coiled and folded to produce a compact body. The point on a chromosome where a particular gene occurs is known as its locus. Most higher organisms have two copies of each chromosome (they are ⟡diploid) but some have only one (they are ⟡haploid). There are 46 chromosomes in a normal human cell. See also ⟡mitosis and ⟡meiosis.

chrysanthemum any plant of the genus *Chrysanthemum* of the family Compositae, with about 200 species. There are hundreds of cultivated varieties, whose exact wild ancestry is uncertain. In the Far East the common chrysanthemum has been cultivated for more than 2,000 years and is the imperial emblem of Japan. Chrysanthemums may be grown from seed, but are more usually propagated by cutting or division.

chub freshwater fish *Leuciscus cephalus* of the carp family. Thickset and cylindrical, it grows up to 60 cm/2 ft, is dark greenish or grey on the back, silvery yellow below, with metallic flashes on the flanks. It lives generally in clean rivers throughout Europe.

Chubu mountainous coastal region of central

church

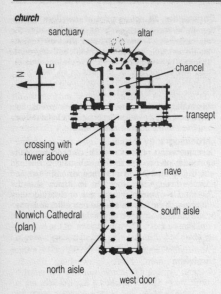

Norwich Cathedral (plan)

sanctuary — altar — chancel — transept — crossing with tower above — nave — south aisle — north aisle — west door

Honshu island, Japan; area 66,774 sq km/ 25,791 sq mi; population (1986) 20,694,000. The chief city is Nagoya.

Chugoku SW region of Honshu island, Japan; area 31,881 sq km/12,314 sq mi; population (1986) 7,764,000. The chief city is Hiroshima.

church building designed as a Christian place of worship; also the Christian community generally, or a specific subdivision of it. Churches were first built in the 3rd century, when persecution of Christians ceased under the Roman emperor Constantine. The original church design was based on the Roman ▷basilica, with a central nave, aisles either side, and an apse at one end. Western churches are built E–W with the altar at the E end, facing the rising Sun.

Churchill Randolph (Henry Spencer) 1849–1895. British Conservative politician, chancellor of the Exchequer and leader of the House of Commons 1886; father of Winston Churchill.

Churchill Winston (Leonard Spencer) 1874–1965. British Conservative politician, prime minister 1940–45 and 1951–55. In Parliament from 1900, as a Liberal until 1923, he held a number of ministerial offices, including First Lord of the Admiralty 1911–15 and chancellor of the Exchequer 1924–29. Absent from the cabinet in the 1930s, he returned Sept 1939 to lead a coalition government 1940–45, negotiating with Allied leaders in World War II to achieve the unconditional surrender of Germany 1945. He led a Conservative government 1951–55. His books include a six-volume history of World War II 1948–54 and a four-volume *History of the English-Speaking Peoples* 1956–58. He was awarded the Nobel Prize for Literature 1953.

Church of England established form of Christianity in England, a member of the Anglican Communion. It was dissociated from the Roman Catholic Church 1534. Usual Sunday attendance in 1991 was 1,154,800.

Church of Scotland established form of Christianity in Scotland, first recognized by the state 1560. It is based on the Protestant doctrines of the reformer Calvin and governed on Presbyterian lines. The church went through several periods of episcopacy in the 17th century, and those who adhered to episcopacy after 1690 formed the Episcopal Church of Scotland, an autonomous church in communion with the Church of England. In 1843, there was a split in the Church of Scotland (the Disruption), in which almost a third of its ministers and members left and formed the Free Church of Scotland. Its membership 1988 was about 850,000.

CIA abbreviation for the US ▷ *Central Intelligence Agency.*

cicada any of several insects of the family Cicadidae. Most species are tropical, but a few occur in Europe and North America. Young cicadas live underground, for up to 17 years in some species. The adults live on trees, whose juices they suck. The males produce a loud, almost continuous, chirping by vibrating membranes in resonating cavities in the abdomen.

Cicero Marcus Tullius 106–43 BC. Roman orator, writer, and politician. His speeches and philosophical and rhetorical works are models of Latin prose, and his letters provide a picture of contemporary Roman life. As consul 63 BC he exposed the Roman politician Catiline's conspiracy in four major orations.

CID abbreviation for ▷ *Criminal Investigation Department.*

Cid, El Rodrigo Díaz de Bivar 1040–1099. Spanish soldier, nicknamed *El Cid* ('the lord') by the ▷Moors. Born in Castile of a noble family, he fought against the king of Navarre and won his nickname *el Campeador* ('the Champion') by killing the Navarrese champion in single combat. Essentially a mercenary, fighting both with and against the Moors, he died while defending Valencia against them, and in subsequent romances became Spain's national hero.

cider in the UK, a fermented drink made from the juice of the apple; in the USA, the term cider usually refers to unfermented (nonalcoholic) apple juice. Cider has been made for more than 2,000 years, and for many centuries has been a popular drink in France and England, which are now its main centres of production.

Cilicia ancient region of Asia Minor, now forming part of Anatolia, Turkey, situated between the Taurus Mountains to the N and W and the Mediterranean to the S.

Cimabue Giovanni (Cenni de Peppi) *c.* 1240–1302.

Italian painter, active in Florence, traditionally styled the 'father of Italian painting'. His paintings retain the golden background of Byzantine art but the figures have a new naturalism. Among the works attributed to him are *Madonna and Child* (Uffizi, Florence), a huge Gothic image of the Virgin that nevertheless has a novel softness and solidity that points forwards to Giotto.

cinchona any shrub or tree of the tropical American genus *Chinchona* of the madder family Rubiaceae. ▷Quinine is produced from the bark of some species, and these are now cultivated in India, Sri Lanka, the Philippines, and Indonesia.

cine camera camera that takes a rapid sequence of still photographs – 24 frames (pictures) each second. When the pictures are projected one after the other at the same speed on to a screen, they appear to show movement, because our eyes hold on to the image of one picture before the next one appears.

cinema 20th-century form of art and entertainment consisting of 'moving pictures' in either black and white or colour, projected on to a screen. Cinema borrows from the other arts, such as music, drama, and literature, but is entirely dependent for its origins on technological developments, including the technology of action photography, projection, sound reproduction, and film processing and printing (see ▷photography).

cinnabar mercuric sulphide, HgS, the only commercially useful ore of mercury. It is deposited in veins and impregnations near recent volcanic rocks and hot springs. The mineral itself is used as a red pigment, commonly known as *vermilion*. Cinnabar is found in the USA (California), Spain (Almadén), Peru, Italy, and Slovenia.

cinnamon dried inner bark of a tree *Cinnamomum zeylanicum* of the laurel family, grown in India and Sri Lanka. The bark is ground to make the spice used in curries and confectionery. Oil of cinnamon is obtained from waste bark and is used as flavouring in food and medicine.

Cinque Ports group of ports in S England, originally five, Sandwich, Dover, Hythe, Romney, and Hastings, later including Rye, Winchelsea, and others. Probably founded in Roman times, they rose to importance after the Norman conquest and until the end of the 15th century were bound to supply the ships and men necessary against invasion.

Circe in Greek mythology, an enchantress living on the island of Aeaea. In Homer's *Odyssey*, she turned the followers of Odysseus into pigs. Odysseus, bearing the herb moly provided by Hermes to protect him from the same fate, forced her to release his men.

circle perfectly round plane shape. Each circle comprises a *centre*, a *radius* (distance from centre to boundary), a *circumference* (the boundary), *diameters* (lines crossing the circle through the

centre), *chords* (lines joining two points on the circumference), *tangents* (lines that touch the circumference at one point only), *sectors* (regions inside the circle between two radii), and *segments* (regions between a chord and the circumference).

circulatory system system of vessels in an animal's body that transports essential substances (blood or other circulatory fluid) to and from the different parts of the body. Except for simple animals such as sponges and coelenterates (jellyfishes, sea anemones, corals), all animals have a circulatory system.

circumcision surgical removal of all or part of the foreskin (prepuce) of the penis, usually performed on the newborn; it is practised among Jews and Muslims. In some societies in Africa and the Middle East, female circumcision or clitoridectomy (removal of the labia minora and/or clitoris) is practised on adolescents as well as babies; it is illegal in the West.

CIS abbreviation for ▷*Commonwealth of Independent States*, established 1992 by 11 former Soviet republics.

circle

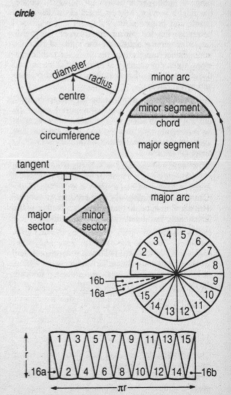

Ciskei, Republic of Bantu homeland in South Africa, which became independent 1981, although this is not recognized by any other country; *area* 7,700 sq km/2,974 sq mi; *capital* Bisho; *features* Ciskei is one of the two homelands of the Xhosa people created by South Africa (the other is Transkei); *government* president (Brig Oupa Gqozo from 1990), with legislative and executive councils; *products* pineapples, timber, metal products, leather, textiles; *population* (1984) 903,681; *language* Xhosa.

Citizens' Advice Bureau (CAB) UK organization established 1939 to provide information and advice to the public on any subject, such as personal problems, financial, house purchase, or consumer rights. If required, the bureau will act on behalf of citizens, drawing on its own sources of legal and other experts. There are more than 900 bureaux located all over the UK.

Citizen's Charter series of proposals aimed at improving public services in the UK, unveiled by Prime Minister John Major 1991. Major's 'programme for a decade' covered the activities of a range of public-sector bodies, including the police, the health service, schools, local authorities, and public and private utility companies. It promised better quality for consumers through the publication of service standards, the right of redress, performance monitoring, penalties for public services, tighter regulation of privatized utilities, and the increased pressures resulting from competition and privatization.

citizenship status as a member of a state. In most countries citizenship may be acquired either by birth or by naturalization. The status confers rights such as voting and the protection of the law and also imposes responsibilities such as military service, in some countries.

citric acid organic acid widely distributed in the plant kingdom; it is found in high concentrations in citrus fruits and has a sharp, sour taste. At one time it was commercially prepared from concentrated lemon juice, but now the main source is the fermentation of sugar with certain moulds.

citrus any tree or shrub of the genus *Citrus*, family Rutaceae. Citruses are found in Asia and other warm parts of the world. They are evergreen and aromatic, and several species – the orange, lemon, lime, citron, and grapefruit – are cultivated for fruit.

city important, or high-order, urban settlement. In the past, a town in Britain needed either a cathedral or a royal charter before it could be called a city, but in modern-day usage a city is a settlement with a population of more than 150,000. Royal charters are still awarded, however.

Ciudad Juárez city on the Rio Grande, in Chihuahua, N Mexico, on the US border; population (1990) 797,650. It is a centre for cotton.

civet small to medium-sized carnivorous mammal found in Africa and Asia, belonging to the family Viverridae, which also includes ◊*mongooses* and ◊*genets*. Distant relations of cats, they generally have longer jaws and more teeth. All have a scent gland in the inguinal (groin) region. Extracts from this gland are taken from the *African civet Civettictis civetta* and used in perfumery.

Civic Forum Czech democratic movement, formed Nov 1989, led by Vaclav ◊Havel. In Dec 1989 it participated in forming a coalition government after the collapse of communist rule in Czechoslovakia. Its Slovak counterpart is ◊Public Against Violence (*Verejnosť proti násiliu*). Both bodies began to splinter during 1991. From Civic Forum emerged the right-of-centre Civic Democratic Party, led by Vaclac Klaus, and the social-democratic Civic Movement, led by Jiri Dienstbier.

civil aviation operation of passenger and freight transport by air. With increasing traffic, control of air space is a major problem, and in 1963 Eurocontrol was established by Belgium, France, West Germany, Luxembourg, the Netherlands, and the UK to supervise both military and civil movement in the air space over member countries. There is also a tendency to coordinate services and other facilities between national airlines; for example, the establishment of Air Union 1963 by France (Air France), West Germany (Lufthansa), Italy (Alitalia), and Belgium (Sabena).

civil engineering branch of engineering that is concerned with the construction of roads, bridges, aqueducts, waterworks, tunnels, canals, irrigation works, and harbours.

civil law legal system based on ◊Roman law. It is one of the two main European legal systems, ◊English (common) law being the other. Civil law may also mean the law relating to matters other than criminal law, such as ◊contract and ◊tort.

civil list in the UK, the annual sum provided from public funds to meet the official expenses of the sovereign and immediate dependents; private expenses are met by the ◊privy purse.

civil rights rights of the individual citizen. In many countries they are specified (as in the Bill of Rights of the US constitution) and guaranteed by law to ensure equal treatment for all citizens. In the USA, the struggle to obtain civil rights for former slaves and their descendants, both through legislation and in practice, has been a major theme since the Civil War. The *civil-rights movement* is a general term for this aspect of US history; see *history* under ◊black.

civil service body of administrative staff appointed to carry out the policy of a government. Members of the UK civil service may not take an active part in politics, and do not change with the government. The two main divisions of the British civil service are the *Home* and *Diplomatic* services.

civil war war between rival groups within the same

country.

Civil War, American also called *War Between the States* war 1861–65 between the Southern or Confederate States of America and the Northern or Union States. The former wished to maintain certain 'states' rights', in particular the right to determine state law on the institution of slavery, and claimed the right to secede from the Union; the latter fought primarily to maintain the Union, with slave emancipation (proclaimed 1863) a secondary issue.

Civil War, English in British history, the conflict between the king and the Royalists (Cavaliers) on one side, and the Parliamentarians (Roundheads) on the other. Hostilities began 1642 and a series of Royalist defeats (Marston Moor 1644, Naseby 1645) culminated in Charles I's capture 1647 and execution 1649. The war continued until the final defeat of Royalist forces at Worcester 1651. Oliver ⇨Cromwell accepted the role of Protector (ruler) 1651 until his death 1658. He was replaced by his son Richard who paved the way for the restoration of the monarchy 1660.

Civil War, Spanish war 1936–39 precipitated by a military revolt led by General Franco against the Republican government. Inferior military capability led to the gradual defeat of the Republicans by 1939 and the establishment of Franco's dictatorship.

clam common name for a ⇨bivalve mollusc. The giant clam *Tridacna gigas* of the Indopacific can grow to 1 m/3 ft across in 50 years and weighs over 250 kg.

clan social grouping based on ⇨kinship. Some traditional societies are organized by clans, which are either matrilineal or patrilineal, and whose members must marry into another clan in order to avoid in-breeding.

Clapton Eric 1945– . English blues and rock guitarist, singer, and composer, member of the Yardbirds 1963–65 and Cream 1966–68. Originally a blues purist, then one of the pioneers of heavy rock with Cream and on the album *Layla* 1970 (released under the name of Derek and the Dominos), he later adopted a more laid-back style in his solo career, as on *Journeyman* 1989.

Clare county on the W coast of the Republic of Ireland, in the province of Munster; area 3,190 sq km/1,231 sq mi; population (1991) 90,800. The coastline is rocky and dangerous, and inland Clare is an undulating plain, with mountains to the E, W, and NW. The principal rivers are the Shannon and its tributary, the Fergus. Shannon airport is here.

Clare John 1793–1864. English poet. His work includes *Poems Descriptive of Rural Life and Scenery* 1820, *The Village Minstrel* 1821, and *The Shepherd's Calendar* 1827. Clare's work was largely rediscovered in the 20th century.

clarinet musical ⇨woodwind instrument, developed in Germany in the 18th century, with a single reed and a cylindrical tube, broadening at the end. At the lower end of its range it has a rich 'woody' tone, which becomes increasingly brilliant towards the upper register. Its ability both to blend and to contrast with other instruments make it popular for chamber music and as a solo instrument. It is also heard in military and concert bands and as a jazz instrument.

Clarke Arthur C(harles) 1917– . English science-fiction and nonfiction writer, who originated the plan for a system of communications satellites in geostationary orbit 1945. His works include *Childhood's End* 1953 and *2001: A Space Odyssey* 1968 (which was made into a film by Stanley Kubrick), and *2010: Odyssey Two* 1982.

Clarke Kenneth (Harry) 1940– . British Conservative politician, member of Parliament from 1970, a cabinet minister from 1985, education secretary 1990–92, and home secretary from 1992.

class in sociology, the main grouping of social stratification in industrial societies, based primarily on economic and occupational factors, but also referring to people's style of living or sense of group identity.

Classicism in art, music, and literature, a style that emphasizes the qualities traditionally considered characteristic of ancient Greek and Roman art, that is, reason, balance, objectivity, restraint, and strict adherence to form. The term Classicism (also ⇨Neo-Classicism) is often used to characterize the culture of 18th-century Europe, and contrasted with 19th-century Romanticism.

classification in biology, the arrangement of organisms into a hierarchy of groups on the basis of their similarities in biochemical, anatomical, or physiological characters. The basic grouping is a ⇨species, several of which may constitute a ⇨genus, which in turn are grouped into families, and so on up through orders, classes, phyla (in plants, sometimes called divisions), to kingdoms.

Claude Lorrain (Claude Gelée) 1600–1682. French landscape painter, active in Rome from 1627. His distinctive, luminous, Classical style had great impact on late 17th- and 18th-century taste. His subjects are mostly mythological and historical, with insignificant figures lost in great expanses of poetic scenery, as in *The Enchanted Castle* 1664 (National Gallery, London).

Claudius Tiberius Claudius Nero 10 BC–AD 54. Nephew of ⇨Tiberius, made Roman emperor by his troops AD 41, after the murder of his nephew Caligula. Claudius was a scholar, historian, and able administrator. During his reign the Roman Empire was considerably extended, and in 43 he took part in the invasion of Britain.

Clause 28 in British law, section 28 of the Local Government Act 1988 that prohibits local authorities promoting homosexuality by publishing material, or by promoting the teaching in state schools of the acceptability of homosexuality as a 'pretended family relationship'. There was widespread opposition to the introduction of the provision.

Clausius Rudolf Julius Emanuel 1822–1888. German physicist, one of the founders of the science of thermodynamics. In 1850 he enunciated its second law: heat cannot pass from a colder to a hotter body.

claustrophobia ◊phobia involving fear of enclosed spaces.

clavichord stringed keyboard instrument, common in Renaissance Europe and in 18th-century Germany. Notes are sounded by a metal blade striking the string. The clavichord was a forerunner of the pianoforte.

Clay Cassius Marcellus, Jr, original name of boxer Muhammad ◊Ali.

clef in music, the symbol used at the beginning of a stave to indicate the pitch of the notes. For example, the treble clef, commonly used, indicates that the second line up of the stave is to be G above middle C; the bass or F clef indicates that the fourth line of the stave is to be F below middle C. The alto, soprano, and tenor clefs all indicate different positions of middle C.

Cleisthenes lived 6th century BC. Ruler of Athens. Inspired by the statesman Solon, he is credited with the establishment of democracy in Athens 507 BC.

clematis any temperate woody climbing plant of the genus *Clematis* with showy flowers. Clematis are a member of the buttercup family, Ranunculaceae. The wild *traveller's joy* or *old man's beard*, *Clematis vitalba*, is the only native British species, although many have been introduced and garden hybrids bred.

Cleopatra c. 68–30 BC. Queen of Egypt 51–48 and 47–30 BC. When the Roman general Julius Caesar arrived in Egypt, he restored her to the throne from which she had been ousted. Cleopatra and Caesar became lovers and she went with him to Rome. After Caesar's assassination 44 BC she returned to Alexandria and resumed her position as queen of Egypt. In 41 BC she was joined there by Mark Antony, one of Rome's rulers. In 31 BC Rome declared war on Egypt and scored a decisive victory in the naval Battle of Actium off the W coast of Greece. Cleopatra fled with her 60 ships to Egypt; Antony abandoned the struggle and followed her. Both he and Cleopatra committed suicide.

Clermont-Ferrand city, capital of Puy-de-Dôme *département*, in the Auvergne region of France; population (1983) 256,000. It is a centre for agriculture, and its rubber industry is the largest in France.

Cleveland county in NE England; *area* 580 sq km/224 sq mi; *towns* Middlesbrough (administrative headquarters), Stockton on Tees, Billingham,

Hartlepool; *features* river Tees, with Seal Sands wildfowl refuge at its mouth; North Yorkshire Moors National Park; *products* steel, chemicals; *population* (1987) 555,000; *famous people* Capt James Cook, Thomas Sheraton, Compton Mackenzie.

Cleveland largest city of Ohio, USA, on Lake Erie at the mouth of the river Cuyahoga; population (1990) 505,600, metropolitan area 2,759,800. Its chief industries are iron and steel and petroleum refining.

Cleveland (Stephen) Grover 1837–1908. 22nd and 24th president of the USA, 1885–89 and 1893–97; the first Democratic president elected after the Civil War, and the only president to hold office for two nonconsecutive terms. He attempted to check corruption in public life, and in 1895 initiated arbitration proceedings that eventually settled a territorial dispute with Britain concerning the Venezuelan boundary.

climate weather conditions at a particular place over a period of time. Climate encompasses all the meteorological elements and the facts that influence them. The primary factors that determine the variations of climate over the surface of the Earth are: (a) the effect of latitude and the tilt of the Earth's axis to the plane of the orbit about the Sun (66.5°); (b) the large-scale movements of different wind belts over the Earth's surface; (c) the temperature difference between land and sea; (d) contours of the ground; and (e) location of the area in relation to ocean currents. Catastrophic variations to climate may be caused by the impact of another planetary body, or by clouds resulting from volcanic activity. The most important local or global metereological changes brought about by human activity are those linked with ◊ozone depleters and the ◊greenhouse effect.

clinical psychology discipline dealing with the understanding and treatment of health problems, particularly mental disorders. The main problems dealt with include anxiety, phobias, depression, obsessions, sexual and marital problems, drug and alcohol dependence, childhood behavioural problems, psychoses (such as schizophrenia), mental handicap, and brain damage (such as dementia).

Clive Robert, Baron Clive of Plassey 1725–1774. British soldier and administrator who established British rule in India by victories over the French 1751 and over the nawab of Bengal 1757. On his return to Britain his wealth led to allegations that he had abused his power. Although acquitted, he committed suicide.

clock any device that measures the passage of time, usually shown by means of pointers moving over a dial or by a digital display. Traditionally a timepiece consists of a train of wheels driven by a spring or weight controlled by a balance wheel or pendulum. The watch is a portable clock.

cloud

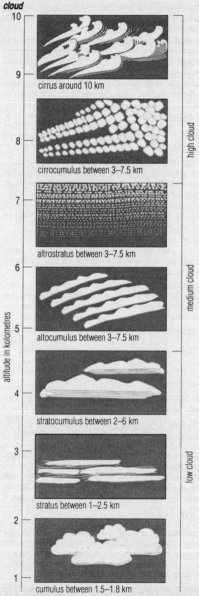

cirrus around 10 km

cirrocumulus between 3–7.5 km

high cloud

altrostratus between 3–7.5 km

altocumulus between 3–7.5 km

medium cloud

stratocumulus between 2–6 km

stratus between 1–2.5 km

low cloud

cumulus between 1.5–1.8 km

altitude in kilometres

closed-circuit television (CCTV) localized television system in which programmes are sent over relatively short distances, the camera, receiver, and controls being linked by cable. Closed-circuit TV systems are used in department stores and large offices as a means of internal security, monitoring people's movements.

closed shop any company or firm, public corporation, or other body that requires its employees to be members of the appropriate trade union. Usually demanded by unions, the closed shop may be preferred by employers as simplifying negotiation, but it was condemned by the European Court of Human Rights in 1981. The European Community's social charter, for which the UK Labour Party announced its support 1989, calls for an end to the closed shop.

cloud water vapour condensed into minute water particles that float in masses in the atmosphere. Clouds, like fogs or mists, which occur at lower levels, are formed by the cooling of air containing water vapour, which generally condenses around tiny dust particles.

clove dried, unopened flower bud of the clove tree *Eugenia caryophyllus*. A member of the myrtle family Myrtaceae, the clove tree is a native of the Moluccas. Cloves are used for flavouring in cookery and confectionery. Oil of cloves, which has tonic and carminative qualities, is employed in medicine.

clover any of an Old World genus *Trifolium* of low-growing leguminous plants, usually with compound leaves of three leaflets and small flowers in dense heads. Many are cultivated as fodder plants for cattle. Sweet clover refers to various species belonging to the related genus *Melilotus*.

Clovis 465–511. Merovingian king of the Franks from 481. He succeeded his father Childeric as king of the Salian (northern) Franks; defeated the Gallo-Romans (Romanized Gauls) near Soissons 486, ending their rule in France; and defeated the Alemanni, a confederation of Germanic tribes, near Cologne 496. He embraced Christianity and subsequently proved a powerful defender of orthodoxy against the Arian Visigoths, whom he defeated at Poitiers 507. He made Paris his capital.

Cluj (German *Klausenberg*) city in Transylvania, Romania, located on the river Somes; population (1985) 310,000. It is a communications centre for Romania and the Hungarian plain. Industries include machine tools, furniture, and knitwear.

clutch any device for disconnecting rotating shafts, used especially in a car's transmission system. In a car with a manual gearbox, the driver depresses the clutch when changing gear, thus disconnecting the engine from the gearbox.

Clwyd county in N Wales. *area* 2,420 sq km/ 934 sq mi; *towns* Mold (administrative headquarters), Flint, Denbigh, Wrexham; seaside resorts: Colwyn Bay, Rhyl, Prestatyn; *physical* rivers: Dee, Clwyd; Clwydian Range of mountains with Offa's Dyke along the main ridge; *features* Chirk, Denbigh, Flint, and Rhuddlan castles; Greenfield Valley, NW of Flint, was in the forefront of the Industrial Revolution before the advent of steam and now has a museum of industrial archaeology;

products dairy and meat products, optical glass, chemicals, limestone, microprocessors, plastics; **population** (1991) 400,500; **language** 19% Welsh, English; **famous people** George Jeffreys, Henry Morton Stanley.

Clyde river in Strathclyde, Scotland; 170 km/ 103 mi long. The Firth of Clyde and Firth of Forth are linked by the Forth and Clyde canal, 56 km/ 35 mi long. The shipbuilding yards have declined in recent years.

Clytemnestra in Greek mythology, the wife of ⟡Agamemnon. With her lover Aegisthus, she murdered her husband on his return from the Trojan War and was in turn killed by her son Orestes.

CND abbreviation for ⟡*Campaign for Nuclear Disarmament.*

Cnossus alternative form of ⟡Knossos, city of ancient Crete.

Cnut alternative spelling of ⟡Canute.

coal black or blackish mineral substance of fossil origin, the result of the transformation of ancient plant matter under progressive compression. It is used as a fuel and in the chemical industry. Coal is classified according to the proportion of carbon and volatiles it contains. The main types are ⟡*anthracite* (shiny, with more than 90% carbon), *bituminous coal* (shiny and dull patches, more than 80% carbon), and *lignite* (woody, grading into ⟡peat, 70% carbon).

coal gas gas produced when coal is destructively distilled or heated out of contact with the air. Its main constituents are methane, hydrogen, and carbon monoxide. Coal gas has been superseded by ⟡natural gas for domestic purposes.

coalition association of political groups, usually for some limited or short-term purpose, such as fighting an election or forming a government when one party has failed to secure a majority in a legislature.

coastguard governmental organization whose members patrol a nation's seacoast to prevent smuggling, assist distressed vessels, watch for oil slicks, and so on. In the UK the HM Coastguard was formed to prevent smuggling after the Napoleonic Wars, and is now administered by the Department of Trade.

coati or *coatimundi* any of several species of carnivores of the genus *Nasua*, in the same family, Procyonidae, as the raccoons. A coati is a good climber and has long claws, a long tail, a good sense of smell, and a long, flexible piglike snout used for digging. Coatis live in packs in the forests of South and Central America.

Cobb Ty(rus Raymond), nicknamed 'the Georgia Peach' 1886–1961. US baseball player, one of the greatest batters and base runners of all time. He played for Detroit and Philadelphia 1905–28, and won the American League batting average championship 12 times. He holds the record for runs scored, 2,254, and batting average, 0.367. He had 4,191 hits in his career – a record that stood for almost 60 years.

COBOL (acronym for *common business-oriented language*) high-level computer-programming language, designed in the late 1950s for commercial data-processing problems; it has become one of the major languages in this field. COBOL features powerful facilities for file handling and business arithmetic. Program instructions written in this language make extensive use of words and look very much like English sentences. This makes COBOL one of the easiest languages to learn and understand.

cobra any of several poisonous snakes, especially the genus *Naja*, of the family Elapidae, found in Africa and S Asia, species of which can grow from 1 m/3 ft to over 4.3 m/14 ft. The neck stretches into a hood when the snake is alarmed. Cobra venom contains nerve toxins powerful enough to kill humans.

coca South American shrub *Erythroxylon coca* of the coca family Erythroxylaceae, whose dried leaves are the source of cocaine. It was used as a holy drug by the Andean Indians.

cockatiel Australian parrot *Nymphicus hollandicus*, about 20 cm/8 in long, with greyish plumage, yellow cheeks, a long tail, and a crest like a cockatoo. Cockatiels are popular as pets and aviary birds.

cockatoo any of several crested parrots, especially of the genus *Cacatua*. They usually have light-coloured plumage with tinges of red, yellow, or orange on the face, and an erectile crest on the head. They are native to Australia, New Guinea, and nearby islands.

Cockcroft John Douglas 1897–1967. British physicist. In 1932 he and the Irish physicist Ernest Walton succeeded in splitting the nucleus of an atom for the first time. In 1951 they were jointly awarded a Nobel prize.

cockle any of over 200 species of bivalve mollusc with ribbed, heart-shaped shells. Some are edible and are sold in W European markets. The common cockle *Cerastoderma edule* is up to 5 cm/2 in across, and is found in sand or mud on shores and in estuaries around N European and Mediterranean coasts.

cockroach any of numerous insects of the family Blattidae, distantly related to mantises and grasshoppers. There are 3,500 species, mainly in the tropics. They have long antennae and biting mouthparts. They can fly, but rarely do so.

cocoa and chocolate food products made from the ⟡cacao (or cocoa) bean, fruit of a tropical tree *Theobroma cacao*, now cultivated mainly in Africa. Chocolate as a drink was introduced to Europe from the New World by the Spanish in the 16th century; eating chocolate was first produced in the late 18th century. Cocoa and chocolate are widely used in confectionery and drinks.

coconut fruit of the coconut palm *Cocos nucifera* of the family Arecaceae, which grows throughout the lowland tropics. The fruit has a large outer husk of fibres, which is split off and used for coconut matting and ropes. Inside this is the nut exported to temperate countries. Its hard shell contains white flesh and coconut milk, both of which are nourishing and palatable.

Cocos Islands or *Keeling Islands* group of 27 small coral islands in the Indian Ocean, about 2,770 km/1,720 mi NW of Perth, Australia; area 14 sq km/5.5 sq mi; population (1986) 616. They are owned by Australia.

Cocteau Jean 1889–1963. French poet, dramatist, and film director. A leading figure in European Modernism, he worked with Picasso, Diaghilev, and Stravinsky. He produced many volumes of poetry, ballets such as *Le Boeuf sur le toit/The Ox on the Roof* 1920, plays, for example, *Orphée/Orpheus* 1926, and a mature novel of bourgeois French life, *Les Enfants terribles/Children of the Game* 1929, which he made into a film 1950.

cod any fish of the family Gadoidea, especially the Atlantic cod, *Gadus morhua* found in the N Atlantic and Baltic. It is brown to grey with spots, white below, and can grow to 1.5 m/5 ft.

coda in music, a concluding section of a movement added to indicate finality.

codeine opium derivative that provides ◊analgesia in mild to moderate pain. It also suppresses the cough centre of the brain. It is an alkaloid, derived from morphine but less toxic and addictive.

Cody (William Frederick) 'Buffalo Bill' 1846–1917. US scout and performer. From 1883 he toured the USA and Europe with a Wild West show which featured the recreation of Indian attacks and, for a time, the cast included Chief ◊Sitting Bull as well as Annie Oakley. His nickname derives from a time when he had a contract to supply buffalo carcasses to railway labourers (over 4,000 in 18 months).

Coe Sebastian 1956– . English middle-distance runner, Olympic 1,500–metre champion 1980 and 1984. He became Britain's most prolific world-record breaker with eight outdoor world records and three indoor world records 1979–81. In 1990 he announced his retirement after failing to win a Commonwealth Games title and is now pursuing a political career with the Conservative party.

coelacanth lobe-finned fish *Latimeria chalumnae* up to 2 m/6 ft long. It has bone and muscle at the base of the fins, and is distantly related to the freshwater lobefins, which were the ancestors of all land animals with backbones. Coelacanths live in deep water (200 m/650 ft) around the Comoros Islands, off the coast of Madagascar. They were believed to be extinct until one was caught in 1938.

cognition in psychology, a general term covering the functions involved in synthesizing information – for example, perception (seeing, hearing, and so on), attention, memory, and reasoning.

cognitive therapy treatment for emotional disorders such as ◊depression and ◊anxiety, developed by Professor Aaron T Beck in the USA. This approach encourages the patient to challenge the distorted and unhelpful thinking that is characteristic of these problems. The treatment includes ◊behaviour therapy and has been most helpful for people suffering from depression.

cohesion in physics, a phenomenon in which interaction between two surfaces of the same material in contact makes them cling together (with two different materials the similar phenomenon is called adhesion). According to kinetic theory, cohesion is caused by attraction between particles at the atomic or molecular level. ◊Surface tension, which causes liquids to form spherical droplets, is caused by cohesion.

cola or *kola* any tropical tree of the genus *Cola*, especially *C. acuminata*, family Sterculiaceae. The nuts are chewed in W Africa for their high-caffeine content, and in the West are used to flavour soft drinks.

cold fusion in nuclear physics, the fusion of atomic nuclei at room temperature. Were cold fusion to become possible it would provide a limitless, cheap, and pollution-free source of energy, and it has therefore been the subject of research around the world. In 1989, Martin Fleischmann (1927–) and Stanley Pons (1943–) of the University of Utah, USA, claimed that they had achieved cold fusion in the laboratory, but their results could not be substantiated.

Colditz town in E Germany, near Leipzig, site of a castle used as a high-security prisoner-of-war camp (Oflag IVC) in World War II. Among daring escapes was that of British Captain Patrick Reid (1910–1990) and others Oct 1942. It became a museum 1989. In 1990 the castle was converted to a hotel.

Cold War ideological, political, and economic tensions 1945–90 between the USSR and Eastern Europe on the one hand and the USA and Western Europe on the other. The Cold War was exacerbated by propaganda, covert activity by intelligence agencies, and economic sanctions; it intensified at times of conflict anywhere in the world. Arms-reduction agreements between the USA and USSR in the late 1980s, and a diminution of Soviet influence in Eastern Europe, symbolized by the opening of the Berlin Wall 1989, led to a reassessment of positions, and the 'war' officially ended 1990.

Coleman Ornette 1930– . US alto saxophonist and jazz composer. In the late 1950s he rejected the established structural principles of jazz for free avant-garde improvisation. He has worked with small and large groups, ethnic musicians of different traditions, and symphony orchestras.

Coleridge Samuel Taylor 1772–1834. English poet, one of the founders of the Romantic movement. A friend of Southey and Wordsworth, he collaborated with the latter on *Lyrical Ballads* 1798. His poems include 'The Rime of the Ancient Mariner', 'Christabel', and 'Kubla Khan'; critical works include *Biographia Literaria* 1817.

Colette Sidonie-Gabrielle 1873–1954. French writer. At 20 she married Henri Gauthier-Villars, a journalist known as 'Willy', under whose name and direction her four 'Claudine' novels, based on her own early life, were written. Divorced 1906, she worked as a striptease and mime artist for a while, but continued to write. Works from this later period include *Chéri* 1920, *La Fin de Chéri/The End of Chéri* 1926, and *Gigi* 1944.

collage technique of pasting paper and other materials to create a picture. Several artists in the early 20th century used collage: Jean (or Hans) Arp, Georges Braque, Max Ernst, and Kurt Schwitters, among others.

collective security system for achieving international stability by an agreement among all states to unite against any aggressor. Such a commitment was embodied in the post-World War I League of Nations and also in the United Nations, although the League was not, and the UN has not yet been, able to live up to the ideals of its founders.

collectivism in politics, a position in which the collective (such as the state) has priority over its individual members. It is the opposite of individualism, which is itself a variant of anarchy.

collie sheepdog originally bred in Britain. The rough and smooth collies are about 60 cm/2 ft tall, and have long narrow heads and muzzles. They may be light to dark brown or silver-grey, with black and white markings. The border collie is a working dog, often black and white, about 50 cm/20 in tall, with a dense coat. The bearded collie is about the same size, and is rather like an Old English sheepdog in appearance.

Collier Lesley 1947– . British ballerina, a principal dancer of the Royal Ballet from 1972. She created roles in Kenneth MacMillan's *Anastasia* 1971 and *Four Seasons* 1975, Hans van Manen's *Four Schumann Pieces* 1975, Frederick Ashton's *Rhapsody*, and Glen Tetley's *Dance of Albiar* both 1980.

Collingwood Cuthbert, Baron Collingwood 1748–1810. British admiral who served with Horatio Nelson in the West Indies against France and blockaded French ports 1803–05; after Nelson's death he took command at the Battle of Trafalgar.

Collins Michael 1890–1922. Irish nationalist. He was a Sinn Féin leader, a founder and director of intelligence of the Irish Republican Army 1919, minister for finance in the provisional government of the Irish Free State 1922 (see ◊Ireland, Republic of), commander of the Free State forces in the civil war, and for ten days head of state before being killed. He and Arthur Griffith (1872–1922) were mainly responsible for the treaty that established the Irish Free State.

Collins (William) Wilkie 1824–1889. English author of mystery and suspense novels. He wrote *The Woman in White* 1860 (with its fat villain Count Fosco), often called the first English detective novel, and *The Moonstone* 1868 (with Sergeant Cuff, one of the first detectives in English literature).

colloid substance composed of extremely small particles of one material (the dispersed phase) evenly and stably distributed in another material (the continuous phase). The size of the dispersed particles (1–1,000 nanometres across) is less than that of particles in suspension but greater than that of molecules in true solution. Colloids involving gases include *aerosols* (dispersions of liquid or solid particles in a gas, as in fog or smoke) and *foams* (dispersions of gases in liquids). Those involving liquids include *emulsions* (in which both the dispersed and the continuous phases are liquids) and *sols* (solid particles dispersed in a liquid). Sols in which both phases contribute to a molecular three-dimensional network have a jellylike form and are known as *gels*; gelatin, starch 'solution', and silica gel are common examples.

Cologne (German **Köln**) industrial and commercial port in North Rhine–Westphalia, Germany, on the left bank of the Rhine, 35 km/22 mi from Düsseldorf; population (1988) 914,000. To the north is the Ruhr coalfield, on which many of Cologne's industries are based. They include motor vehicles, railway wagons, chemicals, and machine tools. Cologne is an important transshipment centre.

Colombia Republic of; country in South America, bordered N and W by the Caribbean and the Pacific and having borders with Panama to the NW, Venezuela to the E and NE, Brazil to the SE, and Peru and Ecuador to the SW; *area* 1,141,748 sq km/440,715 sq mi; *capital* Bogotá; *physical* Andes Mountains run N–S; flat coastland in W and plains in E; Magdalena River runs N to Caribbean Sea; *head of state and government* Cesar Gaviria Trujillo from 1990; *political system* emergent democratic republic; *exports* emeralds (world's largest producer), coffee (world's second largest producer), cocaine (country's largest export), bananas, cotton, meat, sugar, oil, skins, hides, tobacco; *population* (1990 est) 32,598,800; *language* Spanish; *recent history* full independence was achieved from Spain 1886. Civil war broke out 1949; the Conservatives and Liberals formed a National Front. Civil unrest continued because of disillusionment with the government; Virgilio Barco Vargas was elected head of state by a record margin 1986; he declared an antidrug war 1989. The new constitution 1991 prohibited extradition of Colombians wanted for trial in other countries; leading drug traffickers were arrested.

Colombo capital and principal seaport of Sri Lanka, on the W coast near the mouth of the Kelani River; population (1990) 615,000, Greater Colombo about 1,000,000. It trades in tea, rubber, and cacao. It has iron- and steelworks and an oil refinery.

Colón second-largest city in Panama, at the Caribbean end of the Panama Canal; population (1990) 140,900. It has a special economic zone created 1948 used by foreign companies to avoid taxes on completed products in their home countries.

Colorado state of W central USA; nicknamed Centennial State; *area* 269,700 sq km/104,104 sq mi; *capital* Denver; *towns* Colorado Springs, Aurora, Lakewood, Fort Collins, Greeley, Pueblo, Boulder; *physical* Great Plains in the E; the main ranges of the Rocky Mountains; high plateaux of the Colorado Basin in the W; *features* Rocky Mountain National Park; Pikes Peak; prehistoric cliff dwellings of the Mesa Verde National Park; Garden of the Gods (natural sandstone sculptures); Dinosaur and Great Sand Dunes national monuments; 'ghost' mining towns; ski resorts, including Aspen and Vail; *products* cereals, meat and dairy products, oil, coal, molybdenum, uranium, iron, steel, machinery; *population* (1990) 3,294,400; *famous people* Jack Dempsey, Douglas Fairbanks; *history* first visited by Spanish explorers in the 16th century; claimed for Spain 1706; E portion passed to the USA 1803 as part of the Louisiana Purchase, the rest 1845 and 1848 as a result of the Mexican War. It attracted fur traders, and Denver was founded following the discovery of gold 1858. Colorado became a state 1876.

coloratura in music, a rapid ornamental vocal passage with runs and trills. A *coloratura soprano* is a light, high voice suited to such music.

Colosseum amphitheatre in ancient Rome, begun by the emperor Vespasian to replace the one destroyed by fire during the reign of Nero, and completed by his son Titus AD 80. It was 187 m/615 ft long and 49 m/160 ft high, and seated 50,000 people. Early Christians were martyred there by lions and gladiators. It could be flooded for mock sea battles.

colour quality or wavelength of light emitted or reflected from an object. Visible white light consists of electromagnetic radiation of various wavelengths, and if a beam is refracted through a prism, it can be spread out into a spectrum, in which the various colours correspond to different wavelengths. From long to short wavelengths (from about 700 to 400 nanometres) the colours are red, orange, yellow, green, blue, indigo, and violet.

colour blindness hereditary defect of vision that

reduces the ability to discriminate certain colours, usually red and green. For example, many colour-blind observers are unable to distinguish red from yellow or yellow from green. The condition is sex-linked, affecting men more than women.

Coltrane John (William) 1926–1967. US jazz saxophonist who first came to prominence 1955 with the Miles ◊Davis quintet, later playing with Thelonious Monk 1957. He was a powerful and individual artist, whose performances featured much experimentation. His 1960s quartet was highly regarded for its innovations in melody and harmony.

Columbia, District of seat of the federal government of the USA, coextensive with the city of Washington, situated on the Potomac River; area 178 sq km/69 sq mi. It was ceded by Maryland as the national capital site 1790.

columbine any plant of the genus *Aquilegia* of the buttercup family Ranunculaceae. All are perennial herbs with divided leaves and flowers with spurred petals. In Britain *A. vulgaris* grows wild in woods and is a familiar garden plant.

Columbus Christopher (Spanish *Cristóbal Colón*) 1451–1506. Italian navigator and explorer who made four voyages to the New World: 1492 to San Salvador Island, Cuba, and Haiti; 1493–96 to Guadaloupe, Montserrat, Antigua, Puerto Rico, and Jamaica; 1498 to Trinidad and the mainland of South America; 1502–04 to Honduras and Nicaragua.

Believing that Asia could be reached by sailing westwards, he eventually won the support of King Ferdinand and Queen Isabella of Spain and set off on his first voyage from Palos 3 Aug 1492 with three small ships, the *Niña*, the *Pinta*, and his flagship the *Santa Maria*. Land was sighted 12 Oct, probably Watling Island (now San Salvador Island), and within a few weeks he reached Cuba and Haiti, returning to Spain March 1493.

column in architecture, a structure, round or polygonal in plan, erected vertically as a support for some part of a building. In Classical architecture there are five principal types of column; see ◊order.

coma in medicine, a state of deep unconsciousness from which the subject cannot be roused and in which the subject does not respond to pain. Possible causes include head injury, liver failure, cerebral haemorrhage, and drug overdose.

Comecon (acronym from *Co*uncil for *M*utual *Econ*omic Assistance, or CMEA) economic organization 1949–91, linking the USSR with Bulgaria, Czechoslovakia, Hungary, Poland, Romania, East Germany (1950–90), Mongolia (from 1962), Cuba (from 1972), and Vietnam (from 1978), with Yugoslavia as an associated member. Albania also belonged 1949–61. Its establishment was prompted by the ◊Marshall Plan.

comedy drama that aims to make its audience laugh, usually with a happy or amusing ending, as opposed to ⟡tragedy. The comic tradition has enjoyed many changes since its Greek roots; the earliest comic tradition developed in ancient Greece, in the farcical satires of Aristophanes. Great comic playwrights include Shakespeare, Molière, Carlo Goldoni, Pierre de Marivaux, George Bernard Shaw, and Oscar Wilde. Genres of comedy include pantomime, satire, farce, black comedy, and ⟡commedia dell'arte.

comet small, icy body orbiting the Sun, usually on a highly elliptical path. A comet consists of a central nucleus a few kilometres across, and has been likened to a dirty snowball because it consists mostly of ice mixed with dust. As the comet approaches the Sun the nucleus heats up, releasing gas and dust which form a tenuous coma, up to 100,000 km/60,000 mi wide, around the nucleus. Gas and dust stream away from the coma to form one or more tails, which may extend for millions of kilometres.

comfrey any plant of the genus *Symphytum*, borage family Boraginaceae, with rough, hairy leaves and small bell-shaped blue, purple-pink, or white flowers, found in Europe and W Asia.

command language in computing, set of commands and the rules governing their use, by which users control a program. For example, an ⟡operating system may have commands such as SAVE and DELETE, or a payroll program may have commands for adding and amending staff records.

commando member of a specially trained, highly mobile military unit. The term originated in South Africa in the 19th century, where it referred to Boer military reprisal raids against Africans and, in the South African Wars, against the British. Commando units have often carried out operations behind enemy lines.

commedia dell'arte popular form of Italian improvised comic drama in the 16th and 17th centuries, performed by trained troupes of actors and involving stock characters and situations. It exerted considerable influence on writers such as Molière and Carlo Goldoni, and on the genres of ⟡pantomime, harlequinade, and the Punch and Judy show. It laid the foundation for a tradition of mime, strong in France, that has continued with the contemporary mime of Jean-Louis Barrault and Marcel Marceau.

commodity something produced for sale. Commodities may be consumer goods, such as radios, or producer goods, such as copper bars. *Commodity markets* deal in raw or semi-raw materials that are amenable to grading and that can be stored for considerable periods without deterioration.

common law that part of the English law not embodied in legislation. It consists of rules of law based on common custom and usage and on judicial decisions. English common law became the basis of law in the USA and many other English-speaking countries.

Commons, House of the lower but more powerful of the two parts of the British and Canadian ⟡parliaments. In the UK, the House of Commons consists of 650 elected members of parliament each of whom represents a constituency. Its functions are to debate and legislate, and to scrutinize the activities of government.

commonwealth body politic founded on law for the common 'weal' or good. Political philosophers of the 17th century, such as Thomas Hobbes and John Locke, used the term to mean an organized political community. In Britain it was specifically applied to the regime (*the Commonwealth*) of Oliver ⟡Cromwell 1649–60.

Commonwealth Games multisport gathering of competitors from British Commonwealth countries, held every four years. The first meeting (known as the British Empire Games) was in Hamilton, Canada, Aug 1930.

Commonwealth of Independent States (CIS) successor body to the ⟡Union of Soviet Socialist Republics, formed 21 Dec 1991 by 11 out of the remaining 12 constituent republics. Georgia did not join. The member republics are Armenia, Azerbaijan, Belarus, Kazakhstan, Kyrgyzstan, Moldova, the Russian Federation (or Russia), Tajikistan, Turkmenistan, Ukraine, and Uzbekistan. It operates mainly in the sporting, military and financial spheres. Its headquarters are in Mensk (Minsk), Belarus.

Commonwealth, the (British) voluntary association of 50 countries and their dependencies that once formed part of the ⟡British Empire and are now independent sovereign states. They are all regarded as 'full members of the Commonwealth'. Additionally, there are some 29 territories that are not completely sovereign and remain dependencies of the UK or another of the fully sovereign members, and are regarded as 'Commonwealth countries'. Heads of government meet every two years, apart from those of Nauru and Tuvalu; however, Nauru and Tuvalu have the right to participate in all functional activities. The Commonwealth has no charter or constitution, and is founded more on tradition and sentiment than political or economic factors.

Commune, Paris two periods of government in France; see ⟡Paris Commune.

communications satellite relay station in space for sending telephone, television, telex, and other messages around the world. Messages are sent to and from the satellites via ground stations. Most communications satellites are in ⟡geostationary orbit, appearing to hang fixed over one point on the Earth's surface.

Communion, Holy in the Christian church, another name for the ⟡Eucharist.

communism revolutionary socialism based on the theories of the political philosophers Karl Marx and Friedrich Engels, emphasizing common ownership of the means of production and a planned economy. The principle held is that each should work according to their capacity and receive according to their needs. Politically, it seeks the overthrow of capitalism through a proletarian revolution. The first communist state was the USSR after the revolution of 1917. Revolutionary socialist parties and groups united to form communist parties in other countries (in the UK 1920). After World War II, communism was enforced in those countries that came under Soviet occupation. China emerged after 1961 as a rival to the USSR in world communist leadership, and other countries attempted to adapt communism to their own needs. The late 1980s saw a movement for more individual freedoms in many communist countries, culminating in the abolition or overthrow of communist rule in Eastern European countries and Mongolia, and further state repression in China. The failed hard-line coup in the USSR against President Gorbachev 1991 resulted in the effective abandonment of communism there.

Commonwealth, British

Country *Capital* (Area in 1,000 sq km)

IN AFRICA

Botswana *Gaborone* (575)
British Indian Ocean Terr. *Victoria* (0.2)
Gambia *Banjul* (11)
Ghana *Accra* (239)
Kenya *Nairobi* (583)
Lesotho *Maseru* (30)
Malawi *Zomba* (117)
Mauritius *Port Louis* (2)
Nigeria *Lagos* (924)
St Helena *Jamestown* (0.1)
Seychelles *Victoria* (65)
Sierra Leone *Freetown* (73)
Swaziland *Mbabane* (17)
Tanzania *Dodoma* (943)
Uganda *Kampala* (236)
Zambia *Lusaka* (752)
Zimbabwe *Salisbury* (391)

IN THE AMERICAS

Anguilla *The Valley* (0.09)
Antigua *St John's* (0.4)
Bahamas *Nassau* (14)
Barbados *Bridgetown* (0.4)
Belize *Belmopan* (23)
Bermuda *Hamilton* (0.05)
Brit. Virgin Is. *Road Town* (0.2)
Canada *Ottawa* (9,976)
Cayman Islands *Georgetown* (0.3)
Dominica *Roseau* (0.7)
Falkland Is. *Stanley* (12)
Grenada *St George's* (0.3)
Guyana *Georgetown* (210)
Jamaica *Kingston* (12)
Montserrat *Plymouth* (0.1)
St Christopher-Nevis *Basseterre Charlestown* (0.4)
St Lucia *Castries* (0.6)
St Vincent and the Grenadines *Kingstown* (0.2)
Trinidad and Tobago *Port of Spain* (0.5)
Turks and Caicos Is. *Grand Turk* (0.4)

IN THE ANTARCTIC

Australian Antarctic Terr. (5,403)
Brit. Antarctic Terr. (390)
Falklands Is. Dependencies (1.6)
(N.Z.) Ross Dependency (453)

Country *Capital* (Area in 1,000 sq km)

IN ASIA

Bangladesh *Dacca* (143)
Brunei *Bandar Seri Begawan* (6)
Cyprus *Nicosia* (9)
Hong Kong *Victoria* (1.2)
India *Delhi* (3,215)
Malaysia, Rep. of *Kuala Lumpur* (332)
Maldives *Malé* (0.3)
Singapore *Singapore* (0.6)
Sri Lanka *Colombo* (66)

IN AUSTRALASIA AND THE PACIFIC

Australia *Canberra* (7,704)
  Norfolk Island (0.03)
  Fiji *Suva* (18)
  Kiribati *Tarawa* (0.7)
*Nauru (0.02)
New Zealand *Wellington* (269)
  Cook Islands (0.2)
  Niue Island (0.3)
  Tokelau Islands (0.01)
Papua New Guinea *Port Moresby* (475)
  Pitcairn (0.005)
Solomon Islands *Honiara* (30)
Tonga *Nuku'alofa* (0.7)
*Tuvalu *Funafuti* (0.02)
  Vanuatu *Vila* (15)
  Western Samoa *Apia* (3)

IN EUROPE

*United Kingdom
  England *London* (131)
  Wales *Cardiff* (21)
  Scotland *Edinburgh* (79)
  N. Ireland *Belfast* (14)
  Isle of Man *Douglas* (0.5)
  Channel Islands (0.2)
Gibraltar *Gibraltar* (0.006)
Malta *Valletta* (0.3)

TOTAL (33,932)

*Special members

community in the social sciences, the sense of identity, purpose, and companionship that comes from belonging to a particular place, organization, or social group. The concept dominated sociological thinking in the first half of the 20th century, and inspired the academic discipline of *community studies*.

Comoros Federal Islamic Republic of; group of islands in the Indian Ocean between Madagascar and the E coast of Africa. Three of them, Njazidja, Nzwani, and Mwali, form the republic of Comoros. The fourth island in the group, Mayotte, is a French dependency; *area* 1,862 sq km/719 sq mi; *capital* Moroni; *physical* the islands are volcanic; they lie at the N end of the Mozambique Channel; *head of state and government* Said Mohammad Djohar (interim administration); *political system* authoritarian nationalism; *exports* copra, vanilla, cocoa, sisal, coffee, cloves, essential oils; *population* (1990 est) 459,000; *languages* Arabic (official); Comorian (Swahili and Arabic dialect), Makua, French; *recent history* independence was achieved 1975, but Mayotte remained part of France; the Comoros joined the United Nations the same year. Two presidents have been killed in attempts to gain control of the government; an interim president is in power.

compact disc disc for storing digital information, about 12 cm/4.5 in across, mainly used for music, when it has up to an hour's playing time on one side. Entirely different from a conventional LP (long-playing) gramophone record, the compact disc is made of aluminium with a transparent plastic coating; the metal disc underneath is etched by a ◇laser beam with microscopic pits that carry a digital code representing the sounds. During playback, a laser beam reads the code and produces signals that are changed into near-exact replicas of the original sounds. Compact discs were launched 1983.

company in economics, a number of people grouped together as a business enterprise. Types of company include public limited companies, partnerships, joint ventures, sole proprietorships, and branches of foreign companies. Most companies are private and, unlike public companies, cannot offer their shares to the general public.

compass any instrument for finding direction. The most commonly used is a magnetic compass, consisting of a thin piece of magnetic material with the north-seeking pole indicated, free to rotate on a pivot and mounted on a compass card on which the points of the compass are marked. When the compass is properly adjusted and used, the north-seeking pole will point to the magnetic north, from which true north can be found from tables of magnetic corrections.

complex in psychology, a group of ideas and feelings that have become repressed because they are distasteful to the person in whose mind they arose, but are still active in the depths of the person's unconscious mind, continuing to affect his or her life and actions, even though he or she is no longer fully aware of their existence. Typical examples include the ◇Oedipus complex and the inferiority complex.

complex number in mathematics, a number written in the form $a + ib$, where a and b are ◇real numbers and i is the square root of -1 (that is, $i^2 = -1$); i used to be known as the 'imaginary' part of the complex number. Some equations in algebra, such as those of the form $x^2 + 5 = 0$, cannot be solved without recourse to complex numbers, because the real numbers do not include square roots of negative numbers.

compost organic material decomposed by bacteria under controlled conditions to make a nutrient-rich natural fertilizer for use in gardening or farming. A well-made compost heap reaches a high temperature during the composting process, killing most weed seeds that might be present.

compound chemical substance made up of two or more ◇elements bonded together, so that they cannot be separated by physical means. Compounds are held together by ionic or covalent bonds.

Compton-Burnett Ivy 1892–1969. English novelist. She used dialogue to show reactions of small groups of characters dominated by the tyranny of family relationships. Her novels, set at the turn of the century, include *Pastors and Masters* 1925, *More Women Than Men* 1933, and *Mother and Son* 1955.

computer programmable electronic device that processes data and performs calculations and other symbol-manipulation tasks. There are three types: the *digital computer*, which manipulates information coded as binary numbers (see ◇binary number system); the ◇*analogue computer*, which works with continuously varying quantities; and the *hybrid computer*, which has characteristics of both analogue and digital computers.

computer-aided design use of computers to create and modify design drawings; see ◇CAD.

computer-aided manufacture use of computers to regulate production processes in industry; see ◇CAM.

computer game or *video game* any computer-controlled game in which the computer (usually) opposes the human player. Computer games typically employ fast, animated graphics on a VDU (visual display unit), and synthesized sound.

computerized axial tomography medical technique, usually known as ◇CAT scan, for looking inside bodies without disturbing them.

computer simulation representation of a real-life situation in a computer program. For example, the program might simulate the flow of customers arriving at a bank. The user can alter variables, such as the number of cashiers on duty, and see the effect.

Comte Auguste 1798–1857. French philosopher

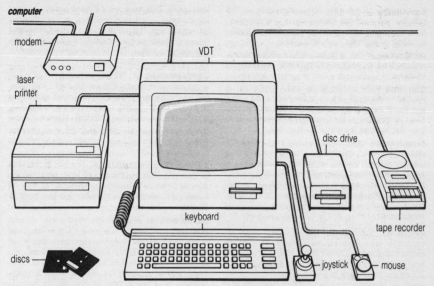

computer

modem

laser printer

VDT

disc drive

tape recorder

keyboard

discs

joystick

mouse

regarded as the founder of sociology, a term he coined 1830. He sought to establish sociology as an intellectual discipline, using a scientific approach ('positivism') as the basis of a new science of social order and social development.

Conakry capital and chief port of the Republic of Guinea; population (1983) 705,300. It is on the island of Tumbo, linked with the mainland by a causeway and by rail with Kankan, 480 km/300 mi to the NE. Bauxite and iron ore are mined nearby.

concentration camp prison camp for civilians in wartime or under totalitarian rule. The first concentration camps were devised by the British during the Second Boer War in South Africa 1899 for the detention of Afrikaner women and children (with the subsequent deaths of more than 20,000 people). A system of approximately 5,000 concentration camps was developed by the Nazis in Germany and occupied Europe (1933–45) to imprison political and ideological opponents after Hitler became chancellor Jan 1933. Several hundred camps were established in Germany and occupied Europe, the most infamous being the extermination camps of Auschwitz, Belsen, Dachau, Maidanek, Sobibor, and Treblinka. The total number of people who died at the camps exceeded 6 million, and some inmates were subjected to medical experimentation before being killed.

concerto composition, usually in three movements, for solo instrument (or instruments) and orchestra. It developed during the 18th century from the *concerto grosso* form for string orchestra, in which a group of solo instruments is contrasted with a full orchestra.

Conchobar in Celtic mythology, king of Ulster whose intended bride, Deirdre, eloped with Noisi. She died of sorrow when Conchobar killed her husband and his brothers.

Concorde the only supersonic airliner, which cruises at Mach 2, or twice the speed of sound, about 2,170 kph/1,350 mph. Concorde, the result of Anglo-French cooperation, made its first flight 1969 and entered commercial service seven years later. It is 62 m/202 ft long and has a wing span of nearly 26 m/84 ft.

concrete building material composed of cement, stone, sand, and water. It has been used since Roman and Egyptian times. During the 20th century, it has been increasingly employed as an economical alternative to materials such as brick and wood.

conditioning in psychology, two major principles of behaviour modification. In *classical conditioning*, described by Ivan Pavlov, a new stimulus can evoke an automatic response by being repeatedly associated with a stimulus that naturally provokes a response. For example, the sound of a bell repeatedly associated with food will eventually trigger salivation, even if sounded without food. In *operant conditioning*, described by Edward Lee Thorndike (1874–1949) and B F Skinner, the frequency of a voluntary response can be increased by following it with a reinforcer or reward.

condom or *sheath* or *prophylactic* barrier contraceptive, made of rubber, which fits over an erect penis and holds in the sperm produced by ejaculation. It is an effective means of preventing pregnancy if used carefully, preferably with a

◊spermicide. A condom with spermicide is 97% effective; one without spermicide is 85% effective. Condoms also give protection against sexually transmitted diseases, including AIDS.

condor large bird, a New World vulture *Vultur gryphus*, with wingspan up to 3 m/10 ft, weight up to 13 kg/28 lb, and length up to 1.2 m/3.8 ft. It is black, with some white on the wings and a white frill at the base of the neck. It lives in the Andes and along the South American coast, and feeds on carrion. The Californian condor *Gymnogyps californianus* is a similar bird, on the verge of extinction.

conductance ability of a material to carry an electrical current, usually given the symbol *G*. For a direct current, it is the reciprocal of resistance: a conductor of resistance *R* has a conductance of 1/ *R*. For an alternating current, conductance is the resistance *R* divided by the impedance Z: $G = R/Z$. Conductance was formerly expressed in reciprocal ohms (or mhos); the SI unit is the siemens (S).

conductor any material that conducts heat or electricity (as opposed to an insulator, or nonconductor). A good conductor has a high electrical or heat conductivity, and is generally a substance rich in free electrons such as a metal. A poor conductor (such as the nonmetals glass and porcelain) has few free electrons. Carbon is exceptional in being nonmetallic and yet (in some of its forms) a relatively good conductor of heat and electricity. Substances such as silicon and germanium, with intermediate conductivities that are improved by heat, light, or voltage, are known as ◊semiconductors.

cone in geometry, a solid or surface consisting of the set of all straight lines passing through a fixed point (the vertex) and the points of a circle or ellipse whose plane does not contain the vertex.

cone in botany, the reproductive structure of the conifers and cycads; also known as a strobilus. It consists of a central axis surrounded by numerous overlapping scalelike modified leaves (sporophylls) that bear the reproductive organs. Usually there are separate male and female cones. The pollen is carried from male to female cones by the wind (anemophily). The seeds develop within the female cone and are released as the scales open in dry atmospheric conditions, which favour seed dispersal.

Confederacy in US history, popular name for the *Confederate States of America*, the government established by 6 (later 11) Southern states Feb 1861 when they seceded from the Union, precipitating the ◊Civil War. Richmond, Virginia, was the capital, and Jefferson Davis the president. The Confederacy fell after its army was defeated 1865 and General Robert E Lee surrendered.

Confederation, Articles of in US history, the initial means by which the 13 former British colonies created a form of national government. Ratified 1781, the articles established a unicameral legislature, Congress, with limited powers of raising revenue, regulating currency, and conducting foreign affairs. But because the individual states retained significant autonomy, the confederation was unmanageable. The articles were superseded by the US Constitution 1788.

Confederation of British Industry (CBI) UK organization of employers, established 1965, combining the former Federation of British Industries (founded 1916), British Employers' Confederation, and National Association of British Manufacturers.

Conference on Security and Cooperation in Europe (CSCE) international forum attempting to reach agreement in security, economics, science, technology, and human rights. The CSCE first met in Helsinki 1975. By the end of June 1992, having admitted the former Soviet republics, as well as Croatia and Slovenia, its membership had risen to 52 states.

confession in religion, the confession of sins practised in Roman Catholic, Orthodox, and most Far Eastern Christian churches, and since the early 19th century revived in Anglican and Lutheran churches. The Lateran Council of 1215 made auricular confession (self-accusation by the penitent to a priest, who in Catholic doctrine is divinely invested with authority to give absolution) obligatory once a year.

confirmation rite practised by a number of Christian denominations, including Roman Catholic, Anglican, and Orthodox, in which a previously baptized person is admitted to full membership of the church. In Reform Judaism there is often a confirmation service several years after the bar or bat mitzvah (initiation into the congregation).

Confucianism body of beliefs and practices based on the Chinese classics and supported by the authority of the philosopher Confucius. The origin of things is seen in the union of *yin* and *yang*, the passive and active principles. Human relationships follow the patriarchal pattern. For more than 2,000 years Chinese political government, social organization, and individual conduct was shaped by Confucian principles. In 1912, Confucian philosophy, as a basis for government, was dropped by the state.

Confucius (Latinized form of *K'ung Tzu*, 'Kong the master') 551–479 BC. Chinese sage whose name is given to Confucianism. He devoted his life to relieving suffering among the poor through governmental and administrative reform. His emphasis on tradition and ethics attracted a growing number of pupils during his lifetime. *The Analects of Confucius*, a compilation of his teachings, was published after his death. Within 300 years of the death of Confucius his teaching was adopted by the Chinese state.

conger any large marine eel of the family Congridae, especially the genus *Conger*. Conger eels live in shallow water, hiding in crevices during the day and active by night, feeding on fish and crabs. They are valued for food and angling. The European conger *C. conger* is found in the N Atlantic and in the Mediterranean. It is often 1.8 m/6 ft long, and sometimes as much as 2.7 m/9 ft.

Congo Republic of; country in W central Africa, bordered N by Cameroon and the Central African Republic, E and S by Zaire, W by the Atlantic Ocean, and NW by Gabon; *area* 342,000 sq km/ 132,012 sq mi; *capital* Brazzaville; *physical* narrow coastal plain rises to central plateau then falls into northern basin; Zaïre (Congo) River on the border with Zaire; half the country is rainforest; *head of state and government* Denis Sassou-Nguesso from 1979; *political system* emergent democracy; *exports* timber, petroleum, coffee, tobacco; *population* (1990 est) 2,305,000 (chiefly Bantu); *languages* French (official); many African languages; *recent history* independence from France was achieved 1960, since when government of the country has been unsettled. A Marxist state, the People's Republic of the Congo, was announced 1970. Multiparty politics were promised 1990. The country was renamed Republic of Congo 1991; a new constitution was adopted, pending a referendum.

Congress national legislature of the USA, consisting of the House of Representatives (435 members, apportioned to the states of the Union on the basis of population, and elected for two-year terms) and the Senate (100 senators, two for each state, elected for six years, one-third elected every two years). Both representatives and senators are elected by direct popular vote. Congress meets in Washington DC, in the Capitol Building. An ▷act of Congress is a bill passed by both houses.

Congreve William 1670–1729. English dramatist and poet. His first success was the comedy *The Old Bachelor* 1693, followed by *The Double Dealer* 1694, *Love for Love* 1695, the tragedy *The Mourning Bride* 1697, and *The Way of the World* 1700. His plays, which satirize the social affectations of the time, are characterized by elegant wit and wordplay.

conic section curve obtained when a conical surface is intersected by a plane. If the intersecting plane cuts both extensions of the cone, it yields a ▷hyperbola; if it is parallel to the side of the cone, it produces a ▷parabola. Other intersecting planes produce ▷circles or ▷ellipses.

conifer tree or shrub of the class Coniferales, in the gymnosperm or naked-seed-bearing group of plants. They are often pyramidal in form, with leaves that are either scaled or made up of needles; most are evergreen. Conifers include pines, spruces, firs, yews, junipers, monkey puzzles, and larches.

conjunction grammatical ▷part of speech that serves to connect words, phrases, and clauses; for example *and* in 'apples and pears' and *but* in 'we're going but they aren't'.

conjunctivitis inflammation of the conjunctiva, the delicate membrane that lines the inside of the eyelids and covers the front of the eye. It may be caused by infection, allergy, or other irritant. Treatment is usually with eyedrops.

Connacht province of the Republic of Ireland, comprising the counties of Galway, Leitrim, Mayo, Roscommon, and Sligo; *area* 17,130 sq km/ 6,612 sq mi; population (1991) 422,900. The chief towns are Galway, Roscommon, Castlebar, Sligo, and Carrick-on-Shannon. Mainly lowland, it is agricultural and stock-raising country, with poor land in the west.

Connecticut state in New England, USA; nicknamed Constitution State/Nutmeg State; *area* 13,000 sq km/5,018 sq mi; *capital* Hartford; *physical* highlands in the NW; Connecticut River; *features* Yale University; *products* dairy, poultry, and market garden products; tobacco, watches, clocks, silverware, helicopters, jet engines, nuclear submarines; *population* (1990) 3,287,100; *famous people* Phineas T Barnum, George Bush, Katharine Hepburn, Harriet Beecher Stowe, Mark Twain; *history* settled by Puritan colonists from Massachusetts 1635, it was one of the Thirteen Colonies, and became a state 1788.

conquistador any of the early Spanish explorers and adventurers in the Americas, such as Hernando Cortés (Mexico) and Francisco Pizarro (Peru).

Conrad Joseph. Pen name of Teodor Jozef Conrad Korzeniowski 1857–1924. English novelist, born in the Ukraine of Polish parents. He joined the French merchant navy at the age of 17 and first learned English at 21. His greatest works include the novels *Lord Jim* 1900, *Nostromo* 1904, *The Secret Agent* 1907, and *Under Western Eyes* 1911, and the short stories 'Heart of Darkness' 1902 and 'The Shadow Line' 1917. These combine a vivid sensuous evocation of various lands and seas with a rigorous, humane scrutiny of moral dilemmas, pitfalls, and desperation.

conservation action taken to protect and preserve the natural world, usually from pollution, over-exploitation, and other harmful features of human activity. The late 1980s saw a great increase in public concern for the environment, with membership of conservation groups, such as Friends of the Earth, rising sharply. Globally the most important issues include the depletion of atmospheric ozone by the action of chlorofluorocarbons (CFCs), the build-up of carbon dioxide in the atmosphere (thought to contribute to an intensification of the ▷greenhouse effect), and the destruction of the tropical rainforests (see ▷deforestation).

conservatism approach to government favouring the maintenance of existing institutions and identified with a number of Western political parties, such as the British Conservative, German Christian Democratic, and Australian Liberal parties. It tends to be explicitly nondoctrinaire and pragmatic but generally emphasizes free-enterprise capitalism, minimal government intervention in the economy, rigid law and order, and the importance of national traditions.

Conservative Party UK political party, one of the two historic British parties; the name replaced *Tory* in general use from 1830 onwards. Traditionally the party of landed interests, it broadened its political base under Benjamin Disraeli's leadership in the 19th century. The present Conservative Party's free-market capitalism is supported by the world of finance and the management of industry.

Constable John 1776–1837. English landscape painter. He painted scenes of his native Suffolk, including *The Haywain* 1821 (National Gallery, London), as well as castles, cathedrals, landscapes, and coastal scenes in other parts of Britain. Constable inherited the Dutch tradition of sombre realism, in particular the style of Jacob ◊Ruisdael, but he aimed to capture the momentary changes of nature as well as to create monumental images of British scenery, such as *The White Horse* 1819 (Frick Collection, New York) and *Flatford Mill* 1825.

Constantine the Great born *c.* AD 280, died 337. First Christian emperor of Rome and founder of Constantinople. He defeated Maxentius, joint emperor of Rome AD 312, and in 313 formally recognized Christianity. As sole emperor of the west of the empire, he defeated Licinius, emperor of the east, to become ruler of the Roman world 324. He presided over the church's first council at Nicaea 325. In 330 Constantine moved his capital to Byzantium, renaming it Constantinople.

Constantinople former name (330–1453) of Istanbul, Turkey. It was named after the Roman emperor Constantine the Great when he enlarged the Greek city of Byzantium 328 and declared it the capital of the ◊Byzantine Empire 330. Its elaborate fortifications enabled it to resist a succession of sieges, but it was captured by crusaders 1204, and was the seat of a Latin (Western European) kingdom until recaptured by the Greeks 1261. An attack by the Turks 1422 proved unsuccessful, but it was taken by another Turkish army 29 May 1453 after nearly a year's siege, and became the capital of the Ottoman Empire.

constellation one of the 88 areas into which the sky is divided for the purposes of identifying and naming celestial objects. The first constellations were simple, arbitrary patterns of stars in which early civilizations visualized gods, sacred beasts, and mythical heroes.

constitution body of fundamental laws of a state, laying down the system of government and defining the relations of the legislature, executive, and judiciary to each other and to the citizens. Since the French Revolution almost all countries (the UK is an exception) have adopted written constitutions; that of the USA (1787) is the oldest. The constitution of the UK does not exist as a single document but as an accumulation of customs and precedents, together with laws defining certain of its aspects.

Constructivism revolutionary art movement founded in Moscow 1917 by the Russians Naum ◊Gabo, his brother Antoine Pevsner (1886–1962), and Vladimir Tatlin (1885–1953). Tatlin's abstract sculptures, using wood, metal, and clear plastic, were hung on walls or suspended from ceilings. Gabo and Pevsner soon left the USSR and joined the European avant-garde.

consul chief magistrate of ancient Rome after the expulsion of the last king 510 BC. The consuls were two annually elected magistrates, both of equal power; they jointly held full civil power in Rome and the chief military command in the field. After the establishment of the Roman Empire the office became purely honorary.

contact lens lens, made of soft or hard plastic, that is worn in contact with the cornea and conjunctiva of the eye, beneath the eyelid, to correct defective vision. In special circumstances, contact lenses may be used as protective shells or for cosmetic purposes, such as changing eye colour.

continent any one of the large land masses of the Earth, as distinct from the oceans. They are Asia, Africa, North America, South America, Europe, Australia, and Antarctica. Continents are constantly moving and evolving (see ◊plate tectonics). A continent does not end at the coastline; its boundary is the edge of the shallow continental shelf (part of the continental crust, made of sial), which may extend several hundred miles or kilometres out to sea.

Continental Congress in US history, the federal legislature of the original 13 states, acting as a provisional government during the ◊American Revolution. It was convened in Philadelphia 1774–89, when the constitution was adopted. The second Continental Congress, convened May 1775, was responsible for drawing up the Declaration of Independence.

continental drift in geology, theory proposed by the German meteorologist Alfred Wegener in 1915 that, about 200 million years ago, Earth consisted of a single large continent (Pangaea) that subsequently broke apart to form the continents known today. Such vast continental movements could not be satisfactorily explained until the study of ◊plate tectonics in the 1960s.

continuo abbreviation for *basso continuo*; in music, the bass line on which a keyboard player, often accompanied by a bass stringed instrument, built up a harmonic accompaniment in 17th-century Baroque music.

Contra member of a Central American right-wing guerrilla force attempting to overthrow the democratically elected Nicaraguan Sandinista government 1979–90. The Contras, many of them mercenaries or former members of the deposed dictator Somoza's guard (see Nicaraguan Revolution), operated mainly from bases outside Nicaragua, mostly in Honduras, with covert US funding, as revealed by the ◊Irangate hearings 1986–87.

contraceptive any drug, device, or technique that prevents pregnancy. The contraceptive pill (the ◊Pill) contains female hormones that interfere with egg production or the first stage of pregnancy. The 'morning-after' pill can be taken up to 72 hours after unprotected intercourse. Barrier contraceptives include ◊condoms (sheaths) and ◊diaphragms, also called caps or Dutch caps; they prevent the sperm entering the cervix (neck of the womb). ◊Intrauterine devices, also known as IUDs or coils, cause a slight inflammation of the lining of the womb; this prevents the fertilized egg from becoming implanted. See also ◊family planning.

contracting out agreement between an employer and employee whereby the employee does not participate in a financial contributory scheme administered by the employer. This usually applies to pension or health insurance schemes, or payment of trade union or other subscriptions from the

continental drift

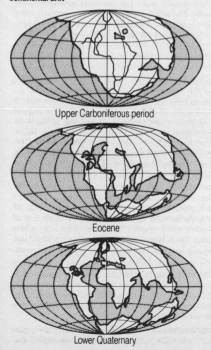

Upper Carboniferous period

Eocene

Lower Quaternary

gross salary.

contralto in music, a low-registered female voice; also called an ◊*alto*.

convection heat energy transfer that involves the movement of a fluid (gas or liquid). According to kinetic theory, molecules of fluid in contact with the source of heat expand and tend to rise within the bulk of the fluid. Less energetic, cooler molecules sink to take their place, setting up convection currents. This is the principle of natural convection in many domestic hot-water systems and space heaters.

conveyancing administrative process involved in transferring title to land, usually on its sale or purchase. In England and Wales, conveyancing is usually done by solicitors, but, since 1985, can also be done by licensed conveyancers. Conveyancing has been simplified by the registration of land with the ◊Land Registry.

convolvulus or *bindweed* any plant of the genus *Convolvulus* of the morning-glory family Convolvulaceae. They are characterized by their twining stems and by their petals, which are united into a funnel-shaped tube. The field bindweed *C. arvensis*, a trailing plant with handsome white or pink-and-white-streaked flowers, is a common weed in Britain.

convulsion series of violent contractions of the muscles over which the patient has no control. It may be associated with loss of consciousness.

Cook Capt James 1728–1779. British naval explorer. As a result of sending his observations of an eclipse of the Sun 1766 to the Royal Society, he was made commander of the first scientific exploration to the Pacific 1768–71, sailing in the *Endeavour* to Tahiti, New Zealand, and Australia. In 1772–75 he sailed to the South Pacific (with the *Resolution* and *Adventure*) and in 1776–79 to the South and North Pacific (with the *Resolution* and *Discovery*), attempting to find the Northwest Passage and charting the Siberian coast. He is credited with preventing scurvy through providing his sailors with fresh fruit. He was killed in Hawaii.

Cook, Mount highest point, 3,764 m/12,353 ft, of the Southern Alps, a range of mountains running through New Zealand.

Cooke Sam 1931–1964. US soul singer and songwriter who began his career as a gospel singer and turned to pop music in 1956. His hits include 'You Send Me' 1957 and 'Wonderful World' 1960 (re-released 1986).

Cook Islands group of six large and a number of smaller Polynesian islands 2,600 km/1,600 mi NE of Auckland, New Zealand; area 290 sq km/112 sq mi; population (1991) 19,000. Their main products include fruit, copra, and crafts. They became a self-governing overseas territory of New Zealand 1965.

Cook Strait strait dividing North Island and South Island, New Zealand. A submarine cable carries electricity from South to North Island.

Coolidge (John) Calvin 1872–1933. 30th president of the USA 1923–29, a Republican. As governor of Massachusetts 1919, he was responsible for crushing a Boston police strike. As Warren ▷Harding's vice president 1921–23, he succeeded to the presidency on Harding's death (2 Aug 1923). He won the 1924 presidential election, and his period of office was marked by great economic prosperity.

coordinate in geometry, a number that defines the position of a point relative to a point or axis. Cartesian coordinates define a point by its perpendicular distances from two or more axes drawn through a fixed point at right angles to each other; polar coordinates define a point in a plane by its distance from a fixed point and direction from a fixed line.

coordinate geometry or **analytical geometry** system of geometry in which points, lines, shapes, and surfaces are represented by algebraic expressions. In plane (two-dimensional) coordinate geometry, the plane is usually defined by two axes at right angles to each other, the horizontal x-axis and the vertical y-axis, meeting at O, the origin. A point on the plane can be represented by a pair of ▷Cartesian coordinates, which define its position in terms of its distance along the x-axis and along the y-axis from O. These distances are respectively the x and y coordinates of the point.

coot any of various freshwater birds of the genus *Fulica* in the rail family. Coots are about 38 cm/ 1.2 ft long, and mainly black. They have a white bill, extending up the forehead in a plate, and big feet with lobed toes. The Old World coot *F. atra* is found on inland waters in Europe, Asia, N Africa, and Australia.

Copenhagen (Danish *København*) capital of Denmark, on the islands of Zealand and Amager; population (1990) 1,337,100 (including suburbs). Copenhagen was a fishing village until 1167, when the bishop of Roskilde built a castle on the site of the present Christiansborg Palace. A settlement grew up and it became the Danish capital 1443. The British fleet under Nelson and Sir Hyde Parker defeated the Danish fleet in a naval battle off Copenhagen 1801; this was within the context of the French Revolutionary Wars.

Copernicus Nicolaus 1473–1543. Polish astronomer who believed that the Sun, not the Earth, is at the centre of the Solar System, thus defying the Christian church doctrine of the time. For 30 years he worked on the hypothesis that the rotation and the orbital motion of the Earth were responsible for the apparent movement of the heavenly bodies. His great work *De Revolutionibus Orbium Coelestium/ About the Revolutions of the Heavenly Spheres* was not published until the year of his death.

Copland Aaron 1900–1990. US composer. His early works, such as his piano concerto 1926, were in the jazz idiom but he gradually developed a gentler style with a regional flavour drawn from American folk music. Among his works are the ballets *Billy the Kid* 1939, *Rodeo* 1942, *Appalachian Spring* 1944 (based on a poem by Hart Crane), and *Inscape for Orchestra* 1967.

copper orange-pink, very malleable and ductile, metallic element, symbol Cu (from Latin *cuprum*), atomic number 29, relative atomic mass 63.546. It is used for its durability, pliability, high thermal and electrical conductivity, and resistance to corrosion.

copra dried meat from the kernel of the ▷coconut, used to make coconut oil.

Copt descendant of those ancient Egyptians who adopted Christianity in the 1st century and refused to convert to Islam after the Arab conquest. They now form a small minority (about 5%) of Egypt's population. **Coptic** is a member of the Hamito-Semitic language family. It is descended from the language of the ancient Egyptians and is the ritual language of the Coptic Christian church. It is written in the Greek alphabet with some additional characters derived from ▷demotic script.

copyright law applying to literary, musical, and artistic works (including plays, recordings, films, photographs, radio and television broadcasts, and, in the USA and the UK, computer programs), which prevents the reproduction of the work, in whole or in part, without the author's consent. In the UK and (since 1989) the USA, copyright lasts for a holder's lifetime plus 50 years, or (in the USA), a flat 75 years for a company copyright.

coral marine invertebrate of the class Anthozoa in the phylum Cnidaria, which also includes sea anemones and jellyfish. It has a skeleton of lime (calcium carbonate) extracted from the surrounding water. Corals exist in warm seas, at moderate depths with sufficient light. Some coral is valued for decoration or jewellery, for example, Mediterranean red coral *Corallum rubrum*. **Barrier reefs** are separated from the shore by a saltwater lagoon, which may be as much as 30 km/20 mi wide; there are usually navigable passes through the barrier into the lagoon. **Atolls** resemble a ring surrounding a lagoon, and do not enclose an island. They are usually formed by the gradual subsidence of an extinct volcano, the coral growing up from where the edge of the island once lay.

Coral Sea or *Solomon Sea* part of the Pacific Ocean bounded by NE Australia, New Guinea, the Solomon Islands, Vanuatu, and New Caledonia. It contains numerous coral islands and reefs. The Coral Sea Islands are a territory of Australia; they comprise scattered reefs and islands over an area of about 1 million sq km/914,000 sq mi.

cor anglais or *English horn* double-reeded musical instrument; the alto member of the ▷oboe family.

Corbusier, Le see ◊Le Corbusier, architect.

Cordilleras, the mountainous western section of North America, with the Rocky Mountains and the coastal ranges parallel to the contact between the North American and the Pacific plates.

Corfu (Greek *Kérkira*) northernmost and second largest of the Ionian islands of Greece, off the coast of Epirus in the Ionian Sea; area 1,072 sq km/ 414 sq mi; population (1981) 96,500. Its businesses include tourism, fruit, olive oil, and textiles. Its largest town is the port of Corfu (Kérkira), population (1981) 33,560. Corfu was colonized by the Corinthians about 700 BC. Venice held it 1386–1797, Britain 1815–64.

corgi either of two breeds of short-legged dogs from Wales. The Pembrokeshire Welsh corgi has a finely textured coat, yellowish or reddish brown, sometimes black and tan. It stands up to 30 cm/12 in at the shoulder. It has almost no tail. The Cardigan Welsh corgi has short, rough hair. The coat colour is usually red and white. It also stands about 30 cm/12 in high and has a long, furry tail. Corgis were originally bred to herd cattle.

coriander pungent fresh herb, the Eurasian plant *Coriandrum sativum*, a member of the parsley family Umbelliferae; also a spice: the dried ripe fruit. The spice is used commercially as a flavouring in meat products, bakery goods, tobacco, gin, liqueurs, chilli, and curry powder. Both are much used in cooking in the Middle East, India, Mexico, and China.

Corinth (Greek *Kórinthos*) port in Greece, on the isthmus connecting the Peloponnese with the mainland; population (1981) 22,650. The rocky isthmus is bisected by the 6.5 km/4 mi Corinth canal, opened 1893. The site of the ancient city-state of Corinth lies 7 km/4.5 mi SW of the port.

Corinthian in Classical architecture, one of the five types of column; see ◊order.

Coriolis effect result of the deflective force of the Earth's west-to-east rotation. Winds, ocean currents, and aircraft are deflected to the right of their direction of travel in the northern hemisphere and to the left in the southern hemisphere.

cork light, waterproof outer layers of the bark of the stems and roots of almost all trees and shrubs. The cork oak *Quercus suber*, a native of S Europe and N Africa, is cultivated in Spain and Portugal; the exceptionally thick outer layers of its bark provide the cork that is used commercially.

Cork largest county of the Republic of Ireland, in the province of Munster; county town Cork; area 7,460 sq km/2,880 sq mi; population (1991) 409,800. It is agricultural, but there is also some copper and manganese mining, marble quarrying, and river and sea fishing. Natural gas and oil fields are found off the S coast at Kinsale.

coriander

corm short, swollen, underground plant stem, surrounded by protective scale leaves, as seen in the genus *Crocus*. It stores food, provides a means of ◊vegetative reproduction, and acts as a ◊perennating organ.

cormorant any of various diving seabirds, mainly of the genus *Phalacrocorax*, about 90 cm/3 ft long, with webbed feet, long neck, hooked beak, and glossy black plumage. There are some 30 species of cormorant worldwide. Some species breed on inland lakes and rivers.

corn main ◊cereal crop of a region – for example, wheat in the UK, oats in Scotland and Ireland, maize in the USA.

corn circle see ◊crop circle.

corncrake bird *Crex crex* of the rail family. About 25 cm/10 in long, it is drably coloured, shy, and has a persistent rasping call. It lives in meadows and crops in temperate regions, but has become rare where mechanical methods of cutting corn are used.

cornet brass band instrument. It is like a shorter, broader trumpet, with a wider bore and mellower tone, and without fixed notes. Notes of different pitch are obtained by overblowing and by means of three pistons.

cornflower plant *Centaurea cyanus* of the family Compositae. It is distinguished from the knapweeds by its deep azure-blue flowers. Formerly a common weed in N European wheat fields, it is now commonly grown in gardens as a herbaceous plant.

Cornish language extinct member of the ◊Celtic languages, a branch of the Indo-European language family, spoken in Cornwall, England, until 1777. Written Cornish first appeared in 10th-century documents; some religious plays were written in Cornish in the 15th and 16th centuries, but later literature is scanty, consisting mainly of folk tales and verses. In recent years the language has been revived in a somewhat reconstructed form by members of the Cornish nationalist movement.

Corn Laws in Britain until 1846, laws used to regulate the export or import of cereals in order to maintain an adequate supply for consumers and a secure price for producers. For centuries the Corn Laws formed an integral part of the mercantile system in England; they were repealed because they became an unwarranted tax on food and a hindrance to British exports.

Cornwall county in SW England including the ▷Scilly Islands (Scillies); *area* (excluding Scillies) 3,550 sq km/1,370 sq mi; *towns* Truro (administrative headquarters), Camborne, Launceston; resorts of Bude, Falmouth, Newquay, Penzance, St Ives; *physical* Bodmin Moor (including Brown Willy 419 m/1,375 ft), Land's End peninsula, St Michael's Mount, rivers Tamar, Fowey, Fal, Camel; *products* electronics, spring flowers, tin (mined since Bronze Age, some workings renewed 1960s, though the industry has all but disappeared), kaolin (St Austell), fish; *population* (1991) 469,300; *famous people* John Betjeman, Humphry Davy, Daphne Du Maurier, William Golding.

coronary artery disease condition in which the fatty deposits of ▷atherosclerosis form in the coronary arteries that supply the heart muscle, making them too narrow.

coronation ceremony of investing a sovereign with the emblems of royalty, as a symbol of inauguration in office. Since the coronation of Harold 1066, English sovereigns have been crowned in Westminster Abbey, London. The kings of Scotland were traditionally crowned in Scone; French kings in Reims.

coroner official who investigates the deaths of persons who have died suddenly by acts of violence or under suspicious circumstances, by holding an inquest or ordering a postmortem examination (autopsy). Coroners may also inquire into instances of ▷treasure trove. In Scotland similar duties are performed by the procurator fiscal.

Corot Jean-Baptiste-Camille 1796–1875. French painter, creator of a distinctive landscape style with cool colours and soft focus. His early work, including Italian scenes in the 1820s, influenced the Barbizon school of painters. Like them, Corot worked outdoors, but he also continued a conventional academic tradition with more romanticized paintings.

corporal punishment physical punishment of wrongdoers – for example, by whipping. It is still used as a punishment for criminals in many countries, especially under Islamic law. Corporal punishment of children by parents is illegal in some countries, including Sweden, Finland, Denmark, and Norway. It was abolished as a punishment for

criminals in Britain 1967 but only became illegal for punishing schoolchildren in state schools 1986.

corporation tax tax levied on a company's profits by public authorities. It is a form of income tax, and rates vary according to country, but there is usually a flat rate. It is a large source of revenue for governments.

Correggio Antonio Allegri da c. 1494–1534. Italian painter of the High Renaissance whose style followed the Classical grandeur of Leonardo and Titian but anticipated the Baroque in its emphasis on movement, softer forms, and contrasts of light and shade. Based in Parma, he created splendid illusionistic visions in the cathedral there, including *The Ascension of the Virgin*.

Corsica (French *Corse*) island region of France, in the Mediterranean off the W coast of Italy, N of Sardinia; it comprises the *départements* of Haute Corse and Corse du Sud; *area* 8,700 sq km/ 3,358 sq mi; *capital* Ajaccio (port); *physical* mountainous; maquis vegetation; *features* Corsica's mountain bandits were eradicated 1931, but the tradition of the vendetta or blood feud lingers. The island is the main base of the Foreign Legion; *government* its special status involves a 61-member regional parliament with the power to scrutinize French National Assembly bills applicable to the island and propose amendments; *products* wine, olive oil; *population* (1986) 249,000, including just under 50% native Corsicans. There are about 400,000 *émigrés*, mostly in Mexico and Central America, who return to retire; *language* French (official); the majority speak Corsican, an Italian dialect; *famous people* Napoleon.

Cortés Hernán (Ferdinand) 1485–1547. Spanish conquistador. He conquered the Aztec empire 1519–21, and secured Mexico for Spain.

corticosteroid any of several steroid hormones secreted by the cortex of the ▷adrenal glands; also synthetic forms with similar properties. Corticosteroids have anti-inflammatory and immunosuppressive effects and may be used to treat a number of conditions including rheumatoid arthritis, severe allergies, asthma, some skin diseases, and some cancers. Side effects can be serious, and therapy must be withdrawn very gradually.

cortisone natural corticosteroid produced by the ▷adrenal gland, now synthesized for its anti-inflammatory qualities and used in the treatment of rheumatoid arthritis.

corundum native aluminium oxide, Al_2O_3, the hardest naturally occurring mineral known apart from diamond (corundum rates 9 on the Mohs' scale of hardness); lack of cleavage also increases its durability. Varieties of gem-quality corundum are *ruby* (red) and *sapphire* (any colour other than red, usually blue). Poorer-quality and synthetic corundum is used in industry – for example, as an ◇abrasive.

Cosgrave Liam 1920– . Irish Fine Gael politician, prime minister of the Republic of Ireland 1973–77. As party leader 1965–77, he headed a Fine Gael–Labour coalition government from 1973. Relations between the Irish and UK governments improved under his premiership.

Cosgrave William Thomas 1880–1965. Irish politician. He took part in the ◇Easter Rising 1916 and sat in the Sinn Féin cabinet of 1919–21. Head of the Free State government 1922–33, he founded and led the Fine Gael opposition 1933–44. His eldest son is Liam Cosgrave.

cosine in trigonometry, a function of an angle in a right-angled triangle found by dividing the length of the side adjacent to the angle by the length of the hypotenuse (the longest side). It is usually shortened to cos.

cosmic radiation streams of high-energy particles from outer space, consisting of protons, alpha particles, and light nuclei, which collide with atomic nuclei in the Earth's atmosphere, and produce secondary nuclear particles (chiefly ◇mesons, such as pions and muons) that shower the Earth.

cosmology study of the structure of the universe. Modern cosmology began in the 1920s with the discovery that the universe is expanding, which suggested that it began in an explosion, the ◇Big Bang. An alternative view, the ◇steady-state theory, claimed that the universe has no origin, but is expanding because new matter is being continually created.

Cossack member of any of several, formerly horse-raising groups of S and SW Russia, the Ukraine, and Poland, predominantly Russian or Ukrainian origin, who took in escaped serfs and lived in independent communal settlements (military brotherhoods) from the 15th to the 19th century. Later they held land in return for military service in the cavalry under Russian and Polish rulers. After 1917, the various Cossack communities were incorporated into the Soviet administrative and collective system.

Costa Rica Republic of; country in Central America, bordered N by Nicaragua, S by Panama, E by the Caribbean, and W by the Pacific Ocean; *area* 51,100 sq km/19,735 sq mi; *capital* San José; *physical* high central plateau and tropical coasts; Costa Rica was once entirely forested but by 1983 only 17% of the forest remained; half of the arable land had been cleared for cattle ranching; *head of state and government* Rafael Calderón from 1990; *political system* liberal democracy; *exports* coffee, bananas, cocoa, sugar, beef; *population* (1990 est) 3,032,000 (including 1,200 Guaymi Indians); *language* Spanish (official); *recent history* independence was achieved from Spain 1821. A new

constitution was adopted 1949. Deterioration in the economy was faced by a harsh austerity programme. Despite US pressure, Costa Rica remained neutral towards the Sandinista regime in Nicaragua during the 1980s. Former president Oscar Arias Sánchez won the Nobel Peace Prize 1987 for devising a Central American peace plan.

Costner Kevin 1955– . US film actor. He first achieved top-ranking success with his role as law-enforcer, Elliot Ness, in the film version of the 60s television series *The Untouchables* 1987. Increasingly identified with the embodiment of idealism and high principle, Costner went on to direct and star in *Dances With Wolves* 1990, a Western sympathetic to the native American Indian, which won several Academy Awards. Subsequent films include *Robin Hood – Prince of Thieves* 1991 and *JFK* 1991.

cost of living cost of goods and services needed for an average standard of living. In Britain the cost-of-living index was introduced 1914 and based on the expenditure of a working-class family of a man, woman, and three children; the standard is 100. Known from 1947 as the Retail Price Index (RPI), it is revised to allow for inflation.

cot death death of an apparently healthy baby during sleep, also known as **sudden infant death syndrome** (SIDS). It is most common in the winter months, and strikes more boys than girls. The cause is not known.

Cotman John Sell 1782–1842. British landscape painter, with John Crome a founder of the **Norwich school**, a group of realistic landscape painters influenced by Dutch examples. His early watercolours were bold designs in simple flat washes of colour, for example *Greta Bridge, Yorkshire* 1805 (British Museum, London).

cotoneaster any shrub or tree of the Eurasian genus *Cotoneaster*, rose family Rosaceae, closely allied to the hawthorn and medlar. The fruits, though small and unpalatable, are usually bright red and conspicuous, often persisting through the winter. Some of the shrubs are cultivated for their attractive appearance.

Cotonou chief port and largest city of Benin, on the Bight of Benin; population (1982) 487,000. Palm products and timber are exported. Although not the official capital, it is the seat of the president, and the main centre of commerce and politics.

Cotopaxi active volcano, situated to the S of Quito in Ecuador. It is 5,897 m/19,347 ft high and was first climbed 1872.

cotton tropical and subtropical herbaceous plant of the genus *Gossypium* of the mallow family Malvaceae. Fibres surround the seeds inside the ripened fruits, or bolls, and these are spun into yarn for cloth. Cotton production represents 5% of world agricultural output.

cotyledon structure in the embryo of a seed plant

that may form a 'leaf' after germination and is commonly known as a seed leaf. The number of cotyledons present in an embryo is an important character in the classification of flowering plants (⟡angiosperms).

couch grass European grass *Agropyron repens* of the family Gramineae. It spreads rapidly by underground stems. It is considered a troublesome weed in North America, where it has been introduced.

cougar another name for the ⟡puma, a large North American cat.

coulomb SI unit (symbol C) of electrical charge. One coulomb is the quantity of electricity conveyed by a current of one ⟡ampere in one second.

council in local government in England and Wales, a popularly elected local assembly charged with the government of the area within its boundaries. Under the Local Government Act 1972, they comprise three types: ⟡county councils, ⟡district councils, and parish councils.

Council of Europe body constituted 1949 in Strasbourg, France (still its headquarters), to secure 'a greater measure of unity between the European countries'. The widest association of European states, it has a *Committee* of foreign ministers, a *Parliamentary Assembly* (with members from national parliaments), and a *European Commission* investigating violations of human rights.

council tax method of raising revenue for local government in Britain, announced by the government April 1991, to replace the community charge, or ⟡poll tax, from 1993. The tax is based on property values but takes some account of the number of people occupying each property.

counselling approach to treating problems, usually psychological ones, in which clients are encouraged to solve their own problems with support from a counsellor. There is some overlap with ⟡psychotherapy although counselling is less concerned with severe psychological disorders.

counterpoint in music, the art of combining different forms of an original melody with apparent freedom and yet to harmonious effect. Giovanni ⟡Palestrina and J S ⟡Bach were masters of counterpoint.

Counter-Reformation movement initiated by the Catholic church at the Council of Trent 1545–63 to counter the spread of the ⟡Reformation. Extending into the 17th century, its dominant forces included the rise of the Jesuits and the deployment of the Spanish ⟡Inquisition in other countries.

country and western or *country music* popular music of the white US South and West; it evolved from the folk music of the English, Irish, and Scottish settlers and has a strong blues influence. Characteristic instruments are the steel guitar, mandolin, and fiddle.

county administrative unit of a country or state. In the UK it is nowadays synonymous with 'shire', although historically the two had different origins. Many of the English counties can be traced back to Saxon times. In the USA a county is a subdivision of a state; the power of counties differs widely between states. The Republic of Ireland has 26 geographical and 27 administrative counties.

county council in the UK, a unit of local government whose responsibilities include broad planning policy, highways, education, personal social services, and libraries; police, fire, and traffic control; and refuse disposal.

coup d'état or *coup* forcible takeover of the government of a country by elements from within that country, generally carried out by violent or illegal means. It differs from a revolution in typically being carried out by a small group (for example, of army officers or opposition politicians) to install its leader as head of government, rather than being a mass uprising by the people.

couplet in literature, a pair of lines of verse, usually of the same length and rhymed.

Courbet Gustave 1819–1877. French artist, a portrait, genre, and landscape painter. Reacting against academic trends, both Classicist and Romantic, he sought to establish a new realism based on contemporary life. His *Burial at Ornans* 1850 (Louvre, Paris), showing ordinary working people gathered round a village grave, shocked the public and the critics with its 'vulgarity'.

courgette small variety of marrow, *Cucurbita pepo*, of the Cucurbitaceae family. It is cultivated as a vegetable and harvested before it is fully mature, at 15–20 cm/6–8 in. In the USA and Canada it is known as a zucchini.

Court Margaret (born Smith) 1942– . Australian tennis player. The most prolific winner in the women's game, she won a record 64 Grand Slam titles, including 25 at singles. She was the first from her country to win the ladies title at Wimbledon 1963 and the second woman after Maureen Connolly to complete the Grand Slam 1970.

court martial court convened for the trial of persons subject to military discipline who are accused of violations of military laws. British courts martial are governed by the code of the service concerned – Naval Discipline, Army, or Air Force acts – and in 1951 an appeal court was established for all three services by the Courts Martial (Appeals) Act.

Cousteau Jacques Yves 1910– . French oceanographer, known for his researches in command of the *Calypso* from 1951, his film and television documentaries, and his many books; he pioneered the invention of the aqualung 1943 and techniques in underwater filming. He is a popular and active environmentalist.

Covenanter in Scottish history, one of the Presbyterian Christians who swore to uphold their forms of worship in a National Covenant, signed 28 Feb 1638, when Charles I attempted to introduce a liturgy on the English model into Scotland.

Coventry industrial city in West Midlands, England; population (1981) 313,800. Manufacturing includes cars, electronic equipment, machine tools, and agricultural machinery. The city originated when Leofric, Earl of Mercia and husband of Lady Godiva, founded a priory here 1043. It was severely bombed in World War II. The cathedral, designed by Basil Spence, incorporates the steeple of the church destroyed in an air raid.

Coward Noël 1899–1973. English playwright, actor, producer, director, and composer, who epitomized the witty and sophisticated man of the theatre. From his first success with *The Young Idea* 1923, he wrote and appeared in plays and comedies on both sides of the Atlantic such as *Hay Fever* 1925, *Private Lives* 1930 with Gertrude Lawrence, *Design for Living* 1933, and *Blithe Spirit* 1941.

cow parsley or *keck* tall perennial plant, *Anthriscus sylvestris*, of the carrot family. It grows in Europe, N Asia, and N Africa. Up to 1 m/3 ft tall, with pinnate leaves, hollow furrowed stems, and heads of white flowers, it is widespread in hedgerows and shady places.

Cowper William 1731–1800. English poet. He trained as a lawyer, but suffered a mental breakdown 1763 and entered an asylum, where he underwent an evangelical conversion. He later wrote hymns (including 'God Moves in a Mysterious Way'). His verse includes the six books of *The Task* 1785.

cowrie marine snail of the family Cypreidae, in which the interior spiral form is concealed by a double outer lip. The shells are hard, shiny, and often coloured. Most cowries are shallow-water forms, and are found in many parts of the world, particularly the tropical Indo-Pacific. Cowries have been used as ornaments and fertility charms, and also as currency, for example the Pacific money cowrie *Cypraea moneta*.

cowslip European plant *Primula veris* of the same genus as the primrose and belonging to the family Primulaceae, with yellow flowers. It is native to temperate regions of the Old World. The oxlip *P. elatior* is closely related to the cowslip.

coyote wild dog *Canis latrans*, in appearance like a small wolf, living from Alaska to Central America and east to New York. Its head and body are about 90 cm/3 ft long and brown, flecked with grey or black. Coyotes live in open country and can run at 65 kph/40 mph. Their main foods are rabbits and rodents. Although persecuted by humans for over a century, the species is very successful.

coypu South American water rodent *Myocastor coypus*, about 60 cm/2 ft long and weighing up to 9 kg/20 lb. It has a scaly, ratlike tail, webbed hind feet, a blunt-muzzled head, and large orange incisors. The fur is reddish brown. It feeds on vegetation, and lives in burrows in rivers and lake banks.

CPU in computing, abbreviation for ▷central processing unit.

CPVE (abbreviation for *Certificate of Pre-Vocational Education*) in the UK, educational qualification introduced 1986 for students over 16 in schools and colleges who want a one-year course of preparation for work or further vocational study.

crab any decapod (ten-legged) crustacean of the division Brachyura, with a broad, rather round, upper body shell (carapace) and a small ▷abdomen tucked beneath the body. Crabs are related to lobsters and crayfish. Mainly marine, some crabs live in fresh water or on land. They are alert carnivores and scavengers. They have a typical sideways walk, and strong pincers on the first pair of legs, the other four pairs being used for walking. Periodically, the outer shell is cast to allow for growth. The European shore crab *Carcinus maenas*, common on British shores between the tidemarks, is dull green, and grows to 4 cm/1.5 in or more. The edible crab *Cancer pagurus* grows to 14 cm/5.5 in long or more, lives down to 100 m/325 ft, and is extensively fished. The name 'crab' is sometimes used for similar arthropods, such as the horseshoe crab, which is neither a true crab nor a crustacean.

crab apple any of 25 species of wild ▷apple trees (genus *Malus*), native to temperate regions of the northern hemisphere. Numerous varieties of cultivated apples have been derived from *M. pumila*, the common native crab apple of SE Europe and central Asia. The fruit of native species is smaller and more bitter than that of cultivated varieties and used in crab-apple jelly.

Crabbe George 1754–1832. English poet. Originally a doctor, he became a cleric 1781, and wrote grimly realistic verse on the poor of his own time: *The Village* 1783, *The Parish Register* 1807, *The Borough* 1810 (which includes the story used in Benjamin Britten's opera *Peter Grimes*), and *Tales of the Hall* 1819.

Crab nebula cloud of gas 6,000 light years from Earth, in the constellation Taurus. It is the remains of a star that exploded as a ▷supernova (observed as a brilliant point of light on Earth 1054). At its centre is a ▷pulsar that flashes 30 times a second. The name comes from its crablike shape.

Cracow alternative form of ▷Kraków, Polish city.

Craig Edward Gordon 1872–1966. British director and stage designer. His innovations and theories on stage design and lighting effects, expounded in *On the Art of the Theatre* 1911, had a profound influence on stage production in Europe and the USA.

Craig James 1871–1940. Ulster Unionist politician, the first prime minister of Northern Ireland 1921–40. Craig became a member of Parliament 1906, and was a highly effective organizer of Unionist resistance to Home Rule. As prime minister he carried out systematic discrimination against the Catholic minority, abolishing proportional representation 1929 and redrawing constituency boundaries to ensure Protestant majorities.

crake any of several small birds related to the ⬦corncrake.

Cranach Lucas 1472–1553. German painter, etcher, and woodcut artist, a leading light in the German Renaissance. He painted many full-length nudes and precise and polished portraits, such as *Martin Luther* 1521 (Uffizi, Florence).

cranberry any of several trailing evergreen plants of the genus *Vaccinium* in the heath family Ericaceae, allied to bilberries and blueberries. They grow in marshy places and bear small, acid, crimson berries, high in vitamin C, used for making sauce and jelly.

crane in zoology, a large, wading bird of the family Gruidae, with long legs and neck, and powerful wings. Cranes are marsh- and plains-dwelling birds, feeding on plants as well as insects and small animals. They fly well and are usually migratory. Their courtship includes frenzied, leaping dances. They are found in all parts of the world except South America. The common crane *Grus grus* is still common in many parts of Europe, and winters in Africa and India. It stands over 1 m/3 ft high.

crane fly or *daddy-longlegs* any fly of the family Tipulidae, with long, slender, fragile legs. They look like giant mosquitoes, but the adults are quite harmless. The larvae live in soil or water. Some species, for example the common crane fly *Tipula paludosa*, have soil-living larvae known as leatherjackets, which cause crop damage by eating roots.

cranesbill any plant of the genus *Geranium*, which contains about 400 species. The plants are named after the long, beaklike protrusion attached to the seed vessels. When ripe, this splits into coiling spirals, which jerk the seeds out, assisting in their distribution.

Cranmer Thomas 1489–1556. English cleric, archbishop of Canterbury from 1533. A Protestant convert, he helped to shape the doctrines of the Church of England under Edward VI. He was responsible for the issue of the Prayer Books of 1549 and 1552, and supported the succession of Lady Jane Grey 1553. Cranmer suggested 1529 that the question of Henry VIII's marriage to Catherine of Aragon should be referred to the universities of Europe rather than to the pope, and in 1533 he declared it null and void.

Crassus Marcus Licinius *c.* 108–53 BC. Roman general who crushed the ⬦Spartacus uprising 71 BC. In 60 BC he joined with Caesar and Pompey in the First Triumvirate and obtained command in the east

55 BC. Invading Mesopotamia, he was defeated by the Parthians at the battle of Carrhae, captured, and put to death.

crater bowl-shaped depression, usually round and with steep sides. Craters are formed by explosive events such as the eruption of a volcano or by the impact of a meteorite. A caldera is a much larger feature.

Crawford Joan. Stage name of Lucille Le Seur 1908–1977. US film actress who became a star with her performance as a 'flapper' in *Our Darling Daughter* 1928. Later she appeared as a sultry, often suffering, mature woman. Her films include *Mildred Pierce* 1945 (for which she won an Academy Award), *Password* 1947, and *Whatever Happened to Baby Jane?* 1962.

crayfish freshwater decapod (ten-limbed) crustacean belonging to several families structurally similar to, but smaller than, the lobster. Crayfish are brownish-green scavengers and are found in all parts of the world except Africa. They are edible, and some species are farmed. The common crayfish *Astacus pallipes*, up to 10 cm/4 in long, is found in rivers in chalky areas of Britain.

Crazy Horse 1849–1877. Sioux Indian chief, one of the Indian leaders at the massacre of Little Bighorn. He was killed when captured.

Crécy, Battle of first major battle of the Hundred Years' War 1346. Philip VI of France was defeated by Edward III of England at the village of Crécy-en-Ponthieu, now in Somme *département*, France, 18 km/11 mi NE of Abbeville.

creed in general, any system of belief; in the Christian church the verbal confessions of faith expressing the accepted doctrines of the church. The different forms are the Apostles' Creed, the ⬦Nicene Creed, and the Athanasian Creed. The only creed recognized by the Orthodox Church is the Nicene Creed.

creeper any small, short-legged passerine bird of the family Certhidae, found in temperate regions of the northern hemisphere. They spiral with a mouse-like movement up tree trunks, searching for insects and larvae with their thin, down-curved beaks.

cremation disposal of the dead by burning. The custom was universal among ancient Indo-European peoples, for example, the Greeks, Romans, and Teutons. It was discontinued among Christians until the late 19th century because of their belief in the bodily resurrection of the dead. Overcrowded urban cemeteries gave rise to its revival in the West. It has remained the usual method of disposal in the East. In the UK, the first crematorium was opened 1885 in Woking, Surrey.

Creole in the West Indies and Spanish America, originally someone of European descent born in the New World; later someone of mixed European and African descent. In Louisiana and other states on the Gulf of Mexico, it applies either to someone of French or Spanish descent or (popularly) to someone of mixed French or Spanish and African descent.

creole language any ⟳pidgin language that has ceased to be simply a trade jargon in ports and markets and has become the mother tongue of a particular community. Many creoles have developed into distinct languages with literatures of their own; for example, Jamaican Creole, Haitian Creole, Krio in Sierra Leone, and Tok Pisin, now the official language of Papua New Guinea.

cress any of several plants of the Cruciferae family, characterized by a pungent taste. The common European garden cress *Lepidium sativum* is cultivated worldwide. The young plants are grown along with white mustard to be eaten while in the seed-leaf stage as 'mustard and cress'.

Cretaceous period of geological time 144–65 million years ago. It is the last period of the Mesozoic era, during which angiosperm (seed-bearing) plants evolved, and dinosaurs and other reptiles reached a peak before almost complete extinction at the end of the period. Chalk is a typical rock type of the second half of the period.

Crete (Greek *Kríti*) largest Greek island in the E Mediterranean Sea, 100 km/62 mi SE of mainland Greece; *area* 8,378 sq km/3,234 sq mi; *capital* Khaniá (Canea); *towns* Iraklion (Heraklion), Rethymnon, Aghios Nikolaos; *products* citrus fruit, olives, wine; *population* (1991) 536,900; *language* Cretan dialect of Greek; *history* it has remains of the ⟳Minoan civilization 3000–1400 BC (see ⟳Knossos) and was successively under Roman, Byzantine, Venetian, and Turkish rule. The island was annexed by Greece 1913.

Crick Francis 1916– . British molecular biologist. From 1949 he researched the molecular structure of DNA, and the means whereby characteristics are transmitted from one generation to another. For this work he was awarded a Nobel prize (with Maurice ⟳Wilkins and James ⟳Watson) 1962.

cricket bat-and-ball game between two teams of 11 players each. It is played with a small solid ball and long flat-sided wooden bats, on a round or oval field, at the centre of which is a finely mown pitch, 20 m/22 yd long. At each end of the pitch is a wicket made up of three upright wooden sticks (stumps), surmounted by two smaller sticks (bails). The object of the game is to score more runs than the opposing team. A run is normally scored by the batsman striking the ball and exchanging ends with his or her partner until the ball is returned by a fielder, or by hitting the ball to the boundary line for an automatic four or six runs.

County cricket has been played since 1873. Test matches have been played since 1877 between member countries of the Commonwealth, where the game has its greatest popularity: Australia, India, New Zealand, Pakistan, England, Sri Lanka, and the West Indies. Test matches last five days, but otherwise the majority of matches last one, three, or four days.

cricket in zoology, an insect belonging to any of various families, especially the Grillidae, of the order Orthoptera. Crickets are related to grasshoppers. They have somewhat flattened bodies and long antennae. The males make a chirping noise by rubbing together special areas on the forewings. The females have a long needlelike egglaying organ (ovipositor). There are some 900 species known worldwide.

Crimea northern peninsula on the Black Sea, an autonomous republic of ⟳Ukraine; formerly a region (1954–91); *area* 27,000 sq km/10,425 sq mi; *capital* Simferopol; *towns* Sevastopol, Yalta; *features* mainly steppe, but southern coast is a holiday resort; *products* iron, oil; *population* 2.5 million (70% Russian, despite return of 150,000 Tatars since 1989); *recent history* under Turkish rule 1475–1774; a subsequent brief independence was ended by Russian annexation 1783. Crimea was the republic of Taurida 1917–20 and the Crimean Autonomous Soviet Republic from 1920 until occupied by Germany 1942–1944. It was then reduced to a region, its Tatar people being deported to Uzbekistan for collaboration. A drift back to their former homeland began 1987 and a federal ruling 1988 confirmed their right to residency. In a referendum 1991, citizens of the Crimean peninsula voted overwhelmingly in favour of restoring Crimea as an autonomous republic independent of the Ukraine. In Feb 1991, the Ukrainian Supreme Soviet voted to restore to the Crimea the status of an autonomous Soviet socialist republic within the Ukraine. In Sept 1991, Crimea declared its independence but this was not recognized by Ukraine.

Crimean War war 1853–56 between Russia and the allied powers of England, France, Turkey, and Sardinia. The war arose from British and French mistrust of Russia's ambitions in the Balkans. It began with an allied Anglo-French expedition to the Crimea to attack the Russian Black Sea city of Sevastopol. The battles of the river Alma, Balaclava (including the Charge of the Light Brigade), and Inkerman 1854 led to a siege which, owing to military mismanagement, lasted for a year until Sept 1855. The war was ended by the Treaty of Paris 1856. The scandal surrounding French and British losses through disease led to the organization of proper military nursing services by Florence Nightingale.

Criminal Investigation Department (CID) detective branch of the London Metropolitan Police, established 1878, comprising a force of about 4,000 men and women recruited entirely from the uniformed police and controlled by an assistant commissioner. In London, some 1,000 of the detectives are stationed at New Scotland Yard. Developed outside London in the later 19th century, criminal investigation departments now exist in all UK forces.

criminal law body of law that defines the public wrongs (crimes) that are punishable by the state and establishes methods of prosecution and punishment. It is distinct from ◊civil law, which deals with legal relationships between individuals (including organizations), such as contract law.

Crippen Hawley Harvey 1861–1910. US murderer of his wife, variety artist Belle Elmore. He buried her remains in the cellar of his London home and tried to escape to the USA with his mistress Ethel le Neve (dressed as a boy). He was arrested on board ship following a radio message, the first criminal captured 'by radio', and was hanged.

critical mass in nuclear physics, the minimum mass of fissile material that can undergo a continuous ◊chain reaction. Below this mass, too many ◊neutrons escape from the surface for a chain reaction to carry on; above the critical mass, the reaction may accelerate into a nuclear explosion.

Croatia Republic of; country in S Europe, on the Adriatic Sea, bordered N by Slovenia and Hungary, and E and S by Yugoslavia; **area** 56,500 sq km/ 21,809 sq mi; **capital** Zagreb; **physical** mountainous, with part of Karst region and Julian and Styrian Alps; some marshland; Adriatic coastline with large islands; **head of state** Franjo Tudjman from 1990; **head of government** Franjo Greguric from 1991; **political system** emergent democracy; **products** cereals, potatoes, tobacco, fruit, livestock, metal goods, textiles; **population** (1985) 4,660,000 (including Croats 75%, Serbs 11%, Hungarians 0.5%); **recent history** became part of Kingdom of Serbs, Croats, and Slovenes 1918; when kingdom became Yugoslavia 1929 Croatia continued its campaign for autonomy. Became a Nazi puppet state following German invasion 1941.

Made a constituent republic within Yugoslav Socialist Federal Republic 1945. Separatist demands resurfaced in 1970s. Formation of opposition parties permitted 1989. Communists defeated 1990 in first free election since 1938. 'Sovereignty' declared and new constitution adopted 1990. Assembly called for Croatia's secession 1991; independence declared. Military conflict with Serbia and internal civil war which intensified through 1991. Croatia formally seceded from Yugoslavia Oct 1991. United Nations peace plan accord reached at Sarajevo; Croatia's independence recognized by European Community 1992.

Crockett Davy 1786–1836. US folk hero, born in Tennessee, a Democratic Congressman 1827–31 and 1833–35. A series of books, of which he may have been part-author, made him into a mythical hero of the frontier, but their Whig associations cost him his office. He died in the battle of the ◊Alamo during the War of Texan Independence.

crocodile large aquatic carnivorous reptile of the family Crocodiliae, found throughout the tropics. Crocodiles are related to alligators and caymans, but distinguished from them by a more pointed snout and a notch in the upper jaw into which the fourth tooth in the lower jaw fits. Crocodiles can grow up to 6 m/20 ft, and have long, powerful tails that propel them when swimming. They can live up to 100 years.

crocus any plant of the genus *Crocus* of the iris family Iridaceae, native to northern parts of the Old World, especially S Europe and Asia Minor. It has single yellow, purple, or white flowers and narrow, pointed leaves.

croft small farm in the Highlands of Scotland, traditionally farming common land cooperatively; the 1886 Crofters Act gave security of tenure to crofters. Today, although grazing land is still shared, arable land is typically enclosed.

Cro-Magnon prehistoric human *Homo sapiens sapiens* believed to be ancestral to Europeans, the first skeletons of which were found 1868 in the Cro-Magnon cave near Les Eyzies, in the Dordogne region of France. They are thought to have superseded the Neanderthals in the Middle East, Africa, Europe, and Asia about 40,000 years ago. Although modern in skeletal form, they were more robust in build than some present-day humans. They hunted bison, reindeer, and horses, and are associated with Upper Palaeolithic cultures, which produced fine flint and bone tools, jewellery, and naturalistic cave paintings.

Crome John 1768–1821. British landscape painter, founder of the *Norwich school* with John Sell Cotman 1803. His works include *The Poringland Oak* 1818 (Tate Gallery, London), showing Dutch influence.

Cromwell Oliver 1599–1658. English general and politician, Puritan leader of the Parliamentary side in the ⟡Civil War. He raised cavalry forces (later called *Ironsides*) which aided the victories at Edgehill 1642 and ⟡Marston Moor 1644, and organized the New Model Army, which he led (with General Fairfax) to victory at Naseby 1645. He declared Britain a republic ('the Commonwealth') 1649, following the execution of Charles I. As Lord Protector (ruler) from 1653, Cromwell established religious toleration and raised Britain's prestige in Europe on the basis of an alliance with France against Spain.

Cromwell Richard 1626–1712. Son of Oliver Cromwell, he succeeded his father as Lord Protector but resigned May 1659, having been forced to abdicate by the army. He lived in exile after the Restoration until 1680, when he returned.

Cromwell Thomas, Earl of Essex *c.* 1485–1540. English politician who drafted the legislation making the Church of England independent of Rome. Originally in Lord Chancellor Wolsey's service, he became secretary to Henry VIII 1534 and the real director of government policy; he was executed for treason.

Cronus or *Kronos* (Roman Saturn) in Greek mythology, youngest of the ⟡Titans who overthrew his father Uranus to become ruler of the world. He devoured his children by his sister Rhea (Cybele) to prevent fulfilment of Uranus' prophesy that he too would be supplanted by his child. Rhea concealed her youngest son, Zeus, who grew up in secrecy and defeated his father as predicted.

crop circle or *corn circle* circular area of flattened grain found in fields especially in SE England, with increasing frequency every summer since 1980. More than 1,000 such formations were reported in the UK 1991. The cause is unknown; suggested explanations range from stationary whirlwinds to the work of pranksters or even alien intelligence.

Crosby Bing (Harry Lillis) 1904–1977. US film actor and singer who achieved world success with his distinctive style of crooning in such songs as 'Pennies from Heaven' 1936 (featured in a film of the same name) and 'White Christmas' 1942. He won an acting Oscar for *Going My Way* 1944, and made a series of film comedies with Dorothy Lamour and Bob Hope, the last being *Road to Hong Kong* 1962.

cross symbol of the Christian religion, in widespread use since the 3rd century. It is a symbol of the crucifixion of Jesus with the central significance of his suffering, death, and resurrection. The Latin cross is the most commonly used; other types are the Greek cross (all four arms of equal length), St Anthony's cross (in the shape of the Greek letter tau, T), and St Andrew's cross (diagonal). Symbolic crosses were used by pre-Christian cultures, for example the ancient Egyptian ankh (St Anthony's cross with a loop at the top), symbol of life, and the swastika, used by Hindus, Buddhists, Celts, and N American Indians before it was adopted by the Nazis.

crossbill species of bird, a ⟡finch of the genus *Loxia*, in which the hooked tips of the upper and lower beak cross one another, an adaptation for extracting the seeds from conifer cones. The red or common crossbill *Loxia curvirostra* is found in parts of Eurasia and North America.

crow any of 35 species of the genus *Corvus*, family Corvidae, which also includes jays and magpies. Ravens belong to the same genus as crows. Crows are usually about 45 cm/1.5 ft long, black, with a strong bill feathered at the base, and omnivorous with a bias towards animal food. They are considered to be very intelligent.

crown colony any British colony that is under the direct legislative control of the crown and does not possess its own system of representative government. Crown colonies are administered by a crown-appointed governor or by elected or nominated legislative and executive councils with an official majority. Usually the crown retains rights of veto and of direct legislation by orders in council.

crucifixion death by fastening to a cross, a form of capital punishment used by the ancient Romans, Persians, and Carthaginians, and abolished by the Roman emperor Constantine. Specifically, *the Crucifixion* refers to the execution by the Romans of ⟡Jesus in this manner.

Cruft Charles 1852–1938. British dog expert. He organized his first dog show 1886, and from that year annual shows bearing his name were held in Islington, London. In 1948 the show's venue moved to Olympia and in 1979 to Earl's Court.

crusade European war against non-Christians and heretics, sanctioned by the pope; in particular, the Crusades, a series of wars 1096–1291 undertaken by European rulers to recover Palestine from the Muslims. Motivated by religious zeal, the desire for land, and the trading ambitions of the major Italian cities, the Crusades were varied in their aims and effects.

crustacean one of the class of arthropods that includes crabs, lobsters, shrimps, woodlice, and barnacles. The external skeleton is made of protein and chitin hardened with lime. Each segment bears a pair of appendages that may be modified as sensory feelers (antennae), as mouthparts, or as swimming, walking, or grasping structures.

cryogenics science of very low temperatures (approaching ⟡absolute zero), including the production of very low temperatures and the exploitation of special properties associated with them, such as the disappearance of electrical resistance (⟡superconductivity).

crystal substance with an orderly three-dimensional arrangement of its atoms or molecules, thereby creating an external surface of clearly defined smooth faces having characteristic angles between them. Examples are table salt and quartz.

CSCE abbreviation for ▷*Conference on Security and Cooperation in Europe*.

CSE (abbreviation for *Certificate of Secondary Education*) in the UK, the examinations taken by the majority of secondary school pupils who were not regarded as academically capable of GCE ▷O level, until the introduction of the common secondary examination system, ▷GCSE, 1988.

Cuba Republic of; island in the Caribbean, the largest of the West Indies, off the S coast of Florida; *area* 110,860 sq km/42,820 sq mi; *capital* Havana; *physical* comprises Cuba and smaller islands including Isle of Youth; low hills; Sierra Maestra mountains in SE; Cuba has deep bays, sandy beaches, coral islands and reefs; *head of state and government* Fidel Castro Ruz from 1959; *political system* communist republic; *exports* sugar, tobacco, coffee, nickel, fish; *population* (1990 est) 10,582,000 (37% are white of Spanish descent, 51% mulatto, and 11% are of African origin); *language* Spanish; *recent history* independence was achieved from Spain 1901. Cuba became a communist state under Fidel Castro. With Soviet help, the country made considerable economic and social progress, also becoming involved in international commitments (Angola, Argentina). Overseas military interventions were reduced 1989; Castro reaffirmed communist orthodoxy. Kremlin announced withdrawal of all Soviet troops 1991.

Cubism revolutionary movement in early 20th-century painting, pioneering abstract art. Its founders, Georges Braque and Pablo Picasso, were admirers of Paul Cézanne and were inspired by his attempt to create a structure on the surface of the canvas. About 1907–10 in France the Cubists began to 'abstract' images from nature, gradually releasing themselves from the imitation of reality. Cubism announced that a work of art exists in its own right rather than as a representation of the real world, and it attracted such artists as Juan Gris, Fernand Léger, and Robert Delaunay.

Cuchulain in Celtic mythology, a legendary hero, the chief figure in a cycle of Irish legends. He is associated with his uncle Conchobar, king of Ulster; his most famous exploits are described in *Taín Bó Cuailnge/The Cattle Raid of Cuchulain*.

cuckoo species of bird, any of about 200 members of the family Cuculidae, especially the Eurasian cuckoo *Cuculus canorus*, whose name derives from its characteristic call. Somewhat hawklike, it is about 33 cm/1.1 ft long, bluish-grey and barred beneath (females sometimes reddish), and has a long, typically rounded tail. It is a 'brood parasite', laying its eggs singly, at intervals of about 48 hours, in the nests of small insectivorous birds. As soon as the young cuckoo hatches, it ejects all other young birds or eggs from the nest and is tended by its 'foster parents' until fledging.

cuckoo flower or *lady's smock* perennial plant *Cardamine pratensis*, family Cruciferae. Native to Britain, it is common in damp meadows and marshy woods. It bears pale lilac flowers, which later turn white, from April to June.

cuckoo-pint or *lords-and-ladies* perennial plant *Arum maculatum* of the Araceae family. The large arrow-shaped leaves appear in early spring, and the flower-bearing stalks are enveloped by a bract, or spathe. In late summer the bright red, berrylike fruits, which are poisonous, make their appearance.

cucumber trailing annual plant *Cucumis sativus* of the gourd family Cucurbitaceae, producing long, green-skinned fruit with crisp, translucent, edible flesh. Small cucumbers, called gherkins, usually the fruit of *C. anguria*, are often pickled.

Culloden, Battle of defeat 1746 of the ▷Jacobite rebel army of the British prince ▷Charles Edward Stuart by the Duke of Cumberland on a stretch of moorland in Inverness-shire, Scotland. This battle effectively ended the military challenge of the Jacobite rebellion.

Cultural Revolution mass movement begun by Chinese Communist Party chair Mao Zedong 1966–69, directed against the upper middle class – bureaucrats, artists, and academics who were killed, imprisoned, humiliated, or 'resettled'. Intended to 'purify' Chinese communism, it was also an attempt by Mao to renew his political and ideological pre-eminence inside China. The resulting bureaucratic and economic chaos had many long-term effects.

culture in sociology and anthropology, the way of life of a particular society or group of people, including patterns of thought, beliefs, behaviour, customs, traditions, rituals, dress, and language, as well as art, music, and literature. Sociologists and anthropologists use culture as a key concept in describing and analysing human societies.

Cumbria county in NW England; *area* 6,810 sq km/2,629 sq mi; *towns* Carlisle (administrative headquarters), Barrow, Kendal, Whitehaven, Workington, Penrith; *physical* Lake District National Park, including Scafell Pike 978 m/3,210 ft, highest mountain in England; Helvellyn 950 m/3,118 ft; Lake Windermere, the largest lake in England, 17 km/10.5 mi long, 1.6 km/1 mi wide; other lakes include Derwentwater and Ullswater; Furness peninsula; *features* nearby Grizedale Forest sculpture project; atomic stations at Calder Hall and Sellafield (reprocessing plant), formerly Windscale; *products* the traditional coal, iron, and steel industries of the coast towns have been replaced by newer industries including chemicals, plastics, and electronics; in the north and east there is dairying, and West Cumberland Farmers is the country's largest agricultural cooperative; *population* (1991) 486,900.

cumin seedlike fruit of the herb *Cuminum*

cyminum of the carrot family Umbelliferae, with a bitter flavour. It is used as a spice in cooking.

cuneiform ancient writing system formed of combinations of wedge-shaped strokes, usually impressed on clay. It was probably invented by the Sumerians, and was in use in Mesopotamia as early as the middle of the 4th millennium BC.

Cunene or *Kunene* river rising near Nova Lisboa in W central Angola. It flows S to the frontier with Namibia, then W to the Atlantic; length 250 km/ 150 mi.

Cupid in Roman mythology, the god of love, identified with the Greek god ⟩Eros. The son of Aphrodite and Ares, Cupid is often represented as a chubby, winged child carrying a bow and arrow with which to pierce the hearts of mortals. He is also represented as a handsome youth.

cupronickel copper alloy (75% copper and 25% nickel), used in hardware products and for coinage. In the UK in 1946, it was substituted for the 'silver' (50% silver, 40% copper, 5% nickel and 5% zinc) previously used in coins.

Curaçao island in the West Indies, one of the ⟩Netherlands Antilles; area 444 sq km/171 sq mi; population (1988) 148,500. The principal industry, dating from 1918, is the refining of Venezuelan petroleum. Curaçao was colonized by Spain 1527, annexed by the Dutch West India Company 1634, and gave its name from 1924 to the group of islands renamed Netherlands Antilles in 1948. Its capital is the port of Willemstad.

curare black, resinous poison extracted from the bark and juices of various South American trees and plants. Originally used on arrowheads by Amazonian hunters to paralyse prey, it blocks nerve stimulation of the muscles. Alkaloid derivatives (called curarines) are used in medicine as muscle relaxants during surgery.

Curie Marie (born Sklodovska) 1867–1934. Polish scientist. In 1898 she reported the possible existence of a new, powerfully radioactive element in pitchblende ores. Her husband, Pierre (1859–1906) abandoned his own researches to assist her, and in the same year they announced the existence of polonium and radium. They isolated the pure elements 1902. Both scientists refused to take out a patent on their discovery and were jointly awarded the Davy Medal 1903 and the Nobel Prize for Physics 1903, with Antoine ⟩Becquerel. Marie Curie wrote a *Treatise on Radioactivity* 1910, and was awarded the Nobel Prize for Chemistry 1911.

curium synthesized, radioactive, metallic element of the actinide series, symbol Cm, atomic number 96, relative atomic mass 247. It is produced by bombarding plutonium or americium with neutrons. Its longest-lived isotope has a half-life of 1.7 x 10^7 years. Curium is used to generate heat and power in satellites or in remote places. It was first synthesized 1944, and named after Pierre and Marie

Curie.

curlew wading bird of the genus Numenius of the sandpiper family, Scolopacidae. The curlew is between 36 cm/14 in and 55 cm/1.8 ft in length, and has mottled brown plumage, long legs, and a long, thin, downcurved bill. Several species live in N Europe, Asia, and North America. The name derives from its haunting flutelike call.

currant berry of a small seedless variety of cultivated grape *Vitis vinifera*. Currants are grown on a large scale in Greece and California and used dried in cooking and baking. Because of the similarity of the fruit, the name currant is also given to several species of shrubs in the genus *Ribes*, family Grossulariaceae. The redcurrant *Ribes rubrum* is a native of S Europe and Asia and occasionally grows wild in Britain. The whitecurrant is a cultivated, less acid variety. The blackcurrant *R. nigrum* is the most widely used for cooking.

current flow of a body of water or air, or of heat, moving in a definite direction. There are three basic types of oceanic current: *drift currents* are broad and slow-moving; *stream currents* are narrow and swift-moving; and *upwelling currents* bring cold, nutrient-rich water from the ocean bottom.

Stream currents include the ⟩Gulf Stream and the ⟩Japan (or Kuroshio) Current. Upwelling currents, such as the Gulf of Guinea Current and the Peru (Humboldt) current, provide food for plankton, which in turn supports fish and sea birds. At approximate five-to-eight-year intervals, the Peru Current that runs from the Antarctic up the west coast of South America, turns warm, with heavy rain and rough seas, and has disastrous results (as in 1982–83) for Peruvian wildlife and for the anchovy industry. The phenomenon is called *El Niño* (Spanish 'the Child') because it occurs towards Christmas.

curry traditional Indian mixture of spices used to flavour a dish of rice, meat, and/or vegetables. Spices include turmeric, fenugreek, cloves, chillies, cumin, cinnamon, ginger, black and cayenne pepper, coriander, and caraway.

Curzon George Nathaniel, 1st Marquess Curzon of Kedleston 1859–1925. British Conservative politician, viceroy of India 1899–1905. During World War I, he was a member of the cabinet 1916–19. As foreign secretary 1919–22, he set up a British protectorate over Persia.

Custer George A(rmstrong) 1839–1876. US Civil War general, the Union's youngest brigadier general as a result of a brilliant war record. Reduced in rank in the regular army at the end of the Civil War, he campaigned against the Sioux from 1874, and was killed with a detachment of his troops by the forces of Sioux chief Sitting Bull in the Battle of Little Bighorn, Montana: also called *Custer's last stand*, 25 June 1876.

Customs and Excise government department

responsible for taxes levied on imports. Excise duties are levied on goods produced domestically or on licences to carry on certain trades (such as sale of wines and spirits) or other activities (theatrical entertainments, betting, and so on) within a country.

cuttlefish any of a family, Sepiidae, of squid-like cephalopods with an internal calcareous shell (cuttlebone). The common cuttle *Sepia officinalis* of the Atlantic and Mediterranean is up to 30 cm/ 1 ft long. It swims actively by means of the fins into which the sides of its oval, flattened body are expanded, and jerks itself backwards by shooting a jet of water from its 'siphon'.

Cuyp Aelbert 1620–1691. Dutch painter of countryside scenes, seascapes, and portraits. His idyllically peaceful landscapes are bathed in golden light; for example, *A Herdsman with Cows by a River* (about 1650, National Gallery, London). His father, *Jacob Gerritsz Cuyp* (1594–1652), was also a landscape and portrait painter.

Cuzco city in S Peru, capital of Cuzco department, in the Andes, over 3,350 m/11,000 ft above sea level and 560 km/350 mi SE of Lima; population (1988) 255,000. It was founded in the 11th century as the ancient capital of the ◊Inca empire and was captured by Francisco Pizarro 1533.

cyanide CN⁻ ion derived from hydrogen cyanide (HCN), and any salt containing this ion (produced when hydrogen cyanide is neutralized by alkalis), such as potassium cyanide (KCN). The principal cyanides are potassium, sodium, calcium, mercury, gold, and copper. Certain cyanides are poisons.

Cybele in Phrygian mythology, an earth goddess, identified by the Greeks with ◊Rhea and honoured in Rome.

cybernetics science concerned with how systems organize, regulate, and reproduce themselves, and also how they evolve and learn. In the laboratory, inanimate objects are created that behave like living systems. Applications range from the creation of electronic artificial limbs to the running of the fully automated factory where decision-making machines operate up to managerial level.

cycad plant of the order Cycadales belonging to the gymnosperms. Some have a superficial resemblance to palms, others to ferns. Their large cones contain fleshy seeds. There are ten genera and about 80–100 species, native to tropical and subtropical countries. The stems of many species yield an edible starchy substance resembling sago. Cycads were widespread during the Mesozoic era.

cyclamen any plant of the genus *Cyclamen* of perennial plants of the primrose family Primulaceae, with heart-shaped leaves and petals that are twisted at the base and bent back. The flowers are usually white or pink, and several species are cultivated.

cycling riding a ◊bicycle for sport, pleasure, or transport. Cycle racing can take place on oval artificial tracks, on the road, or across country (cyclo-cross). *Stage races* are run over gruelling terrain and can last anything from three days to three and a half weeks, as in the Tour de France, Tour of Italy, and Tour of Spain. *Criteriums* are fast, action-packed races around the closed streets of town or city centres. Each race lasts about an hour. *Road races* are run over a prescribed circuit, which the riders will lap several times. Such a race will normally cover a distance of approximately 160 km/100 mi. *Track racing* takes place on a concrete or wooden banked circuit, either indoors or outdoors. In *time trialling* each rider races against the clock, with all the competitors starting at different intervals.

cyclone area of low atmospheric pressure. Cyclones are formed by the mixture of cold, dry polar air with warm, moist equatorial air. These masses of air meet in temperate latitudes; the warm air rises over the cold, resulting in rain.

Cyclops in Greek mythology, one of a legendary nation of giants who lived in Sicily, had one eye in the middle of the forehead, and lived as shepherds; Odysseus fought and overcame them in Homer's *Odyssey*.

cylinder in geometry, a tubular solid figure with a circular base. In everyday use, the term applies to a *right cylinder*, the curved surface of which is at right angles to the base.

cymbal ancient musical instrument of percussion, consisting of a shallow circular brass dish held at the centre; either used in pairs clashed together or singly, struck with a beater. Smaller finger cymbals or *crotala*, used by Debussy and Stockhausen, are more solid and pure in tone. Turkish

cylinder

volume = $\pi r^2 h$

area of curved
surface = $2\pi rh$

total surface area
= $2\pi r(r + h)$

or 'buzz' cymbals have loose rivets to extend the sound.

Cymbeline or *Cunobelin* 1st century AD. King of the Catuvellauni AD 5–40, who fought unsuccessfully against the Roman invasion of Britain. His capital was at Colchester.

Cymru Welsh name for ♢Wales.

Cynewulf early 8th century Anglo-Saxon poet. He is thought to have been a Northumbrian monk and is the undoubted author of 'Juliana' and part of the 'Christ' in the Exeter Book (a collection of poems now in Exeter Cathedral), and of the 'Fates of the Apostles' and 'Elene' in the Vercelli Book (a collection of Old English manuscripts housed in Vercelli, Italy).

Cynic school of Greek philosophy (Cynicism), founded in Athens about 400 BC by Antisthenes, a disciple of Socrates, who advocated a stern and simple morality and a complete disregard of pleasure and comfort. His followers, led by ♢Diogenes, despised all human affection as a source of weakness. Their 'snarling contempt' for ordinary people earned them the name of Cynic (Greek 'doglike').

cypress any coniferous tree or shrub of the genera *Cupressus* and *Chamaecyparis*, family Cupressaceae. There are about 20 species, originating from temperate regions of the northern hemisphere. They have minute, scalelike leaves and small cones made up of woody, wedge-shaped scales and containing an aromatic resin.

Cyprus Greek Republic of (in S), Turkish Republic of Northern Cyprus (in N); island in the Mediterranean, off the S coast of Turkey; *area* 9,251 sq km/3,571 sq mi, 37% in Turkish hands; *capital* Nicosia (divided between Greeks and Turks); *physical* central plain between two E–W mountain ranges; beaches; *heads of state*

and government Georgios Vassilou (Greek) from 1988, Rauf Denktaş (Turkish) from 1976; *political system* democratic divided republic; *exports* citrus, grapes, raisins, Cyprus sherry, potatoes, clothing, footwear; *population* (1990 est) 708,000 (Greek Cypriot 78%, Turkish Cypriot 18%); *languages* Greek and Turkish (official); English; *recent history* independence was achieved from Britain 1960. The Turks set up their own government in N Cyprus; fighting broke out between the Greek and Turkish communities. A UN peacekeeping force was installed 1964. Talks began 1988 on future reunification, under UN auspices. Peace talks were abandoned 1989; a Turkish offer of peace talks 1991 was rejected by Cyprus and Greece.

Cyrano de Bergerac Savinien 1619–1655. French writer. He joined a corps of guards at 19 and performed heroic feats which brought him fame. He is the hero of a classic play by Edmond Rostand, in which his excessively long nose is used as a counterpoint to his chivalrous character.

Cyrenaic member of a school of Greek hedonistic philosophy founded about 400 BC by Aristippus of Cyrene. He regarded pleasure as the only absolutely worthwhile thing in life but taught that self-control and intelligence were necessary to choose the best pleasures.

Cyrus the Great died 529 BC. Founder of the Persian Empire. As king of Persia, he was originally subject to the Medes, whose empire he overthrew 550 BC. He captured Croesus, the king of Lydia, 546, and conquered all Asia Minor, adding Babylonia (including Syria and Palestine) to his empire 539, allowing exiled Jews to return to Jerusalem. He died fighting in Afghanistan.

cystic fibrosis hereditary disease involving defects of various tissues, including the sweat glands, the mucous glands of the bronchi (air passages), and the pancreas. The sufferer experiences repeated chest infections and digestive disorders and generally fails to thrive. In 1989 the gene for cystic fibrosis was identified by teams of researchers in Michigan, USA, and Toronto, Canada. This discovery promises more reliable diagnosis of the disease in babies before birth.

cytoplasm part of the cell outside the ♢nucleus. Strictly speaking, this includes all the ♢organelles (mitochondria, chloroplasts, and so on), but often cytoplasm refers to the jellylike matter in which the organelles are embedded (correctly termed the cytosol).

czar alternative form of ♢*tsar*, an emperor of Russia.

Czechoslovakia Czech and Slovak Federative Republic; country in E central Europe, bordered NE by Poland, E by Ukraine, S by Hungary and Austria, W and NW by Germany; *area* 127,903 sq km/ 49,371 sq mi; *capital* Prague; *physical* Carpathian

Mountains, rivers Morava, Labe (Elbe), Vltava (Moldau); hills and plateau; Danube plain in S; *head of state* Václav Havel from 1989; *head of government* Marián Calfa from 1989 (resigned from Communist Party 1990 but remains premier); *political system* emergent democracy; *exports* machinery, vehicles, timber, ceramics, glass, textiles, lignite, magnesite, mercury; *population* (1990 est) 15,695,000 (Czech 63%, Slovak 31%, with Hungarian, Polish, German, Russian, and other minorities); *languages* Czech and Slovak (official); *recent history* independence was achieved from the Austro-Hungarian Empire 1918. Czechoslovakia was occupied by Germany 1938–45 and the USSR from 1968. The Communist monopoly of power ended in the bloodless revolution of 1989; complete withdrawal of Soviet troops was agreed by May 1991. Bill of rights passed 1991; new parties emerged; Czech and Slovak friction increased from 1991.

dab small marine flatfish of the flounder family, especially the genus *Limanda*. Dabs live in the N Atlantic and around the coasts of Britain and Scandinavia.

Dacca alternative name for ▷Dhaka, capital of Bangladesh.

dace freshwater fish *Leuciscus leuciscus* of the carp family. Common in England and mainland Europe, it is silvery and grows up to 30 cm/1 ft.

Dachau site of a Nazi ▷concentration camp during World War II, in Bavaria, Germany.

dachshund small dog of German origin, bred originally for digging out badgers. It has a long body and short legs. Several varieties are bred: standard size (up to 10 kg/22 lb), miniature (5 kg/11 lb or less), long-haired, smooth-haired, and wire-haired.

Dacia ancient region forming much of modern Romania. The various Dacian tribes were united around 60 BC, and for many years posed a threat to the Roman Empire; they were finally conquered by the Roman emperor Trajan AD 101–06, and the region became a province of the same name. It was abandoned to the invading Goths in about 275.

Dada or *Dadaism* artistic and literary movement founded 1915 in Zürich, Switzerland, by the Romanian poet Tristan Tzara (1896–1963) and others in a spirit of rebellion and disillusionment during World War I. Other Dadaist groups were soon formed by the artists Marcel ▷Duchamp and ▷Man Ray in New York and Francis Picabia in Barcelona. Dada had a considerable impact on early 20th-century art, questioning established artistic rules and values.

daddy-longlegs popular name for a ▷crane fly.

Daedalus in Greek mythology, an Athenian artisan supposed to have constructed for King Minos of Crete the labyrinth in which the ▷Minotaur was imprisoned. When Minos became displeased with him, Daedalus fled from Crete with his son ▷Icarus using wings made by them from feathers fastened with wax.

daffodil any of several Old World species of the genus *Narcissus*, family Amaryllidaceae, distinguished by their trumpet-shaped flowers. The common daffodil of N Europe *N. pseudonarcissus* has large yellow flowers and grows from a large bulb. There are numerous cultivated forms.

Dagestan autonomous republic of S Russia, situated E of the ▷Caucasus, bordering the Caspian Sea; capital Makhachkala; area 50,300 sq km/19,421 sq mi; population (1982) 1,700,000. It is mountainous, with deep valleys, and its numerous ethnic groups speak a variety of distinct languages. Annexed 1723 from Iran, which strongly resisted Russian conquest, it became an autonomous republic in 1921.

Daguerre Louis Jacques Mande 1789–1851. French pioneer of photography. Together with Joseph Niépce, he is credited with the invention of photography (though others were reaching the same point simultaneously). In 1838 he invented the daguerreotype, a single image process superseded ten years later by ▷Talbot's negative/positive process.

Dahl Roald 1916–1990. British writer, known for short stories with a twist, for example, *Tales of the Unexpected* 1979, and for children's books, including *Charlie and the Chocolate Factory* 1964. He also wrote the screenplay for the James Bond film *You Only Live Twice* 1967.

dahlia any perennial plant of the genus *Dahlia*, family Compositae, comprising 20 species and many cultivated forms. Dahlias are stocky plants with showy flowers that come in a wide range of colours. They are native to Mexico and Central America.

Dahomey former name (until 1975) of the People's Republic of ▷Benin.

Dáil Eireann lower house of the legislature of the Republic of Ireland. It consists of 166 members elected by adult suffrage on a basis of proportional representation.

Daimler Gottlieb 1834–1900. German engineer who pioneered the modern car. In 1886 he produced his first motor vehicle and a motor bicycle. He later joined forces with Karl ▷Benz and was one of the pioneers of the high-speed four-stroke petrol engine.

daisy any of numerous species of perennial plants in the family Compositae, especially the field daisy of Europe *Chrysanthemum leucanthemum* and the English common daisy *Bellis perennis*, with a single white or pink flower rising from a rosette of leaves.

Dakar capital and chief port (with artificial harbour) of Senegal; population (1984) 1,000,000. It is an industrial centre, and there is a university, established 1957.

Dakhla port and capital of Western Sahara; population (1982) 17,800. First established as a Spanish trading port 1476, it was known as *Villa Cisneros*.

Dalai Lama 14th incarnation 1935– . Spiritual and temporal head of the Tibetan state until 1959, when he went into exile in protest against Chinese annexation and oppression. Tibetan Buddhists believe that each Dalai Lama is a reincarnation of his predecessor and also of Avalokiteśvara.

Dali Salvador 1904–1989. Spanish painter. In 1928 he collaborated with Luis Buñuel on the film *Un Chien andalou*. In 1929 he joined the Surrealists and became notorious for his flamboyant eccentricity. Influenced by the psychoanalytic theories of Freud, he developed a repertoire of dramatic images, such as the distorted human body, limp watches, and burning giraffes in such pictures as *The Persistence of Memory* 1931 (Museum of Modern Art, New York). They are painted with a meticulous, polished clarity. He also used religious themes and painted many portraits of his wife Gala.

Dallas commercial city in Texas, USA; population (1990) 1,006,900, metropolitan area (with Fort Worth) 3,885,400. Industries include banking, insurance, oil, aviation, aerospace, and electronics. Dallas–Fort Worth Regional Airport (opened 1973) is one of the world's largest. John F ◊Kennedy was assassinated here 1963.

Dalmatian breed of dog, about 60 cm/2 ft tall at the shoulder, white with spots that are black or brown. Dalmatians are born white; the spots appear later.

Dalton John 1766–1844. British chemist who proposed the theory of atoms, which he considered to be the smallest parts of matter. He produced the first list of relative atomic masses in *Absorption of Gases* 1805 and put forward the law of partial pressures of gases (Dalton's law).

dam structure built to hold back water in order to prevent flooding, provide water for irrigation and storage, and to provide hydroelectric power. There are two basic types of dam: the gravity dam, which relies upon the weight of its material to resist the forces imposed upon it, and the arch dam, which uses an arch shape to take the forces in a horizontal direction into the sides of the river valley. Buttress dams are used to hold back very wide rivers or lakes.

Damascus (Arabic *Dimashq*) capital of Syria, on the river Barada, SE of Beirut; population (1981) 1,251,000. It produces silk, wood products, and brass and copper ware. Said to be the oldest continuously inhabited city in the world, Damascus was an ancient city even in Old Testament times; most notable of the old buildings is the Great Mosque, completed as a Christian church in the 5th century.

damson cultivated variety of plum tree *Prunus domestica* var. *institia*, distinguished by its small, oval, edible fruits, which are dark purple or blue to black in colour.

dance rhythmic movement of the body, usually performed in time to music. Its primary purpose may be religious, magical, martial, social, or artistic–the last two being characteristic of non-traditional societies. The pre-Christian era had a strong tradition of ritual dance, and ancient Greek dance still exerts an influence on dance movement today. Although Western folk and social dances have a long history, the Eastern dance tradition long predates the Western. The European Classical tradition dates from the 15th century in Italy, the first printed dance text from 16th-century France, and the first dance school in Paris from the 17th century. The 18th century saw the development of European Classical ballet as we know it today, and the 19th century saw the rise of Romantic ballet. In the 20th century modern dance established itself as a separate dance idiom.

dandelion plant *Taraxacum officinale* belonging to the Compositae family. The stalk rises from a rosette of leaves that are deeply indented like a lion's teeth, hence the name (from French *dent de lion*). The flower heads are bright yellow. The fruit is surmounted by the hairs of the calyx, which constitute the familiar dandelion 'clock'.

Danelaw 11th-century name for the area of N and E England settled by the Vikings in the 9th century. It occupied about half of England, from the river Tees to the river Thames. Within its bounds, Danish law, customs, and language prevailed. Its linguistic influence is still apparent.

Danish language member of the North Germanic group of the Indo-European language family, spoken in Denmark and Greenland and related to Icelandic, Faroese, Norwegian, and Swedish. It has had a particularly strong influence on Norwegian. As one of the languages of the Vikings, who invaded and settled in parts of Britain during the 9th to 11th centuries, Old Danish had a strong influence on English.

Dante Alighieri 1265–1321. Italian poet. His masterpiece *La divina commedia/The Divine Comedy* 1307–21 is an epic account in three parts of his journey through Hell, Purgatory, and Paradise, during which he is guided part of the way by the poet Virgil; on a metaphorical level the journey is also one of Dante's own spiritual development. Other works include the philosophical prose treatise *Convivio/The Banquet* 1306–08, the first major work of its kind to be written in Italian rather than Latin.

Danton Georges Jacques 1759–1794. French revolutionary who organized the uprising 10 Aug 1792 that overthrew Louis XVI and the monarchy, roused the country to expel the Prussian invaders, and in April 1793 formed the revolutionary tribunal and the Committee of Public Safety, of which he was the leader until July of that year. Thereafter he lost power to the ◊Jacobins, and, when he attempted to recover it, was arrested and guillotined.

Danube (German *Donau*) second longest of European rivers, rising on the E slopes of the Black Forest, and flowing 2,858 km/1,776 mi across Europe to enter the Black Sea in Romania by a swampy delta.

Danzig German name for the Polish port of ▷Gdańsk.

Daphne in Greek mythology, a nymph who was changed into a laurel tree to escape from Apollo's amorous pursuit.

Dardanelles (ancient name Hellespont, Turkish name *Canakkale Boğazi*) Turkish strait connecting the Sea of Marmara with the Aegean Sea; its shores are formed by the ▷Gallipoli peninsula on the NW and the mainland of Turkey-in-Asia on the SE. It is 75 km/47 mi long and 5–6 km/3–4 mi wide.

Dar es Salaam chief seaport in Tanzania, on the Indian Ocean, and capital of Tanzania until its replacement by ▷Dodoma in 1974; population (1985) 1,394,000.

Darwin Charles Robert 1809–1882. English scientist who developed the modern theory of ▷evolution and proposed, with Alfred Russel Wallace, the principle of ▷natural selection. After research in South America and the Galápagos Islands as naturalist on HMS *Beagle* 1831–36, Darwin published *On the Origin of Species by Means of Natural Selection or the Preservation of Favoured Races in the Struggle for Life* 1859. This explained the evolutionary process through the principles of natural and sexual selection. It aroused bitter controversy because it disagreed with the literal interpretation of the Book of Genesis in the Bible.

Darwin capital and port in Northern Territory, Australia, in NW Arnhem Land; population (1986) 69,000. It serves the uranium-mining site at Rum Jungle to the south. Destroyed 1974 by a cyclone, the city was rebuilt on the same site.

database structured collection of data. The database makes data available to the various programs that need it, without the need for those programs to be aware of how the data are stored. There are three main types (or 'models'): hierarchical, network, and relational, of which relational is the most widely used. A *free-text database* is one that holds the unstructured text of articles or books in a form that permits rapid searching.

date palm tree of the genus *Phoenix*. The female tree produces the fruit, dates, in bunches weighing 9–11 kg/20–25 lb. Dates are an important source of food in the Middle East, being rich in sugar; they are dried for export. The tree also supplies timber, and materials for baskets, rope, and animal feed.

dating science of determining the age of geological structures, rocks, and fossils, and placing them in the context of geological time. Dating can be carried out by identifying fossils of creatures that lived only at certain times (marker fossils), by looking at the physical relationships of rocks to other rocks of a known age, or by measuring how much of a rock's radioactive elements have changed since the rock was formed, using the process of radiometric dating.

Daumier Honoré 1808–1879. French artist. His sharply dramatic and satirical cartoons dissected Parisian society. He produced over 4,000 lithographs and, mainly after 1860, powerful satirical oil paintings that were little appreciated in his lifetime.

dauphin title of the eldest son of the kings of France, derived from the personal name of a count, whose lands, the *Dauphiné*, traditionally passed to the heir to the throne from 1349 to 1830.

David *c.* 1060–970 BC. Second king of Israel. According to the Old Testament he played the harp for King Saul to banish Saul's melancholy; he later slew the Philistine giant Goliath with a sling and stone. After Saul's death David was anointed king at Hebron, took Jerusalem, and made it his capital.

David Jacques Louis 1748–1825. French painter in the Neo-Classical style. He was an active supporter of and unofficial painter to the republic during the French Revolution, for which he was imprisoned 1794–95. In his *Death of Marat* 1793, he turned political murder into a Classical tragedy. Later he devoted himself to the empire in paintings such as the enormous, pompous *Coronation of Napoleon* 1805–07 (Louvre, Paris).

David I 1084–1153. King of Scotland from 1124. The youngest son of Malcolm III Canmore and S ▷Margaret, he was brought up in the English court of Henry I, and in 1113 married ▷Matilda, widow o the 1st earl of Northampton. He invaded England 1138 in support of Queen Matilda, but was defeated at Northallerton in the Battle of the Standard, and again 1141.

David II 1324–1371. King of Scotland from 1329 son of ▷Robert I (the Bruce). David was married a the age of four to Joanna, daughter of Edward II o England. In 1346 David invaded England, was captured at the battle of Neville's Cross and imprisoned for 11 years.

David, St or *Dewi* 5th–6th century. Patron sain of Wales, Christian abbot and bishop. According t legend he was the son of a prince of Dyfed and uncl of King Arthur; he was responsible for the adoption of the leek as the national emblem of Wales, but his own emblem is a dove. Feast day 1 March.

da Vinci see ▷Leonardo da Vinci, Italian Renaissance artist.

Davis Bette 1908–1989. US actress. She entered films in 1930, and established a reputation as a forceful dramatic actress with *Of Human Bondage* 1934. Later films included *Dangerous* 1935 and *Jezebel* 1938, both winning her Academy Awards *All About Eve*, which won the 1950 Academy Award for best picture, and *Whatever Happened to Baby Jane?* 1962.

Davis Jefferson 1808–1889. US politician, president of the short-lived Confederate States of America 1861–65. He was a leader of the Southern Democrats in the US Senate from 1857, and a defender of 'humane' slavery; in 1860 he issued a declaration in favour of secession from the USA. During the Civil War he assumed strong political leadership, but often disagreed with military policy.

Davis Miles (Dewey, Jr) 1926–1991. US jazz trumpeter, composer, and bandleader. He recorded bebop with Charlie Parker 1945, pioneered cool jazz in the 1950s and jazz-rock fusion beginning in the late 1960s. His albums include *Birth of the Cool* 1957 (recorded 1949 and 1950), *Sketches of Spain* 1959, and *Bitches' Brew* 1970.

Davis Steve 1957– . English snooker player who has won every major honour in the game since turning professional 1978. He has been world champion six times.

Davy Humphry 1778–1829. English chemist. He discovered, by electrolysis, the metallic elements sodium and potassium in 1807, and calcium, boron, magnesium, strontium, and barium in 1808. In addition, he established that chlorine is an element and proposed that hydrogen is present in all acids. He invented the 'safety lamp' for use in mines where methane was present, enabling miners to work in previously unsafe conditions.

Day Lewis Cecil 1904–1972. Irish poet, British poet laureate 1968–1972. With W H Auden and Stephen Spender, he was one of the influential left-wing poets of the 1930s. He also wrote detective novels under the pseudonym *Nicholas Blake*.

DCC abbreviation for ▷*digital compact cassette*.

D-day 6 June 1944, the day of the Allied invasion of Normandy under the command of General Eisenhower, with the aim of liberating Western Europe from German occupation in World War II. The Anglo-American invasion fleet landed on the Normandy beaches between the Orne River and St Marcouf. Two artificial harbours, known as 'Mulberries', were towed across the Channel so that equipment and armaments could be unloaded onto the beaches.

DDT abbreviation for *dichloro-diphenyl-trichloroethane* ($ClC_6H_4)_2CHCCl_3$, an insecticide discovered 1939 by Swiss chemist Paul Müller. It is useful in the control of insects that spread malaria, but resistant strains develop. DDT is highly toxic and persists in the environment and in living tissue. Its use is now banned in most countries, but it continues to be used on food plants in Latin America.

deadly nightshade another name for ▷bella-donna, a poisonous plant.

Dead Sea large lake, partly in Israel and partly in Jordan, lying 394 m/1,293 ft below sea level; area 1,020 sq km/394 sq mi. The chief river entering it is the Jordan; it has no outlet and the water is very salty.

Dead Sea Scrolls collection of ancient scrolls (rolls of writing) and fragments of scrolls found 1947–56 in caves 2 km/1 mi from the north end of the Dead Sea, at Qumran. The documents date mainly from about 150 BC–AD 68 and include copies of Old Testament books 1,000 years older than those previously known.

Dean James (Byron) 1931–1955. US actor. Killed in a car accident after the public showing of his first film, *East of Eden* 1955, he posthumously became a cult hero with *Rebel Without a Cause* 1955 and *Giant* 1956.

death permanent ending of all the functions that keep an organism alive. Death used to be pronounced when a person's breathing and heartbeat stopped. The advent of mechanical aids has made this point sometimes difficult to determine, and in controversial cases a person is now pronounced dead when the brain ceases to control the vital functions even if breath and heartbeat are maintained.

death cap fungus *Amanita phalloides*, the most poisonous mushroom known. The fruiting body has a scaly white cap and a collarlike structure near the base of the stalk.

Death Valley depression 225 km/140 mi long and 6–26 km/4–16 mi wide in SE California, USA. At 85 m/280 ft below sea level, it is the lowest point in North America. Bordering mountains rise to 3,000 m/10,000 ft. It is one of the world's hottest and driest places, with temperatures sometimes exceeding 51.7°C/125°F and an annual rainfall of less than 5 cm/2 in. Borax, iron ore, tungsten, gypsum, and salts are extracted.

deathwatch beetle any wood-boring beetle of the family Anobiidae, especially *Xestobium rufovillosum*. The larvae live in oaks and willows, and sometimes cause damage by boring in old furniture or structural timbers. To attract the female, the male beetle produces a ticking sound by striking his head on a wooden surface, and this is taken by the superstitious as a warning of approaching death.

de Broglie see ▷Broglie, de.

debt something that is owed by a person or organization, usually money, goods, or services. Debt usually occurs as a result of borrowing *credit*. Debt *servicing* is the payment of interest on a debt. The *national debt* of a country is the total money owed by the national government to private individuals, banks, and so on; *international debt*, the money owed by one country to another, began on a large scale in the late 19th to early 20th centuries and became a global problem as a result of the oil crisis of the 1970s.

Debussy (Achille-) Claude 1862–1918. French

composer. He broke with the dominant tradition of German Romanticism and introduced new qualities of melody and harmony based on the whole-tone scale, evoking oriental music. His work includes *Prélude à l'après-midi d'un faune* 1894 and the opera *Pelléas et Mélisande* 1902.

decathlon two-day athletic competition for men consisting of ten events: 100 metres, long jump, shot put, high jump, 400 metres (day one); 110 metres hurdles, discus, pole vault, javelin, 1,500 metres (day two). Points are awarded for performances and the winner is the athlete with the greatest aggregate score. The decathlon is an Olympic event.

decibel unit (symbol dB) of measure used originally to compare sound densities and subsequently electrical or electronic power outputs; now also used to compare voltages. An increase of 10 dB is equivalent to a 10-fold increase in intensity or power, and a 20-fold increase in voltage. A whisper has an intensity of 20 dB; 140 dB (a jet aircraft taking off nearby) is the threshold of pain.

deciduous of trees and shrubs, shedding leaves before the onset of winter or a dry season (see ▷abscission). In temperate regions there is little water available during winter, and leaf fall is an adaptation to reduce ▷transpiration, the loss of water by evaporation. Examples of deciduous trees are oak and beech.

decimal fraction ▷fraction expressed by the use of the decimal point, that is, a fraction in which the denominator is any higher power of 10. Thus $^3/_{10}$, $^{51}/_{100}$, $^{23}/_{1000}$ are decimal fractions and are normally expressed as 0.3, 0.51, 0.023. The use of decimals greatly simplifies addition and multiplication of fractions, though not all fractions can be expressed exactly as decimal fractions.

Declaration of Independence historic US document stating the theory of government on which the USA was founded, based on the right 'to life, liberty, and the pursuit of happiness'. The statement was issued by the American Continental Congress 4 July 1776, renouncing all allegiance to the British crown and ending the political connection with Britain.

Declaration of Rights in Britain, the statement issued by the Convention Parliament Feb 1689, laying down the conditions under which the crown was to be offered to ▷William III and Mary. Its clauses were later incorporated in the ▷Bill of Rights.

dedicated computer computer built into another device for the purpose of controlling or supplying information to it. Its use has increased dramatically since the advent of the ▷microprocessor: washing machines, digital watches, cars, and video recorders all now have their own processors.

Dee river in Grampian region, Scotland; length 139 km/87 mi. From its source in the Cairngorms, it flows east into the North Sea at Aberdeen (by an artificial channel). Also a river in Wales and England; length 112 km/70 mi. Rising in Lake Bala, Gwynedd, it flows into the Irish Sea west of Chester. There is another Scottish river Dee (61 km/38 mi) in Kirkcudbright.

deed legal document that passes an interest in property or binds a person to perform or abstain from some action. Deeds are of two kinds: indenture and deed poll. **Indentures** bind two or more parties in mutual obligations. A *deed poll* is made by one party only, such as when a person changes his or her name.

deep-sea trench another term for ▷ocean trench.

deer any of various ruminant, even-toed, hoofed mammals belonging to the family Cervidae. The male typically has a pair of antlers, shed and regrown each year. Most species of deer are forest-dwellers and are distributed throughout Eurasia and North America, but are absent from Australia and Africa S of the Sahara. Native to Britain are red deer *Cervus elaphus* and roe deer *Capreolus capreolus*.

deerhound large, rough-coated dog, formerly used for hunting and killing deer. Slim and long-legged, it grows to 75 cm/2.5 ft or more, usually with a bluish-grey coat.

Defence, Ministry of British government department created 1964 from a temporary Ministry of Defence established after World War II together with the Admiralty, Air Ministry, and War Office. It is headed by the secretary of state for defence with ministers of state for the armed forces and defence procurement. This centralization was influenced by the example of the US Department of ▷Defense.

Defense, Department of US government department presided over by the secretary of defense, with headquarters in the ▷Pentagon. The secretary holds a seat in the president's cabinet; each of the three military services has a civilian secretary, not of cabinet rank, at its head. It was established when the army, navy, and air force were unified by the National Security Act 1947.

deflation in economics, a reduction in the level of economic activity, usually caused by an increase in interest rates and reduction in the money supply, increased taxation, or a decline in government expenditure.

Defoe Daniel 1660–1731. English writer. His *Robinson Crusoe* 1719, though purporting to be a factual account of shipwreck and solitary survival, was influential in the development of the novel. The fictional *Moll Flanders* 1722 and the partly factual *A Journal of the Plague Year* 1722 are still read for their concrete realism. A prolific journalist and pamphleteer, he was imprisoned 1702–04 for the ironic *The Shortest Way with Dissenters* 1702.

deforestation destruction of forest for timber, fuel, charcoal burning, and clearing for agriculture and extractive industries, such as mining, without planting new trees to replace those lost (reafforestation) or working on a cycle that allows the natural forest to regenerate. Deforestation causes fertile soil to be blown away or washed into rivers, leading to ⟡soil erosion, drought, flooding, and loss of wildlife.

Degas (Hilaire Germain) Edgar 1834–1917. French Impressionist painter and sculptor. He devoted himself to lively, informal studies, often using pastels, of ballet, horse racing, and young women working. From the 1890s he turned increasingly to sculpture, modelling figures in wax in a fluent, naturalistic style.

de Gaulle Charles (André Joseph Marie) 1890–1970. French general and first president of the Fifth Republic 1958–69. He organized the Free French troops fighting the Nazis 1940–44, was head of the provisional French government 1944–46, and leader of his own Gaullist party. In 1958 the national assembly asked him to form a government during France's economic recovery and to solve the crisis in Algeria. He became president at the end of 1958, having changed the constitution to provide for a presidential system, and served until 1969.

degree in mathematics, a unit (symbol °) of measurement of an angle or arc. A circle is divided into 360°; a degree is subdivided into 60 minutes (symbol ′). *Temperature* is also measured in degrees, which are divided on a decimal scale. See also ⟡Celsius, ⟡Fahrenheit, and ⟡circle.

De Havilland Geoffrey 1882–1965. British aircraft designer who designed and whose company produced the Moth biplane, the Mosquito fighter-bomber of World War II, and the postwar Comet, the world's first jet-driven airliner to enter commercial service.

deism belief in a supreme being; but the term usually refers to a movement of religious thought in the 17th and 18th centuries, characterized by the belief in a rational 'religion of nature' as opposed to the orthodox beliefs of Christianity. Deists believed that God is the source of natural law but does not intervene directly in the affairs of the world, and that the only religious duty of humanity is to be virtuous.

de Klerk F(rederik) W(illem) 1936– . South African National Party politician, president from 1989. He served in the cabinets of B J Vorster and P W Botha 1978–89, and replaced Botha as National Party leader and state president. In Feb 1990 he ended the ban on the ⟡African National Congress opposition movement and released its effective leader, Nelson Mandela. In 1991 de Klerk repealed all racially discriminating laws. In March 1992 a whites-only referendum gave him a clear mandate to proceed with constitutional reform to end white minority rule.

Delacroix Eugène 1798–1863. French Romantic painter. His prolific output included religious and historical subjects and portraits of friends, among

them the musicians Paganini and Chopin. Against French academic tradition, he evolved a highly coloured, fluid style, as in *The Death of Sardanapalus* 1827 (Louvre, Paris).

de la Mare Walter 1873–1956. English poet, known for his verse for children, such as *Songs of Childhood* 1902, and the novels *The Three Royal Monkeys* 1910 for children and, for adults, *The Memoirs of a Midget* 1921.

Delaunay Robert 1885–1941. French painter, a pioneer in abstract art. With his wife Sonia Delaunay-Terk, he invented Orphism, an early variation on Cubism, focusing on the effects of pure colour.

Delaware state in NE USA; nickname First State/Diamond State; *area* 5,300 sq km/2,046 sq mi; *capital* Dover; *towns* Wilmington, Newark; *physical* divided into two physical areas, one hilly and wooded, the other gently undulating; *features* one of the most industrialized states; headquarters of the Dupont chemical firm; Rehoboboth Beach; *products* dairy, poultry, and market-garden produce; chemicals, motor vehicles, and textiles; *population* (1990) 666,200; *famous people* J P Marquand; *history* the first settlers were Dutch 1631 and Swedes 1638, but the area was captured by the British 1664. Delaware was made a separate colony 1704 and organized as a state 1776, one of the original 13 states of the USA.

de Lesseps Ferdinand, Vicomte. French engineer; see de ⟡Lesseps.

Delhi Union Territory of the Republic of India from 1956; capital New Delhi; area 1,500 sq km/579 sq mi; population (1991) 9,370,400. It produces grain, sugar cane, fruit, and vegetables.

della Robbia Italian family of artists; see ⟡Robbia, della.

Delors Jacques 1925– . French socialist politician, finance minister 1981–84. As president of the European Commission from 1984 he has overseen significant budgetary reform and the move towards a free European Community market in 1993, with increased powers residing in Brussels.

Delphi city of ancient Greece, situated in a rocky valley north of the gulf of Corinth, on the southern slopes of Mount Parnassus, site of an ⟡oracle in the temple of Apollo. The oracle was interpreted by priests from the inspired utterances of the Pythian priestess until it was closed down by the Roman emperor Theodosius AD 390.

delphinium any plant of the genus *Delphinium* belonging to the buttercup family Ranunculaceae. There are some 250 species, including the butterfly or Chinese delphinium *D. grandiflorum*, an Asian form and one of the ancestors of the garden delphinium. Most species have blue, purple, or white flowers on a long spike.

del Sarto Andrea 1486–1531. Italian Renaissance painter; see ⟡Andrea del Sarto.

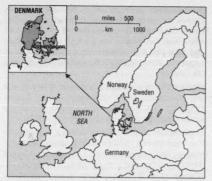

delta roughly fanlike tract of land at a river's mouth, formed by deposited silt or sediment. Familiar examples of large deltas are those of the Mississippi, Ganges and Brahmaputra, Rhône, Po, Danube, and Nile; the shape of the Nile delta is like the Greek letter *delta* Δ, and thus gave rise to the name.

dementia mental deterioration as a result of physical changes in the brain. It may be due to degenerative change, circulatory disease, infection, injury, or chronic poisoning. *Senile dementia*, a progressive loss of mental abilities such as memory and orientation, is typically a problem of old age, and can be accompanied by ◊depression.

Demeter in Greek mythology, the goddess of agriculture (identified with Roman ◊Ceres), daughter of Kronos and Rhea, and mother of Persephone by Zeus. She is identified with the Egyptian goddess Isis and had a temple dedicated to her at Eleusis, where ◊mystery religions were celebrated.

De Mille Cecil B (lount) 1881–1959. US film director and producer. He entered films 1913 with Jesse L Lasky (with whom he later established Paramount Pictures), and was one of the founders of Hollywood. He specialized in biblical epics, such as *The Sign of the Cross* 1932 and *The Ten Commandments* 1923; remade 1956. He also made the 1952 Academy Award-winning *The Greatest Show on Earth*.

Demirel Suleyman 1924– . Turkish politician. Leader from 1964 of the Justice Party, he was prime minister 1965–71, 1975–77, and 1979–80. He favoured links with the West, full membership in the European Community, and foreign investment in Turkish industry.

democracy government by the people, usually through elected representatives. In the modern world, democracy has developed from the American and French revolutions.

Democratic Party one of the two main political parties of the USA. It tends to be the party of the working person, as opposed to the Republicans, the party of big business, but the divisions between the two are not clear cut. Its stronghold since the Civil War has traditionally been industrial urban centres and the Southern states, but conservative Southern Democrats were largely supportive of Republican positions and helped elect President Reagan.

demography study of the size, structure, dispersement, and development of human populations to establish reliable statistics on such factors as birth and death rates, marriages and divorces, life expectancy, and migration.

Demosthenes *c.* 384–322 BC. Athenian orator and politician. From 351 BC he led the party that advocated resistance to the growing power of ◊Philip of Macedon, and in his *Philippics* incited the Athenians to war. This policy resulted in the defeat of Chaeronea 338, and the establishment of Macedonian supremacy. After the death of Alexander he organized a revolt; when it failed, he killed himself.

Demotic Greek common or vernacular variety of the modern ◊Greek language.

demotic script cursive (joined) writing derived from Egyptian hieratic script, itself a cursive form of ◊hieroglyphic. Demotic documents are known from the 6th century BC to about AD 470. It was written horizontally, from right to left.

Deng Xiaoping or *Teng Hsiao-ping* 1904– Chinese political leader. A member of the Chinese Communist Party (CCP) from the 1920s, he took part in the Long March 1934–36. He was in the Politburo from 1955 until ousted in the Cultural Revolution 1966–69. Reinstated in the 1970s, he gradually took power and introduced a radical economic modernization programme. He retired from the Politburo 1987 and from his last official position (as chair of State Military Commission) March 1990, but remained influential behind the scenes.

Den Haag Dutch form of The ◊Hague, city in the Netherlands.

De Niro Robert 1943– . US actor. He won Oscars for his performances in *The Godfather II* 1974 and *Raging Bull* 1979. His other films, many of them directed by Martin Scorsese, include *Taxi Driver* 1976, *The Deer Hunter* 1978, *The King of Comedy* 1982, and *Cape Fear* 1992.

Denktaş Rauf R 1924– . Turkish-Cypriot nationalist politician. In 1975 the Turkish Federated State of Cyprus (TFSC) was formed in the northern third of the island, with Denktaş as its head, and in 1983 he became president of the breakaway Turkish Republic of Northern Cyprus (TRNC).

Denmark Kingdom of; peninsula and islands in N Europe, bordered N by the Skagerrak, E by the Kattegat, S by Germany, and W by the North Sea; *area* 43,075 sq km/16,627 sq mi; *capital* Copenhagen; *physical* comprises the Jutland peninsula and about 500 islands (100 inhabited);

the land is flat and cultivated; sand dunes and lagoons on the W coast and long inlets (fjords) on the E; *head of state* Queen Margarethe II from 1972; *head of government* Poul Schlüter from 1982; *exports* bacon, dairy produce, eggs, fish, mink pelts, car and aircraft parts, electrical equipment, textiles, chemicals; *population* (1990 est) 5,134,000; *language* Danish (official); *recent history* occupied by Germany 1940. Recognized the independence of Iceland 1945 and granted home rule to the Faeroe Islands 1948. Founder member of NATO 1949; member of European Free Trade Association (EFTA) 1960–1973; joined European Community 1973. In 1972 Margrethe II became Denmark's first queen in nearly 600 years; inconclusive general elections, minority governments and coalitions have dogged Danish politics since 1987.

Denpasar capital town of Bali in the Lesser Sunda Islands of Indonesia; population (1980) 88,100.

density measure of the compactness of a substance; it is equal to its mass per unit volume and is measured in kg per cubic metre/lb per cubic foot. Density is a scalar quantity. Relative density is the ratio of the density of a substance to that of water at 4°C.

dentistry care and treatment of the teeth and gums. *Orthodontics* deals with the straightening of the teeth for aesthetic and clinical reasons, and *periodontics* with care of the supporting tissue (bone and gums).

Denver city and capital of Colorado, USA, on the South Platte River, near the foothills of the Rocky Mountains; population (1990) 467,600, Denver-Boulder metropolitan area 1,848,300. It is a processing and distribution centre for a large agricultural area and for natural resources (minerals, oil, gas). It was the centre of a gold and silver boom in the 1870s and 1880s, and for oil in the 1970s.

depreciation in economics, the decline of a currency's value in relation to other currencies. Depreciation also describes the fall in value of an asset (such as factory machinery) resulting from age, wear and tear, or other circumstances. It is an important factor in assessing company profits and tax liabilities.

depression in economics, a period of low output and investment, with high unemployment. Specifically, the term describes two periods of crisis in world economy: 1873–96 and 1929–mid-1930s.

depression or *low* in meteorology, a region of low atmospheric pressure. It produces unstable weather since air spirals into it, in an anticlockwise direction in the northern hemisphere and a clockwise direction in the southern, generating winds. Depressions form as warm air from the tropics spirals round cold polar air, producing cold and warm fronts. The warm air rising where cold and warm fronts converge produces the lowering of pressure; the rising air produces rain.

depression in psychology, an emotional state characterized by sadness, unhappy thoughts, apathy, and dejection. Sadness is a normal response to major losses such as bereavement or unemployment. After childbirth, postnatal depression is common. However, clinical depression, which is prolonged or unduly severe, often requires treatment, such as antidepressant medication or ▷cognitive therapy.

De Quincey Thomas 1785–1859. English author whose works include *Confessions of an English Opium-Eater* 1821 and the essays 'On the Knocking at the Gate in Macbeth' 1823 and 'On Murder Considered as One of the Fine Arts' 1827. He was a friend of the poets Wordsworth and Coleridge.

Derby industrial city in Derbyshire, England; population (1991) 214,000. Products include rail

depression

a typical depression showing low pressure at the centre

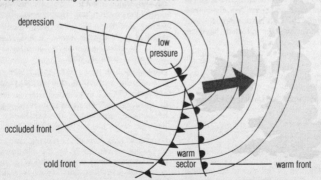

depression

low pressure

occluded front

warm sector

cold front

warm front

the fronts are associated with belts of rain (frontal rainfall)

locomotives, Rolls-Royce cars and aero engines, chemicals, paper, electrical, mining, and engineering equipment. The museum collections of Crown Derby china, the Rolls-Royce collection of aero engines, and the Derby Playhouse are here.

Derby blue riband of the English horse-racing season. It is run over 2.4 km/1.5 mi at Epsom, Surrey, every June. It was established 1780 and named after the 12th Earl of Derby. The USA has an equivalent horse race, the *Kentucky Derby*.

Derby Edward (George Geoffrey Smith) Stanley, 14th Earl of Derby 1799–1869. British politician, prime minister 1852, 1858–59, and 1866–68. Originally a Whig, he became secretary for the colonies 1830, and introduced the bill for the abolition of slavery. He joined the Tories 1834, and the split in the Tory Party over Robert Peel's free-trade policy gave Derby the leadership for 20 years.

Derbyshire county in N central England; *area* 2,630 sq km/1,015 sq mi; *towns* Matlock (administrative headquarters), Derby, Chesterfield, Ilkeston; *features* Peak District National Park (including Kinder Scout 636 m/2,088 ft); rivers: Derwent, Dove, Rother, Trent; Chatsworth House, Bakewell (seat of the Duke of Devonshire); Haddon Hall; *products* cereals; dairy and sheep farming; there have been pit and factory closures, but the area is being redeveloped, and there are large reserves of fluorite; *population* (1991) 915,000; *famous people* Thomas Cook, Marquess Curzon of Kedleston, Samuel Richardson.

deregulation US term for freeing markets from protection, with the aim of improving competitiveness. It often results in greater monopoly control.

Derg, Lough lake in County Donegal, NW Ireland, with an island (Station Island or St Patrick's Purgatory) that is the country's leading place of pilgrimage. Associated with St Patrick, a monastery flourished here from early times.

Derry county of Northern Ireland; *area* 2,070 sq km/799 sq mi; *towns* Derry (county town, formerly Londonderry), Coleraine, Portstewart; *features* rivers Foyle, Bann, and Roe; borders Lough Neagh; *products* mainly agricultural, but farming is hindered by the very heavy rainfall; flax, cattle, sheep, food processing, textiles, light engineering; *population* (1981) 187,000; *famous people* Joyce Cary.

Derry former name (1610–1984) of *Londonderry* historic city and port on the river Foyle, County Derry, Northern Ireland; population (1981) 89,100. Derry dates from the foundation of a monastery by St Columba AD 546. James I of England granted the borough and surrounding land to the citizens of London and a large colony of imported Protestants founded the present city. Textiles and chemicals are produced.

Derwent river in N Yorkshire, NE England; length

112 km/70 mi. Rising in the N Yorkshire moors, it joins the river Ouse SE of Selby. Other rivers of the same name in the UK are found in Derbyshire (96 km/60 mi), Cumbria (56 km/35 mi), and Northumberland (26 km/16 mi).

Descartes René 1596–1650. French philosopher and mathematician. He believed that commonly accepted knowledge was doubtful because of the subjective nature of the senses, and attempted to rebuild human knowledge using as his foundation *cogito ergo sum* ('I think, therefore I am'). He also believed that the entire material universe could be explained in terms of mathematical physics, and founded coordinate geometry as a way of defining and manipulating geometrical shapes by means of algebraic expressions. ⟡Cartesian coordinates are the means by which points are represented in this system. Descartes also established the science of optics, and helped to shape contemporary theories of astronomy and animal behaviour.

desert arid area without sufficient rainfall and, consequently, vegetation to support human life. The term includes the ice areas of the polar regions (known as cold deserts). Almost 33% of Earth's land surface is desert, and this proportion is increasing.

destroyer small, fast warship designed for anti-submarine work. Destroyers played a critical role in the convoy system in World War II. Modern destroyers often carry guided missiles and displace 3,700–5,650 tonnes.

détente (French) reduction of political tension and the easing of strained relations between nations, for example, the ending of the Cold War 1989–90, although it was first used in the 1970s to describe the easing East–West relations, trade agreements, and cultural exchanges.

detergent surface-active cleansing agent. The common detergents are made from ⟡fats (hydrocarbons) and sulphuric acid, and their long-chain molecules have a type of structure similar to that of soap molecules: a salt group at one end attached to a long hydrocarbon 'tail'. Unlike soap, they do not produce scum.

determinism in philosophy, the view that denies human freedom of action. Everything is strictly governed by the principle of cause and effect, and human action is no exception. It is the opposite of free will, and rules out moral choice and responsibility.

de Tocqueville Alexis. French politician; see ⟡Tocqueville, Alexis de.

Detroit city in Michigan, USA, situated on Detroit River; population (1990) 1,028,000, metropolitan area 4,665,200. It is an industrial centre with the headquarters of Ford, Chrysler, and General Motors, hence its nickname, Motown (from 'motor town'). Other manufactured products include metal products, machine tools, chemicals, office machines, and pharmaceuticals. Detroit is a port on the St Lawrence Seaway.

deuterium naturally occurring heavy isotope of hydrogen, mass number 2 (one proton and one neutron), discovered by Harold Urey 1932. It is sometimes given the symbol D. In nature, about one in every 6,500 hydrogen atoms is deuterium. Combined with oxygen, it produces 'heavy water' (D_2O), used in the nuclear industry.

de Valera Eamon 1882–1975. Irish nationalist politician, prime minister of the Irish Free State/Eire/Republic of Ireland 1932–48, 1951–54, and 1957–59, and president 1959–73. Repeatedly imprisoned, he participated in the Easter Rising 1916 and was leader of the nationalist ◊Sinn Féin party 1917–26, when he formed the republican ◊Fianna Fáil party; he directed negotiations with Britain 1921 but refused to accept the partition of Ireland until 1937.

de Valois Ninette. Stage name of Edris Stannus 1898– . Irish dancer, choreographer, and teacher. A pioneer of British national ballet, she worked with Sergei Diaghilev in Paris in the 1920s. Collaborating with Lilian Baylis at the Old Vic, she founded the Vic-Wells Ballet 1931, which later became the Royal Ballet and Royal Ballet School. Among her works are *Job* 1931 and *Checkmate* 1937.

devaluation in economics, the lowering of the official value of a currency against other currencies, so that exports become cheaper and imports more expensive. Used when a country is badly in deficit in its balance of trade, it results in the goods the country produces being cheaper abroad, so that the economy is stimulated by increased foreign demand.

devil in Jewish, Christian, and Muslim theology, the supreme spirit of evil (*Beelzebub*, *Lucifer*, *Iblis*), or an evil spirit generally.

devil ray any of several large rays of the genera *Manta* and *Mobula*, fish in which two 'horns' project forwards from the sides of the huge mouth. These flaps of skin guide the plankton on which the fish feed into the mouth. The largest of these rays can be 7 m/23 ft across, and weigh 1,000 kg/2,200 lb. They live in warm seas.

Devil's Island (French *Ile du Diable*) smallest of the Iles du Salut, off French Guiana, 43 km/27 mi NW of Cayenne. The group of islands was collectively and popularly known by the name Devil's Island and formed a penal colony notorious for its terrible conditions.

devolution delegation of authority and duties; in the later 20th century, the movement to decentralize governmental power, as in the UK, where a bill for the creation of Scottish and Welsh assemblies was introduced 1976 (rejected by referendums in Scotland and Wales 1979).

Devon or *Devonshire* county in SW England; *area* 6,720 sq km/2,594 sq mi; *towns* Exeter (administrative headquarters), Plymouth; resorts: Paignton, Torquay, Teignmouth, and Ilfracombe; *features* rivers: Dart, Exe, Tamar; national parks: Dartmoor, Exmoor; Lundy bird sanctuary and marine nature reserve in the Bristol Channel; *products* mainly agricultural, with sheep and dairy farming; cider and clotted cream; kaolin in the south; Honiton lace; Dartington glass; *population* (1991) 1,008,300; *famous people* Francis Drake, John Hawkins, Charles Kingsley, Robert F Scott.

Devonian period of geological time 408–360 million years ago, the fourth period of the Palaeozoic era. Many desert sandstones from North America and Europe date from this time. The first land plants flourished in the Devonian period, corals were abundant in the seas, amphibians evolved from air-breathing fish, and insects developed on land.

dew precipitation in the form of moisture that collects on the ground. It forms after the temperature of the ground has fallen below the dew point of the air in contact with it. As the temperature falls during the night, the air and its water vapour become chilled, and condensation takes place on the cooled surfaces.

Dewar James 1842–1923. Scottish chemist and physicist who invented the vacuum flask (Thermos) 1872 during his research into the properties of matter at extremely low temperatures.

Dhaka or *Dacca* capital of Bangladesh from 1971, in Dhaka region, west of the river Meghna; population (1984) 3,600,000. It trades in jute, oilseed, sugar, and tea and produces textiles, chemicals, glass, and metal products.

Dhofar mountainous western province of ◊Oman, on the border with Yemen; population (1982) 40,000. South Yemen supported guerrilla activity here in the 1970s, while Britain and Iran supported the government's military operations. The capital is Salalah, which has a port at Rasut.

diabetes disease *diabetes mellitus* in which a disorder of the islets of Langerhans in the ◊pancreas prevents the body producing the hormone ◊insulin, so that sugars cannot be used properly. Treatment is by strict dietary control and oral or injected insulin. In 1989, it was estimated that 4% of the world's population had diabetes.

Diaghilev Sergei Pavlovich 1872–1929. Russian ballet impresario who in 1909 founded the Ballets Russes/Russian Ballet (headquarters in Monaco), which he directed for 20 years. Through this company he brought Russian ballet to the West, introducing and encouraging a dazzling array of dancers, choreographers, and composers, such as Anna Pavlova, Vaslav Nijinsky, Mikhail Fokine, Léonide Massine, George Balanchine, Igor Stravinsky, and Sergey Prokofiev.

dialect variation of a spoken language shared by those in a particular area or a particular social group or both. The term is used both objectively, to indicate a geographical area ('northern dialects') or social group ('black dialect'), and subjectively, in a judgemental and sometimes dismissive way.

dialectic Greek term, originally associated with the philosopher Socrates' method of argument through dialogue and conversation. *Hegelian dialectic*, named after the German philosopher ▷Hegel, refers to an interpretive method in which the contradiction between a thesis and its antithesis is resolved through synthesis.

dialysis in medicine, the process used to mimic the effects of the kidneys. It may be life-saving in some types of poisoning. Dialysis is usually performed to compensate for failing kidneys; there are two main methods, haemodialysis and peritoneal dialysis.

diameter straight line dividing a circle into two equal halves. Every diameter of a circle passes through the centre.

diamond generally colourless, transparent mineral, the hard crystalline form of carbon. It is regarded as a precious gemstone, and is the hardest natural substance known (10 on the ▷Mohs' scale). Industrial diamonds are used for cutting, grinding, and polishing.

Diana in Roman mythology, the goddess of chastity, hunting, and the Moon (Greek ▷Artemis), daughter of Jupiter and twin of Apollo.

Diana Princess of Wales 1961– . The daughter of the 8th Earl Spencer, she married Prince Charles in St Paul's Cathedral, London 1981, the first English bride of a royal heir since 1659. She is descended from the only sovereigns from whom Prince Charles is not descended, Charles II and James II.

diaphragm muscular sheet separating the thorax from the abdomen in mammals. Its rhythmical movements affect the size of the thorax and cause the pressure changes within the lungs that result in breathing.

diaphragm or *cap* or *Dutch cap* barrier ▷contraceptive that is pushed into the vagina and fits over the cervix (neck of the uterus), preventing sperm from entering the uterus. For a cap to be effective, a ▷spermicide must be used and the diaphragm left in place for 6–8 hours after intercourse. This method is 97% effective if practised correctly.

diarrhoea excessive action of the bowels so that the faeces are fluid or semifluid. It is caused by intestinal irritants (including some drugs and poisons), infection with harmful organisms (as in dysentery, salmonella, or cholera), or allergies.

Diaspora dispersal of the Jews, initially from Palestine after the Babylonian conquest 586 BC, and then following the Roman sack of Jerusalem AD 70 and their crushing of the Jewish revolt of 135. The

term has come to refer to all the Jews living outside Israel.

Diaz Bartolomeu *c.* 1450–1500. Portuguese explorer, the first European to reach the Cape of Good Hope 1488, and to establish a route around Africa. He drowned during an expedition with Pedro Cabral.

Dickens Charles 1812–1870. English novelist, popular for his memorable characters and his portrayal of the social evils of Victorian England. In 1836 he published the first number of the *Pickwick Papers*, followed by *Oliver Twist* 1838, the first of his 'reforming' novels; *Nicholas Nickleby* 1839; *Barnaby Rudge* 1840; *The Old Curiosity Shop* 1841; and *David Copperfield* 1849. Among his later books are *A Tale of Two Cities* 1859 and *Great Expectations* 1861.

Dickinson Emily 1830–1886. US poet. Born in Amherst, Massachusetts, she lived in near seclusion there from 1862. Very few of her many short, mystical poems were published during her lifetime, and her work became well known only in the 20th century.

dicotyledon major subdivision of the ▷angiosperms, containing the great majority of flowering plants. Dicotyledons are characterized by the presence of two seed leaves, or ▷cotyledons, in the embryo, which is usually surrounded by an endosperm. They generally have broad leaves with netlike veins.

dictatorship term or office of an absolute ruler, overriding the constitution. (In ancient Rome a dictator was a magistrate invested with emergency powers for six months.) Although dictatorships were common in Latin America during the 19th century, the only European example during this period was the rule of Napoleon III. The crises following World War I produced many dictatorships, including the regimes of Atatürk and Pilæsudski (nationalist); Mussolini, Hitler, Primo de Rivera, Franco, and Salazar (all right-wing); and Stalin (communist).

Diderot Denis 1713–1784. French philosopher. He is closely associated with the Enlightenment, the European intellectual movement for social and scientific progress, and was editor of the enormously influential ▷*Encyclopédie* 1751–80.

Dido Phoenician princess, legendary founder of Carthage, N Africa, who committed suicide to avoid marrying a local prince. In the Latin epic *Aeneid*, Virgil claims that it was because ▷Aeneas deserted her.

diesel engine ▷internal-combustion engine that burns a lightweight fuel oil. The diesel engine operates by compressing air until it becomes sufficiently hot to ignite the fuel. It is a piston-in-cylinder engine, like the ▷petrol engine, but only air (rather than an air-and-fuel mixture) is taken into the cylinder on the first piston stroke (down). The piston moves up and compresses the air until it is at a very high temperature. The fuel oil is then injected into the hot air, where it burns, driving the piston down on its power stroke. For this reason the engine is called a compression-ignition engine.

Dietrich Marlene (Maria Magdalene) 1904–1992. German-born US actress and singer who appeared in both the German and American versions of the film *The Blue Angel* 1930, directed by Josef von Sternberg. She stayed in Hollywood, becoming a US citizen in 1937. Her husky, sultry singing voice added to her appeal. Her other films include *Blonde Venus* 1932, *Destry Rides Again* 1939, and *Just a Gigolo* 1978.

diffraction spreading of a wave motion (such as light or sound) as it passes an obstacle and expands into a region not exposed directly to incoming waves behind the obstacle. This accounts for interference phenomena observed at the edges of opaque objects, or discontinuities between different media in the path of a wave train. The phenomena give rise to slight spreading of light into coloured bands at the shadow of a straight edge.

diffusion spontaneous and random movement of molecules or particles in a fluid (gas or liquid) from a region in which they are at a high concentration to a region in which they are at a low concentration, until a uniform concentration is achieved throughout. No mechanical mixing or stirring is involved.

digestive system mouth, stomach, intestine, and associated glands of animals, which are responsible for digesting food. The food is broken down by physical and chemical means in the ⟢stomach; digestion is completed, and most nutrients are absorbed in the small intestine; what remains is stored and concentrated into faeces in the large intestine. In birds, additional digestive organs are the crop and gizzard.

Diggers also called *true* ⟢*Levellers* English 17th-century radical sect that attempted to cultivate common land. The Diggers became prominent April 1649 when, headed by Gerrard Winstanley (c. 1609–1660), they set up communal colonies near Cobham, Surrey, and elsewhere. These colonies were attacked by mobs and, being pacifists, the Diggers made no resistance. The support they attracted alarmed the government and they were dispersed 1650. Their ideas influenced the early ⟢Quakers.

digit in mathematics, any of the numbers from 0 to 9 in the decimal system. Different bases have different ranges of digits. For example, the ⟢hexadecimal system has digits 0 to 9 and A to F, whereas the binary system has two digits (or ⟢bits), 0 and 1.

digestive system

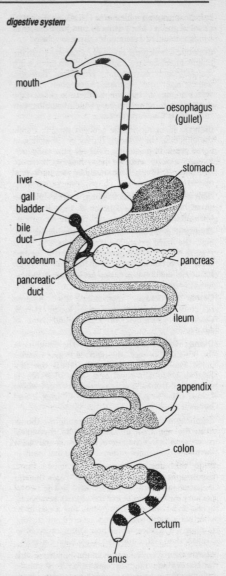

digital audio tape (DAT) digitally recorded audio tape produced in cassettes that can carry two hours of sound on each side and are about half the size of standard cassettes. DAT players/recorders were developed 1987 but not marketed in the UK until 1989. Prerecorded cassettes are copy-protected. The first DAT for computer data was introduced 1988.

digital compact cassette (DCC) digitally recorded audio cassette that is roughly the same size as a standard cassette. It cannot be played on a normal tape recorder, though standard tapes can be played on a DCC machine; this is known as 'backwards compatibility'. The playing time is 90 minutes.

digitalis plant of the genus *Digitalis* of the figwort family Scrophulariaceae, which includes the ▷foxgloves. The leaves of the common foxglove *Digitalis purpurea* are the source of the drug *digitalis* used in the treatment of heart disease.

digital recording technique whereby the pressure of sound waves is sampled more than 30,000 times a second and the values converted by computer into precise numerical values. These are recorded and, during playback, are reconverted to sound waves.

dik-dik any of several species of tiny antelope, genus *Madoqua*, found in Africa S of the Sahara in dry areas with scattered brush. Dik-diks are about 60 cm/2 ft long and 35 cm/1.1 ft tall, and often seen in pairs. Males have short, pointed horns. The dik-dik is so named because of its alarm call.

dill herb *Anethum graveolens* of the carrot family Umbelliferae, whose bitter seeds and aromatic feathery leaves are used for culinary and medicinal purposes. A native plant of Asia and E Europe, it is now common throughout much of Europe.

dimension in science, any directly measurable physical quantity such as mass (M), length (L), and time (T), and the derived units obtainable by multiplication or division from such quantities. For example, acceleration (the rate of change of velocity) has dimensions (LT^{-2}), and is expressed in such units as km s^{-2}. A quantity that is a ratio, such as relative density or humidity, is dimensionless.

Dinesen Isak 1885–1962. Pen name of Danish writer Karen ▷Blixen, born Karen Christentze Dinesen.

dingo wild dog of Australia. Descended from domestic dogs brought from Asia by Aborigines thousands of years ago, it belongs to the same species *Canis familiaris* as other domestic dogs. It is reddish brown with a bushy tail, and often hunts at night. It cannot bark.

Dinkins David 1927– . Mayor of New York City from Jan 1990, a Democrat. He won a reputation as a moderate and consensual community politician and was Manhattan borough president before succeeding Edward Koch to become New York's first black mayor.

dinosaur any of a group (sometimes considered as two separate orders) of extinct reptiles living between 230 million and 65 million years ago. Their closest living relations are crocodiles and birds, the latter perhaps descended from the dinosaurs. Many species of dinosaur evolved during the millions of years they were the dominant large land animals. Most were large (up to 27 m/90 ft), but some were as small as chickens. They disappeared 65 million years ago for reasons not fully understood, although many theories exist.

Diocletian Gaius Valerius Diocletianus AD 245–313. Roman emperor 284–305, when he abdicated in favour of Galerius. He reorganized and subdivided the empire, with two joint and two subordinate emperors, and in 303 initiated severe persecution of Christians.

diode combination of a cold anode and a heated cathode (or the semiconductor equivalent, which incorporates a *p–n* junction). Either device allows the passage of direct current in one direction only, and so is commonly used in a ▷rectifier to convert alternating current (AC) to direct current (DC).

Diogenes *c.* 412–323 BC. Ascetic Greek philosopher of the ▷Cynic school. He believed in freedom and self-sufficiency for the individual, and that the virtuous life was the simple life; he did not believe in social mores. His writings do not survive.

Dionysius two tyrants of the ancient Greek city of Syracuse in Sicily. *Dionysius the Elder* (432–367 BC) seized power in 405 BC. His first two wars with Carthage further extended the power of Syracuse, but in a third (383–378 BC) he was defeated. He was a patron of ▷Plato. He was succeeded by his son, *Dionysius the Younger* (c. 390–344 BC), who was driven out of Syracuse by Dion in 356; he was tyrant again in 353, but in 343 returned to Corinth.

Dionysus in Greek mythology, the god of wine (son of Semele and Zeus), and also of orgiastic excess, who was attended by women called maenads, who were believed to be capable of tearing animals to pieces with their bare hands when under his influence. He was identified with the Roman ▷Bacchus, whose rites were less savage.

Diouf Abdou 1935– . Senegalese left-wing politician, president from 1980. He became prime minister 1970 under President Leopold Senghor and, on his retirement, succeeded him, being re-elected in 1983 and 1988. His presidency has been characterized by authoritarianism.

diphtheria infection of the upper air passages, caused by the bacillus *Corynebacterium diphtheriae*. It multiplies usually in the nose or throat, forming a grey membrane and causing swelling at the site of infection. A toxin is produced and is carried by the blood throughout the body. Symptoms are fever, severe prostration and difficulty in breathing. Treatment is by injections of antitoxin serum and penicillin. Cases are rare, due to immunization.

diplodocus plant-eating sauropod dinosaur that lived about 145 million years ago, the fossils of which have been found in the W USA. Up to 27 m/88 ft long, most of which was neck and tail, it weighed about 11 tonnes. It walked on four elephantine legs, had nostrils on top of the skull, and peglike teeth at the front of the mouth.

diploid having two sets of ◊chromosomes in each cell. In sexually reproducing species, one set is derived from each parent, the ◊gametes, or sex cells, of each parent being ◊haploid (having only one set of chromosomes) due to ◊meiosis (reduction cell division).

dipper any of various passerine birds of the family Cinclidae, found in hilly and mountainous regions across Eurasia and North America, where there are clear, fast-flowing streams. It can swim, dive, or walk along the bottom, using the pressure of water on its wings and tail to keep it down, while it searches for insect larvae and other small animals.

Dirac Paul Adrien Maurice 1902–1984. British physicist who worked out a version of quantum mechanics consistent with special ◊relativity. The existence of the positron (positive electron) was one of its predictions. He shared the Nobel Prize for Physics 1933 with Austrian physicist Erwin Schrödinger (1887–1961).

Dire Straits UK rock group formed 1977 by guitarist, singer, and songwriter Mark Knopfler (1949–). Their tasteful musicianship was tailormade for the new compact-disc audience, and their 1985 LP *Brothers in Arms* went on to sell 20 million copies.

dirigible another name for ◊airship.

disarmament reduction of a country's weapons of war. Most disarmament talks since World War II have been concerned with nuclear-arms verification and reduction, but biological, chemical, and conventional weapons have also come under discussion at the United Nations and in other forums. Attempts to limit the arms race between the USA and (until its demise) the USSR included the ◊Strategic Arms Limitation Talks (SALT) of the 1970s and the ◊Strategic Arms Reduction Talks (START) of the 1980s–90s.

disc in computing, a common medium for storing large volumes of data (an alternative is magnetic tape.) A magnetic disc is rotated at high speed in a disc-drive unit as a read/write (playback or record) head passes over its surfaces to record or 'read' the magnetic variations that encode the data. There are several types, including ◊floppy discs, ◊hard discs, and ◊CD-ROM.

Discman Sony trademark for a portable compact-disc player; the equivalent of a Walkman, it also comes in a model with a liquid-crystal display for data discs.

discus circular disc thrown by athletes who rotate the body to gain momentum from within a circle 2.5 m/8 ft in diameter. The men's discus weighs 2 kg/4.4 lb and the women's 1 kg/2.2 lb. Discus throwing was a competition in ancient Greece at gymnastic contests, such as those of the Olympic Games. It is an event in the modern Olympics and athletics meetings.

disinfectant agent that kills, or prevents the growth of, bacteria and other microorganisms. Chemical disinfectants include carbolic acid (phenol, used by Joseph ◊Lister in surgery in the 1870s), ethanal, methanal, chlorine, and iodine.

Disney Walt(er Elias) 1901–1966. US filmmaker and animator, a pioneer of family entertainment. He established his own studio in Hollywood 1923, and his first Mickey Mouse cartoons appeared 1928. In addition to short cartoons, the studio made feature-length animated films, including *Snow White and the Seven Dwarfs* 1938, *Pinocchio* 1940, and *Dumbo* 1941. Disney's cartoon figures, for example Donald Duck, also appeared in comic books worldwide. In 1955, Disney opened the first theme park, Disneyland, in California.

dispersion in optics, the splitting of white light into a spectrum; for example, when it passes through a prism or a diffraction grating. It occurs because the prism (or grating) bends each component wavelength to a slightly different extent. The natural dispersion of light through raindrops creates a rainbow.

Disraeli Benjamin, Earl of Beaconsfield 1804–1881. British Conservative politician and novelist. Elected to Parliament 1837, he was chancellor of the Exchequer under Lord ◊Derby 1852, 1858–59, and 1866–68, and prime minister 1868 and 1874–80. His imperialist policies brought India directly under the crown, and he was personally responsible for purchasing control of the Suez Canal. The central Conservative Party organization is his creation. His popular, political novels reflect an interest in social reform and include *Coningsby* 1844 and *Sybil* 1845.

distemper any of several infectious diseases of animals characterized by catarrh, cough, and general weakness. Specifically, it refers to a virus disease in young dogs, also found in wild animals, which can now be prevented by vaccination. In 1988 an allied virus killed over 10,000 common seals in the Baltic and North seas.

distillation technique used to purify liquids or to separate mixtures of liquids possessing different boiling points. *Simple distillation* is used in the purification of liquids (or the separation of substances in solution from their solvents) – for example, in the production of pure water from a salt solution.

district council unit of local government in England and Wales. District-council responsibilities cover housing, local planning and development, roads (excluding trunk and classified), bus services, environmental health (refuse collection, clean air, food safety and hygiene, and enforcement of the Offices, Shops and Railway Premises Act), poll tax, museums and art galleries, parks and playing fields, swimming baths, cemeteries, and so on. In metropolitan district councils education, personal social services, and libraries are also included.

District of Columbia federal district of the USA comprising ◊Washington DC.

diuretic any drug that rids the body of fluid accumulated in the tissues by increasing the output of urine by the kidneys. It may be used in the treatment of heart disease, high blood pressure, kidney or liver disease, and some endocrine disorders. A potassium supplement is prescribed where potassium loss would be dangerous.

diver also called *loon* any of four species of bird specialized for swimming and diving, found in northern regions of the northern hemisphere. They have straight bills and long bodies, and feed on fish, crustaceans, and some water plants.

dividend in business, the amount of money that company directors decide should be taken out of profits for distribution to shareholders. It is usually declared as a percentage or fixed amount per share.

divine right of kings Christian political doctrine that hereditary monarchy is the system approved by God, hereditary right cannot be forfeited, monarchs are accountable to God alone for their actions, and rebellion against the lawful sovereign is therefore blasphemous.

diving sport of entering water either from a springboard (1 m/3 ft or 3 m/10 ft above the water) or from a platform, or highboard (10 m/33 ft above the water). Various differing starts are adopted, facing forward or backward, and somersaults, twists, and other combinations thereof are performed in midair before entering the water. A minimum pool depth of 5 m/16.5 ft is needed for high or platform diving.

Diwali Hindu festival in Oct/Nov celebrating Lakshmi, goddess of light and wealth. It is marked by the lighting of lamps and candles, feasting, and the exchange of gifts.

Dixieland jazz jazz style that originated in New Orleans, USA, in the early 20th century, dominated by cornet, trombone, and clarinet. The trumpeter Louis Armstrong emerged from this style. The *trad jazz* movement in the UK in the 1940s–50s was a Dixieland revival.

Djakarta variant spelling of ◊Jakarta, capital of Indonesia.

Djibouti chief port and capital of the Republic of Djibouti, on a peninsula 240 km/149 mi SW of Aden and 565 km/351 mi NE of Addis Ababa; population (1988) 290,000.

Djibouti Republic of; country on the E coast of Africa, at the S end of the Red Sea, bordered E by the Gulf of Aden, SE by the Somali Republic, and S, W, and N by Ethiopia; *area* 23,200 sq km/ 8,955 sq mi; *capital* (and chief port) Djibouti;

physical mountains divide an inland plateau from a coastal plain; climate hot and arid; *head of state and government* Hassan Gouled Aptidon from 1977; *political system* authoritarian nationalism; *exports* acts mainly as a transit port for Ethiopia; *population* (1990 est) 337,000 (Issa 47%, Afar 37%, European 8%, Arab 6%); *languages* French (official); Somali, Afar, Arabic; *recent history* achieved independence from France 1977. In 1979 all political parties combined to form the People's Progress Assembly (RPP), made the only legal party in a new constitution 1981

DNA (*deoxyribonucleic acid*) complex two-stranded molecule that contains, in chemically coded form, all the information needed to build, control, and maintain a living organism. DNA is a ladderlike double-stranded nucleic acid that forms the basis of genetic inheritance in all organisms, except for a few viruses that have only ◊RNA. In ◊eukaryotic organisms, it is organized into ◊chromosomes and contained in the cell nucleus.

Dnepropetrovsk city in Ukraine, on the right bank of the river Dnieper; population (1987) 1,182,000. It is the centre of a major industrial region, with iron, steel, chemical, and engineering industries. It is linked with the Dnieper Dam, 60 km/37 mi downstream.

Dnieper or *Dnepr* river rising in the Smolensk region of Russia and flowing south through Belarus, Ukraine to enter the Black Sea east of Odessa. Total length 2,250 km/1,400 mi.

Dobermann or *Dobermann pinscher* smooth-coated dog with a docked tail, much used as a guard dog. It stands up to 70 cm/2.2 ft tall, has a long head with a flat, smooth skull, and is often black with brown markings. It takes its name from the person who bred it in 19th-century Germany.

dock or *sorrel* in botany, any of a number of plants of the genus *Rumex* of the buckwheat family Polygonaceae. They are tall, annual to perennial herbs, often with lance-shaped leaves and small, greenish flowers. Native to temperate regions, there are 30 North American and several British species.

Dodgson Charles Lutwidge. Real name of writer Lewis ◊Carroll.

dodo extinct bird *Raphus cucullatus* formerly found on the island of Mauritius, but exterminated before the end of the 17th century. Although related to the pigeons, it was larger than a turkey, with a bulky body and very short wings and tail. Flightless and trusting, it was easy prey to humans.

Dodoma capital (replacing Dar-es-Salaam in 1974) of Tanzania; 1,132 m/3,713 ft above sea level; population (1985) 85,000. Centre of communications, linked by rail with Dar-es-Salaam and Kigoma on Lake Tanganyika, and by road with Kenya to the north and Zambia and Malawi to the south.

dog any carnivorous mammal of the family Canidae, including wild dogs, wolves, jackals, coyotes, and foxes. Specifically, the domestic dog *Canis familiaris*, the earliest animal to be domesticated (more than 10,000 years ago, when hunters used them to stalk game), descended from the wolf or jackal. Dogs migrated with humans to all the continents. They have been selectively bred into many different varieties for use as working animals and pets.

doge chief magistrate in the ancient constitutions of Venice and Genoa. The first doge of Venice was appointed 697 with absolute power (modified 1297), and from his accession dates Venice's prominence in history. The last Venetian doge, Lodovico Manin, retired 1797 and the last Genoese doge 1804.

dogfish any of several small sharks found in the NE Atlantic, Pacific, and Mediterranean. The sandy dogfish *Scyliorhinus caniculus* is found around the coasts of Britain, Scandinavia, and Europe. Bottom-living, it grows to about 75 cm/2.5 ft, and is known in restaurants as 'rock eel' or 'rock salmon'.

dogwood any of a genus *Cornus* of trees and shrubs of the dogwood family (Cornaceae), native to temperate regions of North America and Eurasia. The flowering dogwood *Cornus florida* of the eastern USA is often cultivated as an ornamental for its beautiful blooms consisting of clusters of small greenish flowers surrounded by four large white or pink petal-like ◊bracts.

Doha (Arabic *Ad Dawḥah*) capital and chief port of Qatar; population (1986) 217,000. Industries include oil refining, refrigeration plants, engineering, and food processing. It is the centre of vocational training for all the Persian Gulf states.

doldrums area of low atmospheric pressure along the equator, largely applied to oceans at the convergence of the NE and SE ◊trade winds. To some extent the area affected moves north and south with seasonal changes.

Dollfuss Engelbert 1892–1934. Austrian Christian Socialist politician. He was appointed chancellor in 1932, and in 1933 suppressed parliament and ruled by decree. In Feb 1934 he crushed a protest by the socialist workers by force, and in May Austria was declared a 'corporative' state. The Nazis attempted a coup d'état on 25 July; the Chancellery was seized and Dollfuss murdered.

dolmen prehistoric monument in the form of a chamber built of large stone slabs, roofed over by a flat stone which they support. Dolmens are grave chambers of the Neolithic period, found in Europe and Africa, and occasionally in Asia as far east as Japan. In Wales they are known as *cromlechs*.

dolomite white mineral with a hexagonal structure, calcium magnesium carbonate ($CaMg (CO_3)_2$). The term also applies to a type of limestone rock

dolphin

where the calcite content is replaced by the mineral dolomite. Dolomite rock may be white, grey, brown, or reddish in colour, commonly crystalline. It is used as a building material. The region of the Alps known as **the Dolomites** is a fine example of dolomite formation.

dolphin any of various highly intelligent aquatic mammals of the family Delphinidae, which also includes porpoises. There are about 60 species. The name 'dolphin' is generally applied to species having a beaklike snout and slender body, whereas the name 'porpoise' is reserved for the smaller species with a blunt snout and stocky body. Dolphins use sound (echolocation) to navigate, to find prey, and for communication. They feed on fish and squid. The common dolphin *Delphinus delphis* is found in all temperate and tropical seas and is up to 2.5 m/8 ft long.

Domesday Book record of the survey of England carried out 1086 by officials of William the Conqueror in order to assess land tax and other dues, ascertain the value of the crown lands, and enable the king to estimate the power of his vassal barons. The name is derived from the belief that its judgement was as final as that of Doomsday.

Domingo Placido 1937– . Spanish tenor who excels in romantic operatic roles. He made his debut in 1960 as Alfredo in Verdi's *La traviata*, then spent four years with the Israel National Opera. He has since performed diverse roles in opera houses worldwide. In 1986 he starred in the film version of *Otello*.

Dominica Commonwealth of; island in the West Indies, between Guadeloupe and Martinique, the largest of the Windward Islands, with the Atlantic to the E and the Caribbean to the W; **area** 751 sq km/290 sq mi; **capital** Roseau; **physical** second largest of the Windward Islands; mountainous central ridge with tropical rainforest; **head of state** Clarence Seignoret from 1983; **head of government** Eugenia Charles from 1980; **exports** bananas, coconuts, citrus, lime, bay oil; **population** (1990 est) 94,200 (mainly black African in origin, a small Carib reserve of some 500); **languages** English (official); Dominican *patois*; **recent history** independence achieved from Britain 1978, with Patrick John as prime minister. After defeat in 1980 general election, John was implicated in a plot to overthrow the government, tried and acquitted 1982, retried and found guilty 1985. Regrouping of left-of-centre parties resulted in new Labour Party of Dominica (DFP), led by Eugenia Charles, re-elected 1985. Integration with Windward Islands proposed 1991.

Dominican Republic country in the West Indies, occupying the eastern two-thirds of the island of Hispaniola, with Haiti to the west. The island is surrounded by the Caribbean Sea; *area* 48,442 sq km/ 18,700 sq mi; *capital* Santo Domingo; *physical* central mountain range with fertile valleys; *head of state and government* Joaquín Ricardo Balaguer from 1986; *exports* sugar, gold, silver, tobacco, coffee, nickel; *population* (1989 est) 7,307,000; *language* Spanish (official); *recent history* military coup established dictatorship under Rafael Trujillo from 1930 until 1961, when Trujillo was assassinated; first democratic elections held 1962. In 1963 elected President Bosch was overthrown in a military coup. A period of political instability and economic difficulties led to pressure from the International Monetary Fund to adopt austerity measures to save the economy 1985.

Don river in Russia, rising to the S of Moscow and entering the NE extremity of the Sea of Azov; length 1,900 km/1,180 mi. In its lower reaches the Don is 1.5 km/1 mi wide, and for about four months of the year it is closed by ice. Its upper course is linked with the river Volga by a canal.

Donatello (Donato di Niccolo) 1386–1466. Italian sculptor of the early Renaissance, born in Florence. He was instrumental in reviving the Classical style, as in his graceful bronze statue of the youthful *David* (Bargello, Florence) and his equestrian statue of the general *Gattamelata* 1443 (Padua). The course of Florentine art in the 15th century was strongly influenced by his style.

Donau German name for the river ◊Danube.

Donegal mountainous county in Ulster province in the NW of the Republic of Ireland, surrounded on three sides by the Atlantic; area 4,830 sq km/ 1,864 sq mi; population (1991) 127,900. The county town is Lifford; the market town and port of Donegal is at the head of Donegal Bay in the SW. Commercial activities include sheep and cattle raising, tweed and linen manufacture, and some deep-sea fishing. The river Erne hydroelectric project (1952) involved the building of large power stations at Ballyshannon.

Donetsk city in Ukraine; capital of Donetsk region, situated in the Donets Basin, a major coal-mining area, 600 km/372 mi SE of Kiev; population (1987) 1,090,000. It has blast furnaces, rolling mills, and other heavy industries.

Donizetti Gaetano 1797–1848. Italian composer who created more than 60 operas, including *Lucrezia Borgia* 1833, *Lucia di Lammermoor* 1835, *La Fille du régiment* 1840, *La Favorite* 1840, and

Don Pasquale 1843. They show the influence of Rossini and Bellini, and are characterized by a flow of expressive melodies.

Don Juan character of Spanish legend, Don Juan Tenorio, supposed to have lived in the 14th century and notorious for his debauchery. Tirso de Molina, Molière, Mozart, Byron, and George Bernard Shaw have featured the legend in their works.

donkey another name for ◊ass.

Donne John 1571–1631. English metaphysical poet. His work consists of love poems, religious poems, verse satires, and sermons, most of which were first published after his death. His religious poems show the same passion and ingenuity as his love poetry. A Roman Catholic in his youth, he converted to the Church of England and finally became dean of St Paul's Cathedral, where he is buried.

Doomsday Book variant spelling of ◊Domesday Book, English survey of 1086.

Doors, the US psychedelic rock group formed 1965 in Los Angeles by Jim Morrison (1943–1971, vocals), Ray Manzarek (1935– , keyboards), Robby Krieger (1946– , guitar), and John Densmore (1944– , drums). Their first hit was 'Light My Fire' from their debut album *The Doors* 1967. They were noted for Morrison's poetic lyrics and flamboyant performance.

doo-wop US pop-music form of the 1950s, a style of harmony singing without instrumental accompaniment or nearly so, almost exclusively by male groups. The name derives from the practice of having the lead vocalist singing the lyrics against a backing of nonsense syllables from the other members of the group. Many of the doo-wop groups were named after birds; for example, the Ravens and the Orioles.

Doppler effect change in the observed frequency (or wavelength) of waves due to relative motion between the wave source and the observer. The Doppler effect is responsible for the perceived change in pitch of a siren as it approaches and then recedes, and for the ◊red shift of light from distant stars. It is named after the Austrian physicist Christian Doppler (1803–1853).

Dordogne river in SW France, rising in Puy-de-Dôme *département* and flowing 490 km/300 mi to join the river Garonne, 23 km/14 mi N of Bordeaux. It gives its name to a *département* and is a major source of hydroelectric power.

Doré Gustave 1832–1883. French artist, chiefly known as a prolific illustrator, and also active as a painter, etcher, and sculptor. He produced closely worked engravings of scenes from, for example, Rabelais, Dante, Cervantes, the Bible, Milton, and Edgar Allan Poe.

Dorian member of a people of ancient Greece. They entered Greece from the north and took most of the Peloponnese from the Achaeans, destroying the

◊Mycenaean civilization; this invasion appears to have been completed before 1000 BC. Their chief cities were Sparta, Argos, and Corinth.

Doric in Classical architecture, one of the five types of column; see ◊order.

dormouse small rodent, of the family Gliridae, with a hairy tail. There are about ten species, living in Europe, Asia, and Africa. They are arboreal (live in trees) and nocturnal, and hibernate during winter in cold regions. The common dormouse *Muscardinus avellanarius* lives all over Europe in thickets and forests with undergrowth.

Dorset county in SW England; *area* 2,650 sq km/ 1,023 sq mi; *towns* Dorchester (administrative headquarters), Poole, Shaftesbury, Sherborne; resorts: Bournemouth, Lyme Regis, Weymouth; *features* Chesil Bank, a shingle bank along the coast 19 km/11 mi long; Isle of Purbeck, a peninsula where china clay and Purbeck 'marble' are quarried, and which includes Corfe Castle and the holiday resort of Swanage; Dorset Downs; Cranborne Chase; rivers Frome and Stour; Maiden Castle; *products* Wytch Farm is the largest onshore oilfield in the UK; *population* (1987) 649,000; *famous people* Anthony Ashley Cooper, Thomas Hardy, Thomas Love Peacock.

Dortmund industrial centre in the ◊Ruhr, Germany, 58 km/36 mi NE of Düsseldorf; population (1988) 568,000. It is the largest mining town of the Westphalian coalfield and the southern terminus of the Dortmund–Ems canal. Industries include iron, steel, construction machinery, engineering, and brewing.

dory marine fish *Zeus faber* found in the Mediterranean and Atlantic. It grows up to 60 cm/2 ft, and has nine or ten long spines at the front of the dorsal fin, and four at the front of the anal fin. It is considered to be an excellent food fish and is also known as *John Dory*.

DOS (acronym for *d*isc *o*perating *s*ystem) computer ◊operating system specifically designed for use with disc storage; also used as an alternative name for a particular operating system, ◊MS-DOS.

Dos Santos José Eduardo 1942– . Angolan leftwing politician, president from 1979, a member of the People's Movement for the Liberation of Angola (MPLA). By 1989, he had negotiated the withdrawal of South African and Cuban forces, and in 1991 a peace agreement to end the civil war.

Dostoevsky Fyodor Mihailovich 1821–1881. Russian novelist. Remarkable for their profound psychological insight, Dostoevsky's novels have greatly influenced Russian writers, and since the beginning of the 20th century have been increasingly influential abroad. In 1849 he was sentenced to four years' hard labour in Siberia, followed by army service, for printing socialist propaganda. *The House of the Dead* 1861 recalls his prison experiences, followed by his major works *Crime and Punishment* 1866, *The Idiot* 1868–69, and *The Brothers Karamazov* 1880.

dotterel bird *Eudromias morinellus* of the plover family, nesting on high moors and tundra in Europe and Asia, and migrating south for the winter. About 23 cm/9 in long, it is clad in a pattern of black, brown, and white in summer, duller in winter, but always with white eyebrows and breastband.

Douala or *Duala* chief port and industrial centre (aluminium, chemicals, textiles, pulp) of Cameroon, on the Wouri River estuary; population (1981) 637,000. Known as *Kamerunstadt* until 1907, it was capital of German Cameroon 1885–1901.

double bass large bowed four-stringed musical instrument, the bass of the ◊violin family, tuned in fourths, and descended from the violone of the ◊viol family.

Douglas capital of the Isle of Man in the Irish Sea; population (1981) 20,000. It is a holiday resort and terminus of shipping routes to and from Fleetwood and Liverpool.

Douglas Kirk. Stage name of Issur Danielovitch 1916– . US film actor. Usually cast as a dynamic and intelligent hero, as in *Spartacus* 1960, he was a major star of the 1950s and 1960s. He is the father of Michael Douglas.

Douglas Michael 1944– . US film actor and producer. One of the biggest box-office draws of the late 1980s and 1990s, Douglas won an Academy Award for his portrayal of a ruthless corporate raider in *Wall Street* 1987. His acting range includes both romantic and heroic leads in films such as *Romancing the Stone* 1984 and *Jewel of the Nile* 1985, both of which he produced. Among his other films are *Fatal Attraction* 1987 and *Basic Instinct* 1991.

Douglas fir any of some six species of coniferous evergreen tree of the family Pinaceae. The most common is *Pseudotsuga menziesii*, native to western North America and E Asia. It grows 60–90 m/200–300 ft, has long, flat, spirally arranged needles and hanging cones, and produces hard, strong timber. *P. taxifolia* was introduced to Britain by Scottish botanist David Douglas (1798–1834).

Douglas-Home Alec. British politician, see ◊Home.

Doulton Henry 1820–1897. English ceramicist. He developed special wares for the chemical, electrical, and building industries, and established the world's first stoneware-drainpipe factory 1846. From 1870 he created art pottery and domestic tablewares in Lambeth, S London, and Burslem, near Stoke-on-Trent.

Douro (Spanish *Duero*) river rising in N central Spain and flowing through N Portugal to the Atlantic at Porto; length 800 km/500 mi. Navigation at the river mouth is hindered by sand bars. There are hydroelectric installations.

dove another name for ⟡pigeon.

dove person who takes a moderate, sometimes pacifist, view on political issues. The term originated in the US during the Vietnam War. Its counterpart is a ⟡hawk. In more general usage today, a dove is equated with liberal policies, and a hawk with conservative ones.

Dover, Strait of (French *Pas-de-Calais*) stretch of water separating England from France, and connecting the English Channel with the North Sea. It is about 35 km/22 mi long and 34 km/21 mi wide at its narrowest part. It is one of the world's busiest sea lanes.

Dowell Anthony 1943– . British ballet dancer in the Classical style. He was principal dancer with the Royal Ballet 1966–86, and director 1986–89.

Dow Jones Index (*Dow Jones Industrial 30 Share Index*) scale for measuring the average share price and percentage change of 30 major US industrial companies. It is widely used as an indicator of general trends and has been published since 1897 by the financial news publisher Dow Jones and Company.

Dowland John 1563–1626. English composer. He is remembered for his songs to lute accompaniment as well as music for lute alone, such as *Lachrymae* 1605.

Down county in SE Northern Ireland, facing the Irish Sea on the east; area 2,470 sq km/953 sq mi; population (1981) 53,000. To the south are the Mourne mountains, to the east Strangford sea lough. The county town is Downpatrick; the main industry is dairying.

Downing Street street in Westminster, London, leading from Whitehall to St James's Park, named after Sir George Downing (died 1684), a diplomat under Cromwell and Charles II. *Number 10* is the official residence of the prime minister and *number 11* is the residence of the chancellor of the Exchequer. *Number 12* is the office of the government whips.

Down's syndrome condition caused by a chromosomal abnormality (the presence of an extra copy of chromosome 21) which in humans produces mental retardation; a flattened face; coarse, straight hair; and a fold of skin at the inner edge of the eye (hence the former name 'mongolism').

Doyle Arthur Conan 1859–1930. British writer, creator of the detective Sherlock Holmes and his assistant Dr Watson, who first appeared in *A Study in Scarlet* 1887 and featured in a number of subsequent stories, including *The Hound of the Baskervilles* 1902. Conan Doyle also wrote historical romances (*Micah Clarke* 1889 and *The White Company* 1891) and the scientific romance *The Lost World* 1912.

D'Oyly Carte Richard 1844–1901. British producer of the Gilbert and Sullivan operas at the Savoy Theatre, London, which he built. The old D'Oyly Carte

Opera Company, founded 1876, was disbanded 1982, but a new one opened 1988 and based itself in Birmingham from 1991.

Drabble Margaret 1939– . British writer. Her novels include *The Millstone* 1966 (filmed as *The Touch of Love*), *The Middle Ground* 1980, *The Radiant Way* 1987, and *A Natural Curiosity* 1989. She edited the 1985 edition of the *Oxford Companion to English Literature*.

Draco 7th century BC. Athenian politician, the first to codify the laws of the Athenian city-state. These were notorious for their severity; hence *draconian*, meaning particularly harsh.

Dracula in the novel *Dracula* 1897 by Bram Stoker, the caped count who, as a vampire, drinks the blood of beautiful women. The original of Dracula is thought to have been Vlad Ţepeş, or Vlad the Impaler, ruler of medieval Wallachia, who used to impale his victims and then mock them.

dragon Euro-Asian mythical reptilian beast, often portrayed as breathing fire. The name is popularly given to various sorts of lizard. These include the flying dragon *Draco volans* of SE Asia; the komodo dragon *Varanus komodoensis* of Indonesia, at over 3 m/10 ft the largest living lizard; and some Australian lizards with bizarre spines or frills.

dragonfly any of numerous insects of the order Odonata, including damselflies. They all have long narrow bodies, two pairs of almost equalsized, glassy wings with a network of veins; short, bristlelike antennae; powerful, 'toothed' mouthparts; and very large compound eyes which may have up to 30,000 facets. They hunt other insects by sight, both as adults and as aquatic nymphs.

Drake Francis *c.* 1545–1596. English buccaneer and explorer. Having enriched himself as a pirate against Spanish interests in the Caribbean 1567–72, he was sponsored by Elizabeth I for an expedition to the Pacific, sailing round the world 1577–80 in the *Golden Hind*, robbing Spanish ships as he went. This was the second circumnavigation of the globe (the first was by the Portuguese explorer Ferdinand Magellan). Drake also helped to defeat the Spanish Armada 1588 as a vice admiral in the *Revenge*.

drama in theatre, any play performed by actors for an audience. The term is also used collectively to group plays into historical or stylistic periods – for example, Greek drama, Restoration drama – as well as referring to the whole body of work written by a dramatist for performance. Drama is distinct from literature in that it is a performing art open to infinite interpretation, the product not merely of the playwright but also of the collaboration of director, designer, actors, and technical staff. See also ⟡comedy, ⟡tragedy, ⟡mime, and ⟡pantomime.

dream series of events or images perceived through the mind during sleep. Their function is unknown, but Sigmund ⬦Freud saw them as wish fulfilment (nightmares being failed dreams prompted by fears of 'repressed' impulses). Dreams occur in periods of rapid eye movement (REM) by the sleeper, when the cortex of the brain is approximately as active as in waking hours. Dreams occupy about a fifth of sleeping time.

Drenthe low-lying northern province of the Netherlands; *area* 2,660 sq km/1,027 sq mi; *population* (1988) 437,000; *towns* capital Assen; Emmen, Hoogeveen; *physical* fenland and moors; well-drained clay and peat soils; *products* livestock, arable crops, horticulture, petroleum; *history* governed in the Middle Ages by provincial nobles and by bishops of Utrecht, Drenthe was eventually acquired by Charles V of Spain in 1536. It developed following land drainage initiated in the mid-18th century and was established as a separate province of the Netherlands in 1796.

Dresden capital of the state of Saxony, Germany; population (1990) 520,000. Industries include chemicals, machinery, glassware, and musical instruments. It was one of the most beautiful German cities until its devastation by Allied fire-bombing 1945. Dresden county has an area of 6,740 sq km/2,602 sq mi and a population of 1,772,000.

Dreyfus Alfred 1859–1935. French army officer, victim of miscarriage of justice, anti-Semitism, and cover-up. Employed in the War Ministry, in 1894 he was accused of betraying military secrets to Germany, court-martialled, and sent to the penal colony on ⬦Devil's Island, French Guiana. When his innocence was discovered 1896 the military establishment tried to conceal it, and the implications of the Dreyfus affair were passionately discussed in the press until he was exonerated in 1906.

dromedary variety of Arabian ⬦camel. The dromedary or one-humped camel has been domesticated since 400 BC. During a long period without water, the dromedary can lose up to one-quarter of its bodyweight without ill effects.

drought period of prolonged dry weather. The area of the world subject to serious droughts, such as the Sahara, is increasing because of destruction of forests, overgrazing, and poor agricultural practices. In the UK, drought is defined as the passing of 15 days with less than 0.2 mm of rain.

drug any of a range of chemicals voluntarily or involuntarily introduced into the bodies of humans and animals in order to enhance or suppress a biological function. Most drugs in use are medicines (pharmaceuticals), used to prevent or treat diseases, or to relieve their symptoms; they include antibiotics, cytotoxic drugs, immunosuppressives, sedatives, and pain-relievers (analgesics).

drug misuse illegal use of drugs for nonmedicinal purposes. Under the UK Misuse of Drugs Acts drugs used illegally comprise: (1) *most harmful*

heroin, morphine, opium, and other narcotics; hallucinogens, such as mescalin and LSD; and injectable amphetamines, such as methedrine; (2) *less harmful* narcotics such as codeine and cannabis; stimulants of the amphetamine type, such as Benzedrine and barbiturates; (3) *least harmful* milder drugs of the amphetamine type. *Designer drugs*, for example ecstasy, are usually modifications of the amphetamine molecule, altered in order to evade the law as well as for different effects, and may be many times more powerful and dangerous. Crack, a smokable form of cocaine, became available to drug users in the 1980s.

Druidism religion of the Celtic peoples of the pre-Christian British Isles and Gaul. The word is derived from Greek *drus* 'oak'. The Druids regarded this tree as sacred; one of their chief rites was the cutting of mistletoe from it with a golden sickle. They taught the immortality of the soul and a reincarnation doctrine, and were expert in astronomy. The Druids are thought to have offered human sacrifices.

drum percussion instrument, essentially a piece of skin (parchment, plastic, or nylon) stretched over a resonator and struck with a stick or the hands. The drum is one of the oldest instruments. Electronic drums, first marketed 1980, are highly touch-and force-sensitive and can also be controlled by computer.

drupe fleshy fruit containing one or more seeds which are surrounded by a hard, protective layer – for example cherry, almond, and plum. The wall of the fruit (pericarp) is differentiated into the outer skin (exocarp), the fleshy layer of tissues (mesocarp), and the hard layer surrounding the seed (endocarp).

Druse or *Druze* religious sect in the Middle East of some 500,000 people. They are monotheists, preaching that the Fatimid caliph al-Hakim (996–1021) is God; their scriptures are drawn from the Bible, the Koran, and Sufi allegories. Druse militia groups form one of the three main factions involved in the Lebanese civil war (the others are Amal Shi'ite Muslims and Christian Maronites). The Druse military leader (from the time of his father's assassination 1977) is Walid Jumblatt.

Dryden John 1631–1700. English poet and dramatist, noted for his satirical verse and for his use of the heroic couplet. His poetry includes the verse satire *Absalom and Achitophel* 1681, *Annus Mirabilis* 1667, and 'St Cecilia's Day' 1687. Plays include the comedy *Marriage à la mode* 1672 and *All for Love* 1678, a reworking of Shakespeare's *Antony and Cleopatra*.

dry ice solid carbon dioxide (CO_2), used as a refrigerant. At temperatures above $-79°C/-110.2°F$, it sublimes (turns into vapour without passing through a liquid stage) to gaseous carbon dioxide.

dry rot infection of timber in damp conditions

by fungi, such as *Merulius lacrymans*, that form a threadlike surface. Whitish at first, the fungus later reddens as reproductive spores are formed. Fungoid tentacles also enter the fabric of the timber, rendering it dry-looking and brittle. Dry rot spreads rapidly through a building.

DTP abbreviation for desktop publishing.

Duarte José Napoleon 1925–1990. El Salvadorean centrist politician, president 1980–82 and 1984–88. He was mayor of San Salvador 1964–70, and was elected president 1972, but exiled by the army 1982. On becoming president again 1984, he sought a negotiated settlement with the left-wing guerrillas 1986, but resigned on health grounds.

Dubai one of the ⟡United Arab Emirates.

Dubček Alexander 1921– . Czechoslovak politician, chair of the federal assembly from 1989. He was a member of the Czech ⟡resistance movement during World War II, and became first secretary of the Communist Party 1967–69. He launched a liberalization campaign (called the Prague Spring) that was opposed by the USSR and led to the Soviet invasion of Czechoslovakia 1968. He was arrested by Soviet troops and expelled from the party 1970. In 1989 he gave speeches at prodemocracy rallies and, after the fall of the hardline regime, returned to elected office.

Dublin county in Leinster province, Republic of Ireland, facing the Irish Sea; area 920 sq km/355 sq mi; population (1986) 1,021,000. It is mostly level and low-lying, but rises in the south to 753 m/2,471 ft in Kippure, part of the Wicklow mountains. The river Liffey enters Dublin Bay. Dublin, the capital of the Republic of Ireland, and Dun Laoghaire are the two main towns.

Dublin (Gaelic *Baile Atha Cliath*) capital and port on the east coast of the Republic of Ireland, at the mouth of the river Liffey, facing the Irish Sea; population (1981) 526,000, Greater Dublin (including Dun Laoghaire) 921,000. It is the site of one of the world's largest breweries (Guinness); other industries include textiles, pharmaceuticals, electrical goods, and machine tools. It was the centre of English rule from 1171 (exercised from Dublin Castle 1220) until 1922.

Duchamp Marcel 1887–1968. US artist, born in France. He achieved notoriety with his *Nude Descending a Staircase* 1912 (Philadelphia Museum of Art), influenced by Cubism and Futurism. An active exponent of ⟡Dada, he invented 'readymades', everyday items like a bicycle wheel on a kitchen stool, which he displayed as works of art.

duck any of several short-legged waterbirds with webbed feet and flattened bills, of the family Anatidae, which also includes the larger geese and swans. Ducks were domesticated for eggs, meat, and feathers by the ancient Chinese and the ancient Maya (see ⟡poultry). Most ducks live in fresh water, feeding on worms and insects as well as vegetable matter. They are generally divided into dabbling ducks and diving ducks. There are over 100 species of duck worldwide.

Dufy Raoul 1877–1953. French painter and designer. He originated a fluent, brightly coloured style in watercolour and oils, painting scenes of gaiety and leisure, such as horse racing, yachting, and life on the beach. He also designed tapestries, textiles, and ceramics.

duiker any of several antelopes of the family Bovidae, common in Africa. Duikers are shy and nocturnal, and grow to 30–70 cm/12–28 in tall.

Duisburg river port and industrial city in North Rhine–Westphalia, Germany, at the confluence of the Rhine and Ruhr rivers; population (1987) 515,000. It is the largest inland river port in Europe. Heavy industries include oil refining and the production of steel, copper, zinc, plastics, and machinery.

Dukas Paul (Abraham) 1865–1935. French composer. His orchestral scherzo *L'Apprenti sorcier/The Sorcerer's Apprentice* 1897 is full of the colour and energy that characterizes much of his work.

dulcimer musical instrument consisting of a shallow soundbox strung with many wires that are struck with small wooden hammers. In Hungary it is called a cimbalom.

Dumas Alexandre 1802–1870. French author, known as Dumas *père* (the father). His romances, the reworked output of a 'fiction-factory' of collaborators, include *Les trois Mousquetaires/The Three Musketeers* 1844 and its sequels. Dumas *fils* was his son.

Dumas Alexandre 1824–1895. French author, known as Dumas *fils* (the son of Dumas *père*) and remembered for the play *La Dame aux camélias/The Lady of the Camellias* 1852, based on his own novel and the source of Verdi's opera *La traviata*.

Du Maurier Daphne 1907–1989. British novelist whose romantic fiction includes *Jamaica Inn* 1936, *Rebecca* 1938, and *My Cousin Rachel* 1951. *Jamaica Inn*, *Rebecca*, and her short story 'The Birds' were made into films by the English director Alfred Hitchcock.

Dumfries and Galloway region of Scotland; *area* 6,500 sq km/2,510 sq mi; *towns* Dumfries (administrative headquarters); *features* Solway Firth; Galloway Hills, setting of John Buchan's *The Thirty-Nine Steps*; Glen Trool National Park; Ruthwell Cross, a runic cross of about 800 at the village of Ruthwell; Stranraer provides the shortest sea route to Ireland; *products* horses and cattle, sheep, timber; *famous people* Robert I (Robert the Bruce), Robert Burns, Thomas Carlyle; *population* (1987) 147,000.

Duncan Isadora 1878–1927. US dancer and teacher. An influential pioneer of Modern dance, she adopted an expressive free form, dancing barefoot and wearing a loose tunic, inspired by the ideal of Hellenic beauty. She toured extensively, often returning to Russia after her initial success there 1905.

Dundee city and fishing port, administrative headquarters of Tayside, Scotland, on the N side of the Firth of Tay; population (1981) 175,000. It is an important shipping and rail centre with marine engineering, watch and clock, and textile industries.

dune mound or ridge of wind-drifted sand. Loose sand is blown and bounced along by the wind, up the windward side of a dune. The sand particles then fall to rest on the lee side, while more are blown up from the windward side. In this way a dune moves gradually downwind.

Dunedin port on Otago harbour, South Island, New Zealand; population (1986) 106,864. It is a road, rail, and air centre, with engineering and textile industries. The city was founded 1848 by members of the Free Church of Scotland.

Dunfermline industrial town near the Firth of Forth in Fife region, Scotland; population (1981) 52,000. It is the site of the naval base of Rosyth; industries include engineering, shipbuilding, electronics, and textiles. Many Scottish kings, including Robert the Bruce, are buried in Dunfermline Abbey. It is the birthplace of the industrialist Andrew Carnegie.

Dun Laoghaire (former name *Kingstown*) port and suburb of Dublin, Republic of Ireland. It is a terminal for ferries to Britain, and there are fishing industries.

dunnock European bird *Prunella modularis* similar in size and colouring to the sparrow, but with a slate-grey head and breast, and more slender bill. It nests in bushes and hedges, and is often called the 'hedge sparrow'.

Duns Scotus John *c.* 1265–*c.* 1308. Scottish monk, a leading figure in the theological and philosophical system of medieval ▷scholasticism. On many points he turned against the orthodoxy of Thomas ▷Aquinas; for example, he rejected the idea of a necessary world, favouring a concept of God as absolute freedom capable of spontaneous activity. The church rejected his ideas, and the word *dunce* is derived from Dunses, a term of ridicule applied to his followers.

Du Pré Jacqueline 1945–1987. English cellist. She was celebrated for her proficient technique and powerful interpretations of the Classical cello repertory, particularly of Edward ▷Elgar. She had an international concert career while still in her teens and made many recordings.

Durban principal port of Natal, South Africa, and second port of the republic; population (1985) 634,000, urban area 982,000. It exports coal, maize, and wool, imports heavy machinery and mining equipment, and is also a holiday resort.

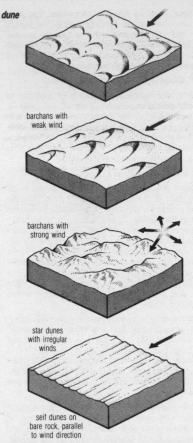

dune

barchans with weak wind

barchans with strong wind

star dunes with irregular winds

seif dunes on bare rock, parallel to wind direction

Dürer Albrecht 1471–1528. German artist, the leading figure of the northern Renaissance. He was born in Nuremberg and travelled widely in Europe. Highly skilled in drawing and a keen student of nature, he perfected the technique of woodcut and engraving, producing woodcut series such as the *Apocalypse* 1498 and copperplate engravings such as *The Knight, Death, and the Devil* 1513, and *Melancholia* 1514; he may also have invented etching

Durham county in NE England; *area* 2,440 sq km/ 942 sq mi; *towns* Durham (administrative headquarters), Darlington, Peterlee, Newton Aycliffe; *features* Beamish open-air industrial museum; *products* sheep and dairy produce; site of one of Britain's richest coalfields; *population* (1987) 599,000; *famous people* Elizabeth Barrett Browning, Anthony Eden.

Durkheim Emile 1858–1917. French sociologist,

one of the founders of modern sociology, who also influenced social anthropology. He worked to establish sociology as a respectable and scientific discipline, capable of diagnosing social ills and recommending possible cures.

Durrell Gerald (Malcolm) 1925– . British naturalist, director of Jersey Zoological Park. He is the author of travel and natural history books, and the humorous memoir *My Family and Other Animals* 1956. He is the brother of Lawrence Durrell.

Durrell Lawrence (George) 1912–1990. British novelist and poet. Born in India, he joined the foreign service and lived mainly in the E Mediterranean, the setting of his novels, including the Alexandria Quartet: *Justine, Balthazar, Mountolive,* and *Clea* 1957–60; he also wrote travel books.

Dushanbe formerly (1929–69) *Stalinabad* capital of Tajikistan, 160 km/100 mi N of the Afghan frontier; population (1987) 582,000. It is a road, rail, and air centre. Industries include cotton mills, tanneries, meat-packing factories, and printing works. A curfew was imposed Feb 1990–Jan 1991 in response to antigovernment rioting and pogroms; a state of emergency remained in force after Jan.

Düsseldorf industrial city of Germany, on the right bank of the river Rhine, 26 km/16 mi NW of Cologne, capital of North Rhine–Westphalia; population (1988) 561,000. It is a river port and the commercial and financial centre of the Ruhr area, with food processing, brewing, agricultural machinery, textile, and chemical industries.

Dutch East India Company trading monopoly of the 17th and 18th centuries; see ◊East India Company, Dutch.

Dutch East Indies former Dutch colony, which in 1945 became independent as ◊Indonesia.

Dutch Guiana former Dutch colony, which in 1975 became independent as ◊Surinam.

Dutch language member of the Germanic branch of the Indo-European language family, often referred to by scholars as Netherlandic and taken to include the standard language and dialects of the Netherlands (excluding Frisian) as well as Flemish (in Belgium and N France) and, more remotely, its offshoot Afrikaans in South Africa.

Duvalier François 1907–1971. Right-wing president of Haiti 1957–71. Known as *Papa Doc*, he ruled as a dictator, organizing the Tontons Macoutes ('bogeymen') as a private security force to intimidate and assassinate opponents of his regime. He rigged the 1961 elections in order to have his term of office extended until 1967, and in 1964 declared himself president for life. He was excommunicated by the Vatican for harassing the church, and was succeeded on his death by his son Jean-Claude Duvalier.

Duvalier Jean-Claude 1951– . Right-wing president of Haiti 1971–86. Known as *Baby Doc*, he

succeeded his father François Duvalier, becoming, at the age of 19, the youngest president in the world. He continued to receive support from the USA but was pressured into moderating some elements of his father's regime, yet still tolerated no opposition. In 1986, with Haiti's economy stagnating and with increasing civil disorder, Duvalier fled to France, taking much of the Haitian treasury with him.

Dvořák Antonin (Leopold) 1841–1904. Czech composer. International recognition came with his series of *Slavonic Dances* 1877–86, and he was director of the National Conservatory, New York, 1892–95. Works such as his *New World Symphony* 1893 reflect his interest in American folk themes, including black and native American. He wrote nine symphonies; tone poems; operas, including *Rusalka* 1900; large-scale choral works; the *Carnival* 1891–92 and other overtures; violin and cello concertos; chamber music; piano pieces; and songs. His Romantic music extends the Classical tradition of Beethoven and Brahms and displays the influence of Czech folk music.

Dyck Anthony Van 1599–1641. Flemish painter. Born in Antwerp, Van Dyck was an assistant to Rubens 1618–20, then briefly worked in England at the court of James I, and moved to Italy 1622. In 1626 he returned to Antwerp, where he continued to paint religious works and portraits. From 1632 he lived in England and produced numerous portraits of royalty and aristocrats, such as *Charles I on Horseback* about 1638 (National Gallery, London).

dye substance that, applied in solution to fabrics, imparts a colour resistant to washing. *Direct dyes* combine with the material of the fabric, yielding a coloured compound; *indirect dyes* require the presence of another substance (a mordant), with which the fabric must first be treated; *vat dyes* are colourless soluble substances that on exposure to air yield an insoluble coloured compound.

Dyfed county in SW Wales; *area* 5,770 sq km/ 2,227 sq mi; *towns* Carmarthen (administrative headquarters), Llanelli, Haverfordwest, Aberystwyth, Cardigan, Lampeter; *features* Pembrokeshire Coast National Park; part of the Brecon Beacons National Park; the Black Mountains; part of the Cambrian Mountains, including Plynlimon Fawr 752 m/2,468 ft; the village of Laugharne, at the mouth of the river Tywi, which was the home of the writer Dylan Thomas; anthracite mines produce about 50,000 tonnes a year; *population* (1987) 343,000; *language* 46% Welsh, English; *famous people* Dafydd ap Gwilym, Giraldus Cambrensis.

Dylan Bob. Adopted name of Robert Allen Zimmerman 1941– . US singer and songwriter whose lyrics provided catchphrases for a generation and influenced innumerable songwriters. He began in the folk-music tradition. His early songs, as on his albums *Freewheelin'* 1963 and *The Times They Are*

A-Changin' 1964, were associated with the US civil-rights movement and antiwar protest. From 1965 he worked in an individualistic rock style, as on the albums *Highway 61 Revisited* 1965 and *Blonde on Blonde* 1966. In 1991, *The Bootleg Years*, a collection of 58 previously unreleased tracks, reasserted his standing.

dynamics or *kinetics* in mechanics, the mathematical and physical study of the behaviour of bodies under the action of forces that produce changes of motion in them.

dysentery infection of the large intestine causing abdominal cramps and painful ⟩diarrhoea with blood. There are two kinds of dysentery: *amoebic* (caused by a protozoan), common in the tropics, which may lead to liver damage; and *bacterial*, the kind most often seen in the temperate zones.

dyslexia malfunction in the brain's synthesis and interpretation of sensory information, popularly known as 'word blindness'. It results in poor ability to read and write, though the person may otherwise excel, for example, in mathematics. A similar disability with figures is called dyscalculia.

dysprosium silver-white, metallic element of the ⟩lanthanide series, symbol Dy, atomic number 66, relative atomic mass 162.50. It is among the most magnetic of all known substances and has a great capacity to absorb neutrons.

eagle any of several genera of large birds of prey of the family Accipitridae, including the golden eagle *Aquila chrysaetos* of Eurasia and North America, which has a 2 m/6 ft wingspan and is dark brown.

ear organ of hearing in animals. It responds to the vibrations that constitute sound, and these are translated into nerve signals and passed to the brain. A mammal's ear consists of three parts: outer ear, middle ear, and inner ear. The *outer ear* is a funnel that collects sound, directing it down a tube to the *ear drum* (tympanic membrane), which separates the outer and *middle ear*. Sounds vibrate this membrane, the mechanical movement of which is transferred to a smaller membrane leading to the *inner ear* by three small bones, the auditory ossicles. Vibrations of the inner ear membrane move fluid contained in the snail-shaped cochlea, which vibrates hair cells that stimulate the auditory nerve connected to the brain. Three fluid-filled canals of the inner ear detect changes of position; this mechanism, with other sensory inputs, is responsible for the sense of balance.

Earhart Amelia 1898–1937. US aviation pioneer and author, who in 1928 became the first woman to fly across the Atlantic. With copilot Frederick Noonan, she attempted a round-the-world flight 1937. Somewhere over the Pacific their plane disappeared.

Earth third planet from the Sun. It is almost spherical, flattened slightly at the poles, and is composed of three concentric layers: the core, the ◇mantle, and the crust. 70% of the surface (including the north and south polar icecaps) is covered with water. The Earth is surrounded by a life-supporting atmosphere and is the only planet on which life is known to exist. *mean distance from the Sun* 149,500,000 km/92,860,000 mi; *equatorial diameter* 12,756 km/7,923 mi; *circumference* 40,070 km/24,900 mi; *rotation period* 23 hr 56 min 4.1 sec; *year* (complete orbit, or sidereal period) 365 days 5 hr 48 min 46 sec. Earth's average speed around the Sun is 30 kps/18.5

ear

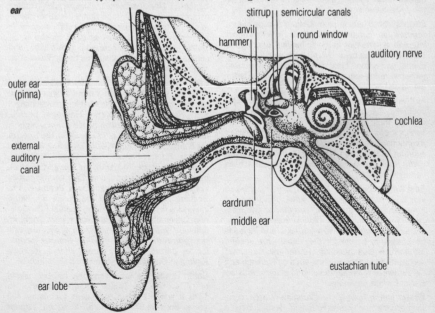

mps; the plane of its orbit is inclined to its equatorial plane at an angle of 23.5°, the reason for the changing seasons; *atmosphere* nitrogen 78.09%; oxygen 20.95%; argon 0.93%; carbon dioxide 0.03%; and less than 0.0001% neon, helium, krypton, hydrogen, xenon, ozone, radon; *surface* land surface 150,000,000 sq km/57,500,000 sq mi (greatest height above sea level 8,872 m/29,108 ft Mount Everest); water surface 361,000,000 sq km/139,400,000 sq mi (greatest depth 11,034 m/36,201 ft ◊Mariana Trench in the Pacific). The interior is thought to be an inner core about 2,600 km/1,600 mi in diameter, of solid iron and nickel; an outer core about 2,250 km/1,400 mi thick, of molten iron and nickel; and a mantle of mostly solid rock about 2,900 km/1,800 mi thick, separated by the ◊Mohorovičić discontinuity from the Earth's crust. The crust and the topmost layer of the mantle form about 12 major moving plates, some of which carry the continents. The plates are in constant, slow motion, called tectonic drift; *satellite* the ◊Moon; *age* 4.6 billion years. The Earth was formed with the rest of the ◊solar system by consolidation of interstellar dust. Life began 3.5–4 billion years ago.

earthquake shaking or convulsion of the Earth's surface, the scientific study of which is called ◊seismology. Earthquakes result from a build-up of stresses within rocks until strained to fracturing point. Most occur along ◊faults (fractures or breaks) in the Earth's crust. Most earthquakes happen under the sea. Their force is measured on the ◊Richter scale.

Earth Summit (official name *United Nations Conference on Environment and Development*) international meeting in Rio de Janeiro, Brazil, June 1992, drawing up measures towards world environmental protection. Treaties were made to combat global warming and protect biodiversity (the latter not signed by the USA).

earthworm ◊annelid worm of the class Oligochaeta. Earthworms are hermaphroditic, and deposit their eggs in cocoons. They live by burrowing in the soil, feeding on the organic matter it contains. They are vital to the formation of humus, aerating the soil and levelling it by transferring earth from the deeper levels to the surface as castings.

East Anglia region of E England, formerly a Saxon kingdom, including Norfolk, Suffolk, and parts of Essex and Cambridgeshire. Norwich is the principal city of East Anglia. The University of East Anglia was founded in Norwich 1962, and includes the Sainsbury Centre for the Visual Arts, opened 1978, which has a collection of ethnographic art and sculpture. East Anglian ports such as Harwich and Felixstowe have greatly developed as trade with the rest of Europe increases.

Easter spring feast of the Christian church, commemorating the Resurrection of Jesus. It is a moveable feast, falling on the first Sunday following

the full moon after the vernal equinox (21 March), thus between 22 March and 25 April.

Easter Island or *Rapa Nui* Chilean island in the S Pacific Ocean, part of the Polynesian group, about 3,500 km/2,200 mi W of Chile; area about 166 sq km/64 sq mi; population (1985) 2,000. It was first reached by Europeans on Easter Sunday 1722. On it stand huge carved statues and stone houses, the work of Neolithic peoples of unknown origin.

Easter Rising or *Easter Rebellion* in Irish history, a republican insurrection that began on Easter Monday, April 1916, in Dublin. It was inspired by the Irish Republican Brotherhood (IRB) in an unsuccessful attempt to overthrow British rule in Ireland. It was led by Patrick Pearse of the IRB and James Connolly of Sinn Féin.

East Germany see ◊Germany, East, former country.

East India Company commercial company 1600–1858 with a monopoly of trade between England and the Far East. In the 18th century the company became, in effect, the ruler of a large part of India, and a form of dual control by the company and a committee responsible to Parliament in London was introduced 1784. The end of the monopoly of China trade came 1834, and after the ◊Indian Mutiny 1857 the crown took complete control of the government of British India.

East India Company, Dutch (*VOC*, or *Vereenigde Oost-Indische Compagnie*) trading company chartered by the States General (parliament) of the Netherlands, and established in N Netherlands 1602. It was given a monopoly on Dutch trade in the Indonesian archipelago, and certain sovereign rights such as the creation of an army and a fleet.

East Sussex county in SE England; *area* 1,800 sq km/695 sq mi; *towns* Lewes (administrative headquarters), Newhaven (cross-channel port), Brighton, Eastbourne, Hastings, Bexhill, Winchelsea, Rye; *features* Beachy Head, highest headland on the S coast at 180 m/590 ft, the E end of the South ◊Downs; the Weald (including Ashdown Forest); Friston Forest; rivers: Ouse, Cuckmere, East Rother; Romney Marsh; the 'Long Man' chalk hill figure at Wilmington, near Eastbourne; castles at Hastings, Herstmonceux, Lewes, Pevensey, and Bodiam; Battle Abbey and the site of the Battle of Hastings; Michelham Priory; Sheffield Park garden; University of Sussex at Falmer, near Brighton, founded 1961; *products* electronics, gypsum, timber; *population* (1987) 698,000; *famous people* former homes of Henry James at Rye, Rudyard Kipling at Burwash, Virginia Woolf at Rodmell.

East Timor disputed territory on the island of ◊Timor in the Malay Archipelago; prior to 1975, it was a Portuguese colony for almost 460 years; *area* 14,874 sq km/5,706 sq mi; *capital* Dili; *products* coffee; *population* (1980) 555,000;

history following Portugal's withdrawal 1975, the left-wing Revolutionary Front of Independent East Timor (Fretilin) occupied the capital, calling for independence. In opposition, troops from neighbouring Indonesia invaded the territory, declaring East Timor (*Loro Sae*) the 17th province of Indonesia July 1976. This claim is not recognized by the United Nations.

ebony any of a group of hardwood trees of the ebony family Ebenaceae, especially some tropical persimmons of the genus *Diospyros*, native to Africa and Asia. Their very heavy, hard, black timber polishes well and is used in cabinetmaking, inlaying, and for piano keys and knife handles.

EC abbreviation for ⟩*European Community*.

echidna or *spiny anteater* any of several species of toothless, egg-laying, spiny mammals of the genera *Tachyglossus* and *Zaglossus* in the order Monotremata, found in Australia and New Guinea. They feed entirely upon ants and termites, which they dig out with their powerful claws and lick up with their prehensile tongues. When attacked, an echidna rolls itself into a ball, or tries to hide by burrowing in the earth.

echinoderm marine invertebrate of the phylum Echinodermata ('spiny-skinned'), characterized by a five-radial symmetry. They have a water-vascular system which transports substances around the body. Echinoderms include starfishes (or sea stars), brittle-stars, sea lilies, sea urchins, and sea cucumbers. The skeleton is external, made of a series of limy plates, and echinoderms generally move by using tube feet – small water-filled sacs that can be protruded or pulled back to the body.

echo repetition of a sound wave, or of a ⟩radar or ⟩sonar signal, by reflection from a surface. By accurately measuring the time taken for an echo to return to the transmitter, and by knowing the speed of a radar signal (the speed of light) or a sonar signal (the speed of sound in water), it is possible to calculate the range of the object causing the echo.

Echo in Greek mythology, a nymph who pined away until only her voice remained, after being rejected by Narcissus.

eclipse passage of an astronomical body through the shadow of another. The term is usually employed for solar and lunar eclipses, which may be either partial or total, but also, for example, for eclipses by Jupiter of its satellites. An eclipse of a star by a body in the solar system is called an occultation.

Eco Umberto 1932– . Italian writer, semiologist, and literary critic. His works include *The Role of the Reader* 1979, and two novels: the 'philosophical thriller' *The Name of the Rose* 1983 and *Foucault's Pendulum* 1988.

ecology study of the relationship among organisms and the environments in which they live, including all living and nonliving components. The term was coined by the biologist Ernst Haeckel 1866.

economics social science devoted to studying the production, distribution, and consumption of wealth. It consists of the disciplines of ⟩*microeconomics*, the study of individual producers, consumers, or markets, and ⟩*macroeconomics*, the study of whole economies or systems (in particular, areas such as taxation and public spending).

ECU abbreviation for *European Currency Unit*, official monetary unit of the EC. It is based on the value of the different currencies used in the ⟩European Monetary System (ERM). In 1990 and 1991, sterling's central rate within the ERM was = 1.43 ECU.

Ecuador Republic of; country in South America, bordered N by Colombia, E and S by Peru, and W by the Pacific Ocean; *area* 270,670 sq km/ 104,479 sq mi; *capital* Quito; *physical* coastal plain rises charply to Andes Mountains which are divided into a series of cultivated valleys; flat, low-lying rainforest in E; *head of state and government* Rodrigo Borja Cevallos from 1988; *political system* emergent democracy; *exports* bananas, cocoa, coffee, sugar, rice, balsa wood, fish, petroleum; *population* (1989 est) 10,490,000 (mestizo (mixed race) 55%, Indian 25%, European 10%, black African 10%); *languages* Spanish (official); Quechuan, Jivaroan; *recent history* independence was achieved from Spain 1830. After a long period of instability, liberal and conservative governments alternated from 1948 until 1963 when the military junta came into power. In 1982, a state of emergency was declared after strikes and demonstrations, followed by austerity measures 1983.

ecumenical movement movement for reunification of the various branches of the Christian church. It began in the 19th century with the extension of missionary work to Africa and Asia, where the divisions created in Europe were incomprehensible; the movement gathered momentum from the need for unity in the face of growing secularism in Christian countries and of the challenge posed by such faiths as Islam. The *World Council of Churches* was founded 1948.

eczema inflammatory skin condition, a form of dermatitis, marked by dryness, rashes, itching, the formation of blisters, and the exudation of fluid. It may be allergic in origin and is sometimes complicated by infection.

Edberg Stefan 1966– . Swedish lawn-tennis player and twice winner of Wimbledon 1988, 1990. He won the junior Grand Slam 1983 and his first senior Grand Slam title, the Australian Open 1985, and three more Grand Slam events by the end of 1991. At Wimbledon in 1987, he became the first male player in 40 years to win a match without conceding a game.

edelweiss perennial alpine plant *Leontopodium alpinum*, family Compositae, with a white, woolly, star-shaped bloom, found in the high mountains of Eurasia.

Eden river in Cumbria, NW England; length 104 km/65 mi. From its source in the Pennines, it flows NW to enter the Solway Firth NW of Carlisle.

Eden Anthony, 1st Earl of Avon 1897–1977. British Conservative politician, foreign secretary 1935–38, 1940–45, and 1951–55; prime minister 1955–57, when he resigned after the failure of the Anglo-French military intervention in the ⟡Suez Crisis.

Edgar the Peaceful 944–975. King of all England from 959. He was the younger son of Edmund I, and strove successfully to unite English and Danes as fellow subjects.

Edinburgh capital of Scotland and administrative centre of the region of Lothian, near the southern shores of the Firth of Forth; population (1985) 440,000. A cultural centre, it holds an annual festival of music and the arts; the university was established 1583. Industries include printing, publishing, banking, insurance, chemical manufactures, distilling, brewing, and some shipbuilding.

Edinburgh, Duke of title of Prince ⟡Philip of the UK.

Edison Thomas Alva 1847–1931. US scientist and inventor, with over 1,000 patents. In Menlo Park, New Jersey, 1876–87, he produced his most important inventions, including the electric light bulb 1879. He constructed a system of electric power distribution for consumers, the telephone transmitter, and the phonograph.

Edmonton capital of Alberta, Canada, on the North Saskatchewan River; population (1986) 576,200. It is the centre of an oil and mining area to the north and also an agricultural and dairying region. Petroleum pipelines link Edmonton with Superior, Wisconsin, USA, and Vancouver, British Columbia.

Edmund II Ironside *c.* 989–1016. King of England 1016, the son of Ethelred II the Unready. He led the resistance to ⟡Canute's invasion 1015, and on Ethelred's death 1016 was chosen king by the citizens of London, whereas the Witan (the king's council) elected Canute. In the struggle for the throne, Edmund was defeated by Canute at Assandun (Ashington), Essex, and they divided the kingdom between them; when Edmund died the same year, Canute ruled the whole kingdom.

education the process, beginning at birth, of developing intellectual capacity, manual skill, and social awareness, especially by instruction. In its more restricted sense, the term refers to the process of imparting literacy, numeracy, and a generally accepted body of knowledge.

Edward (full name Edward Antony Richard Louis) 1964– . Prince of the UK, third son of Queen Elizabeth II. He is seventh in line to the throne after Charles, Charles's two sons, Andrew, and Andrew's two daughters.

Edward the *Black Prince* 1330–1376. Prince of Wales, eldest son of Edward III of England. The epithet (probably posthumous) may refer to his black armour. During the Hundred Years' War he fought at the Battle of Crécy 1346 and captured the French king at Poitiers 1356. He ruled Aquitaine 1360–71; during the revolt that eventually ousted him, he caused the massacre of Limoges 1370.

Edward I 1239–1307. King of England from 1272, son of Henry III. Edward led the royal forces against Simon de Montfort in the ⟡Barons' War 1264–67, and was on a crusade when he succeeded to the throne. He established English rule over all Wales 1282–84, and secured recognition of his overlordship from the Scottish king, although the Scots (under Wallace and Bruce) fiercely resisted actual conquest. In his reign Parliament took its approximate modern form with the ⟡Model Parliament 1295.

Edward II 1284–1327. King of England from 1307. Son of Edward I and born at Caernarvon Castle, he was created the first Prince of Wales 1301. His invasion of Scotland 1314 to suppress revolt resulted in defeat at ⟡Bannockburn. He was deposed 1327 by his wife Isabella (1292–1358), daughter of Philip IV of France, and her lover Roger de ⟡Mortimer, and murdered.

Edward III 1312–1377. King of England from 1327, son of Edward II. He assumed the government 1330 from his mother, through whom in 1337 he laid claim to the French throne and thus began the ⟡Hundred Years' War. He was succeeded by Richard II. During his last years his son John of Gaunt acted as head of government.

Edward IV 1442–1483. King of England 1461–70 and from 1471. He was the son of Richard, Duke of York, and succeeded Henry VI in the Wars of the ⟡Roses, temporarily losing the throne to Henry when Edward fell out with his adviser ⟡Warwick, but regaining it at the Battle of Barnet 1471. He was succeeded by his son Edward V.

Edward V 1470–1483. King of England 1483. Son of Edward IV, he was deposed three months after his accession in favour of his uncle (⟡Richard III), and is traditionally believed to have been murdered (with his brother) in the Tower of London on Richard's orders.

Edward VI 1537–1553. King of England from 1547, son of Henry VIII and Jane Seymour. The government was entrusted to his uncle the Duke of Somerset (who fell from power 1549), and then to the Earl of Warwick, later created Duke of Northumberland. He was succeeded by his sister, Mary I.

Edward VII 1841–1910. King of Great Britain and

Ireland from 1901. As Prince of Wales he was a prominent social figure, but his mother Queen Victoria considered him too frivolous to take part in political life. In 1860 he made the first tour of Canada and the USA ever undertaken by a British prince.

Edward VIII 1894–1972. King of Great Britain and Northern Ireland Jan–Dec 1936, when he renounced the throne to marry Wallis Warfield ◊Simpson. He was created Duke of Windsor and was governor of the Bahamas 1940–45, subsequently settling in France. He was succeeded by his brother, George VI.

Edward the Confessor c. 1003–1066. King of England from 1042, the son of Ethelred II. He lived in Normandy until shortly before his accession. During his reign power was held by Earl Godwin and his son ◊Harold, while the king devoted himself to religion, including the rebuilding of Westminster Abbey (consecrated 1065), where he is buried. His childlessness led ultimately to the Norman Conquest 1066. He was canonized 1161.

Edward the Elder c. 870–924. King of the West Saxons. He succeeded his father ◊Alfred the Great 899. He reconquered SE England and the Midlands from the Danes, uniting Wessex and ◊Mercia with the help of his sister, Athelflad. By the time Edward died, his kingdom was the most powerful in the British Isles. He was succeeded by his son ◊Athelstan.

Edward the Martyr c. 963–978. King of England from 975. Son of King Edgar, he was murdered at Corfe Castle, Dorset, probably at his stepmother Aelfthryth's instigation (she wished to secure the crown for her son, Ethelred). He was canonized 1001.

eel any fish of the order Anguilliformes. Eels are snakelike, with elongated dorsal and anal fins. They include the freshwater eels of Europe and North America (which breed in the Atlantic), the marine conger eels, and the morays of tropical coral reefs.

eelgrass or *tape grass* or *glass wrack* any of several flowering plants of the genus *Zostera*, especially *Zostera marina*, of the pondweed family Zosteraceae. Eelgrass is found in tidal mud flats and is one of the few flowering plants to adapt to marine conditions, being completely submerged at high tide.

EFTA acronym for ◊*European Free Trade Association*.

egg in animals, the ovum, or female ◊gamete (reproductive cell). After fertilization by a sperm cell, it begins to divide to form an embryo. Eggs may be deposited by the female (ovipary) or they may develop within her body (◊vivipary and ovovivipary). In the oviparous reptiles and birds, the egg is protected by a shell, and well supplied with nutrients in the form of yolk.

ego in psychology, a general term for the processes concerned with the self and a person's conception of himself or herself, encompassing values and attitudes. In Freudian psychology, the term refers specifically to the element of the human mind that represents the conscious processes concerned with reality, in conflict with the ◊id (the instinctual element) and the ◊superego (the ethically aware element).

egret any of several herons with long feathers on the head or neck. The great white egret *Egretta alba* of SE Europe and other parts of the Old World, which grows to a length of 1 m/3 ft, develops snowy-white plumes, formerly used for hat ornaments.

Egypt Arab Republic of; country in NE Africa, bordered N by the Mediterranean, E by the Suez Canal and Red Sea, S by Sudan, and W by Libya; *area* 1,001,450 sq km/386,990 sq mi; *capital* Cairo; *physical* mostly desert; hills in E; fertile land along river Nile; cultivated and settled area is about 35,500 sq km/13,700 sq mi; *head of state and government* Hosni Mubarak from 1981; *political system* democratic republic; *exports* cotton and textiles, petroleum, fruit and vegetables; *population* (1989 est) 54,779,000; *language* Arabic (official); *recent history* independence was achieved from Britain 1936. President General Neguib declared Egypt a republic 1953. In 1956, President Nasser announced the nationalization of the Suez Canal, resulting in the Six-Day War with Israel and the occupation of the Sinai and Gaza strip. The Camp David talks with Israel led to the exclusion of Egypt from the Arab League. President Sadat was assassinated and replaced by Hosni Mubarak 1981. Egypt was readmitted into the Arab League 1987 and diplomatic relations with Arab countries were subsequently restored. In 1991 Egypt participated in the ◊Gulf War on the US-led side and played a major role in convening a Middle East peace conference 1991.

Ehrlich Paul 1854–1915. German bacteriologist and immunologist who produced the first cure for ◊syphilis, developing the arsenic compounds used

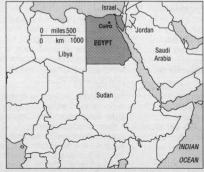

until the discovery of antibiotics. He shared the 1908 Nobel Prize for Medicine with Ilya Mechnikov for his work on immunity.

eider large marine ◊duck, *Somateria mollissima*, highly valued for its soft down, which is used in quilts and cushions for warmth. It is found on the northern coasts of the Atlantic and Pacific Oceans.

Einstein Albert 1879–1955. German-born US physicist who formulated the theories of ◊relativity, and worked on radiation physics and thermodynamics. In 1905 he published the special theory of relativity, and in 1915 issued his general theory of relativity. He received the Nobel Prize for Physics 1921. His latest conception of the basic laws governing the universe was outlined in his ◊unified field theory, made public 1953.

einsteinium synthesized, radioactive, metallic element of the actinide series, symbol Es, atomic number 99, relative atomic mass 254.

Eire Gaelic name for the Republic of ◊Ireland.

Eisenhower Dwight D (avid 'Ike') 1890–1969. 34th president of the USA 1953–61, a Republican. A general in World War II, he commanded the Allied forces in Italy 1943, then the Allied invasion of Europe, and from Oct 1944 all the Allied armies in the West. As president he promoted business interests at home and conducted the ◊Cold War abroad. His vice president was Richard Nixon.

eisteddfod traditional Welsh gathering lasting up to a week and dedicated to the encouragement of the bardic arts of music, poetry, and literature; it dates from pre-Christian times.

eland largest species of ◊antelope, *Taurotragus oryx*. Pale fawn in colour, it is about 2 m/6 ft high,

and both sexes have spiral horns about 45 cm/18 in long. It is found in central and southern Africa.

Elbe one of the principal rivers of Germany, 1,166 km/725 mi long, rising on the southern slopes of the Riesengebirge, Czechoslovakia, and flowing NW across the German plain to the North Sea.

Elbruz or *Elbrus* highest mountain (5,642 m/ 18,517 ft) on the continent of Europe, in the Caucasus, Georgia.

elder small tree or shrub of the genus *Sambucus*, family Caprifoliaceae. The common *Sambucus nigra* of Europe, N Africa, and W Asia has pinnate leaves and heavy heads of small, sweet-scented, white flowers in early summer. These are succeeded by clusters of small, black berries.

Eleanor of Aquitaine *c*. 1122–1204. Queen of France 1137–51 as wife of Louis VII, and of England from 1154 as wife of Henry II. Henry imprisoned her 1174–89 for supporting their sons, the future Richard I and King John, in revolt against him.

Eleanor of Castile *c*. 1245–1290. Queen of Edward I of England, the daughter of Ferdinand III of Castile. She married Prince Edward 1254, and accompanied him on his crusade 1270. She died at Harby, Nottinghamshire, and Edward erected stone crosses in towns where her body rested on the funeral journey to London. Several *Eleanor Crosses* are still standing, for example at Northampton.

election process of appointing a person to public office or a political party to government by voting. Elections were occasionally held in ancient Greek democracies; Roman tribunes were regularly elected. In England elections have been used as a parliamentary process since the 13th century.

Egypt, ancient

5000 BC	Egyptian culture well established in the Nile Valley, with Neolithic farming villages.
3200 BC	Menes united Lower Egypt (the delta) with his own kingdom of Upper Egypt.
2800 BC	The architect Imhotep built the step pyramid at Sakkara.
c.2600 BC	Old Kingdom reached the height of its power and the kings of the 4th dynasty built the pyramids at Giza.
c.2200–1800 BC	Middle Kingdom, under which the unity lost towards the end of the Old Kingdom was restored.
1730 BC	Invading Asian Hyksos people established their kingdom in the Nile Delta.
c.1580 BC	New Kingdom established by the 18th dynasty, following the eviction of the Hyksos, with its capital at Thebes. High point of ancient Egyptian civilization under pharaohs Thothmes, Hatshepsut, Amenhotep, Ikhnaton (who moved the capital to Akhetaton), and Tutankhamen.
c.1321 BC	19th dynasty: Ramses I built a temple at Karnak, Ramses II the temple at Abu Simbel.
1191 BC	Ramses III defeated the Indo-European Sea Peoples, but after him there was decline; power passed from the pharaohs to the priests of Ammon.
1090–663 BC	Late New Kingdom Egypt was often divided between two or more dynasties; the nobles became virtually independent.
8th–7th centuries BC	Brief interlude of rule by kings from Nubia.
666 BC	The Assyrians under Ashurbanipal occupied Thebes.
663–609 BC	Psammetichus I restored Egypt's independence and unity.
525 BC	Egypt was conquered by Cambyses and became a Persian province.
c.405–340 BC	A period of independence.
332 BC	Conquest by Alexander the Great. On the division of his empire, Egypt went to one of his generals, Ptolemy I, and his descendants, the Macedonian dynasty.
30 BC	Death of Cleopatra, last of the Macedonians, and conquest by the Roman emperor Augustus; Egypt became a province of the Roman and Byzantine empires.

electricity supply

coal-fired power station (highly simplified)

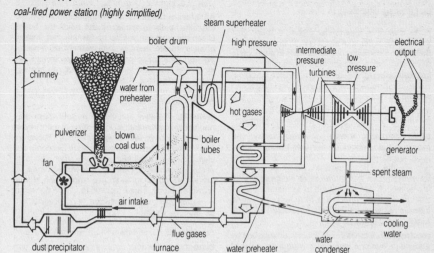

The secret ballot was adopted 1872. All registered members of the public aged 18 and over may vote in local, parliamentary, and European Parliament elections.

electoral system see ▷vote and ▷proportional representation.

electric charge property of some bodies that causes them to exert forces on each other. Two bodies both with positive or both with negative charges repel each other, whereas bodies with opposite or 'unlike' charges attract each other, since each is in the electric field of the other. In atoms, ▷electrons possess a negative charge, and ▷protons an equal positive charge. The ▷SI unit of electric charge is the coulomb (symbol C).

electric current the flow of electrically charged particles through a conducting circuit due to the presence of a ▷potential difference. The current at any point in a circuit is the amount of charge flowing per second; its SI unit is the ampere (coulomb per second).

electricity all phenomena caused by ▷electric charge, whether static or in motion. Electric charge is caused by an excess or deficit of electrons in the charged substance, and an electric current by the movement of electrons around a circuit. Substances may be electrical conductors, such as metals, which allow the passage of electricity through them, or insulators, such as rubber, which are extremely poor conductors. Substances with relatively poor conductivities that can be improved by the addition of heat or light are known as ▷semiconductors.

electrocardiogram (ECG) graphic recording of the electrical changes in the heart muscle, as detected by electrodes placed on the chest. Electrocardiography is used in the diagnosis of heart disease.

electroconvulsive therapy (ECT) or *electroshock therapy* treatment for ▷schizophrenia and ▷depression, given under anaesthesia and with a muscle relaxant. An electric current is passed through the brain to induce alterations in the brain's electrical activity. The treatment can cause distress and loss of concentration and memory, and so there is much controversy about its use and effectiveness.

electrocution death caused by electric current. It is used as a method of execution in some US states. The condemned person is strapped into a special chair and a shock of 1,800–2,000 volts is administered. See ▷capital punishment.

electrode any terminal by which an electric current passes in or out of a conducting substance; for example, the anode or cathode in a battery or the carbons in an arc lamp. The terminals that emit and collect the flow of electrons in thermionic ▷valves (electron tubes) are also called electrodes: for example, cathodes, plates, and grids.

electroencephalogram (EEG) graphic record of the electrical discharges of the brain, as detected by electrodes placed on the scalp. The pattern of electrical activity revealed by electroencephalography is helpful in the diagnosis of some brain disorders, such as epilepsy.

electrolysis the production of chemical changes by passing an electric current through a solution or molten salt (the electrolyte), resulting in the migration of ions to the electrodes: positive ions (cations) to the negative electrode (cathode) and negative ions (anions) to the positive electrode (anode).

electromagnetic field in physics, the agency by which a particle with an ◊electric charge experiences a force in a particular region of space. If it does so only when moving, it is in a pure **magnetic field**; if it does so when stationary, it is in an **electric field**. Both can be present simultaneously.

electromagnetic force one of the four fundamental ◊forces of nature, the other three being gravity, the strong nuclear force, and the weak nuclear force. The ◊elementary particle that is the carrier for the electromagnetic (em) force is the photon.

electromagnetic waves oscillating electric and magnetic fields travelling together through space at a speed of nearly 300,000 km/186,000 mi per second. The (limitless) range of possible wavelengths or ◊frequencies of electromagnetic waves, which can be thought of as making up the **electromagnetic spectrum**, includes radio waves, infrared radiation, visible light, ultraviolet radiation, X-rays, and gamma rays.

electromotive force (emf) the energy supplied by a source of electric power in driving a unit charge around an electrical circuit. The unit is the ◊volt.

electron stable, negatively charged ◊elementary particle; it is a constituent of all atoms, and a member of the class of particles known as ◊leptons. The electrons in each atom surround the nucleus in groupings called shells; in a neutral atom the number of electrons is equal to the number of protons in the nucleus. This electron structure is responsible for the chemical properties of the atom (see ◊atomic structure).

electronic music studio-based serial music composed entirely of electronically generated and modified tones, as opposed to **concrete music**, which arranges prerecorded sounds by intuition. The term was later broadened to include prerecorded vocal and instrumental sounds, although always implying a serial basis. Bruno Maderna, Karlheinz ◊Stockhausen, and Milton Babbitt were among the pioneers of electronic music in the 1950s.

electronics branch of science that deals with the emission of ◊electrons from conductors and ◊semiconductors, with the subsequent manipulation of these electrons, and with the construction of electronic devices. The first electronic device was the thermionic ◊valve, or vacuum tube, in which electrons moved in a vacuum. This led to such inventions as radio, television, radar, and the digital computer. Replacement of valves with the comparatively tiny and reliable transistor in 1948 revolutionized electronic development. Modern electronic devices are based on minute integrated circuits (silicon chips), wafer-thin crystal slices holding tens of thousands of electronic components.

electron microscope instrument that produces a magnified image by using a beam of ◊electrons instead of light rays, as in an optical ◊microscope. An **electron lens** is an arrangement of electromagnetic coils that control and focus the beam. Electrons are not visible to the eye, so instead of an eyepiece there is a fluorescent screen or a photographic plate on which the electrons form an image. The wavelength of the electron beam is much shorter than that of light, so much greater magnification and resolution (ability to distinguish detail) can be achieved.

element substance that cannot be split chemically into simpler substances. The atoms of a particular element all have the same number of protons in their nuclei (their atomic number). Elements are classified in the periodic table (see ◊periodic table of the elements). Of the 109 known elements, 95 are known to occur in nature (those with atomic numbers 1–95). Those from 96 to 109 do not occur in nature and are synthesized only, produced in particle accelerators. Eighty-one of the elements are stable; all the others, which include atomic numbers 43, 61, and from 84 up, are radioactive.

elementary particle in physics, a subatomic particle that is not made up of smaller particles, and so can be considered one of the fundamental units of matter. There are three groups of elementary particles: quarks, leptons, and gauge bosons.

elephant the two surviving species of the order Proboscidea: the Asian elephant *Elephas maximus* and the African elephant *Loxodonta africana*. Elephants can grow to 4 m/13 ft and weigh up to 8 tonnes; they have a thick, grey, wrinkled skin, a large head, a long trunk used to obtain food and water, and upper incisors or tusks, which grow to a considerable length. The African elephant has very large ears and a flattened forehead, and the Asian species has smaller ears and a convex forehead.

Elgar Edward (William) 1857–1934. English composer. His *Enigma Variations* appeared 1899, and although his oratorio setting of John Henry Newman's *The Dream of Gerontius* was initially a failure, it was well received in Düsseldorf, Germany, in 1902. Many of his earlier works were then performed, including the *Pomp and Circumstance* marches.

Elijah *c.* mid-9th century BC. In the Old Testament, a Hebrew prophet during the reigns of the Israelite kings Ahab and Ahaziah. He came from Gilead. He defeated the prophets of ◊Baal, and was said to have been carried up to heaven in a fiery chariot in a whirlwind. In Jewish belief, Elijah will return to Earth to herald the coming of the Messiah.

Eliot George. Pen name of Mary Ann Evans 1819–1880. English novelist whose works include the pastoral *Adam Bede* 1859, *The Mill on the Floss* 1860, with its autobiographical elements, *Silas Marner* 1861, which contains elements of the folktale, and *Daniel Deronda* 1876. *Middlemarch*, published serially 1871–72, is considered her greatest novel for its confident handling of numerous characters and central social and moral issues.

Eliot T(homas) S(tearns) 1888–1965. US poet, playwright, and critic who lived in London from 1915. His first volume of poetry, *Prufrock and Other Observations* 1917, introduced new verse forms and rhythms; further collections include *The Waste Land* 1922, *The Hollow Men* 1925, and *Old Possum's Book of Practical Cats* 1939. His plays include *Murder in the Cathedral* 1935 and *The Cocktail Party* 1949. Nobel Prize for Literature 1948.

Elizabeth the **Queen Mother** 1900– . Wife of King George VI of England. She was born Lady Elizabeth Angela Marguerite Bowes-Lyon, and on 26 April 1923 she married Albert, Duke of York. Their children are Queen Elizabeth II and Princess Margaret.

Elizabeth I 1533–1603. Queen of England 1558–1603, the daughter of Henry VIII and Anne Boleyn. Through her Religious Settlement of 1559 she enforced the Protestant religion by law. She had ⟶Mary Queen of Scots executed 1587. Her conflict with Roman Catholic Spain led to the defeat of the ⟶Spanish Armada 1588. The Elizabethan age was expansionist in commerce and geographical exploration, and arts and literature flourished.

Elizabeth II 1926– . Queen of Great Britain and Northern Ireland from 1952, the elder daughter of George VI. She married her third cousin Philip, the Duke of Edinburgh, 1947. They have four children: Charles, Anne, Andrew, and Edward.

elk large deer *Alces alces* inhabiting N Europe, Asia, Scandinavia, and North America, where it is known as the moose. It is brown in colour, stands about 2 m/6 ft at the shoulders, has very large palmate antlers, a fleshy muzzle, short neck, and long legs. It feeds on leaves and shoots. In North America, the ⟶wapiti is called an elk.

Ellice Islands former name of ⟶Tuvalu, a group of islands in the W Pacific Ocean.

Ellington Duke (Edward Kennedy) 1899–1974. US pianist, composer, and arranger, one of the founders of big-band jazz and a leading figure in American music for 55 years. He wrote numerous pieces for his own jazz orchestra, accentuating the strengths of individual virtuoso instrumentalists. His compositions include 'Mood Indigo', 'Sophisticated Lady', 'Solitude', and 'Black and Tan Fantasy'.

ellipse curve joining all points (loci) around two fixed points (foci) such that the sum of the distances from those points is always constant. The diameter passing through the foci is the major axis, and the diameter bisecting this at right angles is the minor axis. An ellipse is one of a series of curves known as ⟶conic sections. A slice across a cone that is not made parallel to, and does not pass through, the

base will produce an ellipse.

Ellis Island island in New York Harbor, USA; area 11 hectares/27 acres. Used as a reception centre for steerage-class immigrants during the immigration waves of 1892–1943, 12 million people passed through it 1892–1924.

elm any tree of the family Ulmaceae, found in temperate regions of the northern hemisphere and in mountainous parts of the tropics. The common English elm *Ulmus procera* is widely distributed throughout Europe. It reaches 35 m/115 ft, with tufts of small, purplish-brown flowers, which appear before the leaves.

El Paso city in Texas, USA, situated at the base of the Franklin Mountains, on the Rio Grande, opposite the Mexican city of Ciudad Juárez; population (1990) 515,000. It is the centre of an agricultural and cattle-raising area, and there are electronics, food processing, packing, and leather industries, as well as oil refineries and industries based on local iron and copper mines.

El Salvador Republic of; country in Central America, bordered N and E by Honduras, S and SW by the Pacific Ocean, and NW by Guatemala; *area* 21,393 sq km/8,258 sq mi; *capital* San Salvador; *physical* narrow coastal plan, rising to mountains in N with central plateau; *head of state and government* Alfredo Cristiani from 1989; *political system* emergent democracy; *exports* coffee, cotton, sugar; *population* (1989 est) 5,900,000 (mainly of mixed Spanish and Indian ancestry; 10% Indian); *languages* Spanish and Nahuatl; *recent history* independence was achieved from Spain 1821. A right-wing government came into power 1961, resulting in left-wing guerrilla activities. Following a coup, pacifist Archbishop Oscar Romero was overthrown and replaced with a military–civilian junta. His assassination 1980 brought the country to the verge of civil war. José Duarte became president in the same year, and a new constitution was written 1983. In 1989 Alfredo Cristiani was elected; guerrilla activities continued until UN-sponsored peace accord signed 1991 and validated 1992.

Elysium in Greek mythology, the Islands of the Blessed, situated at the western end of the Earth, near the river Oceanus, to which favoured heroes are sent by the gods to enjoy a life after death. Later a region in ⟶Hades.

Emancipation Proclamation in US history, President Abraham Lincoln's Civil War announcement on 22 Sept 1862 that from the beginning of 1863 all black slaves in states still engaged in rebellion against the federal government would be free. Slaves in border states still remaining loyal to the Union were excluded.

embryo early development stage of an animal or a plant following fertilization of an ovum (egg cell), or activation of an ovum by ⟶parthenogenesis. In humans, the term embryo describes the fertilized egg during its first seven weeks of existence; from the eighth week onwards it is referred to as a fetus.

emerald clear, green gemstone variety of the mineral beryl. It occurs naturally in Colombia, the Ural Mountains in Russia, Zimbabwe, and Australia. Synthetic emeralds are manufactured by a secret process in Germany, France, and the USA.

Emerson Ralph Waldo 1803–1882. US philosopher, essayist, and poet. He settled in Concord, Massachusetts, which he made a centre of transcendentalism, and wrote *Nature* 1836, which states the movement's main principles emphasizing the value of self-reliance and the godlike nature of human souls. His two volumes of *Essays* (1841, 1844) made his reputation.

emery greyish-black opaque metamorphic rock consisting of ◊corundum and magnetite, together with other minerals such as hematite. It is used as an ◊abrasive. Emery occurs on the island of Naxos, Greece, and in Turkey.

Emilia-Romagna region of N central Italy including much of the Po valley; area 22,100 sq km/ 8,531 sq mi; population (1988) 3,924,000. The capital is Bologna; other towns include Reggio, Rimini, Parma, Ferrara, and Ravenna. Agricultural produce includes fruit, wine, sugar beet, beef, and dairy products; oil and natural-gas resources have been developed in the Po valley.

emu flightless bird *Dromaius novaehollandiae* native to Australia. It stands about 1.8 m/6 ft high and has coarse brown plumage, small rudimentary wings, short feathers on the head and neck, and powerful legs, well adapted for running and kicking.

emulsion stable dispersion of a liquid in another liquid – for example, oil and water in some cosmetic lotions.

enamel vitrified (glasslike) coating of various colours used for decorative purposes on a metallic or porcelain surface. In *cloisonné* the various sections of the design are separated by thin metal wires or strips. In *champlevé* the enamel is poured into engraved cavities in the metal surface.

enclosure appropriation of common land as private property, or the changing of open-field systems to enclosed fields (often used for sheep). This process began in Britain in the 14th century and became widespread in the 15th and 16th centuries. It caused poverty, homelessness, and rural depopulation, and resulted in revolts 1536, 1569, and 1607.

endive cultivated annual plant *Cichorium endivia*, family Compositae, the leaves of which are used in salads and cooking. One variety has narrow, curled leaves; another has wide, smooth leaves. It is related to ◊chicory.

endocrine gland gland that secretes hormones into the bloodstream to regulate body processes. Endocrine glands are most highly developed in vertebrates, but are also found in other animals,

notably insects. In humans the main endocrine glands are the pituitary, thyroid, parathyroid, adrenal, pancreas, ovary, and testis.

endorphin natural substance (a polypeptide) that modifies the action of nerve cells. Endorphins are produced by the pituitary gland and hypothalamus of vertebrates. They lower the perception of pain by reducing the transmission of signals between nerve cells.

endosperm nutritive tissue in the seeds of most flowering plants. It surrounds the embryo and is produced by an unusual process that parallels the ◊fertilization of the ovum by a male gamete. A second male gamete from the pollen grain fuses with two female nuclei within the ◊embryo sac. Thus endosperm cells are triploid (having three sets of chromosomes); they contain food reserves such as starch, fat, and protein that are utilized by the developing seedling.

Endymion in Greek mythology, a beautiful young man loved by Selene, the Moon goddess. He was granted eternal sleep in order to remain for ever young. Keats's poem *Endymion* 1818 is an allegory of searching for perfection.

energy capacity for doing ◊work. Potential energy (PE) is energy deriving from position; thus a stretched spring has elastic PE, and an object raised to a height above the Earth's surface, or the water in an elevated reservoir, has gravitational PE. A lump of coal and a tank of petrol, together with the oxygen needed for their combustion, have chemical energy. Other sorts of energy include electrical and nuclear energy, and light and sound. Moving bodies possess kinetic energy (KE). Energy can be converted from one form to another, but the total quantity stays the same (in accordance with the conservation of energy principle that governs many natural phenomena). For example, as an apple falls, it loses gravitational PE but gains KE.

energy, alternative energy from sources that are renewable and ecologically safe, as opposed to sources that are nonrenewable with toxic by-products, such as coal, oil, or gas (fossil fuels), and uranium (for nuclear power). The most important alternative energy source is flowing water, harnessed as hydroelectric power. Other sources include the oceans' tides and waves (see ◊tidal power station and ◊wave power), wind (harnessed by windmills and wind turbines), the Sun (◊solar energy), and the heat trapped in the Earth's crust (◊geothermal energy).

Engels Friedrich 1820–1895. German social and political philosopher, a friend of, and collaborator with, Karl ◊Marx on *The Communist Manifesto* 1848 and other key works. His later interpretations of Marxism, and his own philosophical and historical studies such as *Origins of the Family, Private Property, and the State* 1884 (which linked patriarchy with the development of private

England: history

5th–7th centuries	Anglo-Saxons overran all England except Cornwall and Cumberland, forming independent kingdoms including Northumbria, Mercia, Kent, and Wessex.
*c.*597	England converted to Christianity by St Augustine.
829	Egbert of Wessex accepted as overlord of all England.
878	Alfred ceded N and E England to the Danish invaders but kept them out of Wessex.
1066	Norman Conquest; England passed into French hands under William the Conqueror.
1172	Henry II became king of Ireland and established a colony there.
1215	King John forced to sign Magna Carta.
1284	Conquest of Wales, begun by the Normans, completed by Edward I.
1295	Model Parliament set up.
1338–1453	Hundred Years' War with France enabled Parliament to secure control of taxation and, by impeachment, of the king's choice of ministers.
1348–49	Black Death killed about 30% of the population.
1381	Social upheaval led to the ◊Peasants' Revolt, which was brutally repressed.
1399	Richard II deposed by Parliament for absolutism.
1414	Lollard revolt repressed.
1455–85	Wars of the Roses.
1497	Henry VII ended the power of the feudal nobility with the suppression of the Yorkist revolts.
1529	Henry VIII became head of the Church of England after breaking with Rome.
1536–43	Acts of Union united England and Wales after conquest.
1547	Edward VI adopted Protestant doctrines.
1553	Reversion to Roman Catholicism under Mary I.
1558	Elizabeth I adopted a religious compromise.
1588	Attempted invasion of England by the Spanish Armada.
1603	James I united the English and Scottish crowns; parliamentary dissidence increased.
1642–52	Civil War between royalists and parliamentarians, resulting in victory for Parliament.
1649	Charles I executed and the Commonwealth set up.
1653	Oliver Cromwell appointed Lord Protector.
1660	Restoration of Charles II.
1685	Monmouth rebellion.
1688	William of Orange invited to take the throne; flight of James II.
1707	Act of Union between England and Scotland under Queen Anne, after which the countries became known as Great Britain.
	For pre-Roman history, see ◊Britain, ancient; for further history, see ◊United Kingdom.

property), developed such concepts as historical materialism. His use of positivism and Darwinian ideas gave Marxism a scientific and deterministic flavour that was to influence Soviet thinking.

engine device for converting stored energy into useful work or movement. Most engines use a fuel as their energy store. The fuel is burned to produce heat energy – hence the name 'heat engine' – which is then converted into movement. Heat engines can be classified according to the fuel they use (◊petrol engine or ◊diesel engine), or according to whether the fuel is burned inside the engine (◊internal-combustion engine) or outside (◊steam engine), or according to whether they produce a reciprocating or rotary motion (◊turbine or ◊Wankel engine).

engineering the application of science to the design, construction, and maintenance of works, machinery, roads, railways, bridges, harbour installations, engines, ships, aircraft and airports, spacecraft and space stations, and the generation, transmission, and use of electrical power. The main divisions of engineering are aerospace, chemical, civil, electrical, electronic, gas, marine, materials, mechanical, mining, production, radio, and structural.

England largest division of the ◊United Kingdom; *area* 130,357 sq km/50,318 sq mi; *capital* London; *towns* Birmingham, Cambridge, Coventry, Leeds, Leicester, Manchester, Newcastle-upon-Tyne, Nottingham, Oxford, Sheffield, York; ports Bristol, Dover, Felixstowe, Harwich, Liverpool, Portsmouth, Southampton; *features* variability of climate and diversity of scenery; among European countries, only the Netherlands is more densely populated; *exports* agricultural (cereals, rape, sugar beet, potatoes); meat and meat products; electronic (software) and telecommunications equipment (main centres Berkshire and Cambridge); scientific instruments; textiles and fashion goods; North Sea oil and gas, petrochemicals, pharmaceuticals, fertilizers; beer; china clay, pottery, porcelain, and glass; film and television programmes, and sound recordings. Tourism is important. There are worldwide banking and insurance interests; *currency* pound sterling; *population* (1986) 47,255,000; *language* English, with more than 100 minority languages; *religion* Christian, with the Church of England as the established church, and various Protestant groups; Roman Catholic; Muslim; Jewish; Sikh; Hindu. For *government* and *history*, see ◊Britain, ancient; ◊England: history; ◊United Kingdom.

English language member of the Germanic branch of the Indo-European language family. It is traditionally described as having passed through four major stages over about 1,500 years: *Old English* or *Anglo-Saxon* (*c.* 500–1050), rooted in the dialects of invading settlers (Jutes, Saxons, Angles, and Frisians); **Middle English** (*c.* 1050–1550), influenced by Norman French after the Conquest 1066 and by ecclesiastical Latin; **Early Modern English** (*c.* 1550–1700), including a standardization of the diverse influences of Middle English; and **Late Modern English** (*c.* 1700 onwards), including in particular the development and spread of current Standard English. English spread worldwide from the 17th century onwards and remains the most important international language of trade and technology.

English law one of the main European legal systems, ◊Roman law being the other. English law has spread to many other countries, including former English colonies such as the USA, Canada, Australia, and New Zealand. A unique feature of English law is the doctrine of judicial precedents, whereby previous court decisions are binding.

Entebbe town in Uganda, on the NW shore of Lake Victoria, 20 km/12 mi SW of Kampala, the capital; 1,136 m/3,728 ft above sea level; population (1983) 21,000. Founded 1893, it was the administrative centre of Uganda 1894–1962.

entropy in ◊thermodynamics, a parameter representing the state of disorder of a system at the atomic, ionic, or molecular level; the greater the disorder, the higher the entropy. Thus the fast-moving disordered molecules of water vapour have higher entropy than those of more ordered liquid water, which in turn have more entropy than the molecules in solid crystalline ice.

Enver Pasha 1881–1922. Turkish politician and soldier. He led the military revolt 1908 that resulted in the Young Turks' revolution (see ◊Turkey). He was killed fighting the Bolsheviks in Turkestan.

environment in ecology, the sum of conditions affecting a particular organism, including physical surroundings, climate, and influences of other living organisms. See ◊habitat.

enzyme biological ◊catalyst produced in cells, and capable of speeding up the chemical reactions necessary for life by converting one molecule (substrate) into another. Enzymes are not themselves destroyed by this process. They are large, complex ◊proteins, and are highly specific, each chemical reaction requiring its own particular enzyme.

Eocene second epoch of the Tertiary period of geological time, 55–38 million years ago. It was originally considered the earliest division of the Tertiary. The name means 'early recent', referring to the early forms of mammals evolving at the time, following the extinction of the dinosaurs.

Eos in Greek mythology, the goddess of the dawn, equivalent to the Roman Aurora.

Ephesus ancient Greek seaport in Asia Minor, a centre of the ◊Ionian Greeks, with a temple of Artemis destroyed by the Goths AD 262.

Now in Turkey, it is one of the world's largest archaeological sites.

epic narrative poem or cycle of poems dealing with some great deed – often the founding of a nation or the forging of national unity – and often using religious or cosmological themes. The two main epic poems in the Western tradition are the ancient Greek Iliad and Odyssey, attributed to Homer, which were probably intended to be chanted in sections at feasts.

Epicureanism system of philosophy that claims soundly based human happiness is the highest good, so that its rational pursuit should be adopted. It was named after the Greek philosopher Epicurus. The most distinguished Roman Epicurean was ◊Lucretius.

Epidaurus or **Epidavros** ancient Greek city and port on the east coast of Argolis, in the NE Peloponnese. The site contains a well-preserved theatre of the 4th century BC; nearby are the ruins of the temple of Aesculapius, the god of healing.

epidermis the outermost layer of ◊cells on an organism's body. In plants and many invertebrates such as insects, it consists of a single layer of cells. In vertebrates, it consists of several layers of cells, of which the outermost are dead, forming a tough, waterproof layer, known as ◊skin.

epilepsy medical disorder characterized by a tendency to develop fits, which are convulsions or abnormal feelings caused by abnormal electrical discharges in the cerebral hemispheres of the ◊brain. Epilepsy can be controlled with a number of anticonvulsant drugs.

Epiphany festival of the Christian church, held 6 Jan, celebrating the coming of the Magi (the three Wise Men) to Bethlehem with gifts for the infant Jesus, and symbolizing the manifestation of Jesus to the world. It is the 12th day after Christmas, and marks the end of the Christmas festivities.

epiphyte any plant that grows on another plant or object above the surface of the ground, and has no roots in the soil. An epiphyte does not parasitize the plant it grows on but merely uses it for support. Its nutrients are obtained from rainwater, organic debris such as leaf litter, or from the air.

episcopacy in the Christian church, a system of government in which administrative and spiritual power over a district (diocese) is held by a bishop. The Roman Catholic, Eastern Orthodox, Anglican, and Episcopal churches (USA) are episcopalian.

epistemology branch of philosophy that examines the nature of knowledge and attempts to determine the limits of human understanding. Central issues include how knowledge is derived and how it is to be validated and tested.

epistle in the New Testament, any of the 21 letters to individuals or to the members of various churches written by Christian leaders, including the 13 written by St ⬦Paul. The term also describes a letter with a suggestion of pomposity and literary affectation, and a letter addressed to someone in the form of a poem, as in the epistles of ⬦Horace and Alexander ⬦Pope.

epoch subdivision of a geological period in the geological time scale. Epochs are sometimes given their own names (such as the Palaeocene, Eocene, Oligocene, Miocene, and Pliocene epochs comprising the Tertiary period), or they are referred to as the late, early, or middle portions of a given period (as the Late Cretaceous or the Middle Triassic epoch).

EPROM (acronym for erasable programmable read-only memory) computer memory device in the form of an ⬦integrated circuit (chip) that can record data and retain it indefinitely. The data can be erased by exposure to ultraviolet light, and new data recorded. Other kinds of computer memory chips are ⬦ROM (read-only memory), ⬦PROM (programmable read-only memory), and ⬦RAM (random-access memory).

Epstein Jacob 1880–1959. British sculptor, born in New York. He experimented with abstract forms, but is chiefly known for his controversial muscular nude figures such as *Genesis* 1931 (Whitworth Art Gallery, Manchester).

equator the *terrestrial equator* is the great circle whose plane is perpendicular to the Earth's axis (the line joining the poles). Its length is 40,092 km/24,901.8 mi, divided into 360 degrees of longitude. The *celestial equator* is the circle in which the plane of the Earth's equator intersects the ⬦celestial sphere.

Equatorial Guinea Republic of; country in W central Africa, bordered N by Cameroon, E and S by Gabon, and W by the Atlantic Ocean; also several small islands off the coast and the larger island of Bioko off the coast of Cameroon; *area* 28,051 sq km/10,828 sq mi; *capital* Malabo (Bioko); *physical* comprises mainland Rio Muni, plus the small islands of Corisco, Elobey Grande and Elobey Chico, and Bioko (formerly Fernando Po) together with Annobón (formerly Pagalu); *head of state and government* Teodoro Obiang Nguema Mbasogo from 1979; *political system* one-party military republic; *exports* cocoa, coffee, timber; *population* (1988 est) 336,000 (plus 110,000 estimated to live in exile abroad); *languages* Spanish (official); pidgin English is widely spoken, and on Pagalu a Portuguese dialect; *recent history* known as Spanish Guinea until 1968 when independence was achieved. In 1979 Teodoro Obiang Nguema Mbasogo overthrew his uncle, dictator Francisco Macias Nguema, establishing a military regime. Macias was tried and executed. 1982 saw a new constitution and 1989 the re-election of Obiang as president.

equestrianism skill in horse riding, as practised under International Equestrian Federation rules. An Olympic sport, there are three main branches of equestrianism: show jumping, dressage, and three-day eventing.

equinox the points in spring and autumn at which the Sun's path, the ecliptic, crosses the celestial equator, so that the day and night are of approximately equal length. The *vernal equinox* occurs about 21 March and the *autumnal equinox* about 23 Sept.

equity system of law supplementing the ordinary rules of law where the application of these would operate harshly in a particular case; sometimes it is regarded as an attempt to achieve 'natural justice'. Equity appears as an element in most legal systems.

era any of the major divisions of geological time, each including several periods, but smaller than an eon. The currently recognized eras all fall within the Phanerozoic eon. The eras in ascending order are the Palaeozoic, Mesozoic, and Cenozoic.

Erasmus Desiderius *c.* 1466–1536. Dutch scholar and leading humanist of the Renaissance era, who taught and studied all over Europe and was a prolific writer. His pioneer translation of the Greek New Testament 1516 exposed the Vulgate as a second-hand document.

erbium soft, lustrous, greyish, metallic element of the lanthanide series, symbol Er, atomic number 68, relative atomic mass 167.26. It occurs with the element yttrium or as a minute part of various minerals. It was discovered 1843 by Carl Mosander (1797–1858), and named after the town of Ytterby, Sweden, where the lanthanides (rare-earth elements) were first found.

Erebus, Mount the world's southernmost active volcano, 3,794 m/12,452 ft high, on Ross Island, Antarctica.

Erebus in Greek mythology, the god of darkness and the intermediate region between upper Earth and ⬦Hades.

ergonomics study of the relationship between people and the furniture, tools, and machinery they use at work. The object is to improve work performance by removing sources of muscular stress and general fatigue.

ergot certain parasitic fungi (especially of the genus *Claviceps*), whose brown or black grainlike masses replace the kernels of rye or other cereals. *C. purpurea* attacks the rye plant. Ergot poisoning is caused by eating infected bread, resulting in burning pains, gangrene, and convulsions.

Erhard Ludwig 1897–1977. West German Christian Democrat politician, chancellor of the Federal Republic 1963–66. The 'economic miracle' of West Germany's recovery after World War II is largely attributed to Erhard's policy of social free enterprise (German *Marktwirtschaft*), which he initiated as federal economics minister (1949–63).

erica any plant of the genus *Erica*, family Ericaceae, including the heathers. There are about 500 species, distributed mainly in South Africa with some in Europe.

Ericsson Leif *c.* AD 1000. Norse explorer, son of Eric the Red, who sailed west from Greenland about 1000 to find a country first sighted by Norsemen in 986. Landing with 35 companions in North America, he called it Vinland, because he discovered grape vines growing there.

Eric the Red 940–1010. Allegedly the first European to find Greenland. According to a 13th-century saga, he was the son of a Norwegian chieftain, and was banished from Iceland about 982 for murder. He then sailed westward and discovered a land that he called Greenland.

Erie, Lake fourth largest of the Great Lakes of North America, connected to Lake Ontario by the Niagara River and bypassed by the Welland Canal; area 9,930 sq mi/25,720 sq km.

Eritrea province of N Ethiopia; *area* 117,600 sq km/45,394 sq mi; *capital* Asmara; *towns* Assab and Massawa (Ethiopia's outlets to the sea); *physical* coastline on the Red Sea 1,000 km/620 mi; narrow coastal plain that rises to an inland plateau; *products* coffee, salt, citrus fruits, grains, cotton; *currency* birr; *population* (1984) 2,615,000; *language* Amharic (official); *religion* Muslim; *history* part of an ancient Ethiopian kingdom until the 7th century; under Ethiopian influence until it fell to the Turks mid-16th century; Italian colony 1889–1941, when it was the base for Italian invasion of Ethiopia; under British 1962, when it became an autonomous part of Ethiopia. From 1962, when it became a region, various secessionist movements arose. During civil war in the 1970s, guerrillas held most of Eritrea; Ethiopian government troops, backed by Soviet and Cuban forces, recaptured most towns 1978. Resistance continued throughout the 1980s, aided by conservative Persian Gulf states and some cooperation with guerrillas in Tigré province. The collapse of Ethiopia's government in 1991 led to the recognition of Eritrea's right to seek independence.

ermine the ⇨stoat during winter, when its coat becomes white. In northern latitudes the coat becomes completely white, except for a black tip on the tail, but in warmer regions the back may remain brownish. The fur is used commercially.

Ernst Max 1891–1976. German artist who worked in France 1922–38 and in the USA from 1941. He was an active Dadaist, experimenting with collage, photomontage, and surreal images, and helped found the Surrealist movement 1924. His paintings are highly diverse.

Eros in Greek mythology, boy-god of love, traditionally armed with bow and arrows. He was the son of Aphrodite (Roman, Venus), and fell in love with

⇨Psyche. He is identified with the Roman Cupid.

erosion processes whereby the rocks and soil (see ⇨soil erosion) of the Earth's surface are loosened, worn away, and transported (weathering does not involve transportation). There are two types, chemical and physical. **Chemical erosion** involves the alteration of the mineral component of the rock, by means of rainwater or the substances dissolved in it, and its subsequent movement. *Physical erosion* involves the breakdown and transportation of exposed rocks by physical forces. In practice the two work together.

Ershad Hussain Mohammad 1930– . Military ruler of Bangladesh 1982–90. He became chief of staff of the Bangladeshi army 1979 and assumed power in a military coup 1982. As president from 1983, Ershad introduced a successful rural-oriented economic programme but faced continuing political opposition, which forced him to resign Dec 1990. He was subsequently convicted of corruption.

escape velocity in physics, minimum velocity with which an object must be projected for it to escape from the gravitational pull of a planetary body. In the case of the Earth, the escape velocity is 11.2 kps/6.9 mps; the Moon 2.4 kps/1.5 mps; Mars 5 kps/3.1 mps; and Jupiter 59.6 kps/37 mps.

Eskimo member of a group of Asian, North American, and Greenland Arctic peoples who migrated east from Siberia about 2,000 years ago, exploiting the marine coastal environment and the tundra. Eskimo languages belong to the Eskimo-Aleut family and form a continuum of dialects from Siberia east to Greenland. Some Arctic peoples, for example the ⇨Inuit, consider the term Eskimo offensive.

ESP abbreviation for ⇨extrasensory perception.

esparto grass *Stipa tenacissima*, native to S Spain, S Portugal, and the Balearics, but now widely grown in dry, sandy locations throughout the world. The plant is just over 1 m/3 ft high, producing greyish-green leaves, which are used for making paper, ropes, baskets, mats, and cables.

Esperanto language devised 1887 by Polish philologist Ludwig L Zamenhof (1859–1917) as an international auxiliary language. For its structure and vocabulary it draws on Latin, the Romance languages, English, and German.

essay short piece of nonfiction, often dealing from a personal point of view with some particular subject. The essay became a recognized genre with the French writer Montaigne's *Essais* 1580. Francis Bacon's *Essays* 1597 are among the most famous in English.

Essen city in North Rhine–Westphalia, Germany; population (1988) 615,000. It is the administrative centre of the Ruhr, with textile, chemical, and electrical industries.

essential oil volatile ⇨oil obtained by distillation

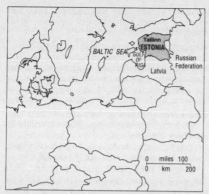

and marked by the odour of the plant or substance from which it is extracted; for example, oil of laurel.

Essequibo the longest river in Guyana, South America, rising in the Guiana Highlands of S Guyana; length 1,014 km/630 mi.

Essex county in SE England; *area* 3,670 sq km/ 1,417 sq mi; *towns* Chelmsford (administrative headquarters), Colchester; ports: Harwich, Tilbury; resorts: Southend, Clacton; *features* former royal hunting ground of Epping Forest (controlled from 1882 by the City of London); the marshy coastal headland of the Naze; Stansted, London's third airport; *products* dairying, cereals, fruit; *population* (1987) 1,522,000; *famous people* William Harvey.

Essex Robert Devereux, 2nd Earl of Essex 1566–1601. English soldier and politician. He became a favourite with Queen Elizabeth I from 1587, but was executed because of his policies in Ireland.

estate in law, the rights that a person has in relation to any property. *Real estate* is an interest in any land; *personal estate* is an interest in any other kind of property.

ester organic compound formed by the reaction between an alcohol and an acid, with the elimination of water. Unlike ◊salts, esters are covalent compounds.

Estonia Republic of; country in NE Europe, bordered E by the Russian Federation, S by Latvia, and N and E by the Baltic Sea; *area* 45,100 sq km/ 17,413 sq mi; *capital* Tallinn; *physical* lakes and marshes in a partly forested plain; 774 km/481 mi of coastline; *head of state* Arnold Rüütel from 1988; *head of government* Tiit Vahl from 1992; *political system* emergent democratic republic; *products* oil and gas (from shale), wood products, chemical fertilizers, construction materials, agricultural and mining machinery, flax, textiles, processed foods, dairy and pig products; *population* (1989 est) 1,573,000 (Estonian 62%, Russian 30%, Ukrainian and Belarusian minorities); *language* Estonian, allied to Finnish; *recent history* independence

from Russian rule was declared 1918; Estonia was incorporated into the USSR 1940. Nationalist dissent grew in the 1980s; own constitution was adopted 1988 and the republic declared 'sovereign' and autonomous. Full independence was achieved 1991 and membership of the United Nations was granted. Prime Minister Edgar Savisaar resigned Jan 1992 because of his government's inability to alleviate food and energy shortages; new government formed by Tiit Vahl.

Estonian member of the largest ethnic group in Estonia. There are 1 million speakers of the Estonian language, a member of the Finno-Ugric branch of the Uralic family. Most live in Estonia.

etching ◊printmaking technique in which the design is made from a metal plate (usually copper or zinc), which is covered with a waxy overlayer (ground) and then drawn on with an etching needle. The exposed areas are then 'etched', or bitten into, by a corrosive agent (acid), so that they will hold ink for printing.

ethane CH_3CH_3 colourless, odourless gas, the second member of the ◊alkane series of hydrocarbons (paraffins).

ethanol common name *ethyl alcohol* C_2H_5OH alcohol found in beer, wine, cider, spirits, and other alcoholic drinks. When pure, it is a colourless liquid with a pleasant odour, miscible with water or ether; it burns in air with a pale blue flame. The vapour forms an explosive mixture with air and may be used in high-compression internal-combustion engines.

Ethelbert *c.* 552–616. King of Kent 560–616. He was defeated by the West Saxons 568 but later became ruler of England south of the river Humber. He married a French princess, Bertha. Ethelbert received the Christian missionary Augustine 597 and later converted to become the first Christian ruler of Anglo-Saxon England. Ethelbert issued the first written code of laws known in England.

Ethelred II *the Unready c.* 968–1016. King of England from 978. He tried to buy off the Danish raiders by paying Danegeld. In 1002, he ordered the massacre of the Danish settlers, provoking an invasion by Sweyn I of Denmark. War with Sweyn and Sweyn's son Canute occupied the rest of Ethelred's reign. He was nicknamed the 'Unready' because of his apparent lack of foresight.

ether in chemistry, any of a series of organic chemical compounds having an oxygen atom linking the carbon atoms of two hydrocarbon radical groups (general formula R-O-R'); also the common name for ethoxyethane $C_2H_5OC_2H_5$ (also called diethyl ether). This is used as an anaesthetic and as an external cleansing agent before surgical operations. It is also used as a solvent, and in the extraction of oils, fats, waxes, resins, and alkaloids.

ethics area of philosophy concerned with human

values, which studies the meanings of moral terms and theories of conduct and goodness; also called **moral philosophy**. It is one of the three main branches of contemporary philosophy.

Ethiopia People's Democratic Republic of (formerly also known as **Abyssinia**); country in E Africa, bordered NE by Djibouti and the Red Sea, E and SE by Somalia, S by Kenya, and W and NW by Sudan; **area** 1,221,900 sq km/471,653 sq mi; **capital** Addis Ababa; **physical** high plateau with central mountain range divided by Rift Valley; plains in E; source of Blue Nile River; **head of state and government** Meles Zenawi from 1991; **political system** transition to democratic socialist republic; **exports** coffee, pulses, oilseeds, hides, skins; **population** (1989 est) 47,709,000 (Oromo 40%, Amhara 25%, Tigré 12%, Sidamo 9%); **languages** Amharic (official); Tigrinya, Orominga, Arabic; **recent history** the annexation of Eritrea 1962 by Emperor Haile Selassie gave birth to a resistance movement. In 1974 a military government was put in place and a socialist state declared by General Teferi Benti. Killed 1977, he was replaced by Col Mengistu Haile Mariam, who embarked on a 'Red Terror' reign killing thousands of people. 1985 saw widespread famine and Western aid was provided although food supplies were blocked by rebel guerrillas. Civil disorder and shortages continued; in 1991 Mengistu was overthrown, cessation of civil war was agreed, Meles Zenawi was elected president, and a transitional government formed until free elections 1993. The independence of Eritrea was agreed 1991.

ethnography the study of living cultures, using anthropological techniques like participant observation (where the anthropologist lives in the society being studied) and a reliance on informants.

ethnology the study of contemporary peoples, concentrating on their geography and culture, as distinct from their social systems. Ethnologists make a comparative analysis of data from different

eucalyptus

cultures to understand how cultures work and why they change, with a view to deriving general principles about human society.

ethology the comparative study of animal behaviour in its natural setting. Ethology is concerned with the causal mechanisms (both the stimuli that elicit behaviour and the physiological mechanisms controlling it), as well as the development of behaviour, its function, and its evolutionary history.

Etna volcano on the east coast of Sicily, 3,323 m/10,906 ft, the highest in Europe. About 90 eruptions have been recorded since 1800 BC, yet because of the rich soil, the cultivated zone on the lower slopes is densely populated, including the coastal town of Catania. The most recent eruption was in Dec 1985.

Etruscan member of an ancient people inhabiting Etruria (modern-day Tuscany and part of Umbria in Italy) from the 8th to 4th centuries BC. The Etruscan dynasty of the Tarquins ruled Rome 616–509 BC. At the height of their civilization, in the 6th century BC, the Etruscans achieved great wealth and power from their maritime strength. They were driven out of Rome 509 BC and eventually dominated by the Romans.

Etruscan art sculpture, painting, pottery, metalwork, jewellery, and design of the first known Italian civilization. Etruscan terracotta coffins (*sarcophagi*), carved with reliefs and topped with portraits of the dead reclining on one elbow, were to influence the later Romans and early Christians.

etymology the study of the origin and history of words within and across languages. It has two major aspects: the study of the phonetic and written forms of words, and of the semantics or meanings of those words.

eucalyptus any tree of the genus *Eucalyptus* of the myrtle family Myrtaceae, native to Australia and Tasmania, where they are commonly known as **gumtrees**. About 90% of Australian timber belongs to the eucalyptus genus, which comprises about 500 species. The trees have dark hardwood timber which is used principally for heavy construction, as in railway and bridge building. They are tall, aromatic, evergreen trees with pendant leaves and white, pink, or red flowers.

Eucharist chief Christian sacrament, in which bread is eaten and wine drunk in memory of the death of Jesus. Other names for it are the **Lord's Supper**, **Holy Communion**, and (among Roman Catholics, who believe that the bread and wine are transubstantiated, that is, converted to the body and blood of Christ) the **Mass**. The doctrine of transubstantiation was rejected by Protestant churches during the Reformation.

Euclid *c.* 330–*c.* 260 BC. Greek mathematician, who lived in Alexandria and wrote the *Stoicheia/Elements* in 13 books, of which nine deal with plane and solid geometry and four with number theory. His great achievement lay in the systematic arrangement of previous discoveries, based on axioms, definitions, and theorems.

eugenics the study of ways in which the physical and mental quality of a people can be controlled and improved by selective breeding, and the belief that this should be done. The idea was abused by the Nazi Party in Germany during the 1930s to justify the attempted extermination of entire groups of people. Eugenics can try to control the spread of inherited genetic abnormalities by counselling prospective parents.

eukaryote in biology, one of the two major groupings into which all organisms are divided. Included are all organisms, except bacteria and cyanobacteria (♢blue-green algae), which belong to the ♢prokaryote grouping.

Eumenides in Greek mythology, appeasing name for the ♢Furies.

eunuch castrated man. Originally eunuchs were bedchamber attendants in harems in the East, but as they were usually castrated to keep them from taking too great an interest in their charges, the term became applied more generally. In China, eunuchs were employed within the imperial harem from some 4,000 years ago and by medieval times wielded considerable political power. Eunuchs often filled high offices of state in India and Persia.

Euphrates (Arabic *Furat*) river, rising in E Turkey, flowing through Syria and Iraq and joining the river Tigris above Basra to form the river Shatt-al-Arab, at the head of the Persian/Arabian Gulf; 3,600 km/ 2,240 mi in length. The ancient cities of Babylon, Eridu, and Ur were situated along its course.

Eureka Stockade incident at Ballarat, Australia, when about 150 goldminers, or 'diggers', rebelled against the Victorian state police and military authorities. They took refuge behind a wooden stockade, which was taken in a few minutes by the military on 3 Dec 1854. Of the 13 tried for treason, all were acquitted, thus marking the emergence of Australian democracy.

Euripides *c.* 484–407 BC. Greek dramatist whose plays deal with the emotions and reactions of ordinary people and social issues rather than with deities and the grandiose themes of his contemporaries. He wrote more than 80 plays, of which 18 survive.

Euro Disney or *Euro Disneyland* theme park in Marne-la-vallé, 32 km/20 mi E of Paris, France, opened by the US Walt Disney Company in April 1992. It covers 56 ha/138 acres, cost about $3 billion to realize, and is the fourth Disney theme park.

Europa in Greek mythology, the daughter of the king of Tyre, carried off by Zeus (in the form of a bull); she personifies the continent of Europe.

Europe second smallest continent, occupying 8% of the Earth's surface; *area* 10,400,000 sq km/ 4,000,000 sq mi; *largest cities* (population over 1.5 million) Athens, Barcelona, Berlin, Birmingham, Bucharest, Budapest, Hamburg, Istanbul, Kharkov, Kiev, Lisbon, London, Madrid, Manchester, Milan, Moscow, Paris, Rome, St Petersburg, Vienna, Warsaw; *physical* conventionally occupying that part of Eurasia to the west of the Ural Mountains, north of the Caucasus Mountains, and north of the Sea of Marmara, Europe lies entirely in the northern hemisphere between 36° N and the Arctic Ocean. About two-thirds of the continent is a great plain which covers the whole of European Russia and spreads westward through Poland to the Low Countries and the Bay of Biscay. To the north lie the Scandinavian highlands, rising to 2,470 m/ 8,110 ft at Glittertind in the Jotunheim Range of Norway. To the south, a series of mountain ranges stretch from east to west (Caucasus, Balkans, Carpathians, Apennines, Alps, Pyrenees, and Sierra Nevada); *features* Mount Elbruz 5,642 m/18,517 ft in the Caucasus Mountains is the highest peak in Europe; Mont Blanc 4,807 m/15,772 ft is the highest peak in the Alps; lakes (over 5,100 sq km/ 2,000 sq mi) include Ladoga, Onega, Vänern; rivers (over 800 km/500 mi) include the Volga, Danube, Dnieper Ural, Don, Pechora, Dneister, Rhine, Loire, Tagus, Ebro, Oder, Prut, Rhône; *products* nearly 50% of the world's cars are produced in Europe (Germany, France, Italy, Spain, Russia, Georgia, Ukraine, Latvia, Belarus, UK); the rate of fertilizer consumption on agricultural land is four times greater than that in any other continent; Europe produces 43% of the world's barley (Germany, Spain, France, UK), 41% of its rye (Poland, Germany), 31% of its oats (Poland, Germany, Sweden, France), and 24% of its wheat (France, Germany, UK, Romania); Italy, Spain, and Greece produce more than 70% of the world's olive oil; *population* (1985) 496 million (excluding Turkey and the ex-Soviet republics); annual growth rate 0.3%, projected population of 512 million by 2000

European Atomic Energy Commission (Euratom) organization established by the second Treaty of Rome 1957, which seeks the cooperation of member states of the European Community in nuclear research and the rapid and large-scale development of nonmilitary nuclear energy.

European Community (EC) political and economic alliance consisting of the European Coal and Steel Community (1952), European Economic Community (EEC, popularly called the Common Market, 1957), and the European Atomic Energy Commission (Euratom, 1957). The original six members – Belgium, France, West Germany, Italy, Luxembourg, and the Netherlands – were joined by the UK, Denmark, and the Republic of Ireland 1974, Greece 1981, and Spain and Portugal 1985. In 1991 association agreements – providing for free trade within ten years and the possibility of full EC membership – were signed between the EC and Czechoslovakia, Hungary, and Poland, subject to ratification. The aims of the EC include the expansion of trade, the abolition of restrictive trading practices, the encouragement of free movement of capital and labour within the community, and the establishment of a closer union among European people.

European Court of Human Rights court that hears cases referred from the European Commission of Human Rights, if the commission has failed to negotiate a friendly settlement in a case where individuals' rights have been violated by a member state. The court sits in Strasbourg and comprises one judge for every state that is a party to the 1950 convention.

European Court of Justice the court of the European Community (EC), which is responsible for interpreting Community law and ruling on breaches by member states and others of such law. It sits in Luxembourg with judges from the member states.

European Free Trade Association (EFTA) organization established 1960 consisting of Austria, Finland, Iceland, Norway, Sweden, Switzerland, and (from 1991) Liechtenstein, previously a nonvoting associate member. There are no import duties between members.

European Monetary System (EMS) attempt by the European Community to bring financial cooperation and monetary stability to Europe. It was established 1979 in the wake of the 1974 oil crisis, which brought growing economic disruption to European economies because of floating exchange rates. Central to the EMS is the ⇨*Exchange Rate Mechanism* (ERM), a voluntary system of semi-fixed exchange rates based on the European Currency Unit (ECU).

European Parliament the parliament of the European Community, which meets in Strasbourg to comment on the legislative proposals of the Commission of the European Communities. Members are elected for a five-year term. The European Parliament has 518 seats, apportioned on the basis of population, of which the UK, France, Germany, and Italy have 81 each, Spain 60, the Netherlands 25, Belgium, Greece, and Portugal 24 each, Denmark 16, the Republic of Ireland 15, and Luxembourg 6.

European Space Agency (ESA) organization of European countries (Austria, Belgium, Denmark, France, Germany, Ireland, Italy, the Netherlands, Norway, Spain, Sweden, Switzerland, and the UK) that engages in space research and technology. It was founded 1975, with headquarters in Paris.

europium soft, greyish, metallic element of the ⇨lanthanide series, symbol Eu, atomic number 63, relative atomic mass 151.96. It is used in lasers and as the red phosphor in colour television sets; its compounds are used to make control rods for nuclear reactors. It was named in 1901 by French chemist Eugène Demarçay (1852–1904) after the continent of Europe, where it was first found.

Eurydice in Greek mythology, the wife of ⇨Orpheus. She was a dryad, or forest nymph, and died from a snake bite. Orpheus attempted unsuccessfully to fetch her back from the realm of the dead.

euthanasia in medicine, mercy killing of someone with a severe and incurable condition or illness. The Netherlands legalized voluntary euthanasia 1983, but is the only country to have done so.

eutrophication the excessive enrichment of rivers, lakes, and shallow sea areas, primarily by nitrate fertilizers washed from the soil by rain, and by phosphates from fertilizers and detergents in municipal sewage. These encourage the growth of algae and bacteria which use up the oxygen in the water, thereby making it uninhabitable for fishes and other animal life.

evangelist person travelling to spread the Christian gospel, in particular the authors of the four Gospels in the New Testament: Matthew, Mark, Luke, and John.

Evans Edith 1888–1976. English character actress who performed on the London stage and on Broadway. Her many imposing performances include the film role of Lady Bracknell in Oscar Wilde's comedy *The Importance of Being Earnest* 1952.

evaporation process in which a liquid turns to a vapour without its temperature reaching boiling point. A liquid left to stand in a saucer eventually evaporates because, at any time, a proportion of its molecules will be fast enough (have enough kinetic energy) to escape through the attractive intermolecular forces at the liquid surface into the atmosphere. The temperature of the liquid tends to fall because the evaporating molecules remove energy from the liquid. The rate of evaporation rises with increased temperature.

Eve in the Old Testament, the first woman, wife of ⇨Adam. She was tempted by Satan (in the form of a snake) to eat the fruit of the Tree of Knowledge of Good and Evil, and then tempted Adam to eat of the fruit as well, thus bringing about their expulsion from the Garden of Eden.

evening primrose any plant of the genus *Oenothera*, family Onagraceae. Some 50 species are native to North America, several of which now also grow in Europe. Some are cultivated for their oil, which is used in treating eczema, premenstrual tension, and chronic fatigue syndrome.

Everest, Mount the world's highest mountain, in the Himalayas, on the China–Nepal frontier; height 8,872 m/29,108 ft (measured by satellite to this new height from the former official height of 8,848 m/29,028 ft). It was first climbed by Edmund Hillary and Tenzing Norgay 1953.

Everglades area of swamps, marsh, and lakes in S ⇨Florida, USA; area 5,000 sq mi/12,950 sq km. A national park covers the southern tip.

evergreen in botany, a plant, such as pine, spruce, or holly, that bears its leaves all year round. Most ▷conifers are evergreen. Plants that shed their leaves in autumn or during a dry season are described as ▷deciduous.

Evert Chris(tine) 1954–   . US tennis player. She won her first Wimbledon title 1974, and has since won 21 Grand Slam titles. She became the first woman tennis player to win $1 million in prize money. She has an outstanding two-handed backhand and is a great exponent of baseline technique. Evert retired from competitive tennis 1989.

evolution slow process of change from one form to another, as in the evolution of the universe from its formation in the Big Bang to its present state, or in the evolution of life on Earth. Some Christians and Muslims deny the theory of evolution as conflicting with the belief that God created all things. The current theory of evolution, called ▷Neo-Darwinism, combines Charles ▷Darwin's theory of natural selection with Gregor ▷Mendel's theories on genetics.

exchange rate the price at which one currency is bought or sold in terms of other currencies, gold, or accounting units such as the special drawing right (SDR) of the ▷International Monetary Fund. Exchange rates may be fixed by international agreement or by government policy; or they may be wholly or partly allowed to 'float' (that is, find their own level) in world currency markets.

Exchange Rate Mechanism (ERM) voluntary system for controlling exchange rates within the European Community's ▷European Monetary System. The member currencies of the ERM are fixed against each other within a narrow band of fluctuation based on a central European Currency Unit (ECU) rate, but floating against those of nonmember countries. If a currency deviates significantly from the central ECU rate, the ▷European Monetary Cooperation Fund and the central banks concerned intervene to stabilize the currency. The UK entered the system Oct 1990.

excise duty levied on certain goods produced within a country; it is collected by the government's ▷Customs and Excise department.

excommunication in religion, exclusion of an offender from the rights and privileges of the Roman Catholic Church; King John, Henry VIII, and Elizabeth I were all excommunicated.

excretion in biology, the removal of waste products from the cells of living organisms. In plants andsimple animals, waste products are removed by diffusion, but in higher animals they are removed by specialized organs. In mammals, carbon dioxide and water are removed via the for example, lungs, and nitrogenous compounds and water via the liver, the kidneys, and the urinary system.

existentialism branch of philosophy based on the concept of an absurd universe where humans have free will. Existentialists argue that philosophy must begin from the concrete situation of the individual in such a world, and that humans are responsible for and the sole judge of their actions as they affect others, though no one else's existence is real to the individual. The origin of existentialism is usually traced back to the Danish philosopher ▷Kierkegaard; among its proponents were Martin Heidegger in Germany and Jean-Paul ▷Sartre in France.

exorcism rite used in a number of religions for the expulsion of so-called evil spirits. In Christianity it is employed, for example, in the Roman Catholic and Pentecostal churches.

exosphere the uppermost layer of the ▷atmosphere. It is an ill-defined zone above the thermosphere, beginning at about 700 km/435 mi and fading off into the vacuum of space. The gases are extremely thin, with hydrogen as the main constituent.

expansion in physics, the increase in size of a constant mass of substance caused by, for example, increasing its temperature (▷thermal expansion) or its internal pressure. The *expansivity*, or coefficient of thermal expansion, of a material is its expansion (per unit volume, area, or length) per degree rise in temperature.

export goods or service produced in one country and sold to another. Exports may be visible (goods physically exported) or invisible (services provided in the exporting country but paid for by residents of another country).

Expressionism style of painting, sculpture, and literature that expresses inner emotions; in particular, a movement in early 20th-century art in northern and central Europe. Expressionists tended to distort or exaggerate natural appearance in order to create a reflection of an inner world. The Norwegian painter Eduard Munch's *Skriket/The Scream* 1893 (National Gallery, Oslo) is an example.

extinction in biology, the complete disappearance of a species. In the past, extinctions are believed to have occurred because species were unable to adapt quickly enough to a naturally changing environment. Today, species are disappearing at the rate of at least one a day, owing to human activity, usually hunting and habitat destruction.

extradition the surrender, by one state or country to another, of a person accused of a criminal offence in the state or country to which that person is extradited.

extrasensory perception (ESP) perception beyond and distinct from the known sensory processes. The main forms of ESP are clairvoyance, precognition, and telepathy, or thought transference. Verification by scientific study has yet to be achieved.

eye

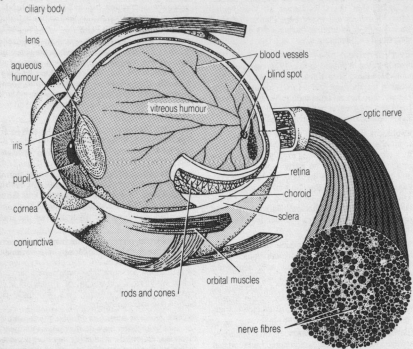

ciliary body
lens
aqueous humour
iris
pupil
cornea
conjunctiva
rods and cones
vitreous humour
blood vessels
blind spot
optic nerve
retina
choroid
sclera
orbital muscles
nerve fibres

Extremadura autonomous region of W Spain including the provinces of Badajoz and Cáceres; area 41,600 sq km/16,058 sq mi; population (1986) 1,089,000. Irrigated land is used for growing wheat; the remainder is either oak forest or used for pig or sheep grazing.

extroversion or *extraversion* personality dimension described by Carl ◊Jung and later by Hans Eysenck. The typical extrovert is sociable, impulsive, and carefree.

Eyck Jan van *c.* 1390–1441. Flemish painter of the early northern Renaissance, one of the first to work in oils. His paintings are technically brilliant and sumptuously rich in detail and colour.

eye the organ of vision. The *human eye* is a roughly spherical structure contained in a bony socket. Light enters it through the *cornea*, and passes through the circular opening (*pupil*) in the iris (the coloured part of the eye). The light is focused by the combined action of the curved cornea, the internal fluids, and the *lens* (the rounded transparent structure behind the iris). The ciliary

muscles act on the lens to change its shape, so that images of objects at different distances can be focused on the *retina*. This is at the back of the eye, and is packed with light-sensitive cells (rods and cones), connected to the brain by the optic nerve. In contrast, the *insect eye* is compound – that is, made up of many separate facets, known as ommatidia, each of which collects light and directs it separately to a receptor to build up an image. Invertebrates, such as some worms and snails, and certain bivalves, have much simpler eyes, with no lens. Among molluscs, cephalopods have complex eyes similar to those of vertebrates.

Eyre Richard (Charles Hastings) 1943– . English stage and film director who succeeded Peter Hall as artistic director of the National Theatre, London, 1988.

Eyre, Lake Australia's largest lake, in central South Australia, which frequently runs dry, becoming a salt marsh in dry seasons; area up to 9,000 sq km/3,500 sq mi. It is the continent's lowest point, 12 m/39 ft below sea level.

Fabergé Peter Carl 1846–1920. Russian goldsmith and jeweller. Among his masterpieces was a series of jewelled Easter eggs, the first of which was commissioned by Alexander III for the tsarina 1884.

Fabian Society UK socialist organization for research, discussion, and publication, founded in London 1884, aiming to attain socialism by a succession of gradual reforms. Early members included the playwright George Bernard Shaw and Beatrice and Sidney Webb. The society helped to found the Labour Representative Committee 1900 which became the Labour Party 1906.

fable story, either in verse or prose, in which animals or inanimate objects are endowed with the mentality and speech of human beings to point out a moral. Fabulists include Aesop, Babrius, Phaedrus, Avianus, and La Fontaine.

facsimile transmission full name for ♢*fax* or *telefax*.

factory farming intensive rearing of poultry or animals for food, usually on high-protein foodstuffs in confined quarters. Chickens (for eggs and meat) and calves (for veal) are commonly factory-farmed. Some countries restrict the use of antibiotics and growth hormones as aids to factory farming, because they can persist in the flesh of the animals after they are slaughtered. Many people object to factory farming for moral as well as health reasons. In the UK in 1990, factory-farmed table chickens numbered 600 million.

FA Cup abbreviation for *Football Association Cup*, the major annual soccer knockout competition in England and Wales, open to all member clubs of the British Football Association. First held 1871–72, it is the oldest football knockout competition.

Faeroe Islands or *Faeroes* alternative spelling of the ♢Faroe Islands, in the N Atlantic.

Fahd 1921– . King of Saudi Arabia from 1982, when he succeeded his half-brother Khalid. As head of government, he has been active in trying to bring about a solution to the Middle East conflicts.

Fahrenheit scale temperature scale invented 1714 by Gabriel Fahrenheit, which was commonly used in English-speaking countries up until the 1970s, after which the ♢Celsius scale was adopted in line with the rest of the world. In the Fahrenheit scale, intervals are measured in degrees (°F); °F = (°C × $^9/_5$) + 32.

Fairbanks Douglas, Sr. Stage name of Douglas Elton Ulman 1883–1939. US actor. He played acrobatic swashbuckling heroes in silent films such as *The Mark of Zorro* 1920, *The Three Musketeers* 1921, *Robin Hood* 1922, *The Thief of Bagdad* 1924, and *Don Quixote* 1925. He was married to film star Mary Pickford ('America's Sweetheart') 1920–33. Together with Charlie Chaplin and D W Griffith they founded United Artists in 1919.

Fairbanks Douglas, Jr 1909– . US actor who appeared in the same type of swashbuckling film roles as his father, Douglas Fairbanks; for example, in *Catherine the Great* 1934 and *The Prisoner of Zenda* 1937.

Fairfax Thomas, 3rd Baron Fairfax of Cameron 1612–1671. English general, commander in chief of the Parliamentary army in the English Civil War. With Oliver Cromwell he formed the ♢New Model Army and defeated Charles I at Naseby. He opposed the king's execution, resigned in protest 1650 against the invasion of Scotland, and participated in the restoration of Charles II after Cromwell's death.

Faisal Ibn Abdul Aziz 1905–1975. King of Saudi Arabia from 1964. He was the younger brother of King Saud, on whose accession 1953 he was declared crown prince. He was prime minister from 1953 to 1960 and from 1962 to 1975. In 1964 he emerged victorious from a lengthy conflict with his brother and adopted a policy of steady modernization of his country. He was assassinated by his nephew.

Faisal I 1885–1933. King of Iraq 1921–33. An Arab nationalist leader during World War I, he was instrumental in liberating the Middle East from Ottoman control and was declared king of Syria in 1918 but deposed by the French in 1920. The British then installed him as king in Iraq, where he continued to foster pan-Arabism.

Faisalabad city in Punjab province, Pakistan; population (1981) 1,092,000. It trades in grain, cotton, and textiles.

falcon any bird of prey of the genus *Falco*, family Falconidae, order Falconiformes. Falcons are the smallest of the hawks (15–60 cm/6–24 in). They nest in high places and kill their prey by 'stooping' (swooping down at high speed). They include the peregrine and kestrel.

Falkland Islands British crown colony in the S Atlantic; *area* 12,173 sq km/4,700 sq mi, made up of two main islands: East Falkland 6,760 sq km/2,610 sq mi, and West Falkland 5,413 sq km/2,090 sq mi; *capital* Stanley; new port facilities opened 1984, Mount Pleasant airport 1985; *features* in addition to the two main islands, there are about 200 small islands, all with wild scenery and rich bird life; *products* wool, alginates (used as dyes and as a food additive) from seaweed beds; *population* (1986) 1,916.

Falklands War war between Argentina and Britain over disputed sovereignty of the Falkland Islands, initiated when Argentina invaded and occupied the islands 2 April 1982. On the following day, the United Nations Security Council passed a resolution calling for Argentina to withdraw. A British task force was immediately dispatched and, after a fierce conflict in which over 1,000 Argentine and British lives were lost, 12,000 Argentine troops surrendered and the islands were returned to British rule 14–15 June 1982.

Falla Manuel de 1876–1946. Spanish composer. His opera *La vida breve/Brief Life* 1905 (performed 1913) was followed by the ballets *El amor brujo/Love the Magician* 1915 and *El sombrero de tres picos/The Three-Cornered Hat* 1919, and his most ambitious concert work, *Noches en los jardines de España/Nights in the Gardens of Spain* 1916.

Fallopian tube or *oviduct* in mammals, one of two tubes that carry eggs from the ovary to the uterus. An egg is fertilized by sperm in the Fallopian tubes, which are lined with cells whose cilia move the egg towards the uterus.

fallout harmful radioactive material released into the atmosphere in the debris of a nuclear explosion and descending to the surface. Such material can enter the food chain, cause ♢radiation sickness, and last for hundreds of thousands of years (see ♢half-life).

Famagusta seaport on the E coast of Cyprus, in the Turkish Republic of Northern Cyprus; population (1985) 19,500. It was the chief port of the island until the Turkish invasion 1974.

family planning spacing or preventing the birth of children. Access to family-planning services (see ♢contraceptive) is a significant factor in women's health as well as in limiting population growth.

famine severe shortage of food affecting a large number of people. Almost 750 million people worldwide (equivalent to double the population of Europe) suffer from hunger and malnutrition. Famines are usually explained as being caused by insufficient food supplies, so most Western famine-relief agencies, such as the International ♢Red Cross, set out to supply food or to increase the local production, rather than becoming involved in politics. Another theory is that famines arise when one group in a society loses its opportunity to exchange its labour or possessions for food.

FAO abbreviation for the United Nations ♢*Food and Agriculture Organization.*

farad SI unit (symbol F) of electrical capacitance (how much electricity a ♢capacitor can store for a given voltage). One farad is a capacitance of one ♢coulomb per volt. For practical purposes the microfarad (one millionth of a farad) is more commonly used. The farad is named after English scientist Michael Faraday.

Faraday Michael 1791–1867. English chemist and physicist. In 1821 he began experimenting with electromagnetism, and ten years later discovered the induction of electric currents and made the first dynamo. He subsequently found that a magnetic field will rotate the plane of polarization of light. Faraday also investigated electrolysis.

farce broad form of comedy involving stereotyped characters in complex, often improbable situations frequently revolving around extramarital relationships (hence the term 'bedroom farce').

Far East geographical term for all Asia east of the Indian subcontinent.

Faroe Islands or *Faeroe Islands* or *Faeroes* (Danish *Faerøerne*, 'Sheep Islands') island group (18 out of 22 inhabited) in the N Atlantic, between the Shetland Islands and Iceland, forming an outlying part of Denmark; *area* 1,399 sq km/540 sq mi; largest islands are Strømoø, Østerø, Vagø, Suderø, Sandø, and Bordø; *capital* Thorshavn on Strømø, population (1986) 15,287; *products* fish, crafted goods; *currency* Danish krone; *population* (1986) 46,000; *languages* Faerøese, Danish; *government* since 1948 the islands have had full self-government; they do not belong to the European Community; *history* first settled by Norsemen in the 9th century, the Faroes were a Norwegian province 1380–1709. Their parliament was restored 1852. They withdrew from the European Free Trade Association 1972.

Farouk 1920–1965. King of Egypt 1936–52. He succeeded his father Fuad I. In 1952 a coup headed by General Muhammed Neguib and Colonel Gamal Nasser compelled him to abdicate, and his son Fuad II was temporarily proclaimed in his place.

fascism political ideology that denies all rights to individuals in their relations with the state; specifically, the totalitarian nationalist movement founded in Italy 1919 by ♢Mussolini and followed by Hitler's Germany 1933. The fascist party, the *Partitio Nazionale Fascista*, controlled Italy 1922–43. Fascism protected the existing social order by forcible suppression of the working-class movement and by providing scapegoats for popular anger such as outsiders who lived within the state: Jews, foreigners, or blacks.

Fassbinder Rainer Werner 1946–1982. West German film director who began as a fringe actor and founded his own 'anti-theatre' before moving into films. His works are mainly stylized indictments of contemporary German society. He made more than 40 films, including *Die bitteren Tränen der Petra von Kant/The Bitter Tears of Petra von Kant* 1972, *Angst essen Seele auf/Fear Eats the Soul* 1974, and *Die Ehe von Maria Braun/The Marriage of Maria Braun* 1979.

fasting the practice of voluntarily going without food. It can be undertaken as a religious observance, a sign of mourning, a political protest (hunger strike), or for slimming purposes.

fast reactor or **fast breeder reactor** ▷nuclear reactor that makes use of fast neutrons to bring about fission. Unlike other reactors used by the nuclear-power industry, it has little or no moderator, to slow down neutrons. The reactor core is surrounded by a 'blanket' of uranium carbide. During operation, some of this uranium is converted into plutonium, which can be extracted and later used as fuel.

fat in the broadest sense, a mixture of ▷lipids – chiefly triglycerides (lipids containing three ▷fatty acid molecules linked to a molecule of glycerol). More specifically, the term refers to a lipid mixture that is solid at room temperature (20°C); lipid mixtures that are liquid at room temperature are called *oils*. The higher the proportion of saturated fatty acids in a mixture, the harder the fat.

Fatah, al- Palestinian nationalist organization founded 1956 to bring about an independent state of Palestine. Also called the Palestine National Liberation Movement, it is the main component of the ▷Palestine Liberation Organization. Its leader is Yassir ▷Arafat.

Fates in Greek mythology, three female figures who determined the destiny of human lives. They were envisaged as spinners: Clotho spun the thread of life, Lachesis twisted the thread, and Atropos cut it off. They are analogous to the Roman Parcae and Norse Norns.

Father's Day day set apart in many countries for honouring fathers, observed on the third Sunday in June in the USA, UK, and Canada. The first Father's Day was celebrated in the USA 1910.

Fatimid dynasty of Muslim Shi'ite caliphs founded 909 by Obaidallah, who claimed to be a descendant of Fatima (the prophet Muhammad's daughter) and her husband Ali, in N Africa. In 969 the Fatimids conquered Egypt, and the dynasty continued until overthrown by Saladin 1171.

fatty acid or **carboxylic acid** organic compound consisting of a hydrocarbon chain, up to 24 carbon atoms long, with a carboxyl group (–COOH) at one end. The covalent bonds between the carbon atoms may be single or double; where a double bond occurs the carbon atoms concerned carry one instead of two hydrogen atoms. Chains with only single bonds have all the hydrogen they can carry,

so they are said to be *saturated* with hydrogen. Chains with one or more double bonds are said to be *unsaturated* (see ▷polyunsaturate).

fatwa in Islamic law, an authoritative legal opinion on a point of doctrine. In 1989 a fatwa calling for the death of English novelist Salman ▷Rushdie was made by the Ayatollah ▷Khomeini of Iran, following publication of Rushdie's controversial and allegedly blasphemous book *The Satanic Verses*.

Faulkner William 1897–1962. US novelist who wrote in an experimental stream-of-consciousness style. His works include *The Sound and the Fury* 1929, dealing with a Southern family in decline; *As I Lay Dying* 1930; and *The Hamlet* 1940, *The Town* 1957, and *The Mansion* 1959, a trilogy. Nobel prize 1949.

fault in geology, a fracture in the Earth's crust along which the two sides have moved as a result of differing strains in the adjacent rock bodies. Displacement of rock masses horizontally or vertically along a fault may be microscopic, or it may be massive, causing major ▷earthquakes.

Faunus in Roman mythology, god of fertility and prophecy, with goat's ears, horns, tail and hind legs, identified with the Greek Pan.

Fauré Gabriel (Urbain) 1845–1924. French composer of songs, chamber music, and a choral *Requiem* 1888. He was a pupil of Saint-Saëns, became professor of composition at the Paris Conservatoire 1896 and was director from 1905 to 1920.

Faust legendary magician who sold his soul to the Devil. The historical Georg Faust appears to have been a wandering scholar and conjurer in Germany at the start of the 16th century. Goethe, Heine, Thomas Mann, and Paul Valéry all used the legend, and it inspired musical works by Schumann, Berlioz, Gounod, Boito, and Busoni.

Fauvism style of painting with a bold use of vivid colours inspired by van Gogh, Cézanne, and Gaugin. A short-lived but influential art movement, Fauvism originated in Paris 1905 with the founding of the Salon d'Automne by Henri ▷Matisse and others, when the critic Louis Vauxcelles called their gallery *'une cage aux fauves'* (a cage of wild beasts).

Fawkes Guy 1570–1606. English conspirator in the ▷Gunpowder Plot to blow up King James I and the members of both Houses of Parliament. Fawkes, a Roman Catholic convert, was arrested in the cellar underneath the House 4 Nov 1605, tortured, and executed. The event is still commemorated in Britain and elsewhere every 5 Nov with bonfires, fireworks, and the burning of the 'guy', an effigy.

fax (common name for *facsimile transmission* or *telefax*) the transmission of images over a ▷telecommunications link, usually the telephone network. When placed on a fax machine, the original image is scanned by a transmitting device and converted into coded signals, which travel via the telephone lines to the receiving fax machine, where an image is created that is a copy of the original.

FBI abbreviation for ⟡*Federal Bureau of Investigation*, agency of the US Department of Justice.

February Revolution the first of the two political uprisings of the ⟡Russian revolution in 1917 that led to the overthrow of the tsar and the end of the ⟡Romanov dynasty.

Federal Bureau of Investigation (FBI) agency of the US Department of Justice that investigates violations of federal law not specifically assigned to other agencies, being particularly concerned with internal security. The FBI was established 1908 and built up a position of powerful autonomy during the autocratic directorship of J Edgar Hoover 1924–72.

federalism system of government in which two or more separate states unite under a common central government while retaining a considerable degree of local autonomy. A federation should be distinguished from a *confederation*, a looser union of states for mutual assistance. Switzerland, the USA, Canada, Australia, and Malaysia are all examples of federal government, and many supporters of the European Community see it as the forerunner of a federal Europe.

feldspar one of a group of rock forming minerals; the chief constituents of ⟡igneous rock. Feldspars all contain silicon, aluminium, and oxygen, linked together to form a framework; spaces within this structure are occupied by sodium, potassium, calcium, or occasionally barium, in various proportions. Feldspars form white, grey, or pink crystals and rank 6 on the ⟡Mohs' scale of hardness.

Fellini Federico 1920– . Italian film director whose films, from his own scripts, combine dream and fantasy sequences with satire and autobiographical details. His films include *I vitelloni/The Young and the Passionate* 1953, *La Strada/The Street* 1954 (Academy Award 1956), *Le notti di Cabiria/ The Nights of Cabiria* 1956, *La dolce vita* 1960, *Otto e mezzo/8½* 1963, *Giulietta degli spiriti/Juliet of the Spirits* 1965, *Satyricon* 1969, and *Amarcord* 1974.

fencing sport of fighting with swords including the *foil*, derived from the light weapon used in practice duels; the *épée*, a heavier weapon derived from the duelling sword proper; and the *sabre*, with a curved handle and narrow V-shaped blade. In sabre fighting, cuts count as well as thrusts. Masks and protective jackets are worn, and hits are registered electronically in competitions.

Fenian movement Irish-American republican secret society, founded 1858 and named after the ancient Irish legendary warrior band of the Fianna. The collapse of the movement began when an attempt to establish an independent Irish republic by an uprising in Ireland 1867 failed, as did raids into Canada 1866 and 1870, and England 1867.

fennel any of several varieties of a perennial plant *Foeniculum vulgare* with feathery green leaves, of the carrot family Umbelliferae. Fennels have an aniseed flavour, and the leaves and seeds are used in seasoning. The thickened leafstalks of sweet fennel *F. vulgare dulce* are eaten.

Fens, the level, low-lying tracts of land in E England, W and S of the Wash, about 115 km/ 70 mi N–S and 55 km/34 mi E–W. They fall within the counties of Lincolnshire, Cambridgeshire, and Norfolk, consisting of a huge area, formerly a bay of the North Sea, but now crossed by numerous drainage canals and forming some of the most productive agricultural land in Britain. The peat portion of the Fens is known as the *Bedford Level*.

Ferdinand 1861–1948. King of Bulgaria 1908–18. Son of Prince Augustus of Saxe-Coburg-Gotha, he was elected prince of Bulgaria 1887 and, in 1908, proclaimed Bulgaria's independence of Turkey and assumed the title of tsar. In 1915 he entered World War I as Germany's ally, and in 1918 abdicated.

Ferdinand I *the Great c.* 1016–1065. King of Castile from 1035. He began the reconquest of Spain from the Moors and united all NW Spain under his and his brothers' rule.

Ferdinand V 1452–1516. King of Castile from 1474, *Ferdinand II* of Aragon from 1479, and *Ferdinand III* of Naples from 1504; first king of all Spain. In 1469 he married his cousin ⟡Isabella I, who succeeded to the throne of Castile 1474; together they were known as *the Catholic Monarchs* because, as a reaction to 700 years of rule by the ⟡Moors, they Catholicized Spain. When Ferdinand inherited the throne of Aragon 1479, the two great Spanish kingdoms were brought under a single government for the first time. They introduced the ⟡Inquisition 1480; expelled the Jews; and in 1492 forced the final surrender of the Moors at Granada and financed Columbus' expedition to the Americas.

Ferdinand I 1503–1564. Holy Roman emperor who succeeded his brother Charles V 1558; king of Bohemia and Hungary from 1526, king of the Germans from 1531. He reformed the German monetary system and reorganized the judicial Aulic council (*Reichshofrat*). He was the son of Philip the Handsome and grandson of Maximilian I.

Ferdinand II 1578–1637. Holy Roman emperor from 1619, when he succeeded his uncle Matthias; king of Bohemia from 1617 and of Hungary from 1618. A zealous Catholic, he provoked the Bohemian revolt that led to the Thirty Years' War. He was a grandson of Ferdinand I.

Fermanagh county in the southern part of Northern Ireland; *area* 1,680 sq km/648 sq mi; *towns* Enniskillen (county town), Lisnaskea, Irvinestown; *physical* in the centre is a broad trough of low-lying land, in which lie Upper and Lower Lough Erne; *products* mainly agricultural; livestock, tweeds, clothing; *population* (1981) 52,000.

Fermat Pierre de 1601–1665. French mathematician, who with Blaise Pascal founded the theory of ▷probability and the modern theory of numbers and who made contributions to analytical geometry.

fermentation the breakdown of sugars by bacteria and yeasts using a method of respiration without oxygen (▷anaerobic). Fermentation processes have long been utilized in baking bread, making beer and wine, and producing cheese, yoghurt, soy sauce, and many other foodstuffs.

Fermi Enrico 1901–1954. Italian-born US physicist who proved the existence of new radioactive elements produced by bombardment with neutrons, and discovered nuclear reactions produced by low-energy neutrons. His theoretical work included study of the weak nuclear force, one of the fundamental forces of nature, and (with Paul Dirac) of the quantum statistics of fermion particles. Nobel prize 1938.

fermion in physics, a subatomic particle whose spin can only take values that are half-integers, such as $1/2$ or $1\frac{1}{2}$. Fermions may be classified as leptons, such as the electron, and baryons, such as the proton and neutron. All elementary particles are either fermions or ▷bosons.

fermium synthesized, radioactive, metallic element of the ▷actinide series, symbol Fm, atomic number 100, relative atomic mass 257. Ten isotopes are known, the longest-lived of which, Fm-257, has a half-life of 80 days. Fermium has been produced only in minute quantities in particle accelerators.

fern plant of the class Filicales, related to horsetails and clubmosses. Ferns are spore-bearing, not flowering, plants, and most are perennial, spreading by low-growing roots. The leaves, known as fronds, vary widely in size and shape. Some taller types, such as tree ferns, grow in the tropics. There are over 7,000 species.

ferret domesticated variety of the Old World ▷polecat. About 35 cm/1.2 ft long, it usually has yellowish-white fur and pink eyes, but may be the dark brown colour of a wild polecat. Ferrets may breed with wild polecats. They have been used since ancient times to hunt rabbits and rats.

fertilization in ▷sexual reproduction, the union of two ▷gametes (sex cells, often called egg and sperm) to produce a ▷zygote, which combines the genetic material contributed by each parent. In self-fertilization the male and female gametes come from the same plant; in cross-fertilization they come from different plants. Self-fertilization rarely occurs in animals; usually even hermaphrodite animals cross-fertilize each other.

fertilizer substance containing some or all of a range of about 20 chemical elements necessary for healthy plant growth, used to compensate for the deficiencies of poor or depleted soil. Fertilizers may be *organic*, for example farmyard manure, composts, bonemeal, blood, and fishmeal; or *inorganic*, in the form of compounds, mainly of nitrogen, phosphate, and potash, which have been used on a very much increased scale since 1945.

Fès or *Fez* former capital of Morocco 808–1062, 1296–1548, and 1662–1912, in a valley N of the Great Atlas mountains, 160 km/100 mi E of Rabat; population (1982) 563,000. Textiles, carpets, and leather are manufactured, and the *fez*, a brimless hat worn in S and E Mediterranean countries, is traditionally said to have originated here.

fetishism in anthropology, belief in the supernormal power of some inanimate object that is known as a fetish. Fetishism in some form is common to most cultures, and often has religio-magical significance.

fetishism in psychology, the transfer of erotic interest to an object, such as an item of clothing whose real or fantasized presence is necessary for sexual gratification.

fetus or *foetus* stage in mammalian ▷embryo development. The human embryo is usually termed a fetus after the eighth week of development, when the limbs and external features of the head are recognizable.

feudalism the main form of social organization in medieval Europe. A system based primarily on land, it involved a hierarchy of authority, rights, and power that extended from the monarch downwards. An intricate network of duties and obligations linked royalty, nobility, lesser gentry, free tenants, villeins, and serfs.

Fianna Fáil Republic of Ireland political party, founded by the Irish nationalist de Valera 1926. It has been the governing party in the Republic of Ireland 1932–48, 1951–54, 1957–73, 1977–81, 1982, and from 1987. It aims at the establishment of a united and completely independent all-Ireland republic.

fibre, dietary or *roughage* plant material that cannot be digested by human digestive enzymes; it consists largely of cellulose, a carbohydrate found in plant cell walls. Fibre adds bulk to the gut contents, assisting the muscular contractions that force food along the intestine. A diet low in fibre causes constipation and is believed to increase the risk of developing diverticulitis, diabetes, gall-bladder disease, and cancer of the large bowel.

fibreglass glass that has been formed into fine fibres, either as long continuous filaments or as a fluffy, short-fibred glass wool. Fibreglass is heat- and fire-resistant and a good electrical insulator. It has applications in the field of fibre optics and as a strengthener for plastics in GRP (glass-reinforced plastics).

fiction in literature, any work in which the content is completely or largely invented. The term describes imaginative works of narrative prose (such as the novel or the short story), and is distinguished from **nonfiction** (such as history, biography, or works on practical subjects), and **poetry**.

fieldfare thrush *Turdus pilaris* of the family Muscicapidae; it has a pale-grey lower back and neck and a dark tail. It is a migrant in Britain, breeding in Scandinavia and N Russia.

Fielding Henry 1707–1754. English novelist. His greatest work, *The History of Tom Jones, a Foundling* 1749 (which he described as 'a comic epic in prose'), realized for the first time in English the novel's potential for memorable characterization, coherent plotting, and perceptive analysis.

Field of the Cloth of Gold site between Guînes and Ardres near Calais, France, where a meeting took place between Henry VIII of England and Francis I of France in June 1520, remarkable for the lavish clothes worn and tent pavilions erected. Francis hoped to gain England's support in opposing the Holy Roman emperor, Charles V, but failed.

Fields W C. Stage name of William Claude Dukenfield 1879–1946. US actor and screenwriter. His distinctive strangled speech and professed attitudes such as hatred of children and dogs gained him enormous popularity in such films as *David Copperfield* 1935, *My Little Chickadee* (co-written with Mae West) and *The Bank Dick* both 1940, and *Never Give a Sucker an Even Break* 1941.

Fife region of E Scotland (formerly the county of Fife), facing the North Sea and Firth of Forth; **area** 1,300 sq km/502 sq mi; **towns** administrative headquarters Glenrothes; Dunfermline, St Andrews, Kirkcaldy, Cupar; **physical** the only high land is the Lomond Hills in the NW; chief rivers Eden and Leven; **products** potatoes, cereals, electronics, petrochemicals (Mossmorran), light engineering; **population** (1991) 339,200.

fifth-generation computer anticipated new type of computer based on emerging microelectronic technologies with high computing speeds. The development of very large-scale integration (◊VLSI) technology, which can put many more circuits on to an ◊integrated circuit (chip) than is currently possible, and developments in computer hardware and software design may produce computers far more powerful that those in current use.

fig any tree of the genus *Ficus* of the mulberry family Moraceae, including the many cultivated varieties of *F. carica*, originally from W Asia. They produce two or three crops of fruit a year. Eaten fresh or dried, figs have a high sugar content and laxative properties. Figs grow extensively in S Europe.

figwort any Old World plant of the genus *Scrophularia* of the figwort family, which also includes foxgloves and snapdragons. Members of the genus have square stems, opposite leaves, and open two-lipped flowers in a cluster at the top of the stem.

Fiji Republic of; country comprising a group of 844 Melanesian and Polynesian islands and islets in the SW Pacific, about 110 of which are inhabited; **area** 18,333 sq km/7,078 sq mi; **capital** Suva; **physical** largest islands Viti Levu (10,429 sq km/4,028 sq mi) and Vanua Levu (5,550 sq km/2,146 sq mi); mountainous, volcanic, with tropical rainforest and grasslands; **head of state** Ratu Sir Penaia Ganilau from 1987; **head of government** Ratu Sir Kamisese Mara from 1970; **political system** democratic republic; **exports** sugar, coconut oil, ginger, timber, canned fish, gold; tourism is important; **population** (1989 est) 758,000 (46% Fijian, holding 80% of the land communally, and 49% Indian, introduced in 19th century to work the sugar crop); **languages** English (official), Fijian, Hindi; **recent history** independence achieved from Britain 1970; Ratu Sir Kamisese Mara elected the first prime minister. In 1987 a general election brought to power an Indian-dominated coalition led by Dr Timoci Bavadra, but two military coups followed in the same year, and Fiji was declared a republic and removed from the Commonwealth, and the constitution was suspended. In Dec civilian government was restored, with Lt-Col Sitivina Rambuka retaining control of security as minister for home affairs.

Fillmore Millard 1800–1874. 13th president of the USA 1850–53, a Whig. Born into a poor farming family in New Cayuga County, New York State, he was Zachary Taylor's vice-president from 1849, and succeeded him on Taylor's death, July 9 1850. Fillmore supported a compromise on slavery 1850 to reconcile North and South.

film, photographic strip of transparent material (usually cellulose acetate) coated with a light-sensitive emulsion, used in cameras to take pictures. The emulsion contains a mixture of light-sensitive silver halide salts (for example, bromide or iodide) in gelatin. Films differ in their sensitivities to light, this being indicated by their speeds. When the emulsion is exposed to light, the silver salts are invisibly altered, giving a latent image, which is then made visible by the process of developing. Colour film consists of several layers of emulsion, each of which records a different colour in the light falling on it.

filtration technique by which suspended solid particles in a fluid are removed by passing the mixture through a porous barrier, usually paper or cloth. The particles are retained by the paper or cloth to form a residue and the fluid passes through to make up the filtrate.

Financial Times Index (FT Index) indicator measuring the daily movement of 30 major industrial share prices on the London Stock Exchange (1935 = 100), issued by the UK *Financial Times* newspaper. Other FT indices cover government securities, fixed-interest securities, gold mine shares, and Stock Exchange activity.

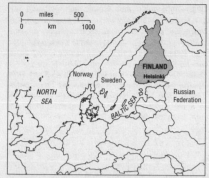

finch any of various songbirds of the family Fringillidae, in the order Passeriformes (perching birds). They are seed-eaters with stout conical beaks, and include chaffinches, sparrows, and canaries.

Fine Gael Republic of Ireland political party founded 1933 by W J ◊Cosgrave and led by Alan Dukes from 1987. It is socially liberal but fiscally conservative.

fingerprint ridge pattern of the skin on a person's fingertips; this is constant through life and no two are exactly alike. Fingerprinting was first used as a means of identifying crime suspects in India, and was adopted by the English police 1901; it is now widely employed in police and security work.

Finland Republic of; country in Scandinavia, bordered N by Norway, E by the Russian Federation, S and W by the Baltic Sea, and NW by Sweden; *area* 338,145 sq km/130,608 sq mi; *capital* Helsinki; *physical* most of the country is forest, with low hills and about 60,000 lakes; one-third is within the Arctic Circle; archipelago in S; *head of state* Mauno Koivisto from 1982; *head of government* Esko Aho from 1991; *political system* democratic republic; *exports* metal, chemical, and engineering products (icebreakers and oil rigs), paper, sawn wood, clothing, fine ceramics, glass, furniture; *population* (1989 est) 4,990,00; *languages* Finnish 93%, Swedish 6% (both official); small Lapp- and Russian-speaking minorities; *recent history* independence achieved from Russia 1917, but defeated by USSR in Winter War of 1939 and later allowed Germany to station troops in Finland to attack USSR; USSR bombed Finland. In 1944 a separate armistice was concluded with USSR. Finland joined the UN and the Nordic Council 1955, signed treaties of trade with the EC 1973, and the USSR 1977, joined the Council of Europe 1989, and applied for EC membership 1992.

Finland, Gulf of eastern arm of the ◊Baltic Sea, separating Finland from Estonia.

Finno-Ugric group or family of more than 20 languages spoken by some 22 million people in scattered communities from Norway in the west to Siberia in the east and to the Carpathian Mountains in the south. Members of the family include Finnish, Lapp, and Hungarian.

fir any ◊conifer of the genus *Abies* in the pine family Pinaceae. The true firs include the balsam fir of N North America and the Eurasian silver fir *A. alba*. Douglas firs of the genus *Pseudotsuga* are native to W North America and the Far East.

firearm weapon from which projectiles are discharged by the combustion of an explosive. Firearms are generally divided into two main sections: ◊*artillery* (ordnance or cannon), with a bore greater than 2.54 cm/1 in, and ◊*small arms*, with a bore of less than 2.54 cm/1 in. Although gunpowder was known in Europe 60 years previously, the invention of guns dates from 1300–25, and is attributed to Berthold Schwartz, a German monk.

Firenze Italian form of ◊Florence.

First World War another name for ◊World War I 1914–18.

fish aquatic vertebrate that uses gills for obtaining oxygen from fresh or sea water. There are three main groups, not closely related: the bony fishes or Osteichthyes (goldfish, cod, tuna); the cartilaginous fishes or Chondrichthyes (sharks, rays); and the jawless fishes or Agnatha (hagfishes, lampreys).

fission in physics, the splitting of a heavy atomic nucleus into two or more major fragments. It is accompanied by the emission of two or three neutrons and the release of large amounts of energy (see ◊nuclear energy).

Fitzgerald Ella 1918– . US jazz singer, recognized as one of the finest, most lyrical voices in jazz, both in solo work and with big bands. She is celebrated for her smooth interpretations of Gershwin and Cole Porter songs.

Fitzgerald F(rancis) Scott (Key) 1896–1940. US novelist and short-story writer. His early autobiographical novel *This Side of Paradise* 1920 made him known in the postwar society of the East Coast, and *The Great Gatsby* 1925 epitomizes the Jazz Age.

FitzGerald Garret 1926– . Irish politician, leader of the Fine Gael party 1977–87. As *Taoiseach* (prime minister) 1981–82 and again 1982–86, he was noted for his attempts to solve the Northern Ireland dispute, ultimately by participating in the Anglo-Irish agreement 1985.

fjord or *fiord* narrow sea inlet enclosed by high cliffs. Fjords are found in Norway, New Zealand, and western parts of Scotland. They are formed when an overdeepened glacial trough is drowned by a rise in sea-level. At the mouth of the fjord there is a characteristic lip causing a shallowing of the water. This is due to reduced glacial erosion at this point.

flamenco music and dance of the Andalusian gypsies of S Spain, evolved from Andalusian and Arabic folk music. The *cante* (song) is sometimes performed as a solo but more often accompanied by guitar music and passionate improvised dance. Male flamenco dancers excel in powerful, rhythmic footwork while the female dancers place emphasis on the graceful and erotic movements of their hands and bodies. Hand clapping, finger clicking (castanets are a more recent addition), and enthusiastic shouts are all features of flamenco.

flamingo long-legged and long-necked wading bird, family Phoenicopteridae, of the stork order Ciconiiformes. Largest of the family is the greater or roseate flamingo *Phoenicopterus ruber*, found in Africa, the Caribbean, and South America, with delicate pink plumage and 1.25 m/4 ft tall.

Flanders region of the Low Countries that in the 8th and 9th centuries extended from Calais to the Scheldt and is now covered by the Belgian provinces of Oost Vlaanderen and West Vlaanderen (East and West Flanders), the French *département* of Nord, and part of the Dutch province of Zeeland. The language is Flemish. East Flanders, capital Ghent, has an area of 3,000 sq km/1,158 sq mi and a population (1991) of 1,335,700. West Flanders, capital Bruges, has an area of 3,100 sq km/1,197 sq mi and a population (1991) of 1,106,800.

flatfish bony fishes of the order Pleuronectiformes, having a characteristically flat, asymmetrical body with both eyes (in adults) on the upper side. Species include flounders, turbots, halibuts, plaice, and the European soles.

flatworm invertebrate of the phylum Platyhelminthes. Some are free-living, but many are parasitic (for example, tapeworms and flukes). The body is simple and bilaterally symmetrical, with one opening to the intestine. Many are hermaphroditic

(with both male and female sex organs), and practise self-fertilization.

Flaubert Gustave 1821–1880. French novelist, author of *Madame Bovary* 1857. *Salammbô* 1862 was followed by *L'Education sentimentale/Sentimental Education* 1869 and *La Tentation de Saint Antoine/The Temptation of St Anthony* 1874. Flaubert also wrote the short stories *Trois contes/Three Tales* 1877. His dedication to art resulted in a meticulous prose style, realistic detail, and psychological depth.

flax any plant of the genus *Linum*, family Linaceae. The species *L. usitatissimum* is the cultivated strain; *linen* is produced from the fibre in its stems. The seeds yield *linseed oil*, used in paints and varnishes. The plant, of almost worldwide distribution, has a stem up to 60 cm/24 in high, small leaves, and bright blue flowers.

flea wingless insect of the order Siphonaptera, with blood-sucking mouthparts. Fleas are parasitic on warm-blooded animals. Some fleas can jump 130 times their own height.

Fleming Alexander 1881–1955. Scottish bacteriologist who discovered the first antibiotic drug, ⟩penicillin, in 1928 (though it did not come into use until 1941). In 1922 he had discovered lysozyme, an antibacterial enzyme present in saliva, nasal secretions, and tears. While studying this, he found an unusual mould growing on a neglected culture dish, which he isolated and grew into a pure culture; this led to his discovery of penicillin. In 1945 he won the Nobel Prize for Physiology and Medicine with Howard W Florey and Ernst B Chain, whose research had brought widespread realization of the value of penicillin.

Flemish art the style of painting developed and practised in Flanders (a region in the Lowlands of NW Europe, largely coinciding with modern

fish

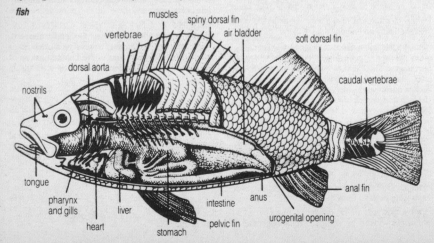

muscles
spiny dorsal fin
vertebrae
air bladder
soft dorsal fin
dorsal aorta
caudal vertebrae
nostrils
tongue
anal fin
pharynx and gills
liver
intestine
anus
heart
stomach
pelvic fin
urogenital opening

Belgium). A Flemish style emerged in the early 15th century. Paintings are distinguished by keen observation, minute attention to detail, bright colours, and superb technique – oil painting was a Flemish invention. Apart from portraits, they depict religious scenes, often placed in contemporary Flemish landscapes, townscapes, and interiors. Flemish sculpture shows German and French influence.

flight or *aviation* method of transport in which aircraft carry people and goods through the air. People first took to the air in ◊balloons and began powered flight 1852 in ◊airships, but the history of flying, both for civilian and military use, is dominated by the ◊aeroplane. The earliest planes were designed for ◊gliding; the advent of the petrol engine saw the first powered flight by the ◊Wright brothers 1903 in the USA. This inspired the development of aircraft throughout Europe. Biplanes were succeeded by monoplanes in the 1930s. The first jet plane (see ◊jet propulsion) was produced 1939, and after the end of World War II the development of jetliners brought about a continuous expansion in passenger air travel. In 1969 came the supersonic aircraft ◊Concorde.

flint compact, hard, brittle mineral (a variety of chert), brown, black, or grey in colour, found in nodules in limestone or shale deposits. It consists of fine-grained silica, SiO_2, in cryptocrystalline form (usually ◊quartz). Flint implements were widely used in prehistory and constitute the basis of all human technology.

Flodden, Battle of the defeat of the Scots by the English under the Earl of Surrey 9 Sept 1513 on a site 5 km/3 mi SE of Coldstream, Northumberland, England; many Scots, including King James IV, were killed.

floppy disc in computing, a storage device consisting of a light, flexible disc enclosed in a cardboard or plastic jacket. The disc is placed in a disc drive, where it rotates at high speed. Data are recorded magnetically on one or both surfaces.

Florence (Italian *Firenze*) capital of ◊Tuscany, N Italy, 88 km/55 mi from the mouth of the river Arno; population (1988) 421,000. It has printing, engineering, and optical industries; many crafts, including leather, gold and silver work, and embroidery; and its art and architecture attract large numbers of tourists.

Florida southeasternmost state of the USA; mainly a peninsula jutting into the Atlantic, which it separates from the Gulf of Mexico; nickname Sunshine State; *area* 152,000 sq km/58,672 sq mi; *capital* Tallahassee; *cities* Miami, Tampa, Jacksonville; *population* (1990) 12,937,900, one of the fastest-growing of the states; including 15% nonwhite; 10% Hispanic, (especially Cuban); *physical* 50% forested; lakes (including Okeechobee 1,000 sq km/695 sq mi; Everglades National Park

(5,000 sq km/1,930 sq mi), with birdlife, cypresses, alligators; *features* Palm Beach island resort, between the lagoon of Lake Worth and the Atlantic; Florida Keys; John F Kennedy Space Center at Cape Canaveral; Disney World theme park; beach resorts on Gulf and on Atlantic; Daytona International Speedway; *products* citrus fruits, melons, vegetables, fish, shellfish, phosphates, chemicals, electrical and electronic equipment, aircraft, fabricated metals; it is a banking centre, handling much cash derived from the traffic in illegal drugs from Latin America; *famous people* Chris Evert, Henry Flagler, James Weldon Johnson, Sidney Poitier, Philip Randolph, Joseph Stilwell; *history* discovered by Ponce de Leon and under Spanish rule from 1513 until its cession to England 1763; was returned to Spain 1783 and purchased by the US 1819, becoming a state 1845.

flounder small flatfish *Platychthys flesus* of the NE Atlantic and Mediterranean, although it sometimes lives in estuaries. It is dully coloured and grows to 50 cm/1.6 ft.

flower the reproductive unit of an ◊angiosperm or flowering plant, typically consisting of four whorls of modified leaves: ◊sepals, petals, ◊stamens, and ◊carpels. These are borne on a central axis or receptacle. The many variations in size, colour, number and arrangement of parts are closely related to the method of pollination. Flowers adapted for wind pollination typically have reduced or absent petals and sepals and long, feathery stigmas that hang outside the flower to trap airborne pollen. In contrast, the petals of insect-pollinated flowers are usually conspicuous and brightly coloured.

flugelhorn alto brass instrument, similar in appearance to the ◊cornet.

fluorescence in scientific usage, very short-lived ◊luminescence (a glow not caused by high temperature). Generally, the term is used for any luminescence regardless of the persistence. See ◊phosphorescence.

fluorine pale yellow, gaseous, nonmetallic element, symbol F, atomic number 9, relative atomic mass 19. It is the first member of the halogen group of elements, and is pungent, poisonous, and highly reactive, uniting directly with nearly all the elements. It occurs naturally as the minerals fluorite (CaF_2) and cryolite (Na_3AlF_6). Hydrogen fluoride is used in etching glass, and the freons, which all contain fluorine, are widely used as refrigerants.

flute member of a group of ◊woodwind musical instruments (although usually made of metal), including the piccolo, the concert flute, and the bass or alto flute. Flutes are cylindrical in shape, with a narrowed end, containing a shaped aperture, across which the player blows. The air vibrations produce the note, which can be altered by placing fingers over lateral holes. Certain keys can be depressed to extend the range of the flute to three octaves.

fly any insect of the order Diptera. A fly has a single pair of wings, antennae, and compound eyes; the hind wings have become modified into knoblike projections (halteres) used to maintain equilibrium in flight. There are over 90,000 species.

flying fish any of a family, Exocoetidae, of marine bony fishes of the order Beloniformes, best represented in tropical waters. They have winglike pectoral fins that can be spread to glide over the water.

flying fox fruit-eating ♢bat of the suborder Megachiroptera.

flying squirrel any of numerous species of squirrel, not closely related to the true squirrels. They are characterized by a membrane along the side of the body from forelimb to hindlimb (in some species running to neck and tail) which allows them to glide through the air. Several genera of flying squirrel are found in the Old World; the New World has the genus *Glaucomys*. Most species are E Asian.

Flynn Errol. Stage name of Leslie Thompson 1909–1959. Australian-born US film actor. He is renowned for his portrayal of swashbuckling heroes.

Foch Ferdinand 1851–1929. Marshal of France during World War I. He was largely responsible for the Allied victory at the first battle of the Marne Sept 1914, and commanded on the NW front Oct 1914–Sept 1916. He was appointed commander in chief of the Allied armies in the spring of 1918, and launched the Allied counter-offensive in July that brought about the negotiation of an armistice to end the war.

fog cloud that collects at the surface of the Earth, composed of water vapour that has condensed on particles of dust in the atmosphere. Cloud and fog are both caused by the air temperature falling below dew point. The thickness of fog depends on the number of water particles it contains. Usually, fog is formed by the meeting of two currents of air, one cooler than the other, or by warm air flowing over a cold surface. Sea fogs commonly occur where warm and cold currents meet and the air above them mixes.

Fokine Mikhail 1880–1942. Russian dancer and choreographer, born in St Petersburg. He was chief choreographer to the Ballets Russes 1909–14, and with ♢Diaghilev revitalized and reformed the art of ballet.

folklore the oral traditions and culture of a people, expressed in legends, riddles, songs, tales, and proverbs. The term was coined 1846 by W J Thoms (1803–1885), but the founder of the systematic study of the subject was Jacob Grimm; see also ♢oral literature.

folk music body of traditional music, originally transmitted orally. Many folk songs originated as a rhythmic accompaniment to manual work or to

mark a specific ritual. Folk song is usually melodic, not harmonic, and the modes used are distinctive of the country of origin; see ♢world music.

Fonda Henry 1905–1982. US actor whose engaging style made him ideal in the role of the American pioneer and honourable man. His many films include the Academy Award-winning *The Grapes of Wrath* 1940, *My Darling Clementine* 1946, and *On Golden Pond* 1981, for which he won the Academy Award for best actor.

Fonda Jane 1937– . US actress. Her films include *Cat Ballou* 1965, *Barefoot in the Park* 1967, *Barbarella* 1968, *They Shoot Horses, Don't They?* 1969, *Julia*, 1977, *The China Syndrome* 1979, *On Golden Pond* 1981, in which she appeared with her father Henry Fonda, and *Agnes of God* 1985. She won Academy Awards for *Klute* 1971 and *Coming Home* 1979. She is active in left-wing politics and in promoting physical fitness.

Fonteyn Margot. Stage name of Margaret Hookham 1919–1991. English ballet dancer. She made her debut with the Vic-Wells Ballet in *Nutcracker* 1934 and first appeared as Giselle 1937, eventually becoming prima ballerina of the Royal Ballet, London. Renowned for her perfect physique, musicality, and interpretive powers, she created many roles in Frederick ♢Ashton's ballets and formed a legendary partnership with Rudolf ♢Nureyev. She did not retire from dancing until 1979.

food anything eaten by human beings and other animals to sustain life and health. The building blocks of food are nutrients, and humans can utilize the following nutrients: *carbohydrates*, as starches found in bread, potatoes, and pasta; as simple sugars in sucrose and honey; as fibres in cereals, fruit, and vegetables; *proteins* as from nuts, fish, meat, eggs, milk, and some vegetables; *fats* as found in most animal products (meat, lard, dairy products, fish), also in margarine, nuts and seeds, olives, and edible oils; *vitamins* are found in a wide variety of foods, except for vitamin B_{12}, which is mainly found in animal foods; *minerals* are found in a wide variety of foods; good sources of calcium are milk and broccoli, for example; iodine from seafood; iron from liver and green vegetables; *water* ubiquitous in nature; *alcohol* is found in fermented distilled beverages, from 40% in spirits to 0.01% in low-alcohol lagers and beers.

Food and Agriculture Organization (FAO) United Nations agency that coordinates activities to improve food and timber production and levels of nutrition throughout the world. It is also concerned with investment in agriculture and dispersal of emergency food supplies. It has headquarters in Rome and was founded 1945.

food chain or *food web* in ecology, the sequence of organisms through which energy and other nutrients are successively transferred. Since many organisms feed at several different levels (for example, omnivores feed on both fruit and meat), the relationships often form a complex web rather than a simple chain. See also ▷ecosystem.

food poisoning any acute illness characterized by vomiting and diarrhoea and caused by eating food contaminated with harmful bacteria (for example, listeriosis), poisonous food (for example, certain mushrooms, puffer fish), or poisoned food (such as lead or arsenic introduced accidentally during processing). A frequent cause of food poisoning is ▷salmonella bacteria. These come in many forms, and strains are found in cattle, pigs, poultry, and eggs.

foot imperial unit of length (symbol ft), equivalent to 0.3048 m, in use in Britain since Anglo-Saxon times. It originally represented the length of a human foot. One foot contains 12 inches and is one-third of a yard.

Foot Michael 1913– . British Labour politician and writer. A leader of the left-wing Tribune Group, he was secretary of state for employment 1974–76, Lord President of the Council and leader of the House 1976–79, and succeeded James Callaghan as Labour Party leader 1980–83.

football, American contact sport similar to the English game of rugby, played between two teams of 11 players, with an inflated oval ball. Players

food chain

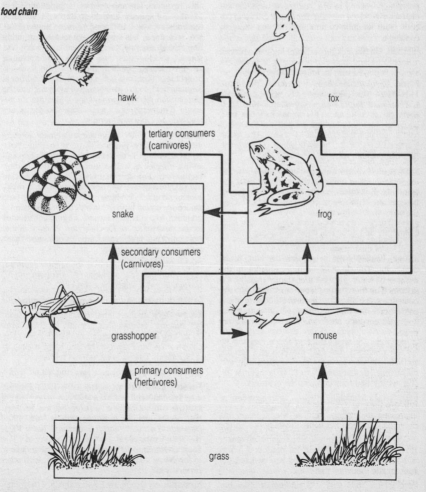

are well padded for protection and wear protective helmets. The first match under Harvard rules was between Harvard University and McGill University, Montréal, Canada, in 1874.

football, association or *soccer* form of football originating in the UK, popular in Europe and Latin America. It is played between two teams each of 11 players, on a field 90–120 m/100–130 yd long and 45–90 m/50–100 yd wide, with an inflated spherical ball of circumference 69 cm/27 in. The object of the game is to kick or head the ball into the opponents' goal, an area 7.31 m/8 yd wide and 2.44 m/8 ft high.

football, Australian Rules game that combines aspects of Gaelic football, rugby, and association football; it is played between two teams of 18 players each, with an inflated oval ball. It is unique to Australia.

football, Gaelic kicking and catching game played mainly in Ireland, between two teams of 15 players each. It is played with an inflated spherical ball, on a field 76–90 m/84–100 yd long and 128–146 m/140–160 yd wide. At each end is a set of goalposts 4.88 m/16 ft high, with a crossbar 2.44 m/8 ft above the ground, and a net across its lower half. Goals are scored by kicking the ball into the net (3 points) or over the crossbar (1 point). The game was first played 1712. The leading tournament is the All-Ireland Championship (first held 1887).

force in physics, any influence that tends to change the state of rest or uniform motion in a straight line of a body. It is measured by the rate of change of momentum of the body on which it acts, that is, the mass of the body multiplied by its acceleration: *F=ma*. Force is a vector quantity, possessing both magnitude and direction; its SI unit is the newton. See also ▷Newton's laws of motion.

forces, fundamental in physics, the four fundamental interactions believed to be at work in the physical universe. There are two long-range forces: *gravity*, which keeps the planets in orbit around the Sun, and acts between all particles that have mass; and the *electromagnetic force*, which stops solids from falling apart, and acts between all particles with ▷electric charge. There are two very short-range forces: the *weak nuclear force*, responsible for the reactions that fuel the Sun and for the emission of ▷beta particles from certain nuclei; and the *strong nuclear force*, which binds together the protons and neutrons in the nuclei of atoms.

Ford Gerald R(udolph) 1913– . 38th president of the USA 1974–77, a Republican. He was elected to the House of Representatives 1949, was nominated to the vice-presidency by Richard Nixon 1973 on the resignation of Spiro Agnew, and became president 1974, when Nixon resigned. He pardoned Nixon and gave amnesty to those who had resisted the draft for the Vietnam War.

Ford Henry 1863–1947. US automobile manufacturer, who built his first car 1896 and founded the Ford Motor Company 1903. His Model T (1908–27) was the first car to be constructed solely by assembly-line methods and to be mass marketed; 15 million of these cars were made and sold.

Foreign Legion volunteer corps of foreigners within a country's army. The French *Légion Etrangère*, formed 1831, is one of a number of such forces. Enlisted volunteers are of any nationality (about half are now French), but the officers are usually French.

forensic science the use of scientific techniques to solve criminal cases. A multidisciplinary field embracing chemistry, physics, botany, zoology, and medicine, forensic science includes the identification of human bodies or traces. Traditional methods such as fingerprinting (see ▷fingerprint) are still used, assisted by computers; in addition, blood analysis, forensic dentistry, voice and speech spectrograms, and genetic fingerprinting are increasingly applied. Ballistics (the study of projectiles, such as bullets), another traditional forensic field, today makes use of tools such as the comparison microscope and the ▷electron microscope. Chemicals, such as poisons and drugs, are analysed by ▷chromatography.

forestry the science of forest management. Recommended forestry practice aims at multipurpose crops, allowing the preservation of varied plant and animal species as well as human uses (lumbering, recreation). Forestry has often been confined to the planting of a single species, such as a rapid-growing conifer providing softwood for paper pulp and construction timber, for which world demand is greatest. In tropical countries, logging contributes to the destruction of ▷rainforests, causing global environmental problems. A small, unplanned forest area is called ▷woodland.

forget-me-not any plant of the genus *Myosotis*, family Boraginaceae, including *M. sylvatica* and *M. scorpioides*, with bright blue flowers.

formaldehyde common name for ▷methanal.

Formentera smallest inhabited island in the Spanish Balearic Islands, lying south of Ibiza; area 93 sq km/36 sq mi; population (1981) 3,500. The chief town is San Francisco Javier and the main port is La Sabina. The main industry is tourism.

formic acid common name for ▷methanoic acid.

Forster E(dward) M(organ) 1879–1970. English novelist, concerned with the interplay of personality and the conflict between convention and instinct. His novels include *A Room with a View* 1908, *Howard's End* 1910, and *A Passage to India* 1924. He also wrote short stories, for example 'The Eternal Omnibus' 1914; criticism, including *Aspects of the Novel* 1927; and essays, including *Abinger Harvest* 1936.

forsythia any temperate E Asian shrub of the genus *Forsythia* of the olive family Oleaceae, which bear yellow bell-shaped flowers in early spring before the leaves appear.

Forth river in SE Scotland, with its headstreams rising on the NE slopes of Ben Lomond. It flows approximately 72 km/45 mi to Kincardine where the *Firth of Forth* begins. The Firth is approximately 80 km/50 mi long, and is 26 km/16 mi wide where it joins the North Sea. At Queensferry near Edinburgh are the Forth rail (1890) and road (1964) bridges. The *Forth and Clyde Canal* (1768–90) across the lowlands of Scotland links the Firth with the river Clyde, Grangemouth to Bowling (53 km/33 mi).

FORTRAN (acronym for *for*mula *tran*slation) high-level computer-programming language suited to mathematical and scientific computations. Developed in the mid-1950s, it is one of the earliest languages still in use. ⬦BASIC was strongly influenced by FORTRAN and is similar in many ways.

Fort Worth city in NE Texas, USA; population (1990) 447,600. Formerly an important cattle area, it is now a grain, petroleum, aerospace, and railway centre serving the S USA.

fossil remains of an animal or plant preserved in rocks. Fossils may be formed by refrigeration (for example, Arctic ⬦mammoths in ice); carbonization (leaves in coal); formation of a cast (dinosaur or human footprints in mud); or mineralization of bones, more generally teeth or shells. The study of fossils is called ⬦palaeontology.

fossil fuel fuel, such as coal, oil, and natural gas, formed from the fossilized remains of plants that lived hundreds of millions of years ago. Fossil fuels are a nonrenewable resource and will eventually run out. Extraction of coal (mining) causes considerable environmental pollution, and burning coal contributes to problems of ⬦acid rain and the ⬦greenhouse effect.

Foster Jodie. Stage name of Alicia Christian Foster 1962– . US film actress who began as a child in a great variety of roles. She starred in *Taxi Driver* 1976 and *Bugsy Malone* both 1976, when only 14. Subsequent films include *The Accused* 1988, for which she won the Academy Award for best actress, and *The Silence of the Lambs* 1991.

Foster Norman 1935– . English architect of the high-tech school. His buildings include the Willis Faber office, Ipswich, 1978, the Sainsbury Centre for Visual Arts at the University of East Anglia 1974 (opened 1978), the headquarters of the Hongkong and Shanghai Bank, Hong Kong, 1986, and Stansted Airport, Essex, 1991.

Foucault Michel 1926–1984. French philosopher who rejected phenomenology and existentialism. He was concerned with how forms of knowledge and forms of human subjectivity are constructed by specific institutions and practices.

Foucault Jean Bernard Léon 1819–1868. French physicist who used a pendulum to demonstrate the rotation of the Earth on its axis, and invented the gyroscope.

four-stroke cycle the engine-operating cycle of most petrol and ⬦diesel engines. The 'stroke' is an upward or downward movement of a piston in a cylinder. In a petrol engine the cycle begins with the induction of a fuel mixture as the piston goes down on its first stroke. On the second stroke (up) the piston compresses the mixture in the top of the cylinder. An electric spark then ignites the mixture, and the gases produced force the piston down on its third, power stroke. On the fourth stroke (up) the piston expels the burned gases from the cylinder into the exhaust.

fowl chicken or chickenlike bird. Sometimes the term is also used for ducks and geese. The red jungle fowl *Gallus gallus* is the ancestor of all domestic chickens. It is a forest bird of S Asia, without the size or egg-laying ability of many domestic strains. ⬦Guinea fowl are of African origin.

fox member of the smaller species of wild dog of the family Canidae, which live in Africa, Asia, Europe, North America, and South America. Foxes feed on a wide range of animals from worms to rabbits, scavenge for food, and also eat berries. They are very adaptable, maintaining high populations close to urban areas.

Fox Charles James 1749–1806. English Whig politician, son of the 1st baron Holland. He entered Parliament 1769 as a supporter of the court, but went over to the opposition 1774. As secretary of state 1782, leader of the opposition to Pitt, and foreign secretary 1806, he welcomed the French Revolution and brought about the abolition of the slave trade.

foxglove any flowering plant of the genus *Digitalis*, family Scrophulariaceae, found in Europe and the Mediterranean region. It bears showy spikes of bell-like flowers, and grows up to 1.5 m/5 ft high.

foxhound small, keen-nosed hound, up to 60 cm/2 ft tall and black, tan, and white in colour. There are two recognized breeds: the English foxhound, bred for some 300 years to hunt foxes, and the American foxhound, not quite as stocky, used for foxes and other game.

fraction in mathematics, a number that indicates one or more equal parts of a whole. Usually, the number of equal parts into which the unit is divided (denominator) is written below a horizontal line, and the number of parts comprising the fraction (numerator) is written above; thus $2/3$ or $3/4$. Such fractions are called *vulgar* or *simple* fractions. The denominator can never be zero.

Fragonard Jean Honoré 1732–1806. French painter, the leading exponent of the Rococo style (along with his master Boucher). His light-hearted subjects include *The Swing* about 1766 (Wallace Collection, London).

France Republic of; country in W Europe, bordered

NE by Belgium and Germany, E by Germany, Switzerland and Italy, S by the Mediterranean, SW by Spain and Andorra, and W by the Atlantic Ocean; *area* (including Corsica) 543,965 sq km/209,970 sq mi; *capital* Paris; *physical* rivers Seine, Loire, Garonne, Rhône, Rhine; mountain ranges Alps, Massif Central, Pyrenees, Jura, Vosges, Cévennes; *territories* Guadeloupe, French Guiana, Martinique, Réunion, St Pierre and Miquelon, Southern and Antarctic Territories, New Caledonia, French Polynesia, Wallis and Futuna Islands; *head of state* François Mitterrand from 1981; *head of government* Pierre Bérégovoy from 1992; *political system* liberal democracy; *exports* fruit (especially apples), wine, cheese, wheat, automobiles, aircraft, iron and steel, petroleum products, chemicals, jewellery, silk, lace; tourism is very important; *population* (1990 est) 56,184,000 (including 4,500,000 immigrants, chiefly from Portugal, Algeria, Morocco, and Tunisia); *language* French (regional dialects include Breton, Catalan, Provençal); *recent history* de Gaulle's provisional government of 1944–46 marked the start of the Fourth Republic; entry into the EC took place 1957; de Gaulle became president 1957, resigned 1969. François Mitterrand, the first socialist president, was elected 1981, and re-elected 1988, when moderate socialist Michel Rocard became prime minister and continued in this post despite the Socialist Party failing to obtain a secure majority in the National Assembly elections. In Sept 1990, after Iraqi violation of the French ambassador's residence in Kuwait, the French government despatched 5,000 troops to Saudi Arabia, and took an important role in the ▷Gulf War and the liberation of Kuwait 1991. Edith Cresson became France's first woman prime minister 1991 but was replaced by Pierre Bérégovoy 1992. National support for the Mitterrand administration continued to decline.

Francesca Piero della. See ▷Piero della Francesca, Italian painter.

Franche-Comté region of E France; area 16,200 sq km/6,253 sq mi; population (1987) 1,086,000. Its capital is Besançon, and it includes the *départements* of Doubs, Jura, Haute Saône, and Territoire de Belfort. In the mountainous Jura, there is farming and forestry, and elsewhere there are engineering and plastics industries.

franchise in politics, the eligibility, right or privilege to vote at public elections, especially for the members of a legislative body. In the UK adult citizens are eligible to vote from the age of 18, with the exclusion of peers, the insane, and criminals.

Francis I 1494–1547. King of France from 1515. He succeeded his cousin Louis XII, and from 1519 European politics turned on the rivalry between him and the Holy Roman emperor Charles V, which led to war 1521–29, 1536–38, and 1542–44. In 1525 Francis was defeated and captured at Pavia and released only after signing a humiliating treaty. At home, he developed absolute monarchy.

Francis II 1544–1560. King of France from 1559 when he succeeded his father, Henry II. He married Mary Queen of Scots 1558. He was completely under the influence of his mother, ▷Catherine de' Medici.

Francis II 1768–1835. Holy Roman emperor 1792–1806. He became Francis I, Emperor of Austria 1804, and abandoned the title of Holy Roman emperor 1806. During his reign Austria was five times involved in war with France, 1792–97, 1798–1801, 1805, 1809, and 1813–14. He succeeded his father Leopold II.

Francis of Assisi, St 1182–1226. Italian founder of the Roman Catholic Franciscan order of friars 1209 and, with St Clare, of the Poor Clares 1212. In 1224 he is said to have undergone a mystical experience during which he received the *stigmata* (five wounds of Jesus). Many stories are told of his ability to charm wild animals, and he is the patron saint of ecologists. His feast day is 4 Oct.

francium radioactive metallic element, symbol Fr, atomic number 87, relative atomic mass 223. It is one of the ▷alkali metals and occurs in nature in small amounts as a decay product of actinium. Its longest-lived isotope has a half-life of only 21 minutes. Francium was discovered and named in 1939 by Marguérite Perey to honour her country.

Franck César Auguste 1822–1890. Belgian composer. His music, mainly religious and Romantic in style, includes the Symphony in D minor 1866–68, *Symphonic Variations* 1885 for piano and orchestra, the Violin Sonata 1886, the oratorio *Les Béatitudes/The Beatitudes* 1879, and many organ pieces.

Franco Francisco (Paulino Hermenegildo Teódulo Bahamonde) 1892–1975. Spanish dictator from 1939. As a general, he led the insurgent Nationalists to victory in the Spanish ▷Civil War 1936–39, supported by Fascist Italy and Nazi Germany,

France: history

5th century BC	France, then called Gaul (*Gallia* by the Romans) was invaded by Celtic peoples.
57–51 BC	Conquest by the Roman general Julius Caesar.
1st–5th centuries AD	During Roman rule the inhabitants of France accepted Roman civilization and the Latin language. As the empire declined, Germanic tribes overran the country and settled.
481–511	A Frankish chief, Clovis, brought the other tribes under his rule, accepted Christianity, and made Paris the capital.
511–751	Under Clovis' successors, the Merovingians, the country sank into anarchy.
741–68	Unity was restored by Pepin, founder of the Carolingian dynasty.
768–814	Charlemagne made France the centre of the Holy Roman empire.
912	The province of Normandy was granted as a duchy to the Viking leader Rollo, whose invading Norsemen had settled there.
987	The first king of the House of Capet assumed the crown. Under Charlemagne's weak successors the great nobles had become semi-independent. The Capets established rule in the district around Paris but were surrounded by vassals stronger than themselves.
11th–13th centuries	The power of the Capets was gradually extended, with the support of the church and the townspeople.
1337–1453	In the Hundred Years' War Charles VII expelled the English from France, aided by Joan of Arc.
1483	Burgundy and Brittany were annexed. Through the policies of Louis XI the restoration of the royal power was achieved.
1503–1697	Charles VIII's Italian wars initiated a struggle with Spain for supremacy in W Europe that lasted for two centuries.
1592–98	Protestantism (Huguenot) was adopted by a party of the nobles for political reasons; the result was a succession of civil wars, fought under religious slogans.
1589–1610	Henry IV restored peace, established religious toleration, and made the monarchy absolute.
1634–48	The ministers Richelieu and Mazarin, by their intervention in the Thirty Years' War, secured Alsace and made France the leading power in Europe.
1643–1763	Louis XIV embarked on an aggressive policy that united Europe against him; in his reign began the conflict with Britain that lost France its colonies in Canada and India in the War of the Spanish Succession (1701–14), War of the Austrian Succession (1756–58), and Seven Years' War (1756–63).
1789–99	The French Revolution abolished feudalism and absolute monarchy, but failed to establish democracy.
1799–1815	Napoleon's military dictatorship was aided by foreign wars (1792–1802, 1803–15). The Bourbon monarchy was restored 1814 with Louis XVIII.
1830	Charles X's attempt to substitute absolute for limited monarchy provoked a revolution, which placed his cousin, Louis Philippe, on the throne.
1848	In the Feb revolution Louis Philippe was overthrown and the Second Republic set up.
1852–70	The president of the republic, Louis Napoleon, Napoleon I's nephew, restored the empire 1852, with the title of Napoleon III. His expansionist foreign policy ended in defeat in the Franco-Prussian War and the foundation of the Third Republic.
1863–1946	France colonized Indochina, parts of N Africa, and the S Pacific.
1914	France entered World War I.
1936–38	A radical-socialist-communist alliance introduced many social reforms.
1939	France entered World War II.
1940	The German invasion allowed the extreme right to set up a puppet dictatorship under Pétain in Vichy, but resistance was maintained by the ◊maquis and the Free French under de Gaulle.
1944	Liberation from the Nazis.
	For postwar history see ◊France.

and established a dictatorship. In 1942 Franco reinstated the Cortes (Spanish parliament), which in 1947 passed an act by which he became head of state for life.

François French form of ◊Francis, two kings of France.

Franco-Prussian War 1870–71. The Prussian chancellor Bismarck put forward a German candidate for the vacant Spanish throne with the deliberate, and successful, intention of provoking the French emperor Napoleon III into declaring war. The Prussians defeated the French at Sedan, then besieged Paris. The Treaty of Frankfurt May 1871 gave Alsace, Lorraine, and a large French indemnity to Prussia. The war established Prussia, at the head of a newly established German empire, as Europe's leading power.

frangipani any tropical American tree of the genus *Plumeria*, especially *P. rubra*, of the dogbane family Apocynaceae. Perfume is made from the strongly scented flowers.

Frank member of a group of Germanic peoples prominent in Europe in the 3rd to 9th centuries. Believed to have originated in Pomerania on the Black Sea, they had settled on the Rhine by the 3rd century, spread into the Roman Empire by the 4th century, and gradually conquered most of Gaul, Italy, and Germany under the ◊Merovingian and ◊Carolingian dynasties. The kingdom of the W Franks became France, the kingdom of the E Franks became Germany.

Frank Anne 1929–1945. German diarist who fled to the Netherlands with her family 1933 to escape Nazi anti-Semitism. During the German occupation of Amsterdam, they and two other families remained in a sealed-off room, protected by Dutch sympathizers 1942–44, when betrayal resulted in their deportation and Anne's death in Belsen concentration camp. Her diary of her time in hiding was published 1947 and has been made into a play and a film publicizing the plight of millions (see the ◊Holocaust).

Frankfurt-am-Main city in Hessen, Germany, 72 km/45 mi NE of Mannheim; population (1988) 592,000. It is a commercial and banking centre, with electrical and machine industries, and an inland port on the river Main. An international book fair is held here annually.

frankincense resin of various African and Asian trees of the genus *Boswellia*, family Burseraceae, burned as incense. Costly in ancient times, it is traditionally believed to be one of the three gifts brought by the Magi to the infant Jesus.

Franklin Benjamin 1706–1790. US printer, publisher, author, scientist, and statesman. He proved that lightning is a form of electricity, distinguished between positive and negative electricity, and invented the lightning conductor. He was the first US ambassador to France 1776–85, and negotiated peace with Britain 1783. As a delegate to the Continental Congress from Pennsylvania 1785–88, he helped to draft the ◊Declaration of Independence and the US ◊Constitution.

Franz Ferdinand or *Francis Ferdinand* 1863–1914. Archduke of Austria. He became heir to his uncle, Emperor Franz Joseph, in 1884 but while visiting Sarajevo 28 June 1914, he and his wife were assassinated by a Serbian nationalist. Austria used the episode to make unreasonable demands on Serbia that ultimately precipitated World War I.

Franz Joseph or *Francis Joseph* 1830–1916. Emperor of Austria-Hungary from 1848, when his uncle, Ferdinand I, abdicated. After the suppression of the 1848 revolution, Franz Joseph tried to establish an absolute monarchy but had to grant Austria a parliamentary constitution 1861 and Hungary equality with Austria 1867. He was defeated in the Italian War 1859 and the Prussian War 1866. In 1914 he made the assassination of his heir and nephew, Franz Ferdinand, the excuse for attacking Serbia, thus precipitating World War I.

Fraser (John) Malcolm 1930– . Australian Liberal politician, prime minister 1975–83; nicknamed 'the Prefect' because of a supposed disregard of subordinates.

fraud in law, an act of deception resulting in injury to another. To establish fraud it has to be demonstrated that (1) a false representation (for example, a factually untrue statement) has been made, with the intention that it should be acted upon; (2) the person making the representation knows it is false or does not attempt to find out whether it is true or not; and (3) the person to whom the representation is made acts upon it to his or her detriment.

Frederick I *Barbarossa* ('red-beard') *c.* 1123–1190. Holy Roman emperor from 1152. Originally duke of Swabia, he was elected emperor 1152, and was engaged in a struggle with Pope Alexander III 1159–77, which ended in his submission; the Lombard cities, headed by Milan, took advantage of this to establish their independence of imperial control. Frederick died on the Third Crusade.

Frederick II 1194–1250. Holy Roman emperor from 1212, called 'the Wonder of the World'. He led a crusade 1228–29 that recovered Jerusalem by treaty, without fighting. He quarrelled with the pope, who excommunicated him three times, and a feud began that lasted at intervals until the end of his reign. Frederick, who was a religious sceptic, is often considered the most cultured man of his age. He was the son of Henry VI.

Frederick II *the Great* 1712–1786. King of Prussia from 1740, when he succeeded his father Frederick William I. In that year he started the War of the ◊Austrian Succession by his attack on Austria. In the peace of 1745 he secured Silesia. The struggle was renewed in the ◊Seven Years' War 1756–63. He acquired West Prussia in the first partition of Poland 1772 and left Prussia as Germany's foremost state. He was an efficient and just ruler in the spirit of the Enlightenment and a patron of the arts.

Frederick William 1620–1688. Elector of Brandenburg from 1640, 'the Great Elector'. By successful wars against Sweden and Poland, he prepared the way for Prussian power in the 18th century.

Free Church the Protestant denominations in England and Wales that are not part of the Church of England; for example, the Methodist Church, Baptist Union, and United Reformed Church (Congregational and Presbyterian). These churches joined for common action in the Free Church Federal Council 1940.

Free Church of Scotland the body of Scottish Presbyterians who seceded from the Established Church of Scotland in the Disruption of 1843. In 1900 all but a small section that retains the old name, and is known as the *Wee Frees*, combined with the United Presbyterian Church to form the United Free Church, which reunited with the Church of Scotland 1929.

free enterprise or *free market* economic system where private capital is used in business with profits going to private companies and individuals. The term has much the same meaning as ◊capitalism.

freehold in England and Wales, ownership of land which is for an indefinite period. It is contrasted with a leasehold, which is always for a fixed period. In practical effect, a freehold is absolute ownership.

Freemasonry the beliefs and practices of a group of linked national organizations open to men over the age of 21, united by a common code of morals and certain traditional 'secrets'. Modern Freemasonry began in 18th-century Europe.

freesia any plant of the South African genus *Freesia* of the iris family Iridaceae, commercially grown for their scented, funnel-shaped flowers.

Freetown capital of Sierra Leone, W Africa; population (1988) 470,000. It has a naval station and a harbour. Industries include cement, plastics, footwear, and oil refining. Platinum, chromite, diamonds, and gold are traded. It was founded as a settlement for freed slaves in the 1790s.

free trade economic system where governments do not interfere in the movement of goods between countries; there are thus no taxes on imports. In the modern economy, free trade tends to hold within economic groups such as the European Community, but not generally, despite such treaties as ▷GATT 1948 and subsequent agreements to reduce tariffs. The opposite of free trade is ▷protectionism.

free verse poetry without metrical form. At the beginning of the 20th century, under the very different influences of Whitman and Mallarmé, many poets believed that the 19th century had accomplished most of what could be done with regular metre, and rejected it, in much the same spirit as Milton had rejected rhyme, preferring irregular metres that made it possible to express thought clearly and without distortion.

free will the doctrine that human beings are free to control their own actions, and that these actions are not fixed in advance by God or fate. Some Jewish and Christian theologians assert that God gave humanity free will to choose between good and evil; others that God has decided in advance the outcome of all human choices (▷predestination), as in Calvinism.

freezing change from liquid to solid state, as when water becomes ice. For a given substance, freezing occurs at a definite temperature, known as the **freezing point**, that is invariable under similar conditions of pressure, and the temperature remains at this point until all the liquid is frozen. The amount of heat per unit mass that has to be removed to freeze a substance is a constant for any given substance, and is known as the latent heat of fusion.

French Guiana (French *Guyane Française*) French administrative region on the N coast of South America, bounded to the W by Suriname and to the E and S by Brazil; **area** 83,500 sq km/ 32,230 sq mi; **capital** Cayenne; **towns** St Laurent;

features Eurospace rocket launch pad at Kourou; Iles du Salut, which include ▷Devil's Island; *products* timber, shrimps, gold; *currency* franc; *population* (1987) 89,000; *languages* 90% Creole, French, Amerindian; *famous people* Alfred ▷Dreyfus; *history* first settled by France 1604, the territory became a French possession 1817; penal colonies, including Devil's Island, were established from 1852; by 1945 the shipments of convicts from France ceased. The status changed to an overseas *département* 1946 and an administrative region 1974.

French horn musical ▷brass instrument.

French language member of the Romance branch of the Indo-European language family, spoken in France, Belgium, Luxembourg, Monaco, and Switzerland in Europe; also in Canada (principally in the province of Québec), various Caribbean and Pacific Islands (including overseas territories such as Martinique and French Guiana), and certain N and W African countries (for example, Mali and Senegal).

French Polynesia French Overseas Territory in the S Pacific, consisting of five archipelagos: Windward Islands, Leeward Islands (the two island groups comprising the ▷Society Islands), ▷Tuamotu Archipelago (including ▷Gambier Islands), ▷Tubuai Islands, and ▷Marquesas Islands; *total area* 3,940 sq km/1,521 sq mi; *capital* Papeete on Tahiti; *products* cultivated pearls, coconut oil, vanilla; tourism is important; *population* (1990) 199,100; *languages* Tahitian (official), French; *government* a high commissioner (Alain Ohrel) and Council of Government; two deputies are returned to the National Assembly in France; *history* first visited by Europeans 1595; French Protectorate 1843; annexed to France 1880–82; became an Overseas Territory, changing its name from French Oceania 1958; self-governing 1977. Following demands for independence in ▷New Caledonia 1984–85, agitation increased also in Polynesia.

French Revolution the period 1789–1799 that saw the end of the French monarchy and its claim to absolute rule, and the establishment of the First Republic. Although the revolution began as an attempt to create a constitutional monarchy, by late 1792 demands for long-overdue reforms resulted in the proclamation of the republic. The violence of the revolution, attacks by other nations, and bitter factional struggles, riots, and counterrevolutionary uprisings consumed the republic. This helped bring the extremists to power, and the bloody Reign of Terror followed. French armies then succeeded in holding off their foreign enemies and one of the generals, ▷Napoleon, seized power 1799.

French Sudan former name (1898–1959) of ▷Mali.

French West Africa group of French colonies administered from Dakar 1895–1958. They are now

Senegal, Mauritania, Sudan, Burkina Faso, Guinea, Niger, Ivory Coast, and Benin.

frequency in physics, the number of periodic oscillations, vibrations, or waves occurring per unit of time. The unit of frequency is the hertz (Hz), one hertz being equivalent to one cycle per second. Human beings can hear sounds from objects vibrating in the range 20–15,000 Hz. Ultrasonic frequencies well above 15,000 Hz can be detected by mammals such as bats.

fresco mural painting technique using water-based paint on wet plaster. Some of the earliest frescoes (about 1750–1400 BC) were found in Knossos, Crete (now preserved in the Heraklion Museum). Fresco reached its finest expression in Italy from the 13th to the 17th centuries. Giotto, Masaccio, Michelangelo, and many other artists worked in the medium.

Freud Lucian 1922– . British painter, whose realistic portraits with the subject staring intently from an almost masklike face include *Francis Bacon* 1952 (Tate Gallery, London). He is a grandson of Sigmund Freud.

Freud Sigmund 1865–1939. Austrian physician who pioneered the study of the unconscious mind. He developed the methods of free association and interpretation of dreams that are basic techniques of ◊psychoanalysis, and formulated the concepts of the id, ego, and ◊superego.

Freya or *Frigga* in Scandinavian mythology, wife of Odin and mother of Thor, goddess of married love and the hearth. Friday is named after her.

friction in physics, the force that opposes the relative motion of two bodies in contact. The *coefficient of friction* is the ratio of the force required to achieve this relative motion to the force pressing the two bodies together.

Friedman Milton 1912– . US economist. The foremost exponent of ◊monetarism, he argued that a country's economy, and hence inflation, can be controlled through its money supply, although most governments lack the 'political will' to control inflation by cutting government spending and thereby increasing unemployment. Nobel Prize for Economics 1976.

Friedrich Caspar David 1774–1840. German Romantic landscape painter, active mainly in Dresden. He imbued his subjects – mountain scenes and moonlit seas – with poetic melancholy and was later admired by Symbolist painters.

Friendly Islands another name for ◊Tonga.

Friends of the Earth (FoE or FOE) environmental pressure group, established in the UK 1971, that aims to protect the environment and to promote rational and sustainable use of the Earth's resources. It campaigns on issues such as acid rain; air, sea, river, and land pollution; recycling; disposal of toxic wastes; nuclear power and renewable energy; the destruction of rainforests; pesticides; and agriculture. FoE has branches in 30 countries.

Friesland maritime province of the N Netherlands, which includes the Frisian Islands and land that is still being reclaimed from the former Zuyder Zee; the inhabitants of the province are called Frisians; *area* 3,400 sq km/1,312 sq mi; *population* (1990) 600,000; *towns* capital Leeuwarden; Drachten, Harlingen, Sneek, Heerenveen; *products* livestock (Friesian cattle originated here), dairy products, small boats; *history* ruled by the Holy Roman Empire during the Middle Ages, Friesland passed to Saxony in 1498 and, after a revolt, to Charles V of Spain. In 1579 it subscribed to the Treaty of Utrecht, opposing Spanish rule. In 1748 its stadholder, Prince William IV of Orange, became stadholder of all the United Provinces of the Netherlands.

Friends, Society of or *Quakers* Christian Protestant sect founded by George ◊Fox in England in the 17th century. They were persecuted for their nonviolent activism, and many emigrated to form communities elsewhere, for example in Pennsylvania and New England, USA. They now form a worldwide movement of about 200,000. Their worship stresses meditation and the freedom of all to take an active part in the service (called a meeting, held in a meeting house). They have no priests or ministers.

frigate escort warship smaller than a destroyer. Before 1975 the term referred to a warship larger than a destroyer but smaller than a light cruiser. In the 18th and 19th centuries a frigate was a small, fast sailing warship.

fringe theatre plays that are anti-establishment or experimental, and performed in informal venues, in contrast to mainstream commercial theatre. In the UK, the term originated in the 1960s from the activities held on the 'fringe' of the Edinburgh Festival. The US equivalent is off-off-Broadway (off-Broadway is mainstream theatre that is not on Broadway).

fritillary in zoology, any of a large grouping of butterflies of the family Nymphalidae. Mostly medium-sized, fritillaries are usually orange and reddish with a black criss-cross pattern or spots above and with silvery spots on the underside of the hindwings.

frog any amphibian of the order Anura (Greek 'tailless'). There are no clear rules for distinguishing between frogs and toads. Frogs usually have squat bodies, hind legs specialized for jumping, and webbed feet for swimming. Many frogs use their long, extensible tongues to capture insects. Frogs vary in size from the tiny North American little grass frog *Limnaoedus ocularis*, 12 mm/0.5 in long, to the giant aquatic frog *Telmatobius culeus*, 50 cm/20 in long, of Lake Titicaca, South America.

Fronde French revolts 1648–53 against the administration of the chief minister ◊Mazarin during Louis XIV's minority. In 1648–49 the Paris *parlement* attempted to limit the royal power, its leaders were arrested, Paris revolted, and the rising

fruit

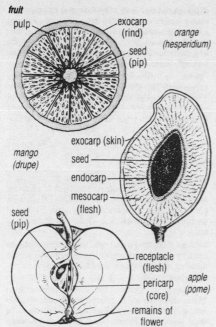

pulp — exocarp (rind)

orange (hesperidium)

seed (pip)

exocarp (skin)

mango (drupe)

seed

endocarp

mesocarp (flesh)

seed (pip)

receptacle (flesh)

pericarp (core)

apple (pome)

remains of flower

was suppressed by the royal army under Louis II Condé. In 1650 Condé led a new revolt of the nobility, but this was suppressed by 1653. The defeat of the Fronde enabled Louis to establish an absolutist monarchy in the later 17th century.

front in meteorology, the interface between two air masses of different temperature or humidity. A *cold front* marks the line of advance of a cold air mass from below, as it displaces a warm air mass; a *warm front* marks the advance of a warm air mass pushing a cold one forward.

frost condition of the weather that occurs when the air temperature is below freezing, 0°C/32°F. Water in the atmosphere is deposited as ice crystals on the ground or exposed objects. As cold air is heavier than warm, ground frost is more common than hoar frost, which is formed by the condensation of water particles in the same way that ▷dew collects.

Frost Robert (Lee) 1874–1963. US poet whose verse, in traditional form, is written with an individual voice and penetrating vision. His poems include 'Mending Wall' ('Something there is that does not love a wall'), 'The Road Not Taken', and 'Stopping by Woods on a Snowy Evening'.

fructose $C_6H_{12}O_6$ a sugar that occurs naturally in honey, the nectar of flowers, and many sweet fruits; it is commercially prepared from glucose.

fruit in botany, the ripened ovary in flowering plants that develops from one or more seeds or carpels and encloses one or more seeds. Its function is to protect the seeds during their development and to aid in their dispersal. Fruits are often edible, sweet, juicy, and colourful. When eaten they provide vitamins, minerals, and enzymes, but little protein. Most fruits are borne by perennial plants.

FT Index abbreviation for ▷*Financial Times Index*, a list of leading share prices.

fuchsia any shrub or herbaceous plant of the genus *Fuchsia* of the evening primrose family Onagraceae. Species are native to South and Central America and New Zealand, and bear red, purple, or pink bell-shaped flowers.

fuel cell cell converting chemical energy directly to electrical energy. It works on the same principle as a battery but is continually fed with fuel, usually hydrogen. Fuel cells are silent and reliable (no moving parts) but expensive to produce.

fugue in music, a contrapuntal form (with two or more melodies) for a number of parts or 'voices', which enter successively in imitation of each other. It was raised to a high art by J S ▷Bach.

Fujian or *Fukien* province of SE China, bordering Taiwan Strait, opposite Taiwan; *area* 123,100 sq km/47,517 sq mi; *capital* Fuzhou; *physical* dramatic mountainous coastline; *features* being developed for tourists; designated a pace-setting province for modernization 1980; *products* sugar, rice, teas, tobacco, timber, fruit; *population* (1990) 30,048,000

Fujimori Alberto 1939– . President of Peru from July 1990. As leader of the newly formed Cambio 90 (Change 90) he campaigned on a reformist ticket and defeated his more experienced Democratic Front opponent. Having no assembly majority, he dismissed the assembly in 1992.

Fujiyama or *Mount Fuji* Japanese volcano and highest peak, on Honshu Island; height 3,778 m/12,400 ft. Extinct since 1707, it has a Shinto shrine and a weather station on its summit. Located near Tokyo, it has long been revered for its picturesque cone-shaped crater peak, and figures prominently in Japanese art, literature, and religion.

Fukuoka formerly *Najime* Japanese industrial port on the NW coast of Kyushu island; population (1989) 1,182,700. It produces chemicals, textiles, paper, and metal goods.

Fuller (Richard) Buckminster 1895–1983. US architect, engineer, and futurist social philosopher who embarked on an unorthodox career in an attempt to maximize energy resources through improved technology. In 1947 he invented the lightweight geodesic dome, a half-sphere of triangular components independent of buttress or vault.

fullerene form of carbon, discovered 1985, based on closed cages of carbon atoms. The molecules of the most symmetrical of the fullerenes are called buckminsterfullerenes. They are perfect spheres made up of 60 carbon atoms linked together in 12 pentagons and 20 hexagons fitted together like those of a spherical football.

fulmar any of several species of petrels of the family Procellariidae, which are similar in size and colour to herring gulls. The northern fulmar *Fulmarus glacialis* is found in the N Atlantic and visits land only to nest, laying a single egg.

fumitory any plant of the genus *Fumeria*, family Fumariaceae, native to Europe and Asia. The common fumitory *F. officinalis* grows to 50 cm/20 in tall, and produces pink flowers tipped with blackish red; it has been used in medicine for stomach and liver complaints.

functionalism in the social sciences, the view of society as a system made up of a number of interrelated parts, all interacting on the basis of a common value system or consensus about basic values and common goals. Every social custom and institution is seen as having a function in ensuring that society works efficiently; deviance and crime are seen as forms of social sickness.

Functionalism in architecture and design, a 20th-century school, also called Modernism or International Style, characterized by the ideal of excluding everything that serves no practical purpose. It developed as a reaction against the 19th-century practice of imitating and combining earlier styles, and its finest achievements are in the realm of industrial architecture and office furnishings.

fundamental constant any physical quantity that is constant in all circumstances throughout the whole universe. Examples are the electric charge of an electron, the speed of light, Planck's constant, and the gravitational constant.

fundamentalism in religion, an emphasis on basic principles or articles of faith. *Christian fundamentalism* emerged in the USA just after World War I (as a reaction to theological modernism and the historical criticism of the Bible) and insisted on belief in the literal truth of everything in the Bible. *Islamic fundamentalism* insists on strict observance of Muslim Shari'a law.

fungicide any chemical ♢pesticide used to prevent fungus diseases in plants and animals. Inorganic and organic compounds containing sulphur are widely used.

fungus (plural *fungi*) any of a group of organisms in the kingdom Fungi. Fungi are not considered plants. They lack leaves and roots; they contain no chlorophyll and reproduce by spores. Moulds, yeasts, rusts, smuts, mildews, and mushrooms are all types of fungus.

funk dance music of black US origin, relying on heavy percussion in polyrhythmic patterns. Leading exponents include James Brown (1928–) and George Clinton (1940–).

fur pelts of certain animals. Fur is used as clothing, although the methods of breeding or trapping animals are often cruel. Mink, chinchilla, and sable are among the most valuable, the wild furs being finer than the farmed. Such fur as mink is made up of a soft, thick, insulating layer called underfur and a top layer of longer, lustrous guard hairs.

Furies in Greek mythology, the Erinyes, appeasingly called the Eumenides ('kindly ones'). They were the daughters of Earth or of Night, represented as winged maidens with serpents twisted in their hair. They punished such crimes as filial disobedience, murder, and inhospitality.

furlong unit of measurement, originating in Anglo-Saxon England, equivalent to 220 yd (201.168 m).

fusion in physics, the fusing of the nuclei of light elements, such as hydrogen, into those of a heavier element, such as helium. The resultant loss in their combined mass is converted into energy. Stars and thermonuclear weapons work on the principle of nuclear fusion.

futures trading buying and selling commodities (usually cereals and metals) at an agreed price for delivery several months ahead.

Futurism literary and artistic movement 1909–14, originating in Paris. The Italian poet Filippo Marinetti published the *Futurist Manifesto* 1909 urging Italian artists to join him in Futurism. In their works the Futurists eulogized the modern world and the 'beauty of speed and energy', trying to capture the dynamism of a speeding car or train by combining the shifting geometric planes of ♢Cubism with vibrant colours.

Fuzhou or *Foochow* industrial port and capital of Fujian province, SE China; population (1989) 1,270,000. It is a centre for shipbuilding and steel production; rice, sugar, tea, and fruit pass through the port. There are joint foreign and Chinese factories.

fuzzy logic in mathematics and computing, a form of knowledge representation suitable for notions (such as 'hot' or 'loud') that cannot be defined precisely but which depend on their context. For example, a jug of water may be described as hot or cold, depending on whether it is to be used to wash one's face or to make tea. The central idea of fuzzy logic is *probability of set membership*. For instance, referring to someone 5 ft 9 in tall, the statement 'this person is tall' (or 'this person is a member of the set of tall people') might be about 70% true if that person is a man, and about 85% true if that person is a woman. Fuzzy logic enables computerized devices to reason more like humans, responding effectively to complex messages from their control panels and sensors.

G7 or *Group of Seven* the seven wealthiest nations in the world: the USA, Japan, Germany, France, the UK, Italy, and Canada. Since 1975 their heads of government have met once a year to discuss economic and, increasingly, political matters.

gabbro basic (low-silica) ⬦igneous rock formed deep in the Earth's crust. It contains pyroxene and calcium-rich feldspar, and may contain small amounts of olivine and amphibole. Its coarse crystals of dull minerals give it a speckled appearance.

Gable (William) Clark 1901–1960. US actor. A star for more than 30 years in 90 films, he was celebrated for his romantic, rakish nonchalance in roles such as Rhett Butler in *Gone With the Wind* 1939. Other films include *The Painted Desert* 1931 (his first), *It Happened One Night* 1934 (Academy Award), *Mutiny on the Bounty* 1935, and *The Misfits* 1961.

Gabo Naum. Adopted name of Naum Neemia Pevsner 1890–1977. US abstract sculptor, born in Russia. One of the leading exponents of ⬦Constructivism, he left the USSR in 1922 for Germany and taught at the Bauhaus in Berlin (a key centre of modern design). He lived in Paris and England in the 1930s, then settled in the USA in 1946. He was one of the first artists to make kinetic (moving) sculpture and often used transparent coloured plastics.

Gabon (Gabonese Republic); country in central Africa, bordered N by Cameroon, E and S by the Congo, W by the Atlantic Ocean, and NW by Equatorial Guinea; *area* 267,667 sq km/103,319 sq mi; *capital* Libreville; *physical* virtually the whole country is tropical rainforest; narrow coastal plain rising to hilly interior with savanna in E and S; Ogooué River flows N–W; *head of state and government* Omar Bongo from 1967; *political system* authoritarian nationalism; *exports* petroleum, manganese, uranium, timber; *population* (1988) 1,226,000 (including 40 Bantu tribes);

languages French (official), Bantu; *recent history* part of the French Congo from 1889 until independence from France achieved 1960. In 1968 President Bongo established a one-party state. Although his regime is authoritarian, Gabon's prosperity has diluted any serious opposition to President Bongo. He was re-elected 1986, and in 1989 an attempted coup against him was defeated by loyal troops. In September 1990 the first multiparty elections were held since 1964 amid claims of widespread fraud.

Gaborone capital of Botswana from 1965, mainly an administrative centre; population (1989) 120,200. Light industry includes textiles.

Gaddafi alternative form of ⬦Khaddhafi, Libyan leader.

gadolinium silvery-white metallic element of the lanthanide series, symbol Gd, atomic number 64, relative atomic mass 157.25. It is found in the products of nuclear fission and used in electronic components, alloys, and products needing to withstand high temperatures.

Gaelic language member of the Celtic branch of the Indo-European language family, spoken in Ireland, Scotland, and (until 1974) the Isle of Man. Gaelic has been in decline for several centuries, discouraged until recently within the British state. There is a small Gaelic-speaking community in Nova Scotia, Canada.

Gagarin Yuri (Alexeyevich) 1934–1968. Soviet cosmonaut who in 1961 became the first human in space aboard the spacecraft *Vostok 1*.

Gaia or *Ge* in Greek mythology, the goddess of the Earth. She sprang from primordial Chaos and herself produced Uranus, by whom she was the mother of the Cyclopes and Titans.

Gaia hypothesis theory that the Earth's living and nonliving systems form an inseparable whole that is regulated and kept adapted for life by living organisms themselves. The planet therefore functions as a single organism, or a giant cell. The Gaia hypothesis was elaborated by British scientist James Lovelock (1919–) in the 1970s.

Gainsborough Thomas 1727–1788. English landscape and portrait painter. In 1760 he settled in Bath and painted society portraits. In 1774 he went to London and became one of the original members of the Royal Academy. He was one of the first British artists to follow the Dutch in painting realistic landscapes rather than imaginative Italianate scenery.

Galahad in Arthurian legend, one of the knights of the Round Table. Galahad succeeded in the quest for the ⬦Holy Grail because of his virtue. He was the son of Lancelot of the Lake.

Galápagos Islands (official name *Archipiélago de Colón*) group of 15 islands in the Pacific, belonging to Ecuador; area 7,800 sq km/3,000 sq mi; population (1982) 6,120. The capital is San Cristóbal on the island of the same name. The islands are a nature reserve. Their unique fauna (including giant tortoises, iguanas, penguins, flightless cormorants, and Darwin's finches), which inspired Charles ▷Darwin to formulate the principle of evolution by natural selection, is under threat from introduced species.

galaxy congregation of millions or billions of stars, held together by gravity. *Spiral galaxies*, such as the ▷Milky Way, are flattened in shape, with a central bulge of old stars surrounded by a disc of younger stars, arranged in spiral arms like a Catherine wheel. The arms of spiral galaxies contain gas and dust from which new stars are still forming. *Elliptical galaxies* contain old stars and very little gas. They include the most massive galaxies known, containing a trillion stars. There are also irregular galaxies. Most galaxies occur in clusters, containing anything from a few to thousands of members.

Galbraith John Kenneth 1908– . Canadian-born US economist; he became a US citizen 1937. His major works include the *Affluent Society* 1958, in which he documents the tendency of the 'invisible hand' of free-market capitalism to create private splendour and public squalor, and *Economics and the Public Purpose* 1974.

Galen c. 130–c. 200. Greek physician whose ideas dominated Western medicine for almost 1,500 years. Central to his thinking were the theories of humours and the threefold circulation of the blood. He remained the highest medical authority until Andreas Vesalius and William Harvey exposed the fundamental errors of his system.

Galicia mountainous but fertile autonomous region of NW Spain, formerly an independent kingdom; area 29,400 sq km/11,348 sq mi; population (1986) 2,785,000. It includes La Coruña, Lugo, Orense, and Pontevedra. Industries include fishing and the mining of tungsten and tin. The language is similar to Portuguese.

Galileo properly Galileo Galilei 1564–1642. Italian mathematician, astronomer, and physicist. He developed the astronomical telescope and was the first to see sunspots, the four main satellites of Jupiter, mountains and craters on the Moon, and the appearance of Venus going through 'phases', thus proving it was orbiting the Sun. In mechanics, Galileo discovered that freely falling bodies, heavy or light, had the same, constant acceleration and that a body moving on a perfectly smooth horizontal surface would neither speed up nor slow down.

gall bladder small muscular sac, part of the digestive system of most, but not all, vertebrates. In humans, it is situated on the underside of the liver and connected to the small intestine by the bile duct. It stores bile from the liver.

Gallipoli port in European Turkey, giving its name to the peninsula (ancient name *Chersonesus*) on

which it stands. In World War I, at the instigation of Winston Churchill, an unsuccessful attempt was made Feb 1915–Jan 1916 by Allied troops to force their way through the Dardanelles and link up with Russia. The campaign was fought mainly by Australian and New Zealand (▷ANZAC) forces, who suffered heavy losses. An estimated 36,000 Commonwealth troops died during the nine-month campaign.

gallium grey metallic element, symbol Ga, atomic number 31, relative atomic mass 69.75. It is liquid at room temperature. Gallium arsenide crystals are used in microelectronics, since electrons travel a thousand times faster through them than through silicon. The element was discovered in 1875 by Lecoq de Boisbaudran (1838–1912).

gallon imperial liquid or dry measure, equal to 4.546 litres, and subdivided into four quarts or eight pints. The US gallon is equivalent to 3.785 litres.

gallstone pebblelike, insoluble accretion formed in the human gall bladder or bile ducts from cholesterol or calcium salts present in bile. Gallstones may be symptomless or they may cause pain, indigestion, or jaundice. They can be dissolved with medication or removed, along with the gall bladder, in an operation known as cholecystectomy.

Galtieri Leopoldo 1926– . Argentine general, president 1981–82. A leading member from 1979 of the ruling right-wing military junta and commander of the army, Galtieri became president in 1981. Under his leadership the junta ordered the seizure 1982 of the Falkland Islands (Malvinas), a British colony in the SW Atlantic claimed by Argentina. After the surrender of his forces he resigned and was imprisoned.

Galway county on the W coast of the Republic of Ireland, in the province of Connacht; area 5,940 sq km/2,293 sq mi; population (1991) 180,300.

Gama Vasco da c. 1469–1524. Portuguese navigator who commanded an expedition in 1497 to discover the route to India around the Cape of Good Hope in modern South Africa. On Christmas Day 1497 he reached land, which he named Natal. He then crossed the Indian Ocean, arriving at Calicut May 1498, and returning to Portugal Sept 1499.

Gambia Republic of The; country in W Africa, surrounded N, E, and S by Senegal and bordered W by the Atlantic Ocean; *area* 10,402 sq km/4,018 sq mi; *capital* Banjul; *physical* banks of the river Gambia flanked by low hills; *head of state and government* Dawda Jawara from 1970; *political system* liberal democracy; *exports* groundnuts, palm oil, fish; *population* (1990 est) 820,000; *languages* English (official), Mandinka, Fula, and other native tongues; *recent history* independence from UK as a constitutional monarchy within the Commonwealth achieved 1965. The Gambia was declared a republic 1970. The Confederation of Senegambia was formed with Senegal 1982; dissolved 1989.

gamete cell that functions in sexual reproduction by merging with another gamete to form a ◊zygote. Examples of gametes include sperm and egg cells. In most organisms, the gametes are haploid (they contain half the number of chromosomes of the parent), owing to reduction division or ◊meiosis.

gamma radiation very-high-frequency electromagnetic radiation, similar in nature to X-rays but of shorter wavelength, emitted by the nuclei of radioactive substances during decay or by the interactions of high-energy electrons with matter. Cosmic gamma rays have been identified as coming from pulsars, radio galaxies, and quasars, although they cannot penetrate the Earth's atmosphere.

Gamsakhurdia Zviad 1939– . Georgian politician, president 1990–92. He was an active anticommunist and became head of state after nationalist success in parliamentary elections. Directly elected to the post by a huge margin in May 1991, Gamsakhurdia's increasingly dictatorial style led to his forced removal and he fled to Armenia.

Gandhi Indira (born Nehru) 1917–1984. Indian politician, prime minister of India 1966–77 and 1980–84, and leader of the ◊Congress Party 1966–77 and subsequently of the Congress (I) party. She was assassinated 1984 by members of her Sikh bodyguard, resentful of her use of troops to clear malcontents from the Sikh temple at ◊Amritsar.

Gandhi Mohandas Karamchand, called *Mahatma* ('Great Soul') 1869–1948. Indian nationalist leader. A pacifist, he led the struggle for Indian independence from the UK by advocating nonviolent noncooperation (*satyagraha*, defence of and by truth) from 1915. He was imprisoned several times by the British authorities and was influential in the Nationalist Congress Party and in the independence negotiations 1947. He was assassinated by a Hindu nationalist in the violence that followed the partition of British India into India and Pakistan.

Gandhi Rajiv 1944–1991. Indian politician, prime minister from 1984 (following his mother Indira Gandhi's assassination) to Nov 1989. As prime minister, he faced growing discontent with his party's elitism and lack of concern for social issues. He was assassinated by a bomb at an election rally.

Ganges (Hindi *Ganga*) major river of India and Bangladesh; length 2,510 km/1,560 mi. It is the most sacred river for Hindus. The Ganges is joined in its delta in Bangladesh by the ◊Brahmaputra.

Gang of Four chief members of the radical faction that tried to seize power in China after the death of Mao Zedong 1976. It included his widow, ◊Jiang Qing; the other members were Zhang Chunjao, Wang Hungwen, and Yao Wenyuan. The coup failed, and they were soon arrested.

gangrene death and decay of body tissue (often of a limb) due to bacterial action; the affected part gradually turns black and causes blood poisoning.

gannet N Atlantic sea bird *Sula bassana* in the same family (Sulidae) as the boobies. When fully grown, it is white with black-tipped wings having a span of 1.7 m/5.6 ft. The young are speckled. It breeds on cliffs in nests made of grass and seaweed. Only one (white) egg is laid.

Gansu or *Kansu* province of NW China. **area** 530,000 sq km/204,580 sq mi; **capital** Lanzhou; **features** subject to earthquakes; the 'Silk Road' (now a motor road) passed through it in the Middle Ages, carrying trade to central Asia; **products** coal, oil, hydroelectric power from the Huang He (Yellow) river; **population** (1990) 22,371,000, including many Muslims.

Garbo Greta. Stage name of Greta Lovisa Gustafsson 1905–1990. Swedish-born US film actress. She went to the USA in 1925, and her captivating beauty and leading role in *The Torrent* 1926 made her one of Hollywood's first stars in silent films. Her later films include *Mata Hari* 1931, *Grand Hotel* 1932, *Queen Christina* 1933, *Anna Karenina* 1935, *Camille* 1936, and *Ninotchka* 1939. Her qualities of ethereality and romantic mystery on the screen intermingled with her seclusion in private life. She retired 1941.

García Lorca Federico, Spanish poet. See ◊Lorca, Federico García.

García Márquez Gabriel 1928– . Colombian novelist. His sweeping novel *Cien años de soledad/One Hundred Years of Solitude* 1967 (which tells the story of a family over a period of six generations) is an example of magic realism, a technique used to heighten the intensity of realistic portrayal of social and political issues by introducing grotesque or fanciful material. Nobel prize 1982.

gardenia any subtropical and tropical tree or shrub of Africa and Asia, genus *Gardenia*, of the madder family Rubiaceae, with evergreen foliage and flattened rosettes of fragrant waxen-looking blooms, often white in colour.

Garfield James A(bram) 1831–1881. 20th president of the USA 1881, a Republican. A compromise candidate for the presidency, he held office for only four months before being assassinated by a disappointed office-seeker. His short tenure was marked primarily by struggles within the Republican party over influence and cabinet posts.

Garibaldi Giuseppe 1807–1882. Italian soldier who played a central role in the unification of Italy by conquering Sicily and Naples 1860. From 1834 a member of the nationalist Mazzini's Young Italy society, he was forced into exile until 1848 and again 1849–54. He fought against Austria 1848–49, 1859, and 1866, and led two unsuccessful expeditions to liberate Rome from papal rule in 1862 and 1867.

Garland Judy. Stage name of Frances Gumm 1922–1969. US singer and actress whose peformances are marked by a compelling intensity. Her films include *The Wizard of Oz* (which featured the tune that was to become her theme song, 'Over the Rainbow'), *Babes in Arms* 1939, *Strike Up the Band* 1940, *Meet Me in St Louis* 1944, *Easter Parade* 1948, *A Star is Born* 1954, and *Judgment at Nuremberg* 1961.

garlic perennial plant *Allium sativum* of the lily family Liliaceae, with white flowers. The bulb, made of small segments, or cloves, is used in cookery, and its pungent essence has an active medical ingredient, allyl methyl trisulphide, which prevents blood clotting.

garnet group of silicate minerals with the formula $X_3Y_2(SiO_4)_3$, when X is calcium, magnesium, iron, or manganese, and Y is iron, aluminium, or chromium. Garnets are used as semiprecious gems (usually pink to deep red) and as abrasives. They occur in metamorphic rocks such as gneiss and schist.

Garrick David 1717–1779. British actor and theatre manager. He was a pupil of Samuel ▷Johnson. From 1747 he became joint licensee of the Drury Lane theatre with his own company, and instituted a number of significant theatrical conventions including concealed stage lighting and banishing spectators from the stage.

Garvey Marcus (Moziah) 1887–1940. Jamaican political thinker and activist, an early advocate of black nationalism. He founded the UNIA (Universal Negro Improvement Association) in 1914, and moved to the USA in 1916, where he established branches in New York and other northern cities, aiming to achieve human rights and dignity for black people through black pride and economic self-sufficiency. He led a Back to Africa movement for black Americans to establish a black-governed country in Africa. The Jamaican cult of ▷Rastafarianism is based largely on his ideas.

gas in physics, a form of matter, such as air, in which the molecules move randomly in otherwise empty space, filling any size or shape of container into which the gas is put.

Gascony ancient province of SW France. With Guienne it formed the duchy of Aquitaine in the 12th century; Henry II of England gained possession of it through his marriage to Eleanor of Aquitaine in 1152, and it was often in English hands until 1451. It was then ruled by the king of France until it was united with the French royal domain 1607 under Henry IV.

gastropod any member of a very large class (Gastropoda) of ▷molluscs. Gastropods are single-shelled (in a spiral or modified spiral form), have eyes on stalks, and move on a flattened, muscular foot. They have well-developed heads and rough, scraping tongues called radulae. Some are marine, some freshwater, and others land creatures, but all tend to inhabit damp places.They include snails, slugs, limpets, and periwinkles.

GATT acronym for ▷General Agreement on Tariffs and Trade.

Gaudí Antonio 1852–1926. Spanish architect distinguished for his flamboyant Art Nouveau style. Gaudí worked exclusively in Barcelona, designing both domestic and industrial buildings. He introduced colour, unusual materials, and audacious technical innovations. His spectacular Church of the Holy Family, Barcelona, begun 1883, is still under construction.

Gaudier-Brzeska Henri (Henri Gaudier) 1891–1915. French artist, active in London from 1911; he is regarded as one of the outstanding sculptors of his generation. He studied art in Bristol, Nuremberg, and Munich and became a member of the English Vorticist movement, which sought to reflect the industrial age by a sense of motion and angularity. From 1913 his sculptures showed the influence of Constantin Brancusi and Jacob Epstein. He was killed in action during World War I.

gauge boson or *field particle* any of the particles that carry the four fundamental forces of nature (see ▷forces, fundamental). Gauge bosons are ▷elementary particles that cannot be subdivided, and include the photon, the graviton, the gluons, and the weakons.

Gauguin Paul 1848–1903. French Post-Impressionist painter. Going beyond the Impressionists' notion of reality, he sought a more direct experience of life in the magical rites and rich colours of the South Sea islands. He disliked theories and rules of painting, and his pictures are ▷Expressionist compositions characterized by his use of pure, unmixed colours. Among his paintings is *Le Christe Jaune* 1889 (Albright-Knox Art Gallery, Buffalo, USA).

Gaul member of the Celtic-speaking peoples who inhabited France and Belgium in Roman times; also their territory. The Romans conquered S Gaul between the Mediterranean and the Cevennes in about 125 BC and the remaining Gauls up to the Rhine were conquered by Julius ▷Caesar 58–51 BC.

Gaulle Charles de. French politician, see Charles ▷de Gaulle.

Gaviria (Trujillo) Cesar 1947– . Colombian Liberal Party politician, president from 1990; he was finance minister 1986–87 and minister of government 1987–89. He supports the extradition of drug traffickers wanted in the USA and seeks more US aid in return for stepping up the drug war.

Gay John 1685–1732. British poet and dramatist. He wrote *Trivia* 1716, a verse picture of 18th-century London. His *The Beggar's Opera* 1728, a 'Newgate pastoral' using traditional songs and telling of the love of Polly for highwayman Captain Macheath, was an extraordinarily popular success. Its satiric political touches led to the banning of *Polly*, a sequel.

Gazankulu ▷Black National State in Transvaal province, South Africa, with self-governing status from 1971; population (1985) 497,200.

gazelle

Gaza Strip strip of Palestine under Israeli administration; capital Gaza; area 363 sq km/140 sq mi; population (1989) 645,000 of which 446,000 are refugees.

gazelle any of a number of species of lightly built, fast-running ◊antelopes found on the open plains of Africa and S Asia, especially those of the genus *Gazella*.

GCSE (*General Certificate of Secondary Education*) in the UK, from 1988, examination for 16-year-old pupils, superseding both GCE O level and CSE, and offering qualifications for up to 60% of school leavers in any particular subject.

Gdańsk (German *Danzig*) Polish port; population (1990) 465,100. Oil is refined, and textiles, televisions, and fertilizers are produced. In the 1980s there were repeated anti-government strikes at the Lenin shipyards.

GDP (abbreviation for *gross domestic product*) the total value of all goods and services produced within a country each year. It is equivalent to GNP less income from investments abroad but including the production of foreign-owned firms within the country.

gecko any lizard of the family Gekkonidae. Geckos are common worldwide in warm climates, and have large heads and short, stout bodies. Many have no eyelids. Their adhesive toe pads enable them to climb vertically and walk upside down on smooth surfaces in their search for flies, spiders, and other prey.

Geiger counter any of a number of devices used for detecting nuclear radiation and/or measuring its intensity by counting the number of ionizing particles produced (see ◊radioactivity). It is named after Hans Geiger.

Geingob Hage Gottfried 1941– . Namibian politician and prime minister. Geingob was appointed founding director of the United Nations Institute for Namibia in Lusaka, 1975. He became first prime minister of an independent Namibia March 1990.

Gelderland (English *Guelders*) province of the E Netherlands; **area** 5,020 sq km/1,938 sq mi; **population** (1991) 1,817,000; **towns** capital Arnhem, Apeldoorn, Nijmegen, Ede; **products** livestock, textiles, electrical goods.

Gell-Mann Murray 1929– . US physicist. In 1964 he formulated the theory of the ◊quark as one of the fundamental constituents of matter. In 1969 he was awarded a Nobel prize for his work on elementary particles and their interaction.

gem mineral valuable by virtue of its durability (hardness), rarity, and beauty, cut and polished for ornamental use, or engraved. Of 120 minerals known to have been used as gemstones, only about 25 are in common use in jewellery today; of these, the diamond, emerald, ruby, and sapphire are classified as precious, and all the others semiprecious, for example the topaz, amethyst, opal, and aquamarine.

Gemeinschaft and **Gesellschaft** German terms (roughly, 'community' and 'association') coined by Ferdinand Tönnies 1887 to contrast social relationships in traditional rural societies with those in modern industrial societies. He saw *Gemeinschaft* (traditional) as intimate and positive, and *Gesellschaft* (modern) as impersonal and negative.

Gemini prominent zodiacal constellation in the northern hemisphere represented as the twins Castor and Pollux. Its brightest star is Pollux; Castor is a system of six stars. The Sun passes through Gemini from late June to late July. Each Dec, the Geminid meteors radiate from Gemini. In astrology, the dates for Gemini are between about 21 May and 21 June (see ◊precession).

gene unit of inherited material, encoded by a strand of ◊DNA, and transcribed by ◊RNA. In higher organisms, genes are located on the ◊chromosomes. The term 'gene', coined 1909 by the Danish geneticist Wilhelm Johannsen (1857–1927), refers to the inherited factor that consistently affects a particular character in an individual – for example, the gene for eye colour. Also termed a Mendelian gene, after Gregor ◊Mendel, it occurs at a particular point or locus on a particular chromosome and may have several variants or ◊alleles, each specifying a particular form of that character – for example, the alleles for blue or brown eyes.

General Agreement on Tariffs and Trade (GATT) organization within the United Nations founded 1948 with the aim of encouraging ◊free trade between nations through low tariffs, abolitions of quotas, and curbs on subsidies.

general strike refusal to work by employees in several key industries, with the intention of paralysing the economic life of a country. In British history, the General Strike was a nationwide strike called by the Trade Union Congress on 3 May 1926 in support of the miners' union.

genet small, nocturnal, meat-eating mammal,

genus *Genetta*, in the mongoose and civet family (Viverridae). Most species live in Africa, but *G. genetta* is also found in Europe and the Middle East. It is about 50 cm/1.6 ft long with a 45 cm/1.5 ft tail, and greyish yellow with rows of black spots. It climbs well.

genetic code the way in which instructions for building proteins, the basic structural molecules of living matter, are 'written' in the genetic material ⟡DNA. This relationship between the sequence of bases (the subunits in a DNA molecule) and the sequence of ⟡amino acids (the subunits of a protein molecule) is the basis of heredity. The code employs codons of three bases each; it is the same in almost all organisms, except for a few minor differences recently discovered in some protozoa.

genetic engineering deliberate manipulation of genetic material by biochemical techniques. It is often achieved by the introduction of new ⟡DNA, usually by means of a virus or plasmid. This can be for pure research or to breed functionally specific plants, animals, or bacteria. These organisms with a foreign gene added are said to be transgenic (see ⟡transgenic organism).

genetics study of inheritance and of the units of inheritance (⟡genes). The founder of genetics was Gregor ⟡Mendel, whose experiments with plants, such as peas, showed that inheritance takes place by means of discrete 'particles', which later came to be called genes.

Geneva (French *Genève*) Swiss city, capital of Geneva canton, on the shore of Lake Geneva; population (1990) city 167,200; canton 376,000. It is a point of convergence of natural routes and is a cultural and commercial centre. Industries include the manufacture of watches, scientific and optical instruments, foodstuffs, jewellery, and musical boxes.

Geneva Convention international agreement 1864 regulating the treatment of those wounded in war, and later extended to cover the types of weapons allowed, the treatment of prisoners and the sick, and the protection of civilians in wartime. The rules were revised at conventions held 1906, 1929, and 1949, and by the 1977 Additional Protocols. The first Geneva Convention founded the ⟡Red Cross.

Geneva, Lake (French *Lac Léman*) largest of the central European lakes, between Switzerland and France; area 580 sq km/225 sq mi.

Genghis Khan *c.* ?1167–1227. Mongol conqueror, ruler of all Mongol peoples from 1206. He began the conquest of N China 1213, and when he died, his empire ranged from the Yellow Sea to the Black Sea; it continued to expand after his death to extend from Hungary to Korea. Genghis Khan controlled probably a larger area than any other individual in history. He was not only a great military leader, but the creator of a stable political system.

Genoa (Italian *Genova*) historic city in NW Italy,

capital of Liguria; population (1989) 706,700. It is Italy's largest port; industries include oil-refining, chemicals, engineering, and textiles.

genome the full complement of ⟡genes carried by a single (haploid) set of ⟡chromosomes. The term may be applied to the genetic information carried by an individual or to the range of genes found in a given species.

genotype the particular set of ⟡alleles (variants of genes) possessed by a given organism. The term is usually used in conjunction with ⟡phenotype, which is the product of the genotype and all environmental effects. See also ⟡environment–heredity controversy.

Genova Italian form of ⟡Genoa, city in Italy.

genre painting painting of scenes from everyday life. Genre paintings were enormously popular in the Netherlands and Flanders in the 17th century (Vermeer, de Hooch, and Brouwer were great exponents). The term 'genre' is also used more broadly to mean a category in the arts, such as landscape painting, or literary forms, such as the detective novel.

Genscher Hans-Dietrich 1927– . German politician, chair of the West German Free Democratic Party (FDP) 1974–85, foreign minister 1974–92. A skilled and pragmatic tactician, Genscher became the reunified Germany's most popular politician.

Gentile da Fabriano *c.* 1370–1427. Italian painter of frescoes and altarpieces in the International Gothic style. Gentile was active in Venice, Florence, Siena, Orvieto, and Rome and collaborated with the artists Pisanello and Jacopo Bellini. *The Adoration of the Magi* 1423 (Uffizi, Florence) is typically rich in detail and crammed with courtly figures.

genus (plural *genera*) group of ⟡species with many characteristics in common. Thus all doglike species (including dogs, wolves, and jackals) belong to the genus *Canis* (Latin 'dog'). Species of the same genus are thought to be descended from a common ancestor species. Related genera are grouped into families.

Geoffrey of Monmouth *c.* 1100–1154. Welsh writer and chronicler. While a canon at Oxford, he wrote *Historia Regum Britanniae/History of the Kings of Britain c.* 1139, which included accounts of the semi-legendary kings Lear, Cymbeline, and Arthur, and *Vita Merlini*, a life of the legendary wizard.

geography science of the Earth's surface; its topography, climate, and physical conditions, and how these factors affect civilization and society. It is usually divided into *physical geography*, dealing with landforms and climates; *biogeography*, dealing with the conditions that affect the distribution of animals and plants; and *human geography*, dealing with the distribution and activities of peoples on Earth.

geological time time scale embracing the history of the Earth from its physical origin to the present day. Geological time is divided into eras (Precambrian, Palaeozoic, Mesozoic, Cenozoic), which in turn are divided into periods, epochs, ages, and finally chrons. We are living in the Recent epoch of the Quaternary period of the Cenozoic era.

geology science of the Earth, its origin, composition, structure, and history. It is divided into several branches: *mineralogy* (the minerals of Earth), *petrology* (rocks), *stratigraphy* (the deposition of successive beds of sedimentary rocks), *palaeontology* (fossils), and *tectonics* (the deformation and movement of the Earth's crust).

geometry branch of mathematics concerned with the properties of space, usually in terms of plane (two-dimensional) and solid (three-dimensional) figures. The subject is usually divided into *pure geometry*, which embraces roughly the plane and solid geometry dealt with in Euclid's *Elements*, and *analytical* or ▷*coordinate geometry*, in which problems are solved using algebraic methods. A third, quite distinct, type includes the non-Euclidean geometries.

George I 1660–1727. King of Great Britain and Ireland from 1714. He was the son of the first elector of Hanover, Ernest Augustus (1629–1698), and a great-grandson of James I. He succeeded to the electorate 1698, and became king on the death of Queen Anne. He attached himself to the Whigs, and spent most of his reign in Hanover, never having learned English.

George II 1683–1760. King of Great Britain and Ireland from 1727, when he succeeded his father, George I. His victory at Dettingen 1743, in the War of the Austrian Succession, was the last battle commanded by a British king. He married Caroline of Anspach 1705.

George III 1738–1820. King of Great Britain and Ireland from 1760, when he succeeded his grandfather George II. His rule was marked by intransigence resulting in the loss of the American colonies, for which he shared the blame with his chief minister Lord North, and the emancipation of Catholics in England. He had repeated attacks of insanity, permanent from 1811. He was succeeded by his son George IV.

George IV 1762–1830. King of Great Britain and Ireland from 1820, when he succeeded his father George III, for whom he had been regent during the king's period of insanity 1811–20. In 1785 he secretly married a Catholic widow, Maria Fitzherbert, but in 1795 also married Princess ▷Caroline of Brunswick, in return for payment of his debts. His prestige was undermined by his treatment of Caroline (they separated 1796), his dissipation, and his extravagance. He was succeeded by his brother, the duke of Clarence, who became William IV.

George V 1865–1936. King of Great Britain from 1910, when he succeeded his father Edward VII. He was the second son, and became heir 1892 on the death of his elder brother Albert, Duke of Clarence. In 1893, he married Princess Victoria Mary of Teck (Queen Mary), formerly engaged to his brother. In 1917, he abandoned all German titles for himself and his family. The name of the royal house was changed from Saxe-Coburg-Gotha (popularly known as Brunswick or Hanover) to Windsor.

George VI 1895–1952. King of Great Britain from 1936, when he succeeded after the abdication of his brother Edward VIII, who had succeeded their father George V. Created Duke of York 1920, he married in 1923 Lady Elizabeth Bowes-Lyon (1900–), and their children are Elizabeth II and Princess Margaret.

George, St patron saint of England. The story of St George rescuing a woman by slaying a dragon, evidently derived from the ▷Perseus legend, first appears in the 6th century. The cult of St George was introduced into W Europe by the Crusaders. His feast day is 23 April.

Georgetown capital and port of Guyana; population (1983) 188,000. Founded 1791 by the British, it was held 1784–1812 by the Dutch, who renamed it *Stabroek*.

Georgetown or *Penang* chief port of the Federation of Malaysia, and capital of Penang, on the island of Penang; population (1980) 250,600. It produces textiles and toys.

Georgia state in SE USA; nickname Empire State of the South/Peach State; *area* 58,904 sq mi/ 152,600 sq km; *capital* Atlanta; *cities* Columbus, Savannah, Macon; *features* Okefenokee National Wildlife Refuge (656 sq mi/1,700 sq km), Sea Islands, historic Savannah; *products* poultry, livestock, tobacco, maize, peanuts, cotton, soya beans, china clay, crushed granite, textiles, carpets, aircraft, paper products; *population* (1990) 6,480,000; *famous people* Jim Bowie; Erskine Caldwell; Jimmy Carter; Ray Charles; Ty Cobb; Bobby Jones; Martin Luther King, Jr; Margaret Mitchell; James Oglethorpe; Jackie Robinson; *history* explored 1540 by Hernando de Soto; claimed by the British and named after George II of England; founded 1733 as a colony for the industrious poor by James Oglethorpe, a philanthropist, and was one of the original 13 states of the USA. In 1864, during the Civil War, General W T Sherman's Union troops cut a wide swath of destruction as they marched from Atlanta to the sea.

Georgia country in SE Europe, on the Black Sea, bordered N by the Russian Federation, E by Azerbaijan, and S by Armenia and Turkey; *area* 69,700 sq km/26,911 sq mi; *capital* Tbilisi; *physical* largely mountainous with a variety of landscape ranging from subtropical Black Sea shores to ice and snow of Caucasus Mountains; rivers Kura and Rioni; *head of state* Eduard Shevardnadze (interim) from 1992; *head of government* Tengiz Sigua from 1992; *political system* transitional;

products tea, citrus and orchard fruits, tung oil, tobacco, vines, silk, hydroelectricity; **population** (1990) 5,500,000 (Georgian 69%, Armenian 9%, Russian 7%, Azeri 5%, Ossetian 3%, Abkhazian 2%); **language** Georgian; **recent history** independent republic 1918–21; uprising quelled by Red Army and Soviet republic established 1921. Linked with Armenia and Azerbaijan as Transcaucasian Republic 1922–36; separate republic within USSR 1936. Increasing demands for autonomy in 1980s. Economic and political sovereignty of Georgia declared 1989. In 1990 S Ossetia declared its independence; not recognized. Ruling Georgian Communist Party announced secession from Communist Party of USSR and called for independence 1990. Independence declared 1991; all relations with USSR severed; state of emergency. Georgia was admitted into ▷Conference on Security and Cooperation in Europe (CSCE) 1992.

Georgian period of English architecture, furniture making, and decorative art between 1714 and 1830. The architecture is mainly Classical in style, although external details and interiors were often rich in Rococo carving. Furniture was frequently made of mahogany and satinwood, and mass production became increasingly common; designers included Thomas Chippendale, George Hepplewhite, and Thomas Sheraton. The silver of this period is particularly fine, and ranges from the earlier, simple forms to the more ornate, and from the Neo-Classical style of Robert Adam to the later, more decorated pre-Victorian taste.

geothermal energy energy extracted for heating and electricity generation from natural steam, hot water, or hot dry rocks in the Earth's crust. Water is pumped down through an injection well where it passes through joints in the hot rocks. It rises to the surface through a recovery well and may be converted to steam or run through a heat exchanger. Dry steam may be directed through turbines to produce electricity.

geranium any plant either of the family

Geraniaceae, having divided leaves and pink or purple flowers, or of the family Pelargonium, having a hairy stem, and red, pink, or white flowers. Some geraniums are also called ▷cranesbill.

gerbil any of numerous rodents of the family Cricetidae with elongated back legs and good hopping or jumping ability. Gerbils range from mouse-to rat-size, and have hairy tails. Many of the 13 genera live in dry, sandy, or sparsely vegetated areas of Africa and Asia.

geriatrics branch of medicine concerned with diseases and problems of the elderly.

Géricault Théodore (Jean Louis André) 1791–1824. French Romantic painter. *The Raft of the Medusa* 1819 (Louvre, Paris) was notorious for exposing a relatively recent scandal in which shipwrecked sailors had been cut adrift and left to drown. He painted *The Derby at Epsom* 1821 (Louvre, Paris) and pictures of cavalry. He also painted portraits.

Germanic languages branch of the Indo-European language family, divided into *East Germanic* (Gothic, now extinct), *North Germanic* (Danish, Faroese, Icelandic, Norwegian, Swedish), and *West Germanic* (Afrikaans, Dutch, English, Flemish, Frisian, German, Yiddish).

German measles or *rubella* mild, communicable virus disease, usually caught by children. It is marked by a sore throat, pinkish rash, and slight fever, and has an incubation period of two to three weeks. If a woman contracts it in the first three months of pregnancy, it may cause serious damage to the unborn child.

German shepherd another name for ▷Alsatian, a breed of dog.

Germany, East (German Democratic Republic) country 1949–90, formed from the Soviet zone of occupation in the partition of Germany following World War II. East Germany became a sovereign state 1954, and was reunified with West Germany Oct 1990. For history before 1949, see ▷Germany, history; for history after 1949, see ▷Germany, Federal Republic of.

Germany Federal Republic of; country in central Europe, bordered N by the North and Baltic Seas and Denmark, E by Poland and Czechoslovakia, S by Austria and Switzerland, and W by France, Belgium, Luxembourg, and the Netherlands; *area* 357,041 sq km/137,853 sq mi; *capital* Berlin; *physical* flat in N, mountainous in S with Alps; rivers Rhine, Weser, Elbe flow N, Danube flows SE, Oder, Neisse flow N along Polish frontier; many lakes, including Müritz; *head of state* Richard von Weizsäcker from 1984; *head of government* Helmut Kohl from 1982; *political system* democratic federal republic; *exports* machine tools (world's leading exporter), cars, commercial vehicles, electronics, industrial goods, textiles, chemicals, iron, steel, wine, lignite (world's largest

producer), uranium, coal, fertilizers, plastics; *population* (1990 est) 78,420,000 (including nearly 5,000,000 guest workers, *Gastarbeiter*, of whom 1,600,000 are Turks; the rest are Yugoslavs, Italians, Greeks, Spanish, and Portuguese); *languages* German, Serbian; *recent history* divided 1945 into four occupation zones (US, French, British, Soviet). Federal Republic (West Germany) and German Democratic Republic (East Germany) established as independent states 1949. Berlin Wall constructed 1961. National borders, including the Wall, were opened 1989 and the official reunification of Germany was declared Oct 1990. Kohl elected chancellor of reunited Germany 1990; his popularity declined as racism and economic hardship increased; metal and engineering workers went on strike for pay rises 1992.

Germany, West (Federal Republic of Germany) country 1949–90, formed from the British, US, and French occupation zones after World War II; reunified with East Germany Oct 1990.

germination in botany, the initial stages of growth in a seed, spore, or pollen grain. Seeds germinate when they are exposed to favourable external conditions of moisture, light, and temperature, and when any factors causing dormancy have been removed.

Gershwin George 1898–1937. US composer who wrote both 'serious' music, such as the tone poem *Rhapsody in Blue* 1924 and *An American in Paris* 1928, and popular musicals and songs, many with lyrics by his brother **Ira Gershwin** (1896–1983), including 'I Got Rhythm', ''S Wonderful', and 'Embraceable You'. His opera *Porgy and Bess* 1935, an ambitious work that incorporated jazz rhythms and popular song styles in an operatic format, was his masterpiece.

Gestapo (contraction of **G**eheime **Sta**ats**po**lizei) Nazi Germany's secret police, formed 1933, and under the direction of Heinrich Himmler from 1936.

gestation in all mammals except the monotremes (duck-billed platypus and spiny anteaters), the period from the time of implantation of the embryo in the uterus to birth. This period varies among species; in humans it is about 266 days, in elephants 18–22 months, in cats about 60 days, and in some species of marsupial (such as opossum) as short as 12 days.

Gethsemane site of the garden where Judas Iscariot, according to the New Testament, betrayed Jesus. It is on the Mount of Olives, E of Jerusalem. When Jerusalem was divided between Israel and Jordan 1948, Gethsemane fell within Jordanian territory.

Getty J(ean) Paul 1892–1976. US oil billionaire, president of the Getty Oil Company from 1947, and founder of the Getty Museum (housing the world's highest-funded art gallery) in Malibu, California. In 1985 his son *John Paul Getty Jr* (1932–) established an endowment fund of £50 million for the National Gallery, London.

Gettysburg site in Pennsylvania of a decisive battle of the American ♢Civil War 1863, won by the North. The site is now a national cemetery, at the dedication of which President Lincoln delivered the *Gettysburg Address* 19 Nov 1863, a speech in which he reiterated the principles of freedom, equality, and democracy embodied in the US Constitution.

geyser natural spring that intermittently discharges an explosive column of steam and hot water into the air.

G-force force that pilots and astronauts experience when their craft accelerate or decelerate rapidly. One G is the ordinary pull of gravity. Early astronauts were subjected to launch and re-entry forces of six G or more; in the space shuttle, more than three G is experienced on liftoff. Pilots and astronauts wear G-suits that prevent their blood 'pooling' too much under severe G-forces, which can lead to unconsciousness.

Ghali Boutros Boutros 1922– . Egyptian diplomat and politician, secretary general of the United Nations from Jan 1992. He was deputy prime minister 1991–92 and worked towards peace in the Middle East in the foreign-ministry posts he held 1977–91.

Ghana Republic of; country in W Africa, bordered N by Burkina Faso, E by Togo, S by the Gulf of Guinea, and W by the Ivory Coast; *area* 238,305 sq km/91,986 sq mi; *capital* Accra; *physical* mostly tropical lowland plains; bisected by river Volta; *head of state and government* Jerry Rawlings from 1981; *political system* military republic; *exports* cocoa, coffee, timber, gold, diamonds, manganese, bauxite; *population* (1990 est) 15,310,000; *languages* English (official), African languages; *recent history* independence achieved from UK 1957; Kwame Nkrumah became president. Republic and one-party state formed 1960.

Nkrumah deposed by military coup 1966. Return to civilian government 1969–72, but ended 1979–1981 by further coups.

Ghats, Eastern and Western twin mountain ranges in S India, to the E and W of the central plateau; a few peaks reach about 3,000 m/9,800 ft. The name is a European misnomer, the Indian word *ghat* meaning 'pass', not 'mountain'.

Ghent (Flemish *Gent,* French *Gand*) city and port in East Flanders, NW Belgium; population (1991) 230,200. Industries include textiles, chemicals, electronics, and metallurgy.

gherkin young or small green ⟡cucumber, used for pickling.

ghetto any deprived area occupied by a minority group. The term first came into use 1516 in Venice and meant the area of a town where Jews were compelled to live, decreed by a law enforced by papal bull 1555. Jewish ghettos were abolished, except in E Europe, in the 19th century, but the concept and practice were revived by the Germans and Italians 1940–45.

Ghiberti Lorenzo 1378–1455. Italian sculptor and goldsmith. In 1401 he won the commission for a pair of gilded bronze doors for Florence's baptistry. He produced a second pair (1425–52), the *Gates of Paradise,* one of the masterpieces of the early Italian Renaissance.

Ghirlandaio Domenico *c.* 1449–1494. Italian fresco painter, head of a large and prosperous workshop in Florence. His fresco cycle 1486–90 in Sta Maria Novella, Florence, includes portraits of many Florentines and much contemporary domestic detail. He also worked in Pisa, Rome, and San Gimignano, and painted portraits.

GI abbreviation for *government issue*; hence (in the USA) a common soldier.

Giacometti Alberto 1901–1966. Swiss sculptor and painter who trained in Italy and Paris. In the 1930s, in his Surrealist period, he began to develop his characteristic spindly constructions. His mature style of emaciated single figures, based on wire frames, emerged in the 1940s.

Giambologna (Giovanni da Bologna or Jean de Boulogne) 1529–1608. Flemish-born sculptor active mainly in Florence and Bologna. In 1583 he completed his public commission for the Loggia dei Lanzi in Florence, *The Rape of the Sabine Women,* a dynamic group of muscular figures and a prime example of Mannerist sculpture.

gibbon any of several small S Asian apes of the genus *Hylobates,* including the subgenus *Symphalangus.* The common or lar gibbon *H. lar* is about 60 cm/2 ft tall, with a body that is hairy except for the buttocks, which distinguishes it from other types of apes. Gibbons have long arms and no tail. They are arboreal in habit, being very agile when swinging from branch to branch. On the ground,

they walk upright, and are more easily caught by predators.

Gibraltar British dependency, situated on a narrow rocky promontory in S Spain. *area* 6.5 sq km/ 2.5 sq mi; *features* strategic naval and air base, with NATO underground headquarters and communications centre; colony of Barbary apes; the frontier zone is adjoined by the Spanish port of La Línea; *exports* mainly a trading centre for the import and re-export of goods; *population* (1988) 30,000; *history* captured from Spain 1704 by English admiral George Rooke (1650–1709), it was ceded to Britain under the Treaty of Utrecht 1713. A referendum 1967 confirmed the wish of the people to remain in association with the UK, but Spain continues to claim sovereignty and closed the border 1969–85.

Gibraltar, Strait of strait between N Africa and Spain, with the Rock of Gibraltar on the north side and Jebel Musa on the south, the so-called Pillars of Hercules.

Gide André 1869–1951. French novelist, born in Paris. His work is largely autobiographical and concerned with the dual themes of self-fulfilment and renunciation. It includes *L'Immoraliste/The Immoralist* 1902, *La Porte étroite/Strait Is the Gate* 1909, *Les Caves du Vatican/The Vatican Cellars* 1914, and *Les Faux-monnayeurs/The Counterfeiters* 1926; and an almost lifelong *Journal.* Nobel prize 1947.

Gielgud John 1904– . English actor and director, renowned as one of the greatest Shakespearean actors of his time. He made his debut at the Old Vic 1921, and his numerous stage appearances ranged from roles in works by Chekhov and Sheridan to those of Alan Bennett, Harold Pinter, and David Storey. Gielgud's films include *Becket* 1964, *Oh! What a Lovely War* 1969, *Providence* 1977, and *Prospero's Books* 1991. He won an Academy Award for his role as a butler in *Arthur* 1981.

gigabyte in computing, a measure of ⟡memory capacity, equal to 1,024 ⟡megabytes. It is also used, less precisely, to mean 1,000 million ⟡bytes.

Gilbert W(illiam) S(chwenk) 1836–1911. British humorist and dramatist who collaborated with composer Arthur ⟡Sullivan, providing the libretti for their series of light comic operas from 1871; they include *HMS Pinafore* 1878, *The Pirates of Penzance* 1879, and *The Mikado* 1885.

Gilbert and Ellice Islands former British colony in the Pacific, known since independence 1978 as the countries of ⟡Tuvalu and ⟡Kiribati.

gill in biology, the main respiratory organ of most fishes and immature amphibians, and of many aquatic invertebrates. In all types, water passes over the gills, and oxygen diffuses across the gill membranes into the circulatory system, while carbon dioxide passes from the system out into the water.

gill imperial unit of volume for liquid measure, equal to one-quarter of a pint or 4 fluid ounces (0.142 litre). It is used in selling alcoholic drinks.

Gill Eric 1882–1940. English sculptor and engraver. He designed the typefaces Perpetua 1925 and Gill Sans (without serifs) 1927, and created monumental stone sculptures with clean, simplified outlines, such as *Prospero and Ariel* 1929–31 (on Broadcasting House, London).

Gillespie Dizzy (John Birks) 1917– . US jazz trumpeter who, with Charlie ◊Parker, was the chief creator and exponent of the ◊bebop style. He influenced many modern jazz trumpeters, including Miles Davis.

gilt-edged securities stocks and shares issued and guaranteed by the British government to raise funds and traded on the Stock Exchange. A relatively risk-free investment, gilts bear fixed interest and are usually redeemable on a specified date. The term is now used generally to describe securities of the highest value.

gin alcoholic drink made by distilling a mash of maize, malt, or rye, with juniper flavouring. It was first produced in the Netherlands. In Britain, the low price of corn led to a mania for gin during the 18th century.

ginger SE Asian reedlike perennial *Zingiber officinale*, family Zingiberaceae; the hot-tasting underground root is used as a condiment and in preserves.

ginkgo or *maidenhair tree* tree *Ginkgo biloba* of the gymnosperm (or naked-seed-bearing) division of plants. It may reach a height of 30 m/100 ft by the time it is 200 years old.

Ginsberg Allen 1926– . US poet. His 'Howl' 1956, an influential poem of the ◊Beat Generation, criticizes the materialism of contemporary US society. In the 1960s Ginsberg travelled widely in Asia and was a key figure in introducing Eastern thought to students of that decade.

ginseng plant *Panax ginseng*, family Araliaceae, with a thick, forked aromatic root used in medicine as a tonic. It is cultivated especially in Korea.

Giorgione del Castelfranco *c.* 1475–1510. Italian Renaissance painter, active in Venice, probably trained by Giovanni Bellini. His work influenced Titian and other Venetian painters. His subjects are imbued with a sense of mystery and treated with a soft technique, reminiscent of Leonardo da Vinci's later works, as in *The Tempest* 1504 (Accademia, Venice).

Giotto di Bondone 1267–1337. Italian painter and architect. He broke away from the conventional Gothic style of the time, and introduced a naturalistic style, painting saints as real people. He painted cycles of frescoes in churches at Assisi, Florence, and Padua.

giraffe world's tallest mammal, *Giraffa camelopardalis*, belonging to the ruminant family Giraffidae.

It stands over 5.5 m/18 ft tall, the neck accounting for nearly half this amount. The giraffe has two to four small, skin-covered, hornlike structures on its head and a long, tufted tail. The skin has a mottled appearance and is reddish brown and cream. Giraffes are found only in Africa, south of the Sahara Desert.

Girl Guide female member of the ◊Scout organization founded 1910 in the UK by Robert Baden-Powell and his sister Agnes. There are three branches: Brownie Guides (age 7–11); Guides (10–16); Ranger Guides (14–20); and Guiders (adult leaders). The World Association of Girl Guides and Girl Scouts (as they are known in the USA) has over 6.5 million members.

Girondin member of the right-wing republican party in the French Revolution, so called because a number of their leaders came from the Gironde region. They were driven from power by the ◊Jacobins 1793.

Giscard d'Estaing Valéry 1926– . French conservative politician, president 1974–81. He was finance minister to de Gaulle 1962–66 and Pompidou 1969–74. As leader of the Union pour la Démocratie Française, which he formed in 1978, Giscard sought to project himself as leader of a 'new centre'.

Giulio Romano *c.* 1499–1546. Italian painter and architect. An assistant to Raphael, he developed a Mannerist style, creating effects of exaggerated movement and using rich colours, for example the frescoes in the Palazzo del Tè (1526, Mantua).

Giza, El or *al-Jizah* site of the Great Pyramids and Sphinx; a suburb of ◊Cairo, Egypt; population (1983) 1,500,000. It has textile and film industries.

glacier body of ice, originating in mountains in snowfields above the snowline, which traverses land surfaces (glacier flow). It moves slowly down a valley or depression, and is constantly replenished from its source. The scenery produced by the erosive action of glaciers is characteristic and includes U-shaped valleys, corries, arêtes, and various features formed by the deposition of moraine (rocky debris).

gladiator in ancient Rome, a trained fighter, recruited mainly from slaves, criminals, and prisoners of war, who fought to the death in arenas for the entertainment of spectators. The custom, which originated in the practice of slaughtering slaves on a chieftain's grave, was introduced into Rome from Etruria in 264 BC and continued until the 5th century AD.

gladiolus any plant of the genus *Gladiolus* of S European and African cultivated perennials of the iris family Iridaceae, with brightly coloured, funnel-shaped flowers, borne in a spike; the swordlike leaves spring from a corm.

Gladstone William Ewart 1809–1898. British Liberal politician, repeatedly prime minister. He

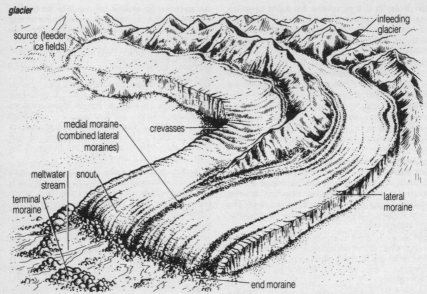

glacier

infeeding glacier

source (feeder ice fields)

medial moraine (combined lateral moraines)

crevasses

meltwater stream

snout

terminal moraine

lateral moraine

end moraine

entered Parliament as a Tory in 1833 and held ministerial office, but left the party 1846 and after 1859 identified himself with the Liberals. He was chancellor of the Exchequer 1852–55 and 1859–66, and prime minister 1868–74, 1880–85, 1886, and 1892–94. He introduced elementary education 1870 and vote by secret ballot 1872 and many reforms in Ireland, although he failed in his efforts to get a Home Rule Bill passed.

Glamorgan (Welsh *Morgannwg*) three counties of S Wales – Mid Glamorgan, South Glamorgan, and West Glamorgan – created in 1974 from the former county of Glamorganshire. All are on the Bristol Channel, and the administrative headquarters of Mid and South Glamorgan is Cardiff; the headquarters of West Glamorgan is Swansea. *Mid Glamorgan*, which also takes in a small area of the former county of Monmouthshire to the east, contains the coalmining towns of Aberdare and Merthyr Tydfil, and the Rhondda in the valleys. The mountains are in the northern part of the county; area 1,019 sq km/394 sq mi; population (1991) 526,500. In *South Glamorgan*, there is mixed farming in the fertile Vale of Glamorgan, and towns include Cardiff, Penarth, and Barry; area 416 sq km/161 sq mi; population (1991) 383,300. *West Glamorgan* includes Swansea, with tin-plating and copper industries, Margam, with large steel-rolling mills, Port Talbot, and Neath; area 815 sq km/315 sq mi; population (1991) 357,500.

gland specialized organ of the body that manufactures and secretes enzymes, hormones, or other chemicals. In animals, glands vary in size from small (for example, tear glands) to large (for example, the pancreas), but in plants they are always small, and may consist of a single cell. Some glands discharge their products internally (▷endocrine glands), others externally (exocrine glands). Lymph nodes are sometimes wrongly called glands.

glandular fever or *infectious mononucleosis* viral disease characterized at onset by fever and painfully swollen lymph nodes (in the neck); there may also be digestive upset, sore throat, and skin rashes. Lassitude persists for months and even years, and recovery is often very slow. It is caused by the Epstein-Barr virus.

Glasgow city and administrative headquarters of Strathclyde, Scotland; population (1991) 654,500. Industries include engineering, chemicals, printing, and distilling.

glasnost (Russian 'openness') Soviet leader Mikhail ▷Gorbachev's policy, introduced 1986, of liberalizing various aspects of Soviet life, such as granting greater freedom of expression and information and opening up relations with Western countries.

glass transparent or translucent substance that is physically neither a solid nor a liquid. Although glass is easily shattered, it is one of the strongest substances known. It is made by fusing certain types of sand (silica); this fusion occurs naturally in volcanic glass.

glaucoma condition in which pressure inside the eye (intraocular pressure) is raised abnormally as excess fluid accumulates. It occurs when the normal flow of intraocular fluid out of the eye is interrupted. As pressure rises, the optic nerve suffers irreversible damage, leading to a reduction in the field of vision and, ultimately, loss of eyesight.

Glendower Owen *c.* 1359–*c.* 1416. Welsh nationalist leader of a successful revolt against the English in N Wales, who defeated Henry IV in three campaigns 1400–02, although Wales was reconquered 1405–13. Glendower disappeared 1416 after some years of guerrilla warfare.

gliding the art of using air currents to fly unpowered aircraft. Technically, gliding involves the gradual loss of altitude; gliders designed for soaring flight (utilizing air rising up a cliff face or hill, warm air rising as a 'thermal' above sun-heated ground, and so on) are known as sailplanes. The sport of ⏵hang gliding was developed in the 1970s.

global warming projected imminent climate change attributed to the ⏵greenhouse effect.

globefish another name for ⏵puffer fish.

Glorious Revolution in British history, the events surrounding the removal of James II from the throne and his replacement by Mary (daughter of Charles I) and William of Orange as joint sovereigns in 1689. James had become increasingly unpopular on account of his unconstitutional behaviour and Catholicism. Various elements in England, including seven prominent politicians, plotted to invite the Protestant William to invade. Arriving at Torbay on 5 Nov 1688, William rapidly gained support and James was allowed to flee to France after the army deserted him. William and Mary then accepted a new constitutional settlement, the ⏵Bill of Rights 1689, which assured the ascendancy of parliamentary power over sovereign rule.

Gloucestershire county in SW England; *area* 2,640 sq km/1,019 sq mi; *towns* Gloucester (administrative headquarters), Stroud, Cheltenham, Tewkesbury, Cirencester; *features* Cotswold Hills; river Severn and tributaries; Berkeley Castle, where Edward II was murdered; Prinknash Abbey; Cotswold Farm Park, near Stow-on-the Wold, which has rare and ancient breeds of farm animals; *products* cereals, fruit, dairy products; engineering, coal in the Forest of Dean; *population* (1991) 520,600.

glow-worm the wingless female of some luminous beetles (fireflies) in the family Lampyridae. The luminous organs situated under the abdomen serve to attract winged males for mating. There are about 2,000 species, distributed worldwide.

glucose or *dextrose* or *grape-sugar* $C_6H_{12}O_6$ sugar present in the blood, and found also in honey and fruit juices. It is a source of energy for the body, being produced from other sugars and starches to form the 'energy currency' of many biochemical reactions also involving ⏵ATP.

gluon in physics, a ⏵gauge boson that carries the strong nuclear force, responsible for binding quarks together to form the strongly interacting subatomic particles known as ⏵hadrons. There are eight kinds of gluon.

glycerine CH another name for ⏵glycerol.

glycerol or *glycerine* or *propan-1,2,3–triol* $HOCH_2CH(OH)CH_2OH$ thick, colourless, odourless, sweetish liquid. It is obtained from vegetable and animal oils and fats (by treatment with acid, alkali, superheated steam, or an enzyme), or by fermentation of glucose, and is used in the manufacture of high explosives, in antifreeze solutions, to maintain moist conditions in fruits and tobacco, and in cosmetics.

gnat small fly of the family Culicidae, the mosquitoes. The eggs are laid in water, where they hatch into wormlike larvae, which pass through a pupal stage to emerge as adult insects.

Gnosticism esoteric cult of divine knowledge (a synthesis of Christianity, Greek philosophy, Hinduism, Buddhism, and the mystery cults of the Mediterranean), which flourished during the 2nd and 3rd centuries and was a rival to, and influence on, early Christianity.

GNP abbreviation for ⏵*gross national product.*

gnu or *wildebeest* either of two species of African ⏵antelope, genus *Connochaetes*, with a cowlike face, a beard and mane, and heavy curved horns in both sexes. The body is up to 1.3 m/4.2 ft at the shoulder and slopes away to the hindquarters.

Goa state of India; *area* 3,700 sq km/1,428 sq mi; *capital* Panaji; *population* (1991) 1,168,600; *history* captured by the Portuguese 1510; the inland area added in the 18th century. Goa was incorporated into India as a Union Territory with ⏵Daman and ⏵Diu 1961 and became a state 1987.

goat ruminant mammal of the genus *Capra* in the family Bovidae, closely related to the sheep. Both males and females have horns and beards. They are sure-footed animals, and feed on shoots and leaves more than on grass.

Gobi Asian desert divided between the Mongolian People's Republic and Inner Mongolia, China; 800 km/500 mi N–S, and 1,600 km/1,000 mi E–W. It is rich in fossil remains of extinct species.

God the concept of a supreme being, a unique creative entity, basic to several monotheistic religions (for example Judaism, Christianity, Islam); in many polytheistic cultures (for example Norse, Roman, Greek), the term 'god' refers to a supernatural being who personifies the force behind an aspect of life (for example Neptune, Roman god of the sea).

Godard Jean-Luc 1930– . French film director, one of the leaders of New Wave cinema. His works are often characterized by experimental editing techniques and an unconventional dramatic form. His films include *A bout de souffle/Breathless* 1959, *Vivre sa Vie* 1962, *Weekend* 1968, and *Je vous salue, Marie* 1985.

Godiva Lady c. 1040–1080. Wife of Leofric, earl of Mercia (died 1057). Legend has it that her husband promised to reduce the heavy taxes on the people of Coventry if she rode naked through the streets at noon. The grateful citizens remained indoors as she did so, but 'Peeping Tom' bored a hole in his shutters and was struck blind.

Godthaab (Greenlandic *Nuuk*) capital and largest town of Greenland; population (1982) 9,700. It is a storage centre for oil and gas, and the chief industry is fish processing.

Godunov Boris 1552–1605. Tsar of Russia from 1598, elected after the death of Fyodor I, son of Ivan the Terrible. He was assassinated by a pretender to the throne who professed to be Dmitri, a brother of Fyodor and the rightful heir. The legend that has grown up around this forms the basis of Pushkin's play *Boris Godunov* 1831 and Mussorgsky's opera of the same name 1874.

Goebbels Paul Josef 1897–1945. German Nazi leader. As minister of propaganda from 1933, he brought all cultural and educational activities under Nazi control and built up sympathetic movements abroad to carry on the 'war of nerves' against Hitler's intended victims. On the capture of Berlin by the Allies, he poisoned himself.

Goering (German *Göring*) Hermann Wilhelm 1893–1946. Nazi leader, German field marshal from 1938. He was part of Hitler's inner circle, and with Hitler's rise to power in 1933, he established the Gestapo and concentration camps. Appointed successor to Hitler in 1939, he built a vast economic empire in occupied Europe, but later lost favour and was expelled from the party in 1945. Tried at Nuremberg for war crimes, he poisoned himself before he could be executed.

Goethe Johann Wolfgang von 1749–1832. German poet, novelist, and dramatist, generally considered the founder of modern German literature, and leader of the Romantic ◊*Sturm und Drang* movement. His works include the autobiographical *Die Leiden des Jungen Werthers/The Sorrows of the Young Werther* 1774 and *Faust* 1808, his masterpiece. A visit to Italy 1786–88 inspired the classical dramas *Iphigenie auf Tauris/Iphigenia in Tauris* 1787 and *Torquato Tasso* 1790.

Gogh Vincent van 1853–1890. Dutch painter, a Post-Impressionist. He tried various careers, including preaching, and began painting in the 1880s. He met Paul ◊Gauguin in Paris, and when he settled in Arles, Provence, 1888, Gauguin joined him there. After a quarrel van Gogh cut off part of his own earlobe, and in 1889 he entered an asylum; the following year he committed suicide. The Arles paintings testify to his intense emotional involvement in his art; among them are *The Yellow Chair* and several *Sunflowers* 1888 (National Gallery, London).

Gogol Nicolai Vasilyevich 1809–1852. Russian writer. His first success was a collection of stories, *Evenings on a Farm near Dikanka* 1831–32, followed by *Mirgorod* 1835. Later works include *Arabesques* 1835, the comedy play *The Inspector General* 1836, and the picaresque novel *Dead Souls* 1842, which satirizes Russian provincial society.

Goh Chok Tong 1941– . Singapore politician, prime minister from 1990. A trained economist, Goh became a member of Parliament for the ruling People's Action Party 1976. Rising steadily through the party ranks, he was appointed deputy prime minister 1985, and subsequently chosen by the cabinet as Lee Kuan Yew's successor.

goitre enlargement of the thyroid gland seen as a swelling on the neck. It is most pronounced in simple goitre, which is caused by iodine deficiency. Much more common is toxic goitre or ◊thyrotoxicosis, caused by overactivity of the thyroid gland.

Golan Heights (Arabic *Jawlan*) plateau on the Syrian border with Israel, bitterly contested in the ◊Arab-Israeli Wars and annexed by Israel on 14 Dec 1981.

gold heavy, precious, yellow, metallic element; symbol Au, atomic number 79, relative atomic mass 197.0. It is unaffected by temperature changes and is highly resistant to acids. For manufacture, gold is alloyed with another strengthening metal (such as copper or silver), its purity being measured in ◊carats on a scale of 24.

goldcrest smallest British bird, *Regulus regulus*, about 9 cm/3.5 in long. It is olive green, with a bright yellow streak across the crown. This warbler builds its nest in conifers.

Golden Fleece in Greek mythology, fleece of the winged ram Chrysomallus, which hung on an oak tree at Colchis and was guarded by a dragon. It was stolen by Jason and the Argonauts.

Golden Horde the invading Mongol-Tatar army that first terrorized Europe from 1237 under the leadership of Batu Khan, a grandson of Genghis Khan. ◊Tamerlane broke their power 1395, and ◊Ivan III ended Russia's payment of tribute to them 1480.

golden section visually satisfying ratio, first constructed by the Greek mathematician ◊Euclid and used in art and architecture. It is found by dividing a line AB at a point O such that the rectangle produced by the whole line and one of the segments is equal to the square drawn on the other segment. The ratio of the two segments is about 8:13, and a rectangle whose sides are in this ratio is called a *golden rectangle*.

goldfinch songbird of the genus *Carduelis*, found in Eurasia, N Africa, and N America. It is about 12 cm/4.5 in long and black, white, and red about the head, with gold and black wings.

goldfish fish *Carassius auratus* of the ◊carp family,

golden section

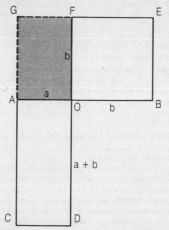

found in E Asia. Greenish-brown in its natural state, it has for centuries been bred by the Chinese, taking on highly coloured and sometimes freakishly shaped forms.

Golding William 1911– . English novelist. His first book, *Lord of the Flies* 1954, was about savagery taking over among a group of English schoolboys marooned on a Pacific island. Later novels include *The Spire* 1964, *Rites of Passage* 1980 (Booker prize), and *The Paper Men* 1984. Nobel prize 1983.

Goldsmith Oliver 1728–1774. Irish writer whose works include the novel *The Vicar of Wakefield* 1766; the poem 'The Deserted Village' 1770; and the play *She Stoops to Conquer* 1773. In 1761 Goldsmith met Samuel Johnson, and became a member of his 'club'. *The Vicar of Wakefield* was sold (according to Johnson's account) to save him from imprisonment for debt.

golf outdoor game in which a small rubber-cored ball is hit with a wooden-or iron-faced club; the object is to sink the ball into a series of holes, usually 18, anywhere between 90 m/100 yd and 457 m/500 yd away, using the least number of strokes. Natural hazards such as trees, bushes, and streams make play more difficult, and there are artificial hazards in the form of sand-filled bunkers. Golf was played as early as the 15th century in Scotland.

Goncourt, de the brothers Edmond 1822–1896 and Jules 1830–1870. French writers. They collaborated in producing a compendium, *L'Art du XVIIIème siècle/18th-Century Art* 1859–75, historical studies, and a *Journal* published 1887–96 that depicts French literary life of their day. Edmond de Goncourt founded the Académie Goncourt, opened 1903, which awards an annual prize, the Prix Goncourt, to the author of the best French novel of the year.

González Márquez Felipe 1942– . Spanish socialist politician, leader of the Socialist Workers' Party (PSOE), prime minister from 1982. Although re-elected in the 1989 election his popularity suffered from economic upheaval and allegations of corruption. Under his administration left-wing members of the Socialist Workers' Party, disenchanted with González's policies, formed a new party called Social Democracy 1990.

Good Friday in the Christian church, the Friday before Easter, which is observed in memory of the Crucifixion (the death of Jesus on the cross).

Goodman Benny (Benjamin David) 1909–1986. US clarinetist, nicknamed the 'King of Swing' for the new jazz idiom he introduced with arranger Fletcher Henderson (1897–1952). Leader of his own swing band 1934–40, and again later, he is associated with such numbers as 'Blue Skies' and 'Let's Dance'.

goose aquatic bird of any of several genera (especially *Anser*) in the family Anatidae, which also includes ducks and swans. Both genders are similar in appearance: they have short, webbed feet, placed nearer the front of the body than in other members of the order Anatidae, and the beak is slightly hooked. They feed entirely on grass and plants.

gooseberry edible fruit of *Ribes uva-crispa*, a low-growing bush related to the currant. It is straggling in its growth, bearing straight sharp spines in groups of three, and rounded, lobed leaves. The flowers are green, and hang on short stalks. The fruits are generally globular, green, and hairy, but there are reddish and white varieties.

Gorbachev Mikhail Sergeyevich 1931– . Soviet president, in power 1985–91. He was a member of the Politburo from 1980. As general secretary of the Communist Party (CPSU) 1985–91, president of the Supreme Soviet 1988–91, and head of state 1989–91, he introduced liberal reforms (◊*perestroika* and ◊*glasnost*) with multiparty democracy, and attempted to halt the arms race. But he faced an economic crisis and strivings for independence in the Soviet republics. After a coup attempt by hardliners Aug 1991 and subsequent international acceptance of independence for the Baltic states, Gorbachev was obliged to relinquish his leadership of the party, renounce communism as a state doctrine, suspend all activities of the Communist Party, and surrender many of his central powers to the states. With the emergence of the ◊Commonwealth of Independent States (CIS), Gorbachev resigned as Soviet leader on 25 Dec 1991. Nobel Peace Prize 1990.

Gordimer Nadine 1923– . South African novelist, an opponent of apartheid. Her first novel, *The Lying Days*, appeared in 1953, and other works include *The Conservationist* 1974, the volume of short stories *A Soldier's Embrace* 1980, and *July's People* 1981. Nobel prize 1991.

Gorgon in Greek mythology, any of three sisters,

Stheno, Euryale, and Medusa, who had wings, claws, enormous teeth, and snakes for hair. Medusa, the only one who was mortal, was killed by ◊Perseus, but even in death her head was still so frightful that it turned the onlooker to stone.

gorilla largest of the apes, *Gorilla gorilla*, found in the dense forests of W Africa and mountains of central Africa. The male stands about 1.8 m/6 ft and weighs about 200 kg/450 lbs. Females are about half the size. The body is covered with blackish hair, silvered on the back in older males. Gorillas live in family groups. They are vegetarian, highly intelligent, and will attack only in self-defence. They are dwindling in numbers, being shot for food by some local people or caught by poachers for zoos.

Göring Hermann. German spelling of ◊Goering, Nazi leader.

Gorky Maxim. Pen name of Alexei Peshkov 1868–1936. Russian writer. Born in Nizhni Novgorod (named Gorky 1932–90 in his honour), he was exiled 1906–13 for his revolutionary principles. His works, which include the play *The Lower Depths* 1902 and the memoir *My Childhood* 1913–14, combine realism with optimistic faith in the potential of the industrial proletariat.

gorse or **furze** or **whin** Eurasian genus of plants *Ulex*, family Leguminosac, consisting of thorny shrubs with spine-shaped leaves densely clustered along the stems, and bright yellow flowers. The gorse bush *U. europaeus* is an evergreen and grows on heaths and sandy areas throughout W Europe.

goshawk or **northern goshawk** woodland hawk *Accipiter gentilis* that is similar in appearance to the peregrine falcon, but with shorter wings and legs. It is used in falconry.

Gospel (Middle English 'good news') in the New Testament generally, the message of Christian salvation; in particular the four written accounts of the life of Jesus by Matthew, Mark, Luke, and John. Although the first three give approximately the same account or synopsis (thus giving rise to the name 'Synoptic Gospels'), their differences from John have raised problems for theologians.

gospel music vocal music developed in the 1920s in the black Baptist churches of the US South from spirituals, which were 18th-and 19th-century hymns joined to the old African pentatonic (five-note) scale.

Göteborg (German *Gothenburg*) port and industrial (ships, vehicles, chemicals) city (Sweden's second largest) on the W coast of Sweden, on the Göta Canal (built 1832), which links it with Stockholm; population (1990) 433,000.

Goth E Germanic people who settled near the Black Sea around the 2nd century AD. There are two branches, the eastern Ostrogoths and the western Visigoths. The *Ostrogoths* were conquered by the Huns 372. They regained their independence 454 and under Theodoric the Great conquered Italy 488–93; they disappeared as a nation after the

Byzantine emperor ◊Justinian I reconquered Italy 535–55. The *Visigoths* migrated to Thrace. Under ◊Alaric they raided Greece and Italy 395–410, sacked Rome, and established a kingdom in S France. Expelled from there by the Franks, they established a Spanish kingdom which lasted until the Moorish conquest of 711.

Gothic architecture style of architecture that flourished in Europe from the mid-12th century to the end of the 15th century. It is characterized by vertical lines of tall pillars, spires, height in interior spaces, the pointed arch, rib vaulting, and the flying buttress.

Gothic art style of painting and sculpture that dominated European art from the late 12th century until the early Renaissance. The great Gothic church façades held hundreds of sculpted figures and profuse ornamentation, and manuscripts were lavishly decorated. Stained glass replaced mural painting to some extent in N European churches. The *International Gothic* style in painting emerged in the 14th century, characterized by delicate and complex ornamentation and increasing realism.

Gounod Charles François 1818–1893. French composer. His operas include *Sappho* 1851, *Faust* 1859, *Philémon et Baucis* 1860, and *Roméo et Juliette* 1867. He also wrote sacred songs, masses, and an oratorio, *The Redemption* 1882. His music has great lyrical appeal and emotional power and it inspired many French composers of the later 19th century.

gourd any of various members of the family Cucurbitaceae, including melons and pumpkins. In a narrower sense, the name applies only to the genus *Lagenaria*, of which the bottle gourd or ◊calabash *Lagenaria siceraria* is best known.

gout disease, a hereditary form of ◊arthritis, marked by an excess of uric acid crystals in the tissues, causing pain and inflammation in one or more joints (usually of the feet or hands). Acute attacks are treated with ◊anti-inflammatories.

government any system whereby political authority is exercised. Modern systems of government distinguish between liberal democracies, totalitarian (one-party) states, and autocracies (authoritarian, relying on force rather than ideology). The Greek philosopher Aristotle was the first to attempt a systematic classification of governments. His main distinctions were between government by one person, by few, and by many (monarchy, oligarchy, and democracy), although the characteristics of each may vary between states and each may degenerate into tyranny (rule by an oppressive elite in the case of oligarchy or by the mob in the case of democracy).

Gower David 1957– . English left-handed cricketer who played for Leicestershire 1975–89 and for Hampshire from 1990. In 1992 during the third test match against Pakistan he became England's highest-scoring batsman in test cricket, surpassing Geoffrey Boycott's 8,114 runs.

Goya Francisco José de Goya y Lucientes 1746–1828. Spanish painter and engraver. He painted portraits of four successive kings of Spain, and his etchings include *The Disasters of War*, depicting the French invasion of Spain 1810–14. Among his last works are the 'black paintings' (Prado, Madrid), with horrific images such as *Saturn Devouring One of His Sons* 1822.

Grace W(illiam) G(ilbert) 1848–1915. English cricketer. By profession a doctor, he became the best batsman in England. He began playing first-class cricket at the age of 16, scored 152 runs in his first test match, and scored the first triple century 1876. Throughout his career, which lasted nearly 45 years, he scored more than 54,000 runs.

Graces in Greek mythology, three goddesses (Aglaia, Euphrosyne, Thalia), daughters of Zeus and Hera, personifications of pleasure, charm, and beauty; the inspirers of the arts and the sciences.

Graf Steffi 1969– . German lawn-tennis player who brought Martina ◊Navratilova's long reign as the world's number-one female player to an end. Graf reached the semi-final of the US Open 1985 at the age of 16, and won five consecutive Grand Slam singles titles 1988–89. She won her fourth Wimbledon singles title 1992, bringing her grand slam total to 11.

grafting in medicine, the operation by which a piece of living tissue is removed from one organism and transplanted into the same or a different organism where it continues growing. In horticulture, it is a technique widely used for propagating plants, especially woody species. A bud or shoot on one plant, termed the *scion*, is inserted into another, the *stock*, so that they continue growing together, the tissues combining at the point of union.

Graham Billy (William Franklin) 1918– . US Protestant evangelist, known for the dramatic staging and charismatic eloquence of his preaching.

Graham Martha 1893–1991. US dancer, choreographer, teacher, and director. A leading exponent of modern dance in the USA, she developed a distinctive vocabulary of movement, the *Graham Technique*, now taught worldwide. Her pioneering technique, designed to express inner emotion and intention through dance forms, represented the first real alternative to classical ballet.

Grahame Kenneth 1859–1932. Scottish author. The early volumes of sketches of childhood, *The Golden Age* 1895 and *Dream Days* 1898, were followed by his masterpiece *The Wind in the Willows* 1908, an animal fantasy created for his young son, dramatized by A A Milne as *Toad of Toad Hall* 1929.

gram metric unit of mass; one-thousandth of a kilogram.

grammar the rules for combining words into phrases, clauses, sentences, and paragraphs. Emphasis on the standardizing impact of print has meant that spoken or colloquial language is often perceived as less grammatical than written language, but all forms of a language, standard or otherwise, have their own grammatical systems of differing complexity. People often acquire several overlapping grammatical systems within one language; for example, one formal system for writing and standard communication and one less formal system for everyday and peer-group communication.

Grampian region of Scotland; *area* 8,600 sq km/ 3,320 sq mi; *towns* Aberdeen (administrative headquarters); *features* part of the Grampian Mountains (the Cairngorms); valley of the river Spey, with whisky distilleries; Balmoral Castle (royal residence); Braemar Highland Games in Aug; *products* beef cattle (Aberdeen Angus and Beef Shorthorn), fishing, North Sea oil service industries, tourism (winter skiing); *population* (1991) 493,200; *famous people* John Barbour, James Ramsay MacDonald, Alexander Cruden.

Gramsci Antonio 1891–1937. Italian Marxist who attempted to unify social theory and political practice. He helped to found the Italian Communist Party 1921 and was elected to parliament 1924, but was imprisoned by the Fascist leader Mussolini from 1926; his *Quaderni di carcere/Prison Notebooks* were published posthumously 1947.

Granada city in the Sierra Nevada in Andalusia, S Spain; population (1986) 281,000. It produces textiles, soap, and paper.

Grand Canal (Chinese *Da Yune*) the world's longest canal. It is 1,600 km/1,000 mi long and runs north from Hangzhou to Tianjin, China; it is 30–61 m/100–200 ft wide, and reaches depths of over 1.5 km/1 mi. The earliest section was completed 486 BC, and the northern section was built AD 1282–92, during the reign of Kublai Khan.

Grand Canyon vast gorge of multicoloured rock strata cut by the Colorado River, N Arizona, USA. It is 350 km/217 mi long, 6–29 km/4–18 mi wide, and reaches depths of over 1.7 km/1.1 mi.

Grand National in horse-racing, any of several steeplechases, such as the one run at Aintree, England, during the Liverpool meeting in March or April over 7,242 m/4.5 mi, with 30 formidable jumps. The highest jump is the Chair at 156 cm/5 ft 2in. The Grand National was first run 1839.

Grand Remonstrance petition passed by the British Parliament in Nov 1641 which listed all the alleged misdeeds of Charles I and demanded Parliamentary approval for the king's ministers and the reform of the church. Charles refused to accept the Grand Remonstrance and countered by trying to arrest five leading members of the House of Commons (Pym, Hampden, Holles, Hesilrige, and Strode). The worsening of relations between king and Parliament led to the outbreak of the English Civil War in 1642.

grand slam in tennis, the four major tournaments:

the Australian Open, the French Open, Wimbledon, and the US Open. In golf, it is also the four major tournaments: the US Open, the British Open, the Masters, and the PGA (Professional Golfers Association). In baseball, a grand slam is a home run with runners on all the bases. A grand slam in bridge is when all 13 tricks are won by one team.

grand unified theory (GUT) in physics, a sought-for theory that would combine the theory of the strong nuclear force (called ⟡quantum chromodynamics) with the theory of the weak nuclear and electromagnetic forces. The search for the grand unified theory is part of a larger programme seeking a ⟡unified field theory, which would combine all the forces of nature (including gravity) within one framework.

granite coarse-grained ⟡igneous rock, typically consisting of the minerals quartz, feldspar, and mica. It may be pink or grey, depending on the composition of the feldspar. Granites are chiefly used as building materials.

Grant Cary. Stage name of Archibald Leach 1904–1986. British-born actor who became a US citizen 1942. His witty, debonair personality made him a screen favourite for more than three decades. He was directed by Alfred ⟡Hitchcock in *Suspicion* 1941, *Notorious* 1946, *To Catch a Thief* 1955, and *North by Northwest* 1959. He received a 1970 Academy Award for general excellence.

Grant Duncan 1885–1978. British painter and designer, a member of the ⟡Bloomsbury group and a pioneer of abstract art in the UK. He lived with Vanessa Bell from about 1914 and worked with her on decorative projects. Later works, such as *Snow Scene* 1921, showed the influence of the Post-Impressionists.

Grant Ulysses S(impson) 1822–1885. American Civil War leader and 18th president of the USA 1869–77. He was a Union general in the American Civil War and commander in chief from 1864. As a Republican president, he carried through a liberal ⟡Reconstruction policy in the South, reformed the civil service, and ratified the Treaty of Washington with Great Britain 1871.

grape fruit of any ⟡vine of the genus *Vitis*.

grapefruit round, yellow, juicy, sharp-tasting fruit of the evergreen tree *Citrus paradisi* of the Rutaceae family. The tree grows up to 10 m/33 ft and has dark shiny leaves and large white flowers. The large fruits grow in grapelike clusters (hence the name). Grapefruits were first established in the West Indies and subsequently cultivated in Florida by the 1880s; they are now also grown in Israel and South Africa. Some varieties have pink flesh.

graphite blackish-grey, laminar, crystalline form of ⟡carbon. It is used as a lubricant and as the active component of pencil lead.

grass plant of the large family Gramineae of monocotyledons, with about 9,000 species distributed worldwide except in the Arctic regions. The majority are perennial, with long, narrow leaves and jointed, hollow stems; hermaphroditic flowers are borne in spikelets; the fruits are grainlike. Included are bluegrass, wheat, rye, maize, sugarcane, and bamboo.

Grass Günter 1927– . German writer. The grotesque humour and socialist feeling of his novels *Die Blechtrommel/The Tin Drum* 1959 and *Der Butt/The Flounder* 1977 are also characteristic of many of his poems.

grasshopper insect of the order Orthoptera, usually with strongly developed hind legs, enabling it to leap. The femur of each hind leg in the male usually has a row of protruding joints that produce the characteristic chirping when rubbed against the hard wing veins. Members of the order include ⟡locusts, ⟡crickets, and katydids.

gravel coarse ⟡sediment consisting of pebbles or small fragments of rock, originating in the beds of lakes and streams or on beaches. Gravel is quarried for use in road building, railway ballast, and for an aggregate in concrete. It is often found mixed with sand or clay. Some gravel deposits also contain metal ores (chiefly tin) or free metals (such as gold and silver).

Graves Robert (Ranke) 1895–1985. English poet and author. He was severely wounded on the Somme in World War I, and his frank autobiography *Goodbye to All That* 1929 is one of the outstanding war books. Other works include the poems *Over the Brazier* 1916; two historical novels of imperial Rome, *I Claudius* and *Claudius the God*, both 1934; and books on myth – for example, *The White Goddess* 1948.

gravity force of attraction that arises between objects by virtue of their masses. On Earth, gravity is the force of attraction between any object in the Earth's gravitational field and the Earth itself. It is regarded as one of the four ⟡fundamental forces of nature, the other three being the ⟡electromagnetic force, the ⟡strong nuclear force, and the ⟡weak nuclear force. The gravitational force is the weakest of the four forces, but it acts over great distances.

gravure one of the three main ⟡printing methods, in which printing is done from a plate etched with a pattern of recessed cells in which the ink is held. The greater the depth of a cell, the greater the strength of the printed ink. Gravure plates are expensive to make, but the process is economical for high-volume printing and reproduces illustrations well.

Gray Thomas 1716–1771. English poet whose 'Elegy Written in a Country Churchyard' 1751 is one of the most quoted poems in English.

grayling freshwater fish *Thymallus thymallus* of the family Salmonidae. It has a long multi-rayed dorsal fin, and a coloration shading from silver to purple. It is found in northern parts of Europe, Asia, and North America, where it was once common in the Great Lakes.

Great Barrier Reef chain of coral reefs and islands about 2,000 km/1,250 mi long, off the E coast of Queensland, Australia, at a distance of 15–45 km/10–30 mi. It is believed to be the world's largest living organism and forms an immense natural breakwater, the coral rock forming a structure larger than all human-made structures on Earth combined. The reef is in danger from large numbers of starfish, which are reported to have infested 35% of the reef. Some scientists fear the entire reef will disappear within 50 years.

Great Bear Lake lake on the Arctic Circle, in the Northwest Territories, Canada; area 31,800 sq km/12,275 sq mi.

Great Britain official name for ▷England, ▷Scotland, and ▷Wales, and the adjacent islands (except the Channel Islands and the Isle of Man) from 1603, when the English and Scottish crowns were united under James I of England (James VI of Scotland). With Northern ▷Ireland it forms the ▷United Kingdom.

Great Dane large, short-haired breed of dog, usually fawn in colour, standing about 76 cm/30 in tall and weighing up to 70 kg/154 lb. It has a long head, a large nose, and small, erect ears. It was used in Europe for hunting boar and stags.

Great Dividing Range E Australian mountain range, extending 3,700 km/2,300 mi N–S from Cape York Peninsula, Queensland, to Victoria. It includes the Carnarvon Range, Queensland, which has many Aboriginal cave paintings, the Blue Mountains in New South Wales, and the Australian Alps.

Great Lakes series of five freshwater lakes along the US–Canada border: Lakes Superior, Michigan, Huron, Erie, and Ontario; total area 245,000 sq km/94,600 sq mi. Interconnecting canals make them navigable by large ships, and they are drained by the St Lawrence River. The whole forms the St Lawrence Seaway. They are said to contain 20% of the world's surface fresh water.

Great Leap Forward change in the economic policy of the People's Republic of China introduced by ▷Mao Zedong under the second five-year plan of 1958–62. The aim was to convert China into an industrially based economy by transferring resources away from agriculture. This coincided with the creation of people's communes. The inefficient and poorly planned allocation of state resources led to the collapse of the strategy by 1960 and a return to more adequate support for agricultural production.

Great Patriotic War (1941–45) during World War II, the war between the USSR and Germany. When Germany invaded the USSR in June 1941, the Soviet troops retreated, carrying out a scorched earth policy. The Allies tried to provide the USSR with vital supplies through Murmansk and Archangel despite German attempts to blockade the ports. In 1942 German troops besieged Leningrad and

Stalingrad, and attempted to take Moscow. The Red Army gradually forced the Germans back; by Feb 1945 Soviet troops had reached the German border and in April 1945 they entered Berlin. In May 1945 the war ended. Some 20 million Soviet people were killed and millions more wounded in the Great Patriotic War.

Great Plains semiarid region to the E of the Rocky Mountains, USA, stretching as far as the 100th meridian of longitude through Oklahoma, Kansas, Nebraska, and the Dakotas. The plains, which cover one-fifth of the USA, extend from Texas in the south over 2,400 km/1,500 mi north to Canada. Ranching and wheat farming have resulted in overuse of water resources to such an extent that available farmland has been reduced by erosion.

Great Rift Valley longest 'split' in the Earth's surface, 8,000 km/5,000 mi long, from the Jordan Valley to central Mozambique in SE Africa; see ▷Rift Valley, Great.

Great Schism in European history, the period 1378–1417 in which rival popes had seats in Rome and in Avignon; it was ended by the election of Martin V during the Council of Constance 1414–17.

Great Slave Lake lake in the Northwest Territories, Canada; area 28,450 sq km/10,980 sq mi. It is the deepest lake (615 m/2,020 ft) in North America.

Great Trek in South African history, the movement of 12,000–14,000 Boer (Dutch) settlers from Cape Colony 1835 and 1845 to escape British rule. They established republics in Natal and the Transvaal. It is seen by many white South Africans as the main event in the founding of the present republic and also as a justification for continuing whites-only rule.

Great Wall of China continuous defensive wall stretching from W Gansu to the Gulf of Liaodong (2,250 km/1,450 mi). It was once even longer. It was built under the Qin dynasty from 214 BC to prevent incursions by the Turkish and Mongol peoples. Some 8 m/25 ft high, it consists of a brick-faced wall of earth and stone, has a series of square watchtowers, and has been carefully restored. It is so large that it can be seen from space.

Great War another name for ▷World War I.

grebe any of 19 species of water birds belonging to the family Podicipedidae. The great crested grebe *Podiceps cristatus*, 50 cm/20 in long, is the largest of the Old World grebes. It lives in ponds and marshes in Eurasia, Africa, and Australia, feeding on fish.

Greco, El (Doménikos Theotokopoulos) 1541–1614. Spanish painter called 'the Greek' because he was born in Crete. He studied in Italy, worked in Rome from about 1570, and by 1577 had settled in Toledo. He painted elegant portraits and intensely emotional religious scenes with increasingly distorted figures and flickering light; for example, *The Burial of Count Orgaz* 1586 (Toledo).

Greece Hellenic Republic; country in SE Europe,

Greece, ancient

1600–1200 BC	Mycenean civilization, influenced by Minoan Crete, established in mainland Greece.
14th century BC	Achaeans invade Greece and Crete.
c. 1180 BC	Siege of Troy.
c. 1100 BC	Dorians settle in the Pelopponese and found Sparta.
750–550 BC	Greeks found colonies in Asia Minor, Sicily, S Italy, S France, Spain and N Africa.
594–507 BC	Development of democracy in Athens and other cities.
545 BC	Persia invades Ionian cities of Asia Minor.
499–449 BC	Persian Wars, ending in defeat of Persia at Salamis (480 BC) and Platea (479 BC). Confederacy of Delos established.
461–429 BC	Pericles attempts to establish Athenian empire.
431–404 BC	Pelopponesian War between Athens and Sparta destroys political power of Athens.
378–371 BC	Sparta rules until defeated by Thebes.
358–336 BC	Philip of Macedon establishes supremacy over Greece.
337–323 BC	Alexander of Macedon defeats Persia, conquers Syria and Egypt, and invades Punjab. After his death, the empire is divided between his generals.
324–212 BC	Achaean and Anatolian leagues attempt to maintain independence of Greek cities against Macedon, Egypt and Rome.
146 BC	Greece annexed by Rome.

comprising the S Balkan peninsula, bordered N by Yugoslavia and Bulgaria, NE by Turkey, E by the Aegean Sea, S by the Mediterranean Sea, W by the Ionian Sea, NW by Albania, and numerous islands to the S and E; *area* 131,957 sq km/ 50,935 sq mi; *capital* Athens; *physical* mountainous; a large number of islands, notably Crete, Corfu, and Rhodes; *head of state* Christos Sartzetakis from 1985; *head of government* Xenophon Zolotas from 1989; *political system* democratic republic; *exports* tobacco, fruit, vegetables, olives, olive oil, textiles, aluminium, iron and steel; *population* (1990 est) 10,066,000; *language* Greek; *recent history* civil war 1946 followed the end of German occupation. The communists were defeated and the monarchy was re-established 1949, but overthrown by a military coup 1967. Martial law and the ban on political parties were lifted 1974 and a new constitution adopted 1975. Greece became a member of the EC 1981. Mounting criticism of Prime Minister Andreas Papandreou led to his defeat 1989.

Greek architecture the architecture of ancient Greece is the base for virtually all architectural developments in Europe. The Greeks invented the entablature, which allowed roofs to be hipped (inverted V-shape), and perfected the design of arcades with support columns. There were three styles, or ◊orders, of ◊columns: Doric, Ionic, and Corinthian.

Greek art sculpture, mosaic, and crafts of ancient Greece (no large paintings survive). It is usually divided into three periods: *Archaic* (late 8th century–480 BC), showing Egyptian influence; *Classical* (480–323 BC), characterized by dignified realism; and *Hellenistic* (323–27 BC), more exuberant or dramatic. Sculptures of human figures dominate all periods, and vase painting was a focus for artistic development for many centuries.

Greek language member of the Indo-European language family, which has passed through at least five distinct phases since the 2nd millennium BC: *Ancient Greek* 14th–12th centuries BC; *Archaic*

Greek, including Homeric epic language, until 800 BC; *Classical Greek* until 400 BC; *Hellenistic Greek*, the common language of Greece, Asia Minor, W Asia, and Egypt to the 4th century AD, and *Byzantine Greek*, used until the 15th century and still the ecclesiastical language of the Greek Orthodox Church. *Modern Greek* is principally divided into the general vernacular (*Demotic Greek*) and the language of education and literature (*Katharevousa*).

Greek Orthodox Church another name for the ◊Orthodox Church.

green belt area surrounding a large city, officially designated not to be built upon but preserved where possible as open space (for agricultural and recreational use). In the UK the first green belts were introduced in 1947 around such conurbations as London in order to prevent urban sprawl.

Greene (Henry) Graham 1904–1991. English writer whose novels of guilt, despair, and penitence are set in a world of urban seediness or political corruption in many parts of the world. They include *Brighton Rock* 1938, *The Power and the Glory* 1940, *The Heart of the Matter* 1948, *The Third Man* 1950, *The Honorary Consul* 1973, and *Monsignor Quixote* 1982.

greenfinch songbird *Carduelis chloris*, common in Europe and N Africa. The male is green with a yellow breast, and the female is a greenish-brown.

greenfly plant-sucking insect, a type of ◊aphid.

greenhouse effect in the Earth's atmosphere, the trapping of solar radiation, which, absorbed by the Earth and re-emitted from the surface, is prevented from escaping by various gases in the air. The result is a rise in the Earth's temperature. The main greenhouse gases are carbon dioxide, methane, and ◊chlorofluorocarbons. Fossil-fuel consumption and forest fires are the main causes of carbon dioxide build-up; methane is a byproduct of agriculture (rice, cattle, sheep). Water vapour is another greenhouse gas. The United Nations Environment

Programme estimates an increase in average world temperatures of 1.5°C/2.7°F with a consequent rise of 20 cm/7.7 in in sea level by 2025.

Greenland (Greenlandic *Kalaalit Nunaat*) world's largest island, lying between the North Atlantic and Arctic Oceans E of North America; *area* 2,175,600 sq km/840,000 sq mi; *capital* Godthaab (Greenlandic *Nuuk*) on the W coast; *features* the whole of the interior is covered by a vast ice sheet (the remnant of the last glaciation, part of the N Polar icecap); the island has an important role strategically and in civil aviation, and shares military responsibilities with the USA; there are lead and cryolite deposits, and offshore oil is being explored; *economy* fishing and fish-processing; *population* (1990) 55,500; Inuit (Ammassalik Eskimoan), Danish, and other European; *language* Greenlandic (Ammassalik Eskimoan); *history* Greenland was discovered about 982 by Eric the Red, who founded colonies on the W coast soon after Eskimos from the North American Arctic had made their way to Greenland. Christianity was introduced to the Vikings about 1000. In 1261 the Viking colonies accepted Norwegian sovereignty, but early in the 15th century all communication with Europe ceased, and by the 16th century the colonies had died out, but the Eskimos had moved on to the E coast. It became a Danish colony in the 18th century, and, after a referendum 1979, attained full internal self-government 1981.

green movement collective term for the individuals and organizations involved in efforts to protect the environment. The movement encompasses political parties such as the ◊Green Party and campaigning nongovernmental organizations like ◊Friends of the Earth and ◊Greenpeace.

Green Paper publication issued by a British government department setting out various aspects of a matter on which legislation is contemplated, and inviting public discussion and suggestions. In due course it may be followed by a ◊White Paper, giving details of proposed legislation. The first Green Paper was published 1967.

Green Party political party aiming to 'preserve the planet and its people', based on the premise that incessant economic growth is unsustainable. The leaderless party structure reflects a general commitment to decentralization. Green parties sprang up in W Europe in the 1970s and in E Europe from 1988. Parties in different countries are linked to one another but unaffiliated to any pressure group. They had parliamentary seats in seven countries in 1992, and 29 members of the European Parliament.

Greenpeace international environmental pressure group, founded 1971, with a policy of nonviolent direct action backed by scientific research. During a protest against French atmospheric nuclear testing in the S Pacific 1985, its ship *Rainbow Warrior* was sunk by French intelligence agents, killing a crew member.

green revolution in agriculture, a popular term for the change in methods of arable farming in Third World countries. The intent is to provide more and better food for their populations, albeit with a heavy reliance on chemicals and machinery. It was instigated in the 1940s and 1950s, but abandoned by some countries in the 1980s. Much of the food produced is exported as ◊cash crops, so that local diet does not always improve.

Greenwich Mean Time (GMT) local time on the zero line of longitude (the *Greenwich meridian*), which passes through the Old Royal Observatory at Greenwich, London. It was replaced 1986 by coordinated universal time (UTC); see ◊time.

Greer Germaine 1939– . Australian feminist who became widely known on the publication of her book *The Female Eunuch* 1970. Later works include *The Obstacle Race* 1979, a study of contemporary women artists, and *Sex and Destiny: The Politics of Human Fertility* 1984. She is also a speaker and activist.

Gregorian chant any of a body of plainsong choral chants associated with Pope Gregory the Great (540–604), which became standard in the Roman Catholic Church.

Gregory I St, *the Great c.* 540–604. Pope from 590 who asserted Rome's supremacy and exercised almost imperial powers. In 596 he sent St ◊Augustine to England. He introduced the choral *Gregorian chant* into the liturgy. Feast day 12 March.

Gregory XIII 1502–1585. Pope from 1572 who introduced the reformed *Gregorian calendar*, still in use, in which a century year is not a leap year unless it is divisible by 400.

Grenada island country in the Caribbean, the southernmost of the Windward Islands; *area* (including the Grenadines, notably Carriacou) 340 sq km/131 sq mi; *capital* St George's; *physical* mountainous; *head of state* Elizabeth II from 1974 represented by governor general; *head of government* Ben Jones from 1989; *political system* emergent democracy; *exports* coca, nutmeg, bananas, mace; *population* (1990 est) 84,000; *languages* English (official), some French patois spoken; *recent history* independence achieved from UK 1974. Constitution suspended and people's revolutionary government established 1979. Relations with USSR and Cuba strengthened. After a coup 1983 the USA invaded and reinstated the 1974 constitution. Integration with the Windward Islands proposed 1991.

Grenadines chain of about 600 small islands in the Caribbean sea, part of the group known as the Windward Islands. They are divided between ◊St Vincent and ◊Grenada.

Grenville George 1712–1770. British Whig politician, prime minister, and chancellor of the Exchequer, whose introduction of the ◊Stamp Act

1765 to raise revenue from the colonies was one of the causes of the American Revolution. His government was also responsible for prosecuting the radical John ◊Wilkes.

Grey Charles, 2nd Earl Grey 1764–1845. British Whig politician. He entered Parliament 1786, and in 1806 became First Lord of the Admiralty, and foreign secretary soon afterwards. As prime minister 1830–34, he carried the Great Reform Bill that reshaped the parliamentary representative system 1832 and the act abolishing slavery throughout the British Empire 1833.

Grey Lady Jane 1537–1554. Queen of England for nine days, 10–19 July 1553, the great-granddaughter of Henry VII. She was married 1553 to Lord Guildford Dudley (died 1554), son of the Duke of ◊Northumberland. Edward VI was persuaded by Northumberland to set aside the claims to the throne of his sisters Mary and Elizabeth. When Edward died on 6 July the same year, Jane reluctantly accepted the crown and was proclaimed queen four days later. Mary, although a Roman Catholic, had the support of the populace, and the Lord Mayor of London announced that she was queen on 19 July. Grey was executed on Tower Green.

greyhound ancient breed of dog, with a long narrow muzzle, slight build, and long legs, renowned for its swiftness. It is up to 78 cm/2 ft 6 in tall, and can exceed 60 kmph/40 mph. Greyhound racing is a popular spectator sport.

Grieg Edvard Hagerup 1843–1907. Norwegian composer. Much of his music is small-scale, particularly his songs, dances, sonatas, and piano works. Among his orchestral works are the *Piano Concerto* 1869 and the incidental music for Ibsen's *Peer Gynt* 1876.

griffin mythical monster, the supposed guardian of hidden treasure, with the body, tail, and hind legs of a lion, and the head, forelegs, and wings of an eagle. It is often found in heraldry.

Griffith D(avid) W(ark) 1875–1948. US film director, one of the most influential figures in the development of cinema as an art. He made hundreds of 'one-reelers' 1908–13, in which he pioneered the techniques of masking, fade-out, flashback, crosscut, close-up, and long shot. After much experimentation with photography and new techniques came his masterpiece as a director, *The Birth of a Nation* 1915, about the aftermath of the Civil War, later criticized as degrading to blacks.

Grimm brothers Jakob Ludwig Karl (1785–1863) and Wilhelm (1786–1859), philologists and collectors of German fairy tales such as Hansel and Gretel and Rumpelstiltskin. Joint compilers of an exhaustive dictionary of German, they saw the study of language and the collecting of folk tales as strands in a single enterprise.

Gromyko Andrei 1909–1989. President of the

USSR 1985–88. As ambassador to the USA from 1943, he took part in the Tehran, Yalta, and Potsdam conferences; as United Nations representative 1946–49, he exercised the Soviet veto 26 times. He was foreign minister 1957–85.

Groningen most northerly province of the Netherlands; *area* 2,350 sq km/907 sq mi; *population* (1991) 554,600; *towns* capital Groningen; Hoogezand-Sappemeer, Stadskanaal, Veendam, Delfzijl, Winschoten; *products* natural gas, arable crops, dairy produce, sheep, horses; *physical* Ems estuary, innermost W Friesian Islands; *history* under the power of the bishops of Utrecht from 1040, Groningen became a member of the Hanseatic League 1284. Taken by Spain 1580, it was recaptured by Maurice of Nassau 1594.

Gropius Walter Adolf 1883–1969. German architect who lived in the USA from 1937. He was an early exponent of the international modern style defined by glass curtain walls, cubic blocks, and unsupported corners – for example, the model factory and office building at the 1914 Cologne Werkbund exhibition. A founder and director of the ◊Bauhaus school in Weimar 1919–28, he advocated teamwork in design and artistic standards in industrial production.

gross of a particular figure or price, calculated before the deduction of specific items such as commission, discounts, interest, and taxes. The opposite is ◊net.

gross domestic product (GDP) value of the output of all goods and services produced within a nation's borders, normally given as a total for the year. It thus includes the production of foreign-owned firms within the country, but excludes the income of domestically owned firms located abroad. See also ◊gross national product. In the UK, the percentage increase in GDP from one year to the next is the standard measure of ◊economic growth.

gross national product (GNP) the most commonly used measurement of the wealth of a country. GNP is defined as the total value of all goods and services produced by firms owned by the country concerned. It is measured as the ◊gross domestic product plus income from abroad, minus income earned during the same period by foreign investors within the country.

Grosz Georg 1893–1959. German Expressionist painter and illustrator, a founder of the Berlin group of the Dada movement 1918. Grosz excelled in savage satirical drawings criticizing the government and the military establishment. After numerous prosecutions he fled his native Berlin 1932 and became a naturalized American 1938.

Grotius Hugo 1583–1645. Dutch jurist and politician, born in Delft. He became a lawyer, and later received political appointments. In 1618 he was arrested as a republican and sentenced to imprisonment for life. His wife contrived his escape 1620, and he settled in France, where he composed the *De Jure Belli et Pacis/On the Law of War and Peace* 1625, the foundation of international law. He was Swedish ambassador in Paris 1634–45.

groundnut another word for ◊peanut.

grouper any of several species of large sea perch (Serranidae), found in warm waters. Some species grow to 2 m/6.5 ft long, and can weigh 300 kg/ 660 lbs.

grouse fowl-like game bird of the subfamily Tetraonidae, in the pheasant family, Phasianidae. The subfamily also includes quail, ptarmigan, and prairie chicken. Grouse are native to North America and N Europe. They are mostly ground-living. During the mating season the males undertake elaborate courtship displays in small individual territories (leks). The grouse-shooting season in the UK is 12 Aug to 10 Dec.

Guadalajara industrial (textiles, glass, soap, pottery) capital of Jalisco state, W Mexico; population (1990) 2,847,000. It is a key communications centre. It has a 16th–17th-century cathedral, the Governor's Palace, and an orphanage with murals by the Mexican painter José Orozco.

Guadalcanal largest of the ◊Solomon Islands; area 6,500 sq km/2,510 sq mi; population (1987) 71,000. Gold, copra, and rubber are produced. During World War II it was the scene of a battle that was won by US forces after six months of fighting.

Guadeloupe island group in the Leeward Islands, West Indies, an overseas *département* of France; area 1,705 sq km/658 sq mi; population (1982) 328,400. The main islands are Basse-Terre, on which is the chief town of the same name, and Grande-Terre. Sugar refining and rum distilling are the main industries.

Guam largest of the ◊Mariana Islands in the W Pacific, an unincorporated territory of the USA. *area* 540 sq km/208 sq mi; *capital* Agaña; *population* (1990) 132,800; *languages* English, Chamorro (basically Malay-Polynesian); *recent history* ceded by Spain to the USA 1898; occupied by Japan 1941–44. Guam achieved full US citizenship and self-government from 1950. A referendum 1982 favoured the status of a commonwealth, in association with the USA.

Guangdong or *Kwantung* province of S China. *area* 231,400 sq km/89,320 sq mi; *capital* Guangzhou; *features* tropical climate; Hainan, Leizhou peninsula, and the foreign enclaves of Hong Kong and Macao in the Pearl river delta; *products* rice, sugar, tobacco, minerals, fish; *population* (1990) 62,829,000.

Guangxi or *Kwangsi Chuang* autonomous region in S China; *area* 220,400 sq km/85,074 sq mi; *capital* Nanning; *products* rice, sugar, fruit; *population* (1990) 42,246,000, including the Zhuang people, allied to the Thai, who form China's largest ethnic minority.

Guangzhou or *Kwangchow* or *Canton* capital of Guangdong province, S China; population (1989) 3,490,000. Its industries include shipbuilding, engineering, chemicals, and textiles.

Guatemala Republic of; country in Central America, bordered N and NW by Mexico, E by Belize and the Caribbean Sea, SE by Honduras and El Salvador, and SW by the Pacific Ocean; *area* 108,889 sq km/42,031 sq mi; *capital* Guatemala City; *physical* mountainous; narrow coastal plains; limestone tropical plateau in N; frequent earthquakes; *head of state and government* Jorge Serrano Elias from 1991; *political system* democratic republic; *exports* coffee, bananas, cotton, sugar, beef; *population* (1990 est) 9,340,000 (Mayaquiche Indian 54%, mestizo (mixed race) 42%); *languages* Spanish (official); 40% speak 18 Indian dialects; *recent history* independence achieved from Spain 1839. A series of coups from 1954 led to widespread violence. A further coup 1983 was followed by amnesty for the guerrillas and the adoption of a new constitution. Diplomatic relations with Belize established 1991.

Guatemala City capital of Guatemala; population (1983) 1,300,000. It produces textiles, tyres, footwear, and cement. It was founded 1776 when its predecessor (Antigua) was destroyed in an earthquake. It was severely damaged by another earthquake 1976.

guava tropical American tree *Psidium guajava* of the myrtle family Myrtaceae; the astringent yellow pear-shaped fruit is used to make guava jelly, or it can be stewed or canned. It has a high vitamin-C content.

Guayaquil largest city and chief port of ◊Ecuador; population (1986) 1,509,100. The economic centre of Ecuador, Guayaquil manufactures machinery and consumer goods, processes food, and refines petroleum. It was founded 1537 by the Spanish explorer Francisco de Orellana.

gudgeon any of an Old World genus *Gobio* of freshwater fishes of the carp family, especially *G. gobio* found in Europe and N Asia on the gravel bottoms of streams. It is olive-brown, spotted with black, and up to 20 cm/8 in long, with a distinctive barbel (a sensory fleshy filament) at each side of the mouth.

Guelph and Ghibelline rival parties in medieval Germany and Italy, which supported the papal party and the Holy Roman emperors respectively.

Guernsey second largest of the ◊Channel Islands; area 63 sq km/24.3 sq mi; population (1986) 55,500. The capital is St Peter Port. Products include electronics, tomatoes, flowers, and more recently butterflies; from 1975 it has been a major financial centre. Guernsey cattle, which are a distinctive pale fawn colour and give rich creamy milk, originated here.

guerrilla irregular soldier fighting in a small

unofficial unit, typically against an established or occupying power, and engaging in sabotage, ambush, and the like, rather than pitched battles against an opposing army. Guerrilla tactics have been used both by resistance armies in wartime (for example, the Vietnam War) and in peacetime by national liberation groups and militant political extremists (for example the ◊PLO; Tamil Tigers).

Guevara 'Che' Ernesto 1928–1967. Latin American revolutionary. He was born in Argentina and trained there as a doctor, but left his homeland 1953 because of his opposition to the right-wing president Perón. In effecting the Cuban revolution of 1959, he was second only to Castro and Castro's brother Raúl. In 1965 he went to the Congo to fight against white mercenaries, and then to Bolivia, where he was killed in an unsuccessful attempt to lead a peasant rising. He was an orthodox Marxist, and renowned for his guerrilla techniques.

Guiana NE part of South America, which includes ◊French Guiana, ◊Guyana, and ◊Surinam.

Guido Reni. Italian painter, see ◊Reni.

guild or *gild* medieval association, particularly of artisans or merchants, formed for mutual aid and protection and the pursuit of a common purpose, religious or economic. Guilds became politically powerful in Europe but after the 16th century their position was undermined by the growth of capitalism.

guillemot diving seabird of the auk family that breeds in large numbers on rocky N Atlantic and Pacific coasts. The common guillemot *Uria aalge* has a sharp bill and short tail, and sooty-brown and white plumage. Guillemots build no nest, but lay one large, almost conical egg.

Guinea Republic of; country in W Africa, bordered N by Senegal, NE by Mali, SE by the Ivory Coast, SW by Liberia and Sierra Leone, W by the Atlantic Ocean, and NW by Guinea-Bissau; *area* 245,857 sq km/94,901 sq mi; *capital* Conakry; *physical* flat coastal plain with mountainous interior; sources of rivers Niger, Gambia, and Senegal; forest in SE; *head of state and government* Lansana Conté from 1984; *political system* military republic; *exports* coffee, rice, palm kernels, alumina, bauxite, diamonds; *population* (1990 est) 7,269,000 (chief peoples are Fulani, Malinke, Susu); *languages* French (official), African languages; *recent history* gained independence from France 1958. Sékou Touré elected president; held office till his death 1984, when a coup established a military government. Attempted coup foiled 1985. Antigovernment general strike called by National Confederation of Guinea Workers 1991.

Guinea-Bissau Republic of; country in W Africa, bordered N by Senegal, E and SE by Guinea, and SW by the Atlantic Ocean; *area* 36,125 sq km/ 13,944 sq mi; *capital* Bissau; *physical* flat coastal plain rising to savanna in E; *head of state*

and government João Bernardo Vieira from 1980; *political system* socialist pluralist republic; *exports* rice, coconuts, peanuts, fish, timber; *population* (1989 est) 929,000; *languages* Portuguese (official), Crioulo (Cape Verdean dialect of Portuguese), African languages; *recent history* formerly part of the Portuguese colony of Guinea and Cape Verde. Gained independence 1974. Cape Verde decided against joining a unified state. In 1980, the president of the state council was deposed and a council of revolution set up. New constitution adopted 1984, making João Bernardo Vieira head of government as well as head of state.

guinea fowl chickenlike African bird of the family Numididae. The group includes the helmet guinea fowl *Numida meleagris*, which has a horny growth on the head, white-spotted feathers, and fleshy cheek wattles. It is the ancestor of the domestic guinea fowl.

guinea pig species of ◊cavy, a type of rodent.

Guinevere Welsh *Gwenhwyfar* in British legend, the wife of King ◊Arthur. Her adulterous love affair with the knight Lancelot of the Lake led ultimately to Arthur's death.

Guinness Alec 1914– . English actor of stage and screen. His films include *Kind Hearts and Coronets* 1949 (in which he played eight parts, including a woman), *The Bridge on the River Kwai* 1957 (Academy Award), and *Star Wars* 1977.

guitar six-stringed, flat-bodied musical instrument, plucked or strummed with the fingers. The *Hawaiian guitar*, laid across the lap, uses a metal bar to produce a distinctive gliding tone; the solid-bodied *electric guitar*, developed in the 1950s, mixes and amplifies vibrations from microphone contacts at different points to produce a range of tone qualities.

Guizhou or *Kweichow* province of S China *area* 174,000 sq km/67,164 sq mi; *capital* Guiyang; *products* rice, maize, nonferrous minerals; *population* (1990) 32,392,000.

Gujarat or *Gujerat* state of W India *area* 196,000 sq km/75,656 sq mi; *capital* Ahmedabad; *features* heavily industrialized; includes most of the Rann of Kutch; the Gir Forest (the last home of the wild Asian lion); *products* cotton, petrochemicals, oil, gas, rice, textiles; *language* Gujarati (Gujerati), Hindi; *population* (1991) 41,174,000.

Gujarati inhabitant of Gujarat on the NW coast of India. The Gujaratis number approximately 30 million and speak their own Indo-European language, Gujarati, which has a long literary tradition. It is written in its own script, a variant of the Devanagari script used for Sanskrit and Hindi. The Gujaratis are predominantly Hindu (90%), with Muslim (8%) and Jain (2%) minorities.

Gulf Cooperation Council (GCC) Arab organization for promoting peace in the Persian Gulf area, established 1981. Its declared purpose is 'to bring about integration, coordination, and cooperation in economic, social, defence, and political affairs among Arab Gulf states'. Its members include Bahrain, Kuwait, Oman, Qatar, Saudi Arabia, and the United Arab Emirates; its headquarters are in Riyadh, Saudi Arabia.

Gulf States oil-rich countries sharing the coastline of the ♢Persian Gulf (Bahrain, Iran, Iraq, Kuwait, Oman, Qatar, Saudi Arabia, and the United Arab Emirates). In the USA, the term refers to those states bordering the Gulf of Mexico (Alabama, Florida, Louisiana, Mississippi, and Texas).

Gulf Stream warm ocean current that flows north from the warm waters of Gulf of Mexico. Part of the current is diverted east across the Atlantic, where it is known as the *North Atlantic Drift*, and warms what would otherwise be a colder climate in the British Isles and NW Europe.

Gulf War 16 Jan–28 Feb 1991 war between Iraq and a coalition of 28 nations led by the USA. (It is also another name for the ♢Iran–Iraq War.) The invasion and annexation of Kuwait by Iraq on 2 Aug 1990 provoked a build-up of US troops in Saudi Arabia, eventually totalling over 500,000. The UK subsequently deployed 42,000 troops, France 15,000, Egypt 20,000, and other nations smaller contingents. An air offensive lasting six weeks, in which 'smart' weapons came of age, destroyed perhaps one-third of Iraqi equipment and inflicted massive casualties. A 100-hour ground war followed, which effectively destroyed the remnants of the 500,000-strong Iraqi army in or near Kuwait.

gull seabird of the family Laridae, especially the genus *Larus*. Gulls are usually 25–75 cm/10–30 in long, white with grey or black on the back and wings, and have large beaks.

gum in botany, complex polysaccharides (carbohydrates) formed by many plants and trees, particularly by those from dry regions. They form four main groups: plant exudates (gum arabic); marine plant extracts (agar); seed extracts; and fruit and vegetable extracts. Some are made synthetically.

gumtree common name for the ♢eucalyptus tree.

gun any kind of ♢firearm or any instrument consisting of a metal tube from which a projectile is discharged.

Gunpowder Plot in British history, the Catholic conspiracy to blow up James I and his parliament on 5 Nov 1605. It was discovered through an anonymous letter. Guy ♢Fawkes was found in the cellar beneath the Palace of Westminster, ready to fire a store of explosives. Several of the conspirators were killed, and Fawkes and seven others were executed.

guppy small fish *Poecilia reticulata* native to fresh, brackish water of Venezuela and adjacent Caribbean islands. It is a popular aquarium fish and comes in many colours, 6 cm/2.5 in long. The guppy bears live young.

guru (Hindi *gurū*) Hindu or Sikh leader, or religious teacher.

Gustavus Vasa or *Gustavus I* 1496–1560. King of Sweden from 1523, when he was elected after leading the Swedish revolt against Danish rule. He united and pacified the country and established Lutheranism as the state religion.

Gustavus Adolphus or *Gustavus II* 1594–1632. King of Sweden from 1611, when he succeeded his father Charles IX. He waged successful wars with Denmark, Russia, and Poland, and in the ♢Thirty Years' War became a champion of the Protestant cause. Landing in Germany 1630, he defeated the German general Wallenstein at Lützen, SW of Leipzig, 6 Nov 1632, but was killed in the battle. He was known as the 'Lion of the North'.

Gutenberg Johann *c.* 1400–1468. German printer, the inventor of printing from movable metal type, based on the Chinese wood-block-type method (although Laurens Janszoon Coster has a rival claim). Gutenberg began work on the process in the 1430s and in 1440 set up a printing business in Mainz. By 1455 he had produced the first printed Bible (known as the Gutenberg Bible).

Guthrie Woody (Woodrow Wilson) 1912–1967. US folk singer and songwriter whose left-wing protest songs, 'dustbowl ballads', and 'talking blues' influenced, among others, Bob Dylan; they include 'Deportees', 'Hard Travelin', and 'This Land Is Your Land'.

Guyana Cooperative Republic of; country in South America, bordered N by the Atlantic Ocean, E by Surinam, S and SW by Brazil, and NW by Venezuela; *area* 214,969 sq km/82,978 sq mi; *capital* Georgetown; *physical* coastal plain rises into rolling highlands with savanna in S; mostly tropical rainforest; *head of state and government* Desmond Hoyte from 1985; *political system* democratic republic; *exports* sugar, rice, rum, timber, diamonds, bauxite, shrimps, molasses; *population* (1989 est) 846,000 (descendants of workers introduced from India to work sugar plantations after abolition of slavery 51%, black 30%, Amerindian 5%); *languages* English (official), Hindi, Amerindian; *recent history* became a British colony 1831 as British Guiana. Internal self-government achieved 1961; independence 1966. Guyana became a republic within the Commonwealth 1970.

Gwent county in S Wales; *area* 1,380 sq km/ 533 sq mi; *towns* Cwmbran (administrative headquarters), Abergavenny, Newport, Tredegar; *products* salmon and trout from the Wye and Usk rivers; iron and steel at Llanwern; *population* (1991) 432,300; *languages* 2.5% Welsh, English; *famous people* Aneurin Bevan and Neil Kinnock, both born in Tredegar; Alfred Russel Wallace.

Gwyn Nell (Eleanor) 1651–1687. English comedy actress from 1665, formerly an orange-seller at Drury Lane Theatre, London. The poet Dryden wrote parts for her, and from 1669 she was the mistress of Charles II.

Gwynedd county in NW Wales; *area* 3,870 sq km/ 1,494 sq mi; *towns* Caernarvon (administrative headquarters), Bangor; *products* cattle, sheep, gold (at Dolgellau), textiles, electronics, slate; *population* (1991) 238,600; *languages* 61% Welsh, English; *features* Snowdonia National Park including Snowdon (the highest mountain in Wales, with a rack railway to the top from Llanberis) 1,085 m/3,561 ft, Cader Idris 892 m/2,928 ft, and the largest Welsh lake, Llyn Tegid (Bala Lake) 6 km/4 mi long; ◊Anglesey, across the Menai Straits; Lleyn Peninsula and Bardsey Island, with a 6th-century ruined abbey, once a centre for pilgrimage; Sergontium Roman Fort Museum; Caernarvon, Criccieth, and Harlech Castles; Bodnant Garden; the fantasy resort of Portmeirion, built by Clough ◊Williams-Ellis; *famous people* Edward II, T E Lawrence.

gymnastics physical exercises, originally for health and training (so called from the way in which men of ancient Greece trained: *gymnos* 'naked'). *Men's gymnastics* includes high bar, parallel bars, horse vault, rings, pommel horse, and floor exercises. *Women's gymnastics* includes asymmetrical bars, side horse vault, balance beam, and floor exercises. Also popular are *sports acrobatics*, performed by gymnasts in pairs, trios, or fours to music, where the emphasis is on dance, balance, and timing, and *rhythmic gymnastics*, choreographed to music and performed by individuals or six-girl teams, with small hand apparatus such as a ribbon, ball, or hoop.

gymnosperm in botany, any plant whose seeds are exposed, as opposed to the structurally more advanced ◊angiosperms, where they are inside an ovary. The group includes conifers and related plants such as cycads and ginkgos, whose seeds develop in ◊cones. Fossil gymnosperms have been found in rocks about 350 million years old.

gynaecology in medicine, a specialist branch concerned with disorders of the female reproductive system.

400–500°C/752–932°F and at 200 atmospheres pressure. The two gases, in the proportions of 1:3 by volume, are passed over a ◊catalyst of finely divided iron. Around 10% of the reactants combine, and the unused gases are recycled. The ammonia is separated either by being dissolved in water or by being cooled to liquid form.

habitat localized ◊environment in which an organism lives, and which provides for all (or almost all) of its needs. The diversity of habitats found within the Earth's ecosystem is enormous, and they are changing all the time. Many can be considered inorganic or physical, for example the Arctic ice cap, a cave, or a cliff face. Others are more complex, for instance a woodland or a forest floor. Some habitats are so precise that they are called *microhabitats*, such as the area under a stone where a particular type of insect lives. Most habitats provide a home for many species.

Habsburg or *Hapsburg* European royal family, former imperial house of Austria-Hungary and Spain. The Habsburgs held the title Holy Roman emperor 1273–91, 1298–1308, 1438–1740, and 1745–1806. The family reached the zenith of its power under Charles V (1519–56), who divided his lands, creating an Austrian Habsburg line and a Spanish line. The Habsburgs ruled Austria 1278–1918, under the title emperor 1806–1918; they ruled Spain to 1700.

haddock marine fish *Melanogrammus aeglefinus* of the cod family found off the N Atlantic coasts. It is brown with silvery underparts and black markings above the pectoral fins. It can grow to a length of 1 m/3 ft. Haddock are important food fish; about 45 million kg/100 million lb are taken annually off the New England fishing banks alone.

Hades in Greek mythology, the underworld where spirits went after death, usually depicted as a cavern or pit underneath the Earth, the entrance of which was guarded by the three-headed dog Cerberus. It was presided over by the god Hades or Pluto (Roman Dis).

Hadrian AD 76–138. Roman emperor from 117. Born in Spain, he was adopted by his relative, the emperor Trajan, whom he succeeded. He abandoned Trajan's conquests in Mesopotamia and adopted a defensive policy, which included the building of Hadrian's Wall in Britain.

Hadrian's Wall Roman fortification built AD 122–126 to mark England's northern boundary and abandoned about 383; its ruins run 185 km/115 mi from Wallsend on the river Tyne to Maryport, W Cumbria. The fort at South Shields, Arbeia, built to defend the eastern end, is being reconstructed.

hadron in physics, a subatomic particle that experiences the strong nuclear force. Each is made up of two or three indivisible particles called quarks. The hadrons are grouped into the baryons (protons, neutrons, and hyperons) and the

Haakon VII 1872–1957. King of Norway from 1905. Born Prince Charles, the second son of Frederick VIII of Denmark, he was elected king of Norway on separation from Sweden, and in 1906 he took the name Haakon. In World War II he carried on the resistance from Britain during the Nazi occupation of his country. He returned 1945.

Haarlem industrial city and capital of North Holland, the Netherlands, 20 km/12 mi W of Amsterdam; population (1991) 149,500. At Velsea to the north a road-rail tunnel runs under the North Sea Canal, linking North and South Holland. Industries include chemicals, pharmaceuticals, textiles, and printing. Haarlem is renowned for flowering bulbs and has a 15th–16th-century cathedral and a Frans Hals museum.

habeas corpus in law, a writ directed to someone who has custody of a person, ordering him or her to bring the person before the court issuing the writ and to justify why the person is detained in custody. Traditional rights to habeas corpus were embodied in the English Habeas Corpus Act 1679. The main principles were adopted in the US Constitution. The Scottish equivalent is the Wrongous Imprisonment Act 1701.

Haber Fritz 1868–1934. German chemist whose conversion of atmospheric nitrogen to ammonia opened the way for the synthetic fertilizer industry. His study of the combustion of hydrocarbons led to the commercial 'cracking' or fractional distillation of natural oil (petroleum) into its components (for example, diesel, petrol, and paraffin). In electrochemistry, he was the first to demonstrate that oxidation and reduction take place at the electrodes; from this he developed a general electrochemical theory.

Haber process or *Haber–Bosch process* industrial process by which ammonia is manufactured by direct combination of its elements, nitrogen and hydrogen. The reaction is carried out at

↪mesons (particles with masses between those of electrons and protons).

haemoglobin protein used by all vertebrates and some invertebrates for oxygen transport because the two substances combine reversibly. In vertebrates it occurs in red blood cells (erythrocytes), giving them their colour.

haemophilia any of several inherited diseases in which normal blood clotting is impaired. The sufferer experiences prolonged bleeding from the slightest wound, as well as painful internal bleeding without apparent cause.

haemorrhage loss of blood from the circulatory system. It is 'manifest' when the blood can be seen, as when it flows from a wound, and 'occult' when the bleeding is internal, as from an ulcer or internal injury.

hafnium (Latin *Hafnia* 'Copenhagen') silvery, metallic element, symbol Hf, atomic number 72, relative atomic mass 178.49. It occurs in nature in ores of zirconium, the properties of which it resembles. Hafnium absorbs neutrons better than most metals, so it is used in the control rods of nuclear reactors; it is also used for light-bulb filaments.

haggis Scottish dish consisting of chopped sheep's heart, lungs, and liver mixed with suet, oatmeal, onion, and spices and contained within the sheep's stomach. It is boiled and served with mashed potatoes and turnips. Haggis is traditionally eaten at Hogmanay (New Year's Eve) and on Burns' Night (25 Jan).

Hague, The (Dutch *'s-Gravenhage* or *Den Haag*) capital of South Holland and seat of the Netherlands government, linked by canal with Rotterdam and Amsterdam; population (1991) 444,200. It is also the seat of the United Nations International Court of Justice.

Hahn Otto 1879–1968. West German physical chemist who discovered nuclear fission (see under ↪nuclear energy). In 1938 with Fritz Strassmann (1902–1980), he discovered that uranium nuclei split when bombarded with neutrons, which led to the development of the atom bomb. He was awarded the Nobel Prize for Chemistry 1944.

hahnium name proposed by US scientists for the element also known as unnilpentium (atomic number 105), in honour of German nuclear physicist Otto Hahn. The symbol is Ha.

Haifa port in NE Israel; population (1988) 222,600. Industries include oil refining and chemicals.

Haig Douglas, 1st Earl Haig 1861–1928. British army officer, commander in chief in World War I. His Somme offensive in France in the summer of 1916 made considerable advances only at enormous cost to human life, and his Passchendaele offensive in Belgium from July to Nov 1917 achieved little at a similar loss. He was created field marshal 1917 and,

after retiring, became first president of the British Legion 1921.

hail precipitation in the form of pellets of ice (hailstones). It is caused by the circulation of moisture in strong convection currents, usually within cumulonimbus ↪clouds.

Haile Selassie Ras (Prince) Tafari ('the Lion of Judah') 1892–1975. Emperor of Ethiopia 1930–74. He pleaded unsuccessfully to the League of Nations against Italian conquest of his country 1935–36, and lived in the UK until his restoration 1941. He was deposed by a military coup 1974 and died in captivity the following year. Followers of the Rastafarian religion (see ↪Rastafarianism) believe that he was the Messiah, the incarnation of God (Jah).

Hainan island in the South China Sea; area 34,000 sq km/13,124 sq mi; population (1990) 6,557,000. The capital is Haikou. In 1987 Hainan was designated a Special Economic Zone; in 1988 it was separated from Guangdong and made a new province. It is China's second largest island.

hair threadlike structure growing from mammalian skin. Each hair grows from a pit-shaped follicle embedded in the second layer of the skin, the dermis. It consists of dead cells impregnated with the protein keratin.

Haiti Republic of; country in the Caribbean, occupying the western part of the island of Hispaniola; to the east is the Dominican Republic; *area* 27,750 sq km/10,712 sq mi; *capital* Port-au-Prince; *physical* mainly mountainous and tropical; seriously deforested; *interim head of state* Joseph Nerette from 1991; *head of government* Jean Jacques Honorat from 1991; *political system* transitional; *population* (1990 est) 6,409,000; *languages* French, creole; *recent history* independence was achieved from France 1804. Haiti was invaded by the USA 1915 and remained under US control until 1934. François Duvalier was elected president 1957; he was made president for life from 1964. He died 1971 and was succeeded by his son, Jean-Claude, who was deposed 1986. Military coups 1988–89; Jean Bertrand Aristide was elected president 1991 but overthrown the same year in a military coup by Brig-Gen Raoul Cedras; Joseph Nerette became interim head of state.

Haitink Bernard 1929– . Dutch conductor of the Concertgebouw Orchestra, Amsterdam, from 1964, and music director of the Royal Opera House, Covent Garden, London, from 1986.

hajj pilgrimage to ↪Mecca that should be undertaken by every Muslim at least once in a lifetime, unless he or she is prevented by financial or health difficulties. A Muslim who has been on hajj may take the additional name Hajji. Many of the pilgrims on hajj also visit Medina, where the prophet Muhammad is buried.

hake any of various marine fishes of the cod family, found in N European, African, and American waters. They have silvery, elongated bodies and attain a length of 1 m/3 ft. They have two dorsal fins and one long anal fin. The silver hake *Merluccius bilinearis* is an important food fish.

Halab Arabic name of ◊Aleppo, a city in Syria.

halal (Arabic 'lawful') conforming to the rules laid down by Islam. The term can be applied to all aspects of life, but usually refers to food permissible under Muslim dietary laws, including meat from animals that have been slaughtered in the correct ritual fashion.

Hale George Ellery 1868–1938. US astronomer who made pioneer studies of the Sun and founded three major observatories. In 1889 he invented the spectroheliograph, a device for photographing the Sun at particular wavelengths. In 1917 he established on Mount Wilson, California, a 2.5–m/100–in reflector, the world's largest telescope until superseded 1948 by the 5–m/200–in reflector on Mount Palomar, which Hale had planned just before he died.

Haley Bill 1927–1981. US pioneer of rock and roll who was originally a western-swing musician. His songs 'Rock Around the Clock' 1954 (recorded with his group the Comets and featured in the 1955 film *Blackboard Jungle*) and 'Shake, Rattle and Roll' 1955 became anthems of the early rock-and-roll era.

half-life in physics, the time taken for half the nuclei in a sample of a radioactive isotope to disintegrate. It may vary from millionths of a second to billions of years, even among different isotopes of the same element.

halibut any of several large flatfishes of the genus *Hippoglossus*, in the family Pleuronectidae, found in the Atlantic and Pacific oceans. The largest of the flatfishes, they may grow to 2 m/6 ft and weigh 90–135 kg/200–300 lb. They are very dark mottled brown or green above and pure white beneath. The Atlantic halibut *H. hippoglossus* is caught offshore at depths of 180–730 m/600–2,400 ft.

Halifax capital of Nova Scotia, E Canada's main port; population (1986) 296,000. Its industries include oil refining and food processing. There are six military bases in Halifax and it is a major centre of oceanography. It was founded by British settlers 1749.

Hall Peter (Reginald Frederick) 1930– . English theatre, opera, and film director. He was director of the Royal Shakespeare Theatre in Stratford-on-Avon 1960–68 and developed the Royal Shakespeare Company 1968–73 until appointed director of the National Theatre 1973–88, succeeding Laurence Olivier. He founded the Peter Hall Company 1988.

Halley's comet comet that orbits the Sun about every 76 years, named after Edmond Halley who calculated its orbit. It is the brightest and most conspicuous of the periodic comets. Recorded sightings go back over 2,000 years. It travels around the Sun in the opposite direction to the planets. Its

orbit is inclined at almost 20° to the main plane of the Solar System and ranges between the orbits of Venus and Neptune. It will next reappear 2061.

Hallowe'en evening of 31 Oct, immediately preceding the Christian feast of Hallowmas or All Saints' Day.

halogen any of a group of five nonmetallic elements with similar chemical bonding properties: fluorine, chlorine, bromine, iodine, and astatine. They form a linked group in the ◊periodic table of the elements, descending from fluorine, the most reactive, to astatine, the least reactive. They combine directly with most metals to form salts, such as common salt (NaCl). Each halogen has seven electrons in its valence shell, which accounts for the chemical similarities displayed by the group.

Hals Frans *c.* 1581–1666. Flemish-born painter of lively portraits, such as the *Laughing Cavalier* 1624 (Wallace Collection, London), and large groups of military companies, governors of charities, and others (many examples in the Frans Hals Museum, Haarlem, the Netherlands). In the 1620s he experimented with genre (domestic) scenes.

Hamburg largest inland port of Europe, in Germany, on the river Elbe; population (1988) 1,571,000. Industries include oil, chemicals, electronics, and cosmetics.

Hamilcar Barca *c.* 270–228 BC. Carthaginian general, father of ◊Hannibal. From 247 to 241 BC he harassed the Romans in Italy and then led an expedition to Spain, where he died in battle.

Hamilton capital (since 1815) of Bermuda, on Bermuda Island; population about (1980) 1,617. It was founded 1612.

Hamilton Emma (born Amy Lyon) 1765–1815. English courtesan. In 1782 she became the mistress of Charles Greville and in 1786 of his uncle Sir William Hamilton, the British envoy to the court of Naples, who married her 1791. After Admiral ◊Nelson's return from the Nile 1798 during the Napoleonic Wars, she became his mistress and their daughter, Horatia, was born 1801.

Hamilton Richard 1922– . English artist, a pioneer of Pop art. His collage *Just what is it that makes today's homes so different, so appealing?* 1956 (Kunsthalle, Tübingen, Germany) is often cited as the first Pop art work.

Hamito-Semitic language any of a family of languages spoken throughout the world. There are two main branches, the *Hamitic* languages of N Africa and the *Semitic* languages originating in Syria, Mesopotamia, Palestine, and Arabia, but now found from Morocco in the west to the Persian Gulf in the east.

Hammarskjöld Dag 1905–1961. Swedish secretary general of the United Nations 1953–61. He opposed Britain over the ◊Suez Crisis 1956. His attempts to solve the problem of the Congo (now Zaire), where he was killed in a plane crash, were criticized by the USSR. He was awarded the Nobel Peace Prize 1961.

hammer in track and field athletics, a throwing event in which only men compete. The hammer is a spherical weight attached to a chain with a handle. The competitor spins the hammer over his head to gain momentum, within the confines of a circle, and throws it as far as he can. The hammer weighs 7.26 kg/16 lb, and may originally have been a blacksmith's hammer.

hammerhead any of several species of shark of the genus *Sphyrna*, found in tropical seas, characterized by having eyes at the ends of flattened extensions of the skull. Hammerheads can grow to 4 m/13 ft.

Hammerstein Oscar, II 1895–1960. Lyricist and librettist who collaborated with Richard ⊳Rodgers on some of the best-known American musicals, including *Oklahoma* 1943 (Pulitzer prize), *Carousel* 1945, *South Pacific* 1949 (Pulitzer prize), *The King and I* 1951, and *The Sound of Music* 1959.

Hammett (Samuel) Daskiell 1894–1961. US crime novelist. His works, *The Maltese Falcon* 1930, *The Glass Key* 1931, and *The Thin Man* 1932 introduced the 'hard-boiled' detective character into fiction.

Hampshire county of S England; **area** 3,770 sq km/1,455 sq mi; **towns** Winchester (administrative headquarters), Southampton, Portsmouth, Gosport; **features** New Forest, area 373 sq km/144 sq mi, a Saxon royal hunting ground; the river Test, which is renowned for its trout fishing; Hampshire Basin, where Britain has onshore and offshore oil; Danebury, 2,500-year-old Celtic hillfort; Beaulieu (including National Motor Museum); Broadlands (home of Lord Mountbatten); Highclere (home of the Earl of Carnarvon, with 'gardens by Capability Brown); Hambledon, where the first cricket club was founded 1750; site of the Roman town of Silchester, the only one in Britain known in such detail; Jane Austen's cottage 1809–17 is a museum; **products** agricultural including watercress growing; oil from refineries at Fawley; chemicals, pharmaceuticals, electronics; **population** (1991) 1,511,900; **famous people** Jane Austen, Charles Dickens, Gilbert White.

hamster rodent of the family Cricetidae with a thickset body, short tail, and cheek pouches to carry food. Several genera are found across Asia and in SE Europe. Hamsters are often kept as pets.

Han member of the majority ethnic group in China, numbering about 990 million. The Hans speak a wide variety of dialects of the same monosyllabic language, a member of the Sino-Tibetan family. Their religion combines Buddhism, Taoism, Confucianism, and ancestor worship.

Handel Georg Friedrich 1685–1759. German composer who became a British subject 1726. His first opera, *Almira*, was performed in Hamburg 1705. In 1710 he was appointed Kapellmeister to the elector of Hanover (the future George I of England). In 1712 he settled in England, where he established his popularity with such works as the *Water Music* 1717 (written for George I). His great choral works include the *Messiah* 1742 and the later oratorios *Samson* 1743, *Belshazzar* 1745, *Judas Maccabaeus* 1747, and *Jephtha* 1752.

Hangchow alternative transcription of ⊳Hangzhou, port in Zhejiang province, China.

hang-gliding technique of unpowered flying using air currents, perfected by US engineer Francis Rogallo in the 1970s. The aeronaut is strapped into a carrier, attached to a sail wing of nylon stretched on an aluminium frame like a paper dart, and jumps into the air from a high place, where updrafts of warm air allow soaring on the 'thermals'. See ⊳gliding.

Hangzhou or *Hangchow* port and capital of Zhejiang province, China; population (1989) 1,330,000. It has jute, steel, chemical, tea, and silk industries.

Hannibal 247–182 BC. Carthaginian general from 221 BC, son of Hamilcar Barca. His siege of Saguntum (now Sagunto, near Valencia) precipitated the 2nd ⊳Punic War with Rome. Following a campaign in Italy (after crossing the Alps in 218 with 57 elephants), Hannibal was the victor at Trasimene in 217 and Cannae in 216, but he failed to take Rome. In 203 he returned to Carthage to meet a Roman invasion but was defeated at Zama in 202 and exiled in 196 at Rome's insistence.

Hanoi capital of Vietnam, on the Red River; population (1989) 1,088,900. Industries include textiles, paper, and engineering.

Hanover industrial city, capital of Lower Saxony, Germany; population (1988) 506,000. Industries include machinery, vehicles, electrical goods, rubber, textiles, and oil refining.

Hansard official report of the proceedings of the British Parliament, named after Luke Hansard (1752–1828), printer of the House of Commons *Journal* from 1774. The publication of the debates is now the responsibility of the Stationery Office. The name *Hansard* was officially adopted 1943.

Hanseatic League confederation of N European trading cities from the 12th century to 1669. At its height in the late 14th century the Hanseatic League included over 160 cities and towns, among them Lübeck, Hamburg, Cologne, Breslau, and Kraków. The basis of the league's power was its monopoly of the Baltic trade and its relations with Flanders and England. The decline of the Hanseatic League from the 15th century was caused by the closing and moving of trade routes and the development of nation states.

haploid having a single set of ⊳chromosomes in each cell. Most higher organisms are ⊳diploid — that is, they have two sets — but their gametes (sex cells) are haploid. Some plants, such as mosses, liverworts, and many seaweeds, are haploid, and male honey bees are haploid because they develop from eggs that have not been fertilized.

Hapsburg English form of ⫌Habsburg, former imperial house of Austria–Hungary.

Harare capital of Zimbabwe, on the Mashonaland plateau, about 1,525 m/5,000 ft above sea level; population (1982) 656,000. It is the centre of a rich farming area (tobacco and maize), with metallurgical and food processing industries.

Harbin or *Haerhpin* or *Pinkiang* port on the Songhua River, NE China, capital of Heilongjiang province; population (1989) 2,800,000. Industries include metallurgy, machinery, paper, food processing, and sugar refining, and it is a major rail junction. Harbin was developed by Russian settlers after Russia was granted trading rights there 1896, and more Russians arrived as refugees after the October Revolution 1917.

hard disc in computing, a storage device consisting of a rigid metal ⫌disc coated with a magnetic material. Data are read from and written to the disc by means of a disc drive. The hard disc may be permanently fixed into the drive or in the form of a disc pack that can be removed and exchanged with a different pack. Hard discs vary from large units with capacities of over 3,000 megabytes, intended for use with mainframe computers, to small units with capacities as low as 20 megabytes, intended for use with microcomputers.

Hardicanute *c.* 1019–1042. King of England from 1040. Son of Canute, he was king of Denmark from 1028. In England he was considered a harsh ruler.

Hardie (James) Keir 1856–1915. Scottish socialist, member of Parliament 1892–95 and 1900–15. He worked in the mines as a boy and in 1886 became secretary of the Scottish Miners' Federation. In 1888 he was the first Labour candidate to stand for Parliament; he entered Parliament independently as a Labour member 1892 and was a chief founder of the Independent Labour Party 1893.

Harding Warren G(amaliel) 1865–1923. 29th president of the USA 1921–23, a Republican. Harding was born in Ohio, and entered the US Senate 1914. As president he concluded the peace treaties of 1921 with Germany, Austria, and Hungary, and in the same year called the Washington Naval Conference to resolve conflicting British, Japanese, and US ambitions in the Pacific. He opposed US membership of the League of Nations.

hardware the mechanical, electrical, and electronic components of a computer system, as opposed to the various programs, which constitute ⫌software.

Hardy Thomas 1840–1928. English novelist and poet. His novels, set in rural 'Wessex' (his native West Country), portray intense human relationships played out in a harshly indifferent natural world. They include *Far From the Madding Crowd* 1874, *The Return of the Native* 1878, *The Mayor of Casterbridge* 1886, *The Woodlanders* 1887, *Tess of the d'Urbervilles* 1891, and *Jude the Obscure* 1895. His poetry includes the *Wessex Poems* 1898, the blank-verse epic of the Napoleonic Wars *The Dynasts* 1904–08, and several volumes of lyrics.

hare mammal of the genus *Lepus* of the family Leporidae (which also includes rabbits) in the order Lagomorpha. Hares are larger than rabbits, with very long, black-tipped ears, long hind legs, and short, upturned tails. Unlike rabbits, hares do not burrow. Their furred, open-eyed young are called leverets. They are cared for in a grassy depression called a form.

harebell perennial plant *Campanula rotundifolia* of the ⫌bellflower family, with bell-shaped blue flowers, found on dry grassland and heaths. It is known in Scotland as the bluebell.

Hare Krishna popular name for a member of the ⫌International Society for Krishna Consciousness, derived from their chant.

Hargreaves James died 1778. English inventor who co-invented a carding machine for combing wool 1760. About 1764 he invented his 'spinning jenny', which enabled a number of threads to be spun simultaneously by one person.

harmonica or *mouth organ* pocket-sized reed organ blown directly from the mouth; it was invented by Charles Wheatstone 1829.

harmonium keyboard reed organ of the 19th century, powered by foot-operated bellows.

harmony in music, any simultaneous combination of sounds, as opposed to melody, which is a succession of sounds. Although the term suggests a pleasant or agreeable sound, it is applied to any combination of notes, whether consonant or dissonant. Harmony deals with the formation of chords and their interrelation and logical progression.

Harold I died 1040. King of England from 1035. The illegitimate son of Canute, known as *Harefoot*, he claimed the throne 1035 when the legitimate heir Hardicanute was in Denmark. He was elected king 1037.

Harold II *c.* 1020–1066. King of England from Jan 1066. He succeeded his father Earl Godwin 1053 as earl of Wessex. In 1063 William of Normandy (⫌William I) tricked him into swearing to support his claim to the English throne, and when the Witan (a council of high-ranking religious and secular men) elected Harold to succeed Edward the Confessor, William prepared to invade. Meanwhile, Harold's treacherous brother Tostig (died 1066) joined the king of Norway, Harald III Hardrada (1015–1066), in invading Northumbria. Harold routed and killed them at Stamford Bridge 25 Sept. Three days later William landed at Pevensey, Sussex, and Harold was killed at the Battle of Hastings 14 Oct 1066.

harp plucked musical string instrument, with the

strings stretched vertically within a wooden frame, normally triangular. The concert harp is now the largest musical instrument to be plucked by hand. It has up to 47 strings, and seven pedals set into the soundbox at the base to alter pitch.

harpsichord keyboard musical instrument common in the 16th–18th centuries, until superseded by the piano. The strings are plucked by quills. It was revived in the 20th century for the authentic performance of early music.

Harpy (plural **Harpies**) in early Greek mythology, a wind spirit; in later legend the Harpies have horrific women's faces and the bodies of vultures.

harrier bird of prey of the genus *Circus*, family Accipitridae. Harriers have long wings and legs, short beaks and soft plumage. They are found throughout the world. Three species occur in Britain: the hen harrier *C. cyaneus*, Montagu's harrier *C. pygargus*, and the marsh harrier *C. aeruginosus*.

Harrier the only truly successful vertical takeoff and landing fixed-wing aircraft, often called the *jump jet*. Built in Britain, it made its first flight 1966. It has a single jet engine and a set of swivelling nozzles. These deflect the jet exhaust vertically downwards for takeoff and landing, and to the rear for normal flight. Designed to fly from confined spaces with minimal ground support, it refuels in midair.

Harris southern part of Lewis with Harris, in the Outer ◊Hebrides; area 500 sq km/193 sq mi; population (1971) 2,900. It is joined to Lewis by a narrow isthmus. Harris tweeds are produced here.

Harrison Benjamin 1833–1901. 23rd president of the USA 1889–93, a Republican. He called the first Pan-American Conference, which led to the establishment of the Pan American Union, to improve inter-American cooperation, and develop commercial ties. In 1948 this became the ◊Organization of American States.

Harrison Rex (Reginald Carey) 1908–1990. English film and theatre actor. He appeared in over 40 films and numerous plays, often portraying sophisticated and somewhat eccentric characters, such as the waspish Professor Higgins in *My Fair Lady* 1964, the musical version of Irish dramatist George Bernard Shaw's play *Pygmalion*. His other films include *Blithe Spirit* 1945, *The Ghost and Mrs Muir* 1947, and *Dr Doolittle* 1967.

hartebeest large African antelope *Alcelaphus buselaphus* with lyre-shaped horns set close on top of the head in both sexes. It may grow to 1.5 m/5 ft at the rather humped shoulders and up to 2 m/6 ft long. Although they are clumsy-looking runners, hartebeest can reach 65 kph/40 mph.

Hartz Mountains range running N to S in Tasmania, Australia, with two remarkable peaks: Hartz Mountain (1,254 m/4,113 ft) and Adamsons Peak (1,224 m/4,017 ft).

Harvey William 1578–1657. English physician who discovered the circulation of blood. In 1628 he published his book *De Motu Cordis/On the Motion of the Heart and the Blood in Animals*. He was court physician to James I and Charles I.

Haryana state of NW India; *area* 44,200 sq km/17,061 sq mi; *capital* Chandigarh; *features* part of the Ganges plain; a centre of Hinduism; *products* sugar, cotton, oilseed, textiles, cement, iron ore; *population* (1991) 16,317,700; *language* Hindi.

Hasdrubal Barca Carthaginian general, son of Hamilcar Barca and brother of Hannibal. He remained in command in Spain when Hannibal invaded Italy and, after fighting there against Scipio until 208, marched to Hannibal's relief. He was defeated and killed in the Metaurus valley, NE Italy.

hashish drug made from the resin contained in the female flowering tops of hemp (◊cannabis).

Hasid or *Hassid, Chasid* (plural *Hasidim, Hassidim, Chasidim*) member of a sect of Orthodox Jews, founded in 18th-century Poland, which stresses intense emotion as a part of worship. Many of their ideas are based on the ◊kabbala.

Hassan II 1929– . King of Morocco from 1961; from 1976 he undertook the occupation of Western Sahara when it was ceded by Spain.

Hastings resort in East Sussex, England; population (1981) 74,803. The chief of the ◊Cinque Ports, it has ruins of a Norman castle. It is adjoined by St Leonard's, developed in the 19th century.

Hastings, Battle of battle 14 Oct 1066 at which William the Conqueror, Duke of Normandy, defeated Harold, King of England. The site is 10 km/6 mi inland from Hastings, at Senlac, Sussex; it is marked by Battle Abbey.

Hathaway Anne 1556–1623. Englishwoman, daughter of a yeoman farmer, who married William ◊Shakespeare 1582. She was born at Shottery, near Stratford, where her cottage can still be seen.

Hathor in ancient Egyptian mythology, the sky goddess, identified with ◊Isis.

Haughey Charles 1925– . Irish Fianna Fáil politician of Ulster descent. Dismissed 1970 from Jack Lynch's cabinet for alleged complicity in IRA gunrunning, he was afterwards acquitted. He was prime minister 1979–81, March–Nov 1982, and 1986–92, when he was replaced by Albert Reynolds.

Haute-Normandie or *Upper Normandy* coastal region of NW France lying between Basse-Normandie and Picardy and bisected by the river Seine; area 12,300 sq km/4,757 sq mi; population (1986) 1,693,000. It comprises the *départements* of Eure and Seine-Maritime; its capital is Rouen. Major ports include Dieppe and Fécamp. The area has many beech forests.

Havana capital and port of Cuba; population (1989) 2,096,100. Products include cigars and tobacco.

Havel Vaclav 1936– . Czech playwright and

politician, president 1989–92. His plays include *The Garden Party* 1963 and *Largo Desolato* 1985, about a dissident intellectual. Havel became widely known as a human-rights activist. He was imprisoned 1979–83 and again 1989 for support of Charter 77 (see ◊Czechoslovakia).

Hawaii Pacific state of the USA; nickname Aloha State; *area* 16,800 sq km/6,485 sq mi; *capital* Honolulu on Oahu; *towns* Hilo; *physical* Hawaii consists of a chain of some 20 volcanic islands, of which the chief are (1) *Hawaii*, noted for Mauna Kea (4,201 m/13,788 ft), the world's highest island mountain (site of a UK infrared telescope) and Mauna Loa (4,170 m/13,686 ft), the world's largest active volcanic crater; (2) *Maui*, the second largest of the islands; (3) *Oahu*, the third largest, with the greatest concentration of population and tourist attractions – for example, Waikiki beach and the Pearl Harbor naval base; (4) *Kauai*; and (5) *Molokai*, site of a historic leper colony; *products* sugar, coffee, pineapples, flowers, women's clothing; *population* (1990) 1,108,200; 34% European, 25% Japanese, 14% Filipino, 12% Hawaiian, 6% Chinese; *language* English; *religion* Christianity; Buddhist minority; *famous people* Father Joseph Damien, Kamehameha I, Queen Liliuokalani, Sanford Dole; *history* a Polynesian kingdom from the 6th century until 1893; Hawaii became a republic 1894; ceded itself to the US 1898, and became a US territory 1900. Japan's air attack on Pearl Harbor 7 Dec 1941 crippled the US Pacific fleet and turned the territory into an armed camp, under martial law, for the remainder of the war. Hawaii became a state 1959. Tourism is the chief source of income.

hawfinch European finch *Coccothraustes coccothraustes* about 18 cm/7 in long. It feeds on berries and seeds, and can crack cherry stones with its large and powerful bill. It is rather uncommon and spends most of its time in the treetops.

hawk any of various small- to medium-sized birds of prey of the family Accipitridae, other than eagles, kites, ospreys, and vultures. The name is used especially to describe the genera *Accipiter* and *Buteo*. Hawks have short, rounded wings compared with falcons, and keen eyesight.

hawk person who believes in the use of military action rather than mediation as a means of solving a political dispute. The term first entered the political language of the USA during the 1960s, when it was applied metaphorically to those advocating continuation and escalation of the Vietnam War. Those with moderate, or even pacifist, views were known as ◊doves.

Hawke Bob (Robert) 1929– . Australian Labor politician, prime minister 1983–91, on the right wing of the party. He was president of the Australian Council of Trade Unions 1970–80. He announced his retirement from politics 1992.

Hawking Stephen 1942– . English physicist who has researched ◊black holes and gravitational field theory. His books include *A Brief History of Time* 1988, in which he argues that our universe is only one small part of a 'super-universe' that has existed for ever and that comprises an infinite number of universes like our own.

hawk moth family of moths (Sphingidae) with more than 1,000 species distributed throughout the world, but found mainly in tropical regions.

Hawksmoor Nicholas 1661–1736. English architect, assistant to Christopher ◊Wren in designing London churches and St Paul's Cathedral; joint architect with John ◊Vanbrugh of Castle Howard and Blenheim Palace. His genius is displayed in a quirky and uncompromising style incorporating elements from both Gothic and Classical sources.

Haworth village in W Yorkshire, home of the ◊Brontë family. It is now part of Keighley.

hawthorn shrub or tree of the genus *Crataegus* of the rose family Rosaceae. Species are most abundant in E North America, but there are also many in Eurasia. All have alternate, toothed leaves and bear clusters of showy white, pink, or red flowers. Small applelike fruits can be red, orange, blue, or black. Hawthorns are popular as ornamentals.

Hayden William (Bill) 1933– . Australian Labor politician. He was leader of the Australian Labor Party and of the opposition 1977–83, and minister of foreign affairs 1983. He became governor general 1989.

Haydn Franz Joseph 1732–1809. Austrian composer. A teacher of Mozart and Beethoven, he was a major exponent of the classical sonata form in his numerous chamber and orchestral works (he wrote more than 100 symphonies). He also composed choral music, including the oratorios *The Creation* 1798 and *The Seasons* 1801. He was the first great master of the string quartet.

hay fever allergic reaction to pollen, causing sneezing, inflammation of the eyes, and asthmatic symptoms. Sufferers experience irritation caused by powerful body chemicals related to histamine produced at the site of entry. Treatment is by antihistamine drugs.

hazel shrub or tree of the genus *Corylus*, family Corylaceae, including the European common hazel or cob *C. avellana*, of which the filbert is the cultivated variety. North American species include the American hazel *C. americana*.

H-bomb abbreviation for ◊*hydrogen bomb*.

HDTV abbreviation for *high-definition* ◊*television*.

Health and Safety Commission UK government organization responsible for securing the health, safety, and welfare of people at work, and for protecting the public against dangers to health and safety arising from work activities. It was established by the Health and Safety at Work Act 1974 and is responsible to the secretary of state for employment.

health, world the health of people worldwide is monitored by the ⟡World Health Organization (WHO). Outside the industrialized world, in particular, poverty and degraded environmental conditions mean that easily preventable diseases are widespread: WHO estimated 1990 that 1 billion people, or 20% of the world's population, were diseased, in poor health, or malnourished. In North Africa and the Middle East, 25% of the population were ill.

Heaney Seamus (Justin) 1939– . Irish poet, born in County Derry, who has written powerful verse about the political situation in Northern Ireland. Collections include *North* 1975, *Field Work* 1979, and *Station Island* 1984. In 1989, he was elected professor of poetry at Oxford University.

heart muscular organ that rhythmically contracts to force blood around the body of an animal with a circulatory system. Annelid worms and some other invertebrates have simple hearts consisting of thickened sections of main blood vessels that pulse regularly. An earthworm has ten such hearts. Vertebrates have one heart. A fish heart has two chambers – the thin-walled *atrium* (once called the auricle) that expands to receive blood, and the thick-walled *ventricle* that pumps it out. Amphibians and most reptiles have two atria and one ventricle; birds and mammals have two atria and two ventricles. The beating of the heart is controlled by the autonomic nervous system and an internal control centre or pacemaker, the sinoatrial node.

heart attack sudden onset of gripping central chest pain, often accompanied by sweating and vomiting, caused by death of a portion of the heart muscle following obstruction of a coronary artery by thrombosis (formation of a blood clot). Half of all heart attacks result in death within the first two hours, but in the remainder survival has improved following the widespread use of streptokinase and aspirin to treat heart-attack victims.

heart disease disorder affecting the heart; for example, ⟡ischaemic heart disease, in which the blood supply through the coronary arteries is reduced by ⟡atherosclerosis; ⟡valvular heart disease, in which a heart valve is damaged; and cardiomyophathy, where the heart muscle itself is diseased.

heat form of internal energy possessed by a substance by virtue of the kinetic energy in the motion of its molecules or atoms. It is measured by ⟡temperature. Heat energy is transferred by conduction, convection, and radiation. It always flows from a region of higher temperature (heat intensity) to one of lower temperature. Its effect on a substance may be simply to raise its temperature, or to cause it to expand, melt (if a solid), vaporize (if a liquid), or increase its pressure (if a confined gas).

heat capacity in physics, the quantity of heat required to raise the temperature of a substance by one degree. The *specific heat capacity* of a substance is the heat capacity per unit of mass, measured in joules per kilogram per kelvin (J kg⁻¹ K⁻¹).

Heath Edward (Richard George) 1916– . British Conservative politician, party leader 1965–75. As prime minister 1970–74 he took the UK into the European Community but was brought down by economic and industrial relations crises at home. He was replaced as party leader by Margaret Thatcher 1975, and became increasingly critical of her policies and her opposition to the UK's full participation in the EC. In 1990 he undertook a mission to Iraq in an attempt to secure the release of British hostages.

heather low-growing evergreen shrub of the heath family, common on sandy or acid soil. The common heather *Calluna vulgaris* is a carpet-forming shrub, growing up to 60 cm/24 in high and bearing pale pink-purple flowers. It is found over much of Europe and has been introduced to North America.

heatstroke or *sunstroke* rise in body temperature caused by excessive exposure to heat. Mild heatstroke is experienced as feverish lassitude, sometimes with simple fainting; recovery is prompt following rest and replenishment of salt lost in sweat. Severe heatstroke causes collapse akin to that seen in acute ⟡shock, and is potentially lethal without prompt treatment of cooling the body carefully and giving fluids to relieve dehydration.

heat treatment in industry, the subjection of metals and alloys to controlled heating and cooling after fabrication to relieve internal stresses and improve their physical properties. Methods include ⟡annealing, quenching, and ⟡tempering.

heaven in Christianity and some other religions, the abode of God and the destination of the virtuous after death. Theologians now usually describe it as a place or state in which the soul experiences the full reality of God.

heavy metal in music, a style of rock characterized by loudness and insensitivity, with extended guitar solos. Heavy metal developed out of the hard rock of the late 1960s and early 1970s, was performed by such groups as Led Zeppelin (1969–80) and Deep Purple (1968–76), and enjoyed a resurgence in the late 1980s. Bands include Van Halen (formed 1974), Def Leppard (formed 1977), and Guns n' Roses (formed 1987).

heavy water or *deuterium oxide* D₂O water containing the isotope deuterium instead of hydrogen (relative molecular mass 20 as opposed to 18 for ordinary water).

Hebe in Greek mythology, the goddess of youth, daughter of Zeus and Hera.

Hebei or *Hopei* or *Hupei* province of N China; *area* 202,700 sq km/78,242 sq mi; *capital* Shijiazhuang; *features* includes special municipalities of Beijing and Tianjin; *products* cereals, textiles, iron, steel; *population* (1990) 61,082,000.

heart

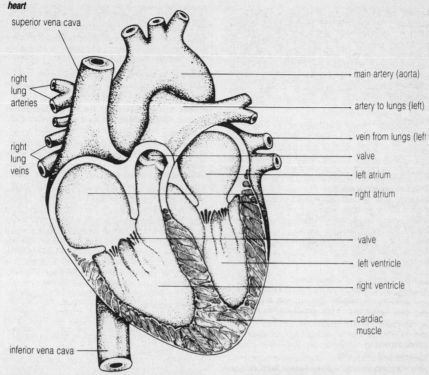

superior vena cava

right lung arteries

right lung veins

inferior vena cava

main artery (aorta)

artery to lungs (left)

vein from lungs (left)

valve

left atrium

right atrium

valve

left ventricle

right ventricle

cardiac muscle

Hebrew member of the Semitic people who lived in Palestine at the time of the Old Testament and who traced their ancestry to ▷Abraham of Ur, a city of Sumer.

Hebrew Bible the sacred writings of Judaism (some dating from as early as 1200 BC), called by Christians the ▷Old Testament. It includes the Torah (the first five books, ascribed to Moses), historical and prophetic books, and psalms, originally written in Hebrew and later translated into Greek and other languages.

Hebrides group of more than 500 islands (fewer than 100 inhabited) off W Scotland; total area 2,900 sq km/1,120 sq mi. The Hebrides were settled by Scandinavians during the 6th to 9th centuries and passed under Norwegian rule from about 890 to 1266.

Hecate in Greek mythology, the goddess of witchcraft and magic, sometimes identified with ▷Artemis and the Moon.

hectare metric unit of area equal to 100 ares or 10,000 square metres (2.47 acres), symbol ha.

Hector in Greek mythology, a Trojan prince, son of King Priam and husband of Andromache, who, in

the siege of Troy, was the foremost warrior on the Trojan side until he was killed by ▷Achilles.

Hecuba in Greek mythology, the wife of King Priam, and mother of Hector and ▷Paris. She was captured by the Greeks after the fall of Troy.

hedgehog insectivorous mammal of the genus *Erinaceus*, native to Europe, Asia, and Africa. The body, including the tail, is 30 cm/1 ft long. It is greyish-brown in colour, has a piglike snout, and is covered with sharp spines. When alarmed it can roll itself into a ball. Hedgehogs feed on insects, slugs and carrion. Long-eared hedgehogs and desert hedgehogs are placed in different genera.

hedge sparrow another name for ▷*dunnock*, a small bird.

hedonism ethical theory that pleasure or happiness is, or should be, the main goal in life. Hedonist sects in ancient Greece were the ▷Cyrenaics, who held that the pleasure of the moment is the only human good, and the ▷Epicureans, who advocated the pursuit of pleasure under the direction of reason. Modern hedonistic philosophies, such as those of the British philosophers Jeremy Bentham and J S Mill, regard the happiness of society, rather than that of the individual, as the aim.

Hegel Georg Wilhelm Friedrich 1770–1831. German philosopher who conceived of consciousness and the external object as forming a unity in which neither factor can exist independently, mind and nature being two abstractions of one indivisible whole. He believed development took place through dialectic: thesis and antithesis (contradiction) and synthesis, the resolution of contradiction. He wrote *The Phenomenology of Spirit* 1807, *Encyclopaedia of the Philosophical Sciences* 1817, and *Philosophy of Right* 1821.

hegemony political dominance of one power over others in a group in which all are supposedly equal. The term was first used for the dominance of Athens over the other Greek city states, later applied to Prussia within Germany, and, in more recent times, to the USA and the USSR with regard to the rest of the world.

Heidegger Martin 1889–1976. German philosopher. In *Sein und Zeit/Being and Time* 1927 (translated 1962) he used the methods of Edmund ▷Husserl's phenomenology to explore the structures of human existence. His later writings meditated on the fate of a world dominated by science and technology.

Heilongjiang or *Heilungkiang* province of NE China, in ▷Manchuria; *area* 463,600 sq km/ 178,950 sq mi; *capital* Harbin; *features* China's largest oilfield, near Anda; *products* cereals, gold, coal, copper, zinc, lead, cobalt; *population* (1990) 35,215,000.

Heilungkiang former name of ▷Heilongjiang, a province of NE China.

Heine Heinrich 1797–1856. German Romantic poet and journalist who wrote *Reisebilder* 1826 and *Buch der Lieder/Book of Songs* 1827. From 1831 he lived mainly in Paris, working as a correspondent for German newspapers. Schubert and Schumann set many of his lyrics to music.

Heisenberg Werner Carl 1901–1976. German physicist who developed ▷quantum theory and formulated the ▷uncertainty principle, which concerns matter, radiation, and their reactions, and places absolute limits on the achievable accuracy of measurement. Nobel prize 1932.

Hejaz former independent kingdom, merged 1932 with Nejd to form ▷Saudi Arabia; population (1970) 2,000,000; the capital is Mecca.

Hel or *Hela* in Norse mythology, the goddess of the underworld.

Helen in Greek mythology, the daughter of Zeus and Leda, and the most beautiful of women. She married Menelaus, King of Sparta, but during his absence, was abducted by Paris, Prince of Troy. This precipitated the Trojan War. Afterwards she returned to Sparta with her husband.

Helicon mountain in central Greece, on which was situated a spring and a sanctuary sacred to the ▷Muses.

helicopter powered aircraft that achieves both lift and propulsion by means of a rotary wing, or rotor, on top of the fuselage. It can take off and land vertically, move in any direction, or remain stationary in the air. It can be powered by piston or jet engine. The ▷autogiro was a precursor.

Heliopolis ancient Egyptian centre (the biblical *On*) of the worship of the sun god Ra, NE of Cairo and near the village of Matariah.

Helios in Greek mythology, the sun god, thought to make his daily journey across the sky in a chariot.

heliotrope decorative plant of the genus *Heliotropium* of the borage family Boraginaceae, with distinctive spikes of blue, lilac, or white flowers, including the Peruvian or cherry pie heliotrope *H. peruvianum*.

helium (Greek *helios* 'Sun') colourless, odourless, gaseous, nonmetallic element, symbol He, atomic number 2, relative atomic mass 4.0026. It is grouped with the ▷inert gases, is nonreactive, and forms no compounds. It is the second most abundant element (after hydrogen) in the universe, and has the lowest boiling ($-268.9°C/-452°F$) and melting points ($-272.2°C/-458°F$) of all the elements. It is present in small quantities in the Earth's atmosphere from gases issuing from radioactive elements in the Earth's crust; after hydrogen it is the second lightest element.

hell in various religions, a place of posthumous punishment. In Hinduism, Buddhism, and Jainism, hell is a transitory stage in the progress of the soul, but in Christianity and Islam it is eternal (purgatory is transitory). Judaism does not postulate such punishment.

hellebore poisonous European herbaceous plant of the genus *Helleborus* of the buttercup family Ranunculaceae. The stinking hellebore *H. foetidus* has greenish flowers early in the spring. The Christmas rose *H. niger* has white flowers from Dec onwards.

helleborine temperate Old World orchid of the genera *Epipactis* and *Cephalanthera*, including the marsh helleborine *E. palustris* and the hellebore orchid *E. helleborine* introduced to North America.

Hellenic period (from *Hellas*, Greek name for Greece) classical period of ancient Greek civilization, from the first Olympic Games 776 BC until the death of Alexander the Great 323 BC.

Hellenistic period period in Greek civilization from the death of Alexander 323 BC until the accession of the Roman emperor Augustus 27 BC. Alexandria in Egypt was the centre of culture and commerce during this period, and Greek culture spread throughout the Mediterranean region.

Hellespont former name of the ▷Dardanelles, the strait that separates Europe from Asia.

Helmholtz Hermann Ludwig Ferdinand von 1821–1894. German physiologist, physicist, and inventor of the ophthalmoscope for examining the inside of the eye. He was the first to explain how the cochlea of the inner ear works, and the first to measure the speed of nerve impulses. In physics he formulated the law of conservation of energy, and worked in thermodynamics.

Héloïse 1101–1164. Abbess of Paraclete in Champagne, France, correspondent and lover of ▷Abelard. She became deeply interested in intellectual study in her youth and was impressed by the brilliance of Abelard, her teacher, whom she secretly married. After her affair with Abelard, and the birth of a son, Astrolabe, she became a nun 1129, and with Abelard's assistance, founded a nunnery at Paraclete. Her letters show her strong and pious character and her devotion to Abelard.

Helsinki (Swedish **Helsingfors**) capital and port of Finland; population (1990) 492,400, metropolitan area 978,000. Industries include shipbuilding, engineering, and textiles. The homes of the architect Eliel Saarinen and the composer Jean Sibelius outside the town are museums.

Helsinki Conference international meeting 1975 at which 35 countries, including the USSR and the USA established the ▷Conference on Security and Cooperation in Europe (CSCE).

hematite principal ore of iron, consisting mainly of iron(III) oxide, Fe_2O_3. It occurs as **specular hematite** (dark, metallic lustre), **kidney ore** (reddish radiating fibres terminating in smooth, rounded surfaces), and as a red earthy deposit.

Hemingway Ernest 1898–1961. US writer. War, bullfighting, and fishing are used symbolically in his work to represent honour, dignity, and primitivism – prominent themes in his short stories and novels, which include *A Farewell to Arms* 1929, *For Whom the Bell Tolls* 1940, and *The Old Man and the Sea* 1952. His deceptively simple writing style attracted many imitators. Nobel prize 1954.

hemlock plant *Conium maculatum* of the carrot family Umbelliferae, native to Europe, W Asia, and N Africa. Reaching up to 2 m/6 ft high, it bears umbels of small white flowers. The whole plant, especially the root and fruit, is poisonous, causing paralysis of the nervous system. The name hemlock is also applied to members of the genus *Tsuga* of North American and Asiatic conifers of the pine family.

hemp annual plant *Cannabis sativa*, family Cannabaceae. Originally from Asia, it is cultivated in most temperate countries for its fibres, produced in the outer layer of the stem, and used in ropes, twines, and, occasionally, in a type of linen or lace. ▷Cannabis is obtained from certain varieties of hemp.

Henan or **Honan** province of E central China; **area** 167,000 sq km/64,462 sq mi; **capital** Zhengzhou; **features** river plains of the Huang He (Yellow River); the ruins of Xibo, the 16th-century BC capital

of the Shang dynasty; **products** cereals, cotton; **population** (1990) 85,510,000.

henbane poisonous plant *Hyoscyamus niger* of the nightshade family Solanaceae, found on waste ground throughout most of Europe and W Asia. A branching plant, up to 80 cm/31 in high, it has hairy leaves and a nauseous smell. The yellow flowers are bell-shaped. Henbane is used in medicine as a source of hyoscyamine and scopolamine.

Hendrix Jimi (James Marshall) 1942–1970. US rock guitarist, songwriter, and singer, legendary for his virtuoso experimental technique and flamboyance. *Are You Experienced?* 1967 was his first album. He greatly expanded the vocabulary of the electric guitar and influenced both rock and jazz musicians.

Hendry Stephen 1970– . Scottish snooker player. He replaced Steve Davis as the top-ranking player during the 1989–90 season as well as becoming the youngest ever world champion.

Hengist 5th century AD. Legendary leader, with his brother Horsa, of the Jutes, who originated in Jutland and settled in Kent about 450, the first Anglo-Saxon settlers in Britain.

henna small shrub *Lawsonia inermis* of the loosestrife family Lythraceae, found in Iran, India, Egypt, and N Africa. The leaves and young twigs are ground to a powder, mixed to a paste with hot water, and applied to fingernails and hair, giving an orange-red hue. The colour may then be changed to black by applying a preparation of indigo.

Henrietta Maria 1609–1669. Queen of England 1625–49. The daughter of Henry IV of France, she married Charles I of England 1625. By encouraging him to aid Roman Catholics and make himself an absolute ruler, she became highly unpopular and was exiled during the period 1644–60. She returned to England at the Restoration but retired to France 1665.

Henry (Charles Albert David) known as **Harry** 1984– . Prince of the UK; second child of the Prince and Princess of Wales.

Henry Joseph 1797–1878. US physicist, inventor of the electromagnetic motor 1829 and of a telegraphic apparatus. He also discovered the principle of electromagnetic induction, roughly at the same time as Michael ▷Faraday, and the phenomenon of self-induction. A unit of inductance (henry) is named after him.

henry SI unit (symbol H) of ▷inductance (the reaction of an electric current against the magnetic field that surrounds it). One henry is the inductance of a circuit that produces an opposing voltage of one volt when the current changes at one ampere per second.

Henry I 1068–1135. King of England from 1100. Youngest son of William I, he succeeded his brother William II. He won the support of the Saxons by granting them a charter and marrying a Saxon princess. An able administrator, he established a professional bureaucracy and a system of travelling judges. He was succeeded by Stephen.

Henry II 1133–1189. King of England from 1154, when he succeeded ⟡Stephen. He was the son of ⟡Matilda and Geoffrey of Anjou (1113–1151). He curbed the power of the barons, but his attempt to bring the church courts under control had to be abandoned after the murder of Thomas à ⟡Becket. During his reign the English conquest of Ireland began. He was succeeded by his son Richard I.

Henry III 1207–1272. King of England from 1216, when he succeeded John, but he did not rule until 1227. His financial commitments to the papacy and his foreign favourites led to de ⟡Montfort's revolt 1264. Henry was defeated at Lewes, Sussex, and imprisoned. He was restored to the throne after the royalist victory at Evesham 1265. He was succeeded by his son Edward I.

Henry IV (Bolingbroke) 1367–1413. King of England from 1399, the son of ⟡John of Gaunt. In 1398 he was banished by ⟡Richard II for political activity but returned 1399 to head a revolt and be accepted as king by Parliament. He was succeeded by his son Henry V.

Henry VII 1457–1509. King of England from 1485, son of Edmund Tudor, Earl of Richmond (c. 1430–1456), and a descendant of ⟡John of Gaunt. He spent his early life in Brittany until 1485, when he landed in Britain to lead the rebellion against Richard III which ended with Richard's defeat and death at ⟡Bosworth. By his marriage to Elizabeth of York 1486 he united the houses of York and Lancaster. Yorkist revolts continued until 1497, but Henry restored order after the Wars of the ⟡Roses by the ⟡Star Chamber and achieved independence from Parliament by amassing a private fortune through confiscations. He was succeeded by his son Henry VIII.

Henry VIII 1491–1547. King of England from 1509, when he succeeded his father Henry VII and married Catherine of Aragon, the widow of his brother. During the period 1513–29 Henry pursued an active foreign policy, largely under the guidance of his Lord Chancellor, Cardinal Wolsey, who was replaced by Thomas More 1529 for failing to persuade the pope to grant Henry a divorce. After 1532 Henry broke with papal authority, proclaimed himself head of the church in England, dissolved the monasteries, and divorced Catherine. His subsequent wives were Anne Boleyn, Jane Seymour, Anne of Cleves, Catherine Howard, and Catherine Parr. He was succeeded by his son Edward VI.

Henry III 1551–1589. King of France from 1574. He fought both the ⟡Huguenots (headed by his successor, Henry of Navarre) and the Catholic League (headed by the Duke of Guise). Guise expelled Henry from Paris 1588 but was assassinated. Henry allied with the Huguenots under Henry of Navarre to besiege the city, but was assassinated by a monk.

Henry IV 1553–1610. King of France from 1589. Son of Antoine de Bourbon and Jeanne, Queen of Navarre, he was brought up as a Protestant and from 1576 led the ⟡Huguenots. On his accession he settled the religious question by adopting Catholicism while tolerating Protestantism. He restored peace and strong government to France and brought back prosperity by measures for the promotion of industry and agriculture and the improvement of communications. He was assassinated by a Catholic extremist.

Henry III *the Black* 1017–1056. King of Germany from 1028, Holy Roman emperor from 1039. He raised the empire to the height of its power, and extended its authority over Poland, Bohemia, and Hungary.

Henry IV 1050–1106. Holy Roman emperor from 1056, who was involved from 1075 in a struggle with the papacy (see ⟡Gregory VII). Excommunicated twice (1076 and 1080), Henry deposed Gregory and set up the antipope Clement III (died 1191) by whom he was crowned Holy Roman emperor 1084.

Henry VI 1165–1197. Holy Roman emperor from 1190. As part of his plan for making the empire universal, he captured and imprisoned Richard I of England and compelled him to do homage.

Henry the Navigator 1394–1460. Portuguese prince, the fourth son of John I. He set up a school for navigators 1419 and under his patronage Portuguese sailors explored and colonized Madeira, the Cape Verde Islands, and the Azores; they sailed down the African coast almost to Sierra Leone.

hepatitis any inflammatory disease of the liver, usually caused by a virus. Other causes include alcohol, drugs, gallstones, ⟡lupus erythematosus and amoebic dysentery. Symptoms include weakness, nausea, and jaundice.

Hephaestus in Greek mythology, the god of fire and metalcraft (Roman Vulcan), son of Zeus and Hera, husband of Aphrodite. He was lame.

Hepworth Barbara 1903–1975. English sculptor. She developed a distinctive abstract style, creating hollowed forms of stone or wood with spaces bridged by wires or strings; many later works are in bronze.

Hera in Greek mythology, a goddess (Roman Juno), sister-consort of Zeus, mother of Hephaestus, Hebe, and Ares; protector of women and marriage.

Heracles in Greek mythology, a hero (Roman Hercules), son of Zeus and Alcmene, famed for strength. While serving Eurystheus, King of Argos, he performed 12 labours, including the cleansing of the Augean stables.

Heraklion alternative name for ⟡*Iráklion.*

herbalism prescription and use of plants and their derivatives for medication. Herbal products are favoured by alternative practitioners as 'natural medicine', as opposed to modern synthesized medicines and drugs, which are regarded with suspicion because of the dangers of side-effects and dependence.

Herbert George 1593–1633. English poet. His volume of religious poems, *The Temple*, appeared in 1633, shortly before his death. His poems depict his intense religious feelings in clear, simple language.

herbivore animal that feeds on green plants (or photosynthetic single-celled organisms) or their products, including seeds, fruit, and nectar. The most numerous type of herbivore is thought to be the zooplankton, tiny invertebrates in the surface waters of the oceans that feed on small photosynthetic algae. Herbivores are more numerous than other animals because their food is the most abundant. They form a vital link in the food chain between plants and carnivores.

Herculaneum ancient city of Italy between Naples and Pompeii. Along with Pompeii, it was buried when Vesuvius erupted AD 79. It was excavated from the 18th century onwards.

Hercules Roman form of ⏽Heracles.

Hereford and Worcester county in W central England; *area* 3,930 sq km/1,517 sq mi; *towns* Worcester (administrative headquarters), Hereford, Kidderminster, Evesham, Ross-on-Wye, Ledbury; *features* rivers: Wye, Severn; Malvern Hills (high point Worcester Beacon, 425 m/1,395 ft) and Black Mountains; fertile Vale of Evesham; *products* mainly agricultural: apples, pears, cider; hops, vegetables, Hereford cattle; carpets; porcelain; some chemicals and engineering; Droitwich, once a Victorian spa, reopened its baths 1985; *population* (1991) 667,800; *famous people* Edward Elgar, A E Housman, William Langland, John Masefield.

Hereward the Wake 11th century. English leader of a revolt against the Normans 1070. His stronghold in the Isle of Ely was captured by William the Conqueror 1071. Hereward escaped, but his fate is unknown.

hermaphrodite organism that has both male and female sex organs. Hermaphroditism is the norm in species such as earthworms and snails, and is common in flowering plants. Cross-fertilization is the rule among hermaphrodites, with the parents functioning as male and female simultaneously, or as one or the other sex at different stages in their development. *Pseudo-hermaphrodites* have the internal sex organs of one sex, but the external appearance of the other. The true sex of the latter becomes apparent at adolescence when the normal hormone activity appropriate to the internal organs begins to function.

Hermes in Greek mythology, a god, son of Zeus and Maia; messenger of the gods; he wore winged sandals, a wide-brimmed hat, and carried a staff around which serpents coiled. Identified with the Roman Mercury and ancient Egyptian Thoth, he protects thieves, travellers, and merchants.

hernia or *rupture* protrusion of part of an internal organ through a weakness in the surrounding muscular wall, usually in the groin or navel. The appearance is that of a rounded soft lump or swelling.

Hero and Leander in Greek mythology, a pair of lovers. Hero was a priestess of Aphrodite at Sestos on the Hellespont, in love with Leander on the opposite shore at Abydos. When he was drowned while swimming across during a storm, she threw herself into the sea.

Herod the Great 74–4 BC. King of the Roman province of Judaea, S Palestine, from 40 BC. With the aid of Mark Antony, he established his government in Jerusalem 37 BC. He rebuilt the Temple in Jerusalem, but his Hellenizing tendencies made him suspect to orthodox Jewry. His last years were a reign of terror, and in the New Testament Matthew alleges that he ordered the slaughter of all the infants in Bethlehem to ensure the death of Jesus, whom he foresaw as a rival. He was the father of Herod Antipas.

Herod Antipas 21 BC–AD 39. Tetrarch (governor) of the Roman province of Galilee, N Palestine, 4 BC–AD 9, son of Herod the Great. He divorced his wife to marry his niece Herodias, who persuaded her daughter Salome to ask for John the Baptist's head when he reproved Herod's action. Jesus was brought before him on Pontius Pilate's discovery that he was a Galilean and hence of Herod's jurisdiction, but Herod returned him without giving any verdict. In AD 38 Herod Antipas went to Rome to try to persuade Emperor Caligula to give him the title of king, but was instead banished.

Herodotus *c.* 484–424 BC. Greek historian. After four years in Athens, he travelled widely in Egypt, Asia, and eastern Europe, before settling at Thurii in S Italy 443 BC. He wrote a nine-book history of the Greek-Persian struggle that culminated in the defeat of the Persian invasion attempts 490 and 480 BC. Herodotus was the first historian to apply critical evaluation to his material.

heron large to medium-sized wading bird of the family Ardeidae, which also includes bitterns, egrets, night herons, and boatbills. Herons have sharp bills, broad wings, long legs, and soft plumage. They are found mostly in tropical and subtropical regions, but also in temperate zones.

herpes any of several infectious diseases caused by viruses of the herpes group. *Herpes simplex I* is the causative agent of a common inflammation, the cold sore. *Herpes simplex II* is responsible for genital herpes, a highly contagious, sexually transmitted disease characterized by painful blisters in the genital area. It can be transmitted in the birth canal from mother to newborn. *Herpes zoster* causes ⏽shingles; another herpes virus causes chickenpox.

Herrick Robert 1591–1674. English poet and

cleric, born in Cheapside, London. He published *Hesperides* 1648, a collection of sacred and pastoral poetry admired for its lyric quality, including 'Gather ye rosebuds' and 'Cherry ripe'.

herring any of various marine fishes of the herring family (Clupeidae), but especially the important food fish *Clupea harengus*. A silvered greenish-blue, it swims close to the surface, and may be 25–40 cm/10–16 in long. Herring travel in schools several miles long and wide. They are found in large quantities off the E coast of North America, and the shores of NE Europe. Overfishing and pollution have reduced their numbers.

Herschel William 1738–1822. German-born English astronomer. He was a skilled telescope maker, and pioneered the study of binary stars and nebulae. He discovered the planet Uranus 1781 and infrared solar rays 1801. He catalogued over 800 double stars, and found over 2,500 nebulae, catalogued by his sister Caroline Herschel; this work was continued by his son John Herschel. By studying the distribution of stars, William established the basic form of our Galaxy, the Milky Way.

Hertfordshire county in SE England; *area* 1,630 sq km/629 sq mi; *cities* Hertford (administrative headquarters), St Albans, Watford, Hatfield, Hemel Hempstead, Bishop's Stortford, Letchworth; *features* rivers: Lea, Stort, Colne; part of the Chiltern Hills; Hatfield House; Knebworth House (home of Lord Lytton); Brocket Hall (home of Palmerston and Melbourne); home of G B ♢Shaw at Ayot St Lawrence; Berkhamsted Castle (Norman); Rothamsted agricultural experimental station; *products* engineering, aircraft, electrical goods, paper and printing; general agricultural goods; *population* (1991) 951,500; *famous people* Graham Greene.

Herzegovina or *Hercegovina* part of ♢Bosnia-Herzegovina (which was formerly, until 1991, a republic of Yugoslavia).

Hess (Walter Richard) Rudolf 1894–1987. German Nazi leader. Imprisoned with Hitler 1923–25, he became his private secretary, taking down *Mein Kampf* from his dictation. In 1932 he was appointed deputy *Führer* to Hitler. On 10 May 1941 he landed by air in the UK with compromise peace proposals and was held as a prisoner of war until 1945, when he was tried at Nuremberg as a war criminal and sentenced to life imprisonment. He died in Spandau prison, Berlin.

Hesse Hermann 1877–1962. German writer who became a Swiss citizen 1923. A conscientious objector in World War I and a pacifist opponent of Hitler, he published short stories, poetry, and novels, including *Peter Camenzind* 1904, *Siddhartha* 1922, and *Steppenwolf* 1927. Later works, such as *Das Glasperlenspiel/The Glass Bead Game* 1943, tend towards the mystical. Nobel prize 1946.

Hessen administrative region (German *Land*) of Germany; *area* 21,100 sq km/8,145 sq mi; *capital* Wiesbaden; *towns* Frankfurt-am-Main, Kassel, Darmstadt, Offenbach-am-Main; *features* valleys of the rivers Rhine and Main; Taunus mountains, rich in mineral springs, as at Homburg and Wiesbaden; see also ♢Swabia; *products* wine, timber, chemicals, cars, electrical engineering, optical instruments; *population* (1988) 5,550,000; *religion* Protestant 61%, Roman Catholic 33%.

hexadecimal number system number system to the base 16, used in computing. In hex (as it is commonly known) the decimal numbers 0–15 are represented by the characters 0, 1, 2, 3, 4, 5, 6, 7, 8, 9, A, B, C, D, E, F. Hexadecimal numbers are easy to convert to the computer's internal ♢binary code and are more compact than binary numbers.

Heyerdahl Thor 1914– . Norwegian ethnologist. He sailed on the ancient-Peruvian-style raft *Kon-Tiki* from Peru to the Tuamotu Archipelago along the Humboldt Current 1947, and in 1969–70 used ancient-Egyptian-style papyrus reed boats to cross the Atlantic. His experimental approach to historical reconstruction is not regarded as having made any important scientific contribution.

Hezbollah or *Hizbollah* (Party of God) extremist Muslim organization founded by the Iranian Revolutionary Guards who were sent to Lebanon after the 1979 Iranian revolution. Its aim is to spread the Islamic revolution of Iran among the Shi'ite population of Lebanon. Hezbollah is believed to be the umbrella movement of the groups that held many of the Western hostages taken since 1984.

Hiawatha 16th-century North American Indian teacher and Onondaga chieftain. He is said to have welded the Five Nations (later joined by a sixth) of the Iroquois into the league of the **Long House**, as the confederacy was known in what is now upper New York State. Hiawatha is the hero of Longfellow's epic poem *The Song of Hiawatha*.

hibiscus any plant of the genus *Hibiscus* of the mallow family. Hibiscuses range from large herbaceous plants to trees. Popular as ornamental plants because of their brilliantly coloured, red to white, bell-shaped flowers, they include *H. syriacus* and *H. rosa-sinensis* of Asia and the rose mallow *H. palustris* of North America.

Hick Graeme 1966– . Rhodesian-born cricketer who became Zimbabwe's youngest professional cricketer at the age of 17. A prolific batsman, he joined Worcestershire, England, in 1984. He achieved the highest score in England in the 20th century in 1988 against Somerset with 405 not out. He made his test debut for England in 1991 after a seven-year qualification period.

hickory tree of the genus *Carya* of the walnut family, native to North America and Asia. It provides a valuable timber, and all species produce nuts, although some are inedible. The pecan *C. illinoensis* is widely cultivated in the southern USA, and the shagbark *C. ovata* in the northern USA.

hieroglyphic Egyptian writing system of the mid-4th millennium BC–3rd century AD, which combines picture signs with those indicating letters. The direction of writing is normally from right to left, the signs facing the beginning of the line. It was deciphered 1822 by the French Egyptologist JYF Champollion (1790–1832) with the aid of the ▷*Rosetta Stone*, which has the same inscription carved in hieroglyphic, demotic, and Greek.

high jump field event in athletics where competitors leap over a horizontal crossbar held between rigid uprights at least 3.66 m/12 ft apart. The bar is placed at increasingly higher levels. Elimination occurs after three consecutive failures to clear the bar.

Highland Clearances forced removal of tenants from large estates in Scotland during the early 19th century, as landowners 'improved' their estates by switching from arable to sheep farming. It led ultimately to widespread emigration to North America.

Highland Region administrative region of Scotland; *area* 26,100 sq km/10,077 sq mi; *towns* Inverness (administrative headquarters), Thurso, Wick; *features* comprises almost half the country; Grampian Mountains; Ben Nevis (highest peak in the UK); Loch Ness, Caledonian Canal; Inner Hebrides; the Queen Mother's castle of Mey at Caithness; John O'Groats' House; Dounreay (with Atomic Energy Authority's prototype fast reactor and a nuclear processing plant); *products* oil services, winter sports, timber, livestock, grouse and deer hunting, salmon fishing; *population* (1991) 209,400; *famous people* Alexander Mackenzie, William Smith.

Highlands one of the three geographical divisions of Scotland, lying to the north of a geological fault line that stretches from Stonehaven in the North Sea to Dumbarton on the Clyde. It is a mountainous region of hard rocks, shallow infertile soils, and high rainfall.

hijacking illegal seizure or taking control of a vehicle and/or its passengers or goods. The term dates from 1923 and originally referred to the robbing of freight lorries. In recent times it (and its derivative, 'skyjacking') has been applied to the seizure of aircraft, usually in flight, by an individual or group, often with some political aim. International treaties (Tokyo 1963, The Hague 1970, and Montreal 1971) encourage international cooperation against hijackers and make severe penalties compulsory.

Hill David Octavius 1802–1870. Scottish photographer who, in collaboration with Robert ▷Adamson, made extensive use of the ▷calotype process in their large collection of portraits taken in Edinburgh 1843–48.

Hillary Edmund Percival 1919– . New Zealand mountaineer. In 1953, with Nepalese Sherpa mountaineer Tenzing Norgay, he reached the summit of Mount Everest, the first to climb the world's highest peak. As a member of the Commonwealth Transantarctic Expedition 1957–58, he was the first person since Scott to reach the South Pole overland, on 3 Jan 1958.

Hilliard Nicholas *c.* 1547–1619. English miniaturist and goldsmith, court artist to Elizabeth I from about 1579. His sitters included the explorers Francis Drake and Walter Raleigh.

Hillsborough Agreement another name for the ▷Anglo-Irish Agreement 1985.

Himachal Pradesh state of NW India; *area* 55,700 sq km/21,500 sq mi; *capital* Simla; *features* mainly agricultural state, one-third forested, with softwood timber industry; *products* timber, grain, rice, fruit; *population* (1991) 5,111,000; mainly Hindu; *language* Pahari; *history* created as a Union Territory 1948, it became a full state 1971.

Himalayas vast mountain system of central Asia, extending from the Indian states of Kashmir in the west to Assam in the east, covering the southern part of Tibet, Nepal, Sikkim, and Bhutan. It is the highest mountain range in the world. The two highest peaks are *Mount* ▷*Everest* and ▷*Kangchenjunga*. Other peaks over 8,000 m/26,000 ft include Makalu, Annapurna, and Nanga Parbat.

Himmler Heinrich 1900–1945. German Nazi leader, head of the ▷SS elite corps from 1929, the police and the ▷Gestapo secret police from 1936, and supervisor of the extermination of the Jews in E Europe. During World War II he replaced Goering as Hitler's second-in-command. He was captured May 1945 and committed suicide.

Hindenburg Paul Ludwig Hans von Beneckendorf und Hindenburg 1847–1934. German field marshal and right-wing politician. During World War I he was supreme commander and, with Ludendorff, practically directed Germany's policy until the end of the war. He was president of Germany 1925–33.

Hindi language member of the Indo-Iranian branch of the Indo-European language family, the official language of the Republic of India, although resisted as such by the Dravidian-speaking states of the south. Hindi proper is used by some 30% of Indians, in such northern states as Uttar Pradesh and Madhya Pradesh.

Hinduism religion originating in N India about 4,000 years ago, which is superficially and in some of its forms polytheistic, but has a concept of the supreme spirit, ▷Brahman, above the many divine manifestations. These include the triad of chief gods (the Trimurti): Brahma, Vishnu, and Siva (creator, preserver, and destroyer). Central to Hinduism are the beliefs in reincarnation and ▷karma; the oldest scriptures are the *Vedas*. Temple worship is almost universally observed and there are many festivals. There are over 805 million Hindus worldwide.

Hindu Kush mountain range in central Asia,

length 800 km/500 mi, greatest height Tirich Mir, 7,690 m/25,239 ft, in Pakistan. The narrow *Khyber Pass* (53 km/33 mi long) separates Pakistan from Afghanistan and was used by ◊Zahir and other invaders of India.

Hindustan ('land of the Hindus') the whole of India, but more specifically the plain of the Ganges and Jumna rivers, or that part of India north of the Deccan.

Hindustani member of the Indo-Iranian branch of the Indo-European language family, closely related to Hindi and Urdu and originating in the bazaars of Delhi. It is a ◊lingua franca in many parts of the Republic of India.

hip-hop popular music originating in New York in the early 1980s. It uses scratching (a percussive effect obtained by manually rotating a vinyl record) and heavily accented electronic drums behind a ◊rap vocal. The term 'hip-hop' also comprises break dancing and graffiti.

Hippocrates *c*. 460–*c*. 370 BC. Greek physician, often called the father of medicine. Important Hippocratic ideas include cleanliness (for patients and physicians), moderation in eating and drinking, letting nature take its course, and living where the air is good. He believed that health was the result of the 'humours' of the body being in balance; imbalance caused disease. These ideas were later adopted by ◊Galen.

Hippolytus in Greek mythology, the son of Theseus. When he rejected the love of his stepmother, Phaedra, she falsely accused him of making advances to her and turned Theseus against him. Killed by Poseidon at Theseus' request, he was restored to life when his innocence was proven.

hippopotamus large herbivorous, even-toed hoofed mammal of the family Hippopotamidae. The common hippopotamus *Hippopotamus amphibius* is found in Africa. It averages over 4 m/13 ft long, 1.5 m/5 ft high, weighs about 4,500 kg/5 tons, and has a brown or slate-grey skin. It is an endangered species.

Hirohito 1901–1989. Emperor of Japan from 1926; era name *Shōwa*. He succeeded his father Yoshihito. After the defeat of Japan in World War II 1945, he was stripped of his divine powers and made constitutional monarch by the US-backed 1946 constitution.

hippopotamus

Hiroshima industrial city and port on the S coast of Honshu, Japan, destroyed by the first wartime use of an atomic bomb 6 Aug 1945. The city has largely been rebuilt since the war; population (1989) 1,057,100.

Hitler Adolf 1889–1945. German Nazi dictator, born in Austria. He was Führer (leader) of the Nazi Party from 1921 and author of *Mein Kampf/My Struggle* 1925–27. As chancellor of Germany from 1933 and head of state from 1934, he created a dictatorship by playing party and state institutions against each other and continually creating new offices and appointments. His position was not seriously challenged until the 'Bomb Plot' 20 July 1944 to assassinate him. In foreign affairs, he reoccupied the Rhineland and formed an alliance with the Italian Fascist Mussolini 1936, annexed Austria 1938, and occupied the Sudetenland under the ◊Munich Agreement. The rest of Czechoslovakia was annexed March 1939. The Hitler–Stalin pact was followed in Sept by the invasion of Poland and the declaration of war by Britain and France (see ◊World War II). He committed suicide as Berlin fell.

Hitler–Stalin pact nonaggression treaty signed by Germany and the USSR 23 Aug 1939. Under the terms of the treaty both countries agreed to remain neutral and to refrain from acts of aggression against each other if either went to war. Secret clauses allowed for the partition of Poland – Hitler was to acquire western Poland, Stalin the eastern part. On 1 Sept 1939 Hitler invaded Poland. The pact ended when Hitler invaded Russia on 22 June 1941. See also ◊World War II.

Hittite member of a group of people who inhabited Anatolia and N Syria from the 3rd millennium to the 1st millennium BC. The city of Hattusas (now Boğazköy in central Turkey) became the capital of a strong kingdom which overthrew the Babylonian Empire. After a period of eclipse the Hittite New Empire became a great power (about 1400–1200 BC), which successfully waged war with Egypt. The Hittite language is an Indo-European language.

HIV abbreviation for *human immunodeficiency virus*, the infectious agent that causes ◊AIDS. It was first discovered in 1983.

Hobart capital and port of Tasmania, Australia; population (1986) 180,000. Products include zinc, textiles, and paper. Founded 1804 as a penal colony, it was named after Lord Hobart, then secretary of state for the colonies.

Hobbes Thomas 1588–1679. English political philosopher and the first thinker since Aristotle to attempt to develop a comprehensive theory of nature, including human behaviour. In *The Leviathan* 1651, he advocates absolutist government as the only means of ensuring order and security; he saw this as deriving from the social contract.

hobby small falcon *Falco subbuteo* found across

Europe and N Asia. It is about 30 cm/1 ft long, with a grey back, streaked front, and chestnut thighs. It is found in open woods and heaths, and feeds on insects and small birds.

Ho Chi Minh adopted name of Nguyen That Tan 1890–1969. North Vietnamese Communist politician, premier and president 1954–69. Having trained in Moscow shortly after the ♢Russian Revolution, he headed the communist Vietminh from 1941 and fought against the French during the Indochina War 1946–54, becoming president and prime minister of the republic at the armistice. Aided by the Communist bloc, he did much to develop industrial potential. He relinquished the premiership 1955, but continued as president. In the years before his death, Ho successfully led his country's fight against US-aided South Vietnam in the Vietnam War 1954–75.

Ho Chi Minh City (until 1976 *Saigon*) chief port and industrial city of S Vietnam; population (1989) 3,169,100. Industries include shipbuilding, textiles, rubber, and food products. Saigon was the capital of the Republic of Vietnam (South Vietnam) from 1954 to 1976, when it was renamed.

Hockney David 1937– . English painter, printmaker, and designer, resident in California. He contributed to the Pop art movement in the early 1960s, then developed an individual figurative style, as in his portrait *Mr and Mrs Clark and Percy* 1971, Tate Gallery, London, and has prolifically experimented with technique. His views of swimming pools reflect a preoccupation with surface pattern and effects of light. He has also produced drawings, etchings, photo collages, and sets for opera.

Hofstadter Robert 1915–1990. US high-energy physicist who revealed the structure of the atomic nucleus. He demonstrated that the nucleus is composed of a high-energy core and a surrounding area of decreasing density. He shared the 1961 Nobel Prize for Physics with Rudolf Mössbauer.

hog member of the ♢pig family.

Hogarth William 1697–1764. English painter and engraver who produced portraits and moralizing genre scenes, such as the series *A Rake's Progress* 1735. His portraits are remarkably direct and full of character, for example *Heads of Six of Hogarth's Servants c.* 1750–55 (Tate Gallery, London).

Hogmanay Scottish name for New Year's Eve.

Hohenstaufen German family of princes, several members of which were Holy Roman emperors 1138–1208 and 1214–54. They were the first German emperors to make use of associations with Roman law and tradition to aggrandize their office, and included Conrad III; Frederick I (Barbarossa), the first to use the title Holy Roman emperor; Henry VI; and Frederick II.

Hohenzollern German family, originating in Württemberg, the main branch of which held the titles of elector of Brandenburg from 1415, king of Prussia from 1701, and German emperor from 1871. The last emperor, Wilhelm II, was dethroned 1918 after the disastrous course of World War I. Another branch of the family were kings of Romania 1881–1947.

Hokkaido northernmost of the four main islands of Japan, separated from Honshu to the south by Tsugaru Strait and from Sakhalin to the north by Soya Strait; area 83,500 sq km/32,231 sq mi; population (1986) 5,678,000, including 16,000 Ainus. The capital is Sapporo.

Hokusai Katsushika 1760–1849. Japanese artist the leading printmaker of his time. He published *Fugaku Sajū-rokkei/36 Views of Mount Fuji* about 1823–29, but he produced outstanding pictures of almost every kind of subject – birds, flowers courtesans, and scenes from everyday life.

Holbein Hans, *the Elder c.* 1464–1524. German painter, active in Augsburg. His works include altarpieces, such as that of *St Sebastian* 1516 (Alte Pinakothek, Munich). He also painted portraits and designed stained glass.

Holbein Hans, *the Younger* 1497/98–1543. German painter and woodcut artist; the son and pupil of Hans Holbein the Elder. Holbein was born in Augsburg. In 1515 he went to Basel, where he became friendly with Erasmus; he painted three portraits of him in 1523, which were strongly influenced by Quentin Massys. He travelled widely in Europe and was court painter to England's Henry VIII from 1536. He also painted portraits of Thomas More and Thomas Cromwell; a notable woodcut series is *Dance of Death* about 1525. He designed title pages for Luther's New Testament and More's *Utopia*.

Holiday Billie. Stage name of Eleanora Gough McKay 1915–1959. US jazz singer, also known as 'Lady Day'. She made her debut in Harlem clubs and became known for her emotionally charged delivery and idiosyncratic phrasing; she brought a blues feel to performances with swing bands. Songs she made her own include 'Strange Fruit' and 'I Cover the Waterfront'.

holistic medicine umbrella term for an approach that virtually all alternative therapies profess, which considers the overall health and lifestyle profile of a patient, and treats specific ailments not primarily as conditions to be alleviated but rather as symptoms of more fundamental disease.

holly tree or shrub of the genus *Ilex*, family Aquifoliaceae, including the English Christmas holly *I. aquifolium*, an evergreen with spiny, glossy leaves, small white flowers, and poisonous scarlet berries on the female tree. Leaves of the Brazilian holly *I. paraguayensis* are used to make the tea *yerba maté*.

Holly Buddy. Stage name of Charles Hardin Holley 1936–1959. US rock-and-roll singer, guitarist, and songwriter, born in Lubbock, Texas. Holly had a distinctive, hiccuping vocal style and was an early experimenter with recording techniques. Many of his hits with his band, the Crickets, such as 'That'll Be the Day' 1957, 'Peggy Sue' 1957, and 'Maybe Baby' 1958, have become classics. He died in a plane crash.

hollyhock plant of the genus *Althaea* of the mallow family Malvaceae. *A. rosea*, originally a native of Asia, produces spikes of large white, yellow, or red flowers, 3 m/10 ft high when cultivated as a biennial.

Holocaust, the the annihilation of more than 16 million people by the Hitler regime 1933–45 in the numerous extermination and ▷concentration camps, most notably Auschwitz, Sobibor, Treblinka, and Maidanek in Poland, and Belsen, Buchenwald, and Dachau in Germany. Of the victims, more than 6 million were Jews (over 67% of European Jewry); 10 million Ukrainian, Polish, and Russian civilians and prisoners of war, Romanies, socialists, homosexuals, and others (labelled 'defectives') were also imprisoned and/or exterminated. Victims were variously starved, tortured, experimented on, and worked to death. Many thousands were executed in gas chambers, shot, or hanged. It was euphemistically termed the final solution.

Holocene epoch of geological time that began 10,000 years ago, the second and current epoch of the Quaternary period. The glaciers retreated, the climate became warmer, and humans developed significantly.

holography method of producing three-dimensional (3–D) images by means of ▷laser light. Holography uses a photographic technique (involving the splitting of a laser beam into two beams) to produce a picture, or hologram, that contains 3–D information about the object photographed. Some holograms show meaningless patterns in ordinary light and produce a 3–D image only when laser light is projected through them, but reflection holograms produce images when ordinary light is reflected from them (as found on credit cards).

Holy Alliance 'Christian Union of Charity, Peace, and Love' initiated by Alexander I of Russia 1815 and signed by every crowned head in Europe. The alliance became associated with Russian attempts to preserve autocratic monarchies at any price, and served as an excuse to meddle in the internal affairs of other states.

Holy Grail in medieval Christian legend, the dish or cup used by Jesus at the Last Supper, supposed to have supernatural powers. Together with the spear with which he was wounded at the Crucifixion, it was an object of quest by King Arthur's knights in certain stories incorporated in the Arthurian legend.

Home Alec Douglas-Home, Baron Home of the

Hirsel 1903– . British Conservative politician. He was foreign secretary 1960–63, and succeeded Harold Macmillan as prime minister 1963. He renounced his peerage (as 14th Earl of Home) to fight (and lose) the general election 1963, and resigned as party leader 1965. He was again foreign secretary 1970–74, when he received a life peerage. His brother is the playwright William Douglas-Home.

Home Counties counties in close proximity to London, England: Hertfordshire, Essex, Kent, Surrey, and formerly Middlesex.

homeland or *Bantustan* before 1980, name for the ▷Black National States in the Republic of South Africa.

Homer lived *c.* 8th century BC. Legendary Greek epic poet. According to tradition, he was a blind minstrel and the author of the *Iliad* and the *Odyssey*, which are probably based on much older stories, passed on orally, concerning war with Troy in the 12th century BC.

Home Rule, Irish movement to repeal the Act of ▷Union 1801 that joined Ireland to Britain and to establish an Irish parliament responsible for internal affairs. In 1870 Isaac Butt (1813–1879) formed the Home Rule Association and the movement was led in Parliament from 1880 by Charles ▷Parnell. After 1918 the demand for an independent Irish republic replaced that for home rule.

homoeopathy or *homeopathy* system of medicine based on the principle that symptoms of disease are part of the body's self-healing processes, and on the practice of administering extremely diluted doses of natural substances found to produce in a healthy person the symptoms manifest in the illness being treated. Developed by German physician Samuel Hahnemann (1755–1843), the system is widely practised today as an alternative to allopathic medicine, and many controlled tests and achieved cures testify its efficacy.

Honan alternative name of ▷*Henan,* a province of China.

Honduras Republic of; country in Central America, bordered N by the Caribbean, SE by Nicaragua, S by the Pacific, SW by El Salvador, and W and NW by Guatemala; *area* 112,100 sq km/ 43,282 sq mi; *capital* Tegucigalpa; *physical* narrow tropical coastal plain with mountainous interior; Bay Islands; *head of state and government* Rafael Leonardo Callejas from 1990; *political system* democratic republic; *exports* coffee, bananas, sugar, timber (including mahogany, rosewood); *population* (1989 est) 5,106,000 (mestizo (mixed race) 90%, Indians and Europeans 10%); *languages* Spanish (official), English, Indian languages; *recent history* independence was achieved from Spain 1838, followed by military rule. A civilian government was elected 1980.

Honecker Erich 1912– . German communist

politician, in power 1973–89, elected chair of the council of state (head of state) 1976. He governed in an outwardly austere and efficient manner and, while favouring East–West détente, was a loyal ally of the USSR. In Oct 1989, following a wave of prodemocracy demonstrations, he was replaced as leader of the Socialist Unity Party (SED) and head of state by Egon ⟡Krenz, and in Dec expelled from the Communist Party.

honey sweet syrup produced by honey ⟡bees from the nectar of flowers. It is stored in honeycombs and made in excess of their needs as food for the winter. Honey comprises various sugars, mainly laevulose and dextrose, with enzymes, colouring matter, acids, and pollen grains. It has antibacterial properties and was widely used in ancient Egypt, Greece, and Rome as a wound salve.

honeysuckle vine or shrub of the genus *Lonicera*, family Caprifoliaceae. The common honeysuckle or woodbine *L. periclymenum* of Europe is a climbing plant with sweet-scented flowers, reddish and yellow-tinted outside and creamy white inside; it now grows in the northeastern USA.

Hong Kong British crown colony SE of China, in the South China Sea, comprising Hong Kong Island, the Kowloon Peninsula and many other islands, of which the largest is Lantau; and the mainland New Territories. It is due to revert to Chinese control 1997. *Area* 1,070 sq km/ 413 sq mi; *capital* Victoria (Hong Kong City); *towns* Kowloon, Tsuen Wan (in the New Territories); *exports* textiles, clothing, electronic goods, clocks, watches, cameras, plastic products; a large proportion of the exports and imports of S China are transshipped here; tourism is important; *currency* Hong Kong dollar; *population* (1986) 5,431,000; 57% Hong Kong Chinese, most of the remainder refugees from the mainland; *languages* English, Chinese; *religion* Confucianist, Buddhist, Taoist, with Muslim and Christian minorities; *government* Hong Kong is a British dependency administered by a crown-appointed governor (Chris Patten from 1992) who presides over an unelected executive council; *history* formerly part of China, Hong Kong Island was occupied by Britain 1841, during the first of the ⟡Opium Wars, and ceded by China under the 1842 Treaty of Nanking. The Kowloon Peninsula was acquired under the 1860 Beijing (Peking) Convention and the New Territories secured on a 99-year lease from 1898. The colony, which developed into a major entrepôt for Sino-British trade during the late 19th and early 20th centuries, was occupied by Japan 1941–45. In an agreement signed 1984, Britain agreed to transfer full sovereignty of the islands and New Territories to China 1997 in return for Chinese assurance that Hong Kong's social and economic freedom and capitalist lifestyle would be preserved for at least 50 years.

Honiara port and capital of the Solomon Islands, on the NW coast of Guadalcanal island; population (1985) 26,000.

Honolulu capital city and port of Hawaii, on the S coast of Oahu; population (1990) 365,300. It is a holiday resort, noted for its beauty and tropical vegetation, with some industry.

Honshu principal island of Japan. It lies between Hokkaido to the NE and Kyushu to the SW; area 231,100 sq km/89,205 sq mi, including 382 smaller islands; population (1986) 97,283,000. A chain of volcanic mountains runs along the island, which is subject to frequent earthquakes. The main cities are Tokyo, Yokohama, Osaka, Kobe, Nagoya, and Hiroshima.

Hooch Pieter de 1629–1684. Dutch painter, active in Delft and, later, Amsterdam. The harmonious domestic interiors and courtyards of his Delft period were influenced by Vermeer.

Hooke Robert 1635–1703. English scientist and inventor, originator of ⟡*Hooke's law*, and considered the foremost mechanic of his time. His inventions included a telegraph system, the spirit level, marine barometer, and sea gauge. He coined the term 'cell' in biology.

hoopoe bird *Upupa epops* in the order Coraciiformes, slightly larger than a thrush, with a long, thin bill and a bright, buff-coloured crest that expands into a fan shape. The wings are banded with black and white, and the rest of the plumage is black, white, and buff. This bird is the 'lapwing' mentioned in the Old Testament.

Hoover Herbert Clark 1874–1964. 31st president of the USA 1929–33, a Republican. He was secretary of commerce 1921–28. Hoover lost public confidence after the stock-market crash of 1929, when he opposed direct government aid for the unemployed in the Depression that followed.

Hoover J(ohn) Edgar 1895–1972. US director of the Federal Bureau of Investigation (FBI) from 1924. He built up a powerful network for the detection of organized crime. His drive against alleged communist activities after World War II, and his opposition to the Kennedy administration and others brought much criticism over abuse of power.

Hopei alternative transcription of ⟡*Hebei*, a province of China.

Hopkins Gerard Manley 1844–1889. English poet and Jesuit priest. His work, marked by its religious themes and use of natural imagery, includes 'The Wreck of the Deutschland' 1876 and 'The Windhover' 1877. His employment of 'sprung rhythm' greatly influenced later 20th-century poetry. His poetry was written in secret, and published 30 years after his death by his friend Robert Bridges.

Horace 65–8 BC. Roman lyric poet and satirist. He became a leading poet under the patronage of Emperor Augustus. His works include *Satires* 35–30 BC; the four books of *Odes* about 25–24 BC; *Epistles*, a series of verse letters; and a critical work,

horse

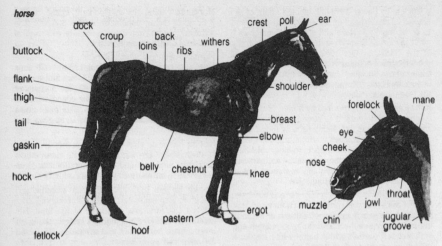

dock, croup, back, loins, ribs, withers, crest, poll, ear, buttock, flank, thigh, tail, gaskin, hock, belly, chestnut, knee, pastern, ergot, hoof, fetlock, shoulder, breast, elbow, forelock, mane, eye, cheek, nose, muzzle, jowl, throat, chin, jugular groove

Ars poetica. They are distinguished by their style, wit, and good sense.

hormone product of the ⯈endocrine glands, concerned with control of body functions. The main glands are the thyroid, parathyroid, pituitary, adrenal, pancreas, uterus, ovary, and testis. Hormones bring about changes in the functions of various organs according to the body's requirements. The pituitary gland, at the base of the brain, is a centre for overall coordination of hormone secretion; the thyroid hormones determine the rate of general body chemistry; the adrenal hormones prepare the organism during stress for 'fight or flight'; and the sexual hormones such as oestrogen govern reproductive functions.

hormone-replacement therapy (HRT) use of oral ⯈oestrogen and progestogen to help limit the effects of the menopause in women. The treatment was first used in the 1970s.

Hormuz or **Ormuz** small island, area 41 sq km/ 16 sq mi, in the Strait of Hormuz, belonging to Iran. It is strategically important because oil tankers leaving the Persian Gulf for Japan and the West have to pass through the strait to reach the Arabian Sea.

hornbeam any tree of the genus *Carpinus* of the birch family Betulaceae. They have oval, serrated leaves and bear pendant clusters of flowers, each with a nutlike seed attached to the base. The trunk is usually twisted, with smooth grey bark.

hornbill bird of the family of Bucerotidae, found in Africa, India, and Malaysia. Omnivorous, it is about 1 m/3 ft long, and has a powerful bill, usually surmounted by a bony growth or casque. During the breeding season, the female walls herself into a hole in a tree, and does not emerge until the young are hatched.

hornet kind of ⯈wasp.

horse hoofed, odd-toed, grazing mammal *Equus caballus* of the family Equidae, which also includes zebras and asses. The many breeds of domestic horse of Euro-Asian origin range in colour from white to grey, brown, and black. The yellow-brown Mongolian wild horse or Przewalski's horse *E. przewalskii*, named after its Polish 'discoverer' about 1880, is the only surviving species of wild horse.

horse chestnut any tree of the genus *Aesculus* of the family Hippocastanaceae, especially *A. hippocastanum*, originally from SE Europe but widely planted elsewhere. Horse chestnuts have large, showy spikes of bell-shaped flowers and bear large, shiny, inedible seeds in capsules (**conkers**). The horse chestnut is not related to the true chestnut. In North America it is called buckeye.

horse racing sport of racing mounted or driven horses. Two popular forms in Britain are **flat racing**, for thoroughbred horses over a flat course, and **National Hunt racing**, in which the horses have to clear obstacles.

horseradish hardy perennial *Armoracia rusticana*, native to SE Europe but naturalized elsewhere, family Cruciferae. The thick, cream-coloured root is strong-tasting and is often made into a condiment.

horsetail plant of the genus *Equisetum*, related to ferns and club mosses; some species are also called **scouring rush**. There are about 35 living species, bearing their spores on cones at the stem tip. The upright stems are ribbed and often have spaced whorls of branches. Today they are of modest size, but hundreds of millions of years ago giant treelike forms existed.

Horus in ancient Egyptian mythology, the hawk-headed sun god, son of Isis and Osiris, of whom the pharaohs were declared to be the incarnation.

hostage person taken prisoner as a means of exerting pressure on a third party, usually with threats of death or injury. It may be a political gesture or ▷kidnapping for gain, or a hostage may be given as security.

Houphouët-Boigny Felix 1905– . Ivory Coast right-wing politician. He held posts in French ministries, and became president of the Republic of the Ivory Coast on independence 1960, maintaining close links with France, which helped to boost an already thriving economy and encourage political stability. He was re-elected for a seventh term 1990 in multiparty elections, amid allegations of ballot rigging and political pressure.

housefly fly of the genus *Musca*, found in and around dwellings, especially *M. domestica*, a common worldwide species. Houseflies are grey, and have mouthparts adapted for drinking liquids and sucking moisture from food and manure.

house music dance music of the 1980s originating in the inner-city clubs of Chicago, USA, combining funk with European high-tech pop, and using dub, digital sampling, and cross-fading. *Acid house* has minimal vocals and melody, instead surrounding the mechanically emphasized 4/4 beat with stripped-down synthesizer riffs and a wandering bass line. Other variants include *hip house*, with rap elements, and *acid jazz*.

House of Representatives lower house of the US ▷Congress, with 435 members elected at regular two-year intervals, every even year, in November.

Houston port in Texas, USA; population (1990) 1,630,600; linked by canal to the Gulf of Mexico. It is a major centre of the petroleum industry and of finance and commerce. It is also one of the busiest US ports. Houston was first settled 1826.

hovercraft vehicle that rides on a cushion of high-pressure air, free from all contact with the surface beneath, invented by British engineer Christopher Cockerell 1959. Hovercraft need a smooth terrain when operating overland and are best adapted to use on waterways. They are useful in places where harbours have not been established.

Howard Catherine *c.* 1520–1542. Queen consort of ▷Henry VIII of England from 1540. In 1541 the archbishop of Canterbury, Thomas Cranmer, accused her of being unchaste before marriage to Henry and she was beheaded 1542 after Cranmer made further charges of adultery.

Howard John 1726–1790. English philanthropist whose work to improve prison conditions is continued today by the *Howard League for Penal Reform*.

Hoxha Enver 1908–1985. Albanian Communist politician, the country's leader from 1954. He founded the Albanian Communist Party 1941, and headed the liberation movement 1939–44. He was prime minister 1944–54, combining with foreign affairs 1946–53, and from 1954 was first secretary

of the Albanian Party of Labour. In policy he was a Stalinist and independent of both Chinese and Soviet communism.

Hsuan Tung name adopted by Henry ▷P'u-i on becoming emperor of China 1908.

Hua Guofeng or *Hua Kuofeng* 1920– . Chinese politician, leader of the Chinese Communist Party (CCP) 1976–81, premier 1976–80. He dominated Chinese politics 1976–77, seeking economic modernization without major structural reform. From 1978 he was gradually eclipsed by Deng Xiaoping. Hua was ousted from the Politburo Sept 1982 but remained a member of the CCP Central Committee.

Huang He or *Hwang-ho* river in China; length 5,464 km/3,395 mi. It takes its name (meaning 'yellow river') from its muddy waters. Formerly known as 'China's sorrow' because of disastrous floods, it is now largely controlled through hydroelectric works and flood barriers.

Hubble Space Telescope (HST) telescope placed into orbit around the Earth, at an altitude of 610 km/380 mi, by the space shuttle *Discovery* in April 1990. It has a main mirror 2.4 m/94 in wide, which suffers from spherical aberration and so cannot be focused properly. Yet, because it is above the atmosphere, the HST outperforms ground-based telescopes.

Hubei or *Hupei* province of central China, through which flow the river Chang Jiang and its tributary the Han Shui; *area* 187,500 sq km/72,375 sq mi; *capital* Wuhan; *features* high land in the W, the river Chang breaking through from Sichuan in gorges; elsewhere low-lying, fertile land; many lakes; *products* beans, cereals, cotton, rice, vegetables, copper, gypsum, iron ore, phosphorous, salt; *population* (1990) 53,969,000.

Hudson river of the NE USA; length 485 km/300 mi. It rises in the Adirondack Mountains and flows south, emptying into a bay of the Atlantic Ocean at New York City.

Hudson Henry *c.* 1565–*c.* 1611. English explorer. Under the auspices of the Muscovy Company 1607–08, he made two unsuccessful attempts to find the Northeast Passage to China. In Sept 1609, commissioned by the Dutch East India Company, he reached New York Bay and sailed 240 km/150 mi up the river that now bears his name, establishing Dutch claims to the area. In 1610, he sailed from London in the *Discovery* and entered what is now the Hudson Strait. After an icebound winter, he was turned adrift by a mutinous crew in what is now Hudson Bay.

Hudson Bay inland sea of NE Canada, linked with the Atlantic Ocean by *Hudson Strait* and with the Arctic Ocean by Foxe Channel; area 1,233,000 sq km/476,000 sq mi. It is named after Henry Hudson, who reached it 1610.

Hudson's Bay Company chartered company founded by Prince ▷Rupert 1670 to trade in furs with North American Indians. In 1783 the rival

North West Company was formed, but in 1851 this became amalgamated with the Hudson's Bay Company. It is still Canada's biggest fur company, but today also sells general merchandise through department stores and has oil and natural gas interests.

Hughes Ted 1930– . English poet, poet laureate from 1984. His work includes *The Hawk in the Rain* 1957, *Lupercal* 1960, *Wodwo* 1967, and *River* 1983, and is characterized by its harsh portrayal of the crueller aspects of nature. In 1956 he married the poet Sylvia Plath.

Hugo Victor (Marie) 1802–1885. French poet, novelist, and dramatist. The *Odes et poésies diverses* appeared 1822, and his verse play *Hernani* 1830 established him as the leader of French Romanticism. More volumes of verse followed between his series of dramatic novels, which included *The Hunchback of Notre Dame* 1831 and *Les Misérables* 1862.

Huguenot French Protestant in the 16th century; the term referred mainly to Calvinists. Severely persecuted under Francis I and Henry II, the Huguenots survived both an attempt to exterminate them (the *Massacre of* ⟡*St Bartholomew* 24 Aug 1572) and the religious wars of the next 30 years. In 1598 Henry IV (himself formerly a Huguenot) granted them toleration under the ⟡*Edict of Nantes.* Louis XIV revoked the edict 1685, attempting their forcible conversion, and 400,000 emigrated. The Huguenots lost military power after the revolt at La Rochelle 1627–29, but were still tolerated by the chief ministers Richelieu and Mazarin. Provoked by Louis XIV they left, taking their industrial skills with them.

Hull officially *Kingston upon Hull* city and port on the north bank of the Humber estuary, where the river Hull flows into it, England; population (1991) 252,200. It is linked with the south bank of the estuary by the Humber Bridge. Industries include fish processing, vegetable oils, flour milling, electrical goods, textiles, paint, pharmaceuticals, chemicals, caravans, and aircraft.

Human Rights, Universal Declaration of charter of civil and political rights drawn up by the United Nations 1948. They include the right to life, liberty, education, and equality before the law; to freedom of movement, religion, association, and information; and to a nationality. Under the European Convention of Human Rights 1950, the Council of Europe established the *European Commission of Human Rights* (headquarters in Strasbourg, France), which investigates complaints by states or individuals, and its findings are examined by the *European Court of Human Rights* (established 1959), whose compulsory jurisdiction has been recognized by a number of states, including the UK.

human species, origins of evolution of humans from ancestral ⟡primates. The African apes (gorilla and chimpanzee) are shown by anatomical and molecular comparisons to be the closest living relatives of humans. Humans are distinguished from apes by the size of their brain and jaw, their bipedalism, and their elaborate culture. Molecular studies put the date of the split between the human and African ape lines at 5–10 million years ago. The oldest known hominids (members of the human group), found in Ethiopia and Tanzania, date from 3.5 to 4 million years ago. These creatures are known as *Australopithecus afarensis*, and they walked upright. They were either direct ancestors or an offshoot of the line that led to modern humans.

Humberside county of NE England; *area* 3,510 sq km/1,355 sq mi; *towns* Hull (administrative headquarters), Grimsby, Scunthorpe, Goole, Cleethorpes; *features* Humber Bridge; fertile Holderness peninsula; Isle of Axholme, bounded by rivers Trent, Don, Idle, and Torne, where medieval open-field strip farming is still practised; *products* petrochemicals, refined oil, processed fish, cereals, root crops, cattle; *population* (1991) 845,200; *famous people* Amy Johnson, Andrew Marvell, John Wesley.

Hume David 1711–1776. Scottish philosopher. *A Treatise of Human Nature* 1739–40 is a central text of British empiricism. Hume denies the possibility of going beyond the subjective experiences of 'ideas' and 'impressions'. The effect of this position is to invalidate metaphysics.

hummingbird any of various birds of the family Trochilidae, found in the Americas. The name is derived from the sound produced by the rapid vibration of their wings. Hummingbirds are brilliantly coloured, and have long, needlelike bills and tongues to obtain nectar from flowers and capture insects. They are the only birds able to fly backwards. The Cuban bee hummingbird *Mellisuga helenae*, the world's smallest bird, is 5.5 cm/2 in long, and weighs less than 2.5 g/0.1 oz.

Hun member of any of a number of nomad Mongol peoples who were first recorded historically in the 2nd century BC, raiding across the Great Wall into China. They entered Europe about AD 372, settled in the area that is now Hungary, and imposed their supremacy on the Ostrogoths and other Germanic peoples. Under the leadership of Attila they attacked the Byzantine Empire, invaded Gaul, and threatened Rome. After Attila's death in 453 their power was broken by a revolt of their subject peoples. The *White Huns*, or Ephthalites, a kindred people, raided Persia and N India in the 5th and 6th centuries.

Hunan province of S central China; *area* 210,500 sq km/81,253 sq mi; *capital* Changsha; *features* Dongting Lake; farmhouse in Shaoshan village where Mao Zedong was born; *products* rice, tea, tobacco, cotton; nonferrous minerals; *population* (1990) 60,660,000.

Hundred Years' War series of conflicts between England and France 1337–1453. Its origins lay

MEDITERRANEAN SEA

with the English kings' possession of Gascony (SW France), which the French kings claimed as their fief, and with trade rivalries over ◊Flanders. English victories in the naval Battle of Sluis 1340, the Battle of Crécy 1346, and the Battle of Poitiers 1356, in which King John of France was captured, culminated in the Treaty of Brétigny–Calais 1360, confirming English possession of Calais. Later, France regained some territory. In 1415 Henry V invaded France and won a victory at Agincourt, followed by conquest of Normandy and leading to the Treaty of Troyes 1419. But after Joan of Arc raised the siege of Orléans 1429, there was a successful French counteroffensive, and in 1453 only Calais was left in English hands.

Hungary Republic of; country in central Europe, bordered N by Czechoslovakia, NE by Ukraine, E by Romania, S by Yugoslavia, and W by Austria; **area** 93,032 sq km/35,910 sq mi; **capital** Budapest; **physical** Great Hungarian Plain covers E half of country; Bakony Forest; Transdanubian Highlands in W; rivers Danube, Tisza; Lake Balaton; **head of state** Arpad Goencz from 1990; **head of government** Jozsef Antall from 1990; **political system** emergent democracy; **exports** machinery, vehicles, iron and steel, chemicals, fruit and vegetables; **population** (1990 est) 10,546,000 (Magyar 92%, Romany 3%, German 2.5%); **language** Hungarian (or Magyar); **recent history** Stalinist regime imposed 1946; Soviet-style constitution adopted 1949. A national uprising 1956 was quelled by the USSR. Reforms 1968–88 were followed by the opening of the border with Austria 1989 and a new 'transitional constitution' was adopted, founded on multiparty democracy and new presidentialist executive. An elected coalition government embarked on a privatization programme 1990; GNP fell by 6% in 1990 and a further 7% in 1991. The last Soviet troops left Hungary 1991.

Hun Sen 1950– . Cambodian political leader, prime minister from 1985. Originally a member of the Khmer Rouge army, he defected in 1977 to join Vietnam-based anti-Khmer Cambodian forces. In Oct 1991, following a peace accord ending 13 years of civil war in Cambodia, Hun Sen agreed to rule the country in conjunction with the United Nations Transitional Authority in Cambodia (UNTAC) and representatives of the warring factions until UN-administered elections 1993.

Hunt William Holman 1827–1910. English painter, one of the founders of the ◊Pre-Raphaelite Brotherhood 1848. Obsessed with realistic detail, he travelled from 1854 onwards to Syria and Palestine to paint biblical subjects. His works include *The Awakening Conscience* 1853 (Tate Gallery, London) and *The Light of the World* 1854 (Keble College, Oxford).

Hupei alternative transcription of ◊Hebei, a province of China.

Hurd Douglas (Richard) 1930– . English Conservative politician, home secretary 1986–89, foreign secretary from 1989. In Nov 1990 he was an unsuccessful candidate in the party leadership contest.

Huron second largest of the Great Lakes of North America, on the US-Canadian border; area 23,160 sq mi/60,000 sq km. It includes Georgian Bay, Saginaw Bay, and Manitoulin Island.

hurricane revolving storm in tropical regions, called **typhoon** in the N Pacific. It originates between 5° and 20° N or S of the equator, when the surface temperature of the ocean is above 27°C/80°F. A central calm area, called the eye, is surrounded by inwardly spiralling winds (anticlockwise in the northern hemisphere) of up to 320 kph/200 mph. A hurricane is accompanied by lightning and torrential rain, and can cause extensive damage. In meteorology, a hurricane is a wind of force 12 or more on the ◊Beaufort scale. The most intense hurricane recorded in the Caribbean/Atlantic sector was Hurricane Gilbert in 1988, with sustained winds of 280 kph/175 mph and gusts of over 320 kph/200 mph.

Husák Gustáv 1913–1991. Leader of the Communist Party of Czechoslovakia (CCP) 1969–87 and president 1975–89. After the 1968 Prague Spring of liberalization, his task was to restore control, purge the CCP, and oversee the implementation of a new, federalist constitution. He was deposed in the popular uprising of Nov–Dec 1989 and expelled from the Communist Party Feb 1990.

husky any of several breeds of sledge dog used in Arctic regions, growing to 70 cm/2 ft high, and weighing about 50 kg/110 lbs, with pricked ears, thick fur, and a bushy tail. The Siberian husky is the best known.

Hussein ibn Talal 1935– . King of Jordan from 1952. Great-grandson of Hussein ibn Ali, he became king following the mental incapacitation of his father, Talal. By 1967 he had lost all his kingdom west of the river Jordan in the ◇Arab-Israeli Wars, and in 1970 suppressed the ◇Palestine Liberation Organization acting as a guerrilla force against his rule on the remaining East Bank territories. In recent years, he has become a moderating force in Middle Eastern politics. After Iraq's annexation of Kuwait 1990 he attempted to mediate between the opposing sides, at the risk of damaging his relations with both sides.

Hussein Saddam 1937– . Iraqi politician, in power from 1968, president from 1979, progressively eliminating real or imagined opposition factions as he gained increasing dictatorial control. Ruthless in the pursuit of his objectives, he fought a bitter war against Iran 1980–88, with US economic aid, and dealt harshly with the population of Kurdish provinces seeking independence. In 1990 he annexed Kuwait but was driven out by a US-dominated coalition army Feb 1991. Defeat in the ◇Gulf War undermined Saddam's position as the country's leader; when the Kurds rebelled again after the end of the war, he sent the remainder of his army to crush them, causing hundreds of thousands of Kurds to flee their homes in N Iraq.

Hutton James 1726–1797. Scottish geologist, known as the 'founder of geology', who formulated the concept of uniformitarianism. In 1785 he developed a theory of the igneous origin of many rocks.

Hutton Len (Leonard) 1916–1990. English cricketer, born in Pudsey, West Yorkshire. He captained England in 23 test matches 1952–56 and was England's first professional captain. In 1938 at the Oval he scored 364 against Australia, a world record test score until beaten by Gary ◇Sobers 1958.

Huxley Aldous (Leonard) 1894–1963. English writer of novels, essays, and verse. From the disillusionment and satirical eloquence of *Crome Yellow* 1921, *Antic Hay* 1923, and *Point Counter Point* 1928, Huxley developed towards the Utopianism exemplified by *Island* 1962. The science fiction novel *Brave New World* 1932 shows human beings massproduced in laboratories and rendered incapable of freedom by indoctrination and drugs. He was the grandson of Thomas Henry Huxley and brother of Julian Huxley.

Huxley Thomas Henry 1825–1895. English scientist and humanist. Following the publication of Charles Darwin's *On the Origin of Species* 1859, he became known as 'Darwin's bulldog', and for many years was a prominent champion of evolution. In 1869, he coined the word 'agnostic' to express his own religious attitude. His grandsons include Aldous, Andrew, and Julian Huxley.

Huysmans J(oris) K(arl) 1848–1907. French novelist of Dutch ancestry. His novel *Marthe* 1876, the story of a courtesan, was followed by other realistic novels, including *A rebours/Against Nature* 1884, a novel of self-absorbed aestheticism that symbolized the 'decadent' movement.

Hwang-Ho alternative transcription of ◇Huang He, a river in China.

hyacinth any bulb-producing plant of the genus *Hyacinthus* of the lily family Liliaceae, native to the E Mediterranean and Africa. The cultivated hyacinth *H. orientalis* has large, scented, cylindrical heads of pink, white, or blue flowers. The ◇water hyacinth, genus *Eichhornia*, is unrelated, a floating plant from South America.

Hyderabad capital city of the S central Indian state of Andhra Pradesh, on the river Musi; population (1981) 2,528,000. Products include carpets, silks, and metal inlay work. It was formerly the capital of the state of Hyderabad. Buildings include the Jama Masjid mosque and Golconda fort.

hydra in zoology, any member of the family Hydridae, or freshwater polyps, of the phylum Cnidaria (coelenterates). The body is a doublelayered tube (with six to ten hollow tentacles around the mouth), 1.25 cm/0.5 in long when extended, but capable of contracting to a small knob. Usually fixed to waterweed, hydras feed on minute animals, that are caught and paralysed by stinging cells on the tentacles.

Hydra in Greek mythology, a huge monster with nine heads. If one were cut off, two would grow in its place. One of the 12 labours of Heracles was to kill it.

hydrangea any flowering shrub of the genus *Hydrangea* of the saxifrage family Hydrangeaceae, native to Japan. Cultivated varieties of *H. macrophylla* normally produce round heads of pink flowers, but these may be blue if certain chemicals, such as alum or iron, are in the soil. The name is from the Greek for 'water vessel', after the cuplike seed capsules.

hydraulics field of study concerned with utilizing the properties of water and other liquids, in particular the way they flow and transmit pressure, and with the application of these properties in engineering. It applies the principles of hydrostatics and hydrodynamics. The oldest type of hydraulic machine is the **hydraulic press**, invented by Joseph ◇Bramah in England 1795. The hydraulic principle of pressurized liquid increasing mechanical efficiency is commonly used on vehicle braking systems, the forging press, and the hydraulic systems of aircraft and excavators.

hydrocarbon any of a class of chemical compounds containing only hydrogen and carbon (for example, the alkanes and alkenes). Hydrocarbons are obtained industrially principally from petroleum and coal tar.

hydrochloric acid HCl solution of hydrogen chloride (a colourless, acidic gas) in water. The concentrated acid is about 35% hydrogen chloride and is corrosive. The acid is a typical strong, monobasic acid forming only one series of salts, the chlorides.

hypotenuse

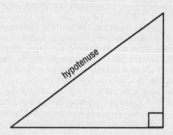

It has many industrial uses, including recovery of zinc from galvanized scrap iron and the production of chlorine. It is also produced in the stomachs of animals for the purposes of digestion.

hydroelectric power (HEP) electricity generated by moving water. In a typical HEP scheme water stored in a reservoir, often created by damming a river, is piped into water ⟡turbines, coupled to electricity generators. In ⟡pumped storage plants, water flowing through the turbines is recycled. A ⟡tidal power station exploits the rise and fall of the tides. About one-fifth of the world's electricity comes from HEP.

hydrofoil wing that develops lift in the water in much the same way that an aeroplane wing develops lift in the air. A hydrofoil boat is one whose hull rises out of the water due to the lift, and the boat skims along on the hydrofoils. The first hydrofoil was fitted to a boat 1906. The first commercial hydrofoil went into operation 1956. One of the most advanced hydrofoil boats is the Boeing ⟡jetfoil.

hydrogen colourless, odourless, gaseous, nonmetallic element, symbol H, atomic number 1, relative atomic mass 1.00797. It is the lightest of all the elements and occurs on Earth chiefly in combination with oxygen as water. Hydrogen is the most abundant element in the universe, where it accounts for 93% of the total number of atoms and 76% of the total mass. It is a component of most stars, including the

Sun, whose heat and light are produced through the nuclear-fusion process that converts hydrogen into helium.

hyena any of three species of carnivorous mammals in the family Hyaenidae, living in Africa and Asia. Hyenas have extremely powerful jaws. They are scavengers, although they will also attack and kill live prey.

Hymen in Greek mythology, either the son of Apollo and one of the Muses, or of Dionysus and Aphrodite. He was the god of marriage, and in painting he is represented as a youth carrying a bridal torch.

hypertension abnormally high ⟡blood pressure due to a variety of causes, leading to excessive contraction of the smooth muscle cells of the walls of the arteries. It increases the risk of kidney disease, stroke, and heart attack.

hypnosis artificially induced state of relaxation in which suggestibility is heightened. The subject may carry out orders after being awakened, and may be made insensitive to pain. Hypnosis is sometimes used to treat addictions to tobacco or overeating, or to assist amnesia victims.

hypotenuse the longest side of a right-angled triangle, opposite the right angle.

hypothermia condition in which the deep (core) temperature of the body spontaneously drops. If it is not discovered, coma and death ensue. Most at risk are the aged and babies (particularly if premature).

hyrax small mammal, forming the order Hyracoidea, that lives among rocks, in deserts, and in forests in Africa, Arabia, and Syria. It is about the size of a rabbit, with a plump body, short legs, short ears, brownish fur, and long, curved front teeth.

hyssop aromatic herb *Hyssopus officinalis* of the mint family Labiatae, found in Asia, S Europe, and around the Mediterranean. It has blue flowers, oblong leaves, and stems that are woody near the ground but herbaceous above.

hysteria according to the work of Sigmund ⟡Freud, the conversion of a psychological conflict or anxiety feeling into a physical symptom, such as paralysis, blindness, recurrent cough, vomiting, and general malaise. The term is little used today in diagnosis.

I

Ibadan city in SW Nigeria and capital of Oyo state; population (1981) 2,100,000. Industries include chemicals, electronics, plastics, and vehicles.

ibex any of various wild goats found in mountainous areas of Europe, NE Africa, and Central Asia. They grow to 100 cm/3.5 ft, and have brown or grey coats and heavy horns. They are herbivorous and live in small groups.

ibis any of various wading birds, about 60 cm/2 ft tall, in the same family, Threskiornidae, as spoonbills. Ibises have long legs and necks, and long, curved beaks. Various species occur in the warmer regions of the world.

Ibiza one of the ◊Balearic Islands, a popular tourist resort; area 596 sq km/230 sq mi; population (1986) 45,000. The capital and port, also called Ibiza, has a cathedral.

Ibo or *Igbo* member of the W African Ibo culture group occupying SE Nigeria and numbering about

ibis

18,000,000. Primarily cultivators, they inhabit the richly forested tableland, bounded by the river Niger to the west and the river Cross to the east. They are divided into five main groups, and their languages belong to the Kwa branch of the Niger-Congo family.

Ibsen Henrik (Johan) 1828–1906. Norwegian playwright and poet, whose realistic and often controversial plays revolutionized European theatre. Driven into exile 1864–91 by opposition to the satirical *Love's Comedy* 1862, he wrote the verse dramas *Brand* 1866 and *Peer Gynt* 1867, followed by realistic plays dealing with social issues, including *Pillars of Society* 1877, ◊*The Doll's House* 1879, ◊*Ghosts* 1881, *An Enemy of the People* 1882, and ◊*Hedda Gabler* 1891. By the time he returned to Norway, he was recognized as the country's greatest living writer.

Icarus in Greek mythology, the son of ◊Daedalus, who with his father escaped from the labyrinth in Crete by making wings of feathers fastened with wax. Icarus plunged to his death when he flew too near the Sun and the wax melted.

ice solid formed by water when it freezes. It is colourless and its crystals are hexagonal. The water molecules are held together by ◊hydrogen bonds.

iceberg floating mass of ice, about 80% of which is submerged, rising sometimes to 100 m/300 ft above sea level. Glaciers that reach the coast become extended into a broad foot; as this enters the sea, masses break off and drift towards temperate latitudes, becoming a danger to shipping.

ice hockey game played on ice between two teams of six, developed in Canada from hockey or bandy. A rubber disc (puck) is used in place of a ball. Players wear skates and protective clothing.

Iceland Republic of; island in the N Atlantic, situated S of the Arctic Circle, between Greenland and Norway; *area* 103,000 sq km/39,758 sq mi; *capital* Reykjavík; *physical* glaciers and lava fields cover 75% of the country; active volcanoes; geysers, hot springs, and new islands created offshore (Surtsey 1963); warmed by the Gulf Stream; *head of state* Vigdís Finnbogadóttir from 1980; *head of government* David Oddsson from 1991; *political system* democratic republic; *exports* cod and other fish products, aluminium, diatomite; *language* Icelandic; *population* (1990 est) 251,000; *recent history* independence was achieved from Denmark 1944. The 1976 'Cod War' with the UK was followed by Iceland's announcement of a 200–mile exclusive fishing zone 1979. Iceland declared itself a nuclear-free zone 1985.

iceman, the nickname given to the preserved body of a prehistoric man discovered 32,810 m/ 10,000 ft up on a glacier in the Otztaler Alps, on the Austrian-Italian border, Sept 1991. On the basis of the clothing and associated artefacts, the body was at first believed to be 4,000 years old, from the Bronze Age. Subsequent carbon dating by Oxford and Zurich universities placed the body in the earlier Stone Age, dating it at about 5,300 years old. The discovery has led to a reappraisal of the prehistoric periods since it has proved that Stone Age civilization was more advanced than previously thought.

Iceni ancient people of E England, who revolted against occupying Romans under ▷Boudicca.

icon in the Greek or Eastern Orthodox Church, a representation of Jesus, Mary, an angel, or a saint, in painting, low relief, or mosaic. The painted icons were traditionally on wood.

iconography in art history, significance attached to symbols that can help to identify subject matter (for example, a saint holding keys usually represents St Peter) and place a work of art in its historical context.

id in Freudian psychology, the instinctual element of the human mind, concerned with pleasure, which demands immediate satisfaction. It is regarded as the ▷unconscious element of the human psyche, and is said to be in conflict with the ▷ego and the ▷superego.

Idaho state of NW USA; nickname Gem State; *area* 216,500 sq km/83,569 sq mi; *capital* Boise; *cities* Pocatello, Idaho Falls; *features* Rocky Mountains; Snake River, which runs through Hell's Canyon (2,330 m/7,647 ft), the deepest in North America, and has the National Reactor Testing Station on the plains of its upper reaches; Sun Valley ski and summer resort; Craters of the Moon National Monument; Nez Percé National Historic Park; *products* potatoes, wheat, livestock, timber, silver, lead, zinc, antimony; *population* (1990) 1,006,700; *history* part of the Louisiana Purchase 1803; first permanently settled 1860 after the discovery of gold, Idaho became a state 1890.

ideology set of ideas, beliefs, and opinions about the nature of people and society, providing a framework for a theory about how people should live, as well as how society is or should be organized. A nation's ideology is usually reflected in the political system it creates.

Ignatius Loyola, St 1491–1556. Spanish noble who founded the ▷Jesuit order 1540, also called the Society of Jesus.

igneous rock rock formed from cooling magma or lava, and solidifying from a molten state. Igneous rocks are classified according to their crystal size, texture, chemical composition, or method of formation. They are largely composed of silica (SiO_2) and they are classified by their silica content into groups: acid (over 66% silica), intermediate (55–66%), basic (45–55%), and ultrabasic (uner 45%). Igneous rocks that crystallize below the Earth's surface are called plutonic or intrusive, depending on the depth of formation. They have large crystals produced by slow cooling; examples include dolerite and granite. Those extruded at

the surface are called extrusive or volcanic. Rapid cooling results in small crystals; basalt is an example.

iguana any lizard, especially the genus *Iguana*, of the family Iguanidae, which includes about 700 species and is chiefly confined to the Americas. The common iguana *I. iguana* of Central and South America is a vegetarian and may reach 2 m/6 ft in length.

IJsselmeer lake in the Netherlands, formed 1932 after the Zuider Zee was cut off by a dyke from the North Sea; freshwater since 1944. Area 1,217 sq km/470 sq mi.

Ikhnaton or *Akhenaton* 14th century BC. King of Egypt of the 18th dynasty (*c.* 1379–1362 BC), who may have ruled jointly for a time with his father Amenhotep III. He developed the cult of the Sun, Aton, rather than the rival cult of ▷Ammon. Some historians believe that his attention to religious reforms rather than imperial defence led to the loss of most of Egypt's possessions in Asia.

Île-de-France region of N France; area 12,000 sq km/4,632 sq mi; population (1986) 10,251,000. It includes the French capital, Paris, and the towns of Versailles, Sèvres, and St-Cloud and comprises the *départements* of Essonne, Val-de-Marne, Val d'Oise, Ville de Paris, Seine-et-Marne, Hauts-de-Seine, Seine-Saint-Denis, and Yvelines. From here the early French kings extended their authority over the whole country.

Iliescu Ion 1930– . Romanian president from 1990. Iliescu became a member of the Romanian Communist Party (PCR) central committee 1968, under the dictator Nicolae Ceaușescu, but fell out of favour. At the outbreak of the 'Christmas revolution' 1989, Iliescu was one of the first leaders to emerge, heading the National Salvation Front, and becoming president of the Provisional Council of National Unity Feb 1990. He won an overwhelming victory in the presidential elections in May 1990.

Illich Ivan 1926– . US radical philosopher and activist, born in Austria. His works, which include *Deschooling Society* 1971, *Towards a History of Need* 1978, and *Gender* 1983, are a critique of contemporary economic development, especially in the Third World.

Illinois midwest state of the USA; nickname Land of Lincoln/Prairie State; *area* 146,100 sq km/56,395 sq mi; *capital* Springfield; *cities* Chicago, Rockford, Peoria, Decatur, Aurora; *features* Lake Michigan; rivers: Mississippi, Illinois, Ohio, Rock; Cahokia Mounds, the largest group of prehistoric earthworks in the USA; the Lincoln Home National Historic Site, Springfield; the University of Chicago; Mormon leader Joseph Smith's home, Nauvoo; the Art Institute and Field Museum, Chicago; *products* soya beans, cereals, meat and dairy products, machinery, electrical and electronic equipment; *population* (1990) 11,430,600;

famous people Jane Addams, Saul Bellow, Mother Cabrini, Clarence Darrow, Enrico Fermi, Ernest Hemingway, Jesse Jackson, Edgar Lee Masters, Ronald Reagan, Louis Sullivan, Frank Lloyd Wright; *history* originally explored by the French in the 17th century, and ceded to Britain by the French 1763, Illinois passed to American control 1783, and became a state 1818.

Imagism movement in Anglo-American poetry that flourished 1912–14 and affected much US and British poetry and critical thinking thereafter. A central figure was Ezra Pound, who asserted the principles of free verse, complex imagery, and poetic impersonality.

imago sexually mature stage of an ⟩insect.

Imhotep *c.* 2800 BC. Egyptian physician and architect, adviser to King Zoser (3rd dynasty). He is thought to have designed the step pyramid at Sakkara, and his tomb (believed to be in the N Sakkara cemetery) became a centre of healing. He was deified as the son of ⟩Ptah and was identified with Aesculapius, the Greek god of medicine.

immunity the protection that organisms have against foreign microorganisms, such as bacteria and viruses, and against cancerous cells (see ⟩cancer). The cells that provide this protection are called white blood cells, or leucocytes, and make up the immune system. They include neutrophils and ⟩macrophages, which can engulf invading organisms and other unwanted material, and natural killer cells that destroy cells infected by viruses and cancerous cells. Some of the most important immune cells are the B cells and T cells.

impala African antelope *Aepyceros melampus* found from Kenya to South Africa in savannas and open woodland. The body is sandy brown. Males have lyre-shaped horns up to 75 cm/2.5 ft long. Impala grow up to 1.5 m/5 ft long and 90 cm/3 ft tall. They live in herds and spring high in the air when alarmed.

impeachment judicial procedure by which government officials are accused of wrongdoing and brought to trial before a legislative body. In the USA the House of Representatives may impeach offenders to be tried before the Senate, as in the case of President Andrew Johnson 1868. Richard Nixon resigned the US presidency 1974 to avoid impeachment. In England the House of Commons from 1376 brought ministers and officers of state to trial before the House of Lords; for example, Francis Bacon 1621, Thomas Strafford 1640, and Warren Hastings 1788.

imperialism policy of extending the power and rule of a government beyond its own boundaries. In the 19th century imperialism was synonymous with the establishment of colonies, as in the British Empire. A country may dominate others by direct rule or by less obvious means such as control of markets for goods or raw materials. The latter is often called neo-colonialism.

imperial system traditional system of units developed in the UK, based largely on the foot, pound, and second (f.p.s.) system. In 1991 it was announced that the acre, pint, troy ounce, mile, yard, foot, and inch would remain in use indefinitely for beer, cider, and milk measures, and in road traffic signs and land registration. Other units, including the fathom and therm, would be phased out by 1994.

import product or service that one country purchases from another for domestic consumption, or for processing and re-exporting (Hong Kong, for example, is heavily dependent on imports for its export business). Imports may be visible (goods) or invisible (services). If an importing country does not have a counterbalancing value of exports, it may experience balance-of-payments difficulties and accordingly consider restricting imports by some form of protectionism (such as an import tariff or imposing import quotas).

Impressionism movement in painting that originated in France in the 1860s and dominated European and North American painting in the late 19th century. The Impressionists wanted to depict real life, to paint straight from nature, and to capture the changing effects of light. The term was first used abusively to describe Monet's painting *Impression, Sunrise* 1872 (stolen from the Musée Marmottan, Paris); other Impressionists were Renoir and Sisley, soon joined by Cézanne, Manet, Degas, and others.

Inca member of an ancient Peruvian civilization of Quechua-speaking Indians that began in the Andean highlands about 1200; by the time of the Spanish Conquest in the 1530s, the Inca ruled from Ecuador in the north to Chile in the south.

incarnation assumption of living form (plant, animal, human) by a deity, for example the gods of Greece and Rome, Hinduism, and Christianity (Jesus as the second person of the Trinity).

inch imperial unit of linear measure, a twelfth of a foot, equal to 2.54 centimetres.

Inchon formerly *Chemulpo* chief port of Seoul, South Korea; population (1990) 1,818,300. It produces steel and textiles.

income support in the UK, ⟩social security benefit payable to people who are unemployed or who work for less than 24 hours per week and whose financial resources fall below a certain level. It replaced supplementary benefit 1988.

income tax direct tax levied on personal income, mainly wages and salaries, but which may include the value of receipts other than in cash. It is one of the main instruments for achieving a government's income redistribution objectives. In contrast, *indirect taxes* are duties payable whenever a specific product is purchased; examples include VAT and customs duties.

Independence Day public holiday in the USA, commemorating the adoption of the ⟩Declaration of Independence 4 July 1776.

Independent Television Commission (ITC) (formerly the Independent Broadcasting Authority) UK corporate body established by legislation to provide commercially funded television (ITV from 1955) and local radio (ILR from 1973) services. During the 1980s, this role was expanded to include the setting-up of Channel 4 (launched 1982) and the provision of satellite television.

index in economics, an indicator of a general movement in wages and prices over a specified period. For example, the Retail Price Index (RPI) records changes in the ⟡cost of living. The *Financial Times* Industrial Ordinary Share Index (FT) indicates the general movement of the London Stock Exchange market in the UK; the US equivalent is the Dow Jones Index.

India Republic of; country in S Asia, bordered N by China, Nepal, and Bhutan; W by Myanmar; NW by Pakistan; and SE, S, and SW by the Indian Ocean; Bangladesh is situated in the NE of India; *area* 3,166,829 sq km/1,222,396 sq mi; *capital* New Delhi; *physical* Himalaya mountains on N border; plains around rivers Ganges, Indus, Brahmaputra; Deccan peninsula S of the Narmada River forms plateau between W and E Ghats mountain ranges; desert in W; Andaman and Nicobar Islands, Lakshadweep Islands; *head of state* R Venkataraman from 1987; *head of government* P V Narasimha Rao from 1991; *political system* federal democratic republic; *exports* tea (world's largest producer), coffee, fish, iron and steel, leather, textiles, polished diamonds; *population* (1991 est) 844,000,000; *languages* Hindi, English, 14 other official languages; *recent history* independence achieved from Britain 1947. War with Pakistan 1971 led to the creation of Bangladesh. Prime Minister Indira Gandhi assassinated 1984. Central rule imposed in Jammu and Kashmir following Muslim separatist violence 1990; central rule imposed in Tamil Nadu 1991. Rajiv Gandhi, leader of the Congress (I) party, assassinated during the 1991

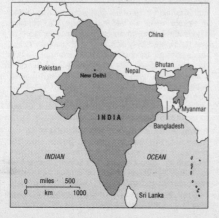

elections. Separatist violence continued. Congress (I) won control of state assembly and majority in parliament in Punjab state elections 1992.

India: history the earliest Indian civilization was that of the Indus Valley *c.* 2500–1600 BC; this may have been built up by the Dravidians, the ancestors of most of the people of S India. Invasions of Aryan people from the NW began *c.* 1500 BC. The subcontinent, except the far south, was first unified under the Mauryan emperors 321–184 BC, and again under the Gupta dynasty *c.* 300–500 AD. Muslim adventurers and traders made inroads from the 11th century and European ones from the 16th century. The Islamic Mogul Empire 1527–1857 grew to encompass virtually the whole subcontinent but declined from 1707. The British East India Company made themselves rulers of India between the mid-18th century and the Indian Mutiny 1857, when rule was transferred to the British crown. Nationalist resistance grew around the India National Congress from 1885 and Mohandas Gandhi from 1915, until in 1947 British India was divided into ⟡India and ⟡Pakistan.

Indiana state of the midwest USA; nickname Hoosier State; *area* 93,700 sq km/36,168 sq mi; *capital* Indianapolis; *cities* Fort Wayne, Gary, Evansville, South Bend; *features* Wabash River; Wyandotte Cavern; Indiana Dunes National Lakeshore; Indianapolis Motor Speedway and Museum; Robert Owen's utopian commune, New Harmony; Lincoln Boyhood National Memorial; *products* maize, pigs, soya beans, limestone, machinery, electrical goods, coal, steel, iron, chemicals; *population* (1990) 5,544,200; *famous people* Hoagy Carmichael, Eugene V Debs, Theodore Dreiser, Michael Jackson, Cole Porter, Wilbur Wright; *history* first white settlements established 1731–35 by French traders; ceded to Britain by the French 1763; passed to American control 1783; became a state 1816.

Indianapolis capital and largest city of Indiana, on the White River; population (1990) 731,300. It is an industrial centre and venue of the 'Indianapolis 500' automobile race.

Indian languages traditionally, the languages of the subcontinent of India; since 1947, the languages of the Republic of India. These number some 200, depending on whether a variety is classified as a language or a dialect. They fall into five main groups, the two most widespread of which are the Indo-European languages (mainly in the north) and the Dravidian languages (mainly in the south).

Indian Mutiny or *Sepoy Rebellion* or *Sepoy Mutiny* revolt 1857–58 of Indian soldiers (Sepoys) against the British in India. The uprising was confined to the north, from Bengal to the Punjab, and central India. The majority of support came from the army and recently dethroned princes, but in some areas it developed into a peasant uprising and general revolt. It included the seizure of Delhi by the rebels, its siege and recapture by the British, and the defence of Lucknow by a British garrison. The mutiny led to the end of rule by the British East India Company and its replacement by direct British crown administration.

Indian Ocean ocean between Africa and Australia, with India to the N, and the S boundary being an arbitrary line from Cape Agulhas to S Tasmania; area 73,500,000 sq km/28,371,000 sq mi; average depth 3,872 m/12,708 ft. The greatest depth is the Java Trench 7,725 m/25,353 ft.

indie (short for *independent*) in music, a record label that is neither owned nor distributed by one of the large conglomerates ('majors') that dominate the industry. Without a corporate bureaucratic structure, the independent labels are often quicker to respond to new trends and more idealistic in their aims. What has become loosely known as *indie music* therefore tends to be experimental, amateurish, or at the cutting edge of street fashion.

indigo violet-blue vegetable dye obtained from plants of the genus *Indigofera*, family Leguminosae, but now replaced by a synthetic product. It was once a major export crop of India.

indium soft, ductile, silver-white, metallic element, symbol In, atomic number 49, relative atomic mass 114.82. It occurs in nature in some zinc ores, is resistant to abrasion, and is used as a coating on metal parts.

Indo-Aryan languages another name for the ◊Indo-European languages.

Indochina French former collective name for ◊Cambodia, ◊Laos, and ◊Vietnam, which became independent after World War II.

Indochina War successful war of independence 1946–54 between the nationalist forces of what was to become Vietnam and France, the occupying colonial power.

Indo-European languages family of languages that includes some of the world's major classical languages (Sanskrit and Pali in India, Zend Avestan in Iran, Greek and Latin in Europe), as well as several of the most widely spoken languages (English worldwide; Spanish in Iberia, Latin America, and elsewhere; and the Hindi group of languages in N India).

Indo-Germanic languages former name for the ◊Indo-European languages.

Indonesia Republic of; country in SE Asia, consisting of many island groups, situated on the equator, between the Indian and Pacific oceans; *area* 1,919,443 sq km/740,905 sq mi; *capital* Jakata; *physical* comprises 13,677 tropical islands of the Greater Sunda group (including Java and Madura, part of Borneo (Kalimantan), Sumatra, Sulawesi, and Belitung) and the Lesser Sundas/Nusa Tenggara (including Bali, Lombok, Sumbawa, Sumba, Flores, and Timor), Malaku/Moluccas and part of New Guinea (Irian Jaya); *head of state and government* T N J Suharto from 1967; *political system* authoritarian nationalist republic; *exports* coffee, rubber, timber, palm oil, coconuts, tin, tea, tobacco, oil, liquid natural gas; *population* (1989 est) 187,726,000 (including 300 ethnic groups); *languages* Indonesian (official); Javanese is most widely spoken dialect; *recent history* unitary constitution established 1950 after the formal transfer of Dutch sovereignty the year before. Western New Guinea (Irian Jaya) ceded by the Netherlands 1963. Forced annexation of former Portuguese colony of East Timor 1976. Massacre of demonstrators in East Timor 1991 severely damaged Indonesia's international reputation.

inductance in physics, a measure of the capability of an electronic circuit or circuit component to form a magnetic field or store magnetic energy when carrying a current. Its symbol is L, and its unit of measure is the ◊henry.

inductor device included in an electrical circuit because of its inductance.

indulgence in the Roman Catholic church, the total or partial remission of temporal punishment for sins which remain to be expiated after penitence and confession have secured exemption from eternal punishment. The doctrine of indulgence began as the commutation of church penances in exchange for suitable works of charity or money gifts to the church, and became a great source of church revenue. This trade in indulgences roused Luther in 1517 to initiate the Reformation. The Council of Trent 1563 recommended moderate retention of indulgences, and they continue, notably in 'Holy Years'.

Indus river in Asia, rising in Tibet and flowing 3,180 km/1,975 mi to the Arabian Sea. In 1960 the use of its waters, including those of its five tributaries, was divided between India (rivers Ravi, Beas, Sutlej) and Pakistan (rivers Indus, Jhelum, Chenab).

Industrial Revolution the sudden acceleration of technical and economic development that began in Britain in the second half of the 18th century. The traditional agrarian economy was replaced by one dominated by machinery and manufacturing, made possible through technical advances such as the steam engine. This transferred the balance of political power from the landowner to the industrial capitalist and created an urban working class. From 1830 to the early 20th century, the Industrial Revolution spread throughout Europe and the USA and to Japan and the various colonial empires.

industry the extraction and conversion of raw materials, the manufacture of goods, and the provision of services. Industry can be either low-technology, unspecialized, and labour-intensive, as in Third World countries, or highly automated, mechanized, and specialized, using advanced technology, as in the industrialized countries. Major trends in industrial activity 1960–90 were the growth of electronic, robotic, and microelectronic technologies and the prominence of Japan and the Pacific region countries in manufacturing and distributing electronics, computers, and motor vehicles. In the UK, the prominent trends in industrial activity from the 1970s onwards have been the growth of the offshore oil and gas industries, the rapid growth of electronic and microelectronic technologies, and a continuous rise in the share of total employment of service industries.

inert gas or *noble gas* any of a group of six elements (helium, neon, argon, krypton, xenon, and radon), so named because they were originally thought not to enter into any chemical reactions. This is now known to be incorrect: in 1962, xenon was made to combine with fluorine, and since then, compounds of argon, krypton, and radon with fluorine and/or oxygen have been described.

inertia in physics, the tendency of an object to remain in a state of rest or uniform motion until an external force is applied, as stated by Isaac Newton's first law of motion (see ⟩Newton's laws of motion).

infection invasion of the body by disease-causing organisms (pathogens, or germs) that become established, multiply, and produce symptoms. Bacteria and viruses cause most diseases, but there are other microorganisms, protozoans, and other parasites.

inferiority complex in psychology, a ⟩complex described by Alfred Adler based on physical inferiority; the term has been popularly used to describe general feelings of inferiority and the overcompensation that often ensues.

infinity mathematical quantity that is larger than any fixed assignable quantity; symbol ∞. By convention, the result of dividing any number by zero is regarded as infinity.

inflation in economics, a rise in the general level of prices. The many causes include *cost-push inflation* that occurred 1974 as a result of the world price increase in oil, thus increasing production costs. *Demand-pull inflation* results when overall demand exceeds supply. Suppressed inflation occurs in controlled economies and is reflected in rationing, shortages, and black market prices. Deflation, a fall in the general level of prices, is the reverse of inflation.

influenza any of various virus infections primarily affecting the air passages, accompanied by systemic effects such as fever, chills, headache, joint and muscle pains, and lassitude. Treatment is with bed rest and analgesic drugs such as aspirin and paracetamol.

information technology collective term for the various technologies involved in processing and transmitting information. They include computing, telecommunications, and microelectronics.

infrared radiation invisible electromagnetic radiation of wavelength between about 0.75 micrometres and 1 millimetre — that is, between the limit of the red end of the visible spectrum and the shortest microwaves. All bodies above the ⟩absolute zero of temperature absorb and radiate infrared radiation. Infrared radiation is used in medical photography and treatment, and in industry, astronomy, and criminology.

infrastructure relatively permanent facilities that service an industrial economy. Infrastructure usually includes roads, railways, other communication networks, energy and water supply, and education and training facilities. Some definitions also include socio-cultural installations such as health-care and leisure facilities.

Ingres Jean Auguste Dominique 1780–1867. French painter, a student of David and leading exponent of the Neo-Classical style. He studied and worked in Rome about 1807–20, where he began the *Odalisque* series of sensuous female nudes, then went to Florence, and returned to France 1824. His portraits painted in the 1840s–50s are meticulously detailed and highly polished.

Inkatha South African political organization formed 1975 by Chief Gatsha ⟩Buthelezi, leader of 6 million Zulus, the country's biggest ethnic group. Inkatha's avowed aims are to create a nonracial democratic political situation. Inkatha has tried to work with the white regime and, as a result, Buthelezi has been widely regarded as a collaborator. Fighting between Inkatha and African National Congress members cost more than 1,000 lives in the first five months of 1990. In 1991, revelations that Inkatha had received covert financial aid from the South African government (at least £50,000 during 1989–90) increased the ANC's distrust of its motives.

INLA abbreviation for ⟩Irish National Liberation Army.

Innocent III 1161–1216. Pope from 1198 who asserted papal power over secular princes, in particular over the succession of Holy Roman Emperors. He also made King ⟩John of England his vassal, compelling him to accept Stephen Langton as archbishop of Canterbury. He promoted the fourth Crusade and crusades against the non-Christian Livonians and Letts, and the Albigensian heretics of S France.

Innsbruck capital of Tirol state, W Austria; population (1981) 117,000. It is a tourist and winter sports centre and a route junction for the Brenner Pass. The 1964 and 1976 Winter Olympics were held here.

Inns of Court four private legal societies in London, England: Lincoln's Inn, Gray's Inn, Inner Temple, and Middle Temple. All barristers (advocates in the English legal system) must belong to one of the Inns of Court. The main function of each Inn is the education, government, and protection of its members.

inoculation injection into the body of dead or weakened disease-carrying organisms or their toxins (vaccine) to produce immunity by inducing a mild form of a disease.

inorganic chemistry branch of chemistry dealing with the chemical properties of the elements and their compounds, excluding the more complex covalent compounds of carbon, which are considered in ⏵organic chemistry.

input device device for entering information into a computer. Input devices include keyboards, joysticks, mice, light pens, touch-sensitive screens, graphics tablets, speech-recognition devices, and vision systems. Compare ⏵output device.

Inquisition tribunal of the Roman Catholic church established 1233 to suppress heresy (dissenting views), originally by excommunication. Sentence was pronounced during a religious ceremony, the ⏵*auto-da-fé*. The Inquisition operated in France, Italy, Spain, and the Holy Roman Empire, and was especially active following the ⏵Reformation; it was later extended to the Americas. Its trials were conducted in secret, under torture, and penalties ranged from fines, through flogging and imprisonment, to death by burning.

insect any member of the class Insecta among the ⏵arthropods or jointed-legged animals. An insect's body is divided into head, thorax, and abdomen. The head bears a pair of feelers or antennae, and attached to the thorax are three pairs of legs and usually two pairs of wings. The scientific study of insects is termed entomology. More than one million species are known, and several thousand new ones are discovered every year. Insects vary in size from 0.02 cm/0.007 in to 35 cm/13.5 in in length.

insecticide any chemical pesticide used to kill insects. Among the most effective insecticides are synthetic organic chemicals such as ⏵DDT and dieldrin, which are chlorinated hydrocarbons. These chemicals, however, have proved persistent in the environment and are also poisonous to all animal life, including humans, and are consequently banned in many countries. Other synthetic insecticides include organic phosphorus compounds such as malathion. Insecticides prepared from plants, such as derris and pyrethrum, are safer to use but need to be applied frequently and carefully.

insemination, artificial see ⏵artificial insemination.

insider trading or *insider dealing* illegal use of privileged information in dealing on a stock exchange, for example when a company takeover bid is imminent. Insider trading is in theory detected by the Securities and Exchange Commission (SEC) in the USA, and by the Securities and Investment Board (SIB) in the UK. Neither agency, however, has any legal powers other than public disclosure and they do not bring prosecutions themselves.

instinct in ⏵ethology, behaviour found in all equivalent members of a given species (for example, all the males, or all the females with young) that is presumed to be genetically determined.

insulin protein ⏵hormone, produced by specialized cells in the islets of Langerhans in the pancreas, that regulates the metabolism (rate of activity) of glucose, fats, and proteins. Insulin was discovered by Canadian physician Frederick ⏵Banting, who pioneered its use in treating ⏵diabetes.

insurance contract indemnifying the payer of a premium against loss by fire, death, accident, and so on, which is known as *assurance* in the case of a fixed sum and *insurance* where the indemnity is proportionate to the loss.

integrated circuit (IC), popularly called *silicon chip*, a miniaturized electronic circuit produced on a single crystal, or chip, of a semiconducting material — usually silicon. It may contain many thousands of components and yet measure only 5 mm square and 1 mm thick. The IC is encapsulated within a plastic or ceramic case, and linked via gold wires to metal pins with which it is connected to a ⏵printed circuit board and the other components that make up such electronic devices as computers and calculators.

intelligence in military and political affairs, information, often secretly or illegally obtained, about other countries. *Counterintelligence* is information on the activities of hostile agents. Much intelligence is gained by technical means, such as satellites and the electronic interception of data. The British secret intelligence service (founded 1909) is M(ilitary) I(ntelligence) 6 and its agents operate abroad; the USA has the Central Intelligence Agency and the National Security Agency. In the USA, the Federal Bureau of Investigation is responsible for counterintelligence; in the UK the counterintelligence service MI5 has as its executive arm Scotland Yard's Special Branch.

intelligence test test that attempts to measure innate intellectual ability, rather than acquired ability. Alfred Binet (1857–1911) devised the first intelligence test in 1905. The concept of intelligence quotient (⏵IQ) was adopted by US psychologist Lewis Terman in 1915. Most psychologists now accept a much broader definition of intelligence, not measured by conventional intelligence tests.

interactive video (IV) computer-mediated system that enables the user to interact with and control information (including text, recorded speech, or moving images) stored on video disc.

interest in finance, a sum of money paid by a borrower to a lender in return for the loan, usually expressed as a percentage per annum. *Simple interest* is interest calculated as a straight percentage of the amount loaned or invested. In *compound interest*, the interest earned over a period of time (for example, per annum) is added to the investment, so that at the end of the next period interest is paid on that total.

interference in physics, the phenomenon of two or more wave motions interacting and combining to produce a resultant wave of larger or smaller amplitude (depending on whether the combining waves are in or out of phase with each other).

interferon naturally occurring cellular protein that makes up part of the body's defences against viral disease. Three types (alpha, beta, and gamma) are produced by infected cells and enter the bloodstream and uninfected cells, making them immune to virus attack.

Intermediate Nuclear Forces Treaty agreement signed 8 Dec 1987 between the USA and the USSR to eliminate all ground-based nuclear missiles in Europe that were capable of hitting only European targets (including European Russia). It reduced the countries's nuclear arsenals by some 2,000 (4% of the total). The treaty included provisions for each country to inspect the other's bases.

internal-combustion engine heat engine in which fuel is burned inside the engine, contrasting with an external combustion engine (such as the steam engine) in which fuel is burned in a separate unit. The diesel and ▷petrol engine are both internal-combustion engines. Gas turbines and jet and rocket engines are sometimes also considered to be internal-combustion engines because they burn their fuel inside their combustion chambers.

International, the coordinating body established by labour and socialist organizations, including the *First International* or *International Working Men's Association* 1864–72, formed in London under Karl ▷Marx; and the *Third (Socialist) International* or *Comintern* 1919–43, formed in Moscow by the Soviet leader Lenin, advocating from 1933 a popular front (communist, socialist, liberal) against the German dictator Hitler.

International Civil Aviation Organization agency of the ▷United Nations, established 1947 to regulate safety and efficiency and air law; headquarters Montréal, Canada.

International Court of Justice main judicial organ of the ▷United Nations, in The Hague, the Netherlands. It superseded the World Court by the UN charter 1945 and hears international law disputes as well as advising UN organs. There are 15 judges, each from a different member state.

International Date Line (IDL) imaginary line that approximately follows the 180° line of longitude. The date is put forward a day when crossing the line going west, and back a day when going east. The IDL was chosen at the International Meridian Conference 1884.

International Gothic late Gothic style of painting prevalent in Europe in the 14th and 15th centuries. It is characterized by increased stylization and strong decorative qualities. Exponents include the Italian Antonio Pisanello (*c.* 1395–1455/56) and the Franco-Flemish Limbourg brothers (active early 15th century).

International Labour Organization (ILO) agency of the United Nations, established 1919, which formulates standards for labour and social conditions. Its headquarters are in Geneva. It was awarded the Nobel Peace Prize 1969.

international law body of rules generally accepted as governing the relations between countries, pioneered by Hugo ▷Grotius, especially in matters of human rights, territory, and war.

International Monetary Fund (IMF) specialized agency of the ▷United Nations, headquarters Washington DC, established under the 1944 ▷Bretton Woods agreement and operational since 1947. It seeks to promote international monetary cooperation and the growth of world trade, and to smooth multilateral payment arrangements among member states.

International Society for Krishna Consciousness (ISKCON) Hindu sect based on the demonstration of intense love for Krishna (an incarnation of the god Vishnu), especially by chanting the mantra 'Hare Krishna'. Members wear distinctive yellow robes, and men often have their heads partly shaven. Their holy books are the Hindu scriptures and particularly the *Bhagavad-Gītā*, which they study daily.

Interpol (acronym for *Inter*national Criminal *Pol*ice Organization) agency founded following the Second International Judicial Police Conference 1923 with its headquarters in Vienna, and reconstituted after World War II with its headquarters in Paris. It has an international criminal register, fingerprint file, and methods index.

intestine in vertebrates, the digestive tract from the stomach outlet to the anus. The human *small intestine* is 6 m/20 ft long, 4 cm/1.5 in in diameter, and consists of the duodenum, jejunum, and ileum; the *large intestine* is 1.5 m/5 ft long, 6 cm/2.5 in in diameter, and includes the caecum, colon, and rectum. Both are muscular tubes comprising an inner lining that secretes alkaline digestive juice, a submucous coat containing fine blood vessels and nerves, a muscular coat, and a serous coat covering all, supported by a strong peritoneum, which carries the blood and lymph vessels, and the nerves. The contents are passed along slowly by peristalsis (waves of involuntary muscular action). The term intestine is also applied to the lower digestive tract of invertebrates.

Intifada Palestinian uprising; also the title of the involved *Liberation Army of Palestine*, a loosely organized group of adult and teenage Palestinians active since 1987 in attacks on Israeli troops in the occupied territories of Palestine. Their campaign for self-determination includes stone-throwing and petrol bombing.

intrusion

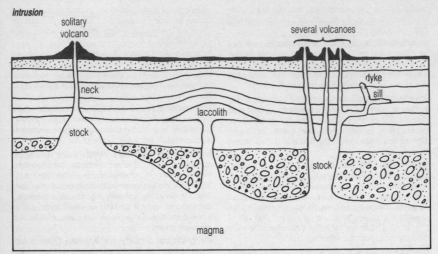

solitary volcano
several volcanoes
neck
dyke
sill
laccolith
stock
stock
magma

intrauterine device IUD or coil, a contraceptive device that is inserted into the womb (uterus). It is a tiny plastic object, sometimes containing copper. By causing a mild inflammation of the lining of the uterus it prevents fertilized eggs from becoming implanted.

intrusion mass of ⟡igneous rock that has formed by 'injection' of molten rock, or magma, into existing cracks beneath the surface of the Earth, as distinct from a volcanic rock mass which has erupted from the surface. Intrusion features include vertical cylindrical structures such as stocks and necks, sheet structures such as dykes that cut across the strata and sills that push between them, and laccoliths, which are blisters that push up the overlying rock.

Inuit people inhabiting the Arctic coasts of North America, the E islands of the Canadian Arctic, and the ice-free coasts of Greenland. Inuktitut, their language, has about 60,000 speakers; it belongs to the Eskimo-Aleut group. The Inuit object to the name Eskimos ('eaters of raw meat') given them by the Algonquin Indians.

Inverness town in Highland region, Scotland, lying in a sheltered site at the mouth of the river Ness; population (1985) 58,000. It is a tourist centre with tweed, tanning, engineering, and distilling industries.

invertebrate animal without a backbone. The invertebrates comprise over 95% of the million or so existing animal species and include sponges, coelenterates, flatworms, nematodes, annelid worms, arthropods, molluscs, echinoderms, and primitive aquatic chordates, such as sea squirts and lancelets.

investment in economics, the purchase of any

asset with the potential to yield future financial benefit to the purchaser (such as a house, a work of art, stocks and shares, or even a private education).

investment trust public company that makes investments in other companies on behalf of its shareholders. It may issue shares to raise capital and issue fixed-interest securities.

in vitro fertilization (IVF) ('fertilization in glass') allowing eggs and sperm to unite in a laboratory to form embryos. The embryos produced may then either be implanted into the womb of the otherwise infertile mother (an extension of ⟡artificial insemination), or used for research. The first baby to be produced by this method was born 1978 in the UK.

iodine greyish-black nonmetallic element, symbol I, atomic number 53, relative atomic mass 126.9044. It is a member of the ⟡halogen group. Its crystals give off, when heated, a violet vapour with an irritating odour resembling that of chlorine. It only occurs in combination with other elements. Its salts are known as iodides, which are found in sea water. As a mineral nutrient it is vital to the proper functioning of the thyroid gland, where it occurs in trace amounts as part of the hormone thyroxine. Iodine is used in photography, in medicine as an antiseptic, and in making dyes.

ion atom, or group of atoms, which is either positively charged (cation) or negatively charged (⟡anion), as a result of the loss or gain of electrons during chemical reactions or exposure to certain forms of radiation.

Iona island in the Inner Hebrides; area 850 hectares/2,100 acres. A centre of early Christianity, it is the site of a monastery founded 563 by St Columba. It later became a burial ground for Irish, Scottish, and Norwegian kings. It has a 13th-century abbey.

Ionesco Eugène 1912– . Romanian-born French dramatist, a leading exponent of the Theatre of the Absurd. Most of his plays are in one act and concern the futility of language as a means of communication. These include *La Cantatrice chauve/The Bald Prima Donna* 1950 and *La Leçon/The Lesson* 1951. Later full-length plays include *Rhinocéros* 1958 and *Le Roi se meurt/Exit the King* 1961.

Ionian member of a Hellenic people from beyond the Black Sea who crossed the Balkans around 1980 BC and invaded Asia Minor. Driven back by the ⟐Hittites, they settled all over mainland Greece, later being supplanted by the Achaeans.

ionosphere ionized layer of Earth's outer ⟐atmosphere (60–1,000 km/38–620 mi) that contains sufficient free electrons to modify the way in which radio waves are propagated, for instance by reflecting them back to Earth. The ionosphere is thought to be produced by absorption of the Sun's ultraviolet radiation.

Iowa state of the midwest USA; nickname Hawkeye State; *area* 145,800 sq km/56,279 sq mi; *capital* Des Moines; *cities* Cedar Rapids, Davenport, Sioux City; *features* Grant Wood Gallery, Davenport; Herbert Hoover birthplace, library, and museum near West Branch; 'Little Switzerland' region in the NE, overlooking the Mississippi River; Effigy Mounds National Monument, near Marquette, a prehistoric Indian burial site; *products* cereals, soya beans, pigs and cattle, chemicals, farm machinery, electrical goods, hardwood lumber, minerals; *population* (1990) 2,776,800; *famous people* 'Bix' Beiderbecke, 'Buffalo Bill' Cody, Herbert Hoover, Glenn Miller, Lillian Russell, Grant Wood; *history* Part of the ⟐Louisiana Purchase 1803, Iowa became a state 1846. It remains an area of small farms.

IQ (abbreviation for *intelligence quotient*) the ratio between a subject's 'mental' and chronological ages, multiplied by 100. A score of 100 ± 10 in an ⟐intelligence test is considered average.

IRA abbreviation for ⟐Irish Republican Army.

Iráklion or *Heraklion* chief commercial port and largest city of Crete, Greece; population (1981) 102,000.

Iran Islamic Republic of (formerly *Persia*); country in SW Asia, bordered N by the CIS and the Caspian Sea, E by Afghanistan and Pakistan, S and SW by the Gulf of Oman, W by Iraq, and NW by Turkey; *area* 1,648,000 sq km/636,128 sq mi; *capital* Tehran; *physical* plateau surrounded by mountains, including Elburz and Zagros; Lake Rezayeh; Dasht-Ekhavir Desert; occupies islands of Abu Musa, Greater Tunb, and Lesser Tunb in the Gulf; *Leader of the Islamic Revolution* Seyed Ali Khamenei from 1989; *head of government* Ali Akbar Hoshemi Rafsanjani from 1989; *political system* authoritarian Islamic republic; *exports* carpets, cotton textiles, metalwork, leather

goods, oil, petrochemicals, fruit; *population* (1989 est) 51,005,000 (including minorities in Azerbaijan, Baluchistan, Khuzestan/Arabistan, and Kurdistan); *languages* Farsi (official); Kurdish, Turkish, Arabic, English, French; *recent history* Ayatollah Khomeini returned to Iran from France 1979 to create Islamic state, replacing the shah. Iran–Iraq War 1980–88, sparked by boundary dispute over the Shatt-al-Arab waterway. Ayatollah Khomeini called for the death of British writer Salman Rushdie 1989. Peace terms with Iraq accepted 1990. In 1991 nearly 1 million Kurds arrived in Iran, fleeing persecution by Saddam Hussein in Iraq after Gulf War.

Irangate US political scandal 1987 involving senior members of the Reagan administration (called this to echo the Nixon administration's ⟐Watergate). Congressional hearings 1986–87 revealed that the US government had secretly sold weapons to Iran in 1985 and traded them for hostages held in Lebanon by pro-Iranian militias, and used the profits to supply right-wing Contra guerrillas in Nicaragua with arms.

Iraq Republic of; country in SW Asia, bordered N by Turkey, E by Iran; S by the Persian Gulf, Kuwait, and Saudi Arabia; SW by Jordan; and W by Syria; *area* 434,924 sq km/167,881 sq mi; *capital* Baghdad; *physical* mountains in N, desert in W; wide valley of rivers Tigris and Euphrates NW–SE; *head of state and government* Saddam Hussein al-Takriti from 1979; *political system* one-party socialist republic; *exports* oil (prior to UN sanctions), dates (80% of world supply), wool; *population* (1989 est) 17,610,000 (Arabs 77%, Kurds 19%, Turks 2%); *languages* Arabic (official); Kurdish, Assyrian, Armenian; *recent history* Iraq became a republic 1958. Iran–Iraq War 1980–88. Saddam Hussein invaded and annexed Kuwait 1990, precipitating the ⟐Gulf War 1991; Iraq was driven out of Kuwait by US-led forces, but Saddam Hussein remained in power.

Ireland one of the British Isles, lying to the west of Great Britain, from which it is separated by the Irish Sea. It comprises the provinces of Ulster, Leinster, Munster, and Connacht, and is divided into the Republic of Ireland (which occupies the south, centre, and northwest of the island) and Northern Ireland (which occupies the northeast corner and forms part of the United Kingdom). The centre of Ireland is a lowland, about 60–120 m/200–400 ft above sea level; hills are mainly around the coasts, although there are a few peaks over 1,000 m/3,000 ft high, the highest being Carrantuohill, 1,040 m/3,415 ft, in Macgillicuddy's Reeks, County Kerry. The entire western coastline is an intricate alternation of bays and estuaries. The lowland bogs that cover parts of central Ireland are intermingled with fertile limestone country where dairy farming is the chief occupation. The bogs are an important source of fuel in the form of ⟐peat.

Ireland, Northern constituent part of the UK;

Ireland: counties

County	Administrative headquarters	Area sq km
Ulster province		
Antrim	Belfast	2,830
Armagh	Armagh	1,250
Down	Downpatrick	2,470
Fermanagh	Enniskillen	1,680
Londonderry	Derry	2,070
Tyrone	Omagh	3,160
	NORTHERN IRELAND	13,460
Cavan	Cavan	1,890
Donegal	Lifford	4,830
Monaghan	Monaghan	1,290
Munster province		
Clare	Ennis	3,190
Cork	Cork	7,460
Kerry	Tralee	4,700
Limerick	Limerick	2,690
Tipperary (N)	Nenagh	2,000
Tipperary (S)	Clonmel	2,260
Waterford	Waterford	1,840
Leinster province		
Carlow	Carlow	900
Dublin	Dublin	920
Kildare	Naas	1,690
Kilkenny	Kilkenny	2,060
Laoighis	Portlaoise	1,720
Longford	Longford	1,040
Louth	Dundalk	820
Meath	Trim	2,340
Offaly	Tullamore	2,000
Westmeath	Mullingar	1,760
Wexford	Wexford	2,350
Wicklow	Wicklow	2,030
Connacht province		
Galway	Galway	5,940
Leitrim	Carrick-on-Shannon	1,530
Mayo	Castlebar	5,400
Roscommon	Roscommon	2,460
Sligo	Sligo	1,800
	REPUBLIC OF IRELAND	68,910

area 13,460 sq km/5,196 sq mi; *capital* Belfast; *towns* Londonderry, Enniskillen, Omagh, Newry, Armagh, Coleraine; *features* Mourne mountains, Belfast Lough and Lough Neagh; Giant's Causeway; comprises the six counties (Antrim, Armagh, Down, Fermanagh, Londonderry, and Tyrone) that form part of Ireland's northernmost province of Ulster; *exports* engineering, especially shipbuilding, textile machinery, aircraft components; linen and synthetic textiles; processed foods, especially dairy and poultry products – all affected by depression and political unrest; *currency* pound sterling; *population* (1986) 1,567,000; *language* English; *religion* Protestant 54%, Roman Catholic 31%; *famous people* Montgomery, Alanbrooke; *government* direct rule from the UK since 1972. Northern Ireland is entitled to send 12 members to the Westminster Parliament; *history* The creation of Northern Ireland dates from 1921 when the mainly Protestant counties of Ulster withdrew from the newly established Irish Free State. Spasmodic outbreaks of violence by the ◊IRA continued, but only in 1968–69 were there serious disturbances arising from Protestant political dominance and discrimination against the Roman Catholic minority in employment and housing. British troops were sent to restore peace and protect Catholics, but disturbances continued and in 1972 the parliament at Stormont was prorogued, and superseded by direct rule from Westminster. Under the ◊Anglo-Irish Agreement 1985, the Republic of Ireland was given a consultative role (via an Anglo-Irish conference) in the government of Northern Ireland, but agreed that there should be no change in its status except by majority consent. The agreement was approved by Parliament, but all 12 Ulster members gave up their seats, so that by-elections could be fought as a form of 'referendum' on the views of the province itself. A similar boycotting of the Northern Ireland Assembly led to its dissolution 1986 by the UK government. Job discrimination was outlawed under the Fair Employment Act 1975, but in 1987 Catholics were two and a half times more likely to be unemployed than their Protestant counterparts — a differential that had not improved since 1971. Between 1969 and 1991 violence had claimed 2,872 lives in Northern Ireland.

Ireland, Republic of country occupying the main part of the island of Ireland, off the NW coast of Europe. It is bordered E by the Irish Sea, S and W by the Atlantic Ocean, and NE by Northern Ireland; *area* 70,282 sq km/27,146 sq mi; *capital* Dublin; *physical* central plateau surrounded by hills; rivers Shannon, Liffey, Boyne; *head of state* Mary Robinson from 1990; *head of government*

Albert Reynolds from 1992; *political system* democratic republic; *exports* livestock, dairy products, Irish whiskey, microelectronic components and assemblies, mining and engineering products, chemicals, clothing; tourism is important; *population* (1989 est) 3,734,00; *languages* Irish Gaelic and English (both official); *recent history* independence achieved from Britain 1937. Eire left the Commonwealth and became Republic of Ireland 1949. Anglo-Irish Agreement signed 1985; relations with UK at low ebb 1988 because of disagreement over extradition decisions.

Irian Jaya the western portion of the island of New Guinea, part of Indonesia; *area* 420,000 sq km/ 162,000 sq mi; *capital* Jayapura; *population* (1989) 1,555,700; *history* part of the Dutch East Indies 1828 as Western New Guinea; retained by the Netherlands after Indonesian independence 1949 but ceded to Indonesia 1963 by the United Nations and remained part of Indonesia by an 'Act of Free Choice' 1969.

iridium hard, brittle, silver-white, metallic element, symbol Ir, atomic number 77, relative atomic mass 192.2. It is twice as heavy as lead and is resistant to tarnish and corrosion. It is one of the so-called platinum group of metals; it occurs in platinum ores and as a free metal (native metal) with osmium in osmiridium, a natural alloy that includes platinum, ruthenium, and rhodium.

iris in anatomy, the coloured muscular diaphragm that controls the size of the pupil in the vertebrate eye. It contains radial muscle that increases the pupil diameter and circular muscle that constricts the pupil diameter. Both types of muscle respond involuntarily to light intensity.

iris in botany, perennial northern temperate flowering plants of the genus *Iris*, family Iridaceae.

Irish Gaelic first official language of the Irish Republic, but much less widely used than the second official language, English. See ◊Gaelic language.

Irish language common name for Irish ◊Gaelic. At one time, especially in the form 'Erse', also a name for the Gaelic of Scotland.

Irish National Liberation Army (INLA) guerrilla organization committed to the end of British rule in Northern Ireland and the incorporation of Ulster into the Irish Republic. The INLA was a 1974 offshoot of the Irish Republican Army (IRA). Among the INLA's activities was the killing of British politician Airey Neave in 1979.

Irish Republican Army (IRA) militant Irish nationalist organization whose aim is to create a united Irish socialist republic including Ulster. The paramilitary wing of ◊Sinn Féin, it was founded 1919 and fought a successful war against Britain 1919–21. It was declared illegal in Eire 1936. The

first bombing campaign in Britain was in 1939. IRA activities intensified from 1968 onwards, as the civil-rights disorders ('the Troubles') in Northern Ireland developed. In 1970 a group in the north broke away to become the *Provisional IRA*; its objective is the expulsion of the British from Northern Ireland. In 1974 a further breakaway occurred, of the left-wing Irish Republican Socialist Party with its paramilitary wing, the Irish National Liberation Army.

iron hard, malleable and ductile, silver-grey, metallic element, symbol Fe (from Latin *ferrum*), atomic number 26, relative atomic mass 55.847. It is the fourth most abundant element (the second most abundant metal, after aluminium) in the Earth's crust.

Iron Age developmental stage of human technology when weapons and tools were made from iron. Iron was produced in Thailand by about 1600 BC but was considered inferior in strength to bronze until about 1000 when metallurgical techniques improved and the alloy steel was produced by adding carbon during the smelting process. In Britain, the Iron Age dates from about 700 BC until the Roman invasion of AD 43.

Iron Curtain in Europe after World War II, the symbolic boundary of the ◊Cold War between capitalist West and communist East. The term was popularized by the UK prime minister Winston Churchill from 1945.

Irrawaddy (Myanmar *Ayeryarwady*) chief river of Myanmar (Burma), flowing roughly N to S for 2,090 km/1,300 mi across the centre of the country into the Bay of Bengal. Its sources are the Mali and N'mai rivers; its chief tributaries are the Chindwin and Shweli.

irrigation artificial water supply for dry agricultural areas by means of dams and channels. Irrigation has been practised for thousands of years, in Eurasia as well as the Americas.

Irving Henry. Stage name of John Brodribb 1838–1905. English actor. He established his reputation from 1871, chiefly at the Lyceum Theatre in London, where he became manager 1878. He staged a series of successful Shakespearean productions, including *Romeo and Juliet* 1882, with himself and Ellen ◊Terry playing the leading roles. He was the first actor to be knighted, in 1895.

Isabella I *the Catholic* 1451–1504. Queen of Castile from 1474, after the death of her brother Henry IV. By her marriage with Ferdinand of Aragon 1469, the crowns of two of the Christian states in the Moorish-held Spanish peninsula were united. In her reign, during 1492, the Moors were driven out of Spain. She introduced the ◊Inquisition into Castile, expelled the Jews, and gave financial encouragement to ◊Columbus. Her youngest daughter was Catherine of Aragon, first wife of Henry VIII of England. In 1992 the Catholic church proposes to beatify her, arousing the indignation of Jewish groups.

Isabella of France 1292–1358. Daughter of King Philip IV of France, wife of King Edward II of England; she intrigued with her lover, Roger Mortimer, to have the king deposed and murdered.

Isaiah 8th century BC. In the Old Testament, the first major Hebrew prophet. The son of Amos, he was probably of high rank, and lived largely in Jerusalem.

Isfahan or **Eṣfahan** industrial (steel, textiles, carpets) city in central Iran; population (1986) 1,001,000. It was the ancient capital (1598–1722) of Abbas I, and its features include the Great Square, Grand Mosque, and Hall of Forty Pillars.

Isherwood Christopher (William Bradshaw) 1904–1986. English novelist. He lived in Germany 1929–33 just before Hitler's rise to power, a period that inspired *Mr Norris Changes Trains* 1935 and *Goodbye to Berlin* 1939, creating the character of Sally Bowles (the basis of the musical *Cabaret* 1968). Returning to England, he collaborated with W H ⟡Auden in three verse plays.

Ishiguro Kazuo 1954– . Japanese-born British novelist. His novel *An Artist of the Floating World* won the 1986 Whitbread Prize, and *The Remains of the Day* won the 1989 Booker Prize.

Ishtar goddess of love and war, worshipped by the Babylonians and Assyrians, and personified as the legendary queen Semiramis.

Isis the principal goddess of ancient Egypt. She was the daughter of Geb and Nut (Earth and Sky), and as the sister-wife of Osiris searched for his body after his death at the hands of his brother, Set. Her son Horus then defeated and captured Set but cut off his mother's head because she would not allow Set to be killed. She was later identified with ⟡Hathor. The cult of Isis ultimately spread to Greece and Rome.

Islam religion founded in the Arabian peninsula in the early 7th century AD. It emphasizes the oneness of God, his omnipotence, benificence, and inscrutability. The sacred book is the *Koran* of the prophet ⟡Muhammad, the Prophet or Messenger of Allah. There are two main Muslim sects: ⟡*Sunni* and ⟡*Shi'ite*. Other schools include *Sufism*, a mystical movement originating in the 8th century.

Islamabad capital of Pakistan from 1967, in the Potwar district, at the foot of the Margala Hills and immediately NW of Rawalpindi; population (1981) 201,000. The city was designed by Constantinos Doxiadis in the 1960s. The Federal Capital Territory of Islamabad has an area of 907 sq km/350 sq mi and a population (1985) of 379,000.

Islamic art art and design of Muslim nations and territories. Because the Koran forbids figurative representation in art, Islamic artistry was channelled into calligraphy and ornament. Despite this, there was naturalistic Persian painting, which inspired painters in the Mogul and Ottoman

empires. Ceramic tiles decorated mosques and palaces from Spain (Alhambra, Granada) to S Russia and Mogul India (Taj Mahal, Agra). Wood, stone, and stucco sculpture ornamented buildings. Islamic artists produced intricate metalwork and, in Persia in the 16th–17th centuries, woven textiles and carpets.

Isle of Man see ⟡Man, Isle of.

Isle of Wight see ⟡Wight, Isle of.

Ismail 1830–1895. Khedive (governor) of Egypt 1866–79. A grandson of Mehemet Ali, he became viceroy of Egypt in 1863 and in 1866 received the title of khedive from the Ottoman sultan. He amassed huge foreign debts and in 1875 Britain, at Prime Minister Disraeli's suggestion, bought the khedive's Suez Canal shares for nearly £4 million, establishing Anglo-French control of Egypt's finances. In 1879 the UK and France persuaded the sultan to appoint Tewfik, his son, khedive in his place.

Ismail I 1486–1524. Shah of Persia from 1501, founder of the *Safavi dynasty*, who established the first national government since the Arab conquest and Shi'ite Islam as the national religion.

isobar line drawn on maps and weather charts linking all places with the same atmospheric pressure (usually measured in millibars). When used in weather forecasting, the distance between the isobars is an indication of the barometric gradient.

isolationism in politics, concentration on internal rather than foreign affairs; a foreign policy having no interest in international affairs that do not affect the country's own interests.

isomer chemical compound having the same molecular composition and mass as another, but with different physical or chemical properties owing to the different structural arrangement of its constituent atoms.

isotope one of two or more atoms that have the same atomic number (same number of protons), but which contain a different number of neutrons, thus differing in their atomic masses. They may be stable or radioactive, naturally occurring or synthesized. The term was coined by English chemist Frederick Soddy, pioneer researcher in atomic disintegration.

Israel State of; country in SW Asia, bordered N by Lebanon, E by Syria and Jordan, S by the Gulf of Aqaba, and W by Egypt and the Mediterranean; *area* 20,800 sq km/8,029 sq mi (as at 1949 armistice); *capital* Jerusalem; *physical* coastal plain of Sharon between Haifa and Tel Aviv noted since ancient times for fertility; central mountains of Galilee, Samariq and Judea; river Jordan Rift Valley along the E is below sea level; Negev Desert in S occupies Golan Heights, West Bank, and Gaza; *head of state* Chaim Herzog from 1983; *head of government* Yitzhak Rabin from 1992; *political system* democratic republic; *exports* citrus and other fruit, avocados, chinese leaves,

fertilizers, diamonds, plastics, petrochemicals, textiles, electronics (military, medical, scientific, industrial), electro-optics, precision instruments, aircraft and missiles; *population* (1989 est) 4,477,000 (including 750,000 Arab Israeli citizens and over 1 million Arabs in occupied territories); *languages* Hebrew and Arabic (official); Yiddish, European, and W Asian languages; *recent history* independent state of Israel proclaimed 1948. Israel invaded Gaza and Sinai 1956. Victory in Six-Day War with Egypt 1967, gaining the West Bank area of Jordan, Jerusalem, the Sinai peninsula in Egypt, and the Golan Heights in Syria. Arab-Israeli war, called the ◊Yom Kippur War, 1973–74. Camp David talks between Egyptian and Israeli leaders 1978. Jerusalem declared capital 1980; Golan Heights formally annexed 1981; Israel withdrew from Sinai 1982. Agreement reached 1983 for withdrawal from Lebanon. Criticism of Israel's handling of Palestinian uprising in occupied territories 1988; Palestine Liberation Organization acknowledged Israel's right to exist. Israel was attacked by Iran during the ◊Gulf War, and later in 1991 the first direct negotiations between Israelis and Palestinians were held.

Istanbul city and chief seaport of Turkey; population (1990) 6,620,200. It produces textiles, tobacco, cement, glass, and leather. Founded as *Byzantium* about 660 BC, it was renamed *Constantinople* AD 330 and was the capital of the ◊Byzantine Empire until captured by the Turks 1453. As *Istamboul* it was capital of the Ottoman Empire until 1922.

Itaipu the world's largest dam, situated on the Paraná River, SW Brazil. A joint Brazilian-Paraguayan venture, it started in 1973; it supplies hydroelectricity to a wide area.

Italian Somaliland former Italian trust territory on the Somali coast of Africa extending to 502,300 sq km/194,999 sq mi. Established 1892, it was extended 1925 with the acquisition of Jubaland

from Kenya; administered from Mogadishu; under British rule 1941–50. Thereafter it reverted to Italian authority before uniting with British Somaliland in 1960 to form the independent state of Somalia.

Italy Republic of; country in S Europe, bordered N by Switzerland and Austria, E by Yugoslavia and the Adriatic Sea, S by the Ionian and Mediterranean seas, and W by the Tyrrhenian Sea and France; *area* 301,300 sq km/116,332 sq mi; *capital* Rome; *physical* mountainous (Maritime Alps, Dolomites, Apennines); rivers Po, Adige, Arno, Tiber, Rubicon; islands of Sicily, Sardinia, Elba, Capri, Ischia, Lipari, Pantelleria; lakes Como, Maggiore, Garda; *head of state* Oscar Luigi Scalfaro from 1992; *head of government* (interim) Giulio Andreotti from 1992; *political system* democratic republic; *exports* wine (world's largest producer), fruit, vegetables, textiles, clothing, leather goods, motor vehicles, electrical goods, chemicals, marble (Carrara), sulphur, mercury, iron, steel; *population* (1990 est) 57,657,000; *language* Italian; *recent history* monarchy replaced by republic 1946. Christian Democrats established a five-party coalition including the Socialists 1988; in 1989 Communists formed 'shadow government'. A referendum 1991 approved electoral reform.

Ithaca (Greek *Ithaki*) Greek island in the Ionian Sea, area 93 sq km/36 sq mi. Important in preclassical Greece, Ithaca was (in Homer's poem) the birthplace of Odysseus.

Ito Hirobumi, Prince 1841–1909. Japanese politician, prime minister 1892–96, 1898, 1900–01. He was a key figure in the modernization of Japan and was involved in the Meiji restoration 1866–68 and in government missions to the USA and Europe in the 1870s.

Ivan III Ivan the Great 1440–1505. Grand duke of Muscovy from 1462, who revolted against Tatar overlordship by refusing tribute to Grand Khan Ahmed 1480. He claimed the title of tsar, and

used the double-headed eagle as the Russian state emblem.

Ivan IV *the Terrible* 1530–1584. Grand duke of Muscovy from 1533; he assumed power 1544 and was crowned as first tsar of Russia 1547. He conquered Kazan 1552, Astrakhan 1556, and Siberia 1581. He reformed the legal code and local administration 1555 and established trade relations with England. In his last years he alternated between debauchery and religious austerities, executing thousands and, in rage, his own son.

ivory the hard white substance of which the teeth and tusks of certain mammals are composed. Most valuable are elephants' tusks, which are of unusual hardness and density. Ivory is used in carving and other decorative work, and is so valuable that poachers continue to destroy the remaining wild elephant herds in Africa to obtain it illegally.

Ivory Coast Republic of; country in W Africa, bordered N by Mali and Burkina Faso, E by Ghana, S by the Gulf of Guinea, and W by Liberia and Guinea; *area* 322,463 sq km/124,471 sq mi; *capital* Yamoussoukro; *physical* tropical rainforest in S; savanna and low mountains in N; *head of state and government* Félix Houphouët-Boigny from 1960; *political system* one-party presidential republic since 1960; *exports* coffee, cocoa, timber, petroleum products; *population* (1990 est) 12,070,000; *languages* French (official); over 60 native dialects; *recent history* independence achieved from France 1960. Name officially changed to Côte d'Ivoire 1986.

ivy any tree or shrub of the genus *Hedera* of the ginseng family Araliaceae. English or European ivy *H. helix* has shiny, evergreen, triangular or oval-shaped leaves, and clusters of small, yellowish-green flowers, followed by black berries. It climbs by means of rootlike suckers put out from its stem, and is injurious to trees.

Iwo Jima largest of the Japanese Volcano Islands in the W Pacific Ocean, 1,222 km/760 mi S of Tokyo; area 21 sq km/8 sq mi. Annexed by Japan 1891, it was captured by the USA 1945 after fierce fighting. It was returned to Japan 1968.

Izmir formerly *Smyrna*. Port and naval base in Turkey; population (1990) 1,757,400. Products include steel, electronics, and plastics. The largest annual trade fair in the Middle East is held here. It is the headquarters of ⟡North Atlantic Treaty Organization SE Command.

J

jacana one of seven species of wading birds, family Jacanidae, with very long toes and claws enabling it to walk on the flat leaves of river plants, hence the name 'lily trotter'. Jacanas are found in Mexico, Central America, South America, Africa, S Asia, and Australia.

jacaranda any tropical American tree of the genus *Jacaranda* of the family Bignoniaceae, with fragrant wood and showy blue or violet flowers, commonly cultivated in the southern USA.

jackal any of several wild dogs of the genus *Canis*, found in S Asia, S Europe, and N Africa. Jackals can grow to 80 cm/2.7 ft long, and have greyish-brown fur and a bushy tail.

jackdaw Eurasian bird *Corvus monedula* of the crow family. It is mainly black, but greyish on sides and back of head, and about 33 cm/1.1 ft long. It nests in tree holes or on buildings.

Jackson Andrew 1767–1845. 7th president of the USA 1829–37, a Democrat. A major general in the War of 1812, he defeated a British force at New Orleans in 1815 (after the official end of the war in 1814) and was involved in the war that led to the purchase of Florida in 1819. The political organization he built as president, with Martin Van Buren, was the basis for the modern ▷Democratic Party.

Jackson Glenda 1936– . English actress, Labour member of Parliament from 1992. She has made many stage appearances, including *Marat/Sade* 1966, and her films include the Oscar-winning *Women in Love* 1969, *Sunday Bloody Sunday* 1971, and *A Touch of Class* 1973. On television she played Queen Elizabeth I in *Elizabeth R* 1971.

Jackson Jesse 1941– . US Democrat politician, a cleric and campaigner for minority rights. He contested his party's 1984 and 1988 presidential nominations in an effort to increase voter registration and to put black issues on the national agenda. He is an eloquent public speaker.

Jackson Michael 1958– . US rock singer and songwriter whose videos and live performances are meticulously choreographed. His first solo hit was 'Got to Be There' 1971; his worldwide popularity peaked with the albums *Thriller* 1982 and *Bad* 1987, followed by *Dangerous* 1991.

Jacksonville port, resort, and commercial centre in Florida, USA; population (1990) 635,200. The port has naval installations and ship-repair yards. To the north the Cross-Florida Barge Canal links the Atlantic with the Gulf of Mexico. Manufactured goods include wood and paper products, chemicals, and processed food.

Jack the Ripper popular name for the unidentified mutilator and murderer of at least five women prostitutes in the Whitechapel area of London in 1888.

Jacob in the Old Testament, Hebrew patriarch, son of Isaac and Rebecca, who obtained the rights of seniority from his twin brother Esau by trickery. He married his cousins Leah and Rachel, serving their father Laban seven years for each, and at the time of famine in Canaan joined his son Joseph in Egypt. His 12 sons were the traditional ancestors of the 12 tribes of Israel.

Jacobin member of an extremist republican club of the French Revolution founded at Versailles 1789, which later used a former Jacobin (Dominican) friary as its headquarters in Paris. Helped by ▷Danton's speeches, they proclaimed the French republic, had the king executed, and overthrew the moderate ▷Girondins 1792–93. Through the Committee of Public Safety, they began the Reign of Terror, led by ▷Robespierre. After his execution 1794, the club was abandoned and the name 'Jacobin' passed into general use for any left-wing extremist.

Jacobite in Britain, a supporter of the royal house of Stuart after the deposition of James II in 1688. They include the Scottish Highlanders, who rose unsuccessfully under Claverhouse in 1689; and those who rose in Scotland and N England under the leadership of ▷James Edward Stuart, the Old Pretender, in 1715, and followed his son ▷Charles Edward Stuart in an invasion of England that reached Derby in 1745–46. After the defeat at ▷Culloden, Jacobitism disappeared as a political force.

Jacquard Joseph Marie 1752–1834. French textile manufacturer who invented a punched-card system for programming designs on a carpet-making loom. In 1804 he constructed looms that used a series of punched cards to control the pattern of longitudinal warp threads depressed before each sideways passage of the shuttle. On later machines the punched cards were joined to form an endless loop that represented the 'program' for the repeating pattern of a carpet.

Jacquerie French peasant uprising 1358, caused

by the ravages of the English army and French nobility during the Hundred Years' War, which reduced the rural population to destitution. The word derives from the nickname for French peasants, Jacques Bonhomme.

Jacuzzi Candido 1903–1986. Italian-born US engineer who invented the Jacuzzi, a pump that produces a whirlpool effect in a bathtub. It was launched commercially in the mid-1950s.

jade semiprecious stone consisting of either jadeite, $NaAlSi_2O_6$ (a pyroxene), or nephrite, $Ca_2(Mg,Fe)_5Si_8O_{22}(OH,F)_2$ (an amphibole), ranging from colourless through shades of green to black according to the iron content. Jade ranks 5.5–6.5 on the Mohs' scale of hardness.

Jaffa (biblical name *Joppa*) port in W Israel, part of ⬦Tel Aviv from 1950.

Jaffna capital of Jaffna district, Northern Province, Sri Lanka; population (1990) 129,000. It was the focal point of Hindu Tamil nationalism and the scene of recurring riots during the 1980s.

jaguar largest species of ⬦cat *Panthera onca* in the Americas, formerly ranging from the SW USA to S South America, but now extinct in most of North America. It can grow up to 2.5 m/8 ft long including the tail. The background colour of the fur varies from creamy white to brown or black, and is covered with black spots.

jaguarundi wild cat *Felis yaguoaroundi* found in forests in Central and South America. Up to 1.1 m/3.5 ft long, it is very slim with rather short legs and short rounded ears. It is uniformly coloured dark brown or chestnut. A good climber, it feeds on birds and small mammals and, unusually for a cat, has been reported to eat fruit.

Jainism ancient Indian religion, sometimes regarded as an offshoot of Hinduism. Jains emphasize the importance of not injuring living beings, and their code of ethics is based on sympathy and compassion for all forms of life. They also believe in ⬦karma but not in any deity. It is a monastic, ascetic religion. There are two main sects: the Digambaras and the Swetambaras. Jainism practises the most extreme form of nonviolence (*ahimsā*) of all Indian sects, and influenced the philosophy of Mahatma Gandhi. Jains number approximately 6 million; the majority live in India.

Jaipur capital of Rajasthan, India; population (1981) 1,005,000. Formerly the capital of the state of Jaipur, which was merged with Rajasthan in 1949. Products include textiles and metal products.

Jakarta or *Djakarta* (former name until 1949 *Batavia*) capital of Indonesia on the NW coast of Java; population (1980) 6,504,000. Industries include textiles, chemicals, and plastics; a canal links it with its port of Tanjung Priok where rubber, oil, tin, coffee, tea, and palm oil are among its exports; also a tourist centre. Jakarta was founded by Dutch traders in 1619.

Jakeš Miloš 1922– . Czech communist politician, a member of the Politburo from 1981 and party leader 1987–89. A conservative, he supported the Soviet invasion of Czechoslovakia in 1968. He was forced to resign in Nov 1989 following a series of pro-democracy mass rallies.

Jamaica island in the Caribbean, S of Cuba and W of Haiti; *area* 10,957 sq km/4,230 sq mi; *capital* Kingston; *physical* mountainous tropical island; *head of state* Elizabeth II from 1962 represented by governor general; *head of government* Percival Patterson from 1992; *political system* constitutional monarchy; *exports* sugar, bananas, bauxite, rum, cocoa, coconuts, liqueurs, cigars, citrus; *population* (1990 est) 2,513,000 (African 76%, mixed 15%, Chinese, Caucasian, East Indian); *languages* English, Jamaican creole; *recent history* internal self-government introduced 1944; independence from Britain within the Commonwealth achieved 1962. The People's National Party (PNP) held power during the 1970s, but economic decline led to a decisive victory for the Jamaica Labour Party (JLP) in the 1980 elections, an end to the JLP's policies of economic self-reliance, and closer relations with the USA.

James Henry 1843–1916. US novelist, who lived in Europe from 1875 and became a naturalized British subject 1915. His novels deal with the impact of sophisticated European culture on the innocent American. They include *The Portrait of a Lady* 1881, *Washington Square* 1881, *The Bostonians* 1886, *The Ambassadors* 1903, and *The Golden Bowl* 1904. He also wrote more than a hundred shorter works of fiction, notably the supernatural tale *The Turn of the Screw* 1898.

James Jesse 1847–1882. US bank and train robber, born in Missouri and a leader, with his brother *Frank James* (1843–1915), of the Quantrill raiders, a Confederate guerrilla band in the Civil War. Frank later led his own gang. Jesse was killed by Bob Ford, an accomplice; Frank remained unconvicted and became a farmer.

James I 1566–1625. King of England from 1603 and Scotland (as *James VI*) from 1567. The son of Mary Queen of Scots and Lord Darnley, he succeeded on his mother's abdication from the Scottish throne, assumed power 1583, established a strong centralized authority, and in 1589 married Anne of Denmark (1574–1619). As successor to Elizabeth I in England, he alienated the Puritans by his High Church views and Parliament by his assertion of ⬦divine right, and was generally unpopular because of his favourites, such as ⬦Buckingham, and his schemes for an alliance with Spain. He was succeeded by his son Charles I.

James II 1633–1701. King of England and Scotland (as *James VII*) from 1685, second son of Charles I. He succeeded Charles II. James married Anne Hyde 1659 (1637–1671, mother of Mary II and Anne) and ⬦Mary of Modena 1673 (mother of

James Edward Stuart). He became a Catholic 1671, which led first to attempts to exclude him from the succession, then to the rebellions of ▷Monmouth and Argyll, and finally to the Whig and Tory leaders' invitation to William of Orange to take the throne in 1688. James fled to France, then led an uprising in Ireland 1689, but after defeat at the Battle of the ▷Boyne 1690 remained in exile in France.

James I 1394–1437. King of Scotland 1406–37, who assumed power 1424. He was a cultured and strong monarch whose improvements in the administration of justice brought him popularity among the common people. He was assassinated by a group of conspirators led by the Earl of Atholl.

James II 1430–1460. King of Scotland from 1437, who assumed power 1449. The only surviving son of James I, he was supported by most of the nobles and Parliament. He sympathized with the Lancastrians during the Wars of the ▷Roses, and attacked English possessions in S Scotland.

James III 1451–1488. King of Scotland from 1460, who assumed power 1469. His reign was marked by rebellions by the nobles, including his brother Alexander, Duke of Albany. He was murdered during a rebellion.

James IV 1473–1513. King of Scotland from 1488, who married Margaret (1489–1541, daughter of Henry VII) in 1503. He came to the throne after his followers murdered his father, James III, at Sauchieburn. His reign was internally peaceful, but he allied himself with France against England, invaded 1513 and was defeated and killed at the Battle of ▷Flodden.

James V 1512–1542. King of Scotland from 1513, who assumed power 1528. During the long period of his minority, he was caught in a struggle between pro-French and pro-English factions. When he assumed power, he allied himself with France and upheld Catholicism against the Protestants. Following an attack on Scottish territory by Henry VIII's forces, he was defeated near the border at Solway Moss 1542.

James VI of Scotland. See ▷James I of England.

James VII of Scotland. See ▷James II of England.

James Edward Stuart 1688–1766. British prince, known as the *Old Pretender* (for the ▷Jacobites, he was James III). Son of James II, he was born at St James's Palace and after the revolution of 1688 was taken to France. He landed in Scotland in 1715 to head a Jacobite rebellion but withdrew through lack of support. In his later years he settled in Rome.

Jameson Leander Starr 1853–1917. British colonial administrator. In South Africa, early in 1896, he led the *Jameson Raid* from Mafeking into Transvaal to support the non-Boer colonists there, in an attempt to overthrow the government (for which he served some months in prison). Returning to South Africa, he succeeded Cecil ▷Rhodes as leader of the Progressive Party of Cape Colony, where he was prime minister 1904–08.

Jammu and Kashmir state of N India; *area* 101,300 sq km/39,102 sq mi; another 78,900 sq km/30,455 sq mi is occupied by Pakistan, 42,700 sq km/16,482 sq mi by China; *capital* Jammu (winter); Srinagar (summer); *towns* Leh; *products* timber, grain, rice, fruit, silk, carpets; *population* (1991) 7,718,700 (Indian-occupied territory); *history* part of the Mogul Empire from 1586, Jammu came under the control of Gulab Singh 1820. In 1947 Jammu was attacked by Pakistan and chose to become part of the new state of India. Dispute over the area caused further hostilities 1971 between India and Pakistan (ended by the Simla agreement 1972).

Janáček Leoš 1854–1928. Czech composer. He became director of the Conservatoire at Brno in 1919 and professor at the Prague Conservatoire in 1920. His music, highly original and influenced by Moravian folk music, includes arrangements of folk songs, operas (*Jenůfa* 1904, *The Cunning Little Vixen* 1924), and the choral *Glagolitic Mass* 1926.

Janus in Roman mythology, god of doorways and passageways, the patron of the beginning of the day, month, and year, after whom January is named; he is represented as having two faces, one looking forwards and one back.

Japan country in E Asia, occupying a group of islands of which the four main ones are Hokkaido, Honshu, Kyushu, and Shikoku. Japan is situated in the N Pacific, E of North and South Korea; *area* 377,535 sq km/145,822 sq mi; *capital* Tokyo; *physical* mountainous, volcanic; comprises over 1,000 islands; *head of state* (figurehead) Emperor Akihito from 1989; *head of government* Kiichi Miyazawa from 1991; *political system* liberal democracy; *exports* televisions, cassette and video recorders, radios, cameras, computers, robots, other electronic and electrical equipment, motor vehicles, ships, iron, steel, chemicals, textiles; *population* (1990 est) 123,778,000; *language* Japanese; *recent history* World War II ended wih

Japanese surrender; an Allied control commission took power and, in 1946, a Peace Constitution was framed. Full sovereignty was regained 1952. Japan joined the United Nations 1958. The postwar period has been marked by rapid economic growth and the opening of extensive foreign markets. Emperor Hirohito died and was succeeded by his son Akihito 1989. In the same year the Recruit corporation insider-trading scandal, and other revelations, led to a number of ministerial resignations, and there were further financial scandals 1992, contributing to a sharp drop in the Tokyo stock market. The rate of economic growth slowed. Japan contributed billions of dollars to the Gulf War 1991 and its aftermath, and pledged 1992 to take the world lead in environmental aid.

Jaruzelski Wojciech 1923– . Polish general, communist leader from 1981, president 1985–90. He imposed martial law for the first year of his rule, suppressed the opposition, and banned trade-union activity, but later released many political prisoners. In 1989, elections in favour of the free trade union Solidarity forced Jaruzelski to speed up democratic reforms, overseeing a transition to a new form of 'socialist pluralist' democracy and stepping down as president 1990.

jasmine any subtropical plant of the genus *Jasminium* of the olive family Oleaceae, with fragrant white or yellow flowers, and yielding jasmine oil, used in perfumes. The common jasmine *J. officinale* has pure white flowers; the Chinese winter jasmine *J. nudiflorum* has bright yellow flowers that appear before the leaves.

Jason in Greek mythology, leader of the Argonauts who sailed in the *Argo* to Colchís in search of the ◊Golden Fleece.

jaundice yellow discoloration of the skin and whites of the eyes caused by an excess of bile pigment in the bloodstream. Mild jaundice is common in newborns, but a serious form occurs in rhesus disease (see ◊rhesus factor).

Java or **Jawa** the most important island of Indonesia, situated between Sumatra and Bali; *area* (with the island of Madura) 132,000 sq km/ 51,000 sq mi; *capital* Jakarta (also capital of Indonesia); *towns* ports include Surabaya and Semarang; *physical* about half the island is under cultivation, the rest being thickly forested; *features* a chain of mountains, some of which are volcanic, runs along the centre, rising to 2,750 m/ 9,000 ft. The highest mountain, Semeru (3,676 m/ 12,060 ft) is in the east; *products* rice, coffee, cocoa, tea, sugar, rubber, quinine, teak, petroleum; *population* (with Madura; 1989) 107,513,800, including people of Javanese, Sundanese, and Madurese origin, with differing languages; *religion* predominantly Muslim; *history* the island's last Hindu kingdom, Majapahit, was destroyed about 1520 and followed by a number of short-lived Javanese kingdoms. The Dutch East India company founded a factory in 1610. Britain took over

during the Napoleonic period, 1811–16, and Java then reverted to Dutch control. Occupied by Japan 1942–45, Java then became part of the republic of ◊Indonesia.

javelin spear used in athletics events. The men's javelin is about 260 cm/8.5 ft long, weighing 800 g/ 28 oz; the women's 230 cm/7.5 ft long, weighing 600 g/21 oz. It is thrown from a scratch line at the end of a run-up. The centre of gravity on the men's javelin was altered 1986 to reduce the vast distances (90 m/100 yd) that were being thrown.

jay any of several birds of the crow family Corvidae, generally brightly coloured and native to Eurasia and the Americas. In the Eurasian common jay *Garrulus glandarius*, the body is fawn with patches of white, blue, and black on the wings and tail.

jazz polyphonic, syncopated music characterized by solo virtuosic improvisation, which developed in the USA at the turn of the 20th century. It had its roots in black American and other popular music and evolved various distinct vocal and instrumental forms. The earliest, Dixieland and swing, were mainly dance music; bebop and cool jazz, developed in the 1940s–50s, were less accessible and the jazz audience shrank with the rise of rock music. Jazz fragmented further into different styles and fusions.

Jedda alternative spelling for the Saudi Arabian port ◊Jiddah.

Jefferson Thomas 1743–1826. 3rd president of the USA 1801–09, founder of the Democratic Republican Party. He published *A Summary View of the Rights of America* 1774 and as a member of the Continental Congresses of 1775–76 was largely responsible for the drafting of the ◊Declaration of Independence. He was governor of Virginia 1779–81, ambassador to Paris 1785–89, secretary of state 1789–93, and vice president 1797–1801.

Jeffreys George, 1st Baron 1648–1689. Welsh judge, popularly known as the hanging judge. He became Chief Justice of the King's Bench in 1683, and presided over many political trials, notably those of Philip Sidney, Titus Oates, and Richard Baxter, becoming notorious for his brutality.

Jehovah's Witness member of a religious organization originating in the USA 1872 under Charles Taze Russell (1852–1916). Jehovah's Witnesses attach great importance to Christ's second coming, which Russell predicted would occur 1914, and which Witnesses still believe is imminent. All Witnesses are expected to take part in house-to-house preaching; there are no clergy.

Jekyll Gertrude 1843–1932. English landscape gardener and writer. She created over 200 gardens, many in collaboration with the architect Edwin ◊Lutyens. In her books, she advocated natural gardens of the cottage type, with plentiful herbaceous borders.

jellyfish marine invertebrate of the phylum Cnidaria (coelenterates) with an umbrella-shaped body composed of a semi-transparent gelatinous substance, with a fringe of stinging tentacles.

Jenner Edward 1749–1823. English physician who pioneered vaccination. In Jenner's day, smallpox was a major killer. His discovery 1796 that inoculation with cowpox gives immunity to smallpox was a great medical breakthrough. He coined the word 'vaccination' from the Latin word for cowpox, *vaccina*.

jerboa small, nocturnal, leaping rodent belonging to the family Dipodidae. There are about 25 species of jerboa, native to N Africa and SW Asia.

Jeremiah 7th–6th century BC. Old Testament Hebrew prophet, whose ministry continued 626–586 BC. He was imprisoned during ♢Nebuchadnezzar's siege of Jerusalem on suspicion of intending to desert to the enemy. On the city's fall, he retired to Egypt.

Jerome, St *c.* 340–420. One of the early Christian leaders and scholars known as the Fathers of the Church. His Latin versions of the Old and New Testaments form the basis of the Roman Catholic Vulgate. He is usually depicted with a lion. Feast day 30 Sept.

Jersey largest of the ♢Channel Islands; capital St Helier; area 117 sq km/45 sq mi; population (1986) 80,000. It is governed by a lieutenant-governor representing the English crown and an assembly. Jersey cattle were originally bred here; the island also gave its name to a woollen garment.

Jerusalem ancient city of Palestine, divided 1948 between Jordan and the new republic of Israel; area (pre-1967) 37.5 sq km/14.5 sq mi, (post-1967) 108 sq km/42 sq mi, including areas of the West Bank; population (1989) 500,000, about 350,000 Israelis and 150,000 Palestinians. In 1950 the western New City was proclaimed as the Israeli capital, and, having captured from Jordan the eastern Old City 1967, Israel affirmed 1980 that the united city was the country's capital; the United Nations does not recognize the claim.

Jerusalem artichoke a variety of ♢artichoke.

jet propulsion

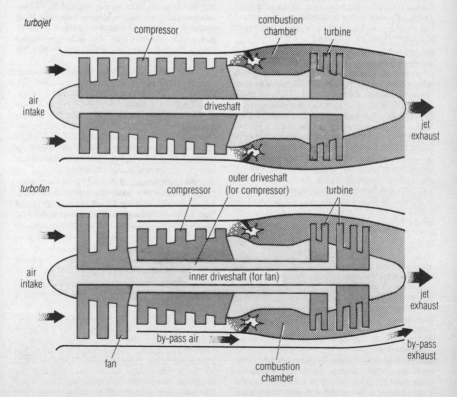

turbojet — compressor — combustion chamber — turbine — air intake — driveshaft — jet exhaust

turbofan — compressor — outer driveshaft (for compressor) — turbine — air intake — inner driveshaft (for fan) — by-pass air — fan — combustion chamber — jet exhaust — by-pass exhaust

Jesuit member of the largest and most influential Roman Catholic religious order (also known as the *Society of Jesus*) founded by ⏵Ignatius Loyola 1534, with the aims of protecting Catholicism against the Reformation and carrying out missionary work. During the 16th and 17th centuries Jesuits were missionaries in Japan, China, Paraguay, and among the North American Indians. The order had about 29,000 members in 1991 (15,000 priests plus students and lay members), and their schools and universities are renowned.

Jesus *c.* 4 BC–AD 29 or 30. Hebrew preacher on whose teachings Christianity was founded. According to the accounts of his life in the four Gospels, he was born in Bethlehem, Palestine, son of God and the Virgin Mary, and brought up by Mary and her husband Joseph as a carpenter in Nazareth. After adult baptism, he gathered 12 disciples, but his preaching antagonized the Roman authorities and he was executed by crucifixion. Three days later there came reports of his resurrection and, later, his ascension to heaven.

jetfoil advanced type of ⏵hydrofoil boat built by Boeing, propelled by water jets. It features horizontal, fully submerged hydrofoils fore and aft and has a sophisticated computerized control system to maintain its stability in all waters.

jet propulsion method of propulsion in which an object is propelled in one direction by a jet, or stream of gases, moving in the other. This follows from Isaac ⏵Newton's third law of motion: 'To every action, there is an equal and opposite reaction.' The most widespread application of the jet principle is in the *jet engine*, the most common kind of aircraft engine. The jet engine is a kind of gas turbine. Air, after passing through a forward-facing intake, is compressed by a compressor, or fan, and fed into a combustion chamber. Fuel (usually kerosene) is sprayed in and ignited. The hot gas produced expands rapidly rearwards, spinning a turbine that drives the compressor before being finally ejected from a rearward-facing tail pipe, or nozzle, at very high speed. Reaction to the jet of gases streaming backwards produces a propulsive thrust forwards, which acts on the aircraft through its engine-mountings, not from any pushing of the hot gas stream against the static air.

Jew follower of ⏵Judaism, the Jewish religion. The term is also used to those who claim descent from the ancient Hebrews, a Semitic people of the Middle East. Today, some may recognize their ethnic heritage but not practise the religious or cultural traditions. The term came into use in medieval Europe, based on the Latin name for Judeans, the people of Judah. Prejudice against Jews is termed ⏵anti-Semitism.

Jiang Zemin 1926– . Chinese political leader. The son-in-law of ⏵Li Xiannian, he joined the Chinese Communist Party's politburo in 1987 after serving in the Moscow embassy and as mayor of Shanghai. He succeeded ⏵Zhao Ziyang as party leader after the Tiananmen Square massacre of 1989. A cautious proponent of economic reform coupled with unswerving adherence to the party's 'political line', he subsequently replaced ⏵Deng Xiaoping as head of the influential central military commission.

Jiang Jie Shi alternate transcription of ⏵Chiang Kai-shek.

Jiang Qing or *Chiang Ching* 1914–1991. Chinese communist politician, third wife of the party leader Mao Zedong. In 1960 she became minister for culture, and played a key role in the 1966–69 Cultural Revolution as the leading member of the Shanghai-based Gang of Four, who attempted to seize power 1976. Jiang was imprisoned 1981.

Jiangsu or *Kiangsu* province on the coast of E China; *area* 102,200 sq km/39,449 sq mi; *capital* Nanjing; *features* the swampy mouth of the Chang Jiang (Yangtze); the special municipality of Shanghai; *products* cereals, rice, tea, cotton, soya beans, fish, silk, ceramics, textiles, coal, iron, copper, cement; *population* (1990) 67,057,000.

Jiangxi or *Kiangsi* province of SE China; *area* 164,800 sq km/63,613 sq mi; *capital* Nanchang; *products* rice, tea, cotton, tobacco, porcelain, coal, tungsten, uranium; *population* (1990) 37,710,000; *history* the province was Mao Zedong's original base in the first phase of the Communist struggle against the Nationalists.

Jiddah or *Jedda* port in Hejaz, Saudi Arabia, on the E shore of the Red Sea; population (1986) 1,000,000. Industries include cement, steel, and oil refining. Pilgrims pass through here on their way to Mecca.

Jilin or *Kirin* province of NE China in central ⏵Manchuria; *area* 187,000 sq km/72,182 sq mi; *capital* Changchun; *population* (1990) 24,659,000.

Jinan or *Tsinan* city and capital of Shandong province, China; population (1989) 2,290,000. It has food-processing and textile industries.

Jinnah Muhammad Ali 1876–1948. Indian politician, Pakistan's first governor general from 1947. He was president of the Muslim League 1916 and from 1934, and by 1940 was advocating the need for a separate state of Pakistan; at the 1946 conferences in London he insisted on the partition of British India into Hindu and Muslim states.

Jinsha Jiang river that rises in SW China and forms the ⏵Chang Jiang (Yangtze) at Yibin.

jive energetic American dance that evolved from the jitterbug, popular in the 1940s and 1950s; a forerunner of rock and roll.

Joan of Arc, St 1412–1431. French military leader. In 1429 at Chinon, NW France, she persuaded Charles VII that she had a divine mission to expel the occupying English from N France (see ⏵Hundred Years' War) and secure his coronation. She raised the siege of Orléans, defeated the English at Patay, north of Orléans, and Charles was crowned in Reims. However, she failed to take Paris and was captured May 1430 by the Burgundians, who sold her to the English. She was found guilty of witchcraft and heresy by a tribunal of French ecclesiastics who supported the English. She was burned to death at the stake in Rouen 30 May 1431. In 1920 she was canonized.

Jodrell Bank site in Cheshire, England, of the Nuffield Radio Astronomy Laboratories of the University of Manchester. Its largest instrument is the 76 m/250 ft radio dish (the Lovell Telescope), completed 1957 and modified 1970. A 38m × 25 m/ 125 ft × 82 ft elliptical radio dish was introduced 1964, capable of working at shorter wavelengths.

Johannesburg largest city of South Africa, situated on the Witwatersrand River in Transvaal; population (1985) 1,609,000. It is the centre of a large gold-mining industry; other industries include engineering works, meat-chilling plants, and clothing factories.

John Elton. Stage name of Reginald Kenneth Dwight 1947–   . English pop singer, pianist, and composer, noted for his melodies and elaborate costumes and glasses. His best-known LP, *Goodbye Yellow Brick Road* 1973, includes the hit 'Bennie and the Jets'. His output is prolific and his hits continued intermittently in the 1980s and 90s.

John *Lackland* 1167–1216. King of England from 1199 and acting king from 1189 during his brother Richard I's (the Lion-Heart) absence on the third Crusade. He lost Normandy and almost all the other English possessions in France to Philip II of France by 1205. His repressive policies and excessive taxation brought him into conflict with his barons, and he was forced to seal the ⟡Magna Carta 1215. Later repudiation of it led to the first Barons' War 1215–17, during which he died.

John I 1357–1433. King of Portugal from 1385. An illegitimate son of Pedro I, he was elected by the Cortes (parliament). His claim was supported by an English army against the rival king of Castile, thus establishing the Anglo-Portuguese Alliance

Johnson Andrew 1808–1875. 17th president of the USA 1865–69, a Democrat. He was a congressman from Tennessee 1843–53, governor of Tennessee 1853–57, senator 1857–62, and vice president 1865. He succeeded to the presidency on Lincoln's assassination (15 April 1865). His conciliatory policy to the defeated South after the Civil War involved him in a feud with the Radical Republicans, culminating 1868 with his impeachment before the Senate, which failed to convict him by one vote.

Johnson Lyndon Baines 1908–1973. 36th president of the USA 1963–69, a Democrat from Texas, elected to Congress 1937–49 and the Senate 1949–60. As vice president, he became president on J F Kennedy's assassination. After the Tonkin Gulf Incident, which precipitated US involvement in the ⟡Vietnam War, support won by Johnson's Great Society legislation (civil rights, education,

alleviation of poverty) dissipated, and he declined to run for re-election 1968.

Johnson Samuel, known as 'Dr Johnson', 1709–1784. English lexicographer, author, and critic, also a brilliant conversationalist and the dominant figure in 18th-century London literary society. His *Dictionary*, published 1755, remained authoritative for over a century, and is still remarkable for the vigour of its definitions. In 1764 he founded the Literary Club, whose members included the painter Joshua Reynolds, the political philosopher Edmund Burke, the playwright Oliver Goldsmith, the actor David Garrick, and James ⟡Boswell, Johnson's biographer.

Johnston Atoll coral island in the mid-Pacific, lying between the ⟡Marshall Islands and Hawaii; area 2.8 sq km. The island is only 2.4 m/8 ft above sea level and subject to hurricanes and tidal waves. It has the status of a National Wildlife Refuge but was contaminated by fallout from nuclear-weapons tests in 1962, and has since 1971 been used as a repository for chemical weapons left over from the Korean and Vietnam wars. An unincorporated territory of the USA, it is administered by the US Defense Nuclear Agency (DNA).

John the Baptist, St *c.* 12 BC–*c.* AD 27. In the New Testament, an itinerant preacher. After preparation in the wilderness, he proclaimed the coming of the Messiah and baptized Jesus in the river Jordan. He was later executed by ⟡Herod Antiplas at the request of Salome, who demanded that his head be brought to her on a platter. As an adult, he is depicted with a shaggy beard and robes.

joint in any animal with a skeleton, a point of movement or articulation. In vertebrates, it is the point where two bones meet. Some joints allow no motion (the sutures of the skull), others allow a very small motion (the sacroiliac joints in the lower back), but most allow a relatively free motion. Of these, some allow a gliding motion (one vertebra of the spine on another), some have a hinge action (elbow and knee), and others allow motion in all directions (hip and shoulder joints), by means of a ball-and-socket arrangement. In invertebrates with an exoskeleton, the joints are places where the exoskeleton is replaced by a more flexible outer covering, the arthrodial membrane, which allows the limb (or other body part) to bend at that point.

Joliot-Curie Irène 1897–1956 and Frédéric (born Frédéric Joliot) 1900–1958. French physicists who made the discovery of artificial radioactivity, for which they were jointly awarded the 1935 Nobel Prize for Chemistry.

Jolson Al. Stage name of Asa Yoelson 1886–1950. Russian-born US singer and entertainer. Formerly a Broadway and vaudeville star, he gained instant film immortality as the star of the first talking picture, *The Jazz Singer* 1927.

Jonah 7th century BC. Hebrew prophet whose name is given to a book in the Old Testament.

According to this, he fled by ship to evade his mission to prophesy the destruction of Nineveh. The crew threw him overboard in a storm, as a bringer of ill fortune, and he spent three days and nights in the belly of a whale before coming to land.

Jones Inigo 1573–c. 1652. English classical architect. Born in London, he studied in Italy and was influenced by the works of Palladio. He was employed by James I to design scenery for Ben Jonson's masques. He designed the Queen's House, Greenwich 1616–35 and his English Renaissance masterpiece, the banqueting room at Whitehall, London, 1619–22.

jonquil species of small daffodil *Narcissus jonquilla*, family Amaryllidaceae, with yellow flowers. Native to Spain and Portugal, it is cultivated elsewhere.

Jonson Ben (jamin) 1572–1637. English dramatist, poet, and critic. *Every Man in his Humour* 1598 established the English 'comedy of humours', in which each character embodies a 'humour', or vice, such as greed, lust, or avarice. This was followed by *Cynthia's Revels* 1600 and *Poetaster* 1601. His first extant tragedy is *Sejanus* 1603, with Burbage and Shakespeare as members of the original cast. The plays of his middle years include *Volpone, or The Fox* 1606, *The Alchemist* 1610, and *Bartholomew Fair* 1614.

Joplin Scott 1868–1917. US ◊ragtime pianist and composer, active in Chicago. His 'Maple Leaf Rag' 1899 was the first instrumental sheet music to sell a million copies, and 'The Entertainer', as the theme tune of the film *The Sting* 1973, revived his popularity. He was an influence on Jelly Roll Morton and other early jazz musicians.

Jordan Hashemite Kingdom of; country in SW Asia, bordered N by Syria, NE by Iraq, E and SE by Saudi Arabia, S by the Gulf of Aqaba, and W by Israel; *area* 89,206 sq km/34,434 sq mi (West Bank incorporated into Jordan 1950 but occupied by Israel since 1967, area 5,879 sq km/2,269 sq mi); *capital* Amman; *physical* desert plateau in E; rift valley separates E and W banks of river Jordan; *head of state* King Hussein ibn Talai from 1952; *head of government* Mudar Badran from 1989; *political system* constitutional monarchy; *exports* potash, phosphates, citrus, vegetables; *population* (1990 est) 3,065,000 (including Palestinian refugees); West Bank (1988) 866,000; *languages* Arabic (official); English; *recent history* independence achieved from Britain as Transjordan 1946; new state of Jordan declared 1949. In 1958 Jordan and Iraq formed Arab Federation, which ended when the Iraqi monarchy was deposed. Since assuming power 1952, and despite the fact that three of Jordan's eight administrative provinces have been occupied by Israel since 1967, King Hussein has tried to act as a mediating influence in Middle Eastern politics; in 1985 he proposed a framework for a Middle East peace settlement; and in 1988 ceased administering the West Bank as part of Jordan, passing responsibility to the Palestine Liberation Organization. In 1989 an 80-member parliament was elected and a prime minister appointed. In 1990 Hussein unsuccessfully tried to mediate after Iraq's invasion of Kuwait, and accepted thousands of refugees who fled to Jordan from Kuwait and Iraq.

Joseph in the New Testament, the husband of the Virgin Mary, a descendant of King David of the Tribe of Judah, and a carpenter by trade. Although Jesus was not the son of Joseph, Joseph was his legal father. According to Roman Catholic tradition, he had a family by a previous wife, and was an elderly man when he married Mary.

Josephine Marie Josèphe Rose Tascher de la Pagerie 1763–1814. As wife of ◊Napoleon Bonaparte, she was empress of France 1796–1809. Born 1386. He married Philippa of Lancaster, daughter of ◊John of Gaunt.

John Bull imaginary figure who is a personification of England, similar to the American Uncle Sam. He is represented in cartoons and caricatures as a prosperous farmer of the 18th century.

John of Gaunt 1340–1399. English politician, born in Ghent, fourth son of Edward III, Duke of Lancaster from 1362. He distinguished himself during the Hundred Years' War. During Edward's last years, and the years before Richard II attained the age of majority, he acted as head of government, and Parliament protested against his corrupt rule.

John Paul II Karol Wojtyla 1920– . Pope from 1978, the first non-Italian to be elected pope since 1522. He was born near Kraków, Poland. He has upheld the tradition of papal infallibility, condemned artificial contraception, women priests, married priests, and modern dress for monks and nuns, and warned against involvement of priests in political activity. All this has aroused criticism from liberalizing elements in the church.

Johns Jasper 1930– . US painter and printmaker who rejected the abstract in favour of such simple subjects as flags, maps, and numbers. He uses pigments mixed with wax (encaustic) to create a rich surface with unexpected delicacies of colour. He has also created collages and lithographs.

John, St 1st century AD. New Testament apostle. Traditionally, he wrote the fourth Gospel and the Johannine Epistles (when he was bishop of Ephesus), and the Book of Revelation (while exiled to the Greek island of Patmos). His emblem is an eagle; his feast day 27 Dec.

Johnson Amy 1903–1941. British aviator. She made a solo flight from England to Australia 1930, in 9½ days, and in 1932 made the fastest ever solo flight from England to Cape Town, South Africa. Her plane disappeared over the English Channel in World War II while she was serving with the Air Transport Auxiliary.

on Martinique, she married in 1779 Alexandre de Beauharnais, who played a part in the French Revolution, and in 1796 Napoleon, who divorced her in 1809 because she had not produced children.

Joseph of Arimathaea, St 1st century AD. In the New Testament, a wealthy Hebrew, member of the Sanhedrin (supreme court), and secret supporter of Jesus. On the evening of the Crucifixion he asked the Roman procurator Pilate for Jesus's body and buried it in his own tomb. Feast day 17 Mar.

joule SI unit (symbol J) of work and energy, replacing the ▷calorie (one joule equals 4.2 calories). It is defined as the work done (energy transferred) by a force of one newton acting over one metre. It can also be expressed as the work done in one second by a current of one ampere at a potential difference of one volt. One watt is equal to one joule per second.

Joule James Prescott 1818–1889. English physicist whose work on the relations between electrical, mechanical, and chemical effects led to the discovery of the first law of ▷thermodynamics.

Joyce James (Augustine Aloysius) 1882–1941. Irish writer, born in Dublin, who revolutionized the form of the English novel with his 'stream of consciousness' technique. His works include *Dubliners* 1914 (short stories), *Portrait of the Artist as a Young Man* 1916, *Ulysses* 1922, and *Finnegans Wake* 1939.

Juan Carlos 1938– . King of Spain. The son of Don Juan, pretender to the Spanish throne, he married Princess Sofia in 1962, eldest daughter of King Paul of Greece. In 1969 he was nominated by ▷Franco to succeed on the restoration of the monarchy intended to follow Franco's death; his father was excluded because of his known liberal views. Juan Carlos became king in 1975.

Juárez Benito 1806–1872. Mexican politician, president 1861–65 and 1867–72. In 1861 he suspended repayments of Mexico's foreign debts, which prompted a joint French, British, and Spanish expedition to exert pressure. French forces invaded and created an empire for Maximilian (1832–1867), brother of the Austrian emperor. After their withdrawal in 1867, Maximilian was executed, and Juárez returned to the presidency.

Judah or *Judaea* district of S Palestine. After the death of King Solomon 937 BC, Judah adhered to his son Rehoboam and the Davidic line, whereas the rest of Israel elected Jeroboam as ruler of the northern kingdom. In New Testament times, Judah was the Roman province of Judaea, and in current Israeli usage it refers to the southern area of the West Bank.

Judaism the religion of the ancient Hebrews and their descendants the Jews, based, according to the Old Testament, on a covenant between God and Abraham about 2000 BC, and the renewal of the covenant with Moses about 1200 BC. It rests on the concept of one eternal invisible God, whose will is revealed in the *Torah* and who has a special relationship with the Jewish people. The Torah comprises the first five books of the Bible (the Pentateuch), which contains the history, laws, and guide to life for correct behaviour. Besides those living in Israel, there are large Jewish populations today in the USA, the former USSR (mostly Russia, Ukraine, Belarus, and Moldova), the UK and Commonwealth nations, and in Jewish communities throughout the world. There are approximately 18 million Jews, with about 9 million in the Americas, 5 million in Europe, and 4 million in Asia, Africa, and the Pacific.

Judas Iscariot 1st century AD. In the New Testament, the disciple who betrayed Jesus Christ. Judas was the treasurer of the group. At the last Passover supper he arranged, for 30 pieces of silver, to point out Jesus to the chief priests so that they could arrest him. Afterwards Judas was overcome with remorse and committed suicide.

judge person invested with power to hear and determine legal disputes. In the UK, judges are chosen from barristers of long standing, but solicitors can be appointed circuit judges. Judges of the High Court, the crown courts, and the county courts are appointed at the advice of the Lord Chancellor, and those of the Court of Appeal and the House of Lords at the advice of the prime minister, although all judges are appointed by the crown. Judges can be removed from office only by a resolution of both houses of Parliament.

judiciary in constitutional terms, the system of courts and body of judges in a country. The independence of the judiciary from other branches of the central authority is generally considered to be an essential feature of a democratic political system. This independence is often written into a nation's constitution and protected from abuse by politicians.

judo form of wrestling of Japanese origin. The two combatants wear loose-fitting, belted jackets and trousers to facilitate holds, and falls are broken by a square mat; when one has established a painful hold that the other cannot break, the latter signifies surrender by slapping the ground with a free hand. Degrees of proficiency are indicated by the colour of the belt: for novices, white; after examination, brown (three degrees); and finally, black (nine degrees).

Jugoslavia alternative spelling of ▷Yugoslavia.

jujube tree of the genus *Zizyphus* of the buckthorn family Thamnaceae, with berrylike fruits.

Julian the Apostate c. 331–363. Roman emperor. Born in Constantinople, the nephew of Constantine the Great, he was brought up as a Christian but early in life became a convert to paganism. Sent by Constantius to govern Gaul in 355, he was proclaimed emperor by his troops in 360, and in 361 was marching on Constantinople when Constantius' death allowed a peaceful succession. He revived pagan worship and refused to persecute heretics.

Julius II 1443–1513. Pope 1503–13. A politician

who wanted to make the Papal States the leading power in Italy, he formed international alliances first against Venice and then against France. He began the building of St Peter's Church in Rome 1506 and was the patron of the artists Michelangelo and Raphael.

July Revolution revolution 27–29 July 1830 in France that overthrew the restored Bourbon monarchy of Charles X and substituted the constitutional monarchy of Louis Philippe, whose rule (1830–48) is sometimes referred to as the July Monarchy.

jumbo jet popular name for a generation of huge wide-bodied airliners including the *Boeing 747*, which is 71 m/232 ft long, has a wingspan of 60 m/196 ft, a maximum takeoff weight of nearly 380 tonnes/400 tons, and can carry more than 400 passengers.

Jung Carl Gustav 1875–1961. Swiss psychiatrist who collaborated with Sigmund ⟡Freud until their disagreement in 1912 over the importance of sexuality in causing psychological problems. Jung studied religion and dream symbolism, saw the unconscious as a source of spiritual insight, and distinguished between introversion and extroversion. His books include *Modern Man in Search of a Soul* 1933.

juniper aromatic evergreen tree or shrub of the genus *Juniperus* of the cypress family Cupressaceae, found throughout temperate regions. Its berries are used to flavour gin. Some junipers are erroneously called ⟡cedars.

junk bond derogatory term for a security officially rated as 'below investment grade'. It is issued in order to raise capital quickly, typically to finance a takeover to be paid for by the sale of assets once the company is acquired. Junk bonds have a high yield, but are a high-risk investment.

Juno principal goddess in Roman mythology (identified with the Greek Hera). The wife of Jupiter, the queen of heaven, she was concerned with all aspects of women's lives.

Jupiter or *Jove* in mythology, chief god of the Romans, identified with the Greek ⟡Zeus. He was god of the sky, associated with lightning and thunderbolts; protector in battle; and bestower of victory. The son of Saturn, he married his sister Juno, and reigned on Mount Olympus as lord of heaven.

Jupiter the fifth planet from the Sun, and the largest in the Solar System (equatorial diameter 142,800 km/88,700 mi), with a mass more than twice that of all the other planets combined, 318 times that of the Earth's. It takes 11.86 years to orbit the Sun, at an average distance of 778 million km/484 million mi, and has at least 16 moons. It is largely composed of hydrogen and helium, liquefied by pressure in its interior, and probably with a rocky core larger than the Earth. Its main feature is the Great Red Spot, a cloud of rising gases, revolving anticlockwise, 14,000 km/8,500 mi wide and some 30,000 km/20,000 mi long.

Jura mountains series of parallel mountain ranges running SW–NE along the French-Swiss frontier between the rivers Rhône and Rhine, a distance of 250 km/156 mi. The highest peak is *Crête de la Neige*, 1,723 m/5,650 ft.

Jurassic period of geological time 213–144 million years ago; the middle period of the Mesozoic era. Climates worldwide were equable, creating forests of conifers and ferns, dinosaurs were abundant, birds evolved, and limestones and iron ores were deposited.

jury body of lay people (usually 12) sworn to decide the facts of a case and reach a verdict in a court of law. Juries, used mainly in English-speaking countries, are implemented primarily in criminal cases, but also sometimes in civil cases; for example, inquests and libel trials.

justice of the peace (JP) in England, an unpaid ⟡magistrate. In the USA, where JPs receive fees and are usually elected, their courts are the lowest in the states, and deal only with minor offences, such as traffic violations; they may also conduct marriages.

Justinian I 483–565. Byzantine emperor from 527. He recovered N Africa from the Vandals, SE Spain from the Visigoths, and Italy from the Ostrogoths, largely owing to his great general Belisarius. He ordered the codification of Roman law, which has influenced European jurisprudence.

jute fibre obtained from two plants of the genus *Corchorus* of the linden family: *C. capsularis* and *C. olitorius*. Jute is used for sacks and sacking, upholstery, webbing, twine, and stage canvas.

Jute member of a Germanic people who originated in Jutland but later settled in Frankish territory. They occupied Kent, SE England, about 450, according to tradition under Hengist and Horsa, and conquered the Isle of Wight and the opposite coast of Hampshire in the early 6th century.

Jutland (Danish *Jylland*) peninsula of N Europe; area 29,500 sq km/11,400 sq mi. It is separated from Norway by the Skagerrak and from Sweden by the Kattegat, with the North Sea to the west. The larger northern part belongs to Denmark, the southern part to Germany.

Juvenal *c.* AD 60–140. Roman satirist and poet. His genius for satire brought him to the unfavourable notice of the emperor Domitian. Juvenal's 16 extant satires give an explicit and sometimes brutal picture of the decadent Roman society of his time.

K2 or *Chogori* second highest mountain above sea level, 8,611 m/28,261 ft, in the Karakoram range, Kashmir, N India. It was first climbed 1954 by an Italian expedition.

kabbala or *cabbala* (Hebrew 'tradition') ancient esoteric Jewish mystical tradition of philosophy containing strong elements of pantheism yet akin to neo-Platonism. Kabbalistic writing reached its peak between the 13th and 16th centuries. It is largely rejected by current Judaic thought as medieval superstition, but is basic to the ▷Hasid sect.

Kabul capital of Afghanistan, 2,100 m/6,900 ft above sea level, on the river Kabul; population (1984) 1,179,300. Products include textiles, plastics, leather, and glass. It commands the strategic routes to Pakistan via the ▷Khyber Pass.

Kádár János 1912–1989. Hungarian Communist leader, in power 1956–88, after suppressing the national uprising. As Hungarian Socialist Workers' Party (HSWP) leader and prime minister 1956–58 and 1961–65, Kádár introduced a series of market-socialist economic reforms, while retaining cordial political relations with the USSR.

Kafka Franz 1883–1924. Czech novelist, born in Prague, who wrote in German. His three unfinished allegorical novels *Der Prozess/The Trial* 1925, *Der Schloss/The Castle* 1926, and *Amerika/America* 1927 were posthumously published despite his instructions that they should be destroyed. His short stories include 'Die Verwandlung/The Metamorphosis' 1915, in which a man turns into a huge insect. His vision of lonely individuals trapped in bureaucratic or legal labyrinths can be seen as a powerful metaphor for modern experience.

Kaiser title formerly used by the Holy Roman emperors, Austrian emperors 1806–1918, and German emperors 1871–1918. The word, like the Russian 'tsar', is derived from the Latin *Caesar*.

Kalahari Desert semi-desert area forming most of Botswana and extending into Namibia, Zimbabwe, and South Africa; area about 900,000 sq km/347,400 sq mi. The only permanent river, the Okavango, flows into a delta in the NW forming marshes rich in wildlife. Its inhabitants are the nomadic Kung.

kale type of ▷cabbage.

Kalgan city in NE China, now known as ▷Zhangjiakou.

Kali in Hindu mythology, the goddess of destruction and death. She is the wife of ▷Siva.

Kālidāsa lived 5th century AD. Indian epic poet and dramatist. His works, in Sanskrit, include the classic drama *Sakuntala*, the love story of King Dushyanta and the nymph Sakuntala.

Kalimantan province of the republic of Indonesia occupying part of the island of Borneo; *area* 543,900 sq km/210,000 sq mi; *towns* Banjermasin and Balikpapan; *physical* mostly low-lying, with mountains in the north; *products* petroleum, rubber, coffee, copra, pepper, timber; *population* (1989 est) 8,677,500.

Kalinin Mikhail Ivanovich 1875–1946. Soviet politician, founder of the newspaper *Pravda*. He was prominent in the 1917 October Revolution, and in 1919 became head of state (president of the Central Executive Committee of the Soviet government until 1937, then president of the Presidium of the Supreme Soviet until 1946).

Kamchatka mountainous peninsula separating the Bering Sea and Sea of Okhotsk, forming (together with the Chukchi and Koryak national districts) a region of E Siberian Russia. Its capital, Petropavlovsk, is the only town; agriculture is possible only in the south. Most of the inhabitants are fishers and hunters.

Kampala capital of Uganda; population (1983) 455,000. It is linked by rail with Mombasa. Products include tea, coffee, textiles, fruit, and vegetables.

Kampuchea former name (1975–89) of ▷Cambodia.

Kananga chief city of Kasai Occidental region, W central Zaire, on the Lulua river; population (1984) 291,000. It was known as *Luluabourg* until 1966.

Kanchenjunga variant spelling of ▷Kangchenjunga, a Himalayan mountain.

Kandinsky Wassily 1866–1944. Russian painter, a pioneer of abstract art. Born in Moscow, he travelled widely, settling in Munich 1896. Around 1910 he produced the first known examples of purely abstract work in 20th-century art. He was an originator of the ▷*Blaue Reiter* movement 1911–12. From 1921 he taught at the ▷Bauhaus school of design. He moved to Paris 1933, becoming a French citizen 1939.

Kandy city in central Sri Lanka, former capital of the kingdom of Kandy 1480–1815; population

(1990) 104,000. Products include tea. One of the most sacred Buddhist shrines is situated in Kandy.

kangaroo any marsupial of the family Macropodidae found in Australia, Tasmania, and New Guinea. Kangaroos are plant-eaters and most live in groups. They are adapted to hopping, the vast majority of species having very large back legs and feet compared with the small forelimbs. The larger types can jump 9 m/30 ft at a single bound. Most are nocturnal. Species vary from small rat kangaroos, only 30 cm/1 ft long, through the medium-sized wallabies, to the large red and great grey kangaroos, which are the largest living marsupials. Red kangaroos may be 2 m/6.5 ft long and grey kangaroos 1.8 m/5.9 ft long with 1.1 m/3.5 ft tails.

Kangchenjunga Himalayan mountain on the Nepal–Sikkim border, 8,598 m/28,208 ft high, 120 km/75 mi SE of Mount Everest. The name means 'five treasure houses of the great snows'. Kangchenjunga was first climbed by a British expedition 1955.

Ka Ngwane black homeland in Natal province, South Africa; achieved self-governing status 1971; population (1985) 392,800.

Kano capital of Kano state in N Nigeria, trade centre of an irrigated area; population (1983) 487,100. Products include bicycles, glass, furniture, textiles, and chemicals. Founded about 1000 BC, Kano is a walled city, with New Kano extending beyond the walls.

Kanpur formerly *Cawnpore* capital of Kanpur district, Uttar Pradesh, India, SW of Lucknow, on the river Ganges; a commercial and industrial centre (cotton, wool, jute, chemicals, plastics, iron, steel); population (1981) 1,688,000.

Kansas state in central USA; nickname Sunflower State; *area* 213,200 sq km/82,296 sq mi; *capital* Topeka; *cities* Kansas City, Wichita, Overland Park; *features* Dodge City, once 'cowboy capital of the world'; Eisenhower Center, Abilene; Fort Larned and Fort Scott; Pony Express station, Hanover; Wichita Cowtown, a frontier-era reproduction; *products* wheat, cattle, coal, petroleum,

kangaroo

natural gas, aircraft, minerals; *population* (1990) 2,477,600; *famous people* Amelia Earhart; Dwight D Eisenhower; William Inge; Buster Keaton; C F William and Karl Menninger; Carry Nation; Charlie Parker; Gordon Parks; William Allen White; *history* explored by Francisco de Coronado for Spain 1541 and La Salle for France 1682; ceded to the USA 1803 as part of the Louisiana Purchase.

Kansas City twin city in the USA at the confluence of the Missouri and Kansas rivers, partly in Kansas and partly in Missouri; population (1990) of Kansas City (Kansas) 149,800, Kansas City (Missouri) 435,100. A market and agricultural distribution centre and one of the chief livestock centres of the USA. Kansas City, Missouri, has car assembly plants and Kansas City, Kansas, has the majority of offices.

Kansu alternative spelling for the Chinese province ⟡Gansu.

Kant Immanuel 1724–1804. German philosopher who believed that knowledge is not merely an aggregate of sense impressions but is dependent on the conceptual apparatus of the human understanding, which is itself not derived from experience. In ethics, Kant argued that right action cannot be based on feelings or inclinations but conforms to a law given by reason, the *categorical imperative*.

Kanto flat, densely populated region of E Honshu island, Japan; population (1988) 37,867,000; area 32,377 sq km/12,505 sq mi. The chief city is Tokyo.

Karachi largest city and chief seaport of Pakistan, and capital of Sind province, NW of the Indus delta; population (1981) 5,208,000. Industries include engineering, chemicals, plastics, and textiles. It was the capital of Pakistan 1947–59.

Karajan Herbert von 1908–1989. Austrian conductor. He was the principal conductor of the Berlin Philharmonic Orchestra 1955–89 and artistic director of the Vienna State Opera 1956–64. He was also the artistic director of the Salzburg Festival from 1956 to 1960. He was associated with the Classical and Romantic repertoire – Beethoven, Brahms, Mahler, and Richard Strauss.

Karakoram mountain range in central Asia, divided among China, Pakistan, and India. Peaks include K2, Masharbrum, Gasharbrum, and Mustagh Tower. *Ladakh* subsidiary range is in NE Kashmir on the Tibetan border.

karaoke amateur singing in public to prerecorded backing tapes. Karaoke originated in Japan and spread to other parts of the world in the 1980s. In Japan, karaoke machines – jukeboxes of backing tracks to well-known popular songs, usually with a microphone attached – have been installed not only in bars but also in taxis.

karate (Japanese 'empty hand') one of the ⟡martial arts. Karate is a type of unarmed combat derived from kempo, a form of the Chinese Shaolin boxing. It became popular in the 1930s.

Karelia autonomous republic of NW Russia; *area*

172,400 sq km/66,550 sq mi; *capital* Petrozavodsk; *town* Vyborg; *physical* mainly forested; *features* Lake Ladoga; *products* fishing, timber, chemicals, coal; *population* (1989) 792,000; *history* Karelia was annexed to Russia by Peter the Great 1721 as part of the grand duchy of Finland. In 1917 part of Karelia was retained by Finland when it gained its independence from Russia. The remainder became an autonomous region 1920 and an autonomous republic 1923 of the USSR. Following the wars of 1939–40 and 1941–44, Finland ceded 46,000 sq km/ 18,000 sq mi to the USSR. Part of this territory was incorporated in the Russian Soviet Republic and part in the Karelian autonomous republic. 400,000 Karelians were evacuated to Finland on Soviet annexation 1940. A Karelian reunification movement emerged in the late 1980s.

Karl-Marx-Stadt former name (1953–90) of Chemnitz, city in Germany.

karma (Sanskrit 'fate') in Hinduism, the sum of a human being's actions, carried forward from one life to the next, resulting in an improved or worsened fate. Buddhism has a similar belief, except that no permanent personality is envisaged, the karma relating only to the physical and mental elements carried on from birth to birth, until the power holding them together disperses in the attainment of nirvana.

Karnataka formerly (until 1973) *Mysore* state in SW India; *area* 191,800 sq km/74,035 sq mi; *capital* Bangalore; *products* mainly agricultural; minerals include manganese, chromite, and India's only sources of gold and silver; *population* (1991) 44,817,400; *language* Kannada; *famous people* Hyder Ali, Tippu Sultan.

Karpov Anatoly 1951– . Russian chess player. He succeeded Bobby Fischer of the USA as world champion 1975, and held the title until losing to Gary Kasparov 1985.

Karroo two areas of semi-desert in Cape Province, South Africa, divided into the *Great Karroo* and *Little Karroo* by the Swartberg mountains. The two Karroos together have an area of about 260,000 sq km/100,000 sq mi.

Kashmir former part of Jammu state in the north of British India with a largely Muslim population, ruled by a Hindu maharajah, who joined it to the republic of India 1947. There was fighting between pro-India and pro-Pakistan factions, the former being the Hindu ruling class and the latter the Muslim majority, and open war between the two countries 1965–66 and 1971. It remains divided: the northwest is occupied by Pakistan, and the rest by India.

Kashmir Pakistan-occupied area, 30,445 sq mi/ 78,900 sq km, in the northwest of the former state of Kashmir; now ▷Jammu and Kashmir. Azad ('free') Kashmir in the west has its own legislative assembly based in Muzaffarabad while Gilgit and Baltistan

regions to the north and east are governed directly by Pakistan. The Northern Areas are claimed by India and Pakistan; *population* 1,500,000; *towns* Gilgit, Skardu; *features* W Himalayan peak Nanga Parbat 8,126 m/26,660 ft, Karakoram Pass, Indus River, Baltoro Glacier.

Kasparov Gary 1963– . Russian chess player. When he beat his compatriot Anatoly Karpov to win the world title 1985, he was the youngest ever champion at 22 years 210 days.

Katmandu or *Kathmandu* capital of Nepal; population (1981) 235,000. Founded in the 8th century on an ancient pilgrim and trade route from India to Tibet and China, it has a royal palace, Buddhist shrines, and monasteries.

Katowice industrial city (anthracite, iron and coal mining, iron foundries, smelting works, machine shops) in Upper Silesia, S Poland; population (1990) 366,800.

Kaunda Kenneth (David) 1924– . Zambian politician, president 1964–91. Imprisoned 1958–60 as founder of the Zambia African National Congress, he became in 1964 the first prime minister of Northern Rhodesia, then the first president of independent Zambia. In 1973 he introduced one-party rule. He supported the nationalist movement in Southern Rhodesia, now Zimbabwe, and survived a coup attempt 1980 thought to have been promoted by South Africa. He was elected chair of the Organization of African Unity 1987. In 1990 he was faced with wide anti-government demonstrations, leading to the acceptance of a multiparty political system. He lost the first multiparty election, in Nov 1991, to Frederick Chiluba.

Kawabata Yasunari 1899–1972. Japanese novelist, translator of Lady ▷Murasaki, and author of *Snow Country* 1947 and *A Thousand Cranes* 1952. His novels are characterized by melancholy and loneliness. He was the first Japanese to win the Nobel Prize for Literature, in 1968.

Kawasaki industrial city (iron, steel, shipbuilding, chemicals, textiles) on Honshu island, Japan; population (1989) 1,128,000.

Kayseri (ancient name *Caesarea Mazaca*) capital of Kayseri province, central Turkey; population (1990) 421,400. It produces textiles, carpets, and tiles. In Roman times it was capital of the province of Cappadocia.

Kazakh or *Kazak* member of a pastoral Kyrgyz people of Kazakhstan. Kazakhs also live in China (Xinjiang, Gansu, and Qinghai), Mongolia, and Afghanistan. There are 5–7 million speakers of Kazakh, a Turkic language belonging to the Altaic family. They are predominantly Sunni Muslim, although pre-Islamic customs have survived. Kazakhs herd horses and make use of camels; they also keep cattle. Traditionally the Kazakhs lived in tents and embarked on seasonal migrations in search of fresh pastures. Collectivized herds were established in the 1920s and 1930s.

Kazakhstan Republic of; country in N Asia, bordered N by the Russian Federation, E by China and Kyrgyzstan, S by Uzbekistan, the Aral Sea, and Turkmenistan, and W by the Caspian Sea; *area* 2,717,300 sq km/1,049,150 sq mi; *capital* Alma-Ata; *physical* Caspian and Aral seas; Lake Balkhash; Steppe region; *head of state* Nursultan Nazarbayev from 1990; *political system* emergent democracy; *products* grain, copper, lead, zinc, manganese, coal, oil; *population* (1990) 16,400,000 (Kazakh 40%, Russian 38%, other 22%); *languages* Russian, Kazakh; *recent history* autonomous republic in USSR 1920; joined USSR and became full union republic 1936. Large influx of Russians in 1960s turned Kazakhs into minority in own republic. Anti-Russian sentiment resulted in riots in capital 1989. Kazakh voters supported maintenance of Union in USSR 1991; Nazarbayev condemned attempted anti-Gorbachev coup. Communist Party abolished, replaced by Independent Socialist Party of Kazakhstan. Joined Commonwealth of Independent States Dec 1991. Independence recognized by USA Jan 1992. Admitted into Conference on Security and Cooperation in Europe 1992.

Kazan capital of Tatarstan, central Russia, on the river Volga; population (1989) 1,094,000. It is a transport, commercial, and industrial centre (engineering, oil refining, petrochemicals, textiles, large fur trade). Formerly capital of a Tatar khanate, Kazan was captured by Ivan IV 'the Terrible' 1552.

Keating Paul 1954– . Australian politician, Labor Party (ALP) leader and prime minister from 1991. He was treasurer and deputy leader of the ALP 1983–91, and also held several posts in Labor's shadow ministry 1976–83.

Keats John 1795–1821. English Romantic poet who produced work of the highest quality and promise before dying at the age of 25. *Poems* 1817, *Endymion* 1818, the great odes (particularly 'Ode to a Nightingale' and 'Ode on a Grecian Urn' 1819), and the narratives 'Lamia', 'Isabella', and 'The Eve of St Agnes' 1820, show his lyrical richness and talent for drawing on both classical mythology and medieval lore.

Kells, Book of 8th-century illuminated manuscript of the Gospels produced at the monastery of Kells in County Meath, Ireland. It is now in Trinity College library, Dublin.

Kelly Grace (Patricia) 1928–1982. US film actress who retired from acting after marrying Prince Rainier III of Monaco 1956. She starred in *High Noon* 1952, *The Country Girl* 1954, for which she received an Academy Award, and *High Society* 1955. She also starred in three Hitchcock classics – *Dial M for Murder* 1954, *Rear Window* 1954, and *To Catch a Thief* 1955.

kelp collective name for large brown seaweeds, such as those of the Fucaceae and Laminariaceae families. Kelp is also a term for the powdery ash of burned seaweeds, a source of iodine.

Kelvin William Thomson, 1st Baron Kelvin 1824–1907. British physicist who introduced the *kelvin scale*, the absolute scale of temperature. His work on the conservation of energy 1851 led to the second law of ▷thermodynamics.

kelvin scale temperature scale used by scientists. It begins at ▷absolute zero (–273.16°C) and increases by the same degree intervals as the Celsius scale; that is, 0°C is the same as 273 K and 100°C is 373 K.

Kemal Atatürk Mustafa. Turkish politician; see ▷Atatürk.

Kempis Thomas à. Medieval German monk and religious writer; see ▷Thomas à Kempis.

Kennedy Edward (Moore) 'Ted' 1932– . US Democratic politician. He aided his brothers John and Robert Kennedy in the presidential campaign of 1960, and entered politics as a senator for Massachusetts 1962. He failed to gain the presidential nomination 1980, largely because of questions about his delay in reporting a car crash at Chappaquiddick Island, near Cape Cod, Massachusetts, in 1969, in which his passenger, Mary Jo Kopechne, was drowned.

Kennedy John F(itzgerald) 'Jack' 1917–1963. 35th president of the USA 1961–63, a Democrat; the first Roman Catholic and the youngest person to be elected president. In foreign policy he carried through the unsuccessful ▷Bay of Pigs invasion of Cuba, and in 1963 secured the withdrawal of Soviet missiles from the island. His programme for reforms at home, called the *New Frontier*, was posthumously executed by Lyndon Johnson. Kennedy was assassinated while on a state visit to Dallas, Texas, on 22 Nov 1963 by Lee Harvey Oswald (1939–1963), who was within a few days shot dead by Jack Ruby (1911–1967).

Kennedy Joseph Patrick 1888–1969. US industrialist and diplomat; ambassador to the UK 1937–40.

A self-made millionaire, he ventured into the film industry, then set up the Securities and Exchange Commission (SEC) for F D Roosevelt. He groomed each of his four sons – Joseph Patrick Kennedy Jr (1915–1944), John F ◊Kennedy, Robert ◊Kennedy, and Edward ◊Kennedy – for a career in politics. His eldest son, Joseph (1915–1944), was killed in action with the naval air force in World War II.

Kennedy Robert (Francis) 1925–1968. US Democratic politician and lawyer. He was presidential campaign manager for his brother John F ◊Kennedy 1960, and as attorney general 1961–64 pursued a racket-busting policy and promoted the Civil Rights Act of 1964. He was also a key aide to his brother. When John Kennedy's successor, Lyndon Johnson, preferred Hubert H Humphrey for the 1964 vice presidential nomination, Kennedy resigned and was elected senator for New York. In 1968 he campaigned for the Democratic party's presidential nomination, but during a campaign stop in California was assassinated by Sirhan Bissara Sirhan (1944–), a Jordanian.

Kennedy Space Center the ◊NASA launch site on Merritt Island, near Cape Canaveral, Florida, used for Apollo and space-shuttle launches. The first flight to land on the Moon (1969) and *Skylab*, the first orbiting laboratory (1973), were launched here.

Kennelly–Heaviside layer former term for the ◊E layer.

Kenneth I *MacAlpin* died 858. King of Scotland from *c*. 844. Traditionally, he is regarded as the founder of the Scottish kingdom (Alba) by virtue of his final defeat of the Picts about 844. He invaded Northumbria six times, and drove the Angles and the Britons over the river Tweed.

Kent county in SE England, nicknamed the 'garden of England'; *area* 3,730 sq km/1,440 sq mi; *towns* Maidstone (administrative headquarters), Canterbury, Chatham, Rochester, Sheerness, Tunbridge Wells; resorts: Folkestone, Margate, Ramsgate; *features* traditionally, a 'man of Kent' comes from east of the Medway and a 'Kentish man' from W Kent; New Ash Green, a new town; Romney Marsh; the Isles of Grain, Sheppey (on which is the resort of Sheerness, formerly a royal dockyard) and Thanet; Weald (agricultural area); rivers: Darent, Medway, Stour; Leeds Castle (converted to a palace by Henry VIII); Hever Castle (where Henry VIII courted Anne Boleyn); Chartwell (Churchill's country home), Knole, Sissinghurst Castle and gardens; the Brogdale Experimental Horticulture Station at Faversham has the world's finest collection of apple and other fruit trees; the former RAF Manston became in Oct 1989 Kent International Airport; *products* hops, apples, soft fruit, coal, cement, paper; *population* (1991) 1,485,600; *famous people* Charles Dickens, Edward Heath, Christopher Marlowe.

Kentucky state in S central USA; nickname Bluegrass State; *area* 104,700 sq km/40,414 sq mi; *capital* Frankfort; *cities* Louisville, Lexington, Owensboro, Covington, Bowling Green; *features* bluegrass country; horse racing at Louisville (Kentucky Derby); Mammoth Cave National Park (main cave 6.5 km/4 mi long, up to 38 m/125 ft high, where Indian councils were once held); Abraham Lincoln's birthplace at Hodgenville; Fort Knox, US gold bullion depository; *products* tobacco, cereals, textiles, coal, whiskey, horses, transport vehicles; *population* (1990) 3,365,300; *famous people* Muhammad Ali, Daniel Boone, Louis D Brandeis, Kit Carson, Henry Clay, D W Griffith, Thomas Hunt Morgan, Harland 'Colonel' Sanders, Robert Penn Warren; *history* the first region west of the Alleghenies settled by American pioneers. Originally part of Virginia, it became a state 1792. Badly divided over the slavery question, the state was racked by guerrilla warfare and partisan feuds during the Civil War.

Kenya Republic of; country in E Africa, bordered N by Sudan and Ethiopia, E by Somalia, SE by the Indian Ocean, SW by Tanzania, and W by Uganda; *area* 582,600 sq km/224,884 sq mi; *capital* Nairobi; *physical* mountains and highlands in W and centre; coastal plain in S; arid interior and tropical coast; Great Rift Valley, Mount Kenya, Lake Nakuru, Lake Turkana, Olduvai Gorge; *head of state and government* Daniel arap Moi from 1978; *political system* authoritarian nationalism; *exports* coffee, tea, pineapples, petroleum products; *languages* Kiswahili (official), English, many local dialects; *recent history* Kenya achieved independence from Britain 1964. Jomo ◊Kenyatta became prime minister and then president after full independence 1964. On his death 1978, he was succeeded by Vice-President Daniel arap Moi. There were widespread calls for more democratic government in 1991 and 1992.

Kenyatta Jomo. Assumed name of Kamau Ngengi *c*. 1894–1978. Kenyan nationalist politician, prime minister from 1963, as well as first president of Kenya from 1964 until his death. He led the Kenya African Union from 1947 (*KANU* from 1963) and was active in liberating Kenya from British rule.

Kepler Johannes 1571–1630. German mathematician and astronomer. He formulated what are now called *Kepler's laws* of planetary motion: (1) the orbit of each planet is an ellipse with the Sun at one of the foci; (2) the radius vector of each planet sweeps out equal areas in equal times; (3) the squares of the periods of the planets are proportional to the cubes of their mean distances from the Sun.

Kerala state of SW India, formed 1956 from the former princely states of Travancore and Cochin; *area* 38,900 sq km/15,015 sq mi; *capital* Trivandrum; *features* most densely populated, and most literate (60%) state of India; strong religious and caste divisions make it politically unstable; *products* tea, coffee, rice, oilseed, rubber, textiles, chemicals, electrical goods; *population* (1991) 29,011,200; *languages* Kannada, Malayalam, Tamil.

Kerekou Mathieu (Ahmed) 1933– . Benin socialist politician and soldier, president from 1980. In 1972, when deputy head of the Dahomey army, he led a coup to oust the ruling president and establish his own military government. He embarked on a programme of 'scientific socialism', changing his country's name to Benin to mark this change of direction. In 1987 he resigned from the army and confirmed a civilian administration. He was re-elected president 1989.

Kerkira Greek form of ▷Corfu, an island in the Ionian Sea.

kerosene thin oil obtained from the distillation of petroleum; a highly refined form is used in jet aircraft fuel. Kerosene is a mixture of hydrocarbons of the ▷paraffin series.

Kerouac Jack 1923–1969. US novelist who named and epitomized the ▷Beat Generation of the 1950s. His books, all autobiographical, include *On the Road* 1957, *Big Sur* 1963, and *Desolation Angel* 1965.

Kerry county of Munster province, Republic of Ireland, E of Cork; *area* 4,700 sq km/1,814 sq mi; *county town* Tralee; *physical* western coastline deeply indented; northern part low-lying, but in the south are the highest mountains in Ireland, including Carrantuohill 1,041 m/3,417 ft, the highest peak in Ireland; many rivers and lakes; *features* Macgillycuddy's Reeks, Lakes of Killarney; *products* engineering, woollens, shoes, cutlery; tourism is important; *population* (1991) 121,700.

kestrel hawk *Falco tinnunculus* of the family Falconidae, which breeds in Europe, Asia, and Africa. About 30 cm/1 ft long, the male has a head and tail of bluish grey, and its back is a light chestnut brown with black spots. The female is slightly larger and reddish brown above, with bars. The kestrel hunts mainly by hovering in midair while searching for prey.

ketone member of the group of organic compounds containing the carbonyl group (C=O) bonded to two atoms of carbon (instead of one carbon and one hydrogen as in ▷aldehydes). Ketones are liquids or low-melting-point solids, slightly soluble in water.

key in music, the ▷diatonic scale around which a piece of music is written; for example, a passage in the key of C major will mainly use the notes of the C major scale. The term is also used for the lever activated by a keyboard player, such as a piano key.

Keynes John Maynard, 1st Baron Keynes 1883–1946. English economist, whose *The General Theory of Employment, Interest, and Money* 1936 proposed the prevention of financial crises and unemployment by adjusting demand through

government control of credit and currency. He is responsible for that part of economics now known as ▷**macroeconomics**.

KGB secret police of the USSR, the *Komitet Gosudarstvennoy Bezopasnosti*/Committee of State Security, in control of frontier and general security and the forced-labour system. KGB officers held key appointments in all fields of daily life, reporting to administration offices in every major town. The KGB was superseded by the Russian Federal Security Agency on the demise of the Soviet Union 1991.

Khachaturian Aram Il'yich 1903–1978. Armenian composer. His use of folk themes is shown in the ballets *Gayaneh* 1942, which includes the 'Sabre Dance', and *Spartacus* 1956.

Khabarovsk territory of SE Siberian Russia, bordering the Sea of Okhotsk and drained by the Amur; area 824,600 sq km/318,501 sq mi; population (1985) 1,728,000. The capital is Khabarovsk. Mineral resources include gold, coal, and iron ore.

Khaddhafi or *Gaddafi* or *Qaddafi*, Moamer al 1942– . Libyan revolutionary leader. Overthrowing King Idris 1969, he became virtual president of a republic, although he nominally gave up all except an ideological role 1974. He favours territorial expansion in N Africa reaching as far as Zaire, has supported rebels in Chad, and has proposed mergers with a number of countries. His theories, based on those of the Chinese communist leader Mao Zedong, are contained in a *Green Book*.

Khama Seretse 1921–1980. Botswanan politician, prime minister of Bechuanaland 1965, and first president of Botswana from 1966 until his death.

Khan Imran 1952– . Pakistani cricketer. He played county cricket for Worcestershire and Sussex in the UK, and made his test debut for Pakistan 1971, subsequently playing for his country 82 times.

Khan Jahangir 1963– . Pakistani squash player who won the world open championship a record six times 1981–85 and 1988. He was nine times British Open champion 1982–90, and World Amateur champion 1979, 1983, and 1985.

Khan Liaquat Ali 1895–1951. Indian politician, deputy leader of the Muslim League 1941–47, first prime minister of Pakistan from 1947. He was assassinated by objectors to his peace policy with India.

Kharkov capital of the Kharkov region, E Ukraine, 400 km/250 mi E of Kiev; population (1987) 1,587,000. It is a railway junction and industrial city (engineering, tractors), close to the Donets Basin coalfield and Krivoy Rog iron mines. Kharkov was founded 1654 as a fortress town.

Khartoum capital and trading centre of Sudan, at the junction of the Blue and White Nile; population (1983) 476,000, and of Khartoum North, across the

Blue Nile, 341,000. ▷Omdurman is also a suburb of Khartoum, giving the urban area a population of over 1.3 million.

Khmer or **Kmer** member of the largest ethnic group in Cambodia, numbering about 7 million. Khmer minorities also live in E Thailand and S Vietnam. The Khmer language belongs to the Mon-Khmer family of Austro-Asiatic languages.

Khmer Republic former name of ▷Cambodia.

Khmer Rouge communist movement in Cambodia (Kampuchea), in power 1975–79, a member of the coalition government from 1991, with a guerrilla army that fought the invading Vietnamese forces from 1978 and the Vietnamese-backed Cambodian government 1979–91, and has not renounced its goal of taking control of the country. Under the leadership of Pol Pot 1976–85, the Khmer Rouge became notorious for mass executions.

Khomeini Ayatollah Ruhollah 1900–1989. Iranian Shi'ite Muslim leader, born in Khomein, central Iran. Exiled for opposition to the Shah from 1964, he returned when the Shah left the country 1979, and established a fundamentalist Islamic republic. His rule was marked by a protracted war with Iraq, and suppression of opposition within Iran, executing thousands of opponents.

Khrushchev Nikita Sergeyevich 1894–1971. Soviet politician, secretary general of the Communist Party 1953–64, premier 1958–64. He emerged as leader from the power struggle following Stalin's death and was the first official to denounce Stalin, in 1956. His destalinization programme gave rise to revolts in Poland and Hungary 1956. Because of problems with the economy and foreign affairs (a breach with China 1960; conflict with the USA in the ▷Cuban missile crisis 1962), he was ousted by Leonid Brezhnev and Alexei Kosygin.

Khwārizmī, al- Muhammad ibn-Mūsā c.780–c.850. Persian mathematician from Khwarizm (now Khiva, Uzbekistan), who lived and worked in Baghdad. He wrote a book on algebra, from part of whose title (al-jabr) comes the word 'algebra', and a book in which he introduced to the West the Hindu-Arabic decimal number system. The word 'algorithm' is a corruption of his name.

Khyber Pass pass 53 km/33 mi long through the mountain range that separates Pakistan from Afghanistan. The Khyber Pass was used by invaders of India. The present road was constructed by the British during the Afghan Wars.

Kiangsi alternative spelling of ▷Jiangxi, province of China.

Kiangsu alternative spelling of ▷Jiangsu, province of China.

kibbutz Israeli communal collective settlement with collective ownership of all property and earnings, collective organization of work, and decision making, and communal housing for children.

A modified version, the *Moshav Shitufi*, is similar to the ▷collective farms that were typical of the former USSR. Other Israeli cooperative rural settlements include the *Moshav Ovdim*, which has equal opportunity, and the similar but less strict *Moshav* settlement.

kidney in vertebrates, one of a pair of organs responsible for water regulation, excretion of waste products, and maintaining the ionic composition of the blood. The kidneys are situated on the rear wall of the abdomen. Each one consists of a number of long tubules; the outer parts filter the aqueous components of blood, and the inner parts selectively reabsorb vital salts, leaving waste products in the remaining fluid (urine), which is passed through the ureter to the bladder.

Kierkegaard Søren (Aabye) 1813–1855. Danish philosopher considered to be the founder of ▷existentialism. Disagreeing with the German dialectical philosopher ▷Hegel, he argued that no system of thought could explain the unique experience of the individual. He defended Christianity, suggesting that God cannot be known through reason, but only through a 'leap of faith'. He believed that God and exceptional individuals were above moral laws.

Kiev capital of Ukraine, industrial centre (chemicals, clothing, leatherwork) and third largest city of the former USSR, on the confluence of the Desna and Dnieper rivers; population (1987) 2,554,000.

Kigali capital of Rwanda, central Africa; population (1981) 157,000. Products include coffee and minerals.

Kikuyu member of Kenya's dominant ethnic group, numbering about three million. The Kikuyu are primarily cultivators, although many are highly educated and have entered the professions. Their language belongs to the Bantu branch of the Niger-Congo family.

Kildare county of Leinster province, Republic of Ireland, S of Meath; *area* 1,690 sq km/652 sq mi; *county town* Naas; *physical* wet and boggy in the north; *features* part of the Bog of Allen; the village of Maynooth, with a training college for Roman Catholic priests; the Curragh, a plain that is the site of the national stud and headquarters of Irish horse racing; *products* oats, barley, potatoes, cattle; *population* (1991) 122,516.

Kilimanjaro volcano in ▷Tanzania, the highest mountain in Africa, 5,900 m/19,364 ft.

Kilkenny county of Leinster province, Republic of Ireland, E of Tipperary; *area* 2,060 sq km/ 795 sq mi; *county town* Kilkenny; *features* river Nore; *products* agricultural, coal; *population* (1991) 73,600.

killer whale or *orca* toothed whale *Orcinus orca* of the dolphin family, found in all seas of the world. It is black on top, white below, and grows up to 9 m/30 ft long. It is the only whale that has been observed to prey on other whales, as well as on seals and seabirds.

kilobyte (K or KB) in computing, a unit of memory equal to 1,024 ⏵bytes. It is sometimes used, less precisely, to mean 1,000 bytes.

kilogram SI unit (symbol kg) of mass equal to 1,000 grams (2.2 lb). It is defined by scientists as a mass equal to that of the international prototype, a platinum-iridium cylinder held at the International Bureau of Weights and Measures at Sèvres, France.

kilometre unit (symbol km) of length equal to 1,000 metres (3,280.89 ft or about ⅝ of a mile).

kilowatt unit (symbol kW) of power equal to 1,000 watts or about 1.34 horsepower.

Kim Il Sung 1912– . North Korean Communist politician and marshal. He became prime minister 1948 and president 1972, retaining the presidency of the Communist Workers' party. He likes to be known as the 'Great Leader' and has campaigned constantly for the reunification of Korea. His son *Kim Jong Il* (1942–), known as the 'Dear Leader', has been named as his successor.

kinetics branch of ⏵dynamics dealing with the action of forces producing or changing the motion of a body; *kinematics* deals with motion without reference to force or mass.

kinetic theory theory describing the physical properties of matter in terms of the behaviour – principally movement – of its component atoms or molecules. The temperature of a substance is dependent on the velocity of movement of its constituent particles, increased temperature being accompanied by increased movement. A gas consists of rapidly moving atoms or molecules and, according to kinetic theory, it is their continual impact on the walls of the containing vessel that accounts for the pressure of the gas. The slowing of molecular motion as temperature falls, according to kinetic theory, accounts for the physical properties of liquids and solids, culminating in the concept of no molecular motion at ⏵absolute zero (0 K/ –273°C). By making various assumptions about the nature of gas molecules, it is possible to derive from the kinetic theory the various gas laws (such as ⏵Avogadro's hypothesis, ⏵Boyle's law, and ⏵Charles's law).

King Martin Luther Jr 1929–1968. US civil-rights campaigner, black leader, and Baptist minister. He first came to national attention as leader of the ⏵Montgomery, Alabama, bus boycott 1955, and was one of the organizers of the massive (200,000 people) march on Washington DC 1963 to demand racial equality. An advocate of nonviolence, he was awarded the Nobel Peace Prize 1964. He was assassinated in Memphis, Tennessee, by James Earl Ray (1928–).

king crab or *horseshoe crab* marine arthropod, class Arachnida, subclass Xiphosura, which lives on the Atlantic coast of North America, and the coasts of Asia. The upper side of the body is entirely covered with a rounded shell, and it has a long spinelike tail. It is up to 60 cm/2 ft long. It is unable to swim, and lays its eggs in the sand at the high-water mark.

kingdom the primary division in biological ⏵classification. At one time, only two kingdoms were recognized: animals and plants. Today most biologists prefer a five-kingdom system, even though it still involves grouping together organisms that are probably unrelated. One widely accepted scheme is as follows: *Kingdom Animalia* (all multicellular animals); *Kingdom Plantae* (all plants, including seaweeds and other algae); *Kingdom Fungi* (all fungi, including the unicellular yeasts, but not slime moulds); *Kingdom Protista* or *Protoctista* (protozoa, diatoms, dinoflagellates, slime moulds, and various other lower organisms with eukaryotic cells); and *Kingdom Monera* (all prokaryotes – the bacteria and cyanobacteria, or ⏵blue-green algae). The first four of these kingdoms make up the eukaryotes.

kingfisher heavy-billed bird of the worldwide family Alcedinidae, found near streams, ponds, and coastal areas. Kingfishers plunge-dive for fish and aquatic insects. The nest is usually a burrow in a river bank.

Kingsley Charles 1819–1875. English author. A rector, he was known as the 'Chartist clergyman' because of such social novels as *Alton Locke* 1850. His historical novels include *Westward Ho!* 1855. He also wrote *The Water-Babies* 1863.

Kingston capital and principal port of Jamaica, West Indies, the cultural and commercial centre of the island; population (1983) 101,000, metropolitan area 525,000. Founded 1693, Kingston became the capital of Jamaica 1872.

Kingston upon Hull official name of ⏵Hull, city in Humberside in NE England.

Kingstown capital and principal port of St Vincent and the Grenadines, West Indies, in the SW of the island of St Vincent; population (1989) 29,400.

Kinki region of S Honshu island, Japan; population (1988) 22,105,000; area 33,070 sq km/12,773 sq mi. The chief city is Osaka.

Kinnock Neil 1942– . British Labour politician, party leader 1983–92. Born and educated in Wales, he was elected to represent a Welsh constituency in Parliament 1970 (Islwyn from 1983). He was further left than prime ministers Wilson and Callaghan, but as party leader (in succession to Michael Foot) adopted a moderate position, initiating a major policy review 1988–89. He resigned as party leader after Labour's defeat in the 1992 general election.

Kinshasa formerly *Léopoldville* capital of Zaire on the river Zaïre, 400 km/250 mi inland from Matadi; population (1984) 2,654,000. Industries include chemicals, textiles, engineering, food processing, and furniture. It was founded by the explorer Henry Stanley 1887.

Kipling (Joseph) Rudyard 1865–1936. English writer, born in India. *Plain Tales from the Hills* 1888, about Anglo-Indian society, contains the earliest of his masterly short stories. His books for children, including *The Jungle Books* 1894–95, *Just So Stories* 1902, *Puck of Pook's Hill* 1906, and the novel *Kim* 1901, reveal his imaginative identification with the exotic. Poems such as 'Danny Deever', 'Gunga Din', and 'If–' express an empathy with common experience, which contributed to his great popularity, together with a vivid sense of 'Englishness' (sometimes denigrated as a kind of jingoist imperialism). His work is increasingly valued for its complex characterization and subtle moral viewpoints. Nobel prize 1907.

Kirchner Ernst Ludwig 1880–1938. German Expressionist artist, a leading member of the group *die ◊Brücke* in Dresden from 1905 and in Berlin from 1911. His Dresden work, which includes woodcuts, shows the influence of African art. In Berlin he turned to city scenes and portraits, using lurid colours and bold diagonal paint strokes recalling woodcut technique. He suffered a breakdown during World War I and settled in Switzerland, where he committed suicide.

Kiribati Republic of; country in the central Pacific, consisting of three groups of coral atolls and a volcanic island; *area* 717 sq km/277 sq mi; *capital* and port Bairiki (on Tarawa Atoll); *physical* comprises 33 Pacific coral islands: the Kiribati (Gilbert), Rawaki (Phoenix), and Line Islands, and Banaba (Ocean Island) and Kiritimati (Christmas Island); *head of state and government* Teatao Teannaki from 1991; *political system* liberal democracy; *exports* copra, fish; *languages* English (official); Gilbertese; *recent history* achieved independence from Britain and became a republic 1979. First political party, opposition Christian Democrats, formed 1985.

Kirin alternative name for ◊Jilin, Chinese province.

Kishinev capital of the Republic of Moldova; population (1989) 565,000. Industries include cement, food processing, tobacco, and textiles.

Kissinger Henry 1923– . German-born US diplomat. Following a brilliant academic career at Harvard University, he was appointed assistant for National Security Affairs 1969 by President Nixon, and was secretary of state 1973–77. His missions to the USSR and China improved US relations with both countries, and he took part in negotiating US withdrawal from Vietnam 1973 and in Arab-Israeli peace negotiations 1973–75. Nobel Peace Prize 1973.

Kitakyushu industrial port city (coal, steel, chemicals, cotton thread, plate glass, alcohol) port city in Japan, on the Hibiki Sea, N Kyushu, formed 1963 by the amalgamation of Moji, Kokura, Tobata, Yawata, and Wakamatsu; population (1989) 1,030,000. A tunnel 1942 links it with Honshu.

Kitchener Horatio Herbert, Earl Kitchener of Khartoum 1850–1916. British soldier and administrator. He defeated the Sudanese dervishes at Omdurman 1898 and reoccupied Khartoum. In South Africa, he was Chief of Staff 1900–02 during the Boer War, and commanded the forces in India 1902–09. He was appointed war minister on the outbreak of World War I, and drowned when his ship was sunk on the way to Russia.

kitchen-sink painters loose-knit group of British artists specializing in social-realistic painting, active in the late 1940s and early 1950s. They depicted drab, ordinary themes with an aggressive technique and brilliant, 'crude' colour. The best known were John Bratby (1928–), Derrick Greaves (1927–), Edward Middleditch (1923–1987), and Jack Smith (1928–). The group disbanded after a few years but interest in them revived in the 1990s.

kite one of about 20 birds of prey in the family Accipitridae, found in all parts of the world. The *red kite Milvus milvus*, found in Europe, has a forked tail and narrow wings, and is about 60 cm/2 ft long. There are 50 known pairs in Wales, the only place in the UK where the kite is found.

kittiwake slender gull *Rissa tridactyla* with a yellow-green bill. It breeds in large colonies in Arctic and northern regions. The cup-shaped nest of moss and seaweed is built on inaccessible cliff ledges.

kiwi flightless bird *Apteryx australis* found only in New Zealand. It has long, hairlike brown plumage and a very long beak with nostrils at the tip. It is nocturnal and insectivorous.

kiwi fruit or *Chinese gooseberry* fruit of a vinelike plant *Actinidithia chinensis*, family Actinidiaceae, commercially grown on a large scale in New Zealand. Kiwi fruits are egg-sized, oval, and of similar flavour to a gooseberry, with a fuzzy brown skin.

Klammer Franz 1953– . Austrian skier who won a record 35 World Cup downhill races between 1974 and 1985. Olympic gold medallist 1976. He was the combined world champion 1974, and the World Cup downhill champion 1975–78 and 1983.

Klee Paul 1879–1940. Swiss painter. He settled in Munich 1906, joined the ◊*Blaue Reiter* group 1912,

kingfisher

and worked at the Bauhaus school of art and design 1920–31, returning to Switzerland 1933. His style in the 1920s and 1930s was dominated by humorous linear fantasies.

kleptomania behavioural disorder characterized by an overpowering desire to possess articles for which one has no need. In kleptomania, as opposed to ordinary theft, there is no obvious need or use for what is stolen and sometimes the sufferer has no memory of the theft.

Klimt Gustav 1862–1918. Austrian painter, influenced by Jugendstil ('youth style', a form of Art Nouveau); a founding member of the Vienna *Sezession* group 1897. His paintings have a jewelled effect similar to mosaics, for example *The Kiss* 1909 (Musée des Beaux-Arts, Strasbourg). His many portraits include *Judith I* 1901 (Osterreichische Galerie, Vienna).

Klondike former gold-mining area in ◊Yukon, Canada, named after the river valley where gold was found 1896. About 30,000 people moved there during the following 15 years. Silver is still mined there.

knapweed any of several weedy plants of the genus *Centaurea*, family Compositae. In the common knapweed *C. nigra*, also known as *hardhead*, the hard bract-covered buds break into purple composite heads. It is native to Europe.

Kneller Godfrey 1646–1723. German-born portrait painter who lived in England from 1674. He was court painter to Charles II, James II, William III, and George I. Among his paintings are the series *Hampton Court Beauties* (Hampton Court, Richmond, Surrey).

knighthood, order of fraternity carrying with it the rank of knight, admission to which is granted as a mark of royal favour or as a reward for public services. During the Middle Ages in Europe, such fraternities fell into two classes, religious and secular. The first class, including the ◊*Templars* and the *Knights of St John*, consisted of knights who had taken religious vows and devoted themselves to military service against the Saracens (Arabs) or other non-Christians. The secular orders probably arose from bands of knights engaged in the service of a prince or great noble.

Knock (also the *Basilica of Our Lady, Queen of Ireland*) Roman Catholic shrine in County Mayo, W Ireland, one of three national places of pilgrimage (with Lough Derg and Croagh Patrick). On 21 Aug 1879 it was the scene of an alleged apparition of the Virgin Mary.

Knossos chief city of ◊Minoan Crete, near present-day Iráklion, 6 km/4 mi SE of Candia. The archaeological site excavated by Arthur ◊Evans 1899–1935, dates from about 2000 BC, and includes the palace throne room and a labyrinth, legendary home of the ◊Minotaur.

knot wading bird *Calidris canutus* of the sandpiper family. It is about 25 cm/10 in long. In the winter, it is grey above and white below, but in the breeding season, it is brick-red on the head and chest and black on the wings and back. It feeds on insects and molluscs.

knot in navigation, unit by which a ship's speed is measured, equivalent to one ◊nautical mile per hour (one knot equals about 1.15 miles per hour). It is also sometimes used in aviation.

knowledge-based system (KBS) computer program that uses an encoding of human knowledge to help solve problems. It was discovered during research into ◊artificial intelligence that adding heuristics (rules of thumb) enabled programs to tackle problems that were otherwise difficult to solve by the usual techniques of computer science.

Knox John *c.* 1505–1572. Scottish Protestant reformer, founder of the Church of Scotland. He spent several years in exile for his beliefs, including a period in Geneva where he met John ◊Calvin. He returned to Scotland 1559 to promote Presbyterianism. His books include *First Blast of the Trumpet Against the Monstrous Regiment of Women* 1558.

koala marsupial *Phascolarctos cinereus* of the family Phalangeridae, found only in E Australia. It feeds almost entirely on eucalyptus shoots. It is about 60 cm/2 ft long, and resembles a bear. The popularity of its greyish fur led to its almost complete extermination by hunters. Under protection since 1936, it has rapidly increased in numbers.

Kobe deep-water port in S Honshu, Japan; population (1989) 1,438,200. *Port Island*, created 1960–68 from the rock of nearby mountains, area 5 sq km/2 sq mi, is one of the world's largest construction projects.

København Danish name for ◊Copenhagen, capital of Denmark.

Kodály Zoltán 1882–1967. Hungarian composer. With Bela ◊Bartók, he recorded and transcribed Magyar folk music, the scales and rhythm of which he incorporated in a deliberately nationalist style. His works include the cantata *Psalmus Hungaricus* 1923, a comic opera *Háry János* 1925–27, and orchestral dances and variations.

Koestler Arthur 1905–1983. Hungarian author. Imprisoned by the Nazis in France 1940, he escaped to England. His novel *Darkness at Noon* 1940, regarded as his masterpiece, is a fictional account of the Stalinist purges, and draws on his experiences as a prisoner under sentence of death during the Spanish Civil War. He also wrote extensively about creativity, parapsychology, politics, and culture. He endowed Britain's first chair of parapsychology at Edinburgh, established 1984.

Kohl Helmut 1930– . German conservative politician, leader of the Christian Democratic Union (CDU) from 1976, West German chancellor (prime minister) 1982–90. He oversaw the reunification of East and West Germany 1989–90 and in 1990 won a resounding victory to become the first chancellor of reunited Germany.

kohlrabi variety of kale *Brassica oleracea*. The leaves of kohlrabi shoot from a globular swelling on the main stem; it is used for food and resembles a turnip.

Kokoschka Oskar 1886–1980. Austrian Expressionist painter and writer who lived in England from 1938. Initially influenced by the Vienna *Sezession* painters, he developed a disturbingly expressive portrait style. His writings include several plays.

kola alternative spelling of ⬦cola, a genus of tropical tree.

Kommunizma, Pik or *Communism Peak* highest mountain in the ⬦Pamirs, a mountain range in Tajikistan; 7,495 m/24,599 ft. As part of the former USSR, it was known as *Mount Garmo* until 1933, and *Mount Stalin* 1933–62.

Kong Zi Pinyin form of ⬦Confucius, Chinese philosopher.

kookaburra or *laughing jackass* largest of the world's ⬦kingfishers *Dacelo novaeguineae*, found in Australia, with an extraordinary laughing call. It feeds on insects and other small creatures. The body and tail measure 45 cm/18 in, the head is greyish with a dark eye stripe, and the back and wings are flecked brown with grey underparts.

Koran (alternatively transliterated as *Quran*) sacred book of ⬦Islam. Written in the purest Arabic, it contains 114 *suras* (chapters), and is stated to have been divinely revealed to the prophet Muhammad about 616.

Korda Alexander 1893–1956. Hungarian-born British film producer and director, a dominant figure during the 1930s and 1940s. His films include *The Private Life of Henry VIII* 1933, *The Third Man* 1950, and *Richard III* 1956.

Korea peninsula in E Asia, divided into ⬦Korea, North, and ⬦Korea, South.

Korea: history the foundation of the Korean state traditionally dates from the Tangun dynasty 2000 BC. From 1122 to the 4th century Korea was ruled by the Chinese Kija dynasty. After centuries of internal war and invasion, Korea was united within its present boundaries in the 10th century AD. In the 16th century Japan invaded Korea for the first time, later withdrawing from a country it had devastated. In 1905 Japan began to treat Korea as a protectorate, annexing the country from 1910. Many Japanese colonists settled in Korea, introducing both industrial and agricultural development. At the end of World War II, in 1945, the Japanese in Korea surrendered, but the occupying forces at the ceasefire – the USSR north of the ⬦38th parallel, and the USA south of it – created a lasting division of the country as North and South Korea (see ⬦Korea, North, and ⬦Korea, South, for history since 1945).

Korea, North Democratic People's Republic of;

country in E Asia, bordered N by China, E by the Sea of Japan, S by South Korea, and W by the Yellow Sea; *area* 120,538 sq km/46,528 sq mi; *capital* Pyongyang; *physical* wide coastal plain in W rising to mountains cut by deep valleys in interior; *head of state* Kim Il Sung from 1972; *head of government* Yon Hyong Muk from 1988; *political system* communism; *exports* coal, iron, copper, textiles, chemicals; *language* Korean; *recent history* North Korea was formed from the zone north of the 38th parallel of latitude, occupied by Soviet troops after Japan's surrender 1945. Declared a Democratic People's Republic 1948, it invaded South Korea 1950 in an attempt at reunification, initiating the three-year Korean War which, after intervention by United Nations forces supported by the USA (on the side of the South) and by China (on the side of the North), ended in stalemate. A UN-patrolled demilitarized buffer zone was created. North Korea has never accepted this agreement and remains committed to reunification. Became a UN member 1991; nonaggression agreement and nuclear-weapons pact were signed by the two Koreas in the same year, signalling a move towards a formal peace treaty.

Korean War war 1950–53 between North Korea (supported by China) and South Korea, aided by the United Nations (the troops were mainly US). North Korean forces invaded the South 25 June 1950, and the Security Council of the United Nations, owing to a walk-out by the USSR, voted to oppose them. To begin with the North Koreans held most of the south but US reinforcements arrived Sept 1950 and forced their way through to the North Korean border with China. The Chinese retaliated, pushing them back to the original boundary Oct 1950; truce negotiations began 1951, although the war did not end until 1953.

Korea, South Republic of; country in E Asia, bordered N by North Korea, E by the Sea of Japan, S by the E China Sea, and W by the Yellow Sea; *area* 98,799 sq km/38,161 sq mi; *capital* Seoul; *physical* S end of a mountainous peninsula separating Sea of Japan from Yellow Sea; *head of state* Roh Tae Woo from 1988; *head of government* Chung Won Shik from 1991; *political system* emergent democracy; *exports* steel, ships, chemicals, electronics, textiles and clothing, plywood, fish; *language* Korean; *recent history* proclaimed a republic 1948, South Korea was invaded by, and at war with, North Korea from 1950 until 1953 when an armistice was signed. In 1961 and 1980 military coups, along with student unrest 1987, led to adoption of a more democratic constitution. In 1991 there were further violent demonstrations against the government. Nonaggression and nuclear pacts were signed between the two Koreas 1991.

Kosciusko highest mountain in Australia (2,229 m/ 7,316 ft), in New South Wales.

kosher conforming to religious law with regard

to the preparation and consumption of food; in Judaism, conforming to the Mosaic law of the Book of Deuteronomy. For example, only animals that chew the cud and have cloven hooves (cows and sheep, but not pigs) may be eaten. There are rules governing their humane slaughter and their preparation (such as complete draining of blood) which also apply to fowl. Only fish with scales and fins may be eaten; shellfish may not. Milk products may not be cooked or eaten with meat or poultry, or until four hours after eating them. Utensils for meat must be kept separate from those for milk as well.

Kosovo autonomous region (1974–90) in S Serbia, Yugoslavia; capital Priština; area 10,900 sq km/ 4,207 sq mi; population (1986) 1,900,000, consisting of about 200,000 Serbs and about 1.7 million Albanians. Products include wine, nickel, lead, and zinc. Since it is largely inhabited by Albanians and bordering on Albania, there are demands for unification with that country, while in the late 1980s Serbians were agitating for Kosovo to be merged with the rest of Serbia. A state of emergency was declared Feb 1990 after fighting broke out between ethnic Albanians, police, and the Slavic minority. The parliament and government were dissolved July 1990 and the Serbian parliament formally annexed Kosovo Sept 1990. In 1991 the Kosovo Assembly, though still technically dissolved, organized a referendum on sovereignty which received 99% support. It elected a provisional government, headed by Bujar Bukoshi, which was recognized by Albania in Oct 1991.

Kossuth Lajos 1802–1894. Hungarian nationalist and leader of the revolution of 1848. He proclaimed Hungary's independence of Habsburg rule, became governor of a Hungarian republic 1849, and, when it was defeated by Austria and Russia, fled first to Turkey and then to exile in Britain and Italy.

Kosygin Alexei Nikolaievich 1904–1980. Soviet politician, prime minister 1964–80. He was elected to the Supreme Soviet 1938, became a member of the Politburo 1946, deputy prime minister 1960, and succeeded Khrushchev as premier (while Brezhnev succeeded him as party secretary). In the late 1960s Kosygin's influence declined.

Kowloon peninsula on the Chinese coast forming part of the British crown colony of Hong Kong; the town of Kowloon is a residential area.

Krajina region on the frontier between Croatia and Bosnia-Herzegovina; the chief town is Knin. Dominated by Serbs, the region proclaimed itself an autonomous Serbian province after Croatia declared its independence from Yugoslavia 1991. Krajina was the scene of intense inter-ethnic fighting during the civil war in Croatia 1991–92 and, following the cease-fire Jan 1992, 10,000 UN troops were deployed here and in E and W Slavonia.

Kraków or *Cracow* city in Poland, on the river Vistula; population (1990) 750,500. It is an industrial centre producing railway wagons, paper, chemicals, and tobacco. It was capital of Poland *c.* 1300–1595.

Krasnodar territory of SW Russia, in the N Caucasus, adjacent to the Black Sea; area 83,600 sq km/32,290 sq mi; population (1985) 4,992,000. The capital is Krasnodar. In addition to stock rearing and the production of grain, rice, fruit, and tobacco, oil is refined.

Krasnoyarsk territory of Russia in central Siberia stretching north to the Arctic Ocean; area 2,401,600 sq km/927,617 sq mi; population (1985) 3,430,000. The capital is Krasnoyarsk. It is drained by the Yenisei river. Mineral resources include gold, graphite, coal, iron ore, and uranium.

Kravchuk Leonid 1934– . Ukrainian politician, president from July 1990. Formerly a member of the Ukrainian Communist Party (UCP), he became its ideology chief in the 1980s. After the suspension of the UCP Aug 1991, Kravchuk became an advocate of independence and market-centred economic reform.

Krebs Hans 1900–1981. German-born British biochemist who discovered the citric acid cycle, also known as the *Krebs cycle*, the final pathway by which food molecules are converted into energy in living tissues. For this work he shared with Fritz Lipmann the 1953 Nobel Prize for Medicine.

Krenz Egon 1937– . German communist politician. A member of the East German Socialist Unity Party (SED) from 1955, he joined its politburo 1983 and was a hardline protégé of Erich ♢Honecker, succeeding him as party leader and head of state 1989 after widespread prodemocracy demonstrations. Pledging a 'new course', Krenz opened the country's western border and promised more open elections, but his conversion to pluralism proved weak in the face of popular protest and he resigned Dec 1989 after only a few weeks as party general secretary and head of state.

krill any of several Antarctic crustaceans of the order Euphausiacea, the most common species being *Euphausia superba*. Shrimplike, it is about 6 cm/2.5 in long, with two antennae, five pairs of legs, seven pairs of light organs along the body, and is coloured orange above and green beneath.

Krishna incarnation of the Hindu god ♢Vishnu. The devotion of the bhakti movement is usually directed towards Krishna; an example of this is the ♢International Society for Krishna Consciousness. Many stories are told of Krishna's mischievous youth, and he is the charioteer of Arjuna in the *Bhagavad-Gītā*.

Krishna Consciousness Movement popular name for the ♢International Society for Krishna Consciousness.

Kronos or *Cronus* in Greek mythology, ruler of the world and one of the ♢Titans. He was the father of Zeus, who overthrew him.

Kruger Stephanus Johannes Paulus 1825–1904. President of the Transvaal 1883–1900. He refused to remedy the grievances of the uitlanders (English and other non-Boer white residents) and so precipitated the Second ▷South African War.

krypton colourless, odourless, gaseous, nonmetallic element, symbol Kr, atomic number 36, relative atomic mass 83.80. It is grouped with the inert gases and was long believed not to enter into reactions, but it is now known to combine with fluorine under certain conditions; it remains inert to all other reagents. It is present in very small quantities in the air (about 114 parts per million). It is used chiefly in fluorescent lamps, lasers, and gas-filled electronic valves.

Kuala Lumpur capital of the Federation of Malaysia; area 240 sq km/93 sq mi; population (1990) 1,237,900. The city developed after 1873 with the expansion of tin and rubber trading; these are now its main industries. Formerly within the state of Selangor, of which it was also the capital, it was created a federal territory 1974.

Kublai Khan 1216–1294. Mongol emperor of China from 1259. He completed his grandfather ▷Genghis Khan's conquest of N China from 1240, and on his brother Mungo's death 1259 established himself as emperor of China. He moved the capital to Beijing and founded the Yuan dynasty, successfully expanding his empire into Indochina, but was defeated in an attempt to conquer Japan 1281.

Kubrick Stanley 1928– . US-born British film director, producer, and screenwriter. His films include *Paths of Glory* 1957, *Dr Strangelove* 1964, *2001: A Space Odyssey* 1968, *A Clockwork Orange* 1971, and *The Shining* 1979.

kudu either of two species of African antelope of the genus *Tragelaphus*. The greater kudu *T. strepsiceros* is fawn-coloured with thin white vertical stripes, and stands 1.3 m/4.2 ft at the shoulder, with head and body 2.4 m/8 ft long. Males have long spiral horns. The greater kudu is found in bush country from Angola to Ethiopia. The similar lesser kudu *T. imberbis* lives in E Africa and is 1 m/3 ft at the shoulder.

Ku Klux Klan US secret society dedicated to white supremacy, founded 1866 in the southern states of the USA to oppose ▷Reconstruction after the American ▷Civil War and to deny political rights to the black population. Members wore hooded white robes to hide their identity, and burned crosses at their night-time meetings. It was publicized in the 1960s for terrorizing civil-rights activists and organizing racist demonstrations.

Kumasi second largest city in Ghana, W Africa, capital of Ashanti region, with trade in cocoa, rubber, and cattle; population (1984) 376,200.

Kumayri formerly (until 1990) *Leninakan*, town in Armenia, 40 km/25 m NW of Yerevan; population (1987) 228,000. Industries include textiles and engineering. It was founded 1837 as a fortress called *Alexandropol*. The city was virtually destroyed by an earthquake 1926 and again 1988.

kumquat small orange-yellow fruit of any of several evergreen trees of the genus *Fortunella*, family Rutaceae. Native to E Asia, kumquats are cultivated throughout the tropics. The tree grows 2.4–3.6 m/8–12 ft and has dark green shiny leaves and white scented flowers. The fruit is eaten fresh (the skin is edible), preserved, or candied.

Kun Béla 1885–1938. Hungarian politician who created a Soviet republic in Hungary March 1919, which was overthrown Aug 1919 by a Western blockade and Romanian military actions. The succeeding regime under Admiral Horthy effectively liquidated both socialism and liberalism in Hungary.

Kundera Milan 1929– . Czech writer, born in Brno. His first novel, *The Joke* 1967, brought him into official disfavour in Prague, and, unable to publish further works, he moved to France. Other novels include *The Book of Laughter and Forgetting* 1979 and *The Unbearable Lightness of Being* 1984.

kung fu Chinese art of unarmed combat (Mandarin *ch'üan fa*), one of the ▷martial arts. It is practised in many forms, the most popular being *wing chun*, 'beautiful springtime'. The basic principle is to use attack as a form of defence. Kung fu dates from the 6th century, and was popularized in the West by the film actor Bruce Lee in the 1970s.

Kunming formerly **Yunnan** capital of Yunnan province, China, on Lake Dian Chi, about 2,000 m/6,500 ft above sea level; population (1989) 1,500,000. Industries include chemicals, textiles, and copper smelted with nearby hydroelectric power.

Kurd member of the Kurdish culture, living mostly in the Taurus and Sagros mountains of W Iran and N Iraq in the region called Kurdistan. Although divided among more powerful states, the Kurds have nationalist aspirations; there are some 8 million in Turkey (where they suffer from discriminatory legislation), 5 million in Iran, 4 million in Iraq, 500,000 in Syria, and 100,000 in Azerbaijan and Armenia. Some 1 million Kurds were made homeless and 25,000 killed as a result of chemical-weapon attacks by Iraq 1984–89, and in 1991 more than 1 million were forced to flee their homes in N Iraq. The Kurdish language is a member of the Indo-Iranian branch of the Indo-European family and the Kurds are a non-Arab, non-Turkic ethnic group. The Kurds are predominantly Sunni Muslims, although there are some Shi'ites in Iran.

Kurdistan or *Kordestan* hilly region in SW Asia near Mount Ararat, where the borders of Iran, Iraq, Syria, Turkey, Armenia, and Azerbaijan meet; area 193,000 sq km/74,600 sq mi; total population around 18 million.

Kuril Islands or *Kuriles* chain of about 50 small islands stretching from the NE of Hokkaido, Japan, to the S of Kamchatka, Russia; area 14,765 sq km/5,700 sq mi; population (1970) 15,000. Some of them are of volcanic origin. Two of the Kurils (Etorofu and Kunashiri) are claimed by Japan and Russia.

Kurosawa Akira 1929– . Japanese director whose film *Rashomon* 1950 introduced Western audiences to Japanese cinema. Epics such as *Shichinin no samurai/Seven Samurai* 1954 combine spectacle with intimate human drama.

Kuwait State of; country in SW Asia, bordered N and NW by Iraq, E by the Persian Gulf, and S and SW by Saudi Arabia; *capital* Kuwait (also chief port); *physical* hot desert and islands of Failaka, Bubiyan, and Warba at NE corner of Arabian Peninsula; *head of state and government* Jabir al-Ahmad al-Sabah from 1977; *political system* absolute monarchy; *exports* oil; *languages* Arabic 78%, Kurdish 10%, Farsi 4%; *recent history* recognized as an independent sovereign state from 1914, Kuwait achieved full independence from Britain 1961. On 2 Aug 1990 President Saddam Hussain of Iraq, reactivating a longstanding territorial dispute, annexed Kuwait. The emir and his family escaped to Saudi Arabia. By March 1991 UN coalition forces had liberated Kuwait (see ▷Gulf War), but by flooding the Gulf with crude oil and firing the oil wells around Kuwait city, the occupying forces had left the country an ecological disaster area. The new government formed 1991 omits any opposition representatives. Trials of alleged Iraqi collaborators have been criticized. Promised elections have been postponed.

Kuwait City (Arabic *Al Kuwayt*) formerly *Qurein* chief port and capital of the state of Kuwait, on the southern shore of Kuwait Bay; population (1985) 44,300, plus the suburbs of Hawalli, population (1985) 145,100, Jahra, population (1985) 111,200, and as-Salimiya, population (1985) 153,400. Kuwait is a banking and investment centre.

Kwa Ndebele black homeland in Transvaal province, South Africa; achieved self-governing status 1981; population (1985) 235,800.

Kwangchow alternative transliteration of ▷Guangzhou, city in China.

Kwangchu or *Kwangju* capital of South Cholla province, SW South Korea; population (1990) 1,144,700. It is at the centre of a rice-growing region.

Kwangsi-Chuang alternative transliteration of ▷Guangxi, region of China.

Kwangtung alternative transliteration of ▷Guang-dong, province of China.

Kwa Zulu black homeland in Natal province, South Africa; population (1985) 3,747,000. It achieved self-governing status 1971.

Kweilin alternative transliteration of ▷Guilin in China.

Kyd Thomas *c.* 1557–1595. English dramatist, author in about 1588 of a bloody revenge tragedy, *The Spanish Tragedy*, which anticipated elements present in Shakespeare's *Hamlet*.

Kyoto former capital of Japan 794–1868 (when the capital was changed to Tokyo) on Honshu island, linked by canal with Biwa Lake; population (1989) 1,407,300. Industries include electrical, chemical, and machinery plants; silk weaving; and the manufacture of porcelain, bronze, and lacquerware.

Kyprianou Spyros 1932– . Cypriot politician, president 1977–88. Foreign minister 1961–72, he founded the Federalist, centre-left Demo-cratic Front (DIKO) 1976. Succeeding Archbishop Makarios, he spent much of his presidency vainly trying to reunite his country.

Kyrgyzstan Republic of; country in N Asia, bordered N by Kazakhstan, E by China, S by Tajiki-stan, and W by Uzbekistan; *area* 198,500 sq km/76,641 sq mi; *capital* Bishkek (formerly Frunze); *physical* mountainous, an extension of Tian Shan range; *head of state* Askar Akayev from 1990; *political system* emergent democracy; *products* cereals, sugar, cotton, coal, oil, sheep, yaks, horses; *population* (1990) 4,300,000 (Kyrgyz 52%, Russian 21%, other 27%); *language* Kyrgyz; *recent history* part of an independent Turkestan republic 1917–24; became autonomous republic in USSR 1924 and full union republic within USSR 1936. Ethnic clashes resulted in state of emergency in capi-tal 1990. Kyrgyz voters endorsed maintenance of Union in USSR referendum 1991; President Akayev condemned anti-Gorbachev coup and suspended Kyrgyz Communist Party, which supported the coup; joined Commonwealth of Independent States Dec 1991. Independence recognized by USA Jan 1992; admitted into Conference on Security and Cooperation in Europe.

Kyushu southernmost of the main islands of Japan, separated from Shikoku and Honshu by Bungo Channel and Suo Bay, but connected to Honshu by bridge and rail tunnel; *area* 42,150 sq km/16,270 sq mi, including about 370 small islands; *capital* Nagasaki; *cities* Fukuoka, Kumamoto, Kagoshima; *physical* mountainous, volcanic, with subtropical climate; *features* the active volcano Aso-take (1,592 m/5,225 ft), with the world's largest crater; *products* coal, gold, silver, iron, tin, rice, tea, timber; *population* (1986) 13,295,000.

Labour Day legal holiday in honour of workers. In Canada and the USA, **Labor Day** is celebrated on the first Monday in September. In many countries it coincides with ▷May Day, the first day of May.

Labour Party UK political party based on socialist principles, originally formed to represent workers. It was founded 1900 and first held office 1924. The first majority Labour government 1945–51 introduced ▷nationalization and the National Health Service, and expanded ▷social security. Labour was again in power 1964–70 and 1974–79. The party leader is elected by Labour members of Parliament.

Labrador area of NE Canada, part of the province of Newfoundland, lying between Ungava Bay on the NW, the Atlantic Ocean on the E, and the Strait of Belle Isle on the SE; area 266,060 sq km/ 102,699 sq mi; population (1986) 28,741. Industries include fisheries, timber and pulp, and many minerals. Hydroelectric resources include Churchill Falls on Churchill River, where one of the world's largest underground power houses is situated.

Labrador breed of dog; see ▷retriever.

La Bruyère Jean de 1645–1696. French essayist. He was born in Paris, studied law, took a post in the revenue office, and in 1684 entered the service of the French commander the Prince of Condé. His *Caractères* 1688, satirical portraits of his contemporaries, made him many enemies.

laburnum any flowering tree or shrub of the genus *Laburnum* of the pea family Leguminosae. The seeds are poisonous. *L. anagyroides*, native to the mountainous parts of central Europe, is often grown as an ornamental tree. The flowers, in long drooping clusters, are bright yellow and appear in early spring; some varieties have purple or reddish flowers.

Laccadive, Minicoy, and Amindivi Islands former name of Indian island group ▷Lakshadweep.

lace delicate, decorative openwork textile fabric. Lace is a European craft with centres in Belgium, Italy, France, Germany, and England. It was first successfully machine-produced by John Heathcote 1809 using a bobbin net machine. Nottingham is the centre of machine-made lace in England.

lacewing insect of the families Hemerobiidae (the brown lacewings) and Chrysopidae (the green lacewings) of the order Neuroptera. Found throughout the world, lacewings are so called because of the intricate veining of their two pairs of semitransparent wings. They have narrow bodies and long thin antennae. The larvae (called aphid lions) are predators, especially on aphids.

Laclos Pierre Choderlos de 1741–1803. French author. An army officer, he wrote a single novel in letter form, *Les Liaisons dangereuses/Dangerous Liaisons* 1782, an analysis of moral corruption.

lacrosse Canadian ball game, adopted from the North American Indians, and named after a fancied resemblance of the lacrosse stick (crosse) to a bishop's crosier. Thongs across the curved end of the crosse form a pocket to carry the small rubber ball. The field is approximately 100 m/110 yd long and a minimum of 55 m/60 yd wide in the men's game, which is played with 10 players per side; the women's field is larger, and there are 12 players per side. The goals are just under 2 m/6 ft square, with loose nets. The world championship were first held in 1967 for men, and in 1969 for women.

lactation secretion of milk from the mammary glands of mammals. In late pregnancy, the cells lining the lobules inside the mammary glands begin extracting substances from the blood to produce milk. The supply of milk starts shortly after birth with the production of colostrum, a clear fluid consisting largely of water, protein, antibodies, and vitamins. The production of milk continues practically as long as the infant continues to suck.

Ladoga (Russian **Ladozhskoye**) largest lake on the continent of Europe, in Russia, just NE of St Petersburg; area 18,400 sq km/7,100 sq mi. It receives the waters of several rivers, including the Svir, which drains Lake Onega and runs to the Gulf of Finland by the river Neva.

ladybird or **ladybug** beetle of the family Coccinellidae, generally red or yellow in colour, with black spots. There are numerous species which, as larvae and adults, feed on aphids and scale-insect pests.

Lady Day Christian festival (25 March) of the Annunciation of the Virgin Mary; until 1752 it was the beginning of the legal year in England, and it is still a quarter day (date for the payment of quarterly rates or dues).

Lafayette Marie Joseph Gilbert de Motier, Marquis de Lafayette 1757–1834. French soldier and politician. He fought against Britain in the American Revolution 1777–79 and 1780–82. During the

French Revolution he sat in the National Assembly as a constitutional royalist and in 1789 presented the Declaration of the Rights of Man. After the storming of the ◊Bastille, he was given command of the National Guard. In 1792 he fled the country after attempting to restore the monarchy and was imprisoned by the Austrians until 1797. He supported Napoleon Bonaparte 1815 and played a leading part in the revolution of 1830.

La Fontaine Jean de 1621–1695. French poet. His works include *Fables* 1668–94 and *Contes* 1665–74, a series of witty and bawdy tales in verse, frequently adapted from Aesop and indirectly attacking French society and human nature. He was a friend of the playwrights Molière and Racine, and the poet Boileau.

lagoon coastal body of shallow salt water, usually with limited access to the sea. The term is normally used to describe the shallow sea area cut off by a coral reef or barrier islands.

Lagos chief port and former capital of Nigeria, located at the western end of an island in a lagoon and linked by bridges with the mainland via Iddo Island; population (1983) 1,097,000. Industries include chemicals, metal products, and fish. One of the most important slaving ports, Lagos was bombarded and occupied by the British 1851, becoming the colony of Lagos 1862. ◊Abuja was established as the new capital 1982.

Lahore capital of the province of Punjab and second city of Pakistan; population (1981) 2,920,000. Industries include engineering, textiles, carpets, and chemicals. It is associated with the Mogul rulers Akbar, Jahangir, and Aurangzeb, whose capital it was in the 16th and 17th centuries.

Laing R(onald) D(avid) 1927–1989. Scottish psychoanalyst, originator of the 'social theory' of mental illness, for example that schizophrenia is promoted by family pressure for its members to conform to standards alien to themselves. His books include *The Divided Self* 1960 and *The Politics of the Family* 1971.

laissez faire theory that the state should not intervene in economic affairs, except to break up a monopoly. The phrase originated with the Physiocrats, 18th-century French economists whose maxim was *laissez faire et laissez passer*, (literally, 'let go and let pass' – that is, leave the individual alone and let commodities circulate freely). The degree to which intervention should take place is still one of the chief problems of economics.

Lake District region in Cumbria, England; area 1,800 sq km/700 sq mi. It contains the principal English lakes, including Windermere, Ullswater, and Derwentwater, which are separated by wild uplands rising to many peaks, including Scafell Pike (978 m/3,210 ft). It is a popular holiday area for walking, climbing, and sailing.

Lakshadweep group of 36 coral islands, 10 inhabited, in the Indian Ocean, 320 km/200 mi off the Malabar coast; area 32 sq km/12 sq mi; population (1991) 51,700. The administrative headquarters are on Kavaratti Island. Products include coir, copra, and fish. The islands were created a Union Territory of the Republic of India 1956. Formerly known as the Laccadive, Minicoy, and Amindivi Islands, they were renamed Lakshadweep 1973.

Lakshmi Hindu goddess of wealth and beauty, consort of Vishnu. She appears in many forms; her festival is Diwali.

Lalique René 1860–1945. French designer and manufacturer of ◊Art Nouveau glass, jewellery, and house interiors. The Lalique factory continues in production at Wingen-sur-Moder, Alsace, under his son Marc and granddaughter Marie-Claude.

Lamarck Jean Baptiste de 1744–1829. French naturalist whose theory of evolution, known as *Lamarckism*, was based on the idea that acquired characteristics (changes acquired in an individual's lifetime) are inherited, and that organisms have an intrinsic urge to evolve into better-adapted forms. His works include *Philosophie Zoologique/ Zoological Philosophy* 1809 and *Histoire naturelle des animaux sans vertèbres/Natural History of Invertebrate Animals* 1815–22.

Lamartine Alphonse de 1790–1869. French poet. He wrote romantic poems, including *Méditations poétiques* 1820, followed by *Nouvelles méditations/ New Meditations* 1823, and *Harmonies* 1830. His *Histoire des Girondins/History of the Girondins* 1847 helped to inspire the revolution of 1848.

Lamb Charles 1775–1834. English essayist and critic. He collaborated with his sister **Mary Lamb** (1764–1847) on *Tales from Shakespeare* 1807, and his *Specimens of English Dramatic Poets* 1808 helped to revive interest in Elizabethan plays. As 'Elia' he contributed essays to the *London Magazine* from 1820 (collected 1823 and 1833).

Lammas medieval festival of harvest, celebrated 1 Aug. At one time it was an English quarter day (date for payment of quarterly rates or dues), and is still a quarter day in Scotland.

lammergeier Old World vulture *Gypaetus barbatus*, also known as the bearded vulture, with a wingspan of 2.7 m/9 ft. It ranges over S Europe, N Africa, and Asia, in wild mountainous areas. It feeds on offal and carrion and drops bones onto rocks to break them and so get at the marrow.

Lamont Norman 1942– . UK Conservative politician, chancellor of the Exchequer from 1990, chief secretary of the Treasury 1989–90. Born in the Shetland Islands and educated at Cambridge, Lamont was elected to Parliament 1972 as member for Kingston-upon-Thames. He masterminded John Major's leadership campaign.

lamprey any of various eel-shaped jawless fishes

belonging to the family Petromyzontidae. A lamprey feeds on other fish by fixing itself by its round mouth to its host and boring into the flesh with its toothed tongue. Lampreys breed in fresh water, and the young live as larvae for about five years before migrating to the sea.

Lancashire county in NW England; *area* 3,040 sq km/1,173 sq mi; *towns* Preston (administrative headquarters), which forms part of Central Lancashire New Town (together with Fulwood, Bamber Bridge, Leyland, and Chorley); Lancaster, Accrington, Blackburn, Burnley; ports Fleetwood and Heysham; seaside resorts Blackpool, Morecambe, and Southport; *features* the river Ribble; the Pennines; Forest of Bowland (moors and farming valleys); Pendle Hill; *products* formerly a world centre of cotton manufacture, now replaced with high-technology aerospace and electronics industries; *population* (1991) 1,365,100.; *famous people* Kathleen Ferrier, Gracie Fields, George Formby, Rex Harrison.

Lancaster Burt (Burton Stephen) 1913– . US film actor, formerly an acrobat. A star from his first film, *The Killers* 1946, he proved himself adept both at action roles and more complex character parts as in such films as *From Here to Eternity* 1953, *The Rose Tatoo* 1955, *Elmer Gantry* 1960, and *The Leopard/Il Gattopardo* 1963. Later films include *The Swimmer* 1968, *Atlantic City* 1981, *Local Hero* 1983, and *Field of Dreams* 1989.

Lancaster, House of English royal house, a branch of the Plantagenets. It originated 1267 when Edmund, the younger son of Henry III, was granted the earldom of Lancaster. Henry IV established the royal dynasty of Lancaster 1399 and he was followed by two more Lancastrian kings, Henry V and Henry VI.

Land federal state (plural *Länder*) of Germany or Austria.

Land League Irish peasant-rights organization, formed 1879 by Michael Davitt and Charles ⊳Parnell to fight against tenant evictions. Through its skilful use of the boycott against anyone who took a farm from which another had been evicted, it forced Gladstone's government to introduce a law in 1881 restricting rents and granting tenants security of tenure.

Land Registry, HM official body set up 1925 to register legal rights to land in England and Wales. There has been a gradual introduction, since 1925, of compulsory registration of land in different areas of the country. This requires the purchaser of land to register details of his or her title and all other rights (such as mortgages and easements) relating to the land. Once registered, the title to the land is guaranteed by the Land Registry, subject to those interests that cannot be registered; this makes the buying and selling of land easier and cheaper. The records are open to public inspection (since Dec 1990).

Landsbergis Vytautas 1932– . President of Lithuania from 1990. He became active in nationalist politics in the 1980s, founding and eventually chairing the anticommunist Sajudis independence movement 1988. When Sajudis swept to victory in the republic's elections March 1990, Landsbergis chaired the Supreme Council of Lithuania becoming, in effect, president. He immediately drafted the republic's declaration of independence from the USSR which, after initial Soviet resistance, was recognized Sept 1991.

Landseer Edwin Henry 1802–1873. English painter, sculptor, and engraver of animal studies. Much of his work reflects the Victorian taste for sentimental and moralistic pictures, for example *Dignity and Impudence* 1839 (Tate Gallery, London). The *Monarch of the Glen* (John Dewar and Sons Ltd) 1850, depicting a highland stag, was painted for the House of Lords. His sculptures include the lions at the base of Nelson's Column in Trafalgar Square, London, 1857–67.

Land's End promontory of W Cornwall, 15 km/9 mi WSW of Penzance, the westernmost point of England.

landslide sudden downward movement of a mass of soil or rocks from a cliff or steep slope. Landslides happen when a slope becomes unstable, usually because the base has been undercut or because materials within the mass have become wet and slippery.

Landsteiner Karl 1868–1943. Austrian-born immunologist who discovered the ABO ⊳blood group system 1900–02, and aided in the discovery of the Rhesus blood factors 1940. He also discovered the polio virus. He was awarded a Nobel prize 1930.

Lange David (Russell) 1942– . New Zealand Labour Party prime minister 1983–89. Labour had a decisive win in the 1984 general election on a non-nuclear military policy, which Lange immediately put into effect, despite criticism from the USA. He introduced a free-market economic policy and was re-elected 1987. He resigned Aug 1989 over a disagreement with his finance minister.

Langland William *c.* 1332–*c.* 1400. English poet. His alliterative *Vision Concerning Piers Plowman* appeared in three versions between about 1362 and 1398, but some critics believe he was only responsible for the first of these. The poem forms a series of allegorical visions, in which Piers develops from the typical poor peasant to a symbol of Jesus, and condemns the social and moral evils of 14th-century England.

language human communication through speech, writing, or both. Different nationalities or ethnic groups typically have different languages or variations on particular languages; for example, Armenians speaking the Armenian language and the British and Americans speaking distinctive varieties of the English language. One language may have various ⊳dialects, which may be seen by

landslide
mudflow landslide

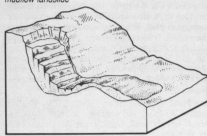

slump landslide

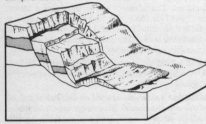

landslip landslide

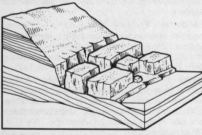

those who use them as languages in their own right. The term is also used for systems of communication with language-like qualities, such as *animal language* (the way animals communicate), *body language* (gestures and expressions used to communicate ideas), *sign language* (gestures for the deaf or for use as a ▷lingua franca, as among American Indians), and *computer languages* (such as BASIC and COBOL).

Languedoc former province of S France, bounded by the river Rhône, the Mediterranean Sea, and the regions of Guienne and Gascony. It was named after the language of its inhabitants.

Languedoc-Roussillon region of S France, comprising the *départements* of Aude, Gard, Hérault, Lozère, and Pyrénées-Orientales; area 27,400 sq km/10,576 sq mi; population (1986) 2,012,000. Its capital is Montpellier, and products include fruit, vegetables, wine, and cheese.

lanthanide any of a series of 15 metallic elements (also known as rare earths) with atomic numbers 57 (lanthanum) to 71 (lutetium). One of its members, promethium, is radioactive. All occur in nature. Lanthanides are grouped because of their chemical similarities (they are all bivalent), their properties differing only slightly with atomic number.

lanthanum soft, silvery, ductile and malleable, metallic element, symbol La, atomic number 57, relative atomic mass 138.91, the first of the lanthanide series. It is used in making alloys. It was named 1839 by Swedish chemist Carl Mosander.

Lanzarote most easterly of the Spanish Canary Islands; area 795 sq km/307 sq mi; capital Arrecife. The desertlike volcanic landscape is dominated by the Montañas de Fuego ('Mountains of Fire') with more than 300 volcanic cones.

Laois or *Laoighis* county in Leinster province, Republic of Ireland; *area* 1,720 sq km/664 sq mi; *county town* Port Laoise; *physical* flat except for the Slieve Bloom mountains in the NW; *products* sugarbeet, dairy products, woollens, agricultural machinery; *population* (1991) 52,300.

Laos Lao People's Democratic Republic; country in SE Asia, bordered N by China, E by Vietnam, S by Cambodia, and W by Thailand; *area* 236,790 sq km/91,400 sq mi; *capital* Vientiane; *physical* high mountains in E; Mekong River in W; jungle covers nearly 60% of land; *head of state* Kaysone Phomvihane from 1991; *head of government* General Khamtay Siphandon from 1991; *political system* communism, one-party state; *exports* hydroelectric power from the Mekong is exported to Thailand; timber, teak, coffee, electricity; *population* (1990 est) 4,024,000 (Lao 48%, Thai 14%, Khmer 25%, Chinese 13%); *languages* Lao (official), French; *recent history* independence was achieved from France 1954. In 1960 civil war followed a right-wing coup. In 1975 a communist-dominated republic was proclaimed. In 1988 the withdrawal was announced of 40% of Vietnamese forces stationed in Laos. The first assembly elections since the communist takeover were held 1989, and a constitution was adopted 1991, containing no references to socialism. Kaysone Phomvihane, premier since 1975 and head of the Communist Party, became executive president.

Lao Zi or Lao Tzu *c.* 604–531 BC. Chinese philosopher, commonly regarded as the founder of ▷Taoism, with its emphasis on the Tao, the inevitable and harmonious way of the universe. Nothing certain is known of his life, and he is variously said to have lived in the 6th or the 4th century BC. The *Tao Tê Ching*, the Taoist scripture, is attributed to him but apparently dates from the 3rd century BC.

La Paz capital city of Bolivia, in Murillo province, 3,800 m/12,400 ft above sea level; population (1988) 1,049,800. Products include textiles and copper.

Founded by the Spanish 1548 as Pueblo Nuevo de Nuestra Senőra de la Paz, it has been the seat of government since 1898.

lapis lazuli rock containing the blue mineral lazurite in a matrix of white calcite with small amounts of other minerals. It occurs in silica-poor igneous rocks and metamorphic limestones found in Afghanistan, Siberia, Iran, and Chile. Lapis lazuli was a valuable pigment of the Middle Ages, also used as a gemstone and in inlaying and ornamental work.

Laplace Pierre Simon, Marquis de Laplace 1749–1827. French astronomer and mathematician. In 1796, he theorized that the Solar System originated from a cloud of gas (the nebular hypothesis). He studied the motion of the Moon and planets, and published a five-volume survey of celestial mechanics, *Traité de méchanique céleste* 1799–1825. Among his mathematical achievements was the development of probability theory.

Lapland region of Europe within the Arctic Circle in Norway, Sweden, Finland, and the Kola Peninsula of NW Russia, without political definition. Its chief resources are chromium, copper, iron, timber, hydroelectric power, and tourism; there is agriculture in summer. The indigenous population are the Saami (formerly known as Lapps), a semi-nomadic herding people. Lapland has three months' continuous daylight in summer and three months' continuous darkness in winter.

La Plata capital of Buenos Aires province, Argentina; population (1980) 560,300. Industries include meat packing and petroleum refining. It was founded 1882.

la Plata, Río de see ▷Plata, Río de la.

lapwing Eurasian bird *Vanellus vanellus* of the plover family, also known as the **green plover** and, from its call, as the **peewit**. Bottle-green above and white below, with a long thin crest and rounded wings, it is about 30 cm/1 ft long. It inhabits moorland in Europe and Asia, making a nest scratched out of the ground.

larch any tree of the genus *Larix*, of the family Pinaceae. The common larch *L. decidua* grows to 40 m/130 ft. It is one of the few ▷conifer trees to shed its leaves annually. The small needlelike leaves are replaced every year by new bright-green foliage, which later darkens.

La Rioja region of N Spain; area 5,000 sq km/1,930 sq mi; population (1986) 263,000. It is famous for its wine.

lark songbird of the family Alaudidae, found mainly in the Old World, but also in North America. Larks are brownish-tan in colour and usually about 18 cm/7 in long; they nest on the ground in the open. The skylark *Alauda arvensis* sings as it rises almost vertically in the air. It breeds in Britain; it is light-brown, and 18 cm/7 in long.

Larkin Philip 1922–1985. English poet. His perfectionist, pessimistic verse includes *The North Ship* 1945, *The Whitsun Weddings* 1964, and *High Windows* 1974. He edited *The Oxford Book of 20th-Century English Verse* 1973. He also wrote two novels.

larkspur plant of the genus ▷delphinium.

La Rochefoucauld François, duc de La Rochefoucauld 1613–1680. French writer. His *Réflexions, ou sentences et maximes morales/Reflections, or Moral Maxims* 1665 is a collection of brief, epigrammatic, and cynical observations on life and society, with the epigraph 'Our virtues are mostly our vices in disguise'.

larva stage between hatching and adulthood in those species in which the young have a different appearance and way of life from the adults. Examples include tadpoles (frogs) and caterpillars (butterflies and moths). Larvae are typical of the invertebrates, some of which (for example, shrimps) have two or more distinct larval stages. Among vertebrates, it is only the amphibians and some fishes that have a larval stage.

larynx in mammals, a cavity at the upper end of the trachea (windpipe), containing the vocal cords. It is stiffened with cartilage and lined with mucous membrane. Amphibians and reptiles have much simpler larynxes, with no vocal cords. Birds have a similar cavity, called the *syrinx*, found lower down the trachea, with well-developed vocal cords.

Lascaux cave system in SW France with prehistoric wall paintings. It is richly decorated with realistic and symbolic paintings of buffaloes, horses, and red deer of the Upper Palaeolithic period, about 18,000 BC. The caves, near Montignac in the Dordogne, were discovered 1940. The opening of the Lascaux caves to tourists led to deterioration of the paintings; the caves were closed 1963 and a facsimile opened 1983.

laser (acronym for *l*ight *a*mplification by *s*timulated *e*mission of *r*adiation) device for producing a narrow beam of light, capable of travelling over vast distances without dispersion, and of being focused to give enormous power densities (10^8 watts per cm^2 for high-energy lasers). The laser operates on a principle similar to that of the ▷maser (a high-frequency microwave amplifier or oscillator). The uses of lasers include communications (a laser beam can carry much more information than can radio waves), cutting, drilling, welding, satellite tracking, medical and biological research, and surgery.

Las Palmas or *Las Palmas de Gran Canaria* tourist resort on the NE coast of Gran Canaria, Canary Islands; population (1991) 347,700. Products include sugar and bananas. There is an 18th-century cathedral.

Las Vegas city in Nevada, USA, known for

its nightclubs and gambling casinos; population (1986) 202,000. Founded 1855 in a ranching area, it is the largest city in Nevada.

latent heat in physics, the heat absorbed or radiated by a substance as it changes state (for example, from solid to liquid) at constant temperature and pressure.

latex fluid of some plants (such as the rubber tree and poppy), an emulsion of resins, proteins, and other organic substances. It is used as the basis for making rubber. The name is also applied to a suspension in water of natural or synthetic rubber (or plastic) particles used in rubber goods, paints, and adhesives.

Latin Indo-European language of ancient Italy. Latin has passed through four influential phases: as

latitude and longitude

Point X lies on longitude 60°W

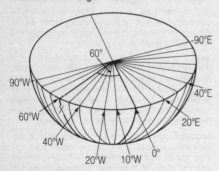

Point X lies on latitude 20°S

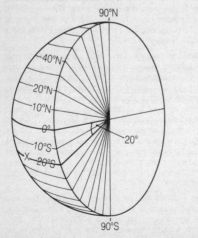

Together longitude 60°W latitude 20°S places point X on a precise position on the globe.

the language of (1) republican Rome, (2) the Roman Empire, (3) the Roman Catholic Church, and (4) W European culture, science, philosophy, and law during the Middle Ages and the Renaissance. During the third and fourth phases, much Latin vocabulary entered the English language. It is the parent form of the ⟩Romance languages, noted for its highly inflected grammar and conciseness of expression.

Latin America countries of South and Central America (also including Mexico) in which Spanish, Portuguese, and French are spoken.

latitude and longitude imaginary lines used to locate position on the globe. Lines of latitude are drawn parallel to the equator, with 0° at the equator and 90° at the north and south poles. Lines of longitude are drawn at right angles to these, with 0° (the Prime Meridian) passing through Greenwich, London.

Latvia Republic of; country in NE Europe, bordered N by Estonia, E by the Russian Federation and Belarus, S by Lithuania, and W by the Baltic Sea; *area* 63,700 sq km/24,595 sq mi; *capital* Riga; *physical* wooded lowland (highest point 312 m/1,024 ft), marshes, lakes; 472 km/293 mi of coastline; *head of state* Anatolijs Gorbunov from 1988; *head of government* Ivacs Godmanis from 1990; *political system* emergent democratic republic; *products* electronic and communications equipment, electric railway carriages, motorcycles, consumer durables, timber, paper and woollen goods, meat and dairy products; *population* (1989 est) 2,681,000 (Latvian 54%, Russian 33%); *language* Latvian; *recent history* independence declared 1918 at end of World War I; incorporated into USSR as constituent republic 1940. Occupied by Germany during World War II; USSR regained control 1944. Nationalist dissent began to grow in 1980s; independence from USSR unilaterally declared May 1990. Soviet paratroopers seized key installations in Riga 1991, but withdrew after protests. Full independence declared after attempted anti-Gorbachev coup and recognized by Soviet government and Western nations. United Nations membership granted; admitted into Conference on Security and Cooperation in Europe (CSCE).

Latynina Larissa Semyonovna 1935– . Soviet gymnast, winner of more Olympic medals than any person in any sport. She won 18 between 1956 and 1964, including nine gold medals. She won a total of 12 individual Olympic and world championship gold medals.

Laud William 1573–1645. English priest; archbishop of Canterbury from 1633. Laud's High Church policy, support for Charles I's unparliamentary rule, censorship of the press, and persecution of the Puritans all aroused bitter opposition, while his strict enforcement of the statutes against enclosures and of laws regulating wages and prices alienated the propertied classes. His attempt to impose the use of the Prayer Book on the Scots

precipitated the English ▷Civil War. He was impeached by Parliament 1640 and beheaded.

laurel any evergreen tree of the European genus *Laurus*, family Lauraceae, with glossy, aromatic leaves, yellowish flowers, and black berries. The leaves of sweet bay or poet's laurel *L. nobilis* are used in cooking. Several species are cultivated worldwide. In classical times *L. nobilis* was used to make wreaths for victorious athletes.

Laurel and Hardy Stan Laurel (stage name of Arthur Stanley Jefferson) (1890–1965) and Oliver Hardy (1892–1957). US film comedians who were one of the most successful comedy teams in film history (Stan was slim, Oliver rotund). Their partnership began in 1927, survived the transition from silent films to sound, and resulted in more than 200 short and feature-length films, which were revived as a worldwide cult in the 1970s. Among these are *Pack Up Your Troubles* 1932, *Our Relations* 1936, and *A Chump at Oxford* 1940.

Lausanne resort and capital of Vaud canton, W Switzerland, above the N shore of Lake Geneva; population (1990) 123,200. Industries include chocolate, scientific instruments, and publishing.

lava molten material that erupts from a ▷volcano and cools to form extrusive ▷igneous rock. A lava high in silica is viscous and sticky and does not flow far, whereas low-silica lava can flow for long distances. Lava differs from its parent ▷magma in that the fluid 'fractionates' on its way to the surface of the Earth; that is, certain heavy or high-temperature minerals settle out and the constituent gases form bubbles and boil away into the atmosphere.

lavender sweet-smelling herb, genus *Lavandula*, of the mint family Labiatae, native to W Mediterranean countries. The bushy low-growing *L. angustifolia* has long, narrow, erect leaves of a silver-green colour. The flowers, borne on a terminal spike, vary in colour from lilac to deep purple and are covered with small fragrant oil glands. The oil is extensively used in pharmacy and the manufacture of perfumes.

Lavoisier Antoine Laurent 1743–1794. French chemist. He proved that combustion needed only a part of the air, which he called oxygen, thereby destroying the theory of phlogiston (an imaginary 'fire element' released during combustion). With Pierre de Laplace, the astronomer and mathematician, he showed that water was a compound of oxygen and hydrogen. In this way he established the basic rules of chemical combination.

law body of rules and principles under which justice is administered or order enforced in a state or nation. In western Europe there are two main systems: ▷Roman law and ▷English law. US law is a modified form of English law.

Law Andrew Bonar 1858–1923. British Conservative politician, born in New Brunswick, Canada. He made a fortune in Scotland as a banker and iron-merchant, and entered Parliament in 1900. Elected leader of the opposition 1911, he became colonial secretary in Asquith's coalition government 1915–16, chancellor of the Exchequer 1916–19, and Lord Privy Seal 1919–21 in Lloyd George's coalition. He formed a Conservative Cabinet in 1922, but resigned on health grounds.

Law Commission in the UK, either of two statutory bodies established 1965 (one for England and Wales and one for Scotland) which consider proposals for law reform and publish their findings. They also keep British law under constant review, systematically developing and reforming it by, for example, the repeal of obsolete and unnecessary enactments.

law courts bodies that adjudicate in legal disputes. Civil and criminal cases are usually dealt with by separate courts. In many countries there is a hierarchy of courts that provide an appeal system.

The courts in England and Wales are: the **House of Lords** (the highest court for the whole of Britain), which deals with both civil and criminal appeals; the **Court of Appeal**, which is divided between criminal and civil appeal courts; the **High Court of Justice** dealing with important civil cases; **crown courts**, which handle criminal cases; and **county courts**, which deal with civil matters. **Magistrates' courts** deal with minor criminal cases and are served by ▷justices of the peace or stipendiary (paid) magistrates; and **juvenile courts** are presided over by specially qualified justices. There are also special courts, such as the Restrictive Practices Court and the Employment Appeal Tribunal.

law lords in England, the ten Lords of Appeal in Ordinary who, together with the Lord Chancellor and other peers, make up the House of Lords in its judicial capacity. The House of Lords is the final court of appeal in both criminal and civil cases. Law lords rank as life peers.

Lawrence D(avid) H(erbert) 1885–1930. English writer whose work expresses his belief in emotion and the sexual impulse as creative and true to human nature. His novels include the semi-autobiographical *Sons and Lovers* 1913, *The Rainbow* 1915, *Women in Love* 1921, and *Lady Chatterley's Lover* 1928. Lawrence also wrote short stories and poetry.

Lawrence T(homas) E(dward), known as *Lawrence of Arabia* 1888–1935. British soldier and writer. Appointed to the military intelligence department in Cairo, Egypt, during World War I, he took part in negotiations for an Arab revolt against the Ottoman Turks, and in 1916 attached himself to the emir Faisal. He became a guerrilla leader of genius, combining raids on Turkish communications with the organization of a joint Arab revolt, described in *The Seven Pillars of Wisdom* 1926.

lawrencium synthesized, radioactive, metallic element, the last of the actinide series, symbol Lr, atomic number 103, relative atomic mass 262. Its only known isotope, Lr-257, has a half-life of 4.3 seconds and was originally synthesized at the University of California at Berkeley 1961 by bombarding californium with boron nuclei. The original symbol, Lw, was officially changed in 1963.

Lawson Nigel 1932– . British Conservative politician. A former financial journalist, he was financial secretary to the Treasury 1979–81, secretary of state for energy 1981–83, and chancellor of the Exchequer 1983. He resigned 1989 after criticism by government adviser Alan Walters over his policy of British membership of the ▷European Monetary System.

laxative substance used to relieve constipation (infrequent bowel movement). Current medical opinion discourages regular or prolonged use. Regular exercise and a diet high in vegetable fibre is believed to be the best means of preventing and treating constipation.

Lazio (Roman *Latium*) region of W central Italy; area 17,200 sq km/6,639 sq mi; capital Rome; population (1990) 5,191,500. Products include olives, wine, chemicals, pharmaceuticals, and textiles. Home of the Latins from the 10th century BC, it was dominated by the Romans from the 4th century BC.

LCD abbreviation for ▷*liquid-crystal display*.

lead heavy, soft, malleable, grey, metallic element, symbol Pb (from Latin *plumbum*), atomic number 82, relative atomic mass 207.19. Usually found as an ore (most often in galena), it occasionally occurs as a free metal (▷native metal), and is the final stable product of the decay of uranium. Lead is the softest and weakest of the commonly used metals, with a low melting point; it is a poor conductor of electricity and resists acid corrosion. As a cumulative poison, lead enters the body from lead water pipes, lead-based paints, and leaded petrol. The metal is an effective shield against radiation and is used in batteries, glass, ceramics, and alloys such as pewter and solder.

leaf lateral outgrowth on the stem of a plant,

and in most species the primary organ of ▷photosynthesis. The chief leaf types are cotyledons (seed leaves), scale leaves (on underground stems), foliage leaves, and bracts (in the axil of which a flower is produced). Leaves that fall in the autumn are termed **deciduous**, while evergreen leaves are termed **persistent**.

leaf insect insect of the order Phasmida, about 10 cm/4 in long, with a green, flattened body, remarkable for closely resembling the foliage on which it lives. It is most common in SE Asia.

League of Nations international organization formed after World War I to solve international disputes by arbitration. Established in Geneva, Switzerland, 1920, the league included representatives from states throughout the world, but was severely weakened by the US decision not to become a member, and had no power to enforce its decisions. It was dissolved 1946, and replaced by the ▷United Nations.

Leakey Louis (Seymour Bazett) 1903–1972. British archaeologist, born in Kenya. In 1958, with his wife Mary Leakey, he discovered gigantic extinct-animal fossils in the ▷Olduvai Gorge in Tanzania, as well as many remains of an early human type.

Leakey Mary 1913– . British archaeologist. In 1948 she discovered, on Rusinga Island, Lake Victoria, E Africa, the prehistoric ape skull known as *Proconsul*, about 20 million years old; and human remains at Laetolil, to the south, about 3,750,000 years old.

Leakey Richard 1944– . British archaeologist. In 1972 he discovered at Lake Turkana, Kenya, an apelike skull, estimated to be about 2.9 million years old; it had some human characteristics and a brain capacity of 800 cu cm. In 1984 his team found an almost complete skeleton of *Homo erectus* some 1.6 million years old. He is the son of Louis and Mary Leakey.

Lean David 1908–1991. British film director. His films, noted for their atmospheric quality, include early work codirected with playwright Noël ▷Coward. *Brief Encounter* 1946 established Lean as a leading talent. Among his later films are such accomplished epics as *The Bridge on the River Kwai* 1957 (Academy Award), *Lawrence of Arabia* 1962 (Academy Award), *Dr Zhivago* 1965, and *A Passage to India* 1984.

Lear Edward 1812–1888. English artist and humorist. His *Book of Nonsense* 1846 popularized the limerick (a five-line humorous verse). He first attracted attention by his paintings of birds, and later turned to landscapes. He travelled to Italy, Greece, Egypt, and India, publishing books on his travels with his own illustrations, and spent most of his later life in Italy.

leather material prepared from the hides and skins of animals, by tanning with vegetable tannins and chromium salts. Leather is a durable and water-resistant material, and is used for bags, shoes, clothing, and upholstery. There are three main stages in the process of converting animal skin into leather: cleaning, tanning, and dressing.

Lebanon Republic of; country in W Asia, bordered N and E by Syria, S by Israel, and W by the Mediterranean Sea; *area* 10,452 sq km/4,034 sq mi; *capital* and port Beirut; *physical* narrow coastal plain; Bekka valley N–S between Lebanon and Anti-Lebanon mountain ranges; *head of state* Elias Hrawi from 1989; *head of government* Rashid al-Solh from 1992; *political system* emergent democratic republic; *exports* citrus and other fruit, vegetables, industrial products to Arab neighbours; *population* (1990 est) 3,340,000 (Lebanese 82%, Palestinian 9%, Armenian 5%); *languages* Arabic, French (both official), Armenian, English; *recent history* independence was achieved from France 1944. In 1964 the Palestine Liberation Organization (PLO) was founded in Beirut. Civil war between Christians and Muslims broke out 1975–76 and resumed 1978 after Israel invaded S Lebanon in search of PLO fighters. By 1985 Lebanon neared chaos. Foreigners were taken hostage. Successive attempts to establish a government failed until 1990, when the government regained control of Beirut and proposals for a new constitution for a Second Republic were discussed. The government extended control to the whole country 1991 and foreign hostages, including Terry Waite, were released. Prime Minister Karami resigned 1992 and was replaced by Rashid al-Solh.

Lebowa black homeland in Transvaal province, South Africa; it achieved self-governing status 1972; population (1985) 1,836,000.

Le Corbusier assumed name of Charles-Edouard Jeanneret 1887–1965. Swiss architect. His functionalist approach to town planning in industrial society was based on the interrelationship between machine forms and the techniques of modern architecture. His concept, *La Ville radieuse*, developed in Marseille, France (1945–50) and Chandigarh, India, placed buildings and open spaces with related functions in a circular formation, with buildings based on standard-sized units mathematically calculated according to the proportions of the human figure (see ◊golden section).

LED abbreviation for ◊*light-emitting diode*.

Leda in Greek mythology, the wife of Tyndareus, and mother of Clytemnestra. Zeus, who came to her as a swan, was the father of her other children, Helen of Troy and the twins Castor and Pollux.

Lee Laurie 1914– . English writer. His works include the autobiographical novel *Cider with Rosie* 1959, a classic evocation of childhood; nature poetry such as *The Bloom of Candles* 1947; and travel writing including *A Rose for Winter* 1955.

Lee Robert E(dward) 1807–1870. US Confederate general in the ◊American Civil War, a military strategist. As military adviser to Jefferson ◊Davis, president of the Confederacy, and as commander of the army of N Virginia, he made several raids into Northern territory, but was defeated at Gettysburg and surrendered at Appomattox 1865.

leech annelid worm forming the class Hirudinea. Leeches inhabit fresh water, and in tropical countries infest damp forests. As bloodsucking animals they are injurious to people and animals, to whom they attach themselves by means of a strong mouth adapted to sucking.

Leeds city in W Yorkshire, England, on the river Aire; population (1991 est) 674,400. Industries include engineering, printing, chemicals, glass, and woollens. It is a centre of communications where road, rail, and canal (to Liverpool and Goole) meet.

leek onionlike plant of the genus *Allium* of the lily family Liliaceae. The cultivated leek is a variety of the wild *A. ampeloprasum* of the Mediterranean area and Atlantic islands. The lower leaf parts form the bulb, which is eaten as a vegetable. The leek is the national emblem of Wales.

Lee Kuan Yew 1923– . Singapore politician, prime minister from 1959. Lee founded the anti-communist Socialist People's Action Party 1954 and entered the Singapore legislative assembly 1955. He was elected the country's first prime minister 1959, and took Singapore out of the Malaysian federation 1965. He remained in power until his resignation 1990. He was succeeded by Goh Chok Tongo.

Lee Teng-hui 1923– . Taiwanese right-wing politician, vice president 1984–88, president and Kuomintang party leader from 1988. Lee, the country's first island-born leader, is viewed as a reforming technocrat.

Leeuwenhoek Anton van 1632–1723. Dutch pioneer of microscopic research. He ground his own lenses, some of which magnified up to 200 times. With these he was able to see individual red blood cells, sperm, and bacteria, achievements not repeated for more than a century.

Leeward Islands (1) group of islands, part of the ◊Society Islands, in ◊French Polynesia, S Pacific; (2) general term for the northern half of the Lesser ◊Antilles in the West Indies; (3) former British colony in the West Indies (1871–1956) comprising Antigua, Montserrat, St Christopher/St Kitts–Nevis, Anguilla, and the Virgin Islands.

left wing in politics, the socialist parties. The term originated in the French National Assembly of 1789, where the nobles sat in the place of honour to the right of the president, and the commons sat to the left. This arrangement has become customary in European parliaments, where the progressives sit on the left and the conservatives on the right. It is also usual to speak of the right, left, and centre, when referring to the different elements composing a single party.

legacy in law, a gift of personal property made by a testator in a will and transferred on the testator's death to the legatee. *Specific legacies* are definite named objects; a *general legacy* is a sum of money or item not specially identified; a *residuary legacy* is all the remainder of the deceased's personal estate after debts have been paid and the other legacies have been distributed.

legionnaire's disease pneumonia-like disease, so called because it was first identified when it broke out at a convention of the American Legion in Philadelphia in 1976. Legionnaire's disease is caused by the bacterium *Legionella pneumophila*, which breeds in warm water (for example, in the cooling towers of air-conditioning systems). It is spread in minute water droplets, which may be inhaled.

Legnano, Battle of defeat of the Holy Roman emperor Frederick I Barbarossa by members of the Lombard League 1176 at Legnano, NW of Milan. It was a major setback to the emperor's plans for imperial domination over Italy and showed for the first time the power of infantry against feudal cavalry.

legume plant of the family Leguminosae, which has a pod containing dry seeds. The family includes peas, beans, lentils, clover, and alfalfa (lucerne). Legumes are important in agriculture because of their specialized roots, which have nodules containing bacteria capable of fixing nitrogen from the air and increasing the fertility of the soil. The edible seeds of legumes are called *pulses*.

Le Havre industrial port (engineering, chemicals, oil refining) in Normandy, NW France, on the river Seine; population (1982) 255,000. It is the largest port in Europe, and has transatlantic passenger links.

Leibniz Gottfried Wilhelm 1646–1716. German mathematician and philosopher. Independently of, but concurrently with, the British scientist Isaac Newton he developed the branch of mathematics known as ◊calculus. In his metaphysical works, such as *The Monadology* 1714, he argued that everything consisted of innumerable units, *monads*, the individual properties of which determined each thing's past, present, and future. Monads, although independent of each other, interacted predictably; this meant that Christian faith and scientific reason need not be in conflict and that 'this is the best of all possible worlds'.

Leicester industrial city (food processing, hosiery, footwear, engineering, electronics, printing, plastics) and administrative headquarters of Leicestershire, England, on the river Soar; population (1991) 270,600.

Leicester Robert Dudley, Earl of Leicester *c.* 1532–

1588. English courtier. Son of the Duke of Northumberland, he was created Earl of Leicester 1564. Queen Elizabeth I gave him command of the army sent to the Netherlands 1585–87 and of the forces prepared to resist the threat of Spanish invasion of 1588. His lack of military success led to his recall, but he retained Elizabeth's favour until his death.

Leicestershire county in central England; *area* 2,550 sq km/984 sq mi; *towns* Leicester (administrative headquarters), Loughborough, Melton Mowbray, Market Harborough; *features* Rutland district (formerly England's smallest county, with Oakham as its county town); Rutland Water, one of Europe's largest reservoirs; Charnwood Forest; Vale of Belvoir (under which are large coal deposits); *products* horses, cattle, sheep, dairy products, coal; *population* (1991) 860,500; *famous people* C P Snow, Thomas Babington Macaulay, Titus Oates.

Leigh Mike 1943– . English playwright and filmmaker, noted for his sharp, carefully improvised social satires. He directs his own plays, which evolve through improvisation before they are scripted. His work for television includes *Nuts in May* 1976 and *Abigail's Party* 1977; his films include *High Hopes* 1989 and *Life Is Sweet* 1991.

Leinster SE province of the Republic of Ireland, comprising the counties of Carlow, Dublin, Kildare, Kilkenny, Laois, Longford, Louth, Meath, Offaly, Westmeath, Wexford, and Wicklow; area 19,630 sq km/7,577 sq mi; capital Dublin; population (1991) 1,860,000.

Leipzig city in W Saxony, Germany, 145 km/90 mi SW of Berlin; population (1986) 552,000. Products include furs, leather goods, cloth, glass, cars, and musical instruments.

Leitrim county in Connacht province, Republic of Ireland, bounded NW by Donegal Bay; *area* 1,530 sq km/591 sq mi; *county town* Carrick-on-Shannon; *features* rivers: Shannon, Bonet, Drowes and Duff; *products* potatoes, cattle, linen, woollens, pottery, coal, iron, lead; *population* (1991) 25,300.

Lely Peter. Adopted name of Pieter van der Faes 1618–1680. Dutch painter, active in England from 1641, who painted fashionable portraits in Baroque style. His subjects included Charles I, Cromwell, and Charles II.

Lemaître Georges Edouard 1894–1966. Belgian cosmologist who in 1927 proposed the ◊Big Bang theory of the origin of the universe. He predicted that the entire universe was expanding, which the US astronomer Edwin Hubble confirmed. Lemaître suggested that the expansion had been started by an initial explosion, the Big Bang, a theory that is now generally accepted.

Léman, Lac French name for Lake ◊Geneva.

Le Mans industrial town in Sarthe *département*,

France; population (1982) 150,000, conurbation 191,000. It has a motor-racing circuit where the annual endurance 24-hour race (established 1923) for sports cars and their prototypes is held.

lemming small rodent of the family Cricetidae, especially the genus *Lemmus*, comprising four species worldwide in northern latitudes. It is about 12 cm/5 in long, with thick brownish fur, a small head, and a short tail. Periodically, when their population exceeds the available food supply, lemmings undertake mass migrations.

lemon sour fruit of the small, evergreen, semitropical lemon tree *Citrus limon*. It may have originated in NW India, and was introduced into Europe by the Spanish Moors in the 12th or 13th century. It is now grown in Italy, Spain, California, Florida, South Africa, and Australia.

lemur prosimian ⟩primate of the family Lemuridae, inhabiting Madagascar and the Comoro Islands. There are about 16 species, ranging from mouse-sized to dog-sized animals. Lemurs are arboreal and some species are nocturnal. They have long, bushy tails, and feed on fruit, insects, and small animals.

Lena longest river in Asiatic Russia, 4,400 km/2,730 mi, with numerous tributaries. Its source is near Lake Baikal, and it empties into the Arctic Ocean through a delta 400 km/240 mi wide. It is ice covered for half the year.

Lendl Ivan 1960– . Czech-born lawn tennis player. He has won eight Grand Slam singles titles, including the US and French titles three times each. He has won more than $15 million in prize money.

Lenin Vladimir Ilyich. Adopted name of Vladimir Ilyich Ulyanov 1870–1924. Russian revolutionary, first leader of the USSR, and communist theoretician. Active in the 1905 Revolution, Lenin had to leave Russia when it failed, settling in Switzerland 1914. He returned to Russia after the February revolution of 1917 (see ⟩Russian Revolution). He led the Bolshevik revolution Nov 1917 and became leader of a Soviet government, concluded peace with Germany, and organized a successful resistance to White Russian (pro-tsarist) uprisings and foreign intervention 1918–20. His modification of traditional Marxist doctrine to fit conditions prevailing in Russia became known as *Marxism–Leninism*, the basis of communist ideology.

Leningrad former name (1924–91) of the Russian city ⟩St Petersburg.

Lennon John (Ono) 1940–1980. UK rock singer, songwriter, and guitarist, in the USA from 1971; a founder member of the ⟩Beatles. Both before the band's break-up 1969 and in his solo career, he collaborated intermittently with his wife **Yoko Ono** (1933–   ). 'Give Peace a Chance', a hit 1969, became an anthem of the peace movement. His solo

work alternated between the confessional and the political, as on the album *Imagine* 1971. He was shot dead by a fan.

lens in optics, a piece of a transparent material, such as glass, with two polished surfaces — one concave or convex, and the other plane, concave, or convex — that modifies rays of light. A convex lens brings rays of light together; a concave lens makes the rays diverge. Lenses are essential to spectacles, microscopes, telescopes, cameras, and almost all optical instruments.

Lent in the Christian church, the 40-day period of fasting that precedes Easter, beginning on Ash Wednesday, but omitting Sundays.

lentil annual Old World plant *Lens culinaris* of the pea family Leguminosae. The plant, which resembles vetch, grows 15–45 cm/6–18 in high and has white, blue, or purplish flowers. The seeds, contained in pods about 1.6 cm/0.6 in long, are widely used as food.

Leo zodiacal constellation in the northern hemisphere represented as a lion. The Sun passes through Leo from mid-Aug to mid-Sept. Its brightest star is first-magnitude Regulus at the base of a pattern of stars called the Sickle. In astrology, the dates for Leo are between about 23 July and 22 Aug (see ⟩precession).

Leo I St *the Great* c. 390–461. Pope from 440 who helped to establish the Christian liturgy. Leo summoned the Chalcedon Council where his Dogmatical Letter was accepted as the voice of St Peter. Acting as ambassador for the emperor Valentinian III (425–455), Leo saved Rome from devastation by the Huns by buying off their king, Attila.

Leo III c. 750–816. Pope from 795. After the withdrawal of the Byzantine emperors, the popes had become the real rulers of Rome. Leo III was forced to flee because of a conspiracy in Rome and took refuge at the court of the Frankish king Charlemagne. He returned to Rome 799 and crowned Charlemagne emperor on Christmas Day 800, establishing the secular sovereignty of the pope over Rome under the suzerainty of the emperor (who became the Holy Roman emperor).

Leo X Giovanni de' Medici 1475–1521. Pope from 1513. The son of Lorenzo the Magnificent of Florence, he was created a cardinal at 13. He bestowed on Henry VIII of England the title of Defender of the Faith. A patron of the arts, he sponsored the rebuilding of St Peter's Church, Rome. He raised funds for this by selling indulgences (remissions of punishment for sin), a sale that led the religious reformer Martin Luther to rebel against papal authority. Leo X condemned Luther and excommunicated him 1521.

Leonardo da Vinci 1452–1519. Italian painter, sculptor, architect, engineer, and scientist, one of the greatest figures of the Italian Renaissance, active in Florence, Milan, and, from 1516, France. As state engineer and court painter to the duke of Milan, he painted the *Last Supper* mural about 1495 (Sta Maria delle Grazie, Milan), and on his return to Florence painted the *Mona Lisa* (Louvre, Paris) about 1503–06. His notebooks and drawings show an immensely inventive and enquiring mind, studying aspects of the natural world from anatomy to aerodynamics.

leopard or ***panther*** cat *Panthera pardus*, found in Africa and Asia. The background colour of the coat is golden, and the black spots form rosettes, that differ according to the variety; black panthers are simply a colour variation and retain the patterning as a 'watered-silk' effect. The leopard is 1.5–2.5 m/ 5–8 ft long, including the tail, which may measure 1 m/3 ft.

Leopold I 1790–1865. King of Belgium from 1831, having been elected to the throne on the creation of an independent Belgium. Through his marriage, when prince of Saxe-Coburg, to Princess Charlotte Augusta, he was the uncle of Queen Victoria of Great Britain and had considerable influence over her.

Leopold II 1835–1909. King of Belgium from 1865, son of Leopold I. He financed the US journalist Henry Stanley's explorations in Africa, which resulted in the foundation of the Congo Free State (now Zaire), from which he extracted a huge fortune by ruthless exploitation.

Leopold III 1901–1983. King of Belgium 1934–51. He surrendered to the German army in World War II 1940. Postwar charges against his conduct led to a regency by his brother Charles and his eventual abdication 1951 in favour of his son Baudouin.

Leopold I 1640–1705. Holy Roman emperor from 1658, in succession to his father Ferdinand III. He warred against Louis XIV of France and the Ottoman Empire.

Leopold II 1747–1792. Holy Roman emperor in succession to his brother Joseph II. He was the son of Empress Maria Theresa of Austria. His hostility to the French Revolution led to the outbreak of war a few weeks after his death.

Léopoldville former name (until 1966) of ⇨Kinshasa, city in Zaire.

Lepanto, Battle of sea battle 7 Oct 1571, fought in the Mediterranean Gulf of Corinth off Lepanto (Italian name of the Greek port of ***Naupaktos***), then in Turkish possession, between the Ottoman Empire and forces from Spain, Venice, Genoa, and the Papal States. The combined western fleets overcame Muslim sea power.

Le Pen Jean-Marie 1928– . French extreme right-wing politician. In 1972 he formed the French National Front, supporting immigrant repatriation and capital punishment; the party gained 14% of the national vote in the 1986 election. Le Pen's openly fascist statements caused his bid for the presidency 1988 to founder. He was elected to the European Parliament 1984.

leprosy or ***Hansen's disease*** chronic, progressive disease caused by a bacterium *Mycobacterium leprae* closely related to that of tuberculosis. The infection attacks the skin and nerves. Once common in many countries, leprosy is now confined almost entirely to the tropics. It is controlled with drugs.

lepton any of a class of light ⇨elementary particles that are not affected by the strong nuclear force; they do not interact strongly with other particles or nuclei. The leptons are comprised of the ⇨electron, muon, and tau, and their ⇨neutrinos (the electron neutrino, muon neutrino, and tau neutrino), plus their six ⇨antiparticles.

lesbianism homosexuality (sexual attraction to one's own sex) between women, so called from the Greek island of Lesbos (now Lesvos), the home of ⇨Sappho the poet and her followers to whom the behaviour was attributed.

Lesbos alternative spelling of ⇨Lesvos, an island in the Aegean Sea.

Lesotho Kingdom of; country in southern Africa, an enclave within South Africa; ***area*** 30,355 sq km/ 11,717 sq mi; ***capital*** Maseru; ***physical*** mountainous with plateau; ***head of state*** King Letsie III from 1990; ***head of government*** Elias Tutsoane Ramaema from 1991; ***political system*** military-controlled monarchy; ***exports*** wool, mohair, diamonds, cattle, wheat, vegetables; ***population*** (1990 est) 1,757,000; ***languages*** Sesotho, English (official), Zulu, Xhosa; ***recent history*** Basutoland, a British protectorate, achieved independence as the Kingdom of Lesotho, within the Commonwealth, 1966. A state of emergency was imposed 1970–73; in 1975 members of the ruling party were attacked by South-Africa-backed guerrillas; and in 1986 South Africa imposed a border blockade, forcing deportation of 60 ANC members. General Lekhanya gained power in a coup and abolished the National Assembly. In 1990 King Moshoeshoe II was dethroned by military council and replaced by his son Mohato as King Letsie III. Lekhanya was ousted in a coup led by Col Elias Tutsoane Ramaema 1991. Political parties were permitted to operate from 1991.

Lesseps Ferdinand, Vicomte de Lesseps 1805–1894. French engineer, constructor of the ⇨Suez Canal 1859–69; he began planning the ⇨Panama Canal 1879, but withdrew 1889 after failing to construct it without locks.

Lessing Doris (May) (née Taylor) 1919– . British novelist, born in Iran. Concerned with social and political themes, particularly the place of women in society, her work includes *The Grass is Singing* 1950, the five-novel series *Children of Violence* 1952–69, *The Golden Notebook* 1962, *The Good Terrorist* 1985, and *The Fifth Child* 1988. She has also written an 'inner space fiction' series *Canopus in Argus Archives* 1979–83, and under the pen name 'Jane Somers', *The Diary of a Good Neighbour* 1981.

Lesvos Greek island in the Aegean Sea, near the coast of Turkey; *area* 2,154 sq km/831 sq mi; *capital* Mytilene; *products* olives, wine, grain; *population* (1981) 104,620; *history* ancient name Lesbos; an Aeolian settlement, the home of the poets Alcaeus and Sappho; conquered by the Turks from Genoa 1462; annexed to Greece 1913.

lettuce annual edible plant *Lactuca sativa*, family Compositae, believed to have been derived from the wild species *L. serriola*. There are many varieties, including the cabbage lettuce, with round or loose heads, and the Cos lettuce, with long, upright heads.

leukaemia any one of a group of cancers of the blood cells, with widespread involvement of the bone marrow and other blood-forming tissue. The central feature of leukaemia is runaway production of white blood cells that are immature or in some way abnormal. These rogue cells, which lack the defensive capacity of healthy white cells, overwhelm the normal ones, leaving the victim vulnerable to infection. Treatment is with radiotherapy and cytotoxic drugs to suppress replication of abnormal cells, or by bone-marrow transplantation.

Levellers democratic party in the English Civil War. The Levellers found wide support among Cromwell's New Model Army and the yeoman farmers, artisans, and small traders, and proved a powerful political force 1647–49. Their programme included the establishment of a republic, government by a parliament of one house, religious toleration, and sweeping social reforms.

lever simple machine consisting of a rigid rod pivoted at a fixed point called the fulcrum, used for shifting or raising a heavy load or applying force in a similar way. Levers are classified into orders according to where the effort is applied, and the load-moving force developed, in relation to the position of the fulcrum.

leveraged buyout in business, the purchase of a controlling proportion of the shares of a company by its own management, financed almost exclusively by borrowing. It is so called because the ratio of a company's long-term debt to its equity (capital assets) is known as its 'leverage'.

Lewis Carl (Frederick Carleton) 1961– . US track and field athlete. At the 1984 Olympic Games he equalled the performance of Jesse ⇄Owens, winning gold medals in the 100 and 200 metres, sprint relay, and long jump. In the 1988 Olympics, he repeated his golds in the 100 metres and long jump, and won a silver in the 200 metres.

Lewis Cecil Day. Irish poet; see ⇄Day Lewis.

Lewis C(live) S(taples) 1898–1963. British academic and writer. A committed Christian, he wrote essays in popular theology, collected in *The Screwtape Letters* 1942 and *Mere Christianity* 1952, and allegorical fiction: a science-fiction trilogy beginning with *Out of the Silent Planet* 1938 and a series of novels for children, set in the magic land of Narnia, beginning with *The Lion, the Witch, and the Wardrobe* 1950. His autobiography is *Surprised by Joy* 1955.

Lewis Jerry Lee 1935– . US rock-and-roll and country singer and pianist. His trademark was the 'pumping piano' style in hits such as 'Whole Lotta Shakin' Going On' and 'Great Balls of Fire' 1957; later recordings include 'What Made Milwaukee Famous' 1968.

Lewis (Percy) Wyndham 1886–1957. English writer and artist who pioneered Vorticism, which with its feeling of movement sought to reflect the age of industry. He had a hard and aggressive style in both his writing and his painting. His literary works include the novels *Tarr* 1918 and *The Childermass* 1928, the essay *Time and Western Man* 1927, and autobiographies.

Lhasa ('the Forbidden City') capital of the autonomous region of Tibet, China, at 5,000 m/16,400 ft; population (1982) 105,000. Products include handicrafts and light industry. The holy city of Lamaism, Lhasa was closed to Westerners until 1904, when members of a British expedition

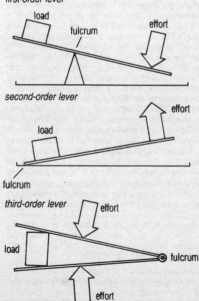

lever

first-order lever

load
fulcrum
effort

second-order lever

effort
load
fulcrum

third-order lever

effort
load
fulcrum
effort

visited the city. It was annexed with the rest of Tibet 1950–51 by China, and the spiritual and temporal head of state, the Dalai Lama, fled in 1959 after a popular uprising against Chinese rule. Monasteries have been destroyed and monks killed, and an influx of Chinese settlers has generated resentment. In 1988 and 1989 nationalist demonstrators were shot by Chinese soldiers.

liability in accounting, a financial obligation. Liabilities are placed alongside assets on a balance sheet to show the wealth of the individual or company concerned at a given date.

Liaoning province of NE China; *area* 151,000 sq km/58,300 sq mi; *capital* Shenyang; *towns* Anshan, Fushun, Liaoyang; *features* one of China's most heavily industrialized areas; *products* cereals, coal, iron, salt, oil; *population* (1990) 39,460,000; *history* developed by Japan 1905–45, including the *Liaodong Peninsula*, whose ports had been conquered from the Russians.

libel in law, defamation published in a permanent form, such as in a newspaper, book, or broadcast. In English law a statement is defamatory if it lowers the plaintiff in the estimation of right-thinking people generally.

Liberal Democrats in UK politics, common name for the ⟡Social and Liberal Democrats.

liberalism political and social theory that favours representative government, freedom of the press, speech, and worship, the abolition of class privileges, the use of state resources to protect the welfare of the individual, and international ⟡free trade. It is historically associated with the Liberal Party in the UK and the Democratic Party in the USA.

Liberal Party British political party, the successor to the ⟡Whig Party, with an ideology of liberalism. In the 19th century, it represented the interests of commerce and industry. Its outstanding leaders were Palmerston, Gladstone, and Lloyd George. From 1914 it declined, and the rise of the Labour Party pushed the Liberals into the middle ground. The Liberals joined forces with the Social Democratic Party (SDP) as the Alliance for the 1983 and 1987 elections. In 1988, a majority of the SDP voted to merge with the Liberals to form the ⟡Social and Liberal Democrats.

Liberia Republic of; country in W Africa, bordered N and NE by Guinea, E by the Ivory Coast, S and SW by the Atlantic Ocean, and NW by Sierra Leone; *area* 111,370 sq km/42,989 sq mi; *capital* and port Monrovia; *physical* forested highlands; swampy coast where six rivers enter the sea; *head of state and government* Amos Sawyer from 1990; *political system* emergent democratic republic; *exports* iron ore, rubber (Africa's largest producer), timber, diamonds, coffee, cocoa, palm oil; *population* (1990 est) 2,644,000 (95% indigenous); *languages* English (official); over 20 Niger-Congo

languages; *recent history* Liberia was founded 1847 as an independent republic. In 1980 President Tolbert, in power since 1971, was assassinated in a coup led by Samuel Doe, who suspended the constitution. A new constitution was approved 1984, when the National Democratic Party of Liberia (NDPL) was founded. In 1985 it won the general election. In 1990 Doe was killed in a civil war between rival rebel factions and an interim government led by Amos Sawyer was formed; Sawyer was elected president 1991.

libido in Freudian psychology, the psychic energy, or life force, that is to be found even in a newborn child. The libido develops through a number of phases, identified by Freud as the *oral stage*, when a child tests everything by mouth, the *anal stage*, when the child gets satisfaction from control of its body, and the *genital stage*, when sexual instincts find pleasure in the outward show of love.

Libra faint zodiacal constellation in the southern hemisphere adjoining Scorpius, and represented as the scales of justice. The Sun passes through Libra during Nov. The constellation was once considered to be a part of Scorpius, seen as the scorpion's claws. In astrology, the dates for Libra are between about 23 Sept and 23 Oct (see ⟡precession).

Libreville capital of Gabon, on the estuary of the river Gabon; population (1988) 352,000. Products include timber, oil, and minerals. It was founded 1849 as a refuge for slaves freed by the French.

Libya Great Socialist People's Libyan Arab Jamahiriya; country in N Africa, bordered N by the Mediterranean Sea, E by Egypt, SE by Sudan, S by Chad and Niger, and W by Algeria and Tunisia; *area* 1,759,540 sq km/679,182 sq mi; *capital* Tripoli; *physical* flat to undulating plains with plateaus and depressions stretch S from Mediterranean coast to extremely dry desert interior; *head of state and government* Moamer al-Khaddhafi from 1969; *political system* one-party socialist state; *exports* oil, natural gas; *population* (1990 est) 4,280,000 (including 500,000 foreign workers); *language* Arabic; *recent history* an Italian colony until 1942, when it was under British and French control. In 1951 Libya achieved independence as the United Kingdom of Libya, under King Idris. Col Khaddhafi deposed the king in a coup 1969, set up a Revolution Command Council and proclaimed the Arab Socialist Union the only legal party. In 1972–81 federations and mergers with Syria, Egypt, and Chad were proposed and abandoned. In 1986, the USA accused Khaddhafi of complicity in terrorist activities and bombed his headquarters; in 1989 it accused him of building a chemical-weapons factory and shot down two Libyan planes. Reconciliation with Egypt 1989.

lichen any organism of the group Lichenes, which consists of a specific fungus and a specific alga existing in a mutually beneficial relationship. Found as coloured patches or spongelike masses adhering to trees, rocks, and other substrates, lichens flourish under adverse conditions.

Lichtenstein Roy 1923– . US Pop artist. He uses advertising imagery and comic-strip techniques, often focusing on popular ideals of romance and heroism, as in *Whaam!* 1963 (Tate Gallery, London). He has also produced sculptures in brass, plastic, and enamelled metal.

Liechtenstein Principality of; country in W central Europe, situated between Austria to the E and Switzerland to the W; *area* 160 sq km/62 sq mi; *capital* Vaduz; *physical* Alpine; includes part of Rhine Valley in W; *head of state* Prince Hans Adam II from 1989; *head of government* Hans Brunhart from 1978; *political system* constitutional monarchy; *exports* microchips, dental products, small machinery, processed foods, postage stamps; *population* (1990 est) 30,000 (33% foreign); *languages* German (official), Alemannic dialect; *recent history* a sovereign state since 1342; the present boundaries were established 1434; former counties of Schellenberg and Vaduz incorporated from 1719. In 1921, Swiss currency was adopted and in 1923 Liechtenstein united in a customs union with Switzerland. Liechtenstein became a member of the United Nations 1990; became seventh member of European Free Trade Association (EFTA) 1991.

lied musical setting of a poem, usually for solo voice and piano; referring to Romantic songs of Schubert, Schumann, Brahms, and Hugo Wolf.

Liège (German *Luik*) industrial city (weapons, textiles, paper, chemicals), capital of Liège province in Belgium, SE of Brussels, on the river Meuse; population (1991) 194,600. The province of Liège has an area of 3,900 sq km/1,505 sq mi and a population (1991) of 999,600.

life ability to grow, reproduce, and respond to such stimuli as light, heat, and sound. It is thought that life on Earth began about 4 billion years ago. The earliest fossil evidence of life is threadlike chains of cells discovered in 1980 in deposits in NW Australia that have been dated as 3.5 billion years old.

life cycle in biology, the sequence of developmental stages through which members of a given species pass. Most vertebrates have a simple life cycle consisting of ▷fertilization of sex cells or ▷gametes, a period of development as an ▷embryo, a period of juvenile growth after hatching or birth, an adulthood including ▷sexual reproduction, and finally death. Invertebrate life cycles are generally more complex and may involve major reconstitution of the individual's appearance (▷metamorphosis) and completely different styles of life. Plants have a special type of life cycle with two distinct phases, known as ▷alternation of generations. In many invertebrates and protozoa there is a sequence of stages in the life cycle, and in parasites different stages often occur in different host organisms.

Liffey river in E Republic of Ireland, flowing from the Wicklow mountains to Dublin Bay; length 80 km/50 mi.

ligament strong flexible connective tissue, made of the protein collagen, which joins bone to bone at moveable joints. Ligaments prevent bone dislocation (under normal circumstances) but permit joint flexion.

light electromagnetic waves in the visible range, having a wavelength from about 400 nanometres in the extreme violet to about 770 nanometres in the extreme red. Light is considered to exhibit particle and wave properties, and the fundamental particle, or quantum, of light is called the photon. The speed of light (and of all electromagnetic radiation) in a vacuum is approximately 300,000 km/186,000 mi per second, and is a universal constant denoted by c.

light-emitting diode (LED) means of displaying symbols in electronic instruments and devices. An LED is made of ▷semiconductor material, such as gallium arsenide phosphide, that glows when electricity is passed through it. The first digital watches and calculators had LED displays, but many later models use ▷liquid-crystal displays.

lightning high-voltage electrical discharge between two charged rainclouds or between a cloud and the Earth, caused by the build-up of electrical charges. Air in the path of lightning ionizes (becomes conducting), and expands; the accompanying noise is heard as thunder. Currents of 20,000 amperes and temperatures of 30,000°C/54,000°F are common.

light year in astronomy, the distance travelled by a beam of light in a vacuum in one year, approximately 9.46 trillion (million million) km/5.88 trillion miles.

Liguria coastal region of NW Italy, which includes the resorts of the Italian Riviera, lying between the western Alps and the Mediterranean Gulf of Genoa. The region comprises the provinces of Genova, La Spezia, Imperia, and Savona, with a population (1990) of 1,719,200 and an area of 5,418 sq km/2,093 sq mi. Genoa is the chief town and port.

lilac any flowering Old World shrub of the genus *Syringa* (such as *S. vulgaris*) of the olive family Oleaceae, bearing panicles (clusters) of small, sweetly scented, white or purplish flowers.

Lilienthal Otto 1848–1896. German aviation pioneer who inspired the US aviators Orville and Wilbur Wright. He made and successfully flew many gliders before he was killed in a glider crash.

Lille (Flemish *Ryssel*) industrial city (textiles, chemicals, engineering, distilling), capital of Nord-Pas-de-Calais, France; population (1982) 174,000, metropolitan area 936,000. The world's first entirely automatic underground system was opened here in 1982.

Lilongwe capital of Malawi since 1975; population (1987) 234,000. Products include tobacco and textiles.

lily plant of the genus *Lilium*, family Liliaceae, of which there are some 80 species, most with showy, trumpet-shaped flowers growing from bulbs. The lily family includes hyacinths, tulips, asparagus, and plants of the onion genus. The term 'lily' is also applied to many lilylike plants of allied genera and families.

lily of the valley plant *Convallaria majalis* of the lily family Liliaceae, growing in woods in Europe, N Asia, and North America. The small, pendant, white flowers are strongly scented. The plant is often cultivated.

Lima capital of Peru, an industrial city (textiles, chemicals, glass, cement) with its port at Callao; population (1988) 418,000, metropolitan area 4,605,000. Founded by the conquistador Pizarro 1535, it was rebuilt after destruction by an earthquake in 1746.

limbo in Christian theology, a region for the souls of those who were not admitted to the divine vision. *Limbus infantum* was a place where unbaptized infants enjoyed inferior blessedness, and *limbus patrum* was where the prophets of the Old Testament dwelt. The word was first used in this sense in the 13th century by St Thomas Aquinas.

Limburg southernmost province of the Netherlands in the plain of the Maas (Meuse); area 2,170 sq km/838 sq mi; population (1991) 1,109,900. Its capital is Maastricht, the oldest city in the Netherlands. The marl soils of S Limburg are used in making cement and fertilizer; other chemicals are also manufactured. Mixed arable farming and horticulture are important.

lime small thorny bush *Citrus aurantifolia* of the rue family Rutaceae, native to India. The white flowers are succeeded by light green or yellow fruits, limes, which resemble lemons but are more globular in shape.

lime or **linden** deciduous tree, genus *Tilia*, of the family Tiliaceae, native to the northern hemisphere. The leaves are heart-shaped and coarsely toothed, and the common lime *T. vulgaris* bears greenish-yellow fragrant flowers in clusters on a winged stalk, succeeded by small round fruits.

lime or **quicklime** CaO (technical name **calcium oxide**) white powdery substance used in making mortar and cement. It is made commercially by heating calcium carbonate ($CaCO_3$), obtained from limestone or chalk, in a lime kiln. Quicklime readily absorbs water to become calcium hydroxide (CaOH), known as slaked lime, which is used to reduce soil acidity.

limerick five-line humorous verse, often nonsensical, which first appeared in England about 1820 and was popularized by Edward ▷Lear. An example is: There was a young lady of Riga, Who rode with a smile on a tiger; They returned from the ride With the lady inside, And the smile on the face of the tiger.

Limerick county town of Limerick, Republic of Ireland, the main port of W Ireland, on the Shannon estuary; population (1991) 52,000. It was founded in the 12th century.

Limerick county in SW Republic of Ireland, in Munster province; *area* 2,690 sq km/1,038 sq mi; *county town* Limerick; *physical* fertile, with hills in the south; *products* dairy products; *population* (1991) 161,900.

limestone sedimentary rock composed chiefly of calcium carbonate $CaCO_3$, either derived from the shells of marine organisms or precipitated from solution, mostly in the ocean. Various types of limestone are used as building stone.

limited company company for whose debts the members are liable only to a limited extent. The capital of a limited company is divided into small units, and profits are distributed according to shareholding. It is the usual type of company formation in the UK and has its origins in the trading companies that began to proliferate in the 16th century.

Limousin former province and modern region of central France; area 16,900 sq km/6,544 sq mi; population (1986) 736,000. It consists of the *départements* of Corréze, Creuse, and Haute-Vienne. The chief town is Limoges. A thinly populated and largely unfertile region, it is crossed by the mountains of the Massif Central. Fruit and vegetables are produced in the more fertile lowlands. Kaolin is mined.

limpet any of various marine ▷snails belonging to several families and genera, especially *Acmaea* and *Patella*. A limpet has a conical shell and adheres firmly to rocks by its disclike foot. Limpets leave their fixed positions only to graze on seaweeds, always returning to the same spot. They are found in the Atlantic and Pacific.

Limpopo river in SE Africa, rising in the Transvaal and reaching the Indian Ocean in Mozambique; length 1,600 km/1,000 mi.

Lincoln Abraham 1809–1865. 16th president of the USA 1861–65, a Republican. In the American ▷Civil War, his chief concern was the preservation of the Union from which the Confederate (Southern) slave states had seceded on his election. In 1863 he announced the freedom of the slaves with the Emancipation Proclamation. He was re-elected in 1864 with victory for the North in sight, but was assassinated at the end of the war.

Lincolnshire county in E England; *area* 5,890 sq km/2,274 sq mi; *towns* Lincoln (administrative headquarters), Skegness; *physical* Lincoln Wolds; marshy coastline; the Fens in the SE; rivers: Witham, Welland; *features* 16th-century Burghley House; Belton House, a Restoration mansion; *products* cattle, sheep, horses, cereals, flower bulbs, oil; *population* (1991) 573,900; *famous people* Isaac Newton, Alfred Tennyson, Margaret Thatcher.

Lindbergh Charles (Augustus) 1902–1974. US aviator who made the first solo nonstop flight in 33.5 hours across the Atlantic (Roosevelt Field, Long Island, New York, to Le Bourget airport, Paris) 1927 in the *Spirit of St Louis*, a Ryan monoplane designed by him.

linden another name for the ⟩lime tree.

linen yarn spun and the textile woven from the fibres of the stem of the ⟩flax plant. Used by the ancient Egyptians, linen was introduced by the Romans to northern Europe, where production became widespread. Religious refugees from the Low Countries in the 16th century helped to establish the linen industry in England, but here and elsewhere it began to decline in competition with cotton in the 18th century.

ling any of several deepwater long-bodied fishes of the cod family found in the N Atlantic. The species *Molva molva* is found off NW Europe. It reaches 2 m/6 ft long and is 20 kg/45 lb in weight.

ling another name for common ⟩heather.

lingua franca any language that is used as a means of communication by groups who do not themselves normally speak that language; for example, English is a lingua franca used by Japanese doing business in Finland, or by Swedes in Saudi Arabia. The term comes from the mixture of French, Italian, Spanish, Greek, Turkish, and Arabic that was spoken around the Mediterranean from the time of the Crusades until the 18th century.

linguistics scientific study of language, from its origins (historical linguistics) to the changing way it is pronounced (phonetics), derivation of words through various languages (etymology), development of meanings (semantics), and the arrangement and modifications of words to convey a message (grammar).

Linnaeus Carolus 1707–1778. Swedish naturalist and physician. His botanical work *Systema naturae* 1735 contained his system for classifying plants into groups depending on shared characteristics (such as the number of stamens in flowers), providing a much-needed framework for identification. He also devised the concise and precise system for naming plants and animals, using one Latin (or Latinized) word to represent the genus and a second to distinguish the species.

linnet Old World finch *Acanthis cannabina*. Mainly brown, the males, noted for their song, have a crimson crown and breast in summer. The linnet nests low in bushes and feeds on weed seeds and some insects. It is about 13 cm/5 in long.

linseed seeds of the flax plant *Linum usitatissimum*, from which linseed oil is expressed, the residue being used as cattle feed. The oil is used in paint, wood treatments and varnishes, and in the manufacture of linoleum.

Linz industrial port (iron, steel, metalworking) on the river Danube in N Austria; population (1981) 199,900.

lion cat *Panthera leo*, now found only in Africa and NW India. The coat is tawny, the young having darker spot markings that usually disappear in the adult. The male has a heavy mane and a tuft at the end of the tail. Head and body measure about 2 m/6 ft, plus 1 m/3 ft of tail, the lioness being slightly smaller. Lions produce litters of two to six cubs, and often live in prides of several adult males and females with several young.

Li Peng 1928– . Chinese communist politician, a member of the Politburo from 1985, and head of government from 1987. During the pro-democracy demonstrations of 1989 he supported the massacre of students by Chinese troops and the subsequent execution of others. He favoured maintaining firm central and party control over the economy, and sought improved relations with the USSR before its demise.

lipid any of a large number of esters of fatty acids, commonly formed by the reaction of a fatty acid with glycerol. They are soluble in alcohol but not in water. Lipids are the chief constituents of plant and animal waxes, fats, and oils.

Li Po 705–762. Chinese poet. He used traditional literary forms, but his exuberance, the boldness of his imagination, and the intensity of his feeling have won him recognition as perhaps the greatest of all Chinese poets. Although he was mostly concerned with higher themes, he is also remembered for his celebratory verses on drinking.

Lippi Filippino 1457–1504. Italian painter of the Florentine school, trained by Botticelli. He produced altarpieces and several fresco cycles, full of detail and drama, elegant and finely drawn. He was the son of Filippo Lippi.

Lippi Fra Filippo 1406–1469. Italian painter whose works include frescoes depicting the lives of St Stephen and St John the Baptist in Prato Cathedral 1452–66. He also painted many altarpieces of Madonnas and groups of saints.

liquefaction the process of converting a gas to a liquid, normally associated with low temperatures and high pressures.

liquid state of matter between a ⟩solid and a ⟩gas. A liquid forms a level surface and assumes the shape of its container. Its atoms do not occupy fixed positions as in a crystalline solid, nor do they have freedom of movement as in a gas. Unlike a gas, a liquid is difficult to compress since pressure applied at one point is equally transmitted throughout (Pascal's principle). ⟩Hydraulics makes use of this property.

liquidation in economics, the termination of a company by converting all its assets into money to pay off its liabilities. Almost 22,500 UK businesses went into liquidation in 1991, with a further 6,500 businesses failing in the first three months of 1991.

liquid-crystal display (LCD) display of numbers (for example, in a calculator) or pictures (such as on a pocket television screen) produced by molecules of a substance in a semiliquid state with some crystalline properties, so that clusters of molecules align in parallel formations. The display is a blank until the application of an electric field, which 'twists' the molecules so that they reflect or transmit light falling on them.

liquorice perennial European herb *Glycyrrhiza glabra*, family Leguminosae. The long, sweet root yields an extract which is made into a hard black paste and used in confectionery and medicines.

Lisbon (Portuguese *Lisboa*) city and capital of SW Portugal, on the tidal lake and estuary formed by the river Tagus; population (1984) 808,000. Industries include steel, textiles, chemicals, pottery, shipbuilding, and fishing. It has been the capital since 1260 and reached its peak of prosperity in the period of Portugal's empire during the 16th century. In 1755 an earthquake killed 60,000 people and destroyed much of the city.

Lister Joseph, 1st Baron Lister 1827–1912. English surgeon and founder of antiseptic surgery, influenced by Louis ⟂Pasteur's work on bacteria. He introduced dressings soaked in carbolic acid and strict rules of hygiene to combat wound sepsis in hospitals.

Liszt Franz 1811–1886. Hungarian pianist and composer. An outstanding virtuoso of the piano, he was an established concert artist by the age of 12. His expressive, romantic, and frequently chromatic works include piano music (*Transcendental Studies* 1851), symphonies, piano concertos, and organ music. Much of his music is programmatic; he also originated the symphonic poem.

litchi or *lychee* evergreen tree *Litchi chinensis* of the soapberry family Sapindaceae. The delicately flavoured ovate fruit is encased in a brownish rough

outer skin and has a hard seed. The litchi is native to S China, where it has been cultivated for 2,000 years.

literature words set apart in some way from ordinary everyday communication. In the ancient oral traditions, before stories and poems were written down, literature had a mainly public function – mythic and religious. As literary works came to be preserved in writing, and, eventually, printed, their role became more private, serving as a vehicle for the exploration and expression of emotion and the human situation.

lithium soft, ductile, silver-white, metallic element, symbol Li, atomic number 3, relative atomic mass 6.941. It is one of the ⟂alkali metals, has a very low density (far less than most woods), and floats on water (specific gravity 0.57); it is the lightest of all metals. Lithium is used to harden alloys, and in batteries; its compounds are used in medicine to treat manic depression.

lithography printmaking technique originated in 1798 by Aloys Senefelder, based on the antipathy of grease and water. A drawing is made with greasy crayon on an absorbent stone, which is then wetted. The wet stone repels ink (which is greasy) applied to the surface and the crayon attracts it, so that the drawing can be printed. Lithographic printing is used in book production and has developed this basic principle into complex processes.

Lithuania Republic of; country in NE Europe, bordered N by Latvia, E by Belarus, S by Poland, and W by the Baltic Sea; *area* 65,200 sq km/ 25,174 sq mi; *capital* Vilnius; *physical* central lowlands with gentle hills in W and higher terrain in SE; 25% forested; some 3,000 small lakes, marshes, and complex sandy coastline; *head of state* Vytautas Landsbergis from 1990; *head of government* Gediminas Vagnorius from 1991; *political system* emergent democratic republic; *products* heavy engineering, electrical goods, shipbuilding, cement, food processing, bacon, dairy products, cereals, potatoes; *population* (1989 est) 3,690,000 (Lithuanian 80%, Russian 9%, Polish, Belarusian, and Ukrainian minorities 8%); *language* Lithuanian; *recent history* independence declared 1918 at end of World War I; incorporated into USSR as constituent republic 1940. German occupation during World War II; USSR resumed control 1944. Lithuanian guerrillas fought against Soviet government during 1940s and 1950s; demonstrations 1972. Nationalist dissent grew 1980, influenced by Polish example. Lithuanian Restructuring Movement formed 1988 to campaign for increased autonomy. Unilateral declaration of independence 1990. Soviet paratroopers seized political and communications buildings in Vilnius 1991 but quickly withdrew. Independence recognized by Soviet government and Western nations Sept 1991. Membership of United Nations granted; admitted into Conference on Security and Cooperation in Europe.

litmus dye obtained from various lichens and used in chemistry as an indicator to test the acidic or alkaline nature of aqueous solutions; it turns red in the presence of acid, and blue in the presence of alkali.

litre metric unit of volume (symbol l), equal to one cubic decimetre (1.76 pints). It was formerly defined as the volume occupied by one kilogram of pure water at 4°C at standard pressure, but this is slightly larger than one cubic decimetre.

liver large organ of vertebrates, which has many regulatory and storage functions. The human liver is situated in the upper abdomen, and weighs about 2 kg/4.5 lbs. It receives the products of digestion, converts glucose to glycogen (a long-chain carbohydrate used for storage), and breaks down fats. It removes excess amino acids from the blood, converting them to urea, which is excreted by the kidneys. The liver also synthesizes vitamins, produces bile and blood-clotting factors, and removes damaged red cells and toxins such as alcohol from the blood.

Liverpool city, seaport, and administrative headquarters of Merseyside, NW England; population (1991 est) 448,300. In the 19th and early 20th centuries it exported the textiles of Lancashire and Yorkshire. Liverpool is the UK's chief Atlantic port with miles of specialized, mechanized quays on the river Mersey.

Liverpool Robert Banks Jenkinson, 2nd Earl Liverpool 1770–1825. British Tory politician. He entered Parliament 1790 and was foreign secretary 1801–03, home secretary 1804–06 and 1807–09, war minister 1809–12, and prime minister 1812–27. His government conducted the Napoleonic Wars to a successful conclusion, but its ruthless suppression of freedom of speech and of the press aroused great opposition.

liverwort plant of the class Hepaticae, of the bryophyte division of nonvascular plants, related to mosses, found growing in damp places.

Livingston industrial new town (electronics, engineering) in W Lothian, Scotland, established 1962; population (1985) 40,000.

Livingstone David 1813–1873. Scottish missionary explorer. In 1841 he went to Africa, reached Lake Ngami 1849, followed the Zambezi to its mouth, saw the Victoria Falls 1855, and went to East and Central Africa 1858–64, reaching Lakes Shirwa and Malawi. From 1866, he tried to find the source of the river Nile, and reached Ujiji in Tanganyika in Oct 1871. British explorer Henry Stanley joined Livingstone in Ujiji.

Livingstone Ken(neth) 1945– . British left-wing Labour politician. He was leader of the Greater London Council (GLC) 1981–86 and a member of Parliament from 1987. He stood as a candidate for the Labour Party leadership elections 1992.

Livonia former region in Europe on the E coast of the Baltic Sea comprising most of present-day Latvia and Estonia. Conquered and converted to Christianity in the early 13th century by the Livonian Knights, a crusading order, Livonia was independent until 1583, when it was divided between Poland and Sweden. In 1710 it was occupied by Russia, and in 1721 was ceded to Peter the Great, Tsar of Russia.

Livy Titus Livius 59 BC–AD 17. Roman historian, author of a *History of Rome* from the city's foundation to 9 BC, based partly on legend. It was composed of 142 books, of which 35 survive, covering the periods from the arrival of Aeneas in Italy to 293 BC and from 218 to 167 BC.

Li Xiannian 1905– . Chinese politician, member of the Chinese Communist Party (CCP) Politburo from 1956. He fell from favour during the 1966–69 Cultural Revolution, but was rehabilitated as finance minister in 1973, supporting cautious economic reform. He was state president 1983–88.

lizard reptile of the suborder Lacertilia, which together with snakes constitutes the order Squamata. Lizards are generally distinguishable from snakes by having four legs, moveable eyelids, eardrums, and a fleshy tongue, but some lizards are legless and snakelike in appearance. There are over 3,000 species of lizard worldwide.

Lizard Point southernmost point of England in Cornwall. The coast is broken into small bays overlooked by two cliff lighthouses.

Ljubljana (German *Laibach*) capital and industrial city (textiles, chemicals, paper, leather goods) of Slovenia; population (1981) 305,200. It has a nuclear research centre and is linked with S Austria by the Karawanken road tunnel under the Alps (1979–83).

llama South American even-toed hoofed mammal *Lama glama* of the camel family, about 1.2 m/4 ft high at the shoulder. Llamas can be white, brown, or dark, sometimes with spots or patches. They are very hardy, and require little food or water. They spit profusely when annoyed.

Llewelyn I 1173–1240. King of Wales from 1194 who extended his rule to all Wales not in Norman hands, driving the English from N Wales 1212, and taking Shrewsbury 1215. During the early part of Henry III's reign, he was several times attacked by English armies. He was married to Joanna, illegitimate daughter of King John.

Llewelyn II *c*. 1225–1282. King of Wales from 1246, grandson of Llewelyn I. In 1277 Edward I of England compelled Llewelyn to acknowledge him as overlord and to surrender S Wales. His death while leading a national uprising ended Welsh independence.

Lloyd George David 1863–1945. Welsh Liberal politician, prime minister of Britain 1916–22. A pioneer of social reform, as chancellor of the

Exchequer 1908–15 he introduced old-age pensions 1908 and health and unemployment insurance 1911. High unemployment, intervention in the Russian Civil War, and use of the military police force, the ⬦Black and Tans, in Ireland eroded his support as prime minister, and the creation of the Irish Free State in 1921 and his pro-Greek policy against the Turks caused the collapse of his coalition government.

Lloyd Webber Andrew 1948– . English composer. His early musicals, with lyrics by Tim Rice, include *Joseph and the Amazing Technicolor Dreamcoat* 1968; *Jesus Christ Superstar* 1970; and *Evita* 1978, based on the life of the Argentinian leader Eva Perón. He also wrote *Cats* 1981 and *The Phantom of the Opera* 1986.

loach carplike freshwater fish, family Cobitidae, with a long narrow body, and no teeth in the small, downward-pointing mouth, which is surrounded by barbels. Loaches are native to Asian and European waters.

loam type of fertile soil, a mixture of sand, silt, clay, and organic material. It is porous, which allows for good air circulation and retention of moisture.

lobby individual or pressure group that sets out to influence government action. The lobby is prevalent in the USA, where the term originated in the 1830s from the practice of those wishing to influence state policy waiting for elected representatives in the lobby of the Capitol. Under the UK lobby system, certain parliamentary journalists are given unofficial access to confidential news.

lobelia any temperate and tropical plant of the genus *Lobelia* of the bellflower family Lobeliaceae, with white to mauve flowers. Lobelias may grow to shrub size but are mostly small annual plants.

lobster large marine crustacean of the order Decapoda. Lobsters are grouped with freshwater ⬦crayfish in the suborder Reptantia ('walking'), although both lobsters and crayfish can also swim, using their fanlike tails. Lobsters have eyes on stalks and long antennae, and are mainly nocturnal. They scavenge and eat dead or dying fish.

local government that part of government dealing mainly with matters concerning the inhabitants of a particular area or town, usually financed at least in part by local taxes. In the USA and UK, local government has comparatively large powers and responsibilities. In the UK in the mid-1980s the Thatcher administration sought to remove many services from the aegis of local authorities and offer them for tender to private companies; thus in many areas school-meals provision was privatized, as were maintenance of council vehicles, street cleaning, and upkeep of parks and sports facilities. In 1987 a code of practice was issued to restrict the ability of local authorities to promote 'partisan' activities.

Locarno, Pact of series of diplomatic documents initialled in Locarno, Switzerland, 16 Oct 1925 and formally signed in London 1 Dec 1925. The pact settled the question of French security, and the signatories – Britain, France, Belgium, Italy, and Germany – guaranteed Germany's existing frontiers with France and Belgium. Following the signing of the pact, Germany was admitted to the League of Nations.

Loch Ness lake in Scotland; see ⬦Ness, Loch.

lock gated chamber installed in canals, rivers, and seaways that allows boats or ships to ascend or descend when the topography is not level. This is important to shipping where canals link oceans of differing levels, such as the Panama Canal, or where falls or rapids are replaced by these adjustable water 'steps'. A lock has gates at each end, and a boat sails in through one gate when the levels are the same. Then water is allowed into (or out of) the lock until the level rises (or falls) to the new level outside the next gate.

Locke John 1632–1704. English philosopher. His *Essay Concerning Human Understanding* 1690 maintained that experience was the only source of knowledge (empiricism), and that 'we can have knowlege no farther than we have ideas' prompted by such experience. *Two Treatises on Government* 1690 helped to form contemporary ideas of liberal democracy.

locomotive engine for hauling railway trains. In 1804 Richard Trevithick built the first steam engine to run on rails. Locomotive design did not radically improve until George Stephenson built the *Rocket* 1829, which featured a multitube boiler and blastpipe, standard in all following **steam locomotives**. Today most locomotives are diesel or electric: **diesel locomotives** have a powerful diesel engine, and **electric locomotives** draw their power from either an overhead cable or a third rail alongside the ordinary track.

locust swarming grasshopper, with short antennae and auditory organs on the abdomen, in the family Acrididae. As winged adults, flying in swarms, locusts may be carried by the wind hundreds of miles from their breeding grounds; on landing they devour all vegetation. Locusts occur in nearly every continent.

locust tree alternative name for the ⬦carob, small tree of the Mediterranean region. It is also the name of several North American trees of the family Leguminosae.

Lódź industrial town (textiles, machinery, dyes) in central Poland, 120 km/75 mi SW of Warsaw; population (1990) 848,300.

Loewe Frederick 1901–1988. US composer of musicals. In 1942 he joined forces with the lyricist Alan Jay Lerner (1918–86), and their joint successes include *Brigadoon* 1947, *Paint Your Wagon* 1951, *My Fair Lady* 1956, *Gigi* 1958, and *Camelot* 1960.

loganberry hybrid between a ▷blackberry and a ▷raspberry with large, tart, dull-red fruit. It was developed by US judge James H Logan in 1881.

logarithm the exponent or index of a number, usually to the base 10. The logarithm of 1000 is 3 because $10^3 = 1000$.

logic branch of philosophy that studies valid reasoning and argument. It is also the way in which one thing may be said to follow from, or be a consequence of, another (deductive logic). Logic is generally divided into the traditional formal logic of Aristotle and the symbolic logic derived from Friedrich Frege and Bertrand Russell.

logical positivism doctrine that the only meaningful propositions are those that can be verified empirically. Metaphysics, religion, and aesthetics are therefore meaningless.

LOGO high-level computer programming language designed to teach mathematical concepts. Developed about 1970 at the Massachusetts Institute of Technology, it became popular in schools and with home computer users because of its 'turtle graphics' feature. This allows the user to write programs that create line drawings on a computer screen, or drive a small mobile robot (a 'turtle' or 'buggy') around the floor.

Loire longest river in France, rising in the Cévennes mountains, at 1,350 m/4,430 ft and flowing for 1,050 km/650 mi first N then W until it reaches the Bay of Biscay at St Nazaire, passing Nevers, Orléans, Tours, and Nantes. It gives its name to the *départements* of Loire, Haute-Loire, Loire-Atlantique, Indre-et-Loire, Maine-et-Loire, and Saône-et-Loire. There are many chateaux and vineyards along its banks.

Lollard follower of the English religious reformer John ▷Wycliffe in the 14th century. The Lollards condemned the doctrine of the transubstantiation of the bread and wine of the Eucharist, advocated the diversion of ecclesiastical property to charitable uses, and denounced war and capital punishment.

Lombard or *Langobard* member of a Germanic people who invaded Italy in 568 and occupied Lombardy (named after them) and central Italy. Their capital was Monza. They were conquered by the Frankish ruler Charlemagne in 774.

Lombardy (Italian *Lombardia*) region of N Italy, including Lake Como; capital Milan; area 23,900 sq km/9,225 sq mi; population (1990) 8,939,400. It is the country's chief industrial area (chemicals, pharmaceuticals, engineering, textiles).

Lomé capital and port of Togo; population (1983) 366,000. It is a centre for gold, silver, and marble crafts; industries include steel production and oil refining.

Lomond, Loch largest freshwater Scottish lake, 37 km/21 mi long, area 70 sq km/27 sq mi,

divided between Strathclyde and Central regions. It is overlooked by the mountain **Ben Lomond** (973 m/3,192 ft) and is linked to the Clyde estuary.

London capital of England and the UK, on the river Thames; area 1,580 sq km/610 sq mi; population (1991) 6,378,600, larger metropolitan area about 9 million. The *City of London* is the financial and commercial centre of the UK. *Greater London* from 1965 comprises the City of London and 32 boroughs. There are recording, broadcasting, television, and film studios; publishing companies; and the works and offices of the national press; as well as various industries on the outskirts. Tourism is important. Popular tourist attractions include the Tower of London, St Paul's Cathedral, Buckingham Palace, and Westminster Abbey. London University is the largest in Britain. The Inns of Court have been the training school for lawyers since the 13th century. London has been the centre of English drama since its first theatre was built by James Burbage in 1576. The City of London has been governed by a corporation from the 12th century. It is headed by the lord mayor. There is no central authority for Greater London. *history* Roman *Londinium* was established soon after the Roman invasion AD 43; by the 11th century, London was the main city of England and gradually extended to link with the originally separate Westminster. Much of the city was destroyed in the Great Fire of 1666.

Londonderry former name (until 1984) of the county and city of ▷Derry in Northern Ireland.

lone pair in chemistry, a pair of electrons in the outermost shell of an atom that are not used in bonding. In certain circumstances, they will allow the atom to bond with atoms, ions, or molecules (such as boron trifluoride, BF_3) that are deficient in electrons, forming coordinate covalent (dative) bonds in which they provide both of the bonding electrons.

Longfellow Henry Wadsworth 1807–1882. US poet, remembered for ballads ('Excelsior', 'The Village Blacksmith', 'The Wreck of the Hesperus') and the mythic narrative epics *Evangeline* 1847, *The Song of* ▷*Hiawatha* 1855, and *The Courtship of Miles Standish* 1858.

Longford county of Leinster province, Republic of Ireland; *area* 1,040 sq km/401 sq mi; *county town* Longford; *features* rivers: Camlin, Inny, Shannon (the W boundary); several lakes; *population* (1991) 30,300.

Long Island island E of Manhattan and SE of Connecticut, USA, separated from the mainland by Long Island Sound and the East River; 120 mi/193 km long by about 30 mi/48km wide; area 1,400 sq mi/3,627 sq km; population (1984) 6,818,480. It includes two boroughs of of New York City (Queens and Brooklyn), John F Kennedy airport, suburbs, and resorts.

longitude see ▷latitude and longitude.

long jump field event in athletics where competitors sprint up to and leap from a take-off board into a sandpit measuring 9 metres in length. The takeoff board is 1 metre from the landing area. Each competitor usually has six trials, and the winner is the one with the longest jump.

Long March in Chinese history, the 10,000 km/6,000 mi trek undertaken 1934–35 by ⇩Mao Zedong and his Communist forces from SE to NW China, under harassment from the Nationalist army.

Long Parliament English Parliament 1640–53 and 1659–60, which continued through the Civil War. After the Royalists withdrew in 1642 and the Presbyterian right was excluded in 1648, the remaining ⇩Rump ruled England until expelled by Oliver Cromwell in 1653. Reassembled 1659–60, the Long Parliament initiated the negotiations for the restoration of the monarchy.

loom any machine for weaving yarn or thread into cloth. The first looms were used to weave sheep's wool about 5000 BC. A loom is a frame on which a set of lengthwise threads (warp) is strung. A second set of threads (weft), carried in a shuttle, is inserted at right angles over and under the warp.

loosestrife any of several plants of the family Primulaceae, including the yellow loosestrife *Lysimachia vulgaris*, with spikes of yellow flowers, and the low-growing creeping jenny *Lysimachia nummularia*. The striking purple loosestrife *Lythrum saclicaria* belongs to the family Lythraceae.

Lope de Vega (Carpio) Feli. Spanish poet and dramatist; see ⇩Vega.

Lorca Federico García 1898–1936. Spanish poet and playwright, born in Granada. His plays include *Bodas de sangre/Blood Wedding* 1933 and *La casa de Bernarda Alba/The House of Bernarda Alba* 1936. His poems include *Lament*, written for the bullfighter Mejías. Lorca was shot by the Falangists during the Spanish Civil War.

Lord Advocate chief law officer of the crown in Scotland who has ultimate responsibility for criminal prosecutions in Scotland. The Lord Advocate does not usually act in inferior courts, where prosecution is carried out by procurators-fiscal acting under the Lord Advocate's instructions.

Lord Chancellor UK state official; see ⇩Chancellor, Lord.

lord mayor in the UK, mayor (principal officer) of a city council.

Lords, House of upper house of the UK ⇩Parliament.

Lorenz Konrad 1903–1989. Austrian ethologist. Director of the Max Planck Institute for the Physiology of Behaviour in Bavaria 1955–73, he wrote the studies of ethology (animal behaviour) *King Solomon's Ring* 1952 and *On Aggression* 1966. In 1973 he shared the Nobel Prize for Medicine with Nikolaas Tinbergen and Karl von Frisch.

loris any of various small prosimian primates of the family Lorisidae. Lorises are slow-moving, arboreal, and nocturnal. They have very large eyes; true lorises have no tails. They climb without leaping, gripping branches tightly and moving on or hanging below them.

Lorrain Claude. French painter; see ⇩Claude Lorrain.

Lorraine region of NE France in the upper reaches of the Meuse and Moselle rivers; bounded to the N by Belgium, Luxembourg, and Germany and to the E by Alsace; area 23,600 sq km/9,095 sq mi; population (1986) 2,313,000. It comprises the *départements* of Meurthe-et-Moselle, Meuse, Moselle, and Vosges, and its capital is Nancy. There are deposits of coal, iron ore, and salt; grain, fruit, and livestock are farmed. In 1871 the region was ceded to Germany as part of Alsace-Lorraine.

Los Angeles city and port in SW California, USA; population (1990) 3,485,400, the metropolitan area of Los Angeles–Long Beach 14,531,530. Industries include aerospace, electronics, motor vehicles, chemicals, clothing, printing, and food processing. Features include Hollywood, centre of the film industry since 1911; observatories at Mount Wilson and Mount Palomar; Disneyland; and the John Paul Getty museum of art. Greater Los Angeles comprises 86 towns, including Long Beach, Redondo Beach, Venice, Santa Monica, Burbank, Compton, Beverly Hills, Glendale, Pasadena, and Pomona. It covers 10,000 sq km/4,000 sq mi.

Lothair I 795–855. Holy Roman emperor from 817 in association with his father Louis I. On Louis's death in 840, the empire was divided between Lothair and his brothers; Lothair took N Italy and the valleys of the rivers Rhône and Rhine.

Lothair II *c.* 1070–1137. Holy Roman emperor from 1133 and German king from 1125. His election as emperor, opposed by the ⇩Hohenstaufen family of princes, was the start of the feud between the ⇩Guelph and Ghibelline factions, who supported the papal party and the Hohenstaufens' claim to the imperial throne respectively.

Lothian region of Scotland; *area* 1,800 sq km/695 sq mi; *towns* Edinburgh (administrative headquarters), Livingston; *features* hills: Lammermuir, Moorfoot, Pentland; Bass Rock in the Firth of Forth, noted for seabirds; *products* bacon, vegetables, coal, whisky, engineering, electronics; *population* (1991) 723,700; *famous people* Alexander Graham Bell, Arthur Conan Doyle, R L Stevenson.

Lotto Lorenzo *c.* 1480–1556. Italian painter, born in Venice, active in Bergamo, Treviso, Venice, Ancona, and Rome. His early works were influenced by Giovanni Bellini; his mature style belongs to the High Renaissance. He painted dignified portraits, altarpieces, and frescoes.

loudspeaker

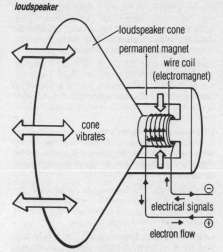

loudspeaker cone
permanent magnet
wire coil
(electromagnet)

cone
vibrates

⊖
electrical signals
⊕
electron flow

lotus any of several different plants, especially the water lily *Nymphaea lotus*, frequent in Egyptian art, and *Nelumbo nucifera*, the pink Asiatic lotus, a sacred symbol in Hinduism and Buddhism, whose flower head floats erect above the water.

loudspeaker electromechanical device that converts electrical signals into sound waves, which are radiated into the air. The most common type of loudspeaker is the ***moving-coil speaker***. Electrical signals from, for example, a radio are fed to a coil of finc wire wound around the top of a cone. The coil is surrounded by a magnet. When signals pass through it, the coil becomes an electromagnet, which by moving causes the cone to vibrate, setting up sound waves.

Lough Derg lake in County Donegal, NW Ireland, with an island (Station Island or St Patrick's Purgatory) that is the country's leading place of Christian pilgrimage. Associated with St Patrick, a monastery flourished here from early times.

Louis Joe. Assumed name of Joseph Louis Barrow 1914–1981. US boxer, nicknamed 'the Brown Bomber'. He was world heavyweight champion between 1937 and 1949 and made a record 25 successful defences (a record for any weight).

Louis III 863–882. King of N France from 879, while his brother Carloman (866–884) ruled S France. Louis countered a revolt of the nobility at the beginning of his reign, and his resistance to the Normans made him a hero of epic poems.

Louis XI 1423–1483. King of France from 1461. He broke the power of the nobility (headed by Charles the Bold) by intrigue and military power.

Louis XII 1462–1515. King of France from 1499. He was duke of Orléans until he succeeded his cousin Charles VIII to the throne. His reign was devoted to Italian wars.

Louis XIII 1601–1643. King of France from 1610 (in succession to his father Henry IV), he assumed royal power in 1617. He was under the political control of Cardinal ⟡Richelieu 1624–42.

Louis XIV *the Sun King* 1638–1715. King of France from 1643, when he succeeded his father Louis XIII; his mother was Anne of Austria. Until 1661 France was ruled by the chief minister, Jules Mazarin, but later Louis took absolute power, summed up in his saying *L'Etat c'est moi* ('I am the state'). Throughout his reign he was engaged in unsuccessful expansionist wars – 1667–68, 1672–78, 1688–97, and 1701–13 (the War of the ⟡Spanish Succession) – against various European alliances, always including Britain and the Netherlands. He was a patron of the arts.

Louis XV 1710–1774. King of France from 1715, with the Duke of Orléans as regent until 1723. He was the great-grandson of Louis XIV. Indolent and frivolous, Louis left government in the hands of his ministers, the Duke of Bourbon and Cardinal Fleury (1653–1743). On the latter's death he attempted to rule alone but became entirely dominated by his mistresses, Madame de Pompadour and Madame Du Barry. His foreign policy led to French possessions in Canada and India being lost to England.

Louis XVI 1754–1793. King of France from 1774, grandson of Louis XV, and son of Louis the Dauphin. He was dominated by his queen, ⟡Marie Antoinette, and French finances fell into such confusion that in 1789 the ⟡States General (parliament) had to be summoned, and the ⟡French Revolution began. Louis lost his personal popularity in June 1791 when he attempted to flee the country, and in Aug 1792 the Parisians stormed the Tuileries palace and took the royal family prisoner. Deposed in Sept 1792, Louis was tried in Dec, sentenced for treason in Jan 1793, and guillotined.

Louis XVII 1785–1795. Nominal king of France, the son of Louis XVI. During the French Revolution he was imprisoned with his parents in 1792 and probably died in prison.

Louis XVIII 1755–1824. King of France 1814–24, the younger brother of Louis XVI. He assumed the title of king in 1795, having fled into exile in 1791 during the French Revolution, but became king only on the fall of Napoleon I in April 1814. Expelled during Napoleon's brief return (the 'hundred days') in 1815, he resumed power after Napoleon's final defeat at Waterloo, pursuing a policy of calculated liberalism until ultra-royalist pressure became dominant after 1820.

Louisiana state in S USA; nickname Pelican State; *area* 135,900 sq km/52,457 sq mi; *capital* Baton Rouge; *cities* New Orleans, Shreveport, Lafayette, Lake Charles; *features* New Orleans French Quarter: jazz, restaurants, Mardi Gras; Cajun country and the Mississippi River delta;

Jean Lafitte National Park and Chalmette National Historical Park; plantation homes near Natchitoches; *products* rice, cotton, sugar, oil, natural gas, chemicals, sulphur, fish and shellfish, salt, processed foods, petroleum products, timber, paper; *population* (1990) 4,219,970; including Cajuns, descendants of 18th-century religious exiles from Canada, who speak a French dialect; *famous people* Louis Armstrong, P G T Beauregard, Huey Long; *history* explored by the Spanish Piñeda 1519, Cabeza de Vaca 1528, and de Soto 1541 and by the French explorer La Salle 1862, who named it after Louis XIV and claimed it for France. It became Spanish 1762–1800, then French, then passed to the USA 1803 under the ◊Louisiana Purchase; admitted to the Union as a state 1812. The Civil War destroyed the plantation economy. Recovery was slow, but in the 1930s Louisiana became one of the world's major centres of petrochemical manufacturing, based on oil wells in the Gulf of Mexico.

Louisiana Purchase purchase by the USA from France 1803 of an area covering about 2,144,000 sq km/828,000 sq mi, including the present-day states of Louisiana, Missouri, Arkansas, Iowa, Nebraska, North Dakota, South Dakota, and Oklahoma.

Louis Philippe 1773–1850. King of France 1830–48. Son of Louis Philippe Joseph, Duke of Orléans 1747–93; both were known as *Philippe Egalité* from their support of the 1792 Revolution. Louis Philipe fled into exile 1793–1814, but became king after the 1830 revolution with the backing of the rich bourgeoisie. Corruption discredited his regime, and after his overthrow, he escaped to the UK and died there.

Lourdes town in SW France, population (1982) 18,000. Its Christian shrine to St ◊Bernadette has a reputation for miraculous cures.

louse parasitic insect of the order Anoplura, which lives on mammals. It has a flat, segmented body without wings, and a tube attached to the head, used for sucking blood from its host.

Louth smallest county of the Republic of Ireland, in Leinster province; county town Dundalk; area 820 sq km/317 sq mi; population (1991) 90,700.

Lovell Bernard 1913– . British radio astronomer, director (until 1981) of ◊Jodrell Bank Experimental Station (now Nuffield radio astronomy laboratories).

Low Countries region of Europe that consists of ◊Belgium and the ◊Netherlands, and usually includes ◊Luxembourg.

Lower Saxony (German *Niedersachsen*) administrative region (German *Land*) of N Germany; *area* 47,400 sq km/18,296 sq mi; *capital* Hanover; *towns* Brunswick, Osnabrück, Oldenburg, Göttingen, Wolfsburg, Salzgitter, Hildesheim; *features*

Lüneburg Heath; *products* cereals, cars, machinery, electrical engineering; *population* (1988) 7,190,000; *religion* 75% Protestant, 20% Roman Catholic; *history* formed 1946 from Hanover, Oldenburg, Brunswick, and Schaumburg-Lippe.

Lowry L(aurence) S(tephen) 1887–1976. English painter. Born in Manchester, he lived mainly in nearby Salford and painted northern industrial townscapes. His characteristic style of matchstick figures and almost monochrome palette emerged in the 1920s.

LSD (lysergic acid diethylamide) psychedelic drug, a hallucinogen. Colourless, odourless, and easily synthesized, it is nonaddictive and nontoxic, but its effects are unpredictable. Its use is illegal in most countries.

LSI (abbreviation for *large-scale integration*) the technology that enables whole electrical circuits to be etched into a piece of semiconducting material just a few millimetres square.

Luanda formerly *Loanda* capital and industrial port (cotton, sugar, tobacco, timber, paper, oil) of Angola; population (1988) 1,200,000. It was founded in 1575 and became a Portuguese colonial administrative centre as well as an outlet for slaves transported to Brazil.

Lubbers Rudolph Franz Marie (Ruud) 1939– . Dutch politician and prime minister of the Netherlands from 1983. Leader of the Christian Democratic Appeal (CDA), he is politically right of centre. He became minister for economic affairs 1973.

lubricant substance used between moving surfaces to reduce friction. Carbon-based (organic) lubricants, commonly called grease and oil, are recovered from petroleum distillation.

Lucerne (German *Luzern*) capital and tourist centre of Lucerne canton, Switzerland, on the river Reuss where it flows out of Lake Lucerne; population (1990) city 59,400, canton 319,500. It developed around the Benedictine monastery, established about 750, and owes its prosperity to its position on the St Gotthard road and railway.

Lucifer in Christian theology, another name for the ◊devil, the leader of the angels who rebelled against God. Lucifer is also another name for the morning star (the planet ◊Venus).

Lucknow capital and industrial city (engineering, chemicals, textiles, many handicrafts) of the state of Uttar Pradesh, India; population (1981) 1,007,000. During the Indian Mutiny against British rule, it was besieged 2 July–16 Nov 1857.

Lucretius (Titus Lucretius Carus) *c.* 99–55 BC. Roman poet and ◊Epicurean philosopher whose *De Rerum natura/On the Nature of Things* envisaged the whole universe as a combination of atoms, and had some concept of evolutionary theory.

Lucullus Lucius Licinius 110–56 BC. Roman

general and consul. As commander against ⇨Mithridates of Pontus 74–66 he proved to be one of Rome's ablest generals and administrators, until superseded by Pompey. He then retired from politics. His wealth enabled him to live a life of luxury, and Lucullan feasts became legendary.

Lüda or *Hüta* industrial port (engineering, chemicals, textiles, oil refining, shipbuilding, food processing) in Liaoning, China, on Liaodong Peninsula, facing the Yellow Sea; population (1986) 4,500,000. It comprises the naval base of Lüshun (known under 19th-century Russian occupation as Port Arthur) and the commercial port of Dalien (formerly Talien/Dairen).

Luddite one of a group of people involved in machine-wrecking riots in N England 1811–16. The organizer of the Luddites was referred to as General Ludd, but may not have existed. Many Luddites were hanged or transported to penal colonies, such as Australia.

Ludwig II 1845–1886. King of Bavaria from 1864, when he succeeded his father Maximilian II. He supported Austria during the Austro-Prussian War 1866, but brought Bavaria into the Franco-Prussian War as Prussia's ally and in 1871 offered the German crown to the king of Prussia. He was the composer Richard Wagner's patron and built the Bayreuth theatre for him. Declared insane in 1886, he drowned himself soon after.

lugworm any of a genus *Arenicola* of marine annelid worms that grow up to 25 cm/10 in long. They are common burrowers between tidemarks and are useful for their cleansing and powdering of the beach sand, of which they may annually bring to the surface about 5,000 tonnes per hectare/2,000 tons per acre.

Lukács Georg 1885–1971. Hungarian philosopher, one of the founders of 'Western' or 'Hegelian' Marxism, a philosophy opposed to the Marxism of the official communist movement.

Luke, St 1st century AD. Traditionally the compiler of the third Gospel and of the Acts of the Apostles in the New Testament. He is the patron saint of painters; his emblem is a winged ox, and his feast day 18 Oct.

lumbago pain in the lower region of the back, usually due to strain or faulty posture. If it occurs with ⇨sciatica, it may be due to pressure on spinal nerves by a displaced vertebra. Treatment includes rest, application of heat, and skilled manipulation. Surgery may be needed in rare cases.

lumbar puncture or *spinal tap* insertion of a hollow needle between two lumbar (lower back) vertebrae to withdraw a sample of cerebrospinal fluid (CSF) for testing. Normally clear and colourless, the CSF acts as a fluid buffer around the brain and spinal cord. Changes in its quantity, colour, or composition may indicate neurological damage or disease.

lumen SI unit (symbol lm) of luminous flux (the amount of light passing through an area per second).

Lumière Auguste Marie 1862–1954 and Louis Jean 1864–1948. French brothers who pioneered cinematography. In 1895 they patented their cinematograph, a combined camera and projector operating at 16 frames per second, and opened the world's first cinema in Paris to show their films.

luminescence emission of light from a body when its atoms are excited by means other than raising its temperature. Short-lived luminescence is called fluorescence; longer-lived luminescence is called phosphorescence.

Lumumba Patrice 1926–1961. Congolese politician, prime minister of Zaïre 1960. Imprisoned by the Belgians, but released in time to attend the conference giving the Congo independence in 1960, he led the National Congolese Movement to victory in the subsequent general election. He was deposed in a coup d'état, and murdered some months later.

lung large cavity of the body, used for gas exchange, or respiration. It is essentially a sheet of thin, moist membrane that is folded so as to occupy less space. Lungs are found in some slugs and snails, particularly those that live on land. Some fishes (lungfish) and most four-limbed vertebrates have a pair of lungs, which occupy the thorax (the upper part of the trunk). Lungs function by bringing inhaled air into close contact with the blood, so that oxygen can pass into the organism and waste carbon dioxide can be passed out; the oxygen is carried by ⇨haemoglobin in red blood cells. The lung tissue, consisting of multitudes of air sacs and blood vessels, is very light and spongy.

lungfish three genera of fleshy-finned bony fishes of the subclass Dipnoi, found in Africa, South America, and Australia. They have elongated bodies, and grow to about 2 m/6 ft, and in addition to gills have 'lungs' with which they can breathe air during periods of drought conditions.

lupin any plant of the genus *Lupinus*, which comprises about 300 species, family Leguminosae. Lupins are native to Mediterranean regions and parts of North and South America, and some species are naturalized in Britain. Their spikes of pealike flowers may be white, yellow, blue, or pink.

Lusaka capital of Zambia from 1964 (of Northern Rhodesia 1935–64), 370 km/230 mi NE of Livingstone; commercial and agricultural centre (flour mills, tobacco factories, vehicle assembly, plastics, printing); population (1988) 870,000.

lute family of stringed musical instruments of the 14th–18th century, including the mandore, theorbo, and chitarrone. Lutes are pear-shaped and are plucked with the fingers. Members of the lute family were used both as solo instruments and for vocal accompaniment, and were often played in

lung

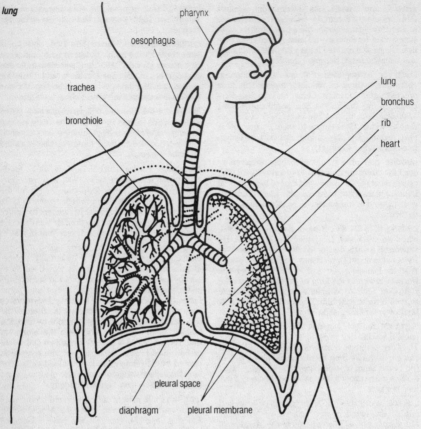

addition to, or instead of, keyboard instruments in larger ensembles and in opera.

lutetium silver-white, metallic element, the last of the ◊lanthanide series, symbol Lu, atomic number 71, relative atomic mass 174.97. It is used in the 'cracking', or breakdown, of petroleum and in other chemical processes. It was named by its discoverer, French chemist Georges Urbain (1872–1938), after his native city.

Luther Martin 1483–1546. German Christian church reformer, a founder of Protestantism. While he was a priest at the University of Wittenberg, he wrote an attack on the sale of indulgences (remissions of punishment for sin) in 95 theses which he nailed to a church door in 1517, in defiance of papal condemnation. The Holy Roman emperor Charles V summoned him to the Diet (meeting of dignitaries of the Holy Roman Empire) of Worms in Germany, in 1521, where he refused to retract his objections. Originally intending reform, his protest

led to schism, with the emergence, following the Augsburg Confession 1530 (a statement of the Protestant faith), of a new Protestant church. Luther is regarded as the instigator of the Protestant revolution, and Lutheranism is now the main religion of many N European countries, including Germany, Sweden, and Denmark.

Lutheranism form of Protestant Christianity derived from the life and teaching of Martin Luther; it is sometimes called Evangelical to distinguish it from the other main branch of European Protestantism, the Reformed. The most generally accepted statement of Lutheranism is that of the *Augsburg Confession* 1530 but Luther's Shorter Catechism also carries great weight. It is the largest Protestant body, including some 80 million persons, of whom 40 million are in Germany, 19 million in Scandinavia, 8.5 million in the USA and Canada, with most of the remainder in central Europe.

Lutyens Edwin Landseer 1869–1944. English

architect. His designs ranged from picturesque to Renaissance-style country houses and ultimately evolved into a Classical style as in the Cenotaph, London, and the Viceroy's House, New Delhi.

lux SI unit (symbol lx) of illuminance or illumination (the light falling on an object). It is equivalent to one ◊lumen per square metre or to the illuminance of a surface one metre distant from a point source of one ◊candela.

Luxembourg capital of Luxembourg; population (1985) 76,000. The 16th-century Grand Ducal Palace, European Court of Justice, and European Parliament secretariat are situated here, but plenary sessions of the parliament are now held only in Strasbourg, in France. Products include steel, chemicals, textiles, and processed food.

Luxembourg Grand Duchy of; country in W Europe, bordered N and W by Belgium, E by Germany, and S by France; *area* 2,586 sq km/998 sq mi; *capital* Luxembourg; *physical* on the river Moselle; part of the Ardennes (Oesling) forest in N; *head of state* Grand Duke Jean from 1964; *head of government* Jacques Santer from 1984; *political system* liberal democracy; *exports* pharmaceuticals, synthetic textiles, steel; *population* (1990 est) 369,000; *languages* French (official), local Letzeburgesch, German; *recent history* a duchy since 1354, under Habsburg control 1482–1797; under French control 1797–1815; a grand duchy under Dutch rule from 1815 until the accession of grand Duke Adolphe of Nassau-Weilburg 1830. Luxembourg formed the Benelux customs union with Belgium and the Netherlands 1948. In 1964 Grand Duchess Charlotte abdicated in favour of her son.

Luxemburg Rosa 1870–1919. Polish-born German communist, a leader of the left wing of the German Social Democratic Party from 1898 and collaborator with Karl Liebknecht in founding the communist Spartacus League in 1918. She was murdered with him by army officers during the Jan 1919 Berlin workers' revolt.

Luxor (Arabic *al-Uqsur*) small town in Egypt on the E bank of the Nile near the ruins of ◊Thebes.

Luzern German name of ◊Lucerne, town in Switzerland.

Luzon largest island of the ◊Philippines; area 108,130 sq km/41,750 sq mi; capital Quezon City; population (1970) 18,001,270. The chief city is Manila, capital of the Philippines. Products include rice, timber, and minerals. It has US military bases.

LW abbreviation for *long wave*, a radio wave with a wavelength of over 1,000 m/3,300 ft; one of the main wavebands into which radio frequency transmissions are divided.

lychee alternative spelling of ◊litchi, a fruit-bearing tree.

Lydia ancient kingdom in Anatolia (7th–6th centuries BC), with its capital at Sardis. The Lydians were the first Western people to use standard coinage. Their last king, Croesus, was conquered by the Persians in 546 BC.

lymph fluid found in the lymphatic system of vertebrates. It carries nutrients, oxygen, and white blood cells to the tissues, and waste matter away from them. It exudes from capillaries into the tissue spaces between the cells and is made up of blood plasma, plus white cells.

lymph nodes small masses of lymphatic tissue in the body that occur at various points along the major lymphatic vessels. Tonsils and adenoids are large lymph nodes. As the lymph passes through them it is filtered, and bacteria and other microorganisms are engulfed by cells known as macrophages.

lymphocyte type of white blood cell with a large nucleus, produced in the bone marrow. Most occur in the ◊lymph and blood, and around sites of infection. *B-lymphocytes* or B cells are responsible for producing ◊antibodies. *T-lymphocytes* or T-cells have several roles in the formation of ◊immunity.

Lynch 'Jack' (John) 1917– . Irish politician, prime minister 1966–73 and 1977–79. A Gaelic footballer and a barrister, in 1948 he entered the parliament of the republic as a Fianna Fáil member.

lynx cat *Felis lynx* found in rocky and forested regions of North America and Europe. About 1 m/3 ft in length, it has a short tail and tufted ears, and the long, silky fur is reddish brown or grey with dark spots. The North American bobcat or bay lynx *Felix rufus* looks similar but is smaller. Some zoologists place the lynx, the bobcat, and the caracal in a separate genus, *Lynx*.

Lyon (English *Lyons*) industrial city (textiles, chemicals, machinery, printing) and capital of Rhône *département*, Rhône-Alpes region, and third largest city of France, at the confluence of the rivers Rhône and Saône, 275 km/170 mi NNW of Marseille; population (1982) 418,476, conurbation 1,221,000. Formerly a chief fortress of France, it was the ancient *Lugdunum*, taken by the Romans in 43 BC.

lyre stringed instrument of great antiquity. It consists of a soundbox with two curved arms extended upwards to a crosspiece to which four to ten strings are attached. It is played with a plectrum or the fingers. It originated in Asia, and was used in Greece and Egypt.

Lysander Spartan general. He brought the Peloponnesian War between Athens and Sparta to a successful conclusion by capturing the Athenian fleet at Aegospotami in 405 BC, and by starving Athens into surrender in the following year. He then aspired to make Sparta supreme in Greece and himself supreme in Sparta; he set up puppet governments in Athens and her former allies, and tried to secure for himself the Spartan kingship, but he was killed in battle with the Thebans.

East and, from March 1942, of the Allied forces in the SW Pacific. After the surrender of Japan he commanded the Allied occupation forces there. During 1950 he commanded the UN forces in Korea, but in April 1951, after expressing views contrary to US and UN policy, he was relieved of all his commands by President Truman.

Macaulay Thomas Babington, Baron Macaulay 1800–1859. English historian, essayist, poet, and politician, secretary of war 1839–41. His *History of England* in five volumes 1849–61 celebrates the Glorious Revolution of 1668 as the crowning achievement of the Whig party.

macaw any of various large, brilliantly coloured, long-tailed tropical American ◊parrots, especially the genus *Ara*.

Macbeth died 1057. King of Scotland from 1040. The son of Findlaech, hereditary ruler of Moray, he was commander of the forces of Duncan I, King of Scotia, whom he killed in battle 1040. His reign was prosperous until Duncan's son Malcolm III led an invasion and killed him at Lumphanan.

McCarthy Joe (Joseph Raymond) 1908–1957. US right-wing Republican politician. His unsubstantiated claim 1950 that the State Department and US army had been infiltrated by communists started a wave of anticommunist hysteria, wild accusations, and blacklists, which continued until he was discredited 1954. He was censured by the US senate for misconduct.

McCartney Paul 1942– . UK rock singer, songwriter, and bass guitarist; former member of the ◊Beatles, and leader of the pop group Wings 1971–81. His subsequent solo hits have included collaborations with Michael Jackson and Elvis Costello. Together with composer Carl Davis, McCartney wrote the *Liverpool Oratorio* 1991, his first work of classical music.

McCullers Carson (Smith) 1917–1967. US novelist. Most of her writing, including her novels *The Heart is a Lonely Hunter* 1940 and *Reflections in a Golden Eye* 1941, is set in the South, where she was born, and deals with spiritual isolation, containing elements of sometimes macabre violence.

McCullin Don(ald) 1935– . British war photographer. He began as a freelance photojournalist for Sunday newspapers and went on to cover hostilities in the Congo, Vietnam, Cambodia, Biafra, India, Pakistan, and Northern Ireland. He has published several books of his work and held many exhibitions.

MacDonald (James) Ramsay 1866–1937. British politician, first Labour prime minister Jan–Oct 1924 and 1929–31. Failing to deal with worsening economic conditions, he left the party to form a coalition government 1931, which was increasingly dominated by Conservatives, until he was replaced by Stanley Baldwin 1935.

Maastricht Summit meeting 9–10 Dec 1991 between leaders of the European Community (EC) nations at Maastricht in the Netherlands to agree on terms for political union. The Maastricht Treaty on European union was formally endorsed by the European Parliament April 1992 but its rejection by the Danish in a 1992 referendum placed its future in jeopardy.

Mabuse Jan. Adopted name of Jan Gossaert *c.* 1478–*c.* 1533. Flemish painter, active chiefly in Antwerp. His visit to Italy 1508 with Philip of Burgundy started a new vogue in Flanders for Italianate ornament and Classical detail in painting, including sculptural nude figures. His works include *The Adoration of the Magi* (National Gallery, London).

macadamia edible nut from the tree *Macadamia ternifolia*, family Proteaceae, native to Australia and cultivated in Hawaii, South Africa, Zimbabwe, and Malawi. The nuts are slow-growing; they are harvested when they drop.

Macao Portuguese possession on the S coast of China, about 65 km/40 mi W of Hong Kong, from which it is separated by the estuary of the Canton River; it consists of a peninsula and the islands of Taipa and Colôane; *area* 17 sq km/7 sq mi; *capital* Macao, on the peninsula; *features* the peninsula is linked to Taipa by a bridge and to Colôane by a causeway, both 2 km/1 mi long; *population* (1986) 426,000; *language* Cantonese; Portuguese (official); *religion* Buddhist, with 6% Catholic minority.

macaque Old World monkey of the genus *Macaca*. Various species of these medium-sized monkeys live in forests from the Far East to N Africa. The ◊rhesus and the ◊Barbary ape are part of this group.

MacArthur Douglas 1880–1964. US general in World War II, commander of US forces in the Far

Macedonia ancient region of Greece, forming parts of modern Greece, Bulgaria, and Yugoslavia. Macedonia gained control of Greece after Philip II's victory at Chaeronea 338 BC. His son, ⇨Alexander the Great, conquered a vast empire. Macedonia became a Roman province 146 BC.

Macedonia (Greek *Makedhonia*) mountainous region of N Greece, part of the ancient country of Macedonia which was divided between Serbia, Bulgaria, and Greece after the Balkan Wars of 1912–13. Greek Macedonia is bounded to the W and N by Albania and Yugoslavia; area 34,177 sq km/13,200 sq mi; population (1991) 2,263,000. The chief city is Thessaloniki. Fertile valleys produce grain, olives, grapes, tobacco, and livestock. Mount Olympus rises to 2,918 m/9,570 ft on the border with Thessaly.

Macedonia (Serbo-Croat *Makedonija*) federal republic of Yugoslavia; *area* 25,700 sq km/9,920 sq mi; *capital* Skopje; *physical* mountainous; rivers: Struma, Vardar; *population* (1981) 2,040,000, 63% Macedonians, 19% Albanians, 4% Turks; *language* Macedonian, closely allied to Bulgarian and written in Cyrillic; *religion* Macedonian Orthodox Christian; *recent history* Macedonia was divided between Serbia, Bulgaria, and Greece after the Balkan Wars of 1912–13. United 1918 in what later became Yugoslavia, nationalist demands for autonomy persisted. During World War II it was occupied by Bulgaria 1941–44. In 1990 Macedonian leaders accused the Serbian republic of plotting to annex Macedonian territory. The ruling League of Communists of Macedonia was voted out of power in multiparty elections 1990. In a referendum 8 Sept 1991, citizens of the republic voted overwhelmingly in favour of independence from Yugoslavia while reserving the right to rejoin a looser Yugoslav federation. In Jan 1992 the republic declared its independence, which Serbia and neighbouring Montenegro rejected, although recognition was granted by Bulgaria. Also in Jan the Albanian community in Macedonia voted for autonomy.

Machel Samora 1933–1986. Mozambique nationalist leader, president 1975–86. Machel was active in the liberation front Frelimo from its conception 1962, fighting for independence from Portugal. He became Frelimo leader 1966, and Mozambique's first president from independence 1975 until his death in a plane crash near the South African border.

Machiavelli Niccolò 1469–1527. Italian politician and author whose name is synonymous with cunning and cynical statecraft. In his most celebrated political writings, *Il principe/The Prince* 1513 and *Discorsi/Discourses* 1531, he discussed ways in which rulers can advance the interests of their states (and themselves) through an often amoral and opportunistic manipulation of other people.

machine device that allows a small force (the effort) to overcome a larger one (the load). There are three basic machines: the inclined plane (ramp), the lever, and the wheel and axle. All other machines are combinations of these three basic types. Simple machines derived from the inclined plane include the wedge and the screw; the spanner is derived from the lever; the pulley from the wheel.

machine code in computing, a set of instructions that a computer's central processing unit (CPU) can understand and obey directly, without any translation. Each type of CPU has its own machine code. Because machine-code programs consist entirely of binary digits (bits), most programmers write their programs in an easy-to-use high-level language. A high-level program must be translated into machine code – by means of a compiler or interpreter program – before it can be executed by a computer.

machine gun rapid-firing automatic gun. The Maxim (named after its inventor, US-born British engineer H S Maxim (1840–1916)) of 1884 was recoil-operated, but some later types have been gas-operated (Bren) or recoil-assisted by gas (some versions of the Browning).

Mach number ratio of the speed of a body to the speed of sound in the undisturbed medium through which the body travels. Mach 1 is reached when a body (such as an aircraft) has a velocity greater than that of sound ('passes the sound barrier'), namely 331 m/1,087 ft per second at sea level. It is named after the Austrian physicist Ernst Mach (1838–1916).

Machu Picchu ruined Inca city in Peru, built about AD 1500, NW of Cuzco, discovered 1911 by Hiram Bingham. It stands at the top of cliffs, 300 m/1,000 ft high, and contains the well-preserved remains of houses and temples.

Mackenzie River river in the Northwest Territories, Canada, flowing NW from Great Slave Lake to the Arctic Ocean; about 1,800 km/1,120 mi long. It is the main channel of the Finlay–Peace–Mackenzie system, 4,241 km/2,635 mi long.

mackerel any of various fishes of the mackerel family Scombroidia, especially the common mackerel *Scomber Scombrus* found in the N Atlantic and Mediterranean. It weighs about 0.7 kg/1.5 lb, and is blue with irregular black bands down its sides, the latter and the under surface showing a metallic sheen.

McKinley William 1843–1901. 25th president of the USA 1897–1901, a Republican. His term as president was marked by the USA's adoption of an imperialist policy, as exemplified by the Spanish-American War 1898 and the annexation of the Philippines. He was first elected to Congress 1876. He was assassinated.

McKinley, Mount or *Denali* peak in Alaska, USA,

the highest in North America, 6,194 m/20,320 ft; named after US president William McKinley.

Mackintosh Charles Rennie 1868–1928. Scottish architect, designer, and painter, whose chief work includes the Glasgow School of Art 1896, various Glasgow tea rooms 1897–about 1911, and Hill House, Helensburg, 1902–03. His early work is Art Nouveau; he subsequently developed a unique style, both rational and expressive.

Macmillan (Maurice) Harold, 1st Earl of Stockton 1894–1986. British Conservative politician, prime minister 1957–63; foreign secretary 1955 and chancellor of the Exchequer 1955–57. In 1963 he attempted to negotiate British entry to the European Economic Community, but was blocked by French president de Gaulle. Much of his career as prime minister was spent trying to maintain a UK nuclear weapon, and he was responsible for the purchase of US Polaris missiles 1962.

MacMillan Kenneth 1929– . Scottish choreographer. He was director of the Royal Ballet 1970–77 and then principal choreographer. He is renowned for his work with the Canadian dancer Lynn Seymour such as *Le Baiser de la fée* 1960 and *Anastasia* 1967–71. Other works include *Elite Syncopations* 1974, *Mayerling* 1978, *Orpheus* 1982, and *Different Drummer* 1984.

MacNeice Louis 1907–1963. British poet, born in Belfast. He made his debut with *Blind Fireworks* 1929 and developed a polished ease of expression, reflecting his classical training, as in *Autumn Journal* 1939. Unlike many of his contemporaries, he was politically uncommitted. Later works include the play *The Dark Tower* 1947, written for radio, for which medium he also wrote features 1941–49; a verse translation of Goethe's *Faust*; and the radio play *The Administrator* 1961.

Macquarie Island outlying Australian territorial possession, a Tasmanian dependency, some 1,370 km/850 mi SE of Hobart; area 170 sq km/65 sq mi; it is uninhabited except for an Australian government research station.

McQueen Steve (Terrence Steven) 1930–1980. US actor, a film star of the 1960s and 1970s, admired for his portrayals of the strong, silent loner, and noted for performing his own stunt work. After television success in the 1950s, he became a film star with *The Magnificent Seven* 1960. His films include *The Great Escape* 1963, *Bullitt* 1968, *Papillon* 1973, and *The Hunter* 1980.

macro in computer programming, a new command created by combining a number of existing ones. For example, if a programming language has separate commands for obtaining data from the keyboard and for displaying data on the screen, the programmer might create a macro that performs both these tasks with one command. A *macro key* on the keyboard combines the effects of pressing several individual keys.

macrobiotics dietary system of organically grown wholefoods. It originates in Zen Buddhism, and attempts to balance the principles of ◊yin and yang, thought to be present in foods in different proportions.

macroeconomics division of economics concerned with the study of whole (aggregate) economies or systems, including such aspects as government income and expenditure, the balance of payments, fiscal policy, investment, inflation, and unemployment. It seeks to understand the influence of all relevant economic factors on each other and thus to quantify and predict aggregate national income.

macrophage type of ◊white blood cell, or leucocyte, found in all vertebrate animals. Macrophages specialize in the removal of bacteria and other microorganisms, or of cell debris after injury. Like phagocytes, they engulf foreign matter, but they are larger than phagocytes and have a longer life span. They are found throughout the body, but mainly in the lymph and connective tissues, and especially the lungs, where they ingest dust, fibres, and other inhaled particles.

Madagascar Democratic Republic of; island country in the Indian Ocean, off the coast of E Africa, about 400 km/280 mi from Mozambique; *area* 587,041 sq km/226,598 sq mi; *capital* Antananarivo; *physical* temperate central highlands; humid valleys and tropical coastal plains; arid in S; *head of state* Didier Ratsiraka from 1975; *head of government* Guy Razanamasy from 1991; *political system* one-party socialist republic; *exports* coffee, cloves, vanilla, sugar, chromite, shrimps; *population* (1990 est) 11,802,000 (mostly of Malayo-Indonesian origin); *languages* Malagasy (official); French, English; *recent history* independence from France achieved 1960. In 1972 the army took control of the government, with Didier Ratsiraka as president; in 1977 the National Front for the Defence of Malagasy Socialist Revolution (FNDR) became the sole legal political organization. Political opposition was legalized 1990; 36 new parties were created. Antigovernment demonstrations 1991; Ratsiraka formed new unity government.

mad cow disease common name for ◊bovine spongiform encephalopathy, an incurable brain condition in cattle.

Madeira group of islands forming an autonomous region of Portugal off the NW coast of Africa, about 420 km/260 mi N of the Canary Islands. Madeira, the largest, and Porto Santo are the only inhabited islands. The Desertas and Selvagens are uninhabited islets. Their mild climate makes them a year-round resort; *area* 796 sq km/308 sq mi; *capital* Funchal, on Madeira; *physical* Pico Ruivo, on Madeira, is the highest mountain at 1,861 m/6,106 ft; *products* Madeira (a fortified wine), sugar cane, fruit, fish, handicrafts;

population (1986) 269,500; *history* Portuguese from the 15th century; occupied by Britain 1801 and 1807–14. In 1980 Madeira gained partial autonomy but remains a Portuguese overseas territory.

Madhya Pradesh state of central India; the largest of the Indian states; *area* 442,700 sq km/ 170,921 sq mi; *capital* Bhopal; *towns* Indore, Jabalpur, Gwalior, Durg-Bhilainagar, Raipur, Ujjain; *products* cotton, oilseed, sugar, textiles, engineering, paper, aluminium; *population* (1991) 66,135,400; *language* Hindi; *history* formed 1950 from the former British province of Central Provinces and Berar and the princely states of Makrai and Chattisgarh; lost some SW districts 1956, including ⟡Nagpur, and absorbed Bhopal, Madhya Bharat, and Vindhya Pradesh. In 1984 some 2,600 people died in ⟡Bhopal from an escape of poisonous gas.

Madison James 1751–1836. 4th president of the USA 1809–17. In 1787 he became a member of the Philadelphia Constitutional Convention and took a leading part in drawing up the US Constitution and the Bill of Rights. He allied himself firmly with Thomas ⟡Jefferson against Alexander ⟡Hamilton in the struggle between the more democratic views of Jefferson and the aristocratic, upper-class sentiments of Hamilton. As secretary of state in Jefferson's government 1801–09, Madison completed the Louisiana Purchase negotiated by James Monroe. During his period of office the War of 1812 with Britain took place.

Madonna Italian name for the Virgin ⟡Mary, meaning 'my lady'.

Madonna stage name of Madonna Louise Ciccone 1958– . US pop singer and actress who presents herself on stage and in videos with exaggerated sexuality and Catholic trappings. Her first hit was 'Like a Virgin' 1984; others include 'Material Girl' 1985 and 'Like a Prayer' 1989. Her films include *Desperately Seeking Susan* 1985 and *Dick Tracy* 1990.

Madras industrial port (cotton, cement, chemicals, iron, and steel) and capital of Tamil Nadu, India, on the Bay of Bengal; population (1981) 4,277,000. Fort St George 1639 remains from the East India Company when Madras was the chief port on the E coast. Madras was occupied by the French 1746–48 and shelled by the German ship *Emden* 1914, the only place in India attacked in World War I.

Madrid industrial city (leather, chemicals, furniture, tobacco, paper) and capital of Spain and of Madrid province; population (1991) 2,984,600. Built on an elevated plateau in the centre of the country, at 655 m/2,183 ft it is the highest capital city in Europe and has excesses of heat and cold. Madrid province has an area of 8,000 sq km/3,088 sq mi and a population of 4,855,000. Madrid began as a Moorish citadel captured by Castile 1083, became important in the times of Charles V and Philip II, and was designated capital 1561.

madrigal form of secular song in four or five parts, usually sung without instrumental accompaniment. It originated in 14th-century Italy. Madrigal composers include Andrea Gabrieli, ⟡Monteverdi, Thomas Morley, and Orlando ⟡Gibbons.

Mafia secret society reputed to control organized crime such as gambling, loansharking, drug traffic, prostitution, and protection; connected with the ⟡Camorra of Naples. It originated in 15th-century Sicily and now operates chiefly there and in countries to which Italians have emigrated, such as the USA and Australia.

magazine publication brought out periodically, typically containing articles, essays, short stories, reviews, and illustrations. The first magazine in the UK was the *Compleat Library* 1691. The US *Reader's Digest* 1922, with editions in many different countries and languages, was the world's best-selling magazine until overtaken by a Soviet journal in the mid-1980s.

Magdeburg industrial city (vehicles, paper, textiles, machinery) and capital of Saxony-Anhalt, Germany, on the river Elbe; population (1990) 290,000. A former capital of Saxony, Magdeburg became capital of Saxony-Anhalt on German reunification 1990. In 1938 the city was linked by canal with the Rhine and Ruhr rivers.

Magellan Ferdinand 1480–1521. Portuguese navigator. In 1519 he set sail in the *Victoria* from Seville with the intention of reaching the East Indies by a westerly route. He sailed through the *Magellan Strait* at the tip of South America, crossed an ocean he named the Pacific, and in 1521 reached the Philippines, where he was killed in a battle with the islanders. His companions returned to Seville 1522, completing the voyage under del Cano. Magellan and his Malay slave, Enrique de Malacca, are considered the first circumnavigators of the globe.

Magellanic Clouds in astronomy, the two galaxies nearest to our own galaxy. They are irregularly shaped, and appear as detached parts of the ⟡Milky Way, in the southern constellations Dorado and Tucana.

maggot soft, plump, limbless larva of flies, a typical example being the larva of the blowfly which is deposited as an egg on flesh.

magic art of controlling the forces of nature by supernatural means such as charms and ritual. The central ideas are that like produces like (*sympathetic magic*) and that influence carries by *contagion* or association; for example, by the former principle an enemy could be destroyed through an effigy, by the latter principle through personal items such as hair or nail clippings.

magic realism in literature, a fantastic situation realistically treated, as in the works of many Latin American writers such as Isabel Allende, Jorge Luis

Borges, and Gabriel García Márquez. In the UK it was practised by, among others, Angela Carter.

Maginot Line French fortification system along the German frontier from Switzerland to Luxembourg built 1929–36 under the direction of the war minister, André Maginot. It consisted of semi-underground forts joined by underground passages, and protected by antitank defences; lighter fortifications continued the line to the sea. In 1940 German forces pierced the Belgian frontier line and outflanked the Maginot Line.

magistrate in English law, a person who presides in a magistrates' court: either a justice of the peace (with no legal qualifications, and unpaid) or a stipendiary magistrate. Stipendiary magistrates are paid, qualified lawyers largely used in London and major cities.

maglev (acronym from **mag**netic **lev**itation) high-speed surface transport using the repellent force of superconductive magnets (see ◊superconductivity) to propel and support, for example, a train above a track. Maglev trains have been developed in Japan, where a Tokyo–Osaka line was being planned 1990, and in Germany. A ship launched Japan 1990 was to be fitted with superconducting thrusters instead of propellers for sea trials 1991.

magma molten rock material beneath the Earth's surface from which ◊igneous rocks are formed. ◊Lava is magma that has reached the surface and solidified, losing some of its components on the way.

Magna Carta in English history, the charter granted by King John 1215, traditionally seen as guaranteeing human rights against the excessive use of royal power. As a reply to the king's demands for excessive feudal dues and attacks on the privileges of the church, Archbishop Langton proposed to the barons the drawing-up of a binding document 1213. John was forced to accept this at Runnymede (now in Surrey) 15 June 1215.

magnesium lightweight, very ductile and malleable, silver-white, metallic element, symbol Mg, atomic number 12, relative atomic mass 24.305. It is one of the ◊alkaline-earth metals, and the lightest of the commonly used metals. Magnesium silicate, carbonate, and chloride are widely distributed in nature. The metal is used in alloys and flash photography. It is a necessary trace element in the human diet, and green plants cannot grow without it since it is an essential constituent of chlorophyll ($C_{55}H_{72}MgN_4O_5$).

magnet any object that forms a magnetic field (displays ◊magnetism), either permanently or temporarily through induction, causing it to attract materials such as iron, cobalt, nickel, and alloys of these. It always has two magnetic poles, called north and south.

magnetic field physical field or region around a

magnetic field

the earth's magnetic field

permanent magnet, or around a conductor carrying an electric current, in which a force acts on a moving charge or on a magnet placed in the field. The field can be represented by lines of force, which by convention link north and south poles and are parallel to the directions of a small compass needle placed on them. Its magnitude and direction are given by the magnetic flux density, expressed in ◊teslas.

magnetic tape narrow plastic ribbon coated with an easily magnetizable material on which data can be recorded. It is used in sound recording, audiovisual systems (videotape), and computing. For mass storage on commercial mainframe computers, large reel-to-reel tapes are used, but for the smaller mini- and microcomputers, tape cassettes and cartridges are more usual.

magnetism phenomena associated with ◊magnetic fields. Magnetic fields are produced by moving charged particles: in electromagnets, electrons flow through a coil of wire connected to a battery; in permanent magnets, spinning electrons within the atoms generate the field.

magnetite black iron ore, iron oxide (Fe_3O_4). Widely distributed, magnetite is found in nearly all igneous and metamorphic rocks. It is strongly magnetic and some deposits, called **lodestone**, are permanently magnetized. Lodestone has been used as a compass since the first millennium BC.

magnetosphere volume of space, surrounding a planet, controlled by the planet's magnetic field, and acting as a magnetic 'shell'. The Earth's magnetosphere extends 64,000 km/40,000 mi towards the Sun, but many times this distance on the side away from the Sun.

magnification measure of the enlargement or reduction of an object in an imaging optical system. **Linear magnification** is the ratio of the size (height) of the image to that of the object. **Angular magnification** is the ratio of the angle subtended at the observer's eye by the image to the angle subtended by the object when viewed directly.

magnitude in astronomy, measure of the brightness of a star or other celestial object. The larger the number denoting the magnitude, the fainter the object. Zero or first magnitude indicates some of the brightest stars. Still brighter are those of negative magnitude, such as Sirius, whose magnitude is −1.46. *Apparent magnitude* is the brightness of an object as seen from Earth; *absolute magnitude*, the brightness at a standard distance of 10 parsecs (32.6 light years).

magnolia tree or shrub of the genus *Magnolia*, family Magnoliaceae, native to North America and E Asia. Magnolias vary in height from 60 cm/2 ft to 30 m/150 ft. The large, fragrant single flowers are white, rose, or purple.

magpie any bird of a genus *Pica* in the crow family. It feeds on insects, snails, young birds, and carrion, and is found in Europe, Asia, N Africa, and W North America. The common magpie *P. pica* is about 45 cm/18 in long, and has black and white plumage, the long tail having a metallic gloss.

Magritte René 1898–1967. Belgian Surrealist painter whose paintings focus on visual paradoxes and everyday objects taken out of context. Recurring motifs include bowler hats, apples, and windows, for example *Golconda* 1953 where men in bowler hats are falling from the sky to a street below. His first Surrealist works date from the mid-1920s. He joined the other Surrealists in Paris 1927; returning to Brussels 1930, he painted murals for public buildings.

Magyar member of the largest ethnic group in Hungary, comprising 92% of the population. Magyars are of mixed Ugric and Turkic origin, and they arrived in Hungary towards the end of the 9th century. The Magyar language (see ◊Hungarian) belongs to the Uralic group.

Mahabad Kurdish town in Azerbaijan, W Iran, population (1983) 63,000. Occupied by Russian troops 1941, it formed the centre of a short-lived republic (1945–46) before being reoccupied by the Iranians. In the 1980s Mahabad was the focal point of resistance by Iranian Kurds against the Islamic republic.

Maharashtra state in W central India; *area* 307,800 sq km/118,811 sq mi; *capital* Bombay; *towns* Pune, Nagpur, Ulhasnagar, Sholapur, Nasik, Thana, Kolhapur, Aurangabad, Sangli, Amravati; *features* cave temples of Ajanta, containing 200 BC–7th century AD Buddhist murals and sculptures; Ellora cave temples 6th–9th century with Buddhist, Hindu, and Jain sculptures; *products* cotton, rice, groundnuts, sugar, minerals; *population* (1991) 78,706,700; *language* Marathi 50%; *religion* Hindu 80%, Parsee, Jain, and Sikh minorities; *history* formed 1960 from the southern part of the former Bombay state.

Mahāyāna one of the two major forms of ◊Buddhism, common in N Asia (China, Korea, Japan, and Tibet). Veneration of bodhisattvas (those who achieve enlightenment but remain on the human plane in order to help other living beings) is a fundamental belief in Mahāyāna, as is the idea that everyone has within them the seeds of Buddhahood.

Mahler Gustav 1860–1911. Austrian composer and conductor whose work displays a synthesis of Romanticism and new uses of chromatic harmonies and musical forms. He composed 14 symphonies, including three unnumbered (as a student), nine massive repertoire symphonies, the titled *Das Lied von der Erde/Song of the Earth* 1909, and the incomplete *Symphony No. 10*. He also wrote song cycles.

Mahmud I 1696–1754. Ottoman sultan from 1730. After restoring order to the empire in Istanbul 1730, he suppressed the Janissary rebellion 1731 and waged war against Persia 1731–46. He led successful wars against Austria and Russia, concluded by the Treaty of Belgrade 1739. He was a patron of the arts and also carried out reform of the army.

mahogany timber from any of several genera of trees found in the Americas and Africa. Mahogany is a tropical hardwood obtained chiefly by rainforest logging. It has a warm red colour and takes a high polish.

maidenhair any fern of the genus *Adiantum*, especially *A. capillus-veneris*, with hairlike fronds terminating in small kidney-shaped, spore-bearing pinnules. It is widely distributed in the Americas, and is sometimes found in the British Isles.

maidenhair tree another name for ◊ginkgo, a surviving member of an ancient group of gymnosperms.

Mailer Norman 1923– . US writer and journalist. He gained wide attention with his novel of World War II *The Naked and the Dead* 1948. A commentator on the US social, literary, and political scene, he has run for mayor of New York City and has expressed radical sexual views.

Maimonides Moses (Moses Ben Maimon) 1135–1204. Jewish rabbi and philosopher, born in Córdoba, Spain. Known as one of the greatest Hebrew scholars, he attempted to reconcile faith and reason.

Maine northeasternmost state of the USA, largest of the New England states; nickname Pine Tree State; *area* 86,200 sq km/33,273 sq mi; *capital* Augusta; *towns* Portland, Lewiston, Bangor; *physical* Appalachian Mountains; 80% of the state is forested; *features* Acadia National Park, including Bar Harbor and most of Mount Desert Island; Baxter State Park, including Mount Katahdin; Roosevelt's Campobello International Park; canoeing along the Allagush Wilderness Waterway;

products dairy and market garden produce, paper, pulp, timber, footwear, textiles, fish, lobster; tourism is important; **population** (1990) 1,228,000; **famous people** Henry Wadsworth Longfellow, Kate Douglas Wiggin, Edward Arlington Robinson, Edna St Vincent Millay; **history** permanently settled by the British from 1623; absorbed by Massachusetts 1691; became a state 1820.

mainframe large computer used for commercial data processing and other large-scale operations. Because of the general increase in computing power, the differences between the mainframe, ◊supercomputer, ◊minicomputer, and ◊microcomputer (personal computer) are becoming less marked.

maintenance in law, payments to support children or a spouse, under the terms of an agreement, or by a court order. In Britain, financial provision orders are made on divorce, but a court action can also be brought for maintenance without divorce proceedings. Applications for maintenance of illegitimate children are now treated in the same way as for legitimate children.

maize (North American *corn*) plant *Zea mays* of the grass family. Grown extensively in all subtropical and warm temperate regions, its range has been extended to colder zones by hardy varieties developed in the 1960s. It is widely used as animal feed.

Major John 1943– . British Conservative politician, prime minister from Nov 1990. He was foreign secretary 1989 and chancellor of the Exchequer 1989–90; as chancellor he led Britain into the European Exchange Rate Mechanism (ERM) Oct 1990. The following month he became prime minister on winning the Conservative Party leadership election in a contest with Michael Heseltine and Douglas Hurd, after the resignation of Margaret Thatcher. His earlier positive approach to European Community (EC) matters was hindered during 1991 by divisions within the Conservative Party. Despite continuing public dissatisfaction with the poll tax, the National Health Service, and the recession, Major was returned to power in the April 1992 general election.

Majorca (Spanish *Mallorca*) largest of the ◊Balearic Islands, belonging to Spain, in the W Mediterranean; **area** 3,640 sq km/1,405 sq mi; **capital** Palma; **features** the highest mountain is Puig Mayor 1,445 m/4,741 ft; **products** olives, figs, oranges, wine, brandy, timber, sheep; tourism is the mainstay of the economy; **population** (1981) 561,215; **history** captured 797 by the Moors, it became the kingdom of Majorca 1276, and was united with Aragon 1343.

Makarios III 1913–1977. Cypriot politician, Greek Orthodox archbishop 1950–77. A leader of the Resistance organization EOKA, he was exiled by the British to the Seychelles 1956–57 for supporting armed action to achieve union with Greece (*enosis*). He was president of the republic of Cyprus 1960–77 (briefly deposed by a Greek military coup July–Dec 1974).

Malabo port and capital of Equatorial Guinea, on the island of Bioko; population (1983) 15,253. It was founded in the 1820s by the British as *Port Clarence*. Under Spanish rule it was known as *Santa Isabel* (until 1973).

Malacca or *Melaka* state of W Peninsular Malaysia; capital Malacca; area 1,700 sq km/656 sq mi; products include rubber, tin, and wire; population (1980) 465,000 (about 70% Chinese). The town originated in the 13th century as a fishing village frequented by pirates, and later developed into a trading port. Portuguese from 1511, then Dutch from 1641, it was ceded to Britain 1824, becoming part of the Straits Settlements.

malachite common copper ore, basic copper carbonate, $Cu_2CO_3(OH)_2$. It is a source of green pigment and is polished for use in jewellery, ornaments, and art objects.

Málaga industrial seaport (sugar refining, distilling, brewing, olive-oil pressing, shipbuilding) and holiday resort in Andalusia, Spain; capital of Málaga province on the Mediterranean; population (1991) 524,800. Founded by the Phoenicians and taken by the Moors 711, Málaga was capital of the Moorish kingdom of Malaga from the 13th century until captured 1487 by the Catholic monarchs Ferdinand and Isabella.

Malagasy inhabitant of or native to Madagascar. The Malagasy language has about 9 million speakers; it belongs to the Austronesian family.

malaria infectious parasitic disease of the tropics transmitted by mosquitoes, marked by periodic fever and an enlarged spleen. When a female mosquito of the *Anopheles* genus bites a human who has malaria, it takes in with the human blood one of four malaria protozoa of the genus *Plasmodium*. This matures within the insect and is then transferred when the mosquito bites a new victim.

Malawi Republic of; country in SE Africa, bordered N and NE by Tanzania; E, S, and W by Mozambique; and W by Zambia; **area** 118,000 sq km/ 45,560 sq mi; **capital** Lilongwe; **physical** narrow plateau with rolling plains; mountainous W of Lake Malawi; one-third of the country is water, including lakes Malawi, Chilara, and Malombe; Great Rift Valley; **head of state and government** Hastings Kamusu Banda from 1966 for life; **political system** one-party republic; **exports** tea, tobacco, cotton, peanuts, sugar; **population** (1990 est) 9,080,000 (nearly 1 million refugees from Mozambique); **languages** English, Chichewa (both official); **recent history** achieved independence from Britain 1964, and became a one-party republic, with Hastings Banda as president, 1966. Banda started programme of moderate liberalization 1977. Nearly

1 million refugees from Mozambique entered the country 1986–89. In 1992 there were industrial riots and calls for greater democracy.

Malawi, Lake or *Lake Nyasa* African lake, bordered by Malawi, Tanzania, and Mozambique, formed in a section of the Great ⬦Rift Valley. It is about 500 m/1,650 ft above sea level and 560 km/350 mi long, with an area of 37,000 sq km/14,280 sq mi. It is intermittently drained to the south by the river Shiré into the Zambezi.

Malay language member of the Western or Indonesian branch of the Malayo-Polynesian language family, used in the Malay peninsula and many of the islands of Malaysia and Indonesia. The Malay language can be written in either Arabic or Roman scripts. The dialect of the S Malay peninsula is the basis of both Bahasa Malaysia and Bahasa Indonesia, the official languages of Malaysia and Indonesia.

Malayo-Polynesian family of languages spoken in Malaysia, better known as ⬦*Austronesian*.

Malaysia country in SE Asia, comprising the Malay Peninsula, bordered N by Thailand, and surrounded E, S, and W by the South China Sea; and the states of Sabah and Sarawak in the northern part of the island of Borneo (S Borneo is part of Indonesia); *area* 329,759 sq km/127,287 sq mi; *capital* Kuala Lumpur; *physical* comprises Peninsular Malaysia (the nine Malay states – Perlis, Kedah, Johore, Selangor, Perak, Negri Sembilan, Kelantan, Trengganu, Pahang – plus Penang and Malacca); and E Malaysia (Sarawak and Sabah); 75% tropical jungle; central mountain range; swamps in E; *head of state* Rajah Azlan Muhibuddin Shah (sultan of Perak) from 1989; *head of government* Mahathir bin Mohamad from 1981; *political system* liberal democracy; *population* (1990 est) 17,053,000 (Malaysian 47%, Chinese 32%, Indian 8%, others 13%); *languages* Bahasa Malaysia (official); English, Chinese, Indian and local languages; *recent history* became a British colony 1826. In 1963 the Federation of Malaysia was formed, including Malaya, Singapore, Sabah and Sarawak; Singapore seceded from the federation 1965. In 1991 the New Development Policy (NDP) economic growth programme was launched, seeking an eightfold increase in national income by 2020.

Malcolm III called *Canmore c.* 1031–1093. King of Scotland from 1054, the son of Duncan I (murdered by ⬦Macbeth 1040). He fled to England when the throne was usurped by Macbeth, but recovered S Scotland and killed Macbeth in battle 1057. He was killed at Alnwick while invading Northumberland, England.

Malcolm X assumed name of Malcolm Little 1926–1965. US black nationalist leader. He campaigned for black separatism, condoning violence in self-defence, but in 1964 modified his views to found the Islamic, socialist Organization of Afro-American Unity, preaching racial solidarity. A year later he was assassinated while addressing a rally in Harlem, New York City. His *Autobiography of Malcolm X* was published 1964.

Maldives Republic of; group of 1,196 islands in the N Indian Ocean, about 640 km/400 mi SW of Sri Lanka, only 203 of which are inhabited; *area* 298 sq km/115 sq mi; *capital* Malé; *physical* coral islands grouped into 12 clusters of atolls, largely flat, none bigger than 13 sq km/5 sq mi, average elevation 1.8 m/6 ft; 203 are inhabited; *head of state and government* Maumoon Abdul Gayoom from 1978; *political system* authoritarian nationalism; *exports* coconuts, copra, bonito (fish related to tuna), garments; *population* (1990 est) 219,000; *languages* Divehi (Sinhalese dialect), English; *recent history* a British protectorate from 1887, the Maldives achieved full independence outside the Commonwealth 1965. In 1968 the sultan was deposed and a republic installed. The Maldives rejoined the Commonwealth 1985. A coup attempt 1988 was foiled by Indian paratroops.

Malé capital of the Maldives in the Indian Ocean; population (1990) 55,100. It trades in copra, breadfruit, and palm products; it is also a tourist centre.

Mali Republic of; country in NW Africa, bordered NE by Algeria, E by Niger, SE by Burkina Faso, S by the Ivory Coast, SW by Senegal and Guinea, and W and N by Mauritania; *area* 1,240,142 sq km/478 695 sq mi; *capital* Bamako; *physical* river Niger and savanna in S; part of Sahara Desert in N; hills in NE; Senegal River and its branches irrigate SW; *head of state and government* Alpha Oumar Konare from 1992; *political system* emergent democratic republic; *exports* cotton, peanuts, livestock, fish; *population* (1990 est) 9,182,000; *languages* French (official); Bambara; *recent history* Mali came under French rule 1895, and became the independent Republic of Mali 1960. Moussa Traoré took power through an army coup 1968, and brought in a new constitution making Mali a one-party state 1974. Demonstrations 1991 against one-party rule were followed by a coup led by Lt-Col Amadou Toumani Toure and the agreement of a new multiparty constitution; a referendum 1992 endorsed the constitution. The multiparty elections 1992 were won by the centrist Alliance for Democracy in Mali (ADEMA) and Alpha Oumar Konare elected president.

mallard common wild duck *Anas platyrhynchos*, found almost worldwide, from which domestic ducks were bred. The male, which can grow to a length of 60 cm/2 ft, usually has a green head and brown breast, while the female is mottled brown. Mallards are omnivorous, dabbling ducks.

Mallarmé Stéphane 1842–1898. French poet who founded the Symbolist school with Paul Verlaine. His belief that poetry should be evocative and suggestive was reflected in *L'Après-midi d'un faune/*

Afternoon of a Faun 1876, which inspired the composer Debussy.

Mallorca Spanish form of ⟡Majorca, an island in the Mediterranean.

mallow any flowering plant of the family Malvaceae, especially of the genus *Malva*, including the European common mallow *M. sylvestris*; the tree mallow *Lavatera arborea*; and the marsh mallow *Althaea officinalis*. Most mallows have pink or purple flowers.

Malmö industrial port (shipbuilding, engineering, textiles) in SW Sweden, situated across the Öresund from Copenhagen, Denmark; population (1990) 233,900. Founded in the 12th century, Malmö is Sweden's third largest city.

Malory Thomas 15th century. English author of the prose romance *Le Morte d'Arthur* about 1470. It is a translation from the French, modified by material from other sources, and it deals with the exploits of King Arthur's knights of the Round Table and the quest for the ⟡Holy Grail.

Malraux André 1901–1976. French writer. An active antifascist, he gained international renown for his novel *La Condition humaine/Man's Estate* 1933, set during the Nationalist/Communist Revolution in China in the 1920s. *L'Espoir/Days of Hope* 1937 is set in Civil War Spain, where he was a bomber pilot in the International Brigade.

malt in brewing, grain (barley, oats, or wheat) artificially germinated and then dried in a kiln. Malts are fermented to make beers or lagers, or fermented and then distilled to produce spirits such as whisky.

Malta Republic of; island country in the Mediterranean Sea, S of Sicily, E of Tunisia, and N of Libya; *area* 320 sq km/124 sq mi; *capital* and port Valletta; *physical* includes islands of Gozo 67 sq km/26 sq mi and Comino 2.5 sq km/1 sq mi; *head of state* Vincent Tabone from 1989; *head of government* Edward Fenech Adami from 1987; *political system* liberal democracy; *recent history* annexed to Britain 1814, Malta achieved self-government 1947; full independence was achieved 1964. Malta applied for European Community membership 1990. The Nationalists were re-elected 1992.

Malta, Knights of another name for members of the military-religious order of the Hospital of St John of Jerusalem.

Malthus Thomas Robert 1766–1834. English economist and cleric. His *Essay on the Principle of Population* 1798 (revised 1803) argued for population control, since populations increase in geometric ratio and food only in arithmetic ratio, and influenced Charles ⟡Darwin's thinking on natural selection as the driving force of evolution. Malthus saw war, famine, and disease as necessary checks on population growth.

Maluku or *Moluccas* group of Indonesian islands; *area* 74,500 sq km/28,764 sq mi; *capital* Ambon, on Amboina; *population* (1989 est) 1,814,000; *history* as the Spice Islands, they were formerly part of the Netherlands East Indies, and the S Moluccas attempted secession from the newly created Indonesian republic from 1949; exiles continue agitation in the Netherlands.

Malvinas Argentine name for the ⟡Falkland Islands.

mamba one of two venomous snakes, genus *Dendroaspis*, of the cobra family Elapidae, found in Africa S of the Sahara. Unlike cobras, they are not hooded.

mammal any vertebrate that suckles its young and has hair. Mammals maintain a constant body temperature in varied surroundings. Most mammals give birth to live young, but the platypus and echidna lay eggs. There are over 4,000 species, adapted to almost every way of life. The smallest shrew weighs only 2 g/0.07 oz, the largest whale up to 150 tonnes.

mammary gland in female mammals, a milk-producing gland derived from epithelial cells underlying the skin, active only after the production of young. In all but monotremes (egg-laying mammals), the mammary glands terminate in teats which aid infant suckling. The number of glands and their position vary between species.

Mammon evil personification of wealth and greed; originally a Syrian god of riches, cited in the New Testament as opposed to the Christian god.

mammoth extinct elephant of genus *Mammuthus*, whose remains are found worldwide. Some were 50% taller than modern elephants. The woolly mammoth *Elephas primigenius*, the size of an Indian elephant, had long fur and large inward-curving tusks. Mammoths were abundant in N Europe in Pleistocene times.

Man, Isle of island in the Irish Sea, a dependency of the British crown, but not part of the UK; *area* 570 sq km/220 sq mi; *capital* Douglas; *towns* Ramsey, Peel, Castletown; *features* Snaefell 620 m/2,035 ft; annual TT (Tourist Trophy) motorcycle races, gambling casinos, Britain's first free port, tax haven; tailless Manx cat; tourism, banking, and insurance are important – the island produces its own coins and notes in UK currency denominations; *government* crown-appointed lieutenant governor, a legislative council, and the representative House of Keys, which together make up the Court of Tynwald, passing laws subject to the royal assent. Laws passed at Westminster only affect the island if specifically so provided; *exports* light engineering products; *population* (1986) 55,500; *language* English (Manx, nearer to Scottish than Irish Gaelic, has been almost extinct since the 1970s); *history* Norwegian until 1266, when the island was ceded to Scotland; it came under UK administration 1765.

management buyout purchase of control of a company by its management, generally with debt funding, making it a ◊leveraged buyout.

Managua capital and chief industrial city of Nicaragua, on the lake of the same name; population (1985) 682,000. It has twice been destroyed by earthquake and rebuilt, 1931 and 1972; it was also badly damaged during the civil war in the late 1970s.

Manama (Arabic *Al Manamah*) capital and free trade port of Bahrain, on Bahrain Island; handles oil and entrepôt trade; population (1988) 152,000.

manatee any plant-eating aquatic mammal of the genus *Trichechus* constituting the family Trichechidae in the order Sirenia (sea cows). Manatees occur in marine bays and sluggish rivers, usually in turbid water; they are found in the Atlantic off Central and South America and off the coast of W Africa.

Manaus capital of Amazonas, Brazil, on the Rio Negro, near its confluence with the Amazon; population (1991) 996,700. It can be reached by sea-going vessels, although it is 1,600 km/1,000 mi from the Atlantic. Formerly a centre of the rubber trade, it developed as a tourist centre in the 1970s.

Manchester city in NW England, on the river Irwell, 50 km/31 mi E of Liverpool. It is a manufacturing (textile machinery, chemicals, rubber, processed foods) and financial centre; population (1991) 397,400. It is linked by the Manchester Ship Canal, built 1894, to the river Mersey and the sea.

Manchester, Greater former (1974–86) metropolitan county of NW England, replaced by a residuary body 1986 that covers some of its former functions; *area* 1,290 sq km/498 sq mi; *towns* Manchester (administrative headquarters), Bolton, Oldham, Rochdale, Salford, Stockport, and Wigan; *features* Manchester Ship Canal links it with the Mersey and the sea; Old Trafford cricket ground at Stretford, and the football ground of Manchester United; *products* industrial; *population* (1991) 2,455,200; *famous people* John Dalton, James Joule, Emmeline Pankhurst, Gracie Fields, Anthony Burgess.

Manchu last ruling dynasty in China, from 1644 until their overthrow 1912; their last emperor was the infant ◊P'u-i. Originally a nomadic people from Manchuria, they established power through a series of successful invasions from the north, then granted trading rights to the USA and Europeans, which eventually brought strife and the ◊Boxer Rebellion.

Manchuria European name for the NE region of China, comprising the provinces of Heilongjiang, Jilin, and Liaoning. It was united with China by the Manchu dynasty 1644, but as the Chinese Empire declined, Japan and Russia were rivals for its control. The Russians were expelled after the ◊Russo-Japanese War 1904–05, and in 1932 Japan

consolidated its position by creating a puppet state, *Manchukuo*, which disintegrated on the defeat of Japan in World War II.

Mandalay chief town of the Mandalay division of Myanmar (formerly Burma), on the river Irrawaddy, about 495 km/370 mi N of Yangon; population (1983) 533,000. Founded by King Mindon Min 1857, it was the capital of Burma 1857–85.

mandarin variety of the tangerine ◊orange *Citrus reticulata*.

mandate in history, a territory whose administration was entrusted to Allied states by the League of Nations under the Treaty of Versailles after World War I. Mandated territories were former German and Turkish possessions (including Iraq, Syria, Lebanon, and Palestine). When the United Nations replaced the League of Nations 1945, mandates that had not achieved independence became known as ◊trust territories.

Mandela Nelson (Rolihlahla) 1918– . South African politician and lawyer, president of the ◊African National Congress (ANC) from 1991. As organizer of the then banned ANC, he was imprisoned 1964. In prison he became a symbol of unity for the worldwide anti-apartheid movement. In Feb 1990 he was released, the ban on the ANC having been lifted, and entered into negotiations with the government about a multiracial future for South Africa.

Mandela Winnie (Nomzamo) 1934– . Civil-rights activist in South Africa and wife of Nelson Mandela. A leading spokesperson for the African National Congress during her husband's imprisonment 1964–90, she has been jailed for a year and put under house arrest several times. In 1989 she was involved in the abduction of four youths, one of whom, Stompie Seipei, was later murdered. Winnie Mandela was convicted of kidnapping and assault, and given a six-year jail sentence May 1991, with the right to appeal.

mandolin musical instrument with four or five pairs of strings tuned like a violin. It takes its name from its almond-shaped body (Italian *mandorla* 'almond').

mandragora or *mandrake* plant of the Old World genus *Mandragora* of almost stemless plants with narcotic properties, of the nightshade family Solanaceae. They have large leaves, pale blue or violet flowers, and globose berries known as devil's apples.

mandrake another name for the plant mandragora.

mandrill large W African forest-living baboon *Mandrillus sphinx*, most active on the ground. It has large canine teeth like the drill *M. leucophaeus*, to which it is closely related. The nose is bright red and the cheeks striped with blue. There are red callosities on the buttocks; the fur is brown, apart from a yellow beard.

Manet Edouard 1832–1883. French painter, active in Paris. Rebelling against the academic tradition, he developed a clear and unaffected Realist style. His subjects were mainly contemporary, such as *Un Bar aux Folies-Bergère/A Bar at the Folies-Bergère* 1882 (Courtauld Art Gallery, London). His *Déjeuner sur l'herbe/Picnic on the Grass* 1863 and *Olympia* 1865 (both Musée d'Orsay, Paris) offended conservative tastes in their matter-of-fact treatment of the nude body. He never exhibited with the Impressionists, although he was associated with them from the 1870s.

manganese hard, brittle, grey-white metallic element, symbol Mn, atomic number 25, relative atomic mass 54.9380. It resembles iron (and rusts), but it is not magnetic and is softer. It is used chiefly in making steel alloys, also alloys with aluminium and copper. It is used in fertilizers, paints, and industrial chemicals. It is a necessary trace element in human nutrition.

mangelwurzel or *mangold* variety of the common beet *Beta vulgaris* used chiefly as feed for cattle and sheep.

mango evergreen tree *Mangifera indica* of the cashew family Anacardiaceae, native to India but now widely cultivated for its oval fruits in other tropical and subtropical areas, such as the West Indies.

mangold another name for ⟩mangelwurzel.

mangrove any of several shrubs and trees, especially of the mangrove family Rhizophoraceae, found in the muddy swamps of tropical coasts and estuaries. By sending down aerial roots from their branches, they rapidly form close-growing mangrove thickets. Their timber is impervious to water and resists marine worms.

Manhattan island 20 km/12.5 mi long and 4 km/2.5 mi wide, lying between the Hudson and East rivers and forming a borough of the city of New York, USA; population (1980) 1,428,000. It includes the Wall Street business centre and Broadway theatres.

manic depression mental disorder characterized by recurring periods of ⟩depression which may or may not alternate with periods of inappropriate elation (mania) or overactivity. Sufferers may be genetically predisposed to the condition. Some cases have been improved by taking prescribed doses of ⟩lithium.

Manichaeism religion founded by the prophet Mani (Latinized as Manichaeus, *c.* 216–276). Despite persecution Manichaeism spread and flourished until about the 10th century. Based on the concept of dualism, it held that the material world is evil, an invasion of the spiritual realm of light by the powers of darkness; particles of divine light imprisoned in evil matter were to be rescued by messengers such as Jesus, and finally by Mani himself.

Manila industrial port (textiles, tobacco, distilling, chemicals, shipbuilding) and capital of the Philippines, on the island of Luzon; population (1990) 1,598,900, metropolitan area (including ⟩Quezon City) 5,926,000.

manioc another name for the plant ⟩cassava.

Manipur state of NE India; *area* 22,400 sq km/8,646 sq mi; *capital* Imphal; *features* Loktak Lake; original Indian home of polo; *products* grain, fruit, vegetables, sugar, textiles, cement; *population* (1991) 1,826,700; *language* Hindi; *religion* Hindu 70%; *history* administered from the state of Assam until 1947 when it became a Union Territory. It became a state 1972.

Manitoba prairie province of Canada; *area* 650,000 sq km/250,900 sq mi; *capital* Winnipeg; *features* lakes Winnipeg, Winnipegosis, and Manitoba (area 4,700 sq km/1,814 sq mi); 50% forested; *exports* grain, manufactured foods, beverages, machinery, furs, fish, nickel, zinc, copper, and the world's largest caesium deposits; *population* (1991) 1,092,600; *history* trading posts and forts were built here by fur traders in the 18th century. What came to be known as the Red River settlement was first colonized 1811 by dispossessed Scottish Highlanders. The colony became the Canadian province of Manitoba 1870 after the Riel Rebellion 1869 ended. The area of the province was extended 1881 and 1912.

Manley Michael (Norman) 1924– . Jamaican politician, leader of the socialist People's National Party from 1969, and prime minister 1972–80 and from 1989. His father, *Norman Manley* (1893–1969), was the founder of the People's National Party and prime minister 1959–62.

Mann Thomas 1875–1955. German novelist and critic, concerned with the theme of the artist's relation to society. His first novel was *Buddenbrooks* 1901, which, followed by *Der Zauberberg/The Magic Mountain* 1924, led to a Nobel prize 1929. Notable among his works of short fiction is *Der Tod in Venedig/Death in Venice* 1913.

Mannerism in painting and architecture, a style characterized by a subtle but conscious breaking of the 'rules' of Classical composition – for example, displaying the human body in an off-centre, distorted pose, and using harsh, non-blending colours. The term was coined by Giorgio ⟩Vasari and used to describe the 16th-century reaction to the peak of Renaissance Classicism as achieved by Raphael, Leonardo da Vinci, and early Michelangelo.

manor basic economic unit in ⟩feudalism in Europe, established in England under the Norman conquest. It consisted of the lord's house and cultivated land, land rented by free tenants, land held by villagers, common land, woodland, and waste land.

Man Ray adopted name of Emmanuel Rudnitsky 1890–1977. US photographer, painter, and sculptor, active mainly in France; associated with the Dada movement. His pictures often showed Surrealist images, for example the photograph *Le Violon d'Ingres* 1924.

Mansell Nigel 1954– . English motor-racing driver who passed the British record of 27 Grand Prix victories with 28 wins 1992. He was runner-up in World Championships in 1986 and 1987.

Mansfield Katherine. Pen name of Kathleen Beauchamp 1888–1923. New Zealand writer who lived most of her life in England. Her delicate artistry emerges not only in her volumes of short stories – such as *In a German Pension* 1911, *Bliss* 1920, and *The Garden Party* 1923 – but also in her *Letters* and *Journal*.

manslaughter in English law, the unlawful killing of a human being in circumstances less culpable than ◊murder – for example, when the killer suffers extreme provocation, is in some way mentally ill (diminished responsibility), did not intend to kill but did so accidentally in the course of another crime or by behaving with criminal recklessness, or is the survivor of a genuine suicide pact that involved killing the other person.

manta another name for ◊devil ray, a large fish.

Mantegna Andrea *c.* 1431–1506. Italian Renaissance painter and engraver, active chiefly in Padua and Mantua, where some of his frescoes remain. Paintings such as *The Agony in the Garden c.* 1455 (National Gallery, London) reveal a dramatic linear style, mastery of perspective, and strongly Classical architectural detail. He worked for the marquis of Gonzaga in Mantua, producing an outstanding fresco series in the Ducal Palace in the 1470s and later *The Triumphs of Caesar* (Hampton Court, near London).

mantis any insect of the family Mantidae, related to cockroaches. Some species can reach a length of 20 cm/8 in. There are about 2,000 species of mantis, mainly tropical.

mantle intermediate zone of the Earth between the crust and the core. It is thought to consist of silicate minerals such as olivine and spinel.

manufacturing base share of the total output in a country's economy contributed by the manufacturing sector. This sector has greater potential

mantis

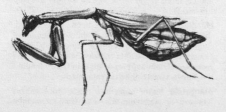

for productivity growth than the service sector, which is labour-intensive; in manufacturing, productivity can be increased by replacing workers with technically advanced capital equipment. It is also significant because of its contribution to exports.

Manx Gaelic ◊Gaelic language of the Isle of Man.

Maoism form of communism based on the ideas and teachings of the Chinese communist leader ◊Mao Zedong. It involves an adaptation of ◊Marxism to suit conditions in China and apportions a much greater role to agriculture and the peasantry in the building of socialism, thus effectively bypassing the capitalist (industrial) stage envisaged by Marx.

Maori member of the indigenous Polynesian people of New Zealand, who numbered 294,200 in 1986, about 10% of the total population. Maori is a member of the Polynesian branch of the Malayo-Polynesian language family.

Mao Zedong or *Mao Tse-tung* 1893–1976. Chinese political leader and Marxist theoretician. A founder of the Chinese Communist Party (CCP) 1921, Mao soon emerged as its leader. He organized the ◊Long March 1934–36 and the war of liberation 1937–49, following which he established a People's Republic and Communist rule in China; he headed the CCP and government until his death. His influence diminished with the failure of his 1958–60 ◊Great Leap Forward, but he emerged dominant again during the 1966–69 ◊Cultural Revolution. Mao adapted communism to Chinese conditions, as set out in the *Little Red Book*.

map projection ways of depicting the spherical surface of the Earth on a flat piece of paper. Traditional projections include the **conic**, **azimuthal**, and **cylindrical**. The most famous cylindrical projection is the ◊Mercator projection, which dates from 1569. The weakness of these systems is that countries in different latitudes are disproportionately large, and lines of longitude and latitude appear distorted. In 1973 German historian Arno Peters devised the **Peters projection** in which the countries of the world retain their relative areas.

maple deciduous tree of the genus *Acer*, family Aceraceae, with lobed leaves and green flowers, followed by two-winged fruits, or samaras. There are over 200 species, chiefly in northern temperate regions. The ◊sycamore *A. pseudoplatanus* is native to Europe. The sugar maple *A. saccharum*, a North American species, is the source of maple syrup.

Maputo formerly (until 1975) *Lourenço Marques* capital of Mozambique, and Africa's second-largest port, on Delagoa Bay; population (1987) 1,006,800. Linked by rail with Zimbabwe and South Africa, it is a major outlet for minerals, steel, textiles, processed foods, and furniture.

marabou stork *Leptoptilos crumeniferus* found in

Africa. It is about 120 cm/4 ft tall, has a bald head, and eats snakes, lizards, insects, and carrion. It is largely dark grey and white and has an inflatable throat pouch.

Maracaibo oil-exporting port in Venezuela, second largest city in the country, on the channel connecting Lake Maracaibo with the Gulf of Venezuela; population (1989) 1,365,308.

Maradona Diego 1960– . Argentine footballer who was voted the best player of the 1980s by the world's press. He helped his country to two successive ♢World Cup finals. He has won 79 international caps; he was South American footballer of the year 1979 and 1980.

Marat Jean Paul 1743–1793. French Revolutionary leader and journalist. He was elected to the National Convention 1792, where he carried on a long struggle with the right-wing ♢Girondins, ending in their overthrow May 1793. In July he was murdered in his bath by Charlotte Corday, a member of the Girondins.

marathon athletics endurance race over 42.195 km/26 mi 385 yd. It was first included in the Olympic Games in Athens 1896. The distance varied until it was standardized 1924. More recently, races have been opened to wider participation, including social runners as well as those competing at senior level. In the 1980s, half marathons, over a distance of 21 km/13 mi 192.5 yd, became very popular.

Marathon, Battle of 490 BC. Fought between the Greeks, who were ultimately victorious, and invading Persians on the plain of Marathon, NE of Athens. Before the battle, news of the Persian destruction of the Greek city of Eretria was taken from Athens to Sparta by a courier, Pheidippides, who fell dead on arrival. His feat is commemorated by the *marathon race*.

Marbella port and tourist resort on the Costa del Sol between Málaga and Algeciras in Andalucia, S Spain; population (1991) 80,645. There are three bullrings, a Moorish castle, and the remains of a medieval defensive wall.

marble metamorphosed ♢limestone that takes and retains a good polish; it is used in building and sculpture. In its pure form it is white and consists almost entirely of calcite $CaCO_3$. Mineral impurities give it various colours and patterns. Carrara, Italy, is known for white marble.

Marches boundary areas of England with Wales, and England with Scotland. In the Middle Ages these troubled frontier regions were held by lords of the Marches, sometimes called *marchiones* and later earls of March. The 1st Earl of March of the Welsh Marches was Roger de Mortimer (*c.* 1286–1330); of the Scottish Marches, Patrick Dunbar (died 1285).

Marciano Rocky (Rocco Francis Marchegiano)

1923–1969. US boxer, world heavyweight champion 1952–56. He retired after 49 professional fights, the only heavyweight champion to retire undefeated.

Marconi Guglielmo 1874–1937. Italian electrical engineer and pioneer in the invention and development of radio. In 1895 he achieved radio communication over more than a mile, and in England 1896 he conducted successful experiments that led to the formation of the company that became Marconi's Wireless Telegraph Company Ltd. He shared the Nobel Prize for Physics 1909.

Marco Polo see ♢Polo, Marco.

Marcos Ferdinand 1917–1989. Filipino right-wing politician, president from 1965 to 1986, when he was forced into exile in Hawaii. He was backed by the USA when in power, but in 1988 US authorities indicted him and his wife Imelda Marcos for racketeering, embezzlement, and defrauding US banks; Marcos was too ill to stand trial.

Marcos Imelda 1930– . Filipino politician and socialite, wife of Ferdinand Marcos, in exile 1986–91. She was acquitted 1990 of defrauding US banks. Under indictment for misuse of Philippine state funds, she returned to Manila Nov 1991 and announced her intention to stand as a candidate in the 1992 presidential elections.

Marcus Aurelius Antoninus AD 121–180. Roman emperor from 161 and Stoic philosopher. Although considered one of the best of the Roman emperors, he persecuted the Christians for political reasons. He wrote the philosophical *Meditations*.

Mardi Gras (French 'fat Tuesday', from the custom of using up all the fat in the household before the beginning of ♢Lent) Shrove Tuesday. A festival was traditionally held on this day in Paris, and there are carnivals in many parts of the world, including New Orleans, Louisiana; Italy; and Brazil.

Margaret (Rose) 1930– . Princess of the UK, younger daughter of George VI and sister of Elizabeth II. In 1960 she married Anthony Armstrong-Jones, later created Lord Snowdon, but they were divorced 1978. Their children are *David, Viscount Linley* (1961–) and *Lady Sarah Armstrong-Jones* (1964–).

Margaret of Anjou 1430–1482. Queen of England from 1445, wife of ♢Henry VI of England. After the outbreak of the Wars of the ♢Roses 1455, she acted as the leader of the Lancastrians, but was defeated and captured at the battle of Tewkesbury 1471 by Edward IV.

Margaret, St 1045–1093. Queen of Scotland, the granddaughter of King Edmund Ironside of England. She went to Scotland after the Norman Conquest, and soon after married Malcolm III. The marriage of her daughter Matilda to Henry I united the Norman and English royal houses.

margarine butter substitute made from animal fats and/or vegetable oils. The French chemist

Hippolyte Mège-Mouriès invented margarine 1889. Today, margarines are usually made with vegetable oils, such as soy, corn, or sunflower oil, giving a product low in saturated fats (see ◊polyunsaturate) and fortified with vitamins A and D.

Margrethe II 1940– . Queen of Denmark from 1972, when she succeeded her father Frederick IX. In 1967, she married the French diplomat Count Henri de Laborde de Monpezat, who took the title Prince Hendrik. Her heir is Crown Prince Frederick (1968–).

marguerite European plant *Leucanthemum vulgare* of the daisy family Compositae. It is a shrubby perennial and bears white daisylike flowers. Marguerite is also the name of a cultivated variety of ◊chrysanthemum.

Mariana Islands or *Marianas* archipelago in the NW Pacific E of the Philippines, divided politically into ◊*Guam* (an unincorporated territory of the USA) and *Northern Marianas* (a commonwealth of the USA with its own internal government, of 16 mountainous islands, extending 560 km/350 mi N from Guam); *area* 480 sq km/185 sq mi; *capital* Garapan on Saipan; *government* own constitutionally elected government; *products* sugar, coconuts, coffee; *population* (1988) 21,000, mainly Micronesian; *languages* Chamorro 55%, English; *religion* mainly Roman Catholic; *history* sold to Germany by Spain 1899. The islands were mandated by the League of Nations to Japan 1918, and taken by US Marines 1944–45 in World War II. The islands were part of the US Trust Territory of the Pacific 1947–78. Since 1978 they have been a commonwealth of the USA.

Mariana Trench lowest region on the Earth's surface; the deepest part of the sea floor. The trench is 2,400 km/1,500 mi long and is situated 300 km/200 mi E of the Mariana Islands, in the NW Pacific Ocean. Its deepest part is the gorge known as the Challenger Deep, which extends 11,034 m/36,201 ft below sea level.

Maria Theresa 1717–1780. Empress of Austria from 1740, when she succeeded her father, the Holy Roman emperor Charles VI; her claim to the throne was challenged and she became embroiled, first in the War of the ◊Austrian Succession 1740–48, then in the ◊Seven Years' War 1756–63; she remained in possession of Austria but lost Silesia. The rest of her reign was peaceful and, with her son Joseph II, she introduced social reforms.

Marie Antoinette 1755–1793. Queen of France from 1774. She was the daughter of Empress Maria Theresa of Austria, and married ◊Louis XVI of France 1770. Her reputation for extravagance helped provoke the ◊French Revolution of 1789. She was tried for treason Oct 1793 and guillotined.

Marie de' Medici 1573–1642. Queen of France, wife of Henry IV from 1600, and regent (after his murder) for their son Louis XIII. She left the government to her favourites, the Concinis, until Louis

XIII seized power and executed them 1617. She was banished, but after she led a revolt 1619, ◊Richelieu effected her reconciliation with her son. When she attempted to oust him again 1630, she was exiled.

marigold any of several plants of the family Compositae, especially the genus *Tagetes*, including pot marigold *Calendula officinalis* and the tropical American *T. patula*, commonly known as French marigold.

marijuana dried leaves and flowers of the hemp plant ◊cannabis, used as a drug; its use is illegal in most countries. Mexico is the world's largest producer.

Mariner spacecraft series of US space probes that explored the planets Mercury, Venus, and Mars 1962–75. *Mariner 11* and *12* were renamed *Voyager 1* and *2* (see ◊Voyager probes).

maritime law that part of the law dealing with the sea: in particular, fishing areas, ships, and navigation. Seas are divided into *internal waters* governed by a state's internal laws (such as harbours, inlets); *territorial waters* (the area of sea adjoining the coast over which a state claims rights); the *continental shelf* (the seabed and subsoil that the coastal state is entitled to exploit beyond the territorial waters); and the *high seas*, where international law applies.

marjoram aromatic herb of the mint family Labiatae. Wild marjoram *Origanum vulgare* is found both in Europe and Asia and has become naturalized in the Americas; the culinary sweet marjoram *O. majorana* is widely cultivated.

Mark Antony Antonius, Marcus 83–30 BC. Roman politician and soldier. He was tribune and later consul under Julius Caesar, serving under him in Gaul. In 44 BC he tried to secure for Caesar the title of king. After Caesar's assassination, he formed the Second Triumvirate with Octavian (◊Augustus) and Lepidus. In 42 he defeated Brutus and Cassius at Philippi. He took Egypt as his share of the empire and formed a liaison with ◊Cleopatra. In 40 he returned to Rome to marry Octavia, the sister of Augustus. In 32 the Senate declared war on Cleopatra. Antony was defeated by Augustus at the battle of Actium 31 BC. He returned to Egypt and committed suicide.

market forces in economics, the forces of demand (a want backed by the ability to pay) and supply (the willingness and ability to supply).

Mark, St 1st century AD. In the New Testament, Christian apostle and evangelist whose name is given to the second Gospel. It was probably written AD 65–70, and used by the authors of the first and third Gospels. He is the patron saint of Venice, and his emblem is a winged lion; feast day 25 April.

Marlborough John Churchill, 1st Duke of Marlborough 1650–1722. English soldier, created a duke 1702 by Queen Anne. He was granted the

Blenheim mansion in Oxfordshire in recognition of his services, which included defeating the French army outside Vienna in the Battle of Blenheim 1704, during the War of the ⟡Spanish Succession.

Marley Bob (Robert Nesta) 1945–1981. Jamaican reggae singer, a Rastafarian whose songs, many of which were topical and political, popularized reggae worldwide in the 1970s. One of his greatest hit songs is 'No Woman No Cry'; his albums include *Natty Dread* 1975 and *Exodus* 1977.

marlin or *spearfish* any of several genera of open-sea fishes known as billfishes, of the family Istiophoridae, order Perciformes. Some 2.5 m/7 ft long, they are found in warmer waters, have elongated snouts, and high-standing dorsal fins. The blue marlin *Makaira nigricans* is the best-known species.

Marlowe Christopher 1564–1593. English poet and dramatist. His work includes the blank-verse plays *Tamburlaine the Great c.* 1587, *The Jew of Malta c.* 1589, *Edward II* and *Dr Faustus*, both *c.* 1592, the poem *Hero and Leander* 1598, and a translation of Ovid's *Amores*.

Marmara, Sea of small inland sea separating Turkey in Europe from Turkey in Asia, connected through the Bosporus with the Black Sea, and through the Dardanelles with the Aegean; length 275 km/170 mi, breadth up to 80 km/50 mi.

marmoset small tree-dwelling monkey in the family Callithricidae, found in South and Central America. Most species have characteristic tufted ears, clawlike nails, and a handsome tail, and some only reach a body length of 18 cm/7 in. The tail is not prehensile. Some are known as tamarins.

marmot any of several large burrowing rodents of the genus *Marmota*, in the squirrel family Sciuridae. There are about 15 species. They eat plants and some insects. Marmots are found throughout Canada and the USA, and from the Alps to the Himalayas. Marmots live in colonies, make burrows (one to each family), and hibernate. In North America they are called **woodchucks** or **groundhogs**. *M. marmota* is the typical marmot of the Central European Alps.

Marquesas Islands (French *Iles Marquises*) island group in ⟡French Polynesia, lying N of the Tuamotu Archipelago; area 1,270 sq km/490 sq mi; population (1988) 7,500. The administrative headquarters is Atuona on Hiva Oa. The islands were annexed by France 1842.

Márquez Gabriel García. Colombian novelist; see ⟡García Márquez.

Marrakesh historic town in Morocco in the foothills of the Atlas Mountains, about 210 km/130 mi S of Casablanca; population (1982) 549,000. It is a tourist centre, and has textile, leather, and food processing industries. Founded 1062, it has a medieval palace and mosques, and was formerly the capital of Morocco.

marram grass coarse perennial grass *Ammophila arenaria*, flourishing on sandy areas. Because of its tough, creeping rootstocks, it is widely used to hold coastal dunes in place.

marriage legally or culturally sanctioned union of one man and one woman (monogamy); one man and two or more women (polygamy); one woman and two or more men (polyandry). The basis of marriage varies considerably in different societies (romantic love in the West; arranged marriages in some other societies), but most marriage ceremonies, contracts, or customs involve a set of rights and duties, such as care and protection, and there is generally an expectation that children will be born of the union to continue the family line, and maintain the family property. In England marriages can be effected according to the rites of the Church of England or those of other faiths, or in a superintendent registrar's office.

marrow trailing vine *Cucurbita pepo*, family Cucurbitaceae, producing large pulpy fruits, used as vegetables and in preserves; the young fruits of one variety are known as courgettes (US zucchini).

Mars in Roman mythology, the god of war, after whom the month of March is named. He is equivalent to the Greek Ares. He is depicted as a fearless warrior.

Mars fourth planet from the Sun, average distance 227.9 million km/141.6 million mi. It revolves around the Sun in 687 Earth days, and has a rotation period of 24 hr 37 min. It is much smaller than Venus or Earth, with a diameter 6,780 km/4,210 mi, and mass 0.11 that of Earth. Mars is slightly pear-shaped, with a low, level northern hemisphere, which is comparatively uncratered and geologically 'young', and a heavily cratered 'ancient' southern hemisphere.

Marseilles (French *Marseille*) chief seaport of France, industrial centre (chemicals, oil refining, metallurgy, shipbuilding, food processing), and capital of the *département* of Bouches-du-Rhône, on the Golfe du Lion, Mediterranean Sea; population (1982) 1,111,000.

Marshall Islands group of islands, the Radak (13 islands) and Ralik (11 islands) chains in the W Pacific; **area** 180 sq km/69 sq mi; **capital** Majuro; **features** include two atolls used for US atom-bomb tests 1946–63, Eniwetok and Bikini (hence the name given to two-piece swimsuits which supposedly had an explosive impact) – radioactivity will last for 100 years, and the people have made claims for rehabilitation; and Kwajalein atoll (the largest) which has a US intercontinental missile range; **government** internally self-governing; **products** copra, phosphates, fish, tourism; **population** (1988) 41,000; **recent history** German 1906–19; administered by Japan until 1946, passed to the USA as part of the Pacific Islands Trust Territory 1947. They were used for many atomic bomb tests 1946–63, and the islanders are demanding compensation. In 1986 a compact of free association with the USA was signed, under which the islands manage their own internal and external affairs but the USA controls military activities in exchange for financial support. In Dec 1990 its membership of the Trust Territory of the Pacific was terminated. It joined the United Nations Sept 1991. The incumbent president Amata Kabua was re-elected 1992 for a further four-year term.

Marshall Plan programme of US financial aid to Europe, set up at the end of World War II, totalling $13,000 billion 1948–52. Officially known as the European Recovery Programme, it was announced by Secretary of State George Marshall in a speech at Harvard June 1947, but it was in fact the work of a State Department group led by Dean ⍔Acheson. The perceived danger of communist takeover in postwar Europe was the main reason for the aid effort.

marsh marigold plant *Caltha palustris* of the buttercup family Ranunculaceae, known as the kingcup in the UK and as the cowslip in the USA. It grows in moist sheltered spots and has five-sepalled flowers of a brilliant yellow.

Marston Moor, Battle of battle fought in the English Civil War 2 July 1644 on Marston Moor, 11 km/7 mi W of York. The Royalists were completely defeated by the Parliamentarians and Scots.

marsupial mammal in which the female has a pouch where she carries her young (born tiny and immature) for a considerable time after birth. Marsupials include omnivorous, herbivorous, and carnivorous species, among them the kangaroo, wombat, opossum, phalanger, bandicoot, dasyure, and wallaby. The marsupial anteater *Myrmecobius* has no pouch.

Martello tower circular tower for coastal defence. Formerly much used in Europe, many were built along the English coast, especially in Sussex and Kent, in 1804, as a defence against the threatened French invasion. The name is derived from a tower on Cape Mortella, Corsica, which was captured by the British with great difficulty 1794, and was taken as a model. They are round towers of solid masonry, sometimes moated, with a flat roof for mounted guns.

marten small bushy-tailed carnivorous mammal of the genus *Martes* in the weasel family Mustelidae. Martens live in North America, Europe, and temperate regions of Asia, and are agile climbers of trees. The pine marten *M. martes*, Britain's rarest mammal, has long, brown fur and is about 75 cm/2.5 ft long.

Martens Wilfried 1936– . Prime minister of Belgium 1979–1992, member of the Social Christian Party (CVP). He was president of the Dutch-speaking CVP 1972–79 and, as prime minister, headed several coalition governments in the period 1979–1992 when he was replaced by Jean-Luc Dehaene heading a new coalition.

martial arts any of several styles of armed and unarmed combat developed in the East from ancient techniques and arts. Common martial arts include aikido, ⍔judo, jujitsu, ⍔karate, kendo, and ⍔kung fu.

martial law replacement of civilian by military authorities in the maintenance of order. In Britain, the legal position of martial law is ill-defined but, in effect, when war or rebellion is in progress in an area, the military authorities maintain order by summary means.

martin any of several species of birds in the swallow family Hirundinidae. The European house martin *Delichon urbica*, a summer migrant from Africa, is blue-black above and white below, distinguished from the swallow by its shorter, less forked tail. The cuplike mud nest is usually constructed under the eaves of buildings. Other species include the brownish European sand martin *Riparia riparia*, also a migrant from Africa, which tunnels to make a nest in sandy banks.

Martinique French island in the West Indies (Lesser Antilles); *area* 1,079 sq km/417 sq mi; *capital* Fort-de-France; *features* several active volcanoes; Napoleon's empress Josephine was born in Martinique, and her childhood home is now a museum; *products* sugar, cocoa, rum, bananas, pineapples; *population* (1984) 327,000; *history* Martinique was reached by Spanish navigators 1493, and became a French colony 1635; since 1972 it has been a French overseas region.

martyr one who voluntarily suffers death for refusing to renounce a religious faith. The first recorded Christian martyr was St Stephen, who was killed in Jerusalem shortly after Jesus' alleged ascension to heaven.

Marvell Andrew 1621–1678. English metaphysical poet and satirist. His poems include 'To His Coy Mistress' and 'Horatian Ode upon Cromwell's Return from Ireland'. He was committed to the parliamentary cause, and was member of Parliament for Hull from 1659. He devoted his last years mainly to verse satire and prose works attacking repressive aspects of government.

Marx Karl (Heinrich) 1818–1883. German philosopher, economist, and social theorist whose account of change through conflict is known as historical, or dialectical, materialism (see ⍔Marxism). His ⍔*Das Kapital/Capital* 1867–95 is the fundamental text of Marxist economics, and his systematic theses on class struggle, history, and the importance of economic factors in politics have exercised an enormous influence on later thinkers and political activists.

Marx Brothers team of US film comedians: Leonard *Chico* (from the 'chicks' – women – he

chased) 1887–1961; Arthur (Adolph), the silent
Harpo (from the harp he played) 1888–1964;
Julius *Groucho* (from his temper) 1890–1977;
Milton *Gummo* (from his gumshoes, or galoshes)
1897–1977, who left the team before films; and
Herbert *Zeppo* (born at the time of the first
zeppelins) 1901–1979, part of the team until 1935.
They made a total of 13 zany films 1929–49 including *Animal Crackers* 1930, *Duck Soup* 1933, *A Night at the Opera* 1935, and *Go West* 1940.

Marxism philosophical system, developed by the
19th-century German social theorists ⟡Marx and
⟡Engels, also known as *dialectical materialism*,
under which matter gives rise to mind (materialism) and all is subject to change (from dialectic;
see ⟡Hegel). As applied to history, it supposes
that the succession of feudalism, capitalism, socialism, and finally the classless society is inevitable.
The stubborn resistance of any existing system to
change necessitates its complete overthrow in the
class struggle – in the case of capitalism, by the
proletariat – rather than gradual modification.

Mary in the New Testament, the mother of Jesus
through divine intervention (see ⟡Annunciation),
wife of ⟡Joseph. The Roman Catholic Church
maintains belief in her Immaculate Conception and
bodily assumption into heaven, and venerates her
as a mediator. Feast day of the Assumption 15 Aug.

Mary Queen of Scots 1542–1587. Queen of Scotland 1542–67. Also known as *Mary Stuart*, she
was the daughter of James V. Mary's connection
with the English royal line from Henry VII made
her a threat to Elizabeth I's hold on the English
throne, especially as she represented a champion
of the Catholic cause. After her forced abdication
she was imprisoned but escaped 1568 to England.
Elizabeth I held her prisoner, while the Roman
Catholics, who regarded Mary as rightful queen of
England, formed many conspiracies to place her on
the throne, and for complicity in one of these she
was executed.

Mary I *Bloody Mary* 1516–1558. Queen of England
from 1553. She was the eldest daughter of Henry
VIII by Catherine of Aragon. When Edward VI died,
Mary secured the crown without difficulty in spite
of the conspiracy to substitute Lady Jane ⟡Grey.
In 1554 Mary married Philip II of Spain, and as a
devout Roman Catholic obtained the restoration of
papal supremacy and sanctioned the persecution of
Protestants. She was succeeded by her half-sister
Elizabeth I.

Mary II 1662–1694. Queen of England, Scotland,
and Ireland from 1688. She was the Protestant elder
daughter of the Catholic ⟡James II, and in 1677 was
married to her cousin ⟡William III of Orange. After
the 1688 revolution she accepted the crown jointly
with William.

Maryland state of E USA; nickname Old Line
State/Free State; *area* 31,600 sq km/12,198 sq mi;

capital Annapolis; *cities* Baltimore, Silver Spring,
Dundalk, Bethesda; *features* Chesapeake Bay, an
inlet of the Atlantic; horse racing (the Preakness
Stakes at Baltimore); yacht racing and the US Naval
Academy at Annapolis; historic Fort McHenry; Fort
Meade, a government electronic-listening centre;
Baltimore harbour; *products* poultry, dairy products, machinery, steel, cars and parts, electric and
electronic equipment, chemicals, fish and shellfish; *population* (1990) 4,781,500; *famous people*
Stephen Decatur, Francis Scott Key, Edgar Allan
Poe, Frederick Douglass, Harriet Tubman, Upton
Sinclair, H L Mencken, Babe Ruth, Billie Holiday;
history one of the original Thirteen Colonies, first
settled 1634; it became a state 1788.

Mary Magdalene, St 1st century AD. In the New
Testament, the woman whom Jesus cured of possession by evil spirits, was present at the Crucifixion
and burial, and was the first to meet the risen Jesus.
She is often identified with the woman of St Luke's
gospel who anointed Jesus' feet, and her symbol is
a jar of ointment; feast day 22 July.

Masaccio (Tomaso di Giovanni di Simone Guidi)
1401–1428. Florentine painter, a leader of the early
Italian Renaissance. His frescoes in Sta Maria del
Carmine, Florence, 1425–28, which he painted with
Masolino da Panicale (*c.* 1384–1447), show a decisive break with Gothic conventions. He was the first
painter to apply the scientific laws of perspective,
newly discovered by the architect Brunelleschi.

Masai member of an E African people whose
territory is divided between Tanzania and Kenya,
and who number about 250,000. They were originally warriors and nomads, breeding humped zebu
cattle, but some have adopted a more settled life.
Their cooperation is being sought by the Kenyan
authorities to help in wildlife conservation.

Masaryk Tomáš (Garrigue) 1850–1937. Czechoslovak nationalist politician. He directed the
revolutionary movement against the Austrian
Empire, founding with Eduard Beneš and Stefanik
the Czechoslovak National Council, and in 1918
was elected first president of the newly formed
Czechoslovak Republic. Three times re-elected, he
resigned 1935 in favour of Beneš.

maser (acronym for *m*icrowave *a*mplification by
*s*timulated *e*mission of *r*adiation) in physics, a
high-frequency microwave amplifier or oscillator in
which the signal to be amplified is used to stimulate
unstable atoms into emitting energy at the same
frequency. Atoms or molecules are raised to a
higher energy level and then allowed to lose this
energy by radiation emitted at a precise frequency.
The principle has been extended to other parts of
the electromagnetic spectrum as, for example, in
the ⟡laser.

Maseru capital of Lesotho, southern Africa, on the
Caledon River; population (1986) 289,000. Founded 1869, it is a centre for trade and diamond
processing.

Masire Quett Ketumile Joni 1925– . President of Botswana from 1980. In 1962, with Seretse ⟡Khama, he founded the Botswana Democratic Party (BDP) and in 1965 was made deputy prime minister. After independence 1966, he became vice president and, on Khama's death 1980, president, continuing a policy of nonalignment.

Mason–Dixon Line in the USA, the boundary line between Maryland and Pennsylvania (latitude 39° 43′ 26.3″ N), named after Charles Mason (1730–1787) and Jeremiah Dixon (died 1777), English astronomers and surveyors who surveyed it 1763–67. It was popularly seen as dividing the North from the South.

masque spectacular and essentially aristocratic entertainment with a fantastic or mythological theme in which music, dance, and extravagant costumes and scenic design figured larger than plot. Originating in Italy, it reached its height of popularity at the English court between 1600 and 1640, with the collaboration of Ben ⟡Jonson as writer and Inigo ⟡Jones as stage designer.

mass in physics, the quantity of matter in a body as measured by its inertia. Mass determines the acceleration produced in a body by a given force acting on it, the acceleration being inversely proportional to the mass of the body. The mass also determines the force exerted on a body by ⟡gravity on Earth, although this attraction varies slightly from place to place. In the SI system, the base unit of mass is the kilogram.

Mass in music, the setting of the invariable parts of the Christian Mass, that is *Kyrie, Gloria, Credo, Sanctus* with *Benedictus*, and *Agnus Dei*. A notable example is Bach's *Mass in B Minor*.

Massachusetts state of USA; nickname Bay State/ Old Colony State; *area* 21,500 sq km/8,299 sq mi; *capital* Boston; *cities* Worcester, Springfield, New Bedford, Brockton, Cambridge; *population* (1990) 6,016,400; *features* Boston landmarks; Harvard University and the Massachusetts Institute of Technology, Cambridge; Cape Cod National Seashore; New Bedford and the islands of Nantucket and Martha's Vineyard, former whaling ports; Berkshire Hills with Tanglewood and other performing-arts centres; the battlefields of Lexington and Concord near Minute Man National Historical Park; Salem, site of witch trials; Plymouth Rock; *products* electronic, communications, and optical equipment; precision instruments; non-electrical machinery; fish; cranberries; dairy products; *famous people* Samuel Adams, Louis Brandeis, Emily Dickinson, Ralph Waldo Emerson, Robert Goddard, Nathaniel Hawthorne, Oliver Wendell Holmes, Winslow Homer, William James, John F Kennedy, Robert Lowell, Paul Revere, Henry Thoreau, Daniel Webster; *history* one of the original Thirteen Colonies, it was first settled 1620 by the Pilgrims at Plymouth. After the ⟡Boston Tea Party 1773, the American Revolution began at Lexington

and Concord 19 April 1775, and the British evacuated Boston the following year. Massachusetts became a state 1788.

massage manipulation of the soft tissue of the body, the muscles, ligaments, and tendons, either to encourage the healing of specific injuries or to produce the general beneficial effects of relaxing muscular tension, stimulating blood circulation, and improving the tone and strength of the skin and muscles.

Massif Central mountainous plateau region of S central France; area 93,000 sq km/36,000 sq mi, highest peak Puy de Sancy 1,886 m/6,188 ft. It is a source of hydroelectricity.

Massine Léonide 1895–1979. Russian choreographer and dancer with the Ballets Russes. He was a creator of comedy in ballet and also symphonic ballet using concert music. His works include the first Cubist-inspired ballet *Parade* 1917, *La Boutique fantasque* 1919, and *The Three-Cornered Hat* 1919.

mastiff breed of powerful dog, usually fawn in colour, that was originally bred in Britain for hunting purposes. It has a large head, wide-set eyes, and broad muzzle. It can grow up to 90 cm/3 ft at the shoulder, and weigh 100 kg/220 lb.

mastodon any of an extinct family (Mastodontidae) of mammals of the elephant order (Proboscidae). They differed from elephants and mammoths in the structure of their grinding teeth. There were numerous species, among which the American mastodon *Mastodon americanum*, about 3 m/10 ft high, of the Pleistocene era, is well known. They were hunted by humans for food.

Mata Hari stage name of Gertrud Margarete Zelle 1876–1917. Dutch courtesan, dancer, and probable spy. In World War I she had affairs with highly placed military and government officials on both sides and told Allied secrets to the Germans. She may have been a double agent, in the pay of both France and Germany. She was shot by the French on espionage charges.

materialism philosophical theory that there is nothing in existence over and above matter and matter in motion. Such a theory excludes the possibility of deities. It also sees mind as an attribute of the physical, denying idealist theories that see mind as something independent of body; for example, Descartes' theory of 'thinking substance'.

mathematics science of spatial and numerical relationships. The main divisions of *pure mathematics* include geometry, arithmetic, algebra, calculus, and trigonometry. Mechanics, statistics, numerical analysis, computing, the mathematical theories of astronomy, electricity, optics, thermodynamics, and atomic studies come under the heading of *applied mathematics*.

Matilda 1102–1167. Claimant to the throne of England. On the death of her father, Henry I, 1135, the barons elected her cousin Stephen to be king. Matilda invaded England 1139, and was crowned by

mathematics signs

$a \rightarrow b$	a implies b
∞	infinity
lim	limiting value
$a \sim b$	numerical difference between a and b
$a \approx b$	a approximately equal to b
$a = b$	a equal to b
$a \equiv b$	a identical with b (for formulae only)
$a > b$	a greater than b
$a < b$	a smaller than b
$a \neq b$	a not equal to b
$b < a < c$	a greater than b and smaller than c, that is a lies between the values b & c but cannot equal either.
$a \geq b$	a equal to or greater than b, that is, a at least as great as b
$a \leq b$	a equal to or less than b, that is, a at most as great as b
$b \leq a \leq c$	a lies between the values b & c and could take the values b and c.
$\|a\|$	absolute value of a; this is always positive, for example $\|-5\| = 5$
$+$	addition sign, positive
$-$	subtraction sign, negative
$\times$ or $\odot$	multiplication sign, times
$:$ or $\div$ or $/$	division sign, divided by
$a + b = c$	$a + b$, read as 'a plus b', denotes the addition of a and b. The result of the addition, c, is also known as the sum.
$\int$	indefinite integral
$_a\int^b f(x)dx$	definite integral, or integral between $x = a$ and $x = b$
$a - b = c$	$a - b$, read as 'a minus b', denotes subtraction of b from a.
	$a - b$, or c, is the difference. Subtraction is the opposite of addition.
$a \times b = c$	
$ab = c$	$a \times b$, read as 'a multiplied by b', denotes multiplication of a by b. $a \times b$, or c, is
$a.b = c$	the product, a and b are factors of c.
$a : b = c$	$a : c$, read as 'a divided by b', denotes division. a is the dividend, b is the divisor; $a:b$, or c, is the quotient.
$a \div b = c$	One aspect of division – repeated subtraction, is the opposite of multiplication – repeated addition.
$a/b = c$	In fractions, or a/b, a is the numerator ($=$ dividend), b the denominator ($=$ divisor).
$a^b = c$	a^b, read as 'a to the power b'; a is the base, b the exponent.
$^b\sqrt{a} = c$	$^b\sqrt{a}$, is the bth root of a, b being known as the root exponent. In the special case of $^2\sqrt{a} = c$, $^2\sqrt{a}$ or c is known as the square root of a, and the root exponent is usually omitted, that is, $^2\sqrt{a} = \sqrt{a}$.
e	exponential constant and is the base of natural (napierian) logarithms $= 2.7182818284.......$
π	ratio of the circumference of a circle to its diameter $= 3.1415925535.......$

her supporters 1141. Civil war ensued until Stephen was finally recognized as king 1153, with Henry II (Matilda's son) as his successor.

Matisse Henri 1869–1954. French painter, sculptor, illustrator, and designer; one of the most original creative forces in early 20th-century art. His work concentrates on designs that emphasize curvaceous surface patterns, linear arabesques, and brilliant colour. Subjects include odalisques (women of the harem), bathers, and dancers; later works include pure abstracts, as in his collages of coloured paper shapes and the designs 1949–51 for the decoration of a chapel for the Dominican convent in Vence, near Nice.

Mato Grosso (Portuguese 'dense forest') area of SW Brazil, now forming two states, with their capitals at Cuiaba and Campo Grande. The forests, now depleted, supplied rubber and rare timbers; diamonds and silver are mined.

matriarchy form of social organization in which women head the family, and descent and relationship are reckoned through the female line. Matriarchy, often associated with polyandry (one wife with several husbands), occurs in certain parts of India, in the South Pacific, Central Africa, and among some North American Indian peoples. In **matrilineal** societies, powerful positions are usually held by men but acceded to through female kin.

matter in physics, anything that has mass and can

be detected and measured. All matter is made up of ◊atoms and ◊elementary particles, and exists ordinarily as a solid, liquid, or gas. The history of science and philosophy is largely taken up with accounts of theories of matter, ranging from the hard 'atoms' of Democritus to the 'waves' of modern quantum theory.

Matterhorn (French *le Cervin*, Italian *il Cervino*) mountain peak in the Alps on the Swiss-Italian border; 4,478 m/14,690 ft.

Matthew, St 1st century AD. Christian apostle and evangelist, the traditional author of the first Gospel. He is usually identified with Levi, who was a tax collector in the service of Herod Antipas, and was called by Jesus to be a disciple as he sat by the Lake of Galilee receiving customs dues. His emblem is a man with wings; feast day 21 Sept.

Maugham (William) Somerset 1874–1965. English writer. His work includes the novels *Of Human Bondage* 1915, *The Moon and Sixpence* 1919, and *Cakes and Ale* 1930; the short-story collections *The Trembling of a Leaf* 1921 and *Ashenden* 1928; and the plays *Lady Frederick* 1907 and *Our Betters* 1923.

Mauna Loa active volcano rising to a height of 4,169 m/13,678 ft on the Pacific island of Hawaii; it has numerous craters, including the second-largest active crater in the world.

Maupassant Guy de 1850–1893. French author who established a reputation with the short story 'Boule de Suif/Ball of Fat' 1880 and wrote some 300 short stories in all. His novels include *Une Vie/A Woman's Life* 1883 and *Bel-Ami* 1885. He was encouraged as a writer by Gustave ◊Flaubert.

Mauriac François 1885–1970. French novelist. His novel *Le Baiser au lépreux/A Kiss for the Leper* 1922 describes the conflict of an unhappy marriage. The

maximum and minimum

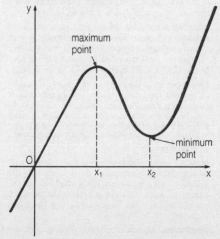

irreconcilability of Christian practice and human nature is examined in *Fleuve de feu/River of Fire* 1923, *Le Désert de l'amour/The Desert of Love* 1925, and *Thérèse Desqueyroux* 1927. He was awarded the Nobel Prize for Literature 1952.

Mauritania Islamic Republic of; country in NW Africa, bordered NE by Algeria, E and S by Mali, SW by Senegal, W by the Atlantic Ocean, and NW by Western Sahara; *area* 1,030,700 sq km/397,850 sq mi; *capital* Nouakchott; *physical* valley of river Senegal in S; remainder flat and arid; *head of state and government* Maaouia Ould Sid Ahmed Taya from 1984; *political system* military republic in state of transition; *exports* iron ore, fish, gypsum; *population* (1990 est) 2,038,000; *languages* French (official); Hasaniya Arabic, black African languages; *recent history* independence was achieved from France 1960. Western Sahara was ceded by Spain 1975; Mauritania occupied the southern area, Morocco the north. Diplomatic relations with Morocco were broken 1981; restored 1985. Violent clashes with the Senegalese occurred 1985. Multiparty elections were promised 1991.

Mauritius Republic of; island country in the Indian Ocean, E of Madagascar; the island of Rodrigues is part of Mauritius; there are several small island dependencies; *area* 1,865 sq km/720 sq mi; *capital* Port Louis; *physical* mountainous, volcanic island surrounded by coral reefs; *head of state* Elizabeth II represented by governor general; *head of government* Aneerood Jugnauth from 1982; *political system* constitutional monarchy; *exports* sugar, knitted goods, tea; *population* (1990 est) 1,141,900; *languages* English (official); French, creole, Indian languages; *recent history* independence was achieved from Britain within the Commonwealth 1968. An attempt to create a republic 1990 failed; Mauritius became a republic 1992.

Maximilian I 1459–1519. Holy Roman emperor from 1493, the son of Emperor Frederick III. He had acquired the Low Countries through his marriage to Mary of Burgundy 1477.

maximum and minimum in ◊coordinate geometry, points at which the slope of a curve representing a function changes from positive to negative (maximum), or from negative to positive (minimum). A tangent to the curve at a maximum or minimum has zero gradient.

Maxwell (Ian) Robert (born Jan Ludvik Hoch) 1923–1991. Czech-born British publishing and newspaper proprietor who owned several UK national newspapers (the *Daily Mirror*, *Sunday Mirror*, *People*, and the weekly *European*), the Macmillan Publishing Company, and the New York *Daily News*. In late 1991 Maxwell, last seen on his yacht off the Canary Islands, was found dead at sea. His sons Kevin and Ian were named as his successors. At the time of his death the Maxwell domain carried debts of some $3.9 billion.

Maxwell James Clerk 1831–1879. Scottish physicist. His main achievement was in the understanding of ▷electromagnetic waves: *Maxwell's equations* bring together electricity, magnetism, and light in one set of relations. He contributed to every branch of physical science – studying gases, optics, and the sensation of colour. His theoretical work in magnetism prepared the way for wireless telegraphy and telephony.

maya (Sanskrit 'illusion') in Hindu philosophy, mainly in the *Vedānta*, the cosmos which Isvara, the personal expression of Brahman, or the ▷atman, has called into being. This is real, yet also an illusion, since its reality is not everlasting.

Maya member of an American Indian civilization originating in the Yucatán Peninsula in Central America about 2600 BC, with later sites in Mexico, Guatemala, and Belize, and enjoying a classical period AD 325–925, after which it declined. Today they are Roman Catholic, and live in Yucatán, Guatemala, Belize, and W Honduras. Many still speak Maya, a member of the Totonac-Mayan (Penutian) language family, as well as Spanish.

May Day first day of May. In many countries it is a public holiday in honour of labour; see also ▷Labour Day.

mayfly any insect of the order Ephemerida (Greek *ephemeros* 'lasting for a day', an allusion to the very brief life of the adult). The larval stage, which can last a year or more, is passed in water, the adult form developing gradually from the nymph through successive moults. The adult has transparent, net-veined wings.

Mayo county in Connacht province, Republic of Ireland; *area* 5,400 sq km/2,084 sq mi; *towns* Castlebar (administrative town) *features* Lough Conn; wild Atlantic coast scenery; Achill Island; the village of Knock, where two women claimed a vision of the Virgin with two saints 1879, now a site of pilgrimage; Croagh Patrick 765 m/2,510 ft, the mountain where St Patrick spent the 40 days of Lent 441; pilgrims climb the mountain on the last Sunday of July each year; *products* sheep and cattle farming; fishing; *population* (1991) 110,700.

mayor title of head of urban administration. In England, Wales, and Northern Ireland, the mayor is the principal officer of a district council that has been granted district-borough status under royal charter. In the USA a mayor is the elected head of a city or town.

mayweed any of several species of the daisy family Compositae native to Europe and Asia, and naturalized elsewhere, including the European dog fennel or stinking daisy *Anthemis cotula*, naturalized in North America, and Eurasian pineapple mayweed *Matricaria matricarioides*. All have finely divided leaves.

Mazarin Jules 1602–1661. French politician who

succeeded Richelieu as chief minister of France 1642. His attack on the power of the nobility led to the ▷Fronde and his temporary exile, but his diplomacy achieved a successful conclusion to the Thirty Years' War, and, in alliance with Oliver Cromwell during the British protectorate, he gained victory over Spain.

Mazowiecki Tadeusz 1927– . Polish politician, founder member of ▷Solidarity, and Poland's first postwar noncommunist prime minister 1989–1990. Forced to introduce unpopular economic reforms, he was knocked out in the first round of the Nov 1990 presidential elections, resigning in favour of his former colleague Lech Walesa.

Mazzini Giuseppe 1805–1872. Italian nationalist. He was a member of the revolutionary society, the Carbonari, and founded in exile the nationalist movement Giovane Italia (Young Italy) 1832. Returning to Italy on the outbreak of the 1848 revolution, he headed a republican government established in Rome, but was forced into exile again on its overthrow 1849. He acted as a focus for the movement for Italian unity (see ▷Risorgimento).

Mbabane capital (since 1902) of Swaziland, 160 km/100 mi W of Maputo, in the Dalgeni Hills; population (1986) 38,000. Mining and tourism are important.

mean in mathematics, a measure of the average of a number of terms or quantities. The simple *arithmetic mean* is the average value of the quantities, that is, the sum of the quantities divided by their number. The *weighted mean* takes into account the frequency of the terms that are summed; it is calculated by multiplying each term by the number of times it occurs, summing the results and dividing this total by the total number of occurrences. The *geometric mean* of n quantities is the nth root of their product. In statistics, it is a measure of central tendency of a set of data.

measles acute virus disease (rubeola), spread by airborne infection. Symptoms are fever, severe catarrh, small spots inside the mouth, and a raised, blotchy red rash appearing for about a week after two weeks' incubation. Prevention is by vaccination.

Meath county in the province of Leinster, Republic of Ireland; *area* 2,340 sq km/903 sq mi; *county town* Trim; *features* Tara Hill, 155 m/509 ft high, was the site of a palace and coronation place of many kings of Ireland (abandoned in the 6th century) and St Patrick preached here; *products* sheep, cattle; *population* (1991) 105,600.

Mecca (Arabic *Makkah*) city in Saudi Arabia and, as birthplace of Muhammad, the holiest city of the Islamic world; population (1974) 367,000. In the centre of Mecca is the Great Mosque, in the courtyard of which is the Kaaba containing the Black Stone revered by Muslims.

mechanics branch of physics dealing with the

motions of bodies and the forces causing these motions, and also with the forces acting on bodies in equilibrium. It is usually divided into ▷dynamics and ▷statics.

Mecklenburg–West Pomerania (German *Mecklenburg-Vorpommern*) administrative *Land* (state) of Germany; *area* 22,887 sq km/8,840 sq mi; *capital* Schwerin; *towns* Rostock, Wismar, Stralsund, Neubrandenburg; *products* fish, ships, diesel engines, electronics, plastics, chalk; *population* (1990) 2,100,000; *history* the state was formerly the two grand duchies of Mecklenburg-Schwerin and Mecklenburg-Strelitz, which became free states of the Weimar Republic 1918–34, and were joined 1946 with part of Pomerania to form a region of East Germany. In 1952 it was split into the districts of Rostock, Schwerin, and Neubrandenburg. Following German reunification 1990, the districts were abolished and Mecklenburg–West Pomerania was reconstructed as one of the five new states of the Federal Republic.

Medan seaport and economic centre of the island of Sumatra, Indonesia; population (1980) 1,379,000. It trades in rubber, tobacco, and palm oil.

Medea in Greek mythology, the sorceress daughter of the king of Colchis. When ▷Jason reached the court, she fell in love with him, helped him acquire the Golden Fleece, and they fled together. When Jason married Creusa, Medea killed his bride with the gift of a poisoned garment, and then killed her own two children by Jason.

Medellín industrial town (textiles, chemicals, engineering, coffee) in the Central Cordillera, Colombia, 1,538 m/5,048 ft above sea level; population (1985) 2,069,000. It is the second city of Colombia, and its drug capital, with 7,000 violent deaths in 1990.

median middle number of an ordered group of numbers. If there is no middle number (because there is an even number of terms), the median is the ▷mean (average) of the two middle numbers. For example, the median of the group 2, 3, 7, 11, 12 is 7; that of 3, 4, 7, 9, 11, 13 is 8 (the average of 7 and 9).

Medici noble family of Florence, the city's rulers from 1434 until they died out 1737. Family members included ▷Catherine de' Medici, Pope ▷Leo X, Pope Clement VII, ▷Marie de' Medici.

Medici Cosimo de' 1389–1464. Italian politician and banker. Regarded as the model for Machiavelli's *The Prince*, he dominated the government of Florence from 1434 and was a patron of the arts. He was succeeded by his inept son *Piero de' Medici* (1416–1469).

Medici Lorenzo de', *the Magnificent* 1449–1492. Italian politician, ruler of Florence from 1469. He was also a poet and a generous patron of the arts.

medicine science of preventing, diagnosing, alleviating, or curing disease, both physical and mental;

also any substance used in the treatment of disease. The basis of medicine is anatomy (the structure and form of the body) and physiology (the study of the body's functions).

medicine, alternative forms of medical treatment that do not use synthetic drugs or surgery in response to the symptoms of a disease, but aim to treat the patient as a whole (▷holism). The emphasis is on maintaining health (with diet and exercise) and on dealing with the underlying causes rather than just the symptoms of illness. It may involve the use of herbal remedies and techniques like ▷acupuncture, ▷homeopathy, and ▷chiropractic. Some alternative treatments are increasingly accepted by orthodox medicine, but the absence of enforceable standards in some fields has led to the proliferation of eccentric or untrained practitioners.

medieval art painting and sculpture of the Middle Ages in Europe and parts of the Middle East, dating roughly from the 4th century to the emergence of the Renaissance in Italy in the 1400s. This includes early Christian, Byzantine, Celtic, Anglo-Saxon, and Carolingian art. The Romanesque style was the first truly international style of medieval times, superseded by Gothic in the late 12th century. Religious sculpture, frescoes, and manuscript illumination proliferated; panel painting came only towards the end of the period.

Medina (Arabic *Madinah*) Saudi Arabian city, about 355 km/220 mi N of Mecca; population (1974) 198,000. It is the second holiest city in the Islamic world, and is believed to contain the tomb of Muhammad. It produces grain and fruit.

meditation act of spiritual contemplation, practised by members of many religions or as a secular exercise. It is a central practice in Buddhism. The Sanskrit term is *dhyāna*. See also ▷transcendental meditation (TM).

Mediterranean Sea inland sea separating Europe from N Africa, with Asia to the E; extreme length 3,700 km/2,300 mi; area 2,966,000 sq km/1,145,000 sq mi. It is linked to the Atlantic (at the Strait of Gibraltar), Red Sea, and Indian Ocean (by the Suez Canal), Black Sea (at the Dardanelles and Sea of Marmara). The main subdivisions are the Adriatic, Aegean, Ionian, and Tyrrhenian seas. It is highly polluted.

medlar small shrub or tree *Mespilus germanica* of the rose family Rosaceae. Native to SE Europe, it is widely cultivated for its fruit, resembling a small brown-green pear or quince. These are palatable when decay has set in.

Medusa in Greek mythology, a mortal woman who was transformed into a ▷Gorgon. Medusa was slain by Perseus; the winged horse ▷Pegasus was supposed to have sprung from her blood.

megabyte (Mb) in computing, a unit of memory equal to 1,024 ▷kilobytes. It is sometimes used, less precisely, to mean 1 million bytes.

megalith prehistoric stone monument of the

medicine: chronology

c. 400 BC	Hippocrates recognized that disease had natural causes.
c. AD 200	Galen, the authority of the Middle Ages, consolidated the work of the Alexandrian doctors.
1543	Andreas Versalius gave the first accurate account of the human body.
1628	William Harvey discovered the circulation of the blood.
1768	John Hunter began the foundation of experimental and surgical pathology.
1785	Digitalis was used to treat heart disease; the active ingredient was isolated 1904.
1798	Edward Jenner published his work on vaccination.
1882	Robert Koch isolated the tuberculosis bacillus.
1884	Edwin Klebs, German pathologist, isolated the diptheria bacillus.
1885	Louis Pasteur produced the rabies vaccine.
1890	Joseph Lister demonstrated antiseptic surgery.
1897	Martinus Beijerinck, Dutch botanist, discovered viruses.
1899	German doctor Felix Hoffman developed aspirin; Sigmund Freud founded psychoanalysis.
1910	Paul Ehrlich synthesized the first specific bacterial agent, salvarsan (cure for syphilis).
1922	Insulin was first used to treat diabetes.
1928	Alexander Fleming discovered the antibiotic penicillin.
1930s	Electro-convulsive therapy (ECT) was developed.
1932	Gerhard Domagk, German bacteriologist and pathologist, began work on the sulphonamide drugs, a kind of antibiotic.
1940s	Lithium treatment for depression was developed.
1950s	Major development of antidepressant drugs and beta blockers for heart disease; Medawar's work on the immune system.
1950–75	Manipulation of the molecules of synthetic chemicals, the main source of new drugs.
1953	Vaccine for polio developed by Jonas Salk.
1960s	Heart-transplant surgery began with the work of Christiaan Barnard; new generation of minor tranquillizers called benzodiazepenes developed.
1971	Viroids, disease-causing organisms smaller than viruses, were isolated outside the living body.
1975	Nuclear medicine, for example positron-emission tomography (Hounsfield), came into use.
1978	Birth of the first 'test-tube baby', Louise Brown, in England.
1980s	AIDS (acquired immune-deficiency syndrome) first recognized in the USA; recognition of the discovery of the transposable gene by Barbara McClintock, US geneticist.
1980	Smallpox eradicated by the World Health Organization.
1984	Vaccine for leprosy developed; discovery of the human immuno-deficiency virus (HIV), responsible for AIDS, at the Institut Pasteur in Paris and in the USA.
1987	World's longest-surviving heart-transplant patient died in France, 18 years after his operation.
1989	Patient with Parkinson's disease first treated by graft of fetal brain tissue.

late Neolithic or early Bronze Age. Most common in Europe, megaliths include single, large uprights (*menhirs*, for example, the Five Kings, Northumberland, England); *rows* (for example, Carnac, Brittany, France); *circles*, generally with a central 'altar stone' (for example, Stonehenge, Wiltshire, England); and the remains of burial chambers with the covering earth removed, looking like a hut (*dolmens*, for example Kits Coty, Kent, England).

Meghalaya state of NE India; *area* 22,500 sq km/8,685 sq mi; *capital* Shillong; *features* mainly agricultural and comprises tribal hill districts; *products* potatoes, cotton, jute, fruit; *minerals* coal, limestone, white clay, corundum, sillimanite; *population* (1991) 1,760,600, mainly Khasi, Jaintia, and Garo; *religion* Hindu 70%; *languages* various.

Mehemet Ali 1769–1849. Pasha (governor) of Egypt from 1805, and founder of the dynasty that ruled until 1953. An Albanian in the Ottoman service, he had originally been sent to Egypt to fight the French. As pasha, he established a European-style army and navy, fought his Turkish overlord 1831 and 1839, and conquered Sudan.

Meiji Mutsuhito 1852–1912. Emperor of Japan from 1867, when he took the title *meiji tennō* ('enlightened sovereign'). During his reign Japan became a world industrial and naval power. He abolished the feudal system and discrimination against the lowest caste, established state schools, and introduced conscription, the Western calendar, and other measures in an attempt to modernize Japan, including a constitution 1889.

meiosis in biology, a process of cell division in which the number of ◊chromosomes in the cell is halved. It only occurs in ◊eukaryotic cells, and is part of a life cycle that involves sexual reproduction because it allows the genes of two parents to be combined without the total number of chromosomes increasing.

Meir Golda 1898–1978. Israeli Labour (*Mapai*) politician. Born in Russia, she emigrated to the USA 1906, and in 1921 went to Palestine. She was foreign minister 1956–66 and prime minister 1969–74. Criticism of the Israelis' lack of preparation for the 1973 Arab-Israeli War led to election losses for Labour and, unable to form a government, she resigned.

Meistersinger one of a group of German lyric

poets, singers, and musicians of the 14th–16th centuries, who formed guilds for the revival of minstrelsy. Hans Sachs was a Meistersinger, and Richard Wagner's opera, *Die Meistersinger von Nürnberg* 1868, depicts the tradition.

Mekele capital of Tigray region, N Ethiopia; population (1984) 62,000. It trades in salt, incense, and resin.

Mekong river rising as the Za Qu in Tibet and flowing to the South China Sea, through a vast delta (about 200,000 sq km/77,000 sq mi); length 4,425 km/2,750 mi. It is being developed for irrigation and hydroelectricity by Cambodia, Laos, Thailand, and Vietnam.

Melaka Malaysian form of ⇩Malacca, state of Peninsular Malaysia.

Melanesia islands in the SW Pacific between Micronesia to the N and Polynesia to the E, embracing all the islands from the New Britain archipelago to Fiji.

melanoma mole or growth containing the dark pigment melanin. Malignant melanoma is a type of skin cancer developing in association with a pre-existing mole. Unlike other skin cancers, it is associated with brief but excessive exposure to sunlight.

Melba Nellie, adopted name of Helen Porter Mitchell 1861–1931. Australian soprano. One of her finest roles was Donizetti's *Lucia*. *Peach melba* (half a peach plus vanilla ice cream and melba sauce, made from sweetened, fresh raspberries) and *melba toast* (crisp, thin toast) are named after her.

Melbourne capital of Victoria, Australia, near the mouth of the river Yarra; population (1990) 3,080,000. It is the second largest city in Australia. Founded 1835, it grew in the wake of the gold rushes and was the seat of the Commonwealth government 1901–27. Industries include engineering, shipbuilding, electronics, chemicals, food processing, clothing, and textiles.

melodrama play or film with romantic and sensational plot elements, often unsubtly acted. The early melodramas used extravagant theatrical effects to heighten violent emotions and actions artificially. By the end of the 19th century, melodrama had become a popular genre of stage play. Beginning with the early work of ⇩Goethe and ⇩Schiller, melodrama was popularized in France by Pixérécourt, and first introduced to England in an unauthorized translation by Thomas Holcroft as *A Tale of Mystery* 1802. Melodramas were frequently played against a Gothic background of mountains or ruined castles.

melody in music, a distinctive sequence of notes. A melody may be a tune in its own right, or it may form a theme running through a longer piece of music.

melon any of several large, juicy, thick-skinned fruits of trailing plants of the gourd family

Cucurbitaceae. The muskmelon *Cucumis melo* and the large red watermelon *Citrullus vulgaris* are two of the many edible varieties.

meltdown melting of the core of a nuclear reactor, due to overheating. To prevent such accidents all reactors have equipment intended to flood the core with water in an emergency. The reactor is housed in a strong containment vessel, designed to prevent radiation escaping into the atmosphere. The result of a meltdown is an area radioactively contaminated for 25,000 years or more.

melting point temperature at which a substance melts, or changes from a solid to liquid form. A pure substance under standard conditions of pressure (usually one atmosphere) has a definite melting point. If heat is supplied to a solid at its melting point, the temperature does not change until the melting process is complete. The melting point of ice is 0°C/32°F.

Melville Herman 1819–1891. US writer whose *Moby-Dick* 1851 was inspired by his whaling experiences in the South Seas. These experiences were also the basis for earlier fiction, such as *Typee* 1846 and *Omoo* 1847. *Billy Budd* was completed just before his death and published 1924. Although most of his works were unappreciated during his lifetime, today he is one of the most highly regarded of US authors.

membrane in living things, a continuous layer, made up principally of fat molecules, that encloses a ⇩cell or ⇩organelles within a cell. Certain small molecules can pass through the cell membrane, but most must enter or leave the cell via channels in the membrane made up of special proteins.

memory in computing, the part of a system used to store data and programs either permanently or temporarily. There are two main types: immediate access memory and backing storage. Memory capacity is measured in ⇩bytes or, more conveniently, in kilobytes (units of 1,024 bytes) or megabytes (units of 1,024 kilobytes).

memory ability to store and recall observations and sensations. Memory does not seem to be based in any particular part of the brain; it may depend on changes to the pathways followed by nerve impulses as they move through the brain. Memory can be improved by regular use as the connections between ⇩nerve cells (neurons) become 'well-worn paths' in the brain. Events stored in *short-term memory* are forgotten quickly, whereas those in *long-term memory* can last for many years, enabling recall of information and recognition of people and places over long periods of time. Research is just beginning to uncover the biochemical and electrical bases of the human memory.

Memphis ruined city beside the Nile, 19 km/ 12 mi S of Cairo, Egypt. Once the centre of the worship of Ptah, it was the earliest capital of a united Egypt under King Menes about 3200 BC, but was superseded by Thebes under the new empire 1570 BC.

Memphis industrial port city (pharmaceuticals, food processing, cotton, timber, tobacco) on the Mississippi River, in Tennessee, USA; population (1990) 610,300. Its musical history includes Beale Street, home of the blues composer W C Handy, and Graceland, the home of Elvis Presley. The French built a fort here 1739, but Memphis was not founded until 1819.

Mendel Gregor Johann 1822–1884. Austrian biologist, founder of ▷genetics. His experiments with successive generations of peas gave the basis for his theory of particulate inheritance rather than blending, involving dominant and recessive characters. His results, published 1865–69, remained unrecognized until the early 20th century.

mendelevium synthesized, radioactive metallic element of the ▷actinide series, symbol Md, atomic number 101, relative atomic mass 258. It was first produced by bombardment of Es-253 with helium nuclei. Its longest-lived isotope, Md-258, has a half-life of about two months. The element is chemically similar to thulium.

Mendeleyev Dmitri Ivanovich 1834–1907. Russian chemist who framed the periodic law in chemistry 1869, which states that the chemical properties of the elements depend on their relative atomic masses. This law is the basis of the ▷periodic table of elements, in which the elements are arranged by atomic number and organized by their related groups.

Mendelism in genetics, the theory of inheritance originally outlined by Gregor Mendel. He suggested that, in sexually reproducing species, all 'characteristics are inherited through indivisible factors' (now identified with ▷genes) contributed by each parent to its offspring.

Mendelssohn (-Bartholdy) (Jakob Ludwig) Felix 1809–1847. German composer, also a pianist and conductor. As a child he composed and performed with his own orchestra and as an adult was helpful to ▷Schumann's career. Among his best-known works are *A Midsummer Night's Dream* 1827; the *Fingal's Cave* overture 1832; and five symphonies, which include the Reformation 1830, the Italian 1833, and the Scottish 1842. He was instrumental in promoting the revival of interest in J S Bach's music.

Menem Carlos (Saul) 1935– . Argentine politician, president from 1989; leader of the Peronist (Justicialist Party) movement. As president, he improved relations with the UK.

Mengistu Haile Mariam 1937– . Ethiopian soldier and socialist politician, head of state 1977–91 (president 1987–91). He seized power in a coup and was confronted with severe problems of drought and secessionist uprisings, but survived with help

from the USSR and the West until he was violently overthrown.

meningitis inflammation of the meninges (membranes) surrounding the brain, caused by bacterial or viral infection. Bacterial meningitis, though treatable by antibiotics, is the more serious threat. Diagnosis is by ▷lumbar puncture.

menopause in women, the cessation of reproductive ability, characterized by menstruation (see ▷menstrual cycle) becoming irregular and eventually ceasing. The onset is at about the age of 50, but varies greatly. Menopause is usually uneventful, but some women suffer from complications such as flushing, excessive bleeding, and nervous disorders. Since the 1950s, ▷hormone replacement therapy (HRT), using ▷oestrogen alone or with ▷progesterone, has been developed to counteract such effects.

Menshevik member of the minority of the Russian Social Democratic Party, who split from the ▷Bolsheviks 1903. The Mensheviks believed in a large, loosely organized party and that, before socialist revolution could occur in Russia, capitalist society had to develop further. During the Russian Revolution they had limited power and set up a government in Georgia, but were suppressed 1922.

menstrual cycle cycle that occurs in female mammals of reproductive age, in which the body is prepared for pregnancy. At the beginning of the cycle, a Graafian (egg) follicle develops in the ovary, and the inner wall of the uterus forms a soft spongy lining. The egg is released from the ovary, and the lining of the uterus becomes vascularized (filled with blood vessels). If fertilization does not occur, the corpus luteum (remains of the Graafian follicle) degenerates, and the uterine lining breaks down, and is shed. This is what causes the loss of blood that marks menstruation. The cycle then begins again. Human menstruation takes place from puberty to menopause, occurring about every 28 days.

mental handicap impairment of intelligence. It can be very mild, but in more severe cases, it is associated with social problems and difficulties in living independently. A person may be born with a mental handicap (for example, ▷Down's syndrome) or may acquire it through brain damage. There are between 90 and 130 million people in the world suffering such disabilities.

mental illness abnormal working of the mind. Since normal working cannot easily be defined, the borderline between mild mental illness and normality is a matter of opinion (not to be confused with normative behaviour). Mild forms are known as *neuroses*, affecting the emotions, whereas more severe forms, *psychoses*, distort conscious reasoning.

menu in computing, a list of options, displayed on screen, from which the user may make a choice –

for example, the choice of services offered to the customer by a bank cash dispenser: withdrawal, deposit, balance, or statement. Menus are used extensively in graphical user-interface (GUI) systems, where the menu options are often selected using a pointing device called a ⟡mouse.

Menuhin Yehudi 1916– . US-born violinist and conductor. A child prodigy, he achieved great depth of interpretation, and was often accompanied on the piano by his sister *Hephzibah* (1921–1981). He made his debut with an orchestra at the age of 11 in New York but moved to London 1959 and became a British subject 1985. He conducted his own chamber orchestra and founded schools in Surrey, England, and Gstaad, Switzerland, for training young musicians.

Mercator Gerardus 1512–1594. Latinized form of the name of the Flemish map-maker Gerhard Kremer. He devised the first modern atlas, showing *Mercator's projection* in which the parallels and meridians on maps are drawn uniformly at 90°. It is often used for navigational charts, because compass courses can be drawn as straight lines, but the true area of countries is increasingly distorted the further north or south they are from the equator.

mercenary soldier hired by the army of another country or by a private army. Mercenary military service originated in the 14th century, when cash payment on a regular basis was the only means of guaranteeing soldiers' loyalty. In the 20th century mercenaries have been common in wars and guerrilla activity in Asia, Africa, and Latin America.

merchant bank financial institution that specializes in the provision of corporate finance and financial and advisory services for business. Originally developed in the UK in the 19th century, merchant banks now offer many of the services provided by the commercial banks.

merchant navy the passenger and cargo ships of a country. Most are owned by private companies. To avoid strict regulations on safety, union rules on crew wages, and so on, many ships are today registered under 'flags of convenience', that is, flags of countries that do not have such rules.

Mercia Anglo-Saxon kingdom that emerged in the 6th century. By the late 8th century it dominated all England S of the Humber, but from about 825 came under the power of ⟡Wessex. Mercia eventually came to denote an area bounded by the Welsh border, the river Humber, East Anglia, and the river Thames.

mercury or *quicksilver* heavy, silver-grey, metallic element, symbol Hg (from Latin *hydrargyrum*), atomic number 80, relative atomic mass 200.59. It is a dense, mobile liquid with a low melting point (–38.87°C/–37.96°F). Its chief source is the mineral cinnabar, HgS, but it sometimes occurs in nature as a free metal.

Mercury Roman god, identified with the Greek

Hermes, and like him represented with winged sandals and a winged staff entwined with snakes. He was the messenger of the gods.

Mercury in astronomy, the closest planet to the Sun, at an average distance of 58 million km/36 million mi. Its diameter is 4,880 km/3,030 mi, its mass 0.056 that of Earth. Mercury orbits the Sun every 88 days, and spins on its axis every 59 days. On its sunward side the surface temperature reaches over 400°C/752°F, but on the 'night' side it falls to –170°C/–274°F. Mercury has an atmosphere with minute traces of argon and helium. In 1974 the US space probe *Mariner 10* discovered that its surface is cratered by meteorite impacts. Mercury has no moons.

merganser any of several diving ducks of the family Mergus with long, serrated bills for catching fish, including the common merganser or goosander *M. merganser* and the red-breasted merganser *M. serrator*. They are widely distributed in the northern hemisphere; most have crested heads.

merger the linking of two or more companies, either by creating a new organization by consolidating the original companies or by absorption by one company of the others. Unlike a takeover, which is not always a voluntary fusion of the parties, a merger is the result of an agreement.

Mérida capital of Yucatán state, Mexico, a centre of the sisal industry; population (1986) 580,000. It was founded 1542, and has a cathedral 1598. Its port on the Gulf of Mexico is Progreso.

meridian half a great circle drawn on the Earth's surface passing through both poles and thus through all places with the same longitude. Terrestrial longitudes are usually measured from the Greenwich Meridian.

merlin small ⟡falcon *Falco columbarius* of Eurasia and North America, where it is also called *pigeon hawk*. The male, 26 cm/10 in long, has a grey-blue back and reddish-brown barred front; the female, 32 cm/13 in long, is brown with streaks.

mermaid mythical sea creature (the male is a *merman*), having a human head and torso and a fish's tail. The dugong and seal are among suggested origins for the idea.

Merovingian dynasty Frankish dynasty, named after its founder, *Merovech* (5th century AD). His descendants ruled France from the time of Clovis (481–511) to 751.

Mersey river in NW England; length 112 km/70 mi. Formed by the confluence of the Goyt and Etherow rivers, it flows W to join the Irish Sea at Liverpool Bay. It is linked to the Manchester Ship Canal. It is polluted by industrial waste, sewage, and chemicals.

Merseyside former (1974–86) metropolitan county of NW England, replaced by a residuary body 1986 which covers some of its former functions; **area** 650 sq km/251 sq mi; **towns** Liverpool (administrative headquarters), Bootle, Birkenhead, St Helens, Wallasey, Southport; **features** river Mersey; Merseyside Innovation Centre (MIC), linked with Liverpool University and Polytechnic; Prescot Museum of clock and watch making; Speke Hall (Tudor), and Croxteth Hall and Country Park (a working country estate open to the public); **products** chemicals, electrical goods, vehicles; **population** (1991) 1,376,800; **famous people** the Beatles, William Ewart Gladstone, George Stubbs.

mescaline psychedelic drug derived from a small, spineless cactus *Lophophora williamsii* of N Mexico and the SW USA, known as ⟡peyote. The tops (called mescal buttons), which scarcely appear above ground, are dried and chewed, or added to alcoholic drinks. Mescaline is a crystalline alkaloid $C_{11}H_{17}NO_3$. It is used by some North American Indians in religious rites.

Mesolithic the Middle Stone Age developmental stage of human technology and of ⟡prehistory.

meson in physics, an unstable subatomic particle made up of two indivisible elementary particles called quarks. It has a mass intermediate between that of the electron and that of the proton, is found in cosmic radiation, and is emitted by nuclei under bombardment by very high-energy particles.

Mesopotamia land between the Tigris and Euphrates rivers, now part of Iraq. Here the civilizations of Sumer and Babylon flourished. Sumer (3500 BC) may have been the earliest civilization.

Mesozoic era of geological time 248–65 million years ago, consisting of the Triassic, Jurassic, and Cretaceous periods. At the beginning of the era, the continents were joined together as Pangaea; dinosaurs and other giant reptiles dominated the sea and air; and ferns, horsetails, and cycads thrived in a warm climate worldwide. By the end of the Mesozoic era, the continents had begun to assume their present positions, flowering plants were dominant, and many of the large reptiles and marine fauna were becoming extinct.

Messiaen Olivier 1908–1992. French composer and organist. His music is mystical in character, vividly coloured, and incorporates transcriptions of birdsong. Among his works are the *Quartet for the End of Time* 1941, the large-scale *Turangalîla Symphony* 1949, and solo organ and piano pieces.

Messina, Strait of channel in the central Mediterranean separating Sicily from mainland Italy; in Greek legend a monster (Charybdis), who devoured ships, lived in the whirlpool on the Sicilian side, and another (Scylla), who devoured sailors, in the rock on the Italian side. The classical hero Odysseus passed safely between them.

metabolism the chemical processes of living organisms: a constant alternation of building up (**anabolism**) and breaking down (**catabolism**). For example, green plants build up complex organic substances from water, carbon dioxide, and mineral salts (photosynthesis); by digestion animals partially break down complex organic substances, ingested as food, and subsequently resynthesize them in their own bodies.

metal any of a class of chemical elements with certain chemical characteristics (⟡metallic character) and physical properties: they are good conductors of heat and electricity; opaque but reflect light well; malleable, which enables them to be cold-worked and rolled into sheets; and ductile, which permits them to be drawn into thin wires.

The following are widely used in commerce: **precious metals**: gold, silver, mercury, and platinum, used principally in jewellery; **heavy metals**: iron, copper, zinc, tin, and lead, the common metals of engineering; **rarer heavy metals**: nickel, cadmium, chromium, tungsten, molybdenum, manganese, cobalt, vanadium, antimony, and bismuth, used principally for alloying with the heavy metals; **light metals**: aluminium and magnesium; **alkali metals**: sodium, potassium, and lithium; and **alkaline-earth metals**: calcium, barium, and strontium, used principally for chemical purposes.

metallic character chemical properties associated with those elements classed as metals. These properties, which arise from the element's ability to lose electrons, are: the displacement of hydrogen from dilute acids; the formation of basic oxides; the formation of ionic chlorides; and their reducing reaction, as in the thermite process (see ⟡reduction).

metalloid or **semimetal** any chemical element having some of but not all the properties of metals; metalloids are thus usually electrically semiconducting. They comprise the elements germanium, arsenic, antimony, and tellurium.

metallurgy science and technology of producing metals, which includes extraction, alloying, and hardening. Extractive or **process metallurgy** is concerned with the extraction of metals from their ⟡ores and refining and adapting them for use. **Physical metallurgy** is concerned with their properties and application. **Metallography** establishes the microscopic structures that contribute to hardness, ductility, and strength.

metamorphic rock rock altered in structure and composition by pressure, heat, or chemically active fluids after original formation. (If heat is sufficient to melt the original rock, technically it becomes an igneous rock upon cooling.)

metamorphosis period during the life cycle of many invertebrates, most amphibians, and some fish, during which the individual's body changes from one form to another through a major reconstitution of its tissues. For example, adult frogs are produced by metamorphosis from tadpoles, and butterflies are produced from caterpillars following metamorphosis within a pupa.

In classical thought and literature, metamorphosis is the transformation of a living being into another shape, either living or inanimate. The Roman poet ♢Ovid wrote about this theme.

metaphysical poet member of a group of 17th-century English poets whose work is characterized by conciseness; ingenious, often highly intricate wordplay; and striking imagery. Among the exponents of this genre are John ♢Donne and George ♢Herbert

metaphysics branch of philosophy that deals with first principles, in particular 'being' (ontology) and 'knowing' (♢epistemology), and that is concerned with the ultimate nature of reality. It has been maintained that no certain knowledge of metaphysical questions is possible.

meteor flash of light in the sky, popularly known as a *shooting* or *falling star*, caused by a particle of dust, a *meteoroid*, entering the atmosphere at speeds up to 70 kps/45 mps and burning up by friction at a height of around 100 km/60 mi. On any clear night, several *sporadic meteors* can be seen each hour.

meteorite piece of rock or metal from space that reaches the surface of the Earth, Moon, or other body. Most meteorites are thought to be fragments from asteroids, although some may be pieces from the heads of comets. Most are stony, although some are made of iron and a few have a mixed rock-iron composition. Thousands of meteorites hit the Earth each year, but most fall in the sea or in remote areas and are never recovered.

meteorology scientific observation and study of the ♢atmosphere, so that weather can be accurately forecast. Data from meteorological stations and weather satellites are collated by computer at central agencies such as the Meteorological Office in Bracknell, near London, and forecast and weather maps based on current readings are issued at regular intervals. Modern analysis can give useful forecasts for up to six days ahead.

methane CH_4 the simplest hydrocarbon of the paraffin series. Colourless, odourless, and lighter than air, it burns with a bluish flame and explodes when mixed with air or oxygen. It is the chief constituent of natural gas and also occurs in the explosive firedamp of coal mines. Methane emitted by rotting vegetation forms marsh gas, which may ignite by spontaneous combustion to produce the pale flame seen over marshland and known as will-o'-the-wisp.

methanol (common name *methyl alcohol*) CH_3OH the simplest of the alcohols. It can be made by the dry distillation of wood (hence it is also known as wood alcohol), but is usually made from coal or natural gas. When pure, it is a colourless, flammable liquid with a pleasant odour, and is highly poisonous.

Methodism evangelical Protestant Christian movement that was founded by John ♢Wesley 1739 within the Church of England, but became a separate body 1795. The Methodist Episcopal Church was founded in the USA 1784. There are over 50 million Methodists worldwide.

Methodist doctrines are contained in Wesley's sermons and *Notes on the New Testament*. A series of doctrinal divisions in the early 19th century were reconciled by a conference in London 1932 that brought Wesleyan methodists, primitive methodists, and United methodists into the Methodist Church. The church government is presbyterian in Britain and episcopal in the USA. Supreme authority is vested in the annual conference (50% ministers, 50% lay people; members are grouped under 'class leaders' and churches into 'circuits'.

methylated spirit alcohol that has been rendered undrinkable, and is used for industrial purposes, as a fuel for spirit burners or as a solvent.

metre SI unit (symbol m) of length, equivalent to 1.093 yards. It is defined by scientists as the length of the path travelled by light in a vacuum during a time interval of 1/299,792,458 of a second.

metre in poetry, the rhythm determined by the number and type of feet (units of stressed and unstressed syllables) in a line. See also ♢verse.

metre in music, accentuation pattern characteristic of a musical line; the regularity underlying musical rhythm.

metric system system of weights and measures developed in France in the 18th century and recognized by other countries in the 19th century. In 1960 an international conference on weights and measures recommended the universal adoption of a revised International System (Système International d'Unités, or SI), with seven prescribed 'base units': the metre (m) for length, kilogram (kg) for mass, second (s) for time, ampere (A) for electric current, kelvin (K) for thermodynamic temperature, candela (cd) for luminous intensity, and mole (mol) for quantity of matter. The UK government agreed to the adoption of SI as the primary system of weights and measures 1965, but compulsion was abandoned 1978.

metropolitan county in England, a group of six counties (1974–86) established under the Local Government Act 1972 in the largest urban areas outside London: Tyne and Wear, South Yorkshire, Merseyside, West Midlands, Greater Manchester, and West Yorkshire. Their elected assemblies were abolished 1986 when their areas of responsibility reverted to district councils.

Metternich Klemens (Wenzel Lothar), Prince von Metternich 1773–1859. Austrian politician, the leading figure in European diplomacy after the fall of Napoleon. As foreign minister 1809–48 (as well as chancellor from 1821), he tried to maintain the

USA

ATLANTIC OCEAN

MEXICO

Mexico City

Cuba

Belize

CARIBBEAN SEA

Guatemala

PACIFIC OCEAN

0 miles 500
0 km 1000

balance of power in Europe, supporting monarchy and repressing liberalism.

Mexican War war between the USA and Mexico 1846–48, begun in territory disputed between Texas (annexed by the USA 1845 but claimed by Mexico) and Mexico. It began when General Zachary Taylor invaded New Mexico after efforts to purchase what are now California and New Mexico failed. Mexico City was taken 1847, and under the Treaty of Guadaloupe Hidalgo that ended the war, the USA acquired New Mexico and California, as well as clear title to Texas in exchange for $15 million.

Mexico United States of; country in Central America, bordered N by the USA, E by the Gulf of Mexico, SE by Belize and Guatemala, and SW and W by the Pacific Ocean; *area* 1,958,201 sq km/756,198 sq mi; *capital* Mexico City; *physical* partly arid central highlands; Sierra Madre mountain ranges E and W; tropical coastal plains; *head of state and government* Carlos Salinas de Gortari from 1988; *political system* federal democratic republic; *exports* silver, gold, lead, uranium, oil, natural gas, handicrafts, fish, shellfish, fruits and vegetables, cotton, machinery; *population* (1990 est) 88,335,000 (mixed descent 60%, Indian 30%, Spanish descent 10%; 50% under 20 years of age); *languages* Spanish (official) 92%; Nahuatl, Maya, Mixtec; *recent history* independence achieved from Spain 1821. Territory was lost in wars with the USA 1846–48. In 1917 a new constitution was introduced, designed to establish permanent democracy. Financial crisis 1983–84; IMF loan agreement signed 1986 to keep country solvent at least until 1988. In 1988 debt reduction accords were negotiated with the USA. In 1991 President Salinas promised constitutional reforms.

Mexico City (Spanish *Ciudad de México*) capital, industrial (iron, steel, chemicals, textiles), and cultural centre of Mexico, 2,255 m/7,400 ft above sea level on the S edge of the central plateau; population (1986) 18,748,000. It is thought to be one of the world's most polluted cities because of its position in a volcanic basin 2,000 m/7,400 ft above sea level. Pollutants gather in the basin causing a smog cloud.

mezuza in Judaism, a small box containing a parchment scroll inscribed with a prayer, the Shema from Deuteronomy 6:4–9; 11:13–21, which is found on the doorpost of every home and every room in a Jewish house, except the bathroom.

mezzo-soprano female singing voice halfway between soprano and contralto.

mezzotint print produced by a method of etching in density of tone rather than line, popular in the 18th and 19th centuries. A copper or steel plate is worked with a tool that raises a burr (rough edge), which will hold ink. The burr is then scraped away to produce a range of lighter tones.

Miami industrial city (food processing, transportation and electronic equipment, clothing, and machinery) and port in Florida, USA; population (1990) 358,500. It is the hub of finance, trade, and air transport for the USA, Latin America, and the Caribbean. There has been an influx of immigrants from Cuba, Haiti, Mexico, and South America since 1959.

mica group of silicate minerals that split easily into thin flakes along lines of weakness in their crystal structure (perfect basal cleavage). They are glossy, have a pearly lustre, and are found in many igneous and metamorphic rocks. Their good thermal and electrical insulation qualities make them valuable in industry.

Michael in the Old Testament, an archangel, referred to as the guardian angel of Israel. In the New Testament Book of Revelation he leads the hosts of heaven to battle against Satan. In paintings, he is depicted with a flaming sword and sometimes a pair of scales. Feast day 29 Sept (Michaelmas).

Michael 1921– . King of Romania 1927–30 and 1940–47. The son of Carol II, he succeeded his grandfather as king 1927 but was displaced when his father returned from exile 1930. In 1940 he was proclaimed king again on his father's abdication, overthrew 1944 the fascist dictatorship of Ion Antonescu (1882–1946), and enabled Romania to share in the victory of the Allies at the end of World War II. He abdicated and left Romania 1947.

Michelangelo Buonarroti 1475–1564. Italian sculptor, painter, architect, and poet, active in his native Florence and in Rome. His giant talent dominated the High Renaissance. In 1496 he completed the *Pietà* (St Peter's, Rome), a technically brilliant sculpture that established his reputation. Also in Rome he began the great tomb of Pope Julius II. The marble *David* 1501–04 (Accademia, Florence) set a new standard in nude sculpture. His massive figure style was translated into fresco in the Sistine

Chapel 1508–12 and 1536–41 (Vatican). Other works in Rome include the dome of St Peter's basilica.

Michelson Albert Abraham 1852–1931. German-born US physicist. In conjunction with Edward Morley, he performed the **Michelson–Morley experiment** 1887 to detect the motion of the Earth through the postulated ether (a medium believed to be necessary for the propagation of light). The failure of the experiment indicated the nonexistence of the ether, and led ▷Einstein to his theory of ▷relativity. Michelson was the first American to be awarded a Nobel prize, 1907.

Michigan state in N central US; nickname Wolverine State/Great Lake State; *area* 151,600 sq km/58,518 sq mi; *capital* Lansing; *cities* Detroit, Grand Rapids, Flint; *features* Great Lakes: Superior, Michigan, Huron, Erie; Porcupine Mountains; Muskegon, Grand, St Joseph, and Kalamazoo rivers; over 50% forested; Isle Royale National Park; Pictured Rocks and Sleeping Bear national seashores; Henry Ford Museum and Greenfield Village, Dearborn; *products* motor vehicles and equipment; nonelectrical machinery; iron and steel; chemicals; pharmaceuticals; dairy products; *population* (1990) 9,295,300; *famous people* Edna Ferber, Gerald Ford, Henry Ford, Jimmy Hoffa, Iggy Pop, Diana Ross; *history* temporary posts established in early 17th century by French explorers Brulé, Marquette, Joliet, and La Salle; first settled 1668 at Sault Sainte Marie; present-day Detroit settled 1701; passed to the British 1763 and to the USA 1796; statehood 1837.

Michigan, Lake lake in N central USA, one of the Great Lakes; area 58,000 sq km/22,390 sq mi. Chicago and Milwaukee are its main ports.

microbiology study of organisms that can only be seen under the microscope, mostly viruses and single-celled organisms such as bacteria, protozoa, and yeasts. The practical applications of microbiology are in medicine (since many microorganisms cause disease); in brewing, baking, and other food and beverage processes, where the microorganisms carry out fermentation; and in genetic engineering, which is creating increasing interest in the field of microbiology.

microchip popular name for the silicon chip, or ▷integrated circuit.

microcomputer or *micro* or *personal computer* small desktop or portable computer, typically designed to be used by one person at a time, although individual computers can be linked in a network so that users can share data and programs. Its central processing unit is a ▷microprocessor, contained on a single integrated circuit.

microeconomics division of economics concerned with the study of individual decision-making units within an economy: a consumer, firm, or industry. Unlike macroeconomics, it looks at how individual markets work and how individual producers and consumers make their choices and with what consequences. This is done by analysing how relevant prices of goods are determined and the quantities that will be bought and sold.

microform generic name for media on which text or images are photographically reduced. The main examples are *microfilm* (similar to the film in an ordinary camera) and *microfiche* (flat sheets of film, generally 105 mm/4 in × 148 mm/6 in, holding the equivalent of 420 A4 sheets). Microform has the advantage of low reproduction and storage costs, but it requires special devices for reading the text. It is widely used for archiving and for storing large volumes of text, such as library catalogues.

microlight aircraft very light aircraft with a small engine, rather like a powered hang-glider.

micrometre one-millionth of a ▷metre (symbol μm).

microminiaturization reduction in size and weight of electronic components. The first size reduction in electronics was brought about by the introduction of the ▷transistor. Further reductions were achieved with ▷integrated circuits and the ▷silicon chip.

Micronesia group of islands in the Pacific Ocean lying N of ▷Melanesia, including the Federated States of Micronesia, Belau, Kiribati, the Mariana and Marshall Islands, Nauru, and Tuvalu.

Micronesia, Federated States of island group in the W Pacific comprising four constituent states – Kosrae, Pohnpei, Chuuk (formerly Truk), and Yap; capital Kolonia, on Pohnpei; area 700 sq km/270 sq mi; population (1988) 86,000. Federal authority resides with an executive president. Its people are Micronesian and Polynesian, and the main languages are Kosrean, Ponapean, Trukese, and Yapese, although the official language is English. Purchased by Germany from Spain 1898, the islands were occupied 1914 by Japan. They were captured by the USA in World War II, and part of the US Trust Territory of the Pacific 1947–90. Micronesia became internally self-governing from 1979, and in free association with the USA from 1986. Although independent from 1990 the USA controls its defence and foreign relations. Micronesia became a member of the United Nations 1991.

microorganism or *microbe* living organism invisible to the naked eye but visible under a microscope. Microorganisms include viruses and single-celled organisms such as bacteria, protozoa, yeasts, and some algae. The term has no taxonomic significance in biology. The study of microorganisms is known as microbiology.

microphone primary component in a sound-reproducing system, whereby the mechanical energy of sound waves is converted into electrical signals by means of a ◊transducer. One of the simplest is the telephone receiver mouthpiece, invented by Alexander Graham Bell 1876; other types of microphone are used with broadcasting and sound-film apparatus.

microprocessor complete computer ◊central processing unit contained on a single ◊integrated circuit, or chip. The appearance of the first microprocessors 1971 heralded the introduction of the microcomputer. The microprocessor has led to a dramatic fall in the size and cost of computers, and ◊dedicated computers can now be found in washing machines, cars, and so on.

microscope instrument for magnification with high resolution for detail. Optical and electron microscopes are the ones chiefly in use; other types include acoustic and X-ray. In 1988 a scanning tunnelling microscope was used to photograph a single protein molecule for the first time. Laser microscopy is under development.

microwave ◊electromagnetic wave with a wavelength in the range 0.3 to 30 cm/0.1 in to 12 in, or 300–300,000 megahertz (between radio waves and ◊infrared radiation). They are used in radar, as carrier waves in radio broadcasting, and in microwave heating and cooking.

microwave heating heating by means of microwaves. Microwave ovens use this form of heating for the rapid cooking or reheating of foods, where heat is generated throughout the food simultaneously. If food is not heated completely, there is a danger of bacterial growth that may lead to food poisoning. Industrially, microwave heating is used for destroying insects in grain and enzymes in processed food, pasteurizing and sterilizing liquids, and drying timber and paper.

Midas in Greek legend, a king of Phrygia who was granted the gift of converting all he touched to gold, and who, for preferring the music of Pan to that of Apollo, was given ass's ears by the latter.

Middle Ages period of European history between the fall of the Roman Empire in the 5th century and the Renaissance in the 15th. Among the period's distinctive features were the unity of W Europe within the Roman Catholic Church, the feudal organization of political, social, and economic relations, and the use of art for largely religious purposes.

Middle East indeterminate area now usually taken to include the Balkan States, Egypt, and SW Asia. Until the 1940s, this area was generally called the Near East, and the term Middle East referred to the area from Iran to Burma (now Myanmar).

Middlesex former English county, absorbed by Greater London 1965. It was settled in the 6th century by Saxons, and its name comes from its position between the kingdoms of the East and West Saxons. Contained within the Thames basin,

it provided good agricultural land before it was built over.

midge common name for many insects resembling ◊gnats, generally divided into biting midges (family Ceratopogonidae) that suck blood, and non-biting midges (family Chironomidae).

Mid Glamorgan (Welsh *Morgannwg Ganol*) county in S Wales; *area* 1,020 sq km/ 394 sq mi; *towns* Cardiff (administrative headquarters); Porthcawl (resort); Aberdare, Merthyr Tydfil, Bridgend, Pontypridd; *features* Caerphilly Castle, with its water defences; *products* the north was formerly a leading coal (Rhondda) and iron and steel area; Royal Mint at Llantrisant; agriculture in the south; Caerphilly mild cheese; *population* (1991) 536,500; *language* 8% Welsh, English; *famous people* Geraint Evans.

Midi-Pyrénées region of SW France, comprising the *départements* of Ariège, Aveyron, Haute-Garonne, Gers, Lot, Haute-Pyrénées, Tarn, and Tarn-et-Garonne; *area* 45,300 sq km/17,486 sq mi; *population* (1986) 2,355,000; *capital* Toulouse; *towns* Montauban, Cahors, Rodez, Lourdes; *products* fruit, wine, livestock; *features* several spa towns, winter resorts, and prehistoric caves; *history* occupied by the Basques since prehistoric times, this region once formed part of the prehistoric province of Gascony that was taken by the English 1154, recaptured by the French 1453, inherited by Henry of Navarre, and reunited with France 1607.

MIDI (acronym for *musical instruments digital interface*) standard ◊interface that enables electronic musical instruments to be connected to a computer. A computer with a MIDI interface can input and store the sounds produced by the connected instruments, and can then manipulate these sounds in many different ways. For example, a single keystroke may change the key of an entire composition.

Midlands area of England corresponding roughly to the Anglo-Saxon kingdom of ◊Mercia. The *E Midlands* comprises Derbyshire, Leicestershire, Northamptonshire, Nottinghamshire. The *W Midlands* covers the former metropolitan county of ◊West Midlands created from parts of Staffordshire, Warwickshire, and Worcestershire; and (often included) the *S Midlands* comprising Bedfordshire, Buckinghamshire, and Oxfordshire.

Midway Islands two islands in the Pacific, 1,800 km/1,120 mi NW of Honolulu; area 5 sq km/ 2 sq mi; population (1980) 500. They were annexed by the USA 1867, and are now administered by the US Navy. The naval *Battle of Midway* 3–6 June 1942, between the USA and Japan, was a turning point in the Pacific in World War II; the US victory marked the end of Japanese expansion in the Pacific.

Midwest or *Middle West* large area of the N central USA. It is loosely defined, but is generally taken to comprise the states of Illinois, Iowa, Wisconsin, Minnesota, Nebraska, Kansas, Missouri, North Dakota, and South Dakota and the portions of Montana, Wyoming, and Colorado that lie E of the Rocky Mountains. Ohio, Michigan, and Indiana are often variously included, as well. Traditionally its economy is divided between agriculture and heavy industry. The main urban Midwest centre is Chicago.

Mies van der Rohe Ludwig 1886–1969. German architect who practised in the USA from 1937. He succeeded Walter ⚬Gropius as director of the ⚬Bauhaus 1929–33. He designed the bronze-and-glass Seagram building in New York City 1956–59 and numerous apartment blocks.

migraine acute, sometimes incapacitating headache (generally only on one side), accompanied by nausea, that recurs, often with advance symptoms such as flashing lights. No cure has been discovered, but ergotamine normally relieves the symptoms. Some sufferers learn to avoid certain foods, such as chocolate, which suggests an allergic factor.

migration the movement, either seasonal or as part of a single life cycle, of certain animals, chiefly birds and fish, to distant breeding or feeding grounds.

Milan (Italian *Milano*) industrial city (aircraft, cars, locomotives, textiles), financial and cultural centre, capital of Lombardy, Italy; population (1988) 1,479,000. Milan became the capital of the Western Roman empire AD 286, of Napoleon's Cisalpine Republic 1799, and of the kingdom of Italy 1805–14. It has a Gothic cathedral *c.* 1450, Leonardo da Vinci's *Last Supper* 1495–97, and La Scala opera house 1778.

mildew any fungus that appears as a destructive growth on plants, paper, leather, or wood when exposed to damp; such fungi usually form a thin white coating.

mile imperial unit of linear measure. A statute mile is equal to 1,760 yards (1.60934 km), and an international nautical mile is equal to 2,026 yards (1,852 m).

Militant Tendency in British politics, left-wing faction originally within the Labour Party, aligned with the publication *Militant*. It became active in the 1970s, with radical socialist policies based on Trotskyism (see ⚬Trotsky), and gained some success in local government, for example in the inner-city area of Liverpool. In the mid-1980s the Labour Party considered it to be a separate organization within the party and banned it.

milk secretion of the ⚬mammary glands of female mammals, with which they suckle their young (during ⚬lactation). Over 85% is water, the remainder comprising protein, fat, lactose (a sugar), calcium, phosphorus, iron, and vitamins. The milk of cows, goats, and sheep is often consumed by humans, but only Western societies drink milk after infancy; for people in most of the world, milk causes flatulence and diarrhoea.

Milky Way faint band of light crossing the night sky, consisting of stars in the plane of our Galaxy. The name Milky Way is often used for the Galaxy itself. It is a spiral ⚬galaxy, about 100,000 light years in diameter, containing at least 100 billion stars. The Sun is in one of its spiral arms, about 25,000 light years from the centre.

Mill John Stuart 1806–1873. English philosopher and economist who wrote *On Liberty* 1859, the classic philosophical defence of liberalism, and *Utilitarianism* 1863, a version of the 'greatest happiness for the greatest number' principle in ethics. His progressive views inspired *On the Subjection of Women* 1869.

Millais John Everett 1829–1896. British painter, a founder member of the ⚬**Pre-Raphaelite Brotherhood** (PRB) 1848. One of his PRB works, *Christ in the House of His Parents* 1850 (Tate Gallery, London) caused an outcry since its realistic detail was considered unfitting to the sacred subject. By the late 1850s he had dropped out of the PRB, and his style became more fluent and less detailed and his subjects more sentimental. Later works include *Bubbles* 1886 (a poster for Pears soap).

Miller Arthur 1915– . US playwright. His plays deal with family relationships and contemporary American values, and include *Death of a Salesman* 1949 and *The Crucible* 1953, based on the Salem witch trials and reflecting the communist witch-hunts of Senator Joe ⚬McCarthy. He was married 1956–61 to the film star Marilyn Monroe, for whom he wrote the film *The Misfits* 1960.

Miller Glenn 1904–1944. US trombonist and, as bandleader, exponent of the big-band swing sound from 1938. He composed his signature tune 'Moonlight Serenade' (a hit 1939). Miller became leader of the US Army Air Force Band in Europe 1942, made broadcasts to troops throughout the world during World War II, and disappeared without trace on a flight between England and France.

millet any of several grasses, family Gramineae, of which the grains are used as a cereal food and the stems as fodder.

Millett Kate 1934– . US radical feminist lecturer, writer, and sculptor whose book *Sexual Politics* 1970 was a landmark in feminist thinking. She was a founding member of the *National Organization of Women* (NOW). Later books include *Flying* 1974, *The Prostitution Papers* 1976, and *Sita* 1977.

millipede any arthropod of the class Diplopoda. It has a segmented body, each segment usually bearing two pairs of legs, and the distinct head bears a pair of short clubbed antennae. Most millipedes are no more than 2.5 cm/1 in long; a few in the tropics are 30 cm/12 in.

Milne A(lan) A(lexander) 1882–1956. English writer. His books for children were based on the teddy bear and other toys of his son Christopher Robin (*Winnie-the-Pooh* 1926 and *The House at Pooh Corner* 1928). He also wrote children's verse (*When We Were Very Young* 1924 and *Now We Are Six* 1927) and plays, including an adaptation of Kenneth Grahame's *The Wind in the Willows* as *Toad of Toad Hall* 1929.

Milosevic Slobodan 1941– . Serbian communist politician, party chief and president of Serbia from 1986; re-elected Dec 1990 in multiparty elections. Milosevic wielded considerable influence over the Serb-dominated Yugoslav federal army during the 1991–92 civil war and continued to back Serbian militia in ◊Bosnia-Herzegovina 1992, although publicly disclaiming any intention to 'carve up' the newly independent republic.

Milton John 1608–1674. English poet whose epic *Paradise Lost* 1667 is one of the landmarks of English literature. Early poems including *Comus* (a masque performed 1634) and *Lycidas* (an elegy, 1638) showed Milton's superlative lyric gift. Latin secretary to Oliver Cromwell during the Commonwealth period, he also wrote many pamphlets and prose works, including *Areopagitica* 1644, which opposed press censorship.

Milwaukee industrial port (meatpacking, brewing, engineering, machinery, electronic and electrical equipment, chemicals) in Wisconsin, USA, on Lake Michigan; population (1990) 628,100. The site was settled 1818 and drew a large influx of German immigrants, beginning in the 1840s.

mimicry imitation of one species (or group of species) by another. The most common form is *Batesian mimicry* (named after H W ◊Bates), where the mimic resembles a model that is poisonous or unpleasant to eat, and has aposematic, or warning, coloration; the mimic thus benefits from the fact that predators have learned to avoid the model. Hoverflies that resemble bees or wasps are an example. Appearance is usually the basis for mimicry, but calls, songs, scents, and other signals can also be mimicked.

mimosa tree, shrub, or herb of the genus *Mimosa* of the family Mimosaceae, found in tropical and subtropical regions. All bear small, fluffy, golden, ball-like flowers.

Mindanao second-largest island of the Philippines; *area* 94,627 sq km/36,526 sq mi; *towns* Davao, Zamboanga; *physical* mountainous rainforest; *features* in 1971, an isolated people, the Tasaday, were reputedly first seen by others (this may be a hoax). The active volcano Apo reaches 2,954 m/9,600 ft, and Mindanao is subject to severe earthquakes. There is a Muslim guerrilla resistance movement; *products* pineapples, coffee, rice, coconut, rubber, hemp, timber, nickel, gold, steel, chemicals, fertilizer; *population* (1980) 10,905,250.

mine explosive charge on land or sea, or in the atmosphere, designed to be detonated by contact, vibration (for example, from an enemy engine), magnetic influence, or a timing device. Countermeasures include metal detectors (useless for plastic types), specially equipped helicopters, and (at sea) minesweepers.

mineral naturally formed inorganic substance with a particular chemical composition and an ordered internal structure. Either in their perfect crystalline form or otherwise, minerals are the constituents of ◊rocks. In more general usage, a mineral is any substance economically valuable for mining (including coal and oil, despite their organic origins).

mineralogy study of minerals. The classification of minerals is based chiefly on their chemical composition and the kind of chemical bonding that holds these atoms together. The mineralogist also studies their crystallographic and physical characters, occurrence, and mode of formation.

Minerva in Roman mythology, the goddess of intelligence, and of the handicrafts and arts, counterpart of the Greek ◊Athena. From the earliest days of ancient Rome, there was a temple to her on the Capitoline Hill, near the Temple of Jupiter.

Mingus Charles 1922–1979. US jazz bassist and composer. He played with Louis Armstrong, Duke Ellington, and Charlie Parker. His experimentation with atonality and dissonant effects opened the way for the new style of free collective jazz improvisation of the 1960s.

miniature painting painting on a very small scale, notably early manuscript paintings, and later miniature portraits, sometimes set in jewelled cases. The art of manuscript painting was developed in classical times in the West and revived in the Middle Ages. Several Islamic countries, for example Persia and India, developed strong traditions of manuscript art. Miniature portrait painting enjoyed a vogue in France and England in the 16th–19th centuries.

minicomputer multiuser computer with a size and processing power between those of a ◊mainframe and a ◊microcomputer.

Mini Disc digital audio disc that resembles a computer floppy disc in a 5 cm/2 in square case, with up to an hour's playing time. The system was developed by Sony for release 1993.

Minimalism movement beginning in the late 1960s in abstract art and music towards a severely simplified composition. In *painting*, it emphasized geometrical and elemental shapes. In *sculpture*, Carl André focused on industrial materials. In *music*, large-scale statements are based on layers of imperceptibly shifting repetitive patterns; its major exponents are Steve ◊Reich and Philip Glass.

mining extraction of minerals from under the land

or sea for industrial or domestic uses. Exhaustion of traditionally accessible resources has led to development of new mining techniques; for example, extraction of oil from offshore deposits and from land shale reserves. Technology is also under development for the exploitation of minerals from entirely new sources such as mud deposits and mineral nodules from the sea bed.

mink two species of carnivores of the weasel family, genus *Mustela*, usually found in or near water. They have rich, brown fur, and are up to 50 cm/1.6 ft long with bushy tails 20 cm/8 in long. They live in Eurasia (*Mustela lutreola*) and North America (*M. vison*).

Minneapolis city in Minnesota, USA, forming with St Paul the Twin Cities area; population (1990) 368,400, metropolitan area 2,464,100. It is at the head of navigation of the Mississippi River. Industries include food processing and the manufacture of machinery, electrical and electronic equipment, precision instruments, transport machinery, and metal and paper products.

Minnesota state in N midwest USA; nickname Gopher State/North Star State; *area* 218,700 sq km/84,418 sq mi; *capital* St Paul; *cities* Minneapolis, Duluth, Bloomington, Rochester; *features* sources of the Mississippi River and the Red River of the North; Voyageurs National Park near the Canadian border; Minnehaha Falls at Minneapolis; Mayo Clinic at Rochester; more than 15,000 lakes; *products* cereals, soya beans, livestock, meat and dairy products, iron ore (about two-thirds of US output), nonelectrical machinery, electronic equipment; *population* (1990) 4,375,100; *famous people* F Scott Fitzgerald, Hubert H Humphrey, Sinclair Lewis, Charles and William Mayo; *history* first European exploration by French fur traders in the 17th century; region claimed for France by Daniel Greysolon, Sieur Duluth, 1679; part E of Mississippi River ceded to Britain 1763 and to the USA 1783; part W of Mississippi passed to the USA under the Louisiana Purchase 1803; became a territory 1849; statehood 1858.

minnow various small freshwater fishes of the carp family Cyprinidae, found in streams and ponds worldwide. Most species are small and dully coloured, but some are brightly coloured. They feed on larvae and insects.

Minoan civilization Bronze Age civilization on the Aegean island of Crete. The name is derived from Minos, the legendary king of Crete, reputed to be the son of the god Zeus. The civilization is divided into three main periods: early Minoan, about 3000–2200 BC, middle Minoan, about 2200–1580 BC; and late Minoan, about 1580–1100 BC. Known from the Minoan civilization are the palaces of Knossos, Phaistos, and Mallia; sophisticated metalwork; and linear scripts. The civilization was suddenly destroyed by earthquake or war.

minor legal term for those under the age of majority, which varies from country to country but is usually between 18 and 21. In the USA (from 1971 for voting, and in some states for nearly all other purposes) and certain European countries (in Britain since 1970) the age of majority is 18.

Minorca (Spanish *Menorca*) second largest of the ◊Balearic Islands in the Mediterranean; *area* 689 sq km/266 sq mi; *towns* Mahon, Ciudadela; *products* copper, lead, iron; tourism is important; *population* (1985) 55,500.

Minotaur in Greek mythology, a monster, half man and half bull, offspring of Pasiphaë, wife of King Minos of Crete, and a bull. It lived in the Labyrinth at Knossos, and its victims were seven girls and seven youths, sent in annual tribute by Athens, until ◊Theseus killed it, with the aid of Ariadne, the daughter of Minos.

Minsk industrial city (machinery, textiles, leather; a centre of the computer industry) and capital of Belarus; population (1987) 1,543,000. It dates back to the 11th century.

mint in botany, any aromatic plant, genus *Mentha*, of the family Labiatae, widely distributed in temperate regions. The plants have square stems, creeping rootstocks, and flowers, usually pink or purplish, that grow in a terminal spike. Mints include garden mint *M. spicata* and peppermint *M. piperita*.

Miocene fourth epoch of the Tertiary period of geological time, 25–5 million years ago. At this time grasslands spread over the interior of continents, and hoofed mammals rapidly evolved.

Mirabeau Honoré Gabriel Riqueti, Comte de 1749–1791. French politician, leader of the National Assembly in the French Revolution. He wanted to establish a parliamentary monarchy on the English model. From May 1790 he secretly acted as political adviser to the king.

miracle play another name for ◊mystery play.

Miró Joan 1893–1983. Spanish Surrealist painter, born in Barcelona. In the mid-1920s he developed a distinctive abstract style with amoeba shapes, some linear, some highly coloured, generally floating on a plain background. During the 1930s his style became more sombre and after World War II he produced larger abstracts. He produced ceramic murals (UNESCO building, Paris 1958) and designed sets for the ballet director Diaghilev.

mirror any polished surface that reflects light; often made from 'silvered' glass (in practice, a mercury-alloy coating of glass). A plane (flat) mirror produces a same-size, erect 'virtual' image located behind the mirror at the same distance from it as the object is in front of it. A spherical concave mirror produces a reduced, inverted real image in front or an enlarged, erect virtual image behind it (as in a shaving mirror), depending on how close the object is to the mirror. A spherical convex mirror produces a reduced, erect virtual image behind it (as in a car's rear-view mirror).

Mishima Yukio 1925–1970. Japanese novelist whose work often deals with sexual desire and perversion, as in *Confessions of a Mask* 1949 and *The Temple of the Golden Pavilion* 1956. He committed hara-kiri (ritual suicide) as a protest against what he saw as the corruption of the nation and the loss of the samurai warrior tradition.

missile rocket-propelled weapon, which may be nuclear-armed (see ♢nuclear warfare). Modern missiles are often classified as surface-to-surface missiles (SSM), air-to-air missiles (AAM), surface-to-air missiles (SAM), or air-to-surface missiles (ASM). A *cruise missile* is in effect a pilotless, computer-guided aircraft; it can be sea-launched from submarines or surface ships, or launched from the air or the ground.

Mississippi river in the USA, the main arm of the great river system draining the USA between the Appalachian and the Rocky mountains. The length of the Mississippi is 3,780 km/2,350 mi; with its tributary the Missouri 6,020 km/3,740 mi.

Mississippi state in SE USA; nickname Magnolia State/Bayou State; *area* 123,600 sq km/ 47,710 sq mi; *capital* Jackson; *cities* Biloxi, Meridian, Hattiesburg; *features* rivers: Mississippi, Pearl, Big Black; Vicksburg National Military Park (Civil War site); Gulf Islands National Seashore; mansions and plantations, many in the Natchez area; *products* cotton, rice, soya beans, chickens, fish and shellfish, lumber and wood products, petroleum and natural gas, transportation equipment, chemicals; *population* (1990) 2,573,200; *famous people* Jefferson Davis, William Faulkner, Elvis Presley, Leontyne Price, Eudora Welty, Tennessee Williams, Richard Wright; *history* first explored by Hernando de Soto for Spain 1540; settled by the French 1699, the English 1763; ceded to USA 1798; statehood achieved 1817.

Missouri state in central USA; nickname Show Me State/Bullion State; *area* 180,600 sq km/ 69,712 sq mi; *capital* Jefferson City; *cities* St Louis, Kansas City, Springfield, Independence; *features* rivers: Mississippi, Missouri; Pony Express Museum at St Joseph; birthplace of Jesse James; Mark Twain and Ozark state parks; Harry S Truman Library at Independence; *products* meat and other processed food, aerospace and transport equipment, lead, zinc; *population* (1990) 5,117,100; *famous people* George Washington Carver, T S Eliot, Jesse James, Joseph Pulitzer, Harry S Truman, Mark Twain; *history* explored by de Soto 1541; acquired by the USA under the Louisiana Purchase 1803; achieved statehood 1821, following the Missouri Compromise of 1820.

Missouri major river in the central USA, a tributary of the Mississippi, which it joins N of St Louis; length 4,320 km/2,683 mi.

mistletoe parasitic evergreen unisexual plant *Viscum album*, native to Europe. It grows on trees as a branched bush with translucent white berries. Used in many Western countries as a Christmas decoration, it also featured in ♢Druidism.

mite minute ♢arachnid of the subclass Acari.

Mithras in Persian mythology, the god of light. Mithras represented the power of goodness, and promised his followers compensation for present evil after death. He was said to have captured and killed the sacred bull, from whose blood all life sprang. Mithraism was introduced into the Roman Empire 68 BC. By about AD 250, it rivalled Christianity in strength.

Mithridates VI Eupator known as *the Great* 132–63 BC. King of Pontus (NE Asia Minor, on the Black Sea) from 120 BC. He massacred 80,000 Romans in overrunning the rest of Asia Minor and went on to invade Greece. He was defeated by ♢Sulla in the First Mithridatic War 88–84; by ♢Lucullus in the Second 83–81; and by ♢Pompey in the Third 74–64. He was killed by a soldier at his own order rather than surrender.

mitosis in biology, the process of cell division. The genetic material of ♢eukaryotic cells is carried on a number of ♢chromosomes. To control their movements during cell division so that both new cells get a full complement, a system of protein tubules, known as the spindle, organizes the chromosomes into position in the middle of the cell before they replicate. The spindle then controls the movement of chromosomes as the cell goes through the stages of division: *interphase*, *prophase*, *metaphase*, *anaphase*, and *telophase*. See also ♢meiosis.

Mitsotakis Constantine 1918– . Greek politician, leader of the conservative New Democracy Party from 1984, prime minister from April 1990. Minister for economic coordination 1965 (a post he held again 1978–80), he was arrested by the military junta 1967, but escaped from house arrest and lived in exile until 1974. In 1980–81 he was foreign minister.

Mitterrand François 1916– . French socialist politician, president from 1981. He held ministerial posts in 11 governments 1947–1958, and founded the French Socialist Party (PS) 1971. In 1985 he introduced proportional representation, allegedly to weaken the growing opposition from left and right. Since 1982 his administrations have combined economic orthodoxy with social reform.

mixed economy type of economic structure that combines the private enterprise of capitalism with a degree of state monopoly. In mixed economies, governments seek to control the public services, the basic industries, and those industries that cannot raise sufficient capital investment from private sources. Thus a measure of economic planning can be combined with a measure of free enterprise. A notable example was US President F D Roosevelt's ♢New Deal in the 1930s.

mixture in chemistry, a substance containing two or more compounds that still retain their separate physical and chemical properties. There is no chemical bonding between them and they can be separated from each other by physical means (compare ⟡compound).

Mizoram state of NE India; *area* 21,100 sq km/ 8,145 sq mi; *capital* Aizawl; *products* rice, hand loom weaving; *population* (1991) 686,200; *religion* 84% Christian; *history* made a Union Territory 1972 from the Mizo Hills District of Assam. Rebels carried on a guerrilla war 1966–76, but acknowledged Mizoram as an integral part of India 1976. It became a state 1986.

Mobutu Sese Seko Kuku Ngbeandu Wa Za Banga 1930– . Zairean president from 1965. He assumed the presidency by coup, and created a unitary state under his centralized government. The harshness of some of his policies and charges of corruption have attracted widespread international criticism. In 1991 opposition leaders forced Mobutu to agree formally to give up some of his powers.

mockingbird North American songbird *Mimus polyglottos* of the mimic thrush family Mimidae, found in the USA and Mexico. About 25 cm/10 in long, it is brownish grey, with white markings on the black wings and tail. It is remarkable for its ability to mimic the songs of other species.

mock orange or *syringa* deciduous shrub of the genus *Philadelphus*, family Philadelphaceae, including *P. coronarius*, which has white, strongly scented flowers, resembling those of the orange.

Model Parliament English parliament set up 1295 by Edward I; it was the first to include representatives from outside the clergy and aristocracy (two from each shire, city, and borough), and was established because Edward needed the support of the whole country against his opponents: Wales, France, and Scotland. His sole aim was to raise money for military purposes, and the parliament did not pass any legislation.

modem (acronym for *mo*dulator/*dem*odulator; also called an *acoustic coupler*) device for transmitting computer data over telephone lines. Such a device is necessary because the digital signals produced by computers cannot, at present, be transmitted directly over the telephone network, which uses analogue signals. The modem converts the digital signals to analogue, and back again. Modems are used for linking remote terminals to central computers and enable computers to communicate with each other anywhere in the world.

modern dance 20th-century dance idiom that evolved in opposition to traditional ballet by those seeking a freer and more immediate means of dance expression. Leading exponents include Martha ⟡Graham and Merce Cunningham in the USA, and Isadora ⟡Duncan and Loie Fuller in Europe.

Modernism in the arts, a general term used to describe the 20th century's conscious attempt to break with the artistic traditions of the 19th century; it is based on a concern with form and the exploration of technique as opposed to content and narrative.

In the visual arts, direct representation gave way to abstraction; in literature, writers experimented with alternatives to orthodox storytelling; in music, the traditional concept of key was challenged by atonality; and in architecture, functionalism ousted decorativeness as a central objective.

Modigliani Amedeo 1884–1920. Italian artist, active in Paris from 1906. He painted and sculpted graceful nudes and portrait studies. His paintings – for example, the portrait of *Jeanne Hebuterne* 1919 (Guggenheim Museum, New York) – have a distinctive elongated, linear style. His life was dramatic and dissolute, and he died of the combined effects of alcoholism, drug addiction, and tuberculosis.

modulation in radio transmission, the intermittent change of frequency, or amplitude, of a radio carrier wave, in accordance with the audio characteristics of the speaking voice, music, or other signal being transmitted. See ⟡pulse-code modulation.

Mogadishu or *Mugdisho* capital and chief port of Somalia; population (1988) 1,000,000. It is a centre for oil refining, food processing, and uranium mining.

Mogul emperors N Indian dynasty 1526–1857, established by ⟡Zahir ('Babur'). Muslim descendants of Tamerlane, the 14th-century Mongol leader, the Mogul emperors ruled until the last one was dethroned and exiled by the British 1857; they included ⟡Akbar, ⟡Aurangzeb, and ⟡Shah Jahan.

Mohács, Battle of Austro-Hungarian defeat of the Turks 1687, which effectively marked the end of Turkish expansion into Europe. It was named after the river port Mohács on the Danube in Hungary, which is also the site of a Turkish victory 1526.

Mohamad Mahathir bin 1925– . Prime minister of Malaysia from 1981 and leader of the United Malays' National Organization (UMNO). His 'look east' economic policy emulates Japanese industrialization.

Mohammed alternative form of ⟡Muhammad, founder of Islam.

Moholy-Nagy Laszlo 1895–1946. US photographer, born in Hungary. He lived in Germany 1923–29, where he was a member of the Bauhaus school, and fled from the Nazis 1935. Through the publication of his illuminating theories and practical experiments, he had great influence on 20th-century photography and design.

Mohorovičić discontinuity also *Moho* or *M-discontinuity* boundary that separates the Earth's crust and mantle, marked by a rapid increase in the speed of earthquake waves. It follows the variations in the thickness of the crust and is found approximately 32 km/20 mi below the continents and about 10 km/6 mi below the oceans. It is named after the Yugoslav geophysicist Andrija Mohorovičić (1857–1936) who suspected its presence after analysing seismic waves from the Kulpa Valley earthquake 1909.

Mohs' scale scale of hardness for minerals (in ascending order): 1 talc; 2 gypsum; 3 calcite; 4 fluorite; 5 apatite; 6 orthoclase; 7 quartz; 8 topaz; 9 corundum; 10 diamond.

Moi Daniel arap 1924– . Kenyan politician, president from 1978. Leader of the Kenya African National Union (KANU), he became minister of home affairs 1964, vice president 1967, and succeeded Jomo Kenyatta as president. He enjoys the support of Western governments but has been widely criticized for Kenya's poor human-rights record.

Mojave Desert arid region in S California, USA, part of the Great Basin; area 38,500 sq km/15,000 sq mi. The US military has appropriated thousands of square kilometres for bombing ranges and test stations, including Edwards Air Force Base, a landing place for space shuttles.

Moldova Republic of; country in SE Europe, bordered N, E, and S by Ukraine, and W by Romania; *area* 33,700 sq km/13,012 sq mi; *capital* Chisinau (Kishinev); *physical* hilly land lying largely between rivers Prut and Dnestr; N Moldova comprises level plain of Beltsy Steppe and uplands; *head of state* Mircea Snegur from 1989; *head of government* Pyotr Paskar from 1991; *political system* emergent democracy; *products* wine, tobacco, canned goods; *population* (1989) 4,341,000 (Moldavian 64%, Ukrainian 14%, Russian 13%, Gagauzi 4%, Jewish 2%); *language* Moldavian; *recent history* Bessarabia in E became part of USSR 1940; W remained in Romania. Bessarabia taken over by Romania-Germany 1941; reconquered by Red Army 1944. Popular front, Democratic Movement for Perestroika, formed 1988, campaigning for accelerated political reform. Nationalist demonstrations in capital 1989; Moldavian language granted official status, triggering clashes between ethnic Russians and Moldavians. Economic and political sovereignty declared 1990; unauthorized elections held for independent parliament. Moldova boycotted USSR's constitutional referendum and declared its independence Aug 1991. Joined Commonwealth of Independent States (CIS) Dec 1991; Civil war followed secession of Trans-Dnestr region between ethnic Romanians and Cossacks and a state of emergency imposed by President Mircea Snegur 1992.

mole burrowing insectivore of the family Talpidae. Moles grow to 18 cm/7 in, and have acute senses of hearing, smell, and touch, but poor vision. They have shovel-like, clawed front feet for burrowing, and eat insects, grubs, and worms. The common

mole of Europe, with soft dark fur, is *Talpa europaea*; it excavates extensive tunnels in its search for food and throws up earth at intervals in molehills.

mole SI unit (symbol mol) of the amount of a substance. One mole of an element that exists as single atoms weighs as many grams as its ◊atomic number (so one mole of carbon weighs 12 g), and it contains 6.022045×10^{23} atoms, which is ◊Avogadro's number.

molecular biology study of the molecular basis of life, including the biochemistry of molecules such as DNA, RNA, and proteins, and the molecular structure and function of the various parts of living cells.

molecule smallest unit of an ◊element or ◊compound that can exist and still retain the characteristics of the element or compound. A molecule of an element consists of one or more like ◊atoms; a molecule of a compound consists of two or more different atoms bonded together. They vary in size and complexity from the hydrogen molecule (H_2) to the large macromolecules of proteins. They are held together by ionic bonds, in which the atoms gain or lose electrons to form ◊ions, or covalent bonds, where electrons from each atom are shared in a new molecular orbital. According to the molecular or ◊kinetic theory of matter, molecules are in a state of constant motion, the extent of which depends on their temperature, and exert forces on one another. The presence of more than one atom in a molecule is denoted by a subscript figure – for example, one molecule of the compound water, having two atoms of hydrogen and one atom of oxygen, is shown as H_2O.

mole rat, naked small subterranean mammal *Heterocephalus glaber*, almost hairless, with a disproportionately large head. The mole rat is of importance to zoologists as one of the very few mammals that are eusocial, that is, living in colonies with sterile workers and one fertile female. This enables study of how under Darwinian evolution it is possible for sterile worker mole rats to be 'reproduced' from one generation to another.

Molière pen name of Jean Baptiste Poquelin 1622–1673. French satirical playwright from whose work modern French comedy developed. One of the founders of the Illustre Théâtre 1643, he was later its leading actor. In 1655 he wrote his first play, *L'Etourdi*, followed by *Les Précieuses ridicules* 1659. His satires include *L'Ecole des femmes* 1662, *Le Misanthrope* 1666, *Le Bourgeois gentilhomme* 1670, and *Le Malade imaginaire* 1673.

Molise mainly agricultural region of S central Italy, comprising the provinces of Campobasso and Isernia; area 4,400 sq km/1,698 sq mi; population (1990) 336,500. Its capital is Campobasso.

mollusc any invertebrate of the phylum Mollusca with a body divided into three parts, a head, a foot, and a visceral mass. The majority of molluscs are marine animals, but some inhabit fresh water, and a few are terrestrial. They include bivalves, mussels, octopuses, oysters, snails, slugs, and squids. The body is soft, limbless, and cold-blooded. There is no internal skeleton, but many species have a hard shell covering the body.

Molotov cocktail home-made weapon consisting of a bottle filled with petrol, plugged with a rag as a wick, ignited, and thrown as a grenade. Resistance groups during World War II named them after Soviet foreign minister Molotov (1890–1986).

Moluccas another name for ⟁Maluku, Indonesia.

molybdenum heavy, hard, lustrous, silver-white, metallic element, symbol Mo, atomic number 42, relative atomic mass 95.94. The chief ore is the mineral molybdenite. The element is highly resistant to heat and conducts electricity easily. It is used in alloys, often to harden steels. It is a necessary trace element in human nutrition. It was named 1781 by Swedish chemist Karl Scheele, after its isolation by P J Helm (1746–1813), for its resemblance to lead ore.

Mombasa industrial port (oil refining, cement) in Kenya (serving also Uganda and Tanzania), built on Mombasa Island and adjacent mainland; population (1984) 481,000. It was founded by Arab traders in the 11th century and was an important centre for ivory and slave trading until the 16th century.

moment of a force in physics, measure of the turning effect, or torque, produced by a force acting on a body. It is equal to the product of the force and the perpendicular distance from its line of action to the point, or pivot, about which the body will turn. Its unit is the newton metre.

moment of inertia in physics, the sum of all the point masses of a rotating object multiplied by the squares of their respective distances from the axis of rotation. It is analogous to the ⟁mass of a stationary object or one moving in a straight line.

momentum in physics, the product of the mass of a body and its linear velocity. The **angular momentum** of a body in rotational motion is the product of its moment of inertia and its angular velocity. The momentum of a body does not change unless it is acted on by an external force; angular momentum does not change unless it is acted upon by a turning force, or torque.

Monaco Principality of; small sovereign state forming an enclave in S France, with the Mediterranean to the S; *area* 1.95 sq km/0.75 sq mi; *capital* Monaco-Ville; *physical* steep and rugged; surrounded landwards by French territory; being expanded by filling in the sea; *head of state* Prince Rainier III from 1949; *head of government* Jean Ausseil from 1986; *political system* constitutional monarchy under French protectorate; *exports* some light industry; economy dependent on tourism and gambling; *population* (1989) 29,000; *languages* French (official); English, Italian; *recent history* became an independent state under French protection 1861. In 1918 France was given a veto over the succession to the throne; Monaco will be incorporated into France if the reigning prince dies without a male heir. Prince Albert, male heir to Prince Rainier III, was born 1958. The 1911 constitution was suspended 1959 and a largely rewritten version adopted 1962.

Monaghan (Irish *Mhuineachain*) county of the NE Republic of Ireland, province of Ulster; area 1,290 sq km/498 sq mi; products include cereals, linen, potatoes, and cattle; population (1991) 51,300. The county town is Monaghan. The county is low and rolling, and includes the rivers Finn and Blackwater.

monasticism devotion to religious life under vows of poverty, chastity, and obedience, known to Judaism (for example Essenes), Buddhism, and other religions, before Christianity. In Islam, the Sufis formed monastic orders from the 12th century.

Mondrian Piet (Pieter Mondriaan) 1872–1944. Dutch painter, a pioneer of abstract art. He lived in Paris 1919–38, then in London, and from 1940 in New York. He was a founder member of the de ⟁Stijl movement and chief exponent of Neo-Plasticism, a rigorous abstract style based on the use of simple geometric forms, straight lines at right angles to each other, and blocks of primary colours against a white background, contained within black outlines.

Monet Claude 1840–1926. French painter, a pioneer of Impressionism and a lifelong exponent of its ideals; his painting *Impression, Sunrise* 1872 gave the movement its name. In the 1870s he began painting the same subjects at different times of day to explore the effects of light on colour and form; the *Haystacks* and *Rouen Cathedral* series followed in the 1890s, and from 1899 he painted a series of *Water Lilies* in the garden of his house at Giverny, Normandy (now a museum).

monetarism economic policy, advocated by the

economist Milton Friedman and the Chicago school of economists, that proposes control of a country's money supply to keep it in step with the country's ability to produce goods, with the aim of curbing inflation. Cutting government spending is advocated, and the long-term aim is to return as much of the economy as possible to the private sector, allegedly in the interests of efficiency.

monetary policy economic policy aimed at controlling the amount of money in circulation, usually through controlling the level of lending or credit. Increasing interest rates is an example of a contractionary monetary policy, which aims to reduce inflation by reducing the rate of growth of spending in the economy.

money any common medium of exchange acceptable in payment for goods or services or for the settlement of debts; legal tender. Money is usually coinage (invented by the Chinese in the second millennium BC) and paper notes (used by the Chinese from about AD 800). Developments such as the cheque and credit card fulfil many of the traditional functions of money.

Mongol member of any of the various Mongol (or Mongolian) ethnic groups of Central Asia. Mongols live in Mongolia, Russia, Inner Mongolia (China), Tibet, and Nepal. The Mongol language belongs to the Altaic family; some groups of Mongol descent speak languages in the Sino-Tibetan family, however.

Mongol Empire empire established by Genghis Khan, who extended his domains from Russia to N China and became khan of the Mongol tribes 1206. His grandson Kublai Khan conquered China and used foreigners such as Marco Polo as well as subjects to administer his empire. The Mongols lost China 1367 and suffered defeats in the West 1380; the empire broke up soon afterwards.

Mongolia State of (formerly *Outer Mongolia* until 1924; *People's Republic of Mongolia* until 1991); country in E Central Asia, bordered N by the Russian Federation and S by China; *area* 1,565,000 sq km/604,480 sq mi; *capital* Ulaanbaatar; *physical* high plateau with desert and steppe (grasslands); *head of state* Punsalmaagiyn Ochirbat from 1990; *head of government* Dashiyn Byambasuren from 1990; *political system* emergent democracy; *exports* meat and hides, minerals, wool, livestock, grain, cement, timber; *population* (1990 est) 2,185,000; *languages* Khalkha Mongolian (official); Chinese, Russian, and Turkic languages; *recent history* Chinese rule overthrown with Soviet help 1921; in 1924 Mongolia was proclaimed a People's Republic. A 20-year friendship, cooperation, and mutual-assistance pact was signed with the USSR 1966; relations with China deteriorated. Mongolia's external contacts broadened as Soviet troops reduced in late 1980s. A democratization campaign was launched by the Mongolian Democratic Union 1990 and

Ochirbat's Mongolian People's Revolutionary Party was elected in free multiparty elections. A massive privatization programme was launched 1991, and a new constitution introduced 1992, but the economic situation is worsening.

Mongolia, Inner (Chinese *Nei Mongol*) autonomous region of NE China from 1947; *area* 450,000 sq km/173,700 sq mi; *capital* Hohhot; *features* strategic frontier area with Russia; known for Mongol herders, now becoming settled farmers; *physical* grassland and desert; *products* cereals under irrigation; coal; reserves of rare earth oxides europium, and yttrium at Bayan Obo; *population* (1990) 21,457,000.

mongoose any of various carnivorous mammals of the family Viverridae, especially the genus *Herpestes*. The Indian mongoose *H. mungo* is greyish in colour and about 50 cm/1.5 ft long, with a long tail. It may be tamed and is often kept for its ability to kill snakes. The white-tailed mongoose *Ichneumia albicauda* of central Africa has a distinctive grey or white bushy tail.

monism in philosophy, the theory that reality is made up of only one substance. This view is usually contrasted with ◊dualism, which divides reality into two substances, matter and mind. The Dutch philosopher Baruch Spinoza saw the one substance as God or Nature. Monism is also sometimes used as a description of a political system in which only one party is permitted to operate.

monitor any of various lizards of the family Varanidae, found in Africa, S Asia, and Australasia. Monitors are generally large and carnivorous, with well-developed legs and claws and a long powerful tail that can be swung in defence.

Monk Thelonious (Sphere) 1917–1982. US jazz pianist and composer who took part in the development of ◊bebop. He had a highly idiosyncratic style, but numbers such as 'Round Midnight' and 'Blue Monk' have become standards.

monkey any of the various smaller, mainly tree-dwelling anthropoid primates, excluding humans and the ◊apes. The 125 species live in tropical Central and South America, Africa, and Asia. New World monkeys have widely-set nostrils; some have prehensile tails. Monkeys eat mainly leaves and fruit, and also small animals. Several species are endangered due to loss of forest habitat, for example the woolly spider monkey and black saki of the Amazonian forest.

monkey puzzle or *Chilean pine* coniferous evergreen tree *Araucaria araucana*, native to Chile; it has whorled branches covered in prickly leaves of a leathery texture.

Monmouth James Scott, Duke of Monmouth 1649–1685. Claimant to the English crown, the illegitimate son of Charles II and Lucy Walter. After James II's accession 1685, Monmouth landed in

England at Lyme Regis, Dorset, claimed the crown, and raised a rebellion, which was crushed at Sedgemoor in Somerset. He was executed with 320 of his accomplices.

monocotyledon angiosperm (flowering plant) having an embryo with a single cotyledon, or seed leaf (as opposed to ▷dicotyledons, which have two). Monocotyledons usually have narrow leaves with parallel veins and smooth edges, and hollow or soft stems. Their flower parts are arranged in threes. Most are small plants such as orchids, grasses, and lilies, but some are trees such as palms.

monomer chemical compound composed of simple molecules from which ▷polymers can be made. Under certain conditions the simple molecules (of the monomer) join together (polymerize) to form a very long chain molecule (macromolecule) called a polymer. For example, the polymerization of ethene (ethylene) monomers produces the polymer polyethene (polyethylene).

monopoly in economics, the domination of a market for a particular product or service by a single company, which can therefore restrict competition and keep prices high. In practice, a company can be said to have a monopoly when it controls a significant proportion of the market (technically an oligopoly).

monosodium glutamate (MSG) $NaC_5H_8NO_4$ a white, crystalline powder, the sodium salt of glutamic acid (an ▷amino acid found in proteins that plays a role in the metabolism of plants and animals). It is used to enhance the flavour of many packaged and 'fast foods', and in Chinese cooking. Ill effects may arise from its overconsumption, and some people are very sensitive to it, even in small amounts. It is commercially derived from vegetable protein.

Monroe James 1758–1831. 5th president of the USA 1817–25, a Democratic Republican. He served in the American Revolution, was minister to France 1794–96, and in 1803 negotiated the ▷Louisiana Purchase. He was secretary of state 1811–17. His name is associated with the ▷Monroe Doctrine.

Monroe Marilyn. Stage name of Norma Jean Mortenson or Baker 1926–1962. US film actress, the voluptuous blonde sex symbol of the 1950s, who made adroit comedies such as *Gentlemen Prefer Blondes* 1953, *How to Marry a Millionaire* 1953, *The Seven Year Itch* 1955, *Bus Stop* 1956, and *Some Like It Hot* 1959. Her second husband was baseball star Joe di Maggio, and her third was playwright Arthur ▷Miller, who wrote *The Misfits* 1961 for her, a serious film that became her last. She committed suicide, taking an overdose of sleeping pills.

Monroe Doctrine declaration by US president James Monroe 1823 that any further European colonial ambitions in the western hemisphere would be threats to US peace and security, made in response to proposed European intervention against newly independent former Spanish colonies in South America. In return the USA would not interfere in European affairs. The doctrine, subsequently broadened, has been a recurrent theme in US foreign policy, although it has no basis in US or international law.

Monrovia capital and port of Liberia; population (1985) 500,000. Industries include rubber, cement, and petrol processing. Founded 1821 for slaves repatriated from the USA, it was originally called Christopolis but was renamed after US president Monroe.

monsoon wind system that dominates the climate of a wide region, with seasonal reversals of direction; in particular, the wind in S Asia that blows towards the sea in winter and towards the land in summer, bringing heavy rain. The monsoon may cause destructive flooding all over India and SE Asia from April to Sept. Thousands of people are rendered homeless each year. The Guinea monsoon is a southwesterly wind that blows in W Africa from April to Sept, throughout the rainy season.

monstera or *Swiss cheese plant* evergreen climbing plant, genus *Monstera*, of the arum family Araceae, native to tropical America. *M. deliciosa* is cultivated as a house plant. Areas between the veins of the leaves dry up, creating deep marginal notches and ultimately holes.

Montaigne Michel Eyquem de 1533–1592. French writer, regarded as the creator of the essay form. In 1580 he published the first two volumes of his *Essais*, the third volume appeared 1588. Montaigne deals with all aspects of life from an urbanely sceptical viewpoint. Through the translation by John Florio 1603, he influenced Shakespeare and other English writers.

Montana state in W USA, on the Canadian border; nickname Treasure State; *area* 318,100 sq km/ 147,143 sq mi; *capital* Helena; *cities* Billings, Great Falls, Butte; *physical* mountainous forests in the west, rolling grasslands in the east; *features* rivers: Missouri, Yellowstone, Little Bighorn; Glacier National Park on the Continental Divide and Yellowstone National Park; Museum of the Plains Indian; Custer Battlefield National Monument; hunting and ski resorts; *products* wheat (under irrigation), cattle, coal, copper, oil, natural gas, lumber, wood products; *population* (1990) 799,100; *famous people* Gary Cooper, Myrna Loy; *history* explored for France by Verendrye early 1740s; passed to the USA 1803 in the Louisiana Purchase; first settled 1809; W Montana obtained from Britain in the Oregon Treaty 1846; influx of gold-seeking immigrants mid-19th century; fierce Indian wars 1867–77, which included 'Custer's Last Stand' at the Little Bighorn with the Sioux; achieved statehood 1889.

Mont Blanc (Italian *Monte Bianco*) highest mountain in the ▷Alps, between France and Italy; height 4,807 m/15,772 ft. It was first climbed 1786.

Monte Carlo town and luxury resort in ⟡Monaco, known for its casino (opened 1861) and the Monte Carlo car rally and Monaco Grand Prix; population (1982) 12,000.

Montenegro (Serbo-Croatian *Crna Gora*) constituent republic of Yugoslavia; *area* 13,800 sq km/ 5,327 sq mi; *capital* Titograd; *town* Cetinje; *features* smallest of the republics; Skadarsko Jezero (Lake Scutari) shared with Albania; *physical* mountainous; *population* (1986) 620,000, including 400,000 Montenegrins, 80,000 Muslims, and 40,000 Albanians; *language* Serbian variant of Serbo-Croat; *religion* Serbian Orthodox; *famous people* Milovan Djilas; *recent history* monarchy founded 1851; became a sovereign principality under the Treaty of Berlin 1878. Montenegro participated in the Balkan Wars 1912 and 1913. It was overrun by Austria in World War I, and in 1918 voted after the deposition of King Nicholas to become part of Serbia. In 1946 Montenegro became a republic of Yugoslavia. In Jan 1989 the entire Communist Party leadership resigned after mass protests which secured the replacement of the party and state leaderships. Later that year the body of the last king, Nicholas I, was brought back to Montenegro and ceremonially reburied in Cetinje. The republic held multiparty elections for the first time Dec 1990; the League of Communists of Montenegro remained in power. A staunch ally of Serbia, Montenegro sided with Serbia in the 1991 conflict with Slovenia and Croatia and approved a Serbian plan which called for a new, overwhelmingly Serb, Yugoslav federation (made up solely of Serbia, Montenegro, and Bosnia-Herzegovina) Aug 1991. Montenegro is the poorest of the Yugoslav republics and had 25% unemployment 1990.

Monterrey industrial city (iron, steel, textiles, chemicals, food processing) in NE Mexico; population (1986) 2,335,000. It was founded 1597.

Montessori Maria 1870–1952. Italian educationalist who developed the *Montessori method*, an educational system based on an informal approach, incorporating instructive play and allowing children to develop at their own pace.

Monteverdi Claudio (Giovanni Antonio) 1567–1643. Italian composer. He contributed to the development of the opera with *Orfeo* 1607 and *The Coronation of Poppea* 1642. He also wrote madrigals, ⟡motets, and sacred music, notably the *Vespers* 1610.

Montevideo capital and chief port (grain, meat products, hides) of Uruguay, on the Rio de la Plata; population (1985) 1,250,000. It was founded 1726.

Montezuma II 1466–1520. Aztec emperor 1502–20. When the Spanish conquistador Cortés invaded Mexico, Montezuma was imprisoned and killed during the Aztec attack on Cortés' force as it tried to leave Tenochtitlán, the Aztec capital city.

Montfort Simon de Montfort, Earl of Leicester *c.* 1208–1265. English politician and soldier. From 1258 he led the baronial opposition to Henry III's misrule during the second ⟡Barons' War and in 1264 defeated and captured the king at Lewes, Sussex. In 1265, as head of government, he summoned the first parliament in which the towns were represented; he was killed at the Battle of Evesham during the last of the Barons' Wars.

Montgolfier Joseph Michel 1740–1810 and Etienne Jacques 1745–1799. French brothers whose hot-air balloon was used for the first successful human flight 21 Nov 1783; they were aloft for 20 minutes above Paris. The Montgolfier experiments with balloons greatly stimulated scientific interest in aviation.

Montgomery Bernard Law, 1st Viscount Montgomery of Alamein 1887–1976. British field marshal. In World War II he commanded the 8th Army in N Africa in the Second Battle of El Alamein 1942. As commander of British troops in N Europe from 1944, he received the German surrender 1945.

Montréal inland port, industrial city (aircraft, chemicals, oil and petrochemicals, flour, sugar, brewing, meat packing) of Québec, Canada, on Montreal island at the junction of the Ottawa and St Lawrence rivers; population (1986) 2,921,000. Established as a French trading post 1611, Ville Marie (later renamed Montréal) was founded 1642; it surrendered to the British 1760.

Montserrat volcanic island in the West Indies, one of the Leeward group, a British crown colony; capital Plymouth; area 110 sq km/42 sq mi; population (1985) 12,000. Practically all buildings were destroyed by hurricane Hugo Sept 1989.

moon in astronomy, any natural ⟡satellite that orbits a planet. Mercury and Venus are the only planets in the Solar System that do not have moons.

Moon natural satellite of Earth, 3,476 km/2,160 mi in diameter, with a mass 0.012 (approximately one-eightieth) that of Earth. Its surface gravity is only 0.16 (one-sixth) that of Earth. Its average distance from Earth is 384,404 km/238,857 mi, and it orbits in a west-to-east direction every 27.32 days (the *sidereal month*). It spins on its axis with one side permanently turned towards Earth. The Moon has no atmosphere or water.

Moonie popular name for a follower of the ⟡Unification Church, a religious sect founded by Sun Myung Moon.

Moor any of the NW African Muslims, of mixed Arab and Berber origin, who conquered Spain and ruled its southern part from 711 to 1492. The name (English form of Latin *Maurus*) was originally applied to an inhabitant of the Roman province of Mauritania, in NW Africa.

Moore Henry 1898–1986. British sculptor. His subjects include the reclining nude, mother and child groups, the warrior, and interlocking abstract forms. Many of his post-1945 works are in bronze or marble, including monumental semi-abstracts such as *Reclining Figure* 1957–58 (outside the UNESCO building, Paris), and often designed to be placed in landscape settings.

moorhen marsh bird *Gallinula chloropus* of the rail family, common in water of swamps, lakes, and ponds in Eurasia, Africa, and North and South America. It is about 33 cm/13 in long, and mainly brown and grey, but with a red bill and forehead, and a vivid white underside to the tail.

moose North American name for ▷elk.

morality play didactic medieval European verse drama, in part a development of the ▷mystery play (or miracle play), in which human characters are replaced by personified virtues and vices, the limited humorous elements being provided by the Devil. Morality plays, such as *Everyman*, flourished in the 15th century. They exerted an influence on the development of Elizabethan drama and comedy.

Moravia (Czech *Morava*) district of central Europe, from 1960 two regions of Czechoslovakia: *South Moravia* (Czech *Jihomoravský*); *area* 15,030 sq km/5,802 sq mi; *capital* Brno; *population* (1991) 2,048,900; *North Moravia* (Czech *Severomoravský*); *area* 11,070 sq km/4,273 sq mi; *capital* Ostrava; *population* (1991) 1,961,500; *features* (N and S) river Morava; 25% forested; *products* maize, grapes, wine in the south; wheat, barley, rye, flax, sugar beet in the north; coal and iron; *history* part of the Avar territory since the 6th century; conquered by Charlemagne's Holy Roman Empire. In 874 the kingdom of Great Moravia was founded by the Slavic prince Sviatopluk, who ruled until 894. It was conquered by the Magyars 906, and became a fief of Bohemia 1029. It was passed to the Habsburgs 1526, and became an Austrian crown land 1849. It was incorporated in the new republic of Czechoslovakia 1918, forming a province until 1949.

Moray Earl of Moray another spelling of ▷Murray, regent of Scotland 1567–70.

More (St) Thomas 1478–1535. English politician and author. From 1509 he was favoured by ▷Henry VIII and employed on foreign embassies. He was a member of the privy council from 1518 and on the fall of Cardinal Wolsey became Lord Chancellor 1529, but resigned 1532 over Henry's break with the pope. He was executed for refusing to accept the king as head of the church. The title of his political book *Utopia* 1516 has come to mean any supposedly perfect society. He was canonized 1935.

Mormon or *Latter-day Saint* member of a Christian sect, the *Church of Jesus Christ of Latter-day Saints*, founded at Fayette, New York, 1830 by Joseph ▷Smith. According to Smith, Mormon was an ancient prophet in North America whose *Book of Mormon*, of which Smith claimed divine revelation, is accepted by Mormons as part of the Christian scriptures. In the 19th century the faction led by Brigham ▷Young was polygamous. It is a missionary church with headquarters in Utah and a worldwide membership of about 6 million.

morning glory any twining or creeping plant of the genus *Ipomoea*, especially *I. purpurea*, family Convolvulaceae, native to tropical America, with dazzling blue flowers. Small quantities of substances similar to the hallucinogenic drug ▷LSD are found in the seeds of some species.

Morocco Kingdom of; country in N Africa, bordered N and NW by the Mediterranean Sea, E and SE by Algeria, and S by Western Sahara; *area* 458,730 sq km/177,070 sq mi; *capital* Rabat; *physical* mountain ranges NE–SW; fertile coastal plains in W; *head of state* Hassan II from 1961; *head of government* Azzedine Laraki from 1985; *political system* constitutional monarchy; *exports* dates, figs, cork, wood pulp, canned fish, phosphates; *population* (1990 est) 26,249,000; *languages* Arabic (official) 75%; Berber 25%, French, Spanish; *recent history* established as a French and Spanish protectorate 1912; independence achieved from France 1956; former Spanish province of Ifni returned to Morocco 1969. Major revision of constitution 1972. Western Sahara ceded by Spain to Morocco and Mauritania 1975; guerrilla war in Western Sahara with Polisario Front, organization seeking independence of region. Morocco agreed to peace formula proposed 1983 but refused to deal directly with Polisario. Ceasefire agreed with Polisario 1987 but fighting continued. Diplomatic relations with Algeria and Syria restored 1988 and 1989.

Moroni capital of the Comoros Republic, on Njazidja (Grand Comore); population (1980) 20,000. It has a small natural harbour from which coffee, cacao, and vanilla are exported.

Morpheus in Greek and Roman mythology, the god of dreams, son of Hypnos or Somnus, god of sleep.

morphine narcotic alkaloid $C_{17}H_{19}NO_3$ derived from ▷opium and prescribed only to alleviate severe pain. Its use produces serious side effects, including nausea, constipation, tolerance, and addiction, but it is highly valued for the relief of the terminally ill. It is a controlled substance in Britain.

Morris William 1834–1896. English designer, founder of the ▷Arts and Crafts movement, socialist, and writer who shared the Pre-Raphaelite painters' fascination with medieval settings. In 1861 he cofounded a firm that designed and produced furniture, carpets, and a wide range of decorative wallpapers, many of which are still produced today. His Kelmscott Press, founded 1890, influenced printing and book design. The prose romances *A Dream of John Ball* 1888 and *News from Nowhere* 1891 reflect his socialist ideology. He also lectured on socialism.

morse code

A B C D E F

G H I J K L

M N O P Q R

S T U V W X

Y Z

1 2 3 4 5

6 7 8 9 0

Morrison Toni 1931– . US novelist whose fiction records black life in the South. Her works include *Song of Solomon* 1978, *Tar Baby* 1981, and *Beloved* 1987, based on a true story about infanticide in Kentucky, which won the Pulitzer Prize 1988.

Morrison Van (George Ivan) 1945– . Northern Irish singer and songwriter whose jazz-inflected Celtic soul style was already in evidence on *Astral Weeks* 1968 and has been highly influential. Among other albums are *Tupelo Honey* 1971, *Veedon Fleece* 1974, and *Avalon Sunset* 1989.

Morse Samuel (Finley Breese) 1791–1872. US inventor. In 1835 he produced the first adequate electric telegraph, and in 1843 was granted $30,000 by Congress for an experimental line between Washington DC and Baltimore. With his assistant Alexander Bain (1810–1877) he invented the Morse code.

Morse code international code for transmitting messages by wire or radio using signals of short (dots) and long (dashes) duration, originated by Samuel Morse for use on his invention, the telegraph.

Mortimer John 1923– . English barrister and writer. His works include the plays *The Dock Brief* 1958 and *A Voyage Round My Father* 1970, the novel *Paradise Postponed* 1985, and the television series *Rumpole of the Bailey*, from 1978, centred on a fictional barrister.

Mortimer Roger de, 8th Baron of Wigmore and 1st Earl of March *c.* 1287–1330. English politician and adventurer. He opposed Edward II and with Edward's queen, Isabella, led a rebellion against him 1326, bringing about his abdication. From 1327 Mortimer ruled England as the queen's lover, until Edward III had him executed.

Morton Jelly Roll. Stage name of Ferdinand Joseph La Menthe 1885–1941. US New Orleans-style jazz pianist, singer, and composer. Influenced by Scott Joplin, he was a pioneer in the development of jazz

from ragtime to swing by improvising and imposing his own personality on the music. His 1920s band was called the Red Hot Peppers.

mosaic design or picture, usually for a floor or wall, produced by inlaying small pieces of marble, glass, or other materials. Mosaic was commonly used by the Romans for their baths and villas (for example Hadrian's Villa at Tivoli) and by the Byzantines, especially for church decoration. More recent examples of mosaic work can be seen in the hall of the Houses of Parliament and in Westminster Cathedral, London.

Moscow (Russian *Moskva*) industrial city, capital of Russia and of the Moskva region, and formerly (1922–91) of the USSR, on the Moskva River 640 km/400 mi SE of St Petersburg; population (1987) 8,815,000. Its industries include machinery, electrical equipment, textiles, chemicals, and many food products. The 12th-century Kremlin is at the centre of the city. Star City (Zvezdnoy Gorodok), the Soviet space centre, is on the outskirts.

Moses *c.* 13th century BC. Hebrew lawgiver and judge who led the Israelites out of Egypt to the promised land of Canaan. On Mount Sinai he claimed to have received from Jehovah the oral and written Law, including the **Ten Commandments** engraved on tablets of stone. The first five books of the Old Testament – in Judaism, the *Torah* – are ascribed to him.

Moslem alternative spelling of *Muslim*, a follower of ◊Islam.

Mosley Oswald (Ernald) 1896–1980. British politician, founder of the British Union of Fascists (BUF). He was a member of Parliament 1918–31, then led the BUF until his internment 1940–43 during World War II. In 1946 Mosley was denounced when it became known that Italy had funded his prewar efforts to establish ◊fascism in Britain, but in 1948 he resumed fascist propaganda with his Union Movement, the revived BUF.

mosque in Islam, a place of worship. Chief features are: the dome; the minaret, a balconied turret from which the faithful are called to prayer; the *mihrab*, or prayer niche, in one of the interior walls, showing the direction of the holy city of Mecca; and an open court surrounded by porticoes.

mosquito any fly of the family Culicidae. The female mosquito has needlelike mouthparts and sucks blood before laying eggs. Males feed on plant juices. Some mosquitoes carry diseases such as ◊malaria.

moss small nonflowering plant of the class Musci (10,000 species), forming with the ◊liverworts and the hornworts the order Bryophyta. The stem of each plant bears rhizoids that anchor it; there are no true roots. Leaves spirally arranged on its lower portion have sexual organs at their tips. Most mosses flourish best in damp conditions where other vegetation is thin. The peat or bog moss *Sphagnum* was formerly used for surgical dressings.

motet sacred, polyphonic music for unaccompanied voices in a form that originated in 13th-century Europe.

moth any of the various families of mainly night-flying insects of the order Lepidoptera, which also includes the butterflies. Their wings are covered with microscopic scales. The mouthparts are formed into a sucking proboscis, but certain moths have no functional mouthparts, and rely upon stores of fat and other reserves built up during the caterpillar stage. At least 100,000 different species of moth are known. The largest British moths are the death's head and convolvulus hawk moths, which have a wingspread ranging from 114 mm/4.5 in to 133 mm/5.25 in.

mother-of-pearl or *nacre* the smooth lustrous lining in the shells of certain molluscs — for example pearl oysters, abalones, and mussels. When this layer is especially heavy it is used commercially for jewellery and decorations. Mother-of-pearl consists of calcium carbonate. See ◊pearl.

Mother's Day or *Mothering Sunday* day set apart in the USA, UK, and many European countries for honouring mothers. It is thought to have originated in Grafton, West Virginia, USA, 1908 when Anna Jarvis observed the anniversary of her mother's death. In the UK it is observed on the fourth Sunday of Lent.

motor anything that produces or imparts motion; a machine that provides mechanical power – for example, an electric motor. Machines that burn fuel (petrol, diesel) are usually called engines, but the internal-combustion engine that propels vehicles has long been called a motor, hence 'motoring' and 'motorcar'. Actually the motor is a part of the car engine.

motorcycle or *motorbike* two-wheeled vehicle propelled by a ◊petrol engine. The first successful motorized bicycle was built in France 1901, and British and US manufacturers first produced motorbikes 1903.

motorcycle racing sport of speed contests on motorcycles. It has many different forms: *road racing* over open roads; *circuit racing* over purpose-built tracks; *speedway* over oval-shaped dirt tracks; *motocross* over natural terrain, incorporating hill climbs; and *trials*, also over natural terrain, but with the addition of artificial hazards. The first motorcycle race was in Richmond, Surrey 1897. The Isle of Man TT races were inaugurated 1907 and are held over the island's roads.

motor neuron disease incurable wasting disease in which the nerve cells (neurons) controlling muscle action gradually die, causing progressive weakness and paralysis. It results from infection in childhood with the ◊polio virus; this is now largely eradicated, and it is thought that motor neuron disease will disappear by 2010.

motor racing competitive racing of motor vehicles.

It has forms as diverse as hill-climbing, stock-car racing, rallying, sports-car racing, and Formula One Grand Prix racing. The first organized race was from Paris to Rouen 1894. In Grand Prix racing, instituted 1906, a world championship for drivers has been in existence since 1950, and for constructors since 1958. The first six drivers and cars in each race are awarded points from nine to one, and the accumulative total at the end of a season (normally 16 races) decides the winners. The 24-hour endurance race at ◊Le Mans, first held 1923, is the foremost race for sports cars and prototypes.

mould mainly saprophytic fungi (see ◊fungus) living on foodstuffs and other organic matter, a few being parasitic on plants, animals, or each other. Many moulds are of medical or industrial importance, for example, penicillin.

moulting periodic shedding of the hair or fur of mammals, feathers of birds, or skin of reptiles. In mammals and birds, moulting is usually seasonal and is triggered by changes of day length.

mountain natural upward projection of the Earth's surface, higher and steeper than a hill. The process of mountain building (orogeny) consists of volcanism, folding, faulting, and thrusting, resulting from the collision and welding together of two tectonic plates. This process deforms the rock and compresses the sediment between the two plates into mountain chains.

mountain ash or *rowan* flowering tree *Sorbus aucuparia* of the family Rosaceae. It grows to 15 m/50 ft and has pinnate leaves and large clusters of whitish flowers, followed by orange-scarlet berries.

mountaineering art and practice of mountain climbing. For major peaks of the Himalayas it was formerly thought necessary to have elaborate support from Sherpas (local people), fixed ropes, and oxygen at high altitudes (*siege-style* climbing). In the 1980s the *Alpine style* was introduced. This dispenses with these aids, and relies on human ability to adapt, Sherpa-style, to high altitude.

mountain lion another name for ◊puma.

Mountbatten Louis, 1st Earl Mountbatten of Burma 1900–1979. British admiral and administrator. In World War II he became chief of combined operations 1942 and commander in chief in SE Asia 1943. As last viceroy of India 1947 and first governor general of India until 1948, he oversaw that country's transition to independence. He was killed by an Irish Republican Army bomb aboard his yacht in the Republic of Ireland.

mouse in computing, an input device used to control a pointer on a computer screen. It is a feature of graphical user-interface (GUI) systems. The mouse, about the size of a pack of playing cards, is connected to the computer by a wire, and incorporates one or more buttons that can be pressed. Moving the mouse across a flat surface causes a corresponding movement of the pointer. In this way, the operator can manipulate objects on the screen and make menu selections.

mouse in zoology, one of a number of small rodents with small ears and a long, thin tail, belonging largely to the Old World family Muridae. The house mouse *Mus musculus* is distributed worldwide. It is 75 mm/3 in long, with a naked tail of equal length, and has a grey-brown body. Common in Britain is the wood mouse *Apodemus sylvaticus*, richer in colour, and normally shy of human habitation. The tiny harvest mouse *Micromys minutus*, 65–75 mm/2.5–3 in long, makes spherical nests of straw supported on grass stems.

movement in music, a section of a large work, such as a symphony, which is often complete in itself.

Mozambique People's Republic of; country in SE Africa, bordered N by Zambia, Malawi, and Tanzania; E by the Indian Ocean; S by South Africa; and E by Swaziland and Zimbabwe; *area* 799,380 sq km/308,561 sq mi; *capital* and chief port Maputo; *physical* mostly flat tropical lowland; mountains in W; *head of state and government* Joaquim Alberto Chissano from 1986; *political system* socialist republic; *exports* prawns, cashews, sugar, cotton, tea, petroleum products, copra; *population* (1990 est) 14,718,000 (mainly indigenous Bantu peoples; Portuguese 50,000); *languages* Portuguese (official); 16 African languages; *recent history* a Portuguese colony from 1505, Mozambique achieved independence as a socialist republic 1975 with Frelimo as sole legal party. Good relations were re-established with Western powers 1983; an accord of nonagression was signed with South Africa 1984. The resistance group Renamo continued attacks on the government; one-party rule ended 1990.

Mozart Wolfgang Amadeus 1756–1791. Austrian composer and performer who showed astonishing precocity as a child and was an adult virtuoso. He was trained by his father, *Leopold Mozart* (1719–1787). From an early age he composed prolifically, his works including 27 piano concertos, 23 string quartets, 35 violin sonatas, and more than 50 symphonies including the E flat K543, G minor K550, and C major K551 ('Jupiter') symphonies, all composed 1788. His operas include *Idomeneo* 1781, *Le Nozze di Figaro/The Marriage of Figaro* 1786, *Don Giovanni* 1787, *Cosi fan tutte/Thus Do All Women* 1790, and *Die Zauberflöte/The Magic Flute* 1791. Strongly influenced by ◊Haydn, Mozart's music marks the height of the Classical age in its purity of melody and form.

MS-DOS (abbreviation for **M**icrosoft **D**isc **O**perating **S**ystem) computer ◊operating system produced by Microsoft Corporation, widely used on ◊microcomputers with 16-bit microprocessors. A version called PC-DOS is sold by IBM specifically

for their range of personal computers. MS-DOS and PC-DOS are usually referred to as DOS. MS-DOS first appeared in the early 1980s, and was based on an earlier system for computers with 8-bit microprocessors, CP/M.

Mubarak Hosni 1928– . Egyptian politician, president from 1981. Vice president to Anwar Sadat from 1975, Mubarak succeeded him on his assassination. He has continued to pursue Sadat's moderate policies, and has significantly increased the freedom of the press and of political association, while trying to repress the growing Islamic fundamentalist movement.

mucous membrane thin skin lining all animal body cavities and canals that come into contact with the air (for example, eyelids, breathing and digestive passages, genital tract). It secretes mucus, a moistening, lubricating, and protective fluid.

mudskipper fish of the goby family, genus *Periophthalmus*, found in brackish water and shores in the tropics, except for the Americas. It can walk or climb over mudflats, using its strong pectoral fins as legs, and has eyes set close together on top of the head. It grows up to 30 cm/12 in long.

Mugabe Robert (Gabriel) 1925– . Zimbabwean politician, prime minister from 1980 and president from 1987. He was in detention in Rhodesia for nationalist activities 1964–74, then carried on guerrilla warfare from Mozambique. As leader of ◊ZANU he was in an uneasy alliance with Joshua ◊Nkomo of ZAPU (Zimbabwe African People's Union) from 1976. The two parties merged 1987.

Muhammad or *Mohammed*, *Mahomet* c. 570–632. Founder of Islam, born in Mecca on the Arabian peninsula. In about 616 he claimed to be a prophet and that the *Koran* was revealed to him by God (it was later written down by his followers), through the angel Jibra'el. He fled from persecution to the town now known as Medina in 622: the flight, *Hegira*, marks the beginning of the Islamic era.

mujaheddin (Arabic *mujahid* 'fighters', from *jihad* 'holy war') Islamic fundamentalist guerrillas of contemporary Afghanistan and Iran. The mujaheddin first rose to prominence during the mid-1970s, opposing the Daud Khan regime and being initially financed by Iran, Libya, and Pakistan, and, after the Soviet invasion of Afghanistan Dec 1979, later received substantial covert support from the USA and China. They secured control over much of the Afghan countryside and so debilitated the Kābul regime that Red Army troops were withdrawn 1989 and the Najibullah administration overthrown 1992.

Mukalla seaport capital of the Hadhramaut coastal region of S Yemen; on the Gulf of Aden 480 km E of Aden; population (1984) 158,000. It is a fishing centre; fish products and boat building are important; coffee and tobacco are exported from Mukalla.

mulberry any tree of the genus *Morus*, family

Moraceae, consisting of a dozen species, including the black mulberry *M. nigra*. It is native to W Asia and has heart-shaped, toothed leaves, and spikes of whitish flowers. It is widely cultivated for its fruit, which, made up of a cluster of small drupes, resembles a raspberry.

mule hybrid animal, usually the offspring of a male ass and a female horse. Mules are used as working animals; they are sterile.

mullet either of two species of fish. The *red mullet Mullus surmuletus* is found in the Mediterranean and warm Atlantic as far north as the English Channel. It is about 40 cm/16 in long, red with yellow stripes, and has long barbels round the mouth. The *grey mullet Crenimugil labrosus* lives in ponds and estuaries. It is greyish above, with longitudinal dark stripes, and grows to 60 cm/24 in.

Mulroney Brian 1939– . Canadian politician, Progressive Conservative Party leader from 1983, prime minister from 1984. He achieved a landslide in the 1984 election, and won the 1988 election on a platform of free trade with the USA, but with a reduced majority. By 1991 his public-opinion standing had fallen to an unprecedented low level.

multinational corporation company or enterprise operating in several countries, usually defined as one that has 25% or more of its output capacity located outside its country of origin.

multiple sclerosis (MS) incurable chronic disease of the central nervous system, occurring in young or middle adulthood. It is characterized by degeneration of the myelin sheath that surrounds nerves in the brain and spinal cord. It is also known as disseminated sclerosis. Its cause is unknown.

multitasking or *multiprogramming* in computing, a system in which one processor appears to run several different programs (or different parts of the same program) at the same time. All the programs are held in memory together and each is allowed to run for a certain period.

mummy any dead body, human or animal, that has been naturally or artificially preserved. Natural mummification can occur through freezing (for example, mammoths in glacial ice from 25,000 years ago), drying, or preservation in bogs or oil seeps. Artificial mummification may be achieved by embalming (for example, the mummies of ancient Egypt) or by freeze-drying.

mumps virus infection marked by fever and swelling of the parotid salivary glands (such as those under the ears). It is usually minor in children, although meningitis is a possible complication. In adults the symptoms are severe and it may cause sterility in adult men.

Munch Edvard 1863–1944. Norwegian painter and printmaker, a forerunner of ⟡Expressionism. He studied in Paris and Berlin, and his major works date from the period 1892–1908, when he lived mainly in Germany. His paintings often focus on neurotic emotional states. The *Frieze of Life* 1890s, a sequence of highly charged, symbolic paintings, includes some of his most characteristic images, such as *Skriket/The Scream* 1893 (National Gallery, Oslo). He later reused these in etchings, lithographs, and woodcuts.

Munich (German *München*) industrial city (brewing, printing, precision instruments, machinery, electrical goods, textiles), capital of Bavaria, Germany, on the river Isar; population (1986) 1,269,400. Dating from the 12th century, the city owes much of its buildings and art treasures to the kings Ludwig I and Maximilian II of Bavaria. It became the centre of the Nazi movement.

Munich Agreement pact signed 29 Sept 1938 by the leaders of the UK (Neville Chamberlain), France (Edouard Daladier), Germany (Hitler), and Italy (Mussolini), under which Czechoslovakia was compelled to surrender its Sudeten-German districts (the *Sudetenland*) to Germany. Chamberlain claimed it would guarantee 'peace in our time', but it did not prevent Hitler from seizing the rest of Czechoslovakia March 1939.

Munster southern province of the Republic of Ireland, comprising the counties of Clare, Cork, Kerry, Limerick, North and South Tipperary, and Waterford; area 24,140 sq km/9,318 sq mi; population (1991) 1,008,400.

muntjac small deer, genus *Muntiacus*, found in SE Asia. There are some six species. Males have short spiked antlers and two sharp canine teeth forming tusks. They are sometimes called 'barking deer' because of their voices. Some have escaped from parks in central England and have become established in the wild.

Murasaki Shikibu *c.* 978–c. 1015. Japanese writer, a lady at the court. Her masterpiece of fiction, *The Tale of Genji*, is one of the classic works of Japanese literature, and may be the world's first novel.

Murcia autonomous region of SE Spain; area 11,300 sq km/4,362 sq mi; population (1986) 1,014,000. It includes the cities Murcia and Cartagena, and produces esparto grass, lead, zinc, iron, and fruit.

murder unlawful killing of one person by another. In British law murder is committed only when the killer acts with malice aforethought, that is, intending either to kill or to cause serious injury, or realizing that this would probably result. It is punishable by life imprisonment. It is the most serious form of ⟡homicide.

Murdoch (Keith) Rupert 1931– . Australian-born US media magnate with worldwide interests. His UK newspapers, generally right-wing, are the *Sun*, the *News of the World*, *The Times* and *Sunday Times*, and *Today*; he (News International) has a 50% share in Sky Television (merged 1990 with

British Satellite Broadcasting to become British Sky Broadcasting, BSkyB). Over 70% of newspapers sold in Australia are controlled by Murdoch. In the USA, he has a 50% share of 20th Century Fox, six Metromedia TV stations, and newspaper and magazine publishing companies.

Murillo Bartolomé Esteban *c*. 1617–1682. Spanish painter, active mainly in Seville. He painted sentimental pictures of the Virgin, such as the *Soult Immaculate Conception* 1678 (Louvre, Paris); he also specialized in studies of street urchins.

Murmansk seaport in NW Russia, on the Barents Sea; population (1987) 432,000. It is the largest city in the Arctic, Russia's most important fishing port, and the base of naval units and the icebreakers that keep the Northeast Passage open.

Murray principal river of Australia, 2,575 km/ 1,600 mi long. It rises in the Australian Alps near Mount Kosciusko and flows west, forming the boundary between New South Wales and Victoria, and reaches the sea at Encounter Bay, South Australia. With its main tributary, the Darling, it is 3,750 km/2,330 mi long.

Murray James Stuart, Earl of Murray, or Moray 1531–1570. Regent of Scotland from 1567, an illegitimate son of James V. He was one of the leaders of the Scottish Reformation, and after the deposition of his half-sister ◊Mary Queen of Scots, he became regent. He was assassinated by one of her supporters.

Muscat or *Masqat* capital of Oman, E Arabia, adjoining the port of Matrah, which has a deepwater harbour; combined population (1982) 80,000. It produces natural gas and chemicals.

muscle contractile animal tissue that produces locomotion and maintains the movement of body substances. Muscle is made of long cells that can contract to between one-half and one-third of their relaxed length.

muscular dystrophy any of a group of inherited chronic muscle disorders marked by weakening and wasting of muscle. Muscle fibres degenerate, to be replaced by fatty tissue, although the nerve supply remains unimpaired. Death occurs in early adult life.

Muses in Greek mythology, the nine daughters of Zeus and Mnemosyne (goddess of memory) and inspirers of creative arts: Calliope, epic poetry; Clio, history; Erato, love poetry; Euterpe, lyric poetry; Melpomene, tragedy; Polyhymnia, hymns; Terpsichore, dance; Thalia, comedy; and Urania, astronomy.

Museveni Yoweri Kaguta 1945– . Ugandan general and politician, president from 1986. He led the opposition to Idi Amin's regime 1971–78 and was minister of defence 1979–80 but, unhappy with Milton Obote's autocratic leadership, formed the National Resistance Army (NRA). When Obote was ousted in a coup 1985, Museveni entered into a brief power-sharing agreement with his successor, Tito Okello, before taking over as president. Museveni leads a broad-based coalition government.

mushroom fruiting body of certain fungi, consisting of an upright stem and a spore-producing cap with radiating gills on the undersurface. There are many edible species belonging to the genus *Agaricus*. See also ◊fungus and ◊toadstool.

music art of combining sounds into a coherent perceptual experience, typically in accordance with fixed patterns and for an aesthetic purpose. Music

muscle

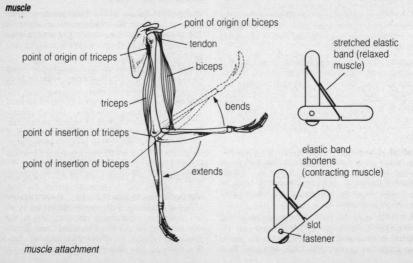

point of origin of biceps

tendon

point of origin of triceps

biceps

triceps

point of insertion of triceps

point of insertion of biceps

bends

extends

stretched elastic band (relaxed muscle)

elastic band shortens (contracting muscle)

slot

fastener

muscle attachment

is generally categorized as classical, ⟡jazz, ⟡pop music, ⟡country and western, and so on.

The various civilizations of the ancient and modern world developed their own musical systems. Eastern music recognizes many more subdivisions of an interval than Western music does and also differs from Western music in that the absence, until recently, of written notation ruled out the composition of major developed works.

musical 20th-century form of dramatic musical performance, combining elements of song, dance, and the spoken word, often characterized by lavish staging and large casts. It developed from the operettas and musical comedies of the 19th century. Well-known musicals include Rodgers and Hammerstein's *Oklahoma!* 1943, Bernstein's *West Side Story* 1957, Lionel Bart's *Oliver!*, Hamlisch and Kleban's *A Chorus Line* 1975, the ⟡Lloyd Webber musicals such as *Phantom of the Opera* 1986, and Alain Boutlil and Claude-Michel Schönberg's *Les Misérables* 1980.

musical instrument digital interface manufacturer's standard for digital music equipment; see ⟡MIDI.

music hall British light theatrical entertainment, in which singers, dancers, comedians, and acrobats perform in 'turns'. The music hall's heyday was at the beginning of the 20th century, with such artistes as Marie Lloyd, Harry Lauder, and George Formby. The US equivalent is vaudeville.

musk in botany, perennial plant *Mimulus moschatus* of the family Scrophulariaceae; its small oblong leaves exude the musky scent from which it takes its name; it is also called *monkey flower*. Also any of several plants with a musky odour, including the musk mallow *Malva moschata* and the musk rose *Rosa moschata*.

musk deer small deer *Moschus moschiferus* native to mountains of central Asia. A solitary animal, it is about 50 cm/20 in high, sure-footed, and has large ears and no antlers. Males have tusklike upper canine teeth. It is hunted and farmed for the musk secreted by an abdominal gland, which is used as medicine or perfume.

musk ox ruminant *Ovibos moschatus* of the family Bovidae, native to the Arctic regions of North America. It displays characteristics of sheep and oxen, is about the size of a small domestic cow, and has long brown hair. At certain seasons it exhales a musky odour.

muskrat rodent *Ondatra zibethicus* of the family Cricetidae, about 30 cm/12 in long, living along streams, rivers, and lakes in North America. It has webbed hind feet, a side-to-side flattened tail, and shiny, light-brown fur. It builds up a store of food, plastering it over with mud, for winter consumption. It is hunted for its fur. Both the animal and its fur are sometimes known as *musquash*.

Muslim or *Moslem*, a follower of ⟡Islam.

mussel one of a number of bivalve molluscs, some of them edible, such as *Mytilus edulis*, found in clusters attached to rocks around the N Atlantic and American coasts. It has a blue-black shell.

Mussolini Benito 1883–1945. Italian dictator 1925–43. As founder of the Fascist Movement (see ⟡fascism) 1919 and prime minister from 1922, he became known as *Il Duce* ('the leader'). He invaded Ethiopia 1935–36, intervened in the Spanish Civil War 1936–39 in support of Franco, and conquered Albania 1939. In June 1940 Italy entered World War II supporting Hitler. Forced by military and domestic setbacks to resign 1943, Mussolini established a breakaway government in N Italy 1944–45, but was killed trying to flee the country.

Mussorgsky Modest Petrovich 1839–1881. Russian composer who was largely self-taught. His opera *Boris Godunov* was completed 1869, although not produced in St Petersburg until 1874. Some of his works were 'revised' by ⟡Rimsky-Korsakov, and only recently has their harsh original beauty been recognized.

mustard any of several annual plants of the family Cruciferae, with sweet-smelling yellow flowers. Brown and white mustard are cultivated as a condiment in Europe and North America. The seeds of brown mustard *Brassica juncea* and white mustard *Sinapis alba* are used in the preparation of table mustard.

mutation in biology, a change in the genes produced by a change in the ⟡DNA that makes up the hereditary material of all living organisms. Mutations, the raw material of evolution, result from mistakes during replication (copying) of DNA molecules. Only a few improve the organism's performance and are therefore favoured by ⟡natural selection. Mutation rates are increased by certain chemicals and by radiation.

mutiny organized act of disobedience or defiance by two or more members of the armed services. In naval and military law, mutiny has always been regarded as one of the most serious of crimes, punishable in wartime by death.

mutualism or ⟡*symbiosis* an association between two organisms of different species whereby both profit from the relationship.

Muybridge Eadweard. Adopted name of Edward James Muggeridge 1830–1904. British photographer. He made a series of animal locomotion photographs in the USA in the 1870s and proved that, when a horse trots, there are times when all its feet are off the ground. He also explored motion in birds and humans.

Muzorewa Abel (Tendekayi) 1925– . Zimbabwean politician and Methodist bishop. He was president of the African National Council 1971–85 and prime minister of Rhodesia/Zimbabwe 1979. He was detained for a year in 1983–84. He is leader of the minority United Africa National Council.

Mwinyi Ali Hassan 1925– . Tanzanian socialist politician, president from 1985, when he succeeded

Julius Nyerere. He began a revival of private enterprise and control of state involvement and spending.

Myanmar Union of (formerly *Burma*); country in SE Asia, bordered NW by India, NE by China, SE by Laos and Thailand, and SW by the Bay of Bengal; *area* 676,577 sq km/261,228 sq mi; *capital* and chief port Yangon (formerly Rangoon); *physical* over half is rainforest; rivers Irrawaddy and Chindwin in central lowlands ringed by mountains in N, W, and E; *head of state and government* Than Shwe from 1992; *political system* military republic; *exports* rice, rubber, jute, teak, jade, rubies, sapphires; *population* (1990 est) 41,279,000 (includes Shan, Karen, Raljome, Chinese, and Indian minorities); *language* Burmese; *recent history* a crown colony in the British Commonwealth from 1937, Burma achieved independence 1948 and left the Commonwealth. Army coup by General Ne Win 1962. Presidential-style 'civilian' constitution adopted 1973–74. General Saw Maung seized power in a military coup 1988; martial law declared 1989; country renamed Myanmar and capital renamed Yangon. Breakaway opposition group formed 'parallel government' on rebel-held territory 1990. Martial law, human-rights abuses, and military offensives continued. Opposition leader, Aung San Suu Kyi, received Nobel Peace Prize 1991. Pogrom against Muslim community in Arakan province 1992 backed by army; Than Shwe replaced General Saw Maung at head of ruling military junta.

mycelium interwoven mass of threadlike filaments or hyphae, forming the main body of most fungi. The reproductive structures, or 'fruiting bodies', grow from the mycelium.

Mycenaean civilization Bronze Age civilization that flourished in Crete, Cyprus, Greece, the Aegean Islands, and W Anatolia about 4000–1000 BC. During this period, magnificent architecture and sophisticated artefacts were produced. The Mycenaeans have been identified with the ▷Achaeans of Homer, and were among the besiegers at ▷Troy. They may also have been the marauding sea peoples of Egyptian records.

mynah any of various tropical starlings, family Sturnidae, of SE Asia. The glossy blackhill mynah *Gracula religiosa* of India is a realistic mimic of sounds and human speech.

myopia short-sightedness, caused either by an eyeball that is too long or a lens that is too strong. Nearby objects are sharply perceived, but distance vision is blurred.

Myron *c.* 500–440 BC. Greek sculptor. His *Discobolus/Discus-Thrower* and *Athene and Marsyas*, much admired in his time, are known through Roman copies. They confirm his ancient reputation for brilliant composition and naturalism.

myrrh gum resin produced by small trees of the genus *Commiphora* of the Bursera family, especially *C. myrrha*, found in Ethiopia and Arabia. In ancient times it was used for incense and perfume and in embalming.

myrtle evergreen shrub of the Old World genus *Myrtus*, family Myrtaceae. The commonly cultivated Mediterranean myrtle *M. communis* has oval opposite leaves and white flowers followed by purple berries, all of which are fragrant.

mystery play or *miracle play* medieval religious drama based on stories from the Bible. Mystery plays were performed around the time of church festivals, reaching their height in Europe during the 15th and 16th centuries. A whole cycle running from the Creation to the Last Judgement was performed in separate scenes on mobile wagons by various town guilds. Four English cycles survive: Coventry, Wakefield (or Townley), Chester, and York. Versions are still performed, such as the York cycle in York.

mystery religion any of various cults of the ancient world, open only to the initiated; for example, the cults of Demeter (see ▷Eleusinian Mysteries), Dionysus, Cybele, Isis, and Mithras. Underlying some of them is a fertility ritual, in which a deity undergoes death and resurrection and the initiates feed on the flesh and blood to attain communion with the divine and ensure their own life beyond the grave. The influence of mystery religions on early Christianity was considerable.

mysticism religious belief or spiritual experience based on direct, intuitive communion with the divine. It does not always involve an orthodox deity, though it is found in all the major religions – for example, kabbalism in Judaism, Sufism in Islam, and the bhakti movement in Hinduism. The mystical experience is often rooted in asceticism and can involve visions, trances, and ecstasies; many religious traditions prescribe meditative and contemplative techniques for achieving mystical experience. Official churches fluctuate between acceptance of mysticism as a form of special grace, and suspicion of it as a dangerous deviation, verging on the heretical.

mythology study and interpretation of the stories symbolically underlying a given culture and of how they relate to similar stories told in other cultures. These stories describe gods and other supernatural beings, with whom humans may have relationships, and are intended to explain the workings of the universe and human history.

myxomatosis contagious, usually fatal, virus infection of rabbits which causes much suffering. It has been deliberately introduced in the UK and Australia since the 1950s to reduce the rabbit population.

N

at 1,660 m/5,450 ft; population (1985) 1,100,000. It has light industry and food processing and is the headquarters of the United Nations Environment Programme. Nairobi was founded 1899.

Najibullah Ahmadzai 1947– . Afghan communist politician, state president 1986–92. A member of the Politburo from 1981, he became leader of the People's Democratic Party of Afghanistan (PDPA) 1986. After the withdrawal of Soviet troops Feb 1989, continuing pressure from the mujaheddin forces for his resignation, and their resistance to any settlement under his regime, resulted in his eventual overthrow. He was captured while attempting to flee the country and placed under UN protection, pending trial by an Islamic court.

Nakhichevan autonomous republic forming part of Azerbaijan, even though it is entirely outside the Azerbaijan boundary, being separated from it by Armenia; area 5,500 sq km/2,120 sq mi; population (1986) 272,000. Taken by Russia in 1828, it was annexed to Azerbaijan in 1924. 85% of the 278,000 population are Muslim Azeris who maintain strong links with Iran to the south. Nakhichevan has been affected by the Armenia–Azerbaijan conflict; many Azeris have fled to Azerbaijan, and in Jan 1990 frontier posts and border fences with Iran were destroyed. The republic is seeking independence from Azerbaijan.

Namib Desert coastal desert region in Namibia between the Kalahari Desert and the Atlantic Ocean. Its sand dunes are among the tallest in the world, reaching heights of 370 m/1,200 ft.

Namibia Republic of (formerly *South West Africa*); country in SW Africa, bordered N by Angola and Zambia, E by Botswana and South Africa, and W by the Atlantic Ocean; **area** 824,300 sq km/318,262 sq mi; **capital** Windhoek; **physical** mainly desert; includes the enclave of Walvis Bay (area 1,120 sq km/432 sq mi); **head of state and government** Sam Nujoma from 1990; **political system** democratic republic; **exports** diamonds, uranium, copper, lead, zinc; **population** (1990 est) 1,372,000 (black African 85%, European 6%); **languages** Afrikaans (spoken by 60% of white population), German, English (all official); several indigenous languages; **recent history** administered by South Africa, under League of Nations mandate, as British South Africa 1920–46. South Africa did not accept the termination of the mandate 1966 by the United Nations and extended apartheid laws to the country. The UN redesignated it Namibia 1968; in 1978 Security Council Resolution 435 for the granting of full sovereignty was accepted by South Africa, then rescinded. SWAPO, formed 1958 to seek full independence and racial equality, pursued an armed resistance campaign for independence until 1989, when a UN peacekeeping force was stationed in Namibia to oversee multiparty elections. These were won by SWAPO. In 1990 Liberal multiparty 'independence'

Nabokov Vladimir 1899–1977. US writer who left his native Russia 1917 and began writing in English in the 1940s. His most widely known book is *Lolita* 1955, the story of the middle-aged Humbert Humbert's infatuation with a precocious girl of 12. His other books include *Laughter in the Dark* 1938, *The Real Life of Sebastian Knight* 1945, *Pnin* 1957, and his memoirs *Speak, Memory* 1947.

Nagaland state of NE India, bordering Myanmar (Burma) on the east; **area** 16,721 sq km/6,456 sq mi; **capital** Kohima; **products** rice, tea, coffee, paper, sugar; **population** (1991) 1,215,600; **history** formerly part of Assam, the area was seized by Britain from Burma (now Myanmar) 1826. The British sent 18 expeditions against the Naga peoples in the north 1832–87. After India attained independence 1947, there was Naga guerrilla activity against the Indian government; the state of Nagaland was established 1963 in response to demands for self-government, but fighting continued sporadically.

Nagasaki industrial port (coal, iron, shipbuilding) on Kyushu island, Japan; population (1989) 442,400. An atom bomb was dropped on it 9 Aug 1945.

Nagoya industrial seaport (cars, textiles, clocks) on Honshu island, Japan; population (1989) 2,101,000. It has a shogun fortress 1610 and a notable Shinto shrine, Atsuta Jingu.

Nagpur industrial city (textiles, metals) in Maharashtra, India; population (1981) 1,298,000.

Nahuatl member of any of a group of Mesoamerican Indian peoples (Mexico and Central America), of which the best-known group were the Aztecs. The Nahuatl are the largest ethnic group in Mexico, and their languages, which belong to the Uto-Aztecan (Aztec-Tanoan) family, are spoken by over a million people today.

naiad in classical mythology, a water nymph.

Nairobi capital of Kenya, in the central highlands

constitution adopted and independence achieved from South Africa. In 1991 joint administration of Walvis Bay was agreed with South Africa.

Nanak 1469–c. 1539. Indian guru and founder of Sikhism, a religion based on the unity of God and the equality of all human beings. He was strongly opposed to caste divisions.

Nanchang industrial (textiles, glass, porcelain, soap) capital of Jiangxi province, China, about 260 km/160 mi SE of Wuhan; population (1989) 1,330,000.

Nanjing or **Nanking** capital of Jiangsu province, China, 270 km/165 mi NW of Shanghai; centre of industry (engineering, shipbuilding, oil refining), commerce, and communications; population (1989) 2,470,000. The bridge 1968 over the Chang Jiang river is the longest in China at 6,705 m/22,000 ft.

nanotechnology the building of devices on a molecular scale. Micromachines, such as gears smaller in diameter than a human hair, have been made at the AT&T Bell laboratories in New Jersey, USA. Building large molecules with useful shapes has been accomplished by research groups in the USA. A robot small enough to travel through the bloodstream and into organs of the body, inspecting or removing diseased tissue, was under development in Japan 1990.

Nansen Fridtjof 1861–1930. Norwegian explorer and scientist. In 1893, he sailed to the Arctic in the *Fram*, which was deliberately allowed to drift north with an iceflow. Nansen, accompanied by F Hjalmar Johansen (1867–1923), continued north on foot and reached 86° 14' N, the highest latitude then attained.

napalm fuel used in flamethrowers and incendiary bombs. Produced from jellied petrol, it is a mixture of *na*phthenic and *palm*itic acids. Napalm causes extensive burns because it sticks to the skin even when aflame. It was widely used by the US Army during the Vietnam War.

naphtha the mixtures of hydrocarbons obtained by destructive distillation of petroleum, coal tar, and shale oil. It is raw material for the petrochemical and plastics industries. The term was originally applied to naturally occurring liquid hydrocarbons.

Napier John 1550–1617. Scottish mathematician who invented ◇logarithms 1614 and 'Napier's bones', an early mechanical calculating device for multiplication and division.

Naples (Italian *Napoli*) industrial port (shipbuilding, cars, textiles, paper, food processing) and capital of Campania, Italy, on the Tyrrhenian Sea; population (1988) 1,201,000. To the south is the Isle of Capri, and behind the city is Mount Vesuvius, with the ruins of Pompeii at its foot.

Naples, Kingdom of the southern part of Italy, alternately independent and united with ◇Sicily in the Kingdom of the Two Sicilies.

Napoleon I Bonaparte 1769–1821. Emperor of the French 1804–14 and 1814–15. A general from 1796 in the ◇Revolutionary Wars, in 1799 he overthrew the ruling Directory (see ◇French Revolution) and made himself dictator. From 1803 he conquered most of Europe (the **Napoleonic Wars**) and installed his brothers as puppet kings (see ◇Bonaparte). After the Peninsular War and retreat from Moscow 1812, he was forced to abdicate 1814 and was banished to the island of Elba. In March 1815 he reassumed power but was defeated by British forces at the Battle of ◇Waterloo and exiled to the island of St Helena. His internal administrative reforms and laws are still evident in France.

Napoleon II 1811–1832. Title given by the Bonapartists to the son of Napoleon I and ◇Marie Louise; until 1814 he was known as the king of Rome and after 1818 as the duke of Reichstadt. After his father's abdication 1814 he was taken to the Austrian court, where he spent the rest of his life.

Napoleon III 1808–1873. Emperor of the French 1852–70, known as *Louis-Napoleon*. After two attempted coups (1836 and 1840) he was jailed, then went into exile, returning for the revolution of 1848, when he became president of the Second Republic but soon turned authoritarian. In 1870 he was manoeuvred by the German chancellor Bismarck into war with Prussia (see ◇Franco-Prussian war); he was forced to surrender at Sedan, NE France, and the empire collapsed.

Napoleonic Wars 1803–15 a series of wars conducted by Napoleon I of France, which were intended to expand and secure French control of Europe. Opposed by a Grand Coalition of European states (Austria, Britain, Russia, Sweden, and Prussia), Napoleon won a series of military victories at Austerlitz (1805), Jena (1806), Eylau and Friedland (1807), but was forced to abandon his campaign against Britain after the naval defeat at Trafalgar. His armies fought an inconclusive war in Spain (Peninsular War) from 1808 but his attempt to invade Russia 1812 proved a disaster, and a further defeat at Leipzig 1813 led to his capture and exile to Elba. Napoleon's escape and return to France 1815 provoked further battles between French armies and Coalition forces, which culminated in a final French defeat at Waterloo.

Narasimha Rao P(amulaparti) V(enkata) 1921– . Indian politician, prime minister of India from 1991 and Congress (I) leader. He governed the state of Andhra Pradesh as chief minister 1971–73, and served in the Congress (I) cabinets of Indira and Rajiv Gandhi. He took over the party leadership after the assassination of Rajiv Gandhi. Elected prime minister the following month, he instituted a reform of the economy.

narcissus any bulbous plant of the genus *Narcissus* family Amaryllidaceae. Species include the daffodil, jonquil, and narcissus. All have flowers with a cup projecting from the centre.

Narcissus in Greek mythology, a beautiful youth who rejected the love of the nymph ⚪Echo and was condemned to fall in love with his own reflection in a pool. He pined away and in the place where he died a flower sprang up that was named after him.

narcotic pain-relieving and sleep-inducing drug. The chief narcotics induce dependency, and include opium, its derivatives and synthetic modifications (such as morphine and heroin); alcohols (such as ethanol); and barbiturates.

Narmada River river that rises in the Maikala range in Madhya Pradesh state, central India, and flows 1,245 km/778 mi WSW to the Gulf of Khambat, an inlet of the Arabian Sea.

narwhal toothed whale *Monodon monoceros*, found only in the Arctic Ocean. It grows to 5 m/16 ft long, has a grey and black body, a small head, and short flippers. The male has a single spirally fluted tusk that may be up to 2.7 m/9 ft long.

NASA (acronym for *National Aeronautics and Space Administration*) US government agency, founded 1958, for spaceflight and aeronautical research. Its headquarters are in Washington DC and its main installation is at the ⚪Kennedy Space Center in Florida. NASA's early planetary and lunar programs included Pioneer spacecraft from 1958, which gathered data for the later crewed missions, the most famous of which took the first people to the Moon in *Apollo 11* on 16–24 July 1969.

Naseby, Battle of decisive battle of the English Civil War 14 June 1645, when the Royalists, led by Prince Rupert, were defeated by Oliver Cromwell and General Fairfax. It is named after the nearby village of Naseby, 32 km/20 mi S of Leicester.

Nash John 1752–1835. English architect. He laid out Regent's Park, London, and its approaches. Between 1813 and 1820 he planned Regent Street (later rebuilt), repaired and enlarged Buckingham Palace (for which he designed Marble Arch), and rebuilt Brighton Pavilion in flamboyant oriental style.

Nash Paul 1889–1946. English painter, an official war artist in world wars I and II. In the 1930s he was one of a group of artists promoting avant-garde styles in the UK. Two of his works are *Totes Meer/Dead Sea* (Tate Gallery, London) and *The Battle of Britain* (Imperial War Museum, London).

Nashville port on the Cumberland river and capital of Tennessee, USA; population (1990) 488,300. It is a banking and commercial centre, and has large printing, music-publishing, and recording industries. Nashville dates from 1778, and the Confederate army was defeated here in 1864 in the American Civil War.

Nassau capital and port of the Bahamas, on New Providence island; population (1980) 135,000. English settlers founded it in the 17th century, and it was a supply base for Confederate blockade runners during the American Civil War.

Nasser Gamal Abdel 1918–1970. Egyptian politician, prime minister 1954–56 and from 1956 president of Egypt (the United Arab Republic 1958–71). In 1952 he was the driving power behind the Neguib coup, which ended the monarchy. His nationalization of the Suez Canal 1956 led to an Anglo-French invasion and the ⚪Suez Crisis, and his ambitions for an Egyptian-led union of Arab states led to disquiet in the Middle East (and in the West). Nasser was also an early and influential leader of the non-aligned movement.

nastic movement plant movement that is caused by an external stimulus, such as light or temperature, but is directionally independent of its source, unlike ⚪tropisms. Nastic movements occur as a result of changes in water pressure within specialized cells or differing rates of growth in parts of the plant.

nasturtium any plant of the genus *Nasturtium*, family Cruciferae, including watercress *N. officinale*, a perennial aquatic plant of Europe and Asia, grown as a salad crop. It also includes plants of the South American family Tropaeolaceae, including the cultivated species *Tropaeolum majus*, with orange or scarlet flowers, and *T. minus*, which has smaller flowers.

Natal province of South Africa, NE of Cape Province, bounded on the east by the Indian Ocean; **area** 91,785 sq km/35,429 sq mi; **capital** Pietermaritzburg; **towns** Durban; **physical** slopes from the Drakensberg to a fertile subtropical coastal plain; **features** Ndumu Game Reserve, Kosi Bay Nature Reserve, Sodwana Bay National Park, Maple Lane Nature Reserve, and St Lucia National Park, which extends from coral reefs of the Indian Ocean N of Umfolozi river (whales, dolphins, turtles, crayfish), over forested sandhills to inland grasslands and swamps of Lake St Lucia, 324 sq km/125 sq mi (reedbuck, buffalo, crocodile, hippopotamus, black rhino, cheetah, pelican, flamingo, stork). It is under threat from titanium mining; **products** sugar cane, black wattle *Acacia mollissima*, maize, fruit, vegetables, tobacco, coal; **population** (1985) 2,145,000.

national curriculum in the UK from 1988, a course of study in ten subjects common to all primary and secondary state schools. The national curriculum is divided into three core subjects – English, maths, and science – and seven foundation subjects: geography, history, technology, a foreign language (for secondary school pupils), art, music, and physical education. There are four stages, on completion of which the pupil's work is assessed. The stages are for ages 5–7, 7–11, 11–14, and 14–16.

national debt debt incurred by the central government of a country to its own people and institutions and also to overseas creditors. A government can borrow from the public by means of selling interest-bearing bonds, for example, or from abroad. Traditionally, a major cause of incurring national debt was the cost of war but in recent decades governments have borrowed heavily in order to finance development or nationalization, to support an ailing currency, or to avoid raising taxes.

National Front in the UK, extreme right-wing political party founded 1967. In 1991, the party claimed 3,000 members. Some of its members had links with the National Socialist Movement of the 1960s (see ⟡Nazi Party).

National Health Service (NHS) UK government medical scheme, established 1948. It includes hospital care, but charges are made for prescriptions, spectacles, and dental treatment, except for children and people on very low incomes. UK expenditure on public health in 1987 was £10,569 million, with an average of 317,000 beds occupied in hospitals. The number of available beds in public hospitals decreased by 25% betwen 1971 and 1987.

national insurance in the UK, state social-security scheme that provides child allowances, maternity benefits, and payments to the unemployed, sick, and retired, and also covers medical treatment. It is paid for by weekly contributions from employees and employers.

nationalism in politics, a movement that consciously aims to unify a nation, create a state, or liberate it from foreign or imperialistic rule. Nationalist movements became a potent factor in European politics during the 19th century; since 1900 nationalism has become a strong force in Asia and Africa and in the late 1980s revived strongly in E Europe. In the second half of the 20th century a strongly national literary and political movement has developed in Scotland and Wales.

nationalization policy of bringing a country's essential services and industries under public ownership. It was pursued, for example, by the UK Labour government 1945–51. In recent years the trend towards nationalization has slowed and in many countries (the UK, France, and Japan) reversed (⟡privatization). Assets in the hands of foreign governments or companies may also be nationalized; for example, Iran's oil industry (see ⟡Abadan), the ⟡Suez Canal, and US-owned fruit plantations in Guatemala, all in the 1950s.

National Rivers Authority UK environmental agency launched Sept 1989. It is responsible for managing water resources, investigating pollution controls, and taking over flood controls and land drainage from the former ten regional water authorities of England and Wales.

National Security Agency (NSA) largest and most secret of US intelligence agencies. Established 1952 to intercept foreign communications as well as to safeguard US transmissions, the NSA collects and analyses computer communications, telephone signals, and other electronic data, and gathers intelligence.

national service ⟡conscription into the armed services in peacetime.

National Socialism official name for the ⟡Nazi movement in Germany; see also ⟡fascism.

National Trust British trust founded 1895 for the preservation of land and buildings of historic interest or beauty, incorporated by act of Parliament 1907. It is the largest private landowner in Britain. The National Trust for Scotland was established 1931.

NATO abbreviation for ⟡*North Atlantic Treaty Organization*.

Natural Environment Research Council (NERC) UK organization established by royal charter 1965 to undertake and support research in the earth sciences, to give advice both on exploiting natural resources and on protecting the environment, and to support education and training of scientists in these fields of study. Research areas include geothermal energy, industrial pollution, waste disposal, satellite surveying, acid rain, biotechnology, atmospheric circulation, and climate.

natural gas mixture of flammable gases found in the Earth's crust, often in association with oil. It is one of the world's three main fossil fuels (with coal and oil). Natural gas is usually transported from its source by pipeline, although it may be liquefied for transport and storage and is, therefore, often used in remote areas where other fuels are scarce and expensive.

natural selection the process whereby gene frequencies in a population change through certain individuals producing more descendants than others because they are better able to survive and reproduce in their environment. The accumulated effect of natural selection is to produce ⟡adaptations such as the insulating coat of a polar bear or the spadelike forelimbs of a mole. The process is slow, relying firstly on random variation in the genes of an organism being produced by ⟡mutation and secondly on the genetic ⟡recombination of sexual reproduction. It was recognized by Charles Darwin and Alfred Russel Wallace as the main process driving ⟡evolution.

nature–nurture controversy or *environment–heredity controversy* long-standing dispute among philosophers and psychologists over the relative importance of environment, that is upbringing, experience and learning ('nurture'), and heredity, that is genetic inheritance ('nature'), in determining the make-up of an organism, as related to human personality and intelligence.

Nauru Republic of; island country in the SW Pacific, in Polynesia, W of Kiribati; *area* 21 sq km/ 8 sq mi; *capital* (seat of government) Yaren District; *physical* plateau circled by coral cliffs and sandy beaches; *head of state and government* Bernard Dowiyogo from 1989; *political system* liberal democracy; *exports* phosphates; *population* (1990 est) 8,100 (mainly Polynesian; Chinese 8%, European 8%); *languages* Nauruan (official);

English; *recent history* administered by Australia, New Zealand, and UK from 1920 until independence, except 1942–45, when it was occupied by Japan. In 1968 independence achieved from Australia, New Zealand, and Britain with 'special member' Commonwealth status.

nautical mile unit of distance used in navigation, an internationally agreed-on standard (since 1959) equalling the average length of one minute of arc on a great circle of the Earth, or 1,852 m/6,076.12 ft. The term formerly applied to various units of distance used in navigation.

nautilus shelled ▷cephalopod, genus *Nautilus*, found in the Indian and Pacific oceans. The pearly nautilus *N. pompilius* has a chambered spiral shell about 20 cm/8 in in diameter. Its body occupies the outer chamber. The nautilus has a large number of short, grasping tentacles surrounding a sharp beak.

Navarre (Spanish *Navarra*) autonomous mountain region of N Spain; *area* 10,400 sq km/4,014 sq mi; *capital* Pamplona; *features* Monte Adi 1,503 m/ 4,933 ft; rivers: Ebro, Arga; *population* (1986) 513,000.

Navarre, Kingdom of former kingdom comprising the Spanish province of Navarre and part of what is now the French *département* of Basses-Pyrénées. It resisted the conquest of the ▷Moors and was independent until it became French 1284 on the marriage of Philip IV to the heiress of Navarre. In 1479 Ferdinand of Aragon annexed Spanish Navarre, with French Navarre going to Catherine of Foix (1483–1512), who kept the royal title. Her grandson became Henry IV of France, and Navarre was absorbed in the French crown lands 1620.

navigation the science and technology of finding the position, course, and distance travelled by a ship, plane, or other craft. Traditional methods include the magnetic ▷compass and ▷sextant. Today the gyrocompass is usually used, together with highly sophisticated electronic methods, employing beacons of radio signals. Satellite navigation uses satellites that broadcast time and position signals.

Navratilova Martina 1956– . Czech tennis player who became a naturalized US citizen 1981. The most outstanding woman player of the 1980s, she had by 1991 55 Grand Slam victories, including 18 singles titles. She has won the Wimbledon singles title a record nine times, including six in succession 1982–87.

Nazarbayev Nursultan 1940– . Soviet politician, executive president of Kazakhstan from 1990. He was leader of the Kazakh Communist Party 1989–91 and prime minister of the republic 1984–89. He advocates free-market policies, yet enjoys the support of the environmentalist lobby.

Nazareth town in Galilee, N Israel, SE of Haifa; population (1981) 64,000. According to the New Testament, it was the boyhood home of Jesus.

Nazism ideology based on racism, nationalism, and the supremacy of the state over the individual. The German Nazi party, the *Nationalsozialistiche Deutsche Arbeiterpartei* (National Socialist German Workers' Party), was formed from the German Workers' Party (founded 1919) and led by Adolf ▷Hitler 1921–45. Nazi-related movements were founded in the UK 1932 by Oswald ▷Mosley and 1962 by Colin Jordan (National Socialist Movement), and in 1967 the ▷National Front was formed. In the USA the American Nazi Party was founded 1958 by George Lincoln Rockwell.

Nazi-Soviet pact see ▷Hitler-Stalin pact.

N'djamena capital of Chad, at the confluence of the Chari and Logone rivers, on the Cameroon border; population (1988) 594,000.

Neagh, Lough lake in Northern Ireland, 25 km/ 15 mi W of Belfast; area 396 sq km/153 sq mi. It is the largest lake in the British Isles.

Neanderthal hominid of the Mid-Late Palaeolithic, named after a skeleton found in the Neander Thal (valley) near Düsseldorf, Germany, in 1856. *Homo sapiens neanderthalensis* lived from about 100,000 to 40,000 years ago and was similar in build to present-day people, but slightly smaller, stockier, and heavier-featured with a strong jaw and prominent brow ridges on a sloping forehead.

Nebraska state in central USA; nickname Cornhusker State/Blackwater State; *area* 200,400 sq km/77,354 sq mi; *capital* Lincoln; *cities* Omaha, Grand Island, North Platte; *population* (1990) 1,578,300; *features* Rocky Mountain foothills; tributaries of the Missouri; Boys' Town for the homeless, near Omaha; the ranch of Buffalo Bill; the only unicameral legislature; *products* cereals, livestock, processed foods, fertilizers, oil, natural gas; *famous people* Fred Astaire, William Jennings Bryan, Johnny Carson, Willa Cather, Henry Fonda, Harold Lloyd, Malcom X; *history* part of the Louisiana Purchase 1803; became a territory 1854 and a state 1867 after the Union Pacific began its transcontinental railroad at Omaha 1865. Nebraska's farm economy was weakened in the 1930s by the Great Depression and dust storms, but World War II brought military airfields and war industries.

Nebuchadnezzar or *Nebuchadrezzar II* king of Babylon from 60 BC. Shortly before his accession he defeated the Egyptians at Carchemish and brought Palestine and Syria into his empire. Judah revolted, with Egyptian assistance, 596 and 587–586 BC; on both occasions he captured Jerusalem and took many Hebrews into captivity. He largely rebuilt Babylon and constructed the hanging gardens.

nebula cloud of gas and dust in space. Nebulae are the birthplaces of stars, but some nebulae are produced by gas thrown off from dying stars (see ▷supernova).

nectar sugary liquid secreted by some plants from

a nectary, a specialized gland usually situated near the base of the flower. Nectar often accumulates in special pouches or spurs, not always in the same location as the nectary. Nectar attracts insects, birds, bats, and other animals to the flower for ◊pollination and is the raw material used by bees in the production of honey.

nectarine smooth, shiny-skinned variety of ◊peach, usually smaller than other peaches and with firmer flesh. It arose from a natural mutation.

needlefish any bony fish of the marine family Belonidae, with an elongated body and long jaws lined with many sharp teeth.

Nefertiti or *Nofretete* queen of Egypt who ruled *c*. 1372–1350 BC; wife of the pharaoh ◊Ikhnaton.

negative/positive in photography, a reverse image, which when printed is again reversed, restoring the original scene. It was invented by Fox ◊Talbot about 1834.

Negev desert in S Israel that tapers to the port of Eilat. It is fertile under irrigation, and minerals include oil and copper.

Nehru Jawaharlal 1889–1964. Indian nationalist politician, prime minister from 1947. Before the partition (the division of British India into India and Pakistan), he led the socialist wing of the Nationalist ◊Congress Party, and was second in influence only to Mohandas ◊Gandhi. He was imprisoned nine times by the British 1921–45 for political activities. As prime minister from the creation of the dominion (later republic) of India in Aug 1947, he originated the idea of nonalignment (neutrality towards major powers). His daughter was Prime Minister Indira ◊Gandhi.

Nelson Horatio, Viscount Nelson 1758–1805. English admiral. He joined the navy in 1770. In the Revolutionary Wars against France he lost the sight in his right eye 1794 and lost his right arm 1797. He became a national hero, and rear admiral, after the victory off Cape St Vincent, Portugal. In 1798 he tracked the French fleet to Aboukir Bay and almost entirely destroyed it in the Battle of the Nile. In 1801 he won a decisive victory over Denmark at the Battle of ◊Copenhagen, and in 1805, after two years of blockading Toulon, another over the Franco-Spanish fleet at the Battle of ◊Trafalgar, near Gibraltar.

nematode unsegmented worm of the phylum Aschelminthes. Nematodes are pointed at both ends, with a tough, smooth outer skin. They include many free-living species found in soil and water, including the sea, but a large number are parasites, such as the roundworms and pinworms that live in humans, or the eelworms that attack plant roots. They differ from ◊flatworms in that they have two openings to the gut (a mouth and an anus).

Nemesis in Greek mythology, the goddess of retribution, who especially punished hubris (Greek *hybris*), the arrogant defiance of the gods.

Neo-Classicism movement in art and architecture in Europe and North America about 1750–1850, a revival of classical art, which superseded the Rococo style. It was partly inspired by the excavation of the Roman cities of Pompeii and Herculaneum. The architect Piranesi was an early Neo-Classicist; in sculpture Antonio ◊Canova and in painting J L ◊David were exponents.

neo-Darwinism the modern theory of ◊evolution, built up since the 1930s by integrating Charles ◊Darwin's theory of evolution through natural selection with the theory of genetic inheritance founded on the work of Gregor ◊Mendel.

neodymium yellowish metallic element of the ◊lanthanide series, symbol Nd, atomic number 60, atomic weight 144.24. Its rose-coloured salts are used in colouring glass, and neodymium is used in lasers.

Neo-Impressionism movement in French painting in the 1880s, an extension of the Impressionists' technique of placing small strokes of different colour side by side. Seurat was the chief exponent; his minute technique became known as 'pointillism'. Signac and Pissarro practised the same style for a few years.

Neolithic last period of the ◊Stone Age, characterized by settled communities based on agriculture and domesticated animals, and identified by sophisticated, finely honed stone tools, and ceramic wares. The earliest Neolithic communities appeared about 9000 BC in the Middle East, followed by Egypt, India, and China. In Europe farming began in about 6500 BC in the Balkans and Aegean, spreading north and east by 1000 BC.

neon colourless, odourless, nonmetallic, gaseous element, symbol Ne, atomic number 10, relative atomic mass 20.183. It is grouped with the ◊inert gases, is non-reactive, and forms no compounds. It occurs in small quantities in the Earth's atmosphere.

neoteny in biology, the retention of some juvenile characteristics in an animal that seems otherwise mature. An example is provided by the axolotl, a salamander that can reproduce sexually although still in its larval form.

Nepal Kingdom of; country in the Himalayan mountain range, bordered N by Tibet, E by Sikkim, and S and W by India; *area* 147,181 sq km/56,850 sq mi; *capital* Katmandu; *physical* descends from the Himalayan mountain range in N through foothills to the river Ganges plain in S; *head of state* King Birendra Bir Bikram Shah Dev from 1972; *head of government* Girija Prasad Koirala from 1991; *political system* constitutional monarchy; *exports* jute, rice, timber, oilseed; *population* (1990 est) 19,158,000 (mainly known by name of predominant clan, Gurkhas; Sherpas are Buddhist minority of NE Nepal); *languages* Nepali (official); 20 dialects spoken; *recent history* independence achieved from Britain 1923; restoration of the monarchy 1951. In 1960 parliament was dissolved by the king, and political parties were banned. A series of popular agitations for greater democracy, followed by referendums and elections, took place throughout the 1980s. Eventually, in 1990, the panchayat system of partyless government collapsed, a new constitution was introduced, and elections were held 1991 when Koirala, leader of the Nepali Congress Party, became head of government. Economic austerity led to demonstrations against the government 1992.

Neptune in Roman mythology, god of the sea, the equivalent of the Greek ⟡Poseidon.

Neptune in astronomy, the eighth planet in average distance from the Sun. Neptune orbits the Sun every 164.8 years at an average distance of 4.497 billion km/2.794 billion mi. It is a giant gas (hydrogen, helium, methane) planet, with a diameter of 48,600 km/30,200 mi and a mass 17.2 times that of Earth. Its rotation period is 16 hours 7 minutes. The methane in its atmosphere absorbs red light and gives the planet a blue colouring. It is believed to have a central rocky core covered by a layer of ice. Neptune has eight known moons.

neptunium silvery, radioactive metallic element of the ⟡actinide series, symbol Np, atomic number 93, relative atomic mass 237.048. It occurs in nature in minute amounts in ⟡pitchblende and other uranium ores, where it is produced from the decay of neutron-bombarded uranium in these ores. The longest-lived isotope, Np-237, has a half-life of 2.2 million years. The element can be produced by bombardment of U-238 with neutrons and is chemically highly reactive.

Nero AD 37–68. Roman emperor from 54. He is said to have murdered his stepfather ⟡Claudius' son Britannicus, his own mother, his wives Octavia and Poppaea, and many others. After the great fire of Rome 64, he persecuted the Christians, who were suspected of causing it. Military revolt followed 68; the Senate condemned Nero to death, and he committed suicide.

Neruda Pablo. Pen name of Neftalí Ricardo Reyes y Basualto 1904–1973. Chilean poet and diplomat. His work includes lyrics and the epic poem of the American continent *Canto General* 1950. He was awarded the Nobel Prize for Literature 1971. He served as consul and ambassador to many countries.

nerve strand of nerve cells enclosed in a sheath of connective tissue joining the ⟡central and the ⟡autonomic nervous systems with receptor and effector organs. A single nerve may contain both ⟡motor and sensory nerve cells, but they act independently.

nerve cell or *neuron* elongated cell, part of the ⟡nervous system, that transmits information between different parts of the body. A nerve

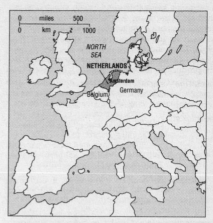

impulse is a travelling wave of chemical and electrical changes that affects the surface membrane of the nerve fibre. Chemical ⟡neurotransmitters pass the impulse from one nerve cell to another. Nerve impulses travel quickly, in humans as fast as 160 m/ 525 ft per second along a nerve cell.

nervous system the system of interconnected ⟡nerve cells of most invertebrates and all vertebrates. It is composed of the ⟡central and ⟡autonomic nervous systems. It may be as simple as the nerve net of coelenterates (for example, jellyfishes) or as complex as the mammalian nervous system, with a central nervous system comprising brain and spinal cord, and a peripheral nervous system connecting up with sensory organs, muscles, and glands.

Ness, Loch lake in Highland region, Scotland, forming part of the Caledonian Canal; 36 km/ 22.5 mi long, 229 m/754 ft deep. There have been unconfirmed reports of a *Loch Ness monster* since the 15th century, and the monster is worth £5 million a year to Scottish tourism.

net of a particular figure or price, calculated after the deduction of specific items such as commission, discounts, interest, and taxes. The opposite is ⟡gross.

net assets either the total ⟡assets of a company less its current liabilities (that is, the capital employed) or the total assets less current liabilities, debt capital, long-term loans and provisions, which would form the amount available to ordinary shareholders if the company were to be wound up.

Netherlands Kingdom of the (popularly referred to as *Holland*); country in W Europe on the North Sea, bordered E by Germany and S by Belgium; *area* 41,863 sq km/16,169 sq mi; *capital* Amsterdam; The Hague is seat of government; *physical* flat coastal lowland (polders (reclaimed land) make up over 40% of land area); rivers Rhine, Schelde

(*Scheldt*), Maas; Frisian Islands; *territories* Aruba, Netherlands Antilles (Caribbean); **head of state** Queen Beatrix Wilhelmina Armgard from 1980; **head of government** Ruud Lubbers from 1989; **political system** constitutional monarchy; *exports* dairy products, flowers, bulbs, vegetables, petrochemicals, electronics; *population* (1990 est) 14,864,000 (including 300,000 of Dutch-Indonesian origin); *language* Dutch; *recent history* occupied by Germany during World War II; joined Benelux Union 1947; founding member of NATO 1949; joined EC 1958. In 1980 Queen Juliana abdicated in favour of her daughter Beatrix. In the 1980s opposition to cruise missiles prevented their being sited on Dutch soil. Prime Minister Lubbers resigned 1989; new Lubbers-led coalition elected.

Netherlands Antilles two groups of Caribbean islands, part of the Netherlands with full internal autonomy, comprising ◊Curaçao and Bonaire off the coast of Venezuela (◊Aruba is considered separately), and St Eustatius, Saba, and the southern part of St Maarten in the Leeward Islands, 800 km/500 mi NE; *area* 797 sq km/308 sq mi; *capital* Willemstad on Curaçao; *products* oil from Venezuela refined here; tourism is important; *language* Dutch (official), Papiamento, English; *population* (1983) 193,000.

nettle any plant of the genus *Urtica*, family Urticaceae. Stinging hairs on the generally ovate leaves can penetrate the skin, causing inflammation. The common nettle *U. dioica* grows on waste ground in Europe and North America, where it was introduced.

network in computing, a method of connecting computers so that they can share data and ◊peripheral devices, such as printers. The main types are classified by the pattern of the connections – star or ring network, for example – or by the degree of geographical spread allowed; for example, local area networks (LANs) for communication within a room or building, and wide area networks (WANs) for more remote systems.

neuralgia sharp or burning pain originating in a nerve and spreading over its area of distribution. Trigeminal neuralgia, a common form, is a severe pain on one side of the face.

neurology the branch of medicine concerned with the study and treatment of the brain, spinal cord, and peripheral nerves.

neuron another name for a ◊nerve cell.

neurosis in psychology, a general term referring to emotional disorders, such as anxiety, depression, and obsessions. The main disturbance tends to be one of mood; contact with reality is relatively unaffected, in contrast to the effects of ◊psychosis.

neurotransmitter chemical that diffuses across a ◊synapse, and thus transmits impulses between ◊nerve cells, or between nerve cells and effector organs (for example, muscles). Common

neurotransmitters are norepinephrine (which also acts as a hormone) and acetylcholine, the latter being most frequent at junctions between nerve and muscle. Nearly 50 different neurotransmitters have been identified.

neutrality the legal status of a country that decides not to choose sides in a war. Certain states, notably Switzerland and Austria, have opted for permanent neutrality. Neutrality always has a legal connotation. In peacetime, neutrality towards the big power alliances is called *nonalignment* (see ◊nonaligned movement).

neutralization in chemistry, a process occurring when the excess acid (or excess base) in a substance is reacted with added base (or added acid) so that the resulting substance is neither acidic nor basic.

neutrino in physics, any of three uncharged ◊elementary particles (and their antiparticles) of the ◊lepton class, having a mass too close to zero to be measured. The most familiar type, the antiparticle of the electron neutrino, is emitted in the beta decay of a nucleus. The other two are the muon neutrino and the tau neutrino.

neutron one of the three main subatomic particles, the others being the proton and the electron. The neutron is a composite particle, being made up of three quarks, and therefore belongs to the baryon group of the ◊hadrons. Neutrons have about the same mass as protons but no electric charge, and occur in the nuclei of all atoms except hydrogen. They contribute to the mass of atoms but do not affect their chemistry.

neutron star very small, 'superdense' star composed mostly of ◊neutrons. They are thought to form when massive stars explode as ◊supernovae, during which the protons and electrons of the star's atoms merge, owing to intense gravitational collapse, to make neutrons. A neutron star may have the mass of up to three Suns, compressed into a globe only 20 km/12 mi in diameter.

Nevada state in W USA; nickname Silver State/Sagebrush State; *area* 286,400 sq km/ 110,550 sq mi; *capital* Carson City; *cities* Las Vegas, Reno; *population* (1990) 1,201,800; *physical* Mojave desert; lakes: Tahoe, Pyramid, Mead; mountains and plateaus alternating with valleys; *features* legal gambling and prostitution (in some counties); entertainment at Las Vegas and Reno casinos; Lehman Caves National Monument; *products* mercury, barite, gold; *history* explored by Kit Carson and John C Fremont 1843–45; ceded to the USA after the Mexican War 1848; first permanent settlement a Mormon trading post 1848. Discovery of silver 1858 led to rapid population growth and statehood 1864. The building of the Hoover Dam in the 1930s provided the water and power needed for the growth of Las Vegas. In 1931 the state created two industries, divorce (Reno) and

neuron

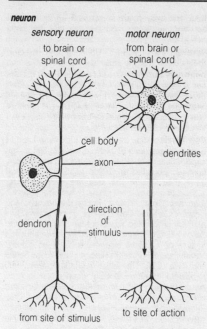

sensory neuron

to brain or
spinal cord

motor neuron

from brain or
spinal cord

cell body

dendrites

axon

dendron

direction
of
stimulus

from site of stimulus

to site of action

intermediate neuron

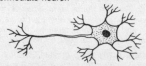

gambling (Las Vegas). Oil was discovered 1954, but gold exceeds all other mineral production. Tourism and gambling now generate more than half of the state's income.

new age movement of the late 1980s characterized by an emphasis on the holistic view of body and mind, alternative (or complementary) medicines, personal growth therapies, and a loose mix of theosophy, ecology, oriental mysticism and a belief in the dawning of an astrological age of peace and harmony.

New Brunswick maritime province of E Canada; *area* 73,400 sq km/28,332 sq mi; *capital* Fredericton; *towns* Saint John, Moncton; *features* Grand Lake, St John river; Bay of Fundy; *products* cereals, wood, paper, fish, lead, zinc, copper, oil, natural gas; *population* (1991) 725,600; 37% French-speaking; *history* first reached by Europeans (Cartier) 1534; explored by Champlain 1604; remained a French colony as part of Nova Scotia until ceded to England 1713. After the American Revolution many United Empire Loyalists settled

there, and it became a province of the Dominion of Canada 1867.

New Caledonia island group in the S Pacific, a French overseas territory between Australia and the Fiji Islands; *area* 18,576 sq km/7,170 sq mi; *capital* Nouméa; *physical* fertile, surrounded by a barrier reef; *products* nickel (the world's third largest producer), chrome, iron; *currency* CFP franc; *population* (1983) 145,300, 37% Kanak (Melanesian), 37% European, 8% Wallisian, 5% Vietnamese and Indonesian, 4% Polynesian; *language* French (official); *religion* Roman Catholic 60%, Protestant 30%; *history* New Caledonia was visited by Captain Cook 1774 and became French 1853.

Newcastle-upon-Tyne industrial port (coal, shipbuilding, marine and electrical engineering, chemicals, metals), commercial and cultural centre in Tyne and Wear, NE England, administrative headquarters of Tyne and Wear and Northumberland; population (1991 est) 263,000. A castle was built here by Henry II 1172–77 on the site of an older castle; the cathedral is chiefly 14th-century; there is a 12th-century church, the Guildhall 1658, and a university 1962. Newcastle is connected with the neighbouring town of Gateshead by several bridges.

New Deal in US history, programme introduced by President F D Roosevelt 1933 to counter the depression of 1929, including employment on public works, farm loans at low rates, and social reforms such as old-age and unemployment insurance, prevention of child labour, protection of employees against unfair practices by employers, and loans to local authorities for slum clearance.

New Delhi city in the Union Territory of Delhi, designed by Lutyens; capital of India since 1912; population (1991) 294,100.

New England region of NE USA, comprising the states of Maine, New Hampshire, Vermont, Massachusetts, Rhode Island, and Connecticut. It is a geographic region rather than a political entity, with an area of 172,681 sq km/66,672 sq mi. Boston is the principal urban centre of the region, and Harvard and Yale its main universities.

Newfoundland breed of dog, said to have originated in Newfoundland. Males can grow to 70 cm/2.3 ft tall, and weigh 65 kg/145 lb; the females are slightly smaller. They have an oily, water-repellent undercoat and are excellent swimmers. Gentle in temperament, their fur is dense, flat, and usually dull black. Newfoundlands that are black and white or brown and white are called *Landseers*.

Newfoundland and Labrador Canadian province on the Atlantic Ocean; *area* 405,700 sq km/156,600 sq mi; *capital* St John's; *towns* Corner Brook, Gander; *physical* Newfoundland island and ▷Labrador on the mainland on the other side of the Straits of Belle Isle; rocky; *features* Grand Banks section of the continental shelf rich in cod; home of the Newfoundland and Labrador dogs; *products* newsprint, fish products, hydroelectric power, iron, copper, zinc, uranium, offshore oil; *population* (1991) 571,600.

New Guinea island in the SW Pacific, N of Australia, comprising Papua New Guinea and the Indonesian province of West Irian (Irian Jaya area); total area about 885,780 sq km/342,000 sq mi. Part of the Dutch East Indies from 1828, West Irian was ceded by the United Nations to Indonesia 1963.

New Hampshire state in NE USA; nickname Granite State; *area* 24,000 sq km/9,264 sq mi; *capital* Concord; *cities* Manchester, Nashua; *population* (1990) 1,109,200; *features* White Mountains, including Mount Washington, the tallest peak E of the Rockies, and Mount Monadnock; the Connecticut River forms boundary with Vermont; earliest presidential-election party primaries every four years; no state income tax or sales tax; ski and tourist resorts; *products* dairy, poultry, fruits and vegetables; electrical and other machinery; pulp and paper; *famous people* Mary Baker Eddy, Robert Frost; *history* settled as a fishing colony near Rye and Dover 1623; separated from Massachusetts colony 1679. As leaders in the Revolutionary cause, its leaders received the honour of being the first to declare independence of Britain on 4 July 1776. It became a state 1788, one of the original thirteen states.

New Hebrides former name (until 1980) of ◊Vanuatu.

New Jersey state in NE USA; nickname Garden State; *area* 20,200 sq km/7,797 sq mi; *capital* Trenton; *cities* Newark, Jersey City, Paterson, Elizabeth; *population* (1985) 7,562,000; *features* about 125 mi/200 km of seashore, including legalized gambling in Atlantic City and the Victorian beach resort of Cape May; Delaware Water Gap; Palisades along the W bank of the Hudson River; Princeton University; Morristown National Historic Park; Edison National Historic Site, Menlo Park; Walt Whitman House, Camden; Statue of Liberty National Monument (shared with New York); the Meadowlands stadium; *products* fruits and vegetables, fish and shellfish, chemicals, pharmaceuticals, soaps and cleansers, transport equipment, petroleum refining; *famous people* Stephen Crane, Thomas Edison, Thomas Paine, Paul Robeson, Frank Sinatra, Bruce Springsteen, Woodrow Wilson; *history* colonized in the 17th century by the Dutch (New Netherlands); ceded to England 1664; became a state 1787. It was one of the original thirteen states.

Newman John Henry 1801–1890. English Roman Catholic theologian. While still an Anglican, he wrote a series of *Tracts for the Times*, which gave their name to the Tractarian Movement (subsequently called the ◊Oxford Movement) for the revival of Catholicism. He became a Catholic

1845 and was made a cardinal 1879. In 1864 his autobiography, *Apologia pro vita sua*, was published.

Newman Paul 1925– . US actor and director, Hollywood's leading male star of the 1960s and 1970s. His films include *Cat on a Hot Tin Roof* 1958, *The Hustler* 1961, *Sweet Bird of Youth* 1962, *Hud* 1963, *Cool Hand Luke* 1967, *Butch Cassidy and the Sundance Kid* 1969, *The Sting* 1973, *The Color of Money* 1986 (for which he won an Academy Award), and *Mr and Mrs Bridge* 1991.

New Mexico state in SW USA; nickname Land of Enchantment; *area* 315,000 sq km/121,590 sq mi; *capital* Santa Fe; *cities* Albuquerque, Las Cruces, Roswell; *population* (1990) 1,515,000; *physical* more than 75% of the area lies over 3,900 ft/1,200 m above sea level; plains, mountains, caverns; *features* Great Plains; Rocky Mountains; Rio Grande; Carlsbad Caverns, the largest known; Los Alamos atomic and space research center; White Sands Missile Range (also used by space shuttle); Sangre de Christos mountains; Taos art colony; Navaho and Hopi Indian reservations; White Sands and Gila Cliff Dwellings national monuments; *products* uranium, potash, copper, oil, natural gas, petroleum and coal products; sheep farming; cotton; pecans; vegetables; *famous people* 'Billy the Kid', Kit Carson, Georgia O'Keeffe; *history* explored by Francisco de Coronado for Spain 1540–42; Spanish settlement 1598 on the Rio Grande; Santa Fe founded 1610; most of New Mexico ceded to the US by Mexico 1848; became a state 1912. The first atomic bomb, a test device, was exploded in the desert near Alamogordo on 16 July 1945. Oil and gas development and tourism now contribute greatly to the state economy.

New Model Army army created 1645 by Oliver Cromwell to support the cause of Parliament during the English ◊Civil War. It was characterized by organization and discipline. Thomas Fairfax was its first commander.

New Orleans commercial and industrial city (banking, oil refining, rockets) and Mississippi River port in Louisiana, USA; population (1990) 496,900. It is the traditional birthplace of jazz.

New South Wales state of SE Australia; *area* 801,600 sq km/309,418 sq mi; *capital* Sydney; *towns* Newcastle, Wollongong, Broken Hill; *physical* Great Dividing Range (including Blue Mountains) and part of the Australian Alps (including Snowy Mountains and Mount Kosciusko); Riverina district, irrigated by the Murray-Darling-Murrumbidgee river system; *features* a radio telescope at Parkes; Siding Spring Mountain 859 m/2,817 ft, NW of Sydney, with telescopes that can observe the central sector of the galaxy. ◊Canberra forms an enclave within the state, and New South Wales administers the dependency of Lord Howe Island; *products* cereals, fruit, sugar, tobacco, wool, meat, hides and skins, gold, silver, copper, tin, zinc, coal; hydroelectric power from the Snowy River; *population* (1987) 5,570,000; 60% in Sydney; *history* convict settlement 1788–1850; opened to free settlement by 1819; achieved self-government 1856; became a state of the Commonwealth of Australia 1901. It was called New Wales by James ◊Cook, who landed at Botany Bay 1770 and thought that the coastline resembled that of Wales.

newspaper daily or weekly publication in the form of folded sheets containing news and comment. News-sheets became commercial undertakings after the invention of printing and were introduced 1609 in Germany, 1616 in the Netherlands. In 1622 the first newspaper appeared in English, the *Weekly News*, edited by Nicholas Bourne and Thomas Archer. Improved ◊printing (steam printing 1814, the rotary press 1846 USA and 1857 UK), newsprint (paper made from woodpulp, used in the UK from the 1880s), and a higher literacy rate led to the growth of newspapers. With the introduction of computer technology, production costs have fallen.

newt small salamander, of the family Salamandridae, found in Eurasia, NW Africa, and North America. The European newts, such as the smooth newt *Triturus vulgaris*, live on land for part of the year but enter a pond or lake to breed in the spring.

New Testament the second part of the ◊Bible, recognized by the Christian church from the 4th century as sacred doctrine. The New Testament includes the Gospels, which tell of the life and teachings of Jesus, the history of the early church, the teachings of St Paul, and mystical writings. It was written in Greek during the 1st and 2nd centuries AD, and the individual sections have been ascribed to various authors by biblical scholars.

newton SI unit (symbol N) of ◊force. One newton is the force needed to accelerate an object with mass of one kilogram by one metre per second per second. To accelerate a car weighing 1,000 kg/2,200 lb from 0 to 60 mph in 30 seconds would take about 2.5×10^5 N.

Newton Isaac 1642–1727. English physicist and mathematician who laid the foundations of physics as a modern discipline. He discovered the law of gravity, created calculus, discovered that white light is composed of many colours, and developed the three standard laws of motion still in use today. During 1665–66, he discovered the binomial theorem, and differential and integral calculus, and also began to investigate the phenomenon of gravitation. In 1685, he expounded his universal law of gravitation. His *Philosophiae naturalis principia mathematica*, usually referred to as *Principia*, was published in 1687, with the aid of Edmund Halley.

Newton's laws of motion in physics, three laws that form the basis of Newtonian mechanics. (1) Unless acted upon by a net force, a body at rest stays at rest, and a moving body continues moving at the same speed in the same straight line. (2) A net force applied to a body gives it a rate of change of ◊momentum proportional to the force and in the direction of the force. (3) When a body A exerts a force on a body B, B exerts an equal and opposite force on A; that is, to every action there is an equal and opposite reaction.

New World the Americas, so called by the first Europeans who reached them. The term also describes animals and plants of the western hemisphere.

New York largest city in the USA, industrial port (printing, publishing, clothing), cultural, financial, and commercial centre, in S New York State, at the junction of the Hudson and East rivers and including New York Bay. It comprises the boroughs of the Bronx, Brooklyn, Manhattan, Queens, and Staten Island; population (1990 census) 7,322,500, white 43.2%, black 25.2%, Hispanic 24.4%. New York is also known as the Big Apple; *features* The Statue of Liberty in the inner harbour of New York Bay; the World Trade Center (412 m/1,350 ft), the Art Deco Empire State Building (381 m/1,250 ft), and the Chrysler Building; headquarters of the United Nations. Columbia University 1754 is the best known of a number of institutions of higher education; *history* The Italian navigator Giovanni da Verrazano (*c.* 1485–*c.* 1528) reached New York Bay 1524, and Henry Hudson explored it 1609. The Dutch established a settlement on Manhattan 1624, named *New Amsterdam* from 1626; this was captured by the English in 1664 and renamed New York. During the War of Independence, British troops occupied New York 1776–84; it was the capital of the USA 1785–89. The five boroughs were linked 1898 to give the city its present extent.

New York state in NE USA; nickname Empire State/Excelsior State; *area* 127,200 sq km/49,099 sq mi; *capital* Albany; *cities* New York, Buffalo, Rochester, Yonkers, Syracuse; *population* (1990) 17,990,400; *physical* mountains: Adirondacks, Catskills; lakes: Champlain, Placid, Erie, Ontario; rivers: Mohawk, Hudson, St Lawrence (with Thousand Islands); Niagara Falls; Long Island; New York Bay; *features* West Point, site of the US Military Academy 1801; horse racing at Belmont, Aqueduct, Saratoga Springs; Washington Irving's home at Philipsburg Manor; Fenimore House (commemorating J F ◊Cooper), Cooperstown; home of F D Roosevelt at Hyde Park; home of Theodore Roosevelt, Oyster Bay; Erie Canal; *products* dairy products, apples, clothing, periodical and book printing and publishing, electronic components and accessories, office machines and computers, communications equipment, motor vehicles and equipment, pharmaceuticals, aircraft and parts; *famous people* James Fenimore Cooper, George Gershwin, Washington Irving, Henry James, Herman Melville, Arthur Miller, Franklin D Roosevelt, Theodore Roosevelt, Walt Whitman; *history* explored by Giovanni da Verrazano for France 1524; explored by Samuel

Champlain for France and Henry Hudson for the Netherlands 1609; colonized by the Dutch from 1614; first permanent settlement at Albany (Fort Orange) 1624; Manhattan Island purchased by Peter Minuit 1625; New Amsterdam annexed by the English 1664. The first constitution was adopted 1777, when New York became one of the original thirteen states.

New Zealand Dominion of; country in the S Pacific, SE of Australia; *area* 268,680 sq km/ 103,777 sq mi; *capital* Wellington; *physical* comprises North Island, South Island, Stewart Island, Chatham Islands, and minor islands; mainly mountainous. On North Island are Ruapehu, highest of three active volcanoes; geysers and hot springs of Rotorua district; Lake Taupo, source of Waikato River. On South Island are Southern Alps and Canterbury Plains; *head of state* Elizabeth II from 1952 represented by governor general; *head of government* Jim Bolger from 1990; *political system* constitutional monarchy; *exports* lamb, beef, wool, leather, dairy products, processed foods, kiwi fruit, seeds and breeding stock, timber, paper, pulp, light aircraft; *population* (1990 est) 3,397,000 (European (mostly British) 87%, Polynesian (mostly Maori) 12%); *languages* English (official); Maori; *recent history* achieved independence from Britain 1931; independence within the Commonwealth confirmed 1947. In 1985 a non-nuclear military policy created disagreements with France and the USA; in 1987 the National Party declared support for the Labour government's non-nuclear policy. A free-trade agreement was signed with Australia 1988. Labour Party defeated by National Party in 1990 general election. Amalgamated Alliance Party formed 1991 to challenge two-party system.

Ney Michael, Duke of Elchingen, Prince of Ney 1769–1815. Marshal of France under ◊Napoleon I, who commanded the rearguard of the French army during the retreat from Moscow, and for his personal courage was called 'the bravest of the brave'. When Napoleon returned from Elba, Ney was sent to arrest him, but instead deserted to him and fought at Waterloo. He was subsequently shot for treason.

Niagara Falls two waterfalls on the Niagara River, on the Canada–USA border, between Lakes Erie and Ontario and separated by Goat Island. The *American Falls* are 51 m/167 ft high, 330 m/ 1,080 ft wide; *Horseshoe Falls*, in Canada, are 49 m/160 ft high, 790 m/2,600 ft across.

Niamey river port and capital of ◊Niger; population (1983) 399,000. It produces textiles, chemicals, pharmaceuticals, and foodstuffs.

Nicaragua Republic of; country in Central America, between the Pacific Ocean and the Caribbean, bordered N by Honduras and S by Costa Rica; *area* 127,849 sq km/49,363 sq mi; *capital* Managua; *physical* narrow Pacific coastal plain separated from broad Atlantic coastal plain by volcanic mountains and lakes Managua and Nicaragua; *head of state and government* Violeta Barrios de Chamorro from 1990; *political system* emergent democracy; *exports* coffee, cotton, sugar, bananas, meat; *population* (1990 est) 3,606,000 (mestizo [mixed race] 70%, Spanish descent 15%, Indian or black 10%); *languages* Spanish (official), Indian, English; *recent history* US military bases established at government's request 1912; guerrilla group under Augusto Sandino opposed their presence. In 1933 US forces withdrew, leaving General Somoza in charge of national guard. Sandinista National Liberation Front (FSLN) formed 1962 to fight Somoza regime; ousted Somoza 1979. USA promoted subversive activity against the government 1982, and actively supported the counterrevolutionary forces (◊Contras); state of emergency declared; USA mined Nicaraguan harbours. US president Reagan denounced Sandinista government, but FSLN won assembly elections. In 1987 a Central American peace agreement was cosigned by Nicaraguan leaders, but the agreement failed 1988. Nicaragua held talks with Contra rebel leaders. Demobilization of rebels and release of former Somozan supporters took place 1989; the ceasefire ended. In 1990 the FSLN was defeated by UNO (National Opposition Union), a US-backed coalition; Violeta Chamorro was elected president; antigovernment riots followed.

Nice city on the French Riviera; population (1982) 449,500. Founded in the 3rd century BC, it repeatedly changed hands between France and the Duchy of Savoy from the 14th to the 19th century. In 1860 it was finally transferred to France.

Nicene Creed one of the fundamental ◊creeds of Christianity, promulgated by the Council of Nicaea 325.

Nicholas I 1796–1855. Tsar of Russia from 1825.

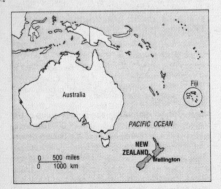

His Balkan ambitions led to war with Turkey 1827–29 and the Crimean War 1853–56.

Nicholas II 1868–1918. Tsar of Russia 1894–1917. He was dominated by his wife, Princess Alix of Hessen (Tsarina ⟩Alexandra), who was under the influence of ⟩Rasputin. His mismanagement of the Russo-Japanese War and of internal affairs led to the revolution of 1905, which he suppressed, although he was forced to grant limited constitutional reforms. He took Russia into World War I in 1914, was forced to abdicate in 1917 (see ⟩Russian Revolution) and was executed with his family.

Nicholas, St also known as *Santa Claus* 4th century AD. In the Christian church, patron saint of Russia, children, merchants, sailors, and pawnbrokers; bishop of Myra (now in Turkey). His legendary gifts of dowries to poor girls led to the custom of giving gifts to children on the eve of his feast day, 6 Dec, still retained in some countries, such as the Netherlands; elsewhere the custom has been transferred to Christmas Day. His emblem is three balls.

Nicholson Ben 1894–1982. English abstract artist. After early experiments influenced by Cubism and de Stijl (see ⟩Mondrian), Nicholson developed a style of geometrical reliefs, notably a series of white reliefs (from 1933).

Nicholson Jack 1937– . US film actor who captured the mood of nonconformist, uncertain young Americans in such films as *Easy Rider* 1969 and *Five Easy Pieces* 1970. He subsequently became a mainstream Hollywood star, appearing in *Chinatown* 1974, *One Flew over the Cuckoo's Nest* (Academy Award) 1975, *The Shining* 1979, *Terms of Endearment* (Academy Award) 1983, and *Batman* 1989.

nickel hard, malleable and ductile, silver-white metallic element, symbol Ni, atomic number 28, relative atomic mass 58.71. It occurs in igneous rocks and as a free metal, occasionally occurring in fragments of iron-nickel meteorites. It is a component of the Earth's core, which is held to consist principally of iron with some nickel. It has a high melting point, low electrical and thermal conductivity, and can be magnetized. It does not tarnish and therefore is much used for alloys, electroplating, and for coinage.

Nicklaus Jack (William) 1940– . US golfer, nicknamed 'the Golden Bear'. He won a record 20 major titles, including 18 professional majors between 1962 and 1986.

Nicobar Islands group of Indian islands, part of the Union Territory of ⟩Andaman and Nicobar Islands.

Nicosia capital of Cyprus, with leather, textile, and pottery industries; population (1987) 165,000. Nicosia was the residence of Lusignan kings of Cyprus 1192–1475. The Venetians, who took Cyprus 1489, surrounded Nicosia with a high wall, which still exists; the city fell to the Turks 1571. It was again partly taken by the Turks in the invasion 1974. The Greek and Turkish sectors are separated by the Attila Line.

nicotine $C_{10}H_{14}N_2$ an ⟩alkaloid (nitrogenous compound) obtained from the dried leaves of the tobacco plant *Nicotiana tabacum* and used as an insecticide. It is the component of cigarette smoke that causes physical addiction. A colourless oil, soluble in water, it turns brown on exposure to the air.

Niemeyer Oscar 1907– . Brazilian architect, joint designer of the United Nations headquarters in New York and of many buildings in Brasília, capital of Brazil.

Nietzsche Friedrich Wilhelm 1844–1900. German philosopher who rejected the accepted absolute moral values and the 'slave morality' of Christianity. He argued that 'God is dead' and therefore people were free to create their own values. His ideal was the *Übermensch*, or 'Superman', who would impose his will on the weak and worthless.

Niger third longest river in Africa, 4,185 km/2,600 mi from the highlands bordering Sierra Leone and Guinea NE through Mali, then SE through Niger and Nigeria to an inland delta on the Gulf of Guinea. Its flow has been badly affected by the expansion of the Sahara Desert. It is sluggish and frequently floods its banks. It was explored by Mungo Park 1795–96.

Niger Republic of; country in W Africa, bordered N by Nigeria and Libya, E by Chad, S by Nigeria and Benin, and W by Burkina Faso and Mali; *area* 1,186,408 sq km/457,953 sq mi; *capital* Niamey; *physical* desert plains between hills in N and savanna in S; river Niger in SW, Lake Chad in SE; *head of state* Ali Saibu from 1987; *head of government* André Salifou from 1991; *political system* military republic; *exports* peanuts, livestock, gum arabic, uranium; *population* (1990 est) 7,691,000; *languages* French (official), Hausa, Djerma, and other minority languages; *recent history* full independence from France achieved 1960; Hamani Diori elected president, but ousted in army coup led by Seyni Kountché 1974. Cooperation agreement signed with France 1977. In 1987 Kountché died and was replaced by Col Ali Saibu. Saibu was stripped of executive powers 1991 and a transitional government formed, which collapsed 1992.

Niger-Congo languages the largest group of languages in Africa. It includes about 1,000 languages and covers a vast area south of the Sahara desert, from the west coast to the east, and down the east coast as far as South Africa. It is divided into groups and subgroups; the most widely spoken Niger-Congo languages are Swahili (spoken on the east coast), the members of the Bantu group (southern Africa), and Yoruba (Nigeria).

Nigeria Federal Republic of; country in W Africa on the Gulf of Guinea, bordered N by Niger, E by Chad and Cameroon, and W by Benin; *area* 923,773 sq km/356,576 sq mi; *capital* and chief port Lagos; Abuja is capital-designate; *physical* arid savanna in N; tropical rainforest in S, with mangrove swamps along the coast; river Niger forms wide delta; mountains in SE; *head of state and government* Ibrahim Babangida from 1985; *political system* military republic pending promised elections; *exports* petroleum (largest oil resources in Africa), cocoa, peanuts, palm oil (Africa's largest producer), cotton, rubber, tin; *population* (1990 est) 118,865,000 (Yoruba in W, Ibo in E, and Hausa-Fulani in N); *languages* English (official); Hausa, Ibo, Yoruba; *recent history* independence achieved from Britain within the Commonwealth 1960; became a republic 1963. A military coup 1966 was followed by a counter-coup and the slaughter of many members of the Ibo tribe in N. Conflict over oil revenues led to declaration of an independent state of Biafra and civil war 1966–70, followed by a series of political coups and counter-coups. In 1989 two new parties were approved. Nine new states were created 1991, bringing the total to 30.

nightingale songbird of the thrush family with a song of great beauty, heard at night as well as by day. About 16.5 cm/6.5 in long, it is dull brown, lighter below, with a reddish-brown tail. It migrates to Europe and winters in Africa. It feeds on insects and small animals.

Nightingale Florence 1820–1910. English nurse, the founder of nursing as a profession. She took a team of nurses to Scutari (now Üsküdar, Turkey) in 1854 and reduced the ▷Crimean War hospital death rate from 42% to 2%. In 1856 she founded the Nightingale School and Home for Nurses in London.

nightjar any of about 65 species of night-hunting birds forming the family Caprimulgidae. They have wide, bristly mouths for catching flying insects. Their distinctive calls have earned them such names as whippoorwill and church-will's-widow. Some are called nighthawks.

nightshade any of several plants in the family Solanaceae, which includes the black nightshade *Solanum nigrum*, bittersweet or woody nightshade *S. dulcamara*, and deadly nightshade or ▷belladonna.

Nihilist member of a group of Russian revolutionaries in the reign of Alexander II 1855–81. The name, popularized by the writer Turgenev, means 'one who approves of nothing' (Latin *nihil*) belonging to the existing order. In 1878 the Nihilists launched a guerrilla campaign leading to the murder of the tsar 1881.

Nijinsky Vaslav 1890–1950. Russian dancer and choreographer. Noted for his powerful but graceful technique, he was a legendary member of ▷Diaghilev's Ballets Russes, for whom he choreographed Debussy's *Prélude à l'Après-midi d'un faune* 1912 and *Jeux* 1913, and Stravinsky's *The Rite of Spring* 1913.

Nile river in Africa, the world's longest, 6,695 km/4,160 mi. The *Blue Nile* rises in Lake Tana, Ethiopia, the *White Nile* at Lake Victoria, and they join at Khartoum, Sudan. It enters the Mediterranean at a vast delta in N Egypt.

Nineveh capital of the Assyrian Empire from the 8th century BC until its destruction by the Medes under King Cyaxares in 612 BC, as forecast by the Old Testament prophet Nahum. It was situated on the river Tigris (opposite the present city of Mosul, Iraq) and was adorned with palaces.

Ningxia or *Ningxia Hui* autonomous region (formerly Ninghsia-Hui) of NW China; *area* 170,000 sq km/65,620 sq mi; *capital* Yinchuan; *physical* desert plateau; *products* cereals and rice under irrigation; coal; *population* (1990) 4,655,000; including many Muslims and nomadic herders.

niobium soft, grey-white, somewhat ductile and malleable, metallic element, symbol Nb, atomic number 41, relative atomic mass 92.906. It occurs in nature with tantalum, which it resembles in chemical properties. It is used in making stainless steel and other alloys for jet engines and rockets and for making superconductor magnets.

Nippon English transliteration of the Japanese name for ▷Japan.

nirvana in Buddhism, the attainment of perfect serenity by the eradication of all desires. To some Buddhists it means complete annihilation, to others it means the absorption of the self in the infinite.

nitrate any salt of nitric acid, containing the NO_3^- ion. Nitrates of various kinds are used in explosives, in the chemical industry, in curing meat, and as inorganic fertilizers. They are the most water-soluble salts known.

nitric acid or *aqua fortis* HNO_3 fuming acid obtained by the oxidation of ammonia or the action of sulphuric acid on potassium nitrate. It is a highly corrosive acid, dissolving most metals, and a strong oxidizing agent. It is used in the nitration and esterification of organic substances, and in the making of sulphuric acid, nitrates, explosives, plastics, and dyes.

nitrite salt or ester of nitrous acid, containing the nitrite ion (NO_2^-). Nitrites are used as preservatives (for example, to prevent the growth of botulism spores) and as colouring agents in cured meats such as bacon and sausages.

nitrogen colourless, odourless, tasteless, gaseous, nonmetallic element, symbol N, atomic number 7, relative atomic mass 14.0067. It forms almost 80% of the Earth's atmosphere by volume and is a constituent of all plant and animal tissues (in proteins and nucleic acids). Nitrogen is obtained for industrial

nitrogen cycle

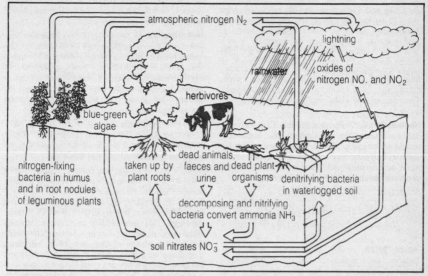

use by the liquefaction and fractional distillation of air. Its compounds are used in the manufacture of foods, drugs, fertilizers, dyes, and explosives.

nitrogen cycle the process of nitrogen passing through the ecosystem. Nitrogen, in the form of inorganic compounds (such as nitrates) in the soil, is absorbed by plants and turned into organic compounds (such as proteins) in plant tissue. A proportion of this nitrogen is eaten by ⊳herbivores, with some of this in turn being passed on to the carnivores, which feed on the herbivores. The nitrogen is ultimately returned to the soil as excrement and when organisms die and are converted back to inorganic form by ⊳decomposers.

nitrogen fixation the process by which nitrogen in the atmosphere is converted into nitrogenous compounds by the action of microorganisms, such as cyanobacteria (see ⊳blue-green algae) and bacteria, in conjunction with certain ⊳legumes. Several chemical processes duplicate nitrogen fixation to produce fertilizers; see ⊳nitrogen cycle.

nitroglycerine $C_3H_5(ONO_2)_3$ flammable, explosive oil produced by the action of nitric and sulphuric acids on glycerol. Although poisonous, it is used in cardiac medicine. It explodes with great violence if heated in a confined space and is used in the preparation of dynamite, cordite, and other high explosives.

nitrous oxide or *dinitrogen oxide* N_2O colourless, nonflammable gas that reduces sensitivity to pain. In higher doses it is an anaesthetic. Well-tolerated, but less potent than some other anaesthetic gases, it is often combined with other drugs to allow lower doses to be used. It may be self-administered; for example, in childbirth. It is popularly known as 'laughing gas'.

Niven David 1909–1983. Scottish-born US film actor, in Hollywood from the 1930s. His films include *Wuthering Heights* 1939, *Separate Tables* 1958 (Academy Award), *The Guns of Navarone* 1961, and *The Pink Panther* 1964. He published two best-selling volumes of autobiography, *The Moon's a Balloon* 1972 and *Bring on the Empty Horses* 1975.

Nixon Richard (Milhous) 1913– . 37th president of the USA 1969–74, a Republican. He attracted attention as a member of the Un-American Activities Committee 1948, and was vice president to Eisenhower 1953–61. As president he was responsible for US withdrawal from Vietnam, and forged new links with China, but at home his culpability in the cover-up of the ⊳Watergate scandal and the existence of a 'slush fund' for political machinations during his re-election campaign 1972 led to his resignation 1974 when threatened with ⊳impeachment.

Nkomo Joshua 1917– . Zimbabwean politician, vice-president from 1988. As president of ZAPU (Zimbabwe African People's Union) from 1961, he was a leader of the black nationalist movement against the white Rhodesian regime. He was a member of Robert ⊳Mugabe's cabinet 1980–82 and from 1987.

Nkrumah Kwame 1909–1972. Ghanaian nationalist politician, prime minister of the Gold Coast

(Ghana's former name) 1952–57 and of newly independent Ghana 1957– 60. He became Ghana's first president 1960 but was overthrown in a coup 1966. His policy of 'African socialism' led to links with the communist bloc.

Nō or *Noh* the classical, aristocratic Japanese drama, which developed from the 14th to the 16th centuries and is still performed. Dance, mime, music, and chanting develop the mythical or historical themes. All the actors are men, some of whom wear masks and elaborate costumes; scenery is limited.

Noah in the Old Testament, the son of Lamech and father of Shem, Ham, and Japheth, who, according to God's instructions, built a ship, the ark, so that he and his family and specimens of all existing animals might survive the Flood. There is also a Babylonian version of the tale, *The Epic of Gilgamesh*.

nobelium synthesized, radioactive, metallic element of the ⟩actinide series, symbol No, atomic number 102, relative atomic mass 259. It is synthesized by bombarding curium with carbon nuclei.

Nobel prize annual international prize, first awarded 1901 under the will of Alfred Nobel, Swedish chemist, who invented dynamite. The interest on the Nobel endowment fund is divided annually among the persons who have made the greatest contributions in the fields of physics, chemistry, medicine, literature, and world peace.

nocturne in music, a lyrical, dreamy piece, often for piano, introduced by John Field (1782–1837) and adopted by Frédéric Chopin.

nonaligned movement countries adopting a strategic and political position of neutrality ('non-alignment') towards major powers, specifically the USA and former USSR. Although originally used by poorer states, the nonaligned position was later adopted by oil-producing nations. The 1989 summit in Belgrade was attended by 102 member states.

Nonconformist in religion, originally a member of the Puritan section of the Church of England clergy who, in the Elizabethan age, refused to conform to certain practices, for example the wearing of the surplice and kneeling to receive Holy Communion. After 1662 the term was confined to those who left the church rather than conform to the Act of Uniformity requiring the use of the Prayer Book in all churches. It is now applied mainly to members of the Free churches.

nonmetal one of a set of elements (around 20 in total) with certain physical and chemical properties opposite to those of metals. Nonmetals accept electrons and are sometimes called electronegative elements.

nonrenewable resource natural resource, such as coal or oil, that takes thousands or millions of years to form naturally and can therefore not be replaced

once it is consumed. The main energy sources used by humans are nonrenewable; ⟩renewable sources, such as solar, tidal, and geothermal power, have so far been less exploited.

noradrenaline in the body, a catecholamine that acts directly on specific receptors to stimulate the sympathetic nervous system. Released by nerve stimulation or by drugs, it causes an increase in blood pressure mainly by constricting arterioles (small, thin-walled divisions of arteries) and so raising total peripheral resistance. It is used therapeutically to treat septic shock.

Nord-Pas-de-Calais region of N France; area 12,400 sq km/4,786 sq mi; population (1986) 3,923,000. Its capital is Lille, and it consists of the *départements* of Nord and Pas-de-Calais.

Norfolk county on the east coast of England; *area* 5,360 sq km/2,069 sq mi; *towns* Norwich (administrative headquarters), King's Lynn; resorts: Great Yarmouth, Cromer, Hunstanton; *physical* rivers: Ouse, Yare, Bure, Waveney; the ⟩Norfolk Broads; Halvergate Marshes wildlife area; *features* traditional reed thatching; Grime's Graves (Neolithic flint mines); shrine of Our Lady of Walsingham, a medieval and present-day centre of pilgrimage; Blickling Hall (Jacobean); residence of Elizabeth II at Sandringham (built 1869–71); *products* cereals, turnips, sugar beets, turkeys, geese, offshore natural gas; *population* (1991) 736,700; *famous people* Fanny Burney, John Sell Cotman, John Crome ('Old Crome'), Rider Haggard, Horatio Nelson, Thomas Paine.

Norfolk Broads area of some 12 interlinked freshwater lakes in E England, created about 600 years ago by the digging out of peat deposits; the lakes are used for boating and fishing.

Noriega Manuel (Antonio Morena) 1940– . Panamanian soldier and politician, effective ruler of Panama from 1982 until deposed by the USA 1989. In the pay of the US Central Intelligence Agency from early in his career, he was known to be involved in drug trafficking as early as 1972. A trial by a US court 1991–92 found him guilty of serious drugs offences.

Norman any of the descendants of the Norsemen (to whose chief, Rollo, Normandy was granted by Charles III of France 911) who adopted French language and culture. During the 11th and 12th centuries they conquered England 1066 (under William the Conqueror), Scotland 1072, parts of Wales and Ireland, S Italy, Sicily, and Malta, and took a prominent part in the Crusades.

Normandy two regions of NW France: ⟩Haute-Normandie and ⟩Basse-Normandie. Its main towns are Alençon, Bayeux, Caen, Cherbourg, Dieppe, Deauville, Lisieux, Le Havre, and Rouen. It was named after the Viking Norsemen (Normans), who conquered and settled in the area in the 9th century. As a French duchy it reached its peak

North America: early history

*c.*35,000 BC	American Indians entered North America from Asia.
*c.*9000 BC	Marmes man, earliest human remains.
*c.*300 BC	Earliest Moundbuilder sites.
*C.*AD 1000	Leif Ericsson reached North America.
12th–14th centuries	Height of the Moundbuilder and Pueblo cultures.
1492	12 Oct Columbus first sighted land in the Caribbean.
1497	Giovanni Caboto reached Canada.
1565	First Spanish settlements in Florida.
1585	First attempted English settlement in North Carolina.
1607	First permanent English settlement, Jamestown, Virginia.

under William the Conqueror and was renowned for its centres of learning established by Lanfranc and St Anselm. Normandy was united with England 1100–35. England and France fought over it during the Hundred Years' War, England finally losing it 1449 to Charles VII. In World War II the Normandy beaches were the site of the Allied invasion on D-day, 6 June 1944.

Norseman early inhabitant of Norway. The term Norsemen is also applied to Scandinavian ◊Vikings who during the 8th–11th centuries raided and settled in Britain, Ireland, France, Russia, Iceland, and Greenland.

North Frederick, 8th Lord North 1732–1792. British Tory politician. He entered Parliament in 1754, became chancellor of the Exchequer in 1767, and was prime minister in a government of Tories and 'king's friends' from 1770. His hard line against the American colonies was supported by George III, but in 1782 he was forced to resign by the failure of his policy. In 1783 he returned to office in a coalition with Charles ◊Fox, and after its defeat retired from politics.

North Oliver 1943– . US Marine lieutenant colonel. In 1981 he was inducted into the National Security Council (NSC), where he supervised the mining of Nicaraguan harbours 1983, an air-force bombing raid on Libya 1986, and an arms-for-hostages deal with Iran 1985 which, when uncovered 1986 (◊Irangate), forced his dismissal and trial.

North America third largest of the continents (including Greenland and Central America), and over twice the size of Europe; *area* 24,000,000 sq km/9,400,000 sq mi; *largest cities* (population over 1 million) Mexico City, New York, Chicago, Toronto, Los Angeles, Montreal, Guadalajara, Monterrey, Philadelphia, Houston, Guatemala City, Vancouver, Detroit, San Diego, Dallas; *physical* the northernmost point on the mainland is the tip of Boothia Peninsula in the Canadian Arctic; the most westerly point on the mainland is Cape Prince of Wales, Alaska; the most easterly point on the mainland lies on the SE coast of Labrador; the highest point is Mount McKinley, Alaska 6,194 m/ 20,320 ft; the lowest point is Badwater in Death Valley –86 m/–282 ft. In Canada and the USA, the Great Plains of the interior separate mountain belts to the east (Appalachians, Laurentian Highlands)

and west (Rocky Mountains, Coast Mountains, Cascade Range, Sierra Nevada). The western range extends south into Mexico as the Sierra Madre. The Mississippi river system drains from the central Great Plains into the Gulf of Mexico; low coastal plains on the Atlantic coast are indented by the Gulf of St Lawrence, Bay of Fundy, Delaware Bay, Chesapeake Bay; the St Lawrence and Great Lakes form a rough crescent (with Lake Winnipeg, Lake Athabasca, the Great Bear, and the Great Slave lakes) around the exposed rock of the great Canadian/Laurentian shield, into which Hudson Bay breaks from the north; Greenland (the largest island in the world next to Australia) is a high, ice-covered plateau with a deeply indented coastline of fjords; *features* Lake Superior (the largest body of freshwater in the world); Grand Canyon on the Colorado River; Redwood National Park, California has some of the world's tallest trees; San Andreas Fault, California; deserts: Death Valley, Mojave, Sonoran; rivers (over 1,600 km/1,000 mi) include Mississippi, Missouri, Mackenzie, Rio Grande, Yukon, Arkansas, Colorado, Saskatchewan-Bow, Columbia, Red, Peace, Snake; *products* with abundant resources and an ever-expanding home market, the USA's fast-growing industrial and technological strength has made it less dependent on exports and a dominant economic power throughout the continent. Canada is the world's leading producer of nickel, zinc, uranium, potash, and linseed, and the world's second largest producer of asbestos, silver, titanium, gypsum, sulphur, and molybdenum; Mexico is the world's leading producer of silver and the fourth largest oil producer; the USA is the world's leading producer of salt and the second largest producer of oil and cotton; nearly 30% of the world's beef and veal is produced in North America; *population* (1990 est) 395 million.

Northamptonshire county in central England; *area* 2,370 sq km/915 sq mi; *towns* Northampton (administrative headquarters), Kettering; *features* river Nene; Canons Ashby, Tudor house, home of the Drydens for 400 years; churches with broached spires; *products* cereals, cattle; *population* (1991) 568,900; *famous people* John Dryden, Richard III, Robert Browne.

North Atlantic Treaty Organization (NATO) association set up 1949 to provide for the collective defence of the major W European and North American states against the perceived threat from the USSR. Its chief body is the Council of Foreign Ministers (who have representatives in permanent session), and there is an international secretariat in Brussels, Belgium, and there is the Military Committee consisting of the Chiefs of Staff. The military headquarters SHAPE (Supreme Headquarters Allied Powers, Europe) is in Chièvres, near Mons, Belgium. After the E European ◊Warsaw Pact was disbanded 1991, an adjunct to NATO, the *North Atlantic Cooperation Council*, was established, including all the former Soviet republics, with the aim of building greater security in Europe.

North Brabant (Dutch *Noordbrabant*) southern province of the Netherlands, lying between the Maas (Meuse) and Belgium; area 4,940 sq km/ 1,907 sq mi; population (1991) 2,209,000. The capital is 's Hertogenbosch. Former heathland is now under mixed farming. Towns such as Breda, Tilburg, and Eindhoven are centres of brewing, engineering, microelectronics, and textile manufacture.

North Cape (Norwegian *Nordkapp*) cape in the Norwegian county of Finnmark; the most northerly point of Europe.

North Carolina state in E USA; nickname Tar Heel State/Old North State; *area* 136,400 sq km/ 52,650 sq mi; *capital* Raleigh; *cities* Charlotte, Greensboro, Winston-Salem; *population* (1990) 6,628,600; *features* Appalachian Mountains (including Blue Ridge and Great Smoky mountains); *products* tobacco, corn, soya beans, livestock, poultry, textiles, clothing, cigarettes, furniture, chemicals, machinery; *famous people* Billy Graham, O Henry, Jesse Jackson, Thomas Wolfe; *history* after England's Roanoke Island colony was unsuccessful 1585 and 1587, permanent settlement was made 1663; it was one of the original thirteen states 1789.

Northcliffe Alfred Charles William Harmsworth, 1st Viscount Northcliffe 1865–1922. British newspaper proprietor, born in Dublin. Founding the *Daily Mail* 1896, he revolutionized popular journalism, and with the *Daily Mirror* 1903 originated the picture paper. In 1908 he also obtained control of *The Times*.

North Dakota state in N USA; nickname Flickertail State/Sioux State; *area* 183,100 sq km/ 70,677 sq mi; *capital* Bismarck; *cities* Fargo, Grand Forks, Minot; *population* (1990) 638,800; *features* fertile Red River valley, Missouri Plateau; Garrison Dam on the Missouri River; Badlands, so called because the pioneers had great difficulty in crossing them (also site of Theodore Roosevelt's Elkhorn Ranch); International Peace Garden, on Canadian border; *products* cereals, meat products, farm equipment, oil, coal; *famous people* Maxwell Anderson, Louis L'Amour; *history* explored by Verendrye's French Canadian expedition 1738–40; acquired by the US partly in the Louisiana Purchase 1803 and partly by treaty with Britain 1813. The earliest settlement was Pembina 1812, by Scottish and Irish families, and it became a state 1889, attracting many German and Norwegian settlers.

North-East India area of India (Meghalaya, Assam, Mizoram, Tripura, Manipur, Nagaland, and Arunachal Pradesh) linked with the rest of India only by a narrow corridor. There is opposition to immigration from Bangladesh and the rest of India, and demand for secession.

Northeast Passage sea route from the N Atlantic, around Asia, to the N Pacific, pioneered by Swedish explorer Nordenskjöld 1878–79 and developed by the USSR in settling N Siberia from 1935. Russia owns offshore islands and claims it as an internal waterway; the USA claims that it is international.

Northern Ireland see ◊Ireland, Northern.

Northern Rhodesia former name (until 1964) of ◊Zambia.

Northern Territory territory of Australia; *area* 1,346,200 sq km/519,633 sq mi; *capital* Darwin (chief port); *towns* Alice Springs; *features* mainly within the tropics, although with wide range of temperature; very low rainfall, but artesian bores are used; Macdonnell Ranges (Mount Zeil 1,510 m/4,956 ft); ◊Cocos and ◊Christmas Islands included in the territory 1984; 50,000–60,000-year-old rock paintings of animals, birds, and fish in Kakadu National Park; *products* beef cattle, prawns, bauxite (Gove), gold and copper (Tennant Creek), uranium (Ranger); *population* (1987) 157,000; *history* originally part of New South Wales, it was annexed 1863 to South Australia but from 1911 until 1978 (when self-government was introduced) was under the control of the Commonwealth of Australia government.

North Holland (Dutch *Noord-Holland*) low-lying coastal province of the Netherlands occupying the peninsula jutting northwards between the North Sea and the IJsselmeer; area 2,670 sq km/ 1,031 sq mi; population (1991) 2,397,000. Most of it is below sea level, protected from the sea by a series of sand dunes and artificial dykes. The capital is Haarlem; other towns are Amsterdam, Hilversum, Den Helder, and the cheese centres Alkmaar and Edam. Famous for its bulbfields, the province also produces grain and vegetables.

North Korea see ◊Korea, North.

North Pole the northern point where an imaginary line penetrates the Earth's surface by the axis about which it revolves; see also ◊Poles and ◊Arctic.

North Rhine–Westphalia (German *Nordrhein-Westfalen*) administrative region (German *Land*) of Germany; *area* 34,100 sq km/13,163 sq mi; *capital* Düsseldorf; *towns* Cologne, Essen, Dortmund, Duisburg, Bochum, Wuppertal, Bielefeld, Bonn, Gelsenkirchen, Münster, Mönchengladbach; *features* valley of the Rhine; Ruhr industrial district; *products* iron, steel, coal, lignite, electrical goods, fertilizers, synthetic textiles; *population*

(1988) 16,700,000; *religion* 53% Roman Catholic, 42% Protestant; *history* see ⟡Westphalia.

North Sea sea to the east of Britain and bounded by the coasts of Belgium, the Netherlands, Germany, Denmark, and Norway; area 523,000 sq km/202,000 sq mi; average depth 55 m/180 ft, greatest depth 660 m/2,165 ft. In the northeast it joins the Norwegian Sea, and in the south it meets the Strait of Dover.

Northumberland county in N England; *area* 5,030 sq km/1,942 sq mi; *towns* Newcastle-upon-Tyne (administrative headquarters), Berwick-upon-Tweed, Hexham; *features* Cheviot Hills; rivers: Tweed, upper Tyne; Northumberland National Park in the west; Holy Island; the Farne island group; part of Hadrian's Wall and Housestead's Fort; Alnwick and Bamburgh castles; large moorland areas are used for military manoeuvres; wild white cattle of Chillingham; *products* sheep; *population* (1991) 300,600.

Northumbria Anglo-Saxon kingdom that covered NE England and SE Scotland, comprising the 6th-century kingdoms of Bernicia (Forth–Tees) and Deira (Tees–Humber), united in the 7th century. Influenced by Irish missionaries, it was a cultural and religious centre until the 8th century with priests such as Bede, Cuthbert, and Wilfrid. It accepted the supremacy of Wessex 827 and was conquered by the Danes in the late 9th century.

Northwest Passage Atlantic–Pacific sea route around the north of Canada. Canada, which owns offshore islands, claims it as an internal waterway; the USA insists that it is an international waterway and sent an icebreaker through without permission 1985.

Northwest Territories territory of Canada; *area* 3,426,300 sq km/1,322,552 sq mi; *capital* Yellowknife; *physical* extends to the North Pole, to Hudson's Bay in the east, and in the west to the edge of the Canadian Shield; *features* Mackenzie River; lakes: Great Slave, Great Bear; Miles Canyon; *products* oil, natural gas, zinc, lead, gold,

tungsten, silver; *population* (1991) 54,000; over 50% native peoples (Indian, Inuit); *history* the area was the northern part of Rupert's Land, bought by the Canadian government from the Hudson's Bay Company 1869. An act of 1952 placed the Northwest Territories under a commissioner acting in Ottawa under the Ministry of Northern Affairs and Natural Resources. In 1990 territorial control of over 350,000 sq km/135,000 sq mi of the Northwest Territories was given to the ⟡Inuit.

North Yorkshire county in NE England; *area* 8,320 sq km/3,212 sq mi; *towns* Northallerton (administrative headquarters), York; resorts: Harrogate, Scarborough, Whitby; *features* England's largest county; including part of the Pennines, the Vale of York, and the Cleveland Hills and North Yorkshire Moors, which form a national park (within which is Fylingdales radar station to give early warning – 4 min – of nuclear attack); and Rievaulx abbey; Yorkshire Dales National Park (including Swaledale, Wensleydale, and Bolton Abbey in Wharfedale); rivers: Derwent, Ouse; Fountains Abbey near Ripon, with Studley Royal Gardens; York Minster; Castle Howard, designed by Vanbrugh, has Britain's largest collection of 18th–20th-century costume; *products* cereals, wool and meat from sheep, dairy products, coal, electrical goods; *population* (1991) 698,000.

Norway Kingdom of; country in NW Europe, on the Scandinavian peninsula, bordered E by Sweden and NE by Finland and the Russian Federation; *area* 387,000 sq km/149,421 sq mi (includes Svalbard and Jan Mayen islands); *capital* Oslo; *physical* mountainous with fertile valleys and coastline deeply indented by fjords; forests cover 25%; extends N of Arctic Circle; glaciers in N; *territories* dependencies in the Arctic (Svalbard and Jan Mayen) and in Antarctica (Bouvet and Peter I Island, and Queen Maud Land); *head of state* Harald V from 1991; *head of government* Gro Harlem Brundtland from 1990; *political system* constitutional monarchy; *exports* petrochemicals from North Sea oil and gas, paper, wood pulp, furniture, iron ore and other minerals, high-tech goods, sports goods, fish; *population* (1990 est) 4,214,000; *languages* Norwegian (official); there are Saami- (Lapp) and Finnish-speaking minorities; *recent history* under Danish rule until 1814, when ceded to Sweden. Independence from Sweden achieved 1905. Occupied by Germany 1940–45; joined NATO 1949, Nordic Council 1952, EFTA 1960; accepted into EC 1972, but application withdrawn after a referendum. In 1988 Gro Harlem Brundtland awarded Third World Prize.

Norwich cathedral city in Norfolk, E England; population (1991) 121,000. Industries include shoes, clothing, chemicals, confectionery, engineering, and printing. It has a Norman castle; 15th-century Guildhall, medieval churches, Tudor houses, Georgian Assembly House.

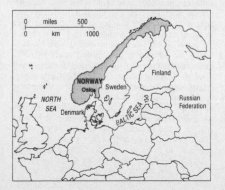

nose in humans, the upper entrance of the respiratory tract; the organ of the sense of smell. The external part is divided down the middle by a septum of ▷cartilage. The whole nasal cavity is lined with a ▷mucous membrane that warms and moistens the air and ejects dirt. In the upper parts of the cavity the membrane contains 50 million olfactory receptor cells (cells sensitive to smell).

Nottingham industrial city (engineering, coal-mining, bicycles, textiles, knitwear, pharmaceuticals, tobacco, lace, electronics) and administrative headquarters of Nottinghamshire, England; population (1991) 261,500.

Nottinghamshire county in central England; **area** 2,160 sq km/834 sq mi; **towns** Nottingham (administrative headquarters), Mansfield, Worksop; **features** river Trent; the remaining areas of Sherwood Forest (home of ▷Robin Hood), formerly a royal hunting ground, are included in the 'Dukeries'; Cresswell Crags (remains of pre-historic humans); D H Lawrence commemorative walk from Eastwood (where he lived) to Old Brinsley Colliery; **products** cereals, cattle, sheep, light engineering, footwear, limestone, ironstone, oil; **population** (1991) 980,600; **famous people** William Booth, D H Lawrence, Alan Sillitoe.

Nouakchott capital of Mauritania; population (1985) 500,000. Products include salt, cement, and insecticides.

noun grammatical ▷part of speech that names a person, animal, object, quality, idea, or time. Nouns can refer to objects such as *house, tree* (**concrete nouns**); specific persons and places such as *John Alden*, the *White House* (**proper nouns**); ideas such as *love, anger* (**abstract nouns**). In English many simple words are both noun and verb (*jump, reign, rain*). Adjectives are sometimes used as nouns ('a *local* man', 'one of the *locals*').

nova (plural *novae*) faint star that suddenly erupts in brightness by 10,000 times or more. Novae are believed to occur in close double star systems, where gas from one star flows to a companion ▷white dwarf. The gas ignites and is thrown off in an explosion at speeds of 1,500 kps/930 mps or more. Unlike a ▷supernova, the star is not completely disrupted by the outburst. After a few weeks or months it subsides to its previous state; it may erupt many more times.

Nova Scotia province of E Canada; **area** 55,500 sq km/21,423 sq mi; **capital** Halifax (chief port); **towns** Dartmouth, Sydney; **features** Cabot Trail (Cape Breton Island); Alexander Graham Bell Museum; Fortress Louisbourg; Strait of Canso Superport, the largest deepwater harbour on the Atlantic coast of North America; **products** coal, gypsum, dairy products, poultry, fruit, forest products, fish products (including scallop and lobster); **population** (1991) 897,500; **history** Nova Scotia was visited by the navigator Giovanni ▷Caboto

1497. A French settlement was established 1604, but expelled 1613 by English colonists from Virginia. The name of the colony was changed from *Acadia* to Nova Scotia 1621. England and France contended for possession of the territory until Nova Scotia (which then included present-day New Brunswick and Prince Edward Island) was ceded to Britain 1713; Cape Breton Island remained French until 1763. Nova Scotia was one of the four original provinces of the Dominion of Canada.

Novgorod industrial (chemicals, engineering, clothing, brewing) city on the Volkhov river, NW Russia; a major trading city in medieval times; population (1987) 228,000.

Novosibirsk industrial city (engineering, textiles, chemicals, food processing) in W Siberian Russia, on the river Ob; population (1987) 1,423,000. Winter lasts eight months here.

Nu U (Thakin) 1907– . Myanmar politician, prime minister of Burma (now Myanmar) for most of the period from 1948 to the military coup of 1962. Exiled from 1966, U Nu returned to the country 1980 and, in 1988, helped found the National League for Democracy opposition movement.

nuclear energy or *atomic energy* energy released from the inner core, or nucleus, of the atom. Energy produced by nuclear fission (the splitting of uranium or plutonium nuclei) has been harnessed since the 1950s to generate electricity, and research continues into the possible controlled use of nuclear fusion (the fusing, or combining, of atomic nuclei).

nuclear physics the study of the properties of the nucleus of the ▷atom, including the structure of nuclei; nuclear forces; the interactions between particles and nuclei; and the study of radioactive decay. See also ▷particle physics.

nuclear reactor device for producing ▷nuclear energy in a controlled manner. There are various types of reactor in use, all using nuclear fission. In a *gas-cooled reactor*, a circulating gas under pressure (such as carbon dioxide) removes heat from the core of the reactor, which usually contains natural uranium. The efficiency of the fission process is increased by slowing neutrons in the core by using a moderator such as carbon. The reaction is controlled with neutron-absorbing rods made of boron. An *advanced gas-cooled reactor* (AGR) generally has enriched uranium as its fuel. A *water-cooled reactor*, such as the steam-generating heavy water (deuterium oxide) reactor, has water circulating through the hot core. The water is converted to steam, which drives turbo-alternators for generating electricity. The most widely used reactor is the *pressurized-water reactor*, which contains a sealed system of pressurized water that is heated to form steam in heat exchangers in an external circuit. The *fast reactor* has no moderator and uses fast neutrons to bring about fission. It uses a mixture of plutonium and uranium oxide as fuel. When operating, uranium is converted to plutonium, which can be extracted and used later as fuel. The *fast breeder* produces more plutonium than it consumes. Heat is removed from the reactor by a coolant of liquid sodium.

Nuclear accidents Public concern over the safety of nuclear reactors has been intensified by explosions and accidental release of radioactive materials: **Chernobyl**, Ukraine. In April 1986 there was an explosive leak, caused by overheating, from a nonpressurized boiling water reactor, one of the largest in Europe. The resulting clouds of radioactive material spread as far as Sweden, and thousands of square kilometres of land were contaminated by fallout; **Three Mile Island**, Harrisburg, Pennsylvania, USA. In 1979, a combination of mechanical and electrical failure, as well as operator error, caused a pressurized water reactor to leak radioactive matter; **Windscale** (now Sellafield), Cumbria, England. In 1957, fire destroyed the core of a reactor, releasing large quantities of radioactive fumes into the atmosphere.

nuclear warfare war involving the use of nuclear weapons. The worldwide total of nuclear weapons in 1990 was about 50,000, and the number of countries possessing nuclear weapons stood officially at five — USA, USSR, UK, France, and China — although some other nations were thought either to have a usable stockpile of these weapons (Israel) or the ability to produce them quickly (Brazil, India, Pakistan, South Africa). The UK nuclear warhead programme costs £607 million a year.

Atom bomb The original weapon relied on use of a chemical explosion to trigger a chain reaction. The first use in war was by the USA against Japan 6 Aug 1945 over Hiroshima and three days later at Nagasaki. *Hydrogen bomb* A much more powerful weapon than the atom bomb, it relies on the release of thermonuclear energy by the condensation of hydrogen nuclei to helium nuclei (as happens in the Sun). The first detonation was at Eniwetok Atoll, Pacific Ocean, 1952 by the USA. *Neutron bomb* or enhanced radiation weapon A very small hydrogen bomb that has relatively high radiation but relatively low blast, designed to kill (in up to six days) by a brief neutron radiation that leaves buildings and weaponry intact.

nuclear waste the radioactive and toxic by-products of the nuclear-energy and nuclear-weapons industries. Reactor waste is of three types: high-level spent fuel, or the residue when nuclear fuel has been removed from a reactor and reprocessed; intermediate, which may be long- or short-lived; and low-level, but bulky, waste from reactors, which has only short-lived radioactivity. Disposal, by burial on land or at sea, has raised problems of safety, environmental pollution, and security. In absolute terms, nuclear waste cannot be safely relocated or disposed of.

nucleus in physics, the positively charged central part of an ⟡atom, which constitutes almost all its mass. Except for hydrogen nuclei, which have only protons, nuclei are composed of both protons and neutrons. Surrounding the nuclei are electrons, which contain a negative charge equal to the protons, thus giving the atom a neutral charge.

nucleus in biology, the central, membrane-enclosed part of a ⟡eukaryotic cell, containing the chromosomes.

Nujoma Sam 1929– . Namibian left-wing politician, president from 1990, founder and leader of ⟡SWAPO (the South-West Africa People's Organization) from 1959. He was exiled in 1960 and controlled guerrillas from Angolan bases until the first free elections were held 1989, taking office early the following year.

Nukua'lofa capital and port of Tonga on Tongatapu; population (1986) 29,000.

number symbol used in counting or measuring. In mathematics, there are various kinds of numbers. The everyday number system is the decimal ('proceeding by tens') system, using the base ten. ⟡Real numbers include all rational numbers (integers, or whole numbers, and fractions) and irrational numbers (those not expressible as fractions). ⟡Complex numbers include the real and unreal numbers (real-number multiples of the square root of –1). The ⟡binary number system, used in computers, has two as its base.

Nuremberg (German *Nürnberg*) industrial city (electrical and other machinery, precision instruments, textiles, toys) in Bavaria, Germany; population (1988) 467,000. From 1933 the Nuremberg rallies were held here, and in 1945 the Nuremberg trials of war criminals.

Nuremberg trials after World War II, the trials of the 24 chief ⟡Nazi war criminals Nov 1945–Oct 1946 by an international military tribunal consisting of four judges and four prosecutors: one of each from the USA, UK, USSR, and France. An appendix accused the German cabinet, general staff, high command, Nazi leadership corps, ⟡SS, ⟡Sturmabteilung, and ⟡Gestapo of criminal behaviour.

Nureyev Rudolf 1938– . Russian dancer and choreographer. A soloist with the Kirov Ballet, he defected to the West during a visit to Paris in 1961. Mainly associated with the Royal Ballet (London) and as Margot ⟡Fonteyn's principal partner, he was one of the most brilliant dancers of the 1960s and 1970s. Nureyev danced in such roles as Prince Siegfried in *Swan Lake* and Armand in *Marguerite and Armand*, which was created specifically for Fonteyn and Nureyev. He also danced and acted in films and on television and choreographed several ballets.

nut any dry, single-seeded fruit that does not split open to release the seed, such as the chestnut. A nut is formed from more than one carpel, but only one seed becomes fully formed, the remainder aborting. The wall of the fruit, the pericarp, becomes hard and woody, forming the outer shell.

nuthatch

nuthatch small bird of the family Sittidae, with a short tail and pointed beak. Nuthatches climb head first up, down, and around tree trunks and branches, foraging for insects and their larvae. The European nuthatch *Sitta europaea* has a blue-grey back and buff breast. It feeds mainly on nuts.

nutmeg kernel of the seed of the evergreen tree *Myristica fragrans*, native to the Moluccas. Both the nutmeg and its secondary covering, known as *mace*, are used as spice in cookery.

Nuuk Greenlandic for ⟡Godthaab, capital of Greenland.

Nyasa former name for Lake ⟡Malawi.

Nyasaland former name (until 1964) for ⟡Malawi.

Nyerere Julius (Kambarage) 1922– . Tanzanian socialist politician, president 1964–85. He devoted himself from 1954 to the formation of the Tanganyika African National Union and subsequent campaigning for independence. He became chief minister 1960, was prime minister of Tanganyika 1961–62, president of the newly formed Tanganyika Republic 1962–64, and first president of Tanzania 1964–85. He was head of the Organization of African Unity 1984.

nylon synthetic long-chain polymer similar in chemical structure to protein. Nylon was the first all-synthesized fibre, made from petroleum, natural gas, air, and water by the Du Pont firm in 1938. It is used in the manufacture of moulded articles, textiles, and medical sutures. Nylon fibres are stronger and more elastic than silk and are relatively insensitive to moisture and mildew.

nymph in entomology, the immature form of insects that do not have a pupal stage — for example, grasshoppers and dragonflies. Nymphs generally resemble the adult (unlike larvae), but do not have fully formed reproductive organs or wings.

oak any tree or shrub of the genus *Quercus* of the beech family Fagaceae, with over 300 known species widely distributed in temperate zones. Oaks are valuable for timber, the wood being durable and straight-grained. Their fruits are called acorns.

oarfish any of a family *Regalecidae* of deep-sea bony fishes, found in warm parts of the Atlantic, Pacific, and Indian oceans. Oarfish are large, up to 9 m/30 ft long, elongated, and compressed, with a fin along the back and a manelike crest behind the head. They have a small mouth, no teeth or scales, and large eyes. They are often reported as sea serpents.

oasis area of land made fertile by the presence of water near the surface in an otherwise arid region. The occurrence of oases affects the distribution of plants, animals, and people in the desert regions of the world.

oat

grain

cross
section of
a grain

oat type of grass, genus *Avena*, a cereal food. The plant has long, narrow leaves and a stiff straw stem; the panicles of flowers, and later of grain, hang downwards. The cultivated oat *Avena sativa* is produced for human and animal food.

Oates Titus 1649–1705. English conspirator. A priest, he entered the Jesuit colleges at Valladolid, Spain, and St Omer, France, as a spy 1677–78, and on his return to England announced he had discovered a 'Popish Plot' to murder Charles II and re-establish Catholicism. Although this story was almost entirely false, many innocent Roman Catholics were executed during 1678–80 on Oates's evidence. In 1685 he was flogged, pilloried, and imprisoned for perjury. He was pardoned and granted a pension after the revolution of 1688.

Ob river in Asian Russia, flowing 3,380 km/2,100 mi from the Altai mountains through the W Siberian Plain to the Gulf of Ob' in the Arctic Ocean. With its main tributary, the **Irtysh**, it is 5,600 km/3,480 mi long.

oboe musical instrument of the ◇woodwind family. Played vertically, it is a wooden tube with a bell, is double-reeded, and has a yearning, poignant tone. Its range is almost three octaves. Oboe concertos have been composed by Vivaldi, Albinoni, Richard Strauss, and others.

Obote (Apollo) Milton 1924– . Ugandan politician who led the independence movement from 1961. He became prime minister 1962 and was president 1966–71 and 1980–85, being overthrown by first Idi ◇Amin and then by Lt-Gen Tito Okello.

observatory site or facility for observing astronomical or meteorological phenomena. The earliest recorded observatory was in Alexandria, N Africa, built by Ptolemy Soter in about 300 BC. The modern observatory dates from the invention of the telescope. Observatories may be ground-based, carried on aircraft, or sent into orbit as satellites, in space stations, and on the space shuttle.

obstetrics medical speciality concerned with the management of pregnancy, childbirth, and the immediate postnatal period.

ocean great mass of salt water. Strictly speaking three oceans exist – the Atlantic, Indian, and Pacific – to which the Arctic is often added. They cover approximately 70% or 363,000,000 sq km/140,000,000 sq mi of the total surface area of the Earth. Water levels recorded in the world's oceans have shown an increase of 10–15 cm/4–6 in over the past 100 years.

Oceania general term for the islands of the central and S Pacific, including Australia, New Zealand, and the eastern half of New Guinea; although situated in the world's largest ocean, Oceania is the smallest continent in the world in terms of land surface; *area* 8,500,000 sq km/3,300,000 sq mi (land area); *largest cities* (population over 500,000) Sydney,

Melbourne, Brisbane, Perth, Adelaide, Auckland; *physical* stretching from the Tropic of Cancer in the N to the S tip of New Zealand, Oceania can be broadly divided into groups of volcanic and coral islands on the basis of the ethnic origins of their inhabitants: Micronesia (Guam, Kiribati, Mariana, Marshall, Caroline Islands), Melanesia (Papua New Guinea, Vanuatu, New Caledonia, Fiji, Solomon Islands) and Polynesia (Tonga, Samoa, Line Islands, Tuvalu, French Polynesia, Pitcairn); Australia (the largest island in the world) occupies more than 90% of the land surface; the highest point is Mount Wilhelm, Papua New Guinea 4,509 m/14,793 ft; the lowest point is Lake Eyre, South Australia –16 m/–52 ft; the longest river is the Murray in SE Australia 2,590 km/1,609 mi; *features* the Challenger Deep in the Mariana Trench –11,034 m/–36,201 ft is the greatest known depth of sea in the world; Ayers Rock in Northern Territory, Australia is the world's largest monolith; the Great Barrier Reef is the longest coral reef in the world; Mount Kosciusko 2,229 m/7,316 ft in New South Wales is the highest peak in Australia; Mount Cook 3,764 m/21,353 ft is the highest peak in New Zealand; *products* with a small home market, Oceania has a manufacturing sector dedicated to servicing domestic requirements and a large export-oriented sector 70% of which is based on exports of primary agricultural or mineral products. Australia is a major producer of bauxite, nickel, silver, cobalt, gold, iron ore, diamonds, lead, and uranium; New Caledonia is a source of cobalt, chromite, and nickel; Papua New Guinea produces gold and copper. Agricultural products include coconuts, copra, palm oil, coffee, cocoa, phosphates (Nauru), rubber (Papua New Guinea), 40% of the world's wool (Australia, New Zealand); New Zealand and Australia are, respectively, the world's second and third largest producers of mutton and lamb; fishing and tourism are also major industries; *population* 26 million, rising to 30 million by 2000; annual growth rate from 1980 to 1985 1.5%; Australia accounts for 65% of the population; 1% of Australia's population are Aboriginal and 9% of the people of New Zealand are Maori.

oceanography study of the oceans, their origin, composition, structure, history, and wildlife (seabirds, fish, plankton, and other organisms). Much oceanography uses computer simulations to plot the possible movements of the waters, and many studies are carried out by remote sensing.

ocean ridge mountain range on the seabed indicating the presence of a constructive plate margin (where tectonic plates are moving apart and magma rises to the surface). An ocean ridge can rise thousands of metres above the surrounding seabed.

ocean trench deep trench in the seabed indicating the presence of a destructive margin (produced by the movements of ⇨plate tectonics). Ocean trenches are found around the edge of the Pacific

Ocean. They represent the deepest parts of the ocean floor, the deepest being the ⇨Mariana Trench, off Japan, which has a depth of 11,034 m/36,201 ft.

ocelot wild cat *Felis pardalis* of the southwestern USA, Mexico, and Central and South America, up to 1 m/3 ft long with a 45 cm/1.5 ft tail. It weighs about 18 kg/40 lbs and has a pale yellowish coat marked with longitudinal stripes and blotches. Hunted for its fur, it is close to extinction.

O'Connell Daniel 1775–1847. Irish politician, called 'the Liberator'. Although ineligible, as a Roman Catholic, to take his seat, he was elected member of Parliament for County Clare 1828 and so forced the government to grant Catholic emancipation. In Parliament he cooperated with the Whigs in the hope of obtaining concessions until 1841, when he launched his campaign for repeal of the union.

octal number system number system to the ⇨base eight, used in computing, in which all numbers are made up of the digits 0 to 7. For example, decimal 8 is represented as octal 10, and decimal 17 as octal 21. Also used in computing is the ⇨hexadecimal number system.

Octavian original name of ⇨Augustus, the first Roman emperor.

October Revolution second stage of the ⇨Russian Revolution 1917, when, on 24 Oct (6 Nov in the Western calendar), the Red Guards under Trotsky, and on orders from Lenin, seized the Winter Palace and arrested members of the Provisional Government. The following day the Second All-Russian Congress of Soviets handed over power to the Bolsheviks.

octopus any of an order (Octopoda) of ⇨cephalopods, genus *Octopus*, having a round or oval body and eight arms with rows of suckers on each. They occur in all temperate and tropical seas, where they feed on crabs and other small animals.

ode lyric poem of complex form, originally chanted to a musical accompaniment. Ancient Greek writers of odes include Sappho, Pindar, Horace, and Catullus; and, among English poets, Spenser, Milton, Dryden, and Keats.

Odessa seaport in Ukraine, on the Black Sea, capital of Odessa region; population (1989) 1,115,000. Products include chemicals, pharmaceuticals, and machinery.

Odin chief god of Scandinavian mythology, the *Woden* or *Wotan* of the Germanic peoples. A sky god, he lives in Asgard, at the top of the world-tree, and from the Valkyries (the divine maidens) receives the souls of heroic slain warriors, feasting with them in his great hall, Valhalla. The wife of Odin is Freya, or Frigga, and Thor is their son.

Odysseus chief character of Homer's *Odyssey*, and mentioned also in the *Iliad* as one of the leaders of the Greek forces at the siege of Troy, a man of courage and ingenuity. He is said to have been the ruler of the island of Ithaca.

oedema any abnormal accumulation of fluid in tissues or cavities of the body; waterlogging of the tissues due to excessive loss of ◊plasma through the capillary walls. It may be generalized (the condition once known as dropsy) or confined to one area, such as the ankles.

Oedipus in Greek legend, king of Thebes who unwittingly killed his father and married his mother, in fulfilment of a prophecy. When he learned what he had done, he put out his eyes. The Greek dramatist Sophocles used the story in two tragedies.

Oedipus complex in psychology, term coined by Sigmund ◊Freud for the unconscious antagonism of a son to his father, whom he sees as a rival for his mother's affection. For a girl antagonistic to her mother, as a rival for her father's affection, the term is *Electra complex*.

oesophagus passage by which food travels from mouth to stomach. The human oesophagus is about 23 cm/9 in long. Its upper end is at the bottom of the pharynx, immediately behind the windpipe.

oestrogen group of hormones produced by the ◊ovaries of vertebrates; the term is also used for various synthetic hormones that mimic their effects. The principal oestrogen in mammals is oestradiol. Oestrogens promote the development of female secondary sexual characteristics; stimulate egg production; and, in mammals, prepare the lining of the uterus for pregnancy.

oestrus in mammals, the period during a female's reproductive cycle (also known as the oestrus cycle or ◊menstrual cycle) when mating is most likely to occur. It usually coincides with ovulation.

Offa died 796. King of Mercia, England, from 757. He conquered Essex, Kent, Sussex, and Surrey; defeated the Welsh and the West Saxons; and established Mercian supremacy over all England south of the river Humber.

Offaly county of the Republic of Ireland, in the province of Leinster, between Galway on the west and Kildare on the east; area 2,000 sq km/772 sq mi; population (1991) 58,500.

Offa's Dyke defensive earthwork along the Welsh border, of which there are remains from the mouth of the river Dee to that of the river Severn. It represents the boundary secured by ◊Offa's wars with Wales.

Official Secrets Act UK act of Parliament 1989, making disclosure of confidential material from government sources by employees subject to disciplinary procedures; it remains an absolute offence for a member or former member of the security and intelligence services (or those working closely with them) to disclose information about their work. There is no public-interest defence, and disclosure

of information already in the public domain is still a crime. Journalists who repeat disclosures may also be prosecuted.

offset printing the most common method of ◊printing, which uses smooth (often rubber) printing plates. It works on the principle of ◊lithography: that grease and water repel one another.

Ogallala Aquifer the largest source of groundwater in the USA, stretching from southern South Dakota to NW Texas. The overexploitation of this water resource has resulted in the loss of over 18% of the irrigated farmland of Oklahoma and Texas in the period 1940–90.

Ogun state of SW Nigeria; population (1988) 3,397,900; area 16,762 sq km/6,474 sq mi; capital Abeokuta.

Ohio state in N central USA; nickname Buckeye State; *area* 107,100 sq km/41,341 sq mi; *capital* Columbus; *cities* Cleveland, Cincinnati, Dayton, Akron, Toledo, Youngstown, Canton; *population* (1990) 10,847,100; *features* Ohio River; Lake Erie; Serpent Mound, a 1.3-m/4-ft embankment, 405 m/1,330 ft long and about 5 m/18 ft across (built by Hopewell Indians about 2nd–1st centuries BC); *products* coal, cereals, livestock, dairy, machinery, chemicals, steel, motor vehicles, automotive and aircraft parts, rubber products, office equipment, refined petroleum; *famous people* Thomas Edison, John Glenn, Paul Newman, General Sherman, Orville Wright; six presidents (Garfield, Grant, Harding, Harrison, Hayes, and McKinley); *history* explored for France by Robert La Salle 1669; ceded to Britain by France 1763; first settled at Marietta (capital of the Northwest Territory) by Europeans 1788; became a state 1803.

ohm SI unit (symbol Ω) of electrical ◊resistance (the property of a substance that restricts the flow of electrons through it).

Ohm's law law that states that the current flowing in a metallic conductor maintained at constant temperature is directly proportional to the potential difference (voltage) between its ends. The law was discovered by Georg Ohm 1827.

oil flammable substance, usually insoluble in water, and composed chiefly of carbon and hydrogen. Oils may be solids (fats and waxes) or liquids. The three main types are: ◊*essential oils*, obtained from plants; *fixed oils*, obtained from animals and plants; and *mineral oils*, obtained chiefly from the refining of ◊petroleum.

oil crop plant from which vegetable oils are pressed from the seeds. Cool temperate areas grow rapeseed and linseed; warm temperate regions produce sunflowers, olives, and soya beans; tropical regions produce groundnuts (peanuts), palm oil, and coconuts. Some of the major vegetable oils, such as soya bean oil, peanut oil, and cottonseed oil, are derived from crops grown primarily for other purposes. Most vegetable oils are used as both edible oils and as ingredients in industrial products such as soaps, varnishes, printing inks, and paints.

oil palm African ◊palm tree *Elaeis guineensis*, the fruit of which yields valuable oils, used as food or processed into margarine, soaps, and livestock feeds.

okapi ruminant *Okapia johnstoni* of the giraffe family, although with much shorter legs and neck, found in the tropical rainforests of central Africa. Purplish brown with a creamy face and black and white stripes on the legs and hindquarters, it is excellently camouflaged. Okapis have remained virtually unchanged for millions of years; now only a few hundred are thought to survive.

O'Keeffe Georgia 1887–1986. US painter, based mainly in New York and New Mexico, known for her large, semi-abstract studies of flowers and skulls.

Okhotsk, Sea of arm of the N Pacific between the Kamchatka Peninsula and Sakhalin and bordered southward by the Kuril Islands; area 937,000 sq km/361,700 sq mi. Free of ice only in summer, it is often fogbound.

Okinawa largest of the Japanese ◊Ryukyu Islands in the W Pacific; *area* 2,250 sq km/869 sq mi; *capital* Naha; *population* (1990) 3,145,500; *history* captured by the USA in the *Battle of Okinawa* 1 Apr–21 June 1945, with 47,000 US casualties (12,000 dead) and 60,000 Japanese (only a few hundred survived as prisoners). During the invasion over 150,000 Okinawans, mainly civilians, died; many massacred by Japanese forces. The island was returned to Japan 1972.

Oklahoma state in S central USA; nickname Sooner State; *area* 181,100 sq km/69,905 sq mi; *capital* Oklahoma City; *towns* Tulsa, Lawton, Norman, Enid; *features* Arkansas, Red, and Canadian rivers; Wichita and Ozark mountain ranges; the

okapi

high plains have Indian reservations (Cherokee, Chickasaw, Choctaw, Creek, and Seminole); American Indian Hall of Fame; Chicasaw National Recreation Area; *products* cereals, peanuts, cotton, livestock, oil, natural gas, helium, machinery and other metal products; *population* (1990) 3,145,500; *famous people* John Berryman, Ralph Ellison, Woody Guthrie, Mickey Mantle, Will Rogers, Jim Thorpe; *history* explored for Spain by Francisco de Coronado 1541; most acquired by the USA from France with the ◊Louisiana Purchase 1803. Part of the present state formed the Territory of Oklahoma from 1890, and was thrown open to settlers with lotteries and other hurried methods of distributing land. Together with what remained of Indian Territory, it became a state 1907.

Oklahoma City industrial city (oil refining, machinery, aircraft, telephone equipment), capital of Oklahoma, USA, on the Canadian River; population (1990) 444,700. On 22 April 1889, a tent city of nearly 10,000 inhabitants was set up overnight as the area was opened to settlement. In 1910 Oklahoma City had 64,000 people and became the state capital.

okra plant *Hibiscus esculentus* belonging to the Old World hibiscus family. Its red-and-yellow flowers are followed by long, sticky, green fruits known as *ladies' fingers* or *bhindi*. The fruits are cooked in soups and stews.

Old English general name for the range of dialects spoken by Germanic settlers in England between the 5th and 11th centuries AD, also known as ◊Anglo-Saxon.

Old Pretender nickname of ◊James Edward Stuart, the son of James II of England.

Old Testament Christian term for the Hebrew ◊Bible, which is the first part of the Christian Bible. It contains 39 (according to Christianity) or 24 (according to Judaism) books, which include the origins of the world, the history of the ancient Hebrews and their covenant with God, prophetical writings, and religious poetry. The first five books (*The five books of Moses*) are traditionally ascribed to Moses and known as the Pentateuch (by Christians) or the Torah (by Jews).

Olduvai Gorge deep cleft in the Serengeti steppe, Tanzania, where Louis and Mary ◊Leakey found prehistoric stone tools in the 1930s. They discovered Pleistocene remains of prehumans and gigantic animals 1958–59. The gorge has given its name to the *Olduvai culture*, a simple stone-tool culture of prehistoric hominids, dating from 2–0.5 million years ago.

oleander or *rose bay* evergreen Mediterranean shrub *Nerium oleander* of the dogbane family Apocynaceae, with pink or white flowers and aromatic leaves that secrete the poison oleandrin.

O level, General Certificate of Education or *Ordinary level* formerly an examination taken by

British school children at age 16. It was superseded by the ⬦GCSE 1988.

oligarchy rule of the few, in their own interests. It was first identified as a form of government by the Greek philosopher, Aristotle. In modern times there have been a number of oligarchies, sometimes posing as democracies; the paramilitary rule of the ⬦Duvalier family in Haiti, 1957–86, is an example.

Oligocene third epoch of the Tertiary period of geological time, 38–25 million years ago. The name, from Greek, means 'a little recent', referring to the presence of the remains of some modern types of animals existing at that time.

olive evergreen tree *Olea europaea* of the family Oleaceae. Native to Asia but widely cultivated in Mediterranean and subtropical areas, it grows up to 15 m/50 ft high, with twisted branches and opposite, lance-shaped silvery leaves. The white flowers are followed by green oval fruits that ripen a bluish black. They are preserved in brine or oil, dried, or pressed to make olive oil.

Olivier Laurence (Kerr), Baron Olivier 1907–1989. English actor and director. For many years associated with the Old Vic theatre, he was director of the National Theatre company 1962–73. His stage roles include Henry V, Hamlet, Richard III, and Archie Rice in John Osborne's *The Entertainer*. His acting and direction of filmed versions of Shakespeare's plays received critical acclaim; for example, *Henry V* 1944 and *Hamlet* 1948.

Olympic Games sporting contests originally held in Olympia, ancient Greece, every four years during a sacred truce; records were kept from 776 BC. Women were forbidden to be present, and the male contestants were naked. The ancient Games were abolished AD 394. The present-day games have been held every four years since 1896. Since 1924 there has been a separate winter Games programme. From 1994 the winter and summer Games will be held two years apart.

Olympus (Greek *Olimbos*) several mountains in Greece and elsewhere, one of which is **Mount Olympus** in N Thessaly, Greece, 2,918 m/9,577 ft high. In ancient Greece it was considered the home of the gods.

Oman Sultanate of; country on the Arabian peninsula, bordered W by the United Arab Emirates, Saudi Arabia, and Yemen, and E by the Arabian Sea; *area* 272,000 sq km/105,000 sq mi; *capital* Muscat; *physical* mountains to N and S of high arid plateau; fertile coastal strip; Kuria Muria islands; exclave on Musandam Peninsula controlling Strait of Hormuz; *head of state and government* Qaboos bin Said from 1970; *political system* absolute monarchy; *exports* oil, dates, silverware, copperware; *population* (1990 est) 1,305,000; *languages* Arabic (official); English, Urdu, other Indian dialects; *recent history* the Sultanate of Muscat and Oman

Olympic venues

summer games/winter games
1896 Athens, Greece
1900 Paris, France
1904 St Louis, USA
1906 Athens, Greece
1908 London, England
1912 Stockholm, Sweden
1920 Antwerp, Belgium
1924 Paris, France/Chamonix, France
1928 Amsterdam, Holland/St Moritz, Switzerland
1932 Los Angeles, USA/Lake Placid, USA
1936 Berlin, Germany/Garmisch-Partenkirchen, Germany
1948 London, England/St Moritz, Switzerland
1952 Helsinki, Finland/Oslo, Norway
1956 Melbourne, Australia*/Cortina d'Ampezzo, Italy
1960 Rome, Italy/Squaw Valley, USA
1964 Tokyo, Japan/Innsbruck, Austria
1968 Mexico City, Mexico/Grenoble, France
1972 Munich, West Germany/Sapporo, Japan
1976 Montreal, Canada/Innsbruck, Austria
1980 Moscow, USSR/Lake Placid, USA
1984 Los Angeles, USA/Sarajevo, Yugoslavia
1988 Seoul, South Korea/Calgary, Canada
1992 Barcelona, Spain/Albertville, France
1994 Lillehammer, Norway (winter games)

*Because of quarantine restrictions, equestrian events were held in Stockholm, Sweden.

achieved full independence from Britain 1951; Treaty of Friendship signed with Britain. In 1970 after 38 years' rule, Sultan Said bin Taimur was replaced in a coup by his son Qaboos bin Said, who instituted a more liberal and expansionist regime and changed the country's name to Sultanate of Oman. A rebellion in the south was defeated 1975. In 1982 a Memorandum of Understanding was signed with the UK, providing for regular consultation on international issues.

Omar 581–644. Adviser of the prophet Muhammad. In 634 he succeeded Abu Bakr as caliph (civic and religious leader of Islam), and conquered Syria, Palestine, Egypt, and Persia. He was assassinated by a slave. The Mosque of Omar in Jerusalem is attributed to him.

Omar Khayyám c. 1050–1123. Persian astronomer, mathematician, and poet. In the West, he is chiefly known as a poet through Edward ⬦Fitzgerald's version of *The Rubaiyat of Omar Khayyám* 1859.

Omayyad dynasty Arabian dynasty of the Islamic empire who reigned as caliphs (civic and religious leaders of Islam) 661–750. They were overthrown by Abbasids, but a member of the family escaped to Spain and in 756 assumed the title of emir of Córdoba. His dynasty, which took the title of caliph in 929, ruled in Córdoba until the early 11th century.

ombudsman official who acts on behalf of the private citizen in investigating complaints against the government. The post is of Scandinavian origin;

it was introduced in Sweden 1809, Denmark 1954, and Norway 1962, and spread to other countries from the 1960s.

omnivore animal that feeds on both plant and animal material. Omnivores have digestive adaptations intermediate between those of ◊herbivores and ◊carnivores, with relatively unspecialized digestive systems and gut microorganisms that can digest a variety of foodstuffs. Examples include the chimpanzee, the cockroach, and the ant.

Omsk industrial city (agricultural and other machinery, food processing, sawmills, oil refining) in Russia, capital of Omsk region, W Siberia; population (1987) 1,134,000. Its oil refineries are linked with Tuimazy in the Bashkir republic by a 1,600-km/1,000-mi pipeline.

onager wild ass *Equus hemionus* found in W Asia. Onagers are sandy brown, lighter underneath, and about the size of a small horse.

oncology branch of medicine concerned with the diagnosis and treatment of neoplasms, especially cancer.

Onega, Lake second largest lake in Europe, NE of St Petersburg, partly in Karelia, Russia; area 9,600 sq km/3,710 sq mi. The *Onega canal*, along its southern shore, is part of the Mariinsk system linking St Petersburg with the river Volga.

O'Neill Eugene (Gladstone) 1888–1953. US playwright, the leading dramatist between World Wars I and II. His plays include *Anna Christie* 1922, *Desire under the Elms* 1924, *The Iceman Cometh* 1946, and the posthumously produced autobiographical drama *Long Day's Journey into Night* 1956 (written 1940). Nobel prize 1936.

onion bulbous plant *Allium cepa* of the lily family Liliaceae. Cultivated from ancient times, it may have originated in Asia. The edible part is the bulb, containing an acrid volatile oil and having a strong flavour.

on-line system in computing, a system that allows the computer to work interactively with its users, responding to each instruction as it is given and prompting users for information when necessary. With the falling cost of computer operation, on-line operation has become increasingly attractive commercially.

Ontario province of central Canada; *area* 1,068,600 sq km/412,480 sq mi; *capital* Toronto; *towns* Hamilton, Ottawa (federal capital), London, Windsor, Kitchener, St Catharines, Oshawa, Thunder Bay, Sudbury; *features* Black Creek Pioneer Village; ◊Niagara Falls; richest, chief manufacturing, most populated, and leading cultural province of English-speaking Canada; *products* nickel, iron, gold, forest products, motor vehicles, iron, steel, paper, chemicals, copper, uranium; *population* (1986) 9,114,000; *history* first explored by the French in the 17th century, it

came under British control 1763 (Treaty of Paris). An attempt 1841 to form a merged province with French-speaking Québec failed, and Ontario became a separate province of Canada 1867. Under the protectionist policies of the new federal government, Ontario gradually became industrialized and urban. Since World War II, more than 2 million immigrants, chiefly from Europe, have settled in Ontario.

Ontario, Lake smallest and easternmost of the Great Lakes, on the US-Canadian border; area 19,200 sq km/7,400 sq mi. It is connected to Lake Erie by the Welland Canal and the Niagara River, and drains into the St Lawrence River. Its main port is Toronto.

onyx semiprecious variety of chalcedonic ◊silica (SiO_2) in which the crystals are too fine to be detected under a microscope, a state known as cryptocrystalline. It has straight parallel bands of different colours: milk-white, black, and red.

Oort Jan Hendrik 1900– . Dutch astronomer. In 1927, he calculated the mass and size of our Galaxy, the Milky Way, and the Sun's distance from its centre, from the observed movements of stars around the Galaxy's centre. In 1950 Oort proposed that comets exist in a vast swarm, now called the *Oort cloud*, at the edge of the solar system.

opal form of ◊silica (SiO_2), often occurring as stalactites and found in many types of rock. The common opal is translucent, milk-white, yellow, red, blue, or green, and lustrous. Precious opal is opalescent, the characteristic play of colours being caused by close-packed silica spheres diffracting light rays within the stone.

Op art movement in modern art, popular in the 1960s. It uses scientifically based optical effects that confuse the spectator's eye. Precisely painted lines or dots are arranged in carefully regulated patterns that create an illusion of surface movement. Exponents include Victor Vasarely and Bridget Riley.

opera dramatic musical work in which singing takes the place of speech. In opera the music accompanying the action has paramount importance, although dancing and spectacular staging may also play their parts. Opera originated in late 16th-century Florence when the musical declamation, lyrical monologues, and choruses of Classical Greek drama were reproduced in current forms.

operating system (OS) in computing, a program that controls the basic operation of a computer. A typical OS controls the ◊peripheral devices, organizes the filing system, provides a means of communicating with the operator, and runs other programs.

operetta light form of opera, with music, dance, and spoken dialogue. The story line is romantic and sentimental, often employing farce and parody.

Operetta developed from the 19th-century *opéra comique* and is intended to amuse. Composers include Jacques Offenbach (*Orphée aux enfers/Orpheus in the Underworld* 1858), Johann Strauss the younger (*Die Fledermaus/The Bat* 1874), Gilbert and Sullivan (*The Pirates of Penzance* 1879, *The Mikado* 1885), Franz Lehár (*Die lustige Witwe/The Merry Widow* 1905), and Victor Herbert (*Babes in Toyland* 1903).

ophthalmology medical speciality concerned with diseases of the eye and its surrounding tissues.

opinion poll attempt to measure public opinion by taking a survey of the views of a representative sample of the electorate; the science of opinion sampling is called *psephology*. The first accurately sampled opinion poll was carried out by the statistician George Gallup during the US presidential election 1936. Opinion polls have encountered criticism on the grounds that their publication may influence the outcome of an election.

opium drug extracted from the unripe seeds of the opium poppy *Papaver somniferum* of SW Asia. An addictive narcotic, it contains several alkaloids, including *morphine*, one of the most powerful natural painkillers and addictive narcotics known, and *codeine*, a milder painkiller.

Opium Wars wars waged in the mid-19th century by the UK against China to enforce the opening of Chinese ports to trade in opium. Opium from British India paid for Britain's imports from China, such as porcelain, silk, and, above all, tea.

Oporto alternative form of ⟡Porto in Portugal.

opossum any of a family (Didelphidae) of marsupials native to North and South America. Most opossums are tree-living, nocturnal animals, with prehensile tails, and hands and feet well adapted for grasping. They range from 10 cm/4 in to 50 cm/20 in in length and are insectivorous, carnivorous, or, more commonly, omnivorous.

optical fibre very fine, optically pure glass fibre through which light can be reflected to transmit an image or information from one end to the other. Optical fibres are increasingly being used to replace copper wire in telephone cables, the messages being coded as pulses of light rather than a fluctuating electric current.

optical illusion scene or picture that fools the eye. An example of a natural optical illusion is that the Moon appears bigger when it is on the horizon than when it is high in the sky, owing to the ⟡refraction of light rays by the Earth's atmosphere.

optics branch of physics that deals with the study of light and vision – for example, shadows and mirror images, lenses, microscopes, telescopes, and cameras. For all practical purposes light rays travel in straight lines, although ⟡Einstein demonstrated that they may be 'bent' by a gravitational field. On striking a surface they are reflected or refracted

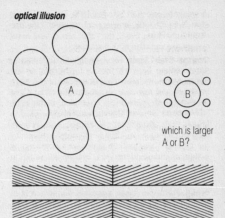

optical illusion

which is larger A or B?

are the two inner lines parallel?

with some absorption of energy, and the study of this is known as geometrical optics.

option in business, a contract giving the owner the right (as opposed to the obligation, as with futures contracts; see ⟡futures trading) to buy or sell a specific quantity of a particular commodity or currency at a future date and at an agreed price, in return for a premium. The buyer or seller can decide not to exercise the option if it would prove disadvantageous.

optoelectronics branch of electronics concerned with the development of devices (based on the ⟡semiconductor gallium arsenide) that respond not only to the ⟡electrons of electronic data transmission, but also to ⟡photons.

oracle Greek sacred site where answers (also called oracles) were given by a deity to enquirers about future events; these were usually ambivalent, so that the deity was proven right whatever happened. The earliest was probably at Dodona (in ⟡Epirus), where priests interpreted the sounds made by the sacred oaks of ⟡Zeus, but the most celebrated was that of Apollo at ⟡Delphi.

oral literature stories that are or have been transmitted in spoken form, such as public recitation, rather than through writing or printing. Most preliterate societies have had a tradition of oral literature, including short folk tales, legends, myths, proverbs, and riddles as well as longer narrative works; and most of the ancient epics – such as the Greek *Odyssey* and the Mesopotamian *Gilgamesh* – seem to have been composed and added to over many centuries before they were committed to writing.

orange any of several evergreen trees of the genus *Citrus*, family Rutaceae, which bear blossom and fruit at the same time. Thought to have originated in SE Asia, orange trees are commercially cultivated in Spain, Israel, the USA, Brazil, South Africa, and elsewhere. The sweet orange *C. sinensis* is the one commonly eaten fresh; the Jaffa, blood, and navel orange are varieties of this species.

Orange Free State province of the Republic of South Africa; *area* 127,993 sq km/49,405 sq mi; *capital* Bloemfontein; *features* plain of the High Veld; Lesotho forms an enclave on the Natal–Cape Province border; *products* grain, wool, cattle, gold, oil from coal, cement, pharmaceuticals; *population* (1987) 1,863,000; 82% ethnic Africans; *history* original settlements from 1810 were complemented by the ▷Great Trek, and the state was recognized by Britain as independent 1854. Following the South African, or Boer, War 1899–1902, it was annexed by Britain until it entered the union as a province 1910.

orang-utan ape *Pongo pygmaeus*, found solely in Borneo and Sumatra. Up to 1.65 m/5.5 ft in height, it is covered with long, red-brown hair and mainly lives a solitary, arboreal life, feeding chiefly on fruit. Now an endangered species, it is officially protected because its habitat is being systematically destroyed by ▷deforestation.

Orasul Stalin name 1948–56 of the Romanian town ▷Braşov.

oratorio musical setting of religious texts, scored for orchestra, chorus, and solo voices, on a scale more dramatic and larger than that of a cantata.

orbit path of one body in space around another, such as the orbit of Earth around the Sun, or the Moon around Earth. When the two bodies are similar in mass, as in a double star, both bodies move around their common centre of mass. The movement of objects in orbit follows Johann ▷Kepler's laws, which apply to artificial satellites as well as to natural bodies.

orchid any plant of the family Orchidaceae, which contains at least 15,000 species and 700 genera, distributed throughout the world except in the coldest areas, and most numerous in damp equatorial regions. The flowers are the most evolved of the plant kingdom, have three sepals and three petals and are sometimes solitary, but more usually borne in spikes, racemes, or panicles, either erect or drooping.

order in classical architecture, the ▷column (including capital, shaft, and base) and the entablature, considered as an architectural whole. The five orders are Doric, Ionic, Corinthian, Tuscan, and Composite.

order in biological classification, a group of related families. For example, the horse, rhinoceros, and tapir families are grouped in the order Perissodactyla, the odd-toed ungulates, because they all have either one or three toes on each foot. The names of orders are not shown in italic (unlike genus and species names) and by convention they have the ending '-formes' in birds and fish; '-a' in

mammals, amphibians, reptiles, and other animals; and '-ales' in fungi and plants. Related orders are grouped together in a ▷class.

ordination religious ceremony by which a person is accepted into the priesthood or monastic life in various religions. Within the Christian church, ordination authorizes a person to administer the sacraments. The Roman Catholic and Eastern Orthodox churches and the Church of England refuse to ordain women.

Ordovician period of geological time 505–438 million years ago; the second period of the ▷Palaeozoic era. Animal life was confined to the sea: reef-building algae and the first jawless fish are characteristic.

ore body of rock or a deposit of sediment that is worth mining for the economically valuable mineral it contains. The term is usually applied to sources of metals. For example, iron ores contain minerals such as iron oxides and carbonates that can be reduced to iron, usually by smelting in a ▷blast furnace.

oregano any of several perennial herbs of the Labiatae family, especially the aromatic *Origanum vulgare*, also known as wild marjoram. It is native to the Mediterranean countries and W Asia and naturalized in the Americas. Oregano is extensively used to season Mediterranean cooking.

Oregon state in NW USA, on the Pacific; nickname Beaver State; *area* 251,500 sq km/97,079 sq mi; *capital* Salem; *cities* Portland, Eugene; *population* (1990) 2,842,300; *features* fertile Willamette River valley; rivers: Columbia, Snake; Crater Lake, deepest in the US (1,933 ft/589 m); mountains: Coast and Cascades; Oregon Dunes National Recreation Area, on Pacific coast; the Oregon Trail (2,000 mi/3,200 km from Independence, Missouri, to the Columbia River) was the pioneer route across the US 1841–60; *products* wheat, livestock, timber, electronics; *famous people* Linus Pauling; *history* settled 1811 by the Pacific Fur Company, Oregon Territory included Washington until 1853; Oregon became a state 1859.

Orestes in Greek legend, the son of ▷Agamemnon and ▷Clytemnestra, who killed his mother because she and her lover Aegisthus had murdered his father.

organ musical wind instrument of ancient origin. It produces sound from pipes of various sizes under applied pressure and has keyboard controls.

organ in biology, part of a living body, such as the liver or brain, that has a distinctive function or set of functions.

organic chemistry branch of chemistry that deals with carbon compounds. Organic compounds form the chemical basis of life and are more abundant than inorganic compounds. In a typical organic compound, each carbon atom forms bonds covalently with each of its neighbouring carbon atoms in a chain or ring, and additionally with other atoms, commonly hydrogen, oxygen, nitrogen, or sulphur.

organic farming farming without the use of synthetic fertilizers (such as ⟡nitrates and phosphates) or ⟡pesticides (herbicides, insecticides and fungicides) or other agrochemicals (such as hormones, growth stimulants, or fruit regulators). Soil erosion is greatly reduced in organic farming.

Organization for Economic Cooperation and Development (OECD) international organization of 24 industrialized countries that provides a forum for discussion and coordination of member states' economic and social policies. Founded 1961, with its headquarters in Paris, the OECD superseded the Organization for European Economic Cooperation, which had been established 1948 to implement the ⟡Marshall Plan.

Organization of African Unity (OAU) association established 1963 to eradicate colonialism and improve economic, cultural, and political cooperation in Africa; headquarters Addis Ababa, Ethiopia. Its membership expanded to 51 countries when Namibia joined after independence 1990. The secretary general is Salim Ahmed Salim of Tanzania.

Organization of American States (OAS) association founded 1948 by a charter signed by representatives of 30 North, Central, and South American states. It aims to maintain peace and solidarity within the hemisphere, and is also concerned with the social and economic development of Latin America.

Organization of Petroleum-Exporting Countries (OPEC) body established 1960 to coordinate price and supply policies of oil-producing states, and also to improve the position of Third World states by forcing Western states to open their markets to the resultant products. Its concerted action in raising prices in the 1970s triggered worldwide recession but also lessened demand so that its influence was reduced by the mid-1980s. OPEC members in 1991 were: Algeria, Ecuador, Gabon, Indonesia, Iran, Iraq, Kuwait, Libya, Nigeria, Qatar, Saudi Arabia, the United Arab Emirates, and Venezuela.

orienteering sport of cross-country running and route-finding. Competitors set off at one-minute intervals and have to find their way, using map and compass, to various checkpoints (approximately 0.8 km/0.5 mi apart), where their control cards are marked. World championships have been held since 1966. Orienteering was invented in Sweden 1918.

Orinoco river in N South America, flowing for about 2,400 km/1,500 mi through Venezuela and forming for about 320 km/200 mi the boundary with

Colombia; tributaries include the Guaviare, Meta, Apure, Ventuari, Caura, and Caroni. It is navigable by large steamers for 1,125 km/700 mi from its Atlantic delta; rapids obstruct the upper river.

oriole any of two families of brightly coloured songbirds. The Old World orioles of Africa and Eurasia belong to the family Oriolidae. New World orioles belong to the family Icteridae.

Orion in astronomy, a very prominent constellation in the equatorial region of the sky, identified with the hunter of Greek mythology. It contains the bright stars Betelgeuse and Rigel, as well as a distinctive row of three stars that make up Orion's belt. Beneath the belt, marking the sword of Orion, is the Orion nebula; nearby is one of the most distinctive dark nebulae, the Horsehead.

Orissa state of NE India; *area* 155,800 sq km/60,139 sq mi; *capital* Bhubaneswar; *towns* Cuttack, Rourkela; *features* mainly agricultural; Chilka lake with fisheries and game; temple of Jagannath or Juggernaut at Puri; *products* rice, wheat, oilseed, sugar, timber, chromite, dolomite, graphite, iron; *population* (1991) 31,512,000; *language* Oriya (official); *religion* 90% Hindu; *history* administered by the British 1803–1912 as a subdivision of Bengal, it joined with Bihar to become a province. In 1936 Orissa became a separate province, and in 1948–49 its area was almost doubled before its designation as a state 1950.

Orkney Islands island group off the NE coast of Scotland; *area* 970 sq km/375 sq mi; *towns* Kirkwall (administrative headquarters), on Mainland (Pomona); *features* comprises about 90 islands and islets, low-lying and treeless; mild climate owing to the Gulf Stream; Skara Brae, a well-preserved Neolithic village on Mainland. Population, long falling, has in recent years risen as the islands' remoteness from the rest of the world attracts new settlers. Scapa Flow, between Mainland and Hoy, was a naval base in both world wars, and the German fleet scuttled itself here 21 June 1919; *products* fishing and farming, wind power (Burgar Hill has the world's most productive wind-powered generator); *population* (1989) 19,400; *famous people* Edwin Muir, John Rae; *history* Harald I (Fairhair) of Norway conquered the islands 876; pledged to James III of Scotland 1468 for the dowry of Margaret of Denmark and annexed by Scotland (the dowry unpaid) 1472.

Orly suburb of Paris in the *département* of Val-de-Marne; population (1982) 17,000. Orly international airport is the busiest in France.

Ormuz alternative name for the Iranian island ⟡Hormuz.

ornithology study of birds. It covers scientific aspects relating to their structure and classification, and their habits, song, flight, and value to agriculture as destroyers of insect pests. There is an International Council for Bird Preservation with its headquarters at the Natural History Museum, London.

Orpheus mythical Greek poet and musician. The son of Apollo and a muse, he married Eurydice, who died from the bite of a snake. Orpheus went down to Hades to bring her back and her return to life was granted on condition that he walk ahead of her without looking back. But he did look back and Eurydice was irretrievably lost. In his grief, he offended the Maenad women of Thrace, and was torn to pieces by them.

Ortega Saavedra Daniel 1945– . Nicaraguan socialist politician, head of state 1981–90. He was a member of the Sandinista Liberation Front (FSLN), which overthrew the regime of Anastasio Somoza 1979. US-sponsored ⟡Contra guerrillas opposed his government from 1982.

Orthodox Church or *Eastern Orthodox Church* or *Greek Orthodox Church* federation of self-governing Christian churches mainly found in SE and E Europe and parts of Asia. The centre of worship is the Eucharist. There is a married clergy, except for bishops; the Immaculate Conception is not accepted. The highest rank in the church is that of ecumenical patriarch, or bishop of Istanbul. Approximately 130 million adherents (1991).

ortolan songbird *Emberiza hortulana* of the bunting family, common in Europe and W Asia, migrating to Africa in the winter. Long considered a delicacy among gourmets, it has become rare and is now a protected species.

Orwell George. Pen name of Eric Arthur Blair 1903–1950. English author. His books include the satire *Animal Farm* 1945, which included such sayings as 'All animals are equal, but some are more equal than others', and the prophetic *Nineteen Eighty-Four* 1949, portraying the dangers of excessive state control over the individual. Other works include *Down and Out in Paris and London* 1933.

oryx any of the genus *Oryx* of large antelopes native to Africa and Asia. The Arabian oryx *O. leucoryx*, at one time extinct in the wild, has been successfully reintroduced into its natural habitat using stocks bred in captivity.

Osaka industrial port (iron, steel, shipbuilding, chemicals, textiles) on Honshu island; population (1989) 2,535,000, metropolitan area 8,000,000. It is the oldest city of Japan and was at times the seat of government in the 4th–8th centuries.

Osborne John (James) 1929– . English dramatist. He became one of the first ⟡Angry Young Men (anti-establishment writers of the 1950s) of British theatre with his debut play, *Look Back in Anger* 1956. Other plays include *The Entertainer* 1957, *Luther* 1960, and *Watch It Come Down* 1976.

oscillator any device producing a desired oscillation (vibration). There are many types of oscillator for different purposes, involving various arrangements of thermionic ⟡valves or components such as ⟡transistors, ⟡inductors, ⟡capacitors, and resistors. An oscillator is an essential part of a radio transmitter, generating the high-frequency carrier signal necessary for radio communication. The ⟡frequency is often controlled by the vibrations set up in a crystal (such as quartz).

oscilloscope or *cathode-ray oscilloscope* (CRO) instrument used to measure electrical voltages that vary over time and to display the waveforms of electrical oscillations or signals, by means of the deflection of a beam of ⟡electrons. Readings are displayed graphically on the screen of a ⟡cathode-ray tube.

Osiris ancient Egyptian god, the embodiment of goodness, who ruled the underworld after being killed by ⟡Set. The sister-wife of Osiris was ⟡Isis or Hathor, and their son ⟡Horus captured his father's murderer.

Oslo capital and industrial port (textiles, engineering, timber) of Norway; population (1991) 461,600. The first recorded settlement was made in the 11th century by Harald III, but after a fire 1624, it was entirely replanned by Christian IV and renamed *Christiania* 1624–1924.

Osman I or *Othman I* 1259–1326. Turkish ruler from 1299. He began his career in the service of the Seljuk Turks, but in 1299 he set up a kingdom of his own in Bithynia, NW Asia, and assumed the title of sultan. He conquered a great part of Anatolia, so founding a Turkish empire. His successors were known as 'sons of Osman', from which the term ⟡Ottoman Empire is derived.

osmium hard, heavy, bluish-white, metallic element, symbol Os, atomic number 76, relative atomic mass 190.2. It is the densest of the elements, and is resistant to tarnish and corrosion. It occurs in platinum ores and as a free metal with iridium in a

osmosis

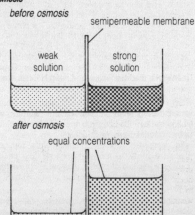

before osmosis

semipermeable membrane

weak solution

strong solution

after osmosis

equal concentrations

natural alloy called osmiridium, containing traces of platinum, ruthenium, and rhodium. Its uses include pen points and light-bulb filaments; like platinum, it is a useful catalyst.

osmosis movement of solvent (liquid) through a semipermeable membrane separating solutions of different concentrations. The solvent passes from the more concentrated solution to the more dilute solution until the two concentrations are equal. Applying external pressure to the solution on the more concentrated side arrests osmosis, and is a measure of the osmotic pressure of the solution.

osprey bird of prey *Pandion haliaetus*, the single member of the family Pandionidae; sometimes erroneously called 'fish hawk'. To catch fish, it plunges feet first into the water. Dark brown above and a striking white below, it measures 60 cm/2 ft with a 2 m/6 ft wingspan. Once extinct in Britain, it is now breeding again in Scotland.

Ossa, Mount the highest peak on the island of Tasmania, Australia; height 1,617 m/5,250 ft.

osteopathy system of alternative medical practice that relies on physical manipulation to treat mechanical stress. It was developed over a century ago by US physician Andrew Taylor Still, who maintained that most ailments can be prevented or cured by techniques of spinal manipulation.

osteoporosis disease in which the bone substance becomes porous and brittle. It is common in older people, affecting more women than men. It may be treated with calcium supplements and etidronate.

Ostia ancient Roman town near the mouth of the Tiber. Founded about 330 BC, it was the port of Rome and had become a major commercial centre by the 2nd century AD. It was abandoned in the 9th century. The present-day seaside resort *Ostia Mare* is situated nearby.

ostrich large flightless bird *Struthio camelus*, found in Africa. The male may be about 2.5 m/8 ft tall and weigh 135 kg/300 lb, and is the largest living bird. It has exceptionally strong legs and feet (two-toed) that enable it to run at high speed, and are also used in defence. It lives in family groups of one cock with several hens.

Ostrogoth member of a branch of the E Germanic people, the ▷Goths.

Otago peninsula and coastal plain on South Island, New Zealand, constituting a district; area 64,230 sq km/ 25,220 sq mi; chief cities include Dunedin and Invercargill.

Othman *c.* 574–656. Third caliph (leader of the Islamic empire) from 644, a son-in-law of the prophet Muhammad. Under his rule the Arabs became a naval power and extended their rule to N Africa and Cyprus, but Othman's personal weaknesses led to his assassination. He was responsible for the compilation of the authoritative version of the Koran, the sacred book of Islam.

Othman I another name for the Turkish sultan ▷Osman I.

otitis inflammation of the ear. *Otitis externa*, occurring in the outer ear canal, is easily treated with antibiotics. Inflamed conditions of the middle ear (*otitis media*) or inner ear (*otitis interna*) are more serious, carrying the risk of deafness and infection of the brain.

Ottawa capital of Canada, in E Ontario, on the hills overlooking the Ottawa river and divided by the Rideau Canal into the Upper (western) and Lower (eastern) towns; population (1986) 301,000, metropolitan area (with adjoining Hull, Québec) 819,000. Industries include timber, pulp and paper, engineering, food processing, and publishing.

otter any of various aquatic carnivores of the weasel family, found on all continents except Australia. Otters have thick, brown fur, short limbs, webbed toes, and long, compressed tails. They are social, playful, and agile. The otter of Europe and Asia *Lutra lutra* has in the UK been hunted to near extinction for its fur, but is slowly making a recovery with the aid of protective legislation.

Otto I 912–973. Holy Roman emperor from 936. He restored the power of the empire, asserted his authority over the pope and the nobles, ended the Magyar menace by his victory at the Lechfeld 955, and refounded the East Mark, or Austria, as a barrier against them.

Otto IV *c.* 1182–1218. Holy Roman emperor, elected 1198. He engaged in controversy with Pope Innocent III, and was defeated by the pope's ally, Philip of France, at Bouvines 1214.

Ottoman Empire Muslim empire of the Turks 1300–1920, the successor of the ▷Seljuk Empire. It was founded by ▷Osman I and reached its height with ▷Suleiman in the 16th century. Its capital was Istanbul (formerly Constantinople).

Otztal Alps range of the Alps in Italy and Austria, rising to 3,774 m/12,382 ft at Wildspitze, Austria's second highest peak.

Ouagadougou capital and industrial centre of Burkina Faso; population (1985) 442,000. Products include textiles, vegetable oil, and soap.

Oughtred William 1575–1660. English mathematician, credited as the inventor of the slide rule 1622. His major work *Clavis mathematicae/The Key to Mathematics* 1631 was a survey of the entire body of mathematical knowledge of his day. It introduced the '×' symbol for multiplication, as well as the abbreviations 'sin' for sine and 'cos' for cosine.

ousel or *ouzel* ancient name of the blackbird. The ring ouzel *Turdus torquatus* is similar to a blackbird, but has a white band across the breast. It is found in Europe in mountainous and rocky country. Water ouzel is another name for the ▷dipper.

Ovamboland region of N Namibia stretching along

the Namibia–Angola frontier; the scene of conflict between SWAPO guerrillas and South African forces in the 1970s and 1980s.

ovary in female animals, the organ that generates the ♦ovum. In humans, the ovaries are two whitish rounded bodies about 25 mm/1 in by 35 mm/1.5 in, located in the abdomen near the ends of the ♦Fallopian tubes. Every month, from puberty to the onset of the menopause, an ovum is released from the ovary. This is called ovulation, and forms part of the ♦menstrual cycle. In botany, an ovary is the expanded basal portion of the ♦carpel of flowering plants, containing one or more ♦ovules. It is hollow with a thick wall to protect the ovules. Following fertilization of the ovum, it develops into the fruit wall or pericarp.

Overijssel province of the E central Netherlands; *area* 3,340 sq km/1,289 sq mi; *towns* capital Zwolle; Enschede, Hengelo, Deventer; *physical* it is generally flat and contains the rivers IJssel and Vecht; *products* livestock, dairy products, textiles; *population* (1991) 1,026,300; *history* ruled by the bishops of Utrecht during the Middle Ages, Overijssel was sold to Charles V of Spain 1527. Joining the revolt against Spanish authority, it became one of the United Provinces of the Netherlands 1579.

overture piece of instrumental music, usually preceding an opera. There are also overtures to suites and plays, ballets, and 'concert' overtures, such as Elgar's *Cockaigne* and John Ireland's descriptive *London Overture*.

Ovid (Publius Ovidius Naso) 43 BC–AD 17. Roman poet whose poetry deals mainly with the themes of love (*Amores* 20 BC, *Ars amatoria/The Art of Love* 1 BC), mythology (*Metamorphoses* AD 2), and exile (*Tristia* AD 9–12).

ovule structure found in seed plants that develops into a seed after fertilization. It consists of an ♦embryo sac containing the female gamete (♦ovum or egg cell), surrounded by nutritive tissue, the nucellus. Outside this there are one or two coverings that provide protection, developing into the testa, or seed coat, following fertilization.

ovum (plural *ova*) female gamete (sex cell) before fertilization. In animals it is called an egg, and is produced in the ovaries. In plants, where it is also known as an egg cell or oosphere, the ovum is produced in an ovule. The ovum is nonmotile. It must be fertilized by a male gamete before it can develop further, except in cases of ♦parthenogenesis.

Owen David 1938– . British politician, Labour foreign secretary 1977–79. In 1981 he was one of the founders of the ♦Social Democratic Party (SDP), and in 1983 became its leader. Opposed to the decision of the majority of the party to merge with the Liberals 1987, Owen stood down, but emerged 1988 as leader of a rump SDP, which was eventually disbanded 1990. In 1992 he retired from active politics.

Owen Wilfred 1893–1918. English poet. His verse, owing much to the encouragement of Siegfried ♦Sassoon, expresses his hatred of war, for example *Anthem for Doomed Youth*, published 1921.

Owens Jesse (James Cleveland) 1913–1980. US track and field athlete who excelled in the sprints, hurdles, and the long jump. At the 1936 Berlin Olympics he won four gold medals.

owl any bird of the order Strigiformes, found worldwide. They are mainly nocturnal birds of prey, with mobile heads, soundless flight, acute hearing, and forward-facing immobile eyes, surrounded by 'facial discs' of rayed feathers. They regurgitate indigestible remains of their prey in pellets (castings).

ox castrated male of domestic species of cattle, used in Third World countries for ploughing and other agricultural purposes. Also the extinct wild ox or ♦aurochs of Europe, and extant wild species such as buffaloes and yaks.

Oxfam (acronym for *Ox*ford Committee for *Fam*ine Relief) charity working to relieve poverty and famine worldwide. It was established in the UK 1942 by Canon Theodore Richard Milford (1896–1987), initially to assist the starving people of Greece.

Oxford Movement also known as *Tractarian Movement* or *Catholic Revival* movement that attempted to revive Catholic religion in the Church of England. Cardinal Newman dated the movement from Keble's sermon in Oxford 1833. The Oxford Movement by the turn of the century had transformed the Anglican communion, and survives today as Anglo-Catholicism.

Oxfordshire county in S central England; *area* 2,610 sq km/1,007 sq mi; *towns* Oxford (administrative headquarters), Abingdon, Banbury, Henley-on-Thames, Witney, Woodstock; *features* river Thames and tributaries; Cotswolds and Chiltern Hills; Vale of the White Horse (chalk hill figure 114 m/374 ft long); Oxford University; Europe's fusion project JET (Joint European Torus), being built at the UK Atomic Energy Authority's fusion laboratories at Culham; *products* cereals, cars, paper, bricks, cement; *population* (1991) 553,800; *famous people* William Davenant, Flora Thompson, Winston Churchill.

oxidation in chemistry, the loss of ♦electrons, gain of oxygen, or loss of hydrogen by an atom, ion, or molecule during a chemical reaction.

oxide compound of oxygen and another element, frequently produced by burning the element or a compound of it in air or oxygen.

oxlip plant closely related to the ♦cowslip.

oxygen colourless, odourless, tasteless, nonmetallic, gaseous element, symbol O, atomic number 8, relative atomic mass 15.9994. It is the most abundant element in the Earth's crust (almost 50%

by mass), forms about 21% by volume of the atmosphere, and is present in combined form in water and many other substances. Life on Earth evolved using oxygen, which is a by-product of ⟡photosynthesis and the basis for ⟡respiration in plants and animals.

oyster bivalve ⟡mollusc constituting the Ostreidae, or true oyster, family, having the upper valve flat, the lower concave, hinged by an elastic ligament. The mantle, lying against the shell, protects the inner body, which includes respiratory, digestive, and reproductive organs. Oysters commonly change their sex annually or more frequently; females may discharge up to a million eggs during a spawning period.

oyster catcher chunky shorebird of the family Haematopodidae, with a laterally flattened, heavy bill that can pry open mollusc shells. The common oyster catcher of European coasts, *Haemotopus ostralegus*, is black and white, with a long red beak.

Ozal Turgut 1927–　. Turkish Islamic right-wing politician, prime minister 1983–89, president from 1989. He has been responsible for improving his country's relations with Greece, but his prime objective has been to strengthen Turkey's alliance with the USA.

Ozark Mountains area in the USA (shared by Arkansas, Illinois, Kansas, Mississippi, Oklahoma) of ridges, valleys, and streams; highest point only 700 m/2,300 ft; area 130,000 sq km/50,000 sq mi. This heavily forested region between the Missouri and Arkansas rivers has agriculture and lead and zinc mines.

ozone O_3 highly reactive pale-blue gas with a penetrating odour. Ozone is an allotrope of oxygen (see ⟡allotropy), made up of three atoms of oxygen. It is formed when the molecule of the stable form of oxygen (O_2) is split by ultraviolet radiation or electrical discharge. It forms a layer in the upper atmosphere, which protects life on Earth from ultraviolet rays, a cause of skin cancer. This layer is rapidly depleting, owing in part to ⟡chlorofluorocarbons (CFCs). At lower atmospheric levels ozone is an air pollutant and contributes to the ⟡greenhouse effect.

ozone depleter any chemical that destroys the ozone in the stratosphere. Most ozone depleters are chemically stable compounds containing chlorine or bromine, which remain unchanged for long enough to drift up to the upper atmosphere. The best known are ⟡chlorofluorocarbons (CFCs), but many other ozone depleters are known, including halons, used in some fire extinguishers; methyl chloroform and carbon tetrachloride, both solvents; some CFC substitutes; and the pesticide methyl bromide.

P

pacemaker medical device implanted in a patient whose heart beats irregularly. It delivers minute electric shocks to stimulate the heart muscles at regular intervals and restores normal heartbeat. The latest pacemakers are powered by radioactive isotopes for long life and weigh no more than 15 grams/0.5 oz. They are implanted under the skin.

Pacific Islands United Nations trust territory in the W Pacific captured from Japan during World War II. The territory comprised over 2,000 islands and atolls and was administered by the USA from 1947. The islands were divided into four governmental units: the Northern Mariana Islands (except Guam), the Federated States of Micronesia (located in the ◊Carolines), the ◊Marshall Islands, and the Palau (now ◊Belau) Islands (also in the Carolines). The Northern Marianas became a self-governing commonwealth in 1975. In 1983 The Marshall Islands and the Federated States of Micronesia were granted free association with the USA. In Dec 1990 the UN Security Council voted to dissolve the trusteeship over the islands with Belau remaining the sole UN trusteeship territory.

Pacific Ocean world's largest ocean, extending from Antarctica to the Bering Strait; area 166,242,500 sq km/64,170,000 sq mi; average depth 4,188 m/13,749 ft; greatest depth of any ocean 11,034 m/36,210 ft in the ◊Mariana Trench.

Pacific War war 1879–83 fought by an alliance of Bolivia and Peru against Chile. Chile seized Antofagasta and the coast between the mouths of the rivers Loa and Paposo, rendering Bolivia landlocked, and also annexed the southern Peruvian coastline from Arica to the mouth of the Loa, including the nitrate fields of the Atacama Desert.

Padua (Italian *Padova*) city in N Italy, 45 km/28 mi W of Venice; population (1988) 224,000. The astronomer Galileo taught at the university, founded 1222.

paediatrics or *pediatrics* medical speciality concerned with the care of children.

Pahlavi dynasty Iranian dynasty founded by Reza Khan (1877–1944), an army officer who seized control of the government 1921 and was proclaimed shah 1925. During World War II, Britain and the USSR were nervous of his German sympathies and occupied Iran 1941–46. They compelled him to abdicate 1941 in favour of his son Muhammad Reza Shah Pahlavi, who took office in 1956, with US support, and was deposed in the Islamic revolution of 1979.

Paine Thomas 1737–1809. English left-wing political writer, active in the American and French revolutions. His pamphlet *Common Sense* 1776 ignited passions in the American Revolution; others include *The Rights of Man* 1791 and *The Age of Reason* 1793. He advocated republicanism, deism, the abolition of slavery, and the emancipation of women.

painting application of colour, pigment, or paint to a surface. The chief methods of painting are: *tempera* emulsion painting, with a gelatinous (for example, egg yolk) rather than oil base; known in ancient Egypt; *fresco* watercolour painting on plaster walls; the palace of Knossos, Crete, contains examples from about 2,000 BC; *ink* developed in China from calligraphy in the Sung period and highly popular in Japan from the 15th century; *oil* ground pigments in linseed, walnut, or other oil; spread from N to S Europe in the 15th century; *watercolour* pigments combined with gum arabic and glycerol, which are diluted with water; the method was developed in the 15th–17th centuries from wash drawings; *acrylic* synthetic pigments developed after World War II; the colours are very hard and brilliant. For the history of painting see ◊ancient art, ◊medieval art, and so on. Individual painters and art movements are listed alphabetically.

Pakistan Islamic Republic of; country in S Asia,

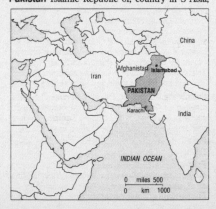

stretching from the Himalayas to the Arabian Sea, bordered W by Iran, NW by Afghanistan, NE by China, and E by India; *area* 796,100 sq km/ 307,295 sq mi; one-third of Kashmir under Pakistani control; *capital* Islamabad; *physical* fertile Indus plain in E; Baluchistan plateau in W, mountains in N and NW; *head of state* Ghulam Ishaq Khan from 1988; *head of government* Nawaz Sharif from 1990; *political system* emergent democracy; *exports* cotton textiles, rice, leather, carpets; *population* (1990 est) 113,163,000 (Punjabi 66%, Sindhi 13%); *languages* Urdu and English (official), Punjabi, Sindhi, Pashto, Baluchi, other local dialects; *recent history* independence was achieved from Britain 1947 and Pakistan was formed following the partition of India; proclaimed a republic 1956. East Pakistan became the separate country of Bangladesh 1971. After civil war, power was transferred to Zulfiqar Ali Bhutto; he was overthrown by General Zia ul-haq 1977 and executed 1979. Agitation for free elections was launched by Benazir Bhutto 1986; she was elected president 1988 (dismissed 1990). Pakistan rejoined the Commonwealth 1989. The Islamic Democratic Alliance government introduced Sharia law and a privatization and economic deregulation programme 1991.

Palaeocene first epoch of the Tertiary period of geological time, 65–55 million years ago. Many types of mammals spread rapidly after the disappearance of the great reptiles of the Mesozoic.

Palaeolithic earliest stage of human technology and development of the Stone Age; see ⟡prehistory.

palaeontology in geology, the study of ancient life that encompasses the structure of ancient organisms and their environment, evolution, and ecology, as revealed by their ⟡fossils.

Palaeozoic era of geological time 590–248 million years ago. It comprises the Cambrian, Ordovician, Silurian, Devonian, Carboniferous, and Permian periods. The Cambrian, Ordovician, and Silurian constitute the Lower Palaeozoic; the Devonian, Carboniferous, and Permian make up the Upper Palaeozoic. The era includes the evolution of hard-shelled multicellular life forms in the sea; the invasion of land by plants and animals; and the evolution of fish, amphibians, and early reptiles. The earliest identifiable fossils date from this era. The climate was mostly warm with short ice ages.

Palatinate (called the *Pfalz* in Germany) historic division of Germany, dating from before the 8th century. It was ruled by a *count palatine* (a count with royal prerogatives) and varied in size.

Palau former name (until 1981) of the Republic of ⟡Belau.

Palermo capital and seaport of Sicily; population (1988) 729,000. Industries include shipbuilding, steel, glass, and chemicals. It was founded by the Phoenicians in the 8th century BC.

Palestine (also called the *Holy Land* because of its links with Judaism, Christianity, and Islam) area between the Mediterranean and the river Jordan, with Lebanon to the north and Sinai to the south. It was in ancient times dominated in turn by Egypt, Assyria, Babylonia, Persia, Macedonia, the Ptolemies, the Seleucids, and the Roman and Byzantine empires. Today it forms part of Israel. The Palestinian people comprise about 500,000 in the West Bank, E Jerusalem, and the Gaza Strip; 1.2 million in Jordan; 1.2 million in Israel; 300,000 in Lebanon; and 100,000 in the USA.

Palestine Liberation Organization (PLO) Arab organization founded 1964 to bring about an independent state of Palestine. It consists of several distinct groupings, the chief of which is al-⟡Fatah, led by Yassir ⟡Arafat, the president of the PLO from 1969. The PLO has pursued diplomatic initiatives, but also operates as a guerrilla army.

Palestrina Giovanni Pierluigi da 1525–1594. Italian composer of secular and sacred choral music. Apart from motets and madrigals, he also wrote 105 masses, including *Missa Papae Marcelli*.

Pali ancient Indo-European language of N India, related to Sanskrit, and a classical language of Buddhism.

Palk Strait channel separating SE India from the island of Sri Lanka; it is 53 km/33 mi at the widest point.

Palladio Andrea 1518–1580. Italian Renaissance architect noted for his harmonious and balanced classical structures. He designed numerous country houses in and around Vicenza, Italy, making use of Roman classical forms, symmetry, and proportion. He also designed churches in Venice and published his studies of classical form in several illustrated books.

palladium lightweight, ductile and malleable, silver-white, metallic element, symbol Pd, atomic number 46, relative atomic mass 106.4. It is one of the so-called platinum group of metals, and is resistant to tarnish and corrosion. It often occurs in nature as a free metal in a natural alloy with platinum. Palladium is used as a catalyst, in alloys of gold (to make white gold) and silver, in electroplating, and in dentistry.

Pallas in Greek mythology, a title of the goddess ⟡Athena.

palm plant of the family Palmae, characterized by a single tall stem bearing a thick cluster of large palmate or pinnate leaves at the top. The majority of the numerous species are tropical or subtropical. Some, such as the coconut, date, sago, and oil palms, are important economically.

Palma (Spanish *Palma de Mallorca*) industrial port (textiles, cement, paper, pottery), resort, and capital of the Balearic Islands, Spain, on Majorca; population (1991) 308,600. Palma was founded

276 BC as a Roman colony. It has a Gothic cathedral begun 1229.

Palmas, Las port in the Canary Islands; see ▷Las Palmas.

Palmer Samuel 1805–1881. English landscape painter and etcher. He lived in Shoreham, Kent, 1826–35 with a group of artists who were all followers of William Blake and called themselves 'the Ancients'. Palmer's expressive landscape style during that period reflected a strongly spiritual inspiration.

Palmerston Henry John Temple, 3rd Viscount Palmerston 1784–1865. British politician. Initially a Tory, in Parliament from 1807, he was secretary-at-war 1809–28. He broke with the Tories 1830 and sat in the Whig cabinets of 1830–34, 1835–41, and 1846–51 as foreign secretary. He was prime minister 1855–58 (when he rectified Aberdeen's mismanagement of the Crimean War, suppressed the ▷Indian Mutiny, and carried through the Second Opium War) and 1859–65 (when he almost involved Britain in the American Civil War on the side of the South).

Palm Sunday in the Christian calendar, the Sunday before Easter and first day of Holy Week, commemorating Jesus' entry into Jerusalem, when the crowd strewed palm leaves in his path.

Palmyra ancient city and oasis in the desert of Syria, about 240 km/150 mi NE of Damascus. Palmyra, the biblical *Tadmor*, was flourishing by about 300 BC. It was destroyed AD 272 after Queen Zenobia had led a revolt against the Romans. Extensive temple ruins exist, and on the site is a village called Tadmor.

Pamirs central Asian plateau mainly in Tajikistan, but extending into China and Afghanistan, traversed by mountain ranges. Its highest peak is Kommunizma Pik (Communism Peak 7,495 m/ 24,600 ft) in the Akademiya Nauk range.

Pampas flat, treeless, Argentine plains, lying between the Andes and the Atlantic and rising gradually from the coast to the lower slopes of the mountains. The E Pampas contain large cattle ranches and the flax- and grain-growing area of Argentina; the W Pampas are arid and unproductive.

pampas grass any grass of the genus *Cortaderia*, native to South America, especially *C. argentea*, which is grown in gardens and has tall leaves and large panicles of white flowers.

Pan in Greek mythology, the god (Roman *Sylvanus*) of flocks and herds, shown as a man with the horns, ears, and hoofed legs of a goat, and playing a shepherd's panpipe (or syrinx).

Pan-Africanist Congress (PAC) militant black South African nationalist group, which broke away from the African National Congress (ANC) 1959. It was outlawed 1960–90. More radical than the ANC,

the Pan-Africanist Congress has a black-only policy for Africa. Since the 1970s, it has been weakened by internal dissent.

Panama Republic of; country in Central America, on a narrow isthmus between the Caribbean and the Pacific Ocean, bordered W by Costa Rica and E by Colombia; *area* 77,100 sq km/29,768 sq mi; *capital* Panama City; *physical* coastal plains and mountainous interior; tropical rainforest in E and NW; Pearl Islands in Gulf of Panama; *head of state and government* Guillermo Endara from 1989; *political system* emergent democratic republic; *exports* bananas, petroleum products, copper, shrimps, sugar; *population* (1990 est) 2,423,000 (mestizo [mixed race] 70%, W Indian 14%, European descent 10%, Indian 6%); *languages* Spanish (official), English; *recent history* independence from Spain was achieved 1821; Panama joined with Colombia until 1903 when full independence was gained. USA–Panama treaties transferred the Panama Canal to Panama 1977. General Noriega, effective ruler of the country from 1983, was charged with drug smuggling by the USA 1988. In 1989 he declared the opposition's electoral victory invalid and was himself declared 'maximum leader' by the assembly. A state of war with the USA was announced; the US invasion 1989 deposed Noriega and installed Guillermo Endara. An attempted coup was foiled 1991; the legislative assembly abolished the army. Noriega was convicted in the USA 1992.

Panama Canal canal across the Panama isthmus in Central America, connecting the Pacific and Atlantic oceans; length 80 km/50 mi, with 12 locks. Built by the USA 1904–14 after an unsuccessful attempt by the French, it was formally opened 1920. The *Panama Canal Zone* was acquired 'in perpetuity' by the USA 1903, comprising land extending about 5 km/3 mi on either side of the canal. The zone passed to Panama 1979, and control of the canal itself was ceded to Panama by the USA in Jan 1990 under the terms of the Panama Canal Treaty 1977. The Canal Zone has several US military bases.

Panama City capital of the Republic of Panama, near the Pacific end of the Panama Canal; population (1990) 584,800. Products include chemicals, plastics, and clothing. An earlier Panama, to the NE, founded 1519, was destroyed 1671, and the city was founded on the present site 1673.

pancreas in vertebrates, an accessory gland of the digestive system located close to the duodenum. When stimulated by the hormone secretin, it secretes enzymes into the duodenum that digest starches, proteins, and fats. In humans, it is about 18 cm/7 in long, and lies behind and below the stomach. It contains groups of cells called the *islets of Langerhans*, which secrete the hormones insulin and glucagon that regulate the blood sugar level.

panda one of two carnivores of different families,

native to NW China and Tibet. The *giant panda Ailuropoda melanoleuca* has black and white fur with black eye patches, and feeds mainly on bamboo shoots. It can grow up to 1.5 m/4.5 ft long, and weigh up to 140 kg/300 lb. It is an endangered species. The *lesser panda Ailurus fulgens*, of the raccoon family, is about 50 cm/1.5 ft long, and is black and chestnut, with a long tail.

Pandora in Greek mythology, the first mortal woman. Zeus sent her to Earth with a box of evils (to counteract the blessings brought to mortals by ◊Prometheus' gift of fire); she opened the box, and the evils all flew out. Only hope was left inside as a consolation.

pangolin or *scaly anteater* any toothless mammal of the order Pholidota. There is only one genus (*Manis*), with seven species found in tropical Africa and SE Asia. They are long-tailed and covered with large, overlapping scales. The elongated skull contains a long, extensible tongue. Pangolins measure up to 1 m/3 ft in length; some are arboreal and others are terrestrial. All live on ants and termites.

Pankhurst Emmeline (born Goulden) 1858–1928. English suffragette. Founder of the Women's Social and Political Union 1903, she launched the militant suffragette campaign 1905. In 1926 she joined the Conservative Party and was a prospective parliamentary candidate. She was supported by her daughters *Christabel Pankhurst* (1880–1958), political leader of the movement, and *Sylvia Pankhurst* (1882–1960).

pansy cultivated violet derived from the European wild pansy, or heartsease, *Viola tricolor*, and including many different varieties and strains. The flowers are usually purple, yellow, cream, or a mixture, and there are many highly developed varieties bred for size, colour, or special markings.

Pantanal large area of swampland in the Mato Grosso of SW Brazil, occupying 220,000 sq km/84,975 sq mi in the upper reaches of the Paraguay River; one of the world's great wildlife refuges; 1,370 sq km/530 sq mi were designated a national park in 1981.

pantheism doctrine that regards all of reality as divine, and God as present in all of nature and the universe. It is expressed in Egyptian religion and Brahmanism; stoicism, Neo-Platonism, Judaism, Christianity, and Islam can be interpreted in pantheistic terms. Pantheistic philosophers include Bruno, Spinoza, Fichte, Schelling, and Hegel.

pantheon originally a temple for worshipping all the gods, such as that in ancient Rome, rebuilt by the emperor Hadrian and still used as a church. In more recent times, the name has been used for a building where famous people are buried (as in the Panthéon, Paris).

panther another name for the ◊leopard.

pantomime in the British theatre, a traditional Christmas entertainment with its origins in the harlequin spectacle of the 18th century and burlesque of the 19th century, which gave rise to the tradition of the principal boy being played by an actress and the dame by an actor. The harlequin's role diminished altogether as themes developed on folktales such as *The Sleeping Beauty* and *Cinderella*, and with the introduction of additional material such as popular songs, topical comedy, and audience participation.

Papal States or *States of the Church* area of central Italy in which the pope was temporal ruler from 756 until the unification of Italy 1870. At one time they included Lazio, Marche, Romagna, Umbria, and part of Tuscany. The ◊Vatican City State is what remains of the Papal States.

Papandreou Andreas 1919– . Greek socialist politician, founder of the Pan-Hellenic Socialist Movement (PASOK), and prime minister 1981–89, when he became implicated in the alleged embezzlement and diversion of funds to the Greek government of $200 million from the Bank of Crete, and as a result lost the election. In Jan 1992 a trial cleared Papandreou of all corruption charges.

papaya tropical tree *Carica papaya* of the family Caricaceae, native from Florida to South America. Varieties are grown throughout the tropics. The edible fruits resemble a melon, with orange-coloured flesh and numerous blackish seeds in the central cavity; they may weigh up to 9 kg/20 lb.

Papeete capital and port of French Polynesia on the NW coast of Tahiti; population (1983) 79,000. Products include vanilla, copra, and mother-of-pearl.

paper thin, flexible material made in sheets from vegetable fibres (such as wood pulp) or rags and used for writing, drawing, printing, packaging, and various household needs. The name comes from papyrus, a form of writing material made from water reed, used in ancient Egypt. The invention of true paper, originally made of pulped fishing nets and rags, is credited to Tsai Lun, Chinese minister of agriculture, AD 105.

Papua New Guinea country in the SW Pacific, comprising the eastern part of the island of New Guinea, the New Guinea Islands, the Admiralty Islands, and part of the Solomon Islands; *area* 462,840 sq km/178,656 sq mi; *capital* Port Moresby (on E New Guinea); *physical* mountainous; includes tropical islands of New Britain, New Ireland, and Bougainville; D'Entrecasteaux and Woodlark Islands, and Louisiade Archipelago; Sepik River; *head of state* Elizabeth II represented by governor general; *head of government* Rabbie Namaliu from 1988; *political system* liberal democracy; *exports* copra, coconut oil, palm oil, tea, copper, gold, coffee; *population* (1989 est) 3,613,000 (Papuans, Melanesians, Pygmies, various minorities); *languages* English (official), pidgin

English, 715 local languages; *recent history* independence was achieved from Australia within the Commonwealth 1975. Joined Solomon Islands and Vanuatu in forming Spearhead Group 1988, aiming to preserve Melanesian cultural traditions and secure independence for French territory of New Caledonia. State of emergency imposed on Bougainville 1989 in response to separatist violence; peace accord signed 1991. Economic boom 1991 as gold production doubled.

papyrus type of paper made by the ancient Egyptians from the stem of the papyrus or paper reed *Cyperus papyrus*, family Cyperaceae.

parachute any canopied fabric device strapped to a person or a package, used to slow down descent from a high altitude, or returning spent missiles or parts to a safe speed for landing, or sometimes to aid (through braking) the landing of a plane or missile. Modern designs enable the parachutist to exercise considerable control of direction, as in skydiving.

paraffin common name for ▷alkane, any member of the series of hydrocarbons with the general formula C_nH_{2n+2}. The lower members are gases, such as methane (marsh or natural gas). The middle ones (mainly liquid) form the basis of petrol, kerosene, and lubricating oils, while the higher ones (paraffin waxes) are used in ointment and cosmetic bases. The fuel commonly sold as paraffin in Britain is more correctly called kerosene.

Paraguay Republic of; country in South America, bordered NE by Brazil, S by Argentina, and NW by Bolivia; *area* 406,752 sq km/157,006 sq mi; *capital* Asunción; *physical* low marshy plain and marshlands; divided by Paraguay River; Paraná River forms SE boundary; *head of state and government* General Andrés Rodríguez from 1989; *political system* emergent democracy; *exports* cotton, soya beans, timber, vegetable oil, maté; *population* (1990 est) 4,660,000 (mixed Guaraní Indian-Spanish 95%); *languages* Spanish (official) 6%, Guaraní 90%; *recent history* independence was achieved from Spain 1811. Much territory was lost during the war with Argentina, Brazil, and Uruguay 1865–70; territory was won from Bolivia during the Chaco War 1932–35. Paraguay has experienced political instability under a series of different presidents since the late 1940s. General Andrés Rodríguez elected president following his overthrow of General Alfredo Stroessner in a coup 1989.

parakeet any of various small ▷parrots.

parallel lines and parallel planes in mathematics, straight lines or planes that always remain a constant distance from one another no matter how far they are extended. This is a principle of Euclidean geometry. Some non-Euclidean geometries, such as elliptical and hyperbolic geometry, however, reject Euclid's parallel axiom.

parallelogram in mathematics, a quadrilateral

parallelogram

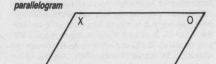

(i) opposite sides & angles are equal

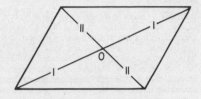

(ii) diagonals bisect each other at 0.

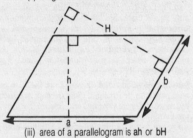

(iii) area of a parallelogram is ah or bH

(four-sided plane figure) with opposite pairs of sides equal in length and parallel, and opposite angles equal. The diagonals of a parallelogram bisect each other. Its area is the product of the length of one side and the perpendicular distance between this and the opposite side. In the special case when all four sides are equal in length, the parallelogram is known as a rhombus, and when the internal angles are right angles, it is a rectangle or square.

parallel processing emerging computer technology that allows more than one computation at the same time. Although in the 1980s this technology enabled only a small number of computer processor units to work in parallel, in theory thousands or millions of processors could be used at the same time.

Paramaribo port and capital of Surinam, South America, 24 km/15 mi from the sea on the river Suriname; population (1980) 193,000. Products include coffee, fruit, timber, and bauxite. It was founded by the French on an Indian village 1540, made capital of British Surinam 1650, and placed under Dutch rule 1816–1975.

Paraná river in South America, formed by the confluence of the Río Grande and Paranaíba; the Paraguay joins it at Corrientes, and it flows into the Río de la Plata with the Uruguay; length 4,500 km/2,800 mi. It is used for hydroelectric power by Argentina, Brazil, and Paraguay.

parapsychology study of phenomena that are not within range of, or explicable by established science, for example, extra-sensory perception. The faculty allegedly responsible for such phenomena, and common to humans and other animals, is known as *psi.*

parasite organism that lives on or in another organism (called the 'host'), and depends on it for nutrition, often at the expense of the host's welfare. Parasites that live inside the host, such as liver flukes and tapeworms, are called *endoparasites*; those that live on the outside, such as fleas and lice, are called *ectoparasites.*

Pareto Vilfredo 1848–1923. Italian economist and political philosopher. A vigorous opponent of socialism and liberalism, he justified inequality of income on the grounds of his empirical observation (*Pareto's law*) that income distribution remained constant whatever efforts were made to change it.

Paris port and capital of France, on the river Seine; *département* in the Île de France region; area 105 sq km/40.5 sq mi; population (1990) 2,175,200. Products include metal, leather, and luxury goods and chemicals, glass, and tobacco.

Paris Commune two periods of government in France: *The Paris municipal government 1789–94* was established after the storming of the ⟡Bastille and remained powerful in the French Revolution until the fall of Robespierre 1794; *The provisional national government 18 March–May 1871* was formed while Paris was besieged by the Germans during the Franco-Prussian War. It consisted of socialists and left-wing republicans, and is often considered the first socialist government in history. Elected after the right-wing National Assembly at Versailles tried to disarm the National Guard, it fell when the Versailles troops captured Paris and massacred 20,000–30,000 people 21–28 May.

parity of a number, the state of being either even or odd. In computing, the term refers to the number of 1s in the binary codes used to represent data. A binary representation has *even parity* if it contains an even number of 1s and *odd parity* if it contains an odd number of 1s.

Park Mungo 1771–1806. Scottish explorer who traced the course of the Niger River 1795– 97 and probably drowned during a second African expedition in 1805–06. He published *Travels in the Interior of Africa* 1799.

Park Chung Hee 1917–1979. President of South Korea 1963–79. Under his rule South Korea had one of the world's fastest-growing economies, but recession and his increasing authoritarianism led to his assassination 1979.

Parker Charlie (Charles Christopher 'Bird', 'Yardbird') 1920–1955. US alto saxophonist and jazz composer, associated with the trumpeter Dizzy Gillespie in developing the ⟡bebop style. His mastery of improvisation inspired performers on all jazz instruments.

Parkinson's disease or *parkinsonism* or *paralysis agitans* degenerative disease of the brain characterized by a progressive loss of mobility, muscular rigidity, tremor, and speech difficulties. The condition is mainly seen in people over the age of 50.

parliament legislative body of a country. The world's oldest parliament is the Icelandic Althing which dates from about 930. The UK Parliament is usually dated from 1265. The legislature of the USA is called ⟡Congress and comprises the ⟡House of Representatives and the ⟡Senate. The English Parliament was united with the Scottish 1707 and with the Irish 1801–1922. The franchise was extended to the middle classes 1832, to the urban working classes 1867, to agricultural labourers 1884, and to women 1918 and 1928. The duration of parliaments was fixed at three years 1694, at seven 1716, and at five 1911. Payment of MPs was introduced 1911.

Parliament, European governing body of the European Community; see ⟡European Parliament.

Parnassus mountain in central Greece, height 2,457 m/8,064 ft, revered by the ancient Greeks as the abode of Apollo and the Muses. The sacred site of Delphi lies on its southern flank.

Parnell Charles Stewart 1846–1891. Irish nationalist politician. He supported a policy of obstruction and violence to attain ⟡Home Rule, and became the president of the Nationalist Party 1877. In 1879 he approved the ⟡Land League, and his attitude led to his imprisonment 1881. His career was ruined 1890 when he was cited as co-respondent in a divorce case.

Parr Catherine 1512–1548. Sixth wife of Henry VIII of England. She had already lost two husbands when in 1543 she married Henry VIII. She survived him, and in 1547 married Lord Seymour of Sudeley (1508–1549).

parrot any bird of the order Psittaciformes, abundant in the tropics, especially in Australia and South America. They are mainly vegetarian, and range in size from the 8.5 cm/3.5 in pygmy parrot to the 100 cm/40 in Amazon parrot. The smaller species are commonly referred to as parakeets. The plumage is often very colourful, and the call is usually a harsh screech. Several species are endangered.

parsec in astronomy, a unit (symbol pc) used for distances to stars and galaxies. One parsec is equal to 3.2616 ⟡light years, 2.063 x 10^5 ⟡astronomical units, and 3.086 x 10^{13} km. It is the distance at which a star would have a parallax (apparent shift in position) of one second of arc when viewed from two points the same distance apart as the Earth's distance from the Sun.

parsley biennial herb *Petroselinum crispum* of the carrot family, Umbelliferae, cultivated for flavouring and its nutrient properties, being rich in vitamin C and minerals. Up to 45 cm/1.5 ft high, it has pinnate, aromatic leaves and yellow umbelliferous flowers.

parsnip temperate Eurasian biennial *Pastinaca sativa* of the carrot family Umbelliferae, with a fleshy edible root.

parthenogenesis development of an ovum (egg) without any genetic contribution from a male. Parthenogenesis is the normal means of reproduction in a few plants (for example, dandelions) and animals (for example, certain fish). Some sexually reproducing species, such as aphids, show parthenogenesis at some stage in their life cycle.

Parthia ancient country in W Asia in what is now NE Iran, capital Ctesiphon. Originating about 248 BC, it reached the peak of its power under Mithridates I in the 2nd century BC, and was annexed to Persia under the Sassanids AD 226. Parthian horsemen feigned retreat and shot their arrows unexpectedly backwards, hence the use of 'Parthian shot' to mean a remark delivered in parting.

particle physics study of the particles that make up all atoms, and of their interactions. More than 300 subatomic particles have now been identified by physicists, categorized into several classes according to their mass, electric charge, spin, magnetic moment, and interaction. Subatomic particles include the *elementary particles* (quarks, leptons, and gauge bosons), which are believed to be indivisible and so may be considered the fundamental units of matter; and the *hadrons* (baryons, such as the proton and neutron, and mesons), which are composite particles, made up of two or three quarks. The proton, electron, and neutrino are the only stable particles (the neutron being stable only when in the atomic nucleus). The unstable particles decay rapidly into other particles, and are known from experiments with particle accelerators and cosmic radiation. See ⟡atomic structure.

particle, subatomic in physics, a particle that is smaller than an atom; see ⟡particle physics.

part of speech grammatical function of a word, described in the grammatical tradition of the Western world, based on Greek and Latin. The four major parts of speech are the noun, verb, adjective, and adverb; the minor parts of speech vary according to schools of grammatical theory, but include the article, conjunction, preposition, and pronoun.

partridge any of various medium-sized ground-dwelling fowl of the family Phasianidae, which also includes pheasants, quail, and chickens. Two species common in the UK are the grey partridge *Perdix perdix*, with mottled brown back, grey speckled breast, and patches of chestnut on the sides, and the French partridge *Alectoris rufa*, distinguished by its red legs, bill, and eyelids.

pascal SI unit (symbol Pa) of pressure, equal to one newton per square metre. It replaces bars and millibars (10^5 Pa equals one bar). It is named after the French scientist Blaise Pascal.

Pascal Blaise 1623–1662. French philosopher and mathematician. He contributed to the development of hydraulics, the ⟡calculus, and the mathematical theory of ⟡probability.

PASCAL (French acronym for *program appliqué à la selection et la compilation automatique de la litterature)* a high-level computer-programming language. Designed by Niklaus Wirth (1934–) in the 1960s as an aid to teaching programming, it is still widely used as such in universities, but is also recognized as a good general-purpose programming language. It was named after 17th-century French mathematician Blaise Pascal.

Pasolini Pier Paolo 1922–1975. Italian poet, novelist, and film director, an influential figure. His writings (making much use of first Friulan and later Roman dialect) include the novels *Ragazzi di vita/ The Ragazzi* 1955 and *Una vita violenta/A Violent Life* 1959, filmed with success as *Accattone!* 1961.

Passchendaele village in W Flanders, Belgium, near Ypres. The Passchendaele ridge before Ypres was the object of a costly and unsuccessful British offensive in World War I, between July and Nov 1917; British casualties numbered nearly 400,000.

passion flower climbing plant of the tropical American genus *Passiflora*, family Passifloraceae. It bears distinctive flower heads comprising a saucer-shaped petal base, a fringelike corona, and a central stalk bearing the stamens and ovary. Some species produce edible fruit.

pass laws South African laws that required the black population to carry passbooks (identity documents) at all times and severely restricted freedom of movement. The laws, a major cause of discontent, formed a central part of the policies of ⟡apartheid. They were repealed 1986.

Passover or *Pesach* in Judaism, an eight-day spring festival which commemorates the exodus of the Israelites from Egypt and the passing over by the Angel of Death of the Jewish houses, so that only the Egyptian firstborn sons were killed.

Pasternak Boris Leonidovich 1890–1960. Russian poet and novelist. His novel *Dr Zhivago* 1957 was banned in the USSR as a 'hostile act', and was awarded a Nobel prize (which Pasternak declined). *Dr Zhivago* has since been unbanned and Pasternak has been posthumously rehabilitated.

Pasteur Louis 1822–1895. French chemist and microbiologist who discovered that fermentation is caused by microorganisms. He also developed a vaccine for ▷rabies, which led to the foundation of the Institut Pasteur in Paris 1888.

pasteurization treatment of food to reduce the number of microorganisms it contains and so protect consumers from disease. Harmful bacteria are killed and the development of others is delayed. For milk, the method involves heating it to 72°C/161°F for 15 seconds followed by rapid cooling to 10°C/50°F or lower. The process also kills beneficial bacteria and reduces the nutritive property of milk.

Patagonia geographic area of South America, south of latitude 40° S, with sheep farming, and coal and oil resources. Sighted by Ferdinand Magellan 1520, it was claimed by both Argentina and Chile until divided between them 1881.

patent or **letters patent** documents conferring the exclusive right to make, use, and sell an invention for a limited period. Ideas are not eligible; neither is anything not new. The earliest known patent for an invention in England is dated 1449 (granted by Henry VI for making stained glass for Eton College).

Pathan member of a people of NW Pakistan and Afghanistan, numbering about 14 million (1984). The majority are Sunni Muslims. The Pathans speak Pashto, a member of the Indo-Iranian branch of the Indo-European family.

pathogen in medicine, a bacterium or virus that causes disease. Most pathogens are ▷parasites, and the diseases they cause are incidental to their search for food or shelter inside the host. Nonparasitic organisms, such as soil bacteria or those living in the human gut and feeding on waste foodstuffs, can also become pathogenic to a person whose immune system or liver is damaged.

pathology medical speciality concerned with the study of disease processes and how these provoke structural and functional changes in the body and its tissues.

Patras (Greek *Pátrai*) industrial city (hydroelectric installations, textiles, paper) in the NW Peloponnese, Greece, on the Gulf of Patras; population (1981) 141,500. The ancient Patrai is the only one of the 12 cities of ▷Achaea to survive.

patriarch in the Old Testament, one of the ancestors of the human race, and especially those of the ancient Hebrews, from Adam to Abraham, Isaac, Jacob, and his sons (who became patriarchs of the Hebrew tribes). In the Eastern Orthodox Church, the term refers to the leader of a national church.

patrician member of a privileged class in ancient Rome, descended from the original citizens. After the 4th century BC the rights formerly exercised by the patricians alone were made available to the ordinary people, the plebeians, and patrician descent became only a matter of prestige.

Patrick, St 389–*c*. 461. Patron saint of Ireland. Born in Britain, probably in S Wales, he was carried off by pirates to six years' slavery in Antrim, Ireland, before escaping either to Britain or Gaul – his poor Latin suggests the former – to train as a missionary. He is variously said to have landed again in Ireland 432 or 456, and his work was a vital factor in the spread of Christian influence there. His symbols are snakes and shamrocks; feast day 17 March.

Patten Chris(topher Francis) 1944– . British Conservative politician, governor of Hong Kong from 1992. He was environment secretary 1989–90 and Conservative Party chair 1990–92, orchestrating the party's campaign for the 1992 general election, in which he lost his Bath parliamentary seat.

Patton George (Smith) 1885–1945. US general in World War II, known as 'Blood and Guts'. He commanded the 2nd Armoured Division 1940, and in 1942 led the Western Task Force that landed at Casablanca, Morocco. After commanding the 7th Army, he led the 3rd Army across France and into Germany, and in 1945 took over the 15th Army.

Pauli Wolfgang 1900–1958. Austrian physicist who originated the *exclusion principle*: in a given system no two fermions (electrons, protons, neutrons, or other elementary particles of half-integral spin) can be characterized by the same set of quantum numbers. He also predicted the existence of neutrinos. He was awarded a Nobel prize 1945 for his work on atomic structure.

Pauling Linus Carl 1901– . US chemist, author of fundamental work on the nature of the chemical bond and on the discovery of the helical structure of many proteins. Nobel Prize for Chemistry 1954.

Paul, St *c*. AD 3–*c*. 68. Christian missionary and martyr; in the New Testament, one of the apostles and author of 13 epistles. He is said to have been converted by a vision on the road to Damascus. His emblems are a sword and a book; feast day 29 June.

Pavarotti Luciano 1935– . Italian tenor whose operatic roles have included Rodolfo in *La Bohème*, Cavaradossi in *Tosca*, the Duke of Mantua in *Rigoletto*, and Nemorino in *L'Elisir d'amore*. He gave his first performance in the title role of *Otello* in Chicago 1991.

Pavlov Ivan Petrovich 1849–1936. Russian physiologist who studied conditioned reflexes in animals. His work had a great impact on behavioural theory and learning theory. See also ▷conditioning. Nobel Prize for Medicine 1904.

Pavlova Anna 1881–1931. Russian dancer. Prima ballerina of the Imperial Ballet from 1906, she left Russia 1913, and went on to become one of the world's most celebrated exponents of classical ballet. With London as her home, she toured extensively with her own company, influencing dancers worldwide with roles such as Mikhail ▷Fokine's *The Dying Swan* solo 1905.

pawpaw or *papaw* small tree *Asimina triloba* of the custard-apple family Annonaceae, native to the eastern USA. It bears oblong fruits 13 cm/5 in long with yellowish, edible flesh. The name pawpaw is also used for the ⟡papaya.

Pax Roman goddess of peace; her Greek counterpart is ⟡Irene.

Paxton Joseph 1801–1865. English architect, garden superintendent to the Duke of Devonshire from 1826 and designer of the Great Exhibition building 1851 (the Crystal Palace), which was revolutionary in its structural use of glass and iron.

Pays de la Loire agricultural region of W France, comprising the *départements* of Loire-Atlantique, Maine-et-Loire, Mayenne, Sarthe, and Vendée; capital Nantes; area 32,100 sq km/12,391 sq mi; population (1986) 3,018,000. Industries include shipbuilding and wine.

Paz Octavio 1914– . Mexican poet and essayist. His works reflect many influences, including Marxism, surrealism, and Aztec mythology. His long poem *Piedra del sol/Sun Stone* 1957 uses contrasting images, centring upon the Aztec Calendar Stone (representing the Aztec universe), to symbolize the loneliness of individuals and their search for union with others. Nobel Prize for Literature 1990.

pea climbing plant *Pisum sativum*, family Leguminosae, with pods of edible seeds, grown since prehistoric times for food. The pea is a popular vegetable and is eaten fresh, canned, dried, or frozen. The sweet pea *Lathyrus odoratus* of the same family is grown for its scented, butterfly-shaped flowers.

Peace Corps organization of trained men and women, established in the USA by President Kennedy 1961, providing skilled volunteer workers for Third World countries, especially in the fields of teaching, agriculture, and health, for a period of two years.

peace movement collective opposition to war. The Western peace movements of the late 20th century can trace their origins to the pacifists of the 19th century and conscientious objectors during World War I. The campaigns after World War II have tended to concentrate on nuclear weapons, but there are numerous organizations devoted to peace, some wholly pacifist, some merely opposed to escalation.

peach tree *Prunus persica*, family Rosaceae. It has ovate leaves and small, usually pink flowers. The yellowish edible fruits have thick velvety skins; the nectarine is a smooth-skinned variety.

peacock technically, the male of any of various large pheasants. The name is most often used for the common peacock *Pavo cristatus*, a bird of the pheasant family, native to S Asia. It is rather larger than a pheasant. The male has a large fan-shaped tail, brightly coloured with blue, green, and purple 'eyes' on a chestnut background. The female (peahen) is brown with a small tail.

peanut or *groundnut* or *monkey nut* South American vinelike annual plant *Arachis hypogaea*, family Leguminosae. After flowering, the flower stalks bend and force the pods into the earth to ripen underground. The nuts are a staple food in many tropical countries and are widely grown in the southern USA. They yield a valuable edible oil and are the basis for numerous processed foods.

pear tree *Pyrus communis*, family Rosaceae, native to temperate regions of Eurasia. It has a succulent edible fruit, less hardy than the apple.

pearl shiny, hard, rounded abnormal growth composed of nacre (or mother-of-pearl), a chalky substance. Nacre is secreted by many molluscs, and deposited in thin layers on the inside of the shell around a parasite, a grain of sand, or some other irritant body. After several years of the mantle (the layer of tissue between the shell and the body mass) secreting this nacre, a pearl is formed.

Pearl Harbor US Pacific naval base in Oahu, Hawaii, USA, the scene of a Japanese attack 7 Dec 1941, which brought the USA into World War II. The attack took place while Japanese envoys were holding so-called peace talks in Washington DC. More than 2,000 members of US armed forces were killed, and a large part of the US Pacific fleet was destroyed or damaged.

Pears Peter 1910–1986. English tenor. A co-founder with Benjamin ⟡Britten of the Aldeburgh Festival, he was closely associated with the composer's work and sang the title role in *Peter Grimes*.

Pearse Patrick Henry 1879–1916. Irish poet prominent in the Gaelic revival, a leader of the ⟡Easter Rising 1916. Proclaimed president of the provisional government, he was court-martialled and shot after its suppression.

Pearson Lester Bowles 1897–1972. Canadian politician, leader of the Liberal Party from 1958, prime minister 1963–68. As foreign minister 1948–57, he represented Canada at the United Nations, playing a key role in settling the ⟡Suez Crisis 1956. Nobel Peace Prize 1957.

Peary Robert Edwin 1856–1920. US polar explorer who, after several unsuccessful attempts, became the first person to reach the North Pole on 6 April 1909. In 1988 an astronomer claimed Peary's measurements were incorrect.

Peasants' Revolt the rising of the English peasantry in June 1381, provoked by the imposition of a poll tax. Led by Wat ⟡Tyler and John ⟡Ball, rebels from SE England marched on London and demanded reforms. The revolt was put down by deceit and force by the authorities.

peat fibrous organic substance found in bogs and formed by the incomplete decomposition of plants such as sphagnum moss. N Asia, Canada, Finland, Ireland, and other places have large deposits, which have been dried and used as fuel from ancient times. Peat can also be used as a soil additive.

pecan nut-producing ⏃hickory tree *Carya illinoensis* or *C. pecan*, native to central USA and N Mexico and now widely cultivated. The tree grows to over 45 m/150 ft, and the edible nuts are smooth-shelled, the kernel resembling a smoothly ovate walnut.

peccary one of two species of the New World genus *Tayassu* of piglike hoofed mammals. A peccary has a gland in the middle of the back which secretes a strong-smelling substance. Peccaries are blackish in colour, covered with bristles, and have tusks that point downwards. Adults reach a height of 40 cm/16 in and a weight of 25 kg/60 lb.

Peel Robert 1788–1850. British Conservative politician. As home secretary 1822–27 and 1828–30, he founded the modern police force and in 1829 introduced Roman Catholic emancipation. He was prime minister 1834–35 and 1841–46, when his repeal of the ⏃Corn Laws caused him and his followers to break with the party.

peepul another name for the ⏃bo tree.

peerage in the UK, holders of the titles of (in descending order) duke, marquess, earl, viscount, and baron. Some of these titles may be held by a woman in default of a male heir. In the late 19th century the peerage was augmented by the Lords of Appeal in Ordinary (the nonhereditary life peers) and, from 1958, by a number of specially created life peers of either sex (usually long-standing members of the House of Commons). Since 1963 peers have been able to disclaim their titles, usually to enable them to take a seat in the Commons (where peers are disqualified from membership).

Pegasus in Greek mythology, the winged horse that sprang from the blood of the Gorgon Medusa. He was transformed into a constellation.

Pei Ieoh Ming 1917–   . Chinese-born US Modernist/high-tech architect, noted for the use of glass walls. His buildings include the Bank of China Tower, Hong Kong, 1987, and the glass pyramid in front of the Louvre, Paris, 1989.

Peking alternative transcription of ⏃Beijing, capital of China.

pekingese breed of long-haired dog with a flat skull and flat face, typically less than 25 cm/10 in tall and weighing less than 5 kg/11 lb.

pelargonium flowering plant of the genus *Pelargonium* of the geranium family Geraniaceae, grown extensively in gardens, where it is familiarly known as the **geranium**. Ancestors of the garden hybrids came from S Africa.

Pelé Adopted name of Edson Arantes do Nascimento 1940–   . Brazilian soccer player. A prolific goal scorer, he appeared in four World Cup competitions 1958–70 and led Brazil to three championships (1958, 1962, 1970).

Pelham Henry 1696–1754. British Whig politician. He held a succession of offices in Robert Walpole's cabinet 1721–42, and was prime minister 1743–54.

pelican any of a family (Pelecanidae) of large, heavy water birds remarkable for the pouch beneath the bill which is used as a fishing net and temporary store for catches of fish. Some species grow up to 1.8 m/6 ft, and have wingspans of 3 m/10 ft.

Pelion mountain in Thessaly, Greece, near Mount Ossa; height 1,548 m/5,079 ft. In Greek mythology it was the home of the centaurs, creatures half human and half horse.

Peloponnese (Greek *Peloponnesos*) peninsula forming the southern part of Greece; area 21,549 sq km/8,318 sq mi; population (1991) 1,077,000. It is joined to the mainland by the narrow isthmus of Corinth and is divided into the nomes (administrative areas) of Argolis, Arcadia, Achaea, Elis, Corinth, Lakonia, and Messenia, representing its seven ancient states.

Peloponnesian War conflict between Athens and Sparta and their allies, 431–404 BC, originating in suspicions about the 'empire-building' ambitions of the Athenian leader Pericles. It was ended by the Spartan general Lysander's capture of the Athenian fleet in 405, and his starving the Athenians into surrender in 404. Sparta's victory meant the destruction of the political power of Athens.

Peltier effect in physics, a change in temperature at the junction of two different metals produced when an electric current flows through them. The extent of the change depends on what the conducting metals are, and the nature of change (rise or fall in temperature) depends on the direction of current flow. It is named after the French physicist Jean Charles Peltier (1785–1845) who discovered it 1834.

Penang (Malay *Pulau Pinang*) state in W Peninsular Malaysia, formed of Penang Island, Province Wellesley, and the Dindings on the mainland; area 1,030 sq km/398 sq mi; capital Penang (George Town); population (1990) 1,142,200. Penang Island was bought by Britain from the ruler of Kedah 1785; Province Wellesley was acquired 1800.

Penda *c*. 577–654. King of Mercia, an Anglo-Saxon kingdom in England, from about 632. He raised Mercia to a powerful kingdom, and defeated and killed two Northumbrian kings, Edwin 632 and Oswald 641. He was killed in battle by Oswy, king of Northumbria.

Penelope in Greek legend, the wife of Odysseus, ruler of Ithaca and one of the leaders of the Greek forces in the Trojan War. During his absence after the siege of Troy she kept her many suitors at bay by asking them to wait until she had woven a shroud for her father-in-law, but unravelled her work each night. When Odysseus returned, after 20 years, he killed her suitors.

penguin any of an order (Sphenisciformes) of marine flightless birds, mostly black and white, found in the southern hemisphere. They range in size from 40 cm/1.6 ft to 1.2 m/4 ft tall, and have thick feathers to protect them from the intense cold. They are awkward on land, but their wings have evolved into flippers, making them excellent swimmers.

penicillin any of a group of ♢antibiotic (bacteria killing) compounds obtained from filtrates of moulds of the genus *Penicillium* (especially *P. notatum*) or produced synthetically. Penicillin was the first antibiotic to be discovered (by Alexander ♢Fleming); it kills a broad spectrum of bacteria, many of which cause disease in humans.

Peninsular War war 1808–14 caused by the French emperor Napoleon's invasion of Portugal and Spain. British expeditionary forces under Sir Arthur Wellesley (Duke of ♢Wellington), combined with Spanish and Portuguese resistance, succeeded in defeating the French at Vimeiro 1808, Talavera 1809, Salamanca 1812, and Vittoria 1813. The results were inconclusive, and the war was ended by Napoleon's abdication.

penis male reproductive organ, used for internal fertilization; it transfers sperm to the female reproductive tract. In mammals, the penis is made erect by vessels that fill with blood, and in most mammals (but not humans) is stiffened by a bone. It also contains the urethra, through which urine is passed. Snakes and lizards have a paired structure that serves as a penis, other reptiles have a single organ. A few birds, mainly ducks and geese, also have a type of penis, as do snails, barnacles, and some other invertebrates. Many insects have a rigid, nonerectile male organ, usually referred to as an intromittent organ.

Penn William 1644–1718. English member of the Society of Friends (Quakers), born in London. He joined the Society 1667, and in 1681 obtained a grant of land in America (in settlement of a debt owed by the king to his father) on which he established the colony of Pennsylvania as a refuge for persecuted Quakers.

Pennines mountain system, 'the backbone of England', broken by a gap through which the river Aire flows to the east and the Ribble to the west; length (Scottish border to the Peaks in Derbyshire) 400 km/250 mi. Britain's first long-distance footpath the *Pennine Way* opened in 1965.

Pennsylvania state in NE USA: nickname Keystone State; *area* 117,400 sq km/45,316, sq mi; *capital* Harrisburg; *cities* Philadelphia, Pittsburgh, Erie, Allentown, Scranton; *features* Allegheny Mountains; rivers: Ohio, Susquehanna, Delaware; Independence National Historic Park, Philadelphia; Valley Forge National Historic Park; Gettysburg Civil War battlefield; Pennsylvania Dutch country; Poconos resort region; *products* hay, cereals, mushrooms, cattle, poultry, dairy products, cement, coal, steel, petroleum products, pharmaceuticals, motor vehicles and equipment, electronic components, textiles; *population* (1990) 11,881,600; *famous people* Marian Anderson, Stephen Foster, Benjamin Franklin, George C Marshall, Robert E Peary, Gertrude Stein, John Updike; *history* founded and named by William ♢Penn 1682, following a land grant by Charles II. It was one of the original thirteen states.

Pentagon the headquarters of the US Department of Defense, Arlington, Virginia. One of the world's largest office buildings (five-sided with a pentagonal central court), it houses the administrative and command headquarters for the US armed forces and has become synonymous with the military establishment bureaucracy.

Pentecost in Judaism, the festival of *Shavuot*, celebrated on the 50th day after ♢Passover in commemoration of the giving of the Ten Commandments to Moses on Mount Sinai, and the end of the grain harvest; in the Christian church, Pentecost is the day on which the apostles experienced inspiration of the Holy Spirit, commemorated on Whit Sunday.

Pentecostal movement Christian revivalist movement inspired by the baptism in the Holy Spirit with 'speaking in tongues' experienced by the apostles at the time of Pentecost. It represents a reaction against the rigid theology and formal worship of the traditional churches. Pentecostalists believe in the literal word of the Bible and disapprove of alcohol, tobacco, dancing, theatre, and so on. It is an intensely missionary faith, and recruitment has been rapid since the 1960s: worldwide membership is more than 10 million.

peony or *paeony* any perennial plant of the genus *Paeonia*, family Paeoniaceae, remarkable for their brilliant flowers. Most popular are the common peony *P. officinalis*, the white peony *P. lactiflora*, and the taller tree peony *P. suffruticosa*.

Pepin the Short c. 714–c. 768. King of the Franks from 751. The son of ♢Charles Martel, he acted as Mayor of the Palace to the last Merovingian king, Childeric III, deposed him and assumed the royal title himself, founding the ♢Carolingian dynasty. He was ♢Charlemagne's father.

pepper climbing plant *Piper nigrum* native to the E Indies, of the Old World pepper family Piperaceae. When gathered green, the berries are crushed to release the seeds for the spice called black pepper. When the berries are ripe, the seeds are removed and their outer skin is discarded, to produce white pepper. Chilli pepper, cayenne or red pepper and the sweet peppers used as a vegetable come from ▷capsicums native to the New World.

peppermint perennial herb *Mentha piperita* of the mint family, native to Europe, with ovate, aromatic leaves and purple flowers. Oil of peppermint is used in medicine and confectionery.

peptide molecule comprising two or more ▷amino acid molecules (not necessarily different) joined by **peptide bonds**, whereby the acid group of one acid is linked to the amino group of the other (–CO.NH). The number of amino acid molecules in the peptide is indicated by referring to it as a di-, tri-, or polypeptide (two, three, or many amino acids).

Pepys Samuel 1633–1703. English diarist. His diary 1659–69 was a unique record of both the daily life of the period and the intimate feelings of the man. Written in shorthand, it was not deciphered until 1825.

percentage way of representing a number as a ▷fraction of 100. Thus 45 percent (45%) equals $45/100$, and 45% of 20 is $45/100 \times 20 = 9$.

Perceval Spencer 1762–1812. British Tory politician. He became chancellor of the Exchequer 1807 and prime minister 1809. He was shot in the lobby of the House of Commons 1812 by a merchant who blamed government measures for his bankruptcy.

perch any of the largest order of spiny-finned bony fishes, the Perciformes, with some 8,000 species. This order includes the sea basses, cichlids, damselfishes, mullets, barracudas, wrasses, and gobies. Perches of the freshwater genus *Perca* are found in Europe, Asia, and North America. They have varied shapes and are usually a greenish colour.

percussion instrument musical instrument played by being struck with the hand or a beater. Percussion instruments can be divided into those that can be tuned to produce a sound of definite pitch, and those without pitch.

Percy Henry 'Hotspur' 1364–1403. English soldier, son of the 1st Earl of Northumberland. In repelling a border raid, he defeated the Scots at Homildon Hill in Durham 1402. He was killed at the battle of Shrewsbury while in revolt against Henry IV.

perennating organ in plants, that part of a biennial plant or herbaceous perennial that allows it to survive the winter; usually a root, tuber, rhizome, bulb, or corm.

perennial plant plant that lives for more than two years. Herbaceous perennials have aerial stems and leaves that die each autumn. They survive the winter by means of an underground storage (perennating) organ, such as a bulb or rhizome. Trees and shrubs or woody perennials have stems that persist above ground throughout the year, and may be either deciduous or ▷evergreen. See also ▷annual plant.

Peres Shimon 1923– . Israeli socialist politician,

prime minister 1984–86. Peres was prime minister, then foreign minister, under a power-sharing agreement with the leader of the Consolidation Party (Likud), Yitzhak ▷Shamir. From 1989 to 1990 he was finance minister in a new Labour–Likud coalition.

perestroika in Soviet politics, the wide-ranging economic and political reforms initiated during Mikhail Gorbachev's leadership that led to the winding-up of the Soviet state. It is also the title of a book by Gorbachev published in 1987.

Pérez de Cuéllar Javier 1920– . Peruvian diplomat, secretary general of the United Nations 1982–91. He raised the standing of the UN by his successful diplomacy in ending the Iran–Iraq War 1988 and securing the independence of Namibia 1989.

Pergamum ancient Greek city in W Asia Minor, which became the capital of an independent kingdom 283 BC. As the ally of Rome it achieved great political importance in the 2nd century BC, and became a centre of art and culture. Close to its site is the modern Turkish town of Bergama.

Pericles *c.* 490–429 BC. Athenian politician who dominated the city's affairs from 461 BC (as leader of the democratic party), and under whom Greek culture reached its height. He created a confederation of cities under the leadership of Athens, but the disasters of the ▷Peloponnesian War led to his overthrow 430 BC. Although quickly reinstated, he died soon after.

periodic table of the elements in chemistry, a table setting out the classification of the elements following the statement by Russian chemist Dmitri Mendeleyev 1869 that 'the properties of elements are in periodic dependence upon their atomic weight'. (Today elements are classified by their atomic number rather than by their relative atomic mass.)

periwinkle in botany, any of several trailing blue-flowered evergreen plants of the genus *Vinca* of the dogbane family Apocynaceae.

periwinkle in zoology, any marine snail of the family Littorinidae, found on the shores of Europe and E North America. Periwinkles have a conical spiral shell, and feed on algae.

Perm industrial city (shipbuilding, oil refining, aircraft, chemicals, sawmills), and capital of Perm region, N Russia, on the Kama near the Ural mountains; population (1987) 1,075,000. It was called Molotov 1940–57.

permafrost condition in which a deep layer of soil does not thaw out during the summer but remains at below 0°C/32°F for at least two years, despite thawing of the soil above. It is claimed that 26% of the world's land surface is permafrost.

Permian period of geological time 286–248 million years ago, the last period of the Palaeozoic era. Its end was marked by a significant change in marine life, including the extinction of many corals and trilobites.

Perón (María Estela) Isabel (born Martínez) 1931– . President of Argentina 1974–76, and third wife of Juan Perón. She succeeded him after he died in office, but labour unrest, inflation, and political violence pushed the country to the brink of chaos. Accused of corruption, she was held under house arrest for five years. She went into exile in Spain.

Perón Evita (María Eva) (born Duarte) 1919–1952. Argentine populist leader. A successful radio actress, she married Juan ◊Perón in 1945. When he became president the following year, she became his chief adviser and virtually ran the health and labour ministries, devoting herself to helping the poor, improving education, and achieving women's suffrage. She was politically astute and sought the vice-presidency 1951, but was opposed by the army and withdrew.

Perón Juan (Domingo) 1895–1974. Argentine politician, dictator 1946–55 and from 1973 until his death. His populist appeal to the poor was enhanced by the charisma and political work of his second wife Eva (Evita) Perón.

Perpendicular period of English Gothic architecture lasting from the end of the 14th century to the mid-16th century. It is characterized by window tracery consisting chiefly of vertical members, two or four arc arches, lavishly decorated vaults and use of traceried panels. Examples include the choir and cloister of Gloucester Cathedral, and King's College Chapel, Cambridge.

perpetual motion the idea that a machine can be designed and constructed in such a way that, once started, it will continue in motion indefinitely without requiring any further input of energy (motive power). Such a device contradicts the two laws of thermodynamics that state that (1) energy can neither be created nor destroyed (the law of conservation of energy) and (2) heat cannot by itself flow from a cooler to a hotter object. As a result, all practical (real) machines require a continuous supply of energy, and no heat engine is able to convert all the heat into useful work.

Perry Matthew Calbraith 1794–1858. US naval officer, commander of the expedition of 1853 that reopened communication between Japan and the outside world after 250 years' isolation. Evident military superiority enabled him to negotiate the Treaty of Kanagawa 1854, giving the USA trading rights with Japan.

Persephone Greek goddess (Roman Proserpina), the daughter of Zeus and Demeter. She was carried off to the underworld as the bride of Pluto, who later agreed that she should spend six months of the year with her mother. The myth symbolizes the growth and decay of vegetation and the changing seasons.

Perseus in Greek mythology, son of Zeus and Danaë. He slew Medusa, the ◊Gorgon, and cut off her head, which he set in his shield, rescued Andromeda, and became king of Tiryns.

Persia, ancient kingdom in SW Asia. The early Persians were a nomadic Aryan people who migrated through the Caucasus to the Iranian plateau.

7th century BC The Persians were established in the present region of Fars, which then belonged to the Assyrians.
550 BC Cyrus the Great overthrew the empire of the Medes, to whom the Persians had been subject, and founded the Persian Empire.
539 BC Having conquered all Anatolia, Cyrus added Babylonia (including Syria and Palestine) to his empire.
529–485 BC Darius I organized an efficient centralized system of administration and extended Persian rule east into Afghanistan and NW India and as far north as the Danube, but the empire was weakened by internal dynastic struggles.
499–449 BC The Persian Wars with Greece ended Persian domination of the ancient world.
331 BC Alexander the Great drove the Persians under Darius III (died 330 BC) into retreat at Arbela on the Tigris, marking the end of the Persian Empire and the beginning of the Hellenistic period under the Seleucids.
AD 226 The Sassanian Empire was established in Persia and annexed Parthia.
637 Arabs took the capital, Ctesiphon, and introduced Islam in place of Zoroastrianism.
For modern history see ◊Iran.

Persian Gulf or *Arabian Gulf* shallow inlet of the Arabian Sea; area 233,000 sq km/90,000 sq mi. It divides the Arabian peninsula from Iran and is linked by the Strait of Hormuz and the Gulf of Oman to the Arabian Sea. Oilfields surround it in the Gulf States of Bahrain, Iran, Iraq, Kuwait, Oman, Qatar, Saudi Arabia, and the United Arab Emirates.

Persian Wars series of conflicts between Greece and Persia 499–449 BC. The eventual victory of Greece marked the end of Persian domination of the ancient world and the beginning of Greek supremacy.

persimmon any tree of the genus *Diospyros* of the ebony family Ebenaceae, especially the common persimmon *D. virginiana* of the southeastern USA. Up to 19 m/60 ft high, the persimmon has alternate oval leaves and yellow-green unisexual flowers. The small, sweet, orange fruits are edible.

Perspex trade name for a clear, lightweight, tough plastic first produced 1930. It is widely used for watch glasses, advertising signs, domestic baths, motorboat windshields, aircraft canopies, and protective shields. Its chemical name is polymethylmethacrylate (PMMA).

Perth capital of Western Australia, with its port at nearby Fremantle on the Swan River; population

(1990) 1,190,100. Products include textiles, cement, furniture, and vehicles. It was founded 1829 and is the commercial and cultural centre of the state.

Peru Republic of; country in South America, on the Pacific, bordered N by Ecuador and Colombia, E by Brazil and Bolivia, and S by Chile; *area* 1,285,200 sq km/496,216 sq mi; *capital* Lima, including port of Callao; *physical* Andes mountains NW–SE cover 27% of Peru, separating Amazon river-basin jungle in NE from coastal plain in W; desert along coast N–S; *head of state and government* Alberto Fujimori from 1990; *political system* democratic republic; *exports* coca, coffee, alpaca, llama, and vicuña wool, fish meal, lead (largest producer in South America), copper, iron, oil; *population* (1990 est) 21,904,000 (Indian, mainly Quechua and Aymara, 46%; mixed Spanish-Indian descent 43%); *languages* Spanish 68%, Quechua 27% (both official), Aymara 3%; *recent history* independence achieved from Spain 1824. Boundary disputes settled with Bolivia 1902, Colombia 1927, and Ecuador 1942; dispute with Ecuador renewed 1981. Peru has been ruled by military and civilian governments alternately since 1948. Civilian rule was restored 1980. In 1992 Fujimori, allying himself with the army, suspended the assembly and dismissed half the senior judges.

Peru Current formerly known as *Humboldt Current* cold ocean ⬦current flowing north from the Antarctic along the west coast of South America to S Ecuador, then west. It reduces the coastal temperature, making the west slopes of the Andes arid because winds are already chilled and dry when they meet the coast.

Peshawar capital of North-West Frontier Province, Pakistan, 18 km/11 mi E of the Khyber Pass; population (1981) 555,000. Products include textiles, leather, and copper.

pesticide any chemical used in farming, gardening or indoors to combat pests. Pesticides are of three main types: *insecticides* (to kill insects), *fungicides* (to kill fungal diseases), and *herbicides* (to kill plants, mainly those considered weeds). The safest pesticides are those made from plants, such as the insecticides pyrethrum and derris. Pesticides cause a number of pollution problems through spray drift onto surrounding areas, direct contamination of users or the public, and as residues on food.

Pétain Henri Philippe 1856–1951. French general and right-wing politician. His defence of Verdun 1916 during World War I made him a national hero. In World War II he became prime minister June 1940 and signed an armistice with Germany. Removing the seat of government to Vichy, a health resort in central France, he established an authoritarian regime. He was imprisoned after the war.

Peter I the Great 1672–1725. Tsar of Russia from 1682 on the death of his brother Tsar Feodor; he assumed control of the government 1689. He attempted to reorganize the country on Western lines; the army was modernized, a fleet was built, the administrative and legal systems were remodelled, education was encouraged, and the church was brought under state control. On the Baltic coast, where he had conquered territory from Sweden, Peter built his new capital, St Petersburg.

Peterloo massacre the events in St Peter's Fields, Manchester, England, 16 Aug 1819, when an open-air meeting in support of parliamentary reform was charged by yeomanry and hussars. Eleven people were killed and 500 wounded. The name was given in analogy with the Battle of Waterloo.

Peter, St Christian martyr, the author of two epistles in the New Testament and leader of the apostles. He is regarded as the first bishop of Rome, whose mantle the pope inherits. His emblem is two keys; feast day 29 June.

Petipa Marius 1818–1910. French choreographer who created some of the most important ballets in the classical repertory. For the Imperial Ballet in Russia he created masterpieces such as *La Bayadère* 1877, *The Sleeping Beauty* 1890, *Swan Lake* 1895 (with Ivanov), and *Raymonda* 1898.

Petra (Arabic *Wadi Musa*) ancient city carved out of the red rock at a site in Jordan, on the eastern slopes of the Wadi el Araba, 90 km/56 mi S of the Dead Sea. An Edomite stronghold and capital of the Nabataeans in the 2nd century, it was captured by the Roman emperor Trajan 106 and destroyed by the Arabs in the 7th century. It was forgotten in Europe until 1812 when the Swiss traveller Jacob Burckhardt (1818–1897) came across it.

Petrarch (Italian *Petrarca*) Francesco 1304–1374. Italian poet, born in Arezzo, a devotee of the Classical tradition. His *Il Canzoniere* is composed of sonnets in praise of his idealized love 'Laura', whom he first saw 1327 (she was a married woman and refused to become his mistress).

petrel any of various families of seabirds, including the worldwide *storm petrels* (family Procellariidae), which include the smallest seabirds (some only 13 cm/5 in long), and the *diving petrels* (family Pelecanoididae) of the southern hemisphere, which feed by diving underwater and are characterized by having nostril tubes. They include ⬦fulmars and ⬦shearwaters.

Petrograd former name (1914–24) of St Petersburg, city in Russia.

petrol mixture of hydrocarbons derived from petroleum, mainly used as a fuel for internal combustion engines. It is colourless and highly volatile. In the USA, petrol is called gasoline.

petrol engine the most commonly used source of power for motor vehicles, introduced by the German engineers Gottlieb Daimler and Karl Benz

petroleum

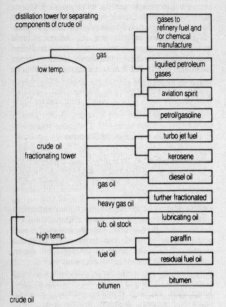

distillation tower for separating
components of crude oil

gas

low temp.

crude oil
fractionating tower

gas oil

heavy gas oil

lub. oil stock

high temp.

fuel oil

bitumen

crude oil

gases to
refinery fuel and
for chemical
manufacture

liquified petroleum
gases

aviation spirit

petrol/gasoline

turbo jet fuel

kerosene

diesel oil

further fractionated

lubricating oil

paraffin

residual fuel oil

bitumen

1885. The petrol engine is a complex piece of machinery made up of about 150 moving parts. It is a reciprocating piston engine, in which a number of pistons move up and down in cylinders. The motion of the pistons rotate a crankshaft, at the end of which is a heavy flywheel. From the flywheel the power is transferred to the car's driving wheels via the transmission system of clutch, gearbox, and final drive.

petroleum or *crude oil* natural mineral oil, a thick greenish-brown flammable liquid found underground in permeable rocks. Petroleum consists of hydrocarbons mixed with oxygen, sulphur, nitrogen, and other elements in varying proportions. It is thought to be derived from ancient organic material that has been converted to, first, bacterial action, then heat and pressure (but its origin may be chemical also). From crude petroleum, various products are made by distillation and other processes; for example, fuel oil, petrol, kerosene, diesel, lubricating oil, paraffin wax, and petroleum jelly.

pewter any of various alloys of mostly tin with varying amounts of lead, copper, or antimony. Pewter has been known for centuries and was once widely used for domestic utensils but is now used mainly for ornamental ware.

peyote spineless cactus *Lophopora williamsii* of N Mexico and the southwestern USA. It has white or pink flowers. Its buttonlike tops contain the hallucinogen **mescaline**, which is used by American Indians in religious ceremonies.

pH scale for measuring acidity or alkalinity. A pH of 7.0 indicates neutrality, below 7 is acid, while above 7 is alkaline.

Phaedra in Greek mythology, a Cretan, daughter of Minos and Pasiphae, married to Theseus of Athens. Her adulterous passion for her stepson Hippolytus led to her death. The story is told in plays by Euripides, Seneca, and Racine.

phagocyte type of white blood cell, or ◊leucocyte, that can engulf a bacterium or other invading microorganism. Phagocytes are found in blood, lymph, and other body tissues, where they also ingest foreign matter and dead tissue. A ◊macrophage differs in size and life span.

Phalangist member of a Lebanese military organization (*Phalanges Libanaises*), since 1958 the political and military force of the Maronite Church in Lebanon. The Phalangists' unbending right-wing policies and resistance to the introduction of democratic institutions helped contribute to the civil war in Lebanon. The Phalangists today form the largest Lebanese political group.

phalarope any of a genus *Phalaropus* of small, elegant shorebirds in the sandpiper family (Scolopacidae). They have the habit of spinning in the water to stir up insect larvae. They are native to North America, the UK, and the polar regions of Europe.

Phanerozoic eon in Earth history, consisting of the most recent 590 million years. It comprises the Palaeozoic, Mesozoic, and Cenozoic eras. The vast majority of fossils come from this eon, owing to the evolution of hard shells and internal skeletons. The name means 'interval of well-displayed life'.

Pharaoh Hebrew form of the Egyptian royal title Per-'o. This term, meaning 'great house', was originally applied to the royal household, and after about 950 BC to the king.

Pharisee member of a conservative Jewish sect that arose in the 2nd century BC in protest against all movements favouring compromise with Hellenistic culture. The Pharisees were devout adherents of the law, both as found in the Torah and in the oral tradition known as the Mishnah.

pharmacology study of the origins, applications, and effects of chemical substances on living organisms. Products of the pharmaceutical industry range from aspirin to anticancer agents.

pheasant any of various large, colourful Asiatic fowls of the family Phasianidae, which also includes grouse, quail, and turkey. The plumage of the male Eurasian ring-necked or common pheasant *Phasianus colchicus* is richly tinted with brownish-green, yellow, and red markings, but the female is a camouflaged brownish colour

phenol member of a group of aromatic chemical compounds with weakly acidic properties, which are characterized by a hydroxyl (OH) group attached directly to an aromatic ring. The simplest of the phenols, derived from benzene, is also known as phenol and has the formula C_6H_5OH. It is sometimes called *carbolic acid* and can be extracted from coal tar.

phenotype in genetics, visible traits, those actually displayed by an organism. The phenotype is not a direct reflection of the ▷genotype because some alleles are masked by the presence of other, dominant alleles. The phenotype is further modified by the effects of the environment (for example, poor nutrition stunts growth).

pheromone chemical signal (such as an odour) that is emitted by one animal and affects the behaviour of others. Pheromones are used by many animal species to attract mates.

Phidias mid-5th century BC. Greek Classical sculptor. He supervised the sculptural programme for the Parthenon (most of it is preserved in the British Museum, London, and known as the *Elgin marbles*). He also executed the colossal statue of Zeus at Olympia, one of the Seven Wonders of the World.

Philadelphia industrial city and port on the Delaware River in Pennsylvania, USA; population (1990) 1,585,600, metropolitan area 5,899,300. Products include refined oil, chemicals, textiles, processed food, printing and publishing. Founded 1682, it was the first capital of the USA 1790–1800.

Philip Duke of Edinburgh 1921– . Prince of the UK, husband of Elizabeth II, a grandson of George I of Greece and a great-great-grandson of Queen Victoria. He was born in Corfu, Greece but brought up in England.

Philip II (Philip Augustus) 1165–1223. King of France from 1180. As part of his efforts to establish a strong monarchy and evict the English from their French possessions, he waged war in turn against the English kings Henry II, Richard I (with whom he also went on the Third Crusade), and John (against whom he won the decisive battle of Bouvines in Flanders 1214).

Philip VI 1293–1350. King of France from 1328, first of the house of Valois, elected by the barons on the death of his cousin, Charles IV. His claim was challenged by Edward III of England, who defeated him at Crécy 1346.

Philip II of Macedon 382–336 BC. King of ▷Macedonia from 359 BC. He seized the throne from his nephew, for whom he was regent, conquered the Greek city states, and formed them into a league whose forces could be united against Persia. He was assassinated while he was planning this expedition, and was succeeded by his son ▷Alexander the Great.

Philip II 1527–1598. King of Spain from 1556. He was born at Valladolid, the son of the Habsburg emperor Charles V, and in 1554 married Queen Mary of England. On his father's abdication 1556 he inherited Spain, the Netherlands, and the Spanish possessions in Italy and the Americas, and in 1580 he annexed Portugal. His intolerance and lack of understanding of the Netherlanders drove them into revolt. Political and religious differences combined to involve him in war with England and, after 1589, with France. The defeat of the ▷Spanish Armada (the fleet sent to invade England in 1588) marked the beginning of the decline of Spanish power.

Philippines Republic of the; country on an archipelago E of the Pacific Ocean and W of the South China Sea; *area* 300,000 sq km/115,800 sq mi; *capital* Manila (on Luzon); *physical* comprises over 7,000 islands; volcanic mountain ranges traverse main chain N–S; 50% still forested. The largest islands are Luzon 108,172 sq km/41,754 sq mi and Mindanao 94,227 sq km/36,372 sq mi; others include Samar, Negros, Palawan, Panay, Mindoro, Leyte, Cebu, and the Sulu group; *head of state and government* Fidel Ramos from 1992; *political system* emergent democracy; *exports* sugar, copra (world's largest producer) and coconut oil, timber, copper concentrates, electronics, clothing; *population* (1990 est) 66,647,000 (Malaysian 93%); *languages* Tagalog (Filipino, official), English, Spanish; *recent history* independence was achieved from the USA 1946. President Ferdinand Marcos was overthrown by Corazon Aquino's People's Power movement 1986; seven coup attempts made between 1987 and 1990 but President Aquino remained in power until she stepped down in 1992. In 1991 the senate refused to renew the US lease of its Subic Bay naval base.

Philip, St 1st century AD. In the New Testament, one of the 12 apostles. He was an inhabitant of Bethsaida (N Israel), and is said to have worked as a missionary in Anatolia. Feast day 3 May.

Philip the Good 1396–1467. Duke of Burgundy from 1419. He engaged in the Hundred Years' War as an ally of England until he made peace with the French at the Council of Arras 1435. He made the Netherlands a centre of art and learning.

Philistine member of a seafaring people of non-Semitic origin who founded city-states on the Palestinian coastal plain in the 12th century BC, adopting a Semitic language and religion. They were at war with the Israelites in the 11th–10th centuries BC (hence the pejorative use of their name in Hebrew records for anyone uncivilized in intellectual and artistic terms). They were largely absorbed into the kingdom of Israel under King David, about 1000 BC.

philosophy branch of learning that includes metaphysics (the nature of being), epistemology (theory of knowledge), logic (study of valid inference), ethics, and aesthetics. Philosophy is concerned with fundamental problems – including the nature of mind and matter, perception, self, free will, causation, time and space, and the existence of moral judgements – which cannot be resolved by a specific method.

phloem tissue found in vascular plants whose main function is to conduct sugars and other food materials from the leaves, where they are produced, to all other parts of the plant.

phlox any plant of the genus *Phlox*, native to North America and Siberia. Phloxes are small with alternate leaves and showy white, pink, red, or purple flowers.

Phnom Penh capital of Cambodia, on the Mekong River, 210 km/130 mi NW of Saigon; population (1989) 800,000. Industries include textiles and food-processing. On 17 April 1975 the entire population (about 3 million) was forcibly evacuated by the ⚪Khmer Rouge communist movement; survivors later returned.

Phoenicia ancient Greek name for N ⚪Canaan on the E coast of the Mediterranean. The Phoenicians lived about 1200–332 BC. Seafaring traders and artisans, they are said to have circumnavigated Africa and established colonies in Cyprus, N Africa (for example Carthage), Malta, Sicily, and Spain. Their cities (Tyre, Sidon, and Byblos were the main ones) were independent states ruled by hereditary kings but dominated by merchant ruling classes. The fall of Tyre to Alexander the Great ended the separate history of Phoenicia.

phoenix mythical Egyptian bird that burned itself to death on a pyre every 500 years and rose rejuvenated from the ashes.

Phoenix capital of Arizona, USA; industrial city (steel, aluminium, electrical goods, food processing) and tourist centre on the Salt River; population (1990) 983,400.

phonetics identification, description, and classification of sounds used in articulate speech. These sounds are codified in the International Phonetic Alphabet (a highly modified version of the English/ Roman alphabet).

phosphate salt or ester of phosphoric acid. Incomplete neutralization of phosphoric acid gives rise to acid phosphates. Phosphates are used as fertilizers, and are required for the development of healthy root systems. They are involved in many biochemical processes, often as part of complex molecules, such as ⚪ATP.

phosphorescence in physics, the emission of light by certain substances after they have absorbed energy, whether from visible light, other electromagnetic radiation such as ultraviolet rays or X-rays, or cathode rays (a beam of electrons).

phosphorus highly reactive, nonmetallic element, symbol P, atomic number 15, relative atomic mass

30.9738. It occurs in nature as phosphates (commonly in the form of the mineral apatite), and is essential to plant and animal life. Compounds of phosphorus are used in fertilizers, various organic chemicals, for matches and fireworks, and in glass and steel.

photochemical reaction any chemical reaction in which light is produced or light initiates the reaction. Light can initiate reactions by exciting atoms or molecules and making them more reactive: the light energy becomes converted to chemical energy. Many photochemical reactions set up a ⚪chain reaction and produce free radicals.

photoelectric effect in physics, the emission of ⚪electrons from a substance (usually a metallic surface) when it is struck by ⚪photons (quanta of electromagnetic radiation), usually those of visible light or ultraviolet radiation.

photography process for reproducing images on sensitized materials by various forms of radiant energy, including visible light, ultraviolet, infrared, X-rays, atomic radiations, and electron beams. Photography was developed in the 19th century; among the pioneers were L J M ⚪Daguerre in France and Fox ⚪Talbot in the UK. Colour photography dates from the early 20th century.

photon in physics, the ⚪elementary particle or 'package' (quantum) of energy in which light and other forms of electromagnetic radiation are emitted. The photon has both particle and wave properties; it has no charge, is considered massless but possesses momentum and energy. It is one of the ⚪gauge bosons, a particle that cannot be subdivided, and is the carrier of the ⚪electromagnetic force, one of the fundamental forces of nature.

photosynthesis process by which green plants trap light energy and use it to drive a series of chemical reactions, leading to the formation of carbohydrates. All animals ultimately depend on photosynthesis because it is the method by which the basic food (sugar) is created. For photosynthesis to occur, the plant must possess ⚪chlorophyll and must have a supply of carbon dioxide and water. Actively photosynthesizing green plants store excess sugar as starch (this can tested for in the laboratory using iodine).

Phrygia former kingdom of W Asia covering the Anatolian plateau. It was inhabited in ancient times by an Indo-European people and achieved great prosperity in the 8th century BC under a line of kings bearing in turn the names Gordius and Midas, but then fell under Lydian rule.

phylloxera any of a family (Phylloxeridae) of small plant-sucking insects (order Homoptera) that attack the leaves and roots of some plants.

phylogeny historical sequence of changes that occurs in a given species during the course of its evolution. It was once erroneously associated with ontogeny (the process of development of a living organism).

phylum (plural *phyla*) major grouping in biological classification. Mammals, birds, reptiles, amphibians, fishes, and tunicates belong to the phylum Chordata; the phylum Mollusca consists of snails, slugs, mussels, clams, squid, and octopuses; the phylum Porifera contains sponges; and the phylum Echinodermata includes starfish, sea urchins, and sea cucumbers. In classifying plants (where the term 'division' often takes the place of 'phylum'), there are between four and nine phyla depending on the criteria used; all flowering plants belong to a single phylum, Angiospermata, and all conifers to another, Gymnospermata. Related phyla are grouped together in a ◊kingdom; phyla are subdivided into ◊classes.

physical chemistry branch of chemistry concerned with examining the relationships between the chemical compositions of substances and the physical properties that they display. Most chemical reactions exhibit some physical phenomenon (change of state, temperature, pressure, or volume, or the use or production of electricity), and the measurement and study of such phenomena has led to many chemical theories and laws.

physics branch of science concerned with the laws that govern the structure of the universe, and the forms of matter and energy and their interactions. For convenience, physics is often divided into branches such as nuclear physics, particle physics, solid- and liquid-state physics, electricity, electronics, magnetism, optics, acoustics, heat, and thermodynamics. Before this century, physics was known as *natural philosophy*.

physiology branch of biology that deals with the functioning of living animals, as opposed to anatomy, which studies their structures.

physiotherapy treatment of injury and disease by physical means such as exercise, heat, manipulation, massage, and electrical stimulation.

piano or *pianoforte* stringed musical instrument, played by felt-covered hammers activated from a keyboard, and capable of soft (piano) or loud (forte) tones, hence its name.

Picardy (French *Picardie*) region of N France, including Aisne, Oise, and Somme *départements*; *area* 19,400 sq km/7,488 sq mi; *population* (1986) 1,774,000; *products* chemicals and metals; *history* in the 13th century the name Picardy was used to describe the feudal smallholdings north of Paris added to the French crown by Philip II. During the Hundred Years' War the area was hotly contested by France and England, but it was eventually occupied by Louis XI in 1477. Picardy once more became a major battlefield in World War I.

Picasso Pablo 1881–1973. Spanish artist, active chiefly in France, one of the most inventive and prolific talents in 20th-century art. His Blue Period 1901–04 and Rose Period 1905–06 preceded the revolutionary *Les Demoiselles d'Avignon* 1907 (Metropolitan Museum of Art, New York), which paved the way for Cubism. In the early 1920s he was considered a leader of the Surrealist movement. In the 1930s his work included metal sculpture, book illustration, and the mural *Guernica* 1937 (Casón del Buen Retiro, Madrid), a comment on the bombing of civilians in the Spanish Civil War. He continued to paint into his eighties.

Pict Roman term for a member of the peoples of N Scotland, possibly meaning 'painted' (tattooed). Of pre-Celtic origin, and speaking a non-Celtic language, the Picts are thought to have inhabited much of England before the arrival of the Celtic Britons. They were united with the Celtic Scots under the rule of Kenneth MacAlpin 844.

pidgin language any of various trade jargons, contact languages, or ◊lingua francas arising in ports and markets where people of different linguistic backgrounds meet for commercial and other purposes.

Piedmont (Italian *Piemonte*) region of N Italy, bordering Switzerland on the N and France on the W, and surrounded, except on the E, by the Alps and the Apennines; area 25,400 sq km/9,804 sq mi; population (1990) 4,356,200. Its capital is Turin, and towns include Alessandria, Asti, Vercelli, and Novara. It also includes the fertile Po river valley. Products include fruit, grain, cattle, cars, and textiles.

Piero della Francesca *c.* 1420–1492. Italian painter, active in Arezzo and Urbino; one of the major artists of the 15th century. His work has a solemn stillness and unusually solid figures, luminous colour, and compositional harmony. It includes a fresco series, *The Legend of the True Cross* (S Francesco, Arezzo), begun about 1452.

piezoelectric effect property of some crystals (for example, quartz) to develop an electromotive force or voltage across opposite faces when subjected to a mechanical strain, and, conversely, to expand or contract in size when subjected to an electromotive force. Piezoelectric crystal ◊oscillators are used as frequency standards (for example, replacing balance wheels in watches), and for producing ◊ultrasound.

pig any even-toed hoofed mammal of the family Suidae. They are omnivorous, and have simple, non-ruminating stomachs and thick hides. The Middle Eastern *wild boar Sus scrofa* is the ancestor of domesticated breeds; it is 1.5 m/4.5 ft long and 1 m/3 ft high, with formidable tusks, but not naturally aggressive. Most British pigs are kept in close-confinement systems.

pigeon any bird of the family Columbidae, sometimes also called doves, distinguished by their large crops, which, becoming glandular in the breeding season, secrete a milky fluid ('pigeon's milk') that aids digestion of food for the young. They are found worldwide.

Piggott Lester 1935– . English jockey. He is regarded as a brilliant tactician and adopted a unique high riding style. A champion jockey 11 times between 1960 and 1982, he has ridden a record nine ♢Derby winners.

pika or *mouse-hare* any small mammal of the family Ochotonidae, belonging to the order Lagomorpha (rabbits and hares). The single genus *Ochotona* contains about 15 species, most of which live in mountainous regions of Asia, although two species are native to North America.

pike any of a family Esocidae in the order Salmoniformes, of slender, freshwater bony fishes with narrow pointed heads and sharp, pointed teeth. The northern pike *Esox lucius*, of North America and Eurasia, may reach 2.2 m/7 ft and 9 kg/20 lb.

Pilate Pontius early 1st century AD. Roman procurator of Judea AD 26–36. The New Testament Gospels describe his reluctant ordering of Jesus' crucifixion, but there has been considerable debate about his actual role in it; many believe that pressure was put on him by Jewish conservative priests.

pilchard any of various small, oily members of the herring family, Clupeidae, especially the commercial sardine of Europe *Sardina pilchardus*, and the California sardine *Sardinops sagax*. Bluish-green above and silvery beneath, the European sardine grows to 25 cm/10 in long. It is most abundant in the W Mediterranean.

Pilgrimage of Grace rebellion against Henry VIII of England 1536–37, originating in Yorkshire and Lincolnshire. The uprising was directed against the policies of the monarch (such as the dissolution of the monasteries and the effects of the enclosure of common land).

Pilgrims the emigrants who sailed from Plymouth, Devon, England, in the *Mayflower* on 16 Sept 1620 to found the first colony in New England at New Plymouth, Massachusetts. Of the 102 passengers fewer than a quarter were Puritan refugees.

pill, the commonly used term for the contraceptive pill, based on female hormones. The combined pill, which contains oestrogen and progesterone, stops the production of eggs, and makes the mucus produced by the cervix hostile to sperm. It is the most effective form of contraception apart from sterilization, being more than 99% effective.

pilotfish small marine fish *Naucrates ductor* of the family Carangidae, which also includes pompanos. It hides below sharks, turtles, or boats, using the shade as a base from which to prey on smaller fish. It is found in all warm oceans and grows to about 36 cm/1.2 ft.

pimento or *allspice* tree found in tropical parts

of the New World. The dried fruits of the species *Pimenta dioica* are used as a spice. Also, a sweet variety of ♢capsicum pepper (more correctly spelled *pimiento*).

pimpernel any plant of the genus *Anagallis* of the primrose family Primulaceae comprising about 30 species mostly native to W Europe. The European scarlet pimpernel *A. arvensis* grows in cornfields, the flowers opening only in full sunshine. It is naturalized in North America.

Pinatubo, Mount active volcano on Luzon Island, the Philippines, 88 km/55 mi N of Manila. Dormant for 600 years, it erupted June 1991, killing 343 people and leaving as many as 200,000 homeless. Surrounding rice fields were covered with 3 m/10 ft of volcanic ash.

Pindling Lynden (Oscar) 1930– . Bahamian prime minister from 1967. After studying law in London, he returned to the island to join the newly formed Progressive Liberal Party and then became the first black prime minister of the Bahamas.

pine evergreen resinous tree of the genus *Pinus* with some 70–100 species, belonging to the Pinaceae, the largest family of conifers. The Scots pine *P. sylvestris* is grown commercially for soft timber and its yield of turpentine, tar, and pitch.

pineal body or *pineal gland* a cone-shaped outgrowth of the vertebrate brain. In some lower vertebrates, it develops a rudimentary lens and retina, which show it to be derived from an eye, or pair of eyes, situated on the top of the head in ancestral vertebrates. The pineal still detects light (through the skull) in some fishes, lizards, and birds. In birds, the pineal detects changes in daylight and stimulates breeding behaviour as spring approaches.

pineapple plant *Ananas comosus* of the bromeliad family, native to South and Central America, but now cultivated in many other tropical areas, such as Hawaii and Queensland, Australia. The mauvish flowers are produced in the second year, and subsequently consolidate with their bracts into a fleshy fruit.

pink any annual or perennial plant of the genus *Dianthus* of the family Carophyllaceae. The stems have characteristically swollen nodes, and the flowers range in colour from white through pink to purple. Members of the pink family include carnations, sweet williams, and baby's breath *Gypsophila paniculata*.

Pinochet (Ugarte) Augusto 1915– . Military ruler of Chile from 1973, when a coup backed by the US Central Intelligence Agency ousted and killed President Salvador Allende. Pinochet took over the presidency and governed ruthlessly, crushing all opposition. He was voted out of power when general elections were held in Dec 1989 but remains head of the armed forces until 1997.

pint imperial dry or liquid measure of capacity equal to 20 fluid ounces, half a quart, one-eighth of a gallon, or 0.568 litre. In the US, a liquid pint is equal to 0.473 litre, while a dry pint is equal to 0.550 litre.

Pinter Harold 1930– . English dramatist, originally an actor. He specializes in the tragicomedy of the breakdown of communication, broadly in the tradition of the Theatre of the Absurd – for example, *The Birthday Party* 1958 and *The Caretaker* 1960. Later plays include *The Homecoming* 1965, *Old Times* 1971, *Betrayal* 1978, and *Mountain Language* 1988.

pinworm ◊nematode worm *Enterobius vermicularis*, an intestinal parasite of humans.

Pinyin Chinese phonetic alphabet approved 1956 by the People's Republic of China, and used since 1979 in transcribing all names of people and places from Chinese ideograms into other languages using the English/Roman alphabet. For example, the former transcription Chou En-lai became Zhou Enlai, Hua Kuo-feng became Hua Guofeng, Teng Hsiao-ping became Deng Xiaoping, Peking became Beijing.

pipit any of various sparrow-sized ground-dwelling songbirds of the genus *Anthus* of the family Motacillidae, which also includes wagtails. The European meadow pipit *Anthus pratensis* is about the size of a sparrow and streaky brown, with a slender bill. It lives in open country and feeds on the ground.

Pirandello Luigi 1867–1936. Italian writer. His plays include *La morsa/The Vice* 1912, *Sei personaggi in cerca d'autore/Six Characters in Search of an Author* 1921, and *Enrico IV/Henry IV* 1922. The themes and treatment of his plays anticipated the work of Brecht, O'Neill, Anouilh, and Genet. Nobel Prize 1934.

piranha any South American freshwater fish of the genus *Serrusalmus*, in the same order as cichlids. They can grow to 60 cm/2 ft long, and have razor-sharp teeth; some species may rapidly devour animals, especially if attracted by blood.

Pisa city in Tuscany, Italy; population (1988) 104,000. It has an 11th–12th-century cathedral. Its famous campanile, the Leaning Tower of Pisa (repaired 1990) is 55 m/180 ft high and about 5 m/ 16.5 ft out of perpendicular. It has foundations only about 3 m/10 ft deep.

pistachio deciduous Eurasian tree *Pistacia vera* of the cashew family Anacardiaceae, with green nuts, which are eaten salted or used to enhance and flavour foods.

pistil general term for the female part of a flower, either referring to one single ◊carpel or a group of several fused carpels.

piston barrel-shaped device used in reciprocating engines (steam, petrol, diesel oil) to harness power. Pistons are driven up and down in cylinders by expanding steam or hot gases. They pass on their motion via a connecting rod and crank to a crankshaft, which turns the driving wheels. In a pump or compressor, the role of the piston is reversed, being used to move gases and liquids. See also ◊internal-combustion engine.

pit bull terrier or *American pit bull terrier* variety of dog that was developed in the USA solely as a fighting dog. It usually measures about 50 cm/20 in at the shoulder and weighs roughly 23 kg/50 lb, but there are no established criteria since it is not recognized as a breed by either the American or the British Kennel Club. Legislation in Britain 1989 and 1991 (see ◊dog, dangerous) has made it illegal to import, breed, or sell pit bull terriers.

Pitcairn Islands British colony in Polynesia, 5,300 km/3,300 mi NE of New Zealand; *area* 27 sq km/ 10 sq mi; *capital* Adamstown; *features* includes the uninhabited Henderson Islands, an unspoiled coral atoll with a rare ecology, and tiny Ducie and Oeno islands, annexed by Britain 1902; *products* fruit and souvenirs to passing ships; *population* (1990) 52; *language* English; *government* the governor is the British high commissioner in New Zealand; *history* first settled 1790 by nine mutineers from the British ship, the *Bounty* together with some Tahitians, their occupation remaining unknown until 1808.

pitch in chemistry, a black, sticky substance, hard when cold, but liquid when hot, used for waterproofing, roofing, and paving. It is made by the destructive distillation of wood or coal tar, and has been used since antiquity for caulking wooden ships.

pitch in music, the position of a note in the scale, dependent on the frequency of the predominant sound wave. In *standard pitch*, A above middle C has a frequency of 440 Hz. *Perfect pitch* is an ability to name or reproduce any note heard or asked for; it does not necessarily imply high musical ability.

pitchblende or *uraninite* brownish-black mineral, the major constituent of uranium ore, consisting mainly of uranium oxide (UO_2). It also contains some lead, and variable amounts of most of the naturally occurring radioactive elements. The uranium yield is 50–80%; it is also a source of radium, polonium, and actinium. Pitchblende was first studied by Pierre and Marie ◊Curie, who found radium and polonium in its residues in 1898.

pitcher plant any of various insectivorous plants of the family Sarraceniaceae, especially the genera *Nepenthes* and *Sarracenia*, the leaves of which are shaped like a pitcher and filled with a fluid that traps and digests insects.

Pitt William, *the Elder*, 1st Earl of Chatham 1708–1778. British Whig politician, 'the Great Commoner'. As paymaster of the forces 1746–55, he broke with tradition by refusing to enrich himself; he was dismissed for attacking the duke of Newcastle, the prime minister. He served effectively as prime minister in coalition governments 1756–61 (successfully conducting the Seven Years' War) and 1766–68.

Pitt William, *the Younger* 1759–1806. British Tory prime minister 1783–1801 and 1804–06. He raised the importance of the House of Commons, clamped down on corruption, carried out fiscal reforms and effected the union with Ireland. He attempted to keep Britain at peace but underestimated the importance of the French Revolution and became embroiled in wars with France from 1793; he died on hearing of Napoleon's victory at Austerlitz.

Pittsburgh industrial city (machinery, chemicals) in the USA and the nation's largest inland port, where the Allegheny and Monongahela rivers join to form the Ohio River in Pennsylvania; population (1990) 369,900, metropolitan area 2,242,800.

pituitary gland major ♢endocrine gland of vertebrates, situated in the centre of the brain. The anterior lobe secretes hormones, some of which control the activities of other glands (thyroid, gonads, and adrenal cortex); others are direct-acting hormones affecting milk secretion and controlling growth. Secretions of the posterior lobe control body water balance and contraction of the uterus. The posterior lobe is regulated by nerves from the hypothalamus, and thus forms a link between the nervous and hormonal systems.

Pius V 1504–1572. Pope from 1566. He excommunicated Elizabeth I of England, and organized the expedition against the Turks that won the victory of ♢Lepanto.

Pius IX 1792–1878. Pope from 1846. He never accepted the incorporation of the Papal States and of Rome in the kingdom of Italy. He proclaimed the dogmas of the Immaculate Conception of the Virgin 1854 and papal infallibility 1870; his pontificate was the longest in history.

Pius XII (Eugenio Pacelli) 1876–1958. Pope from 1939. He was conservative in doctrine and politics, and condemned ♢Modernism. He proclaimed the dogma of the bodily assumption of the Virgin Mary 1950 and in 1951 restated the doctrine (strongly criticized by many) that the life of an infant must not be sacrificed to save a mother in labour. He failed to speak out against atrocities committed by the Germans during World War II and has been accused of collusion with the Nazis.

pixel (acronym for *pic*ture *el*ement) single dot on a computer screen. All screen images are made up of a collection of pixels, with each pixel being either off (dark) or on (illuminated, possibly in colour). The number of pixels available determines the screen's resolution.

Pizarro Francisco *c.* 1475–1541. Spanish conquistador who took part in the expeditions of Vasco Núñez de Balboa and others. He explored the NW coast

of South America in 1526–27, and conquered Peru 1531 with 180 followers. The Inca king Atahualpa was seized and murdered. In 1535 Pizarro founded the Peruvian city of Lima. Internal feuding led to Pizarro's assassination.

placebo any harmless substance, often called a 'sugar pill', that has no chemotherapeutic value and yet produces physiological changes.

placenta in mammals, the organ that attaches the developing ♢fetus to the ♢uterus. It links the blood supply of the fetus to the blood supply of the mother, allowing the exchange of nutrients, wastes, and gases. The two blood systems are not in direct contact, but are separated by thin membranes, with materials diffusing across from one system to the other. The placenta also produces hormones that maintain and regulate pregnancy. It is shed as part of the afterbirth.

plague disease transmitted by fleas (carried by the black rat) which infect the sufferer with the bacillus *Pasteurella pestis*. An early symptom is swelling of lymph nodes, usually in the armpit and groin; such swellings are called 'buboes', hence *bubonic* plague. It causes virulent blood poisoning and the death rate is high.

plaice fish *Pleuronectes platessa* belonging to the flatfish group, abundant in the N Atlantic. It is white beneath and brownish with orange spots on the 'eyed' side. It can grow to 75 cm/2.5 ft long, and weigh about 2 kg/4.5 lb.

Plaid Cymru Welsh nationalist political party established 1925, dedicated to an independent Wales. In 1966 the first Plaid Cymru member of Parliament was elected.

Planck Max 1858–1947. German physicist who framed the quantum theory 1900. His research into the manner in which heated bodies radiate energy led him to report that energy is emitted only in indivisible amounts, called quanta, the magnitudes of which are proportional to the frequency of the radiation. His discovery ran counter to classical physics and is held to have marked the commencement of the modern science. Nobel Prize for Physics 1918.

plane in botany, any tree of the genus *Platanus*. Species include the oriental plane *P. orientalis*, a favourite plantation tree of the Greeks and Romans and the American plane or buttonwood *P. occidentalis*. A hybrid of these two is the London plane *P. x acerifolia*, with palmate, usually five-lobed leaves, which is widely planted in cities for its resistance to air pollution.

planet large celestial body in orbit around a star, composed of rock, metal, or gas. There are nine planets in the solar system: Mercury, Venus, Earth, Mars, Jupiter, Saturn, Neptune, Uranus, and Pluto.

plankton small, often microscopic forms of plant and animal life that live in the upper layers of fresh or salt water, and are an important source of food for larger animals. Marine plankton concentrate in areas where upwelling currents bring mineral salts to the surface; for example, the Grand Banks off Newfoundland.

plant organism that carries out ◁photosynthesis, has cellulose cell walls and complex cells, and is immobile. A few parasitic plants have lost the ability to photosynthesize but are still considered to be plants. Plants are autotrophs, that is, they make carbohydrates from water and carbon dioxide, and are the primary producers in all food chains, so that all animal life is dependent on them. They play a vital part in the carbon cycle, removing carbon dioxide from the atmosphere and generating oxygen. The study of plants is known as botany.

Plantagenet English royal house, reigning 1154–1399, whose name comes from the nickname of Geoffrey, Count of Anjou (1113–1151), father of Henry II, who often wore in his hat a sprig of broom, *planta genista*. In the 1450s, Richard, Duke of York, took 'Plantagenet' as a surname to emphasize his superior claim to the throne over Henry VI's.

plantain any plant of the genus *Plantago*, family Plantaginaceae. *P. lanceolata* is native to Europe and Asia and a widespread weed in Australia, Europe, and America. Many other species are troublesome weeds. A type of ◁banana is also known as plantain.

plant classification taxonomy or classification of plants. Originally the plant kingdom included bacteria, diatoms, dinoflagellates, fungi, and slime moulds, but these are not now thought of as plants. The groups that are always classified as plants are the bryophytes (mosses and liverworts), pteridophytes (ferns, horsetails, and club mosses), gymnosperms (conifers, yews, cycads, and ginkgos), and angiosperms (flowering plants). The angiosperms are split into monocotyledons (for example, orchids, grasses, lilies) and dicotyledons (for example, oak, buttercup, geranium, and daisy).

plasma in biology, the liquid part of the ◁blood.

plasma in physics, an ionized gas produced at extremely high temperatures, as in the Sun and other stars, which contains positive and negative charges in approximately equal numbers. It is a good electrical conductor. In thermonuclear reactions the plasma produced is confined through the use of magnetic fields.

platypus

plastic any of the stable synthetic materials that are fluid at some stage in their manufacture, when they can be shaped, and that later set to rigid or semi-rigid solids. Plastics today are chiefly derived from petroleum. Most are polymers, made up of long chains of identical molecules.

Plata, Río de la (English *River Plate*) estuary in South America into which the rivers Paraná and Uruguay flow; length 320 km/200 mi and width up to 240 km/150 mi. The basin drains much of Argentina, Bolivia, Brazil, Uruguay, and Paraguay, which all cooperate in its development.

plate tectonics concept that attributes ◁continental drift and ◁seafloor spreading to the continual formation and destruction of the outermost layer of the Earth. This layer is seen as consisting of major and minor plates, curved to the planet's spherical shape and with a jigsaw fit to one another. Convection currents within the Earth's mantle produce upwellings of new material along joint lines at the surface, forming ridges (for example, the ◁Mid-Atlantic Ridge). The new material extends the plates, and these move away from the ridges. Where two plates collide, one overrides the other and the lower is absorbed back into the mantle. These subduction zones occur in the ocean trenches.

Plath Sylvia 1932–1963. US poet and novelist whose powerful, highly personal poems, often expressing a sense of desolation, are distinguished by their intensity and sharp imagery. Her *Collected Poems* 1981 was awarded a Pulitzer Prize. Her autobiographical novel *The Bell Jar* 1961 deals with the events surrounding a young woman's emotional breakdown.

platinum heavy, soft, silver-white, malleable and ductile, metallic element, symbol Pt, atomic number 78, relative atomic mass 195.09. It is the first of a group of six metallic elements (platinum, osmium, iridium, rhodium, ruthenium, and palladium) that possess similar traits, such as resistance to tarnish, corrosion, and attack by acid, and that often occur as free metals. They often occur in natural alloys with each other, the commonest of which is osmiridium. Both pure and as an alloy, platinum is used in dentistry, jewellery, and as a catalyst.

Plato *c.* 428–347 BC. Greek philosopher, pupil of Socrates, teacher of Aristotle, and founder of the Academy school of philosophy. He was the author of philosophical dialogues on such topics as metaphysics, ethics, and politics. Central to his teachings is the notion of Forms, which are located outside the everyday world – timeless, motionless, and absolutely real.

platypus monotreme, or egg-laying, mammal *Ornithorhynchus anatinus*, found in Tasmania and E Australia. Semiaquatic, it has small eyes, and no external ears, and jaws resembling a duck's beak. It lives in long burrows along river banks, where it lays two eggs in a rough nest. It feeds on water worms and insects, and when full-grown is 60 cm/ 2 ft long.

plebeian member of the unprivileged class in ancient Rome, composed of aliens, freed slaves, and their descendants. During the 5th–4th centuries BC, plebeians waged a long struggle to win political and social equality with the patricians, eventually securing admission to the offices formerly reserved for patricians.

Pleiades in astronomy, a star cluster about 400 light years away in the constellation Taurus, identified with the Seven Sisters of Greek mythology. Its brightest stars (highly luminous, blue-white giants only a few million years old) are visible to the naked eye, but there are many fainter ones.

Pleistocene first epoch of the Quaternary period of geological time, beginning 1.8 million years ago and ending 10,000 years ago. Glaciers were abundant during the ice age of this period, and humans evolved into modern *Homo sapiens sapiens* about 100,000 years ago.

pleurisy inflammation of the pleura, the thin, secretory membrane that covers the lungs and lines the space in which they rest. Pleurisy is nearly always due to bacterial or viral infection, which can be treated with antibiotics. It renders breathing painful.

Plimsoll line loading mark painted on the hull of merchant ships, first suggested by Samuel Plimsoll. It shows the depth to which a vessel may be safely (and legally) loaded.

Pliny the Elder (Gaius Plinius Secundus) *c.* AD 23–79. Roman scientist and historian; only his works on astronomy, geography, and natural history survive. He was killed in an eruption of Vesuvius, the volcano near Naples.

Pliocene fifth and last epoch of the Tertiary period of geological time, 5–1.8 million years ago. The earliest hominid, the humanlike ape 'australopithecines', evolved in Africa.

PLO abbreviation for ▷*Palestine Liberation Organization*.

plough agricultural implement used for tilling the soil. The plough dates from about 3500 BC, when oxen were used to pull a simple wooden blade, or ard. In about 500 BC the iron ploughshare came into use.

Plovdiv industrial city (textiles, chemicals, leather, tobacco) in Bulgaria, on the river Maritsa; population (1990) 379,100. Conquered by Philip of Macedon in the 4th century BC, it was known as *Philippopolis* ('Philip's city').

plover any shore bird of the family Charadriidae, found worldwide. Plovers are usually black or brown above and white below, and have short bills. The European *golden plover Pluviatilis apricaria*,

of heathland and sea coast, is about 28 cm/11 in long.

plum tree *Prunus domestica*, bearing edible fruits that are smooth-skinned with a flat kernel. There are many varieties, including the Victoria, czar, egg-plum, greengage, and damson; the sloe *P. spinosa* is closely related. Dried plums are known as prunes.

Plutarch *c.* AD 46–120. Greek biographer whose *Parallel Lives* has the life stories of pairs of Greek and Roman soldiers and politicians, followed by comparisons between the two. Thomas North's 1579 translation inspired Shakespeare's Roman plays.

Pluto in astronomy, the smallest and, usually, outermost planet of the solar system. The existence of Pluto was predicted by calculation by Percival Lowell and the planet was located by Clyde ▷Tombaugh 1930. It orbits the Sun every 248.5 years at an average distance of 5.9 billion km/ 3.6 billion mi. Its highly elliptical orbit occasionally takes it within the orbit of Neptune, as in 1979–99. Pluto has a diameter of about 2,300 km/1,400 mi, and a mass about 0.002 of that of Earth. It is of low density, composed of rock and ice, with frozen methane on its surface and a thin atmosphere.

Pluto in Greek mythology, the lord of the underworld (Roman Dis). He was the brother of Zeus and Poseidon.

plutonium silvery-white, radioactive, metallic element of the ▷actinide series, symbol Pu, atomic number 94, relative atomic mass 239.13. It occurs in nature in minute quantities in pitchblende and other ores, but is produced in quantity only synthetically. It has six allotropic forms (see ▷allotropy) and is one of three fissile elements (elements capable of splitting into other elements — the others are thorium and uranium). The element has awkward physical properties and is the most toxic substance known.

Plymouth city and seaport in Devon, England, at the mouth of the river Plym, with dockyard, barracks, and a naval base at Devonport; population (1981) 244,000.

pneumatic drill drill operated by compressed air, used in mining and tunnelling, for drilling shot holes (for explosives), and in road repairs for breaking up pavements. It contains an air-operated piston that delivers hammer blows to the drill bit many times a second. The French engineer Germain Sommeiller (1815–1871) developed the pneumatic drill 1861 for tunnelling in the Alps.

pneumonia inflammation of the lungs, generally due to bacterial or viral infection but also to particulate matter or gases. It is characterized by a build-up of fluid in the alveoli, the clustered air sacs (at the end of the air passages) where oxygen exchange takes place.

Pnom Penh alternative form of ▷Phnom Penh, capital of Cambodia.

pochard any of various diving ducks found in Europe and North America, especially the genus *Aythya*. The male *common pochard Aythya ferina* has a red head, black breast, whitish body and wings with black markings, and is about 45 cm/ 1.5 ft long. The female is greyish brown, with greyish white below.

Poe Edgar Allan 1809–1849. US writer and poet. His short stories are renowned for their horrific atmosphere, as in 'The Fall of the House of Usher' 1839 and 'The Masque of the Red Death' 1842, and for their acute reasoning (ratiocination), as in 'The Gold Bug' 1843 and 'The Murders in the Rue Morgue' 1841 (in which the investigators Legrand and Dupin anticipate Conan Doyle's Sherlock Holmes). His poems include 'The Raven' 1845. His novel, *The Narrative of Arthur Gordon Pym of Nantucket* 1838, has attracted critical attention.

poet laureate poet of the British royal household, so called because of the laurel wreath awarded to eminent poets in the Graeco-Roman world. Early poets with unofficial status were Geoffrey Chaucer, John Skelton, Edmund Spenser, Samuel Daniel, and Ben Jonson. Ted Hughes became poet laureate 1984.

poetry the imaginative expression of emotion, thought, or narrative, frequently in metrical form and often using figurative language. Poetry has traditionally been distinguished from prose (ordinary written language) by rhyme or the rhythmical arrangement of words (metre), although the distinction is not always clear-cut.

pogrom unprovoked violent attack on an ethnic group, particularly Jews, carried out with official sanction. The Russian pogroms against Jews began 1881, after the assassination of Tsar Alexander II, and again in 1903–06; persecution of the Jews remained constant until the Russian Revolution. Later there were pogroms in E Europe, especially in Poland after 1918, and in Germany under Hitler (see ◊Holocaust).

poikilothermy the condition in which an animal's body temperature is largely dependent on the temperature of the air or water in which it lives. It is characteristic of all animals except birds and mammals, which maintain their body temperatures by homeothermy (they are 'warm-blooded'). Poikilotherms have behavioural means of temperature control; they can warm themselves up by basking in the sun, or shivering, and can cool themselves down by sheltering from the sun under a rock or by bathing in water.

poinsettia or *Christmas flower* winter-flowering shrub *Euphorbia pulcherrima*, with large red leaves encircling small greenish-yellow flowers. It is native to Mexico and tropical America and is a popular houseplant in North America and Europe.

Pointe-Noire chief port of the Congo, formerly (1950–58) the capital; population (1984) 297,000. Industries include oil refining and shipbuilding.

pointer breed of dog, often white mixed with black, tan, or dark brown, about 60 cm/2 ft tall, and weighing 28 kg/62 lb.

Pointillism technique in oil painting developed in the 1880s by the Neo-Impressionist Georges Seurat. He used small dabs of pure colour laid side by side to create an impression of shimmering light when viewed from a distance.

Poitou-Charentes region of W central France, comprising the *départements* of Charente, Charente-Maritime, Deux-Sèvres, and Vienne; *capital* Poitiers; *area* 25,800 sq km/9,959 sq mi; *population* (1986) 1,584,000; *products* dairy products, wheat, chemicals, metal goods; brandy is made at Cognac; *history* once part of the Roman province of Aquitaine, this region was captured by the Visigoths in the 5th century and taken by the Franks AD 507. The area was contested by the English and French until the end of the Hundred Years' War in 1453, when it was incorporated into France by Charles II.

Poland Republic of; country in E Europe, bordered N by the Baltic Sea, NE by Lithuania, E by the CIS, S by Czechoslovakia, and W by Germany; *area* 312,700 sq km/120,733 sq mi; *capital* Warsaw; *physical* part of the great plain of Europe; Vistula, Oder, and Neisse rivers; Sudeten, Tatra, and Carpathian mountains on S frontier; *head of state* Lech Walesa from 1990; *head of government* Jan Olszewski from 1991; *political system* emergent democracy; *exports* coal, softwood timber, chemicals, machinery, ships, vehicles, meat, copper (Europe's largest producer); *population* (1990 est) 38,363,000; *languages* Polish (official), German; *recent history* Poland was revived as an independent republic 1918; occupied by the Germans 1939–44; the Polish boundaries were redrawn at the Potsdam Conference 1945. The Communist People's Republic was proclaimed 1947. Solidarity emerged as a free trade union 1980 following the Gdańsk riots. Martial law was imposed by General Jaruzelski 1981–83. In 1988, following Solidarity strikes and demonstrations, pay increases were granted and the government held a church–state–union conference 1989 when a new 'socialist pluralist' constitution was drawn up. Solidarity swept the board in national assembly elections 1989; the Social Democrat Party and breakaway Union of Social Democrats came to power and Lech Walesa was elected head of state 1990. GNP fell by 12% in 1990 and by a further 7% 1991. A multiparty general election was held 1991, and a coalition government formed. A treaty agreeing complete withdrawal of Soviet troops was signed the same year.

Polanski Roman 1933– . Polish film director, born in Paris. His generally sinister films include *Repulsion* 1965, *Cul de Sac* 1966, *Rosemary's Baby* 1968, *Tess* 1979, and *Frantic* 1988.

polar reversal changeover in polarity of the Earth's magnetic poles. Studies of the magnetism retained

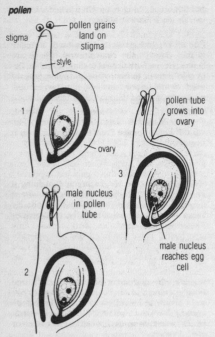

pollen

pollen grains land on stigma

stigma

style

1

ovary

3

pollen tube grows into ovary

male nucleus in pollen tube

2

male nucleus reaches egg cell

in rocks at the time of their formation have shown that in the past the Earth's north magnetic pole repeatedly became the south magnetic pole, and vice versa.

polder area of flat reclaimed land that used to be covered by a river, lake, or the sea. Polders have been artificially drained and protected from flooding by building dykes. They are common in the Netherlands, where the total land area has been increased by nearly one-fifth since AD 1200. Such schemes as the Zuider Zee project have provided some of the best agricultural land in the country.

pole either of the geographic north and south points of the axis about which the Earth rotates. The magnetic poles are the points towards which a freely suspended magnetic needle will point; however, they vary continually.

polecat Old World weasel *Mustela putorius* with a brown back and dark belly and two yellow face patches. The body is about 50 cm/20 in long and it has a strong smell from anal gland secretions. It is native to Asia, Europe, and N Africa. In North America, ▷skunks are sometimes called polecats.

police civil law-and-order force. In the UK it is responsible to the Home Office, with 56 autonomous police forces, generally organized on a county basis. The predecessors of these forces were the ineffective medieval watch and London's Bow Street runners, introduced 1749 by Henry

▷Fielding, which formed a model for the London police force established by Robert ▷Peel's government 1829 (hence 'peelers' or 'bobbies'); the system was introduced throughout the country from 1856.

polio (*poliomyelitis*) viral infection of the central nervous system affecting nerves that activate muscles. The disease used to be known as infantile paralysis. The World Health Organization expects that polio will be eradicated by 2000.

Polish language member of the Slavonic branch of the Indo-European language family, spoken mainly in Poland. Polish is written in the Roman and not the Cyrillic alphabet and its standard form is based on the dialect of Poznań in W Poland.

Polk James Knox 1795–1849. 11th president of the USA 1845–49, a Democrat, born in North Carolina. He allowed Texas admission to the Union, and forced the war on Mexico that resulted in the annexation of California and New Mexico.

pollen the grains of ▷seed plants that contain the male gametes. In ▷angiosperms (flowering plants) pollen is produced within ▷anthers; in most ▷gymnosperms (cone-bearing plants) it is produced in male cones. A pollen grain is typically yellow and, when mature, has a hard outer wall. Pollen of insect-pollinated plants (see ▷pollination) is often sticky and spiny and larger than the smooth, light grains produced by wind-pollinated species.

pollination the process by which fertilization occurs in the sexual reproduction of higher plants. The male ▷gametes are contained in pollen grains, which must be transferred from the anther to the stigma in ▷angiosperms (flowering plants), and from the male cone to the female cone in ▷gymnosperms (cone-bearing plants). Self-pollination occurs when pollen is transferred to a stigma of the same flower, or to another flower on the same plant; cross-pollination occurs when pollen is transferred to another plant. This involves external pollen-carrying agents, such as wind, water, insects, birds, bats, and other small mammals.

Pollock Jackson 1912–1956. US painter, a pioneer of Abstract Expressionism and the foremost exponent of the technique of ▷action painting, a style he developed around 1946.

poll tax tax levied on every individual, without reference to income or property. Being simple to administer, it was among the earliest sorts of tax (introduced in England 1377), but because of its indiscriminate nature (it is a regressive tax, in that it falls proportionately more on poorer people) it has often proved unpopular. The *community charge*, which was a poll tax, was introduced in Scotland by the British government in April 1989, and in England and Wales 1990; but its unpopularity led to the announcement 1991 of its replacement, a 'council tax', based both on property values and on the size of households, to be introduced 1993–94.

The combined cost of collection and abolition of the poll tax is estimated at £4 billion.

pollution the harmful effect on the environment of by-products of human activity, principally industrial and agricultural processes; for example, noise, smoke, car emissions, chemical and radioactive effluents in air, seas, and rivers, pesticides, radiation, sewage, and household waste. Pollution contributes to the ♢greenhouse effect. In the UK in 1987 air pollution caused by carbon monoxide emission from road transport was measured at 5.26 million tonnes.

polo stick-and-ball game played between two teams of four on horseback. It originated in Iran, spread to India and was first played in England 1869. Polo is played on the largest pitch of any game, measuring up to 274 m/300 yd by 182 m/200 yd. A small solid ball is struck with the side of a long-handled mallet through goals at each end of the pitch. A typical match lasts about an hour, and is divided into 'chukkas' of 7½ minutes each. No pony is expected to play more than two chukkas in the course of a day.

Polo Marco 1254–1324. Venetian traveller and writer. He travelled overland to China 1271–75, and served the emperor Kublai Khan until he returned to Europe by sea 1292–95. He was captured while fighting for Venice against Genoa, and, while in prison 1296–98, dictated an account of his travels.

polonium radioactive, metallic element, symbol Po, atomic number 84, relative atomic mass 210. Polonium occurs in nature in small amounts and was isolated from pitchblende. It is the element having the largest number of isotopes (27) and is 5,000 times as radioactive as radium, liberating considerable amounts of heat. It was the first element to have its radioactive properties recognized and investigated.

Pol Pot (also known as *Saloth Sar, Tol Saut,* and *Pol Porth*) 1925– . Cambodian politician and leader of the ♢Khmer Rouge communist movement that overthrew the government 1975. After widespread atrocities against the civilian population, his regime was deposed by a Vietnamese invasion 1979. Pol Pot continued to help lead the Khmer Rouge until their withdrawal in 1989.

polyester synthetic resin formed by the condensation of polyhydric alcohols (alcohols containing more than one hydroxyl group) with dibasic acids (acids containing two replaceable hydrogen atoms). Polyesters are thermosetting ♢plastics, used in making synthetic fibres, such as Dacron and Terylene, and constructional plastics. With glass fibre added as reinforcement, polyesters are used in car bodies and boat hulls.

polyethylene or *polyethene* polymer of the gas ethylene (technically called ethene, C_2H_4). It is a tough, white, translucent, waxy thermoplastic (which means it can be repeatedly softened by heating). It is used for packaging, bottles, toys, electric cable, pipes and tubing. In the UK it is better known under the trademark Polythene.

polymer compound made up of a large, long-chain or branching matrix composed of many repeated simple units (*monomers*). There are many polymers, both natural (cellulose, chitin, lignin) and synthetic (polyethylene and nylon, types of plastic). Synthetic polymers belong to two groups: thermosoftening and thermosetting (see ♢plastic).

Polynesia islands of Oceania E of 170° E latitude, including Hawaii, Kiribati, Tuvalu, Fiji, Tonga, Tokelau, Samoa, Cook Islands, and French Polynesia.

Polynesian languages part of the family of ♢Austronesian languages.

polyunsaturate type of ♢fat or oil containing a high proportion of triglyceride molecules whose ♢fatty-acid chains contain several double bonds. By contrast, the fatty-acid chains of the triglycerides in saturated fats (such as lard) contain only single bonds. Polyunsaturated fats are generally considered healthier for human nutrition than are saturated fats, and are widely used in margarines and cooking oils.

pomegranate deciduous shrub or small tree *Punica granatum*, family Punicaceae, native to SW Asia but cultivated widely in tropical and subtropical areas. The round, leathery, reddish-yellow fruit contains numerous seeds that can be eaten fresh or made into wine.

pomeranian small breed of dog, about 15 cm/6 in long, weighing about 3 kg/6.5 lb. It has long straight hair with a neck frill, and the tail is carried over the back.

Pompadour Jeanne Antoinette Poisson, Marquise de Pompadour 1721–1764. Mistress of ♢Louis XV of France from 1744, born in Paris. She largely dictated the government's ill-fated policy of reversing France's anti-Austrian policy for an anti-Prussian one. She acted as the patron of the Enlightenment philosophers Voltaire and Diderot.

Pompeii ancient city in Italy, near the volcano ♢Vesuvius, 21 km/13 mi SE of Naples. In AD 63 an earthquake destroyed much of the city, which had been a Roman port and pleasure resort; it was completely buried beneath volcanic ash when Vesuvius erupted AD 79. Over 2,000 people were killed. Pompeii was rediscovered 1748 and the systematic excavation begun 1763 still continues.

Pompey the Great (Gnaeus Pompeius Magnus) 106–48 BC. Roman soldier and politician, consul 70–60 BC. From 60 BC to 53 BC, he was a member of the First Triumvirate with Julius ♢Caesar and Marcus Lucius ♢Crassus, but took the opposite side in the civil war from 49 BC.

Pompidou Georges 1911–1974. French conservative politician, president 1969–74. He negotiated a settlement with the Algerians 1961 and, as prime minister 1962–68, with the students in the revolt of May 1968.

Pondicherry Union Territory of SE India; area 480 sq km/185 sq mi; population (1991) 789,400. Its capital is Pondicherry, and products include rice, peanuts, cotton, and sugar. Pondicherry was founded by the French 1674 and changed hands several times among the French, Dutch, and British before being returned to France 1814 at the close of the Napoleonic wars. Together with Karaikal, Yanam, and Mahé (on the Malabar Coast) it formed a French colony until 1954 when all were transferred to the government of India; since 1962 they have formed the Union Territory of Pondicherry. Languages spoken include French, English, Tamil, Telegu, and Malayalam.

pond-skater water ◊bug (insect of the Hemiptra order with piercing mouth parts) that rows itself across the surface by using its middle legs. It feeds on smaller insects.

pondweed any aquatic plant of the genus *Potamogeton* that either floats on the water or is submerged. The leaves of floating pondweeds are broad and leathery, whereas leaves of the submerged forms are narrower and translucent; the flowers grow in green spikes.

pony small horse under 1.47 m/4.5 ft (14.2 hands) shoulder height. Although of Celtic origin, all the pony breeds have been crossed with thoroughbred and Arab stock, except for the smallest – the hardy Shetland, with less than 105 cm/42 in shoulder height.

poodle breed of dog, including standard (above 38 cm/15 in at shoulder), miniature (below 38 cm/15 in), and toy (below 28 cm/11 in) varieties. The long, curly coat, usually cut into an elaborate style, is often either black or white, although greys and browns are also bred.

Poona former English spelling of ◊Pune, city in India; after independence in 1947 the form Poona was gradually superseded by Pune.

poor law English system for poor relief, established by the Poor Relief Act 1601. Each parish was responsible for its own poor, paid for by a parish tax. Relief today is provided by national social-security benefits.

Pop art movement of young artists in the mid-1950s and 1960s, reacting against the elitism of abstract art. Pop art used popular imagery drawn from advertising, comic strips, film, and television. It originated in Britain 1956 with Richard Hamilton, Peter Blake (1932–), and others, and broke through in the USA with the paintings of flags and numbers by Jasper Johns 1958 and Andy Warhol's first series of soup tins 1962.

Pope Alexander 1688–1744. English poet and satirist. He established his reputation with the precocious *Pastorals* 1709 and *Essay on Criticism* 1711,

which were followed by a parody of the heroic epic *The Rape of the Lock* 1712–14 and 'Eloisa to Abelard' 1717. Other works include a highly Neo-Classical translation of Homer's *Iliad* and *Odyssey* 1715–26.

poplar deciduous tree of the genus *Populus* with characteristically broad leaves. The white poplar *P. alba* has a smooth grey trunk and leaves with white undersides.

pop music or *popular music* any contemporary music not classifiable as jazz or classical. Pop became distinct from folk music with the advent of sound-recording techniques, and has incorporated blues, country and western, and music-hall elements; electronic amplification and other technological innovations have played a large part in the creation of new styles. The traditional format is a song of roughly three minutes with verse, chorus, and middle eight bars.

Popocatépetl (Aztec 'smoking mountain') volcano in central Mexico, 50 km/30 mi SE of Mexico City; 5,340 m/17,526 ft. It last erupted 1920.

Popper Karl (Raimund) 1902– . Austrian philosopher of science. His theory of falsificationism says that although scientific generalizations cannot be conclusively verified, they can be conclusively falsified by a counterinstance; therefore, science is not certain knowledge but a series of 'conjectures and refutations', approaching, though never reaching, a definitive truth.

poppy any plant of the genus *Papaver*, family Papaveraceae, that bears brightly coloured, often dark-centred, flowers and yields a milky sap. Species include the crimson European field poppy *P. rhoeas* and the Asian ◊opium poppies. Closely related are the California poppy *Eschscholtzia californica* and the yellow horned or sea poppy *Glaucium flavum*.

porcelain (hard-paste) translucent ceramic material with a shining finish; see ◊pottery and porcelain.

porcupine any ◊rodent with quills on its body, belonging to either of two families: Old World porcupines (family Hystricidae), terrestrial in habit and having long black-and-white quills; or New World porcupines (family Erethizontidae), tree-dwelling, with prehensile tails and much shorter quills.

porpoise any small whale of the family Delphinidae that, unlike dolphins, have blunt snouts without beaks. Common porpoises of the genus *Phocaena* can grow to 1.8 m/6 ft long; they feed on fish and crustaceans.

Port-au-Prince capital and industrial port (sugar, rum, textiles, plastics) of Haiti; population (1982) 763,000.

Porter Cole (Albert) 1892–1964. US composer and lyricist, mainly of musical comedies. His witty, sophisticated songs like 'Let's Do It' 1928, 'I Get a Kick Out of You' 1934, and 'Don't Fence Me In'

1944 have been widely recorded and admired. His shows, many of which were made into films, include *The Gay Divorcee* 1932 and *Kiss Me Kate* 1948.

Portland William Henry Cavendish Bentinck, 3rd Duke of Portland 1738–1809. British politician, originally a Whig, who in 1783 became nominal prime minister in the Fox–North coalition government. During the French Revolution he joined the Tories, and was prime minister 1807–09.

Port Laoise or *Portlaoighise* (formerly *Maryborough*) county town of County Laois, Republic of Ireland, 80 km/50 mi WSW of Dublin; population (1981) 7,756. It has woollen and flour-milling industries, and is the site of a top-security prison.

Port Louis capital of Mauritius, on the island's NW coast; population (1987) 139,000. Exports include sugar, textiles, watches, and electronic goods.

Port Moresby capital and port of Papua New Guinea on the S coast of New Guinea; population (1987) 152,000.

Porto (English *Oporto*) industrial city (textiles, leather, pottery) in Portugal, on the river Douro, 5 km/3 mi from its mouth; population (1984) 327,000. It exports port.

Pôrto Alegre port and capital of Rio Grande do Sul state, S Brazil; population (1991) 1,254,600. It is a freshwater port for ocean-going vessels, and is Brazil's major commercial centre.

Port-of-Spain port and capital of Trinidad and Tobago, on Trinidad; population (1988) 58,000.

Porto Novo capital of Benin, W Africa; population (1982) 208,258. It was a former Portuguese centre for the slave and tobacco trade with Brazil and became a French protectorate 1863.

Port Said port in Egypt, on reclaimed land at the northern end of the ⟡Suez Canal; population (1983) 364,000. During the 1967 Arab-Israeli war the city was damaged and the canal blocked; Port Said was evacuated by 1969 but by 1975 had been largely reconstructed.

Portsmouth city and naval port in Hampshire, England, opposite the Isle of Wight; population (1991) 174,700.

Portugal Republic of; country in SW Europe, on the Atlantic coast, bordered N and E by Spain; *area* 92,000 sq km/35,521 sq mi (including Azores and Madeira); *capital* Lisbon; *physical* mountainous in N, plains in S; rivers Minho, Douro, Tagus (Tejo), Guadiana; *head of state* Mario Alberto Nobre Lopes Soares from 1986; *head of government* Anibal Cavaco Silva from 1985; *political system* democratic republic; *exports* wine, olive oil, resin, cork, sardines, textiles, pottery, pulpwood; *population* (1990 est) 10,528,000; *language* Portuguese; *recent history* Portugal was a military dictatorship 1928–68 under António de Oliveira Salazar. Its African colonies became independent

1975 and 1976 a new constitution, providing for return to civilian rule, was adopted. A new draft constitution was approved 1982, reducing the powers of the presidency. In 1986 Mario Soares was elected the first civilian president for 60 years. Portugal joined the European Community in the same year.

Portuguese East Africa former name of ⟡Mozambique.

Portuguese Guinea former name of ⟡Guinea-Bissau in W Africa.

Portuguese language member of the Romance branch of the Indo-European language family; spoken by 120–135 million people worldwide, it is the national language of Portugal, closely related to Spanish and strongly influenced by Arabic. Portuguese is also spoken in Brazil, Angola, Mozambique, and other former Portuguese colonies.

Portuguese man-of-war any of a genus *Physalia* of phylum *Coelenterata*. They live in the sea, in colonies, and have a large air-filled bladder (or 'float') on top and numerous hanging tentacles made up of feeding, stinging, and reproductive individuals. The float can be 30 cm/1 ft long.

Portuguese West Africa former name of ⟡Angola.

Poseidon Greek god (Roman Neptune), the brother of Zeus and Pluto. The brothers dethroned their father, Kronos, and divided his realm, Poseidon taking the sea; he was also worshipped as god of earthquakes. His son was the merman sea god Triton.

positivism theory that confines genuine knowledge within the bounds of science and observation. The theory is associated with the French philosopher Auguste Comte and ⟡empiricism. *Logical positivism* developed in the 1920s. It rejected any metaphysical world beyond everyday science and common sense, and confined statements to those of formal logic or mathematics.

positron in physics, the antiparticle of the electron; an ⟩elementary particle having the same magnitude of mass and charge as an electron but exhibiting a positive charge. The positron was discovered in 1932 by US physicist Carl Anderson at Caltech, USA, its existence having been predicted by the British physicist Paul Dirac 1928.

possum another name for the ⟩opossum, a marsupial animal with a prehensile tail found in North, Central and South America. The name is also used for many of the smaller marsupials found in Australia.

Post-Impressionism various styles of painting that followed ⟩Impressionism in the 1880s and 1890s. The term was first used by the British critic Roger Fry in 1911 to describe the works of Paul Cézanne, Vincent van Gogh, and Paul Gauguin. These painters moved away from the spontaneity of Impressionism, attempting to give their work more serious meaning and permanence.

Post-Modernism late 20th-century movement in the arts and architecture that rejects the preoccupation of ⟩Modernism and ⟩Functionalism with pure form and technique rather than content. Post-Modern designers use an amalgam of style elements from the past, such as the Classical and the Baroque, and apply them to spare modern forms. Their slightly off-key familiarity creates a more immediate appeal than the austerities of Modernism.

potash general name for any potassium-containing mineral, most often applied to potassium carbonate (K_2CO_3) or potassium hydroxide (KOH). Potassium carbonate, originally made by roasting plants to ashes in earthenware pots, is commercially produced from the mineral sylvite (potassium chloride, KCl) and is used mainly in making artificial fertilizers, glass, and soap.

potassium soft, waxlike, silver-white, metallic element, symbol K (Latin *kalium*), atomic number 19, relative atomic mass 39.0983. It is one of the ⟩alkali metals and has a very low density – it floats on water, and is the second lightest metal (after lithium). It oxidizes rapidly when exposed to air and reacts violently with water. Of great abundance in the Earth's crust, it is widely distributed with other elements and found in salt and mineral deposits in the form of potassium aluminium silicates.

potato perennial plant *Solanum tuberosum*, family Solanaceae, with edible tuberous roots that are rich in starch. Used by the Andean Indians for at least 2,000 years before the Spanish Conquest, the potato was introduced to Europe by the mid-16th century, and reputedly to England by the explorer Walter Raleigh.

potential, electric in physics, the relative electrical state of an object. A charged conductor, for example, has a higher potential than the Earth, whose potential is taken by convention to be zero. An electric ⟩cell (battery) has a potential in relation to emf

(⟩electromotive force), which can make current flow in an external circuit. The difference in potential between two points – the *potential difference* – is expressed in ⟩volts; that is, a 12 V battery has a potential difference of 12 volts between its negative and positive terminals.

potential energy ⟩energy possessed by an object by virtue of its relative position or state (for example, as in a compressed spring). It is contrasted with kinetic energy, the form of energy possessed by moving bodies.

Potter Beatrix 1866–1943. English writer and illustrator of children's books, beginning with *Peter Rabbit* 1900 and *The Tailor of Gloucester* 1902.

pottery and porcelain ⟩ceramics in domestic and ornamental use including: *earthenware* made of porous clay and fired, whether unglazed (when it remains porous, for example, flowerpots, winecoolers) or glazed (most tableware); *stoneware* made of nonporous clay with a high silica content, fired at high temperature, which is very hard; *bone china* (softpaste) semi-porcelain made of 5% bone ash and ⟩china clay; first made in the West in imitation of Chinese porcelain; *porcelain* (hardpaste) characterized by its hardness, ringing sound when struck, translucence, and shining finish, like that of a cowrie shell (Italian *porcellana*); made of kaolin and petuntse (fusible ⟩feldspar consisting chiefly of silicates reduced to a fine, white powder); first developed in China. Porcelain is high-fired at 1,400° C/2,552° F.

potto arboreal, nocturnal, African prosimian primate *Perodicticus potto* belonging to the ⟩loris family. It has a thick body, strong limbs, and grasping feet and hands, and grows to 40 cm/16 in long, with horny spines along its backbone, which it uses in self-defence. It climbs slowly, and eats insects, snails, fruit, and leaves.

pound imperial unit (abbreviation lb) of mass. The commonly used avoirdupois pound, also called the *imperial standard pound* (7,000 grains/0.45 kg), differs from the *pound troy* (5,760 grains/0.37 kg), which is used for weighing precious metals. It derives from the Roman *libra*, which weighed 0.327 kg.

pound British standard monetary unit, issued as a gold sovereign before 1914, as a note 1914–83, and as a circular yellow metal alloy coin from 1983.

Pound Ezra 1885–1972. US poet who lived in London from 1908. His *Personae* and *Exultations* 1909 established the principles of ⟩Imagism. His largest work was the series of *Cantos* 1925–1969 (intended to number 100), which attempted a massive reappraisal of history.

Poussin Nicolas 1594–1665. French painter, active chiefly in Rome; court painter to Louis XIII 1640–43. He was one of France's foremost landscape painters in the 17th century. He painted mythological and literary scenes in a strongly Classical style; for example, *Rape of the Sabine Women* about 1636–37 (Metropolitan Museum of Art, New York).

Powell Colin (Luther) 1937– . US general, chair of the Joint Chiefs of Staff from 1989 and, as such, responsible for the overall administration of the Allied forces in Saudi Arabia during the ◊Gulf War 1991. A Vietnam War veteran, he first worked in government 1972 and was national security adviser 1987–89.

Powell Michael 1905–1990. English film director and producer. Some of his most memorable films were made in collaboration with Hungarian screenwriter Emeric Pressburger. Their richly imaginative films include *A Matter of Life and Death* 1946, *Black Narcissus* 1947, and *The Red Shoes* 1948.

power in mathematics, that which is represented by an exponent or index, denoted by a superior small numeral. A number or symbol raised to the power of 2, that is, multiplied by itself, is said to be squared (for example, 3^2, x^2), and when raised to the power of 3, it is said to be cubed (for example, 2^3, y^3).

power in physics, the rate of doing work or consuming energy. It is measured in watts (joules per second) or other units of work per unit time.

Powys county in central Wales; *area* 5,080 sq km/ 1,961 sq mi; *towns* Llandrindod Wells (administrative headquarters); *features* Brecon Beacons National Park; Black Mountains; rivers: Wye, Severn, which both rise on Plynlimon in Dyfed; Lake Vyrnwy, artificial reservoir supplying Liverpool and Birmingham, alternative technology centre near Machynlleth; *products* agriculture, dairy cattle, sheep; *population* (1991) 116,500; *language* 20% Welsh, English; *famous people* George Herbert, Robert Owen.

Prague (Czech *Praha*) city and capital of Czechoslovakia on the river Vltava; population (1991) 1,212,000. Industries include cars, aircraft, chemicals, paper and printing, clothing, brewing, and food processing. It became the capital 1918.

Praia port and capital of the Republic of Cape Verde, on the island of São Tiago (Santiago); population (1980) 37,500. Industries include fishing and shipping.

prairie the central North American plain, formerly grass-covered, extending over most of the region between the Rockies on the west and the Great Lakes and Ohio River on the east.

prairie dog any of the North American genus *Cynomys* of burrowing rodents in the squirrel family (Sciuridae). They grow to 30 cm/12 in, plus a short 8 cm/3 in tail. Their 'towns' can contain up to several thousand individuals. Their barking cry has given them their name. Persecution by ranchers has brought most of the five species close to extinction.

Prasad Rajendra 1884–1963. Indian politician. A follower of Mahatma Gandhi, he was national president of the Indian National Congress several times between 1934 and 1948 and India's first president after independence 1950–62.

praseodymium silver-white, malleable, metallic element of the ◊lanthanide series, symbol Pr, atomic number 59, relative atomic mass 140.907. It occurs in nature in the minerals monzanite and bastnasite, and its green salts are used to colour glass and ceramics. It was named in 1885 by Austrian chemist Carl von Welsbach (1858–1929).

prawn any of various ◊shrimps of the suborder Natantia ('swimming'), of the crustacean order Decapoda, as contrasted with lobsters and crayfishes, which are able to 'walk'. Species called prawns are generally larger than species called shrimps. The larger **Norway lobster** or **Dublin Bay prawn** *Nephrops norwegicus* is sold as 'scampi'.

Praxiteles mid-4th century BC. Greek sculptor, active in Athens. His *Aphrodite of Knidos* about 350 BC (known through Roman copies) is thought to have initiated the tradition of life-size freestanding female nudes in Greek sculpture.

Precambrian in geology, the time from the formation of Earth (4.6 billion years ago) up to 590 million years ago. Its boundary with the succeeding Cambrian period marks the time when animals first developed hard outer parts (exoskeletons) and so left abundant fossil remains. It comprises about 85% of geological time and is divided into two periods: the Archaean and the Proterozoic.

precession slow wobble of the Earth on its axis, like that of a spinning top. The gravitational pulls of the Sun and Moon on the Earth's equatorial bulge cause the Earth's axis to trace out a circle on the sky every 25,800 years. The position of the celestial poles (see ◊celestial sphere) is constantly changing owing to precession, as are the positions of the equinoxes (the points at which the celestial equator intersects the Sun's path around the sky). This is why the dates of the astrological signs of the zodiac no longer correspond to the times of year when the Sun actually passes through the constellations.

precipitation in chemistry, the formation of a suspension of solid, insoluble particles in a liquid as a result of a reaction within the liquid between two or more soluble substances. If the particles settle, they form a *precipitate*; if the particles are very small and remain in suspension, they form a *colloidal precipitate* (see ◊colloid).

predestination in Christian theology, the doctrine asserting that God has determined all events beforehand, including the ultimate salvation or damnation of the individual human soul. Today Christianity in general accepts that humanity has free will, though some forms, such as Calvinism, believe that salvation can only be attained by the gift of God. The concept of predestination is also found in Islam.

pregnancy in humans, the period during which

Prime Ministers of Britain

Sir Robert Walpole	(Whig)	1721	Lord J Russell	(Liberal)	1865
Earl of Wilmington	(Whig)	1742	Earl of Derby	(Conservative)	1866
Henry Pelham	(Whig)	1743	Benjamin Disraeli	(Conservative)	1868
Duke of Newcastle	(Whig)	1754	W E Gladstone	(Liberal)	1868
Duke of Devonshire	(Whig)	1756	Benjamin Disraeli	(Conserative)	1874
Duke of Newcastle	(Whig)	1757	W E Gladstone	(Liberal)	1880
Earl of Bute	(Tory)	1762	Marquess of Salisbury	(Conservative)	1885
George Grenville	(Whig)	1763	W E Gladstone	(Liberal)	1886
Marquess of Rockingham	(Whig)	1765	Marquess of Salisbury	(Conservative)	1886
Duke of Grafton	(Whig)	1766	W E Gladstone	(Liberal)	1892
Lord North	(Tory)	1770	Earl of Roseberry	(Liberal)	1894
Marquess of Rockingham	(Whig)	1782	Marquess of Salisbury	(Conservative)	1895
Earl of Shelbourne	(Whig)	1782	Sir H Campbell-Bannerman	(Liberal)	1905
Duke of Portland	(Coalition)	1783	H H Asquith	(Liberal)	1908
William Pitt	(Tory)	1783	H H Asquith	(Coalition)	1915
Henry Addington	(Tory)	1801	D Lloyd George	(Coalition)	1916
William Pitt	(Tory)	1804	A Bonar Law	(Conservative)	1922
Lord Grenville	(Whig)	1806	Stanley Baldwin	(Conservative)	1923
Duke of Portland	(Tory)	1807	Ramsay MacDonald	(Labour)	1924
Spencer Percival	(Tory)	1809	Stanley Baldwin	(Conservative)	1924
Earl of Liverpool	(Tory)	1812	Ramsay MacDonald	(Labour)	1929
George Canning	(Tory)	1827	Ramsay MacDonald	(National)	1931
Viscount Goderich	(Tory)	1827	Stanley Baldwin	(National)	1935
Duke of Wellington	(Tory)	1828	N Chamberlain	(National)	1937
Earl Grey	(Whig)	1830	Sir Winston Churchill	(Coalition)	1940
Viscount Melbourne	(Whig)	1834	Clement Attlee	(Labour)	1945
Sir Robert Peel	(Conservative)	1834	Sir Winston Churchill	(Conservative)	1951
Viscount Melbourne	(Whig)	1835	Sir Anthony Eden	(Conservative)	1955
Sir Robert Peel	(Conservative)	1841	Harold Macmillan	(Conservative)	1957
Lord J Russell	(Liberal)	1846	Sir Alec Douglas-Home	(Conservative)	1963
Earl of Derby	(Conservative)	1852	Harold Wilson	(Labour)	1964
Lord Aberdeen	(Peelite)	1852	Edward Heath	(Conservative)	1970
Viscount Palmerston	(Liberal)	1855	Harold Wilson	(Labour)	1974
Earl of Derby	(Conservative)	1858	James Callaghan	(Labour)	1976
Viscount Palmerston	(Liberal)	1859	Margaret Thatcher	(Conservative)	1979

an embryo grows within the womb. It begins at conception and ends at birth, and the normal length is 40 weeks. Menstruation usually stops on conception. About one in five pregnancies fails, but most of these failures occur very early on, so the woman may notice only that her period is late. After the second month, the breasts become tense and tender, and the areas round the nipples become darker. Enlargement of the uterus can be felt at about the end of the third month, and thereafter the abdomen enlarges progressively. Pregnancy in animals is called ¢gestation.

prelude in music, a composition intended as the preface to further music, to set a mood for a stage work, as in Richard Wagner's *Lohengrin*; as used by Frédéric Chopin, a short piano work.

Premadasa Ranasinghe 1924– . Sri Lankan politician, a United National Party member of Parliament

from 1960, prime minister from 1978, and president from 1988, having gained popularity through overseeing a major house-building and poverty-alleviation programme. He has sought peace talks with the Tamil Tiger guerrillas.

premenstrual tension (PMT) or *premenstrual syndrome* medical condition caused by hormone changes and comprising a number of physical and emotional features that occur cyclically before menstruation and disappear with its onset. Symptoms include mood changes, breast tenderness, a feeling of bloatedness, and headache.

Pre-Raphaelite Brotherhood (PRB) group of British painters 1848–53; Dante Gabriel Rossetti, John Everett Millais, and Holman Hunt were founding members. They aimed to paint serious subjects, to study nature closely, and to shun the influence of the styles of painters after Raphael. Their subjects were mainly biblical and literary, painted with obsessive naturalism. Artists associated with the group include Edward Burne-Jones and William Morris.

Presbyterianism system of Christian Protestant church government, expounded during the Reformation by John Calvin, which gives its name to the established Church of Scotland, and is also practised in England, Wales, Ireland, Switzerland, North America, and elsewhere. There is no compulsory form of worship and each congregation is governed by presbyters or elders (clerical or lay), who are of equal rank. Congregations are grouped in presbyteries, synods, and general assemblies.

Presley Elvis (Aaron) 1935–1977. US singer and guitarist, the most influential performer of the rock-and-roll era. With his recordings for Sun Records in Memphis, Tennessee, 1954–55 and early hits such as 'Heartbreak Hotel', 'Hound Dog', and 'Love Me Tender', all 1956, he created an individual vocal style, influenced by Southern blues, gospel music, country music, and rhythm and blues. His records continued to sell in their millions into the 1990s.

press gang method used to recruit soldiers and sailors into the British armed forces in the 18th and early 19th centuries. In effect it was a form of kidnapping carried out by the services or their agents, often with the aid of armed men. This was similar to the practice of 'shanghaiing' sailors for duty in the merchant marine, especially in the Far East.

pressure measure of the force acting normally (at right angles) to a body per unit surface area. The pressure p exerted by a force F newtons acting at right angles over an area of A m² is given by $p = F/A$. The SI unit of pressure is the pascal (newton per square metre).

Pretoria administrative capital of the Republic of South Africa from 1910 and capital of Transvaal province from 1860; population (1985) 741,300. Industries include engineering, chemicals, iron, and steel. Founded 1855, it was named after Boer leader Andries Pretorius (1799–1853).

Previn André (George) 1929– . US conductor and composer, born in Berlin. After a period working as a composer and arranger in the US film industry, he concentrated on conducting. He was principal conductor of the London Symphony Orchestra 1968–79. He was appointed music director of Britain's Royal Philharmonic Orchestra 1985 (a post he relinquished the following year, staying on as principal conductor), and of the Los Angeles Philharmonic in 1986.

Priapus Greek god of fertility, son of Dionysus and Aphrodite, represented as grotesquely ugly, with an exaggerated phallus. He was also a god of gardens, where his image was frequently used as a scarecrow.

prickly pear cactus of the genus *Opuntia*, native to Central and South America, mainly Mexico and Chile, but naturalized in S Europe, N Africa, and Australia, where it is a pest. The common prickly pear *Opuntia vulgaris* is low-growing, with flat, oval, stem joints, bright yellow flowers, and prickly, oval fruit; the flesh and seeds of the peeled fruit have a pleasant taste.

Priestley J(ohn) B(oynton) 1894–1984. English novelist and playwright. His first success was a novel about travelling theatre, *The Good Companions* 1929. He followed it with a realist novel about London life, *Angel Pavement* 1930. As a playwright he was often preoccupied with theories of time, as in *An Inspector Calls* 1945.

primary in presidential election campaigns in the USA, a statewide election to decide the candidates for the two main parties. Held in 35 states, primaries begin with New Hampshire in Feb and continue until June; they operate under varying complex rules.

primate in zoology, any member of the order of mammals that includes monkeys, apes, and humans (together called *anthropoids*, as well as lemurs, bushbabies, lorises, and tarsiers, together called *prosimians*). Generally, they have forward-directed eyes, gripping hands and feet, opposable thumbs, and big toes. They tend to have nails rather than claws, with gripping pads on the ends of the digits – all adaptations to the arboreal, climbing mode of life.

prime minister or *premier* head of a parliamentary government, usually the leader of the largest party.

prime number a number that can be divided only by 1 or itself, that is, having no other factors. There is an infinite number of primes, the first ten of which are 2, 3, 5, 7, 11, 13, 17, 19, 23, and 29 (by definition, the number 1 is excluded from the set of prime numbers). The number 2 is the only even prime because all other even numbers have 2 as a factor.

Primorye territory of Russia, SE Siberia, on the Sea of Japan; area 165,900 sq km/64,079 sq mi; population (1985) 2,136,000; capital Vladivostok. Timber and coal are produced.

primrose any plant of the genus *Primula*, family Primulaceae, with showy five-lobed flowers. The common primrose *P. vulgaris* is a woodland plant, native to Europe, bearing pale yellow flowers in spring. Related to it is the ⟩cowslip.

Prince stage name of Prince Rogers Nelson 1960– . US pop musician who composes, arranges, and produces his own records and often plays all the instruments. His albums, including *1999* 1982 and *Purple Rain* 1984, contain elements of rock, funk, and jazz. His stage shows are energetic and extravagant.

Prince Edward Island province of E Canada; *area* 5,700 sq km/2,200 sq mi; *capital* Charlottetown; *features* named after Prince Edward of Kent, father

printing

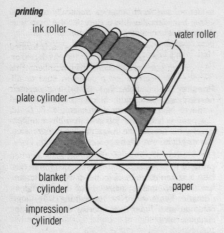

ink roller
water roller
plate cylinder
blanket cylinder
paper
impression cylinder

of Queen Victoria; Prince Edward Island National Park; Summerside Lobster Carnival; *products* potatoes, dairy products, lobsters, oysters, farm vehicles; *population* (1991) 129,900; *history* first recorded visit by Cartier 1534, who called it Isle St-Jean; settled by French; taken by British 1758; annexed to Nova Scotia 1763; separate colony 1769; settled by Scottish 1803; joined Confederation 1873.

Prince William Sound channel in the Gulf of Alaska, extending 200 km/125 mi NW from Kayak Island. In March 1989 the oil tanker *Exxon Valdez* ran aground here, spilling 12 million gallons of crude oil in what was then reckoned to be the world's greatest oil-pollution disaster.

printed circuit board (PCB) electrical circuit created by laying (printing) 'tracks' of a conductor such as copper on one or both sides of an insulating board. The PCB was invented in 1936 by Austrian scientist Paul Eisler, and was first used on a large scale in 1948.

printer in computing, an output device for producing printed copies of text or graphics. Types include the *daisywheel printer*, which produces good-quality text but no graphics; the *dot-matrix printer*, which produces text and graphics by printing a pattern of small dots; the ▷*ink-jet printer*, which creates text and graphics by spraying a fine jet of quick-drying ink onto the paper; and the ▷*laser printer*, which uses electrostatic technology very similar to that used by a photocopier to produce high-quality text and graphics.

printing reproduction of text or illustrative material on paper, as in books or newspapers, or on an increasing variety of materials; for example, on plastic containers. The first printing used woodblocks, followed by carved wood type or moulded metal type and hand-operated presses. Modern printing is effected by electronically controlled machinery. Current printing processes include electronic phototypesetting with ▷offset printing, and ▷gravure print.

printmaking creating a picture or design by printing from a plate (block, stone, or sheet) that holds ink or colour. The oldest form of print is the woodcut, common in medieval Europe, followed by line ▷engraving (from the 15th century), and ▷etching (from the 17th); coloured woodblock prints flourished in Japan from the 18th century. ▷Lithography was invented 1796.

prism in optics, a triangular block of transparent material (plastic, glass, silica) commonly used to 'bend' a ray of light or split a beam into its spectral colours. Prisms are used as mirrors to define the optical path in binoculars, camera viewfinders, and periscopes. The dispersive property of prisms is used in the spectroscope.

prison place of confinement for those convicted of contravening the laws of the state; most countries claim to aim at rehabilitation. The average number of people in prison in the UK (1990) was 43,314 (about 97 people per 100,000 of the population) with almost 20% of these under the age of 21. About 22% were on ▷remand (awaiting trial or sentence). The US prison population (1988) was 800,000 (about 426 per 100,000 people). There are an estimated 10 million prisoners in Chinese prisons (1991).

privateer privately owned and armed ship commissioned by a state to attack enemy vessels. The crews of such ships were, in effect, legalized pirates; they were not paid but received a share of the spoils. Privateering existed from ancient times until the 19th century, when it was declared illegal by the Declaration of Paris 1856.

privatization policy or process of selling or transferring state-owned or public assets and services (notably nationalized industries) to private investors. Privatization of services involves the government contracting private firms to supply services previously supplied by public authorities. The policy has been pursued by the post-1979 Conservative administration in the UK, and by recent governments in France, Japan, Italy, New Zealand and elsewhere. By 1988 the practice had spread worldwide with communist countries such as China and Cuba selling off housing to private tenants.

privet any evergreen shrub of the genus *Ligustrum* of the olive family Oleaceae, with dark green leaves, including the European common privet *L. vulgare*, with white flowers and black berries, naturalized in North America, and the native North American California privet *L. ovalifolium*, also known as hedge privet.

Privy Council council composed originally of the chief royal officials of the Norman kings in Britain; under the Tudors and early Stuarts it became the chief governing body. It was replaced from 1688 by the ▷cabinet, originally a committee of the council, and the council itself now retains only formal powers in issuing royal proclamations and orders-in-council. Cabinet ministers are automatically members, and it is presided over by the Lord President of the Council.

probability likelihood, or chance, that an event will occur, often expressed as odds, or in mathematics, numerically as a fraction or decimal. In general, the probability that n particular events will happen out of a total of m possible events is n/m. A certainty has a probability of 1; an impossibility has a probability of 0. Empirical probability is defined as the number of successful events divided by the total possible number of events.

probate formal proof of a will. In the UK, if a will's validity is unquestioned, it is proven in 'common form'; the executor, in the absence of other interested parties, obtains at a probate registry a grant upon his or her own oath. Otherwise, it must be proved in 'solemn form': its validity established at a probate court (in the Chancery Division of the High Court), those concerned being made parties to the action.

procurator fiscal officer of a Scottish sheriff's court who (combining the role of public prosecutor and coroner) inquires into suspicious deaths and carries out the preliminary questioning of witnesses to crime.

Procyon or *Alpha Canis Minoris* brightest star in the constellation Canis Minor and the eighth brightest star in the sky. Procyon is a white star 11.4 light years from Earth, with a mass of 1.7 Suns. It has a ⬦white dwarf companion that orbits it every 40 years.

productivity in economics, the output produced by a given quantity of labour, usually measured as output per person employed in the firm, industry, sector, or economy concerned. Productivity is determined by the quality and quantity of the fixed ⬦capital used by labour, and the effort of the workers concerned.

progesterone ⬦steroid hormone that occurs in vertebrates. In mammals, it regulates the menstrual cycle and pregnancy. Progesterone is secreted by the corpus luteum (the ruptured Graafian follicle of a discharged ovum).

programming writing instructions in a programming language for the control of a computer. *Applications programming* is for end-user programs, such as accounts programs or word-processing packages. *Systems programming* is for operating systems and the like, which are concerned more with the internal workings of the computer.

programming language in computing, a special notation in which instructions for controlling a computer are written. Programming languages are designed to be easy for people to write and read, but

must be capable of being mechanically translated (by a compiler or an interpreter) into the ⬦machine code that the computer can execute.

progression sequence of numbers each formed by a specific relationship to its predecessor. An *arithmetic progression* has numbers that increase or decrease by a common sum or difference (for example, 2, 4, 6, 8); a *geometric progression* has numbers each bearing a fixed ratio to its predecessor (for example, 3, 6, 12, 24); and a *harmonic progression* has numbers whose reciprocals are in arithmetical progression, for example 1, ½, ⅓, ¼.

Prohibition in US history, the period 1920–33 when alcohol was illegal. It represented the culmination of a long campaign by church and women's organizations, temperance societies, and the Anti-Saloon League. Banning led to bootlegging (the illegal distribution of liquor, often illicitly distilled), to the financial advantage of organized crime, and public opinion insisted on repeal 1933.

prokaryote in biology, an organism whose cells lack organelles (specialized segregated structures such as nuclei, mitochondria, and chloroplasts). Prokaryote DNA is not arranged in chromosomes but forms a coiled structure called a *nucleoid*. The prokaryotes comprise only the *bacteria* and *cyanobacteria* (see ⬦blue-green algae); all other organisms are eukaryotes.

Prokofiev Sergey (Sergeyevich) 1891–1953. Soviet composer. His music includes operas such as *The Love for Three Oranges* 1921; ballets for Sergei ⬦Diaghilev, including *Romeo and Juliet* 1935; seven symphonies including the *Classical Symphony* 1916–17; music for films; piano and violin concertos; songs and cantatas (for example, that composed for the 30th anniversary of the October Revolution); and *Peter and the Wolf* 1936.

proletariat in Marxist theory, those classes in society that possess no property, and therefore depend on the sale of their labour or expertise (as opposed to the capitalists or bourgeoisie, who own the means of production, and the petty bourgeoisie, or working small-property owners). They are usually divided into the industrial, agricultural, and intellectual proletariat.

PROLOG (acronym for *programming in logic*) high-level computer-programming language based on logic. Invented in 1971 at the University of Marseille, France, it did not achieve widespread use until more than ten years later. It is used mainly for ⬦artificial-intelligence programming.

PROM (acronym for *programmable read-only memory*) in computing, a memory device in the form of an integrated circuit (chip) that can be programmed after manufacture to hold information permanently. PROM chips are empty of information when manufactured, unlike ROM (read-only memory) chips, which have information built into them. Other memory devices are ⟡EPROM (erasable programmable read-only memory) and ⟡RAM (random-access memory).

Prometheus in Greek mythology, a ⟡Titan who stole fire from heaven for the human race. In revenge, Zeus had him chained to a rock where an eagle came each day to feast on his liver, which grew back each night, until he was rescued by the hero Heracles.

promethium radioactive, metallic element of the ⟡lanthanide series, symbol Pm, atomic number 61, relative atomic mass 145. It occurs in nature only in minute amounts, produced as a fission product/by-product of uranium in pitchblende and other uranium ores; for a long time it was considered not to occur in nature. The longest-lived isotope has a half-life of slightly more than 20 years.

pronghorn ruminant mammal *Antilocapra americana* constituting the family Antilocapridae, native to the western USA. It is not a true antelope. It is light brown and about 1 m/3 ft high. It sheds its horns annually and can reach speeds of 100 kph/60 mph. The loss of prairies to agriculture, combined with excessive hunting, has brought this unique animal close to extinction.

propane C_3H_8 gaseous hydrocarbon of the ⟡alkane series, found in petroleum and used as fuel.

propanone CH_3COCH_3 (common name *acetone*) colourless flammable liquid used extensively as a solvent, as in nail-varnish remover. It boils at 56.5°C/133.7°F, mixes with water in all proportions, and has a characteristic odour.

propellant substance burned in a rocket for propulsion. Two propellants are used: oxidizer and fuel are stored in separate tanks and pumped independently into the combustion chamber. Liquid oxygen (oxidizer) and liquid hydrogen (fuel) are common propellants, used, for example, in the space-shuttle main engines. The explosive charge that propels a projectile from a gun is also called a propellant.

propeller screwlike device used to propel some ships and aeroplanes. A propeller has a number of curved blades that describe a helical path as they rotate with the hub, and accelerate fluid (liquid or gas) backwards during rotation. Reaction to this backward movement of fluid sets up a propulsive thrust forwards.

property the right to control the use of a thing (such as land, a building, a work of art, or a computer program). In English law, a distinction is made between *real property*, which involves a degree of geographical fixity, and *personal property*, which does not. Property is never absolute, since any society places limits on an individual's property (such as the right to transfer that property to another). Different societies have held widely varying interpretations of the nature of

property and the extent of the rights of the owner of that property.

proportion two variable quantities x and y are proportional if, for all values of x, $y = kx$, where k is a constant. This means that if x increases, y increases in a linear fashion. A graph of x against y would be a straight line passing through the origin (the point $x = 0, y = 0$). y is inversely proportional to x if the graph of y against $1/x$ is a straight line through the origin. The corresponding equation is $y = k/x$. Many laws of science relate quantities that are proportional (for example, ⟡Boyle's law).

proportional representation (PR) electoral system in which distribution of party seats corresponds to their proportion of the total votes cast, and minority votes are not wasted (as opposed to a simple majority, or 'first past the post', system). Forms include: *party list* (PLS) or additional member system (AMS). As recommended by the Hansard Society 1976 for introduction in the UK, three-quarters of the members would be elected in single-member constituencies on the traditional majority-vote system, and the remaining seats be allocated according to the overall number of votes cast for each party (a variant of this is used in Germany); *single transferable vote* (STV), in which candidates are numbered in order of preference by the voter, and any votes surplus to the minimum required for a candidate to win are transferred to second preferences, as are second-preference votes from the successive candidates at the bottom of the poll until the required number of elected candidates is achieved (this is in use in the Republic of Ireland).

prose spoken or written language without metrical regularity; in literature, prose corresponds more closely to the patterns of everyday speech than ⟡poetry. In modern literature, the distinction between verse and prose is not always clear cut.

Proserpina Roman equivalent of ⟡Persephone, goddess of the underworld.

Prost Alain 1955– . French motor-racing driver who was world champion 1985, 1986, and 1989, the first French world drivers' champion. To the start of 1991 he had won a record 44 Grands Prix from 169 starts.

prostaglandin any of a group of complex fatty acids that act as messenger substances between cells. Effects include stimulating the contraction of smooth muscle (for example, of the womb during birth), regulating the production of stomach acid, and modifying hormonal activity. In excess, prostaglandins may produce inflammatory disorders such as arthritis. Synthetic prostaglandins are used to induce labour in humans and domestic animals.

prostate gland gland surrounding and opening into the urethra at the base of the ⟡bladder in male mammals.

prosthesis replacement of a body part with an artificial substitute. Prostheses include artificial limbs, hearing aids, false teeth and eyes, and for the heart, a ⟡pacemaker and plastic heart valves and blood vessels.

protactinium silver-grey, radioactive, metallic element of the ⟡actinide series, symbol Pa, atomic number 91, relative atomic mass 231.036. It occurs in nature in very small quantities, in pitchblende and other uranium ores. It has 14 known isotopes; the longest-lived, Pa-231, has a half-life of 32,480 years.

protectionism in economics, the imposition of heavy duties or import quotas by a government as a means of discouraging the import of foreign goods likely to compete with domestic products. Price controls, quota systems, and the reduction of surpluses are among the measures taken for agricultural products in the European Community (see ⟡agriculture). The opposite practice is ⟡free trade.

protectorate formerly in international law, a small state under the direct or indirect control of a larger one. The 20th-century equivalent was a ⟡trust territory. In English history the rule of Oliver and Richard ⟡Cromwell 1653–59 is referred to as *the Protectorate*.

protein complex, biologically important substance composed of amino acids joined by peptide bonds. Other types of bond, such as sulphur–sulphur bonds, hydrogen bonds, and cation bridges between acid sites, are responsible for creating the protein's characteristic three-dimensional structure, which may be fibrous, globular, or pleated.

Proterozoic period of geological time, 2.5 billion to 590 million years ago, the second division of the Precambrian era. It is defined as the time of simple life, since many rocks dating from this eon show traces of biological activity, and some contain the fossils of bacteria and algae.

Protestantism one of the main divisions of Christianity, which emerged from Roman Catholicism at the ⟡Reformation. The chief denominations are the Anglican Communion (Episcopalian in the USA), Baptists, Lutherans, Methodists, Pentecostals, and Presbyterians, with a total membership of about 300 million.

protist in biology, a single-celled organism which has a eukaryotic cell, but which is not a member of the plant, fungal, or animal kingdoms. The main protists are ⟡protozoa.

proton in physics, a positively charged subatomic particle, a constituent of the nucleus of all atoms. It belongs to the baryon subclass of the ⟡hadrons. A proton is extremely long-lived, with a lifespan of at least 10^{32} years. It carries a unit positive charge equal to the negative charge of an ⟡electron. Its mass is almost 1,836 times that of an electron, or 1.67×10^{-24} g. The number of protons in the atom of an element is equal to the atomic number of that element.

protoplasm contents of a living cell. Strictly speaking it includes all the discrete structures (organelles) in a cell, but it is often used simply to mean the jellylike material in which these float. The contents of a cell outside the nucleus are called ⟡cytoplasm.

protozoa group of single-celled organisms without rigid cell walls. Some, such as amoeba, ingest other cells, but most are saprotrophs or parasites. The group is polyphyletic (containing organisms which have different evolutionary origins).

Proust Marcel 1871–1922. French novelist and critic. His immense autobiographical work *A la recherche du temps perdu/Remembrance of Things Past* 1913–27, consisting of a series of novels, is the expression of his childhood memories coaxed from his subconscious; it is also a precise reflection of life in France at the end of the 19th century.

Provence-Alpes-Côte d'Azur region of SE France, comprising the *départements* of Alpes-de-Haute-Provence, Hautes-Alpes, Alpes-Maritimes, Bouches-du-Rhône, Var, and Vaucluse; area 31,400 sq km/12,120 sq mi; capital Marseille; population (1986) 4,059,000. The *Côte d'Azur*, on the Mediterranean, is a tourist centre. Provence was an independent kingdom in the 10th century, and the area still has its own language, Provençal.

Prussia N German state 1618–1945 on the Baltic coast. It was an independent kingdom until 1867, when it became, under Otto von ⟡Bismarck, the military power of the North German Confederation and part of the German Empire 1871 under the Prussian king Wilhelm I. West Prussia became part of Poland under the Treaty of ⟡Versailles, and East Prussia was largely incorporated into the USSR after 1945.

Prut river that rises in the Carpathian Mountains of SW Ukraine, and flows 900 km/565 mi to meet the Danube at Reni. For part of its course it follows the eastern frontier of Romania.

Przhevalsky Nikolai Mikhailovitch 1839–1888. Russian explorer and soldier. In 1870 he crossed the Gobi Desert to Beijing and then went on to the upper reaches of the Chang Jiang River. His attempts to penetrate Tibet as far as Lhasa failed on three occasions, but he continued to explore the mountain regions between Tibet and Mongolia, where he made collections of plants and animals, including a wild camel and a wild horse (the species is now known as *Przhevalsky's horse*).

pseudocarp fruitlike structure that incorporates tissue that is not derived from the ovary wall. The additional tissues may be derived from floral parts such as the receptacle and ⟡calyx. For example, the coloured, fleshy part of a strawberry develops from the receptacle and the true fruits are small achenes – the 'pips' embedded in its outer surface. Different types of pseudocarp include pineapples, figs, apples, and pears.

Psilocybe genus of mushroom with hallucinogenic properties, including the Mexican sacred mushroom *P. mexicana*, which contains compounds with effects similar to LSD (lysergic acid diethylamide, a hallucinogen). A related species *P. semilanceata* is found in N Europe.

psoriasis chronic, recurring skin disease characterized by raised, red, scaly patches, usually on the scalp, back, arms, and/or legs. Tar preparations, steroid creams, and ultraviolet light are used to treat it, and sometimes it disappears spontaneously. Psoriasis may be accompanied by a form of arthritis (inflammation of the joints).

Psyche late Greek personification of the soul as a winged girl or young woman. The goddess Aphrodite was so jealous of Psyche's beauty that she ordered her son Eros, the god of love, to make Psyche fall in love with the worst of men. Instead, he fell in love with her himself.

psychiatry branch of medicine dealing with the diagnosis and treatment of mental disorder. It is normally divided into types of neurosis (anxiety, depression, hysteria, and so on) and psychosis (for example, schizophrenia). Treatment is by drugs and electroconvulsive therapy.

psychoanalysis theory and treatment method for neuroses, developed by Sigmund ◇Freud. The main treatment method involves the free association of ideas, and their interpretation by patient and analyst. It is typically prolonged and expensive and its effectiveness has been disputed.

psychology systematic study of human and animal behaviour. The first psychology laboratory was founded 1879 by Wilhelm Wundt (1832–1920) at Leipzig, Germany. The subject includes diverse areas of study and application, among them the roles of instinct, heredity, environment, and culture; the processes of sensation, perception, learning and memory; the bases of motivation and emotion; and the functioning of thought, intelligence, and language.

psychosis or *psychotic disorder* general term for a serious mental disorder where the individual commonly loses contact with reality and may experience hallucinations (seeing or hearing things that do not exist) or delusions (fixed false beliefs). For example, in a paranoid psychosis, an individual may believe that others are plotting against him or her. A major type of psychosis is ◇schizophrenia (which may be biochemically induced).

psychotherapy treatment approaches for psychological problems involving talking rather than surgery or drugs. Examples include ◇cognitive therapy and ◇psychoanalysis.

ptarmigan any of a genus (Lagopus) of hardy, northern ground-dwelling birds (family Phasianidae, which also includes ◇grouse), with feathered legs and feet. The rock ptarmigan *L.*

mutus is found in mountainous areas above the tree line in N Europe. About 36 cm/1.2 ft long, it has a white coat in winter.

pteridophyte simple type of vascular plant. The pteridophytes comprise four classes: the Psilosida, including the most primitive vascular plants, found mainly in the tropics; the Lycopsida, including the club mosses; the Sphenopsida, including the horsetails; and the Pteropsida, including the ferns. They do not produce seeds.

pterodactyl genus of ◇pterosaur.

pterosaur extinct flying reptile of the order Pterosauria, existing in the Mesozoic age. They ranged from starling size to a 12 m/40 ft wingspan. Some had horns on their heads, which, in flight, made a whistling to roaring sound.

Ptolemy (Claudius Ptolemaeus) *c.* 100–170 AD. Egyptian astronomer and geographer who worked in Alexandria. His *Almagest* developed the theory that Earth is the centre of the universe, with the Sun, Moon, and stars revolving around it. In 1543 the Polish astronomer ◇Copernicus proposed an alternative to the *Ptolemaic system*. Ptolemy's *Geography* was a standard source of information until the 16th century.

puberty stage in human development when the individual becomes sexually mature. It may occur from the age of ten upwards. The sexual organs take on their adult form and pubic hair grows. In girls, menstruation begins, and the breasts develop; in boys, the voice breaks and becomes deeper, and facial hair develops.

public limited company (plc) a registered company in which shares and debentures may be offered to the public. It must have a minimum of seven shareholders and there is no upper limit. The company's financial records must be available for any member of the public to scrutinize, and the company's name must carry the words 'public limited company' or initials 'plc'. A public company can raise enormous financial resources to fuel its development and expansion by inviting the public to buy shares.

public-sector borrowing requirement (PSBR) the amount of money needed by a government to cover any deficit in financing its own activities. The PSBR is financed chiefly by sales of debt to the public outside the banking system (gilt-edged stocks, national savings, and local-authority stocks and bonds), by external transactions with other countries, and by borrowing from the banking system.

Puccini Giacomo (Antonio Domenico Michele Secondo Maria) 1858–1924. Italian opera composer whose music shows a strong gift for melody and dramatic effect and whose operas combine exotic plots with elements of *verismo* (realism). They include *Manon Lescaut* 1893, *La Bohème*

1896, *Tosca* 1900, *Madame Butterfly* 1904, and the unfinished *Turandot* 1926.

Puerto Rico (the Commonwealth of) easternmost island of the Greater Antilles, situated between the US Virgin Islands and the Dominican Republic; *area* 9,000 sq km/3,475 sq mi; *capital* San Juan; *towns* ports Mayagüez, Ponce; *features* highest per capita income in Latin America; *exports* sugar, tobacco, rum, pineapples, textiles, plastics, chemicals, processed foods; *currency* US dollar; *population* (1990) 3,522,000; *languages* Spanish and English (official); *religion* Roman Catholic; *government* under the constitution of 1952, similar to that of the USA, with a governor elected for four years, and a legislative assembly with a senate and house of representatives; *history* visited 1493 by Columbus; annexed by Spain 1509; ceded to the USA after the ⬦Spanish-American War 1898; achieved commonwealth status with local self-government 1952.

Puerto Sandino major port on the Pacific W coast of Nicaragua, known as *Puerto Somoza* until 1979.

puffball globulous fruiting body of certain fungi (see ⬦fungus) that cracks with maturity, releasing the enclosed spores in the form of a brown powder; for example, the common puffball *Lycoperdon perlatum*.

puffer fish fish of the family Tetraodontidae. As a means of defence it inflates its body with air or water until it becomes spherical and the skin spines become erect. Puffer fish are mainly found in warm waters, where they feed on molluscs, crustaceans, and coral.

puffin any of various sea birds of the genus *Fratercula* of the ⬦auk family, found in the N Atlantic and Pacific. The puffin is about 35 cm/14 in long, with a white face and front, red legs, and a large deep bill, very brightly coloured in summer. Having short wings and webbed feet, puffins are poor fliers but excellent swimmers. They nest in rock crevices, or make burrows, and lay a single egg.

pug breed of small dog with short wrinkled face, chunky body, and tail curled over the hip. It weighs 6–8 kg/13–18 lb.

Puget Sound inlet of the Pacific Ocean on the W coast of Washington State, USA.

Pugin Augustus Welby Northmore 1812–1852. English architect, collaborator with Charles ⬦Barry in the detailed design of the Houses of Parliament. He did much to revive Gothic architecture in England.

Puglia (English *Apulia*) region of Italy, the south eastern 'heel'; area 19,300 sq km/7,450 sq mi; capital Bari; population (1990) 4,081,500. Products include wheat, grapes, almonds, olives, and vegetables. The main industrial centre is Taranto.

P'u-i (or *Pu-Yi*) Henry 1906–1967. Last emperor of China (as Hsuan Tung) from 1908 until his deposition 1912; he was restored for a week 1917. After his deposition he chose to be called Henry. He was president 1932–34 and emperor 1934–45 of the Japanese puppet state of Manchukuo (see ⬦Manchuria).

pulley simple machine consisting of a fixed, grooved wheel, sometimes in a block, around which a rope or chain can be run. A simple pulley serves only to change the direction of the applied effort (as in a simple hoist for raising loads). The use of more than one pulley results in a mechanical advantage, so that a given effort can raise a heavier load.

pulsar celestial source that emits pulses of energy at regular intervals, ranging from a few seconds to a few thousandths of a second. Pulsars were discovered 1967, and are thought to be rapidly rotating ⬦neutron stars, which flash at radio and other wavelengths as they spin. Over 400 radio pulsars are known in our Galaxy, although a million or so may exist.

pulse crop such as peas and beans. Pulses are grown primarily for their seeds, which provide a concentrated source of vegetable protein, and make a vital contribution to human diets in poor countries where meat is scarce, and among vegetarians. Soya beans are the chief temperate protein crop in the West; most are used for oil production or for animal feed. In Asia, most are processed into soya milk and beancurd. Groundnuts dominate pulse production in the tropical world and are generally consumed as human food.

pulse impulse transmitted by the heartbeat throughout the arterial systems of vertebrates. When the heart muscle contracts, it forces blood into the ⬦aorta (the chief artery). Because the arteries are elastic, the sudden rise of pressure causes a throb or sudden swelling through them. The actual flow of the blood is about 60 cm/2 ft a second in humans. The pulse rate is generally about 70 per minute. The pulse can be felt where an artery is near the surface, for example in the wrist or the neck.

puma or *cougar* or *mountain lion* large wild cat *Felis concolor* found in North and South America. Tawny-coated, it is 1.5 m/4.5 ft long with a 1 m/3 ft tail. Cougars live alone, with each male occupying a distinct territory; they eat deer, rodents, and cattle. They have been hunted nearly to extinction.

pump any device for moving liquids and gases, or compressing gases. Some pumps, such as the traditional *lift pump* used to raise water from wells, work by a reciprocating (up-and-down) action. Movement of a piston in a cylinder with a one-way valve creates a partial vacuum in the cylinder, thereby sucking water into it.

pumpkin gourd *Cucurbita pepo* of the family Cucurbitaceae. The large, spherical fruit has a thick, orange rind, pulpy flesh, and many seeds.

Pune formerly *Poona* city in Maharashtra, India; population (1985) 1,685,000. Products include chemicals, rice, sugar, cotton, paper, and jewellery.

Punic Wars three wars between ⟡Rome and ⟡Carthage: *First* 264–241 BC, resulted in the defeat of the Carthaginians under ⟡Hamilcar Barca and the cession of Sicily to Rome; *Second* 218–201 BC, Hannibal invaded Italy, defeated the Romans under Fabius Maximus at Cannae, but was finally defeated by ⟡Scipio Africanus Major at Zama (now in Algeria); *Third* 149–146 BC, ended in the destruction of Carthage, and its possessions becoming the Roman province of Africa.

Punjab (Sanskrit 'five rivers': the Indus tributaries Jhelum, Chenab, Ravi, Beas, and Sutlej) former state of British India, now divided between India and Pakistan. Punjab was annexed by Britain 1849, after the Sikh Wars 1845–46 and 1848–49, and formed into a province with its capital at Lahore. Under the British, W Punjab was extensively irrigated, and land was granted to Indians who had served in the British army.

Punjab state of NW India; *area* 50,400 sq km/ 19,454 sq mi; *capital* Chandigarh; *towns* Amritsar; *features* mainly agricultural, crops chiefly under irrigation; longest life expectancy rates in India (59 for women, 64 for men); Harappa has ruins from the Indus Valley civilization 2500 to 1600 BC; *population* (1991) 20,190,800; *language* Punjabi; *religion* 60% Sikh, 30% Hindu; there is friction between the two groups.

Punjab state of NE Pakistan; *area* 205,344 sq km/ 79,263 sq mi; *capital* Lahore; *features* wheat cultivation (by irrigation); *population* (1981) 47,292,000; *languages* Punjabi, Urdu; *religion* Muslim.

Punjabi member of the majority ethnic group living in the Punjab. Approximately 37 million live in the Pakistani half of Punjab, while another 14 million live on the Indian side of the border. In addition to Sikhs, there are Rajputs in Punjab, some of whom have adopted Islam. The Punjabi language belongs to the Indo-Iranian branch of the Indo-European family. It is considered by some to be a variety of Hindi, by others to be a distinct language.

Punjab massacres in the violence occurring after the partition of India 1947, more than a million people died while relocating in the Punjab. The eastern section became an Indian state, while the western area, dominated by the Muslims, went to Pakistan. Violence occurred as Muslims fled from eastern Punjab, and Hindus and Sikhs moved from Pakistan to India.

punk movement of disaffected youth of the late 1970s, manifesting itself in fashions and music designed to shock or intimidate. *Punk rock* began

in the UK and stressed aggressive performance within a three-chord, three-minute format, as exemplified by the Sex Pistols.

pupa nonfeeding, largely immobile stage of some insect life cycles, in which larval tissues are broken down, and adult tissues and structures are formed.

Purcell Henry 1659–1695. English Baroque composer. His work can be highly expressive, for example, the opera *Dido and Aeneas* 1689 and music for Dryden's *King Arthur* 1691 and for *The Fairy Queen* 1692. He wrote more than 500 works, ranging from secular operas and incidental music for plays to cantatas and church music.

purdah seclusion of women practised by some Islamic and Hindu peoples. It had begun to disappear with the adoption of Western culture, but the fundamentalism of the 1980s revived it; for example, the wearing of the chador (an all-enveloping black mantle) in Iran.

Puritan from 1564, a member of the Church of England who wished to eliminate Roman Catholic survivals in church ritual, or substitute a presbyterian for an episcopal form of church government. The term also covers the separatists who withdrew from the church altogether. The Puritans were identified with the parliamentary opposition under James I and Charles I, and after the Restoration were driven from the church, and more usually known as Dissenters or ⟡Nonconformists.

Pusan or *Busan* chief industrial port (textiles, rubber, salt, fishing) of South Korea; population (1985) 3,797,600. It was invaded by the Japanese 1592 and opened to foreign trade 1883.

Pushkin Aleksandr 1799–1837. Russian poet and writer. His works include the novel in verse *Eugene Onegin* 1823–31 and the tragic drama *Boris Godunov* 1825. Pushkin's range was wide, and his willingness to experiment freed later Russian writers from many of the archaic conventions of the literature of his time.

Puttnam David (Terence) 1941– . English film producer who played a major role in reviving the British film industry internationally in the 1980s. Films include *Chariots of Fire* 1981, *The Killing Fields* 1984 (both of which won several Academy Awards), and *Memphis Belle* 1990. He was briefly head of Columbia Pictures.

Pu-Yi alternative transliteration of the name of the last Chinese emperor, Henry ⟡P'u-i.

Pygmy (sometimes *Negrillo*) member of any of several groups of small-statured, dark-skinned peoples of the rainforests of equatorial Africa. They were probably the aboriginal inhabitants of the region, before the arrival of farming peoples from elsewhere. They live nomadically in small groups, as hunter-gatherers; they also trade with other, settled people in the area.

Pyongyang capital and industrial city (coal,

Pythagoras' theorem
for right-angled triangles

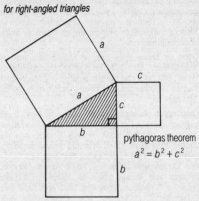

pythagoras theorem
$$a^2 = b^2 + c^2$$

iron, steel, textiles, chemicals) of North Korea; population (1984) 2,640,000.

pyramid four-sided building with triangular sides. They were used in ancient Egypt to enclose a royal tomb; for example, the Great Pyramid of Khufu/ Cheops at Gîza, near Cairo, 230 m/755 ft square and 147 m/481 ft high. In Babylon and Assyria broadly stepped pyramids (ziggurats) were used as the base for a shrine to a god: the Tower of Babel (see ◊Babylon) was probably one of these. Truncated pyramidal temple mounds were also built by the ◊Aztecs and ◊Mayas of Central and South America.

Pyrenees (French *Pyrénées*; Spanish *Pirineos*) mountain range in SW Europe between France and Spain; length about 435 km/270 mi; highest peak Aneto (French Néthon) 3,404 m/11,172 ft. ◊Andorra is entirely within the range. Hydroelectric power has encouraged industrial development in the foothills.

pyrethrum popular name for some flowers of the genus *Chrysanthemum*, family Compositae. The ornamental species *C. coccineum*, and hybrids derived from it, are commonly grown in gardens. Pyrethrum powder, made from the dried flower heads of some species, is a powerful contact pesticide for aphids and mosquitoes.

Pyrrhus *c.* 318–272 BC. King of ◊Epirus, Greece, from 307, who invaded Italy 280, as an ally of the Tarentines against Rome. He twice defeated the Romans but with such heavy losses that a *Pyrrhic victory* has come to mean a victory not worth winning. He returned to Greece 275 after his defeat at Beneventum, and was killed in a riot in Argos.

Pythagoras *c.* 580–500 BC. Greek mathematician and philosopher who formulated Pythagoras' theorem.

Pythagoras' theorem in geometry, a theorem stating that in a right-angled triangle, the area of the square on the hypotenuse (the longest side) is equal to the sum of the areas of the squares drawn on the other two sides. If the hypotenuse is *h* units long and the lengths of the other sides are *a* and *b*, then $h^2 = a^2 + b^2$.

python any constricting snake of the Old World subfamily Pythoninae of the family Boidae, which also includes ◊boas and the ◊anaconda. Pythons are found in the tropics of Africa, Asia, and Australia. Unlike boas, they lay eggs rather than produce living young. Some species are small, but the reticulated python *Python reticulatus* of SE Asia can grow to 10 m/33 ft.

Qaboos bin Said 1940– . Sultan of Oman, the 14th descendant of the Albusaid family. Opposed to the conservative views of his father, he overthrew him 1970 in a bloodless coup and assumed the sultanship. Since then he has followed more liberal and expansionist policies, while maintaining his country's position of international nonalignment.

Qaddafi alternative form of ◊Khaddhafi, Libyan leader.

Qadisiya, Battle of battle fought in S Iraq 637. A Muslim Arab force defeated a larger Zoroastrian Persian army and ended the ◊Sassanian Empire. The defeat is still resented in Iran, where Muslim Arab nationalism threatens to break up the Iranian state.

qat shrub *Catha edulis* of the staff-tree family Celastraceae. The leaves are chewed as a mild narcotic in some Arab countries. Its use was banned in Somalia 1983.

Qatar State of; country in the Middle East, occupying Qatar peninsula in the Arabian Gulf, bordered SW by Saudi Arabia and S by United Arab Emirates; *area* 11,400 sq km/4,402 sq mi; *capital* and chief port Doha; *physical* mostly flat desert with salt flats in S; *head of state and government* Sheik Khalifa bin Hamad al-Thani from 1972; *political system* absolute monarchy; *exports* oil, natural gas, petrochemicals, fertilizers, iron, steel; *population* (1990 est) 498,000 (half in Doha; Arab 40%, Indian 18%, Pakistani 18%); *languages* Arabic (official), English; *recent history* independence was achieved from Britain 1971. Emir Sheik Ahmad was replaced 1972 in a bloodless coup by his cousin, Crown Prince Sheik Khalifa, who embarked on an ambitious programme of social and economic reform, curbing the extravagances of the royal family.

Qinghai or *Tsinghai* province of NW China; *area* 721,000 sq km/278,306 sq mi; *capital* Xining; *features* mainly desert, with nomadic herders; *products* oil, livestock, medical products; *population* (1990) 4,457,000; minorities include 900,000 Tibetans (mostly nomadic herders); Tibetan nationalists regard the province as being under colonial rule.

Qom or *Qum* holy city of Shi'ite Muslims, in central Iran, 145 km/90 mi S of Tehran; population (1986) 551,000. The Islamic academy of Madresseh Faizieh 1920 became the headquarters of Ayatollah ◊Khomeini.

Quadruple Alliance in European history, three military alliances of four nations: *the Quadruple Alliance 1718* Austria, Britain, France, and the United Provinces (Netherlands) joined forces to prevent Spain from annexing Sardinia and Sicily; *the Quadruple Alliance 1813* Austria, Britain, Prussia, and Russia allied to defeat the French emperor Napoleon; renewed 1815 and 1818 (see Congress of ◊Vienna); *the Quadruple Alliance 1834* Britain, France, Portugal, and Spain guaranteed the constitutional monarchies of Spain and Portugal against rebels in the Carlist War.

quail any of several genera of small ground-dwelling birds of the family Phasianidae, which also includes grouse, pheasants, bobwhites, and prairie chickens. The common or European quail *Coturnix coturnix* is about 18 cm/7 in long, reddish-brown, with a white throat and yellowish belly. It is found in Europe, Asia, and Africa, and has been introduced to North America.

Quaker popular name, originally derogatory, for a member of the Society of ◊Friends.

quango (acronym for quasi-autonomous nongovernmental organization) any administrative body that is nominally independent but relies on government funding; for example, the Equal Opportunities Commission (1975). Many quangos (such as the Location of Offices Bureau) were abolished by the Thatcher government 1979–90.

quantum theory or *quantum mechanics* in physics, the theory that ◊energy does not have a continuous range of values, but is, instead, absorbed or radiated discontinuously, in multiples of definite, indivisible units called quanta. Just as earlier theory showed how light, generally seen as a wave motion, could also in some ways be seen as composed of discrete particles (◊photons), quantum theory shows how atomic particles such as electrons may also be seen as having wavelike properties. Quantum theory is the basis of particle physics, modern theoretical chemistry, and the solid-state physics that describes the behaviour of the silicon chips used in computers.

quark in physics, the ◊elementary particle that is the fundamental constituent of all hadrons (baryons, such as neutrons and protons, and mesons). There are six types, or 'flavours': up, down, top, bottom, strange, and charm, each of which has three varieties, or 'colours': red, yellow, and blue (visual colour is not meant, although the analogy is useful in many ways). To each quark there is an antiparticle, called an antiquark.

quartz crystalline form of ◊silica SiO_2, one of the most abundant minerals of the Earth's crust (12% by volume). Quartz occurs in many different kinds of rock, including sandstone and granite. It ranks 7 on the Mohs' scale of hardness and is resistant to chemical or mechanical breakdown. Quartzes vary according to the size and purity of their crystals. Crystals of pure quartz are coarse, colourless, and transparent, and this form is usually called rock crystal. Impure coloured varieties, often used as gemstones, include ◊agate, citrine quartz, and ◊amethyst. Quartz is used in ornamental work and industry.

quasar (from *quasi*-stellar object or QSO) one of the most distant extragalactic objects known, discovered 1964–65. Quasars appear starlike, but each emits more energy than 100 giant galaxies. They are thought to be at the centre of galaxies, their brilliance emanating from the stars and gas falling towards an immense ◊black hole at their nucleus.

quassia any tropical American tree of the genus *Quassia*, family Simaroubaceae, with a bitter bark and wood. The heartwood of *Q. amara* is a source of quassiin, an infusion of which was formerly used as a tonic; it is now used in insecticides.

Quaternary period of geological time that began about 2 million years ago and is still in process. It is divided into the ◊Pleistocene and ◊Holocene epochs.

Quayle (J) Dan(forth) 1947– . US Republican politician, vice president from 1989. A congressman for Indiana 1977–81, he became a senator 1981. He is on the right of the party.

Quebec capital and industrial port (textiles, leather, timber, paper, printing, and publishing) of Québec province, on the St Lawrence River, Canada; population (1986) 165,000, metropolitan area 603,000. It was founded 1608.

Québec province of E Canada; *area* 1,540,700 sq km/594,710 sq mi; *capital* Québec; *towns* Montréal, Laval, Sherbrooke, Verdun, Hull, Trois-Rivières; *features* immense water-power resources (for example, the James Bay project); *products* iron, copper, gold, zinc, cereals, potatoes, paper, textiles, fish, maple syrup (70% of world's output); *population* (1991) 6,811,800; *language* French (the only official language since 1974, although 17% speak English). Language laws 1989 prohibit the use of English on street signs; *history* known as New France 1534–1763; captured by the British and became province of Québec 1763–90, Lower Canada 1791–1846, Canada East 1846–67; one of the original provinces 1867. Nationalist feelings 1960s

(despite existing safeguards for Québec's French-derived civil law, customs, religion, and language) led to the foundation of the Parti Québecois by René Lévesque 1968. There was an uprising by Québec Liberation Front (FLQ) separatists 1970; Parti Québecois won power; a referendum on 'sovereignty-association' (separation) was defeated 1980. The Parti Québecois was defeated by the Liberal Party 1989. Robert Bourassa and Liberals returned to power 1985 and enacted restrictive English-language legislation.

Quechua or *Quichua* or *Kechua* member of the largest group of South American Indians. The Quechua live in the Andean region. Their ancestors included the Inca, who established the Quechua language in the region. Quechua is the second official language of Peru and is widely spoken as a lingua franca in Ecuador, Bolivia, Columbia, Argentina, and Chile; it belongs to the Andean-Equatorial family.

Queen Maud Land region of Antarctica W of Enderby Land, claimed by Norway since 1939.

Queens mainly residential borough and county at the W end of Long Island, New York City, USA; population (1980) 1,891,300.

Queensland state in NE Australia; *area* 1,727,200 sq km/666,699 sq mi; *capital* Brisbane; *towns* Townsville, Toowoomba, Cairns; *features* Great Dividing Range, including Mount Bartle Frere 1,657 m/5,438 ft; Great Barrier Reef (collection of coral reefs and islands about 2,000 km/1,250 mi long off the E coast); Gold Coast 32 km/20 mi long S of Brisbane; Mount Isa mining area; Sunshine Coast, a 100-km/60-mi stretch of coast N of Brisbane, between Rainbow Beach and Bribie Island, including the resorts of Noosa Heads, Coolum Beach, and Caloundra; *products* sugar, pineapples, beef, cotton, wool, tobacco, copper, gold, silver, lead, zinc, coal, nickel, bauxite, uranium, natural gas; *population* (1987) 2,650,000; *history* part of New South Wales until 1859, when it became self-governing. In 1989 the ruling National Party was defeated after 32 years in power and replaced by the Labor Party.

quetzal long-tailed Central American bird *Pharomachus mocinno* of the ◊trogon family. The male is brightly coloured, with green, red, blue, and white feathers, and is about 1.3 m/4.3 ft long including tail. The female is smaller and lacks the tail and plumage.

Quezon City former capital of the Philippines 1948–76, NE part of metropolitan ◊Manila (the present capital), on Luzon Island; population (1990) 1,166,800. It was named after the Philippines' first president, Manuel Luis Quezon (1878–1944).

quince small tree *Cydonia oblonga*, family

Rosaceae, native to W Asia. The bitter, yellow, pear-shaped fruit is used in preserves. Flowering quinces, genus *Chaenomeles*, are cultivated for their flowers.

quinine antimalarial drug extracted from the bark of the cinchona tree. Peruvian Indians taught French missionaries how to use the bark 1630, but quinine was not isolated until 1820. It is a bitter alkaloid $C_{20}H_{24}N_2O_2$.

Quisling Vidkun 1887–1945. Norwegian politician. Leader from 1933 of the Norwegian Fascist Party, he aided the Nazi invasion of Norway 1940 by delaying mobilization and urging non-resistance. He was made premier by Hitler 1942, and was arrested and shot as a traitor by the Norwegians 1945. His name became a generic term for a traitor who aids an occupying force.

Quito capital and industrial city (textiles, chemicals, leather, gold, silver) of Ecuador, about 3,000 m/9,850 ft above sea level; population (1986) 1,093,300. It was an ancient settlement, taken by the Incas about 1470 and by the Spanish 1534. It has a temperate climate all year round.

Qum alternative spelling of ▷Qom, city of Iran.

QwaQwa black homeland of South Africa that achieved self-governing status 1974; population (1985) 181,600.

Rabat capital of Morocco, industrial port (cotton textiles, carpets, leather goods) on the Atlantic coast, 177 km/110 mi W of Fez; population (1982) 519,000, Rabat-Salé 842,000. It is named after its original *ribat* or fortified monastery.

rabbit any of several genera of hopping mammals of the order Lagomorpha, which together with ◊hares constitute the family Leporidae. Rabbits differ from hares in bearing naked, helpless young and in occupying burrows. The common rabbit is greyish-brown, long-eared, has legs and feet adapted for running and hopping, and large front teeth. It can grow up to 40 cm/16 in long.

Rabelais François 1495–1553. French satirist, monk, and physician whose name has become synonymous with bawdy humour. He was educated in the Renaissance humanist tradition and was the author of satirical allegories, including *La Vie inestimable de Gargantua/The Inestimable Life of Gargantua* 1535 and *Faits et dits héroïques du grand Pantagruel/Deeds and Sayings of the Great Pantagruel* 1533.

rabies or *hydrophobia* disease of the central nervous system that can afflict all warm-blooded creatures. It is almost invariably fatal once symptoms have developed. Its transmission to humans is generally by a bite from an infected dog.

Rabin Yitzhak 1922– . Israeli Labour politician, prime minister 1974–77, 1992– . Rabin was minister for defence under the conservative Likud coalition government 1984–90. It was his policy of favouring Palestinian self-government in the occupied territories that contributed to the success of the centre-left party in the 1992 elections.

raccoon any of several New World species of carnivorous mammals of the genus *Procyon*, in the family Procyonidae. The common raccoon *P. lotor* is about 60 cm/2 ft long, with a grey-brown body, a black-and-white ringed tail, and a black 'mask' around its eyes.

race in anthropology, term sometimes applied to a physically distinctive group of people, on the basis of their difference from other groups in skin colour, head shape, hair type, and physique. Formerly anthropologists divided the human race into three hypothetical racial groups: Caucasoid, Mongoloid, and Negroid. However, scientific studies have produced no proof of definite genetic racial divisions. Many anthropologists today, therefore, completely reject the concept of race, and social scientists tend to prefer the term ethnic group.

Rachmaninov Sergei (Vasilevich) 1873–1943. Russian composer, conductor, and pianist. After the 1917 Revolution he went to the USA. His dramatically emotional Romantic music has a strong melodic basis and includes operas, such as *Francesca da Rimini* 1906, three symphonies, four piano concertos, piano pieces, and songs.

Racine Jean 1639–1699. French dramatist and exponent of the classical tragedy in French drama. His subjects came from Greek mythology and he observed the rules of classical Greek drama. Most of his tragedies have women in the title role, for example *Andromaque* 1667, *Iphigénie* 1674, and *Phèdre* 1677. After the failure of *Phèdre* in the theatre he no longer wrote for the secular stage, but influenced by Madame de ◊Maintenon wrote two religious dramas, *Esther* 1689 and *Athalie* 1691, which achieved posthumous success.

racism belief in, or set of implicit assumptions about, the superiority of one's own ◊race or ethnic group, often accompanied by prejudice against members of an ethnic group different from one's own. Racism may be used to justify ◊discrimination, verbal or physical abuse, or even genocide, as in Nazi Germany, or as practised by European settlers against American Indians in both North and South America.

rad unit of absorbed radiation dose, now replaced in the SI system by the gray (one rad equals 0.01 gray), but still commonly used. It is defined as the dose when one kilogram of matter absorbs 0.01 joule of radiation energy (formerly, as the dose when one gram absorbs 100 ergs).

radar (acronym for radio direction and ranging) device for locating objects in space, direction finding, and navigation by means of transmitted and reflected high-frequency radio waves.

radar astronomy bouncing of radio waves off objects in the Solar System, with reception and analysis of the 'echoes'. Radar contact with the Moon was first made 1945 and with Venus 1961. The travel time for radio reflections allows the distances of objects to be determined accurately. Analysis of the reflected beam reveals the rotation period and allows the object's surface to be mapped.

radian SI unit (symbol rad) of plane angles, an alternative unit to the ◊degree. It is the angle at the centre of a circle when the centre is joined to the two ends of an arc (part of the circumference) equal in length to the radius of the circle. There are 2p (approximately 6.284) radians in a full circle (360°).

radiation in physics, emission of radiant ◊energy as particles or waves – for example, heat, light, alpha particles, and beta particles (see ◊electromagnetic waves and ◊radioactivity). See also ◊atomic radiation.

radiation sickness sickness resulting from exposure to radiation, including X-rays, gamma rays, neutrons, and other nuclear radiation, as from weapons and fallout. Such radiation ionizes atoms in the body and causes nausea, vomiting, diarrhoea, and other symptoms. The body cells themselves may be damaged even by very small doses, causing ◊leukaemia; genetic changes may be induced in the germ plasm, causing infants to be born damaged or mutated.

radical in chemistry, a group of atoms forming part of a molecule, which acts as a unit and takes part in chemical reactions without disintegration, yet often cannot exist alone; for example, the methyl radical –CH_3, or the carboxyl radical –COOH.

Radical in Britain, supporter of parliamentary reform before the Reform Bill 1832. As a group the Radicals later became the progressive wing of the Liberal Party. During the 1860s (led by Cobden, Bright, and J S Mill) they campaigned for extension of the franchise, free trade, and ◊laissez faire, but after 1870, under the leadership of Joseph Chamberlain and Charles Dilke, they adopted a republican and semi-socialist programme. With the growth of ◊socialism in the later 19th century, Radicalism ceased to exist as an organized movement.

radio transmission and reception of radio waves. In radio transmission a microphone converts ◊sound waves (pressure variations in the air) into ◊electromagnetic waves that are then picked up by a receiving aerial and fed to a loudspeaker, which converts them back into sound waves.

radioactive decay process of continuous disintegration undergone by the nuclei of radioactive elements, such as radium and various isotopes of uranium and the transuranic elements. This changes the element's atomic number, thus transmuting one element into another, and is accompanied by the emission of radiation. Alpha and beta decay are the most common forms.

radioactivity spontaneous alteration of the nuclei of radioactive atoms, accompanied by the emission of radiation. It is the property exhibited by the radioactive ◊isotopes of stable elements and all isotopes of radioactive elements, and can be either natural or induced. See ◊radioactive decay.

radio astronomy study of radio waves emitted naturally by objects in space, by means of a ◊radio telescope. Radio emission comes from hot gases (**thermal radiation**); electrons spiralling in magnetic fields (**synchrotron radiation**); and specific wavelengths (**lines**) emitted by atoms and molecules in space, such as the 21 cm/8 in line emitted by hydrogen gas.

radiocarbon dating or **carbon dating** method of dating organic materials (for example, bone or wood), used in archaeology. Plants take up carbon dioxide gas from the atmosphere and incorporate it into their tissues, and some of that carbon dioxide contains the radioactive isotope of carbon, carbon-14. This decays at a known rate (half of it decays every 5,730 years); the time elapsed since the plant died can therefore be measured in a laboratory. Animals take carbon-14 into their bodies from eating plant tissues and their remains can be similarly dated. After 120,000 years so little carbon-14 is left that no measure is possible (see ◊half-life).

radio frequencies and wavelengths classification of, see ◊electromagnetic waves.

radiography branch of science concerned with the use of radiation (particularly ◊X-rays) to produce images on photographic film or fluorescent

 radio

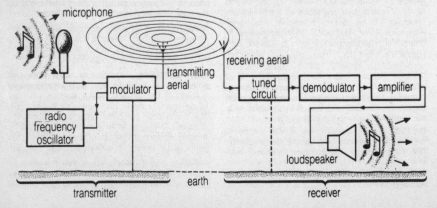

screens. X-rays penetrate matter according to its nature, density, and thickness. In doing so they can cast shadows on photographic film, producing a radiograph. Radiography is widely used in medicine for examining bones and tissues and in industry, for example, to check welded seams in pipelines.

radioisotope (contraction of *radioactive* ▷*isotope*) in physics, a naturally occurring or synthetic radioactive form of an element. Most radioisotopes are made by bombarding a stable element with neutrons in the core of a nuclear reactor. The radiations given off by radioisotopes are easy to detect (hence their use as tracers), can in some instances penetrate substantial thicknesses of materials, and have profound effects (such as genetic ▷mutation on living matter. Although dangerous, radioisotopes are used in the fields of medicine, industry, agriculture, and research.

radio telescope instrument for detecting radio waves from the universe in ▷radio astronomy. Radio telescopes usually consist of a metal bowl that collects and focuses radio waves the way a concave mirror collects and focuses light waves. Radio telescopes are much larger than optical telescopes, because the wavelengths they are detecting are much longer than the wavelength of light. The largest single dish is 305 m/1,000 ft across, at Arecibo, Puerto Rico.

radiotherapy treatment of disease by ▷radiation from X-ray machines or radioactive sources. Radiation, which reduces the activity of dividing cells, is of special value for its effect on malignant tissues, certain nonmalignant tumours, and some diseases of the skin. Similarly, certain radioactive substances may be administered to patients; for example, radioactive iodine for thyroid disease.

radish annual herb *Raphanus sativus*, family Cruciferae. Native to Europe and Asia, it is cultivated for its fleshy, pungent, edible root, which is usually reddish but sometimes white or black.

radium white, radioactive, metallic element, symbol Ra, atomic number 88, relative atomic mass 226.02. It is one of the ▷alkaline earth elements, found in nature in pitchblende and other uranium ores. Of the 16 isotopes, the commonest, Ra-226, has a half-life of 1.622 years. The element was discovered and named in 1898 by Pierre and Marie ▷Curie, who were investigating the residues of pitchblende.

radon colourless, odourless, gaseous, radioactive, nonmetallic element, symbol Rn, atomic number 86, relative atomic mass 222. It is grouped with the ▷inert gases and was formerly considered non-reactive, but is now known to form some compounds with fluorine. Of the 20 known isotopes, only three occur in nature; the longest half-life is 3.82 days.

Raffles Thomas Stamford 1781–1826. British colonial administrator, born in Jamaica. He served in the British East India Company, took part in the capture of Java from the Dutch 1811, and while governor of Sumatra 1818–23 was responsible for the acquisition and founding of Singapore 1819.

Rafsanjani Hojatoleslam Ali Akbar Hashemi 1934– . Iranian politician and cleric, president from 1989. When his former teacher Ayatollah ▷Khomeini returned after the revolution of 1979–80, Rafsanjani became the speaker of the Iranian parliament and, after Khomeini's death, state president and effective political leader.

ragtime syncopated music ('ragged time') in 2/4 rhythm, usually played on piano. It developed in the USA among black musicians in the late 19th century; it was influenced by folk tradition, minstrel shows, and marching bands, and was later incorporated into jazz. Scott ▷Joplin was a leading writer of ragtime pieces, called 'rags'.

ragwort any of several European perennial plants of the genus *Senecio*, family Compositae, usually with yellow-rayed flower heads; some are poisonous.

raï Algerian pop music developed in the 1970s from the Bedouin song form *melhoun*, using synthesizers and electronic drums. Singers often take the name Cheb or Cheba ('young'); Cheb Khaled is an example.

rail any wading bird of the family Rallidae, including the rails proper (genus *Rallus*), coots, moorhens, and gallinules. Rails have dark plumage, a short neck and wings, and long legs. They are 10–45 cm/4–18 in long.

railway method of transport in which trains convey passengers and goods along a twin rail track (at first made of wood but later of iron or steel with ties wedging them apart and relatively parallel). Following the work of English steam pioneers such as James ▷Watt, George ▷Stephenson built the first public steam railway, from Stockton to Darlington, 1825. This heralded extensive railway building in Britain, continental Europe, and North America, providing a fast and economical means of transport and communication. After World War II, steam engines were replaced by electric and diesel engines. At the same time, the growth of road building, air services, and car ownership destroyed the supremacy of the railways. From the 1970s national railway companies began investing in faster intercity services: in the UK, the diesel high-speed train (HST) was introduced; elsewhere such trains run on specially built tracks such as the Shinkansen (Japan) and TGV (France) networks.

rainforest dense forest found on or near the ▷equator where the climate is hot and wet. Over half the tropical rainforests are in Central and South America, the rest in SE Asia and Africa. Although covering approximately 6% of the Earth's land surface, they comprise about 50% of all growing wood on the planet, and harbour at least 40% of the Earth's species (plants and animals). Rainforests are being destroyed at an increasing rate as their valuable timber is harvested and land cleared for agriculture, causing problems of ▷deforestation, ▷soil erosion, and flooding. They also provide the bulk of the oxygen needed for plant and animal respiration. Tropical rainforest once covered 14% of the Earth's land surface. By 1991 over 50% of the world's rainforest had been removed.

Rajasthan state of NW India; *area* 342,200 sq km/ 132,089 sq mi; *capital* Jaipur; *features* includes the larger part of the Thar Desert, where India's first nuclear test was carried out; in the SW is the Ranthambhor wildlife reserve; *products* oilseed, cotton, sugar, asbestos, copper, textiles, cement, glass *population* (1991) 43,880,600; *languages* Rajasthani, Hindi; *religions* 90% Hindu, 3% Muslim; *history* formed 1948; enlarged 1956.

Raleigh or *Ralegh* Walter c. 1552–1618. English adventurer. He made colonizing and exploring voyages to North America 1584–87 and South America 1595, and naval attacks on Spanish ports. His aggressive actions against Spanish interests brought him into conflict with the pacific James I. He was imprisoned for treason 1603–16 and executed on his return from an unsuccessful final expedition to South America.

RAM (acronym for *random-access memory*) in computing, a memory device in the form of a collection of integrated circuits (chips), frequently used in microcomputers. Unlike ▷ROM (read-only memory) chips, RAM chips can be both read from and written to by the computer, but their contents are lost when the power is switched off. Microcomputers of the 1990s may have 10–20 megabytes of RAM.

Rama incarnation of ▷Vishnu, the supreme spirit of Hinduism. He is the hero of the epic poem the *Rāmāyana*, and he is regarded as an example of morality and virtue.

Ramadan in the Muslim ▷calendar, the ninth month of the year. Throughout Ramadan a strict fast is observed during the hours of daylight; Muslims are encouraged to read the whole Koran in commemoration of the Night of Power (which falls during the month) when, it is believed, Muhammad first received his revelations from the angel Gabriel.

Ramakrishna 1834–1886. Hindu sage, teacher, and mystic (one dedicated to achieving oneness with or a direct experience of God or some force beyond the normal world). Ramakrishna claimed that mystical experience was the ultimate aim of religions, and that all religions which led to this goal were equally valid.

Rāmāyana Sanskrit epic of c. 300 BC, in which Rama (an incarnation of the god Vishnu) and his friend Hanuman (the monkey chieftain) strive to recover Rama's wife, Sita, abducted by the demon king Ravana.

Rambert Marie. Adopted name of Cyvia Rambam

1888–1982. Polish-born British ballet dancer and teacher. One of the major innovative and influential figures in modern ballet, she was with the Diaghilev ballet 1912–13, opened the Rambert School 1920, and in 1926 founded the *Ballet Rambert* which she directed. It became a modern dance company from 1966, and was renamed the Rambert Dance Company 1987.

Rameses alternative spelling of ▷Ramses, name of kings of ancient Egypt.

Ramsay William 1852–1916. Scottish chemist who, with Lord Rayleigh, discovered argon 1894. In 1895 Ramsay produced helium and in 1898, in cooperation with Morris Travers, identified neon, krypton, and xenon. In 1903, with Frederick Soddy, he noted the transmutation of radium into helium, which led to the discovery of the density and relative atomic mass of radium. He was awarded the Nobel Prize for Chemistry 1904.

Ramses II or *Rameses II* king of Egypt about 1304–1236 BC, the son of Seti I. He campaigned successfully against the Hittites, and built two rock temples at ▷Abu Simbel in Upper Egypt.

Ramses III or *Rameses III* king of Egypt about 1200–1168 BC. He won a naval victory over the Philistines and other Middle Eastern peoples, and asserted his control over Palestine.

Rangoon former name (until 1989) of ▷Yangon, capital of Myanmar (Burma).

Rao P(amulaparti) V(enkata) Narasimha 1921– Indian politician, see ▷Narasimah Rao.

rape in botany, two plant species of the mustard family Cruciferae, *Brassica rapa* and *B. napus*, grown for their seeds, which yield a pungent edible oil. The common turnip is a variety of the former, and the swede turnip of the latter.

rape in law, sexual intercourse without the consent of the subject. Most cases of rape are of women by men. In 1991 rape within marriage became a criminal offence (as was already the case in Scotland and the Republic of Ireland).

Raphael (Raffaello Sanzio) 1483–1520. Italian painter, one of the greatest of the High Renaissance, active in Perugia, Florence, and Rome (from 1508), where he painted frescoes in the Vatican, including *School of Athens* and the *Disputa* (1508–11). His religious and mythological scenes are harmoniously composed; his portraits enhance the character of his sitters and express dignity. Many of his designs were engraved.

rap music rapid, rhythmic chant over a prerecorded repetitive backing track. Rap emerged in New York 1979 as part of the ▷hip-hop culture, although the macho, swaggering lyrics that initially predominated have roots in ritual boasts and insults. Different styles were flourishing by the 1990s: jazz rap, funk rap, reggae rap, and so on.

rare-earth element alternative name for ▷lanthanide.

raspberry prickly cane plant of the genus *Rubus* of the Rosaceae family, native to Eurasia and North America, with white flowers followed by red fruits. These are eaten fresh and used for jam and wine.

Rasputin (Russian 'dissolute') Grigory Efimovich 1871–1916. Siberian Eastern Orthodox mystic who acquired influence over the tsarina ▷Alexandra, wife of ▷Nicholas II, and was able to make political and ecclesiastical appointments. His abuse of power and notorious debauchery (reputedly including the tsarina) led to his murder by a group of nobles.

Rastafarianism religion originating in the West Indies, based on the ideas of Marcus ▷Garvey, who called on black people to return to Africa and set up a black-governed country there. When Haile Selassie (*Ras Tafari*, 'Lion of Judah') was crowned emperor of Ethiopia 1930, this was seen as a fulfilment of prophecy and Rastafarians acknowledged him as the Messiah, the incarnation of God (*Jah*). The use of ganja (marijuana) is a sacrament. There are no churches.

rat any of numerous long-tailed ▷rodents (especially of the families Muridae and Cricetidae) larger than mice and usually with scaly, naked tails. The genus *Rattus* in the family Muridae includes the rats found in human housing.

rates in the UK, a tax levied on industrial and commercial property (and until the introduction of the ▷poll tax 1989–90, also on residential property) by ▷local government to pay for local amenities such as roads, footpaths, refuse collection and disposal, and community and welfare activities.

ratio measure of the relative size of two quantities or of two measurements (in similar units), expressed as a proportion. For example, the ratio of vowels to consonants in the alphabet is 5:21; the ratio of 500 m to 2 km is 500:2,000, or 1:4.

rationalism in theology, the belief that human reason rather than divine revelation is the correct means of ascertaining truth and regulating behaviour. In philosophy, rationalism takes the view that self-evident propositions deduced by reason are the sole basis of all knowledge (disregarding experience of the senses).

rattlesnake any of various New World pit ▷vipers of the genera *Crotalus* and *Sistrurus* (the massasaugas and pygmy rattlers), distinguished by horny flat segments of the tail, which rattle when vibrated as a warning to attackers. They can grow to 2.5 m/8 ft long. The venom injected by some rattlesnakes can be fatal.

Rauschenberg Robert 1925– . US Pop artist, a creator of happenings (art in live performance) and incongruous multimedia works such as *Monogram* 1959 (Moderna Museet, Stockholm), a car tyre around the body of a stuffed goat daubed with paint. In the 1960s he returned to painting and used the silk-screen printing process to transfer images to canvas. He also made collages.

Ravel (Joseph) Maurice 1875–1937. French composer. His work is characterized by its sensuousness, unresolved dissonances, and 'tone colour'. Examples are the piano pieces *Pavane pour une infante défunte* 1899 and *Jeux d'eau* 1901, and the ballets *Daphnis et Chloë* 1912 and *Boléro* 1928.

raven any of several large ▷crows (genus *Corvus*). The common raven *C. corax* is about 60 cm/ 2 ft long, and has black, lustrous plumage. It is a scavenger, and is found only in the northern hemisphere.

Rawalpindi city in Punjab province, Pakistan, in the foothills of the Himalayas; population (1981) 928,400. Industries include oil refining, iron, chemicals, and furniture.

ray any of several orders (especially Ragiformes) of cartilaginous fishes with a flattened body, winglike pectoral fins, and a whiplike tail.

Ray Satyajit 1921–1992. Indian film director, internationally known for his trilogy of life in his native Bengal: *Pather Panchali*, *Unvanquished*, and *The World of Apu* 1955–59. Later films include *The Music Room* 1958, *Charulata* 1964, *The Chess Players* 1977, and *The Home and the World* 1984.

rayon any of various shiny textile fibres and fabrics made from cellulose. It is produced by pressing whatever cellulose solution is used through very small holes and solidifying the resulting filaments. A common type is viscose, which consists of regenerated filaments of pure cellulose. Acetate and triacetate are kinds of rayon consisting of filaments of cellulose acetate and triacetate.

razorbill North Atlantic sea bird *Alca torda* of the auk family, which breeds on cliffs and migrates south in winter. It has a curved beak and is black above and white below. It uses its wings as paddles when diving. Razorbills are common off Newfoundland.

razor-shell or *razor-fish*; US name *razor clam* any bivalve mollusc in two genera *Ensis* and *Solen* with narrow, elongated shells, resembling an old-fashioned razor handle and delicately coloured. They can burrow rapidly into sand and are good swimmers.

reaction in chemistry, the coming together of two or more atoms, ions, or molecules with the result that a chemical change takes place. The nature of the reaction is portrayed by a chemical equation.

Reagan Ronald (Wilson) 1911– . 40th president of the USA 1981–89, a Republican. He was governor of California 1966–74, and a former Hollywood actor. Reagan was a hawkish and popular president. He adopted an aggressive policy in Central America, attempting to overthrow the government of Nicaragua, and invading ▷Grenada 1983. In 1987, ▷Irangate was investigated by the Tower Commission; Reagan admitted that USA–Iran negotiations had become an 'arms for hostages deal', but denied knowledge of resultant funds being illegally sent to the Contras in Nicaragua. He increased military spending (sending the national budget deficit to record levels), cut social programmes, introduced deregulation of domestic markets, and cut taxes. His ▷Strategic Defense Initiative, announced 1983, proved controversial owing to the cost and unfeasibility. He was succeeded by George ▷Bush.

realism in medieval philosophy, the theory that 'universals' have existence, not simply as names for entities but as entities in their own right. It is thus opposed to nominalism. In contemporary philosophy, the term stands for the doctrine that there is an intuitively appreciated reality apart from what is presented to the consciousness. It is opposed to idealism.

receiver in law, a person appointed by a court to collect and manage the assets of an individual, company, or partnership in serious financial difficulties. In the case of bankruptcy, the assets may be sold and distributed by a receiver to creditors.

recession in economics, a fall in business activity lasting more than a few months, causing stagnation in a country's output. A serious recession is called a *slump*.

recessive gene in genetics, an allele (alternative form of a gene) that will show in the phenotype (observed characteristics of an organism) only if its partner allele on the paired chromosome is similarly recessive. Such an allele will not show if its partner is dominant, that is if the organism is heterozygous for a particular characteristic. Alleles for blue eyes in humans, and for shortness in pea plants are recessive. Most mutant alleles are recessive and therefore are only rarely expressed (see haemophilia and sickle cell disease).

Recife industrial seaport (cotton textiles, sugar refining, fruit canning, flour milling) and naval base in Brazil; capital of Pernambuco state, at the mouth of the river Capibaribe; population (1991) 1,335,700. It was founded 1504.

recombination in genetics, any process that recombines, or 'shuffles', the genetic material, thus increasing genetic variation in the offspring. The two main processes of recombination both occur during meiosis (reduction division of cells). One is *crossing over*, in which chromosome pairs exchange segments; the other is the random reassortment of chromosomes that occurs when each gamete (sperm or egg) receives only one of each chromosome pair.

Reconstruction in US history, the period 1865–77 after the Civil War during which the nation was reunited under the federal government after the defeat of the Southern Confederacy.

recorder in music, a pure-toned instrument of the ▷woodwind family, in which the single reed is integrated with the mouthpiece. Recorders are played in a consort (ensemble) of matching tone and comprise sopranino, descant, treble, tenor, and bass.

Record Office, Public government office containing the English national records since the Norman Conquest, brought together from courts of law and government departments, including the Domesday Book, the Gunpowder Plot papers, and the log of HMS *Victory* at Trafalgar. It was established 1838 in Chancery Lane, London; records dating from the 18th century onwards have been housed at Kew, London, since 1976.

record player device for reproducing recorded sound stored as a spiral groove on a vinyl disc. A motor-driven turntable rotates the record at a constant speed, and a stylus or needle on the head of a pick-up is made to vibrate by the undulations in the record groove. These vibrations are then converted to electrical signals by a transducer in the head (often a ▷piezoelectric crystal). After amplification, the signals pass to one or more loudspeakers, which convert them into sound. Alternative formats are ▷compact disc and ▷tape recording, magnetic.

recycling processing of industrial and household waste (such as paper, glass, and some metals and plastics) so that it can be reused. This saves expenditure on scarce raw materials, slows down the depletion of ▷nonrenewable resources, and helps to reduce pollution. Most British recycling schemes are voluntary, and rely on people taking waste items to a central collection point.

red blood cell or *erythrocyte* the most common type of blood cell, responsible for transporting oxygen around the body. It contains haemoglobin, which combines with oxygen from the lungs to form oxyhaemoglobin. When transported to the tissues, these cells are able to release the oxygen because the oxyhaemoglobin splits into its original constituents. Mammalian erythrocytes are disc-shaped with a depression in the centre and no nucleus; they are manufactured in the bone marrow and, in humans, last for only four months before being destroyed in the liver and spleen. Those of other vertebrates are oval and nucleated.

Red Cross international relief agency founded by the Geneva Convention 1864 at the instigation of the Swiss doctor Henri Dunant to assist the wounded and prisoners in war. Its symbol is a symmetrical red cross on a white ground. In addition to dealing with associated problems of war, such as refugees and the care of the disabled, the Red Cross is increasingly concerned with victims of natural disasters – floods, earthquakes, epidemics, and accidents.

red dwarf any star that is cool, faint, and small (about one-tenth the mass and diameter of the Sun). Red dwarfs burn slowly, and have estimated lifetimes of 100 billion years. They may be the most abundant type of star, but are difficult to see because they are so faint. Two of the closest stars to the Sun, Proxima Centauri and ▷Barnard's Star, are red dwarfs.

Redford (Charles) Robert 1937– . US actor and film director. His first starring role was in *Barefoot In The Park* 1967, followed by *Butch Cassidy and the Sundance Kid* 1969, and *The Sting* (both with Paul ▷Newman). His other films as an actor include *All the President's Men* 1976 and *Out of Africa* 1985. He directed *Ordinary People* 1980 and *The Milagro Beanfield War* 1988.

red giant any large bright star with a cool surface. It is thought to represent a late stage in the evolution of a star like the Sun, as it runs out of hydrogen fuel at its centre. Red giants have diameters between 10 and 100 times that of the Sun. They are very bright because they are so large, although their surface temperature is lower than that of the Sun, about 2,000–3,000K (1,700°C/3,000°F–2,700°C/5,000°F)

Redgrave Michael 1908–1985. British actor. His stage roles included Hamlet and Lear (Shakespeare), Uncle Vanya (Chekhov), and the schoolmaster in Rattigan's *The Browning Version* (filmed 1951). On screen he appeared in *The Lady Vanishes* 1938, *The Importance of Being Earnest* 1952, and *Goodbye Mr Chips* 1959. He was the father of Vanessa and Lynn Redgrave, both actresses.

Redgrave Vanessa 1937– . British actress. She has played Shakespeare's Lady Macbeth and Cleopatra on the stage, and the title role in the film *Julia* 1976 (Academy Award). Recent plays include *Three Sisters* 1990 and *When She Danced* 1991; recent films include *Orpheus Descending* 1990 and *Howard's End* 1992. She is active in left-wing politics. She is the daughter of Michael Redgrave.

Red Guard one of the school and college students, wearing red armbands, active in the ▷Cultural Revolution in China 1966–69. The armed workers who took part in the ▷Russian Revolution of 1917 were also called Red Guards.

Red Sea submerged section of the ▷Great Rift Valley (2,000 km/1,200 mi long and up to 320 km/ 200 mi wide). Egypt, Sudan, and Ethiopia (in Africa) and Saudi Arabia (Asia) are on its shores.

red shift in astronomy, the lengthening of the wavelengths of light from an object as a result of the object's motion away from us. It is an example of the Doppler effect. The red shift in light from galaxies is evidence that the universe is expanding.

redstart any bird of the genus Phoenicurus. A member of the thrush family, it winters in Africa and spends the summer in Eurasia. The male has a dark grey head (with white mark on the forehead and black face) and dark grey back, brown wings with lighter underparts, and a red tail.

reduction in chemistry, the gain of electrons, loss of oxygen, or gain of hydrogen by an atom, ion, or molecule during a chemical reaction.

redwood giant coniferous tree, one of the two types of ▷sequoia.

reed any of various perennial tall, slender grasses of wet or marshy environments; in particular, species of the genera *Phragmites* and *Arundo*; also the stalk of any of these plants. The common reed *P. australis* attains a height of 3 m/10 ft.

Reed Lou 1942– . US rock singer, songwriter, and guitarist; former member (1965–70) of the New York avant-garde group **the Velvet Underground**, perhaps the most influential band of the period. His solo work deals largely with urban alienation and angst, and includes the albums *Berlin* 1973, *Street Hassle* 1978, and *New York* 1989.

referendum procedure whereby a decision on proposed legislation is referred to the electorate for settlement by direct vote of all the people.

reflection throwing back or deflection of waves, such as ◁light or ▷sound waves, when they hit a surface. The *law of reflection* states that the angle of incidence (the angle between the ray and a perpendicular line drawn to the surface) is equal to the angle of reflection (the angle between the reflected ray and a perpendicular to the surface).

reflex in animals, a very rapid automatic response to a particular stimulus. It is controlled by the ▷nervous system. A reflex involves only a few nerve cells, unlike the slower but more complex responses produced by the many processing nerve cells of the brain.

reflex camera camera that uses a mirror and prisms to reflect light passing through the lens into the viewfinder, showing the photographer the exact scene that is being shot. When the shutter button is released the mirror springs out of the way, allowing light to reach the film. The most common type is the single-lens reflex (▷SLR) camera. The twin-lens reflex (▷TLR) camera has two lenses: one has a mirror for viewing, the other is used for exposing the film.

Reform Acts UK acts of Parliament 1832, 1867, and 1884 that extended voting rights and redistributed parliamentary seats; also known as ▷Representation of the People Acts.

Reformation religious and political movement in 16th-century Europe to reform the Roman Catholic church, which led to the establishment of Protestant churches. Anticipated from the 12th century by the Waldenses, Lollards, and Hussites, it became effective in the 16th century when the absolute monarchies gave it support by challenging the political power of the papacy and confiscating church wealth. Martin Luther began the Reformation in Wittenburg, Germany 1517 when he protested against the sale of indulgences; Henry VIII renounced papal supremacy and proclaimed himself head of the Church of England 1533; John Calvin founded the doctrine of Calvinism in

refrigeration

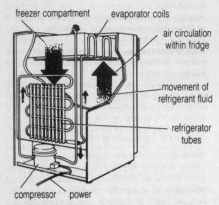

freezer compartment · evaporator coils · air circulation within fridge · movement of refrigerant fluid · refrigerator tubes · compressor · power

Switzerland 1541; John Knox founded the Church of Scotland 1559. The ▷Counter-Reformation was initiated by the Roman Catholic church at the Council of Trent 1545–63.

refraction bending of a wave of light, heat, or sound when it passes from one medium to another. Refraction occurs because waves travel at different velocities in different media.

refractory (of a material) able to resist high temperature, for example ▷ceramics made from clay, minerals, or other earthy materials. Furnaces are lined with refractory materials such as silica and dolomite. Alumina (aluminium oxide) is an excellent refractory, often used for the bodies of spark plugs. Titanium and tungsten are often called refractory metals because they are temperature resistant.

refrigeration use of technology to transfer heat from cold to warm, against the normal temperature gradient, so that a body can remain substantially colder than its surroundings. Refrigeration equipment is used for the chilling and deep freezing of food in food technology, and in air conditioners and industrial processes.

refugee person fleeing from oppressive or dangerous conditions (such as political, religious, or military persecution) and seeking refuge in a foreign country. In 1991 there were an estimated 17 million refugees worldwide, whose resettlement and welfare were the responsibility of the United Nations High Commission for Refugees (UNHCR).

Regency in Britain, the years 1811–20 during which ▷George IV (then Prince of Wales) acted as regent for his father ▷George III.

Regency style style of architecture and interior furnishings popular in England during the late 18th and early 19th centuries. The style is characterized by its restrained simplicity and its imitation of ancient classical elements, often Greek. Architects

of this period include Decimus Burton (1800–81), Henry Holland (1746–1806), and John ▷Nash.

regeneration in biology, regrowth of a new organ or tissue after the loss or removal of the original. It is common in plants, where a new individual can often be produced from a 'cutting' of the original. In animals, regeneration of major structures is limited to lower organisms; certain lizards can regrow their tails if these are lost, and new flatworms can grow from a tiny fragment of an old one.

reggae predominant form of West Indian popular music of the 1970s and 1980s, characterized by a heavily accented offbeat and a thick bass line. The lyrics often refer to ▷Rastafarianism. Musicians include Bob Marley, Lee 'Scratch' Perry (1940– , performer and producer), and the group Black Uhuru (1974–). Reggae is also played in the UK, South Africa, and elsewhere.

Reich Steve 1936– . US composer. His Minimalist music consists of simple patterns carefully superimposed and modified to highlight constantly changing melodies and rhythms; examples are *Phase Patterns* for four electronic organs 1970, *Music for Mallet Instruments, Voices, and Organ* 1973, and *Music for Percussion and Keyboards* 1984.

Reims (English *Rheims*) capital of Champagne-Ardenne region, France; population (1982) 199,000. It is the centre of the champagne industry and has textile industries as well. Ceded to England 1420 under the Treaty of Troyes, it was retaken by Joan of Arc, who had Charles VII consecrated in the 13th-century cathedral. In World War II, the German High Command formally surrendered here to US general Eisenhower 7 May 1945.

reincarnation belief that after death the human soul or the spirit of a plant or animal may live again in another human or animal. It is part of the teachings of many religions and philosophies, for example ancient Egyptian and Greek (the philosophies of Pythagoras and Plato), Buddhism, Hinduism, Jainism, certain Christian heresies (such as the Cathars), and theosophy. It is also referred to as *transmigration* or metempsychosis.

reindeer or *caribou* deer *Rangifer tarandus* of Arctic and subarctic regions, common to North America and Eurasia. About 120 cm/4 ft at the shoulder, it has a thick, brownish coat and broad hooves well adapted to travel over snow. It is the only deer in which both sexes have antlers; these can grow to 150 cm/5 ft long, and are shed in winter.

relative atomic mass mass of an atom relative to one-twelfth the mass of an atom of carbon-12. It depends on the number of protons and neutrons in the atom, the electrons having negligible mass. If more than one ▷isotope of the element is present, the relative atomic mass is calculated by taking an average that takes account of the relative proportions of each isotope, resulting in values that are not whole numbers. The term *atomic weight*, although commonly used, is incorrect.

relativity in physics, the theory of the relative rather than absolute character of motion and mass, and the interdependence of matter, time, and space, as developed by Albert ▷Einstein in two phases: *special theory* (1905) Starting with the premises that (1) the laws of nature are the same for all observers in unaccelerated motion, and (2) the speed of light is independent of the motion of its source, Einstein postulated that the time interval between two events was longer for an observer in whose frame of reference the events occur in different places than for the observer for whom they occur at the same place.

general theory of relativity (1915) The geometrical properties of space–time were to be conceived as modified locally by the presence of a body with mass. A planet's orbit around the Sun (as observed in three-dimensional space) arises from its natural trajectory in modified space–time; there is no need to invoke, as Isaac Newton did, a force of ▷gravity coming from the Sun and acting on the planet. Einstein's theory predicted slight differences in the orbits of the planets from Newton's theory, which were observable in the case of Mercury. The new theory also said light rays should bend when they pass by a massive object, owing to the object's effect on local space–time. The predicted bending of starlight was observed during the eclipse of the Sun 1919, when light from distant stars passing close to the Sun was not masked by sunlight.

relay in electrical engineering, an electromagnetic switch. A small current passing through a coil of wire wound around an iron core attracts an ▷armature whose movement closes a pair of sprung contacts to complete a secondary circuit, which may carry a large current or activate other devices. The solid-state equivalent is a thyristor switching device.

relief in architecture, carved figures and other forms that project from the background. The Italian terms *basso-rilievo* (low relief), *mezzo-rilievo* (middle relief), and *alto-rilievo* (high relief) are used according to the extent to which the sculpture projects. The French term *bas-relief* is commonly used to mean low relief.

religion code of belief or philosophy, which often involves the worship of a ▷God or gods. Belief in a supernatural power is not essential (absent in, for example, Buddhism and Confucianism), but faithful adherence is usually considered to be rewarded, for example by escape from human existence (Buddhism), by a future existence (Christianity, Islam), or by worldly benefit (Sōka Gakkai Buddhism).

rem acronym of *roentgen equivalent man* SI unit of radiation dose equivalent. The rem has now been replaced in the SI system by the ▷sievert (one rem equals 0.01 sievert), but remains in common use.

REM acronym for rapid eye movement; see ▷REM sleep.

remand in law, the committing of an accused but not convicted person into custody or to release on bail pending a court hearing. In the UK, *remand in custody* is made for not more than eight days at a time but can be renewed for further eight-day periods if the court so decides.

Rembrandt Harmensz van Rijn 1606–1669. Dutch painter and etcher, one of the most prolific and significant artists in Europe of the 17th century. Between 1629 and 1669 he painted some 60 penetrating self-portraits. He also painted religious subjects, and produced about 300 etchings and over 1,000 drawings. His group portraits include *The Anatomy Lesson of Dr Tulp* 1632 (Mauritshuis, The Hague) and *The Night Watch* 1642 (Rijksmuseum, Amsterdam). He is known for his skilful handling of light and shadow and his warm browns and yellows and flesh tones. Although he enjoyed great prosperity during his life, Rembrandt became bankrupt 1656 and died in poverty.

remora any of a family of warm-water fishes that have an adhesive disc on the head, by which they attach themselves to whales, sharks, and turtles. These provide the remora with shelter and transport, as well as food in the form of parasites on the host's skin.

remote sensing gathering and recording information from a distance. Space probes have sent back photographs and data about planets as distant as Neptune. In archaeology, surface survey techniques provide information without disturbing subsurface deposits.

REM sleep (acronym for rapid-eye-movement sleep) phase of sleep that recurs several times nightly in humans and is associated with dreaming. The eyes flicker quickly beneath closed lids.

Renaissance period and intellectual movement in European cultural history that is traditionally seen as ending the Middle Ages and beginning modern times. The Renaissance started in Italy in the 14th century and flourished in W Europe until about the 17th century. The aim of Renaissance education was to produce the 'complete human being' (*Renaissance man*), conversant in the humanities, mathematics, and science (including their application in war), the arts and crafts, and athletics and sport; to enlarge the bounds of learning and geographical knowledge; to encourage the growth of scepticism and free thought, and the study and imitation of Greek and Latin literature and art. The revival of interest in classical Greek and Roman culture inspired artists such as Leonardo da Vinci, Michelangelo, and Dürer, architects such as Brunelleschi and Alberti, writers such as Petrarch and Boccaccio. Scientists and explorers proliferated as well.

Renaissance art movement in European art of the 15th and 16th centuries. It began in Florence, Italy, with the rise of a spirit of humanism and a new appreciation of the Classical past. In painting and sculpture this led to greater naturalism and interest in anatomy and perspective. Renaissance art peaked around 1500 with the careers of Leonardo da Vinci, Raphael, Michelangelo, and Titian in Italy and Dürer in Germany.

René France-Albert 1935– . Seychelles left-wing politician, the country's first prime minister after independence and president from 1977 after a coup. He has followed a non-nuclear policy of nonalignment.

renewable energy power from any source that replenishes itself. Most renewable systems rely on ⟡solar energy directly or through the weather cycle as ⟡wave power, ⟡hydroelectric power, or wind power via ⟡wind turbines, or solar energy collected by plants (alcohol fuels, for example). In addition, the gravitational force of the Moon can be harnessed through tidal power stations, and the heat trapped in the centre of the Earth is used via ⟡geothermal energy systems.

renewable resource natural resource that is replaced by natural processes in a reasonable amount of time. Soil, water, forests, plants, and animals are all renewable resources as long as they are properly conserved. Solar, wind, wave, and geothermal energies are based on renewable resources.

Reni Guido 1575–1642. Italian painter, active in Bologna and Rome (about 1600–14), who is considered one of the greatest Italian artists of the 17th century. His work includes the fresco *Phoebus and the Hours Preceded by Aurora* 1613 (Casino Rospigliosi, Rome). His workshop in Bologna produced numerous religious images, including Madonnas.

Rennes industrial city (oil refining, chemicals, electronics, cars) and capital of Ille-et-Vilaine *département*, W France, at the confluence of the Ille and Vilaine, 56 km/35 mi SE of St Malo; population (1982) 234,000. It was the old capital of Brittany.

rennet extract, traditionally obtained from a calf's stomach, that contains the enzyme rennin, used to coagulate milk in the cheesemaking process. The enzyme can now be chemically produced.

Renoir Jean 1894–1979. French director whose films, characterized by their profound humanism, include *Boudu sauvé des eaux/Boudu Saved from Drowning* 1932, *La Grande Illusion* 1937, and *La Règle du jeu/The Rules of the Game* 1939. In 1975 he received an honorary Academy Award for his life's work. He was the son of the painter Pierre-Auguste Renoir.

Renoir Pierre-Auguste 1841–1919. French Impressionist painter. He met Monet and Sisley in the early 1860s, and together they formed the nucleus of the Impressionist movement. He developed a lively, colourful painting style with feathery brushwork and painted many pictures of people at leisure

outdoors and voluptuous female nudes, such as *The Bathers* about 1884–87 (Philadelphia Museum of Art, USA). Other well-known paintings include *Luncheon of the Boating Party* 1881 and *Umbrellas* about 1881–84. In his later years he turned to sculpture.

replication in biology, production of copies of the genetic material, DNA; it occurs during cell division (⟡mitosis and ⟡meiosis). Most mutations are caused by mistakes during replication.

Representation of the People Acts series of UK acts of Parliament from 1867 that extended voting rights, creating universal suffrage in 1928.

reproduction in biology, process by which a living organism produces other organisms similar to itself. There are two kinds: ⟡asexual reproduction and ⟡sexual reproduction.

reptile any member of a class (Reptilia) of vertebrates, dating back over 300 million years. Unlike amphibians, reptiles have hard-shelled, yolk-filled eggs that are laid on land and from which fully formed young are born. Some snakes and lizards retain their eggs and give birth to live young. Reptiles are cold-blooded, produced from eggs, and the skin is usually covered with scales.

republic country where the head of state is not a monarch, either hereditary or elected, but usually a president whose role may or may not include political functions.

Republican Party one of the USA's two main political parties, formed 1854. It is a right-wing party, favouring capital and big business and opposing state subvention and federal controls. In the late 20th century most presidents have come from the Republican Party but in Congress Republicans have been outnumbered.

reserve currency in economics, a country's holding of internationally acceptable means of payment (major foreign currencies or gold); central banks also hold the ultimate reserve of money for their domestic banking sector. On the asset side of company balance sheets, undistributed profits are listed as reserves.

resin substance exuded from pines, firs, and other trees in gummy drops that harden in air. Varnishes are common products of the hard resins, and ointments come from the soft resins.

resistance in physics, that property of a substance that restricts the flow of electricity through it, associated with the conversion of electrical energy to heat; also the magnitude of this property. Resistance depends on many factors, such as the nature of the material, its temperature, dimensions, and thermal properties; degree of impurity; the nature and state of illumination of the surface; and the frequency and magnitude of the current. The SI unit of resistance is the ohm.

resistance movement opposition movement in a

country occupied by an enemy or colonial power, especially in the 20th century; for example, the French resistance to Nazism in World War II.

resonance rapid and uncontrolled increase in the size of a vibration when the vibrating object is subject to a force varying at its natural frequency. In a trombone, for example, the length of the air column in the instrument is adjusted until it resonates with the note being sounded. Resonance effects are also produced by many electrical circuits. Tuning a radio, for example, is done by adjusting the natural frequency of the receiver circuit until it coincides with the frequency of the radio waves falling on the aerial.

respiration biochemical process whereby food molecules are progressively broken down (oxidized) to release energy in the form of ◊ATP. In most organisms this requires oxygen, but in some bacteria the oxidant is the nitrate or sulphate ion instead. In all higher organisms, respiration occurs in the ◊mitochondria. Respiration is also used to mean breathing, although this is more accurately described as a form of gas exchange.

Restoration in English history, the period when the monarchy, in the person of Charles II, was reestablished after the English Civil War and the fall of the ◊Protectorate 1660.

Restoration comedy style of English theatre, dating from the Restoration. It witnessed the first appearance of women on the English stage, most notably in the 'breeches part', specially created in order to costume the actress in male attire, thus revealing her figure to its best advantage. The genre placed much emphasis on sexual antics. Examples include Wycherley's *The Country Wife* 1675, Congreve's *The Way of the World* 1700, and Farquhar's *The Beaux' Stratagem* 1707.

restrictive trade practices agreements between people in a particular trade or business that keep the cost of goods or services artificially high (for example, an agreement to restrict output) or provide barriers to outsiders entering the trade or business.

resurrection in Christian, Jewish, and Muslim belief, the rising from the dead that all souls will experience at the Last Judgement. The Resurrection also refers to Jesus rising from the dead on the third day after his crucifixion, a belief central to Christianity and celebrated at Easter.

resuscitation steps taken to revive anyone on the brink of death. The most successful technique for life-threatening emergencies, such as electrocution, near-drowning, or heart attack, is mouth-to-mouth resuscitation. Medical and paramedical staff are trained in cardiopulmonary resuscitation: the use of specialized equipment and techniques to attempt to restart the breathing and/or heartbeat and stabilize the patient long enough for more definitive treatment.

retail price index (RPI) indicator of variations in the ◊cost of living, superseded in the USA by the consumer price index.

retriever any of several breeds of hunting dogs developed for retrieving birds and other small game. The commonest breeds are the **Labrador retriever**, large, smooth-coated, and usually black or yellow; and the **golden retriever**, with either flat or wavy coat. They can grow to 60 cm/2 ft high and weigh 40 kg/90 lbs. They are used in police work and as guide dogs for the blind; they are popular companion dogs.

retrovirus any of a family (*Retroviridae*) of ◊viruses containing the genetic material ◊RNA rather than the more usual ◊DNA.

Réunion French island of the Mascarenes group, in the Indian Ocean, 650 km/400 mi E of Madagascar and 180 km/110 mi SW of Mauritius; *area* 2,512 sq km/970 sq mi; *capital* St Denis; *physical* forested, rising in Piton de Neiges to 3,069 m/10,072 ft; *features* administers five uninhabited islands, also claimed by Madagascar; *products* sugar, maize, vanilla, tobacco, rum; *population* (1987) 565,000; *history* explored by Portuguese (the first European visitors) 1513; annexed by Louis XIII of France 1642; overseas *département* of France 1946; overseas region 1972.

Revere Paul 1735–1818. American revolutionary, a Boston silversmith, who carried the news of the approach of British troops to Lexington and Concord (see ◊American Revolution) on the night of 18 April 1775. On the next morning the first shots of the Revolution were fired at Lexington. Longfellow's poem 'The Midnight Ride of Paul Revere' commemorates the event.

revisionism political theory derived from Marxism that moderates one or more of the basic tenets of Marx, and is hence condemned by orthodox Marxists.

revolution any rapid, far-reaching, or violent change in the political, social, or economic structure of society. It is usually applied to political change: examples include the American Revolution, where colonists broke free from their colonial ties and established a sovereign, independent nation; the French Revolution, where an absolute monarchy was overthrown by opposition from inside the country and a popular uprising; and the Russian Revolution, where a repressive monarchy was overthrown by those seeking to institute widespread social and economic changes based on a socialist model. See also ◊revolutions of 1989.

Revolutionary Wars series of wars 1791–1802 between France and the combined armies of England, Austria, Prussia, and others, during the period of the ◊French Revolution.

revolutions of 1989 popular uprisings in many countries of Eastern Europe against communist rule, prompted by internal reforms in the USSR that permitted dissent within its sphere of influence. By 1990 nearly all the Warsaw Pact countries had moved from one-party to pluralist political systems, in most cases peacefully but with growing hostility between various nationalist and ethnic groups.

revolutions of 1848 series of revolts in various parts of Europe against monarchical rule. While some of the revolutionaries had republican ideas, many more were motivated by economic grievances. The revolution began in France with the overthrow of Louis Philippe and then spread to Italy, the Austrian Empire, and Germany, where the short-lived Frankfurt Parliament put forward ideas about political unity in Germany. None of the revolutions enjoyed any lasting success, and most were violently suppressed within a few months.

revue stage presentation involving short satirical and topical items in the form of songs, sketches, and monologues; it originated in the late 19th century. By the 1920s and 30s the 'intimate revue' had become increasingly popular, employing writers such as Noël Coward. During the 1960s the satirical revue took off with the Cambridge Footlights' production *Beyond the Fringe*, establishing the revue tradition among the young and at fringe theatrical events.

Reykjavik capital (from 1918) and chief port of Iceland, on the SW coast; population (1988) 93,000. Fish processing is the main industry. Reykjavik is heated by underground mains fed by volcanic springs. It was a seat of Danish administration from 1801 to 1918.

Reynolds Albert 1933– . Irish politician, prime minister from 1992. He joined Fianna Fáil 1977, and held various ministerial posts including minister for industry and commerce 1987–88 and minister of finance 1989–92. He became prime minister after Charles ⟡Haughey was forced to resign 1992.

Reynolds Joshua 1723–1792. English portrait painter, active in London from 1752. He became the first president of the Royal Academy 1768. His portraits display a facility for striking and characterful compositions in a consciously grand manner. He often borrowed classical poses, for example *Mrs Siddons as the Tragic Muse* 1784 (San Marino, California, USA). His *Discourses on Art* 1769–91 contain his theories on the aims of academic art.

rhapsody in music, instrumental fantasia, often based on folk melodies, such as Liszt's *Hungarian Rhapsodies* 1853–54. Rhapsodies are usually emotionally charged and do not adhere to any strict structure.

Rheims English version of ⟡Reims, city in France.

Rheinland-Pfalz German name for the ⟡Rhineland-Palatinate region, Germany.

rhenium heavy, silver-white, metallic element, symbol Re, atomic number 75, relative atomic mass 186.2. It has chemical properties similar to those of manganese and a very high melting point (5,756°F/3,180°C) that makes it valuable as an ingredient in alloys. It was identified 1925 and named after the Rhine river.

rhesus factor ⟡protein on the surface of red blood cells of humans, which is involved in the rhesus blood group system. Most individuals possess the main rhesus factor (Rh+), but those without this factor (Rh–) produce ⟡antibodies if they come into contact with it. The name comes from rhesus monkeys, in whose blood rhesus factors were first found.

rhesus monkey macaque monkey *Macaca mulatta* found in N India and SE Asia. It has a pinkish face, red buttocks, and long, straight, brown-grey hair. It can grow up to 60 cm/2 ft long, with a 20 cm/8 in tail.

rheumatic fever or *acute rheumatism* acute or chronic illness characterized by fever and painful swelling of joints. Some victims also experience involuntary movements of the limbs and head.

Rhine (German *Rhein*, French *Rhin*) European river rising in Switzerland and reaching the North Sea via Germany and the Netherlands; length 1,320 km/820 mi. Tributaries include the Moselle and the Ruhr. The Rhine is linked with the Mediterranean by the Rhine–Rhône Waterway, and with the Black Sea by the Rhine–Main–Danube Waterway. It is the longest, and the dirtiest, river in Europe.

Rhineland-Palatinate (German *Rheinland-Pfalz*) administrative region (German *Land*) of Germany; *area* 19,800 sq km/7,643 sq mi; *capital* Mainz; *towns* Ludwigshafen, Koblenz, Trier, Worms; *physical* wooded mountain country, river valleys of Rhine and Moselle; *products* wine (75% of German output), tobacco, chemicals, machinery, leather goods, pottery; *population* (1992) 3,702,000.

rhinoceros odd-toed hoofed mammal of the family Rhinocerotidae. The one-horned Indian rhinoceros *Rhinoceros unicornis* is up to 2 m/6 ft high at the shoulder, with a tubercled skin, folded into shield-like pieces; the African rhinoceroses are smooth skinned and two-horned. All are endangered.

rhizome horizontal underground plant stem. It is a ⟡perennating organ in some species, where it is generally thick and fleshy, while in other species it is mainly a means of ⟡vegetative reproduction, and is therefore long and slender, with buds all along it that send up new plants. The potato is a rhizome that has two distinct parts, the tuber being the swollen end of a long, cordlike rhizome.

Rhode Island (officially Rhode Island and Providence Plantations) state in NE USA; the smallest state of the USA; nickname Ocean State; *area* 3,100 sq km/1,197 sq mi; *capital* Providence; *towns* Cranston, Woonsocket; *features* Narrangansett Bay, with America's Cup yacht races; mansions of Newport; Block Island; Brown University; Rhode Island School of Design; University of Rhode Island; **products** poultry (Rhode Island Reds), jewellery, silverware, textiles, machinery, primary metals, rubber products, submarine assembly; **population** (1987) 986,000; **history** founded 1636 by Roger Williams, exiled from Massachusetts Bay colony for religious dissent; one of the original 13 states and still the smallest one in the area.

Rhodes (Greek *Rodhos*) Greek island, largest of the Dodecanese, in the E Aegean Sea; **area** 1,412 sq km/545 sq mi; **capital** Rhodes; **products** grapes, olives; **population** (1981) 88,000; **history** settled by Greeks about 1000 BC; the Colossus of Rhodes (fell 224 BC) was one of the ◊Seven Wonders of the World; held by the Knights Hospitallers of St John 1306–1522; taken from Turkish rule by the Italian occupation 1912; ceded to Greece 1947.

Rhodes Cecil (John) 1853–1902. South African politician, born in the UK, prime minister of Cape Colony 1890–96. Aiming at the formation of a South African federation and the creation of a block of British territory from the Cape to Cairo, he was responsible for the annexation of Bechuanaland (now Botswana) in 1885. He formed the British South Africa Company in 1889, which occupied Mashonaland and Matabeleland, thus forming *Rhodesia* (now Zambia and Zimbabwe).

Rhodesia former name of ◊Zambia (Northern Rhodesia) and ◊Zimbabwe (Southern Rhodesia).

rhodium hard, silver-white, metallic element, symbol Rh, atomic number 45, relative atomic mass 102.905. It is one of the so-called platinum group of metals and is resistant to tarnish, corrosion, and acid. It occurs as a free metal in the natural alloy osmiridium and is used in jewellery, electroplating, and thermocouples.

rhododendron any of numerous shrubs of the genus *Rhododendron* of the heath family Ericaceae. Most species are evergreen. The leaves are usually dark and leathery, and the large racemes of flowers occur in all colours except blue. They thrive on acid soils. ◊Azaleas belong to the same genus.

Rhône river of S Europe; length 810 km/500 mi. It rises in Switzerland and flows through Lake Geneva to Lyon in France, where at its confluence with the Saône the upper limit of navigation is reached. The river turns due S, passes Vienne and Avignon, and takes in the Isère and other tributaries. Near Arles it divides into the *Grand* and *Petit Rhône*, flowing respectively SE and SW into the Mediterranean W of Marseille.

Rhône-Alpes region of E France in the upper reaches of the Rhône; area 43,700 sq km/ 16,868 sq mi; population (1992) 5,344,000. It consists of the *départements* of Ain, Ardèche, Drôme, Isère, Loire, Rhône, Savoie, and Haute-Savoie. The chief town is Lyon. There are several notable wine-producing areas, including Chenas, Fleurie, and Beaujolais. Industrial products include chemicals, textiles, and motor vehicles.

rhubarb perennial plant *Rheum rhaponticum* of the buckwheat family Polygonaceae, grown for its pink, edible leaf stalks. The leaves contain oxalic acid, and are poisonous. There are also wild rhubarbs native to Europe and Asia.

rhythm and blues (R & B) US popular music of the 1940s–60s, which drew on swing and jump-jazz rhythms and blues vocals, and was a progenitor of rock and roll. It diversified into soul, funk, and other styles. R & B artists include Bo Diddley (1928–), Jackie Wilson (1934–84), and Etta James (c. 1938–).

riboflavin or *vitamin B₂* ◊vitamin of the B complex whose absence in the diet causes stunted growth.

ribonucleic acid full name of ◊RNA.

ribosome in biology, the protein-making machinery of the cell. Ribosomes are located on the endoplasmic reticulum (ER) of eukaryotic cells, and are made of proteins and a special type of ◊RNA, ribosomal RNA. They receive messenger RNA (copied from the ◊DNA) and ◊amino acids, and 'translate' the messenger RNA by using its chemically coded instructions to link amino acids in a specific order, to make a strand of a particular protein.

Ricardo David 1772–1823. English economist, author of *Principles of Political Economy* 1817. Among his discoveries were the principle of comparative advantage (that countries can benefit by specializing in goods they produce efficiently and trading internationally to buy others), and the law of diminishing returns (that continued increments of capital and labour applied to a given quantity of land will eventually show a declining rate of increase in output).

rice principal cereal of the wet regions of the tropics. It is unique among cereal crops in that it is grown standing in water. The yield is very large, and rice is said to be the staple food of one-third of the world population. New varieties with greatly increased protein content have been developed and yields are higher than ever before (see ◊green revolution).

Richard I *the Lion-Heart* (French *Coeur-de-Lion*) 1157– . King of England from 1189, who spent all but six months of his reign abroad. He was the third son of Henry II, against whom he twice rebelled. In the third ◊Crusade 1191–92 he won victories at Cyprus, Acre, and Arsuf (against ◊Saladin), but failed to recover Jerusalem. While returning overland he was captured by the Duke of Austria, who handed him over to the emperor Henry VI, and he was held prisoner until a large ransom was raised. He then returned briefly to England, where his brother John I had been ruling in his stead. His later years were spent in warfare in France, where he was killed.

Richard II 1367–1400. King of England from 1377, effectively from 1389, son of Edward the Black Prince. He reigned in conflict with Parliament; they executed some of his associates 1388, and he executed some of the opposing barons 1397, whereupon he made himself absolute. Two years later, forced to abdicate in favour of ◊Henry IV, he was jailed and probably assassinated.

Richard III 1452–1485. King of England from 1482. The son of Richard, Duke of York, he was created duke of Gloucester by his brother Edward IV, and distinguished himself in the Wars of the ◊Roses. On Edward's death 1483 he became protector to his nephew Edward V, and soon secured the crown for himself on the plea that Edward IV's sons were illegitimate. He proved a capable ruler, but the suspicion that he had murdered Edward V and his brother undermined his popularity. In 1485 Henry, Earl of Richmond (later ◊Henry VII), raised a rebellion, and Richard III was defeated and killed at ◊Bosworth.

Richards Viv (Isaac Vivian Alexander) 1952– . West Indian cricketer, captain of the West Indies team from 1986. He has played for the Leeward Islands and, in the UK, for Somerset and Glamorgan. A prolific run-scorer, he holds the record for the greatest number of runs made in test cricket in one calendar year (1,710 runs in 1976).

Richardson Ralph (David) 1902–1983. English actor. He played many stage parts, including Falstaff (Shakespeare), Peer Gynt (Ibsen), and Cyrano de Bergerac (Rostand). He shared the management of the Old Vic theatre with Laurence Olivier 1944–50. In later years he revealed himself as an accomplished deadpan comic.

Richardson Samuel 1689–1761. English novelist, one of the founders of the modern novel. *Pamela* 1740–41, written in the form of a series of letters and containing much dramatic conversation, was sensationally popular all across Europe, and was followed by *Clarissa* 1747–48 and *Sir Charles Grandison* 1753–54.

Richelieu Armand Jean du Plessis de 1585–1642. French cardinal and politician, chief minister from 1624. He aimed to make the monarchy absolute; he ruthlessly crushed opposition by the nobility and destroyed the political power of the ◊Huguenots, while leaving them religious freedom. Abroad, he sought to establish French supremacy by breaking the power of the Habsburgs; he therefore supported the Swedish king Gustavus Adolphus and the German Protestant princes against Austria and in 1635 brought France into the Thirty Years' War.

Richter scale scale based on measurement of seismic waves, used to determine the magnitude of

an ◊earthquake at its epicentre. The magnitude of an earthquake differs from its intensity, measured by the ◊Mercalli scale, which is subjective and varies from place to place for the same earthquake. The scale is named after US seismologist Charles Richter (1900–1985).

rickets defective growth of bone in children due to an insufficiency of calcium deposits. The bones, which do not harden adequately, are bent out of shape. It is usually caused by a lack of vitamin D and insufficient exposure to sunlight. Renal rickets, also a condition of malformed bone, is associated with kidney disease.

Rift Valley, Great volcanic valley formed 10–20 million years ago by a crack in the Earth's crust and running about 8,000 km/5,000 mi from the Jordan Valley, through the Red Sea to central Mozambique in SE Africa. At some points its traces have been lost by erosion, but elsewhere, as in S Kenya, cliffs rise thousands of metres. It is marked by a series of lakes, including Lake Turkana (formerly Lake Rudolf), and volcanoes, such as Mount Kilimanjaro.

Riga capital and port of Latvia; population (1987) 900,000. A member of the ◊Hanseatic League from 1282, Riga has belonged in turn to Poland 1582, Sweden 1621, and Russia 1710. It was the capital of independent Latvia 1918–40 and was occupied by Germany 1941–44, before being annexed by the USSR. It again became independent Latvia's capital 1991.

Rigel or *Beta Orionis* brightest star in the constellation Orion. It is a blue-white supergiant, with an estimated diameter 50 times that of the Sun. It is 900 light years from Earth, and is about 100,000 times more luminous than our Sun. It is the seventh brightest star in the sky.

rights issue in finance, new shares offered to existing shareholders to raise new capital. Shareholders receive a discount on the market price while the company benefits from not having the costs of a relaunch of the new issue.

Rights of Man and the Citizen, Declaration of the historic French document. According to the statement of the French National Assembly 1789, these rights include representation in the legislature; equality before the law; equality of opportunity; freedom from arbitrary imprisonment; freedom of speech and religion; taxation in proportion to ability to pay; and security of property. In 1946 were added equal rights for women; right to work, join a union, and strike; leisure, social security, and support in old age; and free education.

right wing the more conservative or reactionary section of a political party or spectrum. It originated in the French national assembly 1789, where the nobles sat in the place of honour on the president's right, whereas the commons were on his left (hence ◊left wing).

Riley Bridget (Louise) 1931– . English Op art

painter. In the early 1960s she invented her characteristic style, arranging hard-edged black and white dots or lines in regular patterns that created disturbing effects of scintillating light and movement; *Fission* 1963 (Museum of Modern Art, New York) is an example. She introduced colour in the late 1960s and experimented with silk-screen prints on Perspex.

Rilke Rainer Maria 1875–1926. Austrian writer. His prose works include the semi autobiographical *Die Aufzeichnungen des Malte Laurids Brigge/Notebook of Malte Laurids Brigge* 1910. His verse is characterized by a form of mystic pantheism that seeks to achieve a state of ecstasy in which existence can be apprehended as a whole.

Rimbaud (Jean Nicolas) Arthur 1854–1891. French Symbolist poet. His verse was chiefly written before the age of 20, notably *Les Illuminations* published 1886. From 1871 he lived with ◊Verlaine.

Rimsky-Korsakov Nikolay Andreyevich 1844–1908. Russian composer. He used Russian folk idiom and rhythms in his Romantic compositions and published a text on orchestration. His operas include *The Maid of Pskov* 1873, *The Snow Maiden* 1882, *Mozart and Salieri* 1898, and *The Golden Cockerel* 1907, a satirical attack on despotism that was banned until 1909.

ringworm any of various contagious skin infections due to related kinds of fungus, usually resulting in circular, itchy, discoloured patches covered with scales or blisters. The scalp and feet (athlete's foot) are generally involved. Treatment is with antifungal preparations.

Rio de Janeiro port and resort in E Brazil; population (1991) 5,487,300. The name (Portuguese 'river of January') commemorates the arrival of Portuguese explorers 1 Jan 1502, but there is in fact no river. Sugar Loaf Mountain stands at the entrance to the harbour. It was the capital of Brazil 1763–1960.

Rio Grande river rising in the Rocky Mountains in S Colorado, USA, and flowing S to the Gulf of Mexico, where it is reduced to a trickle by irrigation demands on its upper reaches; length 3,050 km/ 1,900 mi. Its last 2,400 km/1,500 mi form the US–Mexican border (Mexican name *Río Bravo del Norte*).

Rio Grande do Sul most southerly state of Brazil, on the frontier with Argentina and Uruguay; capital Pôrto Alegre; area 282,184 sq km/108,993 sq mi; population (1990) 9,348,300.

Río Muni mainland portion of ◊Equatorial Guinea.

RISC (acronym for reduced instruction-set computer) in computing, a microprocessor (processor on a single chip) that carries out fewer instructions than other microprocessors in common use in the 1990s. Because of the low number of ◊machine-code instructions, the processor carries out those instructions very quickly.

Risorgimento movement for Italian national unity and independence from 1815. Leading figures in the movement included ◊Cavour, ◊Mazzini, and ◊Garibaldi. Uprisings 1848–49 failed, but with help from France in a war against Austria – to oust it from Italian provinces in the north – an Italian kingdom was founded 1861. Unification was finally completed with the addition of Venetia 1866 and the Papal States 1870.

river long water course that flows down a slope along a channel. It originates at a point called its *source*, and enters a sea or lake at its *mouth*. Along its length it may be joined by smaller rivers called *tributaries*. A river and its tributaries are contained within a drainage basin.

Rivera Diego 1886–1957. Mexican painter, active in Europe until 1921. He received many public commissions for murals exalting the Mexican revolution. A vast cycle on historical themes (National Palace, Mexico City) was begun 1929. In the 1930s he visited the USA and with Ben Shan produced murals for the Rockefeller Center, New York (later

major rivers

Name and location	km	mi
Nile (NE Africa)	6,695	4,160
Amazon (South America)	6,570	4,080
Chiang Jiang (China)	6,300	3,900
Mississippi-Missouri (USA)	6,020	3,740
Ob-Irtysh (USSR)	5,600	3,480
Huang He (China)	5,464	3,395
Zaïre (Africa)	4,500	2,800
Mekong (Asia)	4,425	2,750
Amur (Asia)	4,416	2,744
Lena (USSR)	4,400	2,730
Mackenzie (Canada)	4,241	2,635
Niger (Africa)	4,185	2,600
Yenisei (USSR)	4,100	2,550
Mississippi (USA)	3,779	2,348
Madeira (Brazil)	3,240	2,013
Sao Francisco (Brazil)	3,199	1,988
Yukon (USA)	3,185	1,979
Indus (Tibet/Pakistan)	3,180	1,975
Rio Grande (USA/Mexico)	3,050	1,900
Purus (Brazil)	2,993	1,860
Parana (Brazil)	2,940	1,827
Danube (Europe)	2,858	1,776
Brahmaputra (Asia)	2,850	1,770
Japura (Brazil)	2,816	1,750
Salween (Burma/China)	2,816	1,750
Euphrates (Iraq)	2,735	1,700
Tocantins (Brazil)	2,699	1,677
Zambezi (Africa)	2,650	1,650
Paraguay (Paraguay)	2,591	1,610
Orinoco (Venezuela)	2,600	1,600
Amu-Dar'ya (USSR)	2,540	1,578
Murray (SE Australia)	2,520	1,566
Ganges (India/Bangladesh)	2,510	1,560

overpainted because he included a portrait of Lenin).

Riviera Mediterranean coast of France and Italy from Marseille to La Spezia.

Riyadh (Arabic *Ar Riyād*) capital of Saudi Arabia and of the Central Province, formerly the sultanate of Nejd, in an oasis, connected by rail with Dammam on the Arabian Gulf; population (1986) 1,500,000.

RNA abbreviation for *ribonucleic acid* nucleic acid involved in the process of translating the genetic material ⬦DNA into proteins. It is usually single-stranded, unlike the double-stranded DNA, and consists of a large number of nucleotides strung together, each of which comprises the sugar ribose, a phosphate group, and one of four bases (uracil, cytosine, adenine, or guanine). RNA is copied from DNA by the formation of ⬦base pairs, with uracil taking the place of thymine.

roach any freshwater fish of the Eurasian genus *Rutilus*, of the carp family, especially *R. rutilus* of N Europe. It is dark green above, whitish below, with reddish lower fins; it grows to 35 cm/1.2 ft.

roadrunner crested North American ground-dwelling bird *Geococcyx californianus* of the ⬦cuckoo family, found in the SW USA and Mexico. It can run at a speed of 25 kph/15 mph.

robbery in law, a variety of theft: stealing from a person, using force, or the threat of force, to intimidate the victim. The maximum penalty in the UK is life imprisonment.

Robbia, della Italian family of sculptors and architects, active in Florence. *Luca della Robbia* (1400–1482) created a number of major works in Florence, notably the marble *cantoria* (singing gallery) in the cathedral 1431–38 (Museo del Duomo), with lively groups of choristers. Luca also developed a characteristic style of glazed terracotta work.

Robbins Jerome 1918– . US dancer and choreographer, codirector of the New York City Ballet 1969–83 (with George Balanchine). His ballets are internationally renowned and he is considered the greatest US-born ballet choreographer. He also choreographed the musicals *The King and I* 1951, *West Side Story* 1957, and *Fiddler on the Roof* 1964.

Robert II *c.* 1054–1134. Eldest son of ⬦William I (the Conqueror), succeeding him as duke of Normandy (but not on the English throne) 1087. His brother ⬦William II ascended the English throne, and they warred until 1096, after which Robert took part in the First Crusade. When his other brother ⬦Henry I claimed the English throne 1100, Robert contested the claim and invaded England unsuccessfully 1101. Henry invaded Normandy 1106, and captured Robert, who remained a prisoner in England until his death.

Robert I *Robert the Bruce* 1274–1329. King of Scotland from 1306, and grandson of Robert de ⬦Bruce. He shared in the national uprising led by William ⬦Wallace, and, after Wallace's execution 1305, rose once more against Edward I of England, and was crowned at Scone 1306. He defeated Edward II at ⬦Bannockburn 1314. In 1328 the treaty of Northampton recognized Scotland's independence and Robert as king.

Robert II 1316–1390. King of Scotland from 1371. He was the son of Walter (1293–1326), steward of Scotland, who married Marjory, daughter of Robert I. He was the first king of the house of Stuart.

Robert III *c.* 1340–1406. King of Scotland from 1390, son of Robert II. He was unable to control the nobles, and the government fell largely into the hands of his brother, Robert, Duke of Albany (*c.* 1340–1420).

Robespierre Maximilien François Marie Isidore de 1758–1794. French politician in the ⬦French Revolution. As leader of the ⬦Jacobins in the National Convention, he supported the execution of Louis XVI and the overthrow of the right-wing republican Girondins, and in July 1793 was elected to the Committee of Public Safety. A year later he was guillotined; many believe that he was a scapegoat for the Reign of ⬦Terror since he ordered only 72 executions personally.

robin migratory songbird *Erithacus rubecula* of the thrush family, found in Europe, W Asia, Africa, and the Azores. About 13 cm/5 in long, both sexes are olive brown with a red breast. The nest is constructed in a sheltered place, and from five to seven white freckled eggs are laid.

Robin Hood legendary English outlaw and champion of the poor against the rich. He is said to have lived in Sherwood Forest, Nottinghamshire, during the reign of Richard I (1189–99). He feuded with the sheriff of Nottingham, accompanied by Maid Marian and a band of followers known as his 'merry men'. He appears in ballads from the 13th century, but his first datable appearance is in Langland's *Piers Plowman* about 1377.

Robinson Mary 1944– . Irish Labour politician, president from 1990. She became a professor of law at 25 and has campaigned for women's rights in Ireland.

Robinson W(illiam) Heath 1872–1944. English cartoonist and illustrator who made humorous drawings of bizarre machinery for performing simple tasks, such as raising one's hat. A clumsily designed apparatus is often described as a 'Heath Robinson' contraption.

Robinson Sugar Ray. Adopted name of Walker Smith 1920–1989. US boxer, world welterweight champion 1945–51, defending his title five times. He defeated Jake LaMotta 1951 to take the middleweight title. He lost the title six times and won it seven times. He retired at the age of 45.

robot

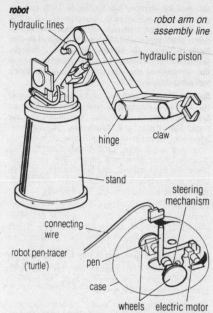

hydraulic lines

robot arm on assembly line

hydraulic piston

hinge

claw

stand

steering mechanism

connecting wire

robot pen-tracer ('turtle')

pen

case

wheels   electric motor

robot any machine controlled by electronic chip or computer that can be programmed to do work (robotics, as opposed to mechanical work, called automation). The most common types are robotic 'arms'; when fixed to the floor or a workbench, they perform functions such as paint spraying or assembling parts in factories. Others include radio-directed or computer-controlled vehicles for carrying materials, and a miscellany of devices from cruise missiles and deep-sea and space-exploration craft to robotic toys.

Rocard Michel 1930– . French socialist politician, prime minister 1988–91. A former radical, he joined the Socialist Party (PS) 1973, emerging as leader of its moderate social-democratic wing. He unsuccessfully challenged François Mitterrand for the party's presidential nomination 1981 and held ministerial office under Mitterrand 1981–85, as minister of planning and regional development 1981–83 and of agriculture 1983–85.

rock and roll pop music born of a fusion of rhythm and blues and country and western and based on electric guitar and drums. In the mid-1950s, with the advent of Elvis Presley, it became the heartbeat of teenage rebellion in the West and also had considerable impact on other parts of the world. It found perhaps its purest form in late-1950s **rockabilly**, the style of white Southerners in the USA; the blanket term 'rock' later came to comprise a multitude of styles. Leading rock-and-roll singers and songwriters of the 1950s included Chuck ⟡Berry, Little

Richard (1932–), Jerry Lee ⟡Lewis, Buddy ⟡Holly, and Gene Vincent (1935–1971).

Rockefeller John D(avison) 1839–1937. US millionaire, founder of Standard Oil 1870 (which achieved control of 90% of US refineries by 1882). He founded the philanthropic *Rockefeller Foundation* 1913, to which his son *John D(avison) Rockefeller Jr* (1874–1960) devoted his life.

rocket projectile driven by the reaction of gases produced by a fast-burning fuel. Unlike jet engines, which are also reaction engines, modern rockets carry their own oxygen supply to burn their fuel and do not require any surrounding atmosphere. For warfare, rocket heads carry an explosive device.

Rocky Mountains or *Rockies* largest North American mountain system. They extend from the junction with the Mexican plateau, northwards through the west central states of the USA, through Canada to S Alaska. The highest mountain is Mount McKinley (6,194 m/20,320 ft).

Rococo movement in the arts and architecture in 18th-century Europe, tending towards lightness, elegance, delicacy, and decorative charm. The term 'Rococo' refers to *rocaille* (rock- or shell-work), a style of interior decoration based on S-curves and scroll-like forms. Watteau's paintings and Sèvres porcelain belong to the French Rococo vogue. In the 1730s the movement became widespread in Europe, notably in the churches and palaces of S Germany and Austria.

rodent any mammal of the worldwide order Rodentia, making up nearly half of all mammal species. Besides ordinary 'cheek teeth', they have a single front pair of incisor teeth in both upper and lower jaw, which continue to grow as they are worn down.

Rodgers Richard (Charles) 1902–1979. US composer. He collaborated with librettist Lorenz Hart (1895–1943) on songs such as 'Blue Moon' 1934 and musicals such as *On Your Toes* 1936, and with Oscar Hammerstein II (1895–1960) wrote musicals such as *Oklahoma!* 1943, *South Pacific* 1949, *The King and I* 1951, and *The Sound of Music* 1959.

Ródhos Greek name for the island of ⟡Rhodes.

Rodin Auguste 1840–1917. French sculptor, often considered the greatest of his day. Through his work he freed sculpture from the idealizing conventions of the time by his realistic treatment of the human figure, introducing a new boldness of style and expression. Examples are *Le Penseur/The Thinker* 1880, *Le Baiser/The Kiss* 1886 (marble version in the Louvre, Paris), and *Les Bourgeois de Calais/The Burghers of Calais* 1884–86 (copy in Embankment Gardens, Westminster, London).

roentgen or *röntgen* unit (symbol R) of radiation exposure, used for X- and gamma rays. It is defined in terms of the number of ions produced in one cubic centimetre of air by the radiation. Exposure to 1,000 roentgens gives rise to an absorbed dose of about 870 rads (8.7 grays), which is a dose equivalent of 870 rems (8.7 sieverts). The annual dose equivalent from natural sources in the UK is 1,100 microsieverts.

Rogers Richard 1933– . British architect. His works include the Centre Pompidou in Paris 1977 (jointly with Renzo Piano) and the Lloyd's building in London 1986.

Roh Tae-woo 1932– . South Korean right-wing politician and general. He held ministerial office from 1981 under President Chun, and became chair of the ruling Democratic Justice Party 1985. He was elected president 1987, amid allegations of fraud and despite being connected with the massacre of about 2,000 anti-government demonstrators 1980.

Roland French hero whose real and legendary deeds of valour and chivalry inspired many medieval and later romances, including the 11th-century *Chanson de Roland* and Ariosto's *Orlando Furioso*. A knight of ▷Charlemagne, Roland was killed 778 with his friend Oliver and the 12 peers of France at Roncesvalles (in the Pyrenees) by Basques. He headed the rearguard during Charlemagne's retreat from his invasion of Spain.

roller any brightly coloured bird of the Old World family Coraciidae, resembling crows but in the same order as kingfishers and hornbills. Rollers grow up to 32 cm/13 in long. The name is derived from the habit of some species of rolling over in flight.

Rolling Stones, the British band formed 1962, once notorious as the 'bad boys' of rock. Original members were Mick Jagger (1943–), Keith Richards (1943–), Brian Jones (1942–1969), Bill Wyman (1936–), Charlie Watts (1941–), and the pianist Ian Stewart (1938–1985). A rock-and-roll institution, the Rolling Stones were still performing and recording in the 1990s.

ROM (acronym for *r*ead-only *m*emory) in computing, a memory device in the form of a collection of integrated circuits (chips), frequently used in microcomputers. ROM chips are loaded with data and programs during manufacture and, unlike ▷RAM (random-access memory) chips, can subsequently only be read, not written to, by computer. However, the contents of the chips are not lost when the power is switched off, as happens in RAM.

Roman art sculpture and painting of ancient Rome, from the 4th century BC to the fall of the empire. Much Roman art was intended for public education, notably the sculpted triumphal arches and giant columns, such as *Trajan's Column* AD 106–113, and portrait sculptures of soldiers, politicians, and emperors. Surviving mural paintings (in Pompeii, Rome, and Ostia) and mosaic decorations show Greek influence. Roman art was to prove a lasting inspiration in the West.

Roman Britain period in British history from the mid-1st century BC to the mid-4th century AD. England was rapidly Romanized, but north of York fewer remains of Roman civilization have been found. Roman towns include London, York, Chester, St Albans, Colchester, Lincoln, Gloucester, and Bath. The most enduring mark of the occupation was the system of military roads radiating from London.

Roman Catholicism one of the main divisions of the Christian religion, separate from the Eastern Orthodox Church from 1054, and headed by the pope. For history and beliefs, see ▷Christianity. Membership is about 585 million worldwide, concentrated in S Europe, Latin America, and the Philippines. Under John Paul II from 1978, power has been more centralized, and bishops and cardinals have been chosen from the more traditionally minded clerics and from the Third World.

romance in literature, tales of love and adventure, in verse or prose, that became popular in France about 1200 and spread throughout Europe. There were Arthurian romances about the legendary King Arthur and his knights, and romances based on the adventures of Charlemagne and on classical themes. In the 20th century the term 'romantic novel' is often used disparagingly, to imply a contrast with a realist novel.

Romance languages branch of Indo-European languages descended from the Latin of the Roman Empire ('popular' or 'vulgar' as opposed to 'classical' Latin). The present-day Romance languages with national status are French, Italian, Portuguese, Romanian, and Spanish.

Roman Empire see ▷Rome, ancient.

Romanesque art style of ▷medieval art.

Romania country in SE Europe, bordered N and E by Ukraine, E by Moldova and the Black Sea, S by Bulgaria, SW by Yugoslavia, and NW by Hungary; *area* 237,500 sq km/91,699 sq mi; *capital* Bucharest; *physical* mountains surrounding a plateau, with river plains S and E; Carpathian Mountains, Transylvanian Alps; river Danube; *head of state* Ion Iliescu from 1989; *head of government* Theodor Stolojan from 1991; *political system* emergent democracy; *exports* petroleum products and oilfield equipment, electrical goods, cars, cereals; *population* (1992 est) 23,152,000 (Romanians 89%, Hungarians 8%, Germans 2%); *languages* Romanian (official), Hungarian, German; *recent history* pro-Nazi Antonescu government overthrown 1944; communist-dominated government appointed 1945; boundaries redrawn, King Michael abdicated, and People's Republic proclaimed 1947. New Soviet-style constitution adopted 1949. Romania joined Comecon 1949 and the Warsaw Pact 1955. Soviet occupation forces were removed 1958. A new constitution was adopted 1965. Nicolae Ceaușescu was created president 1974. In 1987 workers demonstrated against austerity programme introduced after two winters of austerity and power cuts. In 'Christmas revolution' 1989 the Ceauşescu regime was overthrown and power assumed by the military-dissident-reform communist National Salvation Front headed by Ion Iliescu. Ceauşescu was tried and executed and the Securitate intelligence removed. Strikes and protests against the effects of the market followed 1990. New constitution endorsed by a referendum 1991.

Romanian language member of the Romance branch of the Indo-European language family, spoken in Romania, Macedonia, Albania, and parts of N Greece. It has been strongly influenced by the Slavonic languages and by Greek. The Cyrillic alphabet was used until the 19th century, when a variant of the Roman alphabet was adopted.

Roman law legal system of ancient Rome that is now the basis of ▷civil law, one of the main European legal systems.

Roman numerals ancient European number system using symbols different from Arabic numerals (the ordinary numbers 1, 2, 3, 4, 5, and so on). The seven key symbols in Roman numerals, as represented today, are I (1), V (5), X (10), L (50), C (100), D (500) and M (1,000). There is no zero, and therefore no place-value as is fundamental to the Arabic system. The first ten Roman numerals are I, II, III, IV (or IIII), V, VI, VII, VIII, IX, and X. When a Roman symbol is preceded by a symbol of equal or greater value, the values of the symbols are added (XVI = 16). When a symbol is preceded by a symbol of less value, the values are subtracted (XL = 40). A horizontal bar over a symbol indicates a factor of 1,000 ($\bar{X}$ = 10,000).

Romanov dynasty rulers of Russia from 1613 to the ▷Russian Revolution 1917. Under the Romanovs, Russia developed into an absolutist empire. The last tsar, Nicholas II, abdicated March 1917 and was murdered July 1918, together with his family.

Romanticism in literature, music, and art, a style that emphasizes the imagination, emotions, and creativity of the individual artist. The term is often used to characterize the culture of 19th-century Europe, as contrasted with 18th-century ▷Classicism.

Romanticism in music, term that generally refers to a preoccupation with the expression of emotion and with nature and folk history as a source of inspiration. Often linked with nationalistic feelings, the Romantic movement reached its height in the late 19th century, as in the works of Schumann and Wagner.

Romany member of a nomadic people, also called *Gypsy* (a corruption of 'Egyptian', since they were erroneously thought to come from Egypt). They are now believed to have originated in NW India, and live throughout the world. The Romany language,

spoken in several different dialects, belongs to the Indic branch of the Indo-European family.

Rome (Italian *Roma*) capital of Italy and of Lazio region, on the river Tiber, 27 km/17 mi from the Tyrrhenian Sea; population (1987) 2,817,000. Rome has few industries but is an important cultural, road, and rail centre. A large section of the population finds employment in government offices. Remains of the ancient city include the Forum, Colosseum, and Pantheon.

Rome, ancient civilization based in Rome, which occupied first the Italian peninsula, then most of Europe, the Near East, and North Africa. It lasted for about 800 years. Traditionally founded 753 BC, Rome became a kingdom, then a self-ruling republic (and free of ▷Etruscan rule) 510 BC. From then, the history of Rome is one of continual expansion, interrupted only by civil wars in the period 133–27 BC, until the murder of Julius ▷Caesar and foundation of the empire under ▷Augustus and his successors. At its peak under Trajan, the Roman Empire stretched from Britain to Mesopotamia and the Caspian Sea. A long train of emperors ruling by virtue of military, rather than civil, power marked the beginning of Rome's long decline; under ▷Diocletian, the empire was divided into two parts – East and West – although temporarily reunited under ▷Constantine, the first emperor formally to adopt Christianity. The end of the Roman Empire is generally dated by the sack of Rome by the Goths AD 410, or by the deposition of the last emperor in the west AD 476. The Eastern Empire continued until 1453 at ▷Constantinople.

Rome, Treaties of two international agreements signed 25 March 1957 by Belgium, France, West Germany, Italy, Luxembourg, and the Netherlands, which established the European Economic Community (▷European Community) and the European Atomic Energy Commission (EURATOM).

Rommel Erwin 1891–1944. German field marshal. He served in World War I, and in World War II he played an important part in the invasions of central Europe and France. He was commander of the N African offensive from 1941 (when he was nicknamed 'Desert Fox') until defeated in the Battles of El ▷Alamein.

Romney George 1734–1802. English portrait painter, active in London from 1762. He became, with Gainsborough and Reynolds, one of the most successful portrait painters of the late 18th century. He painted several portraits of Lady Hamilton, Admiral Nelson's mistress.

Romulus in Roman mythology, legendary founder and first king of Rome, the son of Mars and Rhea Silvia, daughter of Numitor, king of Alba Longa. Romulus and his twin brother Remus were thrown into the Tiber by their great-uncle Amulius, who had deposed Numitor, but were suckled by a she-wolf and rescued by a shepherd. On reaching adulthood they killed Amulius and founded Rome.

Rondônia state in NW Brazil; the centre of Amazonian tin and gold mining and of experiments in agricultural colonization; area 243,044 sq km/ 93,876 sq mi; population (1991) 1,373,700. Known as the Federal Territory of *Guaporé* until 1956, it became a state 1981.

rook gregarious European ⬦crow *Corvus frugilegus*. The plumage is black and lustrous and the face bare; a rook can grow to 45 cm/18 in long. Rooks nest in colonies at the tops of trees.

Roosevelt Franklin D(elano) 1882–1945. 32nd president of the USA 1933–45, a Democrat. He served as governor of New York 1929–33. Becoming president during the ⬦Depression, he launched the ⬦*New Deal* economic and social reform programme, which made him popular with the people. After the outbreak of World War II he introduced ⬦lend lease for the supply of war materials and services to the Allies and drew up the Atlantic Charter of solidarity. Once the USA had entered the war 1941, he spent much time in meetings with Allied leaders (see ⬦Yalta conference).

Roosevelt Theodore 1858–1919. 26th president of the USA 1901–09, a Republican. After serving as governor of New York 1898–1900 he became vice president to ⬦McKinley, whom he succeeded as president on McKinley's assassination 1901. He campaigned against the great trusts (associations of enterprises that reduce competition), while carrying on a jingoist foreign policy designed to enforce US supremacy over Latin America.

root part of a plant that is usually underground, and whose primary functions are anchorage and the absorption of water and dissolved mineral salts. Roots usually grow downwards and towards water (that is, they are positively geotropic and hydrotropic; see ⬦tropism). Plants such as epiphytic orchids, which grow above ground, produce aerial roots that absorb moisture from the atmosphere. Others, such as ivy, have climbing roots arising from the stems, which serve to attach the plant to trees and walls.

root of an equation, a value that makes the equation true. For example, $x = 0$ and $x = 5$ are roots of the equation $x^2 - 5x = 0$.

root crop plant cultivated for its swollen edible root (which may or may not be a true root). Potatoes are the major temperate root crop; the major tropical root crops are cassava, yams, and sweet potatoes. Together they are second in importance only to cereals as human food. Roots have a high carbohydrate content, but their protein content rarely exceeds 2%. Consequently, communities relying almost exclusively upon roots may suffer from protein deficiency.

roots music term originally denoting ⬦reggae,

later encompassing any music indigenous to a particular culture.

Roscommon (originally Ros-Comain, 'wood around a monastery') county of the Republic of Ireland in the province of Connacht; *area* 2,460 sq km/ 950 sq mi; *towns* county town Roscommon; *physical* bounded on the E by the river Shannon; lakes: Gara, Key, Allen; rich pastures; *features* remains of a castle put up in the 13th century by English settlers; *population* (1991) 51,900.

rose any shrub or climber of the genus *Rosa*, family Rosaceae, with prickly stems and fragrant flowers in many colours. Numerous cultivated forms have been derived from the Eurasian sweetbrier or eglantine *R. rubiginosa* and dog rose *R. canina*. There are many climbing varieties, but the forms more commonly cultivated are bush roses and standards (cultivated roses grafted on to a brier stem).

Roseau formerly *Charlotte Town* capital of ⬦Dominica, West Indies; population (1981) 20,000.

Rosebery Archibald Philip Primrose, 5th Earl of Rosebery 1847–1929. British Liberal politician. He was foreign secretary 1886 and 1892–94, when he succeeded Gladstone as prime minister, but his government survived less than a year. After 1896 his imperialist views gradually placed him further from the mainstream of the Liberal Party.

rosemary evergreen shrub *Rosemarinus officinalis* of the mint family Labiatae, native to the Mediterranean and W Asia, with small, scented leaves. It is widely cultivated as a culinary herb and for the aromatic oil extracted from the clusters of pale blue or purple flowers.

Roses, Wars of the civil wars in England 1455–85 between the houses of ⬦Lancaster (badge, red rose) and ⬦York (badge, white rose), both of whom claimed the throne through descent from the sons of Edward III. As a result of ⬦Henry VI's lapse into insanity, Richard, Duke of York, was installed as protector of the realm. Upon his recovery, Henry forced York to take up arms in self-defence.

Rosetta Stone slab of basalt with inscriptions from 197 BC, found near the town of Rosetta, Egypt, 1799. Giving the same text in three versions – Greek, hieroglyphic, and demotic script – it became the key to deciphering other Egyptian inscriptions.

Rosh Hashanah two-day holiday that marks the start of the Jewish New Year (first new moon after the autumn equinox), traditionally announced by blowing a ram's horn (a shofar).

Rosicrucians group of early 17th-century philosophers who claimed occult powers and employed the terminology of ⬦alchemy to expound their mystical doctrines. Several societies have been founded in Britain and the USA that claim to be their successors, such as the Rosicrucian Fraternity (1614 in Germany, 1861 in the USA).

Ross James Clark 1800–1862. English explorer who discovered the magnetic North Pole 1831. He also went to the Antarctic 1839; Ross Island, Ross Sea, and Ross Dependency are named after him.

Ross Dependency all the Antarctic islands and territories between 160° E and 150° W longitude and S of 60° S latitude; it includes Edward VII Land, Ross Sea and its islands, and parts of Victoria Land.

Rossellini Roberto 1906–1977. Italian film director. His World War II trilogy, *Roma città aperta/Rome, Open City* 1945, *Paisà/Paisan* 1946, and *Germania anno zero/Germany Year Zero* 1947, is considered a landmark of European cinema. He and actress Ingrid ♢Bergman were the parents of actress Isabella Rossellini (1952–).

Rossetti Christina (Georgina) 1830–1894. English poet, sister of Dante Gabriel Rossetti and a devout High Anglican (see ♢Oxford movement). Her verse includes *Goblin Market and Other Poems* 1862 and expresses unfulfilled spiritual yearning and frustrated love. She was a skilful technician and made use of irregular rhyme and line length.

Rossetti Dante Gabriel 1828–1882. British painter and poet, a founding member of the ♢*Pre-Raphaelite Brotherhood* (PRB) with ♢Millais and ♢Hunt 1848. As well as romantic medieval scenes, he produced many idealized portraits of women. His verse includes 'The Blessed Damozel' 1850. His sister was the poet Christina Rossetti.

Rossini Gioacchino (Antonio) 1792–1868. Italian composer. His first success was the opera *Tancredi* 1813. In 1816 his 'opera buffa' *Il barbiere di Siviglia/The Barber of Seville* was produced in Rome. During 1815–23 he produced 20 operas, and created (with ♢Donizetti and ♢Bellini) the 19th-century Italian operatic style.

Rothermere Vere (Harold Esmond Harmsworth), 3rd Viscount 1925– . British newspaper proprietor. As chair of Associated Newspapers (1971–) he controls the right-wing *Daily Mail* (founded by his great-uncle Lord ♢Northcliffe) and *Mail on Sunday* (launched 1982), the London *Evening Standard*, and a string of regional newspapers.

Rothko Mark 1903–1970. Russian-born US painter, an Abstract Expressionist and a pioneer of *Colour Field* painting (abstract, dominated by areas of unmodulated, strong colour). Rothko produced several series of paintings in the 1950s and 1960s, including one at Harvard University; one in the Tate Gallery, London; and one for a chapel in Houston, Texas, 1967–69.

rotifer any of the tiny invertebrates, also called 'wheel animalcules', of the phylum Rotifera. Mainly freshwater, some marine, rotifers have a ring of cilia that carries food to the mouth and also provides propulsion. They are the smallest of multicellular animals, few reach 0.05 cm/0.02 in.

Rotterdam industrial port (brewing, distilling, shipbuilding, sugar and petroleum refining, margarine, tobacco) in the Netherlands and one of the foremost ocean cargo ports in the world, in the Rhine–Maas delta, linked by canal 1866–90 with the North Sea; population (1991) 582,266.

Rottweiler breed of dog originally developed in Rottweil, Germany, as a herding and guard dog, and subsequently used as a police dog. Powerfully built, the dog is about 63–66 cm/25–27 in high at the shoulder, black with tan markings, a short coat and docked tail. Although popular as a family pet in many countries, its natural guarding instincts and powerful bite have placed it at the centre of the debate concerning the regulation of dangerous dogs (see ♢dog, dangerous).

Rouault Georges 1871–1958. French painter, etcher, illustrator, and designer. Early in his career he was associated with the ♢Fauves but created his own style using heavy, dark colours and bold brushwork. His subjects included sad clowns, prostitutes, and evil lawyers; from about 1940 he painted mainly religious works.

Roundhead member of the Parliamentary party during the English Civil War 1640–60, opposing the royalist Cavaliers. The term referred to the short hair then worn only by men of the lower classes.

Rousseau Henri 'Le Douanier' 1844–1910. French painter, a self-taught naive artist. His subjects included scenes of the Parisian suburbs and exotic junglescapes, painted with painstaking detail; for example, *Surprised! Tropical Storm with a Tiger* 1891 (National Gallery, London).

Rousseau Jean-Jacques 1712–1778. French social philosopher and writer whose *Du Contrat social/Social Contract* 1762, emphasizing the rights of the people over those of the government, was a significant influence on the French Revolution. In the novel *Emile* 1762 he outlined a new theory of education.

rowan another name for the European ♢mountain ash tree.

rowing propulsion of a boat by oars, either by one rower with two oars (sculling) or by crews (two, four, or eight persons) with one oar each, often with a coxswain. Major events include the world championship, first held in 1962 for men and 1974 for women, and the Boat Race, first held in 1829, rowed by crews from Oxford and Cambridge rowing clubs between Putney and Mortlake on the river Thames.

Rowlandson Thomas 1756–1827. English painter and illustrator, a caricaturist of Georgian social life. He published the series of drawings *Tour of Dr Syntax in Search of the Picturesque* 1809 and its two sequels 1812–21.

royal assent in the UK, formal consent given by a British sovereign to the passage of a bill through Parliament, after which it becomes an ♢act of Parliament. The last instance of a royal refusal was the rejection of the Scottish Militia Bill of 1702 by Queen Anne.

royal commission in the UK and Canada, a group of people appointed by the government (nominally by the sovereign) to investigate a matter of public concern and make recommendations on any actions to be taken in connection with it, including changes in the law. In cases where agreement on recommendations cannot be reached, a minority report can be submitted by dissenters.

Royal Greenwich Observatory national astronomical observatory of the UK, founded 1675 at Greenwich, E London, England, to provide navigational information for sailors. After World War II it was moved to Herstmonceux Castle, Sussex; in 1990 it was transferred to Cambridge. It also operates telescopes on La Palma in the Canary Islands, including the 4.2-m/165-in William Herschel Telescope, commissioned 1987.

royalty in law, payment to the owner for rights to use or exploit literary or artistic copyrights and patent rights in new inventions of all kinds.

RSFSR abbreviation for *Russian Soviet Federal Socialist Republic*, the largest republic of the former Soviet Union; since 1991 known as the ⟡Russian Federation.

Ruanda part of the former Belgian territory of Ruanda-Urundi until it achieved independence as ⟡Rwanda, country in central Africa.

rubber coagulated latex of a variety of plants, mainly from the New World. Most important is Para rubber, which derives from the tree *Hevea brasiliensis* of the spurge family. It was introduced from Brazil to SE Asia, where most of the world supply is now produced, the chief exporters being Peninsular Malaysia, Indonesia, Sri Lanka, Cambodia, Thailand, Sarawak, and Brunei. At about seven years the tree, which may grow to 20 m/60 ft, is ready for 'tapping'. Small incisions are made in the trunk and the latex drips into collecting cups. In pure form, rubber is white and has the formula $(C_5H_8)_n$.

rubber plant Asiatic tree *Ficus elastica* of the mulberry family Moraceae, native to Asia and N Africa, producing latex in its stem. It has shiny, leathery, oval leaves, and young specimens are grown as house plants.

rubella technical term for ⟡German measles.

Rubens Peter Paul 1577–1640. Flemish painter, who brought the exuberance of Italian Baroque to N Europe, creating, with an army of assistants, innumerable religious and allegorical paintings for churches and palaces. These show mastery of drama in large compositions, and love of rich colour. He also painted portraits and, in his last years, landscapes. His *Raising of the Cross* 1610 and *Descent from the Cross* 1611–14, both in Antwerp cathedral, show his brilliant painterly style.

Rubicon ancient name of the small river flowing into the Adriatic which, under the Roman Republic, marked the boundary between Italy proper and Cisalpine Gaul. When ⟡Caesar led his army across it 49 BC he therefore declared war on the republic; hence to 'cross the Rubicon' means to take an irrevocable step.

rubidium soft, silver-white, metallic element, symbol Rb, atomic number 37, relative atomic mass 85.47. It is one of the ⟡alkali metals, ignites spontaneously in air, and reacts violently with water. It is used in photoelectric cells and vacuum-tube filaments.

ruby red transparent gem variety of the mineral ⟡corundum Al_2O_3, aluminium oxide. Small amounts of chromium oxide, Cr_2O_3, substituting for aluminium oxide, give ruby its colour. Natural rubies are found mainly in Myanmar (Burma), but rubies can also be produced artificially and such synthetic stones are used in ⟡lasers.

rudd freshwater fish *Scardinius erythrophthalmus*, a type of minnow, belonging to the carp family Cypridae, common in lakes and slow rivers of Europe; now introduced in the USA. Brownish green above and silvery below, with red fins and golden eyes, it can reach a length of 45 cm/1.5 ft, and a weight of 1 kg/2.2 lbs.

Rudolf former name of Lake ⟡Turkana in E Africa.

Rudolph I 1218–1291. Holy Roman emperor from 1273. Originally count of Habsburg, he was the first Habsburg emperor and expanded his dynasty by investing his sons with the duchies of Austria and Styria.

Rudolph II 1552–1612. Holy Roman emperor from 1576, when he succeeded his father Maximilian II. His policies led to unrest in Hungary and Bohemia, which led to the surrender of Hungary to his brother Matthias 1608 and religious freedom for Bohemia.

rue shrubby perennial herb *Ruta graveolens*, family Rutaceae, native to S Europe and temperate Asia. It bears clusters of yellow flowers. An oil extracted from the strongly scented, blue-green leaves is used in perfumery.

ruff bird *Philomachus pugnax* of the sandpiper family Scolopacidae. The name is taken from the frill of erectile feathers developed in the breeding season around the neck of the male. The ruff is found across N Europe and Asia, and migrates south in winter.

Rugby League professional form of rugby football founded in England 1895 as the Northern Union when a dispute about pay caused northern clubs to break away from the Rugby Football Union. The game is similar to Rugby Union, but the number of players was reduced from 15 to 13 in 1906, and other rule changes have made the game more open and fast-moving.

Rugby Union amateur form of rugby football in which there are 15 players on each side. 'Tries' are scored by 'touching down' the ball beyond the goal line or by kicking goals from penalties. The Rugby Football Union was formed 1871 and has its headquarters in England (Twickenham, Middlesex).

Ruhr river in Germany; it rises in the Rothaargebirge and flows W to join the Rhine at Duisburg. The *Ruhr valley* (228 km/142 mi), a metropolitan industrial area (petrochemicals, cars; iron and steel at Duisburg and Dortmund) was formerly a coalmining centre.

Ruisdael or *Ruysdael* Jacob van *c.* 1628–1682. Dutch landscape painter, active in Amsterdam from about 1655. He painted rural scenes near his native town of Haarlem and in Germany, and excelled in depicting gnarled and weatherbeaten trees. The few figures in his pictures were painted by other artists.

rum spirit fermented and distilled from sugar cane. Scummings from the sugar-pans produce the best rum, molasses the lowest grade. Puerto Rico and Jamaica are the main producing countries.

ruminant any even-toed hoofed mammal with a rumen, the 'first stomach' of its complex digestive system. Plant food is stored and fermented before being brought back to the mouth for chewing (chewing the cud) and then is swallowed to the next stomach. Ruminants include cattle, antelopes, goats, deer, and giraffes, all with a four-chambered stomach.

Rump, the English parliament formed between Dec 1648 and Nov 1653 after ⟡Pride's purge of the ⟡Long Parliament to ensure a majority in favour of trying Charles I. It was dismissed 1653 by Cromwell, who replaced it with the ⟡Barebones Parliament.

rune character in the oldest Germanic script, chiefly adapted from the Latin alphabet, the earliest examples being from the 3rd century, and found in Denmark. Runes were scratched on wood, metal, stone, or bone.

Rupert Prince 1619–1682. English Royalist general and admiral, born in Prague, son of the Elector Palatine Frederick V (1596–1632) and James I's daughter Elizabeth. Defeated by Cromwell at ⟡Marston Moor and ⟡Naseby in the Civil War, he commanded a privateering fleet 1649–52, until routed by Admiral Robert Blake, and, returning after the Restoration, was a distinguished admiral in the Dutch Wars.

rush any grasslike plant of the genus *Juncus*, family Juncaceae, found in wet places in cold and temperate regions. The round stems and flexible leaves of some species have been used for making mats and baskets since ancient times.

Rushdie (Ahmed) Salman 1947– . British writer, born in India of a Muslim family. His novel *The Satanic Verses* 1988 (the title refers to verses deleted from the Koran) offended many Muslims with alleged blasphemy. In 1989 the Ayatollah Khomeini of Iran called for Rushdie and his publishers to be killed. His earlier novels in the magic-realist style include *Midnight's Children* 1981 (Booker Prize) and *Shame* 1983.

Ruskin John 1819–1900. English art critic and social critic. He published five volumes of *Modern Painters* 1843–60 and *The Seven Lamps of Architecture* 1849, in which he stated his philosophy of art. His writings hastened the appreciation of painters considered unorthodox at the time, such as J M W ⟡Turner and the ⟡Pre-Raphaelite Brotherhood. His later writings were concerned with social and economic problems.

Russell Bertrand (Arthur William), 3rd Earl Russell 1872–1970. English philosopher and mathematician who contributed to the development of modern mathematical logic and wrote about social issues. His works include *Principia Mathematica* 1910–13 (with A N Whitehead), in which he attempted to show that mathematics could be reduced to a branch of logic; *The Problems of Philosophy* 1912; and *A History of Western Philosophy* 1946. He was an outspoken liberal pacifist.

Russell John, 1st Earl Russell 1792–1878. British Liberal politician, son of the 6th Duke of Bedford. He entered the House of Commons 1813 and supported Catholic emancipation and the Reform Bill. He held cabinet posts 1830–41, became prime minister 1846–52, and was again a cabinet minister until becoming prime minister again 1865–66. He retired after the defeat of his Reform Bill 1866.

Russia originally the name of the pre-revolutionary Russian Empire (until 1917), now accurately restricted to the ⟡Russian Federation.

Russian member of the majority ethnic group living in Russia. Russians are also often the largest minority in neighbouring republics. The Russian language is a member of the East Slavonic branch of the Indo-European language family and was the official language of the USSR, with 130–150 million speakers. It is written in the Cyrillic alphabet.

Russian Federation or *Russia* country in E Europe and N Asia, bordered N by the Arctic Ocean, E by the Bering Sea and Sea of Okhotsk, S by China, Mongolia, Kazakhstan, Azerbaijan, and Georgia, and W by Ukraine, Belarus, Lithuania, Latvia, Estonia, Finland, and Norway, with coastlines on the Black Sea and Caspian Sea to the S and the Gulf of Finland to the W; *area* 17,075,000 sq km/6,592,658 sq mi; *capital* Moscow; *physical* extensive forests; Ural Mountains with large mineral resources; fertile Black Earth district; *head of state* Boris Yeltsin from 1991; *head of government* Yegor Gaider from 1992; *political system* emergent democracy; *products* iron ore, coal, oil, gold, platinum and other minerals, agricultural produce; *population* (1992 est) 147,386,000

(Russian 83%); *language* Great Russian; *recent history* became founding member of United Nations 1945. Democratic Union formed in Moscow 1988 as political party opposed to totalitarianism. Boris Yeltsin elected to USSR Congress of People's Deputies 1989; elected president of republic 1990. Economic and political sovereignty declared. Yeltsin elected executive president 1991. During failed anti-Gorbachev coup Aug 1991 Yeltsin emerged as the key power-broker within the Soviet Union. He banned Communist Party of the Soviet Union (CPSU) and Russian Communist Party and negotiated formation of new confederal Commonwealth of Independent States (CIS) Dec 1991. Russian Federation's independence recognized by USA and other Western powers Jan 1992; admitted into Conference on Security and Cooperation in Europe (CSCE) and assumed former USSR permanent seat on UN Security Council. Prices freed; Yeltsin proposed further major reductions in strategic nuclear weapons.

Russian Revolution two revolutions Feb–March and Oct–Nov 1917. Food shortages, war weariness, and a breakdown in government control created mass demonstrations in Petrograd, which led to the overthrow of Tsar Nicholas II and the Romanov dynasty. The resulting provisional government, led by Kerensky, proved incapable of solving the pressing economic and social problems of the state. The Bolsheviks, under ◊Lenin attracted widespread support for their policies which included ending the war and redistributing land to the peasantry. In October, Bolshevik workers and sailors seized government buildings and took over power. Lenin's success in maintaining control, ending the war with the Central Powers and defeating pro-Tsarist forces culminated in the establishment of the Union of Soviet Socialist Republics.

Russo-Japanese War war between Russia and Japan 1904–05, which arose from conflicting ambitions in Korea and ◊Manchuria, specifically, the Russian occupation of Port Arthur (modern Dalian) 1896 and of the Amur province 1900. Japan successfully besieged Port Arthur May 1904–Jan 1905, took Mukden (modern Shenyang) 29 Feb–10 March, and on 27 May defeated the Russian Baltic fleet, which had sailed halfway around the world to

Tsushima Strait. A peace was signed 23 Aug 1905. Russia surrendered its lease on Port Arthur, ceded S Sakhalin to Japan, evacuated Manchuria, and recognized Japan's interests in Korea.

rust reddish-brown oxide of iron formed by the action of moisture and oxygen on the metal. It consists mainly of hydrated iron(III) oxide ($Fe_2O_3.H_2O$ and iron(III) hydroxide ($Fe(OH)_3$).

rust in botany, common name for the minute parasitic fungi of the order Uredinales which appear on the leaves of their hosts as orange-red spots, later becoming darker. The commonest is the wheat rust *Puccinia graminis*.

Ruthenia or *Carpathian Ukraine* region of central Europe, on the southern slopes of the Carpathian Mountains, home of the Ruthenes or Russniaks. Dominated by Hungary from the 10th century, it was part of Austria-Hungary until World War I. Divided between Czechoslovakia, Poland, and Romania 1918, it was independent for a single day in 1938, immediately occupied by Hungary, captured by the USSR 1944, and 1945–47 became incorporated into Ukraine Republic, USSR. Ukraine became an independent republic 1991.

ruthenium hard, brittle, silver-white, metallic element, symbol Ru, atomic number 44, relative atomic mass 101.07. It is one of the so-called platinum group of metals; it occurs in platinum ores as a free metal and in the natural alloy osmiridium. It is used as a hardener in alloys and as a catalyst; its compounds are used as colouring agents in glass and ceramics.

Rutherford Ernest 1871–1937. New Zealand physicist, a pioneer of modern atomic science. His main research was in the field of radioactivity, and he discovered alpha, beta, and gamma rays. He named the nucleus, and was the first to recognize the ionizing nature of the atom. He was awarded the Nobel Prize for Physics 1908.

rutherfordium name proposed by US scientists for the element currently known as unnilquadium (atomic number 104), to honour New Zealand physicist Ernest Rutherford.

Rutland formerly the smallest English county, now part of Leicestershire.

Ruysdael Jacob van. See ◊Ruisdael, Dutch painter.

Rwanda Republic of; country in central Africa, bordered N by Uganda, E by Tanzania, S by Burundi, and W by Zaire; *area* 26,338 sq km/ 10,173 sq mi; *capital* Kigali; *physical* high savanna and hills with volcanic mountains in NW; part of Lake Kivu; Kagera River (headwaters are source of the Nile); *head of state and government* Maj-Gen Juvenal Habyarimana from 1973; *political system* one-party military republic; *exports* coffee, tea, pyrethrum; *population* (1990 est) 7,603,000 (Hutu 90%, Tutsi 9%, Twa 1%); *languages* Kinyarwanda, French (official), Kiswahili; *recent*

history League of Nations mandated Rwanda and Burundi to Belgium as Territory of Ruanda-Urundi 1916. Independence from Belgium achieved 1962. Military coup led by Maj-Gen Juvenal Habyarimana ousted President Kayibanda 1973; new constitution approved 1978; Rwanda remained a military-controlled state. Civilian rule adopted 1980. Rwandan Patriotic Army attacked government 1990; constitutional reforms promised.

Rybinsk port and industrial city (engineering) in NW Russia, on the Volga, NE of Moscow; population (1987) 254,000. In 1984 it was renamed ***Andropov***, commemorating the death that year of the president of the USSR. It reverted to its former name in March 1989.

rye cereal *Secale cereale* grown extensively in N Europe and other temperate regions. The flour is used to make dark-coloured ('black') breads. Rye is grown mainly as a forage crop, but the grain is also used to make whisky and breakfast cereals.

Ryle Martin 1918–1984. English radioastronomer. He developed the technique of sky-mapping using 'aperture synthesis', combining smaller dish aerials to give the characteristics of one large one. His work on the distribution of radio sources in the universe brought confirmation of the ⟡Big Bang theory. He won, with Antony Hewish, the Nobel Prize for Physics 1974.

Ryukyu Islands southernmost island group of Japan, stretching towards Taiwan and including Okinawa, Miyako, and Ishigaki; *area* 2,254 sq km/870 sq mi; *capital* Naha, on Okinawa; *features* 73 islands, some uninhabited; subject to typhoons; *products* sugar, pineapples, fish; *population* (1985) 1,179,000; *history* originally an independent kingdom; ruled by China from the late 14th century until seized by Japan 1609 and controlled by the Satsuma feudal lords until 1868, when the Japanese government took over. Chinese claims to the islands were relinquished 1895. In World War II the islands were taken by USA 1945 (see under ⟡Okinawa); northernmost group, Oshima, restored to Japan 1953, the rest 1972.

S

Saarland (French *Sarre*) *Land* (state) of Germany; *area* 2,570 sq km/992 sq mi; *capital* Saarbrücken; *features* one-third forested; crossed northwest to south by the river Saar; *products* cereals and other crops; cattle, pigs, poultry. Former flourishing coal and steel industries survive only by government subsidy; *population* (1988) 1,034,000; *history* in 1919, the Saar district was administered by France under the auspices of the League of Nations; a plebiscite returned it to Germany 1935; Hitler gave it the name Saarbrücken. Part of the French zone of occupation 1945, it was included in the economic union with France 1947. It was returned to Germany 1957.

Sabah Sheik Jabir al Ahmadal Jabir al- 1928– . Emir of Kuwait from 1977. He suspended the national assembly 1986, after mounting parliamentary criticism, ruling in a feudal, paternalistic manner. On the invasion of Kuwait by Iraq 1990 he fled to Saudi Arabia, returning to Kuwait in March 1991.

Sabine member of an ancient people of central Italy, conquered by the Romans and amalgamated with them in the 3rd century BC. The so-called *rape of the Sabine women* — a mythical attempt by ◊Romulus in the early days of Rome to carry off the Sabine women to colonize the new city — is frequently depicted in art.

sable marten *Martes zibellina*, about 50 cm/20 in long and usually brown. It is native to N Eurasian forests, but now found mainly in E Siberia. The sable has diminished in numbers because of its valuable fur, which has long attracted hunters. Conservation measures and sable farming have been introduced to save it from extinction.

saccharide another name for a ◊sugar molecule.

saccharin or *ortho-sulpho benzimide* $C_7H_5NO_3S$ sweet, white, crystalline solid derived from coal tar and substituted for sugar. Since 1977 it has been regarded as potentially carcinogenic.

Its use is not universally permitted and it has been largely replaced by other sweetening agents.

sacrament in Christian usage, observances forming the visible sign of inward grace. In the Roman Catholic Church there are seven sacraments: baptism, Holy Communion (Eucharist or mass), confirmation, rite of reconciliation (confession and penance), holy orders, matrimony, and the anointing of the sick.

Sadat Anwar 1918–1981. Egyptian politician. Succeeding ◊Nasser as president 1970, he restored morale by his handling of the Egyptian campaign in the 1973 war against Israel. In 1974 his plan for economic, social, and political reform to transform Egypt was unanimously adopted in a referendum. In 1977 he visited Israel to reconcile the two countries, and shared the Nobel Peace Prize with Israeli prime minister Menachem Begin 1978. He was assassinated by Islamic fundamentalists.

Sade Donatien Alphonse François, Comte de, known as the *Marquis de Sade* 1740–1814. French author who was imprisoned for sexual offences and finally committed to an asylum. He wrote plays and novels dealing explicitly with a variety of sexual practices, including sadism.

safflower Asian plant *Carthamus tinctorius*, family Compositae. It is thistlelike, and widely grown for the oil from its seeds, which is used in cooking, margarine, and paints and varnishes; the seed residue is used as cattle feed.

saffron plant *Crocus sativus* of the iris family, probably native to SW Asia, and formerly widely cultivated in Europe; also the dried orange-yellow stigmas of its purple flowers, used for colouring and flavouring.

saga prose narrative written down in the 11th–13th centuries in Norway and Iceland. The sagas range from family chronicles, such as the *Landnamabok* of Ari (1067–1148), to legendary and anonymous works such as the *Njala* saga.

sage perennial herb *Salvia officinalis* with grey-green aromatic leaves used for flavouring. It grows up to 50 cm/20 in high and has bluish-lilac or pink flowers.

Sagittarius zodiac constellation in the southern hemisphere, represented as a centaur aiming a bow and arrow at neighbouring Scorpius. The Sun passes through Sagittarius from mid-Dec to mid-Jan, including the winter solstice, when it is farthest south of the equator. The constellation contains many nebulae and globular clusters, and open ◊star clusters. Kaus Australis and Nunki are its brightest stars. The centre of our Galaxy, the Milky Way, is marked by the radio source Sagittarius A. In astrology, the dates for Sagittarius are between about 22 Nov and 21 Dec (see ◊precession).

sago starchy material obtained from the pith of the sago palm *Metroxylon sagu*. It forms a nutritious food and is used for manufacturing glucose and sizing textiles.

Sahara largest desert in the world, occupying 5,500,000 sq km/2,123,000 sq mi of N Africa from the Atlantic to the Nile, covering: W Egypt; part of W Sudan; large parts of Mauritania, Mali, Niger, and Chad; and southern parts of Morocco, Algeria, Tunisia, and Libya. Small areas in Algeria and Tunisia are below sea level, but it is mainly a plateau with a central mountain system, including the Ahaggar Mountains in Algeria, the Aïr Massif in Niger, and the Tibesti Massif in Chad, of which the highest peak is Emi Koussi 3,415 m/11,208 ft. The area of the Sahara expanded by 650,000 sq km/251,000 sq mi 1940–90, but reafforestation is being attempted in certain areas.

saiga antelope *Saiga tartarica* of E European and W Asian steppes and deserts. Buff-coloured, whitish in winter, it stands 75 cm/30 in at the shoulder, with a body about 1.5 m/5 ft long. Its nose is unusually large and swollen, an adaptation which may help warm and moisten the air inhaled, and keep out the desert dust. The saiga can run at 80 kph/50 mph.

Saigon former name (until 1976) of ▷Ho Chi Minh City, Vietnam.

saint holy man or woman respected for their wisdom, spirituality, and dedication to their faith. Within the Roman Catholic church a saint is officially recognized through ▷canonization by the pope. In the Orthodox church, saints are recognized by the patriarch and Holy Synod after recommendation by local churches. The term is also used in Buddhism for individuals who have led a virtuous and holy life. For individual saints, see under forename, for example ▷Paul, St.

St Andrews town at the eastern tip of Fife, Scotland, 19 km/12 mi SE of Dundee; population (1981) 11,400. Its university (1411) is the oldest in Scotland, and the Royal and Ancient Club (1754) is the ruling body in the sporting world of golf.

St Bartholomew, Massacre of slaughter of ▷Huguenots (Protestants) in Paris, 24 Aug–17 Sept 1572, and until 3 Oct in the provinces. About 25,000 people are believed to have been killed. When ▷Catherine de' Medici's plot to have Admiral Coligny assassinated failed, she resolved to have all the Huguenot leaders killed, persuading her son Charles IX it was in the interest of public safety.

St Bernard breed of large, heavily built dog 70 cm/30 in high at the shoulder, weight about 70 kg/150 lb. They have pendulous ears and lips, large feet, and drooping lower eyelids. They are usually orange and white.

St Christopher (St Kitts)-Nevis Federation of; country comprising two islands in the West Indies, in the E Caribbean Sea; part of the Leeward Islands; *area* 269 sq km/104 sq mi (St Christopher

176 sq km/68 sq mi, Nevis 93 sq km/36 sq mi); *capital* Basseterre (on St Christopher); *physical* both islands are volcanic; fertile plains on coast; black beaches; *head of state* Elizabeth II from 1983 represented by governor general; *head of government* Kennedy Simmonds from 1980; *political system* federal constitutional monarchy; *exports* sugar, molasses, electronics, clothing; *population* (1990 est) 45,800; *language* English; *recent history* granted internal self-government within the British Commonwealth 1967; full independence within the Commonwealth was achieved 1983.

Saint-Exupéry Antoine de 1900–1944. French author who wrote the autobiographical *Vol de nuit/Night Flight* 1931 and *Terre des hommes/Wind, Sand, and Stars* 1939. His children's book *Le petit prince/The Little Prince* 1943 is also an adult allegory.

St George's port and capital of ▷Grenada; population (1986) 7,500, urban area 29,000.

St Helena British island in the S Atlantic; 1,900 km/1,200 mi W of Africa; area 122 sq km/47 sq mi; population (1987) 5,600. Its capital is Jamestown, and it exports fish and timber. Ascension and Tristan da Cunha are dependencies.

St Helens, Mount volcanic mountain in Washington State, USA. When it erupted 1980 after being quiescent since 1857, it devastated an area of 600 sq km/230 sq mi and its height was reduced from 2,950 m/9,682 ft to 2,560 m/8,402 ft.

Saint John largest city of New Brunswick, Canada, on the Saint John River; population (1986) 121,000. It is a fishing port and has shipbuilding, timber, fish-processing, petroleum, refining, and textile industries. Founded by the French as *Saint-Jean* 1635, it was taken by the British 1758.

St John's capital and chief port of Newfoundland, Canada; population (1986) 96,000, urban area 162,000. The main industry is fish processing; other products include textiles, fishing equipment, furniture, and machinery.

St John's port and capital of Antigua and Barbuda, on Antigua; population (1982) 30,000.

Saint-Just Louis Antoine Léon Florelle de 1767–1794. French revolutionary. A close associate of ▷Robespierre, he became a member of the Committee of Public Safety 1793, and was guillotined with Robespierre.

St Kitts-Nevis contracted form of ▷St Christopher-Nevis.

St Lawrence river in E North America. From ports on the ▷Great Lakes it forms, with linking canals (which also give great hydroelectric capacity to the river), the St Lawrence Seaway for oceangoing ships, ending in the Gulf of St Lawrence. It is 745 mi/1,200 km long and is icebound annually for four months.

St Louis city in Missouri, USA, on the Mississippi River; population (1990) 396,700, metropolitan area 2,444,100. Its products include aerospace equipment, aircraft, vehicles, chemicals, electrical goods, steel, and beer.

Saint Lucia country in the West Indies, in the E Caribbean Sea; one of the Windward Islands; *area* 617 sq km/238 sq mi; *capital* Castries; *physical* mountainous island with fertile valleys; mainly tropical forest; volcanic peaks; *head of state* Elizabeth II from 1979 represented by governor general; *head of government* John Compton from 1982; *political system* constitutional monarchy; *exports* coconut oil, bananas, cocoa, copra; *population* (1990 est) 153,000; *languages* English, French patois; *recent history* internal self-government acquired as a West Indies associated state 1967. Independence from Britain achieved 1979; St Lucia remains within the Commonwealth. Integration with the Windward Islands proposed 1991.

St Petersburg former name (1914–24) *Petrograd* and (1924–91) *Leningrad* capital of the St Petersburg region, Russia, at the head of the Gulf of Finland; population (1987) 4,948,000. Industries include shipbuilding, machinery, chemicals, and textiles. Founded 1703, it was capital of the Russian Empire 1709–1918. During World War II, the city withstood a German siege 1941–44, in which a million inhabitants died.

St Pierre and Miquelon territorial dependency of France, eight small islands off the S coast of Newfoundland, Canada; *area* St Pierre group 26 sq km/10 sq mi; Miquelon-Langlade group 216 sq km/83 sq mi; *capital* St Pierre.

Saint-Saëns (Charles) Camille 1835–1921. French composer, pianist and organist. Among his many lyrical Romantic pieces are concertos, the symphonic poem *Danse macabre* 1875, the opera *Samson et Dalila* 1877, and the orchestral *Carnaval des animaux/Carnival of the Animals* 1886.

St Vincent and the Grenadines country in the West Indies, E Caribbean Sea; part of the Windward Islands; *area* 388 sq km/150 sq mi, including islets of Northern Grenadines (43 sq km/17 sq mi); *capital* Kingstown; *physical* volcanic mountains, thickly forested; *head of state* Elizabeth II from 1979 represented by governor general; *head of government* James Mitchell from 1984; *political system* constitutional monarchy; *exports* bananas, taros, sweet potatoes, arrowroot, copra; *population* (1990 est) 106,000; *languages* English, French patois; *recent history* achieved internal self-government 1969 and full independence from Britain within the Commonwealth 1979. A proposal was made 1991 to join the Windward Islands federation.

Sakhalin (Japanese *Karafuto*) island in the Pacific, N of Japan, that since 1947, with the Kurils, forms a region of Russia; capital Yuzhno-Sakhalinsk (Japanese *Toyohara*); area 74,000 sq km/28,564 sq mi; population (1981) 650,000, including aboriginal Ainu and Gilyaks. There are two parallel mountain ranges, rising to over 1,525 m/5,000 ft, which extend throughout its length, 965 km/600 mi. The economy is based on dairy farming, leguminous crops, oats, barley, and sugar beet. In the milder south, there is also timber, rice, wheat, fish, some oil, and coal. The island was settled by both Russians and Japanese from the 17th century. In 1875 the south was ceded by Japan to Russia, but Japan regained it 1905, only to cede it again 1945. It has a missile base.

Sakharov Andrei Dmitrievich 1921–1989. Soviet physicist, known both as the 'father of the Soviet H-bomb' and as an outspoken human-rights campaigner. In 1948 he joined Igor Tamm in developing the hydrogen bomb; he later protested against Soviet nuclear tests and was a founder of the Soviet Human Rights Committee, winning the Nobel Peace Prize 1975. In 1980 he was sent to internal exile in Gorky (now Nizhni-Novgorod) for criticizing Soviet action in Afghanistan. At the end of 1986 he was allowed to return to Moscow and resume his place in the Soviet Academy of Sciences.

Saki pen name of H(ugh) H(ector) Munro 1870–1916. Burmese-born British writer of ingeniously witty and bizarre short stories, often with surprise endings.

Saladin or *Sala-ud-din* 1138–1193. Born a Kurd, sultan of Egypt from 1175, in succession to the Atabeg of Mosul, on whose behalf he conquered Egypt 1164–74. He subsequently conquered Syria 1174–87 and precipitated the third ▷Crusade by his recovery of Jerusalem from the Christians 1187. Renowned for knightly courtesy, Saladin made peace with Richard I of England 1192.

salamander any tailed amphibian of the order *Urodela*. They are sometimes confused with lizards, but unlike lizards they have no scales or claws. Salamanders have smooth or warty moist skin. The order includes some 300 species, arranged in nine families, and found mainly in the northern hemisphere.

Salamis, Battle of naval battle off the coast of the island of Salamis in which the Greeks defeated the Persians 480 BC.

Salazar Antonio de Oliveira 1889–1970. Portuguese prime minister 1932–68 who exercised a virtual dictatorship. During World War II he maintained Portuguese neutrality but fought long colonial wars in Africa (Angola and Mozambique) that impeded his country's economic development as well as that of the colonies.

Salinas de Gortiari Carlos 1948– . Mexican politician, president from 1988, a member of the dominant Institutional Revolutionary Party (PRI).

Salinger J(erome) D(avid) 1919– . US writer, author of the classic novel of mid-20th-century adolescence *The Catcher in the Rye* 1951. He also wrote short stories about a Jewish family named Glass, including *Franny and Zooey* 1961.

Salisbury city and market town in Wiltshire, England, 135 km/84 mi SW of London; population (1981) 35,355. Salisbury is an agricultural centre, and industries include brewing and carpet manufacture (in nearby Wilton). The cathedral of St Mary, built 1220–66, is an example of Early English architecture; its decorated spire 123 m/404 ft is the highest in England; its clock (1386) is one of the oldest still working. The cathedral library contains one of only four copies of the *Magna Carta*.

Salisbury former name (until 1980) of ◊Harare, capital of Zimbabwe.

Salisbury Robert Cecil, 1st Earl of Salisbury. Title conferred on Robert ◊Cecil, secretary of state to Elizabeth I of England.

• **Salisbury** Robert Arthur Talbot Gascoyne-Cecil, 3rd Marquess of Salisbury 1830–1903. British Conservative politician. He entered the Commons 1853 and succeeded to his title 1868. As foreign secretary 1878–80, he took part in the Congress of Berlin, and as prime minister 1885–86, 1886–92, and 1895–1902 gave his main attention to foreign policy, remaining also as foreign secretary for most of this time.

Salk Jonas Edward 1914– . US physician and microbiologist. In 1954 he developed the original vaccine that led to virtual eradication of paralytic ◊polio in industrialized countries. He was director of the Salk Institute for Biological Studies, University of California, San Diego, 1963–75.

Sallust Gaius Sallustius Crispus 86–*c.* 34 BC. Roman historian, a supporter of Julius Caesar. He wrote accounts of Catiline's conspiracy and the Jugurthine War in an epigrammatic style.

salmon any of the various bony fishes of the family Salmonidae. More specifically the name is applied to several species of game fishes of the genera Salmo and Oncorhynchus of North America and Eurasia that mature in the ocean but, to spawn, return to the freshwater streams where they were born. Their normal colour is silvery with a few dark spots, but the colour changes at the spawning season.

Salmonella very varied group of bacteria. They can be divided into three broad groups. One of these causes typhoid and paratyphoid fevers, while a second group causes salmonella ◊food poisoning, which is characterized by stomach pains, vomiting, diarrhoea, and headache. It can be fatal in elderly people, but others usually recover in a few days without antibiotics. Most cases are caused by contaminated animal products, especially poultry meat.

salsa Latin big-band dance music popularized by Puerto Ricans in New York City in the 1980s and by, among others, the Panamanian singer Rubén Blades (1948–).

salsify or *vegetable oyster* hardy biennial *Tragopogon porrifolius*, family Compositae. Its white fleshy roots and spring shoots are cooked and eaten.

SALT abbreviation for ◊*Strategic Arms Limitation Talks*, a series of US–Soviet negotiations 1969–79.

salt in chemistry, any compound formed from an acid and a base through the replacement of all or part of the hydrogen in the acid by a metal or electropositive radical. *Common salt* is sodium chloride (see ◊salt, common).

salt, common or *sodium chloride* NaCl white crystalline solid, found dissolved in sea water and as rock salt (halite) in large deposits and salt domes. Common salt is used extensively in the food industry as a preservative and for flavouring, and in the chemical industry in the making of chlorine and sodium.

Salt Lake City capital of Utah, USA, on the river Jordan, 18 km/11 mi SE of the Great Salt Lake; population (1990) 159,900. Founded 1847, it is the headquarters of the ◊Mormon Church. Mining, construction, and other industries are being replaced by high technology.

saltpetre former name for potassium nitrate (KNO_3), the compound used in making gunpowder (from about 1500). It occurs naturally, being deposited during dry periods in places with warm climates, such as India.

saluki breed of dog resembling the greyhound. It is about 65 cm/26 in high and has a silky coat, which is usually fawn, cream, or white.

Salvador port and naval base in Bahia state, NE Brazil, on the inner side of a peninsula separating Todos Santos Bay from the Atlantic; population (1991) 2,075,400. Products include cocoa, tobacco, and sugar. Founded 1510, it was the capital of Brazil 1549–1763.

Salvador, El republic in Central America; see ◊El Salvador.

Salzburg capital of the state of Salzburg, W Austria, on the river Salzach; population (1981) 139,400. The city is dominated by the Hohensalzburg fortress. It is the seat of an archbishopric founded by St Boniface about 700 and has a 17th-century cathedral. The birthplace of the composer Wolfgang Amadeus Mozart, it has hosted an annual music festival since 1920.

Salzburg federal province of Austria; area 7,200 sq km/2,779 sq mi; population (1987) 462,000. Its capital is Salzburg. Industries include stock rearing, dairy farming, forestry, and tourism.

Samara former name (1935–91) *Kuibyshev* capital of Kuibyshev region, W central Russia, and port at the junction of the rivers Samara and Volga, situated in the centre of the fertile middle Volga plain; industries include aircraft, locomotives, cables, synthetic rubber, textiles, fertilizers, petroleum refining, and quarrying; population (1987) 1,280,000.

Samaria region of ancient Israel. The town of Samaria (now Sebastiyeh) on the west bank of the river Jordan was the capital of Israel in the 10th–8th centuries BC. It was renamed Sebarte in the 1st century BC by the Roman administrator Herod the Great. Extensive remains have been excavated.

Samaritan member or descendant of the colonists forced to settle in Samaria (now N Israel) by the Assyrians after their occupation of the ancient kingdom of Israel 722 BC. Samaritans adopted a form of Judaism, but accepted only the Pentateuch, the five books of Moses of the Old Testament, and regarded their temple on Mount Gerizim as the true sanctuary.

samarium hard, brittle, grey-white, metallic element of the ⟩lanthanide series, symbol Sm, atomic number 62, relative atomic mass 150.4. It is widely distributed in nature and is obtained commercially from the minerals monzanite and bastnasite. It is used only occasionally in industry, mainly as a catalyst in organic reactions.

Samarkand city in E Uzbekistan, capital of Samarkand region, near the river Zerafshan, 217 km/135 mi E of Bukhara; population (1987) 388,000. Industries include cotton-ginning, silk manufacture, and engineering.

samizdat in the USSR and eastern Europe before the 1989 uprisings, written material circulated underground to evade state censorship; for example, reviews of Solzhenitzyn's banned novel *August 1914* 1972.

Samoa volcanic island chain in the SW Pacific. It is divided into Western Samoa and American Samoa.

Samoa, American group of islands 4,200 km/2,610 mi S of Hawaii, administered by the USA; *area* 200 sq km/77 sq mi; *capital* Fagatogo on Tutuila; *features* five volcanic islands, including Tutuila, Tau, and Swain's Island, and two coral atolls. National park (1988) includes prehistoric village of Saua, virgin rainforest, flying foxes; *exports* canned tuna, handicrafts; *currency* US dollar; *population* (1990) 46,800; *language* Samoan and English; *religion* Christian; *government* as a non-self-governing territory of the USA, under Governor A P Lutali, it is constitutionally an unincorporated territory of the USA, administered by the Department of the Interior; *history* the islands were acquired by the USA in Dec 1899 by agreement with Britain and Germany under the Treaty of Berlin. A constitution was adopted 1960 and revised 1967.

Samoa, Western Independent State of; country in the SW Pacific, in Polynesia, NE of Fiji; *area* 2,830 sq km/1,093 sq mi; *capital* Apia (on Upolu island); *physical* comprises South Pacific islands of Savai'i and Upolu, with two smaller tropical islands and islets; mountain ranges on main islands;

lava flows on Savai'i; *head of state* King Malietoa Tanumafili II from 1962; *head of government* Tofilau Eti Alesana from 1988; *political system* liberal democracy; *exports* coconut oil, copra, cocoa, fruit juice, cigarettes, timber; *population* (1989 est) 169,000; *languages* English, Samoan (official); *recent history* independence was achieved within the Commonwealth 1962. Tupuola Taisi Efi was the country's first nonroyal prime minister 1975; universal adult suffrage was introduced 1990; and Fiame Naome became the first woman in the cabinet 1991.

samoyed breed of dog, originating in Siberia. It weighs about 25 kg/60 lb and is 58 cm/23 in tall. It resembles a ⟩chow chow, but has a more pointed face and a white or cream coat.

samphire or *glasswort* or *sea asparagus* perennial plant *Crithmum maritimum* found on sea cliffs in Europe. The aromatic leaves are fleshy and sharply pointed; the flowers grow in yellow-green umbels. It is used in salads, or pickled.

Samson 11th century BC. In the Old Testament, a hero of Israel. He was renowned for exploits of strength against the Philistines, which ended when his lover Delilah cut off his hair, the source of his strength, as told in the Book of Judges.

samurai member of the military caste in Japan from the mid-12th century until 1869, when the feudal system was abolished and all samurai pensioned off by the government. A samurai was an armed retainer of a *daimyō* (large landowner) with specific duties and privileges and a strict code of honour.

Sana'a capital of Yemen, SW Arabia, 320 km/200 mi N of Aden; population (1986) 427,000. A walled city, with fine mosques and traditional architecture, it is rapidly being modernized.

San Andreas fault geological fault line stretching for 1,125 km/700 mi in a NW–SE direction through the state of California, USA.

San Antonio city in S Texas, USA; population (1990) 936,000. It is a commercial and financial centre; industries include aircraft maintenance, oil refining, and meat packing. Founded 1718, it grew up round the site of the ⟩Alamo fort.

sand loose grains of rock, sized 0.02–2.00 mm/0.0008–0.0800 in in diameter, consisting chiefly of ⟩quartz, but owing their varying colour to mixtures of other minerals. Sand is used in cement-making, as an abrasive, in glass-making, and for other purposes.

Sand George. Pen name of Amandine Aurore Lucie Dupin 1804–1876. French author whose prolific literary output was often autobiographical. In 1831 she left her husband after nine years of marriage and, while living in Paris as a writer, had love affairs with Alfred de Musset, Frédéric ⟩Chopin, and others. Her first novel, *Indiana* 1832, was a plea for women's right to independence.

sandalwood fragrant heartwood of any of certain

Asiatic and Australian trees of the genus *Santalum*, family Santalaceae, used for ornamental carving, in perfume, and burned as incense.

sandgrouse any bird of the family Pteroclidae. They look like long-tailed grouse, but are actually closely related to pigeons. They live in warm, dry areas of Europe, Asia, and Africa and have long wings, short legs, and thick skin.

sand hopper or *beachflea* any of various small crustaceans belonging to the order Amphipeda, with laterally compressed bodies, that live in beach sand and jump like fleas. The eastern sand hopper *Orchestia agilis* of North America is about 1.3 cm/0.5 in long.

San Diego city and military and naval base in California, USA; population (1990) 1,110,600, metropolitan area 2,498,000. It is an important Pacific Ocean fishing port. Manufacturing includes aerospace and electronic equipment, metal fabrication, printing and publishing, seafood canning, and shipbuilding. ⟡Tijuana adjoins San Diego across the Mexican border.

Sandinista member of the socialist movement that carried out the ⟡Nicaraguan Revolution.

sandpiper any of various shorebirds belonging to the family Scolopacidae, which includes godwits, ⟡curlews, and ⟡snipes. The common sandpiper *Tringa hypoleucos* is a small graceful bird with long slender bill and short tail, drab above and white below. It is common in the northern hemisphere except North America.

sandstone sedimentary rocks formed from the consolidation of sand, with sand-sized grains (0.0625–2 mm/0.0025–0.08 in) in a matrix or cement. The principal component is quartz. Sandstones are classified according to the matrix or cement material (whether derived from clay or silt, for example as calcareous sandstone, ferruginous sandstone, siliceous sandstone).

Sandwich Islands former name of ⟡Hawaii, a group of islands in the Pacific.

San Francisco chief Pacific port of the USA, in California; population (1990) 724,000, metropolitan area of San Francisco and Oakland 3,686,600. The city stands on a peninsula south of the Golden Gate strait, which gives access to San Francisco Bay and is spanned by the world's second longest single-span bridge (1937). Manufactured goods include textiles, metal products, electrical equipment, petroleum products, chemicals, and pharmaceuticals. A Spanish fort and mission were established here 1776, called **Yerba Buena** until 1846. When gold was discovered nearby in 1848, its population increased from about 800 to about 25,000 in two years. In 1906 the city was almost destroyed by an earthquake and subsequent fire; another earthquake rocked the city 1989.

Sanger Frederick 1918– . English biochemist,

the first person to win a Nobel Prize for Chemistry twice: the first in 1958 for determining the structure of insulin, and the second in 1980 for work on the chemical structure of genes.

San José capital of Costa Rica; population (1989) 284,600. Products include coffee, cocoa, and sugar cane. Founded 1737; capital since 1823.

San José city in Santa Clara Valley, California, USA; population (1990) 782,200. It is the centre of 'Silicon Valley', the site of many high-technology electronic firms. There are also electrical, aerospace, missile, rubber, metal, and machine industries, and it is a commercial and transportation centre for orchard crops and wines produced in the area. It was the first capital of California 1849–51.

San Juan capital of Puerto Rico; population (1990) 437,750. It is a port and industrial city. Products include chemicals, pharmaceuticals, machine tools, electronic equipment, textiles, plastics, and rum.

San Luis Potosí silver-mining city and capital of San Luis Potosí state, central Mexico; population (1986) 602,000.

San Marino Republic of; country within N central Italy; *area* 61 sq km/24 sq mi; *capital* San Marino; *physical* on the slope of Mount Titano; *head of state and government* two captains regent, elected for a six-month period; *political system* direct democracy; *exports* wine, ceramics, paint, chemicals, building stone; *population* (1990 est) 23,000; *language* Italian; *recent history* independence was recognized under Italy's protection 1862. Governed by a series of left-wing and centre-left coalitions 1947–86; Communist and Christian Democrat 'grand coalition' formed 1986.

San Martín Jose de 1778–1850. South American revolutionary leader. He served in the Spanish army during the Peninsular War, but after 1812 he devoted himself to the South American struggle for independence, playing a large part in the liberation of Argentina, Chile, and Peru from Spanish rule.

San Pedro Sula main industrial and commercial city in NW Honduras, the second-largest city in the country; population (1989) 300,900. It trades in bananas, coffee, sugar, and timber and manufactures textiles, plastics, furniture, and cement.

San Salvador capital of El Salvador 48 km/30 mi from the Pacific, at the foot of San Salvador volcano (2,548 m/8,360 ft); population (1984) 453,000. Industries include food processing and textiles. Since its foundation 1525, it has suffered from several earthquakes.

Sanskrit the dominant classical language of the Indian subcontinent, a member of the Indo-Iranian group of the Indo-European language family, and the sacred language of Hinduism. The oldest form of Sanskrit is *Vedic*, the variety used in the *Vedas* and *Upanishads* (about 1500–700 BC).

Santa Anna Antonio López de 1795–1876. Mexican revolutionary who became general and dictator of Mexico for most of the years between 1824 and 1855. He led the attack on the ⇨Alamo fort in Texas 1836.

Santiago capital of Chile; population (1990) 4,385,500. Industries include textiles, chemicals, and food processing. It was founded 1541.

Santo Domingo capital and chief sea port of the Dominican Republic; population (1982) 1,600,000. Founded 1496 by Bartolomeo, brother of Christopher Columbus, it is the oldest colonial city in the Americas. Its cathedral was built 1515–40.

São Paulo city in Brazil, 72 km/45 mi NW of its port Santos; population (1991) 9,700,100, metropolitan area 15,280,000. It is 900 m/3,000 ft above sea level, and 2° S of the Tropic of Capricorn. It is South America's leading industrial city, producing electronics, steel, and chemicals; it has meat-packing plants and is the centre of Brazil's coffee trade. It originated as a Jesuit mission in 1554.

São Tomé e Príncipe Democratic Republic of; country in the Gulf of Guinea, off the coast of W Africa; *area* 1,000 sq km/386 sq mi; *capital* São Tomé; *physical* comprises two main islands and several smaller ones, all volcanic; thickly forested and fertile; *head of state and government* Miguel Trovoada from 1991; *political system* emergent democracy; *exports* cocoa, copra, coffee, palm oil and kernels; *population* (1990 est) 125,000; *languages* Portuguese (official); Fang (Bantu); *recent history* internal self-government achieved 1973; independence from Portugal achieved 1975, with Manuel Pinto da Costa as president. The first multiparty elections were held 1991.

sap the fluids that circulate through vascular plants, especially woody ones. Sap carries water and food to plant tissues. Sap contains alkaloids, protein, and starch; it can be milky (as in rubber trees), resinous (as in pines), or syrupy (as in maples).

sapphire deep-blue, transparent gem variety of the mineral ⇨corundum Al_2O_3, aluminium oxide. Small amounts of iron and titanium give it its colour. A corundum gem of any colour except red (which is a ruby) can be called a sapphire; for example, yellow sapphire.

Sappho *c.* 612–580 BC. Greek lyric poet, friend of the poet Alcaeus and leader of a female literary coterie at Mytilene (now **Lesvos**, hence ⇨lesbianism). Legend says she committed suicide when her love for the boatman Phaon was unrequited. Only fragments of her poems have survived.

Saracen ancient Greek and Roman term for an Arab, used in the Middle Ages by Europeans for all Muslims. The equivalent term used in Spain was ⇨Moor.

Saragossa English spelling of ⇨Zaragoza, city in Aragon, Spain.

Sarajevo capital of ⇨Bosnia-Herzegovina; population (1982) 449,000. Industries include engineering, brewing, chemicals, carpets, and ceramics. It was the site of the 1984 Winter Olympics. Since Jan 1992 the city has been the subject of attacks from Serb militia units opposed to Bosnia-Herzegovina's moves towards independence; the conflict worsened following EC recognition of the republic's independence in April.

Saratov industrial port (chemicals, oil refining) on the river Volga in W central Russia; population (1987) 918,000. It was established in the 1590s as a fortress to protect the Volga trade route.

Sarawak state of Malaysia, on the NW corner of the island of Borneo; *area* 124,400 sq km/48,018 sq mi; *capital* Kuching; *products* it has a tropical climate and produces timber, oil, rice, pepper, rubber, and coconuts; *population* (1991) 1,669,000; 24 ethnic groups make up almost half this number; *physical* mountainous; the rainforest, which may be 10 million years old, contains several thousand tree species. A third of all its plant species are endemic to Borneo. 30% of the forest was cut down 1963–89; timber expected to run out 1995–2001; *history* Sarawak was granted by the Sultan of Brunei to James Brooke 1841, who became 'Rajah of Sarawak'. It was a British protectorate from 1888 until captured by the Japanese in World War II. It was a crown colony from 1946 until 1963, when it became part of Malaysia.

sarcoma malignant ⇨tumour arising from the fat, muscles, bones, cartilage, or blood and lymph vessels and connective tissues. Sarcomas are much less common than ⇨carcinomas.

sardine common name for various small fishes (⇨pilchards) in the herring family.

Sardinia (Italian *Sardegna*) mountainous island, special autonomous region of Italy; area 24,100 sq km/9,303 sq mi; population (1990) 1,664,400. Its capital is Cagliari, and it exports cork and petro-chemicals. It is the second-largest Mediterranean island and includes Costa Smeralda (Emerald Coast) tourist area in the northeast and *nuraghi* (fortified Bronze Age dwellings). After centuries of foreign rule, it became linked 1720 with Piedmont, and this dual kingdom became the basis of a united Italy 1861.

Sargasso Sea part of the N Atlantic (between 40° and 80°W and 25° and 30°N) left static by circling ocean currents, and covered with floating weed *Sargassum natans*.

Sark one of the ⇨Channel Islands, 10 km/6 mi E of Guernsey; area 5 sq km/2 sq mi; there is no town or village. It is divided into Great and Little Sark, linked by an isthmus, and is of great natural beauty. The Seigneurie of Sark was established by Elizabeth I, the ruler being known as Seigneur/Dame, and has its own parliament, the Chief Pleas. There is no income tax, and cars are forbidden; immigration is controlled.

Sartre Jean-Paul 1905–1980. French author and philosopher, a leading proponent of ▷existentialism. He published his first novel, *La Nausée/Nausea*, 1937, followed by the trilogy *Les Chemins de la Liberté/Roads to Freedom* 1944–45 and many plays, including *Huis Clos/In Camera* 1944. *L'Etre et le néant/Being and Nothingness* 1943, his first major philosophical work, sets out a radical doctrine of human freedom. In the later work *Critique de la raison dialectique/Critique of Dialectical Reason* 1960 he tried to produce a fusion of existentialism and Marxism.

Saskatchewan province of W Canada; *area* 652,300 sq km/251,788 sq mi; *capital* Regina; *towns* Saskatoon, Moose Jaw, Prince Albert; *physical* prairies in the south; to the north, forests, lakes, and subarctic tundra; Prince Albert National Park; *products* more than 60% of Canada's wheat; oil, natural gas, uranium, zinc, potash (world's largest reserves), copper, helium (the only western reserves outside the USA); *population* (1991) 995,300; *history* once inhabited by Indians speaking Athabaskan, Algonquin, and Sioux languages, who depended on caribou and moose in the north and buffalo in the south. French trading posts established about 1750; owned by Hudson's Bay Company, first permanent settlement 1774; ceded to Canadian government 1870 as part of Northwest Territories; became a province 1905.

Sassanian Empire Persian empire founded AD 224 by Ardashir, a chieftain in the area of what is now Fars, in Iran, who had taken over ▷Parthia; it was named after his grandfather, Sasan. The capital was Ctesiphon, near modern ▷Baghdad, Iraq. After a rapid period of expansion, when it contested supremacy with Rome, it was destroyed in 637 by Muslim Arabs at the Battle of ▷Qadisiya.

Sassau-Nguesso Denis 1943– . Congolese socialist politician, president from 1979. He progressively consolidated his position within the ruling left-wing Congolese Labour Party (PCT), at the same time as improving relations with France and the USA. In 1990, in response to public pressure, he agreed that the PCT should abandon Marxism-Leninism and that a multiparty system should be introduced.

Sassoon Siegfried 1886–1967. English writer, author of the autobiography *Memoirs of a Foxhunting Man* 1928. His *War Poems* 1919 express the disillusionment of his generation.

satellite any small body that orbits a larger one, either natural or artificial. Natural satellites that orbit planets are called moons. The first *artificial satellite*, *Sputnik 1*, was launched into orbit around the Earth by the USSR 1957. Artificial satellites are used for scientific purposes, communications, weather forecasting, and military applications. The largest artificial satellites can be seen by the naked eye.

satellite television transmission of broadcast signals through artificial communications satellites. Mainly positioned in ▷geostationary orbit, satellites have been used since the 1960s to relay television pictures around the world. Higher-power satellites have more recently been developed to broadcast signals to cable systems or directly to people's homes.

Satie Erik (Alfred Leslie) 1866–1925. French composer. His piano pieces, such as *Gymnopédies* 1888, often combine wit and melancholy. His orchestral works include *Parade* 1917, among whose sound effects is a typewriter. He was the mentor of the group of composers known as ▷*Les Six*.

satire poem or piece of prose that uses wit, humour, or irony, often through ▷allegory or extended metaphor, to ridicule human pretensions or expose social evils. Satire is related to *parody* in its intention to mock, but satire tends to be more subtle and to mock an attitude or a belief, whereas parody tends to mock a particular work (such as a poem) by imitating its style, often with purely comic intent.

Saturn in astronomy, the second-largest planet in the solar system, sixth from the Sun, and encircled by bright and easily visible equatorial rings. Viewed through a telescope it is ochre. Saturn orbits the Sun every 29.46 years at an average distance of 1,427,000,000 km/886,700,000 mi. Its equatorial diameter is 120,000 km/75,000 mi, but its polar diameter is 12,000 km/7,450 mi smaller, a result of its fast rotation and low density, the lowest of any planet. Saturn spins on its axis every 10 hours 14 minutes at its equator, slowing to 10 hours 40 minutes at high latitudes. Its mass is 95 times that of Earth, and its magnetic field 1,000 times stronger.

largest natural planetary satellites

Planet	Satellite	Diameter in km	Mean distance from centre of primary in km	Orbital period in days	Reciprocal mass (planet = 1)
Jupiter	Ganymede	5,270	1,070,000	7.16	12,800
Saturn	Titan	5,150	1,221,900	15.95	4,200
Jupiter	Callisto	4,820	1,880,000	16.69	17,700
Jupiter	Io	3,630	421,600	1.77	21,400
Earth	Moon	3,476	384,400	27.32	81.3
Jupiter	Europa	3,132	670,900	3.55	39,000
Neptune	Triton	2,720	354,000	5.88	750

Saturn is believed to have a small core of rock and iron, encased in ice and topped by a deep layer of liquid hydrogen. There are over 20 known moons, its largest being ⇔Titan.

Saturn in Roman mythology, the god of agriculture (Greek *Kronos*), whose period of rule was the ancient Golden Age. He was dethroned by his sons Jupiter, Neptune, and Pluto. At his festival, the Saturnalia in Dec, gifts were exchanged, and slaves were briefly treated as their masters' equals.

satyr in Greek mythology, a lustful, drunken woodland creature characterized by pointed ears, two horns on the forehead, and a tail. Satyrs attended the god of wine, ⇔Dionysus.

Saudi Arabia Kingdom of; country on the Arabian peninsula, stretching from the Red Sea to the Arabian Gulf, bordered N by Jordan, Iraq, and Kuwait; E by Qatar and the United Arab Emirates; SE by Oman; and S by Yemen; *area* 2,200,518 sq km/849,400 sq mi; *capital* Riyadh; *physical* desert, sloping to the Persian Gulf from a height of 2,750 m/9,000 ft in the W; Naful Desert in N and the Rub'ai Khali (Empty Quarter) in S; *head of state and government* King Fahd Ibn Abdul Aziz from 1982; *political system* absolute monarchy; *exports* oil, petroleum products; *population* (1990 est) 16,758,000 (16% nomadic); *language* Arabic; *recent history* the territories were united and the kingdom established 1926–32. Rioting by Iranian pilgrims 1987 led to severing of diplomatic relations with Iran. In 1990 when Iraqi troops invaded Kuwait and massed on the Saudi Arabian border King Fahd called for help from US and UK forces; the subsequent ⇔Gulf War 1991 ensured Saudi Arabia's security.

Saul in the Old Testament, the first king of Israel. He warred successfully against the neighbouring Ammonites and Philistines, but fell from God's favour in his battle against the Amalekites. After being wounded in battle with the Philistines, in which his three sons died, he committed suicide.

savanna or **savannah** extensive open tropical grasslands, with scattered trees and shrubs. Savannas cover large areas of Africa, North and South America, and N Australia.

Savimbi Jonas 1934– . Angolan soldier and right-wing revolutionary, founder and leader of the National Union for the Total Independence of Angola (UNITA). From 1975 UNITA under Savimbi's leadership tried to overthrow the government. An agreement between the two parties was reached 1991.

Savonarola Girolamo 1452–1498. Italian reformer, a Dominican friar and an eloquent preacher. His crusade against political and religious corruption won him popular support, and in 1494 he led a revolt in Florence that expelled the ruling Medici family and established a democratic republic. His denunciations of Pope ⇔Alexander VI led to his excommunication in 1497, and in 1498 he was arrested, tortured, hanged, and burned for heresy.

Savoy area of France between the Alps, Lake Geneva, and the river Rhône. A medieval duchy, it was made into the *départements* of Savoie and Haute-Savoie, in the Rhône-Alpes region.

sawfish any fish of an order *Pristiformes* of large, sharklike ⇔rays, characterized by a flat, sawlike snout edged with teeth. The common sawfish *P. pectinatus*, also called the smalltooth, is more than 6 m/19 ft long. It has some 24 teeth along an elongated snout (2 m/6 ft) that can be used as a weapon.

sawfly any of several families of insects of the order Hymenoptera, related to bees, wasps, and ants, but lacking a 'waist' on the body. The egg-laying tube (ovipositor) of the female is surrounded by a pair of sawlike organs, which it uses to make a slit in a plant stem to lay its eggs. Horntails are closely related.

Saw Maung 1929– . Myanmar (Burmese) soldier and politician. Appointed head of the armed forces in 1985 by ⇔Ne Win, he led a coup to remove Ne Win's successor, Maung Maung, in 1988 and became leader of a totalitarian 'emergency government', which remained in office despite being defeated in the May 1990 election. In April 1992 he was replaced as chair of the ruling military junta, prime minister, and commander of the armed forces by Than Shwe.

Saxe-Coburg-Gotha Saxon duchy. Albert, the Prince Consort of Britain's Queen Victoria, was a son of the 1st Duke, Ernest I (1784–1844), who was succeeded by Albert's elder brother, Ernest II (1818–1893). It remained the name of the British royal house until 1917, when it was changed to Windsor.

saxifrage any plant of the genus *Saxifraga*, family Saxifragaceae, occurring in rocky, mountainous, and alpine situations in the northern hemisphere. They are low plants with groups of small white, pink, or yellow flowers.

Saxon member of a Teutonic people who invaded Britain in the early Middle Ages; see ⇔Anglo-Saxon.

Saxony (German *Sachsen*) administrative *Land* (state) of Germany; *area* 17,036 sq km/ 6,580 sq mi; *capital* Dresden; *towns* Leipzig, Chemnitz, Zwickau; *physical* on the plain of the river Elbe north of the Erzgebirge mountain range; *products* electronics, textiles, vehicles, machinery, chemicals, coal; *population* (1990) 5,000,000; *history* Conquered by Charlemagne 792, Saxony became a powerful medieval German duchy. The electors of Saxony were also kings of Poland 1697–1763. Saxony was part of East Germany 1946–90, forming a region with Anhalt.

Saxony-Anhalt administrative *Land* (state) of Germany; *area* 20,450 sq km/10,000 sq mi; *capital*

Magdeburg; **towns** Halle, Dessau; **products** chemicals, electronics, rolling stock, footwear, cereals, vegetables; **population** (1990) 3,000,000; **history** Anhalt became a duchy 1863 and a member of the North German Confederation 1866. Between 1946 and 1990 it was joined to the former Prussian province of Saxony as a region of East Germany.

saxophone large family of wind instruments combining woodwind and brass features, the single reed of the clarinet and the wide bore of the bugle. Patented in 1846 by Adolphe Sax (1814–1894), a Belgian instrument maker, the saxophone is a lively and versatile instrument that has played a prominent part in the history of jazz. Four of the original eight sizes remain in common use: soprano, alto, tenor, and baritone.

Say's law in economics, the 'law of markets' formulated by Jean-Baptiste Say (1767–1832) to the effect that supply creates its own demand and that resources can never be underused.

scabies contagious infection of the skin caused by the parasitic itch mite *Sarcoptes scaboi*, which burrows under the skin to deposit eggs. Treatment is by antiparasitic creams and lotions.

scabious any plant of the Eurasian genus *Scabiosa* of the teasel family Dipsacaceae, with many small, usually blue, flowers borne in a single head on a tall stalk. The small scabious *S. columbaria* and the Mediterranean sweet scabious *S. atropurpurea* are often cultivated.

scale in music, a sequence of pitches that establishes a key, and in some respects the character of a composition. A scale is defined by its starting note and may be **major** or **minor** depending on the order of intervals. A **chromatic** scale is the full range of 12 notes: it has no key because there is no fixed starting point.

scale insect any small plant-sucking insect (order *Homoptera*) of the superfamily Coccidea. Some species are major pests – for example, the citrus mealy bug (genus *Pseudococcus*), which attacks citrus fruits in North America. The female is often wingless and legless, attached to a plant by the head and with the body covered with a waxy scale. The rare males are winged.

scallop any marine bivalve ◊mollusc of the family Pectinidae, with a fan-shaped shell. There are two 'ears' extending from the socketlike hinge. Scallops use water-jet propulsion to move through the water to escape predators such as starfish. The giant Pacific scallop found from Alaska to California can reach 20 cm/8 in width.

Scandinavia peninsula in NW Europe, comprising Norway and Sweden; politically and culturally it also includes Denmark, Iceland, the Faroe Islands and Finland.

scandium silver-white, metallic element of the ◊lanthanide series, symbol Sc, atomic number 21, relative atomic mass 44.956. Its compounds are found widely distributed in nature, but only in minute amounts. The metal has little industrial importance. The element was discovered and named in 1879 by Swedish chemist Lars Nilson (1840–1899).

scanning in medicine, the noninvasive examination of body organs to detect abnormalities of structure or function. Detectable waves – for example, ◊ultrasound, magnetic, or ◊X-rays – are passed through the part to be scanned. Their absorption pattern is recorded, analysed by computer, and displayed pictorially on a screen.

scarab any of a family Scarabaeidae of beetles, often brilliantly coloured, and including cockchafers, June beetles, and dung beetles. The *Scarabeus sacer* was revered by the ancient Egyptians as the symbol of resurrection.

Scargill Arthur 1938– . British trade-union leader. Elected president of the National Union of Miners (NUM) 1981, he embarked on a collision course with the Conservative government of Margaret Thatcher. The damaging strike of 1984–85 split the miners' movement.

Scarlatti (Giuseppe) Domenico 1685–1757. Italian composer, eldest son of Alessandro ◊Scarlatti, who lived most of his life in Portugal and Spain in the service of the Queen of Spain. He wrote highly original harpsichord sonatas.

Scarlatti (Pietro) Alessandro (Gaspare) 1660–1725. Italian Baroque composer, Master of the Chapel at the court of Naples, who developed the opera form. He composed more than 100 operas, including *Tigrane* 1715, as well as church music and oratorios.

scarlet fever or **scarlatina** acute infectious disease, especially of children, caused by the bacterium *Streptococcus pyogenes*. It is marked by a sore throat and a bright red rash spreading from the upper to the lower part of the body. The rash is followed by the skin peeling in flakes. It is treated with antibiotics.

scarp and dip in geology, the two slopes formed when a sedimentary bed outcrops as a landscape feature. The scarp is the slope that cuts across the bedding plane; the dip is the opposite slope which follows the bedding plane. The scarp is usually steep, while the dip is a gentle slope.

scepticism ancient philosophical view that absolute knowledge of things is ultimately unobtainable, hence the only proper attitude is to suspend judgement. Its origins lay in the teachings of the Greek philosopher Pyrrho, who maintained that peace of mind lay in renouncing all claims to knowledge.

scherzo in music, a lively piece, usually in rapid triple (3/4) time; often used for the third movement of a symphony, sonata, or quartet.

Schiele Egon 1890–1918. Austrian Expressionist

artist. Originally a landscape painter, he was strongly influenced by Art Nouveau and developed a contorted linear style. His subject matter included portraits and nudes. In 1911 he was arrested for alleged obscenity.

Schiller Johann Christoph Friedrich von 1759–1805. German dramatist, poet, and historian. He wrote *Sturm und Drang* ('storm and stress') verse and plays, including the dramatic trilogy *Wallenstein* 1798–99. Much of his work concerns the aspirations for political freedom and the avoidance of mediocrity.

schist ⟡metamorphic rock containing ⟡mica or another platy or elongate mineral, whose crystals are aligned to give a foliation (planar texture) known as schistosity. Schist may contain additional minerals such as ⟡garnet.

schizophrenia mental disorder, a psychosis of unknown origin, which can lead to profound changes in personality and behaviour including paranoia and hallucinations. Contrary to popular belief, it does not involve a split personality. Modern treatment approaches include drugs, family therapy, stress reduction, and rehabilitation.

Schleswig-Holstein administrative region (*Land*) of Germany; *area* 15,700 sq km/6,060 sq mi; *capital* Kiel; *towns* Lübeck, Flensburg, Schleswig; *features* river Elbe, Kiel Canal, Heligoland; *products* shipbuilding, mechanical and electrical engineering, food processing; *population* (1988) 2,613,000; *religion* 87% Protestant; 6% Catholic; *history* Schleswig (Danish *Slesvig*) and Holstein were two duchies held by the kings of Denmark from 1460, but were not part of the kingdom; a number of the inhabitants were German, and Holstein was a member of the Confederation of the Rhine formed 1815. In 1866 Prussia annexed the two duchies. A plebiscite held 1920 gave the northern part of Schleswig to Denmark, which made it the province of Haderslev and Aabenraa; the rest, with Holstein, remained part of Germany.

Schliemann Heinrich 1822–1890. German archaeologist. He earned a fortune in business, retiring in 1863 to pursue his lifelong ambition to discover a historical basis for Homer's *Iliad*. In 1871 he began excavating at Hissarlik, Turkey, a site which yielded the ruins of nine consecutive cities and was indeed the site of Troy. His later excavations were at Mycenae 1874–76, where he discovered the ruins of the ⟡Mycenaean civilization.

Schmidt Helmut 1918– . German socialist politician, member of the Social Democratic Party (SPD), chancellor of West Germany 1974–83. As chancellor, Schmidt introduced social reforms and continued Brandt's policy of Ostpolitik. With the French president Giscard d'Estaing, he instigated annual world and European economic summits. He was a firm supporter of ⟡NATO and of the deployment of US nuclear missiles in West Germany during the early 1980s.

Schoenberg Arnold (Franz Walter) 1874–1951. Austro-Hungarian composer, a US citizen from 1941. After Romantic early works such as *Verklärte Nacht/Transfigured Night* 1899 and the *Gurrelieder/Songs of Gurra* 1900–11, he experimented with ⟡atonality (absence of key), producing works such as *Pierrot Lunaire* 1912 for chamber ensemble and voice, before developing the 12-tone system of musical composition. This was further developed by his pupils Alban ⟡Berg and Anton ⟡Webern.

Schopenhauer Arthur 1788–1860. German philosopher whose *The World as Will and Idea* 1818 expounded an atheistic and pessimistic world view: an irrational will is considered as the inner principle of the world, producing an ever-frustrated cycle of desire, of which the only escape is aesthetic contemplation or absorption into nothingness.

Schrödinger Erwin 1887–1961. Austrian physicist who advanced the study of wave mechanics (see ⟡quantum theory). Born in Vienna, he became senior professor at the Dublin Institute for Advanced Studies 1940. He shared (with Paul Dirac) a Nobel prize 1933.

Schubert Franz (Peter) 1797–1828. Austrian composer. His ten symphonies include the incomplete eighth in B minor (the 'Unfinished') and the 'Great' in C major. He wrote chamber and piano music, including the 'Trout Quintet', and over 600 lieder (songs) combining the Romantic expression of emotion with pure melody. They include the cycles *Die schöne Müllerin/The Beautiful Maid of the Mill* 1823 and *Die Winterreise/The Winter Journey* 1827.

Schumacher Fritz (Ernst Friedrich) 1911–1977. German economist who believed that the increasing size of institutions, coupled with unchecked economic growth, created a range of social and environmental problems. He argued his case in books like *Small is Beautiful* 1973, and tested it practically through establishing the Intermediate Technology Development Group.

Schumann Robert Alexander 1810–1856. German Romantic composer. His songs and short piano pieces show simplicity combined with an ability to portray mood and emotion. Among his compositions are four symphonies, a violin concerto, a piano concerto, sonatas, and song cycles, such as *Dichterliebe/Poet's Love* 1840. Mendelssohn championed many of his works.

Schwarzkopf (H) Norman (nicknamed 'Stormin' Norman') 1934– . US general who was supreme commander of the Allied forces in the ⟡Gulf War 1991. He planned and executed a blitzkrieg campaign, Desert Storm, sustaining remarkably few casualties in the liberation of Kuwait. He was a battalion commander in the Vietnam War and deputy commander of the 1983 US invasion of Grenada.

sciatica persistent pain in the leg, along the sciatic nerve and its branches. Causes of sciatica include inflammation of the nerve or pressure on, or inflammation of, a nerve root leading out of the lower spine.

science fiction or *speculative fiction* (also known as *SF* or *sci-fi*) genre of fiction and film with an imaginary scientific, technological, or futuristic basis. It is sometimes held to have its roots in the works of Mary Shelley, notably *Frankenstein* 1818. Often taking its ideas and concerns from current ideas in science and the social sciences, science fiction aims to shake up standard perceptions of reality.

Scientology 'applied religious philosophy' based on dianetics, founded in California in 1954 by L Ron Hubbard as the **Church of Scientology**. It claims to 'increase man's spiritual awareness', but its methods of recruiting and retaining converts have been criticized. Its headquarters from 1959 have been in Sussex, England.

scilla any bulbous plant of the genus *Scilla*, family Liliaceae, bearing blue, pink, or white flowers, and including the spring squill *S. verna*.

Scilly Islands group of 140 islands and islets lying 40 km/25 mi SW of Land's End, England; administered by the Duchy of Cornwall; area 16 sq km/6.3 sq mi; population (1981) 1,850. The five inhabited islands are *St Mary's*, the largest, on which is Hugh Town, capital of the Scillies; *Tresco*, the second largest, with subtropical gardens; *St Martin's*, noted for beautiful shells; *St Agnes*; and *Bryher*.

Scipio Africanus Major 237–c. 183 BC. Roman general. He defeated the Carthaginians in Spain 210–206, invaded Africa 204, and defeated Hannibal at Zama 202.

Scotland, history for early history, see also ◊Britain, ancient; ◊Celt; ◊Pict.
4th century BC Celts reached British Isles.
1st century AD Romans prevented by Picts from penetrating far into Scotland.
5th–6th centuries Christianity introduced from Ireland.
9th century Kenneth MacAlpin united kingdoms of Scotland.
946 Malcolm I conquered Strathclyde.
1015 Malcolm II conquered Lothian.
1263 Defeat of Haakon, king of Norway, at Battle of Largs.
1266 Scotland gained Hebrides from Norway at Treaty of Perth.
1292 Scottish throne granted by Edward I (attempting to annex Scotland) to John Baliol.
1297 Defeat of England at Stirling Bridge by Wallace.
1314 Robert Bruce defeated English at Bannockburn.
1328 Scottish independence recognized by England.
1371 First Stuart king, Robert II.
1513 James IV killed at Battle of Flodden.
1540s–1550s Knox introduced Calvinism to Scotland
1565 Mary Queen of Scots married Darnley.

Scipio Africanus Minor *c.* 185–129 BC. Roman general, the adopted grandson of Scipio Africanus Major, also known as *Scipio Aemilianus*. He destroyed Carthage 146, and subdued Spain 134. He was opposed to his brothers-in-law, the Gracchi, and his wife is thought to have shared in his murder.

scorpion any arachnid of the order Scorpiones. Common in the tropics and subtropics, scorpions have large pincers and long tails ending in upcurved poisonous stings, though the venom is not usually fatal to a healthy adult human. Some species reach 25 cm/10 in. They produce live young rather than eggs, and hunt chiefly by night.

Scorsese Martin 1942– . US director whose films concentrate on complex characterization and the themes of alienation and guilt. His influential and invariably powerful work includes *Mean Streets* 1973, *Taxi Driver* 1976, *Raging Bull* 1980, *The Last Temptation of Christ* 1988, and *Cape Fear* 1991.

Scotland the northernmost part of Britain, formerly an independent country, now part of the UK; *area* 78,470 sq km/30,297 sq mi; *capital* Edinburgh; *towns* Glasgow, Dundee, Aberdeen; *features* the Highlands in the north (with the Grampian Mountains); central Lowlands, including valleys of the Clyde and Forth, with most of the country's population and industries; Southern Uplands (including the Lammermuir Hills); and islands of the Orkneys, Shetlands, and Western Isles; the world's greatest concentration of nuclear weapons are at the UK and US bases on the Clyde,

1566 Rizzio murdered.
1567 Darnley murdered.
1568 Mary fled to England.
1578 James VI took over government.
1587 Mary beheaded.
1592 Presbyterianism established.
1603 James VI became James I of England.
1638 Scottish rebellion against England.
1643 Solemn League and Covenant.
1651–1660 Cromwell conquered Scotland.
1679 Covenanters defeated at Bothwell Brig.
1689 Jacobites defeated at Killiecrankie.
1692 Massacre of Glencoe.
1707 Act of Union with England.
1715, 1745 Failed Jacobite risings against England.
18th and 19th centuries Highland Clearances: tenant farmers evicted to make way for sheep.
1945 First Scottish member of Parliament elected.
1979 Referendum rejected Scottish directly elected assembly.
1989 Local rates replaced by 'poll tax' despite wide opposition.
1990 350,000 warrants issued by Mar for nonpayment of poll tax.

near Glasgow; 8,000-year-old pinewood forests once covered 1,500,000 hectares/3,706,500 acres, now reduced to 12,500 hectares/30,900 acres; *industry* electronics, marine and aircraft engines, oil, natural gas, chemicals, textiles, clothing, printing, paper, food processing, tourism; *currency* pound sterling; *population* (1987) 5,113,000; *language* English; Gaelic spoken by 1.3%, mainly in the Highlands; *religion* Presbyterian (Church of Scotland), Roman Catholic; *famous people* Robert Bruce, Walter Scott, Robert Burns, Robert Louis Stevenson, Adam Smith; *government* Scotland sends 72 members to the UK Parliament at Westminster. Local government is on similar lines to that of England but there is a differing legal system (⇨Scots law). There is a movement for an independent or devolved Scottish assembly.

Scots language the form of the English language as traditionally spoken and written in Scotland, regarded by some scholars as a distinct language. Scots derives from the Northumbrian dialect of Anglo-Saxon or Old English, and has been a literary language since the 14th century.

Scots law the legal system of Scotland. Owing to its separate development, Scotland has a system differing from the rest of the UK, being based on ⇨civil law. Its continued separate existence was guaranteed by the Act of Union with England in 1707.

Scott (George) Gilbert 1811–1878. English architect. As the leading practical architect in the mid-19th-century Gothic revival in England, Scott was responsible for the building or restoration of many public buildings, including the Albert Memorial, the Foreign Office, and St Pancras Station, all in London.

Scott Robert Falcon (known as *Scott of the Antarctic*) 1868–1912. English explorer who commanded two Antarctic expeditions, 1901–04 and 1910–12. On 18 Jan 1912 he reached the South Pole, shortly after Norwegian Roald ⇨Amundsen, but on the return journey he and his companions died in a blizzard only a few miles from their base camp. His journal was recovered and published in 1913.

Scott Walter 1771–1832. Scottish novelist and poet. His first works were translations of German ballads, followed by poems such as 'The Lady of the Lake' 1810 and 'Lord of the Isles' 1815. He gained a European reputation for his historical novels such as *Heart of Midlothian* 1818, *Ivanhoe* 1819, and *The Fair Maid of Perth* 1828. His last years were marked by frantic writing to pay off his debts, after the bankruptcy of his publishing company in 1826.

Scottish Gaelic language see ⇨Gaelic language.

Scout member of a worldwide youth organization that emphasizes character, citizenship, and outdoor life. It was founded (as the Boy Scouts) in England 1908 by Robert ⇨Baden-Powell. His book *Scouting for Boys* 1908 led to the incorporation in the UK of

the Boy Scout Association by royal charter in 1912. There are four branches: Beaver Scouts (aged 6–8), Cub Scouts (aged 8–10½), Scouts (10½–15½), and Venture Scouts (15½–20).

scuba acronym for self-contained breathing apparatus, another name for ⇨aqualung.

Scudamore Peter 1958– . British National Hunt jockey who was champion jockey 1982 (shared with John Francome) and from 1986 to 1991 inclusive. In 1988–89 he rode a record 221 winners, and after the 1990–91 season his total of winners stood at a world record 1,374.

sculpture the artistic shaping in relief or in the round of materials such as wood, stone, metal, and, more recently, plastic and other synthetics. The earliest sculptures are Palaeolithic stone, bone, and ivory carvings. All ancient civilizations, including the Assyrian, Egyptian, Indian, Chinese, and Mayan, have left examples of sculpture. Traditional European sculpture descends from that of Greece, Rome, and Renaissance Italy. The indigenous tradition of sculpture in Africa (see ⇨African art), South America, and the Caribbean has inspired much contemporary sculpture.

scurvy disease caused by deficiency of vitamin C (ascorbic acid), which is contained in fresh vegetables and fruit. The signs are weakness and aching joints and muscles, progressing to bleeding of the gums and then other organs, and drying-up of the skin and hair. Treatment is by giving the vitamin.

Scylla and Charybdis in classical mythology, a sea monster and a whirlpool, between which Odysseus had to sail. Later writers located them in the Straits of Messina, between Sicily and Italy.

Scythia region north of the Black Sea between the Carpathian mountains and the river Don, inhabited by the Scythians 7th–1st centuries BC. From the middle of the 4th century, they were slowly superseded by the Sarmatians. The Scythians produced ornaments and vases in gold and electrum with animal decoration.

SDLP abbreviation for ⇨*Social Democratic Labour Party* (Northern Ireland).

SDP abbreviation for ⇨*Social Democratic Party*.

sea anemone invertebrate marine animal of the class Cnidaria with a tubelike body attached by the base to a rock or shell. The other end has an open 'mouth' surrounded by stinging tentacles, which capture crustaceans and other small organisms. Many sea anemones are beautifully coloured, especially those in tropical waters.

sea cucumber any echinoderm of the class Holothuroidea with a cylindrical body that is tough-skinned, knobbed, or spiny. The body may be several feet in length. Sea cucumbers are sometimes called 'cotton-spinners' from the sticky filaments they eject from the anus in self-defence.

sea horse any marine fish of several related genera, especially *Hippocampus*, of the family Syngnathidae, which includes the pipefishes. The body is small and compressed and covered with bony plates raised into tubercles or spines. The tail is prehensile, and the tubular mouth sucks in small shellfish and larvae as food. The head and foreparts, usually carried upright, resemble those of a horse.

seakale perennial plant *Crambe maritima* of the family Cruciferae. In Europe the young shoots are cultivated as a vegetable.

seal aquatic carnivorous mammal of the families Otariidae and Phocidae (sometimes placed in a separate order, the Pinnipedia). The eared seals or sea lions (Otariidae) have small external ears, unlike the true seals (Phocidae). Seals have a streamlined body with thick blubber for insulation, and front and hind flippers. They feed on fish, squid, or crustaceans, and are commonly found in Arctic and Antarctic seas, but also in Mediterranean, Caribbean, and Hawaiian waters.

sea lily any ⟩echinoderm of the class Crinoidea. In most, the rayed, cuplike body is borne on a sessile stalk (permanently attached to a rock) and has feathery arms in multiples of five encircling the mouth. However, some sea lilies are free-swimming and unattached.

sea lion any of several genera of ⟩seals of the family Otariidae (eared seals), which also includes the fur seals. These streamlined animals have large fore flippers which they use to row themselves through the water. The hind flippers can be turned beneath the body to walk on land.

sea slug any of an order (Nudibranchia) of marine gastropod molluscs in which the shell is reduced or absent. The order includes some very colourful forms, especially in the tropics. They are largely carnivorous, feeding on hydroids and ⟩sponges. British species include the shore-living common grey sea slug *Aeolidia papillosa* up to 8 cm/3 in and the yellow sea lemon *Archidoris pseudoargus*.

season period of the year having a characteristic climate. The change in seasons is mainly due to the change in attitude of the Earth's axis in relation to the Sun, and hence the position of the Sun in the sky at a particular place.

Seattle port (grain, timber, fruit, fish) of the state of Washington, USA, situated between Puget Sound and Lake Washington; population (1990) 516,300, metropolitan area (with Everett) 2,559,200. It is a centre for the manufacture of jet aircraft (Boeing), shipbuilding, and paper industries.

sea urchin any of various orders of the class Echinoidea among the ⟩echinoderms. They all have a globular body enclosed with plates of lime and covered with spines. Sometimes the spines are anchoring organs, and they also assist in locomotion. Sea urchins feed on seaweed and the animals frequenting them, and some are edible.

seaweed any of a vast collection of marine and freshwater, simple, multicellular plant forms belonging to the ⟩algae and found growing from about high-water mark to depths of 100–200 m/300–600 ft. Some have holdfasts, stalks, and fronds, sometimes with air bladders to keep them afloat, and are green, blue-green, red, or brown.

Sebastiano del Piombo *c.* 1485–1547. Italian painter, born in Venice, one of the great painters of the High Renaissance. Sebastiano was a pupil of ⟩Giorgione and developed a similar style of painting. In 1511 he moved to Rome, where his friendship with Michelangelo (and rivalry with Raphael) inspired him to his greatest works, such as

season

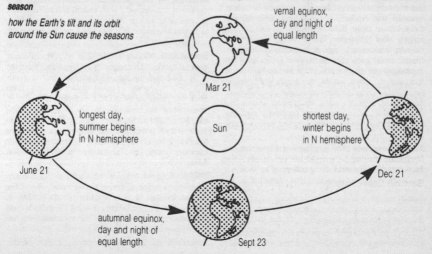

how the Earth's tilt and its orbit around the Sun cause the seasons

vernal equinox, day and night of equal length

Mar 21

longest day, summer begins in N hemisphere

June 21

Sun

shortest day, winter begins in N hemisphere

Dec 21

autumnal equinox, day and night of equal length

Sept 23

The Raising of Lazarus 1517–19 (National Gallery, London). He also painted powerful portraits.

Sebastian, St Roman soldier, traditionally a member of Emperor Diocletian's bodyguard until his Christian faith was discovered. He was martyred by being shot with arrows. Feast day 20 Jan.

second basic SI unit (symbol sec or s) of time, one-sixtieth of a minute. It is defined as the duration of 9,192,631,770 periods of the radiation corresponding to the transition between two hyperfine levels of the ground state of the caesium-133 isotope. In mathematics, the second is a unit (symbol ″) of angular measurement, equalling one-sixtieth of a minute, which in turn is one-sixtieth of a degree.

Second World War alternative name for ▷World War II, 1939–45.

secretary bird ground-hunting, long-legged, mainly grey-plumaged bird of prey *Sagittarius serpentarius*, about 1.2 m/4 ft tall, with an erectile head crest. It is protected in southern Africa because it eats poisonous snakes.

secretary of state in the UK, a title held by a number of ministers; for example, the secretary of state for foreign and commonwealth affairs.

sedge any perennial grasslike plant of the family Cyperaceae, especially the genus *Carex*, usually with three-cornered solid stems, common in low water or on wet and marshy ground.

sediment any loose material that has 'settled' – deposited from suspension in water, ice, or air, generally as the water current or wind speed decreases. Typical sediments are, in order of increasing coarseness, clay, mud, silt, sand, gravel, pebbles, cobbles, and boulders.

sedimentary rock rock formed by the accumulation and cementation of deposits that have been laid down by water, wind, ice, or gravity. Sedimentary rocks cover more than two-thirds of the Earth's surface and comprise three major categories: *clastic, chemically precipitated,* and *organic.* Clastic sediments are the largest group and are composed of fragments of pre-existing rocks; they include clays, sands, and gravels. Chemical precipitates include limestones such as chalk, and evaporated deposits such as gypsum and halite (rock salt). Coal, oil shale, and limestone made of fossil material are examples of organic sedimentary rocks.

seed the reproductive structure of higher plants (▷angiosperms and ▷gymnosperms). It develops from a fertilized ovule and consists of an embryo and a food store, surrounded and protected by an outer seed coat, called the testa. The food store is contained either in a specialized nutritive tissue, the ▷endosperm, or in the ▷cotyledons of the embryo itself. In angiosperms the seed is enclosed within a ▷fruit, whereas in gymnosperms it is usually naked and unprotected, once shed from the female cone.

Following ▷germination the seed develops into a new plant.

seed plant any seed-bearing plant; also known as a **spermatophyte**. The seed plants are subdivided into two classes, the ▷angiosperms, or flowering plants, and the ▷gymnosperms, principally the cycads and conifers. Together, they comprise the major types of vegetation found on land.

Seine French river rising on the Langres plateau NW of Dijon, and flowing 774 km/472 mi in a NW direction to join the English Channel near Le Havre, passing through Paris and Rouen.

seismology study of earthquakes and how their shock waves travel through the Earth. By examining the global pattern of waves produced by an earthquake, seismologists can deduce the nature of the materials through which they have passed. This leads to an understanding of the Earth's internal structure.

select committee any of several long-standing committees of the UK House of Commons, such as the Environment Committee and the Treasury and Civil Service Committee. Select committees represent the chief parliamentary reform of the 20th century, and a possible means – through their all-party membership – of avoiding the automatic repeal of one government's measures by its successor.

Selene in Greek mythology, the goddess of the Moon. She was the daughter of Titan, and the sister of Helios and Eos. In later times she was identified with ▷Artemis.

selenium grey, nonmetallic element, symbol Se, atomic number 34, relative atomic mass 78.96. It belongs to the sulphur group and occurs in several allotropic forms that differ in their physical and chemical properties. It is an essential trace element in human nutrition. Obtained from many sulphide ores and selenides, it is used as a red colouring for glass and enamel.

Seleucus I Nicator *c.* 358–280 BC. Macedonian general under Alexander the Great and founder of the *Seleucid Empire.* After Alexander's death 323 BC, Seleucus became governor and then (312 BC) ruler of Babylonia, founding the city of Seleucia on the river Tigris. He conquered Syria and had himself crowned king 306 BC, but his expansionist policies brought him into conflict with the Ptolemies of Egypt, and he was assassinated by Ptolemy Ceraunus. He was succeeded by his son Antiochus I.

Seljuk Empire empire of the Turkish people (converted to Islam during the 7th century) under the leadership of the invading Tatars or Seljuk Turks. The Seljuk Empire 1055–1243 included all Anatolia and most of Syria. It was succeeded by the ▷Ottoman Empire.

Sellafield site of a nuclear power station on the

coast of Cumbria, NW England. It was known as **Windscale** until 1971, when the management of the site was transferred from the UK Atomic Energy Authority to British Nuclear Fuels Ltd. The plant is the world's greatest discharger of radioactive waste: between 1968 and 1979 180 kg of plutonium was discharged into the Irish Sea.

Sellers Peter 1925–1980. English comedian and film actor. He made his name in the madcap British radio programme *The Goon Show* 1949–60; his films include *The Ladykillers* 1955, *I'm All Right Jack* 1960, *Dr Strangelove* 1964, five *Pink Panther* films 1964–78 (as the bumbling Inspector Clouseau), and *Being There* 1979.

Selznick David O (liver) 1902–1965. US film producer whose early work includes *King Kong*, *Dinner at Eight*, and *Little Women* all 1933. His independent company, Selznick International (1935–40), made such lavish films as *Gone With the Wind* 1939, *Rebecca* 1940, and *Duel in the Sun* 1946.

semaphore visual signalling code in which the relative positions of two moveable pointers or handheld flags stand for different letters or numbers. The system is used by ships at sea and for railway signals.

Semarang port in N Java, Indonesia; population (1980) 1,027,000. There is a shipbuilding industry, and exports include coffee, teak, sugar, tobacco, kapok, and petroleum from nearby oilfields.

semiconductor crystalline material with an electrical conductivity between that of metals (good) and insulators (poor). The conductivity of semiconductors can usually be improved by minute additions of different substances or by other factors. Silicon, for example, has poor conductivity at low temperatures, but this is improved by the application of light, heat, or voltage; hence silicon is used in transistors, rectifiers, and integrated circuits (silicon chips).

semiology or *semiotics* the study of the function of signs and symbols in human communication, both in language and by various nonlinguistic means. Beginning with the notion of the Swiss linguist Ferdinand de Saussure that no word or other sign (*signifier*) is intrinsically linked with its meaning (*signified*), it was developed as a scientific discipline, especially by Claude Lévi-Strauss and Roland ⟡ Barthes.

Semite member of any of the peoples of the Middle East originally speaking a Semitic language, and traditionally said to be descended from Shem, a son of Noah in the Bible. Ancient Semitic peoples include the Hebrews, Ammonites, Moabites, Edomites, Babylonians, Assyrians, Chaldaeans, Phoenicians, and Canaanites. The Semitic peoples founded the monotheistic religions of Judaism, Christianity, and Islam.

Semitic languages branch of the ⟡ Hamito-Semitic language.

Semtex plastic explosive, manufactured in Czechoslovakia. It is safe to handle (it can only be ignited by a detonator) and difficult to trace, since it has no smell. It has been used by extremist groups in the Middle East and by the IRA in Northern Ireland.

senate in ancient Rome, the 'council of elders'. Originally consisting of the heads of patrician families, it was recruited from ex-magistrates and persons who had rendered notable public service, but was periodically purged by the censors. Although nominally advisory, it controlled finance and foreign policy.

Sendak Maurice 1928– . US writer and book illustrator, whose children's books with their deliberately arch illustrations include *Where the Wild Things Are* 1963, *In the Night Kitchen* 1970, and *Outside Over There* 1981.

Seneca Lucius Annaeus *c.* 4 BC–65 AD. Roman Stoic playwright, author of essays and nine tragedies. He was tutor to the future emperor Nero but lost favour after the latter's accession to the throne and was ordered to commit suicide. His tragedies were accepted as classical models by 16th-century dramatists.

Senegal Republic of; country in W Africa, on the Atlantic Ocean, bordered N by Mauritania, E by Mali, S by Guinea and Guinea-Bissau, and enclosing Gambia on three sides; *area* 196,200 sq km/75,753 sq mi; *capital* and chief port Dakar; *physical* plains rising to hills in SE; swamp and tropical forest in SW; river Senegal; *head of state and government* Abdou Diouf from 1981; *political system* emergent socialist democratic republic; *exports* peanuts, cotton, fish, phosphates; *population* (1990 est) 7,740,000; *languages* French (official), African dialects; *recent history* independence was achieved from France 1960. Military assistance was provided to Gambia 1980–81; the confederation of Senegambia came into effect 1982 but was abandoned 1989.

Senghor Léopold (Sédar) 1906– . Senegalese politician and writer, first president of independent Senegal 1960–80. He was Senegalese deputy to the French National Assembly 1946–58, and founder of the Senegalese Progressive Union. He was also a well-known poet and a founder of *négritude*, a black literary and philosophical movement.

senile dementia ⟡ dementia associated with old age, often caused by ⟡ Alzheimer's disease.

Senna Ayrton 1960– . Brazilian motor-racing driver. He had his first Grand Prix win in the 1985 Portuguese Grand Prix, and has progressed to the world driver's title in 1988, 1990, and 1991. He had 26 wins in 100 starts, which he improved with a record four consecutive victories at the start of the 1991 campaign.

Sennacherib died 681 BC. King of Assyria from

705 BC. Son of Sargon II, he rebuilt the city of Nineveh on a grand scale, sacked Babylon 689, and defeated Hezekiah, king of Judah, but failed to take Jerusalem. He was assassinated by his sons, and one of them, Esarhaddon, succeeded him.

Seoul or *Sŏul* capital of South ◊Korea (Republic of Korea), near the Han River, and with its chief port at Inchon; population (1985) 10,627,800. Industries include engineering, textiles, food processing, electrical and electronic equipment, chemicals, and machinery.

sepal part of a flower, usually green, that surrounds and protects the flower in bud. The sepals are derived from modified leaves, and collectively known as the ◊calyx.

Sephardi (plural *Sephardim*) Jew descended from those expelled from Spain and Portugal in the 15th century, or from those forcibly converted during the Inquisition to Christianity (Marranos). Many settled in N Africa and in the Mediterranean countries, as well as in the Netherlands, England, and Dutch colonies in the New World. Sephardim speak Ladino, a 15th-century Romance dialect, as well as the language of their nation.

Sepoy Rebellion alternative name for the ◊Indian Mutiny, a revolt of Indian soldiers against the British in India 1857–58.

septicaemia technical term for blood poisoning.

sequencing in biochemistry, determining the sequence of chemical subunits within a large molecule. Techniques for sequencing amino acids in proteins were established in the 1950s, insulin being the first for which the sequence was completed. Efforts are now being made to determine the sequence of base pairs within ◊DNA.

sequoia two species of conifer in the redwood family Taxodiaceae, native to western USA. The redwood *Sequoia sempervirens* is a long-lived timber tree, and one specimen is the world's tallest tree at 110 m/361 ft. The giant sequoia *Sequoiadendron giganteum* reaches up to 30 m/100 ft in circumference at the base and grows almost as tall as the redwood. It is also (except for the bristlecone pine) the oldest living tree, some specimens being estimated at over 3,500 years of age.

Serb member of Yugoslavia's largest ethnic group, found mainly in Serbia, but also in the neighbouring independent republics of Bosnia-Herzegovina and Croatia. Their language, generally recognized to be the same as Croat and hence known as Serbo-Croatian, belongs to the Slavic branch of the Indo-European family. It has more than 17 million speakers.

Serbia (Serbo-Croatian *Srbija*) constituent republic of Yugoslavia, which includes Kosovo and Vojvodina; *area* 88,400 sq km/34,122 sq mi; *capital* Belgrade; *physical* fertile Danube plains in the north, mountainous in the south; *features* includes

set

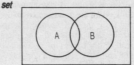

A and B are overlapping sets

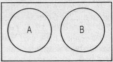

A and B are disjoint sets

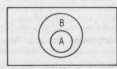

A is the subset of B

the autonomous provinces of ◊Kosovo, capital Priština, of which the predominantly Albanian population demands unification with Albania, and ◊*Vojvodina*, capital Novi Sad, largest town Subotica, with a predominantly Serbian population; *population* (1986) 9,660,000; *language* the Serbian variant of Serbo-Croatian; *religion* Serbian Orthodox.

serenade musical piece for chamber orchestra or wind instruments in several movements, originally intended for evening entertainment, such as Mozart's *Eine kleine Nachtmusik/A Little Night Music*.

serfdom the legal and economic status of peasants under ◊feudalism. Serfs could not be sold like slaves, but they were not free to leave their master's estate without his permission. They had to work the lord's land without pay for a number of days every week and pay a percentage of their produce to the lord every year. They also served as soldiers in the event of conflict. Serfs also had to perform extra labour at harvest time and other busy seasons; in return they were allowed to cultivate a portion of the estate for their own benefit.

serum clear fluid that remains after blood clots. It is blood plasma with the anticoagulant proteins removed, and contains ◊antibodies and other proteins, as well as the fats and sugars of the blood. It can be produced synthetically, and is used to protect against disease.

service tree deciduous Eurasian tree *Sorbus domestica* of the rose family Rosaceae, with alternate pinnate leaves, white flowers, and small, edible, oval fruit. The European wild service tree *Sorbus torminalis* has oblong rather than pointed leaflets. It is related to the ◊mountain ash.

sesame annual plant *Sesamum indicum* of the

family Pedaliaceae, probably native to SE Asia. It produces oily seeds used for food and soap making.

set or **class** in mathematics, any collection of defined things (elements), provided the elements are distinct and that there is a rule to decide whether an element is a member of a set. It is usually denoted by a capital letter and indicated by curly brackets { }.

Set in Egyptian mythology, the god of night, the desert, and of all evils. He was the murderer of ⋗Osiris, portrayed as a grotesque animal.

setter any of various breeds of gun dog, about 66 cm/2.2 ft high and weighing about 25 kg/55 lb. They have a long, smooth coat, feathered tails, and spaniel-like faces. They are called 'setters' because they were trained in crouching or 'setting' on the sight of game to be pursued.

Settlement, Act of in Britain, a law passed 1701 during the reign of King William III, designed to ensure a Protestant succession to the throne by excluding the Roman Catholic descendants of James II in favour of the Protestant House of Hanover. Elizabeth II still reigns under this act.

Seurat Georges 1859–1891. French artist. He originated, with Paul Signac, the Neo-Impressionist technique of ⋗*Pointillism* (painting with small dabs rather than long brushstrokes). Examples of his work are *Bathers at Asnières* 1884 (National Gallery, London) and *Sunday on the Island of La Grande Jatte* 1886 (Art Institute of Chicago).

seven deadly sins in Christian theology, anger, avarice, envy, gluttony, lust, pride, and sloth.

Seven Weeks' War war 1866 between Austria and Prussia, engineered by the German chancellor ⋗Bismarck. It was nominally over the possession of ⋗Schleswig-Holstein, but it was actually to confirm Prussia's superseding Austria as the leading German state. The Battle of Sadowa was the culmination of General von Moltke's victories.

Seven Wonders of the World in antiquity, the pyramids of Egypt, the hanging gardens of Babylon, the temple of Artemis at Ephesus, the statue of Zeus at Olympia, the mausoleum at Halicarnassus, the Colossus of Rhodes, and the Pharos (lighthouse) at Alexandria.

Seven Years' War (in North America known as the *French and Indian War*) war 1756–63 arising from the conflict between Austria and Prussia, and between France and Britain over colonial supremacy. Britain and Prussia defeated France, Austria, Spain, and Russia; Britain gained control of India and many of France's colonies, including Canada. Spain ceded Florida to Britain in exchange for Cuba. Fighting against great odds, Prussia was eventually successful in becoming established as one of the great European powers. The war ended with the Treaty of Paris 1763, signed by Britain, France, and Spain.

Severn river of Wales and England, rising on the NE side of Plynlimmon, N Wales, and flowing 338 km/210 mi through Shrewsbury, Worcester, and Gloucester to the Bristol Channel. The *Severn bore* is a tidal wave up to 2 m/6 ft high.

Seville (Spanish *Sevilla*) city in Andalusia, Spain, on the Guadalquivir River, 96 km/60 mi N of Cadiz; population (1991) 683,500. Products include machinery, spirits, porcelain, pharmaceuticals, silk, and tobacco.

sewing machine apparatus for the mechanical sewing of cloth, leather, and other materials by a needle, powered by hand, treadle, or belted electric motor. The popular lockstitch machine, using a double thread, was invented independently in the USA by both Walter Hunt 1834 and Elias ⋗Howe 1846. Howe's machine was the basis of the machine patented 1851 by Isaac Singer.

sex determination process by which the sex of an organism is determined. In many species, the sex of an individual is dictated by the two sex chromosomes (X and Y) it receives from its parents. In mammals, some plants, and a few insects, males are XY, and females XX; in birds, reptiles, some amphibians, and butterflies the reverse is the case. In bees and wasps, males are produced from unfertilized eggs, females from fertilized eggs. Environmental factors can affect some fish and reptiles, such as turtles, where sex is influenced by the temperature at which the eggs develop.

sextant navigational instrument for determining latitude by measuring the angle between some heavenly body and the horizon. It was invented by John Hadley (1682–1744) in 1730 and can be used only in clear weather.

sexually transmitted disease (STD) any disease transmitted by sexual contact, involving transfer of body fluids. STDs include not only traditional ⋗venereal disease, but also a growing list of conditions, such as ⋗AIDS and scabies, which are known to be spread primarily by sexual contact. Other diseases that are transmitted sexually include viral ⋗hepatitis.

sexual reproduction reproductive process in organisms that requires the union, or ⋗fertilization, of gametes (such as eggs and sperm). These are usually produced by two different individuals, although self-fertilization occurs in a few ⋗hermaphrodites such as tapeworms. Most organisms other than bacteria and cyanobacteria (⋗blue-green algae) show some sort of sexual process. Except in some lower organisms, the gametes are of two distinct types called eggs and sperm. The organisms producing the eggs are called females, and those producing the sperm, males. The fusion of a male and female gamete produces a *zygote*, from which a new individual develops.

Seychelles Republic of; country in the Indian Ocean, off E Africa, N of Madagascar; *area* 453 sq km/175 sq mi; *capital* Victoria (on

Mahé island); **physical** comprises two distinct island groups, one concentrated, the other widely scattered, totalling over 100 islands and islets; Aldabra atoll, containing world's largest tropical lagoon; **head of state and government** France-Albert René from 1977; **political system** one-party socialist republic; **exports** copra, cinnamon; tourism is important; **population** (1990 est) 71,000; **languages** creole (Asian, African, European mixture) 95%, English, French (all official); **recent**

Shakespeare: the plays

Title	Performed
Early Plays	
Henry VI Part I	1589–92
Henry VI Part II	1589–92
Henry VI Part III	1589–92
The Comedy of Errors	1592–93
The Taming of the Shrew	1593–94
Titus Andronicus	1593–94
The Two Gentlemen of Verona	1594–95
Love's Labour's Lost	1594–95
Romeo and Juliet	1594–95
Histories	
Richard III	1592–93
Richard II	1593–96
King John	1596–97
Henry IV Part I	1597–98
Henry IV Part II	1597–98
Henry V	1599
Roman Plays	
Julius Caesar	1599–1600
Antony and Cleopatra	1607–08
Coriolanus	1607–08
The 'Great' or 'Middle' Comedies	
A Midsummer Night's Dream	1595–96
The Merchant of Venice	1596–97
Much Ado About Nothing	1598–99
As You Like It	1599–1600
The Merry Wives of Windsor	1600–01
Twelfth Night	1601–02
The Great Tragedies	
Hamlet	1600–01
Othello	1604–05
King Lear	1605–06
Macbeth	1605–06
Timon of Athens	1607–08
The 'Dark' Comedies	
Troilus and Cressida	1601–02
All's Well That Ends Well	1602–03
Measure for Measure	1604–05
Late Plays	
Pericles	1608–09
Cymbeline	1609–10
The Winter's Tale	1610–11
The Tempest	1611–12
Henry VIII	1612–13

history independence was achieved from Britain as a republic within the Commonwealth 1976. France-Albert René ousted former president Mancham in an armed coup and took over the presidency 1977; a new constitution was adopted 1979 with the Seychelles People's Progressive Front (SPPF) as the sole legal party. Further coups 1981 and 1987 failed.

Seymour Jane *c.* 1509–1537. Third wife of Henry VIII, whom she married in 1536. She died soon after the birth of her son Edward VI.

Shaanxi or **Shensi** province of NW China; **area** 195,800 sq km/75,579 sq mi; **capital** Xian; **physical** mountains; Huang He valley, one of the earliest settled areas of China; **products** iron, steel, mining, textiles, fruit, tea, rice, wheat; **population** (1990) 32,882,000.

Shackleton Ernest 1874–1922. Irish Antarctic explorer. In 1907–09, he commanded an expedition that reached 88° 23' S latitude, located the magnetic South Pole, and climbed Mount ◊Erebus.

shad any of several marine fishes, especially the genus *Alosa*, the largest (60 cm/2 ft long and 2.7 kg/6 lb in weight) of the herring family (Clupeidae). They migrate in shoals to breed in rivers.

Shaftesbury market town and agricultural centre in Dorset, England, 30 km/19 mi SW of Salisbury; population (1985) 6,000. King Alfred is said to have founded an abbey on the site 880; Canute died at Shaftesbury 1035.

Shaftesbury Anthony Ashley Cooper, 1st Earl of Shaftesbury 1621–1683. English politician, a supporter of the Restoration of the monarchy. He became Lord Chancellor in 1672, but went into opposition in 1673 and began to organize the ◊Whig Party. He headed the Whigs' demand for the exclusion of the future James II from the succession, secured the passing of the Habeas Corpus Act 1679, then, when accused of treason 1681, fled to Holland.

shah (more formally, **shahanshah** 'king of kings') traditional title of ancient Persian rulers, and also of those of the recent ◊Pahlavi dynasty in Iran.

Shah Jahan 1592–1666. Mogul emperor of India 1628–58. During his reign the Taj Mahal and the Pearl Mosque at Agra were built. From 1658 he was a prisoner of his son Aurangzeb.

Shaka or **Chaka** *c.* 1787–1828. Zulu chief who formed a Zulu empire in SE Africa. He seized power from his half-brother 1816 and then embarked on a bloody military campaign to unite the Zulu clans. He was assassinated by his two half-brothers.

Shakespeare William 1564–1616. English dramatist and poet. Established in London by 1589 as an actor and a playwright, he was England's unrivalled dramatist until his death, and is considered the greatest English playwright. His plays were written in blank verse. He also wrote numerous sonnets.

shale fine-grained and finely layered ⟡sedimentary rock composed of silt and clay, usually formed in lowland areas. It is a weak rock, splitting easily along bedding planes to form thin, even slabs (by contrast, mudstone splits into irregular flakes). Oil shale contains kerogen, a solid bituminous material that yields ⟡petroleum when heated.

shallot small onion *Allium ascalonicum* in which bulbs are clustered like garlic; used for cooking and in pickles.

shaman ritual leader who acts as intermediary between society and the supernatural world in many indigenous cultures of Asia, Africa, and the Americas. Also known as a *medicine man, seer,* or *sorcerer,* the shaman is expected to use special powers to cure illness and control good and evil spirits. The term is used for any tribal sorcerer or medicine man regardless of geography.

Shamir Yitzhak 1915– . Polish-born Israeli right-wing politician; prime minister 1983–84 and 1986–92; leader of the Likud (Consolidation Party). He was foreign minister under Menachem Begin 1980–83, and again foreign minister in the ⟡Peres unity government 1984–86.

shamrock several trifoliate plants of the family Leguminosae, including ⟡clovers. St Patrick is said to have used one to illustrate the doctrine of the Holy Trinity, and it was made the national badge of Ireland.

Shandong or *Shantung* province of NE China; *area* 153,300 sq km/59,174 sq mi; *capital* Jinan; *towns* ports: Yantai, Weihai, Qingdao, Shigiusuo; *features* crossed by the Huang He River and the ⟡Grand Canal; Shandong Peninsula; *products* cereals, cotton, wild silk, varied minerals; *population* (1990) 84,393,000.

Shanghai port on the Huang-pu and Wusong rivers, Jiangsu province, China, 24 km/15 mi from the Chang Jiang estuary; population (1986) 6,980,000, the largest city in China. The municipality of Shanghai has an area of 5,800 sq km/2,239 sq mi and a population of 13,342,000. Industries include textiles, paper, chemicals, steel, agricultural machinery, precision instruments, shipbuilding, flour and vegetable-oil milling, and oil refining. It handles about 50% of China's imports and exports.

Shankar Ravi 1920– . Indian composer and musician. A virtuoso of the ⟡sitar, he has composed film music and founded music schools in Bombay and Los Angeles.

Shannon longest river in Ireland, rising in County Cavan and flowing 386 km/240 mi through loughs Allen and Ree and past Athlone, to reach the Atlantic through a wide estuary below Limerick. It is also the greatest source of electric power in the republic, with hydroelectric installations at and above Ardnacrusha, 5 km/3 mi N of Limerick.

Shanxi or *Shansi* province of NE China; *area* 157,100 sq km/60,641 sq mi; *capital* Taiyuan; *features* a drought-ridden plateau, partly surrounded by the ⟡Great Wall; *products* coal, iron, fruit; *population* (1990) 28,759,000; *history* saw the outbreak of the Boxer Rebellion 1900.

share in finance, that part of the capital of a company held by a member (shareholder). Shares may be numbered and are issued as units of definite face value; shareholders are not always called on to pay the full face value of their shares, though they bind themselves to do so.

Shari'a the law of ⟡Islam believed by Muslims to be based on divine revelation, and drawn from a number of sources, including the Koran, the Hadith, and the consensus of the Muslim community. Under this law, *qisās,* or retribution, allows a family to exact equal punishment on an accused; *diyat,* or blood money, is payable to a dead person's family as compensation. From the latter part of the 19th century, the role of the Shari'a courts in the majority of Muslim countries began to be taken over by secular courts, and the Shari'a to be largely restricted to family law.

Sharjah or *Shariqah* third largest of the seven member states of the ⟡United Arab Emirates, situated on the Arabian Gulf NE of Dubai; area 2,600 sq km/1,004 sq mi; population (1985) 269,000. Since 1952 it has included the small state of Kalba.

shark any member of various orders of cartilaginous fishes (class Chondrichthyes), found throughout the oceans of the world. There are about 400 known species of shark. They have tough, usually grey, skin covered in denticles (small toothlike scales). Most sharks are fish-eaters, and a few will attack humans. They range from several feet in length to the great *white shark Carcharodon carcharias,* 9 m/30 ft long, and the harmless plankton-eating *whale shark Rhincodon typus,* over 15 m/50 ft in length.

Sharpeville black township in South Africa, 65 km/40 mi S of Johannesburg and N of Vereeniging; 69 people were killed here when police fired on a crowd of anti-apartheid demonstrators 21 March 1960.

Shatt-al-Arab (Persian *Arvand*) the waterway formed by the confluence of the rivers ⟡Euphrates and ⟡Tigris; length 190 km/120 mi to the Persian Gulf. Basra, Khorramshahr, and Abadan stand on it.

Shaw George Bernard 1856–1950. Irish dramatist. He was also a critic and novelist, and an early member of the socialist ⟡Fabian Society. His plays combine comedy with political, philosophical, and polemic aspects, aiming to make an impact on his audience's social conscience as well as their emotions. They include *Arms and the Man* 1894, *Devil's Disciple* 1897, *Man and Superman* 1905, *Pygmalion* 1913, and *St Joan* 1924. Nobel prize 1925.

shearwater any sea bird of the genus *Puffinus,*

in the same family (Procellariidae) as the diving ◊petrels.

Sheba ancient name for south ◊Yemen (Sha'abijah). It was once renowned for gold and spices. According to the Old Testament, its queen visited Solomon; until 1975 the Ethiopian royal house traced its descent from their union.

sheep any of several ruminant, even-toed, hoofed mammals of the family Bovidae. Wild species survive in the uplands of central and eastern Asia, N Africa, southern Europe and North America. The domesticated breeds are all classified as *Ovis aries*.

sheepdog any of several breeds of dog, bred originally for herding sheep. The Old English sheepdog is grey or blue-grey, with white markings, and is about 56 cm/22 in tall at the shoulder. The Shetland sheepdog is much smaller, 36 cm/14 in tall, and shaped more like a long-coated collie. The dog now most commonly used by shepherds and farmers to tend sheep is the border collie.

Sheffield industrial city on the river Don, South Yorkshire, England; population (1991 est) 499,700. From the 12th century, iron smelting was the chief industry, and by the 14th century, Sheffield cutlery, silverware, and plate were made. During the Industrial Revolution the iron and steel industries developed rapidly. It now produces alloys and special steels, cutlery of all kinds, permanent magnets, drills, and precision tools. Other industries include electroplating, type-founding, and the manufacture of optical glass.

sheik the leader or chief of an Arab family or village.

Shelburne William Petty FitzMaurice, 2nd Earl of Shelburne 1737–1805. British Whig politician. He was an opponent of George III's American policy, and as prime minister in 1783, he concluded peace with the USA.

shelduck duck *Tadorna tadorna* with a dark-green head and red bill, with the rest of the plumage strikingly marked in black, white, and chestnut. Widely distributed in Europe and Asia, it lays 10–12 white eggs in rabbit burrows on sandy coasts, and is usually seen on estuary mudflats.

Shelley Mary Wollstonecraft 1797–1851. English writer, the daughter of Mary Wollstonecraft and William Godwin. In 1814 she eloped with the poet Percy Bysshe Shelley, whom she married in 1816. Her novels include *Frankenstein* 1818, *The Last Man* 1826, and *Valperga* 1823.

Shelley Percy Bysshe 1792–1822. English lyric poet, a leading figure in the Romantic movement. Expelled from Oxford University for atheism, he fought all his life against religion and for political freedom. This is reflected in his early poems such as *Queen Mab* 1813. He later wrote tragedies including *The Cenci* 1818, lyric dramas such as *Prometheus Unbound* 1820, and lyrical poems such as 'Ode to the West Wind'. He drowned while sailing in Italy.

shellfish popular name for molluscs and crustaceans, including the whelk and periwinkle, mussel, oyster, lobster, crab, and shrimp.

Shenzen special economic zone established in 1980 opposite Hong Kong on the coast of Guangdong province, S China. Its population rose from 20,000 in 1980 to 600,000 in 1989. Part of the population is 'rotated': newcomers from other provinces return to their homes after a few years spent learning foreign business techniques.

Sheraton Thomas *c.* 1751–1806. English designer of elegant inlaid furniture. He was influenced by his predecessors Hepplewhite and ◊Chippendale.

Sheridan Philip Henry 1831–1888. Union general in the American ◊Civil War. Recognizing Sheridan's aggressive spirit, General Ulysses S ◊Grant gave him command of his cavalry in 1864, and soon after of the Army of the Shenandoah Valley, Virgina. Sheridan laid waste to the valley, cutting off grain supplies to the Confederate armies. In the final stage of the war, Sheridan forced General Robert E ◊Lee to retreat to Appomattox and surrender.

Sherman William Tecumseh 1820–1891. Union general in the American ◊Civil War. In 1864 he captured and burned Atlanta; continued his march eastward, to the sea, laying Georgia waste; and then drove the Confederates northward. He was US Army chief of staff 1869–83.

Sherpa member of a people in NE Nepal related to the Tibetans and renowned for their mountaineering skill. They frequently work as support staff and guides for climbing expeditions. A Sherpa, Tensing Norgay, was one of the first two people to climb to the summit of Everest.

Sherwood Forest hilly stretch of parkland in W Nottinghamshire, England, area about 520 sq km/ 200 sq mi. Formerly a royal forest, it is associated with the legendary outlaw ◊Robin Hood.

Shetland Islands islands off N coast of Scotland, beyond the Orkneys; *area* 1,400 sq km/541 sq mi; *towns* Lerwick (administrative headquarters), on Mainland, largest of 19 inhabited islands; *physical* over 100 islands including Muckle Flugga (latitude 60° 51' N) the northernmost of the British Isles; *products* processed fish, handknits from Fair Isle and Unst, miniature ponies. Europe's largest oil port is Sullom Voe, Mainland; *population* (1987) 22,000; *language* dialect derived from Norse, the islands having been a Norse dependency from the 8th century until 1472.

Shevardnadze Eduard 1928– . Georgian politician, interim head of state of Georgia from 1992, and foreign minister of the USSR 1985–91. A supporter of ◊Gorbachev, he was first secretary of the Georgian Communist Party from 1972 and an advocate of economic reform. In 1985 he became a member of the Politburo, working for détente and disarmament. In July 1991, he resigned from the Communist Party (CPSU) and established the Democratic Reform Movement.

Shiah or ◊*Shi'ite* member of one of the two main sects of ◊Islam.

Shi Huangdi or *Shih Huang Ti* 259–210 BC. Emperor of China who succeeded to the throne of the state of Qin in 246 and reunited China as an empire by 228. He burned almost all existing books in 213 to destroy ties with the past; rebuilt the ◊Great Wall; and was buried at Xian in a tomb complex guarded by 10,000 life-size terracotta warriors (excavated by archaeologists in the 1980s).

Shi'ite or *Shiah* member of a sect of Islam who believe that ◊Ali was ◊Muhammad's first true successor. They are doctrinally opposed to the Sunni Muslims. They developed their own law differing only in minor directions, such as inheritance and the status of women. Holy men have greater authority in the Shi'ite sect than in the Sunni sect. They are prominent in Iran, the Lebanon, and Indo-Pakistan, and are also found in Iraq and Bahrain.

Shikoku smallest of the four main islands of Japan, S of Honshu, E of Kyushu; area 18,800 sq km/7,257 sq mi; population (1986) 4,226,000; chief town Matsuyama. Products include rice, wheat, soya beans, sugar cane, orchard fruits, salt, and copper.

shingles common name for ◊herpes zoster, a disease characterized by infection of sensory nerves, with pain and eruption of blisters along the course of the affected nerves.

Shinto the indigenous religion of Japan. It combines an empathetic oneness with natural forces and loyalty to the reigning dynasty as descendants of the Sun goddess, Amaterasu-Omikami. Traditional Shinto followers stressed obedience and devotion to the emperor, and an aggressive nationalistic aspect was developed by the Meiji rulers. Today Shinto has discarded these aspects.

ship large seagoing vessel. The Greeks, Phoenicians, Romans, and Vikings used ships extensively for trade, exploration, and warfare. The 14th century was the era of European exploration by sailing ship, largely aided by the invention of the compass. In the 15th century Britain's Royal Navy was first formed, but in the 16th–19th centuries Spanish and Dutch fleets dominated the shipping lanes of both the Atlantic and Pacific. The ultimate sailing ships, the fast US and British tea clippers, were built in the 19th century. Also in the 19th century, iron was first used for some shipbuilding instead of wood. Steam-propelled ships of the late 19th century were followed by compound engine and turbine-propelled vessels from the early 20th century.

Shiva alternative spelling of ◊Siva, Hindu god.

Shockley William 1910–1989. US physicist and amateur geneticist who worked with John Bardeen and Walter Brattain on the invention of the ◊transistor. They were jointly awarded a Nobel prize 1956. During the 1970s Shockley was criticized for his claim that blacks were genetically inferior to whites in terms of intelligence.

shogun in Japanese history, title of a series of military dictators 1192–1867 who relegated the emperor's role to that of figurehead. Technically an imperial appointment, the office was treated as hereditary and was held by the Minamoto clan 1192–1219, by the Ashikaga 1336–1573, and by the Tokugawa 1603–1867. The shogun held legislative, judicial, and executive power.

Shona member of a Bantu-speaking people of southern Africa, comprising approximately 80% of the population of Zimbabwe. They also occupy the land between the Save and Pungure rivers in Mozambique, and smaller groups are found in South Africa, Botswana, and Zambia. The Shona are mainly farmers, living in scattered villages. The Shona language belongs to the Niger-Congo family.

short circuit direct connection between two points in an electrical circuit. Its relatively low resistance means that a large current flows through it, bypassing the rest of the circuit, and this may cause the circuit to overheat dangerously.

Short Parliament the English Parliament that was summoned by Charles I on 13 April 1640 to raise funds for his war against the Scots. It was succeeded later in the year by the ◊Long Parliament.

short-sightedness or *myopia* defect of the eye in which a person can see clearly only those objects that are close up. It is caused either by the eyeball being too long or by the cornea and lens system of the eye being too powerful, both of which cause the images of distant objects to be formed in front of the retina. Short-sightedness can be corrected by wearing spectacles fitted with diverging lenses, or by wearing diverging (concave meniscus) contact lenses.

Shostakovich Dmitry (Dmitriyevich) 1906–1975. Soviet composer. His music is tonal, expressive, and sometimes highly dramatic; it has not always been to official Soviet taste. He wrote 15 symphonies, chamber music, ballets, and operas, the latter including *Lady Macbeth of Mtsensk* 1934, which was suppressed as 'too divorced from the proletariat', but revived as *Katerina Izmaylova* 1963.

shot put or *putting the shot* in athletics, the sport of throwing (or putting) overhand from the shoulder a metal ball (or shot). Standard shot weights are 7.26 kg/16 lb for men and 4 kg/8.8 lb for women.

shoveler fresh-water duck *Anas clypeata*, so named after its long and broad flattened beak. Spending the summer in N Europe or North America, it winters further south.

shrew insectivorous mammal of the family Soricidae, found in Eurasia and the Americas. It is mouselike, but with a long nose and pointed teeth. Its high metabolic rate means that it must eat almost constantly. The common shrew *Sorex araneus* is about 7.5 cm/3 in long.

shrike 'butcher-bird' of the family Laniidae, of which there are over 70 species, living mostly in Africa, but also in Eurasia and North America. They often impale insects and small vertebrates on thorns. They can grow to 35 cm/14 in long, and have grey, black, or brown plumage.

shrimp crustacean related to the ▷prawn. It has a cylindrical, semitransparent body, with ten jointed legs. Some shrimps grow as large as 25 cm/10 in long.

Shropshire county in W England. Sometimes abbreviated to *Salop*, it was officially known as Salop from 1974 until local protest reversed the decision 1980; *area* 3,490 sq km/1,347 sq mi; *towns* Shrewsbury (administrative headquarters), Telford, Oswestry, Ludlow; *physical* bisected, on the Welsh border, NW to SE by the river Severn; Ellesmere, the largest of several lakes; the Clee Hills rise to about 610 m/1,800 ft in the SW; *features* Ironbridge Gorge open-air museum of industrial archaeology, with the Iron Bridge 1779; *products* chiefly agricultural: sheep and cattle; *population* (1991) 401,600; *famous people* Charles Darwin, Wilfred Owen, Gordon Richards.

Shushkevich Stanislav 1934– . Belarus politician, president from 1991 after the attempted Soviet coup in Moscow. He was elected to parliament as a 'reform communist' 1990 and played a key role in the creation of the ▷Commonwealth of Independent States.

siamang the largest ▷gibbon *Symphalangus syndactylus*, native to Malaysia and Sumatra. Siamangs have a large throat pouch to amplify the voice, making the territorial 'song' extremely loud.

Sibelius Jean (Christian) 1865–1957. Finnish composer. His works include nationalistic symphonic poems such as *En saga* 1893 and *Finlandia* 1900, a violin concerto 1904, and seven symphonies.

Siberia Asian region of Russia, extending from the Urals to the Pacific; *area* 12,050,000 sq km/4,650,000 sq mi; *towns* Novosibirsk, Omsk, Krasnoyarsk, Irkutsk; *features* long and extremely cold winters; *products* hydroelectric power from rivers Lena, Ob, and Yenisei; forestry; mineral resources, including gold, diamonds, oil, natural gas, iron, copper, nickel, cobalt.

Sibyl in Roman mythology, priestess of Apollo. She offered to sell ▷Tarquinius Superbus nine collections of prophecies, the *Sibylline Books*, but the price was too high. When she had destroyed all but three, he bought those for the identical price, and these were kept for consultation in emergency at Rome.

Sichuan or *Szechwan* province of central China; *area* 569,000 sq km/219,634 sq mi; *capital* Chengdu; *towns* Chongqing; *features* surrounded by mountains, it was the headquarters of the Nationalist government 1937–45, and China's nuclear research centres are here. It is China's most populous administrative area; *products* rice, coal, oil, natural gas; *population* (1990) 107,218,000.

Sicily (Italian *Sicilia*) largest Mediterranean island, an autonomous region of Italy; area 25,700 sq km/9,920 sq mi; population (1990) 5,196,800. Its capital is Palermo, and towns include the ports of Catania, Messina, Syracuse, and Marsala. It exports Marsala wine, olives, citrus, refined oil and petrochemicals, pharmaceuticals, potash, asphalt, and marble. The autonomous region of Sicily also includes the islands of Lipari, Egadi, Ustica, and Pantelleria. Etna, 3,323 m/10,906 ft high, is the highest volcano in Europe; its last major eruption was in 1971.

Sickert Walter (Richard) 1860–1942. English artist. His Impressionist cityscapes of London and Venice, portraits, and domestic and music-hall interiors capture subtleties of tone and light, often with a melancholy atmosphere.

sickle-cell disease hereditary chronic blood disorder common among people of black African descent; also found in the E Mediterranean, parts of the Persian Gulf, and in NE India. It is characterized by distortion and fragility of the red blood cells, which are lost too rapidly from the circulation. This often results in ▷anaemia.

sidewinder rattlesnake *Crotalus cerastes* that lives in the deserts of the SW USA and Mexico, and moves by throwing its coils into a sideways 'jump' across the sand. It can grow up to 75 cm/2 ft 6 in long.

Sidney Philip 1554–1586. English poet and soldier, author of the sonnet sequence *Astrophel and Stella* 1591, *Arcadia* 1590, a prose romance, and *Apologie for Poetrie* 1595, the earliest work of English literary criticism.

Siegfried or *Sigurd* legendary Germanic hero. It is uncertain whether his story has a historical basis, but it was current about AD 700. A version of the story is in the German ▷*Nibelungenlied/Song of the Nibelung*. In the poems of the Norse *Elder Edda* and in the prose *Völsunga Saga*, Siegfried appears under the name of Sigurd.

siemens SI unit (symbol S) of electrical conductance, the reciprocal of the impedance of an electrical circuit. One siemens equals one ampere per volt. It was formerly called the mho or reciprocal ohm.

Sierra Leone Republic of; country in W Africa, on the Atlantic coast, bordered N and E by Guinea and SE by Liberia; *area* 71,740 sq km/27,710 sq mi; *capital* Freetown; *physical* mountains in E; hills and forest; coastal mangrove swamps; *head of state and government* Valentine Strasser from 1992; *political system* transitional; *exports* palm kernels, cocoa, coffee, ginger, diamonds, bauxite, rutile; *population* (1990 est) 4,168,000; *languages* English (official), local languages; *recent history* independence was achieved from Britain within the Commonwealth 1961. An army revolt 1968 was followed by a new constitution 1971, making Sierra Leone a republic with Siaka Stevens as president. Stevens retired 1985. An attempted coup against his successor Joseph Momoh 1989 was foiled. A referendum 1991 endorsed multiparty politics and in 1992 an army coup removed Momoh.

Sierra Madre chief mountain system of Mexico, consisting of three ranges, enclosing the central plateau of the country; highest point Pico de Orizaba 5,700 m/18,700 ft. The Sierra Madre del Sur ('of the south') runs along the SW Pacific coast.

Sigismund 1368–1437. Holy Roman emperor from 1411. He convened and presided over the council of Constance 1414–18, where he promised protection to the religious reformer Huss, but imprisoned him after his condemnation for heresy and acquiesced in his burning. King of Bohemia from 1419, he led the military campaign against the Hussites.

Sigurd in Norse mythology, a hero who appears in both the ◊*Nibelungenlied/Song of the Nibelung* (under his German name of ◊Siegfried) and the Edda.

Sihanouk Norodom 1922– . Cambodian politician, head of state from 1991; he was king 1941–55 and prime minister 1955–70, when his government was overthrown by a military coup led by Lon Nol. Sihanouk formed an alliance with the ◊Khmer Rouge, which overthrew Lon Nol 1975 and briefly restored Sihanouk as prime minister 1975–76. He was then forced into exile, returning Nov 1991 under the auspices of a United Nations-brokered peace settlement to head the Supreme National Council, a new coalition comprising all Cambodia's warring factions, including the Khmer Rouge.

Sikhism religion professed by 14 million Indians, living mainly in the Punjab. Sikhism was founded by Nanak (1469–*c.* 1539). Sikhs believe in a single God who is the immortal creator of the universe and who has never been incarnate in any form, and in the equality of all human beings; Sikhism is strongly opposed to caste divisions. Their holy book is the *Guru Granth Sahib*. Guru Gobind Singh (1666–1708) instituted the *Khanda-di-Pahul*, the baptism of the sword, and established the Khalsa ('pure'), the company of the faithful. The Khalsa wear the five Ks: *kes*, long hair; *kangha*, a comb; *kirpan*, a sword; *kachh*, short trousers; and *kara*, a steel bracelet. Sikh men take the last name 'Singh' ('lion') and women 'Kaur' ('princess').

Sikkim or *Denjong* state of NE India; formerly a protected state, it was absorbed by India 1975,

the monarchy being abolished. China does not recognize India's sovereignty; *area* 7,300 sq km/ 2,818 mi; *capital* Gangtok; *features* Mount Kangchenjunga; wildlife including birds, butterflies, and orchids; *products* rice, grain, tea, fruit, soya beans, carpets, cigarettes, lead, zinc, copper; *population* (1991) 403,600; *language* Bhutia, Lepecha, Khaskura (Nepali) – all official; *religion* Mahayana Buddhism, Hinduism; *history* ruled by the Namgyol dynasty from the 14th century to 1975, when the last chogyal, or king, was deposed. Allied to Britain in 1886, Sikkim became a protectorate of India 1950 and a state of India 1975.

Sikorski Wladyslaw 1881–1943. Polish general and politician; prime minister 1922–23, and 1939–43 of the Polish government in exile in London during World War II. He was killed in an aeroplane crash near Gibraltar in controversial circumstances.

Sikorsky Igor 1889–1972. Ukrainian-born US engineer who built the first successful helicopter. He emigrated to the USA 1918, where he first constructed multi-engined flying boats. His first helicopter (the VS300) flew 1939 and a commercial version (the R3) went into production 1943.

Silesia region of Europe that has long been disputed because of its geographical position, mineral resources, and industrial potential; now in Poland and Czechoslovakia. Dispute began in the 17th century with claims on the area by both Austria and Prussia. It was seized by Prussia's Frederick the Great, which started the War of the ◊Austrian Succession; this was finally recognized by Austria 1763, after the Seven Years' War. After World War I, it was divided in 1919 among newly formed Czechoslovakia, revived Poland, and Germany, which retained the largest part. In 1945, after World War II, all German Silesia east of the Oder-Neisse line was transferred to Polish administration; about 10 million inhabitants of German origin, both there and in Czechoslovak Silesia, were expelled.

silica silicon dioxide, SiO_2, the composition of the most common mineral group, of which the most familiar form is quartz. Other silica forms are ◊chalcedony, chert, opal, tridymite, and cristobalite.

silicon brittle, nonmetallic element, symbol Si, atomic number 14, relative atomic mass 28.086. It is the second most abundant element (after oxygen) in the Earth's crust and occurs in amorphous and crystalline forms. In nature it is found only in combination with other elements, chiefly with oxygen in silica (silicon dioxide, SiO_2) and the silicates. These form the mineral ◊quartz, which makes up most sands, gravels, and beaches.

silicon chip ◊integrated circuit with microscopically small electrical components on a piece of silicon crystal only a few millimetres square.

Silicon Valley region in S California, USA, with a high concentration of high-tech industries connected with microchip production.

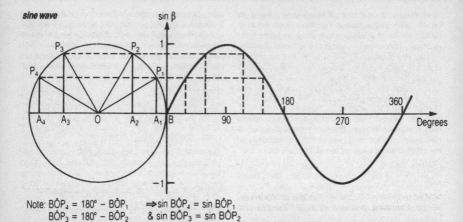

sine wave

Note: $B\hat{O}P_4 = 180° - B\hat{O}P_1$ $\Rightarrow \sin B\hat{O}P_4 = \sin B\hat{O}P_1$
$B\hat{O}P_3 = 180° - B\hat{O}P_2$ $\&\ \sin B\hat{O}P_3 = \sin B\hat{O}P_2$

silk fine soft thread produced by the larva of the ◇silkworm moth when making its cocoon. It is soaked, carefully unwrapped, and used in the manufacture of textiles. The introduction of synthetics originally harmed the silk industry, but rising standards of living have produced an increased demand for real silk. It is manufactured in China, India, Japan, and Thailand.

Silk Road ancient and medieval overland route of about 6,400 km/4,000 mi by which silk was brought from China to Europe in return for trade goods; it ran west via the Gobi Desert, Samarkand, and Antioch to Mediterranean ports in Greece, Italy, the Middle East, and Egypt.

silk-screen printing or *serigraphy* method of ◇printing based on stencils. It can be used to print on most surfaces, including paper, plastic, cloth, and wood. An impermeable stencil (either paper or photographic) is attached to a finely meshed silk screen that has been stretched on a wooden frame, so that the ink passes through to the area beneath only where the image is required. The design can also be painted directly on the screen with varnish. A series of screens can be used to add successive layers of colour to the design.

silkworm usually the larva of the *common silkworm moth Bombyx mori*. After hatching from the egg and maturing on the leaves of white mulberry trees (or a synthetic substitute), it spins a protective cocoon of fine silk thread 275 m/900 ft long. To keep the thread intact, the moth is killed before emerging from the cocoon, and several threads are combined to form the commercial silk thread woven into textiles.

Silurian period of geological time 438–408 million years ago, the third period of the Palaeozoic era. Silurian sediments are mostly marine and consist of shales and limestone. Luxuriant reefs were built by coral-like organisms. The first land plants began

to evolve during this period, and there were many ostracoderms (armoured jawless fishes). The first jawed fishes (called acanthodians) also appeared.

silver white, lustrous, extremely malleable and ductile, metallic element, symbol Ag (from Latin *argentum*), atomic number 47, relative atomic mass 107.868. It occurs in nature in ores and as a free metal; the chief ores are sulphides, from which the metal is extracted by smelting with lead. It is one of the best metallic conductors of both heat and electricity; its most useful compounds are the chloride and bromide, which darken on exposure to light and are the basis of photographic emulsions.

silverfish wingless insect, a type of ◇bristletail.

Simenon Georges 1903–1989. Belgian crime writer. Initially a pulp fiction writer, in 1931 he created Inspector Maigret of the Paris Sûreté who appeared in a series of detective novels.

Simon Paul 1942– . US pop singer and songwriter. In a folk-rock duo with Art Garfunkel (1942–), he had such hits as 'Mrs Robinson' 1968 and 'Bridge Over Troubled Water' 1970. Simon's solo work includes the critically acclaimed album *Graceland* 1986, for which he drew on Cajun and African music.

Simpson Wallis Warfield, Duchess of Windsor 1896–1986. US socialite, twice divorced. She married ◇Edward VIII 1937, who abdicated in order to marry her. He was given the title Duke of Windsor by his brother, George IV, who succeeded him.

Sinai Egyptian peninsula, at the head of the Red Sea; area 65,000 sq km/25,000 sq mi. Resources include oil, natural gas, manganese, and coal; irrigation water from the river Nile is carried under the Suez Canal.

Sinan 1489–1588. Ottoman architect, chief architect from 1538 to Suleiman the Magnificent. Among the hundreds of buildings he designed are the

Suleimaniye in Istanbul, a mosque complex, and the Topkapi Saray, palace of the sultan (now a museum).

Sinatra Frank (Francis Albert) 1915– . US singer and film actor. Celebrated for his phrasing and emotion, especially on love ballads, he is particularly associated with the song 'My Way'. His films from 1941 include *From Here to Eternity* 1953 (Academy Award) and *Guys and Dolls* 1955.

Sinclair Clive 1940– . British electronics engineer who produced the first widely available pocket calculator, pocket and wristwatch televisions, a series of home computers, and the innovative but commercially disastrous 'C5' personal transport (a low cyclelike three-wheeled vehicle powered by a washing-machine motor).

Sindhi member of the majority ethnic group living in the Pakistani province of Sind. The Sindhi language is spoken by about 15 million people. Since the partition of India and Pakistan 1947, large numbers of Urdu-speaking refugees have moved into the region from India, especially into the capital, Karachi.

sine in trigonometry, a function of an angle in a right-angled triangle which is defined as the ratio of the length of the side opposite the angle to the length of the hypotenuse (the longest side).

sinfonietta orchestral work that is of a shorter, lighter nature than a ▷symphony. Also the name for a small orchestra specializing in such works.

Singapore Republic of; country in SE Asia, off the tip of the Malay Peninsula; *area* 622 sq km/240 sq mi; *capital* Singapore City; *physical* comprises Singapore Island, low and flat, and 57 small islands; *head of state* Wee Kim Wee from 1985; *head of government* Goh Chok Tong from 1990; *political system* liberal democracy with strict limits on dissent; *exports* electronics, petroleum products, rubber, machinery, vehicles; *population* (1990 est) 2,703,000 (Chinese 75%, Malay 14%, Tamil 7%); *languages* Malay (national tongue), Chinese, Tamil, English (all official); *recent history* independence from Britain was achieved 1959. Singapore joined the new Federation of Malaysia 1963 but left to become an independent republic 1965. The ruling conservative party exercises an increasingly authoritarian rule.

Singer Isaac Bashevis 1904–1991. Polish-born US novelist and short-story writer, in the USA from 1935. His works, written in Yiddish, often portray traditional Jewish life in Poland and the USA, and the loneliness of old age. They include *The Family Moskat* 1950 and *Gimpel the Fool and Other Stories* 1957. Nobel prize 1978.

Singh Vishwanath Pratap 1931– . Indian politician, prime minister 1989–90. As a member of the Congress (I) Party, he held ministerial posts under Indira Gandhi and Rajiv Gandhi, and from 1984 led

an anti-corruption drive. When he unearthed an arms-sales scandal in 1988, he was ousted from the government and party and formed a broad-based opposition alliance, the *Janata Dal*, which won the Nov 1989 election. Mounting caste and communal conflict split the Janata Dal and forced him out of office in Nov 1990.

singularity in astrophysics, the point at the centre of a ▷black hole at which it is predicted that the infinite gravitational forces will compress the infalling mass of the collapsing star to infinite density. It is a point in space-time at which the known laws of physics break down. It is also thought, in the ▷Big Bang theory of the origin of the universe, to be the point from which the expansion of the universe began.

Sinhalese member of the majority ethnic group of Sri Lanka (70% of the population). Sinhalese is the official language of Sri Lanka; it belongs to the Indo-Iranian branch of the Indo-European family, and is written in a script derived from the Indian Pali form. The Sinhalese are Buddhists. Since 1971 they have been involved in a violent struggle with the Tamil minority, who are seeking independence.

Sinn Féin Irish nationalist party founded by Arthur Griffith (1872–1922) in 1905; in 1917 Eamon ▷de Valera became its president. It is the political wing of the Irish Republican Army, and is similarly split between comparative moderates and extremists. In 1985 it gained representation in 17 out of 26 district councils in Northern Ireland.

Sino-Japanese Wars two wars waged by Japan against China 1894–95 and 1931–45 to expand to the mainland. Territory gained in the First Sino-Japanese War (Korea) and in the 1930s (Manchuria, Shanghai) was returned at the end of World War II.

Sino-Tibetan languages group of languages spoken in SE Asia. This group covers a large area, and includes Chinese and Burmese, both of which have numerous dialects. Some classifications include the Tai group of languages (including Thai and Lao) in the Sino-Tibetan family.

sinusitis painful inflammation of one of the sinuses, or air spaces, that surround the nasal passages. Most cases clear with antibiotics and nasal decongestants, but some require surgical drainage.

siren in Greek mythology, a sea nymph who lured sailors to their deaths along rocky coasts by her singing. ▷Odysseus, in order to hear the sirens safely, tied himself to the mast of his ship and stuffed his crew's ears with wax.

Sirius or *Dog Star* or *Alpha Canis Majoris* the brightest star in the sky, 8.6 light years from Earth in the constellation Canis Major. Sirius is a white star with a mass 2.3 times that of the Sun, a diameter 1.8 times that of the Sun, and a luminosity of 23 Suns. It is orbited every 50 years by a white dwarf, Sirius B, also known as the Pup.

sisal strong fibre made from various species of ▷agave, such as *Agave sisalina*.

siskin greenish-yellow bird *Carduelis spinus* in the finch family Fringillidae, about 12 cm/5 in long, found in Eurasia.

Sisulu Walter 1912– . South African civil-rights activist, one of the first full-time secretary generals of the African National Congress (ANC), in 1964, with Nelson Mandela. He was imprisoned following the 1964 Rivonia Trial for opposition to the apartheid system and released, at the age of 77, as a gesture of reform by President F W ▷de Klerk 1989. In 1991, when Mandela became ANC president, Sisulu became his deputy.

Sisyphus in Greek mythology, king of Corinth who, after his evil life, was condemned in the underworld to roll a huge stone uphill, which always fell back before he could reach the top.

sitar Indian stringed instrument. It has a pear-shaped body, long neck, and an additional gourd resonator at the opposite end. A principal solo instrument, it has seven metal strings extending over movable frets and two concealed strings that provide a continuous singing drone.

sitatunga antelope *Tragelaphus spekei* found in several swamp regions in Central Africa. Its hooves are long and splayed to help progress on soft surfaces. It grows to about 1.2 m/4 ft high at the shoulder; the males have thick horns up to 90 cm/3 ft long.

Sitting Bull *c*. 1834–1893. North American Indian chief who agreed to Sioux resettlement 1868. When the treaty was broken by the US, he led the Sioux against Lieutenant Colonel ▷Custer at the Battle of the Little Bighorn 1876.

situationism in ethics, the doctrine that any action may be good or bad depending on its context or situation. Situationists argue that no moral rule can apply in all situations and that what may be wrong in most cases may be right if the end is sufficiently good. In general, situationists believe moral attitudes are more important than moral rules.

Sitwell Edith 1887–1964. English poet whose series of poems *Façade* was performed as recitations to the specially written music of William ▷Walton from 1923.

SI units (French *Système International d'Unités*) standard system of scientific units used by scientists worldwide. Originally proposed in 1960, it replaces the m.k.s., ▷c.g.s., and f.p.s. systems. It is based on seven basic units: the metre (m) for length, kilogram (kg) for weight, second (s) for time, ampere (A) for electrical current, kelvin (K) for temperature, mole (mol) for amount of substance, and candela (cd) for luminosity.

Siva or *Shiva* in Hinduism, the third chief god (with Brahma and Vishnu). As Mahadeva (great lord), he is the creator, symbolized by the phallic *lingam*, who restores what as Mahakala he destroys. He is often sculpted as Nataraja, performing his fruitful cosmic dance. His consort or female principle (*sakti*) is Parvati, otherwise known as Durga or Kali.

Six-Day War another name for the third ▷Arab-Israeli War.

skate any of several species of flatfish of the ray group. The common skate *Raja batis* is up to 1.8 m/6 ft long and greyish, with black specks. Its egg cases ('mermaids' purses') are often washed ashore by the tide.

skating self-propulsion on ice by means of bladed skates, or on other surfaces by skates with small rollers (wheels of wood, metal, or plastic). The chief competitive ice-skating events are figure skating, for singles or pairs, ice-dancing, and simple speed skating. The first world ice-skating championships were held in 1896.

skeleton the rigid or semirigid framework that supports an animal's body, protects its internal organs, and provides anchorage points for its muscles. The skeleton may be composed of bone and cartilage (vertebrates), chitin (arthropods), calcium carbonate (molluscs and other invertebrates), or silica (many protists).

skiing self-propulsion on snow by means of elongated runners (skis) for the feet, slightly bent upward at the tip. It is a popular recreational sport, as cross-country ski touring or as downhill runs on mountain trails; events include downhill; slalom, in which a series of turns between flags have to be negotiated; cross-country racing; and ski jumping, when jumps of over 150 m/490 ft are achieved from ramps up to 90 m/295 ft high. Speed-skiing uses skis approximately one-third longer and wider than normal with which speeds of up to 200 kph/125 mph have been recorded.

skin the covering of the body of a vertebrate. In mammals, the outer layer (epidermis) is dead and protective, and its cells are constantly being rubbed away and replaced from below. The lower layer (dermis) contains blood vessels, nerves, hair roots, and sweat and sebaceous glands, and is supported by a network of fibrous and elastic cells.

skink lizard of the family Scincidae, a large family of about 700 species found throughout the tropics and subtropics. The body is usually long and the legs are reduced. Some skinks are legless and rather snakelike. Many are good burrowers, or can 'swim' through sand, like the *sandfish* genus *Scincus* of N Africa. Some skinks lay eggs, others bear live young.

Skinner B(urrhus) F(rederic) 1903–1990. US psychologist, a radical behaviourist who rejected mental concepts, seeing the organism as a 'black box' where internal processes are not significant in predicting behaviour. He studied operant conditioning and maintained that behaviour is shaped and maintained by its consequences. His works include *Walden Two* 1948 and *Beyond Freedom and Dignity* 1971.

Skopje capital and industrial city of Macedonia, Yugoslavia; population (1981) 506,547. Industries include iron, steel, chromium mining, and food processing.

skua dark-coloured gull-like seabird living in Arctic and Antarctic waters. Skuas can grow up to 60 cm/2 ft long, and are good fliers. They are aggressive scavengers, who seldom fish for themselves but force gulls to disgorge their catch, and will also eat chicks of other birds.

skull in vertebrates, the collection of flat and irregularly shaped bones (or cartilage) that enclose the brain and the organs of sight, hearing, and smell, and provide support for the jaws. In mammals, the skull consists of 22 bones joined by sutures. The floor of the skull is pierced by a large hole for the spinal cord and a number of smaller apertures through which other nerves and blood vessels pass.

skunk North American mammal of the weasel family. The common skunk *Mephitis mephitis* has a long, arched body, short legs, a bushy tail, and black fur with white streaks on the back. In self-defence, it discharges a foul-smelling fluid.

Skye largest island of the Inner Hebrides, Scotland; area 1,740 sq km/672 sq mi; population (1987) 8,100. It is separated from the mainland by the Sound of Sleat. The chief port is Portree. The economy is based on crofting, tourism, and livestock.

Skylab US space station, launched 14 May 1973, made from the adapted upper stage of a Saturn V rocket. At 75 tonnes, it was the heaviest object ever put into space, and was 25.6 m/84 ft long. *Skylab* contained a workshop for carrying out experiments in weightlessness, an observatory for monitoring the Sun, and cameras for photographing the Earth's surface.

skylark a type of ◊lark.

slander spoken defamatory statement; if broadcast on radio or television it constitutes ◊libel. Like libel, slander must be made to some other person than the one defamed, and in the UK it is actionable only if pecuniary loss may result.

slash and burn simple agricultural method whereby natural vegetation is cut and burned, and the clearing then farmed for a few years until the soil loses its fertility, whereupon farmers move on and leave the area to regrow. Although this is possible with a small, widely dispersed population, it becomes unsustainable with more people and is now a form of ◊deforestation.

slate fine-grained, usually grey metamorphic rock that splits readily into thin slabs along its cleavage plane. It is the metamorphic equivalent of ◊shale.

Slav member of an Indo-European people in central

and E Europe, the Balkans, and parts of N Asia, speaking closely related ◊Slavonic languages. The ancestors of the Slavs are believed to have included the Sarmatians and ◊Scythians. Moving west from central Asia, they settled in E and SE Europe during the 2nd and 3rd millennia BC. The present Slavonic nations emerged around the 5th and 6th centuries AD to become the predominant population of E and SE Europe. During the 9th century they adopted Christianity, and in the course of the Middle Ages were expelled from E Germany.

slavery enforced servitude of one person (a slave) to another or one group to another. A slave has no personal rights and is the property of another person through birth, purchase, or capture. Slavery goes back to prehistoric times but declined in Europe after the fall of the Roman Empire. During the imperialism of Spain, Portugal, and Britain in the 16th–18th centuries and in the American South in the 17th–19th centuries, slavery became a mainstay of an agricultural factory economy, with millions of Africans sold to work on plantations in North and South America. Millions more died in the process, but the profits from this trade were enormous. Slavery was abolished in the British Empire 1833 and in the USA at the end of the Civil War 1863–65, but continues illegally in some countries.

Slavonia region of E Croatia bounded by the Sava, Drava, and Danube rivers; Osijek is the largest town. Slavonia was the scene of fierce fighting between Croatian forces and Serb-dominated Yugoslav federal troops 1991–92. Following Croatia's declaration of independence from Yugoslavia 1991, Eastern and Western Slavonia declared themselves autonomous provinces of Serbia. After the cease-fire 1992, 10,000 United Nations troops were deployed in Slavonia.

Slavonic languages (or *Slavic languages*) branch of the Indo-European language family spoken in central and E Europe, the Balkans, and parts of N Asia. The family comprises the *southern group* (Slovene, Serbo-Croatian, Macedonian, and Bulgarian); the *western group* (Czech and Slovak, Sorbian in Germany, and Polish and its related dialects); and the *eastern group* (Russian, Ukrainian, and Belarusian).

SLD abbreviation for ◊*Social and Liberal Democrats*.

sleep state of reduced awareness and activity that occurs at regular intervals in most mammals and birds, though there is considerable variation in the amount of time spent sleeping. Sleep differs from hibernation in that it occurs daily rather than seasonally, and involves less drastic reductions in metabolism. The function of sleep is unclear. People deprived of sleep become irritable, uncoordinated, forgetful, hallucinatory, and even psychotic.

Sligo county in the province of Connacht, Republic

of Ireland, situated on the Atlantic coast of NW Ireland; area 1,800 sq km/695 sq mi; population (1991) 54,700. The county town is Sligo; there is livestock and dairy farming.

slime mould or *myxomycete* extraordinary organism that shows some features of ▷fungus and some of ▷protozoa. Slime moulds are not closely related to any other group, although they are often classed, for convenience, with the fungi. There are two kinds, cellular slime moulds and plasmodial slime moulds, differing in their complex life cycle.

sloe fruit of the ▷blackthorn.

sloth South American mammal, about 70 cm/2.5 ft long, of the order Edentata. Sloths are greyish brown and have small rounded heads, rudimentary tails, and prolonged forelimbs. Each foot has long curved claws adapted to clinging upside down from trees. They are vegetarian.

Slovakia one of the two republics forming the Federative Republic of ▷Czechoslovakia. It was settled in the 5th–6th centuries by Slavs; occupied by the Magyars in the 10th century; part of the kingdom of Hungary until 1918, when it became a province of Czechoslovakia. Slovakia was a puppet state under German domination 1939–45, and was abolished as an administrative division in 1949. Its capital and chief town is Bratislava.

Slovenia Republic of; country in S Europe, bordered N by Austria, E by Hungary, S by Croatia, and E by Italy, with a coastline on the Adriatic Sea to the E; *area* 20,300 sq km/7,836 sq mi; *capital* Ljubljana; *physical* mountainous; rivers Sava, Drava; *head of state* Milan Kucan from 1990; *head of government* Lojze Peterle from 1991; *political system* emergent democracy; *products* grain, sugarbeet, livestock, timber, cotton and woollen textiles, steel, vehicles; *population* (1986) 1,930,000 (Slovenes 89%); *language* Slovene;

recent history united with Serbia and Croatia 1918; kingdom of Serbs, Croats, and Slovenes renamed Yugoslavia 1929. Became constituent republic of Yugoslav Socialist Federal Republic 1945. Constitution changed 1989 to allow secession from federation. Following multiparty elections 1990, Slovenia declared its sovereignty and independence was overwhelmingly approved in a referendum. Independence declared June 1991; federal army intervened; cease-fire brokered by European Community; army withdrew. Slovenia's independence recognized by EC 1992.

slow-worm harmless species of lizard *Anguis fragilis*, once common in Europe, now a protected species in Britain. Superficially resembling a snake, it is distinguished by its small mouth and movable eyelids. It is about 30 cm/1 ft long, and eats worms and slugs.

SLR abbreviation for *single-lens reflex*, a type of ▷camera in which the image can be seen through the lens before a picture is taken.

slug air-breathing gastropod related to the snails, but with absent or much reduced shell. The grey field slug *Deroceras reticulatum* is a common British species, and a pest to crops and garden plants.

smallpox acute, highly contagious viral disease, marked by aches, fever, vomiting, and skin eruptions leaving pitted scars. Widespread vaccination programmes have almost eradicated this often fatal disease.

smart card plastic card with an embedded microprocessor and memory. It can store, for example, personal data, identification, and bank-account details, to enable it to be used as a credit or debit card. The card can be loaded with credits, which are then spent electronically, and reloaded as needed. Possible other uses range from hotel door 'keys' to passports.

smart drug any drug containing nutrients said to enhance the functioning of the brain, increase mental energy, lengthen the span of attention, and improve the memory; also described as a brain tonic. Smart drugs, developed in the USA, have not been approved by the British Department of Health.

smart weapon programmable missile that can be guided to its target by laser technology, TV homing technology, or terrain-contour matching (TERCOM). A smart bomb or missile relies on its pinpoint accuracy to destroy a target rather than on the size of its warhead.

smell sense that responds to chemical molecules in the air. It works by having receptors for particular chemical groups, into which the airborne chemicals must fit to trigger a message to the brain.

smelt small fish, usually marine, although some species are freshwater. They occur in Europe and North America. The most common European smelt is the sparling *Osmerus eperlanus*.

smelting processing a metallic ore in a furnace to produce the metal. Oxide ores such as iron ore are smelted with coke (carbon), which reduces the ore into metal and also provides fuel for the process.

Smetana Bedřich 1824–1884. Czech composer whose music has a distinct national character, as in, for example, the operas *The Bartered Bride* 1866 and *Dalibor* 1868, and the symphonic suite *My Country* 1875–80. He conducted the National Theatre of Prague 1866–74.

Smith Adam 1723–1790. Scottish economist, often regarded as the founder of political economy. His *The Wealth of Nations* 1776 defined national wealth in terms of labour. The cause of wealth is explained by the division of labour – dividing a production process into several repetitive operations, each carried out by different workers. Smith advocated the free working of individual enterprise, and the necessity of 'free trade'.

Smith Ian (Douglas) 1919– . Rhodesian politician. He was a founder of the Rhodesian Front 1962 and prime minister 1964–79. In 1965 he made a unilateral declaration of Rhodesia's independence and, despite United Nations sanctions, maintained his regime with tenacity. In 1979 he was succeeded as prime minister by Bishop Abel Muzorewa, when the country was renamed Zimbabwe. He was suspended from the Zimbabwe parliament April 1987 and resigned in May as head of the white opposition party.

Smith John 1938– . British Labour politician, party leader from 1992. He held ministerial posts in the Labour governments of the 1970s and became a member of the shadow cabinet 1979, its Treasury spokesperson from 1987. He is a Scottish lawyer.

Smith John 1580–1631. English colonist. After an adventurous early life he took part in the colonization of Virginia, acting as president of the North American colony 1608–09. He explored New England in 1614, which he named, and published pamphlets on America and an autobiography. His trade with the Indians may have kept the colonists alive in the early years.

Smith Stevie (Florence Margaret) 1902–1971. British poet and novelist. She published her first book *Novel on Yellow Paper* 1936, and her first collection of poems *A Good Time Was Had by All* 1937. She wrote a further eight volumes of eccentrically direct verse including *Not Waving but Drowning* 1957, and two more novels. *Collected Poems* was published 1975.

Smith William 1769–1839. British geologist, the founder of stratigraphy. Working as a canal engineer, he observed while supervising excavations that different beds of rock could be identified by their fossils, and so established the basis of stratigraphy. He also produced the first geological maps of England and Wales.

Smiths, the English four-piece rock group (1982–

87) from Manchester. Their songs, with lyrics by singer Morrissey (1959–) and tunes by guitarist Johnny Marr (1964–), drew on diverse sources such as rockabilly, Mersey beat, and the Byrds, with confessional humour and images of urban desolation. They were Britain's main cult band in the 1980s.

Smollett Tobias George 1721–1771. Scottish novelist who wrote the picaresque novels *Roderick Random* 1748, *Peregrine Pickle* 1751, *Ferdinand Count Fathom* 1753, *Sir Launcelot Greaves* 1760–62, and *Humphrey Clinker* 1771.

Smuts Jan Christian 1870–1950. South African politician and soldier; prime minister 1919–24 and 1939–48. He supported the Allies in both world wars and was a member of the British imperial war cabinet 1917–18. He was a segregationalist, voting in favour of legislation that took away black rights and land ownership.

snail air-breathing gastropod mollusc, with a spiral shell. There are thousands of species, on land and in water. The typical snails of the genus *Helix* have two species in Europe. The common garden snail *Helix aspersa* is very destructive to plants.

snake reptile of the suborder Serpentes of the order Squamata, which also includes lizards. Snakes are characterized by an elongated limbless body, possibly evolved because of subterranean ancestors. One of the striking internal modifications is the absence or greatly reduced size of the left lung. The skin is covered in scales, which are markedly wider underneath where they form. There are 3,000 species found in the tropical and temperate zones, but none in New Zealand, Ireland, Iceland, and near the poles. Only three species are found in Britain: the adder, smooth snake, and grass snake.

snapdragon perennial herbaceous plant of the genus *Antirrhinum*, family Scrophulariaceae, with spikes of brightly coloured two-lipped flowers.

snipe European marsh bird of the family Scolopacidae, order Charadriiformes; species include common snipe *Gallinago gallinago* and the rare great snipe *G. media*, of which the males hold spring gatherings to show their prowess. It is closely related to the ⧫woodcock.

snooker indoor game derived from ⧫billiards It is played with 22 balls: 15 red, one each of yellow, green, brown, blue, pink, and black, and one white cueball. Red balls are worth one point when sunk, while the coloured balls have ascending values from two points for the yellow to seven points for the black. The world professional championship was first held in 1927. The world amateur championship was first held 1963.

snowdrop bulbous plant *Galanthus nivalis*, family Amaryllidaceae, native to Europe, with white, bell-shaped flowers, tinged with green, in early spring.

snow leopard a type of ▷leopard.

soap mixture of the sodium salts of various ▷fatty acids; palmitic, stearic, and oleic acid. It is made by the action of sodium hydroxide (caustic soda) or potassium hydroxide (caustic potash) on fats of animal or vegetable origin. Soap makes grease and dirt disperse in water in a similar manner to a ▷detergent.

Soares Mario 1924– . Portuguese socialist politician, president from 1986. Exiled 1970, he returned to Portugal 1974, and, as leader of the Portuguese Socialist Party, was prime minister 1976–78. He resigned as party leader 1980, but in 1986 he was elected Portugal's first socialist president.

Sobchak Anatoly 1937– . Soviet centrist politician, mayor of St Petersburg from 1990, cofounder of the Democratic Reform Movement (with former foreign minister ▷Shevardnadze), and member of the Soviet parliament 1989–91. He prominently resisted the abortive anti-Gorbachev coup of Aug 1991.

Sobers Gary (Garfield St Aubrun) 1936– . West Indian test cricketer. One of the game's great all-rounders, he scored more than 8,000 test runs, took over 200 wickets, held more than 100 catches, and holds the record for the highest test innings, 365 not out.

Social and Liberal Democrats official name for the British political party formed 1988 from the former Liberal Party and most of the Social Democratic Party. The common name for the party is the *Liberal Democrats*. Its leader (from July 1988) is Paddy ▷Ashdown.

social democracy political ideology or belief in the gradual evolution of a democratic ▷socialism within existing political structures. The earliest was the German Sozialdemokratische Partei (SPD), today one of the two main German parties, created in 1875 from August Bebel's earlier German Social Democratic Workers' Party, founded 1869. Parties along the lines of the German model were founded in the last two decades of the 19th century in a number of countries, including Austria, Belgium, the Netherlands, Hungary, Poland, and Russia. The British Labour Party is in the social democratic tradition.

Social Democratic Labour Party (SDLP) Northern Irish left-wing political party, formed in 1970. It aims ultimately at Irish unification, but distances itself from the violent tactics of the Irish Republican Army (IRA), adopting a constitutional, conciliatory role. The SDLP, led by John Hume (1937–), was responsible for setting up the New Ireland Forum in 1983.

Social Democratic Party (SDP) British centrist political party 1981–90 formed by members of Parliament who resigned from the Labour Party. The 1983 and 1987 general elections were fought in alliance with the Liberal Party as the *Liberal/SDP Alliance*. A merger of the two parties was voted for by the SDP 1987, and the new party became the ▷Social and Liberal Democrats, leaving a rump SDP that folded 1990.

socialism movement aiming to establish a classless society by substituting public for private ownership of the means of production, distribution, and exchange. The term has been used to describe positions as widely apart as anarchism and social democracy. Socialist ideas appeared in classical times; in early Christianity; among later Christian sects such as the ▷Anabaptists and ▷Diggers; and, in the 18th and early 19th centuries, were put forward as systematic political aims by Jean-Jacques Rousseau, Claude Saint-Simon, François Fourier, and Robert Owen, among others. See also Karl ▷Marx and Friedrich ▷Engels.

Social Realism in painting, art that realistically depicts subjects of social concern, such as poverty and deprivation. The French artist Courbet provides a 19th-century example of the genre. Subsequently, in the USA, the Ashcan school and Ben Shahn are among those described as Social Realists.

social science the group of academic disciplines that investigate how and why people behave the way they do, as individuals and in groups. The term originated with the 19th-century French thinker Auguste ▷Comte. The academic social sciences are generally listed as sociology, economics, anthropology, political science, and psychology.

social security state provision of financial aid to alleviate poverty. The term 'social security' was first applied officially in the USA, in the Social Security Act 1935. In Britain it was first used officially 1944, and following the Beveridge Report 1942 a series of acts was passed from 1945 to widen the scope of social security. Basic entitlements of those paying National Insurance contributions in Britain include an old-age pension, unemployment benefit, widow's pension, and payment during a period of sickness in one's working life. Other benefits include family credit, child benefit, and attendance allowance for those looking after sick or disabled people.

Society Islands (French *Archipel de la Société*) archipelago in ▷French Polynesia, divided into Windward Islands and Leeward Islands; area 1,685 sq km/650 sq mi; population (1983) 142,000. The administrative headquarters is Papeete on ▷Tahiti. The *Windward Islands* (French *Iles du Vent*) have an area of 1,200 sq km/460 sq mi and a population (1983) of 123,000. They comprise Tahiti, Moorea (area 132 sq km/51 sq mi; population 7,000), Maio (or Tubuai Manu; 9 sq km/3.5 sq mi; population 200), and the smaller Tetiaroa and Mehetia. The *Leeward Islands* (French *Iles sous le Vent*) have an area of 404 sq km/156 sq mi and a population of 19,000. They comprise the volcanic islands of Raiatea (including the main town of Uturoa), Huahine, Bora-Bora, Maupiti, Tahaa, and four small atolls. Claimed by France 1768, the group became a French protectorate 1843 and a colony 1880.

sociobiology study of the biological basis of all social behaviour, including the application of population genetics to the evolution of behaviour. It builds on the concept of inclusive fitness, encapsulated in the notion of the 'selfish gene'. Contrary to some popular interpretations, it does not assume that all behaviour is genetically determined.

sociology systematic study of society, in particular of social order and social change, social conflict and social problems. It studies institutions such as the family, law, and the church, as well as concepts such as norm, role, and culture. Sociology attempts to study people in their social environment according to certain underlying moral, philosophical, and political codes of behaviour.

Socrates *c.* 469–399 BC. Athenian philosopher. He wrote nothing but was immortalized in the dialogues of his pupil Plato. In his desire to combat the scepticism of the ▷sophists, Socrates asserted the possibility of genuine knowledge. In ethics, he put forward the view that the good person never knowingly does wrong. True knowledge emerges through dialogue and systematic questioning and an abandoning of uncritical claims to knowledge.

Socratic method method of teaching used by Socrates, in which he aimed to guide pupils to clear thinking on ethics and politics by asking questions and then exposing their inconsistencies in cross-examination. This method was effective against the ▷sophists.

sodium soft, waxlike, silver-white, metallic element, symbol Na (from Latin *natrium*), atomic number 11, relative atomic mass 22.898. It is one of the ▷alkali metals and has a very low density, being light enough to float on water. It is the sixth most abundant element (the fourth most abundant metal) in the Earth's crust. Sodium is highly reactive, oxidizing rapidly when exposed to air and reacting violently with water. Its most familiar compound is sodium chloride (common salt), which occurs naturally in the oceans and in salt deposits left by dried-up ancient seas.

Sofia or *Sofiya* capital of Bulgaria since 1878; population (1990) 1,220,900. Industries include textiles, rubber, machinery, and electrical equipment. It lies at the foot of the Vitosha Mountains.

software in computing, a collection of programs and procedures for making a computer perform a specific task, as opposed to hardware, the physical components of a computer system. Software is created by programmers and is either distributed on a suitable medium, such as the floppy disc, or built into the computer in the form of firmware.

softwood any coniferous tree, or the wood from it.

In general this type of wood is softer and easier to work, but in some cases less durable, than wood from flowering (or angiosperm) trees.

soil loose covering of broken rocky material and decaying organic matter overlying the bedrock of the Earth's surface. Various types of soil develop under different conditions: deep soils form in warm wet climates and in valleys; shallow soils form in cool dry areas and on slopes. *Pedology*, the study of soil, is significant because of the relative importance of different soil types to agriculture.

soil erosion the wearing away and redistribution of the Earth's soil layer. It is caused by the action of water, wind, and ice, and also by improper methods of ▷agriculture. If unchecked, soil erosion results in the formation of deserts. It has been estimated that 20% of the world's cultivated topsoil was lost between 1950 and 1990.

solar energy energy derived from the Sun's radiation. The amount of energy falling on just 1 sq km/0.3861 sq mi is about 4,000 megawatts, enough to heat and light a small town. In one second the Sun gives off 13 million times more energy than all the electricity used in the USA in one year. *Solar heaters* have industrial or domestic uses. They usually consist of a black (heat-absorbing) panel containing pipes through which air or water, heated by the Sun, is circulated, either by thermal ▷convection or by a pump. Solar energy may also be harnessed indirectly using *solar cells* (photovoltaic cells) made of panels of ▷semiconductor material (usually silicon), which generate electricity when illuminated by sunlight.

solar radiation radiation given off by the Sun, consisting mainly of visible light, ▷ultraviolet radiation, and ▷infrared radiation, although the whole spectrum of ▷electromagnetic waves is present, from radio waves to X-rays. High-energy charged particles such as electrons are also emitted, especially from solar flares. When these reach the Earth, they cause magnetic storms (disruptions of the Earth's magnetic field), which interfere with radio communications.

solar system the Sun (a star) and all the bodies orbiting it: the nine planets (Mercury, Venus, Earth, Mars, Jupiter, Saturn, Uranus, Neptune, and Pluto), their moons, the asteroids, and the comets. It is thought to have formed from a cloud of gas and dust in space about 4.6 billion years ago. The Sun contains 99% of the mass of the solar system. The edge of the solar system is not clearly defined, marked only by the limit of the Sun's gravitational influence, which extends about 1.5 light years, almost halfway to the nearest star, Alpha Centauri, 4.3 light years away.

solar wind stream of atomic particles, mostly protons and electrons, from the Sun's corona, flowing outwards at speeds of between 300 kps/200 mps and 1,000 kps/600 mps.

solar system

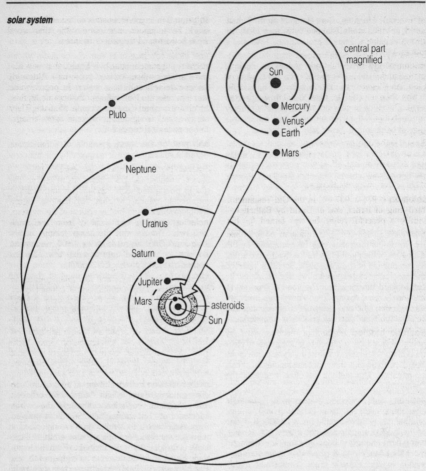

central part magnified

Sun

Mercury
Venus
Earth
Mars

Pluto

Neptune

Uranus

Saturn

Jupiter

Mars

asteroids

Sun

solder any of various alloys used when melted for joining metals such as copper, its common alloys (brass and bronze), and tin-plated steel, as used for making food cans.

sole flatfish found in temperate and tropical waters. The *common sole Solea solea*, also called *Dover sole*, is found in the southern seas of NW Europe. Up to 50 cm/20 in long, it is a prized food fish, as is the *sand* or *French sole Pegusa lascaris* further south.

solenoid coil of wire, usually cylindrical, in which a magnetic field is created by passing an electric current through it (see ▷electromagnet). This field can be used to move an iron rod placed on its axis. Mechanical valves attached to the rod can be operated by switching the current on or off, so converting electrical energy into mechanical energy.

Solenoids are used to relay energy from the battery of a car to the starter motor by means of the ignition switch.

solicitor in the UK, a member of one of the two branches of the English legal profession, the other being a ▷barrister. A solicitor is a lawyer who provides all-round legal services (making wills, winding up estates, conveyancing, divorce, and litigation). A solicitor cannot appear at High Court level, but must brief a barrister on behalf of his or her client. Solicitors may become circuit judges and recorders. In the USA the general term is lawyer or attorney.

solid in physics, a state of matter that holds its own shape (as opposed to a liquid, which takes up the shape of its container, or a gas, which totally fills its container). According to ▷kinetic theory, the atoms or molecules in a solid are not free to move but merely vibrate about fixed positions, such as those in crystal lattices.

Solidarity (Polish *Solidarność*) national confederation of independent trade unions in Poland, formed under the leadership of Lech ◊Wałesa Sept 1980. An illegal organization from 1981 to 1989, it was then elected to head the Polish government. Divisions soon emerged in the leadership. Solidarity had 2.8 million members in 1991.

solipsism in philosophy, a view that maintains that the self is the only thing that can be known to exist. It is an extreme form of ◊scepticism. The solipsist sees himself or herself as the only individual in existence, assuming other people to be a reflection of his or her own consciousness.

Solomon *c.* 974–*c.* 937 BC. In the Old Testament, third king of Israel, son of David by Bathsheba. During a peaceful reign, he was famed for his wisdom and his alliances with Egypt and Phoenicia. The much later biblical Proverbs, Ecclesiastes, and Song of Songs are attributed to him. He built the temple in Jerusalem with the aid of heavy taxation and forced labour, resulting in the revolt of N Israel.

Solomon Islands country in the W Pacific, E of New Guinea, comprising many hundreds of islands; *area* 27,600 sq km/10,656 sq mi; *capital* Honiara (on Guadalcanal); *physical* comprises all but the northernmost islands (which belong to Papua New Guinea) of a Melanesian archipelago stretching nearly 1,500 km/900 mi. The largest is Guadalcanal (area 6,500 sq km/2,510 sq mi); others are Malaita, San Cristobal, New Georgia, Santa Isabel, Choiseul; mainly mountainous and forested; *head of state* Elizabeth II represented by governor general; *head of government* Solomon Mamaloni from 1989; *political system* liberal democracy; *exports* fish products, palm oil, copra, cocoa, timber; *population* (1990 est) 314,000 (Melanesian 95%, Polynesian 4%); *languages* English (official), 120 Melanesian dialects; *recent history* independence was achieved from Britain within the Commonwealth 1978 with Peter Kenilorea as prime minister.

Solomon's seal any perennial plant of the genus *Polygonatum* of the lily family Liliaceae, native to Europe and found growing in moist, shady woodland areas. They have bell-like white or greenish-white flowers drooping from the leaf axils of arching stems, followed by blue or black berries.

Solon *c.* 638–558 BC. Athenian statesman. As one of the chief magistrates about 594 BC, he carried out the revision of the constitution that laid the foundations of Athenian democracy.

solstice either of the points at which the Sun is farthest north or south of the celestial equator each year. The *summer solstice*, when the Sun is farthest north, occurs around June 21; the *winter solstice* around Dec 22.

solution two or more substances mixed to form a single, homogenous phase. One of the substances is the *solvent* and the others (*solutes*) are said to be dissolved in it.

solvent substance, usually a liquid, that will dissolve another substance (see ◊solution). Although the commonest solvent is water, in popular use the term refers to low-boiling-point organic liquids, which are harmful if used in a confined space. They can give rise to respiratory problems, liver damage, and neurological complaints.

Solyman I alternative spelling of ◊Suleiman, Ottoman sultan.

Solzhenitsyn Alexander (Isayevich) 1918– . Soviet novelist, a US citizen from 1974. He was in prison and exile 1945–57 for anti-Stalinist comments. Much of his writing is semi-autobiographical and highly critical of the system, including *One Day in the Life of Ivan Denisovich* 1962, which deals with the labour camps under Stalin, and *The Gulag Archipelago* 1973, an exposé of the whole Soviet labour-camp network. This led to his expulsion from the USSR 1974.

Somalia Somali Democratic Republic; country in NE Africa (the Horn of Africa), on the Indian Ocean, bordered NW by Djibouti, W by Ethiopia and SW by Kenya; *area* 637,700 sq km/246,220 sq mi; *capital* Mogadishu; *physical* mainly flat, with hills in N; *head of state* Ali Mahdi Mohammed from 1991; *head of government* Omar Arte from 1991; *political system* one-party socialist republic; *exports* livestock, skins, hides, bananas, fruit; *population* (1990 est) 8,415,000 (including 350,000 refugees from Ethiopia and 50,000 in Djibouti); *languages* Somali, Arabic (both official); Italian, English; *recent history* independence was achieved from Britain and Italy 1960. Following an army coup 1969, the constitution was suspended, a Supreme Revolutionary Council was set up, and the name of the country was changed to Somali Democratic Republic. After defeat in an eight-month war with Ethiopia 1978, armed insurrection began in the north, leading to civil war and the eventual capture of Mogadishu by rebels 1991. The secession of NE Somalia, as the Somaliland Republic, was announced 1991; a cease-fire was agreed and peace talks began.

Somaliland region of Somali-speaking peoples in E Africa including the former British Somaliland Protectorate (established 1887) and Italian Somaliland (made a colony 1927, conquered by Britain 1941 and administered by Britain until 1950) – which both became independent 1960 as the Somali Democratic Republic, the official name for ◊Somalia – and former French Somaliland, which was established 1892, became known as the Territory of the Afars and Issas 1967, and became independent as ◊Djibouti 1977.

Somerset county in SW England; *area* 3,460

sq km/1,336 sq mi; *towns* administrative head-quarters Taunton; Wells, Bridgwater, Glastonbury, Yeovil; *physical* rivers Avon, Parret, and Exe; marshy coastline on the Bristol Channel; Mendip Hills (including Cheddar Gorge and Wookey Hole, a series of limestone caves where Old Stone Age flint implements and bones of extinct animals have been found); the Quantock Hills; Exmoor; *products* engineering, dairy products, cider, Exmoor ponies; *population* (1991) 459,100; *famous people* Ernest Bevin, Henry Fielding, John Pym.

Somerset Edward Seymour, 1st Duke of Somerset *c.* 1506–1552. English politician. Created Earl of Hertford after Henry VIII's marriage to his sister Jane, he became Duke of Somerset and protector (regent) for Edward VI in 1547. His attempt to check ⟡enclosure (the transfer of land from common to private ownership) offended landowners and his moderation in religion upset the Protestants, and he was beheaded on a fake treason charge in 1552.

Somme, Battle of the Allied offensive in World War I July–Nov 1916 at Beaumont-Hamel-Chaulnes, on the river Somme in N France, during which severe losses were suffered by both sides. It was planned by the Marshal of France, Joseph Joffre, and UK commander in chief Douglas Haig; the Allies lost over 600,000 soldiers and advanced 32 km/20 mi. It was the first battle in which tanks were used. The German offensive around St Quentin March–April 1918 is sometimes called the Second Battle of the Somme.

sonar (acronym for *so*und *na*vigation and *r*anging) method of locating underwater objects by the reflection of ultrasonic waves. The time taken for an acoustic beam to travel to the object and back to the source enables the distance to be found since the velocity of sound in water is known. Sonar devices, or *echo sounders*, were developed 1920.

sonata piece of instrumental music written for a soloist or a small ensemble and consisting of a series of related movements.

Sondheim Stephen (Joshua) 1930– . US composer and lyricist. He wrote the lyrics of Leonard Bernstein's *West Side Story* 1957 and composed witty and sophisticated musicals, including *A Little Night Music* 1973, *Pacific Overtures* 1976, *Sweeney Todd* 1979, *Into the Woods* 1987, and *Sunday in the Park with George* 1989.

song composition for one or more singers, often with instrumental accompaniment, such as madrigals and chansons. Common forms include folk song and ballad. The term 'song' is used for secular music, whereas motet and cantata tend to be forms of sacred music.

Songhai Empire former kingdom of NW Africa, founded in the 8th century, which developed into a powerful Muslim empire under the rule of Sonni Ali

(reigned 1464–92). It superseded the ⟡Mali Empire and extended its territory, occupying an area that included parts of present-day Guinea, Burkina Faso, Senegal, Gambia, Mali, Mauritania, Niger, and Nigeria. In 1591 it was invaded and overthrown by Morocco.

sonnet fourteen-line poem of Italian origin introduced to England by Thomas Wyatt in the form used by Petrarch (rhyming *abba abba cdcdcd* or *cdecde*) and followed by Milton and Wordsworth; Shakespeare used the form *abab cdcd efef gg.*

sophist one of a group of 5th-century BC lecturers on culture, rhetoric, and politics. Sceptical about the possibility of achieving genuine knowledge, they applied bogus reasoning and were concerned with winning arguments rather than establishing the truth. ⟡Plato regarded them as dishonest and *sophistry* came to mean fallacious reasoning.

Sophocles 495–406 BC. Greek dramatist who, with Aeschylus and Euripides, is one of the three great tragedians. He modified the form of tragedy by introducing a third actor and developing stage scenery. He wrote some 120 plays, of which seven tragedies survive. These are *Antigone* 441 BC, *Oedipus Tyrannus*, *Electra*, *Ajax*, *Trachiniae*, *Philoctetes* 409 BC, and *Oedipus at Colonus* 401 BC.

sorghum or *great millet* or *Guinea corn* any cereal grass of the genus *Sorghum*, native to Africa but cultivated widely in India, China, the USA, and S Europe. The seeds are used for making bread. Durra is a member of the genus.

sorrel any of several plants of the genus *Rumex* of the buckwheat family Polygonaceae. *R. acetosa* is grown for its bitter salad leaves. ⟡Dock plants are of the same genus.

Sotho member of a large ethnic group in southern Africa, numbering about 7 million (1987) and living mainly in Botswana, Lesotho, and South Africa. The Sotho are predominantly farmers, living in small village groups. They speak a variety of closely related languages belonging to the Bantu branch of the Niger-Congo family. With English, Sotho is the official language of Lesotho.

soul music emotionally intense style of ⟡rhythm and blues sung by, among others, Sam Cooke (1931–1964), Aretha Franklin (1942–), and Al Green (1946–). A synthesis of blues, gospel music, and jazz, it emerged in the 1950s. Sometimes all popular music made by Afro-Americans is labelled soul music.

sound physiological sensation received by the ear, originating in a vibration (pressure variation in the air) that communicates itself to the air, and travels in every direction, spreading out as an expanding sphere. All sound waves in air travel with a speed dependent on the temperature; under ordinary conditions, this is about 330 m/1,070 ft per second. The pitch of the sound depends on the number of vibrations imposed on the air per second, but the speed is unaffected. The loudness of a sound is dependent primarily on the amplitude of the vibration of the air.

sound barrier concept that the speed of sound, or sonic speed (about 1,220 kph/760 mph at sea level), constitutes a speed limit to flight through the atmosphere, since a badly designed aircraft suffers severe buffeting at near sonic speed owing to the formation of shock waves. US test pilot Chuck Yeager first flew through the 'barrier' in 1947 in a Bell X-1 rocket plane. Now, by careful design, such aircraft as Concorde can fly at supersonic speed with ease, though they create in their wake a ◇sonic boom.

soundtrack band at one side of a cine film on which the accompanying sound is recorded. Usually it takes the form of an optical track (a pattern of light and shade). The pattern is produced on the film when signals from the recording microphone are made to vary the intensity of a light beam. During playback, a light is shone through the track on to a photocell, which converts the pattern of light falling on it into appropriate electrical signals. These signals are then fed to loudspeakers to recreate the original sounds.

South Africa Republic of; country on the S tip of Africa, bordered N by Namibia, Botswana, and Zimbabwe and NE by Swaziland and Mozambique; *area* 1,223,181 sq km/472,148 sq mi (includes Walvis Bay and independent black homelands); *capital* Cape Town (legislative), Pretoria (administrative), Bloemfontein (judicial); *physical* S end of large plateau, fringed by mountains and lowland coastal margin; Drakensberg Mountains, Table Mountain; Limpopo and Orange rivers; the Veld and the Karroo; part of Kalahari Desert; *territories* Marion Island and Prince Edward Island in the Antarctic; *head of state and government* F W de Klerk from 1989; *political system* racist, nationalist republic, restricted democracy; *exports* maize, sugar, fruit, wool, gold (world's largest producer), platinum, diamonds, uranium, iron and

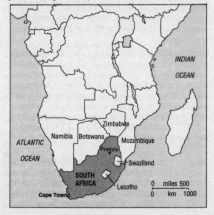

steel, copper; mining and minerals are largest export industry, followed by arms manufacturing; *population* (1990 est) 39,550,000 (73% black: Zulu, Xhosa, Sotho, Tswana; 18% white; 3% mixed; 3% Asiatic); *languages* Afrikaans and English (both official); Bantu; *recent history* the Union of South Africa was formed 1910 from two British colonies and two Boer republics. The apartheid system of racial discrimination was initiated 1948 by Daniel Malan, leader of the National Party (NP). In 1960 the African National Congress (ANC) was banned. South Africa withdrew from the Commonwealth and became a republic 1961. Harsh repression of black South Africans continued; important landmarks were the sentencing to life imprisonment of ANC leaders 1964, violent suppression of the Soweto uprising 1976, and the death in custody of Pan African Congress activist Steve Biko 1977. In 1984 a new constitution was adopted, giving segregated representation to 'coloureds'; the black majority still have no vote. Violence continued to grow in black townships. The Commonwealth agreed on limited sanctions 1986. President F W de Klerk lifted the ban on the ANC 1990 and repealed apartheid laws 1991. Nelson Mandela became ANC leader 1991. Suspicions that the government was sponsoring Inkatha violence against ANC supporters soured talks between de Klerk and Mandela towards a power-sharing arrangement.

South African Wars two wars between the Boers (settlers of Dutch origin) and the British; essentially fought for the gold and diamonds of the Transvaal. The *War of 1881* was triggered by the attempt of the Boers of the ◇Transvaal to reassert the independence surrendered 1877 in return for British aid against African peoples. The British were defeated at Majuba, and the Transvaal again became independent. The *War of 1899–1902*, also known as the *Boer War*, was preceded by the armed Jameson Raid into the Boer Transvaal; a failed attempt, inspired by the Cape Colony prime minister Rhodes, to precipitate a revolt against Kruger, the Transvaal president. The *uitlanders* (non-Boer immigrants) were still not given the vote by the Boers, negotiations failed, and the Boers invaded British territory, besieging Ladysmith, Mafeking (now Mafikeng), and Kimberley. The war ended with the Peace of Vereeniging following the Boer defeat.

South America fourth largest of the continents, nearly twice as large as Europe (13% of the world's land surface), extending south from ◇Central America; *area* 17,864,000 sq km/6,900,000 sq mi; *largest cities* (population over 3.5 million) Buenos Aires, São Paulo, Rio de Janeiro, Bogotá, Santiago, Lima, Caracas; *physical* occupying the southern part of the landmass of the western hemisphere, the South American continent stretches from Point Gallinas on the Caribbean coast of Colombia to Cape Horn at the southern tip of Horn Island, which lies adjacent to Tierra del Fuego; the most southerly point on the mainland is Cape Froward on the Brunswick peninsula, S Chile; at its maximum width (5,120 km/3,200 mi) the continent stretches from Point Pariñas, Peru, in the extreme west to Point Coqueiros, just N of Recife, Brazil, in the east; five-sixths of the continent lies in the southern hemisphere and two-thirds within the tropics; *features* Lake Titicaca (world's highest navigable lake); La Paz (highest capital city in the world); Atacama Desert; Inca ruins at Machu Picchu; rivers include the Amazon (world's largest and second longest), Parana, Madeira, São Francisco, Purus, Paraguay, Orinoco, Araguaia, Negro, Uruguay; *products* produces 44% of the world's coffee (Brazil, Colombia), 22% of its cocoa (Brazil), 35% of its citrus fruit, meat (Argentina, Brazil), soya beans (Argentina, Brazil), cotton (Brazil), linseed (Argentina); Argentina is the world's second largest producer of sunflower seed; Brazil is the world's largest producer of bananas, its second largest producer of tin, and its third largest producer of manganese, tobacco, and mangoes; Peru is the world's second largest producer of silver; Chile is the world's largest producer of copper; *population* (1988) 285 million, rising to 550 million (est) by 2000; annual growth rate from 1980 to 1985 2.3%.

Southampton port in Hampshire, S England; population (1981) 204,604. Industries include engineering, chemicals, plastics, flour-milling, and tobacco; it is also a passenger and container port.

South Australia state of the Commonwealth of Australia; *area* 984,000 sq km/379,824 sq mi; *capital* Adelaide (chief port); *towns* Whyalla, Mount Gambier; *features* Murray Valley irrigated area, including vine-growing Barossa Valley; lakes: ◊Eyre, Torrens; mountains: Mount Lofty, Musgrave, Flinders; parts of the Nullarbor Plain, and Great Victoria and Simpson deserts; experimental rocket range in the arid north at Woomera; *products* meat and wool (80% of area cattle and sheep grazing), wines and spirits, dried and canned fruit, iron (Middleback Range), coal (Leigh Creek), copper, uranium (Roxby Downs), oil and natural gas in the northeast, lead, zinc, iron, opals, household and electrical goods, vehicles; *population* (1987) 1,388,000; 1% Aborigines; *history* possibly known to the Dutch in the 16th century; surveyed by Dutch navigator Abel Tasman 1644; first European settlement 1834; province 1836; state 1901. In British nuclear tests made 1963 at Maralinga, Aborigines are said to have died.

South Carolina state in SE USA; nickname Palmetto State; *area* 80,600 sq km/31,112 sq mi; *capital* Columbia; *cities* Charleston, Greenville-Spartanburg; *population* (1990) 3,486,700; *features* large areas of woodland; subtropical climate in coastal areas; antebellum Charleston; Myrtle Beach and Hilton Head Island ocean resorts; *products* tobacco, soya beans, lumber, textiles, clothing, paper, wood pulp, chemicals,

nonelectrical machinery, primary and fabricated metals; *famous people* John C Calhoun, 'Dizzy' Gillespie; *history* first Spanish settlers 1526; Charles I gave the area (known as Carolina) to Robert Heath (1575–1649), attorney general 1629; Declaration of Independence, one of the original thirteen states 1776; joined the Confederacy 1860; readmitted to Union 1868.

South Dakota state of the USA; nickname Coyote or Sunshine State; *area* 199,800 sq km/77,123 sq mi; *capital* Pierre; *cities* Sioux Falls, Rapid City; *physical* Great Plains; Black Hills (which include granite Mount Rushmore, on whose face giant relief portrait heads of former presidents Washington, Jefferson, Lincoln, and T Roosevelt are carved); Badlands; *products* cereals, hay, livestock, gold (second-largest US producer), meat products; *population* (1990) 696,000; *famous people* Crazy Horse, Sitting Bull, Ernest O Lawrence; *history* claimed by French 18th century; first white settlements 1794; state 1889.

Southeast Asia Treaty Organization (SEATO) collective military system 1954–77 established by Australia, France, New Zealand, Pakistan, the Philippines, Thailand, the UK, and the USA, with Vietnam, Cambodia, and Laos as protocol states. After the Vietnam War, SEATO was phased out. Its nonmilitary aspects were assumed by the ◊Association of Southeast Asian Nations (ASEAN).

Southern Uplands one of the three geographical divisions of Scotland, occupying most of the hilly Scottish Borderland to the south of a geological fault line that stretches from Dunbar on the North Sea to Girvan on the Firth of Clyde. The Southern Uplands, largely formed by rocks of the Silurian and Ordovician age, are intersected by the broad valleys of the Nith and Tweed rivers.

South Georgia island in the S Atlantic, a British crown colony administered with the South Sandwich Islands; area 3,757 sq km/1,450 sq mi. South Georgia lies 1,300 km/800 mi SE of the Falkland Islands, of which it was a dependency until 1985. The British Antarctic Survey has a station on nearby Bird Island.

South Glamorgan (Welsh *De Morgannwg*) county in S Wales; *area* 420 sq km/162 sq mi; *towns* Cardiff (administrative headquarters), Barry, Penarth; *features* fertile Vale of Glamorgan; Welsh Folk Museum at St Fagans, near Cardiff; *products* dairy farming, industry (steel, plastics, engineering) in the Cardiff area; *population* (1991) 383,300; *language* English; 6% are Welsh-speaking; *famous people* Sarah Siddons, Shirley Bassey, R S Thomas.

South Holland (Dutch *Zuid-Holland*) low-lying coastal province of the Netherlands; *area* 2,910 sq km/1,123 sq mi; *population* (1991) 3,245,300; *capital* The Hague; *towns* Rotterdam, Dordrecht, Leiden, Delft, Gouda; *products* bulbs, horticulture, livestock, dairy products, chemicals, textiles; **history** once part of the former county of Holland, which was divided into two provinces in 1840.

South Korea see ◊Korea, South.

South Sea Bubble financial crisis in Britain in 1720. The South Sea Company, founded 1711, which had a monopoly of trade with South America, offered in 1719 to take over more than half the national debt in return for further concessions. Its £100 shares rapidly rose to £1,000, and an orgy of speculation followed. When the 'bubble' burst, thousands were ruined. The discovery that cabinet ministers had been guilty of corruption led to a political crisis.

South West Africa former name (until 1968) of ◊Namibia.

South Yorkshire metropolitan county of England, created 1976, originally administered by an elected council; its powers reverted to district councils from 1986; **area** 1,560 sq km/602 sq mi; **towns** Barnsley, Sheffield, Doncaster; **features** river Don; part of Peak District National Park; **products** metal work, coal, dairy, sheep, arable farming; **population** (1991) 1,269,300; **famous people** Ian Botham, Arthur Scargill.

sovereignty absolute authority within a given territory. The possession of sovereignty is taken to be the distinguishing feature of the state, as against other forms of community. The term has an internal aspect, in that it refers to the ultimate source of authority within a state, such as a parliament or monarch, and an external aspect, where it denotes the independence of the state from any outside authority.

soviet originally a strike committee elected by Russian workers in the 1905 revolution; in 1917 these were set up by peasants, soldiers, and factory workers. The soviets sent delegates to the All-Russian Congress of Soviets to represent their opinions to a future government. They were later taken over by the Bolsheviks.

Soviet Union alternative name for the former ◊Union of Soviet Socialist Republics (USSR).

Soweto (*South West Township*) racially segregated urban settlement in South Africa, SW of Johannesburg; population (1983) 915,872. It has experienced civil unrest because of the ◊apartheid regime.

soya bean leguminous plant *Glycine max*, native to E Asia, in particular Japan and China. Originally grown as a forage crop, it is increasingly used for human consumption in cooking oils and margarine, as a flour, soya milk, soy sauce, or processed into tofu, miso, or textured vegetable protein.

Soyinka Wole 1934– . Nigerian author who was a political prisoner in Nigeria 1967–69. His works include the play *The Lion and the Jewel* 1963; his prison memoirs *The Man Died* 1972; *Aké, The Years of Childhood* 1982, an autobiography, and *Isara*, a fictionalized memoir 1989. He was the first African to receive the Nobel Prize for Literature, in 1986.

Soyuz Soviet series of spacecraft, capable of carrying up to three cosmonauts. Soyuz spacecraft consist of three parts: a rear section containing engines; the central crew compartment; and a forward compartment that gives additional room for working and living space. They are now used for ferrying crews up to space stations, though they were originally used for independent space flight.

space the void that exists beyond Earth's atmosphere. Above 120 km/75 mi, very little atmosphere remains, so objects can continue to move quickly without extra energy. The space between the planets is not entirely empty, but filled with the tenuous gas of the ◊solar wind as well as dust specks.

Spacelab small space station built by the European Space Agency, carried in the cargo bay of the US space shuttle, in which it remains throughout each flight, returning to Earth with the shuttle. Spacelab consists of a pressurized module in which astronauts can work, and a series of pallets, open to the vacuum of space, on which equipment is mounted.

space probe any instrumented object sent beyond Earth to collect data from other parts of the solar system and from deep space. The first probe was the Soviet *Lunik 1*, which flew past the Moon 1959. The first successful planetary probe was the US *Mariner 2*, which flew past Venus 1962, using transfer orbit. The first space probe to leave the solar system was *Pioneer 10* 1983. Space probes include *Giotto*, the Moon probes, and the Mariner, Pioneer, Viking, and Voyager series. Japan launched its first space probe 1990.

space shuttle reusable crewed spacecraft. The first was launched 12 April 1981 by the USA. It was developed by NASA to reduce the cost of using space for commercial, scientific, and military purposes. After leaving its payload in space, the space-shuttle orbiter can be flown back to Earth to land on a runway, and is then available for reuse.

space-time in physics, combination of space and time used in the theory of ◊relativity. When developing relativity, Einstein showed that time was in many respects like an extra dimension (or direction) to space. Space and time can thus be considered as entwined into a single entity, rather than two separate things.

Spain country in SW Europe, on the Iberian Peninsula between the Atlantic and the Mediterranean, bordered N by France and W by Portugal; **area** 504,750 sq km/194,960 sq mi; **capital** Madrid; **physical** central Iberian Plateau (Meseta) with mountain ranges Pyrenees, Cantabrian Mountains, Andalusian Mountains, Sierra Nevada; lowlands

in S; rivers Ebro, Douro, Tagus, Guadiana, Guadalquivir; **territories** Balearic and Canary Islands; in N Africa: Ceuta, Melilla, Alhucemas, Chafarinas Is, Peñon de Vélez; **head of state** Juan Carlos I from 1975; **head of government** Felipe González Márquez from 1982; **political system** constitutional monarchy; **exports** citrus fruits, grapes, pomegranates, vegetables, wine, sherry, olive oil, canned fruit and fish, iron ore, cork, vehicles, textiles, petroleum products, leather goods, ceramics; **population** (1990 est) 39,623,000; **languages** Spanish (Castilian, official); Basque, Catalan, Galician, Valencian, Majorcan; **recent history** civil war 1936–39; General Francisco Franco became head of state and government, with the fascist Falange party as the only legal political organization until his death 1975, when the monarchy was restored. The Socialist Workers' Party (PSOE) won a sweeping electoral victory 1982. Spain joined the European Community 1986 and the Western European Union 1988.

spaniel any of several breeds of dog, characterized by large, drooping ears and a wavy, long, silky coat. The **Sussex spaniel** is believed to be the oldest variety, weighs 20 kg/45 lb, is 40 cm/15 in tall, and is a golden liver colour.

Spanish-American War brief war 1898 between Spain and the USA over Spanish rule in Cuba and the Philippines; the complete defeat of Spain made the USA a colonial power. The Treaty of Paris ceded the Philippines, Guam, and Puerto Rico to the USA; Cuba became independent. The USA paid $20 million to Spain. Thus ended Spain's colonial presence in the Americas.

Spanish Armada fleet sent by Philip II of Spain against England in 1588. Consisting of 130 ships, it sailed from Lisbon and carried on a running fight up the Channel with the English fleet of 197 small ships under Howard of Effingham and Francis ▷Drake. The Armada anchored off Calais but fireships forced it to put to sea, and a general action followed off Gravelines. What remained of

the Armada escaped around the N of Scotland and W of Ireland, suffering many losses by storm and shipwreck on the way. Only about half the original fleet returned to Spain.

Spanish Civil War 1936–39. See ▷Civil War, Spanish.

Spanish Guinea former name of the Republic of ▷Equatorial Guinea.

Spanish language member of the Romance branch of the Indo-European language family, traditionally known as Castilian and originally spoken only in NE Spain. As the language of the court, it has been the standard and literary language of the Spanish state since the 13th century. It is now a world language, spoken in Mexico and all South and Central American countries (except Brazil, Guyana, Surinam, and French Guiana) as well as in the Philippines, Cuba, Puerto Rico, and much of the USA.

Spanish Sahara former name for ▷Western Sahara.

Spanish Succession, War of the war 1701–14 of Britain, Austria, the Netherlands, Portugal, and Denmark (the Allies) against France, Spain, and Bavaria. It was caused by Louis XIV's acceptance of the Spanish throne on behalf of his grandson, Philip V of Spain, in defiance of the Partition Treaty of 1700, under which it would have passed to Archduke Charles of Austria (later Holy Roman emperor Charles VI).

Spark Muriel 1918– . Scottish novelist. Her enigmatic satires include *The Ballad of Peckham Rye* 1960, *The Prime of Miss Jean Brodie* 1961, *The Only Problem* 1984, and *Symposium* 1990.

sparrow any of a family (Passeridae) of small Old World birds of the order Passeriformes with short, thick bills, including the now worldwide house or English sparrow *Passer domesticus*. Many numbers of the New World family Emberizidae, which includes ▷warblers, orioles, and buntings are also called sparrows; for example, the North American song sparrow *Melospize melodia*.

sparrow hawk small woodland ▷hawk *Accipiter nisus* found in Eurasia and N Africa. It has a long tail and short wings. The male grows to 28 cm/11 in long, and the female to 38 cm/15 in. It hunts small birds.

Sparta ancient Greek city-state in the S Peloponnese (near Sparte), developed from Dorian settlements in the 10th century BC. The Spartans, known for their military discipline and austerity, took part in the Persian and Peloponnesian wars.

Spartacus Thracian gladiator who in 73 BC led a revolt of gladiators and slaves in Capua, near Naples. He was eventually caught by Roman general ▷Crassus and crucified.

Speaker presiding officer charged with the preservation of order in the legislatures of various countries. In the UK the equivalent of the Speaker in the House of Lords is the Lord Chancellor; in the House of Commons the Speaker is elected for each parliament, usually on an agreed basis among the parties, but often holds the office for many years. The original appointment dates from 1377.

Special Air Service (SAS) specialist British regiment recruited from regiments throughout the army. It has served in Malaysia, Oman, Yemen, the Falklands, Northern Ireland, and during the 1991 Gulf War, as well as against international urban guerrillas, as in the siege of the Iranian embassy in London 1980.

Special Branch section of the British police originally established 1883 to deal with Irish Fenian activists. All 42 police forces in Britain now have their own Special Branches. They act as the executive arm of MI5 (British ⟡intelligence) in its duty of preventing or investigating espionage, subversion, and sabotage; carry out duties at air and sea ports in respect of naturalization and immigration; and provide armed bodyguards for public figures.

species in biology, a distinguishable group of organisms that resemble each other or consist of a few distinctive types (as in polymorphism), and that can all interbreed to produce fertile offspring. Species are the lowest level in the system of biological classification.

specific gravity alternative term for ⟡relative density.

specific heat capacity in physics, quantity of heat required to raise unit mass (1 kg) of a substance by one ⟡kelvin (1°C). The unit of specific heat capacity in the SI system is the ⟡joule per kilogram kelvin (J kg^{-1} K^{-1}).

Spector Phil 1940– . US record producer, known for the 'wall of sound', created using a large orchestra, distinguishing his work in the early 1960s with vocal groups such as the Crystals and the Ronettes. He withdrew into semi-retirement in 1966 but his influence can still be heard.

spectroscopy study of spectra (see ⟡spectrum) associated with atoms or molecules in solid, liquid, or gaseous phase. Spectroscopy can be used to identify unknown compounds and is an invaluable tool in science, medicine, and industry (for example, in checking the purity of drugs).

spectrum (plural *spectra*) in physics, an arrangement of frequencies or wavelengths when electromagnetic radiations are separated into their constituent parts. Visible light is part of the electromagnetic spectrum and most sources emit waves over a range of wavelengths that can be broken up or 'dispersed'; white light can be separated into red, orange, yellow, green, blue, indigo, and violet. The visible spectrum was first studied by Isaac ⟡Newton, who showed in 1672 how white light could be broken up into different colours.

speech synthesis or *voice output* computer-based technology for generating speech. A speech synthesizer is controlled by a computer, which supplies strings of codes representing basic speech sounds (phonemes); together these make up words. Speech-synthesis applications include children's toys, car and aircraft warning systems, and talking books for the blind.

speed of light speed at which light and other ⟡electromagnetic waves travel through empty space. Its value is 299,792,458 metres per second/ 186,281 miles per second. The speed of light is the highest speed possible, according to the theory of ⟡relativity, and its value is independent of the motion of its source and of the observer. It is impossible to accelerate any material body to this speed because it would require an infinite amount of energy.

speed of sound speed at which sound travels through a medium, such as air or water. In air at a temperature of 0°C/32°F, the speed of sound is 331 metres/1,087 feet per second. At higher temperatures, the speed of sound is greater; at 18°C/64°F it is 342 metres/1,123 feet per second. It is greater in liquids and solids; for example, in water it is around 1,440 metres/4,724 feet per second, depending on the temperature.

speedway sport of motorcycle racing on a dirt track. Four riders compete in each heat over four laps. A series of heats make up a match or competition. In Britain there are two leagues, the British League and the National League. World championships exist for individuals, pairs (first held 1970), four-rider teams (first held 1960), long-track racing, and ice speedway.

speedwell any flowering plant of the genus *Veronica* of the snapdragon family Scrophulariaceae. Of the many wild species, most are low-growing with small, bluish flowers.

speleology scientific study of caves, their origin, development, physical structure, flora, fauna, folklore, exploration, mapping, photography, cave-diving, and rescue work. *Potholing*, which involves following the course of underground rivers or streams, has become a popular sport.

Spence Basil 1907–1976. British architect. He was professor of architecture at the Royal Academy, London, 1961–68, and his works include Coventry Cathedral, Sussex University, and the British embassy in Rome.

Spencer Stanley 1891–1959. English painter who was born and lived in Cookham-on-Thames, Berkshire, and recreated the Christian story in a Cookham setting. His detailed, dreamlike compositions had little regard for perspective and used generalized human figures.

Spender Stephen (Harold) 1909– . English poet and critic. His earlier poetry has a left-wing political content, as in *Twenty Poems* 1930, *Vienna* 1934, *The Still Centre* 1939, and *Poems of Dedication* 1946. Other works include the verse drama *Trial of a Judge* 1938, the autobiography *World within World* 1951, and translations. His *Journals 1939–83* were published 1985.

Spenser Edmund *c.* 1552–1599. English poet, who has been called the 'poet's poet' because of his rich imagery and command of versification. His major work is the moral allegory *The Faerie Queene*, of which six books survive (three published 1590 and three 1596). Other books include *The Shepheard's Calendar* 1579, *Astrophel* 1586, the love sonnets *Amoretti* and the *Epithalamion* 1595.

sperm or **spermatozoon** in biology, the male ⧓gamete of animals. Each sperm cell has a head capsule containing a nuclcus, a middle portion containing ⧓mitochondria (which provide energy), and a long tail (flagellum). See ⧓sexual reproduction.

spermicide any cream, jelly, pessary, or other preparation that kills the ⧓sperm cells in semen. Spermicides are used for contraceptive purposes, usually in combination with a ⧓condom or ⧓diaphragm. Sponges impregnated with spermicide have been developed but are not yet in widespread use. Spermicide used alone is only 75% effective in preventing pregnancy.

Sphinx mythological creature, represented in Egyptian, Assyrian, and Greek art as a lion with a human head. In Greek myth the Sphinx was female and killed travellers who failed to answer a riddle; she killed herself when ⧓Oedipus gave the right answer.

spider any arachnid (eight-legged animal) of the order Araneae. There are about 30,000 known species. Unlike insects, spiders have the head and breast merged to form the cephalothorax, connected to the abdomen by a characteristic narrow waist. There are eight legs, and usually eight simple eyes. On the undersurface of the abdomen are spinnerets, usually six, which exude a viscid fluid. This hardens on exposure to the air to form silky threads, used to make silken egg cases, silk-lined tunnels, or various kinds of webs and snares for catching prey that is then wrapped. The fangs of spiders inject substances to subdue and digest prey, the juices of which are then sucked into the stomach by the spider.

spider plant African plant of the genus *Chlorophytum* of the lily family. Two species, *C. comosum* and *C. elatum*, are popular house plants. They have long narrow variegated leaves and produce flowering shoots from which the new plants grow. The flowers are small and white. Spider plants absorb toxins from the air and therefore have a purifying action on the local atmosphere.

Spielberg Steven 1947– . US director, writer, and producer of such films as *Jaws* 1975, *Close*

Encounters of the Third Kind 1977, *Raiders of the Lost Ark* 1981, and *ET* 1982. Immensely successful, his films usually combine cliff-hanging suspense with heartfelt sentimentality.

spin in physics, the intrinsic angular momentum of a subatomic particle, nucleus, atom, or molecule, which continues to exist even when the particle comes to rest. A particle in a specific energy state has a particular spin, just as it has a particular electric charge and mass. According to quantum theory, this is restricted to discrete and indivisible values, specified by a spin quantum number. Because of its spin, a charged particle acts as a small magnet and is affected by magnetic fields.

spina bifida congenital defect in which part of the spinal cord and its membranes are exposed, due to incomplete dcvclopmcnt of the spine (vertebral column).

spinach annual plant *Spinacia oleracea* of the goosefoot family Chenopodiaceae. It is native to Asia and widely cultivated for its leaves, which are eaten as a vegetable.

spine backbone of vertebrates. In most mammals, it contains 26 small bones called vertebrae, which enclose and protect the spinal cord (which links the peripheral nervous system to the brain). The spine connects with the skull, ribs, back muscles, and pelvis.

spinning machine machine for drawing out fibres and twisting them into a long thread, or yarn. Spinning was originally done by hand, then with the spinning wheel, and in about 1767 in England James ⧓Hargreaves built the spinning jenny, a machine that could spin 8, then 16, bobbins at once. Later, Samuel ⧓Crompton's spinning mule 1779 had a moving carriage carrying the spindles and is still in use today.

Spinoza Benedict or Baruch 1632–1677. Dutch philosopher who believed in a rationalistic pantheism that owed much to Descartes' mathematical appreciation of the universe. Mind and matter are two modes of an infinite substance that he called God or Nature, good and evil being relative. He was a determinist, believing that human action was motivated by self-preservation.

spiny anteater alternative name for ⧓echidna.

spiraea any herbaceous plant or shrub of the genus *Spiraea*, family Rosaceae, which includes many cultivated species with ornamental panicles of flowers.

spiritualism belief in the survival of the human personality and in communication between the living and those who have 'passed on'. The spiritualist movement originated in the USA in 1848. Adherents to this religious denomination practise *mediumship*, which claims to allow clairvoyant knowledge of distant events and spirit healing. The writer Arthur Conan Doyle and the Victorian prime minister Gladstone were converts.

Spitsbergen main island in the Norwegian archipelago of ▷Svalbard.

spleen organ in vertebrates, part of the lymphatic system, which helps to process ▷lymphocytes. It also regulates the number of red blood cells in circulation by destroying old cells, and stores iron. It is situated behind the stomach.

Split (Italian *Spalato*) port in Croatia, on the Adriatic; population (1981) 236,000. Industries include engineering, cement, and textiles, and it is also a tourist resort.

Spode Josiah 1754–1827. English potter. Around 1800, he developed bone porcelain (made from bone ash, china stone, and china clay), which was produced at all English factories in the 19th century. He became potter to King George III in 1806.

sponge any saclike simple invertebrate of the phylum Porifera, usually marine. A sponge has a hollow body, its cavity lined by cells bearing flagellae, whose whiplike movements keep water circulating, bringing in a stream of food particles. The body walls are strengthened with protein (as in the bath sponge) or small spikes of silica, or a framework of calcium carbonate.

spoonbill any of several large wading birds of the Ibis family (Threskiornithidae), characterized by a long, flat bill, dilated at the tip in the shape of a spoon. Spoonbills are white or pink, and up to 90 cm/3 ft tall. The Eurasian spoonbill *Platalea leucorodia* of Europe, S Asia, and Africa is found in shallow open water, which it sifts for food.

spore small reproductive or resting body, usually consisting of just one cell. Unlike a ▷gamete, it does not need to fuse with another cell in order to develop into a new organism. Plant spores are haploid and are produced by the sporophyte, following ▷meiosis, in ▷alternation of generations. Spores are produced by the lower plants, most fungi, some bacteria, and certain protozoa. They are generally light and easily dispersed by wind movements.

Spratly Islands (Chinese *Nanshan Islands*) group of small islands, coral reefs, and sandbars dispersed over a distance of 965 km/600 mi in the South China Sea. Used as a submarine base by the Japanese during World War II, the islands are claimed in whole or part by the People's Republic of China, Taiwan, Malaysia, Vietnam (which calls the islands *Truong Sa*), and the Philippines (which calls them *Kalayaan*). The islands are of strategic importance, commanding the sea passage from Japan to Singapore, and in 1976 oil was discovered.

spreadsheet in computing, a program that mimics a sheet of ruled paper, divided into columns and rows. The user enters values in the sheet, then instructs the program to perform some operation on them, such as totalling a column or finding the average of a series of numbers. Highly complex numerical analyses may be built up from these simple steps.

spring in geology, a natural flow of water from the ground, formed where the water table meets the ground's surface. The source of water is rain that has percolated through the overlying rocks. During its underground passage, the water may have dissolved mineral substances, which may then be precipitated at the spring (hence, a mineral spring).

springbok South African antelope *Antidorcas marsupialis* about 80 cm/30 in at the shoulder, with head and body 1.3 m/4 ft long. It may leap 3 m/10 ft or more in the air when startled or playing, and has a fold of skin along the middle of the back which is raised to a crest in alarm. Springboks once migrated in herds of over a million, but are now found only in small numbers where protected.

Springsteen Bruce 1949– . US rock singer, songwriter, and guitarist, born in New Jersey. His music combines melodies in traditional rock idiom and reflective lyrics about working-class life on albums such as *Born to Run* 1975, *Born in the USA* 1984 maturing into the 1992 albums of *Human Touch* and *Lucky Town*.

spruce coniferous tree of the genus *Picea* of the pine family, found over much of the northern hemisphere. Pyramidal in shape, spruces have rigid, prickly needles and drooping, leathery cones. Some are important forestry trees, such as sitka spruce *P. sitchensis*, native to W North America, and the Norway spruce *P. abies*, now planted widely in North America.

Sputnik series of ten Soviet Earth-orbiting satellites. *Sputnik 1* was the first artificial satellite, launched 4 Oct 1957. It weighed 84 kg/185 lb, with a 58 cm/23 in diameter, and carried only a simple radio transmitter which allowed scientists to track it as it orbited Earth. It burned up in the atmosphere 92 days later. Sputniks were superseded in the early 1960s by the Cosmos series.

square root in mathematics, a number that when squared (multiplied by itself) equals a given number. For example, the square root of 25 (written 25) is ± 5, because $5 \times 5 = 25$, and $(-5) \times (-5) = 25$. As an exponent, a square root is represented by $1/2$, for example, $16^{1/2} = 4$.

squash or *squash rackets* racket-and-ball game usually played by two people on an enclosed court, derived from rackets. Squash became a popular sport in the 1970s and then a fitness craze as well as a competitive sport. There are two forms of squash: the American form, which is played in North and some South American countries, and the English, which is played mainly in Europe and Commonwealth countries such as Pakistan, Australia, and New Zealand.

squill bulb-forming perennial plant of the genus

Scilla, family Liliaceae, found growing in dry places near the sea in W Europe. Cultivated species usually bear blue flowers either singly or in clusters at the top of the stem.

squint or *strabismus* common condition in which one eye deviates in any direction. A squint may be convergent (with the bad eye turned inward), divergent (outward), or, in rare cases, vertical. A convergent squint is also called *cross-eye*.

squirrel rodent of the family Sciuridae. Squirrels are found worldwide except for Australia, Madagascar, and polar regions. Some are tree dwellers; these generally have bushy tails, and some, with membranes between their legs, are called flying squirrels. Others are terrestrial, generally burrowing forms called ground squirrels; these include chipmunks, gophers, marmots, and prairie dogs. In Britain, the red squirrel *Sciurus vulgaris* has been replaced in most areas by the introduced grey squirrel *Sciurus carolinensis* from North America.

Sri Lanka Democratic Socialist Republic of (formerly *Ceylon*); island in the Indian Ocean, off the SE coast of India; *area* 65,600 sq km/ 25,328 sq mi; *capital* and chief port Colombo; *physical* flat in N and around coast; hills and mountains in S and central interior; Adam's Peak 2,243 m/7,538 ft; *head of state* Ranasinghe Premadsa from 1989; *head of government* Dingiri Banda Wijetunge from 1989; *political system* liberal democratic republic; *exports* tea, rubber, coconut products, graphite, sapphires, rubies, other gemstones; *population* (1990 est) 17,135,000 (Sinhalese 74%, Tamils 17%, Moors 7%); *languages* Sinhala, Tamil, English; *recent history* independence from Britain within the Commonwealth was achieved 1948. The Socialist Republic of Sri Lanka was proclaimed 1972. Tamil guerrilla violence escalated 1983; a ceasefire was policed by Indian troops but left-wing guerrillas campaigned against an Indo-Sri Lankan peace pact 1988. India agreed to withdraw its peace-keeping forces 1990; violence continued.

SS Nazi elite corps (German *Schutz-Staffel* 'protective squadron') established 1925. Under ▷Himmler its 500,000 membership included the full-time *Waffen-SS* (armed SS), which fought in World War II, and spare-time members. The SS performed state police duties and was brutal in its treatment of the Jews and others in the concentration camps and occupied territories. It was condemned at the Nuremberg Trials of war criminals.

Staffordshire county in W central England; *area* 2,720 sq km/1,050 sq mi; *towns* Stafford (administrative headquarters), Stoke-on-Trent; *features* largely flat, comprising the Vale of Trent and its tributaries; Cannock Chase; Keele University 1962; Staffordshire bull terriers; *products* coal in the north; china and earthenware in the Potteries and the upper Trent basin; *population* (1991)

1,020,300; *famous people* Arnold Bennett, Peter de Wint, Robert Peel.

stainless steel widely used ▷alloy of iron, chromium, and nickel that resists rusting. Its chromium content also gives it a high tensile strength. It is used for cutlery and kitchen fittings. Stainless steel was first produced in the UK 1913 and in Germany 1914.

stalactite and stalagmite cave structures formed by the deposition of calcite dissolved in ground water. *Stalactites* grow downwards from the roofs or walls and can be icicle-shaped, straw-shaped, curtain-shaped, or formed as terraces. *Stalagmites* grow upwards from the cave floor and can be conical, fir-cone-shaped, or resemble a stack of saucers. Growing stalactites and stalagmites may meet to form a continuous column from floor to ceiling.

Stalin Joseph. Adopted name (Russian 'steel') of Joseph Vissarionovich Djugashvili 1879–1953. Soviet politician. A member of the October Revolution Committee 1917, Stalin became general secretary of the Communist Party 1922. After ▷Lenin's death 1924, Stalin sought to create 'socialism in one country' and clashed with ▷Trotsky, who denied the possibility of socialism inside Russia until revolution had occurred in W Europe. Stalin won this ideological struggle by 1927, and a series of five-year plans was launched to collectivize industry and agriculture from 1928. All opposition was eliminated in the Great Purge 1936–38. During World War II, Stalin intervened in the military direction of the campaigns against Nazi Germany. His role was denounced after his death by Khrushchev and other members of the Soviet regime.

Stalingrad former name (1925–61) of the Russian city of ▷Volgograd.

Stamboul old part of the Turkish city of ▷Istanbul, the area formerly occupied by ▷Byzantium.

stamen male reproductive organ of a flower. The stamens are collectively referred to as the ▷androecium. A typical stamen consists of a stalk, or filament, with an anther, the pollen-bearing organ, at its apex, but in some primitive plants, such as *Magnolia*, the stamen may not be markedly differentiated.

Stamp Act UK act of Parliament in 1765 that sought to raise enough money from the American colonies to cover the cost of their defence. Refusal to use the required tax stamps and a blockade of British merchant shipping in the colonies forced repeal of the act the following year. It was a precursor of the ▷American Revolution.

standard temperature and pressure (STP) in chemistry, a standard set of conditions for experimental measurements, to enable comparisons to be made between sets of results. Standard temperature is 0°C and standard pressure 1 atmosphere (101,325 Pa).

Stanislavsky Konstantin Sergeivich 1863–1938. Russian actor, director, and teacher of acting. He rejected the declamatory style of acting in favour of a more realistic approach, concentrating on the psychological basis for the development of character. The Actors Studio is based on this approach.

Stanley town on E Falkland, capital of the ◊Falkland Islands; population (1986) 1,200. After changing its name only once between 1843 and 1982, it was renamed five times in the space of six weeks during the Falklands War April–June 1982.

Stanley Henry Morton. Adopted name of John Rowlands 1841–1904. Welsh-born US explorer and journalist who made four expeditions to Africa. He and David ◊Livingstone met at Ujiji 1871 and explored Lake Tanganyika. He traced the course of the river Zaïre (Congo) to the sea 1874–77, established the Congo Free State (Zaire) 1879–84, and charted much of the interior 1887–89.

Stansfield Lisa 1965– . English pop singer whose slick soul recordings have won her several of the UK record industry's Brit Awards. She had a UK number-one hit with 'All Around the World' 1989. Her albums *Affection* 1989 and *Real Love* 1992 also enjoyed chart success in the UK and USA.

star luminous globe of gas, producing its own heat and light by nuclear reactions. Stars are born from ◊nebulae, and consist mostly of hydrogen and helium gases. Surface temperatures range from 2,000°C/3,600°F to above 30,000°C/54,000°F and the corresponding colours range from red to blue-white. Temperatures at the centre are typically 8,000,000–33,000,000°C/14,000,000–59,000,000°F. The brightest stars have the highest masses, 100 times that of the Sun, and emit as much light as millions of suns; they live for less than a million years before exploding as ◊supernovae. The faintest stars are the ◊red dwarfs, less than one-thousandth the brightness of the Sun.

starch widely distributed, high-molecular-mass ◊carbohydrate, produced by plants as a food store; main dietary sources are cereals, legumes, and tubers, including potatoes. It consists of varying proportions of two ◊glucose polymers (◊polysaccharides): straight-chain (amylose) and branched (amylopectin) molecules.

Star Chamber in English history, a civil and criminal court, named after the star-shaped ceiling decoration of the room in the Palace of Westminster, London, where its first meetings were held. Created in 1487 by Henry VII, the Star Chamber comprised some 20 or 30 judges. It was abolished 1641 by the ◊Long Parliament.

starfish or *seastar* any ◊echinoderm of the subclass Asteroidea with arms radiating from a central body. Usually there are five arms, but some species have more. They are covered with spines and small pincerlike organs. There are also a number of small tubular processes on the skin surface that assist in locomotion and respiration. Starfish are predators, and vary in size from 1.2 cm/0.5 in to 90 cm/3 ft.

star fruit fruit of the ◊carambola tree.

starling any member of a large, widespread Old World family (Sturnidae) of chunky, dark, generally gregarious birds of the order Passeriformes. The European starling *Sturnus vulgaris* is common in N Eurasia and has been naturalized in North America from the late 19th century. The black, speckled plumage is glossed with green and purple. Its own call is a bright whistle, but it is a mimic of the songs of other birds. It is about 20 cm/8 in long.

Star Wars popular term for the ◊Strategic Defense Initiative announced by US president Reagan in 1983.

States General former French parliament that consisted of three estates – nobility, clergy, and commons. First summoned 1302, it declined in importance as the power of the crown grew. It was not called at all 1614–1789 when the crown needed to institute fiscal reforms to avoid financial collapse. Once called, the demands made by the States General formed the first phase in the ◊French Revolution. States General is also the name of the Dutch parliament.

static electricity ◊electric charge that is stationary, usually acquired by a body by means of electrostatic induction or friction. Rubbing different materials can produce static electricity, as seen in the sparks produced on combing one's hair or removing a nylon shirt. In some processes static electricity is useful, as in paint spraying where the parts to be sprayed are charged with electricity of opposite polarity to that on the paint droplets, and in ◊xerography.

statics branch of mechanics concerned with the behaviour of bodies at rest and forces in equilibrium, and distinguished from ◊dynamics.

statistics branch of mathematics concerned with the collection and interpretation of data. For example, to determine the ◊mean age of the children in a school, a statistically acceptable answer might be obtained by calculating an average based on the ages of a representative sample, consisting, for example, of a random tenth of the pupils from each class. ◊Probability is the branch of statistics dealing with predictions of events.

Stavropol territory of the Russian Federation, lying N of the Caucasus mountains; area 80,600 sq km/31,128 sq mi; population (1985) 2,715,000. The capital is Stavropol. Irrigated land produces grain and sheep are also reared. There are natural gas deposits.

steady-state theory theory that the universe appears the same wherever (and whenever) viewed. This seems to be refuted by the existence of ◊cosmic background radiation.

steam engine engine that uses the power of steam

to produce useful work. It was the principal power source during the British Industrial Revolution in the 18th century. The first successful steam engine was built 1712 by Thomas Newcomen, and it was developed further by James Watt from 1769 and by Richard Trevithick, whose high-pressure steam engine 1802 led to the development of the steam locomotive.

steel alloy or mixture of iron and up to 1.7% carbon, sometimes with other elements, such as manganese, phosphorus, sulphur, and silicon. The USA, Russia, Ukraine, and Japan are the main steel producers. Steel has innumerable uses, including ship and automobile manufacture, skyscraper frames, and machinery of all kinds.

Steele Richard 1672–1729. Irish essayist who founded the journal *The Tatler* 1709–11, in which Joseph ⟩Addison collaborated. They continued their joint work in *The Spectator*, also founded by Steele, 1711–12, and *The Guardian* 1713.

Stein Gertrude 1874–1946. US writer who influenced authors Ernest ⟩Hemingway, Sherwood Anderson, and F Scott ⟩Fitzgerald with her conversational tone, cinematic technique, use of repetition, and absence of punctuation: devices intended to convey immediacy and realism. Her work includes the self-portrait *The Autobiography of Alice B Toklas* 1933.

Steinbeck John (Ernst) 1902–1968. US novelist. His realist novels, such as *In Dubious Battle* 1936, *Of Mice and Men* 1937, and *The Grapes of Wrath* 1939 (Pulitzer prize 1940), portray agricultural life in his native California, where migrant farm laborers from the Oklahoma dust bowl struggled to survive. Nobel prize 1962.

Steinem Gloria 1934– . US journalist and liberal feminist who emerged as a leading figure in the US women's movement in the late 1960s.

Steiner Rudolf 1861–1925. Austrian philosopher, originally a theosophist and follower of Helena Blavatsky. He developed his own mystic and spiritual teaching, **anthroposophy**, designed to develop the whole human being. A number of Steiner schools follow a curriculum laid down by him, with a strong emphasis on the arts, although the pupils can also take state exams.

Stendhal pen name of Marie Henri Beyle 1783–1842. French novelist. His novels *Le Rouge et le noir/The* ⟩*Red and the Black* 1830 and *La Chartreuse de Parme/The Charterhouse of Parma* 1839 were pioneering works in their treatment of disguise and hypocrisy; a review of the latter by fellow novelist ⟩Balzac in 1840 furthered Stendhal's reputation.

Stephen *c.* 1097–1154. King of England from 1135. A grandson of William I, he was elected king 1135, although he had previously recognized Henry I's daughter ⟩Matilda as heiress to the throne.

Matilda landed in England 1139, and civil war disrupted the country until 1153, when Stephen acknowledged Matilda's son, Henry II, as his own heir.

Stephen, St died *c.* AD 35. The first Christian martyr; he was stoned to death. Feast day 26 Dec.

Stephenson George 1781–1848. English engineer who built the first successful steam locomotive, and who also invented a safety lamp in 1815. He was appointed engineer of the Stockton and Darlington Railway, the world's first public railway, in 1821, and of the Liverpool and Manchester Railway in 1826. In 1829 he won a £500 prize with his locomotive *Rocket*.

Stephenson Robert 1803–1859. English civil engineer who constructed railway bridges such as the high-level bridge at Newcastle upon Tyne, England, and the Menai and Conway tubular bridges in Wales. He was the son of George Stephenson.

steppe the temperate grasslands of Europe and Asia. Sometimes the term refers to other temperate grasslands and semi-arid desert edges.

steradian SI unit (symbol sr) of measure of solid (three-dimensional) angles, the three-dimensional equivalent of the ⟩radian. One steradian is the angle at the centre of a sphere when an area on the surface of the sphere equal to the square of the sphere's radius is joined to the centre.

Sterea Ellas-Evvoia region of central Greece and Euboea, occupying the southern part of the Greek mainland between the Ionian and Aegean seas and including the island of Euboea; population (1991) 1,235,600; area 24,391 sq km/9,421 sq mi. The chief city is Athens.

sterilization any surgical operation to terminate the possibility of reproduction. In women, this is normally achieved by sealing or tying off the ⟩Fallopian tubes (tubal ligation) so that fertilization can no longer take place. In men, the transmission of sperm is blocked by ⟩vasectomy.

sterling silver ⟩alloy containing 925 parts of silver and 75 parts of copper. The copper hardens the silver, making it more useful.

Sterne Laurence 1713–1768. Irish writer, creator of the comic anti-hero Tristram Shandy. *The Life and Opinions of Tristram Shandy, Gent* 1760–67, an eccentrically whimsical and bawdy novel, foreshadowed many of the techniques and devices of 20th-century novelists, including James Joyce. His other works include *A Sentimental Journey through France and Italy* 1768.

steroid in biology, any of a group of cyclic, unsaturated alcohols (lipids without fatty acid components), which, like sterols, have a complex molecular structure consisting of four carbon rings. Steroids include the sex hormones, such as ⟩testosterone, the corticosteroid hormones produced by the ⟩adrenal gland, bile acids, and ⟩cholesterol. The term is commonly used to refer to ⟩anabolic steroid.

Stevens Wallace 1879–1955. US poet. An insurance company executive, he was not recognized as a major poet until late in life. His volumes of poems include *Harmonium* 1923, *The Man with the Blue Guitar* 1937, and *Transport to Summer* 1947. *The Necessary Angel* 1951 is a collection of essays. An elegant and philosophical poet, he won the Pulitzer Prize 1954 for his *Collected Poems*.

Stevenson Robert Louis 1850–1894. Scottish novelist and poet, author of the adventure novel *Treasure Island* 1883. Later works included the novels *Kidnapped* 1886, *The Master of Ballantrae* 1889, *Dr Jekyll and Mr Hyde* 1886, and the anthology *A Child's Garden of Verses* 1885.

stick insect insect of the order Phasmida, closely resembling a stick or twig. Many species are wingless. The longest reach a length of 30 cm/1 ft.

stickleback any fish of the family Gasterosteidae, found in marine and fresh waters of the northern hemisphere. It has a long body that can grow to 18 cm/7 in. The spines along a stickleback's back take the place of the first dorsal fin, and can be raised to make the fish difficult to eat for predators. The male builds a nest for the female's eggs, which he then guards.

Stijl, De group of 20th-century Dutch artists and architects led by ▷Mondrian from 1917. They believed in the concept of the 'designer'; that all life, work, and leisure should be surrounded by art; and that everything functional should also be aesthetic. The group had a strong influence on the ▷Bauhaus school.

stimulant any drug that acts on the brain to increase alertness and activity; for example, ▷amphetamine. When given to children, stimulants may have a paradoxical, calming effect. Stimulants cause liver damage, are habit-forming, have limited therapeutic value, and are now prescribed only to treat narcolepsy and to reduce the appetite in dieting.

Stirling James 1926– . British architect, associated with collegiate and museum architecture. His works include the engineering building at Leicester University, and the Clore Gallery (the extension to house the ▷Turner collection) at the Tate Gallery, London, opened in 1987.

stoat carnivorous mammal *Mustela erminea* of the northern hemisphere, in the weasel family, about 37 cm/15 in long including the black-tipped tail. It has a long body and a flattened head. The upper parts and tail are red-brown, and the underparts are white. In the colder regions, the coat turns white (*ermine*) in winter. Stoats live in Europe, Asia, and North America; they have been introduced to New Zealand.

stock in botany, any of several herbaceous plants of the genus *Matthiola* of the crucifer family, commonly grown as garden ornamentals. Many cultivated varieties, including simple-stemmed, queen's, and ten-week, have been derived from the wild stock *M. incana*; *M. bicornis* becomes aromatic at night and is known as night-scented (or evening) stock.

stock exchange institution for the buying and selling of stocks and shares (securities). The world's largest stock exchanges are London, New York (Wall Street), and Tokyo. The oldest stock exchanges are Antwerp 1460, Hamburg 1558, Amsterdam 1602, New York 1790, and London 1801. The former division on the London Stock Exchange between brokers (who bought shares from jobbers to sell to the public) and jobbers (who sold them only to brokers on commission, the 'jobbers' turn') was abolished in 1986.

Stockhausen Karlheinz 1928– . German composer of avant-garde music who has continued to explore new musical sounds and compositional techniques since the 1950s. His major works include *Gesang der Jünglinge* 1956 and *Kontakte* 1960 (electronic music); and *Sirius* 1977.

Stockholm capital and industrial port of Sweden; population (1990) 674,500. It is built on a number of islands. Industries include engineering, brewing, electrical goods, paper, textiles, and pottery.

stocks and shares investment holdings (securities) in private or public undertakings. Although distinctions have become blurred, in the UK stock usually means fixed-interest securities – for example, those issued by central and local government – whereas shares represent a stake in the ownership of a trading company that, if they are ordinary shares, yield to the owner dividends reflecting the success of the company. In the USA the term stock generally signifies what in the UK is an ordinary share.

stoicism Greek school of philosophy, founded about 300 BC by Zeno of Citium. The stoics were pantheistic materialists who believed that happiness lay in accepting the law of the universe. They emphasized human brotherhood, denounced slavery, and were internationalist.

stomach the first cavity in the digestive system of animals. In mammals it is a bag of muscle situated just below the diaphragm. Food enters it from the oesophagus, is digested by the acid and ▷enzymes secreted by the stomach lining, and then passes into the duodenum. Some plant-eating mammals have multichambered stomachs that harbour bacteria in one of the chambers to assist in the digestion of ▷cellulose. The gizzard is part of the stomach in birds.

Stone Age the developmental stage of humans in ▷prehistory before the use of metals, when tools and weapons were made chiefly of stone, especially flint. The Stone Age is subdivided into the Old or Palaeolithic, the Middle or Mesolithic, and the New or Neolithic. The people of the Old Stone Age were hunters and gatherers, whereas the Neolithic people took the first steps in agriculture, the domestication of animals, weaving, and pottery.

stonecrop any of several plants of the genus *Sedum* of the orpine family Crassulaceae, a succulent herb with fleshy leaves and clusters of starlike flowers. Stonecrops are characteristic of dry, rocky places and some grow on walls.

Stonehenge megalithic monument dating from about 2800 BC on Salisbury Plain, Wiltshire, England. It consisted originally of a circle of 30 upright stones, their tops linked by lintel stones to form a continuous circle about 30 m/100 ft across. Within the circle was a horseshoe arrangement of five trilithons (two uprights plus a lintel, set as five separate entities), and a so-called 'altar stone' – an upright pillar – on the axis of the horseshoe at the open, NE end, which faces in the direction of the rising sun. It has been suggested that it served as an observatory.

Stoppard Tom 1937– . Czechoslovak-born British playwright whose works use wit and wordplay to explore logical and philosophical ideas. His play *Rosencrantz and Guildenstern are Dead* 1966 was followed by comedies including *The Real Inspector Hound* 1968, *Jumpers* 1972, *Travesties* 1974, *Dirty Linen* 1976, *The Real Thing* 1982, and *Hapgood* 1988. He has also written for radio, television, and the cinema.

stork any of a family (Ciconiidea) of long-legged, long-necked wading birds with long, powerful wings, and long bills used for spearing prey. Some species grow up to 1.5 m/5 ft tall.

Strachey (Giles) Lytton 1880–1932. English critic and biographer, a member of the ◊Bloomsbury Group of writers and artists. The mocking and witty treatment of Cardinal Manning, Florence Nightingale, Thomas Arnold, and General Gordon in *Eminent Victorians* 1918 won him recognition. His biography of *Queen Victoria* 1921 was more affectionate.

Stradivari Antonio (Latin form *Stradivarius*) 1644–1737. Italian stringed instrument maker, generally considered the greatest of all violin makers. He was born in Cremona and studied there with Niccolo ◊Amati. He produced more than 1,100 instruments from his family workshops, over 600 of which survive.

Strafford Thomas Wentworth, 1st Earl of Strafford 1593–1641. English politician, originally an opponent of Charles I, but from 1628 on the Royalist side. He ruled despotically as Lord Deputy of Ireland 1632–39, when he returned to England as Charles's chief adviser and received an earldom. He was impeached in 1640 by Parliament, abandoned by Charles as a scapegoat, and beheaded.

Strasbourg city on the river Ill, in Bas-Rhin *département*, capital of Alsace, France; population

(1982) 373,000. Industries include car manufacture, tobacco, printing and publishing, and preserves. The ◊Council of Europe meets here, and sessions of the European Parliament alternate between Strasbourg and Luxembourg.

Strategic Arms Limitation Talks (SALT) series of US-Soviet discussions 1969–79 aimed at reducing the rate of nuclear-arms build-up (as opposed to ◊disarmament, which would reduce the number of weapons, as discussed in ◊Strategic Arms Reduction Talks (START).

Strategic Arms Reduction Talks (START) phase in US-Soviet peace discussions dealing with ◊disarmament. START began with talks in Geneva 1983, leading to the signing of the ◊Intermediate Nuclear Forces (INF) Treaty 1987. Reductions of about 30% in strategic nuclear weapons systems were agreed 1991.

Strategic Defense Initiative (SDI) also called *Star Wars* attempt by the USA to develop a defence system against incoming nuclear missiles, based in part outside the Earth's atmosphere. It was announced by President Reagan in March 1983, and the research had by 1990 cost over $16.5 billion. In 1988, the joint Chiefs of Staff announced that they expected to be able to intercept no more than 30% of incoming missiles. Scientists maintain that the system is basically unworkable.

Stratford-upon-Avon market town on the river Avon, in Warwickshire, England; population (1981) 21,000. It is the birthplace of William ◊Shakespeare.

Strathclyde region of Scotland; *area* 13,900 sq km/5,367 sq mi; *towns* Glasgow (administrative headquarters), Paisley, Greenock, Kilmarnock, Clydebank, Hamilton, Coatbridge, Prestwick; *features* includes some of Inner ◊Hebrides; river Clyde; part of Loch Lomond; Glencoe, site of the massacre of the Macdonald clan; Breadalbane; islands: Arran, Bute, Mull; *products* dairy, pig, and poultry products; shipbuilding; engineering; coal from Ayr and Lanark; oil-related services; *population* (1991) 2,218,200, half the population of Scotland; *famous people* William Burrell, James Keir Hardie, David Livingstone.

stratosphere that part of the atmosphere 10–40 km/6–25 mi from Earth, where the temperature slowly rises from a low of –55°C/–67°F to around 0°C/32°F. The air is rarefied and at around 25 km/ 15 mi much ◊ozone is concentrated.

Strauss Johann (Baptist) 1825–1899. Austrian conductor and composer, the son of composer Johann Strauss (1804–1849). In 1872 he gave up conducting and wrote operettas, such as *Die Fledermaus* 1874, and numerous waltzes, such as *The Blue Danube* and *Tales from the Vienna Woods*, which gained him the title 'the Waltz King'.

Strauss Richard (Georg) 1864–1949. German composer and conductor. He followed the German

Romantic tradition but had a strongly personal style, characterized by his bold, colourful orchestration. He first wrote tone poems such as *Don Juan* 1889, *Till Eulenspiegel's Merry Pranks* 1895, and *Also sprach Zarathustra* 1896. He then moved on to opera with *Salome* 1905 and *Elektra* 1909, both of which have elements of polytonality. He reverted to a more traditional style with *Der Rosenkavalier* 1911.

Stravinsky Igor 1882–1971. Russian composer, later of French (1934) and US (1945) nationality. He studied under ◊Rimsky-Korsakov and wrote the music for the Diaghilev ballets *The Firebird* 1910, *Petrushka* 1911, and *The Rite of Spring* 1913 (controversial at the time for their unorthodox rhythms and harmonies). His versatile work ranges from his Neo-Classical ballet *Pulcinella* 1920 to the choral-orchestral *Symphony of Psalms* 1930. He later made use of serial techniques in such works as the *Canticum Sacrum* 1955 and the ballet *Agon* 1953–57.

strawberry low-growing perennial plant of the genus *Fragaria*, family Rosaceae, widely cultivated for its red, fleshy fruits, which are rich in vitamin C. Commercial cultivated forms bear one crop of fruit in summer and multiply by runners.

Streep Meryl 1949– . US actress known for her strong character roles. She became a leading star of the 1980s, winning numerous awards. Her films include *The Deer Hunter* 1978, *Kramer vs Kramer* 1979 (Academy Award), *The French Lieutenant's Woman* 1980, *Sophie's Choice* 1982 (Academy Award), *Out of Africa* 1985, *Ironweed* 1988, and *A Cry in the Dark* 1989.

strike stoppage of work by employees, often as members of a trade union, to obtain or resist change in wages, hours, or conditions. A *lockout* is a weapon of an employer to thwart or enforce such change by preventing employees from working. Another measure is **work to rule**, when production is virtually brought to a halt by strict observance of union rules.

Strindberg August 1849–1912. Swedish playwright and novelist. His plays, influential in the development of dramatic technique, are in a variety of styles including historical plays, symbolic dramas (the two-part *Dödsdansen/The Dance of Death* 1901) and 'chamber plays' such as *Spöksonaten/The Ghost [Spook] Sonata* 1907. *Fadren/The Father* 1887 and *Fröken Julie/Miss Julie* 1888 are among his works.

stroke or **cerebrovascular accident** or **apoplexy** interruption of the blood supply to part of the brain due to a sudden bleed in the brain (cerebral haemorrhage) or embolism or ◊thrombosis. Strokes vary in severity from producing almost no symptoms to proving rapidly fatal. In between are those (often recurring) that leave a wide range of impaired function, depending on the size and location of the event.

Strong Maurice (Frederick) 1929– . Canadian diplomat and entrepreneur, secretary general of the ◊Earth Summit 1992. He became Canadian representative at the United Nations 1967 and went on to establish the UN Environment Programme. He is chair of Petro Canada, an oil company.

strong nuclear force one of the four fundamental ◊forces of nature, the other three being the electromagnetic force, gravity, and the weak nuclear force. The strong nuclear force was first described by Japanese physicist Hideki Yukawa 1935. It is the strongest of all the forces, acts only over very small distances (within the nucleus of the atom), and is responsible for binding together ◊quarks to form ◊hadrons, and for binding together protons and neutrons in the atomic nucleus. The particle that is the carrier of the strong nuclear force is the ◊gluon, of which there are eight kinds, each with zero mass and zero charge.

strontium soft, ductile, pale-yellow, metallic element, symbol Sr, atomic number 38, relative atomic mass 87.62. It is one of the ◊alkaline-earth metals, widely distributed in small quantities only as a sulphate or carbonate. Strontium salts burn with a red flame and are used in fireworks and signal flares.

structuralism 20th-century philosophical movement that has influenced such areas as linguistics, anthropology, and literary criticism. Inspired by the work of the Swiss linguist Ferdinand de Saussure, structuralists believe that objects should be analysed as systems of relations, rather than as positive entities.

strychnine $C_{21}H_{22}O_2N_2$ bitter-tasting, poisonous alkaloid. It is a poison that causes violent muscular spasms, and is usually obtained by powdering the seeds of plants of the genus *Strychnos* (for example *Strychnos nux vomica*). Curare is a related drug.

Stuart or **Stewart** royal family who inherited the Scottish throne in 1371 and the English throne in 1603.

Stubbs George 1724–1806. English artist, known for paintings of horses. After the publication of his book of engravings *The Anatomy of the Horse* 1766, he was widely commissioned as an animal painter.

sturgeon any of a family (Acipenseridae) of large, primitive, bony fishes with five rows of bony plates, small sucking mouths, and chin barbels used for exploring the bottom of the water for prey. The *common sturgeon Acipenser sturio* of the Atlantic and Mediterranean reaches a length of 3.5 m/12 ft.

Sturmabteilung (SA) German terrorist militia, also known as **Brownshirts**, of the ◊Nazi Party, established 1921 under the leadership of Ernst Röhm, in charge of physical training and political indoctrination.

Stuttgart capital of Baden-Württemberg, Germany; population (1988) 565,000. Industries include publishing and the manufacture of vehicles and electrical goods.

Styx in Greek mythology, the river surrounding the underworld.

subatomic particle in physics, a particle that is smaller than an atom. Such particles may be indivisible ▷elementary particles, such as the electron and quark, or they may be composites, such as the proton, neutron, and alpha particle. See also ▷particle physics.

sublimation in chemistry, the conversion of a solid to vapour without passing through the liquid phase.

submarine underwater warship. The first underwater boat was constructed for James I of England by the Dutch scientist Cornelius van Drebbel (1572–1633) in 1620. A naval submarine, or submersible torpedo boat, the *Gymnote*, was launched by France 1888. The conventional submarine of World War I was driven by diesel engine on the surface and by battery-powered electric motors underwater. The diesel engine also drove a generator that produced electricity to charge the batteries.

submersible vessel designed to operate under water, especially a small submarine used by engineers and research scientists as a ferry craft to support diving operations.

subpoena in law, an order requiring someone who might not otherwise come forward of his or her own volition to give evidence before a court or judicial official at a specific time and place. A witness who fails to comply with a subpoena is in ▷contempt of court.

substitution reaction in chemistry, the replacement of one atom or functional group in an organic molecule by another.

succession in ecology, a series of changes that occur in the structure and composition of the vegetation in a given area from the time it is first colonized by plants (*primary succession*), or after it has been disturbed by fire, flood, or clearing (*secondary succession*).

Sucre legal capital and judicial seat of Bolivia; population (1988) 95,600. It stands on the central plateau at an altitude of 2,840 m/9,320 ft.

sucrose or *cane sugar* or *beet sugar* $C_{12}H_{22}O_{10}$ a sugar found in the pith of sugar cane and in sugar beets. It is popularly known as ▷sugar.

Sudan Democratic Republic of; country in NE Africa, S of Egypt, with a Red Sea coast; it is the largest country in Africa; *area* 2,505,800 sq km/967,489 sq mi; *capital* Khartoum; *physical* fertile valley of river Nile separates Libyan Desert in W from high rocky Nubian Desert in E; *head of state and government* General Omar Hassan Ahmed el-Bashir from 1989; *political system* military republic; *exports* cotton, gum arabic, sesame seed, peanuts, sorghum; *population* (1990 est) 25,164,000; *languages* Arabic (official), local languages; *recent history* Sudan achieved independence from Britain and Egypt as a republic 1956;

the name was changed to the Democratic Republic of Sudan 1969. A new constitution was adopted 1971 and a national assembly established 1974. *Sharia* (Islamic law) was introduced 1983. Following a series of unsatisfactory governments and coups since 1956, the country reached a state of virtual civil war with the Sudan People's Liberation Movement (SPLM) 1987; a peace pact was signed 1988 but civil war continued with a new SPLM offensive 1990. In 1991 a federal system was introduced, with division of the country into nine states.

Sudetenland mountainous region of N Czechoslovakia, annexed by Germany under the ▷Munich Agreement 1938; it was returned to Czechoslovakia 1945.

Suetonius (Gaius Suetonius Tranquillus) *c*. AD 69–140. Roman historian, author of *Lives of the Caesars* (Julius Caesar to Domitian).

Suez Canal artificial waterway, 160 km/100 mi long, from Port Said to Suez, linking the Mediterranean and Red seas, separating Africa from Asia, and providing the shortest eastwards sea route from Europe. It was opened 1869, nationalized 1956, blocked by Egypt during the Arab-Israeli war 1967, and not re-opened until 1975.

Suez Crisis military confrontation Oct–Dec 1956 following the nationalization of the Suez Canal by President Nasser of Egypt. In an attempt to reassert international control of the canal, Israel launched an attack, after which British and French troops landed. Widespread international censure (Soviet protest, US non-support, and considerable domestic opposition) forced the withdrawal of British and French troops. The crisis resulted in the resignation of British prime minister Eden. British, French, and Australian relations with the USA were greatly strained during this period.

Suffolk county of E England; *area* 3,800 sq km/1,467 sq mi; *towns* Ipswich (administrative headquarters), Bury St Edmunds, Lowestoft, Felixstowe; *physical* low undulating surface and flat coastline; rivers: Waveney, Alde, Deben, Orwell, Stour; part of the Norfolk Broads; *features* Minsmere marshland bird reserve, near Aldeburgh; site of Sutton Hoo (7th-century ship-burial); site of Sizewell B nuclear reactor (plans approved 1987); *products* cereals, sugar beet, working horses (Suffolk punches), fertilizers, agricultural machinery; *population* (1991) 629,900

suffragette or *suffragist* woman fighting for the right to vote. In the UK, women's suffrage bills were repeatedly introduced and defeated in Parliament between 1886 and 1911, and a militant campaign was launched 1906 by Emmeline ▷Pankhurst and her daughters. In 1918 women were granted limited franchise; in 1928 it was extended to all women over 21.

Sufism mystical movement of ▷Islam that originated in the 8th century. Sufis believe that deep intuition is the only real guide to knowledge. The movement has a strong strain of asceticism. The name derives from Arabic *suf*, a rough woollen robe worn as an indication of disregard for material things. There are a number of groups or brotherhoods within Sufism, each with its own method of meditative practice, one of which is the whirling dance of the dervishes.

sugar or *sucrose* sweet, soluble crystalline carbohydrate found in the pith of sugar cane and in sugar beet. It is a disaccharide sugar, each of its molecules being made up of two simple-sugar (monosaccharide) units: glucose and fructose. Sugar is easily digested and forms a major source of energy in humans, being used in cooking and in the food industry as a sweetener and, in high concentrations, as a preservative. A high consumption is associated with obesity and tooth decay.

sugar maple E North American ⟡maple tree *Acer saccharum*.

Suharto Raden 1921– . Indonesian politician and general. He ousted Sukarno to become president in 1967. He ended confrontation with Malaysia, invaded East Timor in 1975, and reached a cooperation agreement with Papua New Guinea 1979. His authoritarian rule has met domestic opposition from the left. He was re-elected in 1973, 1978, 1983, and 1988.

suite in music, formerly a grouping of old dance forms; later the term came to be used to describe a set of instrumental pieces, sometimes assembled from a stage work, such as Tchaikovsky's *Nutcracker Suite* 1891–92.

Sukarno Achmed 1901–1970. Indonesian nationalist, president 1945–67. During World War II he cooperated in the local administration set up by the Japanese, replacing Dutch rule. After the war he became the first president of the new Indonesian republic, becoming president-for-life in 1966; he was ousted by ⟡Suharto.

Sulawesi formerly *Celebes* island in E Indonesia, one of the Sunda Islands; area (with dependent islands) 190,000 sq km/73,000 sq mi; population (1980) 10,410,000. It is mountainous and forested and produces copra and nickel.

Suleiman or *Solyman* 1494–1566. Ottoman sultan from 1520, known as *the Magnificent* and *the Lawgiver*. Under his rule, the Ottoman Empire flourished and reached its largest extent. He made conquests in the Balkans, the Mediterranean, Persia, and N Africa, but was defeated at Vienna in 1529 and Valletta (on Malta) in 1565. He was a patron of the arts, a poet, and an administrator.

Sulla Lucius Cornelius 138–78 BC. Roman general and politician, a leader of the senatorial party. Forcibly suppressing the democrats in 88 BC, he departed for a successful campaign against ⟡Mithridates VI of Pontus. The democrats seized

power in his absence, but on his return Sulla captured Rome and massacred all opponents. The reforms he introduced as dictator, which strengthened the Senate, were backward-looking and short-lived. He retired 79 BC.

Sullivan Arthur (Seymour) 1842–1900. English composer who wrote operettas in collaboration with William Gilbert, including *HMS Pinafore* 1878, *The Pirates of Penzance* 1879, and *The Mikado* 1885. Their partnership broke down in 1896. Sullivan also composed serious instrumental, choral, and operatic works – for example, the opera *Ivanhoe* 1890 – which he valued more highly than the operettas.

sulphate $SO_4{}^{2-}$ salt or ester derived from sulphuric acid. Most sulphates are water soluble (the exceptions are lead, calcium, strontium, and barium sulphates), and require a very high temperature to decompose them.

sulphite $SO_3{}^{2-}$ salt or ester derived from sulphurous acid.

sulphur brittle, pale-yellow, nonmetallic element, symbol S, atomic number 16, relative atomic mass 32.064. It occurs in three allotropic forms: two crystalline (called rhombic and monoclinic, following the arrangements of the atoms within the crystals) and one amorphous. It burns in air with a blue flame and a stifling odour. Insoluble in water but soluble in carbon disulphide, it is a good electrical insulator. Sulphur is widely used in the manufacture of sulphuric acid (used to treat phosphate rock to make fertilizers) and in making paper, matches, gunpowder and fireworks, in vulcanizing rubber, and in medicines and insecticides.

sulphur dioxide SO_2 pungent gas produced by burning sulphur in air or oxygen. It is widely used for disinfecting food vessels and equipment, and as a preservative in some food products. It occurs in industrial flue gases and is a major cause of ⟡acid rain.

sulphuric acid or *oil of vitriol* H_2SO_4 a dense, viscous, colourless liquid that is extremely corrosive. It gives out heat when added to water and can cause severe burns. Sulphuric acid is used extensively in the chemical industry, in the refining of petrol, and in the manufacture of fertilizers, detergents, explosives, and dyes. It forms the acid component of car batteries.

Sumatra or *Sumatera* second largest island of Indonesia, one of the Sunda Islands; area 473,600 sq km/182,800 sq mi; population (1989) 36,882,000. East of a longitudinal volcanic mountain range is a wide plain; both are heavily forested. Products include rubber, rice, tobacco, tea, timber, tin, and petroleum.

Sumerian civilization the world's earliest civilization, dated about 3500 BC, and located at the confluence of the Tigris and Euphrates rivers in lower Mesopotamia (present-day Iraq). It was a city-state with priests as secular rulers. After 2000 BC, Sumer was absorbed by the Babylonian empire.

Sun the ☼star at the centre of the solar system. Its diameter is 1,392,000 km/865,000 mi; its temperature at the surface is about 5,800K (5,530°C/9,980°F), and at the centre 15,000,000K (15,000,000°C/27,000,000°F). It is composed of about 70% hydrogen and 30% helium, with other elements making up less than 1%. The Sun's energy is generated by nuclear fusion reactions that turn hydrogen into helium at its centre. The gas core is far denser than mercury or lead on Earth. The Sun is about 4.7 billion years old, with a predicted lifetime of 10 billion years.

Sundanese member of the second largest ethnic group in the Republic of Indonesia. There are more than 20 million speakers of Sundanese, a member of the western branch of the Austronesian family. Like their neighbours, the Javanese, the Sundanese are predominantly Muslim. They are known for their performing arts, especially *jaipongan* dance traditions, and distinctive batik fabrics.

sundew any insectivorous plant of the genus *Drosera*, family Droseraceae, with viscid hairs on the leaves for catching prey.

sunfish marine fish *Mola mola* with disc-shaped body 3 m/10 ft long found in all temperate and tropical oceans. The term also applies to fish of the North American freshwater Centrarchidae family, which have compressed, almost circular bodies, up to 80 cm/30 in long, and are nestbuilders and avid predators.

sunflower tall plant of the genus *Helianthus*, family Compositae. The common sunflower *H. annuus*, probably native to Mexico, grows to 4.5 m/15 ft in favourable conditions. It is commercially cultivated in central Europe, the USA, Russia, Ukraine, and Australia for the oil-bearing seeds that follow the yellow-petalled flowers.

Sunni member of the larger of the two main sects of ☼Islam, with about 680 million adherents. Sunni Muslims believe that the first three caliphs were all legitimate successors of the prophet Muhammad, and that guidance on belief and life should come from the Koran and the Hadith, and from the Shari'a, not from a human authority or spiritual leader.

Imams in Sunni Islam are educated lay teachers of the faith and prayer leaders. The name derives from the *Sunna*, Arabic 'code of behaviour', the body of traditional law evolved from the teaching and acts of Muhammad.

sunspot dark patch on the surface of the Sun, actually an area of cooler gas, thought to be caused by strong magnetic fields that block the outward flow of heat to the Sun's surface. Sunspots consist of a dark central **umbra**, about 4,000K (3,700°C/6,700°F), and a lighter surrounding **penumbra**, about 5,500K (5,200°C/9,400°F). They last from several days to over a month, ranging in size from 2,000 km/1,250 mi to groups stretching for over 100,000 km/62,000 mi. The number of sunspots visible at a given time varies from none to over 100 in a cycle averaging 11 years.

Sun Yat-sen or **Sun Zhong Shan** 1867–1925. Chinese revolutionary leader, founder of the Guomindang (Nationalist party) 1894, and provisional president of the Republic of China 1912 after playing a vital part in deposing the emperor. He was president of a breakaway government from 1921.

supercomputer the fastest, most powerful type of computer, capable of performing its basic operations in picoseconds (thousand-billionths of a second), rather than nanoseconds (billionths of a second), like most other computers.

superconductivity in physics, increase in electrical conductivity at low temperatures. The resistance of some metals and metallic compounds decreases uniformly with decreasing temperature until at a critical temperature (the superconducting point), within a few degrees of absolute zero (0 K/–273.16°C/–459.67°F), the resistance suddenly falls to zero. The phenomenon was discovered by Dutch scientist Heike Kamerlingh-Onnes (1853–1926) in 1911.

supergiant the largest and most luminous type of star known, with a diameter of up to 1,000 times that of the Sun and absolute magnitudes of between –5 and –9.

superheterodyne receiver the most widely used type of radio receiver, in which the incoming signal

sun

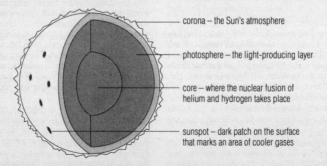

corona – the Sun's atmosphere

photosphere – the light-producing layer

core – where the nuclear fusion of helium and hydrogen takes place

sunspot – dark patch on the surface that marks an area of cooler gases

is mixed with a signal of fixed frequency generated within the receiver circuits. The resulting signal, called the intermediate-frequency (i.f.) signal, has a frequency between that of the incoming signal and the internal signal. The intermediate frequency is near the optimum frequency of the amplifier to which the i.f. signal is passed. This arrangement ensures greater gain and selectivity. The super-heterodyne system is also used in basic television receivers.

Superior, Lake largest and deepest of the ▷Great Lakes of North America, and the second largest lake in the world; area 83,300 sq km/32,200 sq mi.

supernova explosive death of a star, which temporarily attains a brightness of 100 million Suns or more, so that it can shine as brilliantly as a small galaxy for a few days or weeks. Very approximately, it is thought that a supernova explodes in a large galaxy about once every 100 years. Many supernovae remain undetected because of obscuring by interstellar dust – astronomers estimate some 50%.

supersonic speed speed greater than that at which sound travels, measured in ▷Mach numbers. In dry air at 0°C/32°F, sound travels at about 1,170 kph/727 mph, but decreases with altitude until, at 12,000 m/39,000 ft, it is only 1,060 kph/658 mph.

superstring theory in physics, a mathematical theory developed in the 1980s to explain the properties of ▷elementary particles and the forces between them (in particular, gravity and the nuclear forces) in a way that combines ▷relativity and ▷quantum theory. In string theory, the fundamental objects in the universe are not pointlike particles but extremely small stringlike objects. These objects exist in a universe of ten dimensions, although, for reasons not yet understood, only three space dimensions and one dimension of time are discernible.

Supreme Court highest US judicial tribunal, composed since 1869 of a chief justice (William Rehnquist from 1986) and eight associate justices. Appointments are made for life by the president, with the advice and consent of the Senate, and justices can be removed only by impeachment. In Britain, the Supreme Court of Judicature is made up of the Court of Appeal and the High Court.

Supremes, the US vocal group, pioneers of the Motown sound, formed 1959 in Detroit. Beginning in 1962, the group was a trio comprising, initially, Diana Ross (1944–), Mary Wilson (1944–), and Florence Ballard (1943–1976). The most successful female group of the 1960s, they had a string of pop hits beginning with 'Where Did Our Love Go?' 1964 and 'Baby Love' 1964. Diana Ross left to pursue a solo career 1969.

Surabaya port on the island of Java, Indonesia; population (1980) 2,028,000. It has oil refineries and shipyards and is a naval base.

surface tension in physics, the property that causes the surface of a liquid to behave as if it were covered with a weak elastic skin; this is why a needle can float on water. It is caused by the exposed surface's tendency to contract to the smallest possible area because of unequal cohesive forces between ▷molecules at the surface. Allied phenomena include the formation of droplets, the concave profile of a meniscus, and the ▷capillary action by which water soaks into a sponge.

surfing sport of riding on the crest of large waves while standing on a narrow, keeled surfboard, usually of light synthetic material such as fibreglass, about 1.8 m/6 ft long (or about 2.4–7 m/8–9 ft known as the Malibu), as first developed in Hawaii and Australia. Windsurfing is a recent development.

Surinam Republic of; country on the N coast of South America, on the Atlantic Ocean, between Guyana and French Guiana; *area* 163,820 sq km/63,243 sq mi; *capital* Paramaribo; *physical* hilly and forested, with flat and narrow coastal plain; Surinam River; *head of state and government* Ronald Venetiaan from 1991; *political system* emergent democratic republic; *exports* alumina, aluminium, bauxite, rice, timber; *population* (1990 est) 408,000 (Hindu 37%, creole 31%, Javanese 15%); *recent history* independence from the Netherlands achieved 1975; 40% of the population emigrated to the Netherlands. Army coup 1980 overthrew the government; led by Lt-Col Desi Bouterse, the army set up a Revolutionary People's Front 1982. New constitution approved 1987; Bouterse rejected peace accord reached by President Shankar with guerrilla insurgents and vowed to continue fighting. Shankar was deposed in army coup 1990; Ronald Venetiaan was elected president 1991.

Surrealism movement in art, literature, and film that developed out of ▷Dada around 1922. Led by André ▷Breton, who produced the *Surrealist Manifesto* 1924, the Surrealists were inspired by the thoughts and visions of the subconscious mind. They explored varied styles and techniques, and the movement became the dominant force in Western art between world wars I and II.

Surrey county in S England; *area* 1,660 sq km/641 sq mi; *towns* Kingston upon Thames (administrative headquarters), Guildford, Woking; *features* rivers: Thames, Mole, Wey; hills: Box and Leith; North Downs; Runnymede, Thameside site of the signing of Magna Carta; Yehudi Menuhin School; Kew Palace and Royal Botanic Gardens; in 1989 it was the most affluent county in Britain — average income 40% above national average; *products* vegetables, agricultural products, service industries; *population* (1991) 997,000; *famous people* Eric Clapton, John Galsworthy, Aldous Huxley, Laurence Olivier.

suspension mixture consisting of small solid particles dispersed in a liquid or gas, which will settle on standing. An example is milk of magnesia, which is a suspension of magnesium hydroxide in water.

Sussex former county of England, on the south

coast, now divided into ◊East Sussex and ◊West Sussex.

Sutherland Graham (Vivian) 1903–1980. English painter, graphic artist, and designer, active mainly in France from the late 1940s. He painted portraits, landscapes, and religious subjects.

sūtra in Buddhism, discourse attributed to the historical Buddha. In Hinduism, the term generally describes any sayings that contain moral instruction.

suttee Hindu custom whereby a widow committed suicide by joining her husband's funeral pyre, often under public and family pressure. Banned in the 17th century by the Mogul emperors, the custom continued even after it was made illegal under British rule 1829. There continue to be sporadic revivals.

Suu Kyi Aung San 1945– . Myanmar (Burmese) politician and human-rights campaigner, leader of the National League for Democracy (NLD), the main opposition to the military junta. When the NLD won the 1990 elections, the junta refused to surrender power, and placed Suu Kyi under house arrest. Nobel Peace Prize 1991. She is the daughter of former Burmese premier ◊Aung San.

Svalbard Norwegian archipelago in the Arctic Ocean. The main island is Spitsbergen; other islands include North East Land, Edge Island, Barents Island, and Prince Charles Forcland.

Sverdlovsk former name 1924–91 of *Ekaterinburg*.

Swabia (German *Schwaben*) historic region of SW Germany, an independent duchy in the Middle Ages. It includes Augsburg and Ulm and forms part of the *Länder* (states) of Baden-Württemberg, Bavaria, and Hessen.

Swahili language belonging to the Bantu branch of the Niger-Congo family, widely used in east and central Africa. Swahili originated on the E African coast as a *lingua franca* used among traders, and contains many Arabic loan words. It is an official language in Kenya and Tanzania.

swallow any bird of the family Hirundinidae of small, insect-eating birds in the order Passeriformes, with long, narrow wings and deeply forked tails. Swallows feed while flying. The common swallow *Hirundo rustica* winters in Africa and visits Europe April–Sept.

swan any of several large, long-necked, aquatic, web-footed birds of the family Anatidae, which also includes ducks and geese. The mute swan *Cygnus olor* is up to 150 cm/5 ft long, has white plumage, an orange bill with a black knob surmounting it, and black legs; the voice is a harsh hiss. It is wild in eastern Europe, and semidomesticated in the west.

SWAPO (*South West Africa People's Organization*) organization formed 1959 in South West Africa (now ◊Namibia) to oppose South African rule. SWAPO guerrillas, led by Sam Nujoma, began attacking with support from Angola. In 1966

SWAPO was recognized by the United Nations as the legitimate government of Namibia, and won the first independent election 1989.

Swaziland Kingdom of; country in SE Africa, bordered by Mozambique and the Transvaal province of South Africa; *area* 17,400 sq km/6,716 sq mi; *capital* Mbabane; *physical* central valley; mountains in W (Highveld); plateau in E (Lowveld and Lubombo plateau); *head of state and government* King Mswati III from 1986; *political system* near-absolute monarchy; *exports* sugar, canned fruit, woodpulp, asbestos; *population* (1990 est) 779,000; *languages* Swazi 90%, English (both official); *recent history* independence achieved from Britain within the Commonwealth 1968. New constitution adopted 1978. King Sobhuza II died 1982; a power struggle ensued between two of his wives. In 1984 the 18-year-old crown prince became king; formally invested 1986. New government elected 1987 with Sotsha Dlamini as prime minister.

swede annual or biennial plant *Brassica napus*, widely cultivated for its edible root, which is purple, white, or yellow. It is similar in taste to the turnip *B. rapa* but is of greater food value, firmer-fleshed, and longer-keeping. The yellow variety is commonly known as *rutabaga*.

Sweden Kingdom of; country in N Europe on the Baltic Sea, bordered W by Norway and NE by Finland; *area* 450,000 sq km/173,745 sq mi; *capital* Stockholm; *physical* mountains in W; plains in S; thickly forested; more than 20,000 islands off the Stockholm coast; lakes, including Vänern, Vättern, Mälarn, Hjälmarn; islands of Oland and Gotland; *head of state* Carl XVI Gustaf from 1973; *head of government* Carl Bildt from 1991; *political system* constitutional monarchy; *exports* aircraft, vehicles, ballbearings, drills, missiles, electronics, petrochemicals, textiles, furnishings, ornamental glass, paper, iron and steel; *population* (1990 est) 8,407,000 (including 17,000 Saami (Lapps) and 1.2 million postwar immigrants from Finland, Turkey, Yugoslavia, Greece, Iran, other Nordic countries); *languages* Swedish; Finnish- and Saami-speaking minorities; *recent history* Sweden remained neutral in both world wars. The Social Democratic Labour Party (SAP) was continuously in power 1951–76, building the Swedish welfare state. The monarch's last constitutional powers were removed 1975. Prime Minister Olof Palme was murdered 1986; the SAP government was re-elected 1988 but resigned 1990. Sweden applied for European Community membership 1991.

Swedish language member of the Germanic branch of the Indo-European language family, spoken in Sweden and Finland and closely related to Danish and Norwegian.

sweet potato tropical American plant *Ipomoea batatas* of the morning-glory family Convolvulaceae; the white-orange tuberous root is used as a source of starch and alcohol and eaten as a vegetable.

sweet william biennial to perennial plant *Dianthus barbatus* of the pink family Caryophyllaceae, native to S Europe. It is grown for its fragrant red, white, and pink flowers.

swift any fast-flying, short-legged bird of the family Apodidae, of which there are about 75 species, found largely in the tropics. They are 9–23 cm/4–11 in long, with brown or grey plumage, long, pointed wings, and usually a forked tail. They are capable of flying 110 kph/70 mph.

Swift Jonathan 1667–1745. Irish satirist and Anglican cleric, author of *Gulliver's Travels* 1726, an allegory describing travel to lands inhabited by giants, miniature people, and intelligent horses. Other works include *The Tale of a Tub* 1704, attacking corruption in religion and learning; contributions to the Tory paper *The Examiner*, of which he was editor 1710–11; the satirical *A Modest Proposal* 1729, which suggested that children of the poor should be eaten; and many essays and pamphlets.

swimming self-propulsion of the body through water. There are four strokes in competitive swimming: freestyle, breaststroke, backstroke, and butterfly. Distances of races vary between 50 and 1,500 m. Olympic-size pools are 50 m/55 yd long and have eight lanes.

Swinburne Algernon Charles 1837–1909. English poet. He attracted attention with the choruses of his Greek-style tragedy *Atalanta in Calydon* 1865, but he and ◊Rossetti were attacked in 1871 as leaders of 'the fleshly school of poetry', and the revolutionary politics of *Songs before Sunrise* 1871 alienated others.

swing music jazz style popular in the 1930s–40s, a big-band dance music with a simple harmonic base of varying tempo from the rhythm section (percussion, guitar, piano), harmonic brass and woodwind sections (sometimes strings), and superimposed solo melodic line from, for example, trumpet, clarinet, or saxophone. Exponents included Benny Goodman, Duke Ellington, and Glenn Miller, who introduced jazz to a mass white audience.

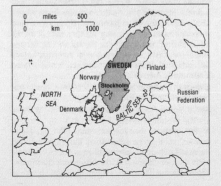

Swiss cheese plant common name for ◊monstera, a plant of the arum family.

Switzerland Swiss Confederation (German *Schweiz*, French *Suisse*, Romansch *Svizzera*); country in W Europe, bordered N by Germany, E by Austria, S by Italy, and W by France; *area* 41,300 sq km/15,946 sq mi; *capital* Bern; *physical* most mountainous country in Europe (Alps and Jura Mountains); highest peak Dufourspitze 4,634 m/15,203 ft in Apennines; lakes Maggiore, Lucerne, Geneva, Constance; *head of state and government* René Felber from 1992; *political system* federal democratic republic; *exports* electrical goods, chemicals, pharmaceuticals, watches, precision instruments, confectionery; *population* (1990 est) 6,628,000; *languages* German 65%, French 18%, Italian 12%, Romansch 1% (all official); *recent history* civil war 1847 resulted in greater centralization of the former Helvetic Republic. Principle of the referendum introduced 1874. Women were given the vote in federal elections 1971. A referendum 1986 rejected a proposal for membership of the United Nations, but the federal government decided 1992 to apply for membership of the European Community.

swordfish marine bony fish *Xiphias gladius*, the only member of its family (Xiphiidae), characterized by a long swordlike beak protruding from the upper jaw. It may reach 4.5 m/15 ft in length and weigh 450 kg/1,000 lb.

sycamore tree *Acer pseudoplatanus* native to Europe. The leaves are five-lobed, and the hanging racemes of flowers are followed by winged fruits. The timber is used for furniture making. In the USA, plane trees are called sycamores.

Sydney capital and port of New South Wales, Australia; population (1990) 3,656,900. Industries include engineering, oil refining, electronics, scientific equipment, chemicals, clothing, and furniture. It is a financial centre, and has three universities. The 19th-century Museum of Applied Arts and Sciences is the most popular museum in Australia.

syllogism set of philosophical statements devised by Aristotle in his work on logic. It establishes the conditions under which a valid conclusion follows or does not follow by deduction from given premises. The following is an example of a valid syllogism: 'All men are mortal, Socrates is a man, therefore Socrates is mortal.'

symbiosis any close relationship between two organisms of different species, and one where both partners benefit from the association. A well-known example is the pollination relationship between insects and flowers, where the insects feed on nectar and carry pollen from one flower to another. This is sometimes known as ◊mutualism. Symbiosis in a broader sense includes commensalism and ◊parasitism.

symbolism in the arts, the use of symbols as a device for concentrating or intensifying meaning. In particular, the term is used for a late 19th-century

movement in French poetry, associated with
Verlaine, Mallarmé, and Rimbaud, who used words
for their symbolic rather than concrete meaning.

Symbolism movement in late 19th-century painting that emerged in France inspired by the trend in
poetry. The subjects were often mythological, mystical, or fantastic. Gustave Moreau was a leading
Symbolist painter.

symmetry exact likeness in shape about a given
line (axis), point, or plane. A figure has symmetry
if one half can be rotated or reflected onto the
other. In a wider sense, symmetry exits if a change
in the system leaves the essential features of the
system unchanged; for example, reversing the sign
of electric charges does not change the electrical
behaviour of an arrangement of charges.

symphonic poem in music, a term originated by
Franz Liszt for his 13 one-movement orchestral
works that interpret a story from literature or history, also used by many other composers. Richard
Strauss preferred the title 'tone poem'.

symphony musical composition for orchestra,
traditionally in four separate but closely related
movements. It developed from the smaller ◊sonata
form, the Italian overture, and the dance suite of the
18th century.

synapse junction between two ◊nerve cells, or
between a nerve cell and a muscle (a neuro-
muscular junction), across which a nerve impulse
is transmitted. The two cells are separated by a
narrow gap called the **synaptic cleft**. The gap is
bridged by a chemical ◊neurotransmitter, released
by the nerve impulse.

syndicalism political movement in 19th-century
Europe that rejected parliamentary activity in
favour of direct action, culminating in a revolutionary general strike to secure worker ownership
and control of industry. After 1918 syndicalism was
absorbed in communism, although it continued to
have an independent existence in Spain until the
late 1930s.

Synge J(ohn) M(illington) 1871–1909. Irish playwright, a leading figure in the Irish dramatic revival
of the early 20th century. His six plays reflect the
speech patterns of the Aran Islands and W Ireland.
They include *In the Shadow of the Glen* 1903, *Riders
to the Sea* 1904, and *The Playboy of the Western World*
1907, which caused riots at the Abbey Theatre,
Dublin, when first performed.

synthesis in chemistry, the formation of a
substance or compound from more elementary
compounds. The synthesis of a drug can involve
several stages from the initial material to the final
product; the complexity of these stages is a major
factor in the cost of production.

synthesizer device that uses electrical components to produce sounds. In **preset synthesizers**,
the sound of various instruments is produced by a
built-in computer-type memory. In **programmable
synthesizers** any number of new instrumental or

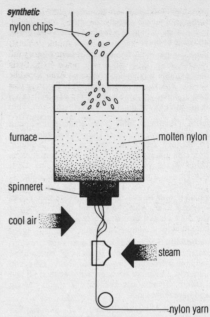

synthetic

other sounds may be produced at the will of the
performer. *Speech synthesizers* can break down
speech into 128 basic elements (allophones), which
are then combined into words and sentences, as in
the voices of electronic teaching aids.

synthetic any material made from chemicals.
Since the 1900s, more and more of the materials
used in everyday life are synthetics, including
plastics (polythene, polystyrene), ◊synthetic fibres
(nylon, acrylics, polyesters), synthetic resins, and
synthetic rubber. Most naturally occurring organic
substances are now made synthetically, especially
pharmaceuticals.

syphilis venereal disease caused by the spiral-
shaped bacterium (spirochete) *Treponema pal-
lidum*. Untreated, it runs its course in three stages
over many years, often starting with a painless hard
sore, or chancre, developing within a month on the
area of infection (usually the genitals). The second
stage, months later, is a rash with arthritis, hepatitis, and/or meningitis. The third stage, years later,
leads eventually to paralysis, blindness, insanity,
and death. The Wassermann test is a diagnostic
blood test for syphilis.

Syria Syrian Arab Republic; country in W Asia,
on the Mediterranean, bordered N by Turkey,
E by Iraq, S by Jordan, and SW by Israel
and Lebanon; *area* 185,200 sq km/71,506 sq mi;
capital Damascus; *physical* mountains alternate
with fertile plains and desert areas; Euphrates
River; Mount Hermon, Golan Heights; *head of*

state and government Hafez-al-Assad from 1971; ***political system*** socialist republic; ***exports*** cotton, cereals, oil, phosphates, tobacco; ***population*** (1990 est) 12,471,000; ***languages*** Arabic (official) 89%, Kurdish 6%, Armenian 3%; ***recent history*** full independence achieved from France 1946. Syria merged with Egypt to form United Arab Republic (UAR) 1958; this disintegrated 1961. Territory was lost to Israel in the Six-Day War of 1967; Israel consolidated its control of Golan Heights after Yom Kippur War 1973. Syrian troops were committed to civil war in Lebanon 1976; further military engagements in Lebanon 1981–82. In 1984 plans for government of national unity in Lebanon were approved by presidents of both countries. President Assad secured release of 39 US hostages from aircraft hijacked by Hezbollah 1985. Attempts to release Western hostages in Lebanon were made 1987. Fighting in Lebanon continued; Syrian forces in Lebanon reinforced 1989. Diplomatic relations were restored with Britain 1990. Syria fought against Iraq in 1991 ⟡Gulf War. President Assad agreed to US Middle East peace plan 1991.

syringa common, but incorrect, name for the ⟡mock orange *Philadelphus*. The genus *Syringa* includes ⟡lilac *Syringa vulgaris*, and is not related to mock orange.

systems analysis in computing, the investigation of a business activity or clerical procedure, with a view to deciding if and how it can be computerized. The analyst discusses the existing procedures with the people involved, observes the flow of data through the business, and draws up an outline specification of the required computer system (see also ⟡systems design).

systems design in computing, the detailed design of an ⟡applications package. The designer breaks the system down into component programs, and designs the required input forms, screen layouts, and printouts. Systems design forms a link between systems analysis and ⟡programming.

Szczecin (German *Stettin*) industrial (shipbuilding, fish processing, synthetic fibres, tools, iron) port on the river Oder, in NW Poland; population (1990) 413,400.

table tennis or *ping pong* indoor game played on a rectangular table by two or four players. It was developed in Britain about 1880 and derived from lawn tennis. World championships were first held 1926.

Tacitus Publius Cornelius *c*. AD 55–*c*. 120. Roman historian. A public orator in Rome, he was consul under Nerva 97–98 and proconsul of Asia 112–113. He wrote histories of the Roman Empire, *Annales* and *Historiae*, covering the years AD 14–68 and 69–97 respectively. He also wrote a *Life of Agricola* 97 (he married Agricola's daughter in 77) and a description of the German tribes, *Germania* 98.

Tadmur Arabic name for the ancient city of ◊Palmyra in Syria.

Taegu largest inland city of South Korea after Seoul; population (1990) 2,228,800.

Taejon capital of South Chungchong province, central South Korea; population (1990) 1,062,100. Korea's tallest standing Buddha and oldest wooden building are found NE of the city at Popchusa in the Mount Songnisan National Park.

Taft William Howard 1857–1930. 27th president of the USA 1909–13, a Republican. He was secretary of war 1904–08 in Theodore Roosevelt's administration, but as president his conservatism provoked Roosevelt to stand against him in the 1912 election.

Tagalog member of the majority ethnic group living around Manila on the island of Luzon, in the Philippines, and numbering about 10 million (1988). The Tagalog live by fishing and trading. In its standardized form, known as Pilipino, Tagalog is the official language of the Philippines, and belongs to the Western branch of the Austronesian family. The Tagalogs' religion is a mixture of animism, Christianity, and Islam.

tagging, electronic long-distance monitoring of the movements of people charged with or convicted

of a crime, thus enabling them to be detained in their homes rather than in prison. In the UK, legislation passed 1991 allowed for its use as an aid to bail and as a means of enforcing punishment; for example, a curfew. The system is in use in the USA.

Taglioni Marie 1804–1884. Italian dancer. A ballerina of ethereal style and exceptional lightness, she was the first to use ◊pointe work, or dancing on the toes, as an expressive part of ballet rather than as sheer technique. She created many roles, including the title role in *La Sylphide* 1832.

Tagore Rabindranath 1861–1941. Bengali Indian writer, born in Calcutta, who translated into English his own verse *Gitanjali* ('song offerings') 1912 and his verse play *Chitra* 1896. Nobel Prize for Literature 1913.

Tahiti largest of the Society Islands, in ◊French Polynesia; area 1,042 sq km/402 sq mi; population (1983) 116,000. Its capital is Papeete. Tahiti was visited by Captain James ◊Cook 1769 and by Admiral ◊Bligh of the *Bounty* 1788. It came under French control 1843 and became a colony 1880.

Taipei or *Taibei* capital and commercial centre of Taiwan; industries include electronics, plastics, textiles, and machinery; population (1990) 2,719,700.

Taiwan (formerly *Formosa*); country in SE Asia, officially the Republic of China, occupying the island of Taiwan between the E China Sea and the S China Sea; *area* 36,179 sq km/13,965 sq mi; *capital* Taipei; *physical* mountainous with lowlands in W; *head of state* Lee Teng-hui from 1988; *head of government* Hao Po-ts'un from 1991; *political system* emergent democracy; *exports* textiles, steel, plastics, electronics, foodstuffs; *population* (1990 est) 20,454,000 (Taiwanese 84%, mainlanders 14%); *languages* Mandarin Chinese (official); Taiwan, Hakka dialects; *recent history* annexed by China 1683, Taiwan was ceded to Japan 1895 but recovered by China 1945. Nationalist government of China led by Chiang Kai-shek fled to Taiwan after Chinese communist revolution 1949 and dominated the island, still claiming sovereignty over mainland until 1970s when no longer recognized by USA and Western nations as legitimate government of China. Chiang Kai-shek died 1975; under his son Chiang Ching-kuo a new programme of gradual democratization and 'Taiwanization' began. Formal opposition party tolerated 1986; in 1989 the Kuomintang (Nationalist Party of China) won the first free assembly elections. End of state of civil war with China announced by President Lee Teng-hui 1991; constitution amended.

Taiyuan capital of Shanxi province, NE China, on the river Fen He; industries include iron, steel, agricultural machinery, and textiles; population (1989) 1,900,000. It is a walled city, founded in the 5th century AD.

Tajik or *Tadzhik* member of the majority ethnic

group living in Tajikistan. Tajiks also live in Afghanistan and parts of Pakistan and W China. The Tajiki language belongs to the West Iranian subbranch of the Indo-European family, and is similar to Farsi; it is written in the Cyrillic script. The Tajiks have long been associated with neighbouring Turkic peoples and their language contains Altaic loan words. The majority of the Tajik people are Sunni Muslims; there is a Shi'ite minority in Afghanistan.

Tajikistan Republic of; country in N Asia, bordered N by Kyrgyzstan, E by China, S by Afghanistan, and E by Uzbekistan; *area* 143,100 sq km/ 55,251 sq mi; *capital* Dushanbe; *physical* mountainous, more than half its territory lying above 3,000 m/10,000 ft; Pik Kommunizma (Communism Peak); huge mountain glaciers, source of many rivers; *head of state and government* Rakhman Nabiyev from 1991; *political system* socialist pluralist; *products* fruit, cereals, cotton, cattle, sheep, silks, carpets, coal, lead, zinc, chemicals, oil, gas; *population* (1990) 5,100,000 (Tajik 62%, Russian 8%, other 30%); *language* Tajik; *recent history* part of Turkestan Soviet Socialist Autonomous Republic 1921; became constituent republic of USSR 1929. Ethnic conflict resulted in rioting in capital against Communist Party 1990; state of emergency. Republic endorsed maintenance of Union in USSR referendum 1991 but Tajik Communist Party broke with Communist Party of Soviet Union and independence from Soviet Union was declared Sept 1991. Joined Commonwealth of Independent States Dec 1991. Admitted into Conference on Security and Cooperation in Europe 1992.

Taj Mahal white marble mausoleum built 1630–53 on the river Jumna near Agra, India. Erected by Shah Jahan to the memory of his favourite wife, it is a celebrated example of Indo-Islamic architecture, the fusion of Muslim and Hindu styles.

takeover in business, the acquisition by one company of a sufficient number of shares in another

company to have effective control of that company – usually 51%, although a controlling stake may be as little as 30%.

Talbot William Henry Fox 1800–1877. English pioneer of photography. He invented the paper-based ◇calotype process, the first negative/positive method. Talbot made photograms several years before Louis Daguerre's invention was announced.

talc Mg₃Si₄O₁₀(OH)₂, mineral, hydrous magnesium silicate. It occurs in tabular crystals, but the massive impure form, known as *steatite* or *soapstone*, is more common. It is formed by the alteration of magnesium compounds, and usually found in metamorphic rocks. Talc is very soft, ranked 1 on the Mohs' scale of hardness. It is used in powdered form in cosmetics, lubricants, and as an additive in paper manufacture.

Talleyrand Charles Maurice de Talleyrand-Périgord 1754–1838. French politician and diplomat. As bishop of Autun 1789–91 he supported moderate reform during the ◇French Revolution, was excommunicated by the pope, and fled to the USA during the Reign of Terror (persecution of anti-revolutionaries). He returned and became foreign minister under the Directory 1797–99 and under Napoleon 1799–1807. He represented France at the Congress of ◇Vienna 1814–15.

Tallinn (German *Reval*) naval port and capital of Estonia; industries include electrical and oil-drilling machinery, textiles, and paper; population (1987) 478,000. Founded 1219, it was a member of the ◇Hanseatic League; it passed to Sweden 1561 and to Russia 1750. Vyshgorod castle (13th century) and other medieval buildings remain. It is a yachting centre.

Tallis Thomas *c.* 1505–1585. English composer in the polyphonic style. He wrote masses, anthems, and other church music. Among his works are the setting for 40 voices of *Spem in alium non habui* (about 1573) and a collection of 34 motets, *Cantiones sacrae*, 1575 (of which 16 are by Tallis and 18 by Byrd). In 1575 Elizabeth I granted Tallis and Byrd the monopoly for printing music and music paper in England.

Talmud the two most important works of post-Biblical Jewish literature. The Babylonian and the Palestinian (or Jerusalem) Talmud provide a compilation of ancient Jewish law and tradition. The Babylonian Talmud was edited at the end of the 5th century AD and is the more authoritative version for later Judaism; both Talmuds are written in a mix of Hebrew and Aramaic.

tamarind evergreen tropical tree *Tamarindus indica*, family Leguminosae, native to the Old World, with pinnate leaves and reddish-yellow flowers, followed by pods. The pulp surrounding the seeds is used medicinally and as a flavouring.

tamarisk any small tree or shrub of the genus

Tamarix, flourishing in warm, salty, desert regions of Europe and Asia where no other vegetation is found. The common tamarisk *T. gallica* has scalelike leaves and spikes of very small, pink flowers.

Tambo Oliver 1917– . South African nationalist politician, in exile 1960–90, president of the African National Congress (ANC) 1977–91.

Tamerlane or *Tamburlaine* or *Timur i Leng* 1336–1405. Mongol ruler of ⟡Samarkand from 1369 who conquered Persia, Azerbaijan, Armenia, and Georgia. He defeated the ⟡Golden Horde 1395, sacked Delhi 1398, invaded Syria and Anatolia, and captured the Ottoman sultan in Ankara 1402; he died invading China.

Tamil member of the majority ethnic group living in the Indian state of Tamil Nadu (formerly Madras). Tamils also live in S India, N Sri Lanka, Malaysia, Singapore, and South Africa, totalling 35–55 million worldwide. Tamil belongs to the Dravidian family of languages; written records in Tamil date from the 3rd century BC. The 3 million Tamils in Sri Lanka are predominantly Hindu, although some are Muslims, unlike the Sinhalese majority, who are mainly Buddhist. The *Tamil Tigers,* most prominent of the various Tamil groupings, are attempting to create a separate homeland in N Sri Lanka through both political and military means.

Tamil Nadu formerly (until 1968) *Madras State* state of SE India; *area* 130,100 sq km/ 50,219 sq mi; *capital* Madras; *products* mainly industrial: cotton, textiles, silk, electrical machinery, tractors, rubber, sugar refining; *population* (1991) 55,638,300; *language* Tamil; *history* the present state was formed 1956. Tamil Nadu comprises part of the former British Madras presidency (later province) formed from areas taken from France and Tipu Sahib, the sultan of Mysore, in the 18th century, which became a state of the Republic of India 1950. The northeast was detached to form Andhra Pradesh 1953; in 1956 other areas went to Kerala and Mysore (now Karnataka), and the Laccadive Islands (now Lakshadweep) became a separate Union Territory.

Tampa port and resort on Tampa Bay in W Florida, USA; industries include fruit and vegetable canning, shipbuilding, and the manufacture of fertilizers, clothing, beer, and cigars; population (1990) 280,000.

Tampere (Swedish *Tammerfors*) city in SW Finland; industries include textiles, paper, footwear, and turbines; population (1990) 172,600, metropolitan area 258,000. It is the second largest city in Finland.

tanager any of various New World birds of the family Emberizidae. There are about 230 species in forests of Central and South America, all brilliantly coloured. They are 10–20 cm/4–8 in long, with plump bodies and conical beaks.

Tanganyika former British colony in E Africa, which now forms the mainland of ⟡Tanzania.

Tanganyika, Lake lake 772 m/2,534 ft above sea level in the Great Rift Valley, E Africa, with Zaire to the W, Zambia to the S, and Tanzania and Burundi to the E. It is about 645 km/400 mi long, with an area of about 31,000 sq km/12,000 sq mi, and is the deepest lake (1,435 m/4,710 ft) in Africa.

tangerine small ⟡orange *Citrus reticulata.*

Tangier or *Tangiers* or *Tanger* port in N Morocco, on the Strait of Gibraltar; population (1982) 436,227. It was a Phoenician trading centre in the 15th century BC. Captured by the Portuguese 1471, it passed to England 1662 as part of the dowry of Catherine of Braganza, but was abandoned 1684, and later became a lair of Barbary Coast pirates. From 1923 Tangier and a small surrounding enclave became an international zone, administered by Spain 1940–45. In 1956 it was transferred to independent Morocco and became a free port 1962.

tank armoured fighting vehicle that runs on tracks and is fitted with weapons systems capable of defeating other tanks and destroying life and property. The term was originally a code name for the first effective tracked and armoured fighting vehicle, invented by the British soldier and scholar Ernest Swinton, and used in the battle of the Somme 1916.

tansy perennial herb *Tanacetum vulgare,* family Compositae, native to Europe. The yellow flower heads grow in clusters on stalks up to 120 cm/4 ft tall, and the aromatic leaves are used in cookery.

tantalum hard, ductile, lustrous, grey-white, metallic element, symbol Ta, atomic number 73, relative atomic mass 180.948. It occurs with niobium in tantalite and other minerals. It can be drawn into wire with a very high melting point and great tenacity, useful for lamp filaments subject to vibration. It is also used in alloys, for corrosion-resistant laboratory apparatus and chemical equipment, as a catalyst in manufacturing synthetic rubber, in tools and instruments, and in rectifiers and capacitors.

Tantalus in Greek mythology, a king whose crimes were punished in Tartarus (a part of the underworld) by the provision of food and drink he could not reach.

Tantrism forms of Hinduism and Buddhism that emphasize the division of the universe into male and female forces that maintain its unity by their interaction; this gives women equal status with men. Tantric Hinduism is associated with magical and sexual yoga practices that imitate the union of Siva and Sakti, as described in religious books known as the *Tantras.* In Buddhism, the *Tantras* are texts attributed to the Buddha, describing methods of attaining enlightenment.

Tanzania United Republic of; country in E Africa,

on the Indian Ocean, bordered N by Uganda and Kenya; S by Mozambique, Malawi, and Zambia; and W by Zaire, Burundi, and Rwanda; *area* 945,000 sq km/364,865 sq mi; *capital* Dodoma; *physical* central plateau; lakes in N and W; coastal plains; lakes Victoria, Tanganyika, and Niasa; *head of state and government* Ali Hassan Mwinyi from 1985; *political system* one-party socialist republic; *exports* coffee, cotton, sisal, cloves, tea, tobacco, cashew nuts, diamonds; *population* (1990 est) 26,070,000; *languages* Kiswahili, English (both official); *recent history* Zanzibar became a British protectorate 1890, then an independent sultanate 1963. Tanganyika, a German colony until 1914, British League of Nations mandate 1920–46, and under United Nations trusteeship from 1946, achieved independence within the Commonwealth 1961, becoming a republic under President Julius Nyerere. In 1964 Tanganyika joined with Zanzibar as the United Republic of Tanzania. The Revolutionary Party of Tanzania (CCM) was proclaimed the only legal party 1977; in 1992 it agreed to abolish one-party rule.

Taoism Chinese philosophical system, traditionally founded by the Chinese philosopher Lao Zi 6th century BC. He is also attributed authorship of the scriptures, *Tao Te Ching*, although these were apparently compiled 3rd century BC. The 'tao' or 'way' denotes the hidden principle of the universe, and less stress is laid on good deeds than on harmonious interaction with the environment, which automatically ensures right behaviour. The magical side of Taoism is illustrated by the *I Ching* or *Book of Changes*, a book of divination.

tape recording, magnetic method of recording electric signals on a layer of iron oxide, or other magnetic material, coating a thin plastic tape. The electrical signals from the microphone are fed to the electromagnetic recording head, which magnetizes the tape in accordance with the frequency and amplitude of the original signal. The impulses may be audio (for sound recording), video (for television), or data (for computer). For playback, the tape is passed over the same, or another, head to convert magnetic into electrical signals, which are then amplified for reproduction.

tapeworm any of various parasitic flatworms of the class Cestoda. They lack digestive and sense organs, can reach 15 m/50 ft in length, and attach themselves to the host's intestines by means of hooks and suckers. Tapeworms are made up of hundreds of individual segments, each of which develops into a functional hermaphroditic reproductive unit capable of producing numerous eggs. The larvae of tapeworms usually reach humans in imperfectly cooked meat or fish, causing anaemia and intestinal disorders.

tapir any of the odd-toed hoofed mammals (perissodactyls) of the single genus *Tapirus*, now constituting the family Tapiridae. There are four

species living in the American and Malaysian tropics. They reach 1 m/3 ft at the shoulder and weigh up to 350 kg/770 lb. Their survival is in danger because of destruction of the forests.

tar dark brown or black viscous liquid obtained by the destructive distillation of coal, shale, and wood. Tars consist of a mixture of hydrocarbons, acids, and bases. ♢Creosote and ♢paraffin are produced from wood tar. See also ♢coal tar.

Taranto naval base and port in Puglia region, SE Italy; population (1988) 245,000. It is an important commercial centre, and its steelworks are part of the new industrial complex of S Italy. It was the site of the ancient Greek *Tarentum*, founded in the 8th century BC by ♢Sparta, and was captured by the Romans 272 BC.

tarantula wolf spider *Lycosa tarantula* with a 2.5 cm/1 in body. It spins no web, relying on its speed in hunting to catch its prey. The name 'tarantula' is also used for any of the numerous large, hairy spiders of the family Theraphosidae, with large poison fangs, native to the SW USA and tropical America.

tariff tax or duty placed on goods when they are imported into a country or trading bloc (such as the European Community) from outside. The aim of tariffs is to reduce imports by making them more expensive.

Tarkovsky Andrei 1932–1986. Soviet film director whose work is characterized by an epic style combined with intense personal spirituality. His films include *Solaris* 1972, *Mirror* 1975, *Stalker* 1979, and *The Sacrifice* 1986.

tarpon large silver-sided fish *Tarpon atlanticus* of the family Megalopidae. It reaches 2 m/6 ft and may weigh 135 kg/300 lb. It lives in warm W Atlantic waters.

tarragon perennial bushy herb *Artemisia dracunculus* of the daisy family Compositae, native to the Old World, growing to 1.5 m/5 ft, with narrow leaves and small green-white flower heads arranged in groups. Tarragon contains an aromatic oil; its leaves are used to flavour salads, pickles, and tartar sauce. It is closely related to wormwood.

tarsier any of three species of the prosimian primates, genus *Tarsius*, of the East Indies and the Philippines. These survivors of early primates are about the size of a rat with thick, light-brown fur, very large eyes, and long feet and hands. They are nocturnal, arboreal, and eat insects and lizards.

Tashkent capital of Uzbekistan; population (1990) 2,100,000. Industries include the manufacture of mining machinery, chemicals, textiles, and leather goods. Founded in the 7th century, it was taken by the Turks in the 12th century and captured by Tamerlane 1361. In 1865 it was taken by the Russians. It was severely damaged by an earthquake 1966.

Tasman Abel Janszoon 1603–1659. Dutch navigator. In 1642, he was the first European to see Tasmania. He also made the first European sightings of New Zealand, Tonga, and Fiji.

Tasmania former name (1642–1856) *Van Diemen's Land* island off the south coast of Australia; a state of the Commonwealth of Australia; *area* 67,800 sq km/26,171 sq mi; *capital* Hobart; *towns* Launceston (chief port); *features* an island state (including small islands in the Bass Strait, and Macquarie Island); Franklin River, a wilderness area saved from a hydroelectric scheme 1983, which also has a prehistoric site; unique fauna including the Tasmanian devil; *products* wool, dairy products, apples and other fruit, timber, iron, tin, coal, copper, silver; *population* (1987) 448,000; *history* the first European to visit here was Abel Tasman 1642; the last of the Tasmanian Aboriginals died 1876. Tasmania joined the Australian Commonwealth as a state 1901.

Tasmanian devil carnivorous marsupial *Sarcophilus harrisii*, in the same family (Dasyuridae) as native 'cats'. It is about 65 cm/2.1 ft long with a 25 cm/10 in bushy tail. It has a large head, strong teeth, and is blackish with white patches on the chest and hind parts. It is nocturnal, carnivorous, and can be ferocious when cornered. It has recently become extinct in Australia and survives only in remote parts of Tasmania.

Tasmanian wolf or *thylacine* carnivorous marsupial *Thylacinus cynocephalus*, in the family Dasyuridae. It is doglike in appearance and can be nearly 2 m/6 ft from nose to tail tip. It was hunted to probable extinction in the 1930s, but there are still occasional unconfirmed reports of sightings.

Tatar or *Tartar* member of a Turkic people, the descendants of the mixed Mongol and Turkic followers of ◊Genghis Khan, called the Golden Horde because of the wealth they gained by plunder. The vast Tatar state was conquered by Russia 1552. The Tatars now live mainly in the Russian autonomous republic of Tatarstan, W Siberia, Turkmenistan, and Uzbekistan (where they were deported from the Crimea 1944). There are over 5 million speakers of the Tatar language, which belongs to the Turkic branch of the Altaic family. The Tatar people are mainly Muslim, although some have converted to the Orthodox Church.

Tatarstan formerly *Tatar Autonomous Republic* autonomous republic of E Russia; *area* 68,000 sq km/26,250 sq mi; *capital* Kazan; *products* oil, chemicals, textiles, timber; *population* (1986) 3,537,000 (48% Tatar, 43% Russian); *history* a territory of Volga-Kama Bulgar state from the 10th century when Islam was introduced; conquered by the Mongols 1236; the capital of the powerful khanate of Kazan until conquered by Russia 1552; an autonomous republic from 1920. It is mainly Muslim and an important industrial and oil-producing area. In Aug 1990 the republic's assembly upgraded

Tatarstan to full republic status, proclaiming its economic and political 'sovereignty', and in June 1991 it refused to participate in the Russian presidential election. The campaign for full independence gathered momentum after the collapse of the Soviet Union.

Taube Henry 1915– . US chemist who established the basis of inorganic chemistry through his study of the loss or gain of electrons by atoms during chemical reactions. Nobel prize 1983.

Taurus zodiacal constellation in the northern hemisphere near Orion, represented as a bull. The Sun passes through Taurus from mid-May to late June. Its brightest star is Aldebaran, seen as the bull's red eye. Taurus contains the Hyades and Pleiades open ◊star clusters, and the Crab nebula. In astrology, the dates for Taurus are between about 20 April and 20 May (see ◊precession).

taxation raising of money from individuals and organizations by the state in order to pay for the goods and services it provides. Taxation can be *direct* (a deduction from income) or *indirect* (added to the purchase price of goods or services, that is, a tax on consumption). The standard form of indirect taxation in Europe is *value-added tax (VAT)*. *Income tax* is the most common form of direct taxation.

taxis (plural *taxes*) or *tactic movement* in botany, the movement of a single cell, such as a bacterium, protozoan, single-celled alga, or gamete, in response to an external stimulus. A movement directed towards the stimulus is described as positive taxis, and away from it as negative taxis. The alga *Chlamydomonas*, for example, demonstrates positive *phototaxis* by swimming towards a light source to increase the rate of photosynthesis. *Chemotaxis* is a response to a chemical stimulus, as seen in many bacteria that move towards higher concentrations of nutrients.

Tay longest river in Scotland; length 189 km/118 mi. Rising in NW Central region, it flows NE through Loch Tay, then E and SE past Perth to the Firth of Tay, crossed at Dundee by the Tay Bridge, before joining the North Sea. The Tay has salmon fisheries; its main tributaries are the Tummel, Isla, and Earn.

Taylor Elizabeth 1932– . English-born US actress whose films include *National Velvet* 1944, *Cat on a Hot Tin Roof* 1958, *Butterfield 8* 1960 (Academy Award), *Cleopatra* 1963, and *Who's Afraid of Virginia Woolf?* 1966 (Academy Award).

Tayside region of Scotland; *area* 7,700 sq km/2,973 sq mi; *towns* Dundee (administrative headquarters), Perth, Arbroath, Forfar; *features* river Tay; Grampian Mountains; Lochs Tay and Rannoch; hills: Ochil and Sidlaw; vales of the North and South Esk; *products* beef and dairy products, soft fruit from the fertile Carse of Gowrie (SW of Dundee); *population* (1991) 385,300;

famous people J M Barrie, John Buchan, Princess Margaret.

Tbilisi formerly *Tiflis* capital of the Republic of Georgia; industries include textiles, machinery, ceramics, and tobacco; population (1987) 1,194,000. Dating from the 5th century, it is a centre of Georgian culture, with fine medieval churches. Anti-Russian demonstrations were quashed here by troops 1981 and 1989; the latter clash followed rejected demands for autonomy from the Abkhazia enclave, and resulted in 19 or more deaths from poison gas (containing chloroacetophenone) and 100 injured.

Tchaikovsky Pyotr Il'yich 1840–1893. Russian composer. His strong sense of melody, personal expression, and brilliant orchestration are clear throughout his many Romantic works, which include six symphonies, three piano concertos, a violin concerto, operas (for example, *Eugene Onegin* 1879), ballets (for example, *The Nutcracker* 1892), orchestral fantasies (for example, *Romeo and Juliet* 1870), and chamber and vocal music.

tea evergreen shrub *Camellia sinensis*, family Theaceae, of which the fermented, dried leaves are infused to make a beverage of the same name. Known in China as early as 2737 BC, tea was first brought to Europe AD 1610 and rapidly became a fashionable drink. In 1823 it was found growing wild in N India, and plantations were later established in Assam and Sri Lanka; producers today include Africa, South America, Georgia, Azerbaijan, Indonesia, and Iran.

teak tropical Asian timber tree *Tectona grandis*, family Verbenaceae, with yellowish wood used in furniture and shipbuilding.

teal any of various small, short-necked dabbling ducks of the genus *Anas*. The drakes generally have a bright head and wing markings. The green-winged teal *A. crecca* is about 35 cm/14 in long.

tear gas any of various volatile gases that produce irritation and tearing of the eyes, used by police against crowds and used in chemical warfare. The gas is delivered in pressurized, liquid-filled canisters or grenades, thrown by hand or launched from a specially adapted rifle. Gases (such as Mace) cause violent coughing and blinding tears, which pass when the victim breathes fresh air, and there are no lasting effects. Blister gases (such as mustard gas) and nerve gases are more harmful and may cause permanent injury or death.

teasel erect, prickly, biennial herb *Dipsacus fullonum*, family Dipsacaceae, native to Eurasia. The dry, spiny seed heads were once used industrially to tease, or raise the nap of, cloth.

tea tree shrub or small tree of the genus *Leptospermum* of Australia and New Zealand. It is thought that some species of leptospermum were used by the explorer Captain Cook to brew tea; it was used in the first years of settlement for this purpose.

technetium silver-grey, radioactive, metallic element, symbol Tc, atomic number 43, relative atomic mass 98.906. It occurs in nature only in extremely minute amounts, produced as a fission product from uranium in pitchblende and other uranium ores. Its longest-lived isotope, Tc-99, has a half-life of 216,000 years. It is a superconductor and is used as a hardener in steel alloys and as a medical tracer.

technology the use of tools, power, and materials, generally for the purposes of production. Almost every human process for getting food and shelter depends on complex technological systems, which have been developed over a 5-million-year period. Significant milestones include the advent of the ◊steam engine 1712, the introduction of ◊electricity and the ◊internal combustion engine in the mid-1800s, and recent developments in communications, ◊electronics, and the nuclear and space industries. The *advanced technology* (highly automated and specialized) on which modern industrialized society depends is frequently contrasted with the *low technology* (labour-intensive and unspecialized) that characterizes some developing countries. *Intermediate technology* is an attempt to adapt scientifically advanced inventions to less developed areas by using local materials and methods of manufacture.

tectonics in geology, the study of the movements of rocks on the Earth's surface. On a small scale tectonics involves the formation of folds and faults, but on a large scale ◊plate tectonics deals with the movement of the Earth's surface as a whole.

Tecumseh 1768–1813. North American Indian chief of the Shawnee. He attempted to unite the Indian peoples from Canada to Florida against the encroachment of white settlers, but the defeat of his brother **Tenskwatawa**, 'the Prophet', at the battle of Tippecanoe in Nov 1811 by W H Harrison, governor of the Indiana Territory, largely destroyed the confederacy built up by Tecumseh.

Teesside industrial area at the mouth of the river Tees, Cleveland, NE England; population (1981) 382,700. Industries include high-technology, capital-intensive steelmaking, chemicals, an oil-fuel terminal, and the main North Sea natural-gas terminal. Middlesbrough is a large port.

Tegucigalpa capital of Honduras; industries include textiles and food-processing; population (1989) 608,000. It was founded 1524 as a gold- and silver-mining centre.

Tehran capital of Iran; industries include textiles, chemicals, engineering, and tobacco; population (1986) 6,043,000. It was founded in the 12th century and made the capital 1788 by Muhammad Shah. Much of the city was rebuilt in the 1920s and 1930s.

telescope

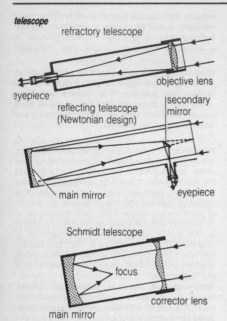

refractory telescope

objective lens

eyepiece

reflecting telescope
(Newtonian design)

secondary
mirror

main mirror   eyepiece

Schmidt telescope

focus

corrector lens

main mirror

Tehran is the site of the Gulistan Palace (the former royal residence).

Te Kanawa Kiri 1944– . New Zealand soprano. Te Kanawa's first major role was the Countess in Mozart's *The Marriage of Figaro* at Covent Garden, London, 1971. Her voice combines the purity and intensity of the upper range with an extended lower range of great richness and resonance. Apart from classical roles, she has also featured popular music in her repertoire, such as the 1984 recording of Leonard Bernstein's *West Side Story*.

Tel Aviv officially *Tel Aviv–Jaffa* city in Israel, on the Mediterranean Sea; industries include textiles, chemicals, sugar, printing, and publishing; population (1987) 320,000. Tel Aviv was founded 1909 as a Jewish residential area in the Arab town of Jaffa, with which it was combined 1949; their ports were superseded 1965 by Ashdod to the south.

telecommunications communications over a distance, generally by electronic means. Long-distance voice communication was pioneered 1876 by Alexander Graham Bell, when he invented the telephone as a result of Faraday's discovery of electromagnetism. Today it is possible to communicate with most countries by telephone cable, or by satellite or microwave link, with over 100,000 simultaneous conversations and several television channels being carried by the latest satellites. Integrated-Services Digital Network (ISDN) makes videophones and high-quality fax possible; the

world's first large-scale centre of ISDN began operating in Japan 1988. The chief method of relaying long-distance calls on land is microwave radio transmission.

Telemann Georg Philipp 1681–1767. German Baroque composer, organist, and conductor at the Johanneum, Hamburg, from 1721. He was exceedingly prolific, producing 25 operas, 1,800 church cantatas, hundreds of other vocal works, and 600 instrumental works.

telephone instrument for communicating by voice over long distances, invented by Alexander Graham ⟡Bell 1876. The transmitter (mouthpiece) consists of a carbon microphone, with a diaphragm that vibrates when a person speaks into it. The diaphragm vibrations compress grains of carbon to a greater or lesser extent, altering their resistance to an electric current passing through them. This sets up variable electrical signals, which travel along the telephone lines to the receiver of the person being called. There they cause the magnetism of an electromagnet to vary, making a diaphragm above the electromagnet vibrate and give out sound waves, which mirror those that entered the mouthpiece originally.

telescope optical instrument that magnifies images of faint and distant objects; any device for collecting and focusing light and other forms of electromagnetic radiation. It is a major research tool in astronomy, is used to sight over land and sea, and small telescopes can be attached to cameras and rifles. A telescope with a large aperture, or opening, can distinguish finer detail and fainter objects than one with a small aperture. The *refracting telescope* uses lenses, and the *reflecting telescope* uses mirrors. A third type, the *catadioptric telescope*, with a combination of lenses and mirrors, is used increasingly. See also ⟡radio telescope.

teletext broadcast system of displaying information on a television screen. The information — typically about news items, entertainment, sport, and finance—is constantly updated. Teletext is a form of ⟡videotext, pioneered in Britain by the British Broadcasting Corporation (BBC) with Ceefax and by Independent Television with Oracle.

television (TV) reproduction at a distance by radio waves of visual images. For transmission, a television camera converts the pattern of light it takes in into a pattern of electrical charges. This is scanned line by line by a beam of electrons from an electron gun, resulting in variable electrical signals that represent the picture. These signals are combined with a radio carrier wave and broadcast as magnetic waves. The TV aerial picks up the wave and feeds it to the receiver (TV set). This separates out the vision signals, which pass to a cathode-ray tube, where a beam of electrons is made to scan across the screen line by line, mirroring the action of the electron gun in the TV camera. The result is a recreation of the pattern of light that entered the camera. The world's first public television service was started from the BBC station at Alexandra Palace in N London, 2 Nov 1936. In 1990 in the UK, the average viewing time per person was 25.5 hours each week.

telex (acronym for *tel*eprinter *ex*change) international telecommunications network that handles telegraph messages in the form of coded signals. It uses teleprinters for transmitting and receiving, and makes use of land lines (cables) and radio and satellite links to make connections between subscribers.

Telford Thomas 1757–1834. Scottish civil engineer who opened up N Scotland by building roads and waterways. He constructed many aqueducts and canals, including the Caledonian canal 1802–23, and erected the Menai road suspension bridge 1819–26, a type of structure scarcely tried previously in England. In Scotland he constructed over 1,600 km/1,000 mi of road and 1,200 bridges, churches, and harbours.

Tell Wilhelm (William) legendary 14th-century Swiss archer, said to have refused to salute the Habsburg badge at Altdorf on Lake Lucerne. Sentenced to shoot an apple from his son's head, he did so, then shot the tyrannical Austrian ruler Gessler, symbolizing his people's refusal to submit to external authority.

tellurium silver-white, semi-metallic (⟁metalloid) element, symbol Te, atomic number 52, relative atomic mass 127.60. Chemically it is similar to sulphur and selenium, and it is considered as one of the sulphur group. It occurs naturally in telluride minerals, and is used in colouring glass blue–brown, in the electrolytic refining of zinc, in electronics, and as a catalyst in refining petroleum.

Telugu language spoken in SE India. It is the official language of Andhra Pradesh, and is also spoken in Malaysia, giving a total number of speakers of around 50 million. Written records in Telugu date from the 7th century AD. Telugu belongs to the Dravidian family.

tempera painting medium in which powdered pigments are bound together, usually with egg yolk and water. A form of tempera was used in ancient Egypt, and egg tempera was the foremost medium for panel painting in late medieval and early Renaissance Europe. It was gradually superseded by oils from the late 15th century onwards.

temperance movement society dedicated to curtailing the consumption of alcohol by total prohibition, local restriction, or encouragement of declarations of personal abstinence ('the pledge'). Temperance movements were first set up in the USA, Ireland, and Scotland, then in the N of England in the 1830s.

temperature state of hotness or coldness of a body,

and the condition that determines whether or not it will transfer heat to, or receive heat from, another body according to the laws of ⟁thermodynamics. It is measured in degrees Celsius (before 1948 called centigrade), kelvin, or Fahrenheit.

Templar member of a Christian military order, founded in Jerusalem 1119, the *Knights of the Temple of Solomon*. The knights took vows of poverty, chastity, and obedience and devoted themselves to the recovery of Palestine from the Muslims.

Temple centre of Jewish national worship in Jerusalem in both ancient and modern days. The Western or *Wailing Wall* is the surviving part of the western wall of the enclosure of Herod's Temple. Since the destruction of the Temple AD 70, Jews have gone there to pray and to mourn their dispersion and the loss of their homeland.

tench European freshwater bony fish *Tinca tinca*, a member of the carp family, now established in North America. It is about 45 cm/18 in long, weighing 2 kg/4.5 lb, coloured olive green above and grey beneath. The scales are small and there is a barbel at each side of the mouth.

Tenerife largest of the ⟁Canary Islands, Spain; area 2,060 sq km/795 sq mi; population (1981) 557,000. *Santa Cruz* is the main town, and *Pico de Teide* is an active volcano.

Teng Hsiao-ping alternative spelling of ⟁Deng Xiaoping, Chinese politician.

Teniers family of Flemish painters, active in Antwerp. *David Teniers the Younger* (David II, 1610–1690) became court painter to Archduke Leopold William, governor of the Netherlands, in Brussels. He painted scenes of peasant life.

Tennessee state in E central USA; nickname Volunteer State; *area* 109,200 sq km/42,151 sq mi; *capital* Nashville; *towns* Memphis, Knoxville, Chattanooga, Clarksville; *features* Tennessee Valley Authority; Great Smoky Mountains National Park; Grand Old Opry, Nashville; Beale Street Historic District and Graceland, estate of Elvis Presley, Memphis; research centres, including Oak Ridge National Laboratory; *products* cereals, cotton, tobacco, soya beans, livestock, timber, coal, zinc, copper, chemicals; *population* (1990) 4,877,200; *famous people* Davy Crockett, David Farragut, W C Handy, Cordell Hull, Andrew Jackson, Andrew Johnson, Dolly Parton, John Crowe Ransom, Bessie Smith; *history* first settled by Europeans 1757; became a state 1796. Tennessee was deeply divided in the Civil War and was a major war theatre, with the battles of Shiloh, Murfreesboro, Chattanooga, and Nashville among those fought in the state.

Tenniel John 1820–1914. English illustrator and cartoonist, known for his illustrations for Lewis Carroll's *Alice's Adventures in Wonderland* 1865 and *Through the Looking-Glass* 1872. He joined the satirical magazine *Punch* 1850, and for over 50 years was one of its leading cartoonists.

tennis, lawn racket-and-ball game invented towards the end of the 19th century, derived from real tennis. Although played on different surfaces (grass, wood, shale, clay, concrete), it is still called 'lawn tennis'. The aim of the two or four players is to strike the ball into the prescribed area of the court, with oval-headed rackets (strung with gut or nylon), in such a way that it cannot be returned. Major events include the *Davis Cup* first contested 1900 for international men's competition, and the annual All England Tennis Club championships (originating 1877), an open event for players of both sexes at Wimbledon.

Tennyson Alfred, 1st Baron Tennyson 1809–1892. English poet, poet laureate 1850–92, whose verse has a majestic, musical quality. His works include 'The Lady of Shalott', 'The Lotus Eaters', 'Ulysses', 'Break, Break, Break', 'The Charge of the Light Brigade'; the longer narratives *Locksley Hall* 1832 and *Maud* 1855; the elegy *In Memoriam* 1850; and a long series of poems on the Arthurian legends *The Idylls of the King* 1857–85.

terbium soft, silver-grey, metallic element of the ◊lanthanide series, symbol Tb, atomic number 81, relative atomic mass 158.925. It occurs in gadolinite and other ores, with yttrium and ytterbium, and is used in lasers, semiconductors, and television tubes. It was named in 1843 by Swedish chemist Carl Mosander (1797–1858) for the town of Ytterby, Sweden, where it was first found.

Terence (Publius Terentius Afer) 190–159 BC. Roman dramatist, born in Carthage and brought as a slave to Rome, where he was freed and came under ◊Scipio Africanus Minor's patronage. His surviving six comedies (including *The Eunuch* 161 BC) are subtly characterized and based on Greek models.

Teresa Mother. Born Agnes Bojaxhiu 1910– . Roman Catholic nun. She was born in Skopje, Albania, and at 18 entered a Calcutta convent and became a teacher. In 1948 she became an Indian citizen and founded the Missionaries of Charity, an order for men and women based in Calcutta that helps abandoned children and the dying. Nobel Peace Prize 1979.

terminal in computing, a device consisting of a keyboard and display screen (VDU) – or, in older systems, a teleprinter – to enable the operator to communicate with the computer. The terminal may be physically attached to the computer or linked to it by a telephone line (remote terminal).

termite any member of the insect order Isoptera. Termites are soft-bodied social insects living in large colonies which include one or more queens (of relatively enormous size and producing an egg every two seconds), much smaller kings, and still smaller soldiers, workers, and immature forms.

Termites build galleried nests of soil particles that may be 6 m/20 ft high.

tern any of various lightly built seabirds placed in the same family (Laridae) as gulls and characterized by pointed wings and bill and usually a forked tail. Terns plunge-dive after aquatic prey. They are 20–50 cm/8–20 in long, and usually coloured in combinations of white and black.

terrapin member of some species of the order Chelonia (◊turtles and ◊tortoises). Terrapins are small to medium-sized, aquatic or semi-aquatic, and are found widely in temperate zones. They are omnivorous, but generally eat aquatic animals. Some species are in danger of extinction owing to collection for the pet trade; most of the animals collected die in transit.

terrier any of various breeds of highly intelligent, active dogs. They are usually small. Types include the bull, cairn, fox, Irish, Scottish, Sealyham, Skye, and Yorkshire terriers. They were originally bred for hunting rabbits and following quarry such as foxes down into burrows.

territory in animal behaviour, a fixed area from which an animal or group of animals excludes other members of the same species. Animals may hold territories for many different reasons; for example, to provide a constant food supply, to monopolize potential mates, or to ensure access to refuges or nest sites. The size of a territory depends in part on its function: some nesting and mating territories may be only a few square metres, whereas feeding territories may be as large as hundreds of square kilometres.

terrorism systematic violence in the furtherance of political aims, often by small ◊guerrilla groups. In English law, under the Prevention of Terrorism Act 1984, people arrested may be detained for 48 hours. The secretary of state can extend the period of detention for a maximum of five further days. By 1991, 18,000 people had been detained but only 250 were charged with offences.

Terror, Reign of period of the ◊French Revolution when the Jacobins were in power (Oct 1793–July 1794) under ◊Robespierre and instituted mass persecution of their opponents. About 1,400 were executed, mainly by guillotine, until public indignation rose and Robespierre was overthrown in July 1794.

Tertiary period of geological time 65–1.8 million years ago, divided into into five epochs: Palaeocene, Eocene, Oligocene, Miocene, and Pliocene. During the Tertiary, mammals took over all the ecological niches left vacant by the extinction of the dinosaurs, and became the prevalent land animals. The continents took on their present positions, and climatic and vegetation zones as we know them became established. Within the geological time column the Tertiary follows the Cretaceous period and is succeeded by the Quaternary period.

tesla SI unit (symbol T) of ◊magnetic flux density. One tesla represents a flux density of one ◊weber per square metre, or 10^4 gauss. It is named after the Croatian engineer Nikola Tesla.

Tesla Nikola 1856–1943. Croatian electrical engineer who emigrated to the USA 1884. He invented fluorescent lighting, the Tesla induction motor, and the Tesla coil, and developed the alternating current (AC) electrical supply system.

TESSA (acronym for *tax-exempt special savings account*) UK scheme, introduced 1991, to encourage longer-term savings by making interest tax-free on deposits of up to £9,000 over five years.

testis (plural *testes*) the organ that produces ◊sperm in male (and hermaphrodite) animals. In vertebrates it is one of a pair of oval structures that are usually internal, but in mammals (other than elephants and marine mammals), the paired testes (or testicles) descend from the body cavity during development, to hang outside the abdomen in a scrotal sac.

test match sporting contest between two nations, the most familiar being those played between the eight nations that play test cricket (England, Australia, New Zealand, West Indies, India, Pakistan, South Africa, and Sri Lanka). Test matches can also be found in Rugby League and Rugby Union. A cricket test match lasts a maximum of five days, and a test series usually consists of four to six matches. The first cricket test match was between Australia and England in Melbourne, Australia, 1877.

testosterone in vertebrates, hormone secreted chiefly by the testes, but also by the ovaries and the cortex of the adrenal glands. It promotes the development of secondary sexual characteristics in males. In animals with a breeding season, the onset of breeding behaviour is accompanied by a rise in the level of testosterone in the blood.

tetanus or *lockjaw* acute disease caused by the toxin of the bacillus *Clostridium tetani*, which usually enters the body through a wound. The bacterium is chiefly found in richly manured soil. Untreated, in seven to ten days tetanus produces muscular spasm and rigidity of the jaw spreading to the other muscles, convulsions, and death. There is a vaccine, and the disease may be treatable with tetanus antitoxin and antibiotics.

Teutonic Knight member of a German Christian military order, the *Knights of the Teutonic Order*, founded 1190 by Hermann of Salza in Palestine. They crusaded against the pagan Prussians and Lithuanians from 1228 and controlled Prussia until the 16th century. Their capital was Marienburg (now Malbork, Poland).

Texas state in SW USA; nickname Lone Star State; *area* 691,200 sq km/266,803 sq mi; *capital* Austin; *towns* Houston, Dallas-Fort Worth, San Antonio, El Paso, Corpus Christi, Lubbock; *features* rivers: Rio Grande, Red; arid Staked Plains, reclaimed by irrigation; the Great Plains; Gulf Coast resorts; Lyndon B Johnson Space Center, Houston; Alamo, San Antonio; Big Bend and Guadalupe Mountains national parks; *products* rice, cotton, sorghum, wheat, hay, livestock, shrimp, meat products, lumber, wood and paper products, petroleum (nearly one-third of US production), natural gas, sulphur, salt, uranium, chemicals, petrochemicals, nonelectrical machinery, fabricated metal products, transportation equipment, electric and electronic equipment; *population* (1990) 16,986,500; *famous people* James Bowie, George Bush, Buddy Holly, Sam Houston, Howard Hughes, Lyndon Johnson, Janis Joplin, Katherine Anne Porter, Tina Turner; *history* settled by the Spanish 1682; part of Mexico 1821–36; Santa Anna massacred the Alamo garrison 1836, but was defeated by Sam Houston at San Jacinto the same year; Texas became an independent republic 1836–45, with Houston as president; in 1845 it became a state of the USA. Texas is the only state in the USA to have previously been an independent republic.

Thackeray William Makepeace 1811–1863. English novelist and essayist, born in Calcutta, India. He was a regular contributor to *Fraser's Magazine* and *Punch*. *Vanity Fair* 1847–48 was his first novel, followed by *Pendennis* 1848, *Henry Esmond* 1852 (and its sequel *The Virginians* 1857–59), and *The Newcomes* 1853–55, in which Thackeray's tendency to sentimentality is most marked.

Thai member of the majority ethnic group living in Thailand and N Myanmar (Burma). Thai peoples also live in SW China, Laos, and N Vietnam. They speak Tai languages, all of which belong to the Sino-Tibetan language family. There are over 60 million speakers, the majority of whom live in Thailand. Most Thais are Buddhists, but the traditional belief in spirits, *phi*, remains.

Thailand Kingdom of; country in SE Asia on the Gulf of Siam, bordered E by Laos and Cambodia, S by Malaysia, and W by Myanmar (formerly Burma); *area* 513,115 sq km/198,108 sq mi; *capital* and chief port Bangkok; *physical* mountainous, semi-arid plateau in NE, fertile central region, tropical isthmus in S; *head of state* King Bhumibol Adulyadej from 1946; *head of government* Somboon Rahong (unelected prime minister) from 1992; *political system* military-controlled emergent democracy; *exports* rice, textiles, rubber, tin, rubies, sapphires, maize, tapioca; *population* (1990 est) 54,890,000 (Thai 75%, Chinese 14%); *languages* Thai and Chinese (both official); regional dialects; *recent history* Anglo-French agreement 1896 recognized Siam as independent buffer state. Constitutional monarchy established 1932; Thailand adopted as name of country 1939. Japanese occupation 1941–44 during World War II. Military seized power in a coup 1947, overthrown 1973, reassumed control 1976. Civilian government

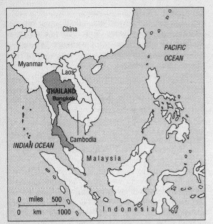

formed 1983 but martial law maintained. Military again seized power in coup 1991; corrupt elections 1992 were followed by appointment of General Suchinda Kraprayoon as unelected prime minister; huge antigovernment demonstrations ensued and more than 100 demonstrators were shot by the army. Somboon Rahong was appointed to replace Kraprayoon.

thallium soft, bluish-white, malleable, metallic element, symbol Tl, atomic number 81, relative atomic mass 204.37. It is a poor conductor of electricity. Its compounds are poisonous and are used as insecticides and rodent poisons; some are used in the optical-glass and infrared-glass industries and in photoelectric cells.

Thames river in S England; length 338 km/210 mi. It rises in the Cotswolds above Cirencester and is tidal as far as Teddington. Below London there is protection from flooding by means of the Thames barrier. The headstreams unite at Lechlade.

Thames Tunnel tunnel extending 365 m/1,200 ft under the river Thames, London, linking Rotherhithe with Wapping; the first underwater tunnel in the world. Designed by Marc Isambard Brunel, it was completed 1843. Today it carries underground trains.

Thanksgiving (Day) national holiday in the US (fourth Thursday in Nov) and Canada (second Monday in Oct), first celebrated by the Pilgrim settlers in Massachusetts after their first harvest 1621.

Thatcher Margaret Hilda (born Roberts) 1925–. British Conservative politician, prime minister 1979–1990. She was education minister 1970–74 and Conservative Party leader from 1975. In 1982 she sent British troops to recapture the Falkland Islands from Argentina. She confronted trade-union power during the miners' strike 1984–85, sold off majority stakes in many public utilities to the private sector, and reduced the influence of local government through such measures as the abolition of metropolitan councils, the control of expenditure through 'rate-capping', and the introduction of the community charge, or ◊poll tax, from 1989. In 1990 splits in the cabinet over the issues of Europe and consensus government forced her resignation. An astute Parliamentary tactician, she tolerated little disagreement, either from the opposition or from within her own party. Life peerage 1992.

Thatcherism political outlook comprising a belief in the efficacy of market forces, the need for strong central government, and a conviction that self-help is preferable to reliance on the state, combined with a strong element of ◊nationalism. The ideology is associated with Margaret Thatcher but stems from an individualist view found in Britain's 19th-century Liberal and 20th-century Conservative parties, and is no longer confined to Britain.

theatre performance by actors for an audience; it may include ◊drama, dancing, music, mime, and puppets. The term is also used for the place or building in which dramatic performances take place. Theatre history can be traced to Egyptian religious ritualistic drama as long ago as 3200 BC. The first known European theatres were in Greece from about 600 BC.

Thebes capital of Boeotia in ancient Greece. In the Peloponnesian War it was allied with Sparta against Athens. For a short time after 371 BC when Thebes defeated Sparta at Leuctra, it was the most powerful state in Greece. Alexander the Great destroyed it 336 BC and although it was restored, it never regained its former power.

Thebes Greek name of an ancient city (*Niut-Ammon*) in Upper Egypt, on the Nile. Probably founded under the first dynasty, it was the centre of the worship of Ammon, and the Egyptian capital under the New Kingdom about 1600 BC. Temple ruins survive near the villages of Karnak and Luxor, and in the nearby *Valley of the Kings* are buried the 18th–20th dynasty kings, including Tutankhamen and Amenhotep III.

Themistocles *c.* 525–*c.* 460 BC. Athenian soldier and politician. Largely through his policies in Athens (creating its navy and strengthening its walls), Greece was saved from Persian conquest. He fought with distinction in the Battle of ◊Salamis 480 BC during the Persian War. About 470 he was accused of embezzlement and conspiracy against Athens, and banished by Spartan influence. He fled to Asia, where Artaxerxes, the Persian king, received him with favour.

theocracy political system run by priests, as was once found in Tibet. In practical terms it means a system where religious values determine political decisions. The closest modern example was Iran during the period when Ayatollah Khomeini was its religious leader, 1979–89. The term was coined by the historian Josephus in the 1st century AD.

Theodora 508–548. Byzantine empress from 527. She was originally the mistress of Emperor Justinian before marrying him in 525. She earned a reputation for charity, courage, and championing the rights of women.

Theodosius I 'the Great' *c.* AD 346–395. Roman emperor AD 388–95. A devout Christian and an adherent of the Nicene creed, he dealt harshly with heretics and in 391 crushed all forms of pagan religion in the empire. He thus founded the orthodox Christian state, acquiring his title. After his reign, the Roman empire was divided into eastern and western halves.

Theravāda one of the two major forms of ⟡Buddhism, common in S Asia (Sri Lanka, Thailand, Cambodia, and Myanmar); the other is the later Mahāyāna.

thermal conductivity in physics, the ability of a substance to conduct heat. Good thermal conductors, like good electrical conductors, are generally materials with many free electrons (such as metals).

thermodynamics branch of physics dealing with the transformation of heat into and from other forms of energy. It is the basis of the study of the efficient working of engines, such as the steam and internal-combustion engines. The three laws of thermodynamics are (1) energy can be neither created nor destroyed, heat and mechanical work being mutually convertible; (2) it is impossible for an unaided self-acting machine to convey heat from one body to another at a higher temperature; and (3) it is impossible by any procedure, no matter how idealized, to reduce any system to the ⟡absolute zero of temperature (0K/–273°C) in a finite number of operations. Put into mathematical form, these laws have widespread applications in physics and chemistry.

thermometer instrument for measuring temperature. There are many types, designed to measure different temperature ranges to varying degrees of accuracy. Each makes use of a different physical effect of temperature.

Thermopylae, Battle of battle during the ⟡Persian Wars 480 BC when Leonidas, king of Sparta, and 1,000 men defended the pass of Thermopylae to the death against a much greater force of Persians. The pass led from Thessaly to Locris in central Greece.

thermosphere layer in the Earth's ⟡atmosphere above the mesosphere and below the exosphere. Its lower level is about 80 km/50 mi above the ground, but its upper level is undefined. The ionosphere is located in the thermosphere. In the thermosphere the temperature rises with increasing height to several thousand degrees Celsius. However, because of the thinness of the air, very little heat is actually present.

Theseus legendary hero of ⟡Attica, supposed to have united the states of the area under a constitutional government in Athens. Ariadne, whom he later abandoned on Naxos, helped him find his way through the Labyrinth to kill the ⟡Minotaur. He also fought the Amazons and was one of the ⟡Argonauts.

Thessaloníki (English **Salonika**) port in Macedonia, NE Greece, at the head of the Gulf of Thessaloníki, the second largest city of Greece; population (1981) 706,200. Industries include textiles, shipbuilding, chemicals, brewing, and tanning. It was founded from Corinth by the Romans 315 BC as **Thessalonica** (to whose inhabitants St Paul addressed two epistles), captured by the Saracens AD 904 and by the Turks 1430, and restored to Greece 1912.

Thessaly (Greek **Thessalia**) region of E central Greece, on the Aegean; area 13,904 sq km/5,367 sq mi; population (1991) 731,200. It is a major area of cereal production. It was an independent state in ancient Greece and later formed part of the Roman province of ⟡Macedonia. It was Turkish from the 14th century until incorporated in Greece 1881.

thiamine or **vitamin B₁** ⟡vitamin of the B complex. Its absence from the diet causes the disease beriberi.

Thimbu or **Thimphu** capital since 1962 of the Himalayan state of Bhutan; population (1987) 15,000.

Third Reich (Third Empire) term used by the

thermometer

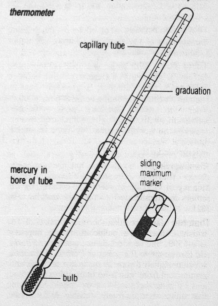

capillary tube

graduation

mercury in bore of tube

sliding maximum marker

bulb

Nazis to describe Germany during the years of Hitler's dictatorship after 1933. The idea of the Third Reich was based on the existence of two previous German empires, the medieval Holy Roman Empire and the second empire 1871–1918.

Third World those countries that are less industrialized than the free-market countries of the West (First World) and the former communist bloc (Second World). Third World countries are the poorest, as measured by their income per head of population, and are concentrated in Asia, Africa, and Latin America; they are also referred to collectively as the South (see ◊North–South divide). They are divided into low-income countries, including China and India; middle-income countries, such as Nigeria, Indonesia, and Bolivia; and upper-middle-income countries, such as Brazil, Algeria, and Malaysia. The Third World has 75% of the world's population but consumes only 20% of its resources. In 1990 the average income per head in the northern hemisphere was $12,500, which is 18 times higher than that in the southern hemisphere.

Thirteen Colonies 13 American colonies that signed the ◊Declaration of Independence from Britain 1776. Led by George Washington, the Continental Army defeated the British army in the ◊American Revolution 1776–81 to become the original 13 United States of America: Connecticut, Delaware, Georgia, Maryland, Massachusetts, New Hampshire, New Jersey, New York, North Carolina, Pennsylvania, Rhode Island, South Carolina, and Virginia. They were united first under the Articles of Confederation and from 1789, the US ◊constitution.

Thirty-Nine Articles set of articles of faith defining the doctrine of the Anglican Church; see under ◊Anglican Communion.

Thirty Years' War major war 1618–48 in central Europe. Beginning as a German conflict between Protestants and Catholics, it gradually became transformed into a struggle to determine whether the ruling Austrian Habsburg family would gain control of all Germany. The war caused serious economic and demographic problems in central Europe.

thistle prickly plant of several genera, such as *Carduus, Carlina, Onopordum,* and *Cirsium,* in the family Compositae. The stems are spiny, the flower heads purple, white, or yellow and cottony, and the leaves deeply indented with prickly margins. The thistle is the Scottish national emblem.

Thomas Clarence 1948– . US Justice of the Supreme Court whose nomination to the Supreme Court 1991 by President Bush caused controversy. He is opposed to the policy of ◊affirmative action, which positively discriminates in favour of minority groups and from which he himself has benefited; and he is thought unlikely to uphold legislation that makes abortion freely available. At the public,

televised Senate confirmation hearings, Anita Hill, a former colleague, accused Thomas of sexually harassing her ten years earlier. He denied the allegations.

Thomas Dylan (Marlais) 1914–1953. Welsh poet. His poems include the celebration of his 30th birthday 'Poem in October' and the evocation of his youth 'Fern Hill' 1946. His 'play for voices' *Under Milk Wood* 1954 describes with humour and compassion a day in the life of the residents of a small Welsh fishing village, Llareggub. The short stories of *Portrait of the Artist as a Young Dog* 1940 are autobiographical.

Thomas à Kempis 1380–1471. German Augustinian monk who lived at the monastery of Zwolle. He took his name from his birthplace Kempen; his real surname was Hammerken. His *De Imitatio Christi/Imitation of Christ* is probably the most widely known devotional work ever written.

Thomas, St in the New Testament, one of the 12 Apostles, said to have preached in S India, hence the ancient churches there were referred to as the 'Christians of St Thomas'. He is not the author of the Gospel of St Thomas, the Gnostic collection of Jesus' sayings.

Thompson Daley (Francis Morgan) 1958– . English decathlete who has broken the world record four times since winning the Commonwealth Games decathlon title 1978. He has won two more Commonwealth titles (1982, 1986), two Olympic gold medals (1980, 1984), three European medals (silver 1978; gold 1982, 1986), and a world title (1983).

Thomson J(oseph) J(ohn) 1856–1940. English physicist who discovered the ◊electron. He was responsible for organizing the Cavendish atomic research laboratory at Cambridge University. His work inaugurated the electrical theory of the atom, and his elucidation of positive rays and their application to an analysis of neon led to Frederick ◊Aston's discovery of ◊isotopes. Nobel prize 1906.

Thor in Norse mythology, god of thunder (his hammer), and represented as a man of enormous strength defending humanity against demons. He was the son of Odin and Freya, and Thursday is named after him.

thorax in tetrapod vertebrates, the part of the body containing the heart and lungs, and protected by the rib cage; in arthropods, the middle part of the body, between the head and abdomen.

Thoreau Henry David 1817–1862. US author and naturalist. His work *Walden, or Life in the Woods* 1854 stimulated the back-to-nature movement, and he completed some 30 volumes based on his daily nature walks. His essay 'Civil Disobedience' 1849, prompted by his refusal to pay taxes, advocated peaceful resistance to unjust laws and had a wide impact, even in the 20th century.

Thoth in Egyptian mythology, god of wisdom and learning. He was represented as a scribe with the head of an ⟩ibis, the bird sacred to him.

Thrace (Greek *Thráki*) ancient empire (6000 BC–AD 300) in the Balkans, SE Europe, formed by parts of modern Greece and Bulgaria. It was held successively by the Greeks, Persians, Macedonians, and Romans.

Three Mile Island island in the Shenandoah River near Harrisburg, Pennsylvania, site of a nuclear power station which was put out of action following a major accident March 1979. Opposition to nuclear power in the USA was reinforced after this accident and safety standards reassessed.

threshing agricultural process of separating cereal grains from the plant. Traditionally, the work was carried out by hand in winter months using the flail, a jointed beating stick. Today, threshing is done automatically inside the combine harvester at the time of cutting.

thrips any of a number of tiny insects of the order Thysanoptera, usually with feathery wings. Many of the 3,000 species live in flowers and suck their juices, causing damage and spreading disease. Others eat fungi, decaying matter, or smaller insects.

thrombosis condition in which a blood clot forms in a vein or artery, causing loss of circulation to the area served by the vessel. If it breaks away, it often travels to the lungs, causing pulmonary embolism.

thrush any bird of the large family Turdidae, order Passeriformes, found worldwide and known for their song. Thrushes are usually brown with speckles of other colours. They are 12–30 cm/5–12 in long.

thrush infection usually of the mouth (particularly in infants), but also sometimes of the vagina, caused by a yeastlike fungus (genus *Candida*). It is seen as white patches on the mucous membranes.

Thucydides 460–400 BC. Athenian historian who exercised command in the ⟩Peloponnesian War with Sparta 424 with so little success that he was banished until 404. In his *History of the Peloponnesian War*, he attempted a scientific impartiality.

thulium soft, silver-white, malleable and ductile, metallic element, of the ⟩lanthanide series, symbol Tm, atomic number 69, relative atomic mass 168.94. It is the least abundant of the rare-earth metals, and was first found in gadolinite and various other minerals. It is used in arc lighting.

Thurber James (Grover) 1894–1961. US humorist. His short stories, written mainly for the *New Yorker* magazine, include 'The Secret Life of Walter Mitty' 1932, and his doodle drawings include fanciful impressions of dogs.

thyme herb, genus *Thymus*, of the mint family

Labiatae. Garden thyme *T. vulgaris*, native to the Mediterranean, grows to 30 cm/1 ft high, and has pinkish flowers. Its aromatic leaves are used for seasoning.

thymus organ in vertebrates, situated in the upper chest cavity in humans. The thymus processes ⟩lymphocyte cells to produce T-lymphocytes (T denotes 'thymus-derived'), which are responsible for binding to specific invading organisms and killing them or rendering them harmless.

thyroid ⟩endocrine gland of vertebrates, situated in the neck in front of the trachea. It secretes several hormones, principally thyroxine, an iodine-containing hormone that stimulates growth, metabolism, and other functions of the body. The thyroid gland may be thought of as the regulator gland of the body's metabolic rate. If it is overactive, as in thyrotoxicosis, the sufferer feels hot and sweaty, has an increased heart rate, diarrhoea, and weight loss. Conversely, an underactive thyroid leads to myxoedema, a condition characterized by sensitivity to the cold, constipation, and weight gain. In infants, an underactive thyroid leads to cretinism, a form of mental retardation.

Tiahuanaco or *Tihuanaco* site of a Peruvian city, S of Lake Titicaca in the Andes, which gave its name to the 8th–14th-century civilization that preceded the Inca and built many of the roads the Inca are credited with building.

Tiananmen Square paved open space in central Beijing (Peking), China, the largest public square in the world (area 0.4 sq km/0.14 sq mi). On 3–4 June 1989 more than 1,000 unarmed protesters were killed by government troops in a massacre that crushed China's emerging prodemocracy movement.

Tianjin or *Tientsin* port and industrial and commercial city in Hubei province, central China; population (1989) 5,620,000. The special municipality of Tianjin has an area of 4,000 sq km/1,544 sq mi and a population (1990) of 8,788,000. Its handmade silk and wool carpets are renowned. Dagan oilfield is nearby. Tianjin was opened to foreign trade 1860 and occupied by the Japanese 1937.

Tian Shan (Chinese *Tien Shan*) mountain system in central Asia. *Pik Pobedy* on the Xinjiang–Kyrgyz border is the highest peak at 7,440 m/24,415 ft.

Tiberius Claudius Nero 42 BC–AD 37. Roman emperor, the stepson, adopted son, and successor of Augustus from AD 14. A distinguished soldier, he was a conscientious ruler under whom the empire prospered.

Tibet autonomous region of SW China (Pinyin form *Xizang*); *area* 1,221,600 sq km/471,538 sq mi; *capital* Lhasa; *features* Tibet occupies a barren plateau bounded south and southwest by the Himalayas and north by the Kunlun Mountains, traversed west to east by the Bukamagna,

Karakoram, and other mountain ranges, and having an average elevation of 4,000–4,500 m/ 13,000–15,000 ft. The Sutlej, Brahmaputra, and Indus rivers rise in Tibet, which has numerous lakes, many of which are salty. The ◊yak is the main domestic animal; **government** Tibet is an autonomous region of China, with its own People's Government and People's Congress. The controlling force in Tibet is the Communist Party of China, represented locally by First Secretary Wu Jinghua from 1985. Tibetan nationalists regard the province as being under colonial rule; **products** wool, borax, salt, horn, musk, herbs, furs, gold, iron pyrites, lapis lazuli, mercury, textiles, chemicals, agricultural machinery; **population** (1988) 2 million Tibetans and 73,000 Han Chinese; there were another 2 million Tibetans in China outside Tibet; **religion** traditionally Lamaist (a form of Mahāyāna Buddhism); **history** Tibet was an independent kingdom from the 5th century AD. It came under nominal Chinese rule about 1700. Independence was regained after a revolt 1912. China regained control 1951 when the historic ruler and religious leader, the ◊Dalai Lama, was driven from the country and the monks (who formed 25% of the population) were forced out of the monasteries. Between 1951 and 1959 the Chinese People's Liberation Army (PLA) controlled Tibet, although the Dalai Lama returned as nominal spiritual and temporal head of state. In 1959 a Tibetan uprising spread from bordering regions to Lhasa and was supported by Tibet's local government. The rebellion was suppressed by the PLA, prompting the Dalai Lama and 9,000 Tibetans to flee to India. The Chinese proceeded to dissolve the Tibet local government, abolish serfdom, collectivize agriculture, and suppress ◊Lamaism. In 1965 Tibet became an autonomous region of China. Chinese rule continued to be resented, however, and the economy languished.

tick any of an arachnid group (Ixodoidea) of large bloodsucking mites. Many carry and transmit diseases to mammals (including humans) and birds.

tide rise and fall of sea level due to the gravitational forces of the Moon and Sun. High water occurs at an average interval of 12 hr 24 min 30 sec. The highest or **spring tides** are at or near new and full Moon; the lowest or **neap tides** when the Moon is in its first or third quarter. Some seas, such as the Mediterranean, have very small tides.

Tiepolo Giovanni Battista 1696–1770. Italian painter, born in Venice. He created monumental Rococo decorative schemes in palaces and churches in NE Italy, SW Germany, and Madrid (1762–70). The style is light-hearted, the palette light and warm, and he made great play with illusion.

Tierra del Fuego island group divided between Chile and Argentina. It is separated from the mainland of South America by the Strait of Magellan, and Cape Horn is at the southernmost point. The chief town, Ushuaia, Argentina, is the world's southernmost town. Industries include oil and sheep farming.

tiger largest of the great cats *Panthera tigris*, formerly found in much of central and S Asia but nearing extinction because of hunting and the destruction of its natural habitat. The tiger can grow to 3.6 m/12 ft long and weigh 300 kg/660 lbs; it has a yellow-orange coat with black stripes. It is solitary, and feeds on large ruminants. It is a good swimmer.

Tigré group of people living in N Ethiopia. The Tigré language is spoken by about 2.5 million people; it belongs to the SE Semitic branch of the Afro-Asiatic family. **Tigrinya** is a closely related language spoken slightly to the south.

Tigré or **Tigray** region in the northern highlands of Ethiopia; area 65,900 sq km/25,444 sq mi. The chief town is Mekele. The region had an estimated population of 2.4 million in 1984, at a time when drought and famine were driving large numbers of people to fertile land in the south or into neighbouring Sudan. Since 1978 a guerrilla group known as the Tigré People's Liberation Front (TPLF) has been fighting for regional autonomy. In 1989 government troops were forced from the province, and the TPLF advanced towards Addis Ababa, playing a key role in the fall of the Ethiopian government in May 1991.

Tigris (Arabic **Shatt Dijla**) river flowing through

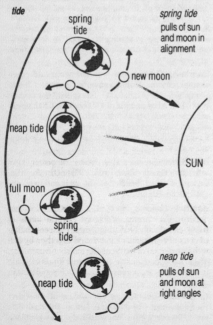

tide

spring
tide

spring tide
pulls of sun
and moon in
alignment

new moon

neap tide

SUN

full moon

spring
tide

neap tide
pulls of sun
and moon at
right angles

neap tide

Turkey and Iraq (see also ⊃Mesopotamia), joining the ⊃Euphrates above Basra, where it forms the ⊃Shatt-al-Arab; length 1,600 km/1,000 mi.

Tijuana city and resort in NW Mexico; population (1990) 742,700; known for horse races and casinos. ⊃San Diego adjoins it across the US border.

timber wood used in construction, furniture, and paper pulp. *Hardwoods* include tropical mahogany, teak, ebony, rosewood, temperate oak, elm, beech, and eucalyptus. All except eucalyptus are slow-growing, and world supplies are almost exhausted. *Softwoods* comprise the ⊃conifers (pine, fir, spruce, and larch), which are quick to grow and easy to work but inferior in quality of grain. *White woods* include ash, birch, and sycamore; all have light-coloured timber, are fast-growing, and can be used as veneers on cheaper timber.

Timbuktu or *Tombouctou* town in Mali; population (1976) 20,500. A camel caravan centre from the 11th century on the fringe of the Sahara, since 1960 it has been surrounded by the southward movement of the desert, and the former canal link with the river Niger is dry. Products include salt.

time continuous passage of existence, recorded by division into hours, minutes, and seconds. Formerly the measurement of time was based on the Earth's rotation on its axis, but this was found to be irregular. Therefore the second, the standard ⊃SI unit of time, was redefined 1956 in terms of the Earth's annual orbit of the Sun, and 1967 in terms of a radiation pattern of the element caesium. The world's standard time zones are calculated from the Greenwich meridian.

Timor largest and most easterly of the Lesser Sunda Islands, part of Indonesia; area 33,610 sq km/12,973 sq mi. *West Timor* (capital Kupang) was formerly Dutch and was included in Indonesia on independence. ⊃*East Timor* (capital Dili), an enclave on the NW coast, and the islands of Atauro and Jaco formed an overseas province of Portugal until it was seized by Indonesia 1975. The annexation is not recognized by the United Nations, and guerrilla warfare by local people seeking independence continues. Since 1975 more than 500,000 Timorese have been killed by Indonesian troops or have resettled in West Timor, according to Amnesty International. Products include coffee, maize, rice, and coconuts.

tin soft, silver-white, malleable and somewhat ductile, metallic element, symbol Sn (from Latin *stannum*), atomic number 50, relative atomic mass 118.69. Tin exhibits allotropy, having three forms: the familiar lustrous metallic form above 55.8°F/13.2°C, a brittle form above 321.8°F/161°C; and a grey powder form below 55.8°F/13.2°C (commonly called tin pest or tin disease). The metal is quite soft (slightly harder than lead) and can be rolled, pressed, or hammered into extremely thin sheets;

it has a low melting point. In nature it occurs rarely as a free metal. It resists corrosion and is therefore used for coating and plating other metals.

tinnitus in medicine, constant internal sounds, inaudible to others. The phenomenon may originate from noisy conditions (drilling, machinery, or loud music) or from infection of the middle or inner ear. The victim may become overwhelmed by the relentless noise in the head.

tinplate milled steel coated with tin, the metal used for most 'tin' cans. The steel provides the strength, and the tin provides the corrosion resistance, ensuring that the food inside is not contaminated. Tinplate may be made by electroplating or by dipping in a bath of molten tin.

Tintoretto real name Jacopo Robusti 1518–1594. Italian painter, active in Venice. His dramatic religious paintings are spectacularly lit and full of movement, such as his canvases of the lives of Christ and the Virgin in the Scuola di San Rocco, Venice, 1564–88.

Tipperary county in the Republic of Ireland, province of Munster, divided into north and south regions. *North Tipperary*: administrative headquarters Nenagh; area 2,000 sq km/772 sq mi; population (1991) 57,800. *South Tipperary*: administrative headquarters Clonmel; area 2,260 sq km/872 sq mi; population (1991) 74,800. It includes part of the Golden Vale, a dairy-farming region.

Tippett Michael (Kemp) 1905– . English composer whose works include the operas *The Midsummer Marriage* 1952, *The Knot Garden* 1970, and *New Year* 1989; four symphonies; *Songs for Ariel* 1962; and choral music including *The Mask of Time* 1984.

Tirana or *Tiranë* capital (since 1920) of Albania; population (1990) 210,000. Industries include metallurgy, cotton textiles, soap, and cigarettes. It was founded in the early 17th century by Turks when part of the Ottoman Empire. Some old districts and mosques have been preserved.

Tirol federal province of Austria; area 12,600 sq km/4,864 sq mi; population (1989) 619,600. Its capital is Innsbruck, and it produces diesel engines, optical instruments, and hydroelectric power. Tirol was formerly a province (from 1363) of the Austrian Empire, divided 1919 between Austria and Italy (see ⊃Trentino–Alto Adige).

tissue in biology, any kind of cellular fabric that occurs in an organism's body. Several kinds of tissue can usually be distinguished, each consisting of cells of a particular kind bound together by cell walls (in plants) or extracellular matrix (in animals). Thus, nerve and muscle are different kinds of tissue in animals, as are parenchyma and sclerenchyma in plants.

tit or *titmouse* any of 65 species of insectivorous, acrobatic bird of the family Paridae. Tits are 8–20 cm/3–8 in long and have grey or black plumage, often with blue or yellow markings. They are found in Eurasia and Africa, and also in North America, where they are called *chickadees*.

Titan in Greek mythology, any of the giant children of Uranus and Gaia, who included Kronos, Rhea, Themis (mother of Prometheus and personification of law and order), and Oceanus. Kronos and Rhea were in turn the parents of Zeus, who ousted Kronos as the ruler of the world.

Titanic British passenger liner, supposedly unsinkable, that struck an iceberg and sank off the Grand Banks of Newfoundland on its first voyage 14–15 April 1912; 1,513 lives were lost. In 1985 it was located by robot submarine 4 km/2.5 mi down in an ocean canyon, preserved by the cold environment. In 1987 salvage operations began.

titanium strong, lightweight, silver-grey, metallic element, symbol Ti, atomic number 22, relative atomic mass 47.90. The ninth most abundant element in the Earth's crust, its compounds occur in practically all igneous rocks and their sedimentary deposits. It is very strong and resistant to corrosion, so it is used in building high-speed aircraft and spacecraft; it is also widely used in making alloys, as it unites with almost every metal except copper and aluminium.

Titian anglicized form of the name of Tiziano Vecellio *c.* 1487–1576. Italian painter, active in Venice, one of the greatest artists of the High Renaissance. In 1533 he became court painter to Charles V, Holy Roman emperor, whose son Philip II of Spain later became his patron. Titian's work is richly coloured, with inventive composition. He produced a vast number of portraits, religious paintings, and mythological scenes, including *Bacchus and Ariadne* 1520–23, *Venus and Adonis* 1554, and the *Entombment of Christ* 1559.

Titicaca lake in the Andes, 3,810 m/12,500 ft above sea level; area 8,300 sq km/3,200 sq mi, the largest lake in South America. It is divided between Bolivia (port at Guaqui) and Peru (ports at Puno and Huancane). It has enormous edible frogs.

Tito adopted name of Josip Broz 1892–1980. Yugoslav soldier and communist politician, in power from 1945. In World War II he organized the National Liberation Army to carry on guerrilla warfare against the German invasion 1941, and was created marshal 1943. As prime minister 1946–53 and president from 1953, he followed a foreign policy of 'positive neutralism'.

Titograd formerly (until 1948) *Podgorica* capital of Montenegro, Yugoslavia; population (1981) 132,300. Industries include metalworking, furniture-making, and tobacco. It was damaged in World War II and after rebuilding was renamed in honour of Marshal Tito. It was the birthplace of the Roman emperor Diocletian.

TNT abbreviation for *trinitrotoluene*,

$CH_3C_6H_2(NO_2)_3$, a powerful high explosive. It is a yellow solid, prepared in several isomeric forms from toluene by using sulphuric and nitric acids.

toad any of the more terrestrial warty-skinned members of the tailless amphibians (order Anura). The name commonly refers to members of the genus *Bufo*, family Bufonidae, which are found worldwide, except for the Australian and polar regions. Toads may grow up to 25 cm/10 in long.

toadstool inedible or poisonous type of ◊fungus with a fleshy, gilled fruiting body on a stalk.

tobacco any large-leaved plant of the genus *Nicotiana* of the nightshade family Solanaceae, native to tropical parts of the Americas. *N. tabacum* is widely cultivated in warm, dry climates for use in cigars and cigarettes, and in powdered form as snuff. The worldwide profits of the tobacco industry are estimated to be over £4 billion a year.

Tobago island in the West Indies; part of the republic of ◊Trinidad and Tobago.

Tobruk Libyan port; population (1984) 94,000. Occupied by Italy 1911, it was taken by Britain 1941 during World War II, and unsuccessfully besieged by Axis forces April–Dec 1941. It was captured by Germany June 1942 after the retreat of the main British force to Egypt, and this precipitated the replacement of Auchinleck by Montgomery as British commander.

toccata in music, a display piece for keyboard instruments, usually for the organ.

Tocqueville Alexis de 1805–1859. French politician and political scientist, author of the first analytical study of the US constitution, *De la Démocratie en Amérique/Democracy in America* 1835, and of a penetrating description of France before the Revolution, *L'Ancien Régime et la Révolution/The Old Regime and the Revolution* 1856.

Togo Republic of; country in W Africa, bordered W by Ghana, E by Benin, and N by Burkina Faso; *area* 56,800 sq km/21,930 sq mi; *capital* Lomé; *physical* two savanna plains, divided by range of hills NE–SW; coastal lagoons and marsh; *head of state* Lt-Gen Etienne Gnassingbé Eyadéma from 1967; *head of government* Joseph Kokou Koffigoh from 1991; *political system* transitional; *exports* phosphates, cocoa, coffee, coconuts; *population* (1990 est) 3,566,000; *languages* French (official), Ewe, Kabre; *recent history* German protectorate as Togoland from 1885 until captured by Anglo-French forces 1914; divided between Britain and France under League of Nations mandate 1922. British Togoland integrated with Ghana 1956; French Togoland achieved independence 1960 as Republic of Togo with Sylvanus Olympio as head of state. A military coup 1963 installed Nicolas Grunitzky as president, replaced 1967 by Lt-Gen Eyadéma in another (bloodless) coup. A further coup attempt 1986 failed. Eyadéma legalized opposition parties 1991.

Tohoku mountainous region of N Honshu island, Japan; population (1988) 9,745,000; area 66,971 sq km/25,867 sq mi. Timber, fruit, fish, and livestock are produced. The chief city is Sendai. Aomori in the north is linked to Hakodate on the island of Hokkaido by the *Seikan tunnel*, the world's longest underwater tunnel.

Tokyo capital of Japan, on Honshu Island; population (1989) 8,099,000, metropolitan area over 12 million. The Sumida River delta separates the city from its suburb of Honjo. It is Japan's main cultural and industrial centre (engineering, chemicals, textiles, electrical goods). Founded in the 16th century as *Yedo* (or *Edo*), it was renamed when the emperor moved his court there from Kyoto 1868. An earthquake 1923 killed 58,000 people and destroyed much of the city, which was again severely damaged by Allied bombing in World War II. The subsequent rebuilding has made it into one of the world's most modern cities.

Toledo city on the river Tagus, Castilla–La Mancha, central Spain; population (1982) 62,000. It was the capital of the Visigoth kingdom 534–711 (see ⟩Goth), then became a Moorish city, and was the Castilian capital 1085–1560.

Tolkien J(ohn) R(onald) R(euel) 1892–1973. English writer who created the fictional world of Middle Earth in *The Hobbit* 1937 and the trilogy *The Lord of the Rings* 1954–55, fantasy novels peopled with hobbits, dwarves, and strange magical creatures. His work developed a cult following in the 1960s and had many imitators.

Tolpuddle Martyrs six farm labourers of Tolpuddle, a village in Dorset, SW England, who were transported to Australia in 1834 for forming a trade union. After nationwide agitation they were pardoned two years later. They returned to England and all but one migrated to Canada.

Tolstoy Leo Nikolaievich 1828–1910. Russian novelist who wrote *War and Peace* 1863–69 and *Anna Karenina* 1873–77. From 1880 Tolstoy underwent a profound spiritual crisis and took up various moral positions, including passive resistance to evil, rejection of authority (religious or civil) and private ownership, and a return to basic mystical Christianity. He was excommunicated by the Orthodox Church, and his later works were banned.

Toltec member of an ancient American Indian people who ruled much of Mexico in the 10th–12th centuries, with their capital and religious centre at Tula, NE of Mexico City. They also constructed a similar city at Chichén Itzá in Yucatán. After the Toltecs' fall in the 13th century, the Aztecs took over much of their former territory, except for the regions regained by the Maya.

tomato annual plant *Lycopersicon esculentum* of the nightshade family Solanaceae, native to South America. It is widely cultivated for the many-seeded red fruit (technically a berry), used in salads and cooking.

ton imperial unit of mass. The *long ton*, used in the UK, is 1,016 kg/2,240 lb; the *short ton*, used in the USA, is 907 kg/2,000 lb. The *metric ton* or *tonne* is 1,000 kg/2,205 lb.

ton in shipping, unit of volume equal to 2.83 cubic metres/100 cubic feet. *Gross tonnage* is the total internal volume of a ship in tons; *net register tonnage* is the volume used for carrying cargo or passengers. *Displacement tonnage* is the weight of the vessel, in terms of the number of imperial tons of seawater displaced when the ship is loaded to its load line; it is used to describe warships.

tone poem in music, another name for ⟩symphonic poem as used, for example, by Richard Strauss.

Tonga Kingdom of (or *Friendly Islands*); country in the SW Pacific, in Polynesia; *area* 750 sq km/290 sq mi; *capital* Nuku'alofa (on Tongatapu island); *physical* three groups of islands, mostly coral formations, but actively volcanic in W; *head of state* King Taufa'ahau Tupou IV from 1965; *head of government* Baron Vaea from 1991; *political system* constitutional monarchy; *population* (1988 est) 95,000; *languages* Tongan (official), English; *recent history* became a British protectorate 1900; independence achieved from Britain within the Commonwealth 1970. Calls for reform of absolutist power 1990.

tonne the metric ton of 1,000 kg/2,204.6 lb; equivalent to 0.9842 of an imperial ⟩ton.

tonsillitis inflammation of the ⟩tonsils.

tonsils in higher vertebrates, masses of lymphoid tissue situated at the back of the mouth and throat (palatine tonsils), and on the rear surface of the tongue (lingual tonsils). The tonsils contain many ⟩lymphocytes and are part of the body's defence system against infection.

Tonton Macoute member of a private army of death squads on Haiti. The Tontons Macoutes were initially organized by François ⟩Duvalier, president of Haiti 1957–71, and continued to terrorize the population under his successor J C Duvalier. It is alleged that the organization continued to operate after Duvalier's exile to France.

tool any implement that gives the user a mechanical advantage, such as a hammer or a saw; a *machine tool* is a tool operated by power. Tools are the basis of industrial production; the chief machine tool is the lathe. The industrial potential of a country is often calculated by the number of machine tools available. Automatic control of machine tools, a milestone in industrial development, is known as ⟩automation, and electronic control is called robotics (see ⟩robot).

tooth in vertebrates, one of a set of hard, bonelike structures in the mouth, used for biting and chewing food, and in defence and aggression. Adult humans have 32 teeth: two incisors, one canine (eye tooth), two premolars, and three molars on each side of each jaw. Each tooth consists of an enamel coat (hardened calcium deposits), dentine (a thick, bonelike layer), and an inner pulp cavity, housing nerves and blood vessels. Mammalian teeth have roots surrounded by cementum, which fuses them into their sockets in the jawbones. The neck of the tooth is covered by the ⚲gum, while the enamel-covered crown protrudes above the gum line.

topaz mineral, aluminium fluosilicate, $Al_2SiO_4(F,OH)_2$. It is usually yellow, but pink if it has been heated, and is used as a gemstone when transparent. It ranks 8 on the Mohs' scale of hardness.

topology branch of geometry that deals with those properties of a figure that remain unchanged even when the figure is transformed (bent, stretched) – for example, when a square painted on a rubber sheet is deformed by distorting the sheet. Topology has scientific applications, as in the study of turbulence in flowing fluids. The map of the London Underground system is an example of the topological representation of a network; connectivity (the way the lines join together) is preserved, but shape and size are not.

Torah in ⚲Judaism, the first five books of the Hebrew Bible (Christian Old Testament), which are ascribed to Moses. It contains a traditional history of the world from the Creation to the death of Moses; it also includes the Hebrew people's ⚲covenant with their one God, rules for religious observance, and guidelines for social conduct, including the Ten Commandments.

tornado extremely violent revolving storm with swirling, funnel-shaped clouds, caused by a rising column of warm air propelled by strong wind. A tornado can rise to a great height, but with a diameter of only a few hundred metres or yards or less. Tornadoes move with wind speeds of 160–480 kph/ 100–300 mph, destroying everything in their path. They are common in the central USA and Australia.

Toronto (North American Indian 'place of meeting') known until 1834 as *York* port and capital of Ontario, Canada, on Lake Ontario; metropolitan population (1985) 3,427,000. It is Canada's main industrial and commercial centre (banking, shipbuilding, cars, farm machinery, food processing, publishing) and also a cultural centre, with theatres and a film industry. A French fort was established 1749, and the site became the provincial capital 1793.

torpedo self-propelled underwater missile, invented 1866 by British engineer Robert Whitehead. Modern torpedoes are homing missiles; some resemble mines in that they lie on the seabed until activated by the acoustic signal of a passing ship. A television camera enables them to be remotely controlled, and in the final stage of attack

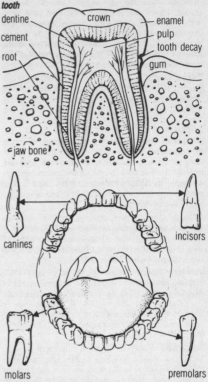

tooth

dentine — crown — enamel
cement — pulp
tooth decay
root — gum

jaw bone

canines — incisors

molars — premolars

they lock on to the radar or sonar signals of the target ship.

torpedo or *electric ray* any species of the order Torpediniformes of mainly tropical rays (cartilaginous fishes), whose electric organs between the pectoral fin and the head can give a powerful shock. They can grow to 180 cm/6 ft in length.

torque the turning effect of force on an object. A turbine produces a torque that turns an electricity generator in a power station. Torque is measured by multiplying the force by its perpendicular distance from the turning point.

Torquemada Tomás de 1420–1498. Spanish Dominican monk, confessor to Queen Isabella I. In 1483 he revived the ⚲Inquisition on her behalf, and at least 2,000 'heretics' were burned; Torquemada also expelled the Jews from Spain 1492, with a resultant decline of the economy.

tort in law, a wrongful act for which someone can be sued for damages in a civil court. It includes such acts as libel, trespass, injury done to someone (whether intentionally or by negligence), and inducement to break a contract (although breach of contract itself is not a tort).

tortoise reptile of the order Chelonia, family Testudinidae, with the body enclosed in a hard shell. Tortoises are related to the ▷terrapins and ▷turtles, and range in length from 10 cm/4 in to 150 cm/5 ft. The shell consists of a curved upper carapace and flattened lower plastron joined at the sides. The head and limbs may be withdrawn into it when the tortoise is in danger. Most land tortoises are herbivorous, feeding on plant material, and have no teeth. The mouth forms a sharp-edged beak. Eggs are laid in warm earth in great numbers, and are not incubated by the mother. Some tortoises are known to live for 150 years.

torture infliction of bodily pain to extort evidence or confession. Legally abolished in England about 1640, torture was allowed in Scotland until 1708 and until 1789 in France. In the 20th century torture is widely (though, in most countries, unofficially) used.

Tory Party the forerunner of the British ▷Conservative Party about 1680–1830. It was the party of the squire and parson, as opposed to the Whigs (supported by the trading classes and Nonconformists). The name is still applied colloquially to the Conservative Party. In the USA a Tory was an opponent of the break with Britain in the War of American Independence 1775–83.

Toscana Italian name for the region of ▷Tuscany.

totalitarianism government control of all activities within a country, overtly political or otherwise, as in fascist or communist dictatorships. Examples of totalitarian regimes are Italy under Benito ▷Mussolini 1922–45; Germany under Adolph ▷Hitler 1933–45; the USSR under Joseph ▷Stalin from the 1930s until his death in 1953; more recently Romania under Nicolae ▷Ceauşescu 1974–89.

totemism the belief in individual or clan kinship with an animal, plant, or object. This totem is sacred to those concerned, and they are forbidden to eat or desecrate it; marriage within the clan is usually forbidden. Totemism occurs among Pacific Islanders and Australian Aborigines, and was formerly prevalent throughout Europe, Africa, and Asia. Most North and South American Indian societies had totems as well.

toucan any South and Central American forest-dwelling bird of the family Ramphastidae. Toucans have very large, brilliantly coloured beaks and often handsome plumage. They live in small flocks and eat fruits, seeds, and insects. They nest in holes in trees, where the female lays 2–4 eggs; both parents care for the eggs and young. There are 37 species, ranging from 30 cm/1 ft to 60cm/2ft in size.

Toulon port and capital of Var *département*, SE France, on the Mediterranean Sea, 48 km/30 mi SE of Marseille; population (1983) 410,000. It is the chief Mediterranean naval station of France. Industries include oil refining, chemicals, furniture, and clothing. Toulon was the Roman *Telo Martius* and was made a port by Henry IV. It was occupied by the British 1793, and Napoleon first distinguished himself in driving them out. In World War II the French fleet was scuttled here to avoid its passing to German control.

Toulouse capital of Haute-Garonne *département*, SW France, on the river Garonne SE of Bordeaux; population (1982) 541,000. The chief industries are textiles and aircraft construction (Concorde was built here). Toulouse was the capital of the Visigoths (see ▷Goth) and later of Aquitaine 781–843.

Toulouse-Lautrec Henri Marie Raymond de 1864–1901. French artist, associated with the Impressionists. He was active in Paris, where he painted entertainers and prostitutes. From 1891 his lithograph posters were a great success.

Toussaint L'Ouverture Pierre Dominique *c.* 1743–1803. Haitian revolutionary leader, born a slave. He joined the insurrection of 1791 against the French colonizers and was made governor by the revolutionary French government. He expelled the Spanish and British, but when the French emperor Napoleon reimposed slavery he revolted, was captured, and died in prison in France.

toxic shock syndrome rare condition marked by rapid onset of fever, vomiting, and low blood pressure, sometimes leading to death. It is caused by a toxin of the bacterium *Staphylococcus aureus*, normally harmlessly present in the body, which may accumulate, for example, if a tampon used by a woman during a period remains unchanged beyond four to six hours.

toxic waste dumped hazardous substance.

trace element chemical element necessary in minute quantities for the health of a plant or animal. For example, magnesium, which occurs in chlorophyll, is essential to photosynthesis, and iodine is needed by the thyroid gland of mammals for making hormones that control growth and body chemistry.

trachea tube that forms an airway in air-breathing animals. In land-living ▷vertebrates, including humans, it is also known as the *windpipe* and runs from the larynx to the upper part of the chest. Its diameter is about 1.5 cm/0.6 in and its length 10 cm/4 in. It is strong and flexible, and reinforced by rings of ▷cartilage. In the upper chest, the trachea branches into two tubes: the left and right bronchi, which enter the lungs. Insects have a branching network of tubes called tracheae, which conduct air from holes (spiracles) in the body surface to all the body tissues. The finest branches of the tracheae are called tracheoles.

trachoma chronic eye infection, resembling severe ▷conjunctivitis. The conjunctiva becomes inflamed, with scarring and formation of pus, and there may be damage to the cornea. It is caused by a viruslike organism (chlamydia), and is a disease of dry tropical regions. Although it responds well to antibiotics, numerically it remains the biggest single cause of blindness worldwide.

Tracy Spencer 1900–1967. US actor distinguished for his understated, seemingly effortless, natural performances. His films include *Captains Courageous* 1937 and *Boys' Town* 1938 (for both of which he won Academy Awards), and he starred with Katharine Hepburn in nine films, including *Adam's Rib* 1949 and *Guess Who's Coming to Dinner* 1967, his final appearance.

tradescantia any plant of the genus *Tradescantia* of the family Commelinaceae, native to North and Central America. The spiderwort *T. virginiana* is a cultivated garden plant; the wandering jew *T. albiflora* is a common house plant, with green oval leaves tinged with pink or purple or silver-striped.

Trades Union Congress (TUC) voluntary organization of trade unions, founded in the UK 1868, in which delegates of affiliated unions meet annually to consider matters affecting their members. In 1991 there were 78 affiliated unions, with an aggregate membership of 10.4 million.

trade union organization of employed workers formed to undertake collective bargaining with employers and to try to achieve improved working conditions for its members. Attitudes of government to unions and of unions to management vary greatly from country to country. Probably the most effective trade-union system is that of Sweden, and the most internationally known is the Polish ◊Solidarity.

trade wind prevailing wind that blows towards the equator from the northeast and southeast. Trade winds are caused by hot air rising at the equator and the consequent movement of air from north and south to take its place. The winds are deflected towards the west because of the Earth's west-to-east rotation. The unpredictable calms known as the ◊doldrums lie at their convergence.

Trafalgar, Battle of battle 21 Oct 1805 in the ◊Napoleonic Wars. The British fleet under Admiral Nelson defeated a Franco-Spanish fleet; Nelson was mortally wounded. The victory laid the foundation for British naval supremacy throughout the 19th century. It is named after Cape Trafalgar, a low headland in SW Spain, near the western entrance to the Straits of Gibraltar.

tragedy in the theatre, a play dealing with a serious theme, traditionally one in which a character meets disaster either as a result of personal failings or circumstances beyond his or her control. Historically the Greek view of tragedy, as defined by Aristotle and expressed by the great tragedians Aeschylus, Euripides, and Sophocles, has been predominant in the western tradition. In the 20th century tragedies in the narrow Greek sense of dealing with exalted personages in an elevated manner have

virtually died out. Tragedy has been replaced by dramas with 'tragic' implications or overtones, as in the work of Ibsen, O'Neill, Tennessee Williams, Pinter, and Osborne, for example, or by the hybrid tragicomedy.

tramway transport system for use in cities, where wheeled vehicles run along parallel rails. Trams are powered either by electric conductor rails below ground or by conductor arms connected to overhead wires. Greater manoeuvrability is achieved with the trolley bus, similarly powered by conductor arms overhead but without tracks.

tranquillizer common name for any drug for reducing anxiety or tension (anxiolytic), such as ◊benzodiazepines, barbiturates, antidepressants, and beta-blockers. The use of drugs to control anxiety is becoming much less popular, because most of the drugs used are capable of inducing dependence.

transcendental meditation (TM) technique of focusing the mind, based in part on Hindu meditation. Meditators are given a mantra (a special word or phrase) to repeat over and over to themselves; such meditation is believed to benefit the practitioner by relieving stress and inducing a feeling of wellbeing and relaxation. It was introduced to the West by Maharishi Mahesh Yogi and popularized by the Beatles in the late 1960s.

transcription in living cells, the process by which the information for the synthesis of a protein is transferred from the ◊DNA strand on which it is carried to the messenger ◊RNA strand involved in the actual synthesis.

transformer device in which, by electromagnetic induction, an alternating current (AC) of one voltage is transformed to another voltage, without change of ◊frequency. Transformers are widely used in electrical apparatus of all kinds, and in particular in power transmission where high voltages and low currents are utilized.

transistor solid-state electronic component, made of ◊semiconductor material, with three or more ◊electrodes, that can regulate a current passing through it. A transistor can act as an amplifier, ◊oscillator, photocell, or switch, and (unlike earlier thermionic valves) usually operates on a very small amount of power. Transistors commonly consist of a tiny sandwich of ◊germanium or ◊silicon, alternate layers having different electrical properties.

transition metal any of a group of metallic elements that have incomplete inner electron shells and exhibit variable valency – for example, cobalt, copper, iron, and molybdenum. They are excellent conductors of electricity, and generally form highly coloured compounds.

Transkei largest of South Africa's Bantustans, or homelands, extending northeast from the Great Kei River, on the coast of Cape Province, to the border of Natal; area 43,808 sq km/16,910 sq mi; population (1985) 3,000,000, including small white and Asian minorities. It became self-governing 1963, and achieved full 'independence' 1976. Its capital is Umtata, and it has a port at Mnganzana. It is one of the two homelands of the Xhosa people (the other is Ciskei), and products include livestock, coffee, tea, sugar, maize, and sorghum. Its government consists of a president (paramount chief Tutor Nyangelizwe Vulinolela Ndamase from 1986) and single-chamber national assembly.

translation in living cells, the process by which proteins are synthesized. During translation, the information coded as a sequence of nucleotides in messenger ⍟RNA is transformed into a sequence of amino acids in a peptide chain. The process involves the 'translation' of the ⍟genetic code. See also ⍟transcription.

transpiration the loss of water from a plant by evaporation. Most water is lost from the leaves through pores known as ⍟stomata, whose primary function is to allow ⍟gas exchange between the plant's internal tissues and the atmosphere. Transpiration from the leaf surfaces causes a continuous upward flow of water from the roots via the ⍟xylem, which is known as the transpiration stream.

transplant in medicine, the transfer of a tissue or organ from one human being to another or from one part of the body to another (skin grafting). In most organ transplants, the operation is for life-saving purposes, though the immune system tends to reject foreign tissue. Careful matching and immunosuppressive drugs must be used, but these are not always successful.

transportation in the UK, a former punishment which involved sending convicted persons to overseas British territories either for life or for shorter periods. It was introduced in England towards the end of the 17th century and was abolished 1857 after many thousands had been transported, mostly to Australia. It was also used for punishment of criminals by France until 1938.

Trans-Siberian Railway railway line connecting the cities of European Russia with Omsk, Novosibirsk, Irkutsk, and Khabarovsk, and terminating at Vladivostok on the Pacific. It was built 1891–1905; from Leningrad to Vladivostok is about 8,700 km/5,400 mi. A 3,102 km/1,928 mi northern line was completed 1984 after ten years' work.

transubstantiation in Christian theology, the doctrine that the whole substance of the bread and wine changes into the substance of the body and blood of Jesus when consecrated in the ⍟Eucharist.

transuranic element or *transuranium element* chemical element with an atomic number of 93 or more – that is, with a greater number of protons in the nucleus than has uranium. All transuranic elements are radioactive. Neptunium and plutonium are found in nature; the others are synthesized in nuclear reactions.

Transvaal province of NE South Africa, bordering Zimbabwe to the north; area 262,499 sq km/101,325 sq mi; population (1985) 7,532,000. Its capital is Pretoria, and towns include Johannesburg, Germiston, Brakpan, Springs, Benoni, Krugersdorp, and Roodepoort. Products include diamonds, coal, iron ore, copper, lead, tin, manganese, meat, maize, tobacco, and fruit. The main rivers are the Vaal and Limpopo with their tributaries. Swaziland forms an enclave on the Natal border. It was settled by *Voortrekkers*, Boers who left Cape Colony in the Great Trek from 1831. Independence was recognized by Britain 1852, until the settlers' difficulties with the conquered Zulus led to British annexation 1877. It was made a British colony after the South African War 1899–1902, and in 1910 became a province of the Union of South Africa.

Transylvania mountainous area of central and NW Romania, bounded to the south by the Transylvanian Alps (an extension of the Carpathians), formerly a province, with its capital at Cluj. It was part of Hungary from about 1000 until its people voted to unite with Romania 1918. It is the home of the vampire legends.

treason act of betrayal, in particular against the sovereign or the state to which the offender owes allegiance. Treason is punishable in Britain by death. It includes: plotting the wounding or death of the sovereign or his or her spouse or heir; levying war against the sovereign in his or her realm; and giving aid or comfort to the sovereign's enemies in wartime.

treasure trove in England, any gold or silver, plate or bullion, found concealed in a house or the ground, the owner being unknown. Normally, treasure originally hidden, and not abandoned, belongs to the crown, but if the treasure was casually lost or intentionally abandoned, the first finder is entitled to it against all but the true owner. Objects buried with no intention of recovering them, for example in a burial mound, do not rank as treasure trove, and belong to the owner of the ground.

treaty written agreement between two or more states. Treaties take effect either immediately on signature or, more often, on ratification. Ratification involves a further exchange of documents and usually takes place after the internal governments have approved the terms of the treaty. Treaties are binding in international law, the rules being laid down in the Vienna Convention on the Law of Treaties 1969.

tree perennial plant with a woody stem, usually a single stem or 'trunk', made up of ⍟wood and protected by an outer layer of ⍟bark. It absorbs water through a ⍟root system. There is no clear dividing line between shrubs and trees, but sometimes a minimum height of 6 m/20 ft is used to define a tree.

tree creeper small, short-legged bird of the family Certhiidae, which spirals with a mouselike movement up tree trunks searching for food with its thin downcurved beak.

trefoil any of several ⟡clover plants of the genus *Trifolium* of the pea family Leguminosae, the leaves of which are divided into three leaflets. The name is also used for other plants with leaves divided into three lobes.

Trent, Council of conference held 1545–63 by the Roman Catholic Church at Trento, N Italy initiating the ⟡Counter-Reformation; see also ⟡Reformation.

Trentino–Alto Adige autonomous region of N Italy, comprising the provinces of Bolzano and Trento; capital Trento; chief towns Trento in the Italian-speaking southern area, and Bolzano-Bozen in the northern German-speaking area of South ⟡Tirol (the region was Austrian until ceded to Italy 1919); area 13,600 sq km/5,250 sq mi; population (1990) 891,400.

Treurnicht Andries Petrus 1921– . South African Conservative Party politician. A former minister of the Dutch Reformed Church, he was elected to the South African parliament as a National Party member 1971 but left it 1982 to form a new right-wing Conservative Party, opposed to any dilution of the ⟡apartheid system.

Trevithick Richard 1771–1833. British engineer, constructor of a steam road locomotive 1801 and the first steam engine to run on rails 1804.

Triassic period of geological time 248–213 million years ago, the first period of the Mesozoic era. The continents were fused together to form the world continent Pangaea. Triassic sediments contain remains of early dinosaurs and other reptiles now extinct. By late Triassic times, the first mammals had evolved.

tribal society way of life in which people govern their own affairs as independent local communities of families and clans without central government organizations or states. They are found in parts of SE Asia, New Guinea, South America, and Africa.

tribunal strictly, a court of justice, but used in English law for a body appointed by the government to arbitrate in disputes, or investigate certain matters. Tribunals usually consist of a lawyer as chair, sitting with two lay assessors.

tribune Roman magistrate of ⟡plebeian family, elected annually to defend the interests of the common people; only two were originally chosen in 494 BC, but there were later ten. They could veto the decisions of any other magistrate.

triceratops any of a genus *Triceratops* of massive, horned dinosaurs of the order Ornithischia. They had three horns and a neck frill and were up to 8 m/25 ft long; they lived in the Cretaceous period.

Trieste port on the Adriatic, opposite Venice, in Friuli-Venezia-Giulia, Italy; population (1988) 237,000, including a large Slovene minority. Trieste was under Austrian rule from 1382 (apart from Napoleonic occupation 1809–14) until transferred to Italy 1918. It was claimed after World War II by

Yugoslavia, and the city and surrounding territory were divided 1954 between Italy and Yugoslavia.

triggerfish any marine bony fish of the family Balistidae, with a laterally compressed body, up to 60 cm/2 ft long, and deep belly. They have small mouths but strong jaws and teeth. The first spine on the dorsal fin locks into an erect position, which allows them to fasten themselves securely in crevices for protection, and can only be moved by depressing the smaller third ('trigger') spine.

triglyceride chemical name for ⟡fat.

trigonometry branch of mathematics that solves problems relating to plane and spherical triangles. Its principles are based on the fixed proportions of sides for a particular angle in a right-angled triangle, the simplest of which are known as the ⟡sine, ⟡cosine, and tangent (so-called trigonometrical ratios). It is of practical importance in navigation, surveying, and simple harmonic motion in physics.

Trimurti the Hindu triad of gods, representing the Absolute Spirit in its three aspects: Brahma, personifying creation; Vishnu, preservation; and Siva, destruction.

Trinidad and Tobago Republic of; country in the West Indies, off the coast of Venezuela; *area* Trinidad 4,828 sq km/1,864 sq mi; Tobago 300 sq km/116 sq mi; *capital* Port-of-Spain; *physical* comprises two main islands and some smaller ones; coastal swamps and hills E–W; *head of state* Noor Hassanali from 1987; *head of government* Patrick Manning from 1991; *political system* democratic republic; *exports* oil, petroleum products, chemicals, sugar, cocoa; *population* (1990 est) 1,270,000 (African descent 40%, Indian 40%, European 16%, Chinese and others 2%); 1.2 million on Trinidad; *languages* English (official), Hindi, French, Spanish; *recent history* Trinidad and Tobago united as British colony 1888; achieved internal self-government 1959. Independence achieved from Britain within the Commonwealth 1962; became a republic 1976. Antigovernment coup 1990 defeated.

Trinity in Christianity, the union of three persons – Father, Son, and Holy Ghost/Spirit – in one godhead. The precise meaning of the doctrine has been the cause of unending dispute, and was the chief cause of the split between the Eastern Orthodox and Roman Catholic churches. *Trinity Sunday* occurs on the Sunday after Pentecost.

triode three-electrode thermionic ⟡valve containing an anode and a cathode (as does a ⟡diode) with an additional negatively biased control grid. Small variations in voltage on the grid bias result in large variations in the current. The triode was commonly used in amplifiers but has now been almost entirely superseded by the ⟡transistor.

Triple Alliance pact from 1882 between Germany, Austria-Hungary, and Italy to offset the power of

Russia and France. It was last renewed 1912, but during World War I Italy's initial neutrality gradually changed and it denounced the alliance 1915. The term also refers to other alliances: 1668 – England, Holland, and Sweden; 1717 – Britain, Holland, and France (joined 1718 by Austria); 1788 – Britain, Prussia, and Holland; 1795 – Britain, Russia, and Austria.

Triple Entente alliance of Britain, France, and Russia 1907–17. In 1911 this became a military alliance and formed the basis of the Allied powers in World War I against the Central Powers, Germany and Austria-Hungary.

triple jump field event in athletics comprising a hop, step and jump sequence from a takeoff board into a sandpit landing area measuring 8 metres (minimum) in length. The takeoff board is usually 13 metres from the landing area. Each competitor has six trials and the winner is the one with the longest jump.

Tripoli (Arabic *Tarabolus al-Gharb*) capital and chief port of Libya, on the Mediterranean; population (1982) 980,000. Products include olive oil, fruit, fish, and textiles. Tripoli was founded about the 7th century BC by Phoenicians from Oea (now Tripoli in Lebanon). It was a base for Axis powers during World War II. In 1986 it was bombed by the US Air Force in retaliation for international guerrilla activity.

Tripura state of NE India since 1972, formerly a princely state, between Bangladesh and Assam; *area* 10,500 sq km/4,053 sq mi; *capital* Agartala; *features* agriculture on a rotation system in the rainforest, now being superseded by modern methods; *products* rice, cotton, tea, sugar cane; steel, jute; *population* (1991) 2,744,800; *language* Bengali; *religion* Hindu.

trireme ancient Greek warship with three banks of oars as well as sails, 38 m/115 ft long. They were used at the battle of Salamis and by the Romans until the 4th century AD.

Tristan hero of Celtic legend who fell in love with Iseult, the bride he was sent to win for his uncle King Mark of Cornwall; the story became part of the Arthurian cycle and is the subject of Wagner's opera *Tristan und Isolde*.

triticale cereal crop of recent origin that is a cross between wheat *Triticum* and rye *Secale*. It can produce heavy yields of high-protein grain, principally for use as animal feed.

triumvir one of a group of three administrators sharing power in ancient Rome, as in the *First Triumvirate* 60 BC: Caesar, Pompey, Crassus; and *Second Triumvirate* 43 BC: Augustus, Antony, and Lepidus.

Trobriand Islands group of coral islands in the Solomon Sea, forming part of the province of Milne Bay, Papua New Guinea; chief town Losuia; area 440 sq km/170 sq mi.

trogon any species of the order Trogoniformes of tropical birds, up to 50 cm/1.7 ft long, with resplendent plumage, living in the Americas and Afro-Asia. Most striking is the ⋄quetzal.

Trojan horse seemingly innocuous but treacherous gift from an enemy. In Greek legend, during the siege of Troy, the Greek army left an enormous wooden horse outside the gate of the city and retreated. When the Trojans had brought it in, Greek soldiers emerged from within the hollow horse and opened the city gates to enable it to be captured.

Trollope Anthony 1815–1882. English novelist who delineated provincial English middle-class society in his Barchester series of novels. *The Warden* 1855 began the series, which includes *Barchester Towers* 1857, *Doctor Thorne* 1858, and *The Last Chronicle of Barset* 1867. His political novels include *Can You Forgive Her?* 1864, *Phineas Finn* 1867–69, and *The Prime Minister* 1875–76.

trombone ⋄brass wind musical instrument developed from the sackbut. It consists of a tube bent double, varied notes being obtained by an inner sliding tube. Usual sizes of trombone are alto, tenor, bass, and contra-bass.

tropics the area between the tropics of Cancer and Capricorn, defined by the parallels of latitude approximately 23°30' N and S of the equator. They are the limits of the area of Earth's surface in which the Sun can be directly overhead. The mean monthly temperature is over 20°C/68°F.

tropism or *tropic movement* the directional growth of a plant, or part of a plant, in response to an external stimulus. If the movement is directed towards the stimulus it is described as positive; if away from it, it is negative. *Geotropism*, the response of plants to gravity, causes the root (positively geotropic) to grow downwards, and the stem (negatively geotropic) to grow upwards. *Phototropism* occurs in response to light, *hydrotropism* to water, *chemotropism* to a chemical stimulus, and *thigmotropism*, or *haptotropism*, to physical contact, as in the tendrils of climbing plants when they touch a support and then grow around it.

troposphere lower part of the Earth's ⋄atmosphere extending about 10.5 km/6.5 mi from the Earth's surface, in which temperature decreases with height to about –60°C/–76°F except in local layers of temperature inversion. The *tropopause* is the upper boundary of the troposphere, above which the temperature increases slowly with height within the atmosphere.

Trotsky Leon. Adopted name of Lev Davidovitch Bronstein 1879–1940. Russian revolutionary. He joined the Bolshevik party and took a leading part in the seizure of power 1917 and raising the Red Army that fought the Civil War 1918–20. In the struggle for power that followed ⋄Lenin's death 1924, ⋄Stalin defeated Trotsky, and this and other differences with the Communist Party led to his exile 1929. He settled in Mexico, where he was assassinated with an ice pick at Stalin's instigation. Trotsky believed in world revolution and in permanent revolution, and was an uncompromising, if liberal, idealist.

Trotskyism form of Marxism advocated by Leon Trotsky. Its central concept is that of *permanent revolution*. In his view a proletarian revolution, leading to a socialist society, could not be achieved in isolation, so it would be necessary to spark off further revolutions throughout Europe and ultimately worldwide. This was in direct opposition to the Stalinist view that socialism should be built and consolidated within individual countries.

troubadour one of a group of poet musicians in Provence and S France in the 12th–13th centuries, which included both nobles and wandering minstrels. The troubadours originated a type of lyric poetry devoted to themes of courtly love and the idealization of women and to glorifying the deeds of their patrons, reflecting the chivalric ideals of the period. Little is known of their music, which was passed down orally.

trout any of various bony fishes in the salmon family, popular for sport and food. They are native to the northern hemisphere. The common trout *Salmo trutta* is widely distributed in Europe, occurring in British fresh and coastal waters. Sea trout are generally silvery and river trout olive-brown, both with spotted fins and sides.

Troy (Latin *Ilium*) ancient city of Asia Minor, besieged in the ten-year Trojan War (mid-13th century BC), which the poet Homer described in the *Iliad*. The city fell to the Greeks, who first used the stratagem of the ♢Trojan horse. The site of Troy was excavated by Heinrich ♢Schliemann 1871–73.

Truffaut François 1932–1984. French New Wave film director and actor, formerly a critic. A popular, romantic, and intensely humane filmmaker, he wrote and directed a series of semi-autobiographical films starring Jean-Pierre Léaud, beginning with *Les Quatre Cent Coups/The 400 Blows* 1959. His other films include *Jules et Jim* 1961, *Fahrenheit 451* 1966, *L'Enfant sauvage/The Wild Child* 1970, and *La Nuit américaine/Day for Night* 1973 (Academy Award).

truffle subterranean fungus of the order Tuberales. Certain species are valued as edible delicacies; in particular, *Tuber melanosporum*, generally found growing under oak trees. It is native to the Périgord region of France but cultivated in other areas as well. It is rounded, blackish brown, covered with warts externally, and with blackish flesh.

Truk group of about 55 volcanic islands surrounded by a coral reef in the E Caroline islands of the W Pacific, forming one of the four states of the Federated States of Micronesia. Fish and copra are the main products.

Truman Harry S 1884–1972. 33rd president of the USA 1945–53, a Democrat. In Jan 1945 he became vice president to F D Roosevelt, and president when Roosevelt died in April that year. He used the atom bomb against Japan, launched the ♢Marshall Plan to restore W Europe's economy, and nurtured the European Community and NATO (including the rearmament of West Germany).

trumpet small high-register ♢brass wind instrument; a doubled tube with valves. Before the 19th century, the trumpet had no valves and was restricted to harmonies.

trumpeter any South American bird of the genus *Psophia*, family Psophiidae, up to 50 cm/20 in tall, related to the cranes. Trumpeters have long legs, a short bill, and dark plumage. The name is also applied to the trumpeter ♢swan.

trust arrangement whereby a person or group of people (the trustee(s)) holds property for others (the beneficiaries) entitled to the beneficial interest. A trust can be a *legal arrangement* under which A is empowered to administer property belonging to B for the benefit of C. A and B may be the same person; B and C may not. A ♢*unit trust* holds and manages a number of marketable securities; by buying a 'unit' in such a trust, the purchaser has a proportionate interest in each of the securities so that his or her risk is spread. Nowadays, an *investment trust* is not a trust, but a public company investing in marketable securities money subscribed by its shareholders who receive dividends from the income earned. A *business trust* is formed by linking several companies to eliminate competition.

trust territory country or area formerly held under the United Nations trusteeship system to be prepared for independence, either former ♢mandates, territories taken over by the Allies in World War II, or those voluntarily placed under the UN by the administering state.

trypanosomiasis any of several debilitating long-term diseases caused by a trypanosome (protozoan of the genus *Trypanosoma*). They include sleeping sickness (nagana) in Africa, transmitted by the bites of ♢tsetse flies, and Chagas' disease in the Americas, spread by assassin bugs.

tsar the Russian imperial title 1547–1721 (although it continued in popular use to 1917), derived from Latin *caesar*.

Tselinograd former name (until 1961) *Akmolinsk* commercial and industrial city in N Kazakhstan, on the river Ishim; population (1983) 253,000. It is situated at a railway junction and produces agricultural machinery, textiles, and chemicals.

tsetse fly blood-feeding insect that carries trypanosomiasis, or sleeping sickness. It is a serious pest in parts of W Africa and is partly responsible for the transhumance (movement from pasture to pasture) of the Fulani people. The disease can kill both animals and people. Moist swampy conditions favour the fly.

Tswana member of the majority ethnic group living in Botswana. The Tswana are divided into four subgroups: the Bakwena, the Bamangwato, the Bangwaketse, and the Batawana. Traditionally they are rural-dwelling farmers, though many now leave their homes to work as migrant labourers in South African industries. The Tswana language belongs to the Bantu branch of the Niger-Congo family.

Tuamotu Archipelago two parallel ranges of 78 atolls, part of ◊French Polynesia; area 690 sq km/266 sq mi; population (1983) 11,800, including the ◊Gambier Islands to the E. The atolls stretch 2,100 km/1,300 mi N and E of the Society Islands. The administrative headquarters is Apataki. The largest atoll is Rangiroa, the most significant is Hao; they produce pearl shell and copra. Mururoa and Fangataufa atolls to the SE have been a French nuclear test site since 1966. Spanish explorers landed 1606, and the islands were annexed by France 1881.

tuba large bass ◊brass wind musical instrument of the cornet family. The *Wagner tuba* combines features of the euphonium and french horn.

tuber swollen region of an underground stem or root, usually modified for storing food. The potato is a *stem tuber*, as shown by the presence of terminal and lateral buds, the 'eyes' of the potato. *Root tubers*, for example dahlias, developed from adventitious roots (growing from the stem, not from other roots), lack these. Both types of tuber can give

tuber

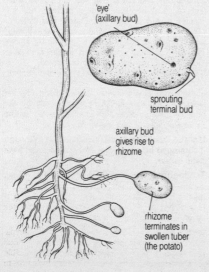

'eye' (axillary bud)

sprouting terminal bud

axillary bud gives rise to rhizome

rhizome terminates in swollen tuber (the potato)

rise to new individuals and so provide a means of ◊vegetative reproduction.

tuberculosis (TB) formerly known as *consumption* or *phthisis* infectious disease caused by the bacillus *Mycobacterium tuberculosis*. It takes several forms, of which pulmonary tuberculosis is by far the most common. A vaccine, ◊BCG, was developed around 1920 and the first antituberculosis drug, streptomycin, in 1944.

Tubuai Islands or *Austral Islands* chain of volcanic islands and reefs 1,300 km/800 mi long in ◊French Polynesia, S of the Society Islands; area 148 sq km/57 sq mi; population (1983) 6,300. The main settlement is Mataura on Tubuai. They were visited by Captain Cook 1777 and annexed by France 1880.

TUC abbreviation for ◊*Trades Union Congress.*

Tudjman Franjo 1922– . Croatian nationalist leader and historian, president from 1990. As leader of the centre-right Croatian Democratic Union (HDZ), he led the fight for Croatian independence. During the 1991–92 civil war his troops were hampered by lack of arms and the military superiority of the Serb-dominated federal army. In Jan 1992, Croatia's independence was recognized by the European Community.

Tudor dynasty English dynasty 1485–1603, descended from the Welsh Owen Tudor (*c.* 1400–1461), second husband of Catherine of Valois (widow of Henry V of England).

tulip plant of the genus *Tulipa*, family Liliaceae, usually with single goblet-shaped flowers on the end of an upright stem and leaves of a narrow oval shape with pointed ends. It is widely cultivated as a garden flower.

tumour overproduction of cells in a specific area of the body, often leading to a swelling or lump. Tumours are classified as *benign* or *malignant* (see ◊cancer).

tuna any of various large marine bony fishes of the mackerel family, especially the genus *Thunnus*, popular as food and game. Tuna may grow up to 2.5 m/8 ft long and weigh 200 kg/440 lbs. *Skipjack* or *bonito tuna Euthynnus pelamis* is one of the most commercially important species. It is a small tuna, up to 1 m/3 ft long.

tundra region of high latitude almost devoid of trees, resulting from the presence of ◊permafrost. The vegetation consists mostly of grasses, sedges, heather, mosses, and lichens. Tundra stretches in a continuous belt across N North America and Eurasia.

tungsten hard, heavy, grey-white, metallic element, symbol W (from German *Wolfram*), atomic number 74, relative atomic mass 183.85. It occurs in the minerals wolframite, scheelite, and hubertite. It has the highest melting point of any metal (6,170°F/3,410°C) and is added to steel to make it harder, stronger, and more elastic; its other uses include high-speed cutting tools, electrical elements, and thermionic couplings. Its salts are used in the paint and tanning industries.

Tunis capital and chief port of Tunisia; population (1984) 597,000. Industries include chemicals and textiles. Founded by the Arabs, it was captured by the Turks in 1533, then occupied by the French 1881 and by the Axis powers 1942–43. The ruins of ancient ◊Carthage are to the northeast.

Tunisia Tunisian Republic; country in N Africa, on the Mediterranean Sea, bordered SE by Libya and W by Algeria; *area* 164,150 sq km/63,378 sq mi; *capital* and chief port Tunis; *physical* arable and forested land in N graduates towards desert in S; *head of state and government* Zine el-Abdine Ben Ali from 1987; *political system* emergent democratic republic; *exports* oil, phosphates, chemicals, textiles, food, olive oil; *population* (1990 est) 8,094,000; *languages* Arabic (official), French; *recent history* a French protectorate from 1883, Tunisia achieved internal self-government 1955 and full independence as a monarchy 1956, with Habib Bourguiba as prime minister. The country became a republic 1957, with Bourguiba as president; he was made president for life 1975. Prime Minister Ben Ali seized power 1987. In the 1989 general elections, the government party, the Constitutional Democratic Rally (RCD), won all assembly seats.

Tunja capital city of Boyacá department, central Colombia, on the Pan-American Highway; population (1985) 93,800.

turbine engine in which steam, water, gas, or air (see ◊windmill) is made to spin a rotating shaft by pushing on angled blades, like a fan. Turbines are among the most powerful machines. Steam turbines are used to drive generators in power stations and ships' propellers; water turbines spin the generators in hydroelectric power plants; and gas turbines (as jet engines; see ◊jet propulsion) power most aircraft and drive machines in industry.

turbot any of various flatfishes of the flounder group prized as food, especially *Scophthalmus maximus* found in European waters. It grows up to 1 m/3 ft long and weighs up to 14 kg/30 lb. It is brownish above and whitish underneath.

Turgenev Ivan Sergeievich 1818–1883. Russian writer, notable for poetic realism, pessimism, and skill in characterization. His works include the play *A Month in the Country* 1849, and the novels *A Nest of Gentlefolk* 1858, *Fathers and Sons* 1862, and *Virgin Soil* 1877. His series *A Sportsman's Sketches* 1852 criticized serfdom.

Turin (Italian *Torino*) capital of Piedmont, NW Italy, on the river Po; population (1988) 1,025,000. Industries include iron, steel, cars, silk and other textiles, fashion goods, chocolate, and wine. It was the first capital of united Italy 1861–64.

Turkana, Lake formerly (to 1979) *Lake Rudolf*

lake in the Great Rift Valley, 375 m/1,230 ft above sea level, with its northernmost end in Ethiopia and the rest in Kenya; area 9,000 sq km/3,475 sq mi. It is saline, and shrinking by evaporation. Its shores were an early human hunting ground, and valuable remains have been found that are accurately datable because of undisturbed stratification.

turkey any of several large game birds of the pheasant family, native to the Americas. The wild turkey *Meleagris galloparvo* reaches a length of 1.3 m/4.3 ft, and is native to North and Central American woodlands. The domesticated turkey derives from the wild species. The ocellated turkey *Agriocharis ocellata* is found in Central America; it has eyespots on the tail.

Turkey Republic of; country between the Black Sea and the Mediterranean, bordered E by Armenia, Georgia, and Iran, SE by Iraq and Syria, W by Greece and the Aegean Sea, and NW by Bulgaria; *area* 779,500 sq km/300,965 sq mi; *capital* Ankara; *physical* central plateau surrounded by mountains; *head of state* Turgut Ozal from 1989; *head of government* Suleyman Demirel from 1991; *political system* democratic republic; *exports* cotton, yarn, hazelnuts, citrus, tobacco, dried fruit, chromium ores; *population* (1990 est) 56,549,000 (Turkish 85%, Kurdish 12%); *languages* Turkish (official), Kurdish, Arabic; *recent history* an independent republic under Mustafa Kemal (Atatürk) since 1923, Turkey held its first free elections 1950; Adnan Menderes became prime minister, but was executed after a military coup 1960. Until 1982, when a new constitution was adopted, the army stayed in nominal control, and harsh repression of political activists attracted international criticism. The ban on political activity was lifted 1983, when Turgut Ozal became prime minister. Ozal was elected president 1989; in the same year Turkey's application for European Community membership was refused. In 1991 Turkey sided with the United Nations coalition against Iraq in the Gulf War. Conflict with Kurdish minority continued.

Turkish language language of central and W Asia, the national language of Turkey. Originally written in Arabic script, it has been written within Turkey in a variant of the Roman alphabet since 1928. Varieties of Turkish are spoken in NW Iran and several of the Central Asian Republics, and all have been influenced by Arabic and Persian.

Turkmenistan Republic of; country in N Asia, bordered N by Kazakhstan and Uzbekistan, SE by Afghanistan, S by Iran, and W by the Caspian Sea; *area* 488,100 sq km/188,455 sq mi; *capital* Ashkhabad; *physical* some 90% of the country comprises desert including Kara Kum 'Black Sands' desert (area about 310,800/120,000 sq mi); river Amu Darya; *head of state* Saparmurad Niyazov from 1991; *head of government* Khan Akhmedov from 1989; *political system* socialist pluralist; *products* silk, karakul, sheep, astrakhan fur, carpets, chemicals, rich deposits of petroleum, natural gas, sulphur, and other industrial materials; *population* (1990) 3,500,000 (Turkmen 72%, Russian 10%, other 18%); *language* West Turkic; *recent history* part of Turkestan Soviet Socialist Autonomous Republic 1925; became constituent republic of USSR 1925. Economic and political sovereignty declared 1990. Turkmenistan endorsed maintenance of Union in USSR referendum 1991; President Niyazov initially supported attempted anti-Gorbachev coup; independence declared Oct 1991 after overwhelming approval in referendum. Joined Commonwealth of Independent States Dec 1991. Admitted into Conference on Security and Cooperation in Europe 1992; joined Economic Cooperative Organization.

Turkoman or *Turkman* member of the majority ethnic group in Turkmenistan. They live to the E of the Caspian Sea, around the Kara Kum desert, and along the borders of Afghanistan and Iran. Traditionally the Turkomen were tent-dwelling pastoral nomads, though the majority are now sedentary farmers. Their language belongs to the Turkic branch of the Altaic family. They are predominantly Sunni Muslims.

Turks and Caicos Islands British crown colony in the West Indies, the SE archipelago of the Bahamas; *area* 430 sq km/166 sq mi; *capital* Cockburn Town on Grand Turk; *features* a group of some 30 islands, of which six are inhabited; *population* (1980) 7,500; *history* secured by Britain 1766 against French and Spanish claims, the islands were a Jamaican dependency 1873–1962, and in 1976 attained internal self-government.

turmeric perennial plant *Curcuma longa* of the ginger family, native to India and the East Indies; also the ground powder from its tuberous rhizomes, used in curries to give a yellow colour, and as a dyestuff.

Turner Joseph Mallord William 1775–1851. English

landscape painter. He travelled widely in Europe, and his landscapes became increasingly Romantic, with the subject often transformed in scale and flooded with brilliant, hazy light. Many later works anticipate Impressionism; for example, *Rain, Steam and Speed* 1844 (National Gallery, London).

Turner Tina. Adopted name of Annie Mae Bullock 1938– . US rhythm-and-blues singer who recorded 1960–76 with her husband *Ike Turner* (1931–), including *River Deep, Mountain High* 1966, produced by Phil ⬦Spector. She achieved success in the 1980s as a solo artist, recording such albums as *Private Dancer* 1984, and as a live performer.

turnip biennial plant *Brassica rapa* cultivated in temperate regions for its edible white- or yellow-fleshed root and the young leaves, which are used as a green vegetable. Closely allied to it is the ⬦swede *Brassica napus*.

turnstone any of a genus *Arenaria* of small wading shorebirds, especially the ruddy turnstone *A. interpres*, which breeds in the Arctic and migrates to the southern hemisphere. It is seen on rocky beaches, turning over stones for small crustaceans and insects.

turquoise mineral, hydrous basic copper aluminium phosphate. Blue-green, blue, or green, it is a gemstone. Turquoise is found in Iran, Turkestan, Mexico, and southwestern USA.

turtle freshwater or marine reptile whose body is protected by a shell. Turtles are related to tortoises, and some species can grow to a length of up to 2.5 m/8 ft. Turtles often travel long distances to lay their eggs on the beaches where they were born, and many species have suffered through destruction of their breeding sites as well as being hunted for food and their shell.

Tuscany (Italian *Toscana*) region of central Italy;

area 23,000 sq km/8,878 sq mi; population (1990) 3,562,500. Its capital is Florence, and towns include Pisa, Livorno, and Siena. The area is mainly agricultural, with many vineyards, such as in the Chianti hills; it also has lignite and iron mines and marble quarries. The Tuscan dialect has been adopted as the standard form of Italian. Tuscany was formerly the Roman *Etruria*, and inhabited by Etruscans around 500 BC. In medieval times the area was divided into small states, united under Florentine rule during the 15th–16th centuries. It became part of united Italy 1861.

Tutankhamen king of Egypt of the 18th dynasty, about 1360–1350 BC. A son of Ikhnaton (also called Amenhotep IV), he was about 11 at his accession. In 1922 his tomb was discovered by the British archaeologists Lord Carnarvon and Howard Carter in the Valley of the Kings at Luxor, almost untouched by tomb robbers. The contents included many works of art and his solid-gold coffin, which are now displayed in a Cairo museum.

Tutu Desmond (Mpilo) 1931– . South African priest, Anglican archbishop of Cape Town and general secretary of the South African Council of Churches 1979–84. One of the leading figures in the struggle against apartheid in the Republic of South Africa, he was awarded the 1984 Nobel Peace Prize.

Tuva (Russian *Tuvinskaya*) autonomous republic (administrative unit) of Russia, northwest of Mongolia; *capital* Kyzyl; *area* 170,500 sq km/ 65,813 sq mi; *population* (1986) 284,000; *features* good pasture; gold, asbestos, cobalt; *history* part of Mongolia until 1911 and declared a Russian protectorate 1914; after the 1917 revolution it became the independent Tannu-Tuva republic 1920, until incorporated in the USSR as an autonomous region 1944. It was made the Tuva Autonomous Republic 1961.

Tuvalu South West Pacific State of (formerly *Ellice Islands*); country in the SW Pacific Ocean, part of Polynesia; *area* 25 sq km/9.5 sq mi; *capital* Funafuti; *physical* nine low coral atolls forming a chain of 579 km/360 mi; *head of state* Elizabeth II from 1978 represented by governor general; *head of government* Bikenibeu Paeniu from 1989; *political system* liberal democracy; *exports* copra, handicrafts, stamps; *population* (1990 est) 9,000 (Polynesian 96%); *languages* Tuvaluan, English; *recent history* became a British protectorate forming part of Gilbert and Ellice Islands group 1892; the islands acquired colonial status 1916. In 1975 the Ellice Islands were separated from the Gilbert Islands. Independence within the Commonwealth was achieved 1978. The islanders rejected a proposal for republican status 1986.

Twain Mark. Pen name of Samuel Langhorne Clemens 1835–1910. US writer. He established

his reputation with the comic masterpiece *The Innocents Abroad* 1869 and two classic American novels, in dialect, *The Adventures of Tom Sawyer* 1876 and *The Adventures of Huckleberry Finn* 1885. He also wrote satire, as in *A Connecticut Yankee at King Arthur's Court* 1889.

two-stroke cycle operating cycle for internal combustion piston engines. The engine cycle is completed after just two strokes (movement up or down) of the piston, which distinguishes it from the more common ◊four-stroke cycle. Power mowers and lightweight motorcycles use two-stroke petrol engines, which are cheaper and simpler than four-strokes.

Tyler Wat died 1381. English leader of the ◊Peasants' Revolt of 1381. He was probably born in Kent or Essex, and may have served in the French wars. After taking Canterbury he led the peasant army to Blackheath and occupied London. At Mile End King Richard II met the rebels and promised to redress their grievances, which included the imposition of a poll tax. At a further conference at Smithfield, Tyler was murdered.

Tyndale William 1492–1536. English translator of the Bible. The printing of his New Testament (the basis of the Authorized Version) was begun in Cologne 1525 and, after he had been forced to flee, completed in Worms. He was strangled and burned as a heretic at Vilvorde in Belgium.

Tyne and Wear metropolitan county in NE England, created 1974, originally administered by an elected metropolitan council; its powers reverted to district councils 1986; *area* 540 sq km/208 sq mi; *towns* Newcastle-upon-Tyne, South Shields, Gateshead, Sunderland; *features* bisected by the rivers Tyne and Wear; includes part of ◊Hadrian's Wall; Newcastle and Gateshead, linked with each other and with the coast on both sides by the Tyne and Wear Metro (a light railway using existing suburban lines, extending 54 km/34 mi); *products* once a centre of heavy industry, it is now being redeveloped and diversified; *population* (1991) 1,087,000.

Tynwald parliament of the ◊Isle of Man.

typewriter keyboard machine that produces characters on paper. The earliest known typewriter design was patented by Henry Mills in England 1714. However, the first practical typewriter was built 1867 in Milwaukee, Wisconsin, USA, by Christopher Sholes, Carlos Glidden, and Samuel Soulé. By 1873 ◊Remington and Sons, US gunmakers, produced under contract the first machines for sale and 1878 patented the first with lower-case as well as upper-case (capital) letters.

typhoid fever acute infectious disease of the digestive tract, caused by the bacterium *Salmonella typhi*, and usually contracted through a contaminated water supply. It is characterized by bowel haemorrhage and damage to the spleen. Treatment is with antibiotics.

typhoon violently revolving storm, a ⟡hurricane in the W Pacific Ocean.

typhus acute infectious disease, often fatal, caused by bacteria transmitted by lice, fleas, mites, and ticks. Symptoms include fever, headache, and rash. Typhus is epidemic among people living in overcrowded conditions. Treatment is by antibiotics.

tyrannosaurus any of a genus *Tyrannosaurus* of gigantic flesh-eating ⟡dinosaurs, order Saurischia, which lived in North America and Asia about 70 million years ago. They had two feet, were up to 15 m/50 ft long, 6.5 m/20 ft tall, weighed 10 tonnes, and had teeth 15 cm/6 in long.

Tyrone county of Northern Ireland; *area* 3,160 sq km/1,220 sq mi; *towns* Omagh (county town), Dungannon, Strabane, Cookstown; *features* rivers: Derg, Blackwater, Foyle; Lough Neagh; *products* mainly agricultural; *population* (1981) 144,000.

Tyrrhenian Sea arm of the Mediterranean surrounded by mainland Italy, Sicily, Sardinia, Corsica, and the Ligurian Sea. It is connected to the Ionian Sea through the Straits of Messina. Islands include Elba, Ustica, Capri, Stromboli, and the Lipari Islands.

Tyson Mike (Michael Gerald) 1966– . US heavyweight boxer, undisputed world champion from Aug 1987 to Feb 1990. He won the World Boxing Council heavyweight title 1986 when he beat Trevor Berbick to become the youngest world heavyweight champion. He beat James 'Bonecrusher' Smith for the World Boxing Association title 1987 and later that year became the first undisputed champion since 1978 when he beat Tony Tucker for the International Boxing Federation title. He was convicted of rape in 1992.

U

U2 Irish rock group formed 1977 by singer Bono Vox (born Paul Hewson, 1960–), guitarist Dave 'The Edge' Evans (1961–), bassist Adam Clayton (1960–), and drummer Larry Mullen (1961–). The band's albums include *The Unforgettable Fire* 1984, *The Joshua Tree* 1987, and *Achtung Baby* 1992.

Uccello Paolo. Adopted name of Paolo di Dono 1397–1475. Italian painter, active in Florence, one of the first to use perspective. His surviving paintings date from the 1430s onwards. Decorative colour and detail dominate his later pictures. His works include *St George and the Dragon* about 1460 (National Gallery, London).

Udmurt (Russian *Udmurtskaya*) autonomous republic in the W Ural foothills, central Russia; *area* 42,100 sq km/16,200 sq mi; *capital* Izhevsk; *products* timber, flax, potatoes, peat, quartz; *population* (1985) 1,559,000; 58% Russian, 33% Udmurt, 7% Tatar; *history* conquered in the 15th–16th centuries; constituted the Votyak Autonomous Region 1920; name changed to Udmurt 1932; Autonomous Republic 1934; part of the independent republic of Russia from 1991.

Uganda Republic of; country in E Africa, bordered N by Sudan, E by Kenya, S by Tanzania and Rwanda, and W by Zaire; *area* 236,000 sq km/91,351 sq mi; *capital* Kampala; *physical* plateau with mountains in W; forest and grassland; arid in NE; *head of state and government* Yoweri Museveni from 1986; *political system* emergent democratic republic; *exports* coffee, cotton, tea, copper; *population* (1990 est) 17,593,000 (largely the Bababanda, from whom country is named; also Langi and Acholi, some surviving Pygmies); *languages* English (official); Kiswahili, Luganda, other African languages; *recent history* independence achieved from Britain within the Commonwealth 1962 with Milton Obote as prime minister; proclaimed a federal republic 1963 with King Mutesa II as president. Obote ousted King Mutesa

1966, ended federal status, and became executive president. Coup led by Maj-Gen Idi Amin overthrew Obote 1971, establishing a ruthlessly dictatorial regime which lasted until 1978. Elections held 1980 returned Obote to power; he was ousted by Brig Tito Okello 1985. Power-sharing agreement between Okello and Yoweri Museveni ended 1986; Museveni became president.

UHF (abbreviation for *ultra high frequency*) referring to radio waves of very short wavelength, used, for example, for television broadcasting.

Ukraine country in E Europe, bordered NW by Belarus, NE and E by the Russian Federation, S by the Black Sea, Moldavia, and Romania, and E by Hungary, Czechoslovakia, and Poland; *area* 603,700 sq km/233,089 sq mi; *capital* Kiev; *physical* Russian plain; Carpathian and Crimean mountains; rivers Dnieper, Donetz, Bug; *head of state* Leonid Kravchuk from 1990; *head of government* Vitold Fokin from 1990; *products* grain, coal, oil, various minerals; *population* (1989) 51,700,000 (Ukrainian 74%, Russian 21%, Russian-speaking Jews 2%; some 1.5 million emigrants in USA, 750,000 in Canada); *language* Ukrainian; *recent history* Independent People's Republic proclaimed 1918; conquered by Red Army 1920. Under Nazi control during World War II; Soviet control re-established 1944. Became a founder member of United Nations 1945. Ukrainian People's Movement established 1989. Ukraine voted to proclaim sovereignty 1990; Kravchuk chosen as president. Independence declared 1991; Communist Party activities suspended; Kravchuk popularly elected president; referendum overwhelmingly endorsed independence. Recognized by Canada and Germany. Joined Commonwealth of Independent States (CIS) Dec 1991. Independence recognized by USA Jan 1992; admitted into Conference on Security and Cooperation in Europe (CSCE).

Ukrainian member of the majority ethnic group living in Ukraine; there are minorities in Siberian Russia, Kazakhstan, Poland, Czechoslovakia, and Romania. There are 40–45 million speakers of Ukrainian, a member of the East Slavonic branch

of the Indo-European family, closely related to Russian. Ukrainian-speaking communities are also found in Canada and the USA.

Ulaanbaatar or *Ulan Bator,* formerly (until 1924) *Urga* capital of the Mongolian Republic; a trading centre producing carpets, textiles, vodka; population (1991) 575,000.

ulcer any persistent breach in a body surface (skin or mucous membrane). It may be caused by infection, irritation, or tumour. Common ulcers include stomach, peptic, mouth (aphthous), intestinal, and varicose.

Ulster former kingdom in Northern Ireland, annexed by England 1461, from Jacobean times a centre of English, and later Scottish, settlement on land confiscated from its owners; divided 1921 into Northern Ireland (counties Antrim, Armagh, Down, Fermanagh, Londonderry, and Tyrone) and the Republic of Ireland (counties Cavan, Donegal, and Monaghan).

ultrasonics study and application of the sound and vibrations produced by ultrasonic pressure waves. In medicine, high-frequency pressure waves are used to investigate various body organs (ultrasound scanning). High-power ultrasound has been used with focusing arrangements to destroy tissue deep in the body, and extremely high frequencies (1,000 MHz or more) are used in ultrasonic microscopes.

ultrasound pressure waves similar in nature to sound waves but occurring at frequencies above 20,000 Hz (cycles per second), the approximate upper limit of human hearing (15–16 Hz is the lower limit).

ultraviolet radiation electromagnetic radiation invisible to the human eye, of wavelengths from about 4×10^{-7} to 5×10^{-9} metres (where the ◊X-ray range begins). Physiologically, ultraviolet radiation is extremely powerful, producing sunburn and causing the formation of vitamin D in the skin.

Ulysses Roman name for ◊Odysseus, Greek mythological hero.

Umayyad alternative spelling of ◊Omayyad dynasty.

umbrella bird bird of tropical South and Central America, family Contingidae. The Amazonian species *Cephalopterus ornatus* has an inflatable wattle at the neck to amplify its humming call, and in display elevates a long crest (12 cm/4 in) lying above the bill so that it rises umbrellalike above the head. These features are less noticeable in the female, which is brownish, whereas the male is blue-black.

Umm al Qaiwain one of the ◊United Arab Emirates.

Umtata capital of the South African Bantu Homeland of Transkei; population (1976) 25,000.

uncertainty principle or *indeterminacy principle* in quantum mechanics, the principle that it is meaningless to speak of a particle's position, momentum, or other parameters, except as results of measurements; measuring, however, involves an interaction (such as a ◊photon of light bouncing off the particle under scrutiny), which must disturb the particle, though the disturbance is noticeable only at an atomic scale. The principle implies that one cannot, even in theory, predict the moment-to-moment behaviour of such a system.

unconscious in psychoanalysis, part of the personality of which the individual is unaware, and which contains impulses or urges that are held back, or repressed, from conscious awareness.

underground (North American *subway*) rail service that runs underground. The first underground line in the world was in London, opened 1863; it was essentially a roofed-in trench. The London Underground is still the longest, with over 400 km/250 mi of routes. Many large cities throughout the world have similar systems, and Moscow's underground, the Metro, handles up to 6.5 million passengers a day.

unemployment lack of paid employment. Unemployment is measured either as a total or as a percentage of those who are available for work, known as the working population or labour force. In Britain, since Sept 1988, it has been measured as the total or percentage of the working population aged 18 or over, unemployed and claiming benefit. This stood at 9.5% in April 1992. Periods of widespread unemployment in Europe and the USA in the 20th century include 1929–1930s and the years since the mid-1970s.

UNESCO acronym for *United Nations Educational, Scientific,* and *Cultural Organization.* Agency of the UN, established 1946, with its headquarters in Paris. The USA, contributor of 25% of its budget, withdrew 1984 on grounds of its 'overpoliticization and mismanagement', and Britain followed 1985.

ungulate general name for any hoofed mammal. Included are the odd-toed ungulates (perissodactyls) and the even-toed ungulates (artiodactyls), along with subungulates such as elephants.

Uniate Church any of the Orthodox churches that accept the Catholic faith and the supremacy of the pope, and are in full communion with the Roman Catholic Church, but retain their own liturgy and separate organization.

unidentified flying object or *UFO* any light or object seen in the sky whose immediate identity is not apparent. Despite unsubstantiated claims, there is no evidence that UFOs are alien spacecraft. On investigation, the vast majority of sightings turn out to have been of natural or identifiable objects, notably bright stars and planets, meteors, aircraft, and satellites, or to have been perpetrated by pranksters. The term *flying saucer* was coined in 1947 and has been in use since.

unified field theory in physics, the theory that

attempts to explain the four fundamental forces (strong nuclear, weak nuclear, electromagnetic, and gravity) in terms of a single unified force (see ◁particle physics).

Union, Act of 1707 Act of Parliament that brought about the union of England and Scotland; that of 1801 united England and Ireland. The latter was revoked when the Irish Free State was constituted in 1922.

Union Movement British political group. Founded as the *New Party* by Oswald ◁Mosley and a number of Labour members of Parliament 1931, it developed into the *British Union of Fascists* 1932. In 1940 the organization was declared illegal and its leaders interned, but at the end of World War II it was revived as the Union Movement, characterized by racist doctrines including anti-Semitism.

Union of Soviet Socialist Republics (USSR) former country (1917–91) in N Asia and E Europe. The USSR was founded as the world's first communist state in the ◁Russian Revolution and became totalitarian under Joseph Stalin, who held power from the mid-1920s. After World War II (known to Soviet citizens as the ◁Great Patriotic War), the USSR consolidated its new empire in E Europe and supported anticolonial movements in the Third World, earning the antagonism of the USA expressed in the ◁Cold War, the nuclear arms race, and the space race. Soviet leaders after the death of Stalin 1953 included Nikita Khrushchev, who confronted the USA in the Cuban missile crisis 1962, and Leonid Brezhnev, under whom Soviet invasions of Czechoslovakia 1968 and Afghanistan 1979 were carried out. Under the reformist leadership of Mikhail Gorbachev 1985–91, the Cold War was formally ended 1989. At home, his policy of ◁*glasnost* allowed to the surface the economic problems that had accumulated and the nationalist tensions that had never been resolved, and the empire began to break up. In Aug 1991, a hardline communist coup that failed gave the Russian president Boris Yeltsin the opportunity to assume far greater powers and he led the way in a rapid dissolution of communist structures. The independence of the Baltic States was acknowledged following the coup. Other republics seceded and the USSR officially broke up 25 Dec 1991; for subsequent history, see ◁Armenia, ◁Azerbaijan, ◁Belarus, ◁Estonia, ◁Georgia, ◁Kazakhstan, ◁Kyrgyzstan, ◁Latvia, ◁Lithuania, ◁Moldova, the ◁Russian Federation, ◁Tajikistan, ◁Turkmenistan, ◁Ukraine, and ◁Uzbekistan.

UNITA *National Union for the Total Independence of Angola*. Angolan nationalist movement backed by South Africa, which continued to wage guerrilla warfare against the ruling MPLA regime after the latter gained control of the country in 1976. The UNITA leader Jonas ◁Savimbi founded the movement 1966. A peace agreement ending the civil war between MPLA–PT was signed May 1991.

United Arab Emirates (UAE); federation of emirates of Abu Dhabi, Ajman, Dubai, Fujairah, Ras al Khaimah, Sharjah, and Umm al Qaiwain in SW Asia, on the Arabian Gulf, bordered SW by Saudi Arabia and SE by Oman; *area* 83,657 sq km/ 32,292 sq mi; *capital* Abu Dhabi; *physical* desert and flat coastal plain; mountains in E; *head of state and government* Sheik Zayed bin al-Nahayan of Abu Dhabi from 1971; *political system* absolutism; *exports* oil, natural gas, fish, dates; *population* (1990 est) 2,250,000 (10% nomadic); *languages* Arabic (official); Farsi, Hindi, Urdu, English; *recent history* in 1952 the seven sheikdoms set up, on British advice and under British protection, the Trucial Council, consisting of all seven rulers, with a view to eventually establishing a federation. In 1968 the British government announced that it was withdrawing its forces within three years. The seven Trucial States, with Bahrain and Qatar, formed the Federation of Arab Emirates; in 1971 Bahrain and Qatar seceded to become independent nations. Six of the Trucial States then combined to form the United Arab Emirates. The remaining sheikdom, Ras al Khaimah, joined 1972. Sheik Zayed bin al-Nahayan became the first president. Diplomatic links with the USSR and China were established 1985; diplomatic relations with Egypt were restored 1987. The UAE opposed the Iraqi invasion of Kuwait 1991 and participated in the Gulf War with the United Nations coalition.

United Arab Republic union formed 1958, broken 1961, between ◁Egypt and ◁Syria. Egypt continued to use the name after the breach until 1971.

United Kingdom of Great Britain and Northern Ireland (UK); country in NW Europe off the coast of France, consisting of England, Scotland, Wales, and Northern Ireland; *area* 244,100 sq km/ 94,247 sq mi; *capital* London; *physical* became separated from European continent about 6000 BC; rolling landscape, increasingly mountainous

towards N, with Grampian mountains in Scotland, Pennines in N England, Cambrian Mountains in Wales; rivers include Thames, Severn, and Spey; *territories* Anguilla, Bermuda, British Antarctic Territory, British Indian Ocean Territory, British Virgin Islands, Cayman Islands, Falkland Islands, Gibraltar, Hong Kong (until 1997), Montserrat, Pitcairn Islands, St Helena and Dependencies (Ascension, Tristan da Cunha), Turks and Caicos Islands; *head of state* Elizabeth II from 1952; *head of government* John Major from 1990; *political system* liberal democracy; *exports* cereals, rape, sugar beet, potatoes, meat and meat products, poultry, dairy products, electronic and telecommunications equipment, engineering equipment and scientific instruments, oil and gas, petrochemicals, pharmaceuticals, fertilizers, film and television programmes, aircraft; *population* (1990 est) 57,121,000 (English 81.5%, Scottish 9.6%, Welsh 1.9%, Irish 2.4%); *languages* English, Welsh, Gaelic; *recent history* Act of Union between England and Scotland 1707; Act of Ireland 1801 united Britain and Ireland. The 1832–67 Reform Acts extended the franchise to the working classes. In 1911 the powers of the House of Lords were curbed. The Home Rule Act 1920 incorporated NE Ireland (Ulster) into the United Kingdom of Great Britain and Northern Ireland. In 1921 Ireland, except for Ulster, became a dominion (Irish Free State, later Eire, 1937). First Labour government led by Ramsay McDonald 1924. General Strike 1926; unemployment reached 3 million 1931. Coalition government under Winston Churchill 1940–45. Welfare state established under Labour government led by Clement Attlee 1945. ⟡Suez Crisis 1956. Direct rule of Northern Ireland from Westminster began 1972. UK joined European Community 1973. Labour replaced Conservative government after coal strike and three-day week 1974; Conservatives returned to power under Margaret Thatcher 1979. Social

Democratic Party (SDP) formed 1981. Unemployment over 3 million; Falklands War 1982. Coal strike (longest in British history) 1984–85. Riots 1990 as poll tax introduced. Troops sent to Persian Gulf following Iraq's invasion of Kuwait 1990; UK joined United Nations forces in ⟡Gulf War against Iraq 1991. In 1990 UK joined European exchange rate mechanism and John Major replaced Margaret Thatcher as prime minister; Conservatives re-elected 1992.

United Nations (UN) association of states for international peace, security, and cooperation, with its headquarters in New York. The UN was established 1945 as a successor to the ⟡League of Nations, and has played a role in many areas, such as refugees, development assistance, disaster relief, and cultural cooperation. Its total proposed budget for 1992/ 93 was $2,006 million. Boutros Boutros ⟡Ghali became secretary general 1992.

United Nations Security Council most powerful body of the UN. It has five permanent members – the USA, Russia, the UK, France, and China – which exercise a veto in that their support is requisite for all decisions, plus ten others, elected for two-year terms by a two-thirds vote of the General Assembly; retiring members are not eligible for re-election.

United States of America (USA); country in North America, extending from the Atlantic to the Pacific oceans, bordered N by Canada and S by Mexico, and including the outlying states of Alaska and Hawaii; *area* 9,368,900 sq km/3,618,770 sq mi; *capital* Washington DC; *physical* tropical (Hawaii) to arctic (Alaska); mountain ranges parallel with E and W coasts; Rocky Mountains separate rivers emptying into the Pacific from those flowing into the Gulf of Mexico; Great Lakes in N; rivers include Hudson, Mississippi, Missouri, Colorado, Columbia, Snake, Rio Grande, Ohio; *territories* commonwealths of Puerto Rico and Northern Marianas; federated states of Micronesia; Guam, US Virgin Islands, American Samoa, Wake Island, Midway Islands, Marshall Islands, Belau, Johnston and Sand Islands; *head of state and government* George Bush from 1989; *political system* liberal democracy; *exports* meat and meat products, oil and gas, petrochemicals, film and television programmes, electronic and telecommunications equipment, engineering equipment, pharmaceuticals; *population* (1990 est) 250,372,000 (white 80%, black 12%, Asian/Pacific islander 3%, Eskimo and Aleut 1%, Hispanic (included in above percentages) 9%); *languages* English, Spanish; *recent history* USA entered World War I 1917–18. In 1919–21 President Wilson's 14 Points became basis for formation of League of Nations. Women achieved the vote 1920; American Indians made citizens by Congress 1924. Wall Street stock-market crash 1929, followed by Depression; Roosevelt's New Deal to counter Depression introduced 1933. USA entered World War II after Japanese attack on Pearl Harbor 1941; ended the war in the Pacific by dropping A-

United States of America

State	Capital	Area sq km	Date of joining the Union
Alabama	Montgomery	134,700	1819
Alaska	Juneau	1,531,100	1959
Arizona	Phoenix	294,100	1912
Arkansas	Little Rock	137,800	1836
California	Sacramento	411,100	1850
Colorado	Denver	269,700	1876
Connecticut	Hartford	13,000	1788
Delaware	Dover	5,300	1787
Florida	Tallahassee	152,000	1845
Georgia	Atlanta	152,600	1788
Hawaii	Honolulu	16,800	1959
Idaho	Boise	216,500	1890
Illinois	Springfield	146,100	1818
Indiana	Indianapolis	93,700	1816
Iowa	Des Moines	145,800	1846
Kansas	Topeka	213,200	1861
Kentucky	Frankfort	104,700	1792
Louisiana	Baton Rouge	135,900	1812
Maine	Augusta	86,200	1820
Maryland	Annapolis	31,600	1788
Massachusetts	Boston	21,500	1788
Michigan	Lansing	151,600	1837
Minnesota	St Paul	218,700	1858
Mississippi	Jackson	123,600	1817
Missouri	Jefferson City	180,600	1821
Montana	Helena	381,200	1889
Nebraska	Lincoln	200,400	1867
Nevada	Carson City	286,400	1864
New Hampshire	Concord	24,000	1788
New Jersey	Trenton	20,200	1787
New Mexico	Santa Fé	315,000	1912
New York	Albany	127,200	1788
North Carolina	Raleigh	136,400	1789
North Dakota	Bismarck	183,100	1889
Ohio	Columbus	107,100	1803
Oklahoma	Oklahoma City	181,100	1907
Oregon	Salem	251,500	1859
Pennsylvania	Harrisburg	117,400	1787
Rhode Island	Providence	3,100	1790
South Carolina	Columbia	80,600	1788
South Dakota	Pierre	199,800	1889
Tennessee	Nashville	109,200	1796
Texas	Austin	691,200	1845
Utah	Salt Lake City	219,900	1896
Vermont	Montpelier	24,900	1791
Virginia	Richmond	105,600	1788
Washington	Olympia	176,700	1889
West Virginia	Charleston	62,900	1863
Wisconsin	Madison	145,500	1848
Wyoming	Cheyenne	253,400	1890
District of Columbia	Washington	180	
Total		9,391,880	

bombs on Hiroshima and Nagasaka, Japan. Became involved in Korean War 1950–53. McCarthy anticommunist investigations became a 'witch hunt'. Civil rights legislation and welfare measures introduced 1954–68. Abortive CIA-backed invasion of Cuba 1961 (see ◊Bay of Pigs). President Kennedy assassinated 1963. USA involvement in Vietnam War 1964–75. In 1969 an American was the first human on the Moon. Economic problems caused by OPEC oil embargo 1973. ◊Watergate scandal 1973–74 led to impeachment of President Nixon. US-Chinese diplomatic relations normalized 1979. US invaded Grenada 1983. Iranian hostage crisis 1979 relieved by President Reagan 1980; Irangate scandal over secret US government arms sales to Iran 1986. Stock-market crash 1988; USA became largest debtor nation. President Reagan signed treaty limiting intermediate nuclear forces 1987. USA invaded Panama 1988. End of Cold War with USSR declared 1989. Troops sent to Persian Gulf following Iraq's invasion of Kuwait 1990; US-led assault drove Iraq from Kuwait in ◊Gulf War 1991. Continuing economic recession.

unit trust company that invests its clients' funds in other companies. The units it issues represent holdings of shares, which means unit shareholders have a wider spread of capital than if they bought shares on the stock market.

universe all of space and its contents, the study of which is called cosmology. The universe is thought to be between 10 billion and 20 billion years old, and is mostly empty space, dotted with ◊galaxies for as far as telescopes can see. The most distant detected galaxies and ◊quasars lie 10 billion light years or more from Earth, and are moving farther apart as the universe expands. Several theories attempt to explain how the universe came into being and evolved, for example, the ◊Big Bang theory of an expanding universe originating in a single explosive event, and the contradictory ◊steady-state theory.

unleaded petrol petrol manufactured without the addition of antiknock. It has a slightly lower octane rating than leaded petrol, but has the advantage of not polluting the atmosphere with lead compounds. Many cars can be converted to running on unleaded petrol by altering the timing of the engine, and most new cars are designed to do so. Cars fitted with a ◊catalytic converter must use unleaded fuel.

unsaturated compound chemical compound in which two adjacent atoms are bonded by a double or triple covalent bond.

Unzen active volcano on the Shimbara peninsula, Kyushu Island, Japan, opposite the city of Kumamoto and 990 km/620 mi SW of Tokyo. Its eruption June 1991 led to the evacuation of 10,000 people.

Updike John (Hoyer) 1932– . US writer. Associated with the *New Yorker* magazine from 1955, he soon established a reputation for polished prose, poetry, and criticism. His novels include *The Poorhouse Fair* 1959, *The Centaur* 1963, *Couples* 1968, *The Witches of Eastwick* 1984, *Roger's Version* 1986, and *S.* 1988, and deal with the tensions and frustrations of contemporary US middle-class life and their effects on love and marriage.

Upper Volta former name (until 1984) of ◊Burkina Faso.

Ur ancient city of the ◊Sumerian civilization, in modern Iraq. Excavations by the British archaeologist Leonard Woolley show that it was inhabited 3500 BC. He discovered evidence of a flood that may have inspired the *Epic of ◊Gilgamesh* as well as the biblical account, and remains of ziggurats, or step pyramids.

Ural Mountains (Russian *Ural'skiy Khrebet*) mountain system running from the Arctic to the Caspian Sea, traditionally separating Europe from Asia. The highest peak is Naradnaya 1,894 m/6,214 ft. It has vast mineral wealth.

uranium hard, lustrous, silver-white, malleable and ductile, radioactive, metallic element of the ◊actinide series, symbol U, atomic number 92, relative atomic mass 238.029. It is the most abundant radioactive element in the Earth's crust, its decay giving rise to essentially all radioactive elements in nature; its final decay product is the stable element lead. Uranium combines readily with most elements to form compounds that are extremely poisonous. The chief ore is pitchblende, in which the element was discovered by German chemist Martin Klaproth in 1789; he named it after the planet Uranus, which had been discovered in 1781.

Uranus in Greek mythology, the primeval sky god. He was responsible for both the sunshine and the rain, and was the son and husband of ◊Gaia, the goddess of the Earth. Uranus and Gaia were the parents of ◊Kronos and the Titans.

Uranus the seventh planet from the Sun, discovered by William ◊Herschel 1781. It is twice as far out as the sixth planet, Saturn. Uranus has a diameter of 50,800 km/31,600 mi and a mass 14.5 times that of Earth. It orbits the Sun in 84 years at an average distance of 2,870 million km/1,783 million mi. The spin axis of Uranus is tilted at 98°, so that one pole points towards the Sun, giving extreme seasons. It has 15 moons, and in 1977 was discovered to have thin rings around its equator.

Urdu language member of the Indo-Iranian branch of the Indo-European language family, related to Hindi and written not in Devanagari but in Arabic script. Urdu is strongly influenced by Farsi (Persian) and Arabic. It is the official language of Pakistan and a language used by Muslims in India.

urea $CO(NH_2)_2$ waste product formed in the mammalian liver when nitrogen compounds are broken down. It is excreted in urine. When purified, it is a white, crystalline solid. In industry it is used to make urea-formaldehyde plastics (or resins), pharmaceuticals, and fertilizers.

uric acid $C_5H_4N_4O_3$ nitrogen-containing waste substance, formed from the breakdown of food and body protein. It is the usual excretory material in insects, reptiles, and birds. (The white part of bird and reptile excrement is uric acid.)

urinary system system of organs that removes nitrogenous waste products and excess water from the bodies of animals. In vertebrates, it consists of a pair of kidneys, which produce urine; ureters, which drain the kidneys; and (in bony fishes, amphibians, some reptiles, and mammals) a bladder, which stores the urine before its discharge. In mammals, the urine is expelled through the urethra; in other vertebrates, the urine drains into a common excretory chamber called a cloaca, and the urine is not discharged separately.

Ursa Major third largest constellation in the sky, in the north polar region. Its seven brightest stars make up the familiar shape of the *Big Dipper* or *Plough*. The second star of the 'handle' of the dipper, called Mizar, has a companion star, Alcor. Two stars forming the far side of the 'bowl' act as pointers to the north pole star, Polaris.

Ursa Minor constellation in the northern sky. It is shaped like a dipper, with the north pole star Polaris at the end of the handle.

Uruguay Oriental Republic of; country in South America, on the Atlantic coast, bordered N by Brazil and W by Argentina; *area* 176,200 sq km/68,031 sq mi; *capital* Montevideo; *physical* grassy plains (Pampas) and low hills; rivers Negro, Uruguay; *head of state and government* Luis Lacalle Herrera from 1989; *political system* democratic republic; *exports* meat and meat products, leather, wool, textiles; *population* (1990 est) 3,002,000 (Spanish, Italian; mestizo [mixed race], mulatto, black); *language* Spanish; *recent history* independence declared from Brazil 1825; first constitution adopted 1930. Repressive rule by army 1976–84; violent antigovernment protests led to agreement 1985 to return to constitutional government; government of national accord established 1986. Luis Lacalle Herrera elected president 1989.

Urumqi or *Urumchi* industrial city and capital of Xinjiang Uygur autonomous region, China, at the northern foot of the Tian Shan mountains; population (1989) 1,110,000. It produces cotton textiles, cement, chemicals, iron, and steel.

Utah state in W USA; nickname Beehive State/Mormon State; *area* 219,900 sq km/84,881 sq mi; *capital* Salt Lake City; *towns* Provo, Ogden; *physical* Colorado Plateau to the east, mountains in centre, Great Basin to the west, Great Salt Lake; *features* Great American Desert; Colorado river system; Dinosaur and Rainbow Bridge national monuments; five national parks: the Arches, Bryce Canyon, Canyonlands, Capitol Reef, Zion; auto racing at Bonneville Salt Flats; Mormon temple and tabernacle, Salt Lake City; *products* wool, gold, silver, copper, coal, salt, steel; *population* (1990) 1,722,900; *famous people* Brigham Young; *history* explored first by Franciscan friars for Spain 1776; Great Salt Lake discovered by US frontier scout Jim Bridger 1824; part of the area ceded by Mexico 1848; developed by Mormons, still by far the largest religious group in the state; territory 1850, but not admitted to statehood until 1896 because of Mormon reluctance to relinquish plural marriage.

uterus hollow muscular organ of female mammals, located between the bladder and rectum, and connected to the Fallopian tubes above and the vagina below. The embryo develops within the uterus, and in placental mammals is attached to it after implantation via the ◊placenta and umbilical cord. The lining of the uterus changes during the ◊menstrual cycle. In humans and other higher primates, it is a single structure, but in other mammals it is paired.

utilitarianism philosophical theory of ethics outlined by the philosopher Jeremy ◊Bentham and developed by John Stuart Mill. According to utilitarianism, an action is morally right if it has consequences that lead to happiness, and wrong if it brings about the reverse. Thus society should aim for the greatest happiness of the greatest number.

Utrecht province of the Netherlands lying SE of Amsterdam, on the Kromme Rijn (crooked Rhine); *area* 1,330 sq km/513 sq mi; *population* (1991) 1,026,800; *capital* Utrecht; *towns* Amersfoort, Zeist, Nieuwegeun, Veenendaal; *products* chemicals, livestock, textiles, electrical goods; *history* ruled by the bishops of Utrecht in the Middle Ages, the province was sold to the emperor Charles V of Spain 1527. It became a centre of Protestant resistance to Spanish rule and, with the signing of the Treaty of Utrecht, became one of the seven United Provinces of the Netherlands 1579.

Uttar Pradesh state of N India; *area* 294,400 sq km/ 113,638 sq mi; *capital* Lucknow; *towns* Kanpur, Varanasi, Agra, Allahabad, Meerut; *features* most populous state; Himalayan peak Nanda Devi 7,817 m/25,655 ft; *population* (1991) 138,760,400; *famous people* Indira Gandhi, Ravi Shankar; *language* Hindi; *religion* 80% Hindu, 15% Muslim; *history* formerly the heart of the Mogul Empire and generating point of the ◊Indian Mutiny 1857 and subsequent opposition to British rule. The regions of Oudh and Agra were joined from 1877, and from 1902 known as the United Provinces of Agra and Oudh, renamed Uttar Pradesh 1950.

Uzbek member of the majority ethnic group (almost 70%) living in Uzbekistan; minorities live in Turkmenistan, Tajikistan, Kazakhstan, and Afghanistan. There are 10–14 million speakers of the Uzbek language, which belongs to the Turkic branch of the Altaic family. Uzbeks are predominantly Sunni Muslims.

Uzbekistan Republic of; country in N Asia, bordered N and W by Kazakhstan, E by Kyrgyzstan and Tajikistan, and S by Afghanistan and Turkmenistan; *area* 447,400 sq km/172,741 sq mi; *capital* Tashkent; *physical* oases in the deserts; rivers Amu Darya, Syr Darya; Fergana Valley; *head of state* Islam Karimov from 1990; *head of government* Abdulkhashim Mutalov from 1991; *political system* socialist pluralist; *products* rice, dried fruit, vines (all grown by irrigation), cotton, silk; *population* (1990) 19,800,000 (Uzbek 71%, Russian 8%, other 21%); *language* Uzbek; *recent history* part of Turkestan Soviet Socialist Autonomous Republic 1921; became a constituent republic of the USSR 1925. Some 160,000 Meskhetian Turks were forcibly transported from their native Georgia to Uzbekistan by Stalin 1944. Uzbek nationalist organization formed 1989; Meskhetian Turks attacked in riots. Economic and political sovereignty declared 1990. Uzbekistan supported 'renewed federation of equal sovereign republics' in USSR referendum 1991; Uzbek Communist Party broke with Communist Party of the Soviet Union; independence declared. Joined Commonwealth of Independent States Dec 1991. Admitted into Conference on Security and Cooperation in Europe 1992; joined Economic Cooperation Organization.

vaccine any preparation of modified viruses or bacteria that is introduced into the body, usually either orally or by a hypodermic syringe, to induce the specific ⟡antibody reaction that produces ⟡immunity against a particular disease. In the UK, children are routinely vaccinated against diphtheria, tetanus, whooping cough, polio, measles, mumps, German measles, and tuberculosis (with ⟡BCG).

vacuum in general, a region completely empty of matter; in physics, any enclosure in which the gas pressure is considerably less than atmospheric pressure (101,325 ⟡pascals).

vagina the front passage in female mammals, linking the uterus to the exterior. It admits the penis during sexual intercourse, and is the birth canal down which the fetus passes during delivery.

Valencia industrial city (wine, fruit, chemicals, textiles, ship repair) in Valencia region, E Spain; population (1991) 777,400. The Community of Valencia, consisting of Alicante, Castellón, and Valencia, has an area of 23,300 sq km/8,994 sq mi and a population of 3,772,000.

Valhalla in Norse mythology, the hall in ⟡Odin's palace where he feasts with the souls of heroes killed in battle.

Valle d'Aosta autonomous region of NW Italy; area 3,300 sq km/1,274 sq mi; population (1990) 116,000, many of whom are French-speaking. It produces wine and livestock. Its capital is Aosta.

Valletta capital and port of Malta; population (1987) 9,000; urban area 101,000.

value-added tax (VAT) tax on goods and services. VAT is imposed by the European Community on member states. The tax varies from state to state. An agreed proportion of the tax money is used to fund the EC.

vanadium silver-white, malleable and ductile, metallic element, symbol V, atomic number 23, relative atomic mass 50.942. It occurs in certain iron, lead, and uranium ores and is widely distributed in small quantities in igneous and sedimentary rocks. It is used to make steel alloys, to which it adds tensile strength.

Van Allen radiation belts two zones of charged particles around the Earth's magnetosphere, discovered 1958 by US physicist James Van Allen. The atomic particles come from the Earth's upper atmosphere and the ⟡solar wind, and are trapped by the Earth's magnetic field.

Vanbrugh John 1664–1726. English Baroque architect and dramatist. He designed Blenheim Palace, Oxfordshire, and Castle Howard, Yorkshire, and wrote the comic dramas *The Relapse* 1696 and *The Provok'd Wife* 1697.

Vancouver industrial city (oil refining, engineering, shipbuilding, aircraft, timber, pulp and paper, textiles, fisheries) in Canada, its chief Pacific seaport, on the mainland of British Columbia; population (1986) 1,381,000.

Vandal member of a Germanic people related to the ⟡Goths. In the 5th century AD the Vandals moved from N Germany to invade Roman ⟡Gaul and Spain, many settling in Andalusia (formerly Vandalitia) and others reaching N Africa 429. They

Van Allen belts

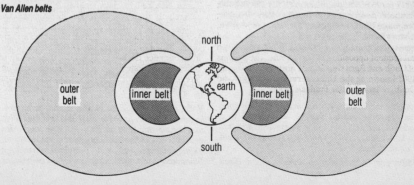

sacked Rome 455 but accepted Roman suzerainty in the 6th century.

van de Graaff Robert Jemison 1901–1967. US physicist who from 1929 developed a high-voltage generator, which in its modern form can produce more than a million volts. It consists of a continuous vertical conveyor belt that carries electrostatic charges (resulting from friction) up to a large hollow sphere supported on an insulated stand. The lower end of the belt is earthed, so that charge accumulates on the sphere. The size of the voltage built up in air depends on the radius of the sphere, but can be increased by enclosing the generator in an inert atmosphere, such as nitrogen.

van der Waals Johannes Diderik 1837–1923. Dutch physicist who was awarded a Nobel prize in 1910 for his theoretical study of gases. He emphasized the forces of attraction and repulsion between atoms and molecules in describing the behaviour of real gases, as opposed to the ideal gases dealt with in ▷Boyle's law and ▷Charles's law.

Van Diemen's Land former name (1642–1855) of ▷Tasmania, Australia. It was named by Dutch navigator Abel Tasman after the governor general of the Dutch East Indies, Anthony van Diemen. The name Tasmania was used from the 1840s and became official 1855.

Vanuatu Republic of; country in the S Pacific, part of Melanesia; *area* 14,800 sq km/5,714 sq mi; *capital* Vila (on Efate island); *physical* comprises 70 islands, including Espiritu Santo, Malekula, and Efate; densely forested, mountainous (three active volcanoes); *head of state* Fred Timakata from 1989; *head of government* Maxime Carlot from 1991; *political system* democratic republic; *exports* copra, fish, coffee, cocoa; tourism is important; *population* (1989) 152,000 (Melanesian 90%); *languages* Bislama 82%, English, French (all official); *recent history* independence achieved from France and Britain within the Commonwealth 1980. Since independence Vanuatu has sought to promote greater cooperation among the states of the Pacific region; with Papua New Guinea and the Solomon Islands, it formed the Spearhead Group 1988, aiming to preserve Melanesian cultural tradition and campaign for New Caledonia's independence.

Varanasi or *Benares* holy city of the Hindus in Uttar Pradesh, India, on the river Ganges; population (1981) 794,000. There are 1,500 golden shrines, and a 5 km/3 mi frontage to the Ganges with sacred stairways (*ghats*) for purification by bathing.

variable in mathematics, a changing quantity (one that can take various values), as opposed to a constant. For example, in the algebraic expression $y = 4x^3 + 2$, the variables are x and y, whereas 4 and 2 are constants.

Varna port in Bulgaria, on an inlet of the Black Sea; population (1990) 320,600. Industries include shipbuilding and the manufacture of chemicals.

Vasari Giorgio 1511–1574. Italian art historian, architect, and painter, author of *Lives of the Most Excellent Architects, Painters and Sculptors* 1550 (enlarged and revised 1568), in which he proposed the theory of a Renaissance of the arts beginning with Giotto and culminating with Michelangelo. He designed the Uffizi Palace, Florence.

vasectomy male sterilization; an operation to cut and tie the duct (vas deferens) that carries sperm from the testes to the penis. Vasectomy does not affect sexual performance, but the semen produced at ejaculation no longer contains sperm.

Vassilou Georgios Vassos 1931– . Greek-Cypriot politician and entrepreneur, president from 1988. A self-made millionaire, he entered politics as an independent and in 1988 won the presidency, with Communist Party support. He has since, with United Nations help, tried unsuccessfully to heal the rift between the Greek and Turkish communities.

VAT abbreviation for ▷value-added tax.

Vatican City State sovereign area in central Rome, Italy; the world's smallest state; *area* 0.4 sq km/109 acres; *physical* forms an enclave in the heart of Rome; *head of state and government* John Paul II from 1978; *political system* absolute Catholicism; *population* (1985) 1,000; *languages* Latin (official); Italian; *recent history* Lateran Treaty recognized sovereignty of pope 1929; new Italian constitution confirmed sovereignty of the city state 1947. John Paul II became first non-Italian pope for more than 400 years 1978.

Vaughan Williams Ralph 1872–1958. English composer. His style was tonal and often evocative of the English countryside through the use of folk themes. Among his works are the orchestral *Fantasia on a Theme by Thomas Tallis* 1910; the opera *Sir John in Love* 1929, featuring the Elizabethan song 'Greensleeves'; and nine symphonies 1909–57.

vector quantity any physical quantity that has both magnitude and direction (such as the velocity or acceleration of an object) as distinct from ▷scalar quantity (such as speed, density, or mass), which has magnitude but no direction. A vector is represented either geometrically by an arrow whose length corresponds to its magnitude and points in an appropriate direction, or by a pair of numbers written vertically and placed within brackets (x) (y) (z).

Veda the most sacred of the Hindu scriptures, hymns written in an old form of Sanskrit; the oldest may date from 1500 or 2000 BC. The four main collections are: the *Rigveda* (hymns and praises); *Yajurveda* (prayers and sacrificial formulae); *Sâmaveda* (tunes and chants); and *Atharvaveda*, or

Veda of the Atharvans, the officiating priests at the sacrifices.

Vedānta school of Hindu philosophy that developed the teachings of the *Upanishads*. One of its teachers was Samkara, who lived in S India in the 8th century AD and is generally regarded as a manifestation of Siva. He taught that there is only one reality, Brahman, and that knowledge of Brahman leads finally to *moksha*, or liberation from reincarnation.

Vega Lope Felix de (Carpio) 1562–1635. Spanish poet and dramatist, one of the founders of modern Spanish drama. He wrote epics, pastorals, odes, sonnets, novels, and, reputedly, over 1,500 plays (of which 426 are still in existence), mostly tragicomedies. He set out his views on drama in *Arte nuevo de hacer comedias/The New Art of Writing Plays* 1609, while reaffirming the classical form. *Fuenteovejuna* 1614 has been acclaimed as the first proletarian drama.

Velázquez Diego Rodríguez de Silva y 1599–1660. Spanish painter, born in Seville, the outstanding Spanish artist of the 17th century. In 1623 he became court painter to Philip IV in Madrid, where he produced many portraits of the royal family as well as occasional religious paintings, genre scenes, and other subjects. *Las Meninas/The Ladies-in-Waiting* 1655 (Prado, Madrid) is a complex group portrait that includes a self-portrait, but nevertheless focuses clearly on the doll-like figure of the Infanta Margareta Teresa.

Venda ◊Black National State from 1979, near the Zimbabwe border, in South Africa; *area* 6,500 sq km/2,510 sq mi; *capital* Thohoyandou; *towns* MaKearela; *features* Homeland of the Vhavenda people; *government* executive president (paramount chief P R Mphephu in office from Sept 1979) and national assembly (not recognized outside South Africa); *products* coal, copper, graphite, construction stone; *population* (1980) 343,500; *language* Luvenda, English.

venereal disease (VD) any disease mainly transmitted by sexual contact, although commonly the term is used specifically for gonorrhoea and syphilis, both occurring worldwide, and chancroid ('soft sore') and lymphogranuloma venerum, seen mostly in the tropics. The term *sexually transmitted diseases* (STDs) is more often used to encompass a growing list of conditions passed on primarily, but not exclusively, in this way.

Veneto region of NE Italy, comprising the provinces of Belluno, Padova (Padua), Treviso, Rovigo, Venezia (Venice), and Vicenza; area 18,400 sq km/7,102 sq mi; population (1990) 4,398,100. Its capital is Venice, and towns include Padua, Verona, and Vicenza. The Veneto forms part of the N Italian plain, with the delta of the river Po; it includes part of the Alps and Dolomites, and Lake Garda. Products include cereals, fruit, vegetables, wine, chemicals, ships, and textiles.

Venezuela Republic of; country in northern South America, on the Caribbean coast, bordered E by Guyana, S by Brazil, and W by Colombia; *area* 912,100 sq km/352,162 sq mi; *capital* Caracas; *physical* Andes Mountains and Lake Maracaibo in NW; central plains (llanos); delta of Orinoco River in E; Guiana Highlands in SE; Angel Falls, world's highest waterfall; *head of state and government* Carlos Andrés Pérez from 1988; *political system* federal democratic republic; *exports* coffee, timber, oil, aluminium, iron ore, petrochemicals; *population* (1990 est) 19,753,000 (mestizo [mixed race] 70%, white (Spanish, Portuguese, Italian) 20%, black 9%, Amerindian 2%); *languages* Spanish (official); Indian languages; *recent history* independence achieved from Spain 1830 after a rebellion led by Simón Bolívar. After a long history of dictatorial rule, a new constitution was adopted 1961; stability increased until economic problems in the 1980s. In 1989 riots were triggered by economic austerity programme; martial law was declared. Protests continued 1991. Attempted coup failed 1992.

Venice (Italian **Venezia**) city, port, and naval base, capital of Veneto, Italy, on the Adriatic; population (1990) 79,000. The old city is built on piles on low-lying islands. Apart from tourism (it draws 8 million tourists a year), industries include glass, jewellery, textiles, and lace. Venice was an independent trading republic from the 10th century, ruled by a doge, or chief magistrate, and was one of the centres of the Italian Renaissance.

Venn diagram in mathematics, a diagram representing a ◊set or sets and the logical relationships between them. The sets are drawn as circles. An area of overlap between two circles (sets) contains elements that are common to both sets, and thus represents a third set. Circles that do not overlap represent sets with no elements in common (disjoint sets). The method is named after the British logician John Venn (1834–1923).

Venus in Roman mythology, the goddess of love and beauty (Greek ◊Aphrodite). The patrician Romans believed that they were descended from Aeneas, the son of the goddess and Anchises, a shepherd. She was venerated as the guardian of the Roman people.

Venus second planet from the Sun. It orbits the Sun every 225 days at an average distance of 108.2 million km/67.2 million mi and can approach the Earth to within 38 million km/24 million mi, closer than any other planet. Its diameter is 12,100 km/7,500 mi and its mass is 0.82 that of Earth. Venus rotates on its axis more slowly than any other planet, once every 243 days and from east to west, the opposite direction to the other planets (except Uranus and possibly Pluto). Venus is shrouded by clouds of sulphuric acid droplets that sweep across the planet from east to west every four days. The atmosphere is almost entirely carbon dioxide, which traps the

Sun's heat by the ▷greenhouse effect and raises the planet's surface temperature to 480°C/900°F, with an atmospheric pressure of 90 times that at the surface of the Earth.

Venus flytrap insectivorous plant *Dionaea muscipula* of the sundew family, native to the SE USA; its leaves have two hinged blades that close and entrap insects.

Verdi Giuseppe (Fortunino Francesco) 1813–1901. Italian opera composer of the Romantic period, who took his native operatic style to new heights of dramatic expression. In 1842 he wrote the opera *Nabucco*, followed by *Ernani* 1844 and *Rigoletto* 1851. Other works include *Il Trovatore* and *La Traviata* both 1853, *Aïda* 1871, and the masterpieces of his old age, *Otello* 1887 and *Falstaff* 1893. His *Requiem* 1874 commemorates Alessandro Manzoni.

Verlaine Paul 1844–1896. French lyric poet who was influenced by the poets Baudelaire and ▷Rimbaud. His volumes of verse include *Poèmes saturniens/Saturnine Poems* 1866, *Fêtes galantes/Amorous Entertainments* 1869, and *Romances sans paroles/Songs without Words* 1874. In 1873 he was imprisoned for attempting to shoot Rimbaud. His later works reflect his attempts to lead a reformed life. He was acknowledged as leader of the ▷Symbolist poets.

Vermeer Jan 1632–1675. Dutch painter, active in Delft. Most of his pictures are ▷genre scenes, with a limpid clarity and distinct air of stillness, and a harmonious palette often focusing on yellow and blue. He frequently depicted solitary women in domestic settings, as in *The Lacemaker* (Louvre, Paris).

Vermont state in NE USA; nickname Green Mountain State; *area* 24,900 sq km/9,611 sq mi; *capital* Montpelier; *towns* Burlington, Rutland, Barre; *features* brilliant autumn foliage and winter sports; Green Mountains; Lake Champlain; *products* apples, maple syrup, dairy products, china clay, granite, marble, slate, business machines, paper and allied products; tourism is important; *population* (1990) 562,800; *famous people* Chester A Arthur, Calvin Coolidge, John Dewey; *history* explored by Champlain from 1609; settled 1724; state 1791.

Verne Jules 1828–1905. French author of tales of adventure that anticipated future scientific developments: *Five Weeks in a Balloon* 1862, *Journey to the Centre of the Earth* 1864, *Twenty Thousand Leagues under the Sea* 1870, and *Around the World in Eighty Days* 1873.

Verona industrial city (printing, paper, plastics, furniture, pasta) in Veneto, Italy, on the Adige; population (1988) 259,000. It also trades in fruit and vegetables. Verona has a large Roman amphitheatre and a 12th-century cathedral.

Veronese Paolo *c.* 1528–1588. Italian painter, born

in Verona, active mainly in Venice (from about 1553). He specialized in grand decorative schemes, such as his ceilings in the Doge's Palace in Venice, with *trompe l'oeil* effects and inventive detail. The subjects are religious, mythological, historical, and allegorical.

Versailles city in N France, capital of Les Yvelines *département*, on the outskirts of Paris; population (1982) 95,240. It grew up around the palace of Louis XV. Within the palace park are two small châteaux, Le Grand and Le Petit Trianon, built for Louis XIV (by Jules-Hardouin Mansart) and Louis XV (by Jacques Gabriel 1698–1782) respectively.

Versailles, Treaty of peace treaty after World War I between the Allies and Germany, signed 28 June 1919. It established the League of Nations. Germany surrendered Alsace-Lorraine to France, and large areas in the east to Poland, and made smaller cessions to Czechoslovakia, Lithuania, Belgium, and Denmark. The Rhineland was demilitarized, German rearmament was restricted, and Germany agreed to pay reparations for war damage. The treaty was never ratified by the USA, which made a separate peace with Germany and Austria 1921.

vertebrate any animal with a backbone. The 41,000 species of vertebrates include mammals, birds, reptiles, amphibians, and fishes. They include most of the larger animals, but in terms of numbers of species are only a tiny proportion of the world's animals. The zoological taxonomic group Vertebrata is a subgroup of the ▷phylum *Chordata*.

Vesalius Andreas 1514–1564. Belgian physician who revolutionized anatomy. His great innovations were to perform postmortem dissections and to make use of illustrations in teaching anatomy.

Vesta in Roman mythology, the goddess of the hearth (Greek *Hestia*). In Rome, the sacred flame in her shrine in the Forum was kept constantly lit by the six *Vestal Virgins*.

Vesuvius (Italian *Vesuvio*) active volcano SE of Naples, Italy; height 1,277 m/4,190 ft. In 79 BC it destroyed the cities of Pompeii, Herculaneum, and Oplonti.

vetch trailing or climbing plant of any of several genera, family Leguminosae, usually having seed pods and purple, yellow, or white flowers, including the fodder crop alfalfa *Medicago sativa*.

VHF (abbreviation for *very high frequency*) referring to radio waves that have very short wavelengths (1 m–10 m). They are used for interference-free FM (frequency-modulated) transmissions. VHF transmitters have a relatively short range because the waves cannot be reflected over the horizon like longer radio waves.

vibraphone electrically amplified musical percussion instrument resembling a ▷xylophone but with metal keys. Spinning discs within resonating tubes under each key give the instrument a vibrato sound that can be controlled in speed with a foot pedal.

viburnum any small tree or shrub of the genus *Viburnum* of the honeysuckle family Caprifoliaceae, found in temperate and subtropical regions, including the wayfaring tree, the laurustinus, and the guelder rose of Europe and Asia, and the North American blackhaws and arrowwoods.

Vichy health resort with thermal springs, known to the Romans, on the river Allier in Allier *département*, central France. During World War II it was the seat of the French general ▷Pétain's government 1940–44 (known also as the Vichy government), which collaborated with the Nazis.

Vico Giambattista 1668–1744. Italian philosopher, considered the founder of the modern philosophy of history. He argued that we can understand history more adequately than nature, since it is we who have made it. He believed that the study of language, ritual, and myth was a way of understanding earlier societies. His cyclical theory of history (the birth, development, and decline of human societies) was put forward in *New Science* 1725.

Victor Emmanuel II 1820–1878. First king of united Italy from 1861. He became king of Sardinia on he abdication of his father Charles Albert 1849. In 1855 he allied Sardinia with France and the UK in the Crimean War. In 1859 in alliance with the French he defeated the Austrians and annexed Lombardy. By 1860 most of Italy had come under his rule, and in 1861 he was proclaimed king of Italy. In 1870 he made Rome his capital.

Victoria state of SE Australia; *area* 227,600 sq km/ 87,854 sq mi; *capital* Melbourne; *towns* Geelong, Ballarat, Bendigo; *physical* part of the Great Dividing Range, running E–W and including the larger part of the Australian Alps; Gippsland lakes; shallow lagoons on the coast; the mallee shrub region; *products* sheep, beef cattle, dairy products, tobacco, wheat, vines for wine and dried fruit, orchard fruits, vegetables, gold, brown coal (Latrobe Valley), oil and natural gas (Bass Strait); *population* (1987) 4,184,000; 70% in the Melbourne area; *history* annexed for Britain by Captain Cook 1770; settled in the 1830s; after being part of New South Wales became a separate colony 1851, named after the queen; became a state 1901.

Victoria industrial port (shipbuilding, chemicals, clothing, furniture) on Vancouver Island, capital of British Columbia, Canada; population (1986) 66,303.

Victoria 1819–1901. Queen of the UK from 1837, when she succeeded her uncle William IV, and empress of India from 1876. In 1840 she married Prince ▷Albert of Saxe-Coburg and Gotha. Her relations with her prime ministers ranged from the affectionate (Melbourne and Disraeli) to the stormy (Peel, Palmerston, and Gladstone). Her golden jubilee 1887 and diamond jubilee 1897 marked a waning of republican sentiment, which had developed with her withdrawal from public life on Albert's death 1861.

Victoria Falls or *Mosi-oa-tunya* waterfall on the river Zambezi, on the Zambia–Zimbabwe border. The river is 1,700 m/5,580 ft wide and drops 120 m/400 ft to flow through a 30–m/100–ft wide gorge.

Victoria, Lake or *Victoria Nyanza* largest lake in Africa; area over 69,400 sq km/26,800 sq mi; length 410 km/255 mi. It lies on the equator at an altitude of 1,136 m/3,728 ft, bounded by Uganda, Kenya, and Tanzania. It is a source of the Nile.

Victorian the mid-and late 19th century in England, covering the reign of Queen Victoria 1837–1901. Victorian style was often very ornate, markedly so in architecture, and Victorian Gothic drew on the original Gothic architecture of medieval times. It was also an era when increasing mass production by machines threatened the existence of crafts and craft skills.

vicuna ▷ruminant mammal *Lama vicugna* of the camel family that lives in herds on the Andean plateau. It can run at speeds of 50 kph/30 mph. It has good eyesight, fair hearing, and a poor sense of smell. It was hunted close to extinction for its meat and soft brown fur, which was used in textile manufacture, but the vicuna is now a protected species; populations are increasing thanks to strict conservation measures. It is related to the ▷alpaca, the guanaco, and the ▷llama.

videotext system in which information (text and simple pictures) is displayed on a television (video) screen. There are two basic systems, known as ▷teletext and viewdata. In the teletext system information is broadcast with the ordinary television signals, whereas in the viewdata system information is relayed to the screen from a central data bank via the telephone network. Both systems require the use of a television receiver with special decoder.

Vienna (German *Wien*) capital of Austria, on the river Danube at the foot of the Wiener Wald (Vienna Woods); population (1986) 1,481,000. Industries include engineering and the production of electrical goods and precision instruments.

Vienna, Congress of international conference held 1814–15 that agreed the settlement of Europe after the Napoleonic Wars. National representatives included the Austrian foreign minister Metternich, Alexander I of Russia, the British foreign secretary Castlereagh and military commander Wellington, and the French politician Talleyrand.

Vientiane (Lao *Vieng Chan*) capital and chief port of Laos on the Mekong River; population (1985) 377,000.

Vietnam Socialist Republic of; country in SE Asia, on the South China Sea, bordered N by China and W by Cambodia and Laos; *area* 329,600 sq km/ 127,259 sq mi; *capital* Hanoi; *physical* Red River and Mekong deltas, centre of cultivation and population; tropical rainforest; mountainous in N and

viper

NW; **head of state** Vo Chi Cong from 1987; **head of government** Vo Van Kiet from 1991; **political system** communism; **exports** rice, rubber, coal, iron, apatite; **population** (1990 est) 68,488,000 (750,000 refugees; many ethnic Chinese left 1975–79); **languages** Vietnamese (official); French, English, Khmer, Chinese, tribal; **recent history** captured by France 1858–84; became part of French colonial possessions of Indochina. Japanese removed at end of World War II 1945. Vietminh War for independence against French commenced 1946; French defeated at Dien Bien Phu 1954. Under the Geneva Convention, the country was divided along the 17th parallel 1954 into separate states of North Vietnam and South Vietnam, but plunged immediately into the Vietnam War, which ended with the declaration of the Socialist Republic of Vietnam 1976. War with Cambodia followed 1978, and border skirmishes with China 1979. Economic crisis led to the murder and robbery at sea of thousands of escaping Vietnamese boat people. Cambodia peace agreement signed 1991; relations with China normalized.

Vietnam War 1954–75. War between communist North Vietnam and US-backed South Vietnam. 200,000 South Vietnamese soldiers, 1 million North Vietnamese soldiers, and 500,000 civilians were killed. 56,555 US soldiers were killed 1961–75, a fifth of them by their own troops. The war destroyed 50% of the country's forest cover and 20% of agricultural land. Cambodia, a neutral neighbour, was bombed by the USA 1969–75, with 1 million killed or wounded.

Viking or **Norseman** medieval Scandinavian sea warrior. They traded with and raided Europe in the 8th–11th centuries, and often settled there. In France the Vikings were given ◊Normandy. Under Sweyn I they conquered England 1013, and his son Canute was king of England as well as Denmark and Norway. In the east they established the first Russian state and founded ◊Novgorod. They reached the Byzantine Empire in the south, and in the west sailed the seas to Ireland, Iceland, Greenland, and North America; see ◊Eric the Red, Leif ◊Ericsson, Vinland.

Vilnius capital of Lithuania; population (1987) 566,000. Industries include engineering and the manufacture of textiles, chemicals, and foodstuffs.

vine or **grapevine** any of various climbing woody plants of the genus *Vitis*, family Vitaceae, especially *V. vinifera*, native to Asia Minor and cultivated from antiquity. Its fruit is eaten or made into wine or other fermented drinks; dried fruits of certain varieties are known as raisins and currants. Many other species of climbing plant are also termed vines.

violet any plant of the genus *Viola*, family Violaceae, with toothed leaves and mauve, blue, or white flowers, such as the heath dog violet *V. canina* and sweet violet *V. odorata*. A ◊pansy is a kind of violet.

violin bowed, four-stringed musical instrument, the smallest and highest-pitched of the violin family. The strings are tuned in fifths (G, D, A, and E), with G as the lowest, tuned below middle C.

viper any front-fanged venomous snake of the family Viperidae. Vipers range in size from 30 cm/1 ft to 3 m/10 ft, and often have diamond or jagged markings. Most give birth to live young.

Virginia state in E USA; nickname Old Dominion; **area** 105,600 sq km/40,762 sq mi; **capital** Richmond; **towns** Norfolk, Virginia Beach, Newport News, Hampton, Chesapeake, Portsmouth; **features** Blue Ridge mountains, which include the Shenandoah National Park; Arlington National Cemetery; Mount Vernon (home of George Washington 1752–99); Monticello (Thomas Jefferson's home near Charlottesville); Stratford Hall (Robert E Lee's birthplace at Lexington); Williamsburg restoration; Jamestown and Yorktown historic sites; **products** sweet potatoes, maize, tobacco, apples, peanuts, coal, ships, lorries, paper, chemicals, processed food, textiles; **population** (1990) 6,187,400; **famous people** Richard E Byrd, Ella Fitzgerald, Patrick Henry, Thomas Jefferson, Robert E Lee, James Madison, George C Marshall, James Monroe, Edgar Allan Poe, John Tyler, Booker T Washington, George Washington, Woodrow Wilson; **history** named in honour of Elizabeth I; Jamestown first permanent English settlement in the New World 1607, slavery was introduced there 1619; settled by planters of indigo and tobacco; took a leading part in the American Revolution; one of the original Thirteen States. It joined the Confederacy in the Civil War, with Richmond the Confederate capital.

Virgin Islands group of about 100 small islands, northernmost of the Leeward Islands in the Antilles, West Indies. Tourism is the main industry. They comprise the **US Virgin Islands** St Thomas (with the capital, Charlotte Amalie), St Croix, St John, and about 50 small islets; area 350 sq km/135 sq mi; population (1990) 101,800; and the **British Virgin Islands** Tortola (with the capital, Road Town), Virgin Gorda, Anegada, and Jost van Dykes, and about 40 islets; area 150 sq km/58 sq mi; population (1987) 13,250. The US Virgin Islands were purchased from Denmark 1917, and form an 'unincorporated territory'. The British Virgin Islands were taken over from the Dutch by British settlers 1666, and have partial internal self-government.

virtual reality advanced form of computer simulation, in which a participant has the illusion of being part of an artificial environment. The participant views the environment through two tiny 3-D television screens built into a visor. Sensors detect movements of the head or body, causing the apparent viewing position to change. Gloves (datagloves) fitted with sensors may be worn, which allow the participant seemingly to pick up and move objects in the environment.

virus infectious particle consisting of a core of nucleic acid (DNA or RNA) enclosed in a protein shell. Viruses are acellular and able to function and reproduce only if they can invade a living cell to use the cell's system to replicate themselves. In the process they may disrupt or alter the host cell's own DNA. The healthy human body reacts by producing an antiviral protein, ◊interferon, which prevents the infection spreading to adjacent cells.

virus in computing, a piece of ◊software that can replicate itself and transfer itself from one computer to another, without the user being aware of it. Some viruses are relatively harmless, but others can damage or destroy data. They are written by anonymous programmers, often maliciously, and are spread along telephone lines or on ◊floppy discs. Antivirus software can be used to detect and destroy well-known viruses, but new viruses continually appear and these may bypass existing antivirus programs.

Visconti Luchino 1906–1976. Italian film, opera, and theatre director. The film *Ossessione* 1942 pioneered neorealist cinema despite being subject to censorship problems from the fascist government; later works include *Rocco and His Brothers* 1960, *The Leopard* 1963, *The Damned* 1969, and *Death in Venice* 1971.

viscosity in physics, the resistance of a fluid to flow, caused by its internal friction, which makes it resist flowing past a solid surface or other layers of the fluid. It applies to the motion of an object moving through a fluid as well as to the motion of a fluid passing by an object.

Vishnu in Hinduism, the second in the triad of gods (with Brahma and Siva) representing three aspects of the supreme spirit. He is the *Preserver*, and is believed to have assumed human appearance in nine *avatāra*s, or incarnations, in such forms as Rama and Krishna. His worshippers are the Vaishnavas.

vitamin any of various chemically unrelated organic compounds that are necessary in small quantities for the normal functioning of the body. Many act as coenzymes, small molecules that enable ◊enzymes to function effectively. They are normally present in adequate amounts in a balanced diet. Deficiency of a vitamin will normally lead to a metabolic disorder ('deficiency disease'), which can be remedied by sufficient intake of the vitamin. They are generally classified as *water-soluble* (B and C) or *fat-soluble* (A, D, E, and K).

Vivaldi Antonio (Lucio) 1678–1741. Italian Baroque composer, violinist, and conductor. He wrote 23 symphonies, 75 sonatas, over 400 concertos, including the *Four Seasons* (about 1725) for violin and orchestra, over 40 operas, and much sacred music. His work was largely neglected until the 1930s.

vivisection literally, cutting into a living animal. Used originally to mean experimental surgery or dissection practised on a live subject, the term is often used by antivivisection campaigners to include any experiment on animals, surgical or otherwise.

Vladivostok port (naval and commercial) in E Siberian Russia, at the Amur Bay on the Pacific coast; population (1987) 615,000. It is kept open by icebreakers during winter. Industries include shipbuilding and the manufacture of precision instruments.

Vojvodina autonomous area in N Serbia, Yugoslavia; area 21,500 sq km/8,299 sq mi; population (1986) 2,050,000, including 1,110,000 Serbs and 390,000 Hungarians. Its capital is Novi Sad. In Sept 1990 Serbia effectively stripped Vojvodina of it autonomous status, causing anti-government and anticommunist riots in early 1991.

volcano vent in the Earth's crust from which molten rock, lava, ashes, and gases are ejected. Usually it is cone-shaped with a pitlike opening at the top called the crater. Some volcanoes, for example, Stromboli and Vesuvius in Italy, eject the material with explosive violence; others, for example on Hawaii, are quiet and the lava simply rises into the crater and flows over the rim.

Volga longest river in Europe; 3,685 km/2,290 mi, 3,540 km/2,200 mi of which are navigable. It drains most of the central and eastern parts of European Russia, rises in the Valdai plateau, and flows into the Caspian Sea 88 km/55 mi below Astrakhan.

Volgograd formerly (until 1925) *Tsaritsyn* and (1925–61) *Stalingrad* industrial city (metal goods, machinery, sawmills, oil refining) in SW Russia, on the river Volga; population (1987) 988,000.

Volta main river in Ghana, about 1,600 km/1,000 mi long, with two main upper branches, the Black and White Volta. It has been dammed to provide power.

Volta, Upper name until 1984 of ◊Burkina Faso.

Volta Alessandro 1745–1827. Italian physicist who invented the first electric cell (the voltaic pile), the electrophorus (an early electrostatic generator), and an electroscope.

Voltaire Pen name of François-Marie Arouet 1694–1778. French writer who believed in ◊deism and devoted himself to tolerance, justice, and humanity. He was threatened with arrest for *Lettres philosophiques sur les Anglais/Philosophical Letters on the English* 1733 (essays in favour of English ways, thought, and political practice) and had to take refuge. Other writings include *Le Siècle de*

Louis XIV/The Age of Louis XIV 1751; *Candide* 1759, a parody on ⟡Leibniz's 'best of all possible worlds'; and *Dictionnaire philosophique* 1764.

volume in geometry, the space occupied by a three-dimensional solid object. A prism (such as a cube) or a cylinder has a volume equal to the area of the base multiplied by the height. For a pyramid or cone, the volume is equal to one-third of the area of the base multiplied by the perpendicular height. The volume of a sphere is equal to $^4/_3\pi r^3$, where r is the radius. Volumes of irregular solids may be calculated by the technique of integration.

von Braun Wernher 1912–1977. German rocket engineer who developed German military rockets (V1 and V2) during World War II and later worked for the space agency NASA in the USA.

Von Neumann John 1903–1957. Hungarian-born US scientist and mathematician who pioneered work on computer design. He invented his 'rings of operators' (called **Von Neumann algebras**) in the late 1930s, and also contributed to set theory, games theory, cybernetics (with his theory of self-reproducing automata, called **Von Neumann machines**), and the development of the atomic and hydrogen bombs.

voodoo set of magical beliefs and practices, followed in some parts of Africa, South America, and the West Indies, especially Haiti. It arose in the 17th century on slave plantations as a combination of Roman Catholicism and W African religious traditions; believers retain membership in the Roman Catholic church.

vote expression of opinion by ⟡ballot, show of hands, or other means. In systems that employ direct vote, the ⟡plebiscite and ⟡referendum are fundamental mechanisms. In parliamentary elections the results can be calculated in a number of ways. The main electoral systems are: *simple plurality* or *first past the post*, with single-member constituencies (USA, UK, India, Canada); *absolute majority*, achieved for example by the *alternative vote*, where the voter, in single-member constituencies, chooses a candidate by marking preferences (Australia), or by the *second ballot*, where, if a clear decision is not reached immediately, a second ballot is held (France, Egypt); ⟡*proportional representation*, achieved for example by the *party list* system (Israel, most countries of Western Europe, and several in South America), the *additional member* system (Germany), the *single transferable vote* (Ireland and Malta), and the *limited vote* (Japan).

Voyager probes two US space probes, originally ⟡Mariners. *Voyager 1*, launched 5 Sept 1977, passed Jupiter March 1979, and reached Saturn Nov 1980. *Voyager 2* was launched earlier, 20 Aug 1977, on a slower trajectory that took it past Jupiter July 1979, Saturn Aug 1981, Uranus Jan 1986, and Neptune Aug 1989. Like the ⟡Pioneer probes, the Voyagers are on their way out of the Solar System. Their tasks now include helping scientists to locate the position of the heliopause, the boundary at which the influence of the Sun gives way to the forces exerted by other stars.

Vranitzky Franz 1937– . Austrian socialist politician, federal chancellor from 1986. A banker, he entered the political arena through the moderate, left-of-centre Socialist Party of Austria (SPÖ), and became minister of finance in 1984. He succeeded Fred Sinowatz as federal chancellor in 1986, heading an SPÖ-ÖVP (Austrian People's Party) coalition.

Vukovar river port in Croatia at the junction of rivers Vuka and Danube, 32 km/20 mi SE of Osijek; population (1981) 81,200. Industries include foodstuffs manufacture, fishing, and agricultural trade. In 1991 the town resisted three months of siege by the Serb-dominated Yugoslav army before capitulating. It suffered the severest damage inflicted to any European city since the bombing of Dresden during World War II.

Vulcan in Roman mythology, the god of fire and destruction, later identified with the Greek god ⟡Hephaestus.

vulcanization technique for hardening rubber by heating and chemically combining it with sulphur. The process also makes the rubber stronger and more elastic. If the sulphur content is increased to as much as 30%, the product is the inelastic solid known as ebonite. More expensive alternatives to sulphur, such as selenium and tellurium, are used to vulcanize rubber for specialized products such as vehicle tyres. The process was discovered accidentally by US inventor Charles Goodyear 1839 and patented 1844.

vulture any of various carrion-eating birds of prey with naked heads and necks and with keen senses of sight and smell. Vultures are up to 1 m/3.3 ft long, with wingspans of up to 3.5 m/11.5 ft. The plumage is usually dark, and the head brightly coloured.

up in political events. His works include *Ashes and Diamonds* 1958, *Man of Marble* 1977, *Man of Iron* 1981, *Danton* 1982, and *Korczak* 1990.

Wales (Welsh *Cymru*) principality; constituent part of the UK, in the west between the British Channel and the Irish Sea; *area* 20,780 sq km/8,021 sq mi; *capital* Cardiff; *towns* Swansea, Wrexham, Newport, Carmarthen; *features* Snowdonia mountains (Snowdon 1,085 m/3,561 ft, the highest point in England and Wales) in the NW and in the SE the Black Mountain, Brecon Beacons, and Black Forest ranges; rivers Severn, Wye, Usk, and Dee; *exports* traditional industries (coal and steel) have declined, but varied modern and high-technology ventures are being developed; Wales has the largest concentration of Japanese-owned plants in the UK. It also has the highest density of sheep in the world and a dairy industry; tourism is important; *currency* pound sterling; *population* (1987) 2,836,000; *language* Welsh 19% (1981), English; *religion* Nonconformist Protestant denominations; Roman Catholic minority; *government* returns 38 members to the UK Parliament.

Wałęsa Lech 1943– . Polish trade-union leader and president of Poland from 1990, founder of ◊Solidarity (Solidarność) in 1980, an organization, independent of the Communist Party, which forced substantial political and economic concessions from the Polish government 1980–81 until being outlawed. Nobel Peace Prize 1983.

Wales, Prince of title conferred on the eldest son of the UK's sovereign. Prince ◊Charles was invested as 21st prince of Wales at Caernarvon in 1969 by his mother, Elizabeth II.

Walker Alice 1944– . US poet, novelist, critic, and essay writer. She was active in the US civil-rights movement in the 1960s and, as a black woman, wrote about the double burden of racist and sexist oppression that such women bear. Her novel *The Color Purple* 1983 (filmed 1985) won the Pulitzer Prize.

Wallace Alfred Russel 1823–1913. English naturalist who collected animal and plant specimens in South America and SE Asia, and independently arrived at a theory of evolution by natural selection similar to that proposed by Charles ◊Darwin.

Wallachia independent medieval principality, founded 1290, with allegiance to Hungary until 1330 and under Turkish rule 1387–1861, when it was united with the neighbouring principality of Moldavia to form Romania.

Waller Fats (Thomas Wright) 1904–1943. US jazz pianist and composer with a forceful stride piano style. His songs, many of which have become jazz standards, include 'Ain't Misbehavin' 1929, 'Honeysuckle Rose' 1929, and 'Viper's Drag' 1934.

wallflower European perennial garden plant *Cheiranthus cheiri*, family Cruciferae, with fragrant red or yellow flowers in spring.

Wall Street street in Manhattan, New York, on

Waddington David Charles, Baron Waddington 1929– . British Conservative politician, home secretary 1989–90. A Conservative whip from 1979, he was a junior minister before becoming chief whip 1987. In 1990 he was made a life peer and became leader of the House of Lords in John Major's government.

wafer in microelectronics, a 'superchip' some 8–10 cm/3–4 in in diameter, for which wafer-scale integration (WSI) is used to link the equivalent of many individual ◊silicon chips, improving reliability, speed, and cooling.

Wagner Richard 1813–1883. German opera composer. He revolutionized the 19th-century conception of opera, envisaging it as a wholly new art form in which musical, poetic, and scenic elements should be unified through such devices as the leitmotif. His operas include *Tannhäuser* 1845, *Lohengrin* 1850, and *Tristan und Isolde* 1865. In 1872 he founded the Festival Theatre in Bayreuth; his masterpiece *Der Ring des Nibelungen/The Ring of the Nibelung*, a sequence of four operas, was first performed there 1876. His last work, *Parsifal*, was produced 1882.

wagtail any slim narrow-billed bird of the genus *Motacilla*, about 18 cm/7 in long, with a characteristic flicking movement of the tail. There are about 30 species, found mostly in Eurasia and Africa.

Waite Terry (Terence Hardy) 1939– . British religious adviser 1980–87 to the archbishop of Canterbury, then Dr Robert Runcie. As the archbishop's special envoy, Waite disappeared 20 Jan 1987 while engaged in secret negotiations to free European hostages in Beirut, Lebanon. He had been taken hostage by an Islamic group and was released 18 Nov 1991.

Wajda Andrzej 1926– . Polish film and theatre director, one of the major figures in postwar European cinema. His films are concerned with the predicament and disillusion of individuals caught

which the stock exchange is situated, and a synonym for stock dealing in the USA. It is so called from a stockade erected 1653.

Wall Street crash 1929 panic selling on the New York Stock Exchange following an artificial boom 1927–29 fed by speculation. On 24 Oct 1929, 13 million shares changed hands, with further heavy selling on 28 Oct and the disposal of 16 million shares on 29 Oct. Many shareholders were ruined, banks and businesses failed, and in the ⟡Depression that followed, unemployment rose to approximately 17 million.

walnut tree *Juglans regia*, probably originating in SE Europe. It can reach 30 m/100 ft, and produces a full crop of nuts about a dozen years from planting; the timber is used in furniture and the oil is used in cooking.

Walpole Robert, 1st Earl of Orford 1676–1745. British Whig politician, the first 'prime minister' as First Lord of the Treasury and chancellor of the Exchequer 1715–17 and 1721–42. He encouraged trade and tried to avoid foreign disputes (until forced into the War of Jenkins's Ear with Spain 1739).

walrus Arctic marine carnivorous mammal *Odobenus rosmarus* of the same family (Otaridae) as the eared ⟡seals. It can reach 4 m/13 ft in length, and weigh up to 1,400 kg/3,000 lb. It has webbed flippers, a bristly moustache, and large tusks. It is gregarious except at breeding time and feeds mainly on molluscs. It has been hunted close to extinction for its ivory tusks, hide, and blubber. The Alaskan walrus is close to extinction.

Wankel engine rotary petrol engine developed by the German engineer Felix Wankel (1902–) in the 1950s. It operates according to the same stages as the ⟡four-stroke petrol engine cycle, but these stages take place in different sectors of a figure-eight chamber in the space between the chamber walls and a triangular rotor. Power is produced once on every turn of the rotor. The Wankel engine is simpler in construction than the four-stroke piston petrol engine, and produces rotary power directly (instead of via a crankshaft). Problems with rotor seals have prevented its widespread use.

wapiti or **elk** species of deer *Cervus canadensis*, native to North America, Europe, and Asia, including New Zealand. It is reddish brown in colour, about 1.5 m/5 ft at the shoulder, weighs up to 450 kg/1,000 lb, and has antlers up to 1.2 m/4 ft long. It is becoming increasingly rare.

Warbeck Perkin *c.* 1474–1499. Flemish pretender to the English throne. Claiming to be Richard, brother of Edward V, he led a rising against Henry VII in 1497, and was hanged after attempting to escape from the Tower of London.

warbler any of two families of songbirds, order Passeriformes. Old World species, which grow up to 25 cm/10 in long and feed on berries and insects, include the chiffchaff, blackcap, goldcrest, and willow warbler.

Warhol Andy. Adopted name of Andrew Warhola

Wales, history

c. **400 BC**	Wales occupied by Celts from central Europe.
AD 50–60	Wales became part of the Roman Empire.
c. **200**	Christianity adopted.
c. **450–600**	Wales became the chief Celtic stronghold in the west since the Saxons invaded and settled in S Britain. The Celtic tribes united against England.
8th century	Frontier pushed back to ⟡Offa's Dyke.
9th–11th centuries	Vikings raided the coasts. At this time Wales was divided into small states organized on a clan basis, although princes such as Rhodri (844–878), Howel the Good (*c.* 904–949), and Griffith ap Llewelyn (1039–1063) temporarily united the country.
11th–12th centuries	Continual pressure on Wales from the Normans across the English border was resisted, notably by ⟡Llewelyn I and II.
1277	Edward I of England accepted as overlord by the Welsh.
1284	Edward I completed the conquest of Wales that had been begun by the Normans.
1294	Revolt against English rule put down by Edward I.
1350–1500	Welsh nationalist uprisings against the English; the most notable was that led by Owen Glendower.
1485	Henry Tudor, a Welshman, became Henry VII of England.
1536–43	Acts of Union united England and Wales after conquest under Henry VIII. Wales sent representatives to the English Parliament; English law was established in Wales; English became the official language.
18th century	Evangelical revival made Nonconformism a powerful factor in Welsh life. A strong coal and iron industry developed in the south.
19th century	The miners and ironworkers were militant supporters of Chartism, and Wales became a stronghold of trade unionism and socialism.
1920s–30s	Wales suffered from industrial depression; unemployment reached 21% 1937, and a considerable exodus of population took place.
post-1945	Growing nationalist movement and a revival of the language, earlier suppressed or discouraged
1966	⟡Plaid Cymru, the Welsh National Party, returned its first member to Westminster.
1979	Referendum rejected a proposal for limited home rule.

1928–1987. US Pop artist and filmmaker. He made his name in 1962 with paintings of Campbell's soup cans, Coca-Cola bottles, and film stars. In his New York studio, the Factory, he produced series of garish silk-screen prints. His films include the semidocumentary *Chelsea Girls* 1966 and *Trash* 1970.

War of 1812 war between the USA and Britain caused by British interference with US trade as part of the economic warfare against Napoleonic France. Tensions with the British in Canada led to plans for a US invasion but these were never realized and success was limited to the capture of Detroit and a few notable naval victories. In 1814, British forces occupied Washington DC and burned many public buildings. A treaty signed in Ghent, Belgium, Dec 1814 ended the conflict.

Warsaw (Polish *Warszawa*) capital of Poland, on the river Vistula; population (1990) 1,655,700. Industries include engineering, food processing, printing, clothing, and pharmaceuticals.

Warsaw Pact military alliance 1955–91 between the USSR and East European communist states, originally established as a response to the admission of West Germany into NATO. Its military structures and agreements were dismantled early in 1991; a political organization remained until the alliance was officially dissolved July 1991.

wart hog African wild ◊pig *Phacochoerus aethiopicus*, which has a large head with a bristly mane, fleshy pads beneath the eyes, and four large tusks. It has short legs and can grow to 80 cm/2.5 ft at the shoulder.

Warwick Richard Neville, Earl of Warwick 1428–1471. English politician, called *the Kingmaker*. During the Wars of the ◊Roses he fought at first on the Yorkist side against the Lancastrians, and was largely responsible for placing Edward IV on the throne. Having quarrelled with him, he restored Henry VI in 1470, but was defeated and killed by Edward at Barnet, Hertfordshire.

Warwickshire county in central England; *area* 1,980 sq km/764 sq mi; *towns* Warwick (administrative headquarters), Leamington, Nuneaton, Rugby, Stratford-upon-Avon; *features* Kenilworth and Warwick castles; remains of the Forest of Arden; site of the Battle of Edgehill; annual Royal Agricultural Show held at Stoneleigh; *products* mainly agricultural, engineering, textiles; *population* (1991) 477,000; *famous people* Rupert Brooke, George Eliot, William Shakespeare.

Wash, the bay of the North Sea between Norfolk and Lincolnshire, England.

Washington state in NW USA; nickname Evergreen State/Chinook State; *area* 176,700 sq km/ 68,206 sq mi; *capital* Olympia; *towns* Seattle, Spokane, Tacoma; *features* Columbia River; national parks: Olympic (Olympic Mountains),

Mount Rainier (Cascade Range), North Cascades; 90 dams; *products* apples and other fruits, potatoes, livestock, fish, timber, processed food, wood products, paper and allied products, aircraft and aerospace equipment, aluminium; *population* (1990) 4,866,700; including 1.4% Indians, mainly of the Yakima people; *famous people* Bing Crosby, Jimi Hendrix, Mary McCarthy, Theodore Roethke; *history* explored by Spanish, British, and Americans in the 18th century; settled from 1811; became a territory 1853 and a state 1889. Mount St Helens erupted 1980.

Washington George 1732–1799. First president of the USA 1789–97. As a strong opponent of the British government's policy, he sat in the ◊Continental Congresses of 1774 and 1775, and on the outbreak of the War of ◊American Independence was chosen commander in chief. After the war he retired to his Virginia estate, Mount Vernon, but in 1787 he re-entered politics as president of the Constitutional Convention. Although he attempted to draw his ministers from all factions, his aristocratic outlook alienated his secretary of state, Thomas Jefferson, who resigned in 1793, thus creating the two-party system.

Washington DC (District of Columbia) national capital of the USA, on the Potomac River; *area* 180 sq km/69 sq mi; *capital* the District of Columbia covers only the area of the city of Washington; *features* designed by a French engineer, Pierre L'Enfant (1754–1825). Among buildings of architectural note are the Capitol, the Pentagon, the White House, and the Lincoln Memorial. The National Gallery has a good collection of paintings; libraries include the Library of Congress, the National Archives, and the Folger Shakespeare Library. The Smithsonian Institution is here; *population* (1983) 623,000 (metropolitan area, extending outside the District of Columbia, 3 million); *history* the District of Columbia, initially land ceded from Maryland and Virginia, was established by Act of Congress 1790–91, and was first used as the seat of Congress 1800. The right to vote in national elections was not granted to residents until 1961. Local self-rule began 1975. In 1988 Washington had the highest murder rate of any large city in the USA.

wasp any of several families of winged stinging insects of the order Hymenoptera, characterized by a thin stalk between the thorax and the abdomen. Wasps can be social or solitary. Among social wasps, the queens devote themselves to egg laying, the fertilized eggs producing female workers; the males come from unfertilized eggs and have no sting. The larvae are fed on insects, but the mature wasps feed mainly on fruit and sugar. In winter, the fertilized queens hibernate, but the other wasps die.

waste materials that are no longer needed and are discarded. Examples are household waste, industrial waste (which often contains toxic chemicals), medical waste (which may contain organisms that cause disease), and ◊nuclear waste (which is radioactive). By ◊recycling, some materials in waste can be reclaimed for further use. In 1990 the industrialized nations generated 2 billion tonnes of waste. Britain generates about 50 million tonnes of waste per year.

waste disposal depositing waste. Methods of waste disposal vary according to the materials in the waste and include incineration, burial at designated sites, and dumping at sea. Organic waste can be treated and reused as fertilizer. ◊Nuclear waste and ◊toxic waste is usually buried or dumped at sea, although this does not negate the danger. The industrial waste dumped every year by the UK in the North Sea includes 550,000 tonnes of fly ash from coal-fired power stations. The Irish Sea receives 80 tonnes of uranium a year, and 300 million gallons of sewage every day. In 1988, 80,000 tonnes of hazardous waste was imported into the UK for processing.

water H_2O liquid without colour, taste, or odour. It is an oxide of hydrogen. Water begins to freeze at 0°C or 32°F, and to boil at 100°C or 212°F. When liquid, it is virtually incompressible; frozen, it expands by $1/11$ of its volume. At 39.2°F/4°C, one cubic centimetre of water has a mass of one gram; this is its maximum density, forming the unit of specific gravity. It has the highest known specific heat, and acts as an efficient solvent, particularly when hot. Most of the world's water is in the sea; less than 0.01% is fresh water.

water boatman any water ◊bug of the family Corixidae that feeds on plant debris and algae. It has a flattened body 1.5 cm/0.6 in long, with oarlike legs.

watercolour painting method of painting with pigments mixed with water, known in China as early as the 3rd century. The art as practised today began in England in the 18th century with the work of Paul Sandby and was developed by Thomas Girtin and J M W Turner. Other watercolourists were Raoul Dufy, Paul Cézanne, and John Marin. The technique of watercolour painting requires great skill since its transparency rules out overpainting.

watercress perennial aquatic plant *Nasturtium officinale* of the crucifer family, found in Europe and Asia, and cultivated as a salad crop.

water cycle in ecology, the natural circulation of water through the ◊biosphere. Water is lost from the Earth's surface to the atmosphere either by evaporation from the surface of lakes, rivers, and oceans or through the transpiration of plants. This atmospheric water forms clouds that condense to deposit moisture on the land and sea as rain or snow. The water that collects on land flows to the ocean in streams and rivers.

water flea any aquatic crustacean in the order Cladocera, of which there are over 400 species. The commonest species is *Daphnia pulex*, used in the pet trade to feed tropical fish.

Waterford county in Munster province, Republic of Ireland; area 1,840 sq km/710 sq mi; population (1991) 91,600. The county town is Waterford. The county includes the rivers Suir and Blackwater, and the Comeragh and Monavallagh mountain ranges in the north and centre. Products include cattle, beer, whiskey, and glassware.

Watergate US political scandal, named after the building in Washington DC that housed the Democrats' campaign headquarters in the 1972 presidential election. Five men, hired by the Republican Committee to Re-elect the President (CREEP), were caught after breaking into the Watergate with complex electronic surveillance equipment. Over the next two years, investigations by the media and a Senate committee revealed that the White House was implicated in the break-in, and that there was a 'slush fund', used to finance unethical activities. In Aug 1974, President ◊Nixon was forced by the Supreme Court to surrender to Congress tape recordings of conversations he had held with administration officials, and these indicated his complicity in a cover-up. Nixon resigned rather than face impeachment for obstruction of justice and other crimes, the only US president to have left office through resignation.

water glass common name for sodium metasilicate (Na_2SiO_3). It is a colourless, jellylike substance that dissolves readily in water to give a solution used for preserving eggs and fireproofing porous materials such as cloth, paper, and wood. It is also used as an adhesive for paper and cardboard and in the manufacture of soap and silica gel, a substance that absorbs moisture.

water hyacinth tropical aquatic plant *Eichhornia crassipes* of the pickerelweed family Pontederiaceae. In one growing season 25 plants can produce 2 million new plants. It is liable to choke waterways, depleting the water of nutrients and blocking the sunlight, but can be used as a purifier of sewage-polluted water as well as in making methane gas, compost, concentrated protein, paper, and baskets. Originating in South America, it now grows in more than 50 countries.

water lily aquatic plant of the family Nymphaeaceae. The fleshy roots are embedded in mud and the large round leaves float on the water. The cup-shaped flowers may be white, pink, yellow, or blue. The white *Nymphaea alba* and yellow *Nuphar lutea* are common in Europe.

Waterloo, Battle of battle on 18 June 1815 in which British forces commanded by Wellington defeated the French army of Emperor Napoleon near the village of Waterloo, 13 km/8 mi S of Brussels, Belgium. Napoleon found Wellington's army isolated from his allies and began a direct offensive to smash them, but the British held on until joined by the

Prussians under General Blücher. Four days later Napoleon abdicated for the second and final time.

watermelon large ◊melon *Citrullus vulgaris* of the gourd family, native to tropical Africa, with pink, white, or yellow flesh studded with black seeds and a green rind. It is widely cultivated in subtropical regions.

water pollution any addition to fresh or sea water that disrupts biological processes or causes a health hazard. Common pollutants include nitrate, pesticides, and sewage, though a huge range of industrial contaminants, such as chemical by-products and residues created in the manufacture of various goods, also enter water – legally, accidentally, and through illegal dumping.

water table the upper level of ground water (water collected underground in porous rocks). Water that is above the water table will drain downwards; a spring forms where the water table cuts the surface of the ground. The water table rises and falls in response to rainfall and the rate at which water is extracted, for example, for irrigation.

Watson James Dewey 1928– . US biologist whose research on the molecular structure of DNA and the genetic code, in collaboration with Francis ◊Crick, earned him a shared Nobel prize in 1962.

watt SI unit (symbol W) of power (the rate of expenditure or consumption of energy). A light bulb may use 40, 100, or 150 watts of power; an electric heater will use several kilowatts (thousands of watts). The watt is named after the Scottish engineer James Watt.

Watt James 1736–1819. Scottish engineer who developed the steam engine. He made Thomas Newcomen's steam engine vastly more efficient by cooling the used steam in a condenser separate from the main cylinder.

Watteau Jean-Antoine 1684–1721. French Rococo painter. He developed a new category of genre painting known as the *fête galante*, scenes of a kind of aristocratic pastoral fantasy world. One of these pictures, *The Embarkation for Cythera* 1717 (Louvre, Paris), won him membership in the French Academy.

wattle certain species of ◊acacia in Australia, where their fluffy golden flowers are the national emblem. The leathery leaves, adapted to drought conditions, further avoid loss of water through transpiration by turning their edges to the direct rays of the sun. Wattles are used for tanning and in fencing.

Waugh Evelyn (Arthur St John) 1903–1966. English novelist. His social satires include *Decline and Fall* 1928, *Vile Bodies* 1930, and *The Loved One* 1948. A Roman Catholic convert from 1930, he developed a serious concern with religious issues in *Brideshead Revisited* 1945. *The Ordeal of Gilbert Pinfold* 1957 is largely autobiographical.

wave in physics, a disturbance travelling through a medium (or space). There are two types: in a

longitudinal wave (such as a ◊sound wave) the disturbance is parallel to the wave's direction of travel; in a **transverse wave** (such as an ◊electromagnetic wave) it is perpendicular. The medium (for example the Earth, for seismic waves) is not permanently displaced by the passage of a wave.

wave in the oceans, a ridge or swell formed by wind. The power of a wave is determined by the strength of the wind and the distance of open water over which the wind blows (the fetch). Waves are the main agents of coastal erosion and deposition: sweeping away or building up beaches, creating spits and berms, and wearing down cliffs by their hydraulic action and by the corrasion of the sand and shingle that they carry.

wavelength the distance between successive crests of a ◊wave. The wavelength of a light wave determines its colour; red light has a wavelength of about 700 nanometres, for example. The complete range of wavelengths of electromagnetic waves is called the electromagnetic ◊spectrum.

wave power power obtained by harnessing the energy of water waves. A number of wave-power devices have been advanced (such as the duck: a floating boom whose segments bob up and down with the waves, driving a generator).

wax solid fatty substance of animal, vegetable, or mineral origin. Waxes are composed variously of ◊esters, ◊fatty acids, free ◊alcohols, and solid hydrocarbons.

waxbill any of a group of small mainly African seed-eating birds in the family Estrildidae, order Passeriformes, which also includes the grass finches of Australia. Waxbills grow to 15 cm/6 in long, are brown and grey with yellow, red, or brown markings, and have waxy-looking red or pink beaks.

Wayne John ('Duke'). Stage name of Marion Morrison 1907–1979. US actor, the archetypal Western hero: plain-speaking, brave, and solitary. His films include *Stagecoach* 1939, *Red River* 1948, *She Wore a Yellow Ribbon* 1949, *The Searchers* 1956, *Rio Bravo* 1959, *The Man Who Shot Liberty Valance* 1962, and *True Grit* 1969 (Academy Award). He was active in conservative politics.

weak nuclear force one of the four fundamental forces of nature, the other three being gravity, the electromagnetic force, and the strong nuclear force. It causes radioactive decay and other subatomic reactions. The particles that carry the weak force are called ◊weakons (or intermediate vector bosons) and comprise the positively and negatively charged W particles and the neutral Z particle.

Wear river in NE England; length 107 km/67 mi. From its source in the Pennines it flows east, past Durham, to meet the North Sea at Sunderland.

weasel any of various small, short-legged, lithe carnivorous mammals with bushy tails, especially the genus *Mustela*, found worldwide except Australia. They feed mainly on small rodents, although some, like the mink *M. vison*, hunt aquatic prey. Most are 12–25 cm/5–10 in long, excluding tail.

weaver any small bird of the family Ploceidae, order Passeriformes, mostly about 15 cm/6 in long, which includes the house ▷sparrow. The majority of weavers are African, a few Asian. The males use grasses to weave elaborate globular nests in bushes and trees. Males are often more brightly coloured than females.

weaving the production of textile fabric by means of a loom. The basic process is the interlacing at right angles of longitudinal threads (the warp) and horizontal threads (the weft), the latter being carried across from one side of the loom to the other by a type of bobbin called a shuttle. The power loom was invented 1786.

Webb (Martha) Beatrice (born Potter) 1858–1943 and Sidney (James), Baron Passfield 1859–1947. English social reformers, writers, and founders of the London School of Economics (LSE) 1895. They were early members of the socialist ▷Fabian Society, and were married in 1892. They argued for social insurance in their minority report (1909) of the Poor Law Commission, and wrote many influential books, including *The History of Trade Unionism* 1894, *English Local Government* 1906–29, and *Soviet Communism* 1935.

Webber Andrew Lloyd. English composer of musicals: see ▷Lloyd Webber.

weber SI unit (symbol Wb) of magnetic flux (the magnetic field strength multiplied by the area through which the field passes). One weber equals 10^8 maxwells.

Weber Carl Maria Friedrich Ernst von 1786–1826. German composer who established the Romantic school of opera with *Der Freischütz* 1821 and *Euryanthe* 1823. He was kapellmeister (chief conductor) at Breslau 1804–06, Prague 1813–16, and Dresden 1816. He died during a visit to London where he produced his opera *Oberon* 1826, written for the Covent Garden theatre.

Weber Max 1864–1920. German sociologist, one of the founders of modern sociology. He emphasized cultural and political factors as key influences on economic development and individual behaviour.

Webern Anton (Friedrich Wilhelm von) 1883–1945. Austrian composer. He was a pupil of Arnold ▷Schoenberg, whose 12–tone technique he adopted. He wrote works of extreme brevity; for example, the oratorio *Das Augenlicht/The Light of Eyes* 1935, and songs to words by Stefan George and poems of Rilke.

Webster John *c.* 1580–1634. English dramatist who ranks after Shakespeare as the greatest tragedian of his time and is the Jacobean whose plays are most frequently performed today. His two great plays

The White Devil 1608 and *The Duchess of Malfi* 1614 are dark, violent tragedies obsessed with death and decay and infused with poetic brilliance.

Weddell Sea arm of the S Atlantic Ocean that cuts into the Antarctic continent SE of Cape Horn; area 8,000,000 sq km/3,000,000 sq mi. Much of it is covered with thick pack ice for most of the year. It is named after the British explorer James Weddell.

Wedgwood Josiah 1730–1795. English pottery manufacturer. He set up business in Staffordshire in the early 1760s to produce his agateware as well as unglazed blue or green stoneware decorated with white Neo-Classical designs, using pigments of his own invention.

weedkiller or *herbicide* chemical that kills some or all plants. Selective herbicides are effective with cereal crops because they kill all broad-leaved plants without affecting grasslike leaves. Those that kill all plants include sodium chlorate and paraquat; see also ▷Agent Orange. The widespread use of weedkillers in agriculture has led to a dramatic increase in crop yield but also to pollution of soil and water supplies and killing of birds and small animals, as well as creating a health hazard for humans.

weevil any of a superfamily (Curculionoidea) of ▷beetles, usually less than 6 mm/0.25 in long, and with a head prolonged into a downward beak, which is used for boring into plant stems and trees for feeding. The adult beetles of *Phyllobius* and *Polydrusus*, the common British genera, are bright green.

weight the force exerted on an object by ▷gravity. The weight of an object depends on its mass – the amount of material in it – and the strength of the Earth's gravitational pull, which decreases with height. Consequently, an object weighs less at the top of a mountain than at sea level. On the Moon, an object has only one-sixth of its weight on Earth, because the pull of the Moon's gravity is one-sixth that of the Earth.

weightlifting sport of lifting the heaviest possible weight above one's head to the satisfaction of judges. In international competitions there are two standard lifts: *snatch* and *jerk*.

Weill Kurt (Julian) 1900–1950. German composer, US citizen from 1943. He wrote chamber and orchestral music and collaborated with Bertolt ▷Brecht on operas such as *Die Dreigroschenoper/ The Threepenny Opera* 1928 and *Aufstieg und Fall der Stadt Mahagonny/The Rise and Fall of the City of Mahagonny* 1930, all attacking social corruption.

Weimar Republic the constitutional republic in Germany 1919–33, which was crippled by the election of antidemocratic parties to the ▷Reichstag (parliament), and then subverted by the Nazi leader Hitler after his appointment as chancellor 1933. It took its name from the city where in Feb 1919 a constituent assembly met to draw up a democratic constitution.

Weizmann Chaim 1874–1952. Zionist leader, the first president of Israel (1948–52), and a chemist. He conducted the negotiations leading up to the Balfour Declaration, by which Britain declared its support for an independent Jewish state.

welding joining pieces of metal (or nonmetal) at faces rendered plastic or liquid by heat or pressure (or both). The principal processes today are gas and arc welding, in which the heat from a gas flame or an electric arc melts the faces to be joined. Additional 'filler metal' is usually added to the joint.

welfare state political system under which the state (rather than the individual or the private sector) has responsibility for the welfare of its citizens. Services such as unemployment and sickness benefits, family allowances and income supplements, pensions, medical care, and education may be provided and financed through state insurance schemes and taxation.

Welles (George) Orson 1915–1985. US actor and film and theatre director, whose first film was *Citizen Kane* 1941, which he produced, directed, and starred in. Using innovative lighting, camera angles and movements, he made it a landmark in the history of cinema, yet he directed very few films subsequently in Hollywood. His performances as an actor include the character of Harry Lime in *The Third Man* 1949.

Wellington capital and industrial port (woollen textiles, chemicals, soap, footwear, bricks) of New Zealand in North Island on Cook Strait; population (1989) 324,600. The harbour was sighted by Captain Cook 1773.

Wellington Arthur Wellesley, 1st Duke of Wellington 1769–1852. British soldier and Tory politician. As commander in the ◊Peninsular War, he expelled the French from Spain 1814. He defeated Napoleon Bonaparte at Quatre-Bras and Waterloo 1815, and was a member of the Congress of Vienna. As prime minister 1828–30, he was forced to concede Roman Catholic emancipation.

Wells H(erbert) G(eorge) 1866–1946. English writer of 'scientific romances' such as *The Time Machine* 1895 and *The War of the Worlds* 1898. His later novels had an anti-establishment, anticonventional humour remarkable in its day, for example *Kipps* 1905 and *Tono-Bungay* 1909. His many other books include *Outline of History* 1920 and *The Shape of Things to Come* 1933, a number of his prophecies from which have since been fulfilled. He also wrote many short stories.

Welsh corgi breed of dog with a foxlike head and pricked ears. The coat is dense, with several varieties of colouring. Corgis are about 30 cm/1 ft at the shoulder, and weigh up to 12 kg/27 lbs.

Welsh language (Welsh **Cymraeg**) member of

the Celtic branch of the Indo-European language family, spoken chiefly in the rural north and west of Wales; it is the strongest of the surviving Celtic languages, and in 1981 was spoken by 18.9% of the Welsh population.

Wesley John 1703–1791. English founder of ◊Methodism. When the pulpits of the Church of England were closed to him and his followers, he took the gospel to the people. For 50 years he rode about the country on horseback, preaching daily, largely in the open air. His sermons became the doctrinal standard of the Wesleyan Methodist Church.

Wessex the kingdom of the West Saxons in Britain, said to have been founded by Cerdic about AD 500, covering present-day Hampshire, Dorset, Wiltshire, Berkshire, Somerset, and Devon. In 829 Egbert established West Saxon supremacy over all England. Thomas ◊Hardy used the term Wessex in his novels for the SW counties of England.

West Mae 1892–1980. US vaudeville, stage, and film actress. She wrote her own dialogue, setting herself up as a provocative sex symbol and the mistress of verbal innuendo. She appeared on Broadway in *Sex* 1926, *Drag* 1927, and *Diamond Lil* 1928, which was the basis of the film (with Cary Grant) *She Done Him Wrong* 1933. Her other films include *I'm No Angel* 1933, *Going to Town* 1934, *My Little Chickadee* 1944 (with W C Fields), *Myra Breckinridge* 1969, and *Sextette* 1977. Both her plays and her films led to legal battles over censorship.

West Rebecca. Pen name of Cicily Isabel Fairfield 1892–1983. British journalist and novelist, an active feminist from 1911. *The Meaning of Treason* 1959 deals with the spies Burgess and Maclean. Her novels have political themes and include *The Fountain Overflows* 1956 and *The Birds Fall Down* 1966.

West Bank area (5,879 sq km/2,270 sq mi) on the west bank of the river Jordan; population (1988) 866,000. The West Bank was taken by the Jordanian army 1948 at the end of the Arab-Israeli war that followed the creation of the state of Israel, and was captured by Israel during the Six-Day War 5–10 June 1967. The continuing Israeli occupation and settlement of the area has created tensions with the Arab population.

West Bengal state of NE India; **area** 87,900 sq km/33,929 sq mi; **capital** Calcutta; **towns** Asansol, Durgapur; **physical** occupies the west part of the vast alluvial plain created by the rivers Ganges and Brahmaputra, with the Hooghly River; annual rainfall in excess of 250 cm/100 in; **products** rice, jute, tea, coal, iron, steel, cars, locomotives, aluminium, fertilizers; **population** (1991) 67,982,700; **history** created 1947 from the former British province of Bengal, with later territories added: Cooch Behar 1950, Chandernagore 1954, and part of Bihar 1956.

Western Australia state of Australia; **area** 2,525,500 sq km/974,843 sq mi; **capital** Perth; **towns** main port Fremantle, Bunbury, Geraldton,

Kalgoorlie-Boulder, Albany; *features* largest state in Australia; Monte Bello Islands; *rivers* Fitzroy, Fortescue, Gascoyne, Murchison, Swan; NW coast subject to hurricanes (willy-willies); Lasseter's Reef; *products* wheat, fresh and dried fruit, meat and dairy products, natural gas (NW shelf) and oil (Canning Basin), iron (the Pilbara), copper, nickel, uranium, gold, diamonds; *population* (1987) 1,478,000; *history* a short-lived convict settlement at King George Sound 1826; the state founded at Perth 1829 by Captain James Stirling (1791–1865); self-government 1890; state 1901.

Western Isles island area of Scotland, comprising the Outer Hebrides (Lewis, Harris, North and South Uist, and Barra); unofficially the Inner and Outer Hebrides generally; *area* 2,900 sq km/1,120 sq mi; *towns* Stornoway on Lewis (administrative headquarters); *features* divided from the mainland by the Minch channel; Callanish monolithic circles of the Stone Age on Lewis; *products* Harris tweed, sheep, fish, cattle; *population* (1991) 29,100; *famous people* Flora MacDonald.

Western Sahara formerly *Spanish Sahara* disputed territory in NW Africa bounded to the N by Morocco, to the W and S by Mauritania, and to the E by the Atlantic Ocean; *area* 266,800 sq km/103,011 sq mi; *capital* Ad Dakhla; *towns* La'Youn, phosphate mining town of Bou Craa; *features* electrically monitored fortified wall 4,000 km/2,500 mi long, enclosing the phosphate area; *exports* phosphates; *currency* dirham; *population* (1988) 181,400; another estimated 165,000 live in refugee camps near Tindouf, SW Algeria. Ethnic composition: Sawrawis (traditionally nomadic herders); *language* Arabic; *religion* Sunni Muslim; *government* administered by Morocco; *history* this 1,000-km-long Saharan coastal region was designated a Spanish 'sphere of influence' 1884 because it lies opposite the Spanish-ruled Canary Islands. On securing its independence 1956, Morocco laid claim to this territory, and within Spanish Sahara a pro-independence nationalist movement (Polisario) developed, from 1973. When Spain withdrew 1975, the territory was partitioned between Morocco and Mauritania. Polisario rejected this partition, declared their own independent Saharan Arab Democratic Republic (SADR), and proceeded to wage a guerrilla war. When Mauritania withdrew 1979 from their southern sector, Morocco occupied it and began building the fortified wall, completed in 1987. In 1988, Morocco and the Polisario Front agreed to United Nations-sponsored plans for a cease-fire and a referendum in Western Sahara. However, sporadic fighting continued. By the end of 1990, 70 countries had granted diplomatic recognition to the SADR.

Western Samoa see ◊Samoa, Western.

West Glamorgan (Welsh *Gorllewin Morgannwg*) county in SW Wales; *area* 820 sq km/ 317 sq mi; *towns* Swansea (administrative headquarters), Port Talbot, Neath; *features* Gower Peninsula; *products* tinplate, copper, steel, chemicals; *population* (1991) 357,800; *language* 16% Welsh, English; *famous people* Richard Burton, Anthony Hopkins, Dylan Thomas.

West Indies archipelago of about 1,200 islands, dividing the Atlantic from the Gulf of Mexico and the Caribbean. The islands are divided into: *Bahamas*; *Greater Antilles* Cuba, Hispaniola (Haiti, Dominican Republic), Jamaica, and Puerto Rico; *Lesser Antilles* Aruba, Netherlands Antilles, Trinidad and Tobago, the Windward Islands (Grenada, Barbados, St Vincent, St Lucia, Martinique, Dominica, Guadeloupe), the Leeward Islands (Montserrat, Antigua, St Christopher (St Kitts)–Nevis, Barbuda, Anguilla, St Martin, British and US Virgin Islands), and many smaller islands.

West Irian former name of ◊Irian Jaya.

Westmeath inland county of Leinster province, Republic of Ireland; *area* 1,760 sq km/679 sq mi; *town* Mullingar (county town); *physical* rivers: Shannon, Inny, Brosna; lakes: Ree, Sheelin, Ennell; *products* agricultural and dairy products, limestone, textiles; *population* (1991) 61,900.

West Midlands metropolitan county in central England, created 1974, originally administered by an elected council; its powers reverted to district councils from 1986; *area* 900 sq km/347 sq mi; *towns* Birmingham; *features* created 1974 from the area around and including Birmingham, and comprising Wolverhampton, Walsall, Dudley, West Bromwich, Smethwick, Coventry; *products* industrial goods; *population* (1991) 2,500,400; *famous people* Edward Burne-Jones, Neville Chamberlain, Philip Larkin.

Westphalia independent medieval duchy, incorporated in Prussia by the Congress of Vienna 1815, and made a province 1816 with Münster as its capital. Since 1946 it has been part of the German *Land* (region) of ◊North Rhine–Westphalia.

Westphalia, Treaty of agreement 1648 ending the ◊Thirty Years' War. The peace marked the end of the supremacy of the Holy Roman Empire and the emergence of France as a dominant power. It recognized the sovereignty of the German states, Switzerland, and the Netherlands; Lutherans, Calvinists, and Roman Catholics were given equal rights.

West Sussex county on the south coast of England; *area* 2,020 sq km/780 sq mi; *towns* Chichester (administrative headquarters), Crawley, Horsham, Haywards Heath, Shoreham (port); resorts: Worthing, Littlehampton, Bognor Regis; *physical* the Weald, South Downs; rivers: Arun, West Rother, Adur; *features* Arundel and Bramber castles; Goodwood, Petworth House (17th century); Wakehurst Place, where the Royal Botanic Gardens, Kew, has additional grounds; the Weald and Downland Open Air Museum at Singleton; *population* (1991) 692,800; *famous people* Richard Cobden, Percy Bysshe Shelley.

whale

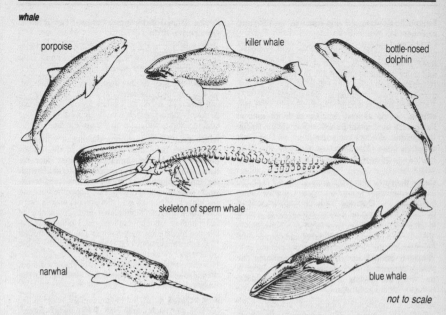

porpoise

killer whale

bottle-nosed dolphin

skeleton of sperm whale

narwhal

blue whale

not to scale

West Virginia state in E central USA; nickname Mountain State; *area* 62,900 sq km/24,279 sq mi; *capital* Charleston; *towns* Huntington, Wheeling; *physical* Allegheny Mountains; Ohio River; *features* port of Harper's Ferry, restored as when John Brown seized the US armoury 1859; *products* apples, maize, poultry, dairy and meat products, coal, natural gas, oil, chemicals, synthetic fibres, plastics, steel, glass, pottery; *population* (1990) 1,793,500; *famous people* Pearl Buck, Thomas 'Stonewall' Jackson, Cyrus Vance; *history* Moundbuilders in the 6th century; explorers and fur traders 1670s; German settlements 1730s; coal discovered on the Coal River 1742; industrial development early 19th century. On the secession of Virginia from the Union 1861, west Virginians dissented and formed a new state 1863. Industrial expansion was accompanied by labour strife in the early 20th century.

West Yorkshire metropolitan county in NE England, created 1976, originally administered by an elected metropolitan council; its powers reverted to district councils from 1986; *area* 2,040 sq km/787 sq mi; *towns* Wakefield, Leeds, Bradford, Halifax, Huddersfield; *features* Ilkley Moor, Haworth Moor, Haworth Parsonage; part of the Peak District National Park; *products* coal, woollen textiles; *population* (1987) 2,052,000; *famous people* the Brontës, David Hockney, Henry Moore, J B Priestley.

Wexford county in the Republic of Ireland, province of Leinster; *area* 2,350 sq km/907 sq mi; *towns*

Wexford (county town), Rosslare; *products* fish, livestock, oats, barley, potatoes; *population* (1991) 102,000.

Weyden Rogier van der *c.* 1399–1464. Netherlandish painter, official painter to the city of Brussels from 1436. He painted portraits and religious subjects, such as *The Last Judgement* about 1450 (Hôtel-Dieu, Beaune). His refined style had considerable impact on Netherlandish painting.

whale any marine mammal of the order Cetacea, with front limbs modified into flippers and with internal vestiges of hind limbs. The order is divided into the toothed whales (Odontoceti) and the baleen whales (Mysticeti). The toothed whales include ◊dolphins and ◊porpoises, along with large forms such as sperm whales. The baleen whales, with plates of modified mucous membrane called baleen in the mouth, are all large in size and include finback and right whales. There were hundreds of thousands of whales at the beginning of the 20th century, but they have been hunted close to extinction (see ◊whaling).

whaling the hunting of whales, largely discontinued 1986. Whales are, or were, killed for whale oil (made from the thick layer of fat under the skin called 'blubber'), used for food and cosmetics; for the large reserve of oil in the head of the sperm whale, used in the leather industry; and for *ambergris*, a waxlike substance from the intestines, used in making perfumes. There are synthetic substitutes for all these products. Whales are also killed for their meat, which is eaten by the

Japanese and was used as pet food in the USA and Europe.

wheat cereal plant derived from the wild *Triticum*, a grass native to the Middle East. It is the chief cereal used in breadmaking and is widely cultivated in temperate climates suited to its growth. Wheat is killed by frost, and damp renders the grain soft, so warm, dry regions produce the most valuable grain.

whelk any of various families of large marine snails with a thick spiral shell, especially the family Buccinidae. Whelks are scavengers, and also eat other shellfish. The largest grow to 40 cm/16 in long. Tropical species, such as the conches, can be very colourful.

Whig Party in the UK, predecessor of the Liberal Party. The name was first used of rebel ⟡Covenanters and then of those who wished to exclude James II from the English succession (as a Roman Catholic). They were in power continuously 1714–60 and pressed for industrial and commercial development, a vigorous foreign policy, and religious toleration. During the French Revolution, the Whigs demanded parliamentary reform in Britain, and from the passing of the Reform Bill in 1832 became known as Liberals.

whip in UK politics, the member of Parliament who ensures the presence of colleagues in the party when there is to be a vote in Parliament at the end of a debate. The written appeal sent by the whips to MPs is also called a whip; this letter is underlined once, twice, or three times to indicate its importance. A *three-line whip* is the most urgent, and every MP is expected to attend and vote with their party.

whippet breed of dog resembling a small greyhound. It grows to 56 cm/22 in at the shoulder, and 9 kg/20 lb in weight.

whip snake any of the various species of nonpoisonous slender-bodied tree-dwelling snakes of the New World genus *Masticophis*, family Colubridae, also called *coachwhips*. They are closely allied to members of the genus *Coluber* of SW North America, Eurasia, Australasia, and N Africa, some of which are called whip snakes in the Old World, but racers in North America.

Whistler James Abbott McNeill 1834–1903. US painter and etcher, active in London from 1859. His riverscapes and portraits show subtle composition and colour harmonies: for example, *Arrangement in Grey and Black: Portrait of the Painter's Mother* 1871 (Louvre, Paris).

White Patrick (Victor Martindale) 1912–1990. Australian writer who did more than any other to put Australian literature on the international map. His partly allegorical novels explore the lives of early settlers in Australia and often deal with misfits or inarticulate people. They include *The Aunt's Story* 1948, *The Tree of Man* 1955, and *Voss* 1957 (based

on the ill-fated 19th-century explorer Leichhardt). Nobel prize 1973.

whitebait any of the fry (young) of various silvery fishes, especially ⟡herring. It is also the name for a Pacific smelt *Osmerus mordax*.

whitebeam tree *Sorbus aria*, native to S Europe, usually found growing on chalk or limestone. It can reach 20 m/60 ft. It takes its name from the pinnately compound leaves, which have a dense coat of short white hairs on the underside.

white blood cell or *leucocyte* one of a number of different cells that play a part in the body's defences and give immunity against disease. Some (phagocytes and macrophages) engulf invading microorganisms, others kill infected cells, while lymphocytes produce more specific immune responses. White blood cells are colourless, with clear or granulated cytoplasm, and are capable of independent amoeboid movement. Unlike mammalian red blood cells, they possess a nucleus. Human blood contains about 11,000 leucocytes to the cubic millimetre — about one to every 500 red cells. However, these cells are not confined to the blood; they also occur in the ⟡lymph and elsewhere in the body's tissues.

white dwarf small, hot ⟡star, the last stage in the life of a star such as the Sun. White dwarfs have a mass similar to that of the Sun, but only 1% of the Sun's diameter, similar in size to the Earth. Most have surface temperatures of 8,000°C/14,400°F or more, hotter than the Sun. Yet, being so small, their overall luminosities may be less than 1% of that of the Sun. The Milky Way contains an estimated 50 billion white dwarfs.

whitefish any of various freshwater fishes, genera *Coregonus* and *Prosopium* of the salmon family, found in lakes and rivers of North America and Eurasia. They include the whitefish *C. clupeaformis* and vendace *C. gracilior*.

White Paper in the UK and some other countries, an official document that expresses government policy on an issue. It is usually preparatory to the introduction of a parliamentary bill (a proposed act of Parliament). Its name derives from its having fewer pages than a government 'blue book', and therefore needing no blue paper cover. ⟡

White Russia English translation of ⟡Belarus.

whitethroat any of several Old World warblers of the genus *Sylvia*, found in scrub, hedges, and wood clearings of Eurasia in summer, migrating to Africa in winter. They are about 14 cm/5.5 in long.

whiting predatory fish *Merlangius merlangus* common in shallow sandy N European waters. It grows to 70 cm/2.3 ft.

Whitman Walt(er) 1819–1892. US poet who published *Leaves of Grass* 1855, which contains the symbolic 'Song of Myself'. It used unconventional free verse (with no rhyme or regular rhythm) and scandalized the public by its frank celebration of sexuality. He preached a particularly American vision of individual freedom and human brotherhood.

Whittle Frank 1907– . British engineer who patented the basic design for the turbojet engine 1930. In the Royal Air Force he worked on jet propulsion 1937–46. In May 1941 the Gloster E 28/39 aircraft first flew with the Whittle jet engine. Both the German (first operational jet planes) and the US jet aircraft were built using his principles.

WHO acronym for ◊ *World Health Organization.*

Who, the English rock group, formed 1964, with a hard, aggressive sound, high harmonies, and a propensity for destroying their instruments on stage. Their albums include *Tommy* 1969, *Who's Next* 1971, and *Quadrophenia* 1973.

whooping cough or *pertussis* acute infectious disease, seen mainly in children, caused by colonization of the air passages by the bacterium *Bordetella pertussis.* There may be catarrh, mild fever, and loss of appetite, but the main symptom is violent coughing, associated with the sharp intake of breath that is the characteristic 'whoop', and often followed by vomiting and severe nose bleeds. The cough may persist for weeks.

whortleberry a form of ◊bilberry.

Wicklow county in the Republic of Ireland, province of Leinster; *area* 2,030 sq km/784 sq mi; *towns* Wicklow (county town); *physical* Wicklow Mountains; rivers: Slane, Liffey; *features* the village of Shillelagh gave its name to rough cudgels of oak or blackthorn made there; *population* (1991) 97,300.

Wiener Norbert 1884–1964. US mathematician, credited with the establishment of the science of cybernetics in his book *Cybernetics* (1948). In mathematics, he laid the foundation of the study of stochastic processes (those dependent on random events), including Brownian movement (evidence of constant random motion of molecules).

Wight, Isle of island and county in S England; *area* 380 sq km/147 sq mi; *towns* Newport (administrative headquarters), resorts: Ryde, Sandown, Shanklin, Ventnor; *features* the Needles, a group of pointed chalk rocks up to 30 m/100 ft high in the sea to the W; the Solent, the sea channel between Hampshire and the island (including the anchorage of Spithead opposite Portsmouth, used for naval reviews); Cowes, venue of Regatta Week and headquarters of the Royal Yacht Squadron; Osborne House, near Cowes, a home of Queen Victoria; *products* chiefly agricultural; tourism is important; *population* (1991) 126,600; *famous people* Thomas Arnold, Robert Hooke.

Wilberforce William 1759–1833. English reformer who was instrumental in abolishing slavery in the British Empire. He entered Parliament 1780; in 1807 his bill for the abolition of the slave trade was passed, and in 1833, largely through his efforts, slavery was abolished throughout the empire.

Wilde Oscar (Fingal O'Flahertie Wills) 1854–1900. Irish writer. With his flamboyant style and quotable conversation, he dazzled London society and, on his lecture tour 1882, the USA. He published his only novel, *The Picture of Dorian Gray*, 1891, followed by witty plays including *A Woman of No Importance* 1893 and *The Importance of Being Earnest* 1895. In 1895 he was imprisoned for two years for homosexual offences; he died in exile.

wildebeest another name for ◊gnu.

Wilder Billy 1906– . Austrian-born accomplished US screenwriter and film director, in the USA from 1934. He directed and coscripted *Double Indemnity* 1944, *The Lost Weekend* (Academy Award for best director) 1945, *Sunset Boulevard* 1950, *Some Like It Hot* 1959, and the Academy Award-winning *The Apartment* 1960.

wild type in genetics, the naturally occurring gene for a particular character that is typical of most individuals of a given species, as distinct from new genes that arise by mutation.

Wilhelm I 1797–1888. King of Prussia from 1861 and emperor of Germany from 1871; the son of Friedrich Wilhelm III. He served in the Napoleonic Wars 1814–15 and helped to crush the 1848 revolution. After he succeeded his brother Friedrich Wilhelm IV to the throne of Prussia, his policy was largely dictated by his chancellor ◊Bismarck, who secured his proclamation as emperor.

Wilhelm II 1859–1941. Emperor of Germany from 1888, the son of Frederick III and Victoria, daughter of Queen Victoria of Britain. In 1890 he forced Chancellor Bismarck to resign and began to direct foreign policy himself, which proved disastrous. He encouraged warlike policies and built up the German navy. In 1914 he first approved Austria's ultimatum to Serbia and then, when he realized war was inevitable, tried in vain to prevent it. In 1918 he fled to Holland, after Germany's defeat and his abdication.

Wilkes John 1727–1797. British Radical politician, imprisoned for his political views; member of Parliament 1757–64 and from 1774. He championed parliamentary reform, religious toleration, and US independence.

Wilkins Maurice Hugh Frederick 1916– . New Zealand-born British scientist. In 1962 he shared the Nobel Prize for Medicine with Francis ◊Crick and James ◊Watson for his work on the molecular structure of nucleic acids, particularly ◊DNA, using X-ray diffraction.

William I *the Conqueror* c. 1027–1087. King of England from 1066. He was the illegitimate son of Duke Robert the Devil and succeeded his father as duke of Normandy 1035. Claiming that his relative King Edward the Confessor had bequeathed him the English throne, William invaded the country 1066, defeating ◇Harold II at Hastings, Sussex, and was crowned king of England.

William II *Rufus, the Red c.* 1056–1100. King of England from 1087, the third son of William I. He spent most of his reign attempting to capture Normandy from his brother ◇Robert II, duke of Normandy. His extortion of money led his barons to revolt and caused confrontation with Bishop Anselm. He was killed while hunting in the New Forest, Hampshire, and was succeeded by his brother Henry I.

William III *William of Orange* 1650–1702. King of Great Britain and Ireland from 1688, the son of William II of Orange and Mary, daughter of Charles I. He was offered the English crown by the parliamentary opposition to James II. He invaded England 1688 and in 1689 became joint sovereign with his wife, ◇Mary II. He spent much of his reign campaigning, first in Ireland, where he defeated James II at the battle of the Boyne 1690, and later against the French in Flanders. He was succeeded by Anne.

William IV 1765–1837. King of Great Britain and Ireland from 1830, when he succeeded his brother George IV; third son of George III. He was created duke of Clarence 1789, and married Adelaide of Saxe-Meiningen (1792–1849) 1818. During the Reform Bill crisis he secured its passage by agreeing to create new peers to overcome the hostile majority in the House of Lords. He was succeeded by Victoria.

William *William the Lion* 1143–1214. King of Scotland from 1165. He was captured by Henry II while invading England 1174, and forced to do homage, but Richard I abandoned the English claim to suzerainty for a money payment 1189. In 1209 William was forced by King John to renounce his claim to Northumberland.

William *the Silent* 1533–1584. Prince of Orange from 1544. Leading a revolt against Spanish rule in the Netherlands from 1573, he briefly succeeded in uniting the Catholic south and Protestant northern provinces, but the former provinces submitted to Spain while the latter formed a federation 1579 which repudiated Spanish suzerainty 1581.

Williams Tennessee (Thomas Lanier) 1911–1983. US playwright, born in Mississippi. His work is characterized by fluent dialogue and searching analysis of the psychological deficiencies of his characters. His plays, usually set in the Deep South against a background of decadence and degradation, include *The Glass Menagerie* 1945, *A Streetcar Named Desire* 1947, and *Cat on a Hot Tin Roof* 1955, the last two of which earned Pulitzer Prizes.

Williamson Malcolm (Benjamin Graham Christopher) 1931– . Australian composer, pianist, and organist, who settled in Britain 1953. His works include operas such as *Our Man in Havana*

1963, symphonies, and chamber music. He became Master of the Queen's Music in 1975.

willow any tree or shrub of the genus *Salix*, family Salicaceae. There are over 350 species, mostly in the northern hemisphere, and they flourish in damp places. The leaves are often lance-shaped, and the male and female catkins are found on separate trees.

willowherb any plant of either of two genera *Epilobium* and *Chamaenerion* of perennial weeds. The rosebay willowherb or fireweed *C. angustifolium* is common in woods and wasteland. It grows to 1.2 m/4 ft with long terminal racemes of red or purplish flowers.

Wilson Charles Thomson Rees 1869–1959. British physicist who in 1911 invented the Wilson ◇cloud chamber, an apparatus for studying subatomic particles. He shared a Nobel prize 1927.

Wilson (James) Harold, Baron Wilson of Rievaulx 1916– . British Labour politician, party leader from 1963, prime minister 1964–70 and 1974–76. His premiership was dominated by the issue of UK admission to membership of the European Community, the social contract (unofficial agreement with the trade unions), and economic difficulties.

Wilson (Thomas) Woodrow 1856–1924. 28th president of the USA 1913–21, a Democrat. He kept the USA out of World War I until 1917, and in Jan 1918 issued his 'Fourteen Points' as a basis for a just peace settlement. At the peace conference in Paris he secured the inclusion of the ◇League of Nations in individual peace treaties, but these were not ratified by Congress, so the USA did not join the League. Nobel Peace Prize 1919.

Wiltshire county in SW England; *area* 3,480 sq km/1,343 sq mi; *towns* Trowbridge (administrative headquarters), Salisbury, Swindon, Wilton; *physical* Marlborough Downs; Savernake Forest; rivers: Kennet, Wylye, Salisbury and Bristol Avons; Salisbury Plain; *features* Salisbury Plain, a military training area used since Napoleonic times; Longleat House (Marquess of Bath); Wilton House (Earl of Pembroke); Stourhead, with 18th-century gardens; Neolithic Stonehenge, Avebury; *products* wheat, cattle, pig and sheep farming, rubber, engineering; *population* (1990) 553,300; *famous people* Isaac Pitman, William Talbot, Christopher Wren.

Windermere largest lake in England, in Cumbria, 17 km/10.5 mi long and 1.6 km/1 mi wide.

wind farm array of windmills or ◇wind turbines used for generating electrical power. A wind farm at Altamont Pass, California, USA, consists of 300 wind turbines, the smallest producing 60 kW and the largest 750 kW of electricity. To produce 1,200 megawatts of electricity (an output comparable with that of a nuclear power station), a wind farm would need to occupy around 370 sq km/140 sq mi.

Windhoek capital of Namibia; population (1988)

115,000. It is just north of the Tropic of Capricorn, 290 km/180 mi from the west coast.

windmill mill with sails or vanes that, by the action of wind upon them, drive machinery for grinding corn or pumping water, for example. Wind turbines, designed to use wind power on a large scale, usually have a propeller-type rotor mounted on a tall shell tower. The turbine drives a generator for producing electricity.

Windscale former name of ▷Sellafield, nuclear power station in Cumbria, England.

wind turbine windmill of advanced aerodynamic design connected to an electricity generator and used in wind-power installations. Wind turbines can be either large propeller-type rotors mounted on a tall tower, or flexible metal strips fixed to a vertical axle at top and bottom. In 1990, over 20,000 wind turbines were in use throughout the world, generating 1,600 megawatts of power.

Windward Islands islands in the path of the prevailing wind, notably: *West Indies* see under ▷Antilles; ▷*Cape Verde Islands*; ▷*French Polynesia* (Tahiti, Moorea, and Makatea).

wine alcoholic beverage, usually made from fermented grape pulp, although wines have also traditionally been made from many other fruits such as damsons and elderberries. *Red wine* is the product of the grape with the skin; *white wine* of the inner pulp of the grape. The sugar content is converted to ethyl alcohol by the yeast *Saccharomyces ellipsoideus*, which lives on the skin of the grape. For *dry wine* the fermentation is allowed to go on longer than for *sweet* or *medium*; ▷Champagne (sparkling wine from the Champagne region of France) is bottled while still fermenting, but other sparkling wines are artificially carbonated. Some wines are fortified with additional alcohol obtained from various sources, and with preservatives. Some of the latter may cause dangerous side effects (see ▷additive). For this reason, organic wines, containing no preservatives, have recently become popular. The largest wine-producing countries are Italy, France, Russia, Georgia, Moldova, Armenia, and Spain; others include almost all European countries, Australia, South Africa, the USA, and Chile.

Winnipeg capital and industrial city (processed foods, transport equipment) in Manitoba, Canada, on the Red River, south of Lake Winnipeg; population (1986) 623,000. Established as Winnipeg 1870 on the site of earlier forts, the city expanded with the arrival of the Canadian Pacific Railroad 1881.

Winnipeg, Lake lake in S Manitoba, Canada, draining much of the Canadian prairies; area 24,500 sq km/9,460 sq mi.

wintergreen any of several plants of the genus *Gaultheria* of the heath family Ericaceae, especially *G. procumbens* of NE North America, creeping underground and sending up tiny shoots. Oil of wintergreen, used in treating rheumatism, is extracted from its leaves. Wintergreen is also the name for various plants of the family Pyrolaceae, including the genus *Pyrola*.

Winter War the USSR's invasion of Finland 30 Nov 1939–12 March 1940, also called the Russo-Finnish War.

Wisconsin state in N central USA; nickname Badger State; *area* 145,500 sq km/56,163 sq mi; *capital* Madison; *cities* Milwaukee, Green Bay, Racine; *features* lakes: Superior, Michigan; Mississippi River; Door peninsula; *products* leading US dairy state; maize, hay, industrial and agricultural machinery, engines and turbines, precision instruments, paper products, cars and lorries, plumbing equipment; *population* (1990) 4,891,800; *famous people* Edna Ferber, Harry Houdini, Joseph McCarthy, Spencer Tracy, Orson Welles, Thornton Wilder, Frank Lloyd Wright; *history* explored by Jean Nicolet for France 1634; originally settled near Ashland by the French; passed to Britain 1763; included in USA 1783. Wisconsin became a territory 1836 and a state 1848.

wisent another name for the European ▷bison.

wisteria any climbing shrub of the genus *Wisteria*, including *W. sinensis*, of the family Leguminosae, native to eastern USA and east Asia. Wisterias have racemes of bluish, white, or pale mauve flowers, and pinnate leaves (leaves on either side of the stem).

witch hazel any flowering shrub or small tree of the genus *Hamamelis* of the witch-hazel family, native to North America and E Asia, especially *H. virginiana*. An astringent extract prepared from the bark or leaves is used in medicine as an eye lotion and a liniment.

Wittgenstein Ludwig 1889–1951. Austrian philosopher. *Tractatus Logico-Philosophicus* 1922 postulated the 'picture theory' of language: that words represent things according to social agreement. He subsequently rejected this idea, and developed the idea that usage was more important than convention.

Witwatersrand or *the Rand* the economic heartland of S Transvaal, South Africa. The chief city of the region is Johannesburg. Forming a watershed between the Vaal and the Olifant rivers, the Rand comprises a series of parallel ranges which extend 100 km/60 mi E–W and rise to 1,525–1,830 m/5,000–6,000 ft. Gold was first found there 1854, and the Rand now produces over half the world's gold.

Wodehouse P(elham) G(renville) 1881–1975. English novelist, a US citizen from 1955, whose humorous novels portray the accident-prone world of such characters as the socialite Bertie Wooster and his invaluable and impeccable manservant Jeeves, and Lord Emsworth of Blandings Castle with his prize pig, the Empress of Blandings.

Woden or *Wodan* the foremost Anglo-Saxon god, whose Norse counterpart is ▷Odin.

wolf any of two species of large wild dogs of the genus *Canis*. The grey or timber wolf *C. lupus*, of North America and Eurasia, is highly social, measures up to 90 cm/3 ft at the shoulder, and weighs up to 45 kg/100 lb. It has been greatly reduced in numbers except for isolated wilderness regions.

Wolfe James 1727–1759. British soldier who served in Canada and commanded a victorious expedition against the French general Montcalm in Québec on the Plains of Abraham, during which both commanders were killed. The British victory established their supremacy over Canada.

Wollongong industrial city (iron, steel) in New South Wales, Australia, 65 km/40 mi S of Sydney; population (1985, with Port Kembla) 238,000.

Wollstonecraft Mary 1759–1797. British feminist, member of a group of radical intellectuals called the English Jacobins, whose book *Vindication of the Rights of Women* 1792 demanded equal educational opportunities for women. She married William Godwin and died giving birth to a daughter, Mary (later Mary ◊Shelley).

Wolsey Thomas *c.* 1475–1530. English cleric and politician. In Henry VIII's service from 1509, he became archbishop of York 1514, cardinal and lord chancellor 1515, and began the dissolution of the monasteries. His reluctance to further Henry's divorce from Catherine of Aragon, partly because of his ambition to be pope, led to his downfall 1529. He was charged with high treason 1530 but died before being tried.

Wolverhampton industrial town (metalworking, chemicals, tyres, aircraft, commercial vehicles) in West Midlands, England, 20 km/12 mi NW of Birmingham; population (1991) 239,800.

wolverine largest land member *Gulo gulo* of the weasel family (Mustelidae), found in Europe, Asia, and North America. It is stocky in build, about 1 m/3.3 ft long. Its long, thick fur is dark brown on the back and belly and lighter on the sides.

wombat any of a family (Vombatidae) of burrowing, herbivorous marsupials, native to Tasmania and S Australia. They are about 1 m/3.3 ft long, heavy, with a big head, short legs and tail, and coarse fur.

women's movement the campaign for the rights of women, including social, political, and economic equality with men. Early European campaigners of the 17th–19th centuries fought for women's right to own property, to have access to higher education, and to vote (see ◊suffragette). Once women's suffrage was achieved in the 20th century, the emphasis of the movement shifted to the goals of equal social and economic opportunities for women, including employment. A continuing area of concern in industrialized countries is the contradiction between the now generally accepted principle of equality and the demonstrable inequalities that remain.

wood the hard tissue beneath the bark of many perennial plants; it is composed of water-conducting cells, or secondary ◊xylem, and gains its hardness and strength from deposits of lignin. **Hardwoods**, such as oak, and **softwoods**, such as pine, have commercial value as structural material and for furniture.

woodcock either of two species of wading birds, genus *Scolopax*, of the family Scolopacidae, which have barred plumage, long bills, and live in wet woodland areas. The Eurasian woodcock *S. rusticola*, is about 35 cm/14 in long, with mottled plumage, a long bill, short legs, and a short tail.

woodcut print made by a woodblock in which a picture or design has been cut in relief. The woodcut is the oldest method of ◊printing, invented in China in the 5th century AD. In the Middle Ages woodcuts became popular in Europe, illustrating early printed books and broadsides.

woodlouse crustacean of the order Isopoda. Woodlice have segmented bodies and flattened undersides. The eggs are carried by the female in a pouch beneath the thorax.

woodpecker bird of the family Picidae, which drills holes in trees to obtain insects. There are about 200 species worldwide. The European green woodpecker or yaffle *Picus viridis* is green with a red crown and yellow rump, and about the size of a jay. The greater and lesser spotted woodpeckers *Dendrocopos major* and *Dendrocopos minor*, also British species, have black, red, and white plumage.

woodwind musical instrument from which sound is produced by blowing into a tube, causing the air within to vibrate. Woodwind instruments include those, like the flute, originally made of wood but now more commonly of metal. The saxophone, made of metal, is an honorary woodwind because it is related to the clarinet. The oboe, bassoon, flute, and clarinet make up the normal woodwind section of an orchestra.

woodworm common name for the larval stage of certain wood-boring beetles. Dead or injured trees are their natural target, but they also attack structural timber and furniture.

Woolf Virginia (born Virginia Stephen) 1882–1941. English novelist and critic. Her first novel, *The Voyage Out* 1915, explored the tensions experienced by women who want marriage and a career. In *Mrs Dalloway* 1925 she perfected her 'stream of consciousness' technique. Among her later books are *To the Lighthouse* 1927, *Orlando* 1928, and *The Years* 1937, which considers the importance of economic independence for women.

word processor in computing, a program that allows the input, amendment, manipulation, storage, and retrieval of text; or a computer system that runs such software. Since word-processing programs became available to microcomputers, the method has been gradually replacing the typewriter for producing letters or other text.

Wordsworth William 1770–1850. English Romantic poet. In 1797 he moved with his sister Dorothy to Somerset to be near ⟁Coleridge, collaborating with him on *Lyrical Ballads* 1798 (which included 'Tintern Abbey'). From 1799 he lived in the Lake District, and later works include *Poems* 1807 (including 'Intimations of Immortality') and *The Prelude* (written by 1805, published 1850). He was appointed poet laureate in 1843.

work in physics, a measure of the result of transferring energy from one system to another to cause an object to move. Work should not be confused with ⟁energy (the capacity to do work, which is also measured in ⟁joules) or with ⟁power (the rate of doing work, measured in joules per second).

World Bank popular name for the *International Bank for Reconstruction and Development*. Specialized agency of the United Nations that borrows in the commercial market and lends on commercial terms. It was established 1945 under the 1944 Bretton Woods agreement, which also

woodwind

created the International Monetary Fund. The *International Development Association* is an arm of the World Bank.

World Cup the most prestigious competition in international soccer; World Cup events are also held in rugby union, cricket, and other sports. The 1990 football World Cup was won by Germany; the 1994 competition will be contested in the USA. The 1991 rugby World Cup was won by Australia and the 1992 cricket World Cup won by Pakistan.

World Health Organization (WHO) agency of the United Nations established 1946 to prevent the spread of diseases and to eradicate them. In 1990–91 it had 4,500 staff and a budget of £843 million. Its headquarters are in Geneva, Switzerland.

World War I 1914–1918. War between the Central European Powers (Germany, Austria-Hungary, and allies) on one side and the Triple Entente (Britain and the British Empire, France, and Russia) and their allies, including the USA (which entered 1917), on the other side. An estimated 10 million lives were lost and twice that number were wounded. It was fought on the eastern and western fronts, in the Middle East, Africa, and at sea. Towards the end of the war Russia withdrew because of the Russian Revolution 1917. The peace treaty of Versailles 1919 was the formal end to the war.

World War II 1939–1945. War between Germany, Italy, and Japan (the Axis powers) on one side, and Britain, the Commonwealth, France, the USA, the USSR, and China (the Allied powers) on the other. An estimated 55 million lives were lost, 20 million of them citizens of the USSR. The world was fought in the Atlantic and Pacific theatres. In 1945, Germany surrendered (May) but Japan fought on until the USA dropped atomic bombs on Hiroshima and Nagasaki (Aug).

World Wide Fund for Nature (WWF, formerly the *World Wildlife Fund*) international organization established 1961 to raise funds for conservation by public appeal. Projects include conservation of particular species, for example, the tiger and giant panda, and special areas, such as the Simen Mountains, Ethiopia.

worm any of various elongated limbless invertebrates belonging to several phyla. Worms include the ⟁flatworms, such as flukes and ⟁tapeworms; the roundworms or ⟁nematodes, such as the eelworm and the hookworm; the marine ribbon worms or nemerteans; and the segmented worms or ⟁annelids.

Worms industrial town in Rhineland-Palatinate, Germany, on the Rhine; population (1984) 73,000. Liebfraumilch wine is produced here. The Protestant reformer Luther appeared before the *Diet* (Assembly) *of Worms* 1521 and was declared an outlaw by the Roman Catholic church.

wormwood any plant of the genus *Artemisia*, family Compositae, especially the aromatic herb *A. absinthium*, the leaves of which are used in absinthe. Tarragon is a member of this genus.

Wounded Knee site on the Oglala Sioux Reservation, South Dakota, USA, of a confrontation between the US Army and American Indians. Sitting Bull was killed, supposedly resisting arrest, on 15 Dec 1890, and on 29 Dec a group of Indians involved in the Ghost Dance Movement (aimed at resumption of Indian control of North America with the aid of the spirits of dead braves) were surrounded and 153 killed.

wrack any of the large brown ⟩seaweeds characteristic of rocky shores. The bladder wrack *Fucus vesiculosus* has narrow, branched fronds up to 1 m/3.3 ft long, with oval air bladders, usually in pairs on either side of the midrib or central vein.

wren any of a family (Troglodytidae) of small birds of order Passeriformes, with slender, slightly curved bills and uptilted tails. The only Old World wren is the species *Troglodytes troglodytes* with a cocked tail. It is about 10 cm/4 in long, has a loud trilling song and feeds on insects and spiders.

Wren Christopher 1632–1723. English architect, designer of St Paul's Cathedral, London, built 1675–1710; many London churches including St Bride's, Fleet Street, and St Mary-le-Bow, Cheapside; the Royal Exchange; Marlborough House; and the Sheldonian Theatre, Oxford.

wrestling sport popular in ancient Egypt, Greece, and Rome, and included in the Olympics from 704 BC. The two main modern international styles are *Greco-Roman*, concentrating on above-waist holds, and *freestyle*, which allows the legs to be used to hold or trip; in both the aim is to throw the opponent to the ground.

Wright Frank Lloyd 1869–1959. US architect who rejected Neo-Classicist styles for 'organic architecture', in which buildings reflected their natural surroundings. Among his buildings are his Wisconsin home Taliesin East 1925; Falling Water, near Pittsburgh, Pennsylvania, 1936, a house built straddling a waterfall; and the Guggenheim Museum, New York, 1959.

Wright Orville 1871–1948 and Wilbur 1867–1912. US inventors; brothers who pioneered piloted, powered flight. Inspired by Otto ⟩Lilienthal's gliding, they perfected their piloted glider 1902. In 1903 they built a powered machine, a 12-hp 341-kg/750-lb plane, and became the first to make a successful powered flight, near Kitty Hawk, North Carolina. Orville flew 36.6 m/120 ft in 12 sec; Wilbur, 260 m/852 ft in 59 sec.

writing any written form of communication using a set of symbols: see ⟩alphabet, ⟩cuneiform,

⟩hieroglyphic. The last two used ideographs (picture writing) and phonetic word symbols side by side, as does modern Chinese. Syllabic writing, as in Japanese, develops from the continued use of a symbol to represent the sound of a short word. Some 8,000-year-old inscriptions, thought to be pictographs, were found on animal bones and tortoise shells in Henan province, China, at a Neolithic site at Jiahu. They are thought to predate by 2,500 years the oldest known writing (Mesopotamian cuneiform of 3,500 BC).

Wroclaw industrial river port in Poland, on the river Oder; population (1990) 643,200. Under the German name of *Breslau*, it was the capital of former German Silesia. Industries include shipbuilding, engineering, textiles, and electronics.

Wuhan river port and capital of Hubei province, China, at the confluence of the Han and Chang Jiang rivers, formed 1950 as one of China's greatest industrial areas by the amalgamation of Hankou, Hanyang, and Wuchang; population (1989) 3,710,000. It produces iron, steel, machine tools, textiles, and fertilizer.

Wycliffe John *c.* 1320–1384. English religious reformer. Allying himself with the party of John of Gaunt, which was opposed to ecclesiastical influence at court, he attacked abuses in the church, maintaining that the Bible rather than the church was the supreme authority. He criticized such fundamental doctrines as priestly absolution, confession, and indulgences, and set disciples to work on translating the Bible into English.

Wye (Welsh *Gwy*) river in Wales and England; length 208 km/130 mi. It rises on Plynlimmon, NE Dyfed, flowing SE and E through Powys, and Hereford and Worcester, then follows the Gwent–Gloucestershire border before joining the river Severn south of Chepstow.

Wyoming state in W USA: nickname Equality State; *area* 253,400 sq km/97,812 sq mi; *capital* Cheyenne; *towns* Casper, Laramie; *features* Rocky Mountains; national parks: Yellowstone (including the geyser Old Faithful), Grand Teton; *products* oil, natural gas, sodium salts, coal, uranium, sheep, beef; *population* (1990) 453,600; *famous people* Buffalo Bill Cody, Jackson Pollock; *history* acquired by USA from France as part of the ⟩Louisiana Purchase 1803; Fort Laramie, a trading post, settled 1834; granted women the vote 1869; state 1890.

WYSIWYG (acronym for *what you see is what you get*) in computing, a program that attempts to display on the screen a faithful representation of the final printed output. For example, a WYSIWYG ⟩word processor would show actual line widths, page breaks, and the sizes and styles of type.

X chromosome larger of the two sex chromosomes, the smaller being the ⟡Y chromosome. These two chromosomes are involved in sex determination. Genes carried on the X chromosome produce the phenomenon of sex linkage.

xenon colourless, odourless, gaseous, nonmetallic element, symbol Xe, atomic number 54, relative atomic mass 131.30. It is grouped with the ⟡inert gases and was long believed not to enter into reactions, but is now known to form some compounds, mostly with fluorine. It is a heavy gas present in very small quantities in the air (about one part in 20 million).

Xenophon *c.* 430–354 BC. Greek historian, philosopher, and soldier. He was a disciple of ⟡Socrates (described in Xenophon's *Symposium*). In 401 he joined a Greek mercenary army aiding the Persian prince Cyrus, and on the latter's death took command. His *Anabasis* describes how he led 10,000 Greeks on a 1,600–km/1,000–mile march home across enemy territory.

xerography dry, electrostatic method of producing images, without the use of negatives or sensitized paper, invented in the USA by Chester Carlson in 1938 and applied in the Xerox ⟡photocopier. Toner powder is sprayed on paper in highly charged areas and fixed with heat.

xerophyte plant adapted to live in dry conditions. Common adaptations to reduce the rate of ⟡transpiration include a reduction of leaf size, sometimes to spines or scales; a dense covering of hairs over the leaf to trap a layer of moist air (as in edelweiss); and permanently rolled leaves or leaves that roll up in dry weather (as in marram grass). Many desert cacti are xerophytes.

Xerxes *c.* 519–465 BC. King of Persia from 485 BC when he succeeded his father Darius and continued the Persian invasion of Greece. In 480, at the head of an army of some 400,000 men and supported by a fleet of 800 ships, he crossed the ⟡Hellespont strait (now the Dardanelles) over a bridge of boats. He defeated the Greek fleet at Artemisium and captured and burned Athens, but Themistocles retaliated by annihilating the Persian fleet at Salamis and Xerxes was forced to retreat. He spent his later years working on a grandiose extension of the capital Persepolis and was eventually murdered in a court intrigue.

Xhosa member of a Bantu people of southern Africa, living mainly in the Black National State of ⟡Transkei. Traditionally, the Xhosa were farmers and pastoralists, with a social structure based on a monarchy. Many are now town-dwellers, and provide much of the unskilled labour in South African mines and factories. Their Bantu language belongs to the Niger-Congo family.

Xian industrial city and capital of Shaanxi province, China; population (1989) 2,710,000. It produces chemicals, electrical equipment, and fertilizers.

Xi Jiang or *Si-Kiang* river in China, that rises in Yunnan and flows into the South China Sea; length 1,900 km/1,200 mi. Guangzhou lies on the N arm of its delta, and Hong Kong island at its mouth. The name means 'west river'.

Xingú region in Pará, Brazil, crossed by branches of the Xingú River which flows for 1,932 km/1,200 mi to the Amazon Delta. In 1989 Xingú Indians protested at the creation of a vast, intrusive lake for the Babaquara and Kararao dams of the Altamira complex.

Xining or *Sining* industrial city and capital of Qinghai province, China; population (1989) 640,000.

Xinjiang Uygur or *Sinkiang Uighur* autonomous region of NW China; **area** 1,646,800 sq km/635,665 sq mi; **capital** Urumqi; **features** largest of Chinese administrative areas; Junggar Pendi (Dzungarian Basin) and Tarim Pendi (Tarim Basin, which includes Lop Nor, China's nuclear testing ground) separated by the Tian Shan mountains; **products** cereals, cotton, fruit in valleys and oases; uranium, coal, iron, copper, tin, oil; **population** (1990) 15,156,000; the region has 13 recognized ethnic minorities, the largest being 6 million Uigurs (Muslim descendants of Turks); **religion** 50% Muslim; **history** under Manchu rule from the 18th century. Large sections were ceded to Russia 1864 and 1881; China has raised the question of their return and regards the 480-km/300-mi frontier between Xinjiang Uygur and Tajikistan as undemarcated.

X-ray band of electromagnetic radiation in the wavelength range 10^{-11} to 10^{-9} m (between gamma rays and ultraviolet radiation; see ⟡electromagnetic waves). Applications of X-rays make use of their short wavelength (such as X-ray crystallography) or their penetrating power (as in medical X-rays of internal body tissues). X-rays are dangerous and can cause cancer.

X-ray astronomy detection of X-rays from intensely hot gas in the universe. Such X-rays are prevented from reaching the Earth's surface by the atmosphere, so detectors must be placed in rockets and satellites. The first celestial X-ray source, Scorpius X-1, was discovered by a rocket flight in 1962.

X-ray diffraction method of studying the atomic and molecular structure of crystalline substances by using ▷X-rays. X-rays directed at such substances spread out as they pass through the crystals owing to ▷diffraction (the slight spreading of waves around the edge of an opaque object) of the rays around the atoms. The method has been used to study substances such as ▷DNA that are found in living material.

xylem tissue found in ▷vascular plants, whose main function is to conduct water and dissolved mineral nutrients from the roots to other parts of the plant. Xylem is composed of a number of different types of cell, and may include long, thin, usually dead cells known as tracheids; fibres (schlerenchyma); thin-walled parenchyma cells; and conducting vessels.

xylophone musical ▷percussion instrument in which wooden bars of varying lengths are arranged according to graded pitch, or as a piano keyboard, over resonators to produce sounds when struck with hammers.

yachting pleasure cruising or racing a small and light vessel, whether sailing or power-driven. At the Olympic Games, seven categories, all sail-driven, exist: Soling, Flying Dutchman, Star, Finn, Tornado, 470, and Windglider or ◊windsurfing (boardsailing). The Finn and Windglider are solo events; the Soling class is for three-person crews; all other classes are for crews of two.

yak species of cattle *Bos grunniens*, family Bovidae, which lives in wild herds at high altitudes in Tibet. It stands about 2 m/6 ft at the shoulder and has long shaggy hair on the underparts. It has large, upward-curving horns and humped shoulders. It is in danger of becoming extinct.

Yakut (Russian *Yakutskaya*) autonomous republic in Siberian Russia; *area* 3,103,000 sq km/ 1,197,760 sq mi; *capital* Yakutsk; *features* one of world's coldest inhabited places; river Lena; *products* furs, gold, natural gas, some agriculture in the south; *population* (1986) 1,009,000; 50% Russians, 37% Yakuts; *history* the nomadic Yakuts were conquered by Russia 17th century; Yakut was a Soviet republic 1922–91. It remained an autonomous republic within the Russian Federation after the collapse of the Soviet Union 1991, since when it has agitated for greater independence.

Yalta Conference in 1945, a meeting at which the Allied leaders Churchill (UK), Roosevelt (USA), and Stalin (USSR) completed plans for the defeat of Germany in World War II and the foundation of the United Nations. It took place in Yalta, a Soviet holiday resort in the Crimea.

yam any climbing plant of the genus *Dioscorea*, family Dioscoreaceae, cultivated in tropical regions; its starchy tubers are eaten as a vegetable. The Mexican yam *D. composita* contains a chemical used in the manufacture of the contraceptive pill.

Yamoussoukro capital of ◊Ivory Coast; population (1986) 120,000. The economy is based on tourism and agricultural trade.

Yangon since 1989 the name for *Rangoon* capital and chief port of Myanmar (Burma) on the Yangon river, 32 km/20 mi from the Indian Ocean; population (1983) 2,459,000. Products include timber, oil, and rice. The city *Dagon* was founded on the site AD 746; it was given the name Rangoon (meaning 'end of conflict') by King Alaungpaya 1755.

Yang Shangkun 1907– . Chinese communist politician. He held a senior position in the party 1956–66 but was demoted during the Cultural Revolution. He was rehabilitated 1978, elected to the Politburo 1982, and to the position of state president 1988.

Yangtze-Kiang alternative transcription of ◊Chang Jiang, the longest river in China.

Yao member of a people living in S China, N Vietnam, N Laos, Thailand, and Myanmar (Burma), and numbering about 4 million (1984). The Yao language may belong to either the Sino-Tibetan or the Thai language family. The Yao incorporate elements of ancestor worship in their animist religion.

Yaoundé capital of Cameroon, 210 km/130 mi E of the port of Douala; population (1984) 552,000. Industry includes tourism, oil refining, and cigarette manufacturing.

yard imperial unit (symbol yd) of length, equivalent to three feet (0.9144 m).

yarrow or *milfoil* perennial herb *Achillea millefolium* of the family Compositae, with feathery, scented leaves and flat-topped clusters of white or pink flowers.

Y chromosome smaller of the two sex chromosomes. In male mammals it occurs paired with the other type of sex chromosome (X), which carries far more genes. The Y chromosome is the smallest of all the mammalian chromosomes and is considered to be largely inert (that is, without direct effect on the physical body). See also ◊sex determination.

yeast one of various single-celled fungi (especially the genus *Saccharomyces*) that form masses of minute circular or oval cells by budding. When placed in a sugar solution the cells multiply and convert the sugar into alcohol and carbon dioxide. Yeasts are used as fermenting agents in baking, brewing, and the making of wine and spirits. Brewer's yeast *S. cerevisiae* is a rich source of vitamin B.

Yeats W(illiam) B(utler) 1865–1939. Irish poet. He was a leader of the Celtic revival and a founder of the Abbey Theatre in Dublin. His early work was romantic and lyrical, as in the poem 'The Lake Isle of Innisfree' and plays *The Countess Cathleen* 1892 and *The Land of Heart's Desire* 1894. His later books of poetry include *The Wild Swans at Coole* 1917 and *The Winding Stair* 1929. He was a senator of the Irish Free State 1922–28. Nobel Prize for Literature 1923.

Yedo or *Edo* former name of ◊Tokyo, Japan, until 1868.

yellow fever or *yellow jack* acute tropical viral disease, prevalent in the Caribbean area, Brazil, and on the west coast of Africa. Its symptoms are a high fever and yellowish skin (jaundice, possibly leading to liver failure); the heart and kidneys may also be affected.

yellowhammer Eurasian bird *Emberiza citrinella* of the bunting family Emberizidae. About 16.5 cm/6.5 in long, the male has a yellow head and underside, a chestnut rump, and a brown-streaked back. The female is duller.

Yellowknife capital of Northwest Territories, Canada, on the N shore of Great Slave Lake; population (1986) 11,753. It was founded 1935 when gold was discovered in the area and became the capital 1967.

Yellow River English name for the ◊Huang He river, China.

Yellow Sea gulf of the Pacific Ocean between China and Korea; area 466,200 sq km/ 180,000 sq mi. It receives the Huang He (Yellow river) and Chang Jiang.

Yellowstone National Park largest US nature reserve, established 1872, on a broad plateau in the Rocky Mountains, chiefly in NW Wyoming, but also in SW Montana and E Idaho; area 8,983 sq km/ 3,469 sq mi. The park contains more than 3,000 geysers and hot springs, including periodically erupting Old Faithful. It is one of the world's greatest wildlife refuges. Much of the park was ravaged by forest fires 1988.

Yeltsin Boris Nikolayevich 1931– . Russian politician, president of the Russian Soviet Federative Socialist Republic (RSFSR) 1990–91, and president and prime minister of the newly independent Russian Federation from 1991. A proponent of price deregulation and accelerated privatization, Yeltsin publicly defied the anti-Gorbachev coup Aug 1991. He then directed the Russian Federation's secession from the USSR and the formation of the ◊Commonwealth of Independent States, with himself as the most powerful leader.

Yemen Republic of; country in SW Asia, bordered N by Saudi Arabia, E by Oman, S by the Arabian Sea, and E by the Red Sea; *area* 531,900 sq km/ 205,367 sq mi; *capital* Sana'a; *physical* hot moist coastal plain, rising to plateau and desert; *head of state and government* Ali Abdullah Saleh from 1990; *political system* authoritarian republic; *exports* cotton, coffee, grapes, vegetables; *population* (1990 est) 11,000,000; *language* Arabic; *recent history* Yemen became independent 1918. North Yemen declared the Yemen Arab Republic (YAR) 1962; People's Republic of South Yemen formed 1967 and renamed People's Democratic Republic of Yemen 1970. War broke out between two Yemens 1971–72; union agreement signed but not kept; at war again 1978. Cease-fire agreed 1979 with commitment to future union. Civil

war in South Yemen 1986. Border between two Yemens opened 1990 and countries formally united May 1990 as Republic of Yemen.

Yemen, North former country in SW Asia. It was united with South Yemen 1990 as the Republic of Yemen.

Yemen, South former country in SW Asia. It was united with North Yemen 1990 as the Republic of Yemen.

Yenisei river in Asian Russia, rising in the Tuva region and flowing across the Siberian plain into the Arctic Ocean; length 4,100 km/2,550 mi.

Yerevan industrial city (tractor parts, machine tools, chemicals, bricks, bicycles, wine, fruit canning) and capital of Armenia, a few miles N of the Turkish border; population (1987) 1,168,000. It was founded in the 7th century and was alternately Turkish and Persian from the 15th century until ceded to Russia 1828. Armenia became an independent republic 1991.

yeti Tibetan for the ◊abominable snowman.

Yevtushenko Yevgeny Aleksandrovich 1933– Soviet poet, born in Siberia. He aroused controversy with his anti-Stalinist 'Stalin's Heirs' 1956, published with Khrushchev's support, and 'Babi Yar' 1961. His autobiography was published in 1963.

yew any evergreen coniferous tree of the genus *Taxus* of the family Taxaceae, native to the northern hemisphere. The leaves and bright red berrylike seeds are poisonous; the wood is hard and close-grained.

Yi member of a people living in S China; there are also Yi populations in Laos, Thailand, and Vietnam, totalling about 5.5 million (1987). The Yi are farmers, producing both crops and livestock. Their language belongs to the Sino-Tibetan family; their religion is animist.

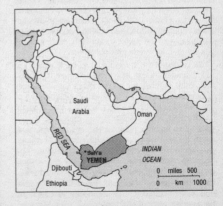

Yiddish language member of the west Germanic branch of the Indo-European language family, deriving from 13th–14th-century Rhineland German and spoken by northern, central, and eastern European Jews, who have carried it to Israel, the USA, and many other parts of the world. It is written in the Hebrew alphabet and has many dialects reflecting European areas of residence, as well as many borrowed words from Polish, Russian, Lithuanian, and other languages encountered.

yield in finance, the annual percentage return from an investment; on ordinary ⟫shares it is the dividend expressed as a percentage.

yin and yang Chinese for 'dark' and 'bright' respectively, referring to the passive (characterized as feminine, negative, intuitive) and active (characterized as masculine, positive, intellectual) principles of nature. Their interaction is believed to maintain equilibrium and harmony in the universe and to be present in all things. In Taoism and Confucianism they are represented by two interlocked curved shapes within a circle, one white, one black, with a spot of the contrasting colour within the head of each.

Yinchuan capital of Ningxia autonomous region, NW China; population (1989) 576,000.

yoga Hindu philosophical system attributed to Patanjali, who lived about 150 BC at Gonda, Uttar Pradesh, India. He preached mystical union with a personal deity through the practice of self-hypnosis and a rising above the senses by abstract meditation, adoption of special postures, and ascetic practices. As practised in the West, yoga is more a system of mental and physical exercise, and of induced relaxation as a means of relieving stress.

Yokohama Japanese port on Tokyo Bay; population (1989) 3,176,000. Industries include shipbuilding, oil refining, engineering, textiles, glass, and clothing.

Yom Kippur War the surprise attack on Israel October 1973 by Egypt and Syria; see ⟫Arab-Israeli Wars. It is named after the Jewish national holiday on which it began, the holiest day of the Jewish year.

York cathedral and industrial city (railway rolling stock, scientific instruments, sugar, chocolate, and glass) in North Yorkshire, N England; population (1991) 100,600. The city is visited by 3 million tourists a year; *features* the Gothic York Minster; part of 14th-century city wall; quarter of medieval streets collectively known as the Shambles (after the slaughterhouse); Jorvik Viking Centre; Theatre Royal, site of a theatre since 1765; the Castle Museum; the National Railway Museum; and the university 1963; *history* traditionally the capital of the N of England, the city became from AD 71 the Roman fortress of *Eboracum*. The first bishop of York (Paulinus) was consecrated 627 in the wooden church that preceded York Minster.

Paulinus baptized King Edwin there 627, and York was created an archbishopric 732. In the 10th century it was a Viking settlement. During the Middle Ages its commercial prosperity depended on the wool trade.

York English dynasty founded by Richard, Duke of York (1411–1460). He claimed the throne through his descent from Lionel, duke of Clarence (1338–1368), third son of Edward III, whereas the reigning monarch, Henry VI of the rival house of Lancaster, was descended from the fourth son. The argument was fought out in the Wars of the ⟫Roses. York was killed at the Battle of Wakefield 1460, but next year his son became King Edward IV, in turn succeeded by his son Edward V and then by his brother Richard III, with whose death at Bosworth the line ended. The Lancastrian victor in that battle was crowned Henry VII and consolidated his claim by marrying Edward IV's eldest daughter, Elizabeth.

York Duke of. Title often borne by younger sons of British sovereigns, for example George V, George VI, and Prince ⟫Andrew from 1986.

Yorkshire former county in NE England on the North Sea divided administratively into N, E, and W ridings (thirds), but reorganized to form a number of new counties 1974: the major part of *Cleveland* and *Humberside*, *North Yorkshire*, *South Yorkshire*, and *West Yorkshire*. Small outlying areas also went to Durham, Cumbria, Lancashire, and Greater Manchester.

Yoruba member of the majority ethnic group living in SW Nigeria; there is a Yoruba minority in E Benin. They number approximately 20 million in all, and their language belongs to the Kwa branch of the Niger-Congo family. The Yoruba established powerful city states in the 15th century, known for their advanced culture which includes sculpture, art, and music.

Young Lester (Willis) 1909–1959. US tenor saxophonist and jazz composer. He was a major figure in the development of his instrument for jazz music from the 1930s and was an accompanist for the singer Billie Holiday, who gave him the nickname 'President', later shortened to 'Pres'.

Young Neil 1945– . Canadian rock guitarist, singer, and songwriter, in the USA from 1966. His high, plaintive voice and loud, abrasive guitar make his work instantly recognizable, despite abrupt changes of style throughout his career. *Rust Never Sleeps* 1979 and *Arc Weld* 1991 (both with the group Crazy Horse) are among his best work.

Young Thomas 1773–1829. British physicist who revived the wave theory of light and identified the phenomenon of ⟫interference in 1801. A child prodigy, he had mastered most European languages and many of the Eastern tongues by the age of 20. He had also absorbed the physics of Newton and the chemistry of Lavoisier. He further displayed his versatility by publishing an account of the Rosetta stone; the work played a crucial role in the stone's eventual decipherment by Jean François Champollion.

Young Pretender nickname of ◊Charles Edward Stuart, claimant to the Scottish and English thrones.

Ypres (Flemish *Ieper*) Belgian town in W Flanders, 40 km/25 mi S of Ostend, a site of three major battles 1914–1917 fought in World War I. The Menin Gate 1927 is a memorial to British soldiers lost in these battles.

ytterbium soft, lustrous, silvery, malleable, and ductile element of the ◊lanthanide series, symbol Yb, atomic number 70, relative atomic mass 173.04. It occurs with (and resembles) yttrium in gadolinite and other minerals, and is used in making steel and other alloys.

yttrium silver-grey, metallic element, symbol Y, atomic number 39, relative atomic mass 88.905. It is associated with and resembles the ◊rare-earth elements (◊lanthanides), occurring in gadolinite, xenotime, and other minerals. It is used in colour-television tubes and to reduce steel corrosion.

Yucatán peninsula in Central America, divided among Mexico, Belize, and Guatemala; area 180,000 sq km/70,000 sq mi. Tropical crops are grown. It is inhabited by Maya Indians and contains the remains of their civilization.

yucca plant of the genus *Yucca*, family Liliaceae, with over 40 species found in Latin America and southwest USA. The leaves are stiff and sword-shaped and the flowers white and bell-shaped.

Yugoslavia (Serbia) country in SE Europe, bordered W by Croatia and the Adriatic Sea, N by Croatia and Hungary, E by Romania and Bulgaria,

and S by Greece and Albania; *area* 88,400 sq km/34,100 sq mi; *capital* Belgrade; *physical* mountainous, with river Danube plains in N and E; limestone (karst) features in NW; *head of state* to be elected; *head of government* central military council, together with leaders of remaining republics; *political system* socialist pluralist republic; *exports* machinery, electrical goods, chemicals, clothing, tobacco; *population* (1981) 9,300,000; *languages* Serbo-Croatian, Macedonian, Slovenian; *recent history* Kingdom of Serbs, Croats, and Slovenes created 1918; name of Yugoslavia adopted 1929. Yugoslav Federal Republic formed under leadership of Tito 1945; communist constitution introduced. Split from USSR 1948; collective leadership assumed power after Tito's death 1980. Economic difficulties led to strikes, high inflation and unemployment; ethnic unrest grew. Multiparty systems were established in Slovenia and Croatia 1990. Several republics called for secession 1991; state president resigned; clashes took place between Serbs and Croats in Croatia. Slovenia and Croatia declared themselves independent; the federal army intervened. Slovenia accepted European Community–sponsored peace pact but fighting continued in Croatia; In 1992 the EC recognized Slovenia and Croatia as independent republics. Serbian aggression continued in Croatia and Bosnia 1992, aiming to create an ethnically pure Great Serbia; the fate of the republic remained uncertain.

Yukon territory of NW Canada; *area* 483,500 sq km/186,631 sq mi; *capital* Whitehorse; *cities* Dawson, Mayo; *features* named after its chief river, the Yukon; includes the highest point in Canada, Mount Logan, 6,050 m/19,850 ft; Klondike Gold Rush International Historical Park, which extends into Alaska; *products* gold, silver, lead, zinc, oil, natural gas, coal; *population* (1991) 26,500; *history* settlement dates from the gold rush 1896–1910, when 30,000 people moved to the ◊Klondike River valley (silver is now worked there). It became separate from the Northwest Territories 1898, with Dawson as the capital 1898–1951. Construction of the Alcan Highway during World War II helped provide the basis for further development.

Yukon River river in North America, 3,185 km/1,979 mi long, flowing from Lake Tagish in Yukon Territory into Alaska, where it empties into the Bering Sea.

Yunnan province of SW China, adjoining Myanmar (Burma), Laos, and Vietnam; *area* 436,200 sq km/168,373 sq mi; *capital* Kunming; *physical* rivers: Chang Jiang, Salween, Mekong; crossed by the Burma Road; mountainous and well forested; *products* rice, tea, timber, wheat, cotton, rubber, tin, copper, lead, zinc, coal, salt; *population* (1990) 36,973,000.

Z

Zagreb industrial city (leather, linen, carpets, paper, and electrical goods) and capital of Croatia, on the Sava river; population (1981) 1,174,512. Zagreb was a Roman city (*Aemona*) and has a Gothic cathedral. Its university was founded 1874.

Zahir ud-din Muhammad 1483–1530. First Great Mogul of India from 1526, called Babur (Arabic 'lion'). He was the great-grandson of the Mongol conqueror Tamerlane and, at the age of 12, succeeded his father, Omar Sheik Mirza, as ruler of Ferghana (Turkestan). In 1526 he defeated the emperor of Delhi at Panipat in the Punjab, captured Delhi and ◇Agra (the site of the Taj Mahal), and established a dynasty that lasted until 1858.

Zaire Republic of (formerly *Congo*); country in central Africa, bordered NW by Congo; N by Central African Republic and Sudan; E by Uganda, Rwanda, Burundi, and Tanzania; S by Zambia; S and SW by Angola with corridor through Angolan territory to Atlantic Ocean where river Zaïre reaches the sea; *area* 2,344,900 sq km/905,366 sq mi; *capital* Kinshasa; *physical* Zaïre river basin has tropical rainforest and savanna; mountains in E and W; *head of state* Mobutu Sese Seko Kuku Ngbendu wa Zabanga from 1965; *head of government* Jean Nguza Karl-i-Bond from 1991; *political system* socialist pluralist republic; *exports* coffee, copper, cobalt (80% of world output), industrial diamonds, palm oil; *population* (1990 est) 35,330,000; *languages* French (official); Swahili, Lingala, other African languages; *recent history* achieved independence from Belgium as the Republic of Congo 1960; became Republic of Zaire 1971. Revolts in Shaba province 1977 and 1978 put down with support of Moroccan forces airlifted to Zaire by France and French and Belgian paratroopers. End of ban on multiparty politics announced 1990; after antigovernment riots Mobutu agreed to share power with opposition 1991. Multiparty elections planned for 1992.

Zaïre River formerly (until 1971) *Congo* second longest river in Africa, rising near the Zambia-Zaire border (and known as the *Lualaba River* in the upper reaches) and flowing 4,500 km/2,800 mi to the Atlantic, running in a great curve that crosses the equator twice, and discharging a volume of water second only to the Amazon. The chief tributaries are the Ubangi, Sangha, and Kasai.

Zambezi river in central and SE Africa; length 2,650 km/1,650 mi from NW Zambia through Mozambique to the Indian Ocean, with a wide delta near Chinde. Major tributaries include the Kafue in Zambia. It is interrupted by rapids, and includes on the Zimbabwe–Zambia border the Victoria Falls (Mosi-oa-tunya) and Kariba Dam, which forms the reservoir of Lake Kariba with large fisheries.

Zambia Republic of; country in S central Africa, bordered N by Zaire and Tanzania, E by Malawi and Mozambique, S by Zimbabwe, Botswana, and Namibia, and W by Angola; *area* 752,600 sq km/ 290,579 sq mi; *capital* Lusaka; *physical* forested plateau cut through by rivers; *head of state and government* Frederick Chiluba from 1991; *political system* socialist pluralist republic; *exports* copper, cobalt, zinc, emeralds, tobacco; *population* (1990 est) 8,119,000; *languages* English (official); Bantu dialects; *recent history* achieved independence from Britain within the Commonwealth 1964 with Kenneth Kaunda as president. Multiparty system introduced 1991; Frederick Chiluba replaced Kaunda.

Zanzibar island region of Tanzania; *area* 1,658 sq km/640 sq mi (80 km/50 mi long); *towns* Zanzibar; *products* cloves, copra; *population* (1985) 571,000; *history* settled by Arab traders in the 7th century; became a sultanate; under British protection 1890–1963. Together with the island of Pemba, some nearby islets, and a strip of mainland territory, it became a republic. It merged with Tanganyika as Tanzania 1964.

Zapata Emiliano 1879–1919. Mexican Indian revolutionary leader. He led a revolt against dictator Porfirio Díaz (1830–1915) from 1911 under the slogan 'Land and Liberty', to repossess for the indigenous Mexicans the land taken by the Spanish. By 1915 he was driven into retreat, and was assassinated.

Zara Italian name for ◇Zadar, port on the Adriatic coast of Croatia.

Zaragoza (English *Saragossa*) industrial city (iron, steel, chemicals, plastics, canned food, electrical goods) in Aragon, Spain; population (1991) 614,400. The medieval city walls and bridges over the river Ebro survive, and there is a 15th-century university.

zebra black and white striped member of the horse genus *Equus* found in Africa; the stripes serve as camouflage or dazzle and confuse predators. It is about 1.5 m/5 ft high at the shoulder, with a stout body and a short, thick mane. Zebras live in family

zebra

groups and herds on mountains and plains, and can run at up to 60 kph/40 mph. Males are usually solitary.

zebu any of a species of ◊cattle *Bos indicus* found domesticated in E Asia, India, and Africa. It is usually light-coloured, with large horns and a large fatty hump near the shoulders. It is used for pulling loads, and is held by some Hindus to be sacred. There are about 30 breeds.

Zeebrugge small Belgian ferry port on the North Sea, linked to Bruges by a 14–km/9–mi canal (built 1896–1907). In March 1987 it was the scene of a disaster in which over 180 passengers lost their lives when the car ferry *Herald of Free Enterprise* put to sea from Zeebrugge with its car-loading doors open.

Zeeland province of the SW Netherlands; *area* 1,790 sq km/691 sq mi; *capital* Middelburg; *towns* Vlissingen, Terneuzen, Goes; *population* (1991) 357,500; *products* cereals, potatoes; *features* mostly below sea level, Zeeland is protected by a system of dykes; *history* disputed by the counts of Flanders and Holland during the Middle Ages, Zeeland was annexed to Holland in 1323 by Count Willam III.

Zeeman Pieter 1865–1943. Dutch physicist who discovered in 1896 that when light from certain elements, such as sodium or lithium (when heated), is passed through a spectroscope in the presence of a strong magnetic field, the spectrum splits into a number of distinct lines. This is known as the *Zeeman effect* and won him a share of the 1902 Nobel Prize for Physics.

Zen form of ◊Buddhism introduced from India to Japan via China in the 12th century. *Kōan* (paradoxical questions), tea-drinking, and sudden enlightenment are elements of Zen practice. Soto Zen was spread by the priest Dōgen (1200–1253), who emphasized work, practice, discipline, and philosophical questions to discover one's Buddha-nature in the 'realization of self'.

Zeno of Elea *c.* 490–430 BC. Greek philosopher who pointed out several paradoxes that raised 'modern' problems of space and time. For example, motion is an illusion, since an arrow in flight must occupy a determinate space at each instant, and therefore must be at rest.

Zeppelin Ferdinand, Count von Zeppelin 1838–1917. German airship pioneer. On retiring from the army in 1891, he devoted himself to the study of aeronautics, and his first airship was built and tested in 1900. During World War I a number of Zeppelin airships bombed England. They were also used for luxury passenger transport but the construction of hydrogen-filled airships with rigid keels was abandoned after several disasters in the 1920s and 1930s. Zeppelin also helped to pioneer large multi-engine bomber planes.

Zeus in Greek mythology, chief of the gods (Roman Jupiter). He was the son of Kronos, whom he overthrew; his brothers included Hades and Poseidon, his sisters Demeter and Hera. As the supreme god he dispensed good and evil and was the father and ruler of all humankind. His emblems are the thunderbolt and aegis (shield), representing the thundercloud.

Zhangjiakou or *Changchiakow* historic town and trade centre in Hebei province, China, 160 km/100 mi NW of Beijing, on the Great Wall; population (1980) 1,100,000. Zhangjiakou is on the border of Inner Mongolia (its Mongolian name is *Kalgan*, 'gate') and on the road and railway to Ulaanbaatar in Mongolia. It developed under the Manchu dynasty, and was the centre of the tea trade from China to Russia.

Zhao Ziyang 1918– . Chinese politician, prime minister 1980–87 and secretary of the Chinese Communist Party 1987–89. His reforms included self-management and incentives for workers and factories. He lost his secretaryship and other posts after the Tiananmen Square massacre in Beijing June 1989.

Zhejiang or *Chekiang* province of SE China; *area* 101,800 sq km/39,295 sq mi; *capital* Hangzhou; *features* smallest of the Chinese provinces; the base of the Song dynasty 12th–13th centuries; densely populated; *products* rice, cotton, sugar, jute, maize; timber on the uplands; *population* (1990) 41,446,000.

Zhelev Zhelyu 1935– . Bulgarian politician, president from 1990. In 1989 he became head of the opposition Democratic Forces coalition. He is a proponent of market-centred economic reform and social peace.

Zhengzhou or *Chengchow* industrial city (light engineering, cotton textiles, foods) and capital (from 1954) of Henan province, China, on the Huang Ho; population (1989) 1,660,000.

Zhivkov Todor 1911– . Bulgarian Communist

Party leader 1954–89, prime minister 1962–71, president 1971–89. His period in office was one of caution and conservatism. In 1991 he was tried for gross embezzlement.

Zhou Enlai or *Chou En-lai* 1898–1976. Chinese politician. Zhou, a member of the Chinese Communist Party from the 1920s, was prime minister 1949–76 and foreign minister 1949–58. He was a moderate Maoist and weathered the Cultural Revolution. He played a key role in foreign affairs.

Zhukov Georgi Konstantinovich 1896–1974. Marshal of the USSR in World War II and minister of defence 1955–57. As chief of staff from 1941, he defended Moscow 1941, counterattacked at Stalingrad (now Volgograd) in 1942, organized the relief of Leningrad (now St Petersburg) 1943, and led the offensive from the Ukraine in March 1944 which ended in the fall of Berlin.

zidovudine (formerly *AZT*) antiviral drug used in the treatment of ◊AIDS. It is not a cure for AIDS but is effective in suppressing the causative virus (HIV) for as long as it is being administered.

Ziegler Karl 1898–1973. German organic chemist. In 1963 he shared the Nobel Prize for Chemistry with Giulio Natta of Italy for his work on the chemistry and technology of large polymers. He combined simple molecules of the gas ethylene (now called ethene) into the long-chain plastic polyethylene (Polythene).

ziggurat in ancient Babylonia and Assyria, a step pyramid of sun-baked brick faced with glazed bricks or tiles on which stood a shrine. The Tower of Babel as described in the Bible may have been a ziggurat.

Zimbabwe Republic of; country in S central Africa, bordered N by Zambia, E by Mozambique, S by South Africa, and W by Botswana; *area* 390,300 sq km/150,695 sq mi; *capital* Harare; *physical* high plateau with central high veld and mountains in E; rivers Zambezi and Limpopo; *head of state and government* Robert Mugabe from 1987; *political system* effectively one-party socialist republic; *exports* tobacco, asbestos, cotton, coffee, gold, silver, copper; *population* (1990 est) 10,205,00 (Shona 80%, Ndbele 19%; about 100,000 whites); *languages* English (official); Shona, Sindebele; *recent history* as Southern Rhodesia, under administration of British South Africa Company 1889–1923 when it became a self-governing British colony. Zimbabwe African People's Union (ZAPU) formed 1961 with Joshua Nkomo as leader; declared illegal 1962. Zimbabwe African National Union (ZANU) formed 1963 with Robert Mugabe as secretary general; banned 1964 when Ian Smith became prime minister. Smith declared unilateral independence 1965; produced new constitution and established new government 1979, denounced by Nkomo and Mugabe. Independence arrangements agreed in London (Lancaster House Agreement)

1979; independence achieved 1980 with Mugabe as prime minister. White-roll seats in assembly abolished 1987, and Mugabe combined posts of head of state and prime minister to become executive president. ZANU and ZAPU formally merged as ZANU-PF 1989, arousing opposition to the creation of a one-party state.

zinc hard, brittle, bluish-white, metallic element, symbol Zn, atomic number 30, relative atomic mass 65.37. The principal ore is sphalerite or zinc blende (zinc sulphide, ZnS). Zinc is little affected by air or moisture at ordinary temperatures; its chief uses are in alloys such as brass and in coating metals (for example galvanized iron). Its compounds include zinc oxide, used in ointments (as an astringent) and cosmetics, paints, glass, and printing ink.

zinnia any annual plant of the genus *Zinnia*, family Compositae, native to Mexico and South America, notably the cultivated hybrids of *Z. elegans*, with brightly coloured, daisylike flowers.

Zinoviev Grigory 1883–1936. Russian communist politician whose name was attached to a forgery, the *Zinoviev letter*, inciting Britain's communists to rise, which helped to topple the Labour government in 1924.

Zion Jebusite (Amorites of Canaan) stronghold in Jerusalem captured by King David, and the hill on which he built the Temple, symbol of Jerusalem and of Jewish national life.

Zionism Jewish political movement for the establishment of a Jewish homeland in Palestine, the 'promised land' of the Bible, with its capital Jerusalem, the 'city of Zion'.

zirconium lustrous, greyish-white, strong, ductile, metallic element, symbol Zr, atomic number 40, relative atomic mass 91.22. It occurs in nature as the mineral zircon (zirconium silicate), from which it is obtained commercially. It is used in some ceramics, alloys for wire and filaments, steel manufacture, and nuclear reactors, where its low neutron absorption is advantageous.

Zi Xi or *Tz'u-hsi* 1836–1908. Dowager empress of China. She was presented as a concubine to the emperor Hsien-feng. On his death 1861 she became regent for her son T'ung Chih and, when he died in 1875, for her nephew Guang Xu (1871–1908).

zodiac zone of the heavens containing the paths of the Sun, Moon, and planets. When this was devised by the ancient Greeks, only five planets were known, making the zodiac about 16° wide. The stars in it are grouped into 12 signs (constellations), each 30° in extent: Aries, Taurus, Gemini, Cancer, Leo, Virgo, Libra, Scorpius, Sagittarius, Capricornus, Aquarius, and Pisces. Because of the ◊precession of the equinoxes, the current constellations do not cover the same areas of sky as the zodiacal signs of the same name.

Zola Emile Edouard Charles Antoine 1840–1902.

French novelist and social reformer. With *La Fortune des Rougon/The Fortune of the Rougons* 1867 he began a series of some 20 naturalistic novels, portraying the fortunes of a French family under the Second Empire. They include *Le Ventre de Paris/ The Underbelly of Paris* 1873, *Nana* 1880, and *La Débâcle/The Debacle* 1892. In 1898 he published *J'accuse/I Accuse*, a pamphlet indicting the persecutors of ⟡Dreyfus, for which he was prosecuted for libel but later pardoned.

zoology branch of biology concerned with the study of animals. It includes description of present-day animals, the study of evolution of animal forms, anatomy, physiology, embryology, behaviour, and geographical distribution.

Zoroastrianism pre-Islamic Persian religion founded by the Persian prophet Zoroaster or Zarathustra in the 6th century BC, and still practised by the Parsees in India. The *Zendavesta* are the sacred scriptures of the faith. The theology is dualistic, *Ahura Mazda* or *Ormuzd* (the good god) being perpetually in conflict with *Ahriman* (the evil god), but the former is assured of eventual victory.

zucchini alternative name for the courgette, a type of ⟡marrow.

Zuider Zee former sea inlet in Holland, cut off from the North Sea by the closing of a dyke in 1932, much of which has been reclaimed as land. The remaining lake is called the ⟡IJsselmeer.

Zulu member of a group of southern African peoples mainly from Natal, South Africa. Their present homeland, Kwa Zulu, represents the nucleus of the once extensive and militaristic Zulu kingdom. Today many Zulus work in the industrial centres around Johannesburg and Durban. The Zulu language, closely related to Xhosa, belongs to the Bantu branch of the Niger-Congo family.

Zululand region in Natal, South Africa, largely corresponding to the Black National State KwaZulu. It was formerly a province, annexed to Natal 1897.

Zürich financial centre and industrial city (machinery, electrical goods, textiles) on Lake Zürich; capital of Zürich canton and the largest city in Switzerland; population (1990) 341,300.

Zwingli Ulrich 1484–1531. Swiss Protestant, born in St Gallen. He was ordained a Roman Catholic priest 1506, but by 1519 was a Reformer and led the Reformation in Switzerland with his insistence on the sole authority of the Scriptures. He was killed in a skirmish at Kappel during a war against the cantons that had not accepted the Reformation.

zydeco dance music originating in Louisiana, USA, similar to ⟡Cajun but more heavily influenced by blues and West Indian music.

zygote ⟡ovum (egg) after ⟡fertilization but before it undergoes cleavage to begin embryonic development.

THE
HUTCHINSON
PAPERBACK ENCYCLOPEDIA

With more than 17,000 entries and over 750 tables, charts, maps and diagrams, *The Hutchinson Paperback Encyclopedia* is the most comprehensive, up-to-date, and easy-to-use paperback encyclopedia on the market. With 50% more entries and double the number of illustrations of its nearest competitor, it is also unrivalled value for money. Derived from the authoritative *Hutchinson Encyclopedia* database, it is ideal for school and college students.

THE
HUTCHINSON
PAPERBACK DICTIONARY OF
BIOGRAPHY

The most famous and infamous names in history, sport, the arts, current affairs and science are covered in this remarkably comprehensive dictionary. Here are Arafat and Aristotle; Beethoven, Botham, and Bush; Winston Churchill, John Cleese and Marie Curie; Angela Davis, Bette Davis, and Miles Davis; Henry VIII and Vaclav Havel; Christine Keeler and Colonel Khaddhafi; Steven Spielberg and Alan Sugar; Lech Walesa, Oscar Wilde, and thousands more. Up to date and authoritative, this compact volume is also illustrated with over 250 photographs.

THE
HUTCHINSON ENCYCLOPEDIA
FAMILY QUIZ BOOK

Over 1,250 questions are included in this unique collection of quizzes for all the family. Based on the enormous range of information contained in *The Hutchinson Encyclopedia*, it includes both general-knowledge and subject-specific questions, at a variety of levels of difficulty. *The Hutchinson Encyclopedia Family Quiz Book* is entirely self-contained, including answers, but interested readers can consult the *Hutchinson Encyclopedia* for further information on any topic contained in the quizzes.